Adolescence

AN INTRODUCTION

Fifth Edition

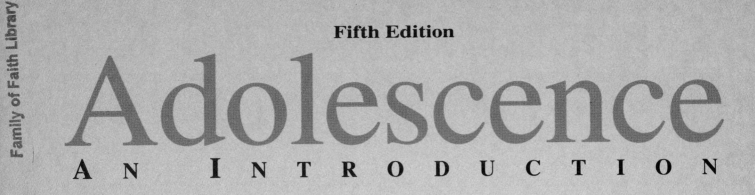

Adolescence

AN INTRODUCTION

John W. Santrock

University of Texas, Dallas

**WCB Brown &
Benchmark**

P U B L I S H E R S

Madison, Wisconsin • Dubuque, Iowa • Indianapolis, Indiana
Melbourne, Australia • Oxford, England

Book Team

Editor *Michael Lange*
Developmental Editor *Sheralee Connors*
Production Editor *Debra DeBord*
Designer *David C. Lansdon*
Art Editor *Rachel Imsland*
Photo Editor *Robin Storm*
Permissions Editor *Vicki Krug*
Art Processor *Rachel Imsland*
Visuals/Design Developmental Consultant *Marilyn A. Phelps*

A Division of Wm. C. Brown Communications, Inc.

Vice President and General Manager *Thomas E. Doran*
Executive Managing Editor *Ed Bartell*
Executive Editor *Edgar J. Laube*
Director of Marketing *Kathy Law Laube*
National Sales Manager *Eric Ziegler*
Marketing Manager *Carla Aspelmeier*
Advertising Manager *Jodi Rymer*
Managing Editor, Production *Colleen A. Yonda*
Manager of Visuals and Design *Faye M. Schilling*

Design Manager *Jac Tilton*
Art Manager *Janice Roerig*
Photo Manager *Shirley Charley*
Publishing Services Manager *Karen J. Slaght*
Permissions/Records Manager *Connie Allendorf*

Wm. C. Brown Communications, Inc.

Chairman Emeritus *Wm. C. Brown*
Chairman and Chief Executive Officer *Mark C. Falb*
President and Chief Operating Officer *G. Franklin Lewis*
Corporate Vice President, Operations *Beverly Kolz*
Corporate Vice President, President of WCB Manufacturing *Roger Meyer*

Cover photo: © Dag Sundberg/The Image Bank

Copyeditor *Mary Monner*

The credits section for this book begins on page 613 and is considered an extension of the copyright page.

Library of Congress Catalog Card Number: 91–74025

ISBN 0–697–12752–4
    0–697–12753–2

Printed in the United States of America by Wm. C. Brown Communications, Inc., 2460 Kerper Boulevard, Dubuque, IA 52001

10 9 8 7 6 5 4 3 2 1

To Tracy and Jennifer, who, as they have matured, have helped me appreciate the marvels of adolescent development.

Brief Contents

Contents

SECTION II

Biological and Cognitive Development

CHAPTER 3

Biological Processes and Physical Development   87

CHAPTER 4

Cognitive Development and Social Cognition   115

CHAPTER 5

Information Processing and Intelligence   145

SECTION III

The Contexts of Adolescent Development

SECTION IV

Social, Emotional, and Personality Development

CHAPTER 10

The Self and Identity 333

CHAPTER 11

Gender 365

CHAPTER 12

Sexuality 395

CHAPTER 13

Moral Development, Values, and Religion 433

CHAPTER 14

Achievement, Careers, and Work 467

SECTION V

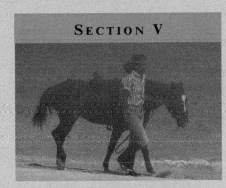

Adolescent Problems, Stress, and Health

CHAPTER 15

Adolescent Problems 499

CHAPTER 16

Stress and Health 541

Box Features

Preface

Fifteen years ago, I agreed to write the first edition of *Adolescence*. My oldest daughter, Tracy, was 12 years old and just embarking on the long, fascinating, and complex journey of making the transition from child to adult. Now 15 years later, *Adolescence* and Tracy have moved through a number of changes. Both have been an important part of my life during the last 15 years. Both are special.

When I wrote the first edition of *Adolescence,* I wanted to construct a book that would portray the study of adolescent development in an interesting and scientific manner. The fifth edition of *Adolescence* continues my effort to both inform and motivate the reader. Because ours is a field of rapidly changing knowledge and research, the second, third, and fourth editions of *Adolescence* represented substantial changes from their predecessors. The fifth edition continues the tradition of extensive research updating.

Highlights of Changes in the Fifth Edition of *Adolescence*

The fifth edition of *Adolescence* has the same number of chapters and sections as the fourth edition. However, as a result of a thorough, painstaking analysis of the current nature of the field, I have added, subtracted, simplified, and integrated information about adolescent development.

Content Changes

Examination of the research taking place in the field of adolescence led to a number of content changes. These changes include an increased emphasis on ethnicity and culture, gender, education and schools, adolescent problems, and social policy.

Ethnicity and Culture

Special attention is given to the roles of ethnicity and culture in adolescent development. This increased coverage reflects the growing interest in ethnic minority and cross-cultural research. A special feature in the fifth edition of *Adolescence* is "Sociocultural Worlds of Adolescence" boxes in every chapter. These first appeared in the fourth edition of the book; they have been expanded and better integrated into the fifth edition. A look through any chapter of the book reveals their special appeal. Reviewers of the fifth edition of *Adolescence* have consistently commented that this book now has far more discussion of ethnicity and culture than any other adolescence text.

Gender

An equally important change in the fifth edition of *Adolescence* is the increased coverage of gender issues and female development. The chapter on gender (Chapter 11) has been expanded to include discussions of developmental changes and gender intensification, the feminist perspective, and adolescence as a critical juncture in the development of females. Carol Gilligan's recent analysis of female adolescent development is extensively examined. Gender issues are also discussed in a number of other places in the text, such as the gender-based criticism of Freud's theory (Chapter 2), gender issues and schools (Chapter 8), Gilligan's recent ideas on the care perspective (Chapter 13), and career development, gender, and ethnicity (Chapter 14).

Education and Schools

The expanded coverage of education includes cross-cultural comparisons of schools; ethnicity and achievement; the importance of adolescence in achievement; mastery versus helpless orientation; culture, schooling, and cognitive development; decision making; critical thinking; computers and adolescents; the snowflake model of creativity and its application to the education of adolescents; Damon's comprehensive moral education approach; and the role of schools in the prevention of and intervention in adolescent problems and disorders.

Problems and Disorders

The majority of adolescents negotiate the transition from childhood to adulthood successfully and competently. However, far too many adolescents still are not getting adequate attention and support. The fifth edition of *Adolescence* provides a very contemporary look at adolescent problems and disorders. Included in the extensively revised and new material on problems and disorders are discussions of the interrelation of problems and disorders in adolescence, high-risk and very-high-risk youth, common components of programs that successfully prevent or reduce adolescent problems, the role of the family in adolescent drug use, juvenile delinquency, support systems, sociocultural factors in adolescent stress, high school dropouts, and adolescent pregnancy.

Social Policy

Another feature of the fifth edition of *Adolescence* is increased coverage of social policy issues. The importance of social policy issues in adolescent development is highlighted in Chapter 1; social policy issues are discussed in a number of other chapters as well, including Chapter 15, which covers problems and disorders.

Increased Coverage of Other Topics

In addition to increased coverage of the topics already mentioned, the following areas have been given more attention in *Adolescence,* fifth edition: AIDS in adolescence, health and nutrition, career development, divorce and stepfamilies, the development of self-understanding, identity development, sexuality, Bronfenbrenner's ecological theory, idealized images of what adolescents should be and society's ambivalent messages to adolescents, the current status of adolescents, working parents, the role of culture and ethnicity in parent-adolescent relationships, peer neglect and rejection, the development of intimacy, the media and music, poverty, and adolescence as a special juncture in the development of ethnic minority individuals.

Pedagogical Changes

One of the main features of the fourth edition of *Adolescence* was its extensive attention to pedagogy. The core of this well-received pedagogical system has been retained, including the useful concept tables, high-interest introductions to chapters, outlines at the beginning of chapters, and chapter summaries. However, to make *Adolescence*'s learning system more effective and challenging, I have incorporated a number of new features that include key-term definitions in text and visual figures and tables.

A very important aspect of *Adolescence*'s improved learning system is the new way key terms are presented. Key terms appear in the text in **boldfaced type,** with their definitions following immediately in *italics*. This provides students with a clear understanding of important concepts in adolescence. The key terms are also listed, with page references, at the end of each chapter and are defined in the page-referenced "Glossary" at the end of the book.

The presentation of figures and tables has also been dramatically improved in the fifth edition of *Adolescence*. Every chapter has a number of visual figures and tables that include both a description of important content information and photographs that illustrate the content. In many instances, the visual figures and tables represent summaries or reviews of important concepts. For example, in Chapter 2, a visual figure summarizes Erikson's eight stages of psychosocial development; in Chapter 4, two visual figures summarize Piaget's concrete and formal operational stages; in Chapter 6, a visual figure summarizes the new look in adolescent family processes; and, in Chapter 11, a visual figure summarizes the overlap hypothesis of gender differences and similarities. The combination of summary descriptions and carefully selected photographs in the form of visual figures and tables presented periodically within each chapter enhances students' retention and makes *Adolescence* an attractive book to study.

Overview of Basic Features in *Adolescence*

In addition to the important changes that have been made in the fifth edition of *Adolescence,* a number of basic features in previous editions have been continued. These features include the book's research system, writing system, learning system, and supplementary materials.

The Research System

The present edition of *Adolescence* is, above all else, an extremely up-to-date presentation of research in the three primary domains of development: biological, cognitive, and social processes. Research on biological, cognitive, and social processes continues to represent the core of *Adolescence*. This core includes both classic and cutting-edge research. More than 40 percent of the references in *Adolescence,* fifth edition, are new. *Adolescence* includes more than 150 references from 1991, 1992, and *in press* sources alone. Scientific knowledge about adolescent development is expanding on many frontiers, and I have tried to capture the excitement of these new discoveries, while presenting the classic studies that are the foundation of the discipline.

The Writing System

With the entire field of adolescence to cover, it was important that this book be written clearly and efficiently. I added, subtracted, integrated, and simplified as I wrote the fifth edition of *Adolescence*. Why spend so much time rewriting this book? Because, when material is simply added without extensive writing, later editions become too choppy and long. With continued expansion of research on many frontiers of adolescence, I found it necessary not only to add material but to start with page one and write the fifth edition as if it were the beginning of a new book. This strategy has the important benefits of allowing me to eliminate ideas and references that have become dated; to retain the theories, concepts, and research ideas that have become the core of the discipline; to add newly developed theories, concepts, and research ideas; and to integrate these changes so that the presentation of the material is clear, efficient, and easy to read. The reviewers of the manuscript for the fifth edition of *Adolescence* consistently commented on the significant improvements in the writing and presentation of the material.

The Learning System

Adolescence incorporates an extremely effective and challenging learning system. Topics are explored in sufficient detail to challenge students, and the complex nature of adolescent development is presented in such a way as to encourage critical thinking. Many questions are asked students throughout the text to encourage their critical thinking.

However, I not only wanted to encourage thinking skills, I also wanted textbook pedagogy to help students learn. Thus, an extensive, carefully designed pedagogical system has been built into *Adolescence,* fifth edition. Critical to this pedagogical system are the concept tables that appear two to three times in every chapter. They are designed to activate students' memory and comprehension of major topics or key concepts that have been discussed to that point. This allows students to get a handle on complex concepts and ideas and to understand how they are interrelated. Concept tables provide a cognitive framework of the most important information in each section.

A very important aspect of *Adolescence*'s learning system is the new way in which key terms are presented. As mentioned previously, key terms appear in the text in **boldfaced type,** with their definition following immediately in *italics*. This provides students with a clear understanding of important concepts in adolescence. The key terms are also listed with page references at the end of each chapter and are defined in the page-referenced "Glossary" at the end of the book.

The new visual figures and tables are also an important addition to the learning system of *Adolescence.* As mentioned earlier, every chapter has a number of visual figures and tables, which include both a description of important content information and photographs to illustrate the content. The combination of summary descriptions and carefully selected photographs enhances students' retention and makes the book more attractive to study.

In addition, an outline at the beginning of each chapter shows the overall hierarchical organization of the material. Then, an imaginative, high-interest piece called "Images of Adolescence" follows, focusing on a topic related to the chapter's content. "Perspective on Adolescent Development" boxes appear in every chapter. A brief glimpse through any chapter reveals the special appeal of these boxes to students. A second type of box, called "Sociocultural Worlds of Adolescence," highlights ethnic, cultural, and gender issues in adolescent development. At the end of each chapter, a detailed "Summary" in outline form provides a helpful review. An annotated list of "Suggested Readings" also appears at the end of each chapter. These elements should help students understand the field of adolescent development.

Supplementary Materials

Brown & Benchmark and the ancillary team have worked together to produce an outstanding, integrated teaching package to accompany *Adolescence.* The authors of the ancillary package are all experienced teachers of the adolescence course. The supplements have been designed to make it as easy as possible to customize the entire package to meet the unique needs of professors and their students.

The *Instructor's Course Planner,* the key to this teaching package, was created by Michael G. Walraven of Jackson Community College. This flexible planner provides a variety of useful tools to enhance your teaching efforts, minimize your work load, and increase your effectiveness. For each chapter of the text, the planner provides a list of learning objectives, key terms, and a chapter summary. These items are also found in the *Student Study Guide.* The planner also contains discussion questions, classroom activities, student activities, questions to promote critical thinking, and essay questions. A listing of films and rental sources follows the final chapter of the planner. The *Instructor's Course Planner* is conveniently housed within an attractive 11-by-13-by-9-inch carrying case. This case is designed to accommodate the complete ancillary package, with each chapter's material within a separate hanging file, allowing you to keep all of your class materials organized at your fingertips.

The *Test Item File* was created by Gregory T. Fouts, University of Calgary. This comprehensive test bank contains over 1,000 new multiple-choice test questions that are keyed to the text and learning objectives and designated as factual, conceptual, or applied.

The *Student Study Guide* was also created by Michael Walraven. For each chapter of the text, the student is provided with learning objectives, a chapter summary, key terms, a guided review, study questions (with answers provided for self-testing), and suggested activities. The study guide begins with "How to Be a Better Student," a section designed to help the student establish goals, build effective study skills, benefit from lectures, and deal with test anxiety.

The *WCB Developmental Psychology Transparency/Slide Set* consists of 100 newly developed acetate transparencies or slides and will be available to adopters of *Adolescence,* fifth edition. These full-color illustrations include graphics from various outside sources. These transparencies, created by Lynne Blesz Vestal, were expressly designed to provide complete coverage of all major topic areas generally covered in a course on developmental psychology. A comprehensive, annotated guide provides a brief description for each transparency and helpful suggestions for use in the classroom.

The *Brown & Benchmark Customized Reader* allows you to select over 80 different journal or magazine articles from a menu provided by your Brown & Benchmark sales representative. These readings will be custom printed for your students and bound into an attractive 8½-by-11-inch book, giving you the opportunity to tailor-make your own student reader.

A large selection of videotapes is also available to adopters based upon the number of textbooks ordered directly from Brown & Benchmark by your bookstore.

The *Test Item File* for *Adolescence* can be used with TestPak 3.0, a complete classroom management system. One of TestPak's most exciting capabilities is its ability to scramble the order of the alternatives, allowing you to use your favorite items frequently and yet have them appear a little differently so that "old forms" cannot be memorized by students or so that you may give alternate versions of the same test in a large classroom setting.

Adopters of *Adolescence,* fifth edition, who use TestPak 3.0 with enhanced quizzing and grading capabilities will find that this convenient system allows them to save hours of test preparation time. This new program allows instructors to print test masters utilizing the TestPak program, construct a test and allow students to take the test on the computer, have the computer automatically grade the exam, give quizzes to help learn material before students take the test, and utilize a gradebook package to compute and graph individual student and total class records.

As another option, an instructor may use our convenient call-in/mail-in/FAX service to generate tests. Using the *Test Item File,* the professor can select the questions to include in the customized test, then simply call in (800–351–7671), mail (Wm. C. Brown Communications/Brown & Benchmark/2460 Kerper Blvd./Dubuque, IA 52001), or FAX (319–589–2955) the request to us. Within two working days of receiving the order, we will send by first-class mail (or FAX) a test master, a student answer sheet, and an answer key for fast and easy grading.

For more information about TestPak 3.0, please contact your local Brown & Benchmark sales representative.

Acknowledgments

A project of this magnitude requires the efforts of many individuals. I owe special thanks to Acquisitions Editor Michael Lange, who has provided outstanding guidance and support. I also thank Developmental Editor Sheralee Connors, who showed a special enthusiasm and competence in monitoring the revision process. The numerous members of the production team did a marvelous job of editing, rearranging, and designing the book—the particular members of the book team are listed at the beginning of the book. Thanks also go to Gregory T. Fouts, University of Calgary, who prepared an excellent *Test Item File* and to Michael G. Walraven, Jackson Community College, who prepared a very useful *Instructor's Course Planner* and *Student Study Guide.* Kathy Skinner did an excellent job of preparing the book's glossary.

I have benefited extensively from the ideas and insights of many colleagues. I would like to thank the following individuals for their feedback on earlier editions of *Adolescence:*

Frank Ascione
Utah State University

Fredda Blanchard-Fields
Louisiana State University

Robert Bornstein
Miami University

James A. Doyle
Roane State Community College

Richard M. Ehlenz
Lakewood Community College

Martin E. Ford
Stanford University

Gregory T. Fouts
University of Calgary

Charles Fry
University of Virginia

William Gnagey
Illinois State University

B. Jo Hailey
University of Southern Mississippi

Dick E. Hammond
Southwest Texas State University

Frances Harnick
University of New Mexico, Indian Children's Program, and Lovelace–Bataan Pediatric Clinic

June V. Irving
Ball State University

Beverly Jennings
University of Colorado–Denver

Joline Jones
Worcester State College

Alfred L. Karlson
University of Massachusetts–Amherst

Lynn F. Katz
University of Pittsburgh

Emmett C. Lampkin
Scott Community College

Royal Louis Lange
Ellsworth Community College

Daniel K. Lapsley
University of Notre Dame

Daniel Lynch
University of Wisconsin–Oshkosh

Ann McCabe
University of Windsor

Susan McCammon
East Carolina University

E. L. McGarry
California State University–Fullerton

Joseph G. Marrone
Siena College

John J. Mirich
Metropolitan State College

Anne Robertson
University of Wisconsin–Milwaukee

Toni E. Santmire
University of Nebraska

Douglas Sawin
University of Texas

Vern Tyler
Western Washington University

Carolyn L. Williams
University of Minnesota

The fifth edition of *Adolescence* also has benefited from a carefully selected board of teaching professionals who provided invaluable feedback by doing extensive user reviews or by analyzing drafts of individual chapters. For their generous help and countless good ideas, I would like to thank:

David K. Bernhardt
Carleton University

Deborah Brown
Friends University

Duane Buhrmester
University of Texas at Dallas

Stephanie M. Clancy
Southern Illinois University at Carbondale

Peggy A. DeCooke
Northern Illinois University

R. Daniel DiSalvi
Kean College

Gene Elliott
Glassboro State University

Robert Enright
University of Wisconsin–Madison

Douglas Fife
Plymouth State College

Gregory T. Fouts
University of Calgary

Margaret J. Gill
Kutztown University

Neal E. Lipsitz
Boston College

Nancey G. Lobb
Alvin Community College

John J. Mitchell
University of Alberta

Joycelyn G. Parish
Kansas State University

A final note of thanks goes to my family—Mary Jo, my wife; Tracy, 25; and Jennifer, 22—whose love and companionship I cherish.

TO THE STUDENT
How the Learning System Works

This book contains a number of learning devices, each of which presents the field of adolescence in a meaningful way. The learning devices in *Adolescence* will help you learn the material more effectively.

Chapter Outlines

Each chapter begins with an outline, showing the organization of topics by heading levels. The outline gives you an overview of the arrangement and structure of the chapter, so you can plan your study time wisely.

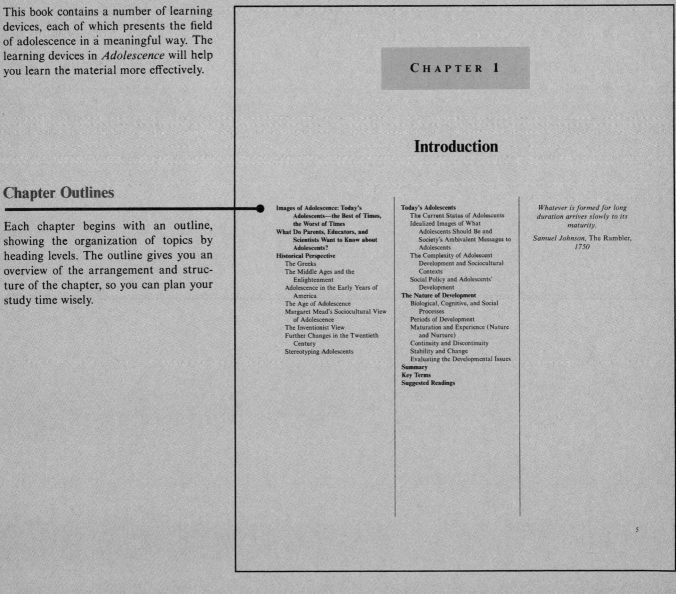

CHAPTER 1

Introduction

Images of Adolescence: Today's
   Adolescents—the Best of Times,
   the Worst of Times
What Do Parents, Educators, and
   Scientists Want to Know about
   Adolescents?
Historical Perspective
   The Greeks
   The Middle Ages and the
      Enlightenment
   Adolescence in the Early Years of
      America
   The Age of Adolescence
   Margaret Mead's Sociocultural View
      of Adolescence
   The Inventionist View
   Further Changes in the Twentieth
      Century
   Stereotyping Adolescents

Today's Adolescents
   The Current Status of Adolescents
   Idealized Images of What
      Adolescents Should Be and
      Society's Ambivalent Messages to
      Adolescents
   The Complexity of Adolescent
      Development and Sociocultural
      Contexts
   Social Policy and Adolescents'
      Development
The Nature of Development
   Biological, Cognitive, and Social
      Processes
   Periods of Development
   Maturation and Experience (Nature
      and Nurture)
   Continuity and Discontinuity
   Stability and Change
   Evaluating the Developmental Issues
Summary
Key Terms
Suggested Readings

*Whatever is formed for long
duration arrives slowly to its
maturity.*

Samuel Johnson, The Rambler,
1750

5

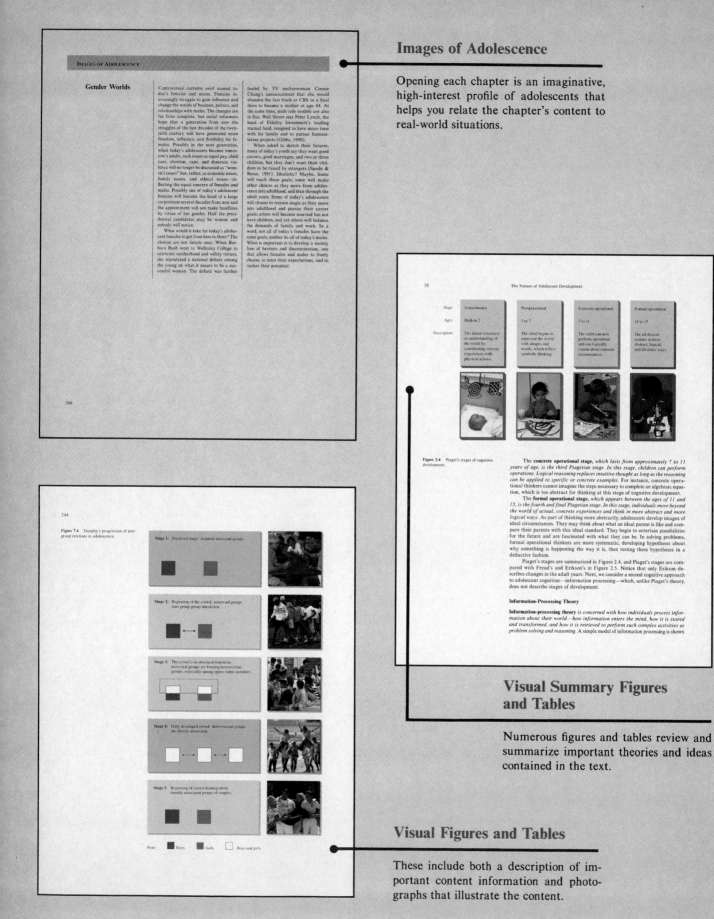

Images of Adolescence

Opening each chapter is an imaginative, high-interest profile of adolescents that helps you relate the chapter's content to real-world situations.

Visual Summary Figures and Tables

Numerous figures and tables review and summarize important theories and ideas contained in the text.

Visual Figures and Tables

These include both a description of important content information and photographs that illustrate the content.

Photographs and Legends

Special attention was given to the choice of photographs for this book. A number of leading researchers in adolescent development willingly sent photographs of themselves to be included. Legends were carefully written with an eye toward further clarification and elaboration of the text.

searchers have found that cooperative learning is associated with enhanced student outcomes, including increases in self-esteem, better academic performance, friendships among classmates, and improved interethnic perceptions (Aronson, 1986; Johnson & Johnson, 1989; Slavin, 1989b).

When the schools of Austin, Texas, were desegregated through extensive busing, the outcome was increased ethnic tension among Blacks, Mexican Americans, and Anglos, producing violence in the schools. The superintendent consulted with Eliot Aronson, a prominent social psychologist, who was a professor at the University of Texas at Austin at the time. Aronson thought it was more important to prevent ethnic tension than to control it. This led him to observe a number of school classrooms in Austin. What he saw was fierce competition between individuals of unequal status.

Aronson stressed that the reward structure of the classrooms needed to be changed from a setting of unequal competition to one of cooperation among equals, without making curriculum changes. To accomplish this, Aronson developed a form of cooperative learning he called the "jigsaw classroom." How does the jigsaw classroom work? Consider a class of 30 students, some Anglo, some Black, some Hispanic. The lesson to be learned focuses on Joseph Pulitzer's life. The class might be broken up into five groups of six students each, with the groups being as equal as possible in ethnic composition and academic achievement level. The lesson about Pulitzer's life could be divided into six parts, with one part given to each member of the six-person group. The parts might be paragraphs from Pulitzer's biography, such as how the Pulitzer family came to the United States, his childhood, his early work, and so on. The components are like the parts of a jigsaw puzzle. They have to be put together to form the complete puzzle.

Each student in the group is given an allotted time to study. Then the group meets, and each member tries to teach a part to the group. After an hour or so, each member is tested on the entire life of Pulitzer, with each member receiving an individual rather than a group score. Each student, therefore, must learn the entire lesson. Learning depends on the cooperation and effort of other members. Aronson believes that this type of learning increases students' interdependence through cooperatively reaching a common goal.

Cooperative learning is an important addition to learning strategies, but esteemed social psychologist Roger Brown (1986) offers a caveat. According to Brown, academic achievement is as much, or more, an individual "sport" as a team "sport." *Individuals* graduate from high school, enter college, and take jobs, not *groups*. A parent with an advantaged adolescent in a cooperative learning classroom thus may react with increased ethnic hostility when the adolescent brings home a lower grade than is typical. The adolescent may tell his father, "The teacher is getting us to teach each other. In my group, we have this kid named Carlos, who can barely speak English." While cooperative learning is an important strategy for reducing interethnic hostility, caution needs to be exercised in its use because of the unequal status of the participants and achievement's individual orientation. Other ways that the educational and achievement orientation of Hispanic students can be improved are described in Sociocultural Worlds of Adolescence 8.2.

Dr. Henry Gaskins began an after-school tutorial program for ethnic minority students in 1983 in Washington, D.C. For four hours every weeknight and all day Saturday, 80 students receive one-on-one assistance from Gaskins and his wife, two adult volunteers, and academically talented peers. Those who can afford it contribute five dollars to cover the cost of school supplies. In addition to tutoring in specific subjects, Gaskins's home-based academy helps students to set personal goals and to commit to a desire to succeed. Many of his students come from families in which the parents are high school dropouts and either cannot or are not motivated to help their adolescents achieve in school. In addition, the academy prepares students to qualify for scholarships and college entrance exams. Gaskins was recently awarded the President's Volunteer Action Award at the White House.

The Subordination and Exploitation of Ethnic Minority Adolescents in Education

American anthropologist John Ogbu (1974, 1986, 1989) proposed the controversial view that ethnic minority youth are placed in a position of subordination and exploitation in the American educational system. He believes that ethnic minority adolescents, especially Black and Hispanic Americans, have inferior educational opportunities, are exposed to teachers and administrators who have low

PERSPECTIVE ON ADOLESCENT DEVELOPMENT 15.1

The Life Skills Training Program

Gilbert Botvin's Life Skills Training Program was selected as one of fourteen showcase programs by the American Psychological Association's Task Force on Promotion, Prevention, and Intervention Alternatives in Psychology (Price & others, 1988). Botvin's (1986) program was the only drug prevention/intervention program selected out of a field of 300 nominees.

According to Botvin, substance use is a socially learned, purposive, and functional behavior. His approach involves attempts to reduce pressure to smoke, to develop general personal competence, and to learn specific skills to resist peer pressure. The Life Skills Training curriculum consists of five main components:

1. Students are given information about the short-term and long-term consequences of substance abuse; biofeedback demonstrates the immediate effects of cigarette smoking.
2. Decision-making skills are taught to foster students' critical thinking. Counterarguments to advertising appeals are formulated.
3. Coping skills are taught so that students deal with stress more effectively.
4. Social skills training for resisting peer pressure is implemented. The training sessions include such topics as dealing with shyness, coping with dating, and assertiveness skills.
5. Self-improvement is emphasized by helping students to develop a positive self-image using learning principles.

The Life Skills Training Program consists of 20 sessions and is designed primarily for middle school and junior high school students. It is directed by a classroom teacher who uses a Teacher's Manual and receives one day of in-service training. Older peers (eleventh- and twelfth-graders) are also used as teachers after extensive training and on-site monitoring by the Life Skills Training staff.

Botvin has conducted a number of evaluations of the Life Skills Training Program and demonstrated that the program is effective in reducing cigarette smoking, alcohol use, and marijuana use. The greatest success has occurred when the sessions are led by older peers (Botvin, 1987).

Counseling about drug abuse should be available throughout the school years.

3. Teacher training is an important element in school-based programs. The best-designed drug abuse curriculum is ineffective in the hands of an inadequately prepared teacher. School systems need to provide time and resources for in-service training and supervision.
4. School skills training, especially focused on coping skills and resistance to peer pressure, is the most promising of the new wave of school-based curricula (Tobler, 1986). However, the effectiveness of these social skills training programs over the long term and whether or not they are as effective with high-risk youth as with others are not known.
5. Peer-led programs are often more effective than teacher-led or counselor-led programs, especially when older students (senior high) are the leaders and role models for younger students (junior high and middle school).
6. Most of the school-based programs have been general programs directed at all students, rather than specific programs targeted at high-risk adolescents. More programs aimed at the high-risk group are needed.
7. The most effective school-based programs are often part of community-wide prevention efforts that involve parents, peers, role models, media, police, courts, businesses, youth-serving agencies, as well as schools (NIAAA, 1984).

Perspective on Adolescent Development 15.1 presents more information on a successful school-based program to prevent substance abuse.

Perspective on Adolescent Development

You'll find one or more of these boxed features in every chapter, giving you an in-depth look at issues confronting adolescents today.

Sociocultural Worlds of Adolescence

Adolescence gives special attention to the cultural, ethnic, and gender worlds of adolescents. Each chapter has one or more boxed inserts that highlight the sociocultural dimensions of adolescent development.

SOCIOCULTURAL WORLDS OF ADOLESCENCE 14.1

Modifying the Math Study Strategies of Black American College Students

Professor Treisman confers with students in a math study group at the University of California-Berkeley. Treisman's research revealed the importance of collaborative learning in helping Black students to succeed in math and science courses.

In 1986, Black and Hispanic Americans were awarded just eight of the more than six hundred doctoral degrees in math in the United States. At every level—high school, college, and graduate school—comparatively smaller percentages of Black and Hispanic American students enroll in math and science courses. The rate of enrollment, especially for Black students, declined in the 1980s. With more than one-fourth of America's college-age population expected to be Black or Hispanic in 1995, increasing the number of Black and Hispanic Americans in math and science is critical.

Motivated to discover why the success rate of Black and Hispanic Americans is so low, University of California-Berkeley mathematician Philip Treisman extensively compared 20 Black and 20 Chinese college students who were enrolled in freshman calculus. At Berkeley, as at many American universities, Asian American students often have the highest rate of success in math. Treisman observed the students in the library, their dormitory rooms, and even their homes. He interviewed their families. The differences in the Black and Chinese students were not due to motivation, income, family support, or academic preparation. Even Black students who came with the best test scores and other positive predictors tended to do poorly in math, for example. The most striking observation was that the Black students were virtually isolated in their study of math. Eighteen of the twenty Black students always studied alone—the two who studied together eventually dropped out to marry each other. Many erected a wall between their intellectual and social lives. Treisman found that, for many graduates of inner-city and predominantly ethnic minority high schools, the self-reliance that may have helped them get into a top college—by buffering them from the distractions at their secondary schools—became their downfall at Berkeley. The students had no way to check out their understanding of math or science, no way to check out what Berkeley as an institution required of them.

Within four weeks after arriving at Berkeley, 13 of the 20 Chinese students found study mates, and several others were still searching. The study groups came together after the students had done extensive individual work. Group study was a final, but very important, step. Studying together, the students picked up solutions they had missed. If no student had solved a problem, members of the group recognized its difficulty and thus avoided self-criticism. In these groups, students tested their perceptions of what professors expected, what the university expected, and how many hours they should be studying. They shared tips for handling the bureaucratic maze and for lining up financial aid and housing. They chatted about how to deal with the White community.

Based on his experiences with the Black and Chinese students, Treisman developed a math workshop with three overriding principles: (1) Help ethnic minority students excel, not just avoid failure; (2) emphasize collaborative learning and small-group teaching methods; and (3) require faculty sponsorship. The accomplishments of the math workshop over seven years of operations include: 55 percent of the workshop's 231 Black students (compared with 21 percent of the 234 Black students not in the workshop) have earned a grade of B− or better in first-year calculus. Black students in the workshop have consistently scored a full grade higher than nonworkshop Black students. Among Black workshop participants who entered Berkeley in 1978 or 1979, 44 percent graduated in math-based majors, while only 10 percent of the nonworkshop Black students did.

Freshman mathematics and science courses have too often been the burial ground for the aspirations of Black and Hispanic American students who have entered college with the goal of majoring in some area of math or science. Programs such as Philip Treisman's reveal how the underachievement of Black and Hispanic American students can be turned into accomplishment (Charles A. Dana Foundation Report, 1988).

Concept Tables

Two or three times in each chapter, you can review what has been discussed so far in that chapter by scanning the information in concept tables. This learning device helps you get a handle on material several times a chapter so you don't wait until the end of the chapter and have too much information to digest.

80

Concept Table 2.3

Research Methods in Adolescent Development

Concept	Processes/Related Ideas	Characteristics/Description
Scientific method	Its steps	The scientific method consists of a series of procedures to obtain accurate information. Its steps include identifying and analyzing a problem, collecting data, drawing conclusions, and revising theories.
Ways of collecting information—methods	Observation	Observation is a key ingredient in adolescent development research that includes laboratory and naturalistic observation.
	Interviews and questionnaires	They are used to assess perceptions and attitudes. Social desirability of responses is a special problem with their use.
	Case studies	They provide an in-depth look at an individual. Caution in generalizing is warranted.
	Standardized tests	They are designed to assess an individual's characteristics relative to those of a large group of similar individuals.
	Cross-cultural research	This research focuses on the culture-universal (etic) and culture-specific (emic) nature of adolescent development.
	Physiological research	This research examines the biological dimensions of the adolescent.
	Multimeasure, multisource, multicontext approach	Increasingly, a strategy in the study of adolescents is to use different measures, obtaining information from different sources, and observing in different contexts.
Strategies for setting up research studies	Correlational strategy	This describes how strongly two or more events or characteristics are related. It does not allow causal statements.
	Experimental strategy	This involves manipulation of influential factors (the independent variables) and measurement of their effect on the dependent variables. Subjects are randomly assigned to experimental and control groups in many studies. The experimental strategy can reveal the causes of behavior and show how one event influenced another.
Time span of inquiry	Cross-sectional approach	This involves comparing individuals of different ages all at one time.
	Longitudinal approach	This involves studying the same individuals over a period of time, usually several years or more.
	Sequential approach	This is a combined cross-sectional, longitudinal approach that evaluates cohort effects in development.
Cohort effects	Their nature	Cohort effects are due to a subject's generation or time of birth but not actually to age. The study of cohort effects underscores the importance of considering the historical dimensions of adolescent development.
Sexist bias	Its nature	A concern is that the vast majority of psychological research has been male-oriented and male-dominated. Some researchers believe that developmentalists need to be challenged to examine adolescents' worlds in a new way, one that incorporates girls' and women's perspectives. Recommendations have been made for conducting nonsexist research.
Ethics in research on adolescent development	Its nature	Researchers are required to ensure the well-being of subjects. The risk of mental and physical harm must be reduced, and informed consent should be obtained.

Summary

At the end of each chapter, a summary in outline form helps you review the main ideas of the entire chapter.

Peers   257

Summary

I. Peer Group Functions
The nature of peer relationships undergoes important changes during adolescence. Peers are individuals who are about the same age or maturity level. Peers provide a means of social comparison and a source of information about the world outside the family. Good peer relations may be necessary for normal social development in adolescence. The inability to "plug in" to a social network in childhood or adolescence is associated with a number of problems and disturbances. Thus, peer influences can be both positive and negative. Both Piaget and Sullivan stressed that peer relations provide the context for learning the symmetrical reciprocity mode of relationships.

II. Peer Conformity, Popularity, Neglect, and Rejection
Conformity occurs when individuals adopt the attitudes or behavior of others because of real or imagined pressure from the others. Conformity to antisocial peer standards peaks around the eighth to ninth grades, then decreases by the twelfth grade. A distinction is made between nonconformists and anticonformists. Listening skills, effective communication, being yourself, being happy, showing enthusiasm and concern for others, and having self-confidence but not being conceited are predictors of peer popularity. Neglected adolescents receive little attention from their peers, while rejected adolescents are disliked by their peers. The risk status of neglected adolescents is unclear. Rejected adolescents are at risk for the development of problems. Training programs focus on improving the peer relations of neglected and rejected adolescents. One issue involving rejected adolescents is whether to initially improve their prosocial skills or reduce their aggressive behavior and improve their self-control. It is important to remember that rejected adolescents reflect a heterogeneous grouping.

III. Social Knowledge, Social Information Processing, and Conglomerate Strategies for Improving Social Skills
Social knowledge and social information-processing skills are associated with improved peer relations. Conglomerate strategies, also referred to as coaching, involve the use of a combination of techniques, rather than a single approach, to improve adolescents' social skills.

IV. Friendships
The functions of friendship include companionship, stimulation, physical support, ego support, social comparison, and intimacy/affection. Harry Stack Sullivan was the most influential theorist to discuss the importance of adolescent friendships. He argued that there is a dramatic increase in the psychological importance and intimacy of close friends during early adolescence. Research findings support many of Sullivan's ideas. Intimacy and similarity are two of the most common characteristics of friendships. Intimacy in friendships is defined narrowly as self-disclosure or sharing of private thoughts. Similarity—in terms of age, sex, ethnicity, and many other factors—is also important to friendships. Adolescents who become close friends with older individuals engage in more deviant behaviors than their counterparts with same-age friends. Early-maturing girls are more likely than their later-maturing counterparts to have older friends, who may encourage deviant behavior.

V. Group Function and Formation
Groups satisfy adolescents' personal needs, reward them, provide information, raise their self-esteem, and give them an identity. Norms are rules that apply to all members of a group. Roles are rules and expectations that govern certain positions in the group. Sherif's classic study documented how adolescents behave in group settings; superordinate tasks reduced adolescents' intergroup hostility.

The Self and Identity 363

that consists of four stages: preencounter, encounter, immersion/emersion, and internalization/commitment. She also proposed a five-stage model of ethnic identity development in White individuals: contact, disintegration, reintegration, pseudo-independence, and autonomy.

XIII. Identity and Intimacy

Intimacy versus isolation is Erikson's sixth developmental stage, which individuals experience during early adulthood. At this time, individuals face the task of forming intimate relationships with others. Orlofsky described five styles of intimate interaction: intimate, preintimate, stereotyped, pseudointimate, and isolated. White proposed a model of relationship maturity in which individuals move through three levels: self-focused, role-focused, and individuated-connected. Surveys often find that the highest levels of loneliness appear during late adolescence and youth. Loneliness is associated with an individual's sex, attachment history, self-esteem, and social skills. The social transition to college is a time when loneliness may develop, as individuals leave behind the familiar world of hometown and family. Weiss distinguished between two types of loneliness: emotional isolation and social isolation.

Key Terms

self-understanding 335	identity foreclosure 349	stereotyped style 357
possible self 336	identity moratorium 349	pseudointimate style 357
self-esteem 338	identity achievement 349	isolated style 357
identity versus identity	individuality 351	self-focused level 357
confusion 345	connectedness 351	role-focused level 357
psychological	intimacy versus	individuated-connected
moratorium 345	isolation 356	level 357
crisis 349	intimate style 357	emotional isolation 359
commitment 349	preintimate style 357	social isolation 359
identity diffusion 349		

Suggested Readings

Erikson, E. H. (1969). *Gandhi's truth.* New York: W. W. Norton.
In this Pulitzer-Prize-winning novel, Erikson weaves an insightful picture of Gandhi's development of identity.
Harter, S. (1990). Self and identity development. In S. S. Feldman & G. R. Elliott (Eds.), *At the threshold: The developing adolescent.* Cambridge, MA: Harvard University Press.
An excellent overview of contemporary theory and research on the nature of self and identity development in adolescence by one of the leading researchers in the area of self-understanding.
Lapsley, D., & Power, F. C. (1988). *Self, ego, and identity.* New York: Springer-Verlag.
An authoritative treatment by leading scholars of issues involved in the nature of the self and identity.
Marcia, J. (1987). The identity status approach to the study of ego identity development. In T. Honess & K. Yardley (Eds.), *Self and identity: Perspectives across the lifespan.* London: Routledge & Kegan Paul.
Marcia presents his concept of the four statuses of identity and describes the complexity of the identity process.
Paul, E. L., & White, K. M. (1990). The development of intimate relationships in late adolescence. *Adolescence, 25,* 375–400.
A recent, authoritative overview of intimacy development in late adolescence, including a description of White's model of relationship maturity.

Key Terms

Listed at the end of each chapter are key terms that are defined throughout the chapter. They are listed with page references and are defined again in a page-referenced glossary at the end of the book to help you review and get ready for exams.

Suggested Readings

A list of readings at the end of each chapter suggests references that can be used for further study of topics covered in the chapter.

328 The Contexts of Adolescent Development

Suggested Readings

Condry, J. C. (1989). *The psychology of television.* Hillsdale, NJ: Erlbaum.
Presents a comprehensive overview of the effects of television on children and adolescents.
Fine, G. A., Mortimer, J. T., & Roberts, D. F. (1990). Leisure, work, and the mass media. In S. S. Feldman & G. R. Elliott (Eds.), *At the threshold: The developing adolescent.* Cambridge, MA: Harvard University Press.
An excellent overview of leisure and mass media influences on adolescent development.
Gibbs, J. T., & Huang, L. N. (Eds.) (1989). *Children of color.* San Francisco: Jossey-Bass.
An excellent overview of the nature of adolescence in ethnic minority groups. Separate chapters on Black adolescents, Mexican American adolescents, American Indian adolescents, Southeast Asia refugee adolescents, Chinese American adolescents, and Puerto Rican adolescents.
Journal of Youth and Adolescence (1989), Vol. 18, No. 6.
This entire issue is devoted to an extensive study of young adolescents' activities by Reed Larson and his colleagues.
Schorr, L. B., with Schorr, D. (1988). *Within our reach: Breaking the cycle of disadvantage and despair.* New York: Doubleday/Anchor.
A penetrating thought-provoking analysis of poverty in America.
Sommer, B. B. (1988). *Puberty and adolescence.* New York: Oxford University Press.
Includes extensive descriptions of rites of passage in primitive cultures.
Spencer, M. B., & Dornbusch, S. M. (1990). Challenges in studying minority youth. In S. S. Feldman & G. R. Elliott (Eds.), *At the threshold: The developing adolescent.* Cambridge, MA: Harvard University Press.
A penetrating, thoughtful insight into the dreams and struggles of ethnic minority adolescents in America today.

Adolescence

AN INTRODUCTION

SECTION I

The Nature of Adolescent Development

In No Order of Things Is Adolescence the Simple Time of Life

Jean Erskine Stewart

A dolescence is a transitional period in the human life cycle, linking childhood and adulthood. Understanding the meaning of adolescence is important because adolescents are the future of any society. This first section contains two chapters: Chapter 1, "Introduction," and Chapter 2, "Theories and Methods."

Introduction

Whatever is formed for long duration arrives slowly to its maturity.

Samuel Johnson, The Rambler, *1750*

Today's Adolescents— the Best of Times, the Worst of Times

It is both the best of times and the worst of times for adolescents. Their world possesses powers and perspectives inconceivable 50 years ago: computers, longer life expectancies, the entire planet accessible through television, satellites, air travel. So much knowledge, though, can be chaotic and dangerous. School curricula have been adapted to teach new topics: AIDS, adolescent suicide, drug and alcohol abuse, incest. The hazards of the adult world— its sometimes fatal temptations—descend upon children and adolescents so early that their ideals may be demolished.

Crack, for example, is far more addictive and deadly than marijuana, the drug of an earlier generation. Strange fragments of violence and sex flash out of the television set and lodge in the minds of youth. The messages are powerful and contradictory. Rock videos suggest orgiastic sex. Public health officials counsel safe sex. Oprah Winfrey and Phil Donahue conduct seminars on lesbian nuns, exotic drugs, transsexual surgery, serial murders. Television pours a bizarre version of reality into the imaginations of adolescents.

Every stable society transmits values from one generation to the next. That is civilization's work. In today's world, there is a special concern about the nature of values being communicated to adolescents. Today's parents are raising adolescents in a world far removed from the era of Ozzie and Harriet 30 years ago, when two out of three American families consisted of a father who was the breadwinner, a mother, and the children and adolescents they were raising. Today fewer than one in five families fits that description. Phrases such as "quality time" have found their way into the American vocabulary. Absence is a motif in the lives of many adolescents. It may be an absence of authority and limits, or of emotional commitment (Morrow, 1988).

Growing up has never been easy. In many ways, the developmental tasks of today's adolescents are no different than the adolescents of Ozzie and Harriet's world. Adolescence is not a time of rebellion, crisis, pathology, and deviance. A far more accurate vision of adolescence is of a time of evaluation, of decision making, of commitment, of carving out a place in the world. Most of the problems of today's youth are not with the youth themselves. What adolescents need is access to a range of legitimate opportunities and to long-term support from adults who care deeply about them.

Each of us has memories of our adolescence—of relationships with parents, peers, and teachers, and of ourselves. This book is a window to the journey of adolescence. The transition from being a child to being an adult is told in words that I hope stimulate you to think about where you have been, where you are, and where you are going in life. You will see yourself and others as adolescents and be motivated to reflect on how the adolescent years influence who we and others are. This book is about life's rhythm and meaning, about turning mystery into understanding, and about weaving a portrait of one of life's most important developmental periods.

A few years ago, it occurred to me that, when I was a teenager, in the early Depression years, there were no teenagers! Teenagers have sneaked up on us in our own lifetime, and yet it seems they always have been with us. . . . The teenager had not yet been invented, though, and there did not yet exist a special class of beings, bounded in a certain way—not quite children and certainly not adults.

P. Musgrove, Youth and Social Order, *Copyright © 1964.*

T hroughout this book, we ask and try to answer many questions about adolescent development. In this first chapter, we evaluate the following questions in turn: What do parents, educators, and scientists want to know about adolescence? What is the nature of interest in adolescence at different points in history? What are today's adolescents like? What is the nature of development?

What Do Parents, Educators, and Scientists Want to Know about Adolescents?

What do you think parents would like to know about their adolescents' development? What do teachers and scientists want to know about adolescents? They all would like to know the most effective ways adults can deal with adolescents.

You have lived through adolescence. I once was an adolescent. No one else experienced adolescence in quite the same way you or I did—your thoughts, feelings, and actions during your adolescent years, like mine, were unique. But we also encountered and handled some experiences in the same ways during adolescence. In high school, we learned many of the same skills that other students learned and grew to care about the same things others cared about. Peers were important to us. And, at one time or another, we probably felt that our parents had no idea what we were all about.

Not only did we feel that our parents misunderstood us, but our parents felt that we misunderstood them. Parents want to know why adolescents have such mercurial moods—happy one moment, sad the next. They want to know why their teenagers talk back to them and challenge their rules and values. They want to know what parenting strategies will help them rear a psychologically healthy, competent adolescent who will become a mature adult. Should they be authoritarian or permissive in dealing with their adolescents? And what should they do when their adolescents increasingly rely on peers to influence their decisions—peers who sometimes have backgrounds and standards the parents detest? Parents worry that their adolescent will have a drinking or smoking problem, take drugs, have sexual intercourse too early, or do poorly in school. They want to know if the situations they are encountering with their adolescents are unique, or if other parents are experiencing the same difficulties and frustrations with their youth.

Educators also have a strong interest in trying to understand adolescents since adolescents spend a large part of their day at school. What is the best way to teach English to a 13-year-old or biology to a 16-year-old? What can educators change about the nature of today's schools that will foster the development of social as well as intellectual competence in adolescents? What can they do in our schools to direct adolescents toward careers that best suit their abilities and desires? And teachers want to know the best strategies for instructing adolescents—for example, should they be more directive or let students be more active in classroom decision making?

BLOOM COUNTY   by Berke Breathed

Growing up has never been easy. However, adolescence is not best viewed as a time of rebellion, crisis, pathology, and deviance. A far more accurate vision of adolescence describes it as a time of evaluation, of decision making, of commitment, and of carving out a place in the world. Most of the problems of today's youth are not with the youth themselves. What adolescents need is access to a range of legitimate opportunities and to long-term support from adults who deeply care about them.

Scientists, as well as parents and educators, are interested in adolescents. They want to know how biological heritage and individual environments influence adolescent behavior. Do the genes inherited some 15 years before still influence how adolescents act, feel, and think? What aspects of family life, peer interaction, school experiences, and cultural standards cause adolescents to become socially responsible or irresponsible?

In answer to these and other questions, scientists develop theories about adolescents. These theories help them to explain why adolescents behave in particular ways, whether they will behave the same way in other circumstances, and what their behavior will be like in the future.

Foremost among the interests of scientists who study adolescents is finding out if adolescents have unique characteristics that set them apart from children and adults. Does the 15-year-old think differently than the 8-year-old? Does the 16-year-old interact differently with her parents than the 10-year-old? Does the 17-year-old view himself differently than the 23-year-old? Do adolescents have problems not found at other points in development? (For example, consider premarital sex and delinquency.)

Scientists are not only interested in what ways adolescents are different from children and adults, but also in how adolescents might be similar to them. Further, scientists would like to know how all adolescents might be similar to each other in some ways and yet different in others.

In their concern for developing a clear demarcation between the child and the adolescent, and between the adolescent and the adult, scientists have debated whether it is appropriate to describe adolescence as a *stage* of development. Does the child's biological, social, and cognitive functioning undergo dramatic transformations at the onset of adolescence, and does something similar occur at the end of adolescence? Or, by contrast, is the child's progress to adolescence smooth (or devoid of abrupt transition) and the adolescent's change to adulthood likewise? Interest in evaluating the unique and stagelike properties of adolescence has led scientists to study youth in a variety of environmental circumstances— adolescents from different historical time periods are compared, as are adolescents who grow up in very different cultures.

Now that we have considered the interests that parents, educators, and scientists have in adolescents, we turn our attention to a historical perspective on adolescence. You will discover that a scientific interest in adolescence developed rather late in history.

Historical Perspective

Our historical view of adolescence begins with an overview of how adolescents were perceived by the early Greeks and then turns to perceptions of adolescents during the Middle Ages and the Enlightenment. Next, we examine the lives of adolescents in America's early years, with special emphasis on the time period 1890–1920. Finally, we evaluate the lives of adolescents in the twentieth century and how easy it is to stereotype the adolescents of any historical time frame.

The Greeks

In early Greece, both Plato and Aristotle commented about the nature of youth. In *The Republic* (fourth century B.C./1968 translation), Plato described three facets of human development (or as he called it, the "soul"): desire, spirit, and reason. According to Plato, reason—the highest of the facets—does not develop in childhood, but rather first appears at about the age period we call adolescence today. Plato argued that, since reason does not mature in childhood, children's education should focus on sports and music. He also emphasized that the onset of rational thought in adolescence requires a change in the educational curricula: Sports and music should be replaced by science and mathematics.

Plato believed that, in the early years of childhood, character, not intellect, should be developed. Even though Plato stressed the importance of early experience in the formation of character, he nonetheless pointed out that experiences in later years could modify character. Arguments about the importance of early experience in human development are still prevalent today. Do the first few years of life determine the adolescent or adult personality? Are later experiences in adolescence just as important in forming and shaping personality as experiences in the early years? We return to the early experience issue later in this chapter.

Aristotle (fourth century B.C./1941 translation) argued that the most important aspect of the age period we now call adolescence is the development of the ability to choose. Aristotle said that this self-determination becomes the hallmark of maturity. Aristotle believed that, at the onset of adolescence, individuals are unstable and impatient, lacking the self-control to be a mature person. But he felt that, by about 21 years of age, most individuals have much better self-control. Aristotle was one of the first individuals to describe specific time periods for stages of human development. He defined three stages: (1) infancy—the first seven years of life; (2) boyhood—age seven to puberty; and (3) young manhood—puberty to age 21. Aristotle's view is not unlike some contemporary views, which use labels like "independence," "identity," and "career choice" to describe the importance of increased self-determination in adolescence.

The Middle Ages and the Enlightenment

Society's view of adolescence changed considerably during the Middle Ages. During the Middle Ages, the child was viewed as a miniature adult. Children and adolescents were believed to entertain the same interests as adults. And since they were simply miniature adults, they were treated as such, with strict, harsh discipline. In the Middle Ages, neither the adolescent nor the child was given status apart from the adult (Muuss, 1989).

During the eighteenth century, Jean Jacques Rousseau offered a more enlightened view of adolescence. Rousseau, a French philosopher, did more than any other individual to restore the belief that a child is not the same as an adult. In *Emile* (1762, 1962 translation), Rousseau argued that treating the child like a miniature adult is potentially harmful. Rousseau believed that, up until the age of 12 or so, children should be free of adult restrictions and allowed to experience their world naturally, rather than having rigid regulations imposed on them.

Rousseau, like Aristotle and Plato, believed that development in childhood and adolescence occurs in a series of stages. From Rousseau's perspective, the four stages of development are:

1. *Infancy* (the first four to five years). The infant is much like an animal with strong physical needs, and the child is hedonistic (dominated by pleasure and pain).

2. *Savage* (5 to 12 years). During this time, sensory development is most important. Sensory experiences, such as play, sports, and games, should be the focus of education. Like Aristotle, Rousseau argued that reason had not developed by the end of this time period.

3. *Stage 3* (12 to 15 years). Reason and self-consciousness develop during this stage, along with an abundance of physical energy. Curiosity should be encouraged in the education of 12- to 15-year-olds by providing a variety of exploratory activities. According to Rousseau, *Robinson Crusoe* is the book to read during this stage of human development because it includes insightful ideas about curiosity and exploratory behavior.

4. *Stage 4* (15 to 20 years). The individual begins to mature emotionally during this time period; interest in others replaces selfishness. Virtues and morals also appear at this point in development.

Rousseau, then, helped to restore the belief that development is stratified, or subject to distinct phases. But his ideas about adolescence were speculative. Other individuals in the nineteenth and twentieth centuries had to bridge the gap between the ideas of philosophers and the empirical approach of scientists.

Adolescence in the Early Years of America

Have adolescents of different eras always had the same interests? Have adolescents always experienced the same kind of academic, work, and family environments as they do today? Today's adolescents spend far more time in school than at work, in structured rather than unstructured environments, and in sessions with their age-mates than did their counterparts of the 1800s and early 1900s. Let's look more closely at what adolescence was like during two time periods in the history of America (Kett, 1977).

The Early Republic, 1790–1840

The migration of young people from the farms to urban life began during the time period 1790–1840. School opportunities became a reality, and career choices grew more varied. However, increasing disorderliness and violence characterized the society.

Work apprenticeships took up much of the day for many adolescent boys, with some apprentices beginning as early as the age of 12, others as late as 16 or 17. Some children left home to become servants even at the age of eight or nine. Many adolescents remained dependent on their families while they engaged in apprentice work experiences. The ages 20 to 25 were then usually filled with indecision. But as in most eras, there were exceptions to this generalization—for example, the man Francis Lieber wrote about in his diary:

> Story from real life. I arrived here in October 1835.
> In January 1836, W ___ and another student were expelled from college on account of a duel. Since that time W ___ has:
> *First:* Shot at this antagonist in the streets of Charleston.
> *Second:* Studied (?) law with Mr. DeSaussure in Charleston.
> *Third:* Married.
> *Fourth:* Been admitted to the Bar.
> *Fifth:* Imprisoned for two months in the above shooting.
> *Sixth:* Become father of fine girl.
> *Seventh:* Practiced law for some time.
> *Eighth:* Been elected a member of the legislature. Now he is only 22 years old. What a state of society this requires and must produce . . . (Perry, 1882, as described in Kett, 1977).

Approaching the Age of Adolescence, 1840–1900

The most important period within the time frame 1840–1900 was from 1880–1900. A gap in economic opportunities developed between lower-class and middle-class adolescents. Middle-class parents were pressed into selecting child-rearing orientations that would ensure the successful placement of their youth in jobs. These child-rearing practices encouraged the adolescent to become passive and conform to societal standards.

To capitalize on the new jobs created by the Industrial Revolution, youth had to stay in school longer and even go on to college. Parents encouraged delay of gratification and self-restraint behaviors because they saw that going to school longer and studying harder meant greater returns for their adolescents in the future.

While college was becoming more of a reality for many youth, it mainly was open to middle-class, but not lower-class, adolescents (Juster & Vinovskis, 1991). Similarly, the youth groups that developed as part of school and church activities were essentially middle class in nature.

The conformity to adult leadership in most of the youth groups coincided with the general orientation of adolescents at this time in America: Adults know what is right; do what they tell you, and you'll get somewhere someday.

The Age of Adolescence

The end of the nineteenth century and the early part of the twentieth century represented an important period in the invention of the concept we now call adolescence. Subsequent changes that adolescents experienced later in the twentieth century also influenced their lives in substantial ways.

The Turn of the Century

Between 1890 and 1920, a number of psychologists, urban reformers, educators, youth workers, and counselors began to mold the concept of adolescence. At this

PERSPECTIVE ON ADOLESCENT DEVELOPMENT 1.1

Adolescence, 1904

G. Stanley Hall's two-volume set, published in 1904, included the following chapters:

Volume I
Chapter

1 Growth in Height and Weight
2 Growth of Parts and Organs during Adolescence
3 Growth of Motor Power and Function
4 Diseases of Body and Mind
5 Juvenile Faults, Immoralities, and Crimes
6 Sexual Development: Its Dangers and Hygiene in Boys
7 Periodicity
8 Adolescence in Literature, Biography, and History

Volume II

9 Changes in the Sense and Voice
10 Evolution and the Feelings and Instincts Characteristic of Normal Adolescence
11 Adolescent Love
12 Adolescent Feelings toward Nature and a New Education in Science
13 Savage Public Initiations, Classical Ideals and Customs, and Church Confirmations
14 The Adolescent Psychology of Conversion
15 Social Instincts and Institutions
16 Intellectual Development and Education
17 Adolescent Girls and their Education
18 Ethnic Psychology and Pedagogy, or Adolescent Races and their Treatment

G. Stanley Hall.

time, young people, especially boys, no longer were viewed as decadent problem causers, but instead were seen as increasingly passive and vulnerable—qualities previously associated only with the adolescent female. When G. Stanley Hall's book on adolescence was published in 1904, as discussed in the next section, it played a major role in restructuring thinking about adolescents. Hall said that, while many adolescents appear to be passive, they are experiencing considerable turmoil within.

Educators, counselors, and psychologists began to develop norms of behavior for adolescents. Hall's storm-and-stress concept influenced these norms considerably. As a result, adults attempted to impose conformity and passivity on adolescents in the 1900–1920 period. Examples of this conformity included the encouragement of school spirit, loyalty, and hero worship on athletic teams.

Hall's strong emphasis on the biological basis of adolescence can be seen in the large number of chapters on physical growth, instincts, and evolution. His concern for education also is evident, as is his interest in religion.

Further insight into Hall's concept of adolescence can be gleaned from his preface to the volumes:

> Development (in adolescence) is less gradual and more saltatory, suggestive of some ancient period of storm and stress when old moorings were broken and a higher level attained. . . . Nature arms youth for conflict with all the resources at her command—speed, power of shoulder, biceps, back, leg, jaw—strengthens and enlarges skull, thorax, hips, makes man aggressive and prepares woman's frame for maternity. . . .
>
> Sex asserts its mastery in field after field, and works its havoc in the form of secret vice, debauch, disease, and enfeebled heredity, cadences the soul to both its normal and abnormal rhythms, and sends many thousand youth a year to quacks, because neither parents, teachers, preachers, or physicians know how to deal with its problems. . . . The social instincts undergo sudden unfoldment and the new life of love awakens. . . . Youth awakes to a new world and understands neither it nor himself. . . .
>
> Never has youth been exposed to such dangers of both perversion and arrest as in our land and day. Urban life has increased temptations, prematurities, sedentary occupations, and passive stimuli, just when an active, objective life is most needed. Adolescents' lives today lack some of the regulations they still have in older lands with more conservative traditions. . . . (Volume I, pp. xi, xiii, xv)

Hall's preoccupation with the evils of adolescence are threaded throughout the texts. This is nowhere more clear than in his comments about masturbation:

> One of the very saddest of all the aspects of human weakness and sin is [masturbation]. . . . Tissot, in 1759, found every pupil guilty. . . . Dr. G. Bachin (1895) argued that growth, especially in the moral and intellectual regions, is dwarfed and stunted [by masturbation]. Bachin also felt that masturbation caused gray hairs, and especially baldness, a stooping and enfeebled gait. . . .
>
> Perhaps masturbation is the most perfect type of individual vice and sin . . . it is the acme of selfishness.
>
> Prominent among predisposing causes are often placed erotic reading, pictures, and theatrical presentations. . . . Schiller protests against trousers pockets for boys, as do others against feather beds, while even horseback riding and the bicycle have been placed under the ban by a few extremist writers.
>
> . . . The medical cures of masturbation that have been prescribed are almost without number: bromide, ergot, lupin, blistering, clitoridectomy, section of certain nerves, small mechanical appliances, of which the Patent Office at Washington has quite a collection. Regimen rather than special treatment must, however, be chiefly relied on. Work reduces temptation, and so does early rising. . . . Good music is a moral tonic. . . . (Volume I, pp. 411–471)

Clearly, our current beliefs about masturbation differ substantially from those of Hall's time. As indicated in the overview of chapters in Hall's volumes, he wrote about many other aspects of adolescence in addition to sex and masturbation. His books are entertaining as well as informative. You are encouraged to look up his original work in your library and compare his comments with those made about adolescence in this text.

G. Stanley Hall

Historians label G. Stanley Hall (1844–1924) the father of the scientific study of adolescence. Hall's ideas were first published in the two-volume set *Adolescence* in 1904. Perspective on Adolescent Development 1.1 provides a sampling of Hall's book.

Hall was strongly influenced by Charles Darwin, the famous evolutionary theorist. Hall applied the scientific and biological dimensions of Darwin's view to the study of adolescent development. Hall believed that all development is controlled by genetically determined physiological factors and that environment plays a minimal role in development, especially during infancy and childhood. He did acknowledge, however, that environment accounts for more change in

Anthropologist Margaret Mead (left) with a Samoan adolescent girl. Mead found that adolescence in Samoa was relatively stress-free, although recently her findings have been challenged. Mead's observations and analysis challenged G. Stanley Hall's biological, storm-and-stress view and called attention to the sociocultural basis of adolescence.

development in adolescence than in earlier periods. Thus, at least with regard to adolescence, Hall believed—as we do today—that heredity interacts with environmental influences to determine the individual's development.

Like Rousseau, Hall subscribed to a four-stage approach to development: infancy, childhood, youth, and adolescence. According to Hall, adolescence is the period from 12 to 23 years of age and is filled with storm and stress. The **storm-and-stress view** *is Hall's concept that adolescence is a turbulent time charged with conflict and mood swings.* Hall borrowed the "storm-and-stress" label from the *Sturm und Drang* descriptions of German writers, such as Goethe and Schiller, who wrote novels full of idealism, commitment to goals, passion, feeling, and revolution. Hall sensed that there was a parallel between the themes of the German authors and the psychological development of adolescents. In Hall's view, adolescents' thoughts, feelings, and actions oscillate between conceit and humility, good and temptation, happiness and sadness. The adolescent may be nasty to a peer one moment, kind the next moment. At one time, the adolescent may want to be alone, but seconds later seek companionship.

Hall's views had implications for the social development and education of adolescents (White, 1985). Hall conceived of development as a biological process that directed social development. In Hall's view, biological changes in adolescence allow for more complicated social arrangements, such as dating. With regard to education, Hall said that such faculties as civility, scientific thinking, and morality should be intensely taught after the age of 15. However, Hall's developmental vision of education rested mainly on highly speculative theory, rather than scientific data. While Hall believed systematic methods should be used to study adolescents, his research efforts resorted to the creation of rather weak and unconvincing questionnaires.

Even though the quality of his research was suspect, Hall was a giant in the field of adolescence. It was he who began the theorizing, the systematizing, and the questioning that went beyond mere speculating and philosophizing. Indeed, we owe the scientific beginnings of adolescent development to Hall.

Margaret Mead's Sociocultural View of Adolescence

Anthropologist Margaret Mead (1928) studied adolescents on the South Sea island of Samoa. She concluded that the basic nature of adolescents is not biological, as Hall envisioned, but rather sociocultural. She argued that, when cultures provide a smooth, gradual transition from childhood to adulthood, which is the way adolescence is handled in Samoa, little storm and stress is associated with the period. Mead's observations of Samoan adolescents revealed that their lives were relatively free of storm and stress. Mead concluded that cultures that allow adolescents to observe sexual relations, see babies born, regard death as natural, do important work, engage in sex play, and know clearly what their adult roles will be promote a relatively stress-free adolescence. However, in cultures like the United States, in which children are considered very different from adults and where adolescence is not characterized by the aforementioned experiences, adolescence is more likely to be stressful.

More than half a century after Mead's Samoan findings, her work was criticized as being biased and error-prone (Freeman, 1983). The current criticism also states that Samoan adolescence is more stressful than Mead observed and that delinquency appears among Samoan adolescents just as it does among Western adolescents. In the current controversy over Mead's findings, some researchers have defended Mead's work (Holmes, 1987).

The Inventionist View

While adolescence has a biological base, as G. Stanley Hall believed, it also has a sociocultural base, as Margaret Mead believed. Indeed, sociohistorical conditions contributed to the emergence of the concept of adolescence. In the quote that opens this chapter, P. Musgrove comments about the teenager sneaking up on us in our own lifetime. At a point not too long ago in history, the teenager had not yet been invented. The **inventionist view** *states that adolescence is a sociohistorical creation. Especially important in the inventionist view of adolescence were the sociohistorical circumstances at the beginning of the twentieth century, a time when legislation was enacted that ensured the dependency of youth and made their move into the economic sphere more manageable.* We discussed many of these sociohistorical circumstances in our overview of the historical background of adolescence. They included the decline in apprenticeship; increased mechanization during the Industrial Revolution, which also involved upgraded skill requirements of labor and specialized divisions of labor; the separation of work and home; the writings of G. Stanley Hall; urbanization; the appearance of youth groups, such as the YMCA and the Boy Scouts; and age-segregated schools.

Schools, work, and economics are important dimensions of the inventionist view of adolescence (Elder, 1975; Field, 1981; Hill, 1980a; Lapsley, Enright, & Serlin, 1985; Lapsley & Rice, 1988b; Mirel, 1991). Some scholars on adolescence argue that the concept of adolescence was invented mainly as a by-product of the motivation to create a system of compulsory public education. In this view, the function of secondary schools is to transmit intellectual skills to youth (Callahan, 1962; Cremin, 1961; Stedman & Smith, 1983). However, other scholars on adolescence argue that the primary purpose of secondary schools is to deploy youth within the economic sphere and to serve as an important cog in the culture's authority structure (Lapsley, Enright, & Serlin, 1985). In this view, the American society "inflicted" the status of adolescence on its youth through child-saving legislation. By developing laws for youth, the adult power structure placed youth in a submissive position that restricted their options, encouraged their dependency, and made their move into the world of work more manageable.

Historians now call the period of 1890–1920 the "age of adolescence" because they believe that it was during this time frame that the concept of adolescence was invented. During this time, a great deal of compulsory legislation aimed at youth was enacted (Tyack, 1976). In virtually every state, laws that excluded youth from most employment and required them to attend secondary school were passed. Extensive enforcement provisions by states characterized much of this legislation.

Two clear changes resulted from this legislation: decreased employment and increased school attendance by youth. From 1910 to 1930, the number of 10- to 15-year-olds who were gainfully employed dropped about 75 percent. In addition, between 1900 and 1930, the number of high school graduates substantially increased (see Table 1.1). Approximately 600 percent more individuals graduated from high school in this 30-year time frame.

A recent analysis of the content of the oldest continuing journal in developmental psychology (*Journal of Genetic Psychology*—earlier called *Pedagogical Seminary*) provided further evidence of history's role in the perception of adolescents (Enright & others, 1987). Four historical periods—the depressions of the 1890s and 1930s, and the two world wars—were evaluated. During the depression periods, scholars talked about the psychological immaturity of youth and their educational needs. In contrast, during the world wars, scholars did not describe youth as immature, but rather underscored their importance as draftees and factory workers.

Table 1.1 Percentage of Growth in High School Graduation, 1870–1940

Year	% Change
1870	
1880	50
1890	83
1900	116
1910	64
1920	112
1930	101
1940	83

Source: Series H598–681, *Historical Statistics of the United States.*

Further Changes in the Twentieth Century

During the three decades from 1920 to 1950, adolescents gained a more prominent status in society as they went through a number of complex changes. The lives of adolescents took a turn for the better in the 1920s but moved through difficult times in the 1930s and 1940s. In the 1920s, the Roaring Twenties atmosphere rubbed off on adolescents. Passivity and conformity to adult leadership were replaced by increased autonomy and conformity to peer values. Adults began to model the styles of youth, rather than vice versa. If a new dance came in vogue, the adolescent girl did it first and her mother learned it from her. Prohibition was the law of the time, but many adolescents drank heavily. More permissive attitudes toward the opposite sex developed, and kissing parties were standard fare. Short skirts even led to a campaign by the YWCA against such abnormal behavior (Lee, 1970).

Just when adolescence was getting to be fun, the Great Depression arrived in the 1930s, followed by World War II in the 1940s. Serious economic and political concerns replaced the hedonistic adolescent values of the 1920s. Radical protest groups that were critical of the government increased in number during the 1930s, and World War II exposed adolescents to another serious, life-threatening event. Military service provided travel and exposure to other youth from different parts of the United States. This experience promoted a broader perspective on life and a greater sense of independence.

By 1950, the development period we refer to as adolescence had come of age—not only did it possess physical and social identity, but legal attention was paid to it as well. Every state had developed special laws for youth between the ages of 16 and 18 or 20. Adolescents in the 1950s have been described as the silent generation (Lee, 1970). Life was much better for adolescents in the 1950s than it had been in the 1930s and 1940s. The government was paying for many individuals' college educations through the GI bill, and television was beginning to invade most homes. Getting a college degree, the key to a good job, was on the minds of many adolescents during the 1950s—so were getting married, having a family, and settling down to the life of luxury displayed in television commercials.

While the pursuit of higher education persisted among adolescents in the 1960s, it became painfully apparent that many Black adolescents not only were being denied a college education, but were receiving an inferior secondary education as well. Ethnic conflicts in the form of riots and "sit-ins" were pervasive, with college-age adolescents among the most vocal participants.

The political protest of adolescents reached a peak in the late 1960s and early 1970s, when millions of adolescents violently reacted to what they saw as unreasonable American participation in the Vietnam War. As parents watched the 1968 Democratic presidential nominating committee, they not only saw political speeches in support of candidates but their adolescents fighting with the police, yelling obscenities at adults, and staging sit-ins.

Parents became more concerned in the 1960s about teenage drug use and abuse than in past eras. Sexual permissiveness in the form of premarital sex, cohabitation, and endorsement of previously prohibited sexual conduct also increased.

By the mid-1970s, much of the radical protest of adolescents had abated and was replaced by increased concern for an achievement-oriented, upwardly mobile career to be attained through hard work in high school, college, or a vocational training school. Material interests began to dominate adolescent motives again, while ideological challenges to social institutions seemed to become less central.

(a)

(b)

(c)

(a) The Roaring Twenties was a time when adolescents began to behave more permissively. Adults began to model the styles of youth. Adolescent drinking increased dramatically. (b) In the 1940s, many youth served in World War II. Military service exposed many youth to life-threatening circumstances and allowed them to see firsthand the way people in other countries live. (c) In the 1950s, many youth developed a stronger orientation toward education. Television was piped into many homes for the first time. One of the fads of the 1950s, shown here, was seeing how many people could squeeze into a phone booth. (d) In the late 1960s, many youth protested U.S. participation in the Vietnam War. Parents became more concerned about adolescent drug use as well. (e) In the 1970s, 1980s, and 1990s, much of the radical protest of youth quieted down. Today's adolescents are achievement-oriented, more likely to be working at a job, experiencing adult roles earlier, showing more interest in equality of the sexes, and heavily influenced by the media.

(d)

(e)

The greatest amount of protest in the 1970s involved the women's movement. The descriptions of adolescents in America in earlier years pertained more to adolescent males than females. The family and career objectives of adolescent females today would barely be recognized by the adolescent females of the 1890s and early 1900s. Later in the text, much more will be said about the increased participation of adolescent females in the work force, including the impact this movement has had on the family and on the female adolescent's relationships with males.

(a)

(b)

In the study by Offer and his colleagues (1988), a healthy self-image characterized at least 73 percent of the adolescents studied around the world, including adolescents from (a) Turkey and (b) Japan.

We have described some important sociohistorical circumstances experienced by adolescents, and we have described how society viewed adolescents at different points in history. As we see next, caution needs to be exercised in generalizing about the adolescents of any era.

Stereotyping Adolescents

It is easy to stereotype a person, groups of people, or classes of people. A **stereotype** *is a broad category that reflects our impressions and beliefs about people. All stereotypes refer to an image of what the typical member of a particular group is like.* We live in a complex world and strive to simplify this complexity. Stereotyping people is one way we do this. We simply assign a label to a group of people—for example, "Youth are promiscuous." Then we have much less to consider when we think about this set of people. Once we assign stereotypes, it is difficult to abandon them, even in the face of contradictory evidence.

Stereotypes about adolescents are plentiful: "They say they want a job, but when they get one, they don't want to work"; "They are all lazy"; "They are all sex fiends"; "They are all into drugs, every last one of them"; "Kids today don't have the moral fiber of my generation"; "The problem with adolescents today is that they all have it too easy"; "They are a bunch of egotistical smart alecks"; and so it goes.

Indeed, during most of the twentieth century, adolescents have been described as abnormal and deviant, rather than normal and nondeviant. Consider Hall's image of storm and stress. Consider also media portrayals of adolescents as rebellious, conflicted, faddish, delinquent, and self-centered—*Rebel without a Cause* in the late 1950s, and *Easy Rider* in the 1960s, for example. Consider also the current image of adolescents as stressed and disturbed, from *Sixteen Candles* and *The Breakfast Club* in the 1980s to *Boyz in the Hood* in the 1990s (Allen & Santrock, 1993). Such stereotyping of adolescents is so widespread that adolescence researcher Joseph Adelson (1979) called it the **adolescent generalization gap,** *meaning that widespread generalizations about adolescents have developed that are based on information about a limited, often highly visible group of adolescents.*

Two studies illustrate the widespread stereotyping of adolescents. In the first study, Daniel Yankelovich (1974) compared the attitudes of adolescents with those of their parents about different values, life-styles, and codes of personal conduct. There was little or no difference in the attitudes of the adolescents and their parents regarding self-control, hard work, saving money, competition, compromise, legal authority, and private property. There was a substantial difference between the adolescents and their parents with regard to religion (89 percent of the parents said that religion was important to them, compared to only 66 percent of the adolescents). But note that a majority of the adolescents still subscribed to the belief that religion is important.

Daniel Offer and his colleagues (1988) also documented a stereotypical view of adolescence as highly stressful and disturbed. The self-images of adolescents around the world—in the United States, Australia, Bangladesh, Hungary, Israel, Italy, Japan, Taiwan, Turkey, and West Germany—were sampled. A healthy self-image characterized at least 73 percent of the adolescents studied. They appeared to be moving toward adulthood with a healthy integration of previous experiences, self-confidence, and optimism about the future. While there were some differences in the adolescents, they were happy most of the time, they enjoyed life, they perceived themselves as able to exercise self-control, they valued work and school, they expressed confidence about their sexual selves, they expressed positive feelings toward their families, and they felt they had the capability to cope with life's stresses—not exactly a storm-and-stress portrayal of adolescence.

Beginning with G. Stanley Hall's portrayal of adolescence as a period of storm and stress, for much of this century in the United States and other Western cultures, adolescence has unfortunately been perceived as a problematic period of the human life cycle that youth, their families, and society had to endure (Offer & Church, 1991a,b). But as the two research studies just described indicate, a large majority of adolescents are not nearly as disturbed and troubled as the popular stereotype of adolescence suggests. Public attitudes about adolescence emerge from a combination of personal experience and media portrayals, neither of which produces an objective picture of how normal adolescents develop (Feldman & Elliott, 1990).

Some of the readiness to assume the worst about adolescents likely involves the short memories of adults. Many adults measure their current perceptions of adolescents by memories of their own adolescence. Adults often portray today's adolescents as more troubled, less respectful, more self-centered, more assertive, and more adventurous than they were.

However, in matters of taste and manners, the youth of every generation have seemed radical, unnerving, and different from adults—different in how they look, how they behave, the music they enjoy, their hairstyles, and the clothing they choose. But it is an enormous error to confuse the adolescent's enthusiasm for trying on new identities and enjoying moderate amounts of outrageous behavior with hostility toward parental and societal standards. Acting-out and boundary-testing are time-honored ways in which adolescents move toward accepting, rather than rejecting, parental values. When my oldest daughter, Tracy, was in her first year of high school, my wife was certain that Tracy was going to waste—she detested Tracy's taste in clothes and hairstyle, didn't like Tracy's friends, didn't care for the boys Tracy was dating, thought she was underachieving in school, and was frightened by some of her escapades. Tracy is now in her early twenties, and observers would be hard-pressed to find vestiges of her earlier so-called immaturity. Tracy's values have become similar to her parents', and her mother no longer worries as much about Tracy's ability to become a competent adult.

As mentioned earlier, stereotypes of adolescence are also generated by media portrayals of youth (Condry, 1989; Feldman & Elliott, 1990). The media often present sensational and "newsworthy" material, which means that they are far more likely to focus on troubled adolescents than normal adolescents. Such media coverage conveys the impression that a majority of youth engage in deviant behaviors, when in fact only a small minority recurrently do. As we see next in our consideration of today's adolescents, not only do media messages convey an image of adolescents as highly troubled, but the messages to adolescents from both adults and the media are often ambivalent.

Today's Adolescents

What is the current status of adolescents compared to the status of their counterparts earlier in history? Do adults have idealized images of adolescents, and does society communicate ambivalent messages to adolescents? How complex is adolescent development today? Should our nation's social policy toward adolescence be changed? We consider each of these questions in turn.

The Current Status of Adolescents

Today's adolescents face demands and expectations, as well as risks and temptations, that appear to be more numerous and complex than did adolescents only a generation ago (Feldman & Elliott, 1990). Nonetheless, contrary to the popular stereotype of adolescents as highly stressed and incompetent, the vast majority of adolescents successfully negotiate the path from childhood to adulthood (Offer & Church, 1991a,b). By some criteria, today's adolescents are doing better than their counterparts from a decade or two earlier. Today, more American adolescents—especially Black adolescents—complete high school. In the last few years, adolescent accidents and homicides have declined somewhat, as have drug use, juvenile delinquency, and adolescent pregnancy rates. Most adolescents today have positive self-conceptions and positive relationships with others. As indicated earlier, such contemporary findings do not support a portrayal of adolescence as a highly disturbed, overly stressful time period in the life cycle. Rather, the majority of adolescents find the transition from childhood to adulthood a time of physical, cognitive, and social development that provides considerable challenge, opportunities, and growth.

Yet, while most adolescents experience the transition from childhood to adulthood more positively than is portrayed by many adults and the media, too many adolescents today are not provided with adequate opportunities and support to become competent adults. In many ways, today's adolescents are presented with a less stable environment than adolescents of a decade or two ago. High divorce rates, high adolescent pregnancy rates, and increased geographic mobility of families contribute to this lack of stability in adolescents' lives. Today's adolescents are exposed to a complex menu of life-style options through the media. And while the adolescent drug rate is beginning to show signs of decline, the rate of adolescent drug use in the United States is the highest of any country in the industrialized Western world. Many of today's adolescents face these temptations, as well as sexual activity, at increasingly young ages.

The previous discussion underscores an important point about adolescents: They are not a homogeneous group of individuals. Most adolescents negotiate the lengthy path to adult maturity successfully, but too large a minority do not. Ethnic, cultural, gender, socioeconomic, age, and life-style differences influence the actual life trajectory of each adolescent. Different portrayals of adolescence often emerge, depending on the particular group of adolescents being described. As we see next, some of the problems faced by today's adolescents involve adults' idealized images of what adolescents should be and society's ambivalent messages to adolescents.

Idealized Images of What Adolescents Should Be and Society's Ambivalent Messages to Adolescents

Adolescent developmental researchers Shirley Feldman and Glenn Elliott (1990) described how American society seems uncertain about what adolescence should be or should not be. The following examples illustrate how adults' idealized images of adolescents and society's ambivalent messages to adolescents may contribute to adolescents' problems:

- Many adults treasure the independence of youth, yet insist that adolescents do not have the maturity to make autonomous, competent decisions about their lives. Some of the ambiguity in messages about adult status and maturity that society communicates to adolescents appears in the form of laws dictating that they cannot drive until they are 16, vote until they are 18, or drink until age 21. Yet, in some states, 14-year-olds now have the legal right to choose the parent with whom they want to live after a parental divorce and to override parental wishes about such medical matters as abortion and psychiatric care.

- Society's sexual messages to adolescents are especially ambiguous. Adolescents are somehow supposed to be sexually naive but become sexually knowledgeable. The message to many adolescents is: "You can experiment with sex and sow your wild oats, but be sure to maintain high standards of maturity and safety." Adolescents must negotiate this formidable task in a society that cannot agree on how much and what kind of explicit sex education adolescents should be given. This same society sanctions alluring messages about the power and attractiveness of sexuality in the media.
- Laws prohibit adolescents from using alcohol, tobacco, or other drugs, and adults decry the high level of drug use by adolescents. Yet, many of the very same adults who stereotype and criticize adolescents for their drug use are themselves drug abusers and heavy cigarette smokers.
- Society promotes education and the development of knowledge as essential to success as an adult. Yet, adolescents frequently observe the rewards society doles out to individuals who develop their athletic skills and business acumen. As adolescents interact with adults who do not value the process of learning, adolescents may attach more importance to simply attaining a diploma than the process of getting one.

We have seen that understanding the current status of adolescents requires consideration of their heterogeneity. In addition, many adults have idealized images of adolescents and communicate ambivalent messages to them. To further understand today's adolescents, we turn our attention to the increased recognition of the complexity of adolescent development.

The Complexity of Adolescent Development and Sociocultural Contexts

As researchers more carefully examine the lives of adolescents, they are recognizing that a single developmental model may not accurately characterize all adolescents (Feldman & Elliott, 1990). The most widely described general model of adolescent development states that adolescence is a transition from childhood to adulthood during which individuals explore alternatives and experiment with choices as part of developing an identity. While this model may accurately fit many White, middle-class adolescents, it is less well suited to adolescents from low-income families, school dropouts, and unemployed adolescents. For many of these youth, development often is more chaotic and restricted. For such youth, social and ethnic barriers too frequently signal the presence of discrimination and prejudice.

Of special importance is the growing interest in the sociocultural contexts of adolescent development (Aber & others, 1992; Dornbusch, Petersen, & Hetherington, 1991; Garnets & others, 1991; Lerner, 1991; Spencer, 1992; Spencer & Dornbusch, 1991). **Contexts** *refer to the settings in which development occurs, settings influenced by historical, economic, social, and cultural factors.* To sense how important contexts are in understanding adolescent development, consider a researcher who wants to discover whether today's adolescents are more racially tolerant than they were a decade ago. Without reference to the historical, economic, social, and cultural aspects of race relations, adolescents' racial tolerance cannot be fully understood. Each adolescent's development occurs against a cul-

Culture, ethnicity, and gender are three important sociocultural contexts in adolescents' lives. How extensively are the ethnic and gender worlds of American adolescents changing?

tural backdrop of contexts. These contexts or settings include homes, schools, peer groups, churches, cities, neighborhoods, communities, university laboratories, the United States, China, Mexico, Japan, Egypt, and many others, each with meaningful historical, economic, social, and cultural legacies.

Three sociocultural contexts that many adolescent researchers believe merit special attention are culture, ethnicity, and gender, each of which we discuss in turn. **Culture** *refers to the behavior patterns, beliefs, and all other products of a particular group of people that are passed on from generation to generation.* The products result from the interaction between groups of people and their environment over many years. A cultural group can be as large as the United States or as small as an African hunter-gatherer group. Whatever its size, the group's culture influences the identity, learning, and social behavior of its members (Brislin, 1990, 1991; Lonner, 1990, 1991; Solantaus, 1992; Whiting & Whiting, 1991). For example, the United States is an achievement-oriented culture with a strong work ethic, but recent comparisons of American and Japanese children and youth revealed that the Japanese were better at math, spent more time working on math in school, and spent more time doing homework than Americans (Stevenson, 1991; Stevenson & others, 1990). **Cross-cultural studies**—*the comparison of a culture with one or more other cultures—provide information about the degree to which adolescent development is similar, or* universal, *across cultures, or the degree to which it is* culture-specific.

Ethnicity *(the word* ethnic *comes from the Greek word for "nation") is based on cultural heritage, nationality characteristics, race, religion, and language.* Ethnicity is central to the development of an **ethnic identity,** *which is a sense of membership based upon the shared language, religion, customs, values, history, and race of an ethnic group.* Each of you is a member of one or more ethnic groups. Your ethnic identity reflects your deliberate decision to identify with an ancestor or ancestral group. If you are of Native American (American Indian) and African slave ancestry, you might choose to align yourself with the traditions and history of Native Americans, although an outsider might believe that your identity is African American. Nowhere are sociocultural changes more profound than in the increasing ethnic diversity of America's adolescents (Allen & Santrock, 1993; Busch-Rossnagel & Zayas, 1991; Gibbs, 1991; Phinney, Espinoza, & Onwughalu, 1992; Ramirez, 1990; Spencer, 1992; Sue, 1990) (see Figure 1.1).

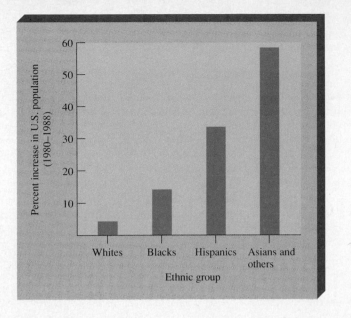

Figure 1.1 The increasing ethnic minority population in the United States. As shown in the graph, from 1980 to 1988, the percentages of Black, Hispanic, and Asian individuals increased dramatically more than that for Whites in the United States. The greatest increase occurred for Asians and Hispanics.

Twenty percent of all American children and adolescents under the age of 17 in 1989 came from ethnic minority groups—Blacks, Hispanics, Native Americans, and Asians. Projections indicate that, by the year 2000, one-third of all school-age children will fall into this category. This changing demographic tapestry promises not only the richness that diversity produces but also difficult challenges in extending the American dream to individuals of all ethnic and minority groups. Historically, ethnic minorities have found themselves at the bottom of the economic and social order. They have been disproportionately represented among the poor and the inadequately educated. Half of all Black adolescents and one-third of all Hispanic adolescents live in poverty. School dropout rates for minority youth reach the alarming figure of 60 percent in some urban areas. More about the nature of ethnic minority adolescents in the United States appears in Sociocultural Worlds of Adolescence 1.1.

Recently, some individuals have voiced dissatisfaction with the use of the term *minority* within the phrase *ethnic minority group*. Some individuals have also objected to using the term *Blacks* or *Black Americans*, preferring instead the term *African Americans* to emphasize their ancestry. Such dissatisfaction and objections stem from traditionally associating the term *minority* with inferiority and deficits. Further, the concept of minority implies that there is a majority. Indeed, it can be argued that there really is no majority in the United States because Whites are actually composed of many different ethnic groups, and Whites are not a majority in the world. When the term *ethnic minority* is used in this text, the use is intentional—not to imply that ethnic minority adolescents should be viewed as inferior or deficient in some way, but to convey the impact that minority status has had on many ethnic minority adolescents. The circumstances of each ethnic group are not solely a function of its own culture. Rather, many ethnic groups have experienced considerable discrimination and prejudice. For example, patterns of alcohol abuse among Native American adolescents cannot be fully understood without considering the exploitation that has accompanied Native Americans' history (Sue, 1990).

A third, very important dimension of sociocultural contexts that is receiving increased attention is gender. **Gender** *is the sociocultural definition of male and female,* while sex refers to the biological dimension of being male or female

Psychologist Rhoda Unger (shown talking with college students) urges psychologists to use the word sex *only when referring to biological mechanisms (such as sex chromosomes or sexual anatomy) and to use the word* gender *only when describing the social, cultural, and psychological aspects of being male or female. Like Unger, psychologist Carolyn Sherif noted some of the problems the word* sex *has brought to the study of gender. Sherif argued that the term* sex roles *uncritically couples a biological concept (sex) with a sociocultural, psychological concept (gender). Sherif stressed that through this coupling many myths about sex may be smuggled into the concept of sociocultural aspects of male and female roles, causing confusion and possible stereotyping.*

The Increasing Ethnic Diversity of Adolescents in the United States

Population trends and U.S. inability to prepare ethnic minority adolescents for full participation in American life have produced an imperative for the social institutions that serve ethnic minorities (Gibbs & Huang, 1989; Spencer, 1991, 1992; Sue, 1990). Schools, colleges, social services, health and mental health agencies, juvenile probation services, and other programs need to become more sensitive to ethnic issues and to provide improved services to ethnic minority and low-income adolescents (Busch-Rossnagel & Zayas, 1991; Fenzel, 1992; Gibbs, 1991).

An especially important idea in considering the nature of cultural and ethnic groups is that not only is there ethnic diversity within a culture—the American culture includes Anglo Americans, Black Americans, Hispanic Americans, Native Americans, Asian Americans, Italian Americans, Polish Americans, and so on—but there is also diversity within each ethnic group. No cultural characteristic is common to all or nearly all Black Americans, or all or nearly all Hispanic Americans, and absent in Anglo Americans, unless it is the experience of being Black or of being Hispanic and the beliefs that develop from that experience (Havighurst, 1987).

Black Americans make up the largest easily visible ethnic minority group in the United States. Black Americans are distributed throughout the social class structure, although they constitute a larger proportion of low-income individuals than the majority Anglo American group (Bell-Scott & Taylor, 1989; McLoyd, in press). The majority of Black youth stay in school, do not take drugs, do not marry prematurely, and grow up to lead productive lives in spite of social and economic disadvantages.

Hispanic Americans also are a diverse group of individuals. Not all Hispanic Americans are Catholic, and not all of them have a Mexican heritage. Many of them have cultural ties with South American countries, with Puerto Rico or other Caribbean countries, or with Spain (Marín & Marín, 1991; Pacheco & Valdez, 1989; Ramirez, 1990; Wall, 1992).

Native Americans also are an extremely diverse and complicated ethnic group (Trimble, 1989), with 511 identifiable tribal units. More than 30 distinct groups are listed under the Asian American designation (Wong, 1982). And within each of the 511 identifiable Native American tribes and 30 distinct Asian American groups is considerable diversity and individual variation.

America has embraced new ingredients from many cultures, and the cultures often mix their beliefs and identities. Some of the culture of origin is retained, some of it is lost, and some of it is mixed with the American culture. As ethnic minority groups continue to expand at a rapidly increasing rate, an important agenda in the next decade is to give increased attention to the role of culture and ethnicity in understanding adolescent development.

The tapestry of American culture has changed dramatically in recent years. Nowhere is the change more noticeable than in the increasing ethnic diversity of America's citizens. Ethnic minority groups—Blacks, Hispanics, Native Americans (American Indians), and Asians, for example—will make up approximately one-third of all individuals under the age of 17 in the United States by the year 2000. One of society's challenges is to become more sensitive to ethnicity and to provide improved services to ethnic minority individuals.

Table 1.2 One Day in the Lives of American Youths

Every day 7 teenagers and 10 young adults are the victims of homicide.

Every day, 10 teenagers and 13 young adults are killed by firearms.

Every day, 39 youths ages 15 to 24 are killed in motor vehicle accidents.

Every day, 604 teenagers contract syphilis or gonorrhea.

Every day, an estimated 1,140 teenagers have abortions.

Every day, teenagers give birth to 1,336 babies and teens younger than 15 give birth to 29 babies.

Every day of the school year, 2,478 teenagers drop out of school.

Every day, 4,901 teenagers and 2,976 young adults are the victims of violent crime.

Every day, 7,742 teenagers become sexually active.

Every day, 8,826 teenagers and 6,235 young adults are the victims of theft.

134,000 teenagers use cocaine once a week or more.

580,000 teenagers use marijuana once a week or more.

454,000 junior and senior high school students are weekly binge drinkers.

8 million junior and senior high school students drink alcohol weekly.

Every month, an average of 1.1 million teenagers and 1.2 million young adults are unemployed.

Adolescent and Young Adult Factbook, p. 2, Children's Defense Fund, Washington, DC, 1991. Used with permission.

(Sherif, 1982). Few aspects of adolescent development are more central to adolescents' identity and to their social relationships than their sex or gender (Linn & Hyde, 1991; Tavris, 1991). Society's gender attitudes are changing. But how much? Is there a limit to how much society can determine what is appropriate behavior for male and female adolescents? A special concern of many feminist writers and scholars is that much of the history of interest in adolescence portrays adolescent development with a "male dominant theme" (DeFour & Paludi, in press; Denmark & Paludi, in press). Just as important themes of this book are to examine cross-cultural issues and the role of ethnicity, an important theme is also to extensively examine gender issues. Chapter 9 is devoted exclusively to culture and ethnicity. Chapter 11 is devoted exclusively to gender. Throughout the book, you also will read about issues involving culture, ethnicity, and gender in "Sociocultural Worlds of Adolescence" boxes and in various chapter discussions. As we see next, increased recognition of the importance of sociocultural contexts dictates that we carefully examine our society's social policy regarding adolescents' development.

Social Policy and Adolescents' Development

Social policy *is a national government's course of action designed to influence the welfare of its citizens.* A current trend is to conduct adolescent development research that will lead to wise and effective decision making in the area of social policy (Gallagher, 1989; Huston, 1991; Klerman, 1991; McLoyd & Wilson, 1991; Scales, 1992). Because more than 25 percent of adolescents and more than half of all ethnic minority adolescents are being raised in poverty, because between 40 and 50 percent of all adolescents will spend at least a portion of their youth in a single-parent home, because children and young adolescents are giving birth, because the use and abuse of drugs is widespread among adolescents, and because the spectre of AIDS is spreading, the United States needs revised social policy related to adolescents (Horowitz & O'Brien, 1989). Table 1.2 vividly portrays one day in the lives of American youths, suggesting the importance of improved social policy for youth.

Adolescents who do not reach their full potential, who are destined to make fewer contributions to society than it needs, and who do not take their place as productive adults diminish the power of that society's future. To help adolescents reach their full potential, shifts in social policy need to be implemented.

The shape and scope of social policies related to adolescents are heavily influenced by the U.S. political system, which is based on negotiation and compromise (Garwood & others, 1989). The values held by individual lawmakers, the nation's economic strengths and weaknesses, and partisan politics all influence the policy agenda and whether the welfare of adolescents will be improved (Spencer, 1990). Developmentalists can play an important role in social policy related to adolescents by helping to develop more positive public opinion for comprehensive legislation involving the welfare of adolescents, by contributing to and promoting research that will benefit adolescents' welfare, and by providing legislators with information that will influence their support of comprehensive welfare legislation that benefits adolescents (Garwood & others, 1989).

Developmentalist Peter Scales (1990) recently described four social policy recommendations for improving the lives of adolescents. He believes that an effective social policy for the prevention of adolescent problems requires that policymakers shift from:

1. Perceiving social problems as separate from each other to perceiving them as interconnected
2. "Throwing money" at crises to investing in broad health promotion, starting early in life and continuing systematically with developmentally appropriate initiatives through late adolescence
3. Expecting immediate program results to anticipating long-term outcomes (which requires a generation of investment—not just a term in office—to determine if programs are working)
4. Viewing policy on adolescents as charity to viewing it as an investment—that is, equating the development of competent adolescents with economic development.

In later chapters, when we discuss such topics as adolescent pregnancy, school dropouts, and substance abuse, social policy implications for reducing such problems are described.

As the twenty-first century approaches, the well-being of adolescents should be one of America's foremost concerns. The future of our youth is the future of our society. Adolescents who do not reach their full potential, who are destined to make fewer contributions to society than it needs, and who do not take their place as productive adults diminish the power of that society's future (Horowitz & O'Brien, 1989).

At this point, we have discussed a number of ideas about the history of interest in adolescence and about today's adolescents. A summary of these ideas is presented in Concept Table 1.1. Next we will turn our attention to a number of issues that confront theorists and researchers as they study adolescent development.

The Nature of Development

Each of us develops in certain ways like all other individuals, like some other individuals, and like no other individuals. Most of the time, our attention focuses on our individual uniqueness, but researchers who study development are drawn to our shared as well as our unique characteristics. As humans, each of us travels some common paths. Each of us—Leonardo da Vinci, Joan of Arc, George Washington, Martin Luther King, Jr., you, and me—walked at about the age of one, talked at about the age of two, engaged in fantasy play as a young child, and became more independent as a youth.

Concept Table 1.1

History of Interest in Adolescence and Today's Adolescents

Concept	Processes/Related Ideas	Characteristics/Description
Early history	The Greeks	Plato argued that reason emerges in adolescence and that childhood experiences influence adolescence. Aristotle believed that the ability to choose is an important aspect of adolescence, that self-determination is the hallmark of adolescent maturity, and that human development has three stages.
	The Middle Ages and the Enlightenment	In the Middle Ages, knowledge about adolescents moved a step backward: children were seen as miniature adults, not adolescents. Neither the adolescent nor the child had status apart from the adult. In the eighteenth century, Rousseau described a more enlightened view of adolescence. He proposed four stages of development. Reason and self-consciousness were thought to develop at 12 to 15 years of age, and emotional maturity was thought to replace selfishness at 15 to 20 years of age.
Adolescence in America	The early years	In the eighteenth and most of the nineteenth century, work apprenticeships took up most of the adolescent male's life. Little has been written about adolescent females during this period.
	The age of adolescence	Between 1890 and 1920, a cadre of psychologists, urban reformers, youth workers, and counselors began to mold the concept of adolescence. G. Stanley Hall's book *Adolescence* in 1904 marked the beginning of the scientific study of adolescence. Hall is known for his storm-and-stress view of adolescence and his belief that biology plays a prominent role in development.
	Margaret Mead's sociocultural view	Margaret Mead's observations of Samoan adolescents revealed that their lives were relatively stress-free. Mead believed that adolescence has a sociocultural basis, in sharp contrast to Hall's biological approach.
	The inventionist view	A number of scholars argue for an inventionist view of adolescence. They believe that legislation ensured the dependency of youth and made adolescents' move into the economic sphere more manageable.
	Further developments in the twentieth century	Adolescents gained a more prominent status in society from 1920 to 1950. By 1950, the developmental period we call adolescence had come of age. It possessed physical and social identity. During the 1960s and early 1970s, adolescent rebelliousness came to the forefront in American society. Much of the radical protest has abated, but today's adolescents face many other issues.
Stereotyping adolescents	Its nature	A stereotype is a broad category reflecting our impressions about people. Many stereotypes about adolescents are inaccurate. Widespread generalizations about adolescents are often based on a limited group of highly visible adolescents. Stereotypes about adolescence often arise from a blend of personal experiences and media portrayals.
Today's adolescents	The current status of adolescents	The majority of adolescents today successfully negotiate the path from childhood to adulthood. By some criteria, today's adolescents also are doing better than their counterparts from a decade or two earlier. However, too many of today's adolescents are not provided with adequate opportunities and support to become competent adults. In many ways, today's adolescents are presented with a less stable environment than a decade or two ago. Adolescents must be viewed as a heterogeneous group because a different portrayal of adolescence emerges, depending on the particular set of adolescents being described.
	Idealized images of what adolescents should be and society's ambivalent messages	American society seems uncertain about what adolescents should be or should not be. In many areas, such as independence, sexuality, laws and values, and education, adults entertain idealized images of adolescents but communicate ambivalent messages to adolescents that may contribute to adolescents' problems.
	The complexity of adolescent development and sociocultural contexts	As researchers carefully examine adolescents' lives, they increasingly recognize the complexity of adolescent development. Because of this complexity, no single developmental model likely fits all adolescents. A special interest today focuses on the contexts of adolescent development, especially the sociocultural contexts of culture, ethnicity, and gender.
	Social policy and adolescents' development	Adolescents are the future of any society. Because too many of today's adolescents are not reaching their full potential, it is important to examine U.S. social policy toward adolescents.

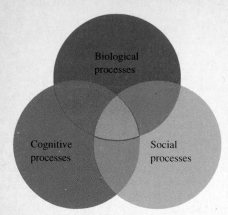

Figure 1.2 Biological, cognitive, and social processes in life-span development. Changes in development are the result of biological, cognitive, and social processes. These processes are interwoven in the development of an individual through the human life cycle.

What do we mean when we speak of an individual's development? **Development** *is the pattern of movement or change that begins at conception and continues through the life cycle. Most development involves growth, although it also includes decay (as in death and dying).* The pattern of movement is complex because it is the product of several processes—biological, cognitive, and social.

Biological, Cognitive, and Social Processes

Biological processes *involve changes in an individual's physical nature.* Genes inherited from parents, the development of the brain, height and weight gains, motor skills, and the hormonal changes of puberty all reflect the role of biological processes in the adolescent's development. Biological processes and physical development in adolescence are discussed extensively in Chapter 3.

Cognitive processes *involve changes in an individual's thought, intelligence, and language.* Memorizing a poem, solving a math problem, and imagining what it would be like to be a movie star all reflect the role of cognitive processes in the adolescent's development. Chapters 4 and 5 discuss cognitive processes in detail.

Social processes *involve changes in an individual's relationships with other people, in emotions, in personality, and in the role of social contexts in development.* Talking back to parents, an aggressive attack on a peer, development of assertiveness, an adolescent's joy at the senior prom, and a society's gender-role orientation all reflect the role of social processes in the adolescent's development. Sections III and IV focus on social processes and adolescent development.

Biological, cognitive, and social processes are intricately interwoven. Social processes shape cognitive processes, cognitive processes advance or restrict social processes, and biological processes influence cognitive processes. Although the various processes involved in adolescent development are discussed in separate sections of the book, keep in mind that you are studying about the development of an integrated human being who has only one interdependent mind and body (see Figure 1.2).

Periods of Development

Development is commonly described in terms of periods. The most widely used classification of developmental periods involves the following sequence: the prenatal period, infancy, early childhood, middle and late childhood, adolescence, early adulthood, middle adulthood, and late adulthood. Approximate age bands are placed on the periods to provide a general idea of when a period first appears and when it ends.

The **prenatal period** *is the time from conception to birth.* It is a time of tremendous growth—from a single cell to an organism complete with brain and behavioral capabilities—in approximately nine months.

Infancy *is the developmental period that extends from birth to 18 or 24 months of age.* Infancy is a time of extreme dependency on adults. Many psychological activities—for example, language, symbolic thought, sensorimotor coordination, social learning, and parent-child relationships—are just beginning.

Early childhood *is the developmental period that extends from the end of infancy to about five or six years of age; sometimes, the period is called the preschool years.* During this time, young children learn to become more self-sufficient and to care for themselves, develop school readiness (following instructions, identifying letters), and spend many hours in play and with peers. First grade typically marks the end of this period.

Middle and late childhood *is the developmental period that extends from about 6 to 11 years of age; sometimes, the period is called the elementary school years.* Children master the fundamental skills of reading, writing, and arithmetic, and they are formally exposed to the larger world and its culture. Achievement becomes a more central theme of the child's world, and self-control increases.

Our major interest in this book is the development of adolescents. However, as our developmental timetable suggests, considerable development and experience have occurred before the individual reaches adolescence. No boy or girl enters adolescence as a blank slate with only a genetic blueprint determining thoughts, feelings, and behaviors. Rather, the combination of a genetic blueprint, childhood experiences, and adolescent experiences determines the course of adolescent development. Keep in mind this point about the continuity of development between childhood and adolescence. More about the issue of continuity and discontinuity in development appears shortly.

A definition of adolescence requires consideration of age and also sociohistorical influences. Remember our earlier discussion of the increased interest in the inventionist view of adolescence. With such limitations in mind, **adolescence** *is defined as the developmental period of transition between childhood and adulthood that involves biological, cognitive, and social changes.* While cultural and historical circumstances limit our ability to place an age range on adolescence, in America and most other cultures today, adolescence begins at approximately 10 to 13 years of age and ends between the ages of 18 and 22 for most individuals. The biological, cognitive, and social changes of adolescence range from the development of sexual functions to abstract thinking processes to independence.

Developmentalists increasingly describe adolescence in terms of early and late periods. **Early adolescence** *corresponds roughly to the middle school or junior high school years and includes most pubertal change.* **Late adolescence** *refers to approximately the latter half of the second decade of life. Career interests, dating, and identity exploration are often more pronounced in late adolescence than in early adolescence.* Researchers who study adolescents increasingly specify whether their results likely generalize to all adolescents or are more specific to early or late adolescence.

Today, developmentalists do not believe that change ends with adolescence (Hetherington, Lerner, & Perlmutter, 1989; Santrock, 1992). Remember that development is defined as a lifelong process. Adolescence is part of the life course, and as such, is not an isolated period of development. While adolescence has some unique characteristics, what takes place in adolescence is interconnected with development and experiences in childhood and adulthood.

Do adolescents abruptly enter adulthood? Sociologist Kenneth Kenniston (1970) thinks not. Faced with a complex world of work and with highly specialized tasks, many post-teenagers spend an extended period of time in technical institutes, colleges, and postgraduate schools to acquire specialized skills, educational experiences, and professional training. For many, this creates an extended period of economic and personal temporariness. Earning levels are often low and sporadic, and established residences may change frequently. Marriage and a family may be shunned. **Youth** *is Kenniston's term for the transitional period between adolescence and adulthood that is a time of economic and personal temporariness.* The transition often lasts for 2 to 8 years, although it is not unusual for it to last a decade or longer.

As singer Bob Dylan asked, how many roads do individuals have to go down before they are called adults? Like childhood, and like adolescence, adulthood is not a homogeneous period of development. Developmentalists often describe three periods of adult development: early adulthood, middle adulthood, and late adulthood. **Early adulthood** *usually begins in the late teens or early twenties and lasts through the thirties.* It is a time of establishing personal and economic independence. Career development becomes a more intensified theme than in adolescence. For many young adults, selecting a mate, learning to live with someone in an intimate way, and starting a family take up a great deal of time. The most widely recognized marker of entry into adulthood is the occasion when an individual first takes a more or less permanent, full-time job. This usually happens when individuals finish school—high school for some, college for others, postgraduate training for others. However, criteria for determining when an individual has left adolescence and entered adulthood are not clear-cut. Economic independence may be considered a criterion of adulthood, but developing this independence is often a long, drawn-out process rather than an abrupt one. Increasingly, college graduates are returning to live with their parents as they attempt to get their feet on the ground economically.

As we have seen, defining when adolescence ends and early adulthood begins is not an easy task. It has been said that adolescence begins in biology and ends in culture. This means that the marker for entry into adolescence is determined by the onset of pubertal maturation and that the marker for entry into adulthood is determined by cultural standards and experiences. As we will discover in Chapter 3, defining entry into puberty is not easy either. For boys, is it the first whisker or the first wet dream? For girls, is it the enlargement of breasts or the first period? For boys and girls, is it a spurt in height? We usually can tell when a boy or girl is in puberty, but its actual onset often goes unnoticed.

Our discussion of developmental periods in the human life cycle continues with a description of the nature of middle adulthood. **Middle adulthood** *is the developmental period entered at approximately 35 to 45 years of age and exited at some point between approximately 55 and 65 years of age.* This period is especially important in the lives of adolescents because their parents either are about to enter this adult period or are already in it. Middle adulthood is a time of increasing interest in transmitting values to the next generation, enhanced concern about one's body, and increased reflection about the meaning of life. In Chapter 6, we study how the maturation of both adolescents and parents contributes to an understanding of parent-adolescent relationships.

Eventually, the rhythm and meaning of the human life cycle wend their way to **late adulthood,** *the developmental period that lasts from approximately 60 to 70 years of age until death.* It is a time of adjustment to decreasing strength and health, and to retirement and reduced income. Reviewing one's life and adapting to changing social roles also characterize late adulthood, as do lessened responsibility, increased freedom, and grandparenthood.

The periods of development are shown in Figure 1.3 along with the processes of development—biological, cognitive, and social. As can be seen in the figure, the interplay of biological, cognitive, and social processes produces the periods of development in the human life cycle.

Maturation and Experience (Nature and Nurture)

We can think of development as produced not only by the interplay of biological, cognitive, and social processes but also by the interplay of maturation and experience. **Maturation** *is the orderly sequence of changes dictated by the genetic blueprint each of us has.* According to the maturational view, just as a sunflower grows in an orderly way—unless flattened by an unfriendly environment—so does the human grow in an orderly way. The range of environments can be vast, but

Figure 1.3 Processes and periods of life-span development. The unfolding of the life cycle's periods of development is influenced by the interplay of biological, cognitive, and social processes.

Periods of development

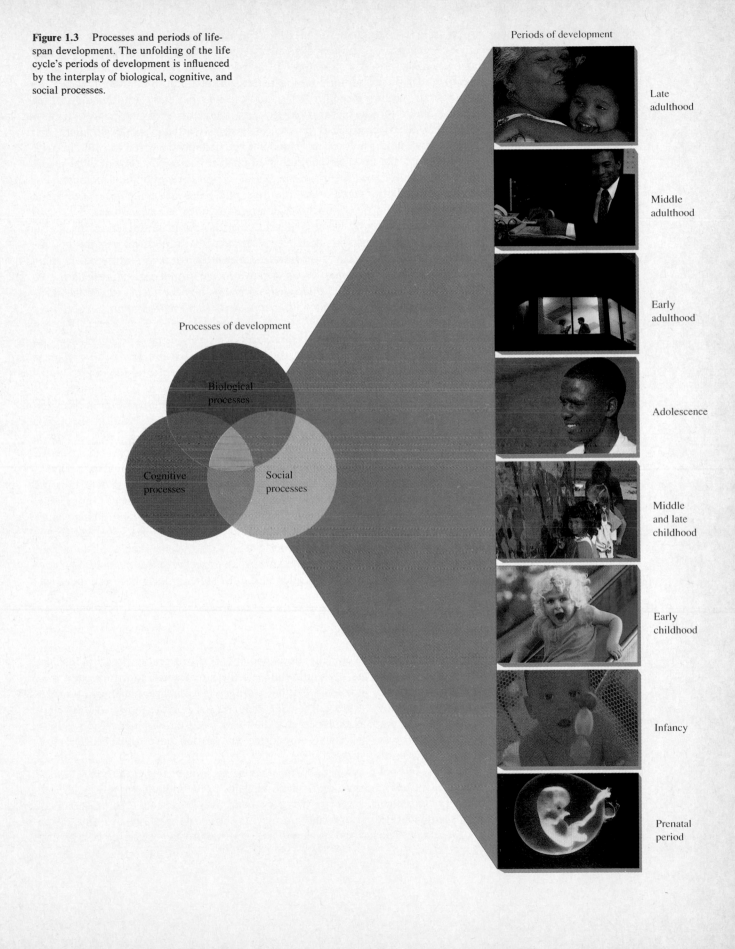

Processes of development

Biological processes

Cognitive processes

Social processes

Late adulthood

Middle adulthood

Early adulthood

Adolescence

Middle and late childhood

Early childhood

Infancy

Prenatal period

the maturational approach argues that the genetic blueprint produces commonalities in our growth and development. We walk before we talk, speak one word before two words, grow rapidly in infancy and less so in early childhood, experience a rush of sexual hormones in puberty after a lull in childhood, reach the peak of our physical strength in late adolescence and early adulthood and then decline, and so on. The maturationists acknowledge that extreme environments—those that are psychologically barren or hostile—can depress development, but they believe that basic growth tendencies are genetically wired into the human.

By contrast, other psychologists emphasize the importance of experiences in development. Experiences run the gamut—from the individual's biological environment (nutrition, medical care, drugs, and physical accidents) to the social environment (family, peers, schools, community, media, and culture).

The debate about whether development is primarily influenced by maturation or by experience has been a part of psychology since its beginning. This debate is often referred to as the **nature-nurture controversy.** Nature *refers to an organism's biological inheritance,* nurture *to environmental experiences. The "nature" proponents claim biological inheritance is the most important influence on development, the "nurture" proponents that environmental experiences are the most important.*

Ideas about development have swung like a pendulum between nature and nurture. In the 1980s, interest in the biological underpinnings of development surged, probably because the pendulum had previously swung too far in the direction of thinking that development was exclusively due to environmental experiences. In the early 1990s, interest in the sociocultural influences on development is increasing, again probably because the pendulum in the 1980s swung so strongly in the biological directions (Bruner, 1989, 1991; Gibbs & Huang, 1989).

Some adolescent development researchers believe that, historically, too much emphasis has been placed on the biological changes of puberty as determinants of adolescent psychological development (Lerner, Petersen, & Brooks-Gunn, 1991; Montemayor & Flannery, 1990). They recognize that biological change is an important dimension of the transition from childhood to adolescence, one that is found in all primate species and in all cultures throughout the world. However, they believe that social contexts (nurture) play important roles in adolescent psychological development as well, roles that until recently have not been given adequate attention.

Continuity and Discontinuity

Think about your development for a moment. Did you gradually grow into the person you are, like the slow, cumulative growth of a seedling into a giant oak, or did you experience sudden, distinct changes in your growth, the way a caterpillar changes into a butterfly? (See Figure 1.4.) For the most part, developmentalists who emphasize experience have described development as a gradual, continuous process; those who emphasize maturation have described development as a series of distinct stages.

Continuity of development *describes development as gradual, cumulative change from conception to death.* A child's first word, while seemingly an abrupt, discontinuous event, is viewed from the continuity perspective as the result of weeks and months of growth and practice. Likewise, puberty, while seemingly an abrupt, discontinuous event, is viewed as a gradual process occurring over several years.

Figure 1.4   Continuity and discontinuity in development. Is development more like a seedling gradually growing into a giant oak or a caterpillar suddenly becoming a butterfly?

Discontinuity of development *describes development as distinct stages in the life span.* According to the discontinuity perspective, each of us passes through a sequence of stages in which change is qualitatively, rather than quantitatively, different. As an oak moves from seedling to giant tree, it becomes *more* oak— its development is continuous. As a caterpillar changes into a butterfly, it becomes not just more caterpillar but a *different* kind of organism—its development is discontinuous. For example, at a certain point, a child moves from not being able to think abstractly about the world to being able to do so. At some point, an adult moves from an individual capable of reproduction to one who is not. These are qualitative, discontinuous changes in development, not quantitative, continuous changes.

Stability and Change

Another important developmental topic is the **stability-change issue,** *which addresses whether development is best characterized mainly by stability or by change. The stability-change issue involves the degree to which we become older renditions of our early experience or whether we can develop into someone different from who we were at an earlier point in development.* Will the shy child who hides behind the sofa when visitors arrive be a wallflower at high school dances, or will the shy child become a sociable, talkative adolescent? Will a fun-loving, carefree adolescent have difficulty holding down a nine-to-five job as an adult or become a straitlaced, serious conformist?

Evaluating the Developmental Issues

Most developmentalists recognize that it is unwise to take an extreme position on the three salient developmental issues—nature and nurture, continuity and discontinuity, and stability and change. Development is not all nature or all nurture, not all continuity or discontinuity, and not all stability or change. Both nature and nurture, continuity and discontinuity, and stability and change characterize our development through adolescence and the human life cycle. In considering the nature-nurture issue, the key to development is the *interaction* of nature and nurture rather than either factor alone (Paikoff & Brooks-Gunn, 1990; Plomin, 1990, 1991). For example, an adolescent's cognitive development is the result of heredity-environment interaction, not heredity or environment alone. Much more about the nature of heredity-environment interaction appears in Chapter 3.

Consider also the behavior of adolescent males and females (Feldman & Elliott, 1990). Nature factors continue to influence differences between adolescent boys and girls in such areas as height, weight, and the age of pubertal onset. On average, girls are shorter and lighter than boys and enter puberty earlier. However, some previously well-established differences between adolescent females and males are diminishing, suggesting an important role for nurture. For example, adolescent females are pursuing careers in math and science in far greater numbers than in the past, and are seeking autonomy in a much stronger fashion. Unfortunately, adolescent females also are increasing their use of drugs and cigarette smoking compared to adolescent females in earlier eras. The shifting patterns of gender similarities and differences underscore the belief that simplistic explanations based only on biological or only on environmental causes are unwise.

While most developmentalists do not take extreme positions on the developmental issues we have discussed, this consensus has not meant the absence of spirited debate about how strongly development is determined by these factors (Dornbusch, Petersen, & Hetherington, 1991; Lerner, 1991; Neiderhiser & others, 1992). Continuing with our example of the behavior of female and male adolescents, are girls less likely to do well in math because of their "feminine" nature or because of society's masculine bias? Consider also the circumstances in which, as children, adolescents experienced a world of poverty, parental neglect, and poor schooling. Could enriched experiences in adolescence remove the "deficits" encountered earlier in development? The answers developmentalists give to such questions reflect their stance on the issues of nature and nurture, continuity and discontinuity, and stability and change. The answers also influence public policy about adolescents and how each of us lives through the human life cycle.

At this point, we have discussed a number of ideas about the nature of development. A summary of these ideas is presented in Concept Table 1.2. In the next chapter, we turn our attention to the scientific orientation in studying adolescent development by examining the theories and methods used by developmentalists who conduct research with adolescents.

Summary

I. The Early Greeks, the Middle Ages, and the Enlightenment

Plato argued that reason emerges in adolescence and that childhood experiences influence adolescence. Aristotle believed that the ability to choose is an important aspect of adolescence, that self-determination is the hallmark of adolescent maturity, and that development has three stages. In the Middle Ages, knowledge about adolescence moved a step backward: children were seen as miniature adults, not adolescents. Neither the adolescent nor the child had status apart from the adult. In the eighteenth century, Rousseau described a more enlightened view of adolescence. He proposed four stages of development. Reason and self-consciousness were thought to develop at 12 to 15 years of age, and emotional maturity was thought to replace selfishness at 15 to 20 years of age.

Concept Table 1.2

The Nature of Development

Concept	Processes/Related Ideas	Characteristics/Description
What is development?	Its nature	Development is the pattern of movement or change that begins at conception and continues throughout the human life cycle. It involves both growth and decline.
Biological, cognitive, and social processes	Biological	These changes involve physical development.
	Cognitive	These changes involve thought, intelligence, and language.
	Social	Changes in relationships with other people, in emotions, in personality, and in social contexts are involved.
Periods of development	Prenatal and infancy	The prenatal period lasts from conception to birth and is a time of dramatic growth. Infancy lasts from birth to about 18 or 24 months of age and is a time of considerable dependence on adults and the emergence of many abilities.
	Early childhood and middle and late childhood	Early childhood lasts from about two to five years of age and also is known as the preschool years. Self-sufficiency increases, as do school-readiness skills and peer relations. During middle and late childhood, which extends from about 6 to 11 years of age, academic skills are mastered, there is formal exposure to the larger world, and self-control increases. This period is often referred to as the elementary school years.
	Adolescence	Adolescence is the developmental period of transition between childhood and adulthood that involves biological, cognitive, and social changes. In most cultures, adolescence begins at about 10 to 13 years of age and ends at about 18 to 22 years of age. Developmentalists increasingly distinguish between early and late adolescence.
	Youth	Youth is Kenniston's term for the transitional period between adolescence and adulthood that is a time of economic and personal temporariness. The period may last for two to eight years or longer.
	Early adulthood and middle adulthood	Early adulthood usually begins in the late teens or early twenties and lasts through the thirties. It is a time of establishing personal and economic independence. Career development and intimacy become more important concerns. Middle adulthood is entered at about 35 to 45 years of age and exited at some point between about 55 and 65 years of age. Transmitting values to the next generation, concern about one's body, and increased reflection on the meaning of life often characterize this period.
	Late adulthood	Late adulthood lasts from approximately 60 to 70 years of age until death. It is a time of adjustment to decreasing health, to retirement, and to reduced income. Reviewing one's life and coping with new social roles also characterize this time.
Developmental issues	Maturation and experience (nature and nurture)	The debate over whether development is due primarily to maturation or to experience is another version of the nature (heredity) versus nurture (environment) controversy.
	Continuity and discontinuity	Some developmentalists describe development as continuous (gradual, cumulative change), others as discontinuous (abrupt, sequence of stages).
	Stability and change	Is development best described as stable or changing? The stability-change issue focuses on the degree to which individuals become older renditions of their early experience or develop into someone different than they were earlier in development.
	Evaluation of the developmental issues	Most developmentalists recognize that extreme positions on the nature-nurture, continuity-discontinuity, and stability-change issues are unwise. Despite this consensus, spirited debate still occurs on these issues.

II. The Early Years in America, the Age of Adolescence, and the Sociocultural, Inventionist Views

In the eighteenth and most of the nineteenth century, work apprenticeships took up most of the adolescent male's life. Little has been written about adolescent females during this period. Between 1890 and 1920, a cadre of psychologists, urban reformers, youth workers, and counselors began to mold the concept of adolescence. G. Stanley Hall's book *Adolescence* in 1904 marked the beginning of the scientific study of adolescence. Hall is known for his storm-and-stress view of adolescence and his belief that biology plays a prominent role in development. Margaret Mead's observations of Samoan adolescents revealed that their lives were relatively stress-free. Mead believed that adolescence has a sociocultural basis, in sharp contrast to Hall's biological view. A number of scholars argue for an inventionist view of adolescence. They believe that legislation ensured the dependency of youth and made adolescents' move into the economic sphere more manageable.

III. Stereotyping Adolescents

A stereotype is a broad category reflecting our impressions about people. Many stereotypes about adolescents are inaccurate. Widespread generalizations about adolescents are often based on a limited group of highly visible adolescents. Stereotypes about adolescence often arise from a blend of personal experiences and media portrayals.

IV. The Current Status of Today's Adolescents, Idealized Images of What Adolescents Should Be, and Society's Ambivalent Messages to Adolescents

The majority of adolescents today successfully negotiate the path from childhood to adulthood. By some criteria, today's adolescents also are doing better than their counterparts from a decade or two earlier. However, too many of today's adolescents are not provided with adequate opportunities and support to become competent adults. In many ways, today's adolescents are presented with a less stable environment than a decade or two ago. Adolescents must be viewed as a heterogeneous group because a different portrayal of adolescence emerges, depending on the particular set of adolescents being described. American society seems uncertain about what adolescents should be or should not be. In many areas, such as independence, sexuality, laws and values, and education, adults entertain idealized images of adolescents but communicate ambivalent messages to adolescents that may contribute to adolescents' problems.

V. The Complexity of Adolescent Development, Sociocultural Contexts, and Social Policy

As researchers carefully examine adolescents' lives, they increasingly recognize the complexity of adolescent development. Because of this complexity, no single developmental model likely fits all adolescents. A special interest today focuses on the contexts of adolescent development, especially the sociocultural contexts of culture, ethnicity, and gender. Adolescents are the future of any society. Because too many of today's adolescents are not reaching their full potential, it is important to examine U.S. social policy toward adolescents.

VI. The Nature of Development and Biological, Cognitive, and Social Processes

Development is a pattern of movement or change that begins at conception and continues throughout the human life cycle. It involves both growth and decline. Development involves the interaction of biological, cognitive, and social processes.

VII. Periods of Development—Childhood

Prenatal development lasts from conception to birth and is a time of dramatic growth. Infancy lasts from birth to about two years of age and is a time of considerable dependence on adults and the emergence of many abilities. Early childhood lasts from about two to five years of age and also is known as the preschool years. Self-sufficiency increases, as do school-readiness skills and peer relations. During middle and late childhood, from about 6 to 11 years of age, academic skills are mastered, there is formal exposure to the larger world, and self-control increases. This period also is called the elementary school years.

VIII. Adolescence and Youth

Adolescence is the transition between childhood and adulthood that involves physical, cognitive, and social changes. Adolescence begins at about 10 to 13 years of age and ends at about 18 to 22 years of age. Developmentalists increasingly distinguish between early and late adolescence. Kenniston proposed that youth is a transitional period between adolescence and adulthood. It is a time of economic and personal temporariness and can last as long as 8 to 10 years.

IX. Adulthood

Adulthood is divided into early, middle, and late periods. Early adulthood covers roughly the third and fourth decades of life and involves themes of career development and intimacy. Taking a more or less permanent job has been a common marker for entrance into adulthood, but this criterion does not always hold up. Middle adulthood is especially important in our study of adolescence because most parents of adolescents are in this period. Late adulthood is the final period of the human life cycle.

X. Developmental Issues

Three important developmental issues involve the degree to which development is due to maturation or experience (nature or nurture), is continuous or discontinuous, and is stable or changing. Most developmentalists recognize that extreme positions on these issues are unwise. Despite this consensus, spirited debate still occurs on these issues.

Key Terms

storm-and-stress view 14
inventionist view 15
stereotype 18
adolescent generalization
    gap 18
contexts 21
culture 22
cross-cultural studies 22
ethnicity 22
ethnic identity 22
gender 23
social policy 25

development 28
biological processes 28
cognitive processes 28
social processes 28
prenatal period 28
infancy 28
early childhood 28
middle and late
    childhood 29
adolescence 29
early adolescence 29
late adolescence 29

youth 29
early adulthood 30
middle adulthood 30
late adulthood 30
maturation 30
nature-nurture
    controversy 32
continuity of
    development 32
discontinuity of
    development 33
stability-change issue 33

Suggested Readings

Child Development, Developmental Psychology, Journal of Early Adolescence, and Journal of Youth and Adolescence.
    Your library will likely have one or more of these research journals that either focus exclusively on adolescents or include many articles about adolescents. Leaf through issues of the journals published within the last several years to obtain a glimpse of the research issues that interest the scientists who study adolescents.

Elder, G. H. (1980). Adolescence in historical perspective. In J. Adelson (Ed.), *Handbook of adolescent psychology.* New York: Wiley.
    Elder provides an intriguing portrayal of how historical time influences the nature of adolescent development.

Feldman, S. S., & Elliott, G. R. (1990). Progress and promise of research on normal adolescent development. In S. S. Feldman & G. Elliott (Eds.), *At the threshold: The developing adolescent.* Cambridge, MA: Harvard University Press.
    The Carnegie Corporation of New York commissioned this book in an effort to pinpoint major gaps in knowledge about normal adolescent development. In this

excellent concluding chapter, Shirley Feldman and Glenn Elliott pull together significant themes in adolescent development, especially describing areas that need further research attention.

Hill, J. P. (1980). *Understanding early adolescence: A framework*. Chapel Hill, NC: University of North Carolina.

This booklet provides an excellent overview of the nature of development in early adolescence. This booklet was written by John Hill, one of the leading scholars in adolescent development.

Lerner, R. M., Petersen, A. C., & Brooks-Gunn, J. (Eds.). (1991). *Encyclopedia of adolescence* (Vols. 1 & 2). New York: Garland.

Many leading researchers contributed to this very up-to-date encyclopedia, which has more than 200 entries. Many of the entries run three to four pages and provide excellent, brief overviews of important topics in adolescent development.

Ross, D. (1972). *G. Stanley Hall: The psychologist as prophet*. Chicago: University of Chicago Press.

Ross provides an intriguing biographical sketch of the father of adolescent psychology, G. Stanley Hall.

CHAPTER 2

Theories and Methods

There is nothing quite so practical as a good theory.

Kurt Lewin

The Youths of Erikson and Piaget

Imagine that you have developed a major theory of adolescent development. What would influence you to construct this theory? A person interested in developing such a theory usually goes through a long university training program that culminates in a doctoral degree. As part of the training, the future theorist is exposed to many ideas about a particular area of development, such as biological, cognitive, or social development. Another factor that could influence you to develop a particular theory is your life experiences. Two important developmental theorists, whose views are described later in the chapter, are Erik Erikson and Jean Piaget. Let's examine a portion of their lives as they were growing up to discover how their experiences might have contributed to the theories they developed.

Erik Homberger Erikson (1902–) was born near Frankfurt, Germany, to Danish parents. Before Erik was born, his parents separated, and his mother left Denmark to live in Germany. At age three, Erik became ill, and his mother took him to see a pediatrician named Homberger. Young Erik's mother fell in love with the pediatrician, married him, and named Erik after his new stepfather.

Erik attended primary school from the ages of 6 to 10 and then the gymnasium (high school) from ages 11 to 18. He studied art and a number of languages rather than science courses, such as biology and chemistry. Erik did not like formal schooling, which was reflected in his grades. Rather than going to college, at age 18, the adolescent Erikson wandered around Europe, keeping a diary of his experiences. After a year of travel through Europe, he returned to Germany and enrolled in art school, became dissatisfied, and enrolled in another. Later, he traveled to Florence, Italy. Psychiatrist Robert Coles (1970) described Erikson at this time:

> To the Italians he was not an unfamiliar sight: the young, tall, thin Nordic expatriate with long, blond hair. He wore a corduroy suit and was seen by his family and friends as not odd or "sick" but as a wandering artist who was trying to come to grips with himself, a not unnatural or unusual struggle. (p. 15)

Jean Piaget (1896–1980) was born in Neuchâtel, Switzerland. Jean's father was an intellectual who taught young Jean to think systematically. Jean's mother was also very bright. His father had an air of detachment from his mother, whom Piaget described as prone to frequent neurotic outbursts.

In his autobiography, Piaget (1952) detailed why he chose to study cognitive development rather than social or abnormal development:

> I started to forego playing for serious work very early. Indeed, I have always detested any departure from reality, an attitude which I relate to my mother's poor mental health. It was this disturbing factor which at the beginning of my studies in psychology made me keenly interested in psychoanalytic and pathological psychology. Though this interest helped me to achieve independence and to widen my cultural background, I have never since felt any desire to involve myself deeper in that particular direction, always much preferring the study of normalcy and the workings of the intellect to that of the tricks of the unconscious. (p. 238)

At the age of 22, Piaget went to work in the psychology laboratory at the University of Zurich. There he was exposed to the insights of Alfred Binet, who developed the first intelligence test. By the time Piaget was 25, his experience in varied disciplines had helped him to see important links between philosophy, psychology, and biology.

These excerpts from Erikson's and Piaget's lives illustrate how personal experiences might influence a theorist's direction. Erikson's wanderings and search for self contributed to his theory of identity development, and Piaget's intellectual experiences with his parents and schooling contributed to his emphasis on cognitive development.

> *Truth is arrived at by the painstaking process of eliminating the untrue.*
>
> *Arthur Conan Doyle,* Sherlock Holmes

I n this chapter, we study two key ingredients of the scientific approach to adolescent development—theories and methods. According to French physicist Henri Poincaré, "Science is built of facts the way a house is built of bricks, but an accumulation of facts is no more science than a pile of bricks a house." Science *does* depend upon the raw material of facts or data, but as Poincaré indicated, science is more than facts, and the nature of theory illustrates this point.

What Is a Theory?

A **theory** *is a coherent set of ideas that helps to explain data and make predictions.* A theory has **hypotheses,** *assumptions that can be tested to determine their accuracy.* For example, a theory of adolescent depression explains observations of depressed adolescents and predicts why adolescents get depressed. A theorist might predict that adolescents get depressed because they fail to focus on their strengths and dwell extensively on their weaknesses. This prediction directs observations by telling the theorist to look for exaggerations of weaknesses and underestimations of strengths and skills.

Erikson's and Piaget's theories are but two of the many theories you will read about in this chapter. The diversity of theories makes understanding adolescent development a challenging undertaking. Just when one theory appears to correctly explain adolescent development, another theory crops up and makes you rethink your earlier conclusion. Remember that adolescent development is complex and multifaceted. While no single theory has been able to account for all aspects of adolescent development, each theory has contributed an important piece to the adolescent development puzzle. Although the theories sometimes disagree about certain aspects of adolescent development, much of their information is *complementary* rather than contradictory. Together, the various theories let us see the total landscape of adolescent development in all its richness. The four main theoretical perspectives we discuss in this chapter are: (1) psychoanalytic, (2) cognitive, (3) behavioral and social learning, and (4) ecological.

Psychoanalytic Theories

According to psychoanalytic theorists, development is primarily unconscious—that is, beyond awareness—and is heavily colored by emotion. Psychoanalytic theorists believe that behavior is merely a surface characteristic and that to truly understand development, we have to analyze the symbolic meanings of behavior and the deep, inner workings of the mind. Psychoanalytic theorists also stress that early experiences with parents extensively shape our development. These characteristics are highlighted in the main psychoanalytic theory, that of Sigmund Freud.

Sigmund Freud.

Freud's Theory

Loved and hated, respected and despised, considered by some the master and considered by others to be misdirected—Sigmund Freud, whether right or wrong in his views, has been one of the most influential thinkers of the twentieth century. Freud was a medical doctor who specialized in neurology. He developed his ideas about psychoanalytic theory from his work with mental patients. He was born in 1856 in Austria and died in London at the age of 83. He spent most of his years in Vienna, although he left the city near the end of his career because of Nazi anti-Semitism.

The Structure of Personality

Freud (1917) believed that personality has three structures: the id, the ego, and the superego. One way to understand the three structures is to consider them as three rulers of a country. The id is king or queen, the ego is prime minister, and the superego is high priest. The id is an absolute monarch, owed complete obedience; it is spoiled, willful, and self-centered. The id wants what it wants right now, not later. The ego as prime minister has the job of getting things done right; it is tuned into reality and is responsive to society's demands. The superego as high priest is concerned with right and wrong; the id may be greedy and needs to be told that nobler purposes should be pursued.

The **id** *is the Freudian structure of personality that consists of instincts, which are an individual's reservoir of psychic energy.* In Freud's view, the id is unconscious; it has no contact with reality. The id works according to the **pleasure principle,** *the Freudian concept that the id always seeks pleasure and avoids pain.* The world would be dangerous and scary if our personalities were all id.

As young children develop, they experience the demands and constraints of reality. They learn, for example, that they cannot slug other children in the face and that they have to use the toilet instead of their diaper. A new structure of personality is formed—the **ego,** *which is the Freudian structure of personality that deals with the demands of reality.* The ego is called the executive branch of personality because it makes rational decisions. The ego abides by the **reality principle,** *the Freudian concept by which the ego tries to bring individuals pleasure within the boundaries of reality.* Few of us are cold-blooded killers or wild wheeler-dealers. We take obstacles that stand in the way of our satisfaction into account. We recognize that our sexual and aggressive impulses cannot go unrestrained. The ego helps adolescents to test reality—to see how far they can go without getting into trouble and hurting themselves. The ego is also partly conscious.

The id and the ego have no morality. The **superego** *is the Freudian structure of personality that is the moral branch of personality. The superego takes into account whether something is right or wrong.* The superego is what we often refer to as our "conscience." Like the id, the superego does not consider reality; it does not deal with what is realistic, only with whether the id's sexual and aggressive impulses can be satisfied in moral terms. You probably are beginning to sense that both the id and the superego make life rough for the ego. An adolescent's ego might say, "I will have sex only occasionally and be sure to take the proper precautions because I don't want the intrusion of a child in the development of my career." The adolescent's id is saying, "I want to be satisfied; sex is pleasurable." The adolescent's superego is at work, too: "I feel guilty about having sex."

Freud considered personality to be like an iceberg: Most of personality exists below our level of awareness, just as the massive part of an iceberg is beneath the water's surface. Figure 2.1 illustrates the iceberg analogy and shows how much of the id, ego, and superego are conscious or unconscious.

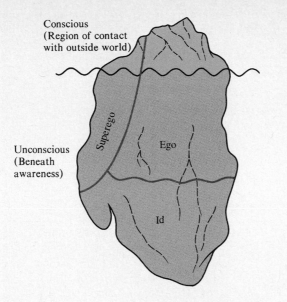

Conscious
(Region of contact
with outside world)

Superego

Ego

Unconscious
(Beneath
awareness)

Id

Figure 2.1 This rather odd-looking diagram illustrates Freud's belief that most of personality's important thoughts occur beneath the level of conscious awareness. Whereas the ego and superego are partly conscious and partly unconscious, the id is completely unconscious, just like the large, submerged part of an iceberg.

Freud believed that adolescents' lives are filled with tension and conflict. To reduce this tension, adolescents keep information locked in their unconscious mind, said Freud. He believed that even trivial behaviors have special significance when the unconscious forces behind them are revealed. A twitch, a doodle, a joke, a smile—each may have an unconscious reason for appearing, according to Freud. For example, 17-year-old Barbara is kissing and hugging Tom. She says, "Oh, *Jeff,* I love you so much." Tom pushes her away and says, "Why did you call me Jeff? I thought you didn't think about him anymore. We need to have a talk!" You probably can remember times when these *Freudian slips* came out in your own behavior.

Freud also believed that dreams are unconscious representations of the conflict and tension in adolescent's everyday lives and hold important clues to adolescents' behavior. Since the conflicts and tension are too painful to handle consciously, they come out in adolescents' dreams. Much of the dream content is disguised in symbolism, requiring extensive analysis and probing to understand. Examples of some of the sexual symbols many psychoanalysts use to interpret dreams are shown in Figure 2.2

Defense Mechanisms

How does the ego resolve the conflict between its demands for reality, the wishes of the id, and the constraints of the superego? Through **defense mechanisms,** *the psychoanalytic term for unconscious methods, the ego distorts reality, thereby protecting itself from anxiety.* In Freud's view, the conflicting demands of the personality structures produce anxiety. For example, when the ego blocks the id's pleasurable pursuits, we feel inner anxiety. This diffuse, distressed state develops when the ego senses that the id is going to cause harm to the individual. The anxiety alerts the ego to resolve the conflict by means of defense mechanisms.

Repression *is the most powerful and pervasive defense mechanism, according to Freud. It pushes unacceptable id impulses out of awareness and back into the unconscious mind.* Repression is the foundation from which all other defense mechanisms work; the goal of every defense mechanism is to *repress,* or push, threatening impulses out of awareness. Freud said that our early childhood experiences, many of which he believed were sexually laden, are too threatening and stressful for us to deal with consciously, and that we reduce the anxiety of this conflict through repression.

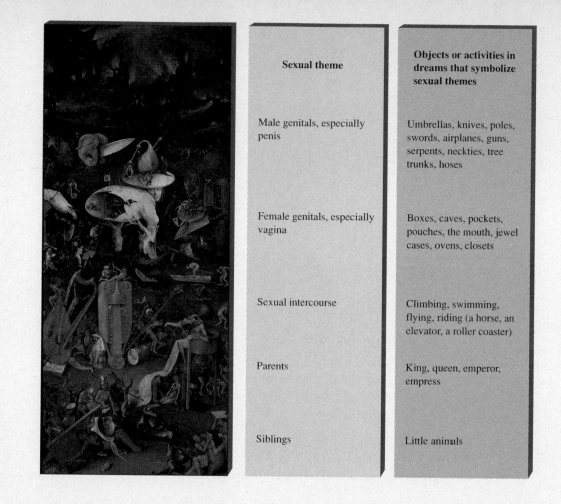

Sexual theme	Objects or activities in dreams that symbolize sexual themes
Male genitals, especially penis	Umbrellas, knives, poles, swords, airplanes, guns, serpents, neckties, tree trunks, hoses
Female genitals, especially vagina	Boxes, caves, pockets, pouches, the mouth, jewel cases, ovens, closets
Sexual intercourse	Climbing, swimming, flying, riding (a horse, an elevator, a roller coaster)
Parents	King, queen, emperor, empress
Siblings	Little animals

Figure 2.2 Psychoanalytic interpretations of sexual symbolism in dreams. The two boxes on the right list some sexual themes of dreams, along with the objects or activities in dreams that symbolize these sexual themes in disguised ways. At left is *The Garden of Delights* by Dutch painter Hieronymus Bosch (1450–1516), which captures some of the sexual symbolism in dreams.

Among other defense mechanisms adolescents use to protect the ego and reduce anxiety are sublimation, rationalization, projection, reaction formation, and regression. **Sublimation** *is the psychoanalytic defense mechanism that occurs when an individual replaces a socially distasteful course of action with a socially useful one.* For example, an individual with strong sexual urges may turn them into socially approved behavior by becoming an artist who paints nudes. **Rationalization** *is the psychoanalytic defense mechanism that occurs when the real motive for an individual's behavior is not accepted by the ego and is replaced by a "cover" motive.* For example, an adolescent is studying hard for a test when a friend calls and says he is having a party in an hour. The adolescent knows that, if he does not study, he will do poorly on tomorrow's exam. However, he says, "I did well on the first test in this class and I have been studying hard all semester; it's time I had some fun." So he goes to the party. The real motive for going to the party is to have some fun. But, the adolescent's ego steps in and "fixes" the motive to make it look better. His ego says that he has worked hard all semester and needs to unwind, and that he probably will do better on the exam if he relaxes a little—a rationale that is more acceptable than just going to have fun. **Projection** *is the psychoanalytic defense mechanism individuals use to attribute their own shortcomings, problems, and faults to others.* For example, an adolescent who manipulates others tells her friend, "The students at our school are so manipulative. They never consider my feelings." When adolescents cannot face their unwanted feelings, they may *project* them onto others and see others as having those traits. **Reaction formation** *is the psychoanalytic defense mech-*

anism that occurs when an individual expresses an unacceptable impulse by transforming it into its opposite. For example, an adolescent boy who likes a particular girl, but doesn't want to acknowledge it, might say that he can't stand the girl when he actually loves her. **Regression** *is the psychoanalytic defense mechanism that occurs when individuals behave in a way that characterizes a previous developmental level.* When anxiety becomes too great, the adolescent may revert to an earlier behavior that provided pleasurable feelings. For example, a girl may run to her mother every time she and her boyfriend have an argument.

Two final points about defense mechanisms are important. First, they are unconscious; adolescents are not aware that they are calling on defense mechanisms to protect their ego and reduce anxiety. Second, when used in moderation or on a temporary basis, defense mechanisms are not necessarily unhealthy. For the most part, though, individuals should not let defense mechanisms dominate their behavior and prevent them from facing the demands of reality. More about defense mechanisms and adolescent development appears in Perspective on Adolescent Development 2.1.

The Development of Personality

As Freud listened to, probed, and analyzed his patients, he became convinced that their problems were the result of experiences early in life. Freud believed that we go through five stages of psychosexual development and that, at each stage, we experience pleasure in one part of the body more than others. **Erogenous zones** *are parts of the body that have especially strong pleasure-giving qualities at each stage of development.*

Freud thought that adult personality is determined by the way in which conflicts between these early sources of pleasure—the mouth, the anus, and then the genitals—and the demands of reality are resolved. When these conflicts are not resolved, people may become fixated at a particular stage of development. **Fixation** *is the psychoanalytic defense mechanism that occurs when an individual remains locked into an earlier developmental stage because his or her needs are under- or overgratified.* For example, a parent may wean a child too early, be too strict in toilet training, punish the child for masturbation, or smother the child with warmth. We will return to the idea of fixation and how it can show up in an adult's personality, but first we need to learn more about the early stages of personality development.

The **oral stage** *is the first Freudian stage of development, occurring during the first 18 months of life, in which an infant's pleasure centers around the mouth.* Chewing, sucking, and biting are the chief sources of pleasure. These actions reduce tension in the infant.

The **anal stage** *is the second Freudian stage of development, occurring between 1 1/2 and 3 years of age, in which the child's greatest pleasure involves the anus or the eliminative functions associated with it.* In Freud's view, the exercise of anal muscles reduces tension.

The **phallic stage** *is the third Freudian stage of development, which occurs between the ages of three and six; its name comes from the Latin word* phallus, *which means "penis." During the phallic stage, pleasure focuses on the genitals, as the child discovers that self-manipulation is enjoyable.*

In Freud's view, the phallic stage has a special importance in personality development because it is during this period that the Oedipus complex appears. This name comes from the Greek mythology, in which Oedipus, the son of the King of Thebes, unwittingly killed his father and married his mother. The **Oedipus complex** *is the Freudian concept in which the young child develops an intense desire to replace the parent of the same sex and enjoy the affections of the opposite-sexed parent.*

THE FAR SIDE By GARY LARSON

"So, Mr. Fenton . . . Let's begin with your mother."

THE FAR SIDE cartoon by Gary Larson is reprinted by permission of Chronicle Features, San Francisco, CA.

The Role of Defense Mechanisms in Adolescent Adjustment: The Views of Peter Blos and Anna Freud

Both Peter Blos (1962, 1989), a British psychoanalyst, and Anna Freud (1958, 1966), Sigmund Freud's daughter, believe that defense mechanisms provide considerable insight into adolescent development. Blos states that regression during adolescence is actually not defensive at all, but rather an integral, normal, inevitable, and universal aspect of puberty. The nature of regression may vary from one adolescent to the next. It may involve childhood autonomy, compliance, and cleanliness, or it may involve a sudden return to the passiveness that characterized the adolescent's behavior during childhood.

In some instances, though, regression can become problematic for adolescents, as it did for 16-year-old John (Adelson & Doehrman, 1980). John entered group therapy with other adolescents at a time when he was recovering from severe depression following the break-off of a serious relationship with his girlfriend. The girl's mother actually referred John to the clinic because she sensed that John's depression had worsened. John was a handsome, intelligent, articulate adolescent who was a leader at school, hardly the type of adolescent who would be a likely candidate for severe depression.

After several therapy sessions, it became apparent that John kept most girls at a distance, especially when they wanted to get seriously involved or to "mother" him. However, he was attracted to girls who were either aloof or tomboyish. John's relationship with girls were characterized by a wish to reestablish a union with his mother, but he had an intense fear of that wish. He was attracted to girls who were standoffish, but once he established a relationship with one of them, he would sink into an uncontrollable dependency on her.

According to Blos and Mahler, defense mechanisms play important roles in understanding many aspects of adolescent development, including dating relationships.

To some degree, then, John's attachments to girls represented a wish to become reunited with his mother. What was John's relationship with his mother like in adolescence? He was often abusive toward her. He complained that she nagged at him all the time; but in truth, he was frightened by his regressive feelings toward her, according to Adelson. The regressive feelings came out clearly in group therapy when his intelligent participation was replaced by sarcasm and then scorn whenever he seemed to be drawn to the "maternal" females in the group. This was particularly true with the woman therapist, who was seen as the group's "mother."

How is the Oedipus complex resolved? At about five to six years of age, children recognize that the same-sex parent might punish them for their incestuous wishes. To reduce this conflict, they identify with the same-sex parent, striving to be like him or her. If the conflict is not resolved, though, the children may become fixated at the phallic stage. Table 2.1 reveals some possible links between adult personality characteristics and fixation, sublimation, and reaction formation involving the phallic stage, as well as the oral and anal stages.

The **latency stage** *is the fourth Freudian stage of development, which occurs between approximately six years of age and puberty; the child represses all interest in sexuality and develops social and intellectual skills.* This activity channels much of the child's energy into emotionally safe areas and helps the child to forget the highly stressful conflicts of the phallic stage.

Anna Freud, Sigmund Freud's daughter, believed that defense mechanisms are an important dimension of the adolescent's development.

Although some psychoanalytic writers, like Blos, consider regression a normal part of adolescent development, for individuals like John, the reappearance of unresolved conflicts from early childhood requires therapy. For most individuals, however, the conflicts are not so serious that therapy is warranted. Thus, the intensity and persistence of the regression determine whether it is a healthy or unhealthy part of adolescent development.

Anna Freud (1958, 1966) developed the idea that defense mechanisms are the key to understanding adolescent adjustment. She believes that the problems of adolescence are not to be unlocked by understanding the id, or instinctual forces, but instead are to be discovered in the existence of "love objects" in the adolescent's past, both Oedipal and Pre-Oedipal. She argues that the attachment to these love objects, usually parents, is carried forward from the infant years and merely toned down or inhibited during the latency years. During adolescence, these pregenital urges may be reawakened, or worse, newly acquired genital (adolescent) urges may combine with the urges that developed in early childhood.

Anna Freud goes on to describe how adolescent defense mechanisms are used to ward off these infantile intrusions. Youth may withdraw from their attachment and identification with their parents and suddenly transfer their love to others—to parent substitutes, to leaders who represent ideals, or to peers. Or, rather than transferring the attachment to someone else, adolescents may reverse their feelings toward the attachment figure—replacing love with hate or dependence with rebellion. Finally, the instinctual fears may even generate unhealthy defensive solutions—for example, the adolescent may withdraw within himself, which could lead to grandiose ideas of triumph or persecution—or regression could occur. Thus, from Anna Freud's perspective, a number of defense mechanisms are essential to the adolescent's handling of conflicts (Draguns, 1991).

The **genital stage** *is the fifth and final Freudian stage of development, occurring from puberty on. The genital stage is a time of sexual reawakening; the source of sexual pleasure now becomes someone outside of the family.* Freud believed that unresolved conflicts with parents reemerge during adolescence. When the conflicts are resolved, the individual becomes capable of developing a mature love relationship and functioning independently as an adult.

Because Freud explored so many new and uncharted regions of development, it is not surprising that many individuals thought that his views needed to be either replaced or revised. One of these individuals was Erik Erikson.

Table 2.1   Possible Links between Adult Personality Characteristics and Fixation at Oral, Anal, and Phallic Stages

Stage	Adult extensions	Sublimations	Reaction formations
Oral	Smoking, eating, kissing, oral hygiene, drinking, chewing gum	Seeking knowledge, humor, wit, sarcasm, being a food or wine expert	Speech purist, food faddist, prohibitionist, dislike of milk
Anal	Notable interest in one's bowel movements, love of bathroom humor, extreme messiness	Interest in painting or sculpture, being overly giving, great interest in statistics	Extreme disgust with feces, fear of dirt, prudishness, irritability
Phallic	Heavy reliance on masturbation, flirtatiousness, expressions of virility	Interest in poetry, love of love, interest in acting, striving for success	Puritanical attitude toward sex, excessive modesty

From *Introduction to Personality* by E. Jerry Phares. Copyright © 1984 by Scott, Foresman and Company. Reprinted by permission of HarperCollins Publishers.

Erikson's Theory

Erikson recognizes Freud's contributions, but he believes that Freud misjudged some important dimensions of human development. For one, Erikson (1950, 1968) says we develop in *psychosocial stages,* in contrast to Freud's psychosexual stages. For another, Erikson emphasizes developmental change throughout the human life cycle, whereas Freud argued that our basic personality is shaped in the first five years of life. The **epigenetic principle** *is Erikson's term for the process that guides development through the life cycle. The epigenetic principle states that anything that grows has a blueprint, with each part having a special time of ascendancy, until all of the parts have arisen to form a functioning whole.* In Erikson's theory, we go through eight stages of development during the life cycle. The first four of these stages appear in childhood, the last four in adolescence and adulthood. Each stage consists of a unique developmental task that confronts individuals with a crisis. According to Erikson, this crisis is not a catastrophe, but a turning point of increased vulnerability and enhanced potential. The more an individual resolves the crises successfully, the healthier development will be (Waterman & Archer, 1991).

Trust versus mistrust *is Erikson's first psychosocial stage, which is experienced in the first year of life.* A sense of trust requires a feeling of physical comfort and a minimal amount of fear and apprehension about the future. Trust in infancy sets the stage for a lifelong expectation that the world will be a good and pleasant place to live.

Autonomy versus shame and doubt *is Erikson's second stage of development, occurring approximately in the second year of life.* After gaining trust in a caregiver(s), infants begin to discover that their behavior is their own. They start to assert this sense of independence, or autonomy. They realize their *will.* If infants are restrained too much or punished too harshly, they are likely to develop a sense of shame and doubt.

Initiative versus guilt *is Erikson's third stage of development, occurring during the preschool years.* As preschool children encounter a widening social world, they are challenged more than when they were infants. Active, purposeful behavior is needed to cope with these challenges. Children are asked to assume responsibility for their bodies, their behavior, their toys, and their pets. Developing a sense of responsibility increases initiative. Uncomfortable guilt feelings may arise, though, if a child is irresponsible and is made to feel overanxious. Erikson has a positive outlook on this stage. He believes that most guilt is quickly compensated for by a sense of accomplishment.

Industry versus inferiority *is Erikson's fourth developmental stage, occurring approximately in the elementary school years.* Children's initiative brings them in contact with a wealth of new experiences. As they move into middle and late childhood, they direct their energy toward mastering knowledge and the intellectual skills. At no other time are children more enthusiastic about learning than at the end of early childhood's expansive imagination. The danger in the elementary school years is the development of a sense of inferiority—of feeling incompetent and unproductive. Erikson believes that teachers have a special responsibility for children's development of industry. Teachers should mildly but firmly coerce children into the adventure of finding out that they can learn to accomplish things they would never have thought of by themselves (Erikson, 1968, p. 127).

Identity versus identity confusion *is Erikson's fifth developmental stage, which individuals experience during the adolescent years.* At this time, individuals face finding out who they are, what they are all about, and where they are going in life. Adolescents are confronted with many new roles and adult statuses—vocational and romantic, for example. Parents need to allow adolescents to explore many different roles and different paths within a particular role. If adolescents explore such roles in a healthy manner and arrive at a positive path to follow in their lives, then a positive identity is achieved. If identities are pushed on adolescents by parents, if the adolescents do not explore many roles, and if a positive future path is not defined, then identity confusion reigns.

Intimacy versus isolation *is Erikson's sixth developmental stage, which individuals experience during the early adulthood years.* At this time, individuals face the developmental task of forming intimate relationships with others. Erikson describes intimacy as finding oneself, yet losing oneself in another. If young adults form healthy friendships and an intimate relationship with another individual, intimacy is achieved; if not, isolation results.

Generativity versus stagnation *is Erikson's seventh developmental stage, which individuals experience during middle adulthood.* A chief concern is to assist the younger generation in developing and leading useful lives—this is what Erikson meant by *generativity.* The feeling of having done nothing to help the next generation is *stagnation.*

Integrity versus despair *is Erikson's eighth and final developmental stage, which individuals experience during late adulthood.* In our later years, we look back and evaluate what we have done with our lives. Through many different routes, the older person may have developed a positive outlook in most or all of the previous developmental stages. If so, the retrospective glances reveal a life well spent, and the person feels a sense of satisfaction—integrity is achieved. If the older adult resolved many of the earlier developmental stages negatively, the retrospective glances likely will yield doubt or gloom—the despair Erikson talks about.

Erikson does not believe that the proper solution to a stage crisis is always completely positive in nature. Some exposure or commitment to the negative end of a person's bipolar conflict is sometimes inevitable—you cannot trust all people under all circumstances and survive, for example. Nonetheless, positive resolutions to stage crises dominate. A summary of Erikson's stages is presented in Figure 2.3.

Erik Erikson developed a theory of life-span development that consists of eight psychosocial stages. In Erikson's theory, the stage that corresponds to adolescence is identity versus identity confusion. As part of their identity development, adolescents search to find out who they are, what they are all about, and where they are going in life.

Figure 2.3 Erikson's eight stages of psychosocial development.

Erikson's stages	Developmental period	Characteristics
Trust versus mistrust	Infancy (first year)	A sense of trust requires a feeling of physical comfort and a minimal amount of fear about the future. The infant's basic needs are met by responsive, sensitive caregivers.
Autonomy versus shame and doubt	Late infancy - toddlerhood (1 to 3 years)	After gaining trust in caregivers, infants start to discover that they have a will of their own. They assert their sense of autonomy or independence. They realize their will. If infants are restrained too much or punishment is too harsh, they are likely to develop a sense of shame and doubt.
Initiative versus guilt	Early childhood (preschool years, ages 3 to 5)	As preschool children encounter a widening social world, they are challenged more and need to develop more purposeful behavior to cope with these challenges. Children are now asked to assume more responsibility. Imaginative play develops. Uncomfortable guilt feelings may arise, though, if the child is irresponsible and is made to feel too anxious.
Industry versus inferiority	Middle and late childhood (elementary school years, 6 to puberty)	At no other time is the child more enthusiastic than at the end of early childhood's expansive imagination. As children move into the elementary school years, they direct their energy toward mastering knowledge and intellectual skills. The danger at this stage involves feeling incompetent and unproductive.

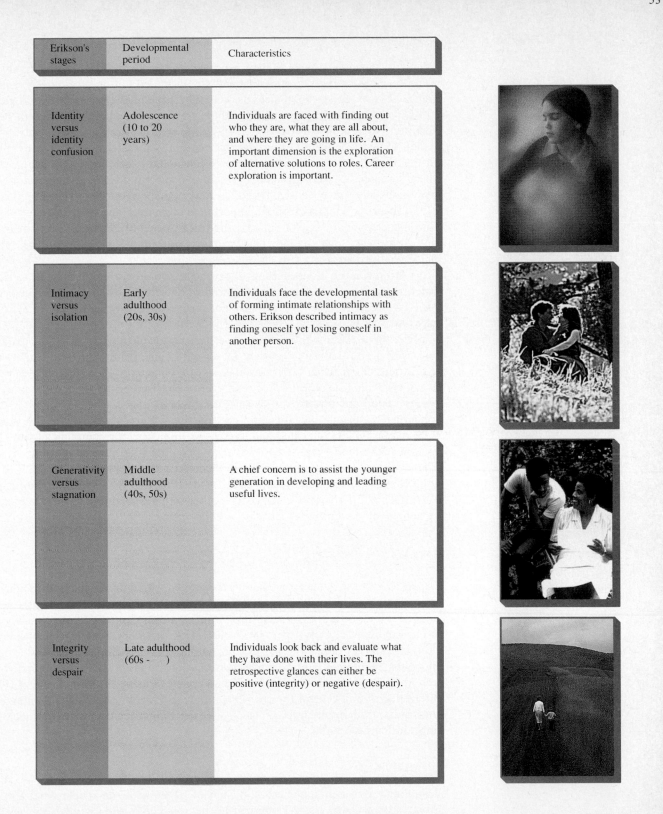

Erikson's stages	Developmental period	Characteristics
Identity versus identity confusion	Adolescence (10 to 20 years)	Individuals are faced with finding out who they are, what they are all about, and where they are going in life. An important dimension is the exploration of alternative solutions to roles. Career exploration is important.
Intimacy versus isolation	Early adulthood (20s, 30s)	Individuals face the developmental task of forming intimate relationships with others. Erikson described intimacy as finding oneself yet losing oneself in another person.
Generativity versus stagnation	Middle adulthood (40s, 50s)	A chief concern is to assist the younger generation in developing and leading useful lives.
Integrity versus despair	Late adulthood (60s -)	Individuals look back and evaluate what they have done with their lives. The retrospective glances can either be positive (integrity) or negative (despair).

Evaluating the Psychoanalytic Theories

While psychoanalytic theories have become heterogeneous, they nonetheless share some core principles: Our development is determined not only by current experiences but by early experiences as well. The principles that early experiences are important determinants of personality and that we can better understand personality by examining it developmentally have withstood the test of time. The belief that environmental experiences are mentally transformed and represented in the mind likewise continues to receive considerable attention. Psychoanalytic theorists forced psychologists to recognize that the mind is not all consciousness; our minds have an unconscious portion that influences our behavior. Psychoanalytic theorists' emphasis on the importance of conflict and anxiety requires us to consider the dark side of our existence, not just its bright side. Adjustment is not always easy, and the individual's inner world often conflicts with the outer demands of reality.

However, the main concepts of psychoanalytic theories are difficult to test. Inference and interpretation are required to determine whether psychoanalytic ideas are accurate. Researchers have not successfully investigated such key concepts as repression in the laboratory. Much of the data used to support psychoanalytic theories come from patients' reconstruction of the past, often the distant past, and are of doubtful accuracy. Other data come from clinicians' subjective evaluations of clients; in such cases, it is easy for clinicians to see what they expect. Some psychologists object that Freud overemphasized sexuality and the unconscious mind, and that the psychoanalytic theories also provide a model of the individual that is too negative and pessimistic. We are not born into the world with only a bundle of sexual and aggressive impulses; our compliance with the external demands of reality does not always conflict with our biological needs. A final criticism of many psychoanalytic theories, especially Freud's theory, is that they contain cultural and gender bias, as described in Sociocultural Worlds of Adolescence 2.1. Next, we consider another important approach to adolescent development—cognitive theories.

Cognitive Theories

Exploration of the human mind has been regarded with a mystical awe throughout much of human history. Now, 10,000 years after the dawn of civilization, a new understanding of mind is flourishing. *Mind* is a complex term, but primarily it is our cognitive activity—perception, attention, memory, language, reasoning, thinking, and the like. Whereas psychoanalytic theorists emphasize unconscious thoughts, cognitive theorists emphasize conscious thoughts. Developing individuals are perceived as rational and logical, capable of using the mind to effectively interact with and control the environment. Jean Piaget's theory has dominated the study of cognitive development. A second important cognitive approach is information processing.

Piaget's Theory

Jean Piaget was a child genius. At the age of 10, he wrote an article about a rare albino sparrow, which was published in the *Journal of the Natural History of Neuchâtel.* The article was so brilliant that the curators of the Geneva Museum of Natural History, who had no idea that the article had been written by a 10-year-old, offered young Piaget a job at the museum. Piaget continued to live in Switzerland as an adult and became one of the most influential forces in child development in the twentieth century. It was said of Piaget following his death at the age of 84 in 1980 that we owe him the present field of cognitive development (Flavell, 1980). What was the theory of this giant in developmental psychology like?

Cognitive developmental theory *is mainly represented by Piaget's theory, which emphasizes that individuals go through four stages of cognitive development in sequence. Piaget's theory emphasizes the organization and adaptation of thought* and is covered in greater detail when we discuss cognitive development in adolescence later in the book. Here, we briefly present the main ideas. Piaget (1952, 1954) stressed that adolescents actively construct their own cognitive world; information is not just poured into their minds from the environment. Two processes underlie adolescents' construction of the world: organization and adaptation. To make sense of our world, we organize our observations and experiences. For example, we separate important ideas from less important ideas. We connect one idea to another. We also *adapt* our thinking to include new ideas because additional information furthers understanding. Piaget (1954) believed that we adapt in two ways: assimilation and accommodation.

Assimilation *occurs when individuals incorporate new information into existing knowledge.* **Accommodation** *occurs when individuals adjust to new information.* Suppose that a 16-year-old girl wants to learn how to type. Her parents buy her a typewriter for her birthday. She has never had the opportunity to use a typewriter. From experience and observation, however, she realizes that a typewriter is to be placed on a table, that it has keys to be punched, and that paper must be inserted into it. Since she realizes each of these things, she sets the typewriter on the table, inserts the paper, and begins to type—incorporating her behavior into a conceptual framework that already exists (assimilation). But as she begins to strike some of the keys, she makes several mistakes. So, she begins to type more slowly. Soon, she realizes that she has to get someone to help her learn to type efficiently or take a class in typing at her high school. These adjustments show her awareness of the need to slightly alter her concept of typing (accommodation).

Piaget also believed that we go through four stages in understanding the world. Each of the stages is age-related and consists of distinct ways of thinking. It is the *different* way of understanding the world that makes one stage more advanced than another; knowing *more* information does not make the adolescent's thinking more advanced in the Piagetian view. This is what Piaget meant when he said that the individual's cognition is *qualitatively* different in one stage compared to another. What are Piaget's four stages of development?

The **sensorimotor stage,** *which lasts from birth to about two years of age, is the first Piagetian stage. In this stage, infants construct an understanding of the world by coordinating sensory experiences (such as seeing and hearing) with physical, motoric actions—hence the term sensorimotor.* At the beginning of this stage, newborns have little more than reflexive patterns with which to work. By the end of this stage, two-year-olds have complex sensorimotor patterns and are beginning to operate with primitive symbols.

The **preoperational stage,** *which lasts from approximately two to seven years of age, is the second Piagetian stage. In this stage, children begin to represent the world with words, images, and drawings. Symbolic thought goes beyond simple connections of sensory information and motoric action.* However, although preschool children can symbolically represent the world, according to Piaget, they still lack the ability to perform operations, the Piagetian term for internalized mental actions that allow individuals to do mentally what was done before physically.

Jean Piaget, famous Swiss developmental psychologist, changed forever the way we think about the development of children's and adolescents' minds. Piaget proposed a series of cognitive stages that individuals go through in sequence. He believed that adolescents think in qualitatively different ways about the world than children do.

Cultural and Gender Bias in Freud's Theory

The Oedipus complex was one of Freud's most influential concepts pertaining to the importance of early psychosexual relationships for later personality development. Freud's theory was developed in the Victorian era of the late 1800s, when males were dominant and females were passive, and when sexual interests, especially females', were repressed. According to Freud, the sequence of events in the phallic stage for girls begins when girls realize that they have no penis. According to Freud, girls recognize that the penis is superior to their own anatomy and thus develop *penis envy*. Since a girl's desire for having a penis can never be satisfied directly, Freud said she develops a wish to become impregnated by her father. Holding her mother responsible for her lack of a penis, she renounces her love for her mother and becomes intensely attached to her father, thus forming her own version of the Oedipus complex, sometimes referred to as the *Electra complex*. Thus, the sequence of events is reversed: For a boy, the Oedipus complex produces castration anxiety, whereas, for a girl, the parallel to castration anxiety—penis envy—occurs first and leads to the formation of the Oedipus complex (Hyde, 1985).

Many psychologists believe that Freud overemphasized behavior's biological determinants and that he did not give adequate attention to sociocultural influences and learning. In particular, his view on the differences between males and females, including their personality development, has a strong biological flavor, relying mainly on anatomical differences. That is, Freud believed that, because they have a penis, boys are likely to develop a dominant, powerful personality, girls a submissive, weak personality. In basing his view of male/female differences in personality development on anatomical differences, Freud ignored the enormous impact of culture and experience in determining male and female personalities.

More than half a century ago, English anthropologist Bronislaw Malinowski (1927) observed the behavior of the Trobriand Islanders of the Western Pacific. He found that the Oedipus complex is not universal but depends on cultural variations in families. The family pattern of the Trobriand Islanders is different from those found in many cultures. In the Trobriand Islands, the biological father is not the head of the household, a role reserved for the mother's brother, who acts as a disciplinarian. Thus, the Trobriand Islanders tease apart the roles played by the same person in Freud's Vienna and in many other cultures. In Freud's view, this different family constellation should make no difference: The Oedipus complex still should emerge, in which the father is the young boy's hated rival for the mother's love. However, Malinowski found no indication of conflict between fathers and sons in the Trobriand Islanders, although he did observe some negative feelings directed by boys toward their maternal uncles. Thus, young boys feared the man who was the authoritarian figure in their life, which in the Trobriand Island culture was the maternal uncle, not the father. In sum, Malinowski's study documented that it was not the sexual relations within the family that created conflict and fear for a child, a damaging finding for Freud's Oedipus complex theory.

The first feminist-based criticism of Freud's theory was proposed by Karen Horney (1967). She developed a model of women with positive feminine qualities and self-valuation. Her critique of Freud's theory included reference to a male-dominant society and culture. Rectification of the male bias in psychoanalytic theory continues

Nancy Chodorow has developed an important contemporary feminist revision of psychoanalytic theory that emphasizes the meaningfulness of emotions for females.

Bwaitalu village carvers in the Trobriand Islands of New Guinea. In the Trobriand Islands, the authoritarian figure in a young boy's life is his maternal uncle, not his father. The young boys in this culture fear the maternal uncle, not the father. Thus, it is not sexual relations in a family that create conflict and fear for a child, a damaging finding for Freud's Oedipus complex theory.

today. For example, Nancy Chodorow (1978, 1989) emphasizes that many more women than men define themselves in terms of their relationships and connections to others. Her feminist revision of psychoanalytic theory also emphasizes the meaningfulness of emotions for women, as well as her belief that many men use the defense mechanism of denial in self-other connections.

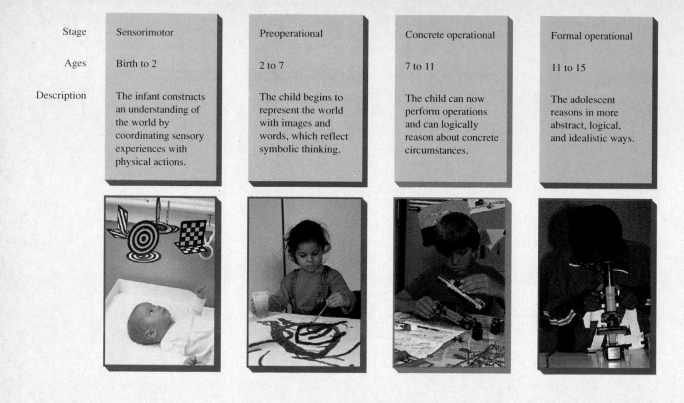

Stage	Sensorimotor	Preoperational	Concrete operational	Formal operational
Ages	Birth to 2	2 to 7	7 to 11	11 to 15
Description	The infant constructs an understanding of the world by coordinating sensory experiences with physical actions.	The child begins to represent the world with images and words, which reflect symbolic thinking.	The child can now perform operations and can logically reason about concrete circumstances.	The adolescent reasons in more abstract, logical, and idealistic ways.

Figure 2.4 Piaget's stages of cognitive development.

The **concrete operational stage,** *which lasts from approximately 7 to 11 years of age, is the third Piagetian stage. In this stage, children can perform operations. Logical reasoning replaces intuitive thought as long as the reasoning can be applied to specific or concrete examples.* For instance, concrete operational thinkers cannot imagine the steps necessary to complete an algebraic equation, which is too abstract for thinking at this stage of cognitive development.

The **formal operational stage,** *which appears between the ages of 11 and 15, is the fourth and final Piagetian stage. In this stage, individuals move beyond the world of actual, concrete experiences and think in more abstract and more logical ways.* As part of thinking more abstractly, adolescents develop images of ideal circumstances. They may think about what an ideal parent is like and compare their parents with this ideal standard. They begin to entertain possibilities for the future and are fascinated with what they can be. In solving problems, formal operational thinkers are more systematic, developing hypotheses about why something is happening the way it is, then testing these hypotheses in a deductive fashion.

Piaget's stages are summarized in Figure 2.4, and Piaget's stages are compared with Freud's and Erikson's in Figure 2.5. Notice that only Erikson describes changes in the adult years. Next, we consider a second cognitive approach to adolescent cognition—information processing—which, unlike Piaget's theory, does not describe stages of development.

Information-Processing Theory

Information-processing theory *is concerned with how individuals process information about their world—how information enters the mind, how it is stored and transformed, and how it is retrieved to perform such complex activities as problem solving and reasoning.* A simple model of information processing is shown

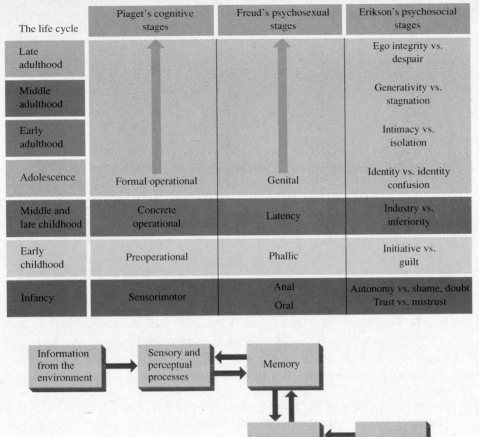

Figure 2.5 Comparison of Piaget's, Freud's, and Erikson's stages.

The life cycle	Piaget's cognitive stages	Freud's psychosexual stages	Erikson's psychosocial stages
Late adulthood			Ego integrity vs. despair
Middle adulthood			Generativity vs. stagnation
Early adulthood			Intimacy vs. isolation
Adolescence	Formal operational	Genital	Identity vs. identity confusion
Middle and late childhood	Concrete operational	Latency	Industry vs. inferiority
Early childhood	Preoperational	Phallic	Initiative vs. guilt
Infancy	Sensorimotor	Anal / Oral	Autonomy vs. shame, doubt / Trust vs. mistrust

Figure 2.6 Model of information processing. In this simplified model, sensory and perceptual processes, memory, thinking, and language are important cognitive processes. Notice the flow of information back and forth between these cognitive processes.

in Figure 2.6. Information processing begins when information from the world is detected through sensory and perceptual processes. Then information is stored, transformed, and retrieved through the processes of memory. Notice in the model that information can flow back and forth between memory and perceptual processes. For example, we are good at remembering the faces we see, yet at the same time, our memory of an individual's face may be different from how the individual actually looks. Keep in mind that our information-processing model is a simple one, designed to illustrate the main cognitive processes and their interrelations. Other arrows could be drawn—between memory and language, between thinking and perception, and between language and perception, for example. Also, the boxes in the figure do not represent sharp, distinct stages in information processing. There is continuity and flow between the cognitive processes as well as overlap.

By the 1940s, serious challenges confronted the claim of behaviorists that people learn primarily through environment-behavior connections. The first successful computer suggested that machines could perform logical operations. This indicated that some mental operations might be modeled by computers, and possibly computers could tell us something about how cognition works. Cognitive psychologists often use the computer to help explain the relation between cognition and the brain. The physical brain is described as the computer's hardware and cognition as its software (see Figure 2.7). The ability to process information has highlighted psychology's cognitive revolution since the 1950s.

Figure 2.7 Computers and cognition: An analogy. Cognitive psychologists often use the computer to help explain the relation between cognition and the brain. The physical brain is described as the computer's hardware and cognition as its software.

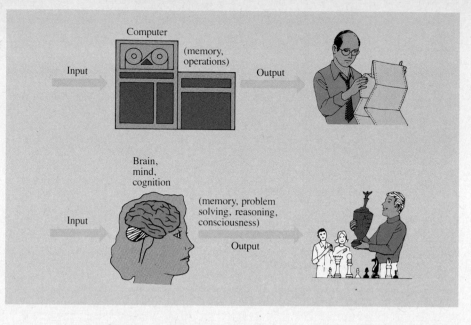

The information-processing approach raises important questions about changes in cognition across the life span. One of these questions is: Does processing speed increase as children grow older and decrease as adults grow older? Speed of processing is an important aspect of the information-processing approach. Many cognitive tasks are performed under real time pressure. For example, at school we have a limited amount of time to add and subtract and take tests; at work we have deadlines for completing a project. A good deal of evidence indicates that processing speed is slower in younger children than in adolescents, and slower in elderly adults than in young adults, but the causes of these differences have not been determined. Although some causes might be biological in origin, they might reflect differences in knowledge about or practice on a task (Bartlett & Santrock, 1986; Keating, 1990).

Evaluating the Cognitive Theories

Both Piaget's cognitive-developmental theory and the information-processing approach contribute in important ways to our knowledge about development. Today, researchers enthusiastically evaluate the accuracy of Piaget's theory. Through such examination, some of Piaget's ideas have remained unscathed, while others are being modified (Beilin, 1989).

The information-processing approach has opened up many avenues of research, offering detailed descriptions of cognitive processes and sophisticated methods for studying cognition (Klahr, 1989). The cognitive theories provide an optimistic view of human development, ascribing to children, adolescents, and adults the ability and motivation to know their world and to cope with it in constructive ways.

Like all theories, the cognitive theories have their weaknesses. There is skepticism about the pureness of Piaget's stages, and his concepts are somewhat loosely defined. The information-processing approach has not yet produced an overall perspective on development. Both the Piagetian and information-

Concept Table 2.1		
The Nature of a Theory, Psychoanalytic Theories, and Cognitive Theories		
Concept	**Processes/Related Ideas**	**Characteristics/Description**
What are theories?	Their nature	Theories are general beliefs that help us to explain what we observe and to make predictions. A good theory has hypotheses, which are assumptions that can be tested.
Psychoanalytic theories	Freud's theory	Freud said that our personality has three structures—id, ego, and superego—that conflict with each other. Most of our thoughts are unconscious in Freud's view, and the id is completely unconscious. The conflicting demands of personality structures produce anxiety; defense mechanisms, especially repression, protect the ego and reduce anxiety. Freud was convinced that problems develop because of childhood experiences. He said that we go through five psychosexual stages—oral, anal, phallic, latency, and genital. During the phallic stage, the Oedipus complex is a main source of conflict.
	Erikson's theory	Erikson's theory emphasizes eight psychosocial stages of development: trust versus mistrust, autonomy versus shame and doubt, initiative versus guilt, industry versus inferiority, identity versus identity confusion, intimacy versus isolation, generativity versus stagnation, and integrity versus despair.
	Evaluating the psychoanalytic theories	The strengths of the psychoanalytic theories are an emphasis on the past, the developmental course of personality, mental representation of environment, unconscious mind, and emphasis on conflict. Weaknesses are the difficulty in testing main concepts, lack of an empirical data base and overreliance on past reports, too much emphasis on sexuality and the unconscious mind, and a negative view of human nature.
Cognitive theories	Piaget's theory	Piaget's theory is responsible for the field of cognitive development. He believed that we are motivated to understand our world and that we use the processes of organization and adaptation (assimilation and accommodation) to do so. Piaget said that we go through four cognitive stages: sensorimotor, preoperational, concrete operational, and formal operational.
	The information-processing approach	The information-processing approach is concerned with how we process information about our world, including how information gets into the mind, how it is stored and transformed, and how it is retrieved to think and solve problems. The development of the computer promoted this approach—the mind as an information-processing system was compared to how a computer processes information. The information-processing approach raises questions about development, among them the rise and decline of information-processing speed.
	Evaluating the cognitive theories	Both the Piagetian and information-processing approaches have made important contributions to understanding adolescent development. They have provided a positive, rational portrayal of human development, although they may underestimate the importance of unconscious thought and environmental experiences. The purity of Piaget's stages has been questioned, and the information-processing approach has not yet produced an overall perspective on development.

processing approaches may have underestimated the importance of the unconscious mind and environmental experiences, especially family experiences, in determining behavior.

At this point, we have discussed what a theory is, psychoanalytic theories, and cognitive theories. A summary of these ideas is presented in Concept Table 2.1. Next, we turn our attention to the behavioral and social learning theories, which emphasize environmental experiences more than the psychoanalytic or cognitive theories.

Behavioral and Social Learning Theories

Fifteen-year-old Tom is going steady with 14-year-old Ann. Both have warm, friendly personalities, and they enjoy being together. Psychoanalytic theorists would say that their warm, friendly personalities are derived from long-standing relationships with their parents, especially their early childhood experiences. They also would argue that the reason for their attraction to each other is unconscious; they are unaware of how their biological heritage and early life experiences have been carried forward to influence their personalities in adolescence.

Behaviorists and social learning theorists would observe Tom and Ann and see something quite different. They would examine the adolescents' experiences, especially their most recent ones, to understand the reason for their attraction. Tom would be described as rewarding Ann's behavior, and vice versa, for example. No reference would be made to unconscious thoughts, the Oedipus complex, defense mechanisms, and so on.

Behaviorists believe that we should examine only what can be directly observed and measured (Baer, 1989; Bijou, 1989). At approximately the same time that Freud was interpreting his patients' unconscious minds through early childhood experiences, behaviorists such as Ivan Pavlov and John B. Watson were conducting detailed observations of behavior in controlled laboratory circumstances. Out of the behavioral tradition grew the belief that development is observable behavior, learned through experience with the environment. The two versions of the behavioral approach that are prominent today are the view of B. F. Skinner and social learning theory.

Skinner's Behaviorism

During World War II, B. F. Skinner constructed a rather strange project—a pigeon-guided missile. A pigeon in the missile warhead operated the flaps on the missile and guided it home by pecking at an image of a target. How could this possibly work? When the missile was in flight, the pigeon pecked the moving image on the screen. This produced corrective signals to keep the missile on its course. The pigeons did their job well in trial runs, but top Navy officials just could not accept pigeons piloting their missiles during a war. Skinner, however, congratulated himself on the degree of control he was able to exercise over the pigeons.

Following the pigeon experiment, Skinner (1948) wrote *Walden Two,* a novel in which he presented his ideas about building a scientifically managed society. Skinner envisioned a utopian society that could be engineered through behavioral control. Skinner viewed existing societies as poorly managed because individuals believe in such myths as free will. He pointed out that humans are no more free than pigeons; denying that our behavior is controlled by environmental forces is to ignore science and reality, he argued. In the long run, Skinner said, we would be much happier when we recognized such truths, especially his concept that we could live a prosperous life under the control of positive reinforcement.

Behaviorism *emphasizes the scientific study of observable behavioral responses and their environmental determinants.* In Skinner's behaviorism, the mind, conscious or unconscious, is not needed to explain behavior and development. For him, development is behavior. For example, observations of Sam reveal that his behavior is shy, achievement-oriented, and caring. Why is Sam's behavior this way? According to Skinner, rewards and punishments in Sam's environment, along with interactions with family members, friends, teachers, and others have caused Sam to *learn* to behave in this fashion.

Since behaviorists believe that development is learned and often changes according to environmental experiences, it follows that rearranging experiences should change the individual's development. According to the behaviorist, shy behavior can be changed into outgoing behavior; aggressive behavior can be shaped into docile behavior; lethargic, boring behavior can be turned into enthusiastic, interesting behavior.

Skinner describes how behavior is controlled in the following way: The individual operates on the environment to produce a change that will lead to a reward (Skinner, 1938). Skinner chose the term *operants* to describe the responses that are actively emitted because of the consequences for the individual. The consequences—rewards and punishments—are *contingent,* or depend on the individual's behavior. For example, an operant might be pressing a lever on a machine that delivers a candy bar; the delivery of the candy bar is contingent on pressing the lever. In sum, **operant conditioning** *is a form of learning in which the consequences of behavior lead to changes in the probability of that behavior's occurrence.*

More needs to be said about reinforcement and punishment. **Reinforcement** *(or reward) is a consequence that increases the probability a behavior will occur.* By contrast, **punishment** *is a consequence that decreases the probability a behavior will occur.* For example, if someone smiles at you and the two of you continue talking for some time, the smile has reinforced your talking. However, if someone you meet frowns at you and you quickly leave the situation, the frown has punished your talking with the individual.

B. F. Skinner.

Social Learning Theory

Some psychologists believe that the behaviorists basically are right when they say that development is learned and is influenced strongly by environmental experiences. But they believe that Skinner went too far in declaring that cognition is unimportant in understanding development. **Social learning theory** *is the view of psychologists who emphasize behavior, environment, and cognition as the key factors in development.*

The social learning theorists say we are not like mindless robots, responding mechanically to others in our environment. And we are not like weather vanes, behaving like a Communist in the presence of a Communist or like a John Bircher in the presence of a John Bircher. Rather, we think, reason, imagine, plan, expect, interpret, believe, value, and compare. When others try to control us, our values and beliefs allow us to restrict their control.

American psychologists Albert Bandura (1977, 1986, 1989, 1991, 1992) and Walter Mischel (1973, 1984) are the main architects of social learning theory's contemporary version, which was labeled *cognitive* social learning theory by Mischel (1973). Bandura believes that we learn by observing what others do. Through observational learning (also called modeling or imitation), we cognitively represent the behavior of others and then possibly adopt this behavior ourselves. For example, a boy may observe his father's aggressive outbursts and hostile interchanges with people; when observed with his peers, the young boy's style of interaction is highly aggressive, showing the same characteristics as his father's behavior. Or, a young female may adopt the dominant and sarcastic style of her boss. When observed interacting with one of her subordinates, the young woman says, "I need this work immediately if not sooner; you are so far behind you think you are ahead!" Social learning theorists believe that we acquire a wide range of such behaviors, thoughts, and feelings through observing others' behavior; these observations form an important part of our development.

Albert Bandura, one of the leading social theorists.

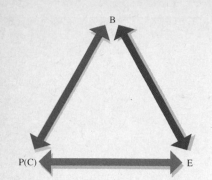

Figure 2.8 Bandura's model of reciprocal influences. The arrows reflect how relations between behavior (B), personal and cognitive factors (P(C)), and environment (E) are reciprocal rather than unidirectional. Examples of personal factors include intelligence, skills, and self-control.

Social learning theorists also differ from Skinner's behavioral view by emphasizing that we can regulate and control our own behavior. For example, another young female executive who observes her boss behave in a dominant and sarcastic manner toward employees may find the behavior distasteful and go out of her way to be encouraging and supportive toward her subordinates. As another example, suppose someone tries to persuade you to join a particular social club on campus and makes you an enticing offer. You reflect about the offer, consider your interests and beliefs, and make the decision not to join. Your *cognition* (your thoughts) leads you to control your behavior and resist environmental influence in this instance.

Bandura's (1986, 1989, 1991, 1992) most recent model of learning and development involves behavior, the person, and the environment. As shown in Figure 2.8, behavior, cognitive and other personal factors, and environmental influences operate interactively. Behavior can influence cognition and vice versa; the person's cognitive activities can influence the environment; environmental influences can change the person's thought processes; and so on.

Let's consider how Bandura's model might work in the case of a college student's achievement behavior. As the student diligently studies and gets good grades, her behavior produces positive thoughts about her abilities. As part of her effort to make good grades, she plans and develops a number of strategies to make her studying more efficient. In these ways, her behavior has influenced her thought and her thought has influenced her behavior. At the beginning of the semester, her college made a special effort to involve students in a study skills program. She decided to join. Her success, along with that of other students who attended the program, has led the college to expand the program next semester. In these ways, environment influenced behavior, and behavior changed the environment. The expectations of the college administrators that the study skills program would work made it possible in the first place. The program's success has spurred expectations that this type of program could work in other colleges. In these ways, cognition changed the environment, and the environment changed cognition. Expectations are an important variable in Bandura's model.

Like Skinner's behavioral approach, the social learning approach emphasizes the importance of empirical research in studying development. This research focuses on the processes that explain development—the social and cognitive factors that influence what we are like as people.

Evaluating the Behavioral and Social Learning Theories

The behavioral and social learning theories emphasize that environmental experiences determine development. These approaches have fostered a scientific climate for understanding development that highlights the observation of behavior. Social learning theory emphasizes both environmental influences and cognitive processes in explaining development; this view also suggests that individuals have the ability to control their environment.

Criticisms of the behavioral and social learning theories are sometimes directed at the behavioral view alone and at other times at both approaches. The behavioral view has been criticized for ignoring the importance of cognition in development and placing too much importance on environmental experiences. Both approaches have been described as being too concerned with change and situational influences on development not paying adequate tribute to the enduring qualities of development. Both views are said to ignore the biological determinants of development. Both are labeled as reductionist, which means that they look at only one or two components of development, rather than at how all of the pieces fit together. And critics have charged that the behavioral and social learning theories are too mechanical. Because these theories are overly concerned with several minute pieces of development, say the detractors, the most exciting and rich dimensions of development are missed.

Behaviorists and social learning theorists believe that the environment plays a powerful role in adolescent development, and they have mainly emphasized the study of behavior in laboratory settings. When humans have been the subjects in behavioral and social learning studies, there has been little or no interest in the sociocultural backdrop of the setting or context. In the next major theoretical approach, the sociocultural setting or context is given considerable importance.

Ecological Theories

Ecological theories *emphasize the role of social contexts in development.* Social contexts are the settings—such as family, peer, school, neighborhood, community, ethnicity, culture, and social class—in which development takes place. The most widely adopted ecological theory was proposed by Cornell University developmental psychologist Urie Bronfenbrenner (1979, 1986, 1989). Bronfenbrenner's ecological theory emphasizes a range of environmental and contextual influences on development, from the fine-grained inputs of direct interactions with social agents, such as parents and teachers, to the more broad-based, distal influences of culture and sociohistorical circumstances.

Urie Bronfenbrenner developed ecological theory, a sociocultural approach to understanding adolescent development.

Bronfenbrenner's Theory

Bronfenbrenner believes that a better understanding of ecological, contextual effects on development involves consideration of five environmental systems—the microsystem, mesosystem, exosystem, macrosystem, and chronosystem—each of which we consider in turn.

The **microsystem** *in Bronfenbrenner's ecological theory is the setting in which the individual lives. These contexts include the person's family, peers, school, and neighborhood. The most direct interactions with social agents— with parents, with peers, and with teachers, for example—occur in the microsystem.* The individual is not viewed as a passive recipient of experiences in these settings, but as someone who helps to construct the settings. Bronfenbrenner points out that most research on sociocultural influences has focused on microsystems.

The **mesosystem** *in Bronfenbrenner's ecological theory involves relations between microsystems or connections between contexts. Examples are the relation of family experiences to school experiences, school experiences to church experiences, and family experiences to peer experiences.* For instance, adolescents whose parents have rejected them may have difficulty developing positive relations with teachers. Developmentalists increasingly believe that it is important to observe behavior in multiple settings—such as family, peer, and school contexts—to obtain a more complete picture of adolescent development.

The **exosystem** *in Bronfenbrenner's ecological theory is involved when experiences in another social setting—in which the individual does not have an active role—influence what the individual experiences in an immediate context.* For example, work experiences may affect a woman's relationship with her husband and their adolescent. The mother may receive a promotion that requires more travel, which might increase marital conflict and change patterns of parent-adolescent interaction. Another example of an exosystem is city government, which is responsible for the quality of parks, recreation centers, and library facilities for children and adolescents.

Cultural standards for dating and marriage often vary considerably. For example, in Xinjiang, China, courtship involves a horseback chase (as shown in the photo). A woman mounts a horse and her suitor must chase her, kiss her, and evade her riding crop—all on the gallop. A new marriage law took effect in China in 1981. The law sets a minimum age for marriage—22 years for males, 20 years for females. Late marriage and late childbirth are critical efforts in China's plans to control population growth.

The **macrosystem** *in Bronfenbrenner's ecological theory involves the culture in which individuals live. Culture refers to the behavior patterns, beliefs, and all other products of a particular group of people that are passed on from generation to generation.* As indicated in Chapter 1, a cultural group can be as large and complex as the United States, or it can be as small as an African hunter-gatherer group. Whatever its size, the group's culture influences the identity, learning, and social behavior of its members (Whiting, 1989). For example, the United States is a very achievement-oriented culture with a strong work ethic, but recent comparisons of American and Japanese children have revealed that Japanese children are better at math, spend more time working on math in school, and spend much more time doing math homework than American children (Stevenson, 1991; Stevenson and others, 1990). Cross-cultural studies, the comparison of one culture with one or more other cultures, provide information about the generality of adolescent development.

The **chronosystem** *in Bronfenbrenner's ecological theory involves the patterning of environmental events and transitions over the life course and their sociohistorical contexts.* For example, in one research investigation, Mavis Hetherington and her colleagues (Hetherington, 1989; Hetherington, Cox, & Cox, 1982; Hetherington & others, 1991) found that the disruptive effects of divorce peaked one year after the divorce, with the effects being more negative for sons than for daughters. By two years after the divorce, family interaction was less

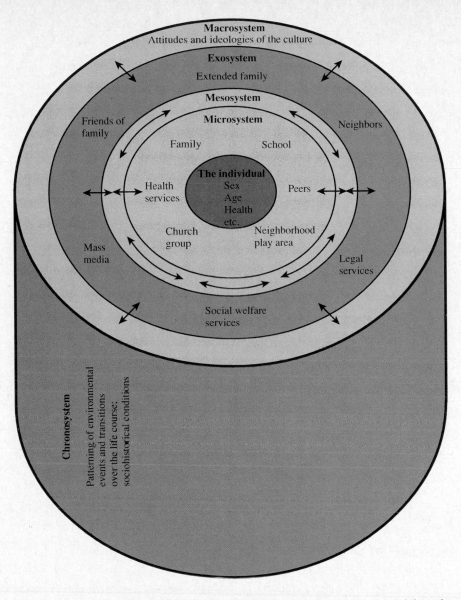

Macrosystem
Attitudes and ideologies of the culture

Exosystem
Extended family

Mesosystem

Microsystem

Friends of family

Neighbors

Family   School

The individual
Sex
Age
Health
etc.

Health services

Peers

Church group

Neighborhood play area

Mass media

Legal services

Social welfare services

Chronosystem
Patterning of environmental events and transitions over the life course; sociohistorical conditions

Figure 2.9 Bronfenbrenner's ecological theory of development consists of five environmental systems: microsystems, mesosystems, exosystems, macrosystems, and chronosystems.

chaotic and more stable. With regard to sociocultural circumstances, girls today are more likely to be encouraged to pursue a career than they were 20 to 30 years ago. In these ways, the chronosystem has a powerful impact on children's lives.

Figure 2.9 summarizes Bronfenbrenner's five environmental systems.

Evaluating Bronfenbrenner's Ecological Theory

Bronfenbrenner's ecological model is one of the few comprehensive frameworks for understanding the environment's role in development. The model includes both micro (molecular) and macro (molar) aspects of environmental, sociocultural influences on development. Bronfenbrenner's most recent addition to the model—the chronosystem—takes into account development over time and sociohistorical influences on development. The main weakness of the ecological model is its failure to adequately account for the influence of both biological and cognitive processes.

Concept Table 2.2

The Behavioral and Social Learning Theories, Ecological Theories, and an Eclectic Theoretical Orientation

Concept	Processes/Related Ideas	Characteristics/Description
Behavioral and social learning theories	Skinner's behaviorism	Skinner emphasized that cognition is unimportant in understanding development and that development is observed behavior, which is determined by rewards and punishments in the environment.
	Social learning theory	Social learning theorists believe that the environment is an important determinant of behavior, but that so are cognitive processes. They also emphasize that we control our own behavior through thoughts, beliefs, and values. Bandura's emphasis on observational learning exemplifies the social learning approach, as does his model of the reciprocal influences of behavior, person (cognition), and environment. The contemporary version of social learning theory is called cognitive social learning theory.
	Evaluating the behavioral and social learning theories	The strengths of both theories include emphases on environmental determinants and a scientific climate for investigating development. Another strength of social learning theory is its focus on cognitive processes and self-control. The behavioral view has been criticized for taking the person out of development and for ignoring cognition. These approaches have not given adequate attention to biological factors and to development as a whole.
Ecological theories	Their nature	Ecological theories emphasize the role of social contexts in development. The most widely adopted ecological theory was proposed by Bronfenbrenner.
	Environmental systems	In Bronfenbrenner's ecological theory, five environmental systems are described: the microsystem, mesosystem, exosystem, macrosystem, and chronosystem.
	Evaluation	Bronfenbrenner's theory is one of the few comprehensive models of environmental influences on development and includes both macro and micro aspects of environmental influence. Criticisms focus on the lack of emphasis on biological and cognitive processes.
An eclectic approach to adolescent development	Its nature	Each of the theories described has a number of strengths and weaknesses, but no single theory is capable of explaining the complexity of adolescent development. For this reason, this text adopts an eclectic approach to adolescent development.

An Eclectic Theoretical Orientation

Which of these theories—psychoanalytic, cognitive, behavioral/social learning, or ecological—is the best way to view adolescent development? Each theory contributes to an understanding of adolescent development, but no single theory provides a complete description and explanation. For these reasons, the four major approaches to adolescent development are presented in this text in an unbiased fashion. As a result, you can view the field of adolescent development as it actually exists—with different theorists drawing different conclusions. Many other theories of adolescent development, not discussed in this chapter, are woven into the discussion of adolescent development in the remainder of the book. For example, Chapter 10 examines the humanistic approach, which emphasizes adolescents' development of self, and Chapter 14 discusses attribution theory, which emphasizes adolescents' motivation for understanding the causes of their own and others' behavior.

At this point, we have discussed a number of ideas about the behavioral and social learning theories, ecological theories, and an eclectic theoretical orientation. A summary of these ideas is presented in Concept Table 2.2. Next, we turn our attention to the methods used to study adolescent development.

Methods

Some individuals have difficulty thinking of adolescent development as a science in the same way physics, chemistry, and biology are sciences. Can a discipline that studies pubertal change, parent-adolescent conflict, peer interaction, and imaginary thoughts be equated with disciplines that investigate how gravity works and the molecular structure of a compound? Science is not defined by *what* it investigates but by *how* it investigates. Whether you are studying photosynthesis, butterflies, Saturn's moons, or adolescent development, it is the way you study that makes the approach scientific or not. Our discussion of the methods used to study adolescent development focuses on the nature of the scientific method, how to collect information about adolescent development, strategies for setting up research studies, the time span of inquiry, cohort effects, reducing sexist research, and ethical issues, each of which we consider in turn.

The Scientific Method

The **scientific method** *is an approach that can be used to discover accurate information about behavior and development and includes the following steps: identify and analyze the problem, collect data, draw conclusions, and revise theories.* For example, suppose that you decide that you want to help aggressive adolescents control their aggression. You have identified the problem, which does not seem like a difficult task. But as part of the first step, you need to go beyond a general description of the problem by isolating, analyzing, narrowing, and focusing on what you hope to investigate. What specific strategies do you want to use to reduce adolescents' aggression? Do you want to look at only one strategy, or several strategies? What aspect of aggression do you want to study—its biological, cognitive, or social characteristics? Gerald Patterson and his colleagues (Patterson, 1982; Patterson, Bank, & Stoolmiller, 1990; Patterson, DeBaryshe, & Ramsey, 1989; Patterson, Capaldi, & Bank, 1991) argue that parents' failure to teach reasonable levels of compliance sets in motion coercive interchanges with family members. In this first step in the scientific method, a problem was identified and analyzed.

After a problem is identified and analyzed, the next step is to collect information (data). Developmentalists observe behavior and draw inferences about thoughts and emotions. For example, in the investigation of aggression, they might observe how effectively parents teach reasonable levels of compliance to their adolescents and the extent to which coercive interchanges occur among family members.

Once data have been collected, researchers attempt to draw conclusions from the data, using statistical procedures. In the investigation of aggression, statistics help the researchers to determine whether or not their observations were due to chance. After data have been collected, researchers compare their data with what others have discovered about the same issue.

The final step in the scientific method is revising theory. Psychologists have devised a number of theories about adolescent development, as we already have seen. Data such as those collected by Patterson and his colleagues force study of existing theories of the development of aggression to see if they are accurate. Over the years, some theories of adolescent development have been discarded and others revised. Theories are an integral part of understanding adolescent development. They are woven through our discussion of adolescent development in the remainder of the book.

Collecting Information about Adolescent Development—Methods

Systematic observations can be conducted in a number of ways. For example, researchers can watch adolescents' behavior in the laboratory or in a more natural setting such as a school, a home, or the neighborhood. They can question adolescents using interviews and surveys, develop and administer standardized tests, conduct case studies, carry out cross-cultural research, or devise physiological measures. To help you understand how developmentalists use these methods, we continue our theme of drawing examples from the study of adolescent aggression.

Observation

Sherlock Holmes chided Watson, "You see but you do not observe." We look at things all the time, but casually watching adolescents interacting with their parents is not scientific observation. Unless you are a trained observer and practice your skills regularly, you may not know what to look for, you may not remember what you saw, what you are looking for may change from one moment to the next, and you may not communicate your observations effectively.

For observations to be effective, researchers have to know what they are looking for, whom they are observing, when and where they will observe, how the observations will be made, and in what form they will be recorded. That is, the observations have to be made in some *systematic* way. Consider aggression. Do we want to study verbal or physical aggression, or both? Do we want to study younger adolescents, or older adolescents or both? Do we want to evaluate them in a university laboratory, at school, at home, in the neighborhood, or at all of these locations? A common way to record observations is to write them down, using shorthand or symbols. However, tape recorders, video cameras, special coding sheets, and one-way mirrors are used increasingly to make observations more efficient.

When researchers observe, it is frequently necessary to *control* certain factors that determine adolescent behavior but that are not the focus of the inquiry. For this reason, some researchers like to observe adolescent behavior in a **laboratory,** *a controlled setting in which many of the complex factors of the "real world" are removed.* For example, Albert Bandura (1965) brought children into the laboratory and had them observe an adult repeatedly hit a plastic, inflated Bobo doll about 3 feet tall. Bandura wondered to what extent the children would imitate the adult's aggressive behavior. The children's imitation of the adult model's aggression was pervasive.

Conducting laboratory research, though, has some disadvantages. First, it is virtually impossible to conduct laboratory research without the participants knowing that they are being studied. Second, the laboratory setting may be *unnatural* and therefore cause *unnatural* behavior. Individuals usually show less aggressive behavior in the laboratory than in a more familiar setting, such as in a park or at home. They also show less aggression when they are aware that they are being observed. Third, some aspects of adolescent development are difficult if not impossible to examine in a laboratory. Certain types of stress are difficult (and unethical) to investigate in the laboratory—for example, recreating the circumstances that stimulate marital conflict or a parent yelling at an adolescent.

In **naturalistic observation,** *scientists observe behavior in real-world settings and make no effort to manipulate or control the situation.* Developmentalists conduct naturalistic observations at schools, parks, hospitals, homes, malls, dances, youth centers, and other places where people live and frequent (Bronfenbrenner, 1989; Schoggen, 1991).

Interviews and Questionnaires

Sometimes, the best and quickest way to get information from adolescents is to ask them for it. Developmentalists use interviews and questionnaires to find out about adolescents' experiences and attitudes. Most interviews occur face-to-face, although they can take place over the telephone. The types of interviews range from highly structured to highly unstructured. Examples of structured interview questions include: "In the last two weeks, how many times did you yell at your friends?" and "How often in the last year have you gotten into a fight with someone at school?" Structure is imposed by the questions themselves, or the interviewer can categorize answers by asking the respondents to choose from several options. For example, in the question about how often an adolescent yells at friends, the adolescent might be asked to choose from: 0, 1–2, 3–5, 6–10, or more than 10 times. An example of an unstructured interview question is: "How aggressive do you see yourself?"

Experienced interviewers know how to put respondents at ease and encourage them to open up. They are sensitive to the way adolescents respond to questions and often probe for more information. An adolescent may respond with fuzzy statements to questions about the nature of parent-adolescent conflict— for example, "Well, I don't know whether we have a lot of conflict or not." A skilled interviewer pushes for more specific, concrete answers, possibly asking, "Tell me the worst things you argue about with your parents." These interviewing strategies force researchers to be involved with, rather than detached from, adolescents, which produces a better understanding of adolescent development.

Interviews are not without drawbacks. Perhaps the most critical is **social desirability,** *a response set in which individuals tell the interviewer what they think is most socially acceptable or desirable, rather than what they truly feel or think.* When asked about parent-adolescent conflict, 16-year-old Scott may not want to divulge that he often gets into fights with his parents. Skilled interviewing techniques and questions to help eliminate such defenses are critical to obtaining accurate information.

Developmentalists also use questionnaires or surveys to question adolescents. A **questionnaire** *is similar to a highly structured interview except that respondents read the questions and mark their answers on paper, rather than responding verbally to an interviewer.* One major advantage of surveys and questionnaires is that they can be given to a large number of adolescents easily. Good surveys have concrete, specific, and unambiguous questions, and assessment of the authenticity of the replies.

Case Studies

A **case study** *is an in-depth look at an individual; it is used mainly by clinical psychologists when the unique aspects of a person's life cannot be duplicated, either for practical or ethical reasons.* A case study provides information about a person's hopes, fears, fantasies, traumatic experiences, family relationships, health, or anything that will help the psychologist understand the adolescent's development. One case study involves a 16-year-old who had damage to the right side of the brain that left him with an inability to express himself emotionally. Another case study involves Genie, a child who was raised almost in complete isolation from the age of 20 months to the age of 13. Genie is proof of human resilience in learning language, although she never learned to ask questions and did not understand much grammar (Curtiss, 1978).

Standardized Tests

Standardized tests *require individuals to answer a series of written or oral questions. They have two distinct features: First, psychologists usually total an individual's score to yield a single score, or set of scores, that reflects something about the individual. Second, psychologists compare the individual's score with the scores of a large group of persons to determine how the individual responded relative to others.* Scores are often described in percentiles. For example, perhaps an adolescent scored in the ninety-second percentile of the Standford-Binet Intelligence Test. This score shows how much lower or higher the adolescent scored than a large group of adolescents who had taken the test previously.

To continue our look at how different measures are used to evaluate aggression, consider the Minnesota Multiphasic Personality Inventory (called the MMPI), which includes a scale to assess delinquency or antisocial tendencies. The items on this scale ask adolescents to respond whether they are rebellious, impulsive, and have trouble with authority figures. This part of the MMPI might be given to adolescents to determine their delinquent and antisocial tendencies.

The main advantage of standardized tests is that they provide information about *individual differences* among people. However, information obtained from standardized tests does not always predict adolescents' behavior in nontest situations. Standardized tests are based on the belief that an individual's behavior is consistent and stable. Although personality and intelligence, two of the primary targets of standardized tests, have some stability, they *can* vary according to the context in which the adolescent is evaluated. Adolescents may perform poorly on a standardized test of intelligence, but when observed in a less anxious setting, such as at home, they may display a much higher level of intelligence. This criticism is especially relevant to ethnic minority group adolescents, some of whom have been inappropriately classified as mentally retarded on the basis of their standardized intelligence test scores. For example, one Black American adolescent from a low-income family scored in the mentally retarded range on a standardized intelligence test, yet he was bright enough to plan an elaborate escape from the institution in which he lived. And cross-cultural psychologists caution that, while many psychological tests may work well in Western cultures, they may not always be appropriate in cultures where they were not developed (Lonner, 1990). Next, we further examine cross-cultural research methods.

Cross-Cultural Research Methods

Researchers who examine adolescent development in different cultures and ethnic groups need to follow certain strategies. When measures are used with cultural and ethnic groups with whom the researcher is unfamiliar, the measures must be constructed to be meaningful for all of the cultural or ethnic groups being studied. To accomplish this goal, researchers use information from all cultures in the investigation to develop a meaningful measure (Berry, 1980; Berry & others, in press).

In conducting developmental research on cultural and ethnic minority issues, investigators distinguish between the emic approach and the etic approach. In the **emic approach,** *the goal is to describe behavior in one culture or ethnic group in terms that are meaningful and important to the people in that culture or* *ethnic group, without regard to other cultures or ethnic groups.* In the **etic approach,** *the goal is to describe behavior so that generalizations can be made across cultures.* That is, the emic approach is culture-specific, the etic approach is more culture-universal. If researchers construct a questionnaire in an emic fashion, the concern is only that the questions are meaningful to the particular culture or ethnic group being studied. If, however, the researchers construct a questionnaire in an etic fashion, they want to include questions that reflect concepts familiar to all cultures involved (Brislin, 1990; Sue, 1990).

How might the emic and etic approaches be reflected in the study of family processes? In the emic approach, the researchers might choose to only focus on White, middle-class families, without regard for whether the information obtained in the study generalizes or is appropriate for ethnic minority groups. In a subsequent study, the researchers may decide to focus on White, lower-income families, Black American families, Hispanic American families, and Asian American families. In studying ethnic minority families, the researchers may discover that the extended family involving a number of relatives is more frequently a support system in ethnic minority families than in White American families. Thus, the emic approach would reveal a different patterning of family interaction than the etic approach, documenting that research with White, middle-class families cannot always be generalized to all ethnic groups.

In keeping with our theme of applying methods to adolescent aggression, cross-cultural researchers have discovered that aggression is a cultural universal, appearing in all cultures studied. Therefore, we can say that aggression is an etic behavior. But how aggression is expressed is sometimes culture-specific, which means that aggression is also an emic behavior (Segall & others, 1990). For example, members of the !Kung culture of southern Africa try to actively dissuade adolescents from behaving aggressively, while in the Yanamamo Indian culture in South America, the members promote aggression. Youth are told that adult status cannot be achieved until they are capable of killing, fighting, and pummeling others.

Physiological Research

Researchers can also use physiological measures to obtain information about adolescent development. Increased research into the biological basis of adolescence has produced some intriguing insights. For example, higher concentrations of some hormones are associated with aggressive behavior in male adolescents (Inoff-Germain & others, 1988; Paikoff & Brooks-Gunn, 1990).

Multimeasure, Multisource, Multicontext Approach

Methods have their strengths and weaknesses. Direct observation is a valuable tool for obtaining information about adolescents, but some things cannot be directly observed in adolescents—their moral thoughts, inner feelings, arguments with parents, how they acquire information about sex, and so on. In such instances, other measures, such as interviews, questionnaires, and case studies, may be valuable. Because every method has limitations, researchers have increasingly turned to multiple measures in assessing adolescent development. For example, a researcher might ask adolescents about their aggressive or delinquent behavior, check with their friends, observe them at home and in the neighborhood, interview their parents, and talk with teachers. Researchers hope that the convergence of multimeasure, multisource, and multicontext information will provide a more comprehensive and valid assessment of adolescent development.

In addition to selecting the methods for obtaining information about adolescent development, researchers also need to determine what kind of strategy will be used to set up the research study.

(a)

(b)

Aggression occurs in both the !Kung culture and in the Yanamamo culture. However, the !Kung of southern Africa (a) discourage aggression, while the Yanamamo of South America (b) actively promote aggression.

Figure 2.10 Examining the correlation between permissive parenting and adolescent self-control. This figure illustrates that an observed correlation between two events cannot be used to conclude that one event causes a second event. It could also be that the second event causes the first, or that a third event causes the correlation between the first two events.

 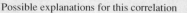

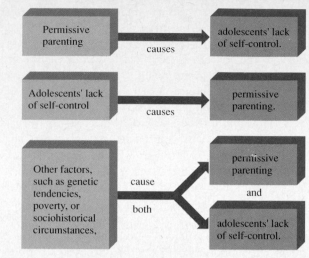

Strategies for Setting Up Research Studies

How can investigators determine if early maturation is related to an adolescent's self-image? How can they determine if lack of parental supervision in the after-school hours is associated with increased peer influence? How can they determine if listening to rock music lowers an adolescent's grades in school? When designing a research study to answer such questions, investigators must decide whether to use a correlational or an experimental strategy.

Correlational Strategy

With the **correlational strategy,** *the goal is to describe the strength of the relation between two or more events or characteristics.* This is a useful strategy because the more strongly events are correlated (related, or associated), the more one can be predicted from the other. For example, if researchers find that, as parents use more permissive ways to deal with their adolescents, the adolescents' self-control decreases, it does not necessarily mean that the parenting style caused the lack of self-control. It also could mean that the adolescents' lack of self-control stimulated parents to simply throw up their arms in despair and give up trying to control the obstreperous adolescents' behavior. Other factors also might be causing this correlation, such as genetic background, poverty, and sociohistorical conditioning. (A few decades ago, a permissive parenting strategy was widely advocated, but today it is no longer in vogue.) Figure 2.10 portrays these possible interpretations of correlational data.

The **correlation coefficient** *is a number based on statistical analysis that is used to describe the degree of association between two variables. The correlation coefficient ranges from −1.00 to +1.00.* A negative number means an inverse relation. For example, today researchers often do find a *negative* correlation between permissive parenting and adolescent self-control. And they often find a *positive* correlation between a parent's involvement in and monitoring of an adolescent's life and the adolescent's self-control. The higher the correlation coefficient (whether positive or negative), the stronger the association between the two variables. A correlation of −0.40 is a stronger correlation than +0.20 because the positive or negative nature of the correlation is disregarded in determining the correlation's magnitude.

Experimental Strategy

Whereas the correlational strategy allows investigators to say only that two events are related, the **experimental strategy** *allows them to precisely determine behavior's causes. Psychologists accomplish this task by performing an* **experiment,** *which is a carefully regulated setting in which one or more of the factors believed to influence the behavior being studied are manipulated and all others are held constant.* If the behavior under study changes when a factor is manipulated, we say that the manipulated factor causes the behavior to change. Experiments establish cause and effect between events, something correlational studies cannot do. *Cause* is the event being manipulated and *effect* is the behavior that changes because of the manipulation. Remember that, in testing correlation, nothing is manipulated; in an experiment, a researcher actively changes an event to see its effect on behavior.

The following example illustrates the nature of an experiment: The problem to be studied was whether a course in time management affects adolescent grades in school. To conduct the experiment researchers needed one group of adolescents who would take the course in time management and one that would not. The adolescents were randomly assigned to these two groups. **Random assignment** *occurs when researchers assign subjects to experimental and control conditions by chance, thus reducing the likelihood that the results of the experiment will be due to preexisting differences in the two groups.* For example, random assignment greatly reduces the probability that the two groups will differ on such factors as age, social class, intelligence, health problems, alertness, and so on.

The **independent variable** *is the manipulated, influential, experimental factor in the experiment.* This variable is *independent* because it can be changed independently of other factors. In the time management study, the time management course was the independent variable. The experimenter manipulated the nature of the course (content, length, instructor, and so on) independently of all other factors. The **dependent variable** *is the factor that is measured in an experiment; it may change because of the manipulation of the independent variable.* The variable is *dependent* because it depends on what happens to the subjects in the experiment. In the time management study, the dependent variable was the adolescents' grades in school. The adolescents' grades depended on the influence of the independent variable (whether or not a time management course was taken). An illustration of the experimental strategy, applied to the time management study, is shown in Figure 2.11.

It might seem as if researchers should always choose an experimental strategy over a correlational strategy, since the experimental strategy gives a better sense of one variable's influence over another. Yet, in three instances, a correlational strategy might be preferred: (1) when the focus of the investigation is so new that there is little knowledge of which factors to manipulate (for example, factors associated with AIDS); (2) when it is physically impossible to manipulate the variables (for example, suicide); and (3) when it is unethical to manipulate the variables (for example, determining the link between parenting strategies and adolescent competence).

Time Span of Inquiry

A special concern of developmentalists is the time span of a research investigation. Studies that focus on the relation of age to some other variable are common in the field of adolescent development. Researchers have several options: they can study different children and adolescents of different ages and compare them; they

Figure 2.11 Principles of the experimental strategy applied to the effects of time management instruction on adolescents' grades in school.

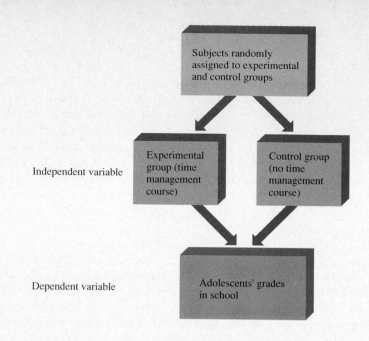

can study the same children and adolescents as they grow older over time; or they can use some combination of these approaches. We consider each of these in turn.

Cross-Sectional Approach

The **cross-sectional approach** *is a research strategy in which individuals of different ages are compared all at one time.* A typical cross-sectional study might include a group of 8-year-olds, 12-year-olds, and 16-year-olds. The different groups can be compared with respect to a number of dependent variables—IQ, memory, peer relations, attachment to parents, identity, hormonal changes, and so on. All of this can be accomplished in a short time—in some studies, data are collected in a single day. Even large-scale cross-sectional studies with hundreds of subjects usually do not take longer than several months to complete data collection.

The main advantage of a cross-sectional study is that researchers do not have to wait for subjects to age. Despite its time efficiency, however, the cross-sectional approach has its drawbacks: It gives no information about how individuals change or about the stability of their characteristics. The increases and decreases—the hills and valleys—of growth and development can become obscured in the cross-sectional approach. Also, because the individuals being studied are of different ages and different groups, they may have experienced different types of parenting and schooling.

Longitudinal Approach

The **longitudinal approach** *is a research strategy in which the same individuals are studied over a period of time, usually several years or more.* In a typical longitudinal study of the same topics discussed under the cross-sectional approach, researchers might structure a test that they administer to children and adolescents when they are 8, 12, and 16 years old. In this example, the same children would be studied over an eight-year time span, allowing investigators to examine patterns of change within each individual child or adolescent. One of the great values of the longitudinal approach is its evaluation of how individual children and adolescents change as they grow up.

Fewer longitudinal than cross-sectional studies are conducted because longitudinal studies are time consuming and costly. A close examination of the longitudinal approach also reveals some additional problems: (1) Since children or adolescents are examined over a long period of time, some of them drop out because they lose interest or move away and cannot be recontacted by the investigator. A fairly common finding is that the remaining adolescents represent a slightly biased sample, in that they tend to be psychologically better or superior to those who have dropped out on almost every dimension the investigator thinks to check out (for example, intelligence, motivation, and cooperativeness). (2) With repeated testing, individual adolescents may become "testwise," which may increase their ability to perform "better" or "more maturely" the next time the investigator interacts with them.

Sequential Approach

Developmentalists also sometimes combine the cross-sectional and longitudinal approaches (Schaie, 1973, 1989, 1991). The **sequential approach** *is the term used to describe the combined cross-sectional, longitudinal design.* In most instances, this approach starts with a cross-sectional study that includes individuals of different ages. A number of months or years after the initial assessment, the same individuals are tested again—this is the longitudinal aspect of the design. At this later time, a new group of subjects is assessed at each age level. The new groups at each level are added at the later time to control for changes that might have occurred in the original group of subjects—for example, some may have dropped out of the study, or retesting might improve their performance. The sequential approach is complex, expensive, and time consuming, but it provides information that is impossible to obtain from the cross-sectional or longitudinal approach alone. The sequential approach has been especially helpful in examining cohort effects in adolescent development, which we discuss next.

Cohort Effects

Cohort effects *are those due to a subject's time of birth or generation but not actually to age.* For example, cohorts can differ in years of education, child-rearing practices, health, attitudes toward sex, religious values, and economic status. Cohort effects can powerfully affect the dependent measures in a study ostensibly concerned with age. Researchers have shown that cohort effects are especially important to investigate in the assessment of intelligence (Willis, 1989; Willis & Schaie, 1986). For example, individuals born at different points in time—such as 1920, 1950, and 1980—have had varying opportunities for education, with individuals born earlier having less access.

Now that we have examined the main ways that developmentalists conduct research, we consider how adolescent development research can become less sexist and ethical considerations in developmental research.

Reducing Sexist Research

Traditional science is presented as being value-free and thus a more valid way of studying mental processes and behavior. However, there is a growing consensus that science in general, and psychology in particular, are not value-free (Doyle & Paludi, 1991). A special concern is that the vast majority of psychological research has been male-oriented and male-dominated. Some researchers believe that male-dominated sciences such as psychology need to be challenged to examine the world in a new way, one that incorporates girls' and women's perspectives and respects their ethnicity, sexual orientation, age, and socioeconomic

Florence Denmark (shown here talking with a group of students) has developed a number of guidelines for nonsexist research. Denmark and others believe that psychology needs to be challenged to examine the world in a new way, one that incorporates girls' and women's perspectives.

status (Denmark & others, 1988; McHugh, Koeske, & Frieze, 1986; Quina, 1986). For example, Florence Denmark and her colleagues (1988) provided the following three recommendations as guidelines for nonsexist research:

1. Research methods
    Problem: The selection of research participants is based on stereotypic assumptions and does not allow for generalizations to other groups.
    Example: On the basis of stereotypes about who should be responsible for contraception, only females are studied.
    Correction: Both sexes should be studied before conclusions are drawn about the factors that determine contraception use.
2. Data analysis
    Problem: Gender differences are inaccurately magnified.
    Example: While only 24 percent of the girls were found to . . . fully 28 percent of the boys were . . .
    Correction: The results should include extensive descriptions of the data so that inappropriate presentations of differences are not exaggerated.
3. Conclusions
    Problem: The title or abstract (a summary) of an article makes no reference to the limitations of the study participants and implies a broader scope of the study than is warranted.
    Example: A study purporting to be about "perceptions of the disabled" uses only blind, White boys.
    Correction: Use more precise titles and clearly describe the sample and its selection criteria in the abstract or summary.

Ethics in Research on Adolescent Development

When Pete and Ann, two 19-year-old college students, agreed to participate in an investigation of dating couples, they did not consider that the questionnaire they filled out would get them to think about issues that might lead to conflict in their relationship and possibly end it. One year after this investigation (Rubin & Mitchell, 1976), nine of the ten participants said that they had discussed their answers with their dating partner. In most instances, the discussions strengthened their relationship. But in some cases, the participants used the questionnaire as a springboard to discuss problems or concerns previously hidden. One participant said, "The study definitely played a role in ending my relationship with Larry." In this circumstance, the couple had different views about how long they expected to be together. She anticipated that the relationship would end much sooner than Larry thought. Discussion of their answers to the questions brought the long-term prospects of the relationship out in the open, and eventually Larry found someone who was more interested in marrying him.

At first glance, you would not think that a questionnaire on dating relationships would have any substantial impact on the participants' behavior. But psychologists increasingly recognize that they must exercise considerable caution to ensure the well-being of the participants in a psychological study. Today, colleges and universities have review boards that evaluate the ethical nature of research conducted at their institutions. Proposed research plans must pass the scrutiny of an ethics research committee before the research can be initiated.

In addition, the American Psychological Association (APA) has developed guidelines for the ethics of its members. The APA code of ethics instructs researchers to protect their subjects from mental and physical harm. The best interests of the subjects need to be kept foremost in the researcher's mind. All subjects, if they are old enough, must give their informed consent to participate in the research study. This requires that subjects know what their participation will entail and any risks that might develop. For example, subjects in an investigation of the effects of divorce on adolescent development should be told beforehand that interview questions might stimulate thought about issues they might not anticipate. The subjects should also be informed that, in some instances, a discussion of the family's experiences might improve family relationships, while in other instances, it might bring up issues that bring the adolescent unwanted stress.

At this point, we have discussed a number of ideas about conducting research on adolescent development. A summary of these ideas is presented in Concept Table 2.3. This concludes Section I of the book. In the next section, we turn our attention to the biological and cognitive changes of adolescent development.

Concept Table 2.3

Research Methods in Adolescent Development

Concept	Processes/Related Ideas	Characteristics/Description
Scientific method	Its steps	The scientific method consists of a series of procedures to obtain accurate information. Its steps include identifying and analyzing a problem, collecting data, drawing conclusions, and revising theories.
Ways of collecting information—methods	Observation	Observation is a key ingredient in adolescent development research that includes laboratory and naturalistic observation.
	Interviews and questionnaires	They are used to assess perceptions and attitudes. Social desirability of responses is a special problem with their use.
	Case studies	They provide an in-depth look at an individual. Caution in generalizing is warranted.
	Standardized tests	They are designed to assess an individual's characteristics relative to those of a large group of similar individuals.
	Cross-cultural research	This research focuses on the culture-universal (etic) and culture-specific (emic) nature of adolescent development.
	Physiological research	This research examines the biological dimensions of the adolescent.
	Multimeasure, multisource, multicontext approach	Increasingly, a strategy in the study of adolescents is to use different measures, obtaining information from different sources, and observing in different contexts.
Strategies for setting up research studies	Correlational strategy	This describes how strongly two or more events or characteristics are related. It does not allow causal statements.
	Experimental strategy	This involves manipulation of influential factors (the independent variables) and measurement of their effect on the dependent variables. Subjects are randomly assigned to experimental and control groups in many studies. The experimental strategy can reveal the causes of behavior and show how one event influenced another.
Time span of inquiry	Cross-sectional approach	This involves comparing individuals of different ages all at one time.
	Longitudinal approach	This involves studying the same individuals over a period of time, usually several years or more.
	Sequential approach	This is a combined cross-sectional, longitudinal approach that evaluates cohort effects in development.
Cohort effects	Their nature	Cohort effects are due to a subject's generation or time of birth but not actually to age. The study of cohort effects underscores the importance of considering the historical dimensions of adolescent development.
Sexist bias	Its nature	A concern is that the vast majority of psychological research has been male-oriented and male-dominated. Some researchers believe that developmentalists need to be challenged to examine adolescents' worlds in a new way, one that incorporates girls' and women's perspectives. Recommendations have been made for conducting nonsexist research.
Ethics in research on adolescent development	Its nature	Researchers are required to ensure the well-being of subjects. The risk of mental and physical harm must be reduced, and informed consent should be obtained.

Summary

I. What Are Theories?

Theories are general beliefs that help us to explain what we observe and to make predictions. A good theory has hypotheses, which are assumptions that can be tested.

II. Psychoanalytic Theories

Freud's and Erikson's theories are two main psychoanalytic theories of adolescent development. Freud said that our personality has three structures—id, ego, and superego—that conflict with each other. Most of our thoughts are unconscious in Freud's view, and the id is completely unconscious. The conflicting demands of personality structures produce anxiety; defense mechanisms, especially repression, protect the ego and reduce anxiety. Freud was convinced that problems develop because of childhood experiences. He said that we go through five psychosexual stages—oral, anal, phallic, latency, and genital. During the phallic stage, the Oedipus complex is a main source of conflict. Erikson's theory emphasizes eight psychosocial stages of development: trust versus mistrust, autonomy versus shame and doubt, initiative versus guilt, industry versus inferiority, identity versus identity confusion, intimacy versus isolation, generativity versus stagnation, and integrity versus despair. Strengths of the psychoanalytic theories are an emphasis on the past, the developmental course of personality, mental representation of the environment, unconscious mind, and emphasis on conflict. Weaknesses are the difficulty in testing main concepts, lack of an empirical data base and overreliance on past reports, too much emphasis on sexuality and the unconscious mind, and a negative view of human nature.

III. Cognitive Theories

Piaget's cognitive developmental theory and the information-processing view are the two main cognitive theories. Piaget's theory is responsible for the field of cognitive development. He believed that we are motivated to understand our world and use the processes of organization and adaptation (assimilation and accommodation) to do so. Piaget said that we go through four cognitive stages: sensorimotor, preoperational, concrete operational, and formal operational. The information-processing approach is concerned with how we process information about our world, including how information gets into our mind, how it is stored and transformed, and how it is retrieved to think and solve problems. The development of the computer promoted this approach—the mind as an information-processing system is compared to how a computer processes information. The information-processing approach raises questions about development, among them the rise and decline of information-processing speed. Both the Piagetian and the information-processing approaches have made important contributions to understanding adolescent development. They have provided a positive, rational portrayal of human development, although they may underestimate the power of unconscious thought and environmental experiences. The purity of Piaget's stages has been questioned, and the information-processing approach has not yet produced an overall perspective on development.

IV. Behavioral and Social Learning Theories

The two main approaches in this theoretical orientation are Skinner's behaviorism and social learning theory. Skinner's behaviorism emphasizes that cognition is not important in understanding development and that development is observed behavior, which is determined by rewards and punishments in the environment. In social learning theory, the environment is an important determinant of behavior, but so are cognitive processes. Social learning theorists believe that we control our own behavior through thoughts, beliefs, and values. Bandura's emphasis on observational learning exemplifies the social learning approach, as does his model of the reciprocal influences of behavior, person (cognition), and environment. The contemporary version of social learning theory is called cognitive social learning theory.

V. Ecological Theories

Ecological theories emphasize the role of social contexts in development. The most widely adopted ecological theory was proposed by Bronfenbrenner. He described five environmental systems: the microsystem, mesosystem, exosystem, macrosystem, and chronosystem. Bronfenbrenner's theory is one of the few comprehensive models of environmental influences on development and includes both macro and micro aspects of environmental influence. Criticisms focus on the lack of emphasis on biological and cognitive processes.

VI. An Eclectic Approach to Adolescent Development

Each of the theories described has a number of strengths and weaknesses, but no single theory is capable of explaining the complexity of adolescent development. For this reason, this text adopts an eclectic approach to adolescent development.

VII. The Scientific Method and Measures

The scientific method is a series of procedures to obtain accurate information. Its steps include identifying and analyzing a problem, collecting data, drawing conclusions, and revising theories. Observation, interviews and questionnaires, case studies, standardized tests, cross-cultural research, and physiological assessment are the main ways developmentalists collect information. Observation is a key ingredient of a scientific approach to development and includes both laboratory and naturalistic observation. Interviews and questionnaires are used to assess perceptions and attitudes. A special problem with their use is social desirability of responses. Case studies provide an in-depth look at an individual; caution in generalizing is warranted. Standardized tests are designed to assess an individual's characteristics relative to those of a large group of similar individuals. Cross-cultural research focuses on the culture-universal (etic) and culture-specific (emic) nature of adolescent development. Physiological research focuses on the biological dimensions of the adolescent. Researchers increasingly study adolescents using multiple measures, multiple sources, and multiple contexts.

VIII. Strategies for Setting Up Research Studies

The two main strategies are correlational and experimental. The correlational strategy describes how strongly two or more events or characteristics are related. It does not allow causal statements. The experimental strategy involves manipulation of influential factors (the independent variables) and measurement of their effect on the dependent variables. Subjects are randomly assigned to experimental and control groups in many studies. The experimental strategy can reveal the cause of behavior and show how one event influenced another.

IX. Time Span of Inquiry and Cohort Effects

The three time spans are cross-sectional, longitudinal, and sequential. In the cross-sectional approach, individuals of different ages are compared all at one time. In the longitudinal approach, the same individuals are studied over a period of time, usually several years or more. The sequential approach is a combined cross-sectional, longitudinal approach that evaluates cohort effects in development. Cohort effects are due to a subject's generation or time of birth but not actually to age.

X. Reducing Sexist Bias; Ethics in Research on Adolescent Development

A special concern is that the vast amount of psychological research has been male-dominated and male-oriented. Some researchers believe that developmentalists need to be challenged to examine adolescents' worlds in a new way, one that incorporates girls' and women's perspectives. Recommendations have been made for conducting nonsexist research. Researchers must ensure the well-being of their subjects. The risk of mental and physical harm must be reduced, and informed consent should be obtained.

Key Terms

theory 43
hypotheses 43
id 44
pleasure principle 44
ego 44
reality principle 44
superego 44
defense mechanisms 45
repression 45
sublimation 46
rationalization 46
projection 46
reaction formation 46
regression 47
erogenous zones 47
fixation 47
oral stage 47
anal stage 47
phallic stage 47
Oedipus complex 47
latency stage 48
genital stage 49
epigenetic principle 50
trust versus mistrust 50
autonomy versus shame
    and doubt 50
initiative versus guilt 50
industry versus
    inferiority 51

identity versus identity
    confusion 51
intimacy versus
    isolation 51
generativity versus
    stagnation 51
integrity versus
    despair 51
cognitive developmental
    theory 55
assimilation 55
accommodation 55
sensorimotor stage 55
preoperational stage 55
concrete operational
    stage 58
formal operational
    stage 58
information-processing
    theory 58
behaviorism 62
operant conditioning 63
reinforcement 63
punishment 63
social learning
    theory 63
ecological theories 65
microsystem 65
mesosystem 65

exosystem 65
macrosystem 66
chronosystem 66
scientific method 69
laboratory 70
naturalistic
    observation 70
social desirability 71
questionnaire 71
case study 71
standardized tests 72
emic approach 72
etic approach 73
correlational
    strategy 74
correlation
    coefficient 74
experimental
    strategy 75
experiment 75
random assignment 75
independent variable 75
dependent variable 75
cross-sectional
    approach 76
longitudinal
    approach 76
sequential approach 77
cohort effects 77

Suggested Readings

Achenbach, T. (1978). *Research in developmental psychology: Concepts, strategies, and methods.* New York: Free Press.
    A well-written introduction to research in developmental psychology with examples of different strategies and designs.
Erikson, Erik. (1968). *Identity: Youth and crisis.* New York: Norton.
    Erikson's most detailed work on adolescents. Exciting reading, with many insights into the lives of individual adolescents that apply to the lives of all adolescents.
Miller, P. H. (1989). Developmental theories of adolescence. In J. Worrell & F. Danner (Eds.). *The adolescent as decision maker.* New York: Academic Press.
    A concise overview of main theories in adolescent development is presented.
Muuss, R. E. (1989). *Theories of adolescence* (5th ed.). New York: Random House.
    Provides a broad overview of theories of adolescence, including those discussed in this chapter, a number of European theories, as well as others.
Vasta, R. (Ed.). (1989). *Six theories of child development: Revised formulations and current issues.* Greenwich, CT: JAI Press.
    A recent overview of major developmental theories by leading experts, including Bandura.

Biological and Cognitive Development

*I think that what is happening to
me is so wonderful and not only
what can be seen on my body, but
all that is taking place inside. I
never discuss myself with anybody;
that is why I have to talk to myself
about them.*

Anne Frank, Diary of
a Young Girl, *1947*

Adolescence is the transition
from childhood to adulthood
that involves biological,
cognitive, and social development.
These strands of development are
interwoven in the adolescent's life.
This section focuses on adolescents'
biological and cognitive development
and consists of three chapters:
Chapter 3, "Biological Processes
and Physical Development";
Chapter 4, "Cognitive Development
and Social Cognition"; and Chapter
5, "Information Processing and
Intelligence."

CHAPTER 3

Biological Processes and Physical Development

*In Youth, We Clothe Ourselves
with Rainbows and Go Brave
As the Zodiac.*

Emerson

Puberty's Mysteries and Curiosities

I am pretty confused. I wonder whether I am weird or normal. My body is starting to change, but I sure don't look like a lot of my friends. I still look like a kid for the most part. My best friend is only 13, but he looks like he is 16 or 17. I get nervous in the locker room during PE class because when I go to take a shower, I'm afraid somebody is going to make fun of me since I'm not as physically developed as some of the others.

Robert, age 12

I don't like my breasts. They are too small, and they look funny. I'm afraid guys won't like me if they don't get bigger.

Angie, age 13

I can't stand the way I look. I have zits all over my face. My hair is dull and stringy. It never stays in place. My nose is too big. My lips are too small. My legs are too short. I have four warts on my left hand, and people get grossed out by them. So do I. My body is a disaster!

Ann, age 14

I'm short and I can't stand it. My father is six feet tall, and here I am only five foot four. I'm 14 already. I look like a kid, and I get teased a lot, especially by other guys. I'm always the last one picked for sides in basketball because I'm so short. Girls don't seem to be interested in me either because most of them are taller than I am.

Jim, age 14

The comments of these four adolescents in the midst of pubertal change underscore the dramatic upheaval in our bodies following the calm, consistent growth of middle and late childhood. Young adolescents develop an acute concern about their bodies. When columnist Bob Greene (1988) dialed a party line called Connections in Chicago to discover what young adolescents were saying to each other, the first things the boys and girls asked for—after first names—were physical descriptions. The idealism of the callers was apparent. Most of the girls described themselves as having long blond hair, being 5 feet, 5 inches tall, and weighing about 110 pounds. Most of the boys said that they had brown hair, lifted weights, were 6 feet tall, and weighed 170 pounds.

*Puberty: The Time of Life When the Two Sexes
Begin to First Become Acquainted.*

Samuel Johnson

P uberty's changes are perplexing to adolescents. But while these changes bring forth doubts, questions, fears, and anxieties, most of us survive them quite well. Our journey through puberty's fascinating moments explores the nature of puberty and its psychological dimensions. But first we evaluate the contributions of heredity to adolescent development.

Genetic Influences on Adolescent Development

Genetic influences are still important some 10 to 20 years after conception. No matter what the species, there must be some mechanism for transmitting characteristics from one generation to the next. Each adolescent carries a genetic code inherited from his or her parents. The genetic codes of all adolescents are alike in one important way—they all contain the human genetic code. Because of the human genetic code, a fertilized human egg cannot grow into an eel, an egret, or an elephant.

The Nature of Genes

We each began life as a single cell weighing 1/20 millionth of an ounce! This tiny piece of matter housed our entire genetic code—the information about whom we would become. These instructions orchestrated growth from that single cell to an adolescent made of trillions of cells, each containing a perfect replica of the original genetic code. Physically, the hereditary code is carried by biochemical agents called genes and chromosomes. Aside from the obvious physical similarity this code produces among adolescents (such as in anatomy, brain structure, and organs), it also accounts for much of our psychological sameness (or universality).

No one possesses all the characteristics that our genetic structure makes possible. A **genotype** *is a person's genetic heritage, the actual genetic material.* However, not all of this genetic material is apparent in our observed and measurable characteristics. A **phenotype** *is the way an individual's genotype is expressed in observed and measurable characteristics.* Phenotypes include physical traits, such as height, weight, eye color, and skin pigmentation, as well as psychological characteristics, such as intelligence, creativity, personality, and social tendencies. For each genotype, a range of phenotypes can be expressed. Imagine that we could identify all of the genes that would make an adolescent introverted or extraverted. Would measured introversion-extraversion be predictable from knowledge of the specific genes? The answer is no, because even if our genetic model was adequate, introversion-extraversion is a characteristic shaped by experience throughout life. For example, a parent may push an introverted child into social situations and encourage the child to become more gregarious.

Genetic codes predispose adolescents to develop in a particular way, and environments are either responsive or unresponsive to this development. For example, the genotype of some adolescents may predispose them to be introverted in an environment that promotes a turning inward of personality, yet in an environment that encourages social interaction and outgoingness, these adolescents

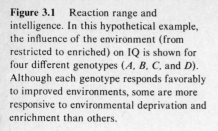

Figure 3.1 Reaction range and intelligence. In this hypothetical example, the influence of the environment (from restricted to enriched) on IQ is shown for four different genotypes (*A, B, C,* and *D*). Although each genotype responds favorably to improved environments, some are more responsive to environmental deprivation and enrichment than others.

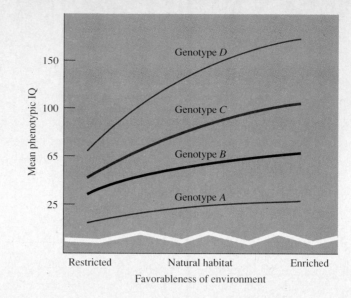

may become more extraverted. However, the adolescent with this introverted genotype is unlikely to become a strong extravert. The term **reaction range** *describes the range of phenotypes for each genotype, suggesting the importance of the environment's restrictiveness or enrichment* (see Figure 3.1).

Sandra Scarr (1984) explains reaction range in the following way: Each of us has a range of potential. For example, an individual may be shorter than average. No matter how well fed the individual is, an individual with "short" genes will never be taller than average. Scarr believes that such characteristics as intelligence and introversion work the same way. That is, there is a range within which the environment can modify intelligence, but intelligence is not completely malleable. Reaction range gives us an estimate of how malleable intelligence is.

Genotypes, in addition to producing many phenotypes, may yield some characteristics that are immune to extensive changes in the environment. These characteristics seem to stay on a particular developmental course regardless of environmental assaults (Waddington, 1957). **Canalization** *is the process by which characteristics take a narrow path or developmental course. Apparently, preservative forces help protect or buffer a person from environmental extremes.* For example, developmental psychologist Jerome Kagan (1984) points to his research on Guatemalan infants who had experienced extreme malnutrition as infants yet showed normal social and cognitive development later in childhood.

Methods Used by Behavior Geneticists

Behavior genetics *is concerned with the degree and nature of behavior's heredity basis.* Behavior geneticists assume that behaviors are jointly determined by the interaction of heredity and environment, and they often use twin studies or adoption studies to investigate heredity's influence on development.

In a **twin study,** *the behavior of identical twins is compared with the behavior of fraternal twins.* **Identical twins** *(called monozygotic twins) develop from a single fertilized egg that splits into two genetically identical replicas, each of which becomes a person.* **Fraternal twins** *(called dyzygotic twins) develop from separate eggs, making them genetically less similar than identical twins.* Although fraternal twins share the same womb, they are no more alike genetically than are nontwin brothers and sisters, and they may be of different sexes. By comparing groups of identical and fraternal twins, behavior geneticists capitalize on the basic knowledge that identical twins are more similar genetically than are fraternal twins. In one twin study, 7,000 pairs of Finnish identical and fraternal twins were compared on the personality traits of extraversion (outgoingness) and neuroticism (psychological instability) (Rose & others, 1988). On both of these personality traits, identical twins were much more similar than fraternal twins, suggesting the role of heredity in both traits. However, several issues crop up in the interpretation of twin studies results. Adults may stress the similarities of identical twins more than those of fraternal twins, and identical twins may perceive themselves as a "set" and play together more than fraternal twins. If so, observed similarities in identical twins could be environmentally influenced.

In an **adoption study,** *the investigators seek to discover whether the behavior and psychological characteristics of adopted adolescents are more like their adoptive parents, who provided a home environment, or their biological parents, who contributed their heredity.* In one investigation, the educational levels attained by biological parents were better predictors of adopted children's IQ scores than were the IQs of children's adopted parents (Scarr & Weinberg, 1983), which implies that heredity influences children's IQ scores.

These identical twins came from a single fertilized egg that split into two genetic replicas. Identical twins are more similar genetically than fraternal twins, who develop from separate eggs.

The concept of heritability is used in many twin and adoption studies. **Heritability** *is the statistical estimate of the degree to which physical, cognitive, and social characteristics among individuals are due to their genetic differences. Heritability is measured by correlational statistical procedures.* The highest degree of heritability is 1.00. A heritability quotient of .80 suggests a strong genetic influence, one of .50 a moderate genetic influence, and one of .20 a much weaker but nonetheless perceptible genetic influence.

The heritability index is not a flawless measure of heredity's influence on development. It is only as good as the information fed into it and the assumptions made about genetic-environmental interaction. First, how varied are the environments being sampled? The narrower the range of the environments, the higher the heritability index; the broader the range of environments, the lower the heritability index. Another important consideration is the validity and reliability of the measure being used in the investigation. That is, what is the quality of the measure? The weaker the measure, the less confidence investigators have in the heritability index. A final consideration is that the heritability index assumes that heredity and environment can be separated, that information can be quantitatively added together to arrive at a discrete influence for each. In reality, heredity and environment interact. Their interaction is lost when the heritability index is computed. Now that we have considered some basic ideas about heredity's role in development, let's turn our attention to a specific human characteristic— temperament—to see biology's role in its development.

Temperament

Temperament *is an individual's behavioral style and characteristic way of responding.* Some adolescents' behavioral style is extremely active, others' more tranquil. Some adolescents show a strong curiosity for exploring their environment for great lengths of time; others show less curiosity. Some adolescents respond warmly to people; others are much more shy. All of these behavioral styles represent an adolescent's temperament.

A widely debated issue in temperament research is defining the key dimensions of temperament. Alexander Chess and Stella Thomas (Chess & Thomas,

Table 3.1 Dimensions and Clusters of Temperament in Chess and Thomas's Research

Temperament Dimension	Description	Temperament Cluster		
		Easy Child	Difficult Child	Slow-to-Warm-Up Child
Rhythmicity	Regularity of eating, sleeping, toileting	Regular	Irregular	
Activity level	Degree of energy movement		High	Low
Approach-withdrawal	Ease of approaching new people and situations	Positive	Negative	Negative
Adaptability	Ease of tolerating change in routine plans	Positive	Negative	Negative
Sensory threshold	Amount of stimulation required for responding			
Predominant quality of mood	Degree of positive or negative affect	Positive	Negative	
Intensity of mood expression	Degree of affect when pleased, displeased, happy, sad	Low to moderate	High	Low
Distractibility/attention span/persistence	Ease of being distracted			

Note: This table shows which of the dimensions were critical in spotting a basic cluster of temperament and what the level of responsiveness was for a critical feature. A blank space indicates that the dimension was not strongly related to a basic cluster of temperament.

1977; Thomas & Chess, 1987) believe that there are three basic types, or clusters, of temperament—easy, difficult, and slow-to-warm-up:

1. An **easy child** *is generally in a positive mood, quickly establishes regular routines, and adapts easily to new experiences.*
2. A **difficult child** *tends to react negatively and fuss a lot, engages in irregular daily routines, and is slow to accept new experiences.*
3. A **slow-to-warm-up child** *has a low activity level, is somewhat negative, shows low adaptability, and displays a low intensity of mood.*

Different dimensions make up these three basic clusters of temperament, as shown in Table 3.1. In their longitudinal study, Chess and Thomas found that 40 percent of the children they studied could be classified as "easy," 10 percent as "difficult," and 15 percent as "slow-to-warm-up."

A number of scholars, including Chess and Thomas, conceive of temperament as a stable characteristic of newborns that comes to be shaped and modified by the child's and adolescent's later experiences (Thomas & Chess, 1987, 1991; Goldsmith, 1988). This raises the question of heredity's role in temperament. Twin and adoption studies conducted to answer this question have found a heritability index in the range of .50 to .60, indicating that heredity has a moderate influence on temperament (Plomin, 1989, 1991a). However, the strength of the association usually declines as infants become older (Goldsmith & Gottesman, 1981), which supports the belief that temperament becomes more malleable with experience. Alternatively, behavioral indicators of temperament may be more difficult to spot in older children.

The **goodness-of-fit model** *states that the adolescent's adaptation is best when there is a congruence, or match, between the adolescent's temperament and the demands of the social environment (for example, the expectations or attitudes of parents, peers, and teachers)* (Lerner & Lerner, 1983; Nitz & Lerner,

1991; Talwar, Nitz, & Lerner, 1990; Thomas & Chess, 1977). A high-strung parent with an adolescent who is difficult and slow to respond to the parent's affection may begin to feel angry or rejected. Parents may withdraw from difficult adolescents, or they may become critical and punish them, which may make the difficult adolescent even more difficult. A more easygoing parent may have a calming effect on a difficult adolescent.

Heredity-Environment Interaction and Development

In temperament and all other characteristics, both genes and environment are necessary for the individual to even exist: No genes, no organism; no environment, no organism (Scarr, 1989; Scarr & Weinberg, 1980; Weinberg, 1989). Heredity and environment operate together—or cooperate—to produce an adolescent's temperament, intelligence, height, weight, ability to pitch a baseball, career interests, and so on. If an attractive, popular, intelligent girl is elected president of her senior class in high school, would we conclude that her success is due to environment or to heredity? Of course, it is both. Because the environment's influence depends on genetically endowed characteristics, the two factors are said to *interact*. (Plomin, 1989, 1991b).

But as we have seen, developmentalists probe further to determine more precisely the influence of heredity and environment on development. What is known about heredity-environment interaction? According to developmental behavior geneticists Sandra Scarr and Kenneth Kidd (1983), we know that literally hundreds of disorders appear because of genetic miscodings. We know that abnormalities in chromosome number adversely affect the development of physical, intellectual, and behavioral features. We know that genotype and phenotype do not map onto each other in one-to-one fashion. We know that it is very difficult to distinguish between genetic and cultural transmission. There usually is a familial concentration of a particular disorder, but familial patterns are considerably different than what would be precisely predicted from simple modes of inheritance. We know that, when we consider the normal range of variation, the stronger the genetic resemblance, the stronger the behavioral resemblance. This holds more strongly for intelligence than personality or interests. The influence of genes on intelligence is present early in children's development and continues through the late adulthood years. We also know that being raised in the same family accounts for some portion of intellectual differences among individuals, but common rearing accounts for little of the variation in personality or interests. One reason for this discrepancy may be that families place similar pressures on their children for intellectual development in the sense that the push is clearly toward the highest level, but they do not direct their children toward similar personalities or interests, in which extremes are not especially desirable. That is, virtually all parents would like their children to have above-average intellect, but there is much less agreement about whether a child should be highly extraverted.

What do we need to know about the role of heredity-environmental interaction in development? Scarr and Kidd (1983) commented that we need to know the pathways by which genetic abnormalities influence development. We need to know more about genetic-environmental interaction in the normal range of development. For example, what accounts for the difference in one individual's IQ of 95 and another individual's IQ of 125? The answer requires information about cultural and genetic influences. We also need to know about heredity's influence across the entire life cycle. For instance, puberty is not an environmentally produced accident (Rowe & Rodgers, 1989); neither is menopause. While puberty and menopause can be influenced by such environmental factors as nutrition, weight, drugs, health, and the like, the basic evolutionary and genetic program

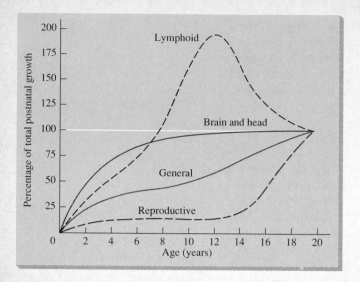

Figure 3.2 Growth and maturity of body systems as a percentage of total postnatal growth.

is wired into the species. It cannot be eliminated; nor should it be ignored. This genetic perspective gives biology its appropriate role in our quest to better understand human development through the life cycle. Next, we consider other dimensions of biology's role in adolescent development and evaluate some general features of physical growth in adolescence.

General Features of Physical Growth in Adolescence

Aspects of adolescents' physical growth that have received the most attention are height and weight, skeletal growth, reproductive functions, and hormonal changes. What is the nature of growth curves for such bodily characteristics? What factors influence these growth curves? We consider each of these questions in turn.

Four Developmental Growth Curves

The developmental growth curves for physical development in general, for the reproductive organs, for the brain and head, and for the lymphoid glands are shown in Figure 3.2. Most skeletal and muscular components of growth, such as height and weight, follow the general curve, as do organs like the liver and kidneys. This growth curve changes gradually in the beginning but rises dramatically at about age 12, characterizing what is commonly referred to as the adolescent growth spurt.

However, the growth curve for the reproductive organs changes even more dramatically than the general curve for height and weight. The prepubertal phase of reproductive development is fairly dormant, but the adolescent phase of the curve is even more precipitous than the adolescent phase of the general height and weight curve. Why is there a difference in the growth curves for height and weight as compared to reproductive functions? The answer lies in an analysis of glandular and hormonal influences. The glands and hormones that control height and weight are not the same ones that regulate reproductive functions. The development of the skeletal and muscular systems, along with that of most organs, is controlled by the pituitary and thyroid glands. On the other hand, the growth of the reproductive organs is regulated by the sex hormones (androgens and estrogens), which show marked increases in activity at the onset of adolescence.

A third growth curve represents the development of the skull, eyes, and ears, which mature sooner than any other parts of the body. At any point during childhood, the head is, in general, more advanced developmentally than any other aspect of the body. And the top parts of the head—the eyes and brain—grow faster than the lower portions, such as the jaw.

Some biologists (Epstein, 1974, 1978) and educators (Toepfer, 1979) argue that the brain does not grow in the relatively smooth, continuous fashion illustrated in Figure 3.2. These same individuals argue that, just as there is a height, weight, and sexual spurt that characterizes puberty, so, too, there is a spurt in brain growth. Brain growth spurts are said to occur between 2 and 4, 6 and 8, 10 and 12, and 14 and 16 years of age. During these spurts, the brain is believed to increase from 5 to 10 percent in size. Since cell formation in the brain is essentially complete at birth, these growth spurts are not due to new cells being formed but to growth within already-formed cells.

The scientists who stress brain growth spurts also believe that these growth spurts affect the brain's synapses (the points of contact between axons (or sending connectors) and dendrites (or receiving connectors). During the growth spurts, the axons and dendrites lengthen. Perspective on Adolescent Development 3.1 presents more information about the importance of the brain in adolescent development and the nature of brain growth spurts.

Factors That Influence Growth Curves

Currently, at least four mechanisms are known to influence growth curves: target-seeking or self-stabilizing factors, maturity gradients, feedback regulation, and body mass (Damon, 1977). Concerning *target-seeking or self-stabilizing factors,* in cases where growth has been stunted by disease or poor nutrition, the individual's growth often catches up with its original path after the negative conditions have been removed. This regulatory force likely has a genetic basis.

Maturity gradients are known to be present in different regions of the body. For example, the head is always more advanced developmentally than the trunk, and the trunk is always more advanced developmentally than the limbs.

Feedback regulation involves biological structures adapting to feedback. For example, the secretions of the pituitary gland influence various other glands, such as the thyroid and the sex glands; the pituitary secretions adjust to the levels of hormones in the other glands. When the other glands' secretions reach appropriate levels, the pituitary regulates its output to continue the equilibrium that has developed.

With regard to *body mass,* Rose Frisch and Roger Revelle (1970; Frisch, 1991) argue that the body has built-in sensors that detect when a certain mass is reached. These detectors then trigger the growth spurt that occurs at the onset of puberty. For young girls, a body weight approximating 106 ± 3 pounds triggers menarche (the first menstruation) and the conclusion of the pubertal growth spurt. Body mass predicts the approximate time female adolescents experience menarche in many different cultures.

At this point, we have discussed a number of ideas about heredity and about general features of growth in adolescence. A summary of these ideas is presented in Concept Table 3.1.

The Adolescent's Brain, Brain Growth Spurts, Cognitive Development, and Education

One biologist, Herman Epstein (1974, 1980), proposed a simple hypothesis: When boys and girls move into one of Piaget's cognitive developmental periods, their brains reveal an unusual amount of growth as well. How did Epstein measure brain growth? He used two methods: growth of the head, particularly its circumference, which is closely linked to brain size, and evaluation of electrical waves through use of the electroencephalograph (EEG). These brain waves are influenced by cognitive activities like thinking and problem solving.

With regard to head circumference, children appear to experience growth at three points in development: at approximately the onset of Piaget's concrete operational period (6 to 7 years of age), at the onset of the formal operational period (about 10 to 12 years of age), and at a second time in the formal operational period (about 14 to 16 years of age). With regard to electrical waves, as shown in Figure 3.A, spurts in electrical activity of the brain coincide with increases in head circumference.

Do the head circumference and electrical activity data document important changes in Piaget's stages of concrete and formal operational thought? Epstein argued that they do. Not only did Epstein suggest that the brain data indicated underlying changes in Piaget's stages, but he and others (Toepfer, 1979) argued that the brain data have implications for how children and adolescents should be educated. For example, based primarily on the head circumference and brain wave data, it was publicized that adolescents between the ages of 12 and 14 are likely to be incapable of learning new skills because this age span reflects little or no growth of the brain. It also was emphasized that adolescents can only consolidate earlier learned skills during this time period, so middle and junior high schools should not attempt to teach new learning skills during this age span.

Did the Epstein data warrant such generalizations and implications for the education of adolescents? Quite clearly they did not! The Epstein data described information about the nature of brain growth and included no measures of cognitive or educational skills. More recent research has revealed that no correlation exists between spurts in head growth and cognitive changes when cognitive skills are actually measured in concert with head growth (McCall & others, 1983). Yet another investigation focused on whether growth spurts in head circumference, as well as other types of growth, such as height and weight, actually correspond to certain developmental growth periods, like 6 to 7 years of age, 10 to 12 years of age, and so forth (Lampl & Emde, 1983). Each boy and girl in the study did show growth spurts, but the growth spurts were not consistently related to developmental time periods.

In sum, there do seem to be some periods of development when brain growth is rapid, although even the consistency of the brain growth spurts have been questioned (Harmon, 1984). The degree to which these brain spurts are closely linked with rapid growth in cognitive skills, such as those associated with the onset of Piagetian stages, has not been documented (Overton & Byrnes, 1991).

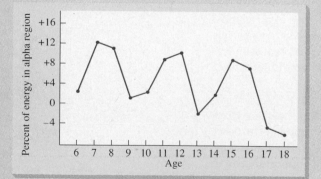

Figure 3.A   Spurts of electrical activity in the brain according to age. According to Epstein, children experience a spurt of brain growth at three points in development—at 6 to 7, 10 to 12, and 14 to 16 years of age. The figure shows the spurts in the electrical activity of the brain as measured by an electroencephalograph. Epstein argued that such spurts in brain growth have implications for how children and adolescents should be educated. What were Epstein's conclusions, and how have they been criticized?

Concept Table 3.1

Heredity and General Dimensions of Physical Growth

Concept	Processes/Related Ideas	Characteristics/Description
Genetic influences on adolescent development	The nature of genes	Each adolescent inherits a genetic code from his or her parents. Physically, the hereditary code is carried by biochemical agents called genes and chromosomes. Genotype refers to each individual's special configuration of genes. Phenotype refers to the individual's observed and measurable characteristics. Introversion-extraversion is moderately influenced by heredity. Genetic transmission is complex, but some principles have been worked out, among them reaction range and canalization.
	Methods used by behavior geneticists	Behavior genetics is the field concerned with the degree and nature of behavior's hereditary basis. Among the most important methods developed by behavior geneticists are the twin study and the adoption study. The concept of heritability is used in many twin and adoption studies, but the heritability index is not flawless.
	Temperament	Temperament refers to an individual's behavioral style. Chess and Thomas believe that there are three basic temperament clusters: easy, difficult, and slow-to-warm-up. Temperament is influenced strongly by biological factors in infancy but becomes more malleable with experience. In the goodness-of-fit model, an adolescent adapts best when there is a congruence, or match, between the adolescent's temperament and the demands of the social environment.
	Heredity-environment interaction and development	No genes, no organism; no environment, no organism. Because the environment's influence depends on genetically endowed characteristics, the two factors are said to interact.
General features of physical growth in adolescence	Four developmental growth curves	The developmental growth curves include a general growth curve, consisting of most aspects of skeletal and muscular growth; a reproductive curve; a curve for the brain and head; and a curve for lymphoid glands. Some biologists argue that the brain grows in spurts; others disagree.
	Factors influencing growth curves	Four mechanisms known to influence growth curves are target-seeking or self-stabilizing factors, maturity gradients, feedback regulation, and body mass.

Puberty

Comedian Bill Cosby once remarked that the problem with his teenage son was not that he grew, but that he did not know when to stop growing. The adolescent growth spurt takes place in puberty.

The Boundaries and Determinants of Puberty

Puberty can be distinguished from adolescence. For most of us, puberty has ended long before adolescence is exited, although puberty is the most important marker of the beginning of adolescence. What is puberty? **Puberty** *is a rapid change to physical maturation involving hormonal and bodily changes that occur primarily during early adolescence.*

Imagine a toddler displaying all the features of puberty—a three-year-old girl with fully developed breasts or a boy just slightly older with a deep male voice. That is what we would see by the year 2250 if the age at which puberty arrives kept getting younger at its present pace. In Norway, **menarche**—*the girl's*

From Penguin Dreams and Stranger Things, *by Berke Breathed. Copyright © 1985 by The Washington Post Company. By permission of Little, Brown and Company.*

Figure 3.3 Median age of menarche in northern European countries and the United States from 1845 to 1969.

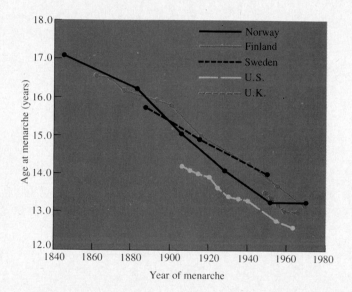

first menstruation—occurs at just over 13 years of age, compared to 17 years of age in the 1840s. In the United States—where children mature up to a year earlier than children in European countries—the average age of menarche has been declining an average of about four months per decade for the past century (see Figure 3.3). Fortunately, however, we are unlikely to see pubescent toddlers, since what has happened in the past century is likely the result of a higher level of nutrition and health (Brooks-Gunn, 1991; Eveleth & Tanner, 1990). The available information suggests that menarche began to occur earlier at about the time of the Industrial Revolution, a period associated with increased standards of living and advances in medical science (Petersen, 1979).

    Genetic factors also are involved in puberty. Puberty is not simply an environmental accident. As indicated earlier, while nutrition, health, and other factors affect puberty's timing and variations in its makeup, the basic genetic program is wired into the nature of the species (Plomin, 1991b; Scarr & Kidd, 1983).

    Another key factor in puberty's occurrence is body mass, as was mentioned earlier (Frisch, 1991; Frisch & Revelle, 1970). Menarche occurs at a relatively consistent weight in girls. A body weight approximating 106 ± 3 pounds can trigger menarche and the end of the pubertal growth spurt. For menarche to begin and continue, fat must make up 17 percent of the girl's body weight. Both teenage anorexics whose weight drops dramatically and female athletes in certain sports (such as gymnastics) may become amenorrheic (having an absence or suppression of menstrual discharge) (Frisch, 1991).

In summary, puberty's determinants include nutrition, health, heredity, and body mass. So far, our discussion of puberty has emphasized its dramatic changes. Keep in mind, though, that puberty is not a single, sudden event (Brooks-Gunn, 1991, 1992). We know when a young boy or girl is going through puberty, but pinpointing its beginning and its end is difficult. Except for menarche, which occurs rather late in puberty, no single marker heralds puberty. For boys, the first whisker or first wet dream are events that could mark its appearance, but both may go unnoticed.

Hormonal Changes

Behind the first whisker in boys and the widening of hips in girls is a flood of **hormones,** *powerful chemical substances secreted by the endocrine glands and carried through the body by the bloodstream.* The endocrine system's role in puberty involves the interaction of the hypothalamus, the pituitary gland, and the gonads (sex glands) (Kulin, 1991). The **hypothalamus** *is a structure in the higher portion of the brain that monitors eating, drinking, and sex.* The **pituitary gland** *is an important endocrine gland that controls growth and regulates other glands.* The **gonads** *are the sex glands—the testes in males, the ovaries in females.* How does this hormonal system work? The pituitary sends a signal via *gonadotropins* (hormones that stimulate the testes or ovaries) to the appropriate gland to manufacture the hormone. Then the pituitary gland, through interaction with the hypothalamus, detects when the optimal level of hormones is reached and responds by maintaining gonadotropin secretion (Petersen & Taylor, 1980).

Two primary classes of hormones are important in pubertal development— androgens and estrogens. **Androgens** *are the main class of male sex hormones.* **Estrogens** *are the main class of female hormones.* Recently, researchers have examined which androgens and which estrogens show the strongest increases during puberty. **Testosterone** *is an androgen that plays an important role in male pubertal development.* Throughout puberty, increasing testosterone levels are associated with a number of physical changes in boys—development of external genitals, increase in height, and voice changes (Fregly & Luttge, 1982; Rabin & Chrousos, 1991). **Estradiol** *is an estrogen that plays an important role in female pubertal development.* As estradiol level rises, breast development, uterine development, and skeletal changes occur. In one study, testosterone levels increased eighteenfold in boys, but only twofold in girls across the pubertal period; estradiol levels increased eightfold in girls, but only twofold in boys during puberty (Nottelman & others, 1987) (see Figure 3.4). Note that both testosterone and estradiol are present in the hormonal makeup of both boys and girls, but that testosterone dominates in male pubertal development, estradiol in female pubertal development.

The same influx of hormones that puts hair on a male's chest and imparts curvature to a female's breast may contribute to psychological development in adolescence (Susman & Dorn, 1991). In one study of 108 normal boys and girls ranging in age from 9 to 14, a higher concentration of testosterone was present in boys who rated themselves more socially competent (Nottelman & others, 1987). In another investigation of 60 normal boys and girls in the same age range, girls with higher estradiol levels expressed more anger and aggression (Inoff-Germain & others, 1988). However, hormonal effects by themselves may account for only a small portion of the variance in adolescent development. For example,

Figure 3.4 Hormone levels by sex and pubertal stage for testosterone and estradiol.

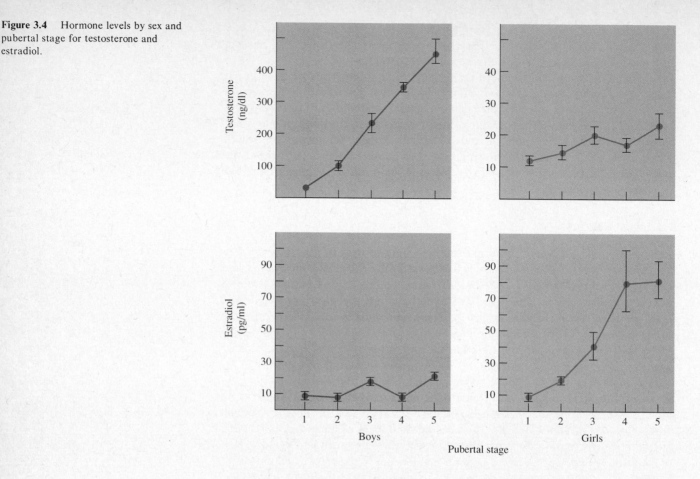

in one recent study, social factors accounted for two to four times as much variance as hormonal factors in young adolescent girls' depression and anger (Brooks-Gunn & Warren, 1989). Also, behavior and moods can affect hormones (Paikoff, Buchanan, & Brooks-Gunn, 1991). Stress, eating patterns, exercise, sexual activity, tension, and depression can activate or suppress various aspects of the hormone system. In sum, the hormone-behavior link is complex.

One additional aspect of the pituitary gland's role in development still needs to be described. Not only does the pituitary gland release gonadotropins that stimulate the testes and ovaries, but through interaction with the hypothalamus, the pituitary gland also secretes hormones that either directly lead to growth and skeletal maturation, or produce such growth effects through interaction with the *thyroid gland,* located in the neck region.

An overview of the location and function of the major endocrine glands is shown in Figure 3.5. Now that we have studied the endocrine system's important role in puberty, we turn our attention to the external physical changes that characterize puberty.

Physical Changes

Among the most noticeable physical changes during puberty are increases in height and weight, and sexual maturation.

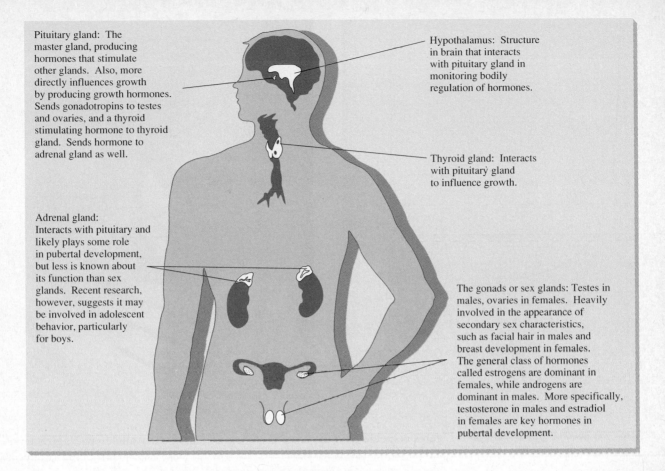

Pituitary gland: The master gland, producing hormones that stimulate other glands. Also, more directly influences growth by producing growth hormones. Sends gonadotropins to testes and ovaries, and a thyroid stimulating hormone to thyroid gland. Sends hormone to adrenal gland as well.

Hypothalamus: Structure in brain that interacts with pituitary gland in monitoring bodily regulation of hormones.

Thyroid gland: Interacts with pituitary gland to influence growth.

Adrenal gland: Interacts with pituitary and likely plays some role in pubertal development, but less is known about its function than sex glands. Recent research, however, suggests it may be involved in adolescent behavior, particularly for boys.

The gonads or sex glands: Testes in males, ovaries in females. Heavily involved in the appearance of secondary sex characteristics, such as facial hair in males and breast development in females. The general class of hormones called estrogens are dominant in females, while androgens are dominant in males. More specifically, testosterone in males and estradiol in females are key hormones in pubertal development.

Figure 3.5 The major endocrine glands involved in pubertal change.

Height and Weight

As indicated in Figure 3.6, the growth spurt occurs approximately two years earlier for girls than for boys (Malina, 1990). The growth spurt for girls begins at approximately 10½ years of age and lasts for about two years. During this time, girls increase in height by about 3½ inches per year. The growth spurt for boys begins at about 12½ years of age and also lasts for about two years. Boys usually grow about four inches per year during this time frame (Faust, 1977; Malina, 1991; Tanner, 1970, 1991).

Boys and girls who are shorter or taller than their peers before adolescence are likely to remain so during adolescence (Tanner, 1970, 1991). In our society, there is a stigma attached to short boys. At the beginning of the adolescent period, girls tend to be as tall or taller than boys their age, but by the end of the junior high years, most boys have caught up or, in many cases, even surpassed girls in height. And even though height in the elementary school years is a good predictor of height later in adolescence, there is still room for the individual's height to change in relation to the height of his or her peers. As much as 30 percent of the height of late adolescents is unexplained by height in the elementary school years (Tanner, 1970, 1991).

The rate at which adolescents gain weight follows approximately the same developmental timetable as the rate at which they gain height. Marked weight

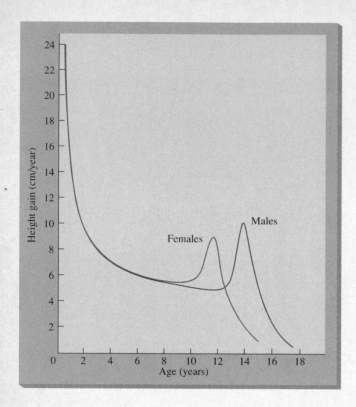

Figure 3.6 The pubertal growth spurt. On the average, the growth spurt that characterizes pubertal change occurs two years earlier for girls (age 10½) than for boys (age 12½).

gains coincide with the onset of puberty. During early adolescence, girls tend to outweigh boys, but by about age 14, just as with height, boys begin to surpass girls (Faust, 1977; Malina, 1991; Tanner, 1970, 1991).

Sexual Maturation

Think back to the onset of your puberty. Of the striking changes that were taking place in your body, what was the first change that occurred? Researchers have found that male pubertal characteristics develop in this order: increase in penis and testicle size, appearance of straight pubic hair, minor voice change, first ejaculation (which usually occurs through masturbation or a wet dream), appearance of kinky pubic hair, onset of maximum growth, growth of hair in armpits, more detectable voice changes, and growth of facial hair (Faust, 1977; Garrison, 1968). Three of the most noticeable areas of sexual maturation in boys are penis elongation, testes development, and growth of facial hair. The normal range and average age of development for these sexual characteristics, along with height spurt, is shown in Figure 3.7. Figure 3.8 shows the typical course of male sexual development during puberty.

What is the order of appearance of physical changes in females? First, either the breasts enlarge or pubic hair appears. Later, hair appears in the armpits. As these changes occur, the female grows in height, and her hips become wider than her shoulders. Her first menstruation comes rather late in the pubertal cycle. Initially, her menstrual cycles may be highly irregular. For the first several years, she may not ovulate every menstrual cycle. In some instances, she does not become fertile until two years after her period begins. No voice changes comparable to those in pubertal males occur in pubertal females. By the end of puberty, the female's breasts have become more fully rounded. Two of the most noticeable

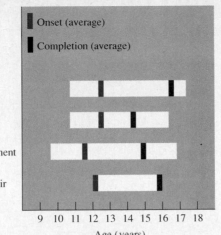

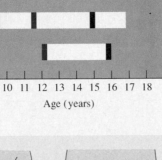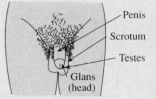

1.
No pubic hair. The testes, scrotum, and penis are about the same size and shape as those of a child.

2.
A little soft, long, lightly colored hair, mostly at the base of the penis. This hair may be straight or a little curly. The testes and scrotum have enlarged, and the skin of the scrotum has changed. The scrotum, the sack holding the testes, has lowered a bit. The penis has grown only a little.

3.
The hair is darker, coarser, and more curled. It has spread to thinly cover a somewhat larger area. The penis has grown mainly in length. The testes and scrotum have grown and dropped lower than in stage 2.

4.
The hair is now as dark, curly, and coarse as that of an adult male. However, the area that the hair covers is not as large as that of an adult male; it has not spread to the thighs. The penis has grown even larger and wider. The glans (the head of the penis) is bigger. The scrotum is darker and bigger because the testes have gotten bigger.

5.
The hair has spread to the thighs and is now like that of an adult male. The penis, scrotum, and testes are the size and shape of those of an adult male.

Figure 3.8 Different stages of male sexual development: the growth of pubic hair, testes, scrotum, and penis.

aspects of female pubertal change are pubic hair and breast development. Figure 3.9 shows the normal range and average development of these sexual characteristics and also provides information about menarche and height gain. Figure 3.10 shows the typical development of the female breast during puberty.

Individual Variation in Puberty

The pubertal sequence may begin as early as 10 years of age or as late as 13½ for most boys. It may end as early as 13 years or as late as 17 years for most boys. The normal range is wide enough that, given two boys of the same chronological age, one may complete the pubertal sequence before the other one has begun it. For girls, the age range of the first menstrual period is even wider. Menarche is considered within a normal range if it appears between the ages of 9 and 15 (Hill, 1980; Brooks-Gunn, 1988; 1991).

Figure 3.9 Normal range and average age of development of sexual characteristics in females.

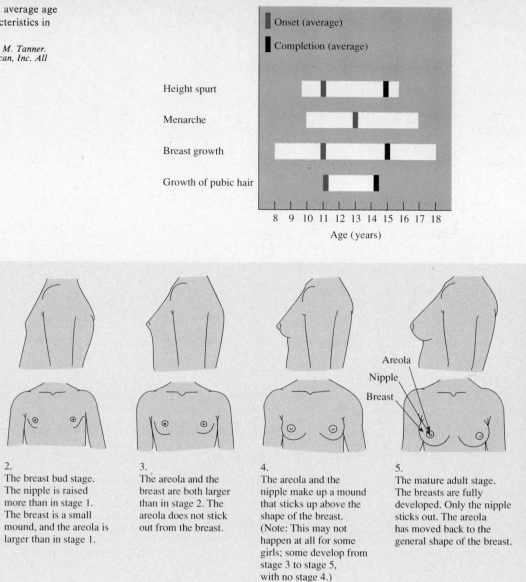

Figure 3.10 Different stages of female sexual development: breast growth.

So far, we have primarily been concerned with the physical dimensions of puberty. As we see next, however, the psychological dimensions of puberty also involve some fascinating changes.

Psychological Dimensions of Puberty

A host of psychological changes accompany an adolescent's pubertal development. Try to remember when you were beginning puberty. Not only did you probably think of yourself differently, but your parents and peers also probably began acting differently toward you. Maybe you were proud of your changing body, even though you were perplexed about what was happening. Perhaps your parents no longer perceived you as someone they could sit in bed with and watch television or as someone who should be kissed goodnight. Among the intriguing

questions posed by developmentalists about puberty's psychological dimensions are the following: What parts of their body image are adolescents most preoccupied with? What are the psychological dimensions of menarche and the menstrual cycle? What are the psychological consequences of early and late maturation? How complex is on-time and off-time in pubertal development? Are the effects of pubertal timing exaggerated? Let's look further at each of these questions.

Body Image

One psychological aspect of physical change in puberty is certain: Adolescents are preoccupied with their bodies and develop individual images of what their bodies are like. Perhaps you looked in the mirror on a daily and sometimes even hourly basis to see if you could detect anything different about your changing body. Preoccupation with one's body image is strong throughout adolescence, but it is especially acute during puberty, a time when adolescents are more dissatisfied with their bodies than in late adolescence (Hamburg, 1974; Wright, 1989).

Being physically attractive and having a positive body image is associated with an overall positive conception of oneself (Adams, 1991). In one investigation, girls who were judged physically attractive and who generally had a positive body image had higher opinions of themselves in general (Lerner & Karabenick, 1974). Other investigators have found that a negative body image is associated with depression in adolescent girls (Rierdan, Koff, & Stubbs, 1989). And in another investigation, breast growth in 9- to 11-year-old girls was associated with a positive body image, positive peer relationships, and superior adjustment (Brooks-Gunn & Warren, 1989).

Was there a part of your body you were preoccupied with during puberty? In one study, boys and girls did not differ much in their preoccupation with various body characteristics (Lerner & Karabenick, 1974). For both males and females, general appearance, the face, facial complexion, and body build were thought to be the most important characteristics in physical attractiveness. Ankles and ears were thought to be the least important. Next, we turn our attention to an important dimension of female pubertal development—menarche and the menstrual cycle.

Menarche and the Menstrual Cycle

The onset of puberty and menarche have often been described as "main events" in most historical accounts of adolescence (Erikson, 1968; Freud, 1958; Hall, 1904; Rousseau, 1962). Basically, these views suggest that pubertal change and events such as menarche produce a different body that requires considerable change in self-conception, possibly resulting in an identity crisis. Only within the last decade has there been empirical research directed at understanding the female adolescent's adaptation to menarche and the menstrual cycle (Brooks-Gunn, 1987; Buchanan, 1989; Hood, 1991; Koff & Rierdan, 1991; Paikoff & Brooks-Gunn, 1990; Stubbs, Rierdan, & Koff, 1989).

In one investigation of 639 girls, a wide range of reactions to menarche appeared (Brooks-Gunn & Ruble, 1982). However, most of the reactions were quite mild, as girls described their first period as a little upsetting, a little surprising, or a little exciting and positive. In this study, 120 of the fifth- and sixth-grade girls were telephoned to obtain more personal, detailed information about their experience with menarche. The most frequent theme of the girls' responses was positive—namely, that menarche was an index of their maturity. Other positive reports indicated that the girls could now have children, were experiencing something that made them more like adult women, and now were more like their friends. The most frequent negative aspects of menarche reported by the girls were its hassle (having to carry supplies around) and its messiness. A minority

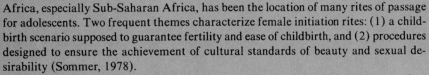

Girls' Initiation Rites and Female Circumcision in Primitive Cultures

Africa, especially Sub-Saharan Africa, has been the location of many rites of passage for adolescents. Two frequent themes characterize female initiation rites: (1) a childbirth scenario supposed to guarantee fertility and ease of childbirth, and (2) procedures designed to ensure the achievement of cultural standards of beauty and sexual desirability (Sommer, 1978).

The female's reproductive capabilities and the onset of menstruation are often the central focus of female rites of passage in primitive cultures. In such rites, female circumcision often occurs, which can take one of two forms. The milder form is practiced in 20 countries, mostly in East, West, and Central Africa. All or part of the clitoris, and sometimes the internal vaginal lips, are removed. In the second, more radical type of operation, all of the external genitalia are removed and the outer lips are sewn shut, leaving just a tiny opening, through which urine and menstrual discharge can pass. In Mali, Sudan, and Somalia, the majority of females undergo this radical procedure.

In Africa alone, more than 75 million females are circumcised. Female circumcision is also practiced in some areas of the Middle East and southeastern Asia. One of the main goals of the operation is to ensure that sex is linked with procreation rather than enjoyment. In many cultures, the female circumcision is carried out as part of the ceremonial ritual signaling membership in the adult community. An increasing number of African women are trying to eliminate female circumcision. In some countries, their efforts are meeting with some success. For example, in Sudan, a survey of female high school students indicated that, while 96 percent had been circumcised, more than 70 percent strongly recommended that their younger sisters, and young girls in general, should not be circumcised (Kenyatta, 1965; Pugh, 1983; Taylor, 1985).

of the girls also indicated that menarche involved physical discomfort, produced behavioral limitations, and created emotional changes.

Questions also were asked about the extent to which the girls communicated with others about the appearance of menarche, the extent to which the girls were prepared for menarche, and how the experience was related to early/late maturation. Virtually all of the girls told their mothers immediately, but most of the girls did not tell anyone else about menarche, with only one in five informing a friend. However, after two or three periods had occurred, most girls had talked with girlfriends about menstruation. Girls not prepared for menarche indicated more negative feelings about menstruation than those who were more prepared for its onset. Girls who matured early had more negative reactions than average or late-maturing girls. In summary, menarche initially may be disruptive, especially for unprepared and early-maturing girls, but it typically does not reach the tumultuous, conflicting proportions described by some early theoreticians.

Female reproductive capabilities are often the central focus of female rites of passage to adult status in primitive cultures. More about girls' initiation rites in primitive cultures and concern about female circumcision in these rites is presented in Sociocultural Worlds of Adolescence 3.1.

For many girls, menarche occurs on time, but for others, it occurs early or late. Next, we examine the effects of early and late maturation on both girls and boys.

Roberta Simmons, shown here interviewing a young adolescent, has conducted a number of important investigations in adolescent development. Her research with Dale Blyth and other colleagues has improved our knowledge of how maturational change (such as early versus late maturation) influences the social and academic lives of adolescents.

Early and Late Maturation

Some of you entered puberty early, others late, and yet others on time. When adolescents mature earlier or later than their peers, might they perceive themselves differently? In the California Longitudinal Study some years ago, early-maturing boys perceived themselves more positively and had more successful peer relations than their late-maturing counterparts (Jones, 1965). The findings for early-maturing girls were similar but not as strong as for boys. When the late-maturing boys were studied in their thirties, however, they had developed a stronger sense of identity than the early-maturing boys (Peskin, 1967). Possibly this occurred because the late-maturing boys had more time to explore life's options or because the early-maturing boys continued to focus on their advantageous physical status instead of career development and achievement.

More recent research, though, confirms that, at least during adolescence, it is advantageous to be an early-maturing rather than a late-maturing boy (Blyth, Bulcroft, & Simmons, 1981; Petersen, 1987; Simmons & Blyth, 1987). Roberta Simmons and Dale Blyth (1987) studied more than 450 individuals for five years, beginning in the sixth grade and continuing through the tenth grade, in Milwaukee, Wisconsin. Students were individually interviewed, and achievement test scores and grade point averages were obtained. The presence or absence of menstruation and the relative onset of menses were used to classify girls as early, middle, or late maturers. The peak of growth in height was used to classify boys according to these categories.

The more recent findings for girls suggest that early maturation is a mixed blessing: These girls experienced more problems in school, but also more independence and popularity with boys (Simmons & Blyth, 1987). The time that maturation was assessed also was a factor. In the sixth grade, early-maturing girls were more satisfied with their figures than late-maturing girls, but by the

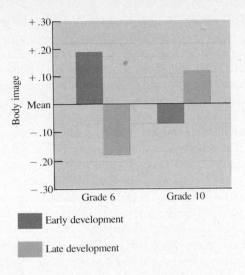

tenth grade, late-maturing girls were more satisfied (see Figure 3.11). The reason for this is that, by late adolescence, early-maturing girls are shorter and stockier, while late-maturing girls are taller and thinner. The late-maturing girls in late adolescence have body images that more closely approximate the current American ideal of feminine beauty—tall and thin.

Complexity of On-Time and Off-Time Pubertal Events in Development

Being on-time or off-time in terms of pubertal events is a complex affair. For example, the dimensions may involve not just biological status and pubertal age, but also chronological age, grade in school, cognitive functioning, and social maturity (Petersen, 1987). Adolescents may be at risk when the demands of a particular social context do not match the adolescents' physical and behavioral characteristics (Lerner, 1987). Dancers whose pubertal status develops on time are one example. In general peer comparisons, on-time dancers should not show adjustment problems. However, they do not have the ideal characteristics for the world of dancers, which generally are those associated with late maturity—a thin, lithe body build. The dancers, then, are on-time in terms of pubertal development for their peer group in general, but there is an asynchrony to their development in terms of their more focused peer group—dancers.

Are Puberty's Effects Exaggerated?

Some researchers have begun to question whether puberty's effects are as strong as once believed (Brooks-Gunn & Warren, 1989; Lerner, Petersen, & Brooks-Gunn, 1991; Montemayor, Adams, & Gulotta, 1990). Have the effects of puberty been exaggerated? Puberty affects some adolescents more strongly than others, and some behaviors more strongly than others. Body image, dating interest, and sexual behavior are quite clearly affected by pubertal change. The recent questioning of puberty's effects, however, suggests that, if we look at overall development and adjustment in the human life cycle, puberty and its variations have less dramatic effects for most individuals than is commonly thought. For some young adolescents, the transition through puberty is stormy, but for most it is not. Each period of the human life cycle has its stresses. Puberty is no different. It imposes new challenges resulting from emerging developmental changes, but the vast majority of adolescents weather these stresses nicely. In addition, the world of adolescents involves not only biological influences on development, but also cognitive and social or environmental influences (Block, 1992; Eccles & Buchanan, 1992). As with all periods of human development, these processes work in concert to produce who we are in adolescence. Singling out biological changes as the dominating change in adolescence may not be a wise strategy.

While extreme early or late maturation may be risk factors in development, we have seen that the overall effects of early or late maturation are often not great. Not all early maturers will date, smoke, and drink, and not all late maturers will have difficulty in peer relations. In some instances, the effects of grade in school are stronger than maturational timing effects (Petersen & Crockett, 1985). Because the adolescent's social world is organized by grade rather than pubertal development, this finding is not surprising. However, this does not mean that maturation has no influence on development. Rather, we need to evaluate puberty's effects within the larger framework of interacting biological, cognitive, and social contexts (Brooks-Gunn, 1988, 1992; Paikoff & Brooks-Gunn, 1990).

At this point, we have discussed a number of ideas about puberty, and a summary of these ideas is presented in Concept Table 3.2. This concludes our discussion of biological processes and physical development during adolescence. In the next chapter, we turn our attention to adolescent cognitive development.

Summary

I. The Nature of Genes

Each adolescent inherits a genetic code from his or her parents. Physically, the hereditary code is carried by biochemical agents called genes and chromosomes. Genotype refers to each individual's special configuration of genes. Phenotype refers to the individual's observed and measurable characteristics. Introversion-extraversion is moderately influenced by heredity. Genetic transmission is complex, but some general principles have been worked out, among them reaction range and canalization.

II. Methods Used by Behavior Geneticists

Behavior genetics is the field concerned with the degree and nature of behavior's hereditary basis. Among the most important methods developed by behavior geneticists are the twin study and the adoption study. The concept of heritability is used in many twin and adoption studies, but the heritability index is not flawless.

III. Temperament

Temperament refers to an individual's behavioral style. Chess and Thomas believe that there are three basic temperament clusters: easy, difficult, and slow-to-warm-up. Temperament is strongly influenced by biological factors in infancy but becomes more malleable with experience. In the goodness-of-fit model, an adolescent adapts best when there is a congruence, or match, between the adolescent's temperament and the demands of the social environment.

IV. Heredity-Environment Interaction

No genes, no organism; no environment, no organism. Because the environment's influence depends on genetically endowed characteristics, the two factors are said to interact.

V. General Features of Physical Growth

The developmental growth curves include a general growth curve, consisting of most aspects of skeletal and muscular growth; a reproductive curve; a curve for the brain and head; and a curve for lymphoid glands. Some biologists argue that the brain grows in spurts; others disagree. Factors that influence growth curves include target-seeking or self-stabilizing factors, maturity gradients, feedback regulation, and body mass.

Concept Table 3.2

Puberty

Concept	Processes/Related Ideas	Characteristics/Description
Boundaries and determinants	Their nature	Puberty is a rapid change to physical maturation involving hormonal and bodily changes that occur primarily during early adolescence. Puberty's determinants include nutrition, health, heredity, and body mass.
Hormonal changes	Hypothalamus, pituitary gland, and gonads	The endocrine system's influence on puberty involves an interaction of the hypothalamus, the pituitary gland, and the gonads (sex glands).
	Androgens and estrogens	Testosterone, a member of the general class of hormones known as androgens, plays a key role in the pubertal development of males. Estradiol, a member of the general class of hormones known as estrogens, plays a key role in the pubertal development of females. Recent research has documented a link between hormonal levels and the adolescent's behavior.
	Pituitary and thyroid glands	The pituitary gland also stimulates growth, either through the thyroid gland, or more directly, through growth hormones.
Physical changes	Height and weight	The growth spurt for boys occurs about two years later than for girls, with 12½ being the average age of onset for boys and 10½ being the average age of onset for girls.
	Sexual maturation	Sexual maturation is a predominant feature of pubertal change and includes a number of changes in physical development, such as penile growth, testicular development, and pubic hair in boys, and pubic hair and breast growth in girls.
	Individual variation	Individual variation in puberty is extensive within a normal range that is wide enough that, given two boys of the same chronological age, one may complete the pubertal sequence before the other has begun it.
Psychological dimensions of puberty	Body image	Adolescents show considerable interest in their body image. Young adolescents are more preoccupied and less satisfied with their body image than are late adolescents.
	Menarche and the menstrual cycle	Menarche is the girl's first period. Menarche and the menstrual cycle produce a wide range of reactions in girls. Those who are not prepared or who mature early tend to have more negative reactions.
	Early and late maturation	Early maturation favors boys, at least during adolescence. As adults, though, late-maturing boys achieve more successful identities. The results for girls are more mixed than for boys.
	On-time and off-time	Being on-time or being off-time in pubertal development is complex. Adolescents may be at risk when the demands of a particular social context do not match adolescents' physical and behavioral characteristics.
	Are puberty's effects exaggerated?	Recently, some scholars have expressed doubt that puberty's effects on development are as strong as once believed. Adolescent development is influenced by an interaction of biological, cognitive, and social factors, rather than being dominated by biology. While extremely early or late maturation may place an adolescent at risk, the overall effects of early and late maturation are not great. This is not the same as saying that puberty and early or late maturation have no effect on development. They do, but puberty's changes always need to be considered in terms of the larger framework of interacting biological, cognitive, and social factors.

VI. Boundaries and Determinants of Puberty

Puberty is a rapid change to physical maturation involving hormonal and bodily changes that occur primarily in early adolescence. Puberty's determinants include nutrition, health, heredity, and body mass.

VII. Hormonal Changes

The endocrine system's influence on puberty involves an interaction of the hypothalamus, the pituitary gland, and the gonads (sex glands). Testosterone, a member of the general class of hormones known as androgens, plays a key role in the pubertal development of males. Estradiol, a member of the general class of hormones known as estrogens, plays a key role in the pubertal development of females. Recent research has documented a link between hormonal levels and the adolescent's behavior. The pituitary gland also stimulates growth, either through the thyroid gland, or more directly, through growth hormones.

VIII. Physical Changes

The growth spurt for boys occurs about two years later than for girls, with 12½ being the average age of onset for boys and 10½ being the average age of onset for girls. Sexual maturation is a predominant feature of pubertal change and includes a number of changes in physical development, such as penile growth, testicular development, and pubic hair in boys, and pubic hair and breast growth in girls. Individual variation in puberty is extensive within a normal range that is wide enough that, given two boys of the same chronological age, one may complete the pubertal sequence before the other has begun it.

IX. Psychological Dimensions of Puberty

Adolescents show considerable interest in their body image. Young adolescents are more preoccupied and less satisfied with their body image than are late adolescents. Menarche is the girl's first period. Menarche and the menstrual cycle produce a wide range of reactions in girls. Those who are not prepared or who mature early tend to have more negative reactions. Early maturation favors boys, at least during adolescence. As adults, though, late-maturing boys achieve more successful identities. The results for girls are more mixed than for boys. Being on-time or being off-time in pubertal development is complex. Adolescents may be at risk when the demands of a particular social context do not match adolescents' physical and behavioral characteristics.

X. Are Puberty's Effects Exaggerated?

Recently, some scholars have expressed doubt that puberty's effects on development are as strong as once believed. Adolescent development is influenced by an interaction of biological, cognitive, and social factors, rather than being dominated by biology. While extreme early or late maturation can place an adolescent at risk, the overall effects of early and late maturation are not great. This is not the same as saying that puberty and early or late maturation have no effect on development. They do, but puberty's changes always need to be considered in terms of the larger framework of interacting biological, cognitive, and social factors.

Key Terms

genotype 89
phenotype 89
reaction range 90
canalization 90
behavior genetics 90
twin study 90
identical twins 90
fraternal twins 90
adoption study 91

heritability 91
temperament 91
easy child 92
difficult child 92
slow-to-warm-up
  child 92
goodness-of-fit
  model 92
puberty 97

menarche 97
hormones 99
hypothalamus 99
pituitary gland 99
gonads 99
androgens 99
estrogens 99
testosterone 99
estradiol 99

Suggested Readings

Adams, G. R., Montemayor, R., & Gullotta, T. P. (Eds.). (1989). *Biology of adolescent behavior and development.* Newbury Park, CA: Sage.
An excellent portrayal of issues involved in the biological basis of adolescent development.

Journal of Youth and Adolescence, 1985, Vol. 14, Nos. 3, 4
These two issues of this research journal have been devoted to the study of maturational timing in adolescence, including many insights into how puberty is experienced.

McCoy, K., & Wibbelsman, C. (1987). *The teenage body book.* Los Angeles, CA: The Body Press.
An award-winning book for youth that answers extensive questions adolescents have about their bodies.

Paikoff, R. L., & Brooks-Gunn, J. (1990). Physiological processes: What role do they play during the transition to adolescence? In R. Montemayor, G. R. Adams, and T. P. Gulotta (Eds.), *From childhood to adolescence: A transitional period.* Newbury Park, CA: Sage.
Presents and evaluates different models for interpreting puberty's effects on adolescent development, along with a very up-to-date research overview of what is known about pubertal changes and psychological development.

Scarr, S., & Kidd, K. K. (1983). Developmental behavior genetics. In P. H. Mussen (Ed.), *Handbook of child psychology* (Vol. 2, 4th ed.). New York: Wiley.
A thorough treatment of heredity's influence on development.

CHAPTER 4

Cognitive Development and Social Cognition

The thirst to know and understand . . . these are the goods in life's rich hand.

Sir William Watson

Sandy's Personal Fable

When you were an adolescent, you probably spent a great deal of time thinking about social matters. As part of this thinking, you likely showed a heightened interest in being unique. In early adolescence, our ideas often are filled with idealistic notions and hypothetical possibilities. And at this point in development, our thoughts reveal an increased ability to step outside of ourselves and anticipate what the reactions of others will be in imaginative circumstances. To retain a sense of personal uniqueness and to preserve the feeling of being perceived in a positive way by others, adolescents may construct a personal fable—a story about themselves. In the following description, Sandy develops a personal fable about a handsome boy named Bob.

> Bob was important to me before I really knew him at all. It began when my mother invited him to a dance at the end of my ninth-grade year. I didn't see much of him at the dance because I was actively pursuing someone else, and my brother's friends from prep school were being very nice to me as little sister. Afterwards, however, he asked me out a couple of times. We didn't get along particularly well. We weren't really attracted or turned off by each other. Then I went away to school.

At school, I found that everyone else had someone "on the outside" to talk about, and, in most cases, to correspond with or even to visit and have visit them. My problem was that I had never been able to bear any of the boys who had shown a great interest in me, probably because I didn't like myself and thought there had to be something basically wrong with anyone who did. Consequently, I had nothing remotely approaching an outside attachment and little hope of forming a spectacular one at school. Still, I was determined to keep up with the competition, so I made up a relationship with Bob. This had the advantage of being based in fact. I had gone out with him, and he was real. Also, he was in school in England, which explained why he never showed up and, to some extent, why he didn't write, since he would have had to ask his parents to find out from my parents where I was. Then, too, his not having shown much interest in me meant that I didn't despise him. This made it easier for me to represent myself as being madly in love with him.

After a few days, I had the other girls convinced, and after a few months, I believed it myself. (Goethals & Klos, 1970)

> *The Thoughts of Youth Are Long, Long Thoughts.*
>
> *Henry Wadsworth Longfellow*

I n this chapter, we explore the fascinating world of adolescents' thoughts. In Chapter 2, we briefly examined Piaget's theory of cognitive development. More than any other theory, Piaget's theory has had the most to say about how adolescents think differently than children. We begin by discussing Piaget's ideas about concrete and formal operational thought, then evaluate whether Piaget's ideas adequately explain adolescent cognition, and finally turn to the intriguing world of adolescents' thoughts about social matters.

Piaget's Theory and Adolescent Cognition

To learn about Piaget's theory of cognitive development, we review the basic ideas presented in Chapter 2, focusing in greater detail on the two stages of thought that Piaget believed primarily characterize the way adolescents think—concrete operational and formal operational.

Overview of Piaget's Theory and Concrete Operational Thought

Piaget's theory is the most well-known, most widely discussed view of adolescent cognitive development. Piaget stressed that adolescents are motivated to understand their world because doing so is biologically adaptive. To understand their world, adolescents use the processes of organization and adaptation (assimilation and accommodation). Piaget believed that individuals develop through four cognitive stages: sensorimotor, preoperational, concrete operational, and formal operational.

According to Piaget, concrete operational thought occurs approximately between the ages of 7 and 11. Piaget said that concrete operational thought involves **operations**—*mental actions that allow the individual to do mentally what was done before physically. And he said that the concrete operational thinker can engage in mental actions that are reversible.* For example, the concrete operational thinker can mentally reverse liquid from one beaker to another and understand that the volume is the same even though the beakers differ in height and width. In Piaget's most famous task, an individual is presented with two identical beakers, each filled with the same amount of liquid (see Figure 4.1). Children are asked if these beakers have the same amount of liquid, and they usually say "yes." Then, the liquid from one beaker is poured into a third beaker, which is taller and thinner than the first two (see Figure 4.1). Children are then asked if the amount of liquid in the tall, thin beaker is equal to that which remains in one of the original beakers. Concrete operational thinkers answer "yes" and justify their answers appropriately. Preoperational thinkers (usually children under the age of seven) often answer "no" and justify their answer in terms of the differing height and width of the beakers. This example reveals the ability of the concrete operational thinker to decenter and coordinate several characteristics (such as height and width), rather than focusing on a single property of an object (such as height).

Conservation *is Piaget's term for an individual's ability to recognize that the length, number, mass, quantity, area, weight, and volume of objects and substances do not change through transformations that alter their appearance.*

Figure 4.1 Piaget's conservation task. The beaker test is a well-known Piagetian test to determine whether the child can think operationally—that is, can mentally reverse actions and show conservation of the substance. (I) Two identical beakers are presented to the child. Then the experimenter pours the liquid from *B* into *C,* which is taller and thinner than *A* or *B*. (II) The child is now asked if these beakers (*A* and *C*) have the same amount of liquid. The preoperational child says no. When asked to point to the beaker that has more liquid, the preoperational child points to the tall, thin beaker.

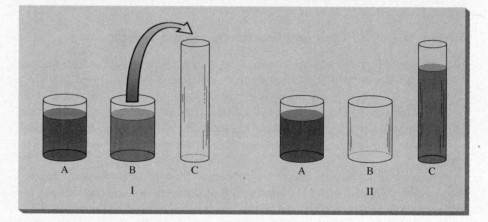

An important aspect of conservation is that children do not conserve all quantities or on all tasks simultaneously. The order of their mastery is: number, length, liquid quantity, mass, weight, and volume. **Horizontal décalage** *is Piaget's concept that describes how similar abilities do not appear at the same time within a stage of development.* Thus, during the concrete operational stage, conservation of number usually appears first and conservation of volume last. An eight-year-old child may know that a long stick of clay can be rolled into a ball but not understand that the ball and the stick weigh the same. At about nine years of age, children often recognize that the ball and stick weigh the same, and eventually, at about 11 to 12 years of age, children often understand that the clay's volume is unchanged by rearranging it. Children initially master tasks that are more visible, mastering those not as visually apparent, such as volume, only later.

Classification, *or class inclusion reasoning, is Piaget's concept of concrete operational thought that requires children to systematically organize objects into hierarchies of classes and subclasses.* Figure 4.2 shows an example of the concrete operational child's classification skills involving a family tree of four generations (Furth & Wachs, 1975). This family tree suggests that the grandfather (*A*) has three children (*B, C,* and *D*), each of whom has two children (*E*

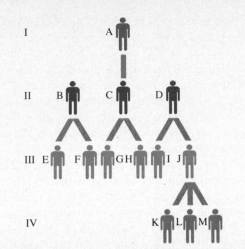

Figure 4.2 Piaget believed that concrete operational thinkers can classify things into different sets or subsets and consider their interrelations. In this family tree of four generations, children who are concrete operational thinkers can move vertically, horizontally, and obliquely within the system.

| Can use operations, mentally reversing action; shows conservation skills | Logical reasoning replaces intuitive reasoning, but only in concrete circumstances | Not abstract (can't imagine steps in algebraic equation, for example) | Classification skills—can divide things into sets and subsets and reason about their interrelations |

through *J*), and that one of these children (*J*) has three children (*K, L,* and *M*). A child who comprehends this classification system can move up and down a level (vertically), across a level (horizontally), and up and down and across (obliquely) within the system. The concrete operational child understands that person *J* can at the same time be father, brother, and grandson, for example.

While concrete operational thought is more advanced than preoperational thought, it has its limitations. Logical reasoning replaces intuitive thought as long as the principles can be applied to specific or *concrete* examples. For example, the concrete operational child cannot imagine the steps necessary to complete an algebraic equation, which is too abstract for thinking at this stage of cognitive development. A summary of the characteristics of concrete operational thought is shown in Figure 4.3.

Figure 4.3 Characteristics of concrete operational thought.

Characteristics of Formal Operational Thought

Adolescents' developing power of thought opens up new cognitive and social horizons. What are the characteristics of formal operational thought, which Piaget believed develops in adolescence? Most significantly, formal operational thought is more *abstract* than concrete operational thought. Adolescents are no longer limited to actual, concrete experiences as anchors for thought. They can conjure up make-believe situations—events that are purely hypothetical possibilities or strictly abstract propositions—and try to reason logically about them.

The abstract quality of the adolescent's thought at the formal operational level is evident in the adolescent's verbal problem-solving ability. While the concrete operational thinker would need to see the concrete elements A, B, and C

"*. . . and give me good abstract-reasoning ability, interpersonal skills, cultural perspective, linguistic comprehension, and high sociodynamic potential.*"

Drawing by Ed Fisher; © 1981 The New Yorker Magazine, Inc.

to be able to make the logical inference that if A = B and B = C, then A = C, the formal operational thinker can solve this problem merely through verbal presentation.

Another indication of the abstract quality of the adolescent's thought is his or her increased tendency to think about thought itself. One adolescent commented, "I began thinking about why I was thinking what I was. Then I began thinking about why I was thinking about why I was thinking about what I was." If this sounds abstract, it is, and it characterizes the adolescent's enhanced focus on thought and its abstract qualities.

Accompanying the abstract nature of formal operational thought in adolescence is thought full of idealism and possibilities. While children frequently think in concrete ways, or in terms of what is real and limited, adolescents begin to engage in extended speculation about ideal characteristics—qualities they desire in themselves and in others. Such thoughts often lead adolescents to compare themselves and others with regard to such ideal standards. And during adolescence, the thoughts of individuals are often fantasy flights into future possibilities. Adolescents may become impatient with these newfound ideal standards and become perplexed over which of many ideal standards to adopt.

At the same time that adolescents think more abstractly and idealistically, they also think more logically. They begin to think more like a scientist thinks, devising plans to solve problems and systematically testing solutions. This type of problem solving has an imposing name. **Hypothetical-deductive reasoning** *is Piaget's formal operational concept that adolescents have the cognitive ability to develop hypotheses, or best guesses, about ways to solve problems, such as an algebraic equation. They then systematically deduce, or conclude, which is the best path to follow in solving the equation.* By contrast, children are more likely to solve problems in a trial-and-error fashion. One example of how hypothetical-deductive reasoning works can be found in a modification of the familiar game "Twenty Questions" (Bruner, 1966). Adolescents are shown a set of 42 color pictures displayed in a rectangular array (six rows of seven pictures each) and are asked to determine which picture the experimenter has in mind (that is, which is "correct"). Adolescents are only allowed to ask questions to which the experimenter can answer "yes" or "no." The object of the game is to select the correct picture by asking as few questions as possible. Adolescents who are deductive-hypothesis testers formulate a plan and test a series of hypotheses, each of which considerably narrows the field of choices. The most effective plan is a "halving" strategy (*Q:* "Is it in the right half of the array?" *A:* "No." *Q:* "Okay—is it in the top half?" and so on). Used correctly, the halving strategy guarantees the questioner the correct solution in seven questions or less, no matter where the correct picture is located in the array. Even if adolescents use a less elegant strategy than "halving," those who are deductive-hypothesis testers understand that, when the experimenter answers "no" to one of their questions, several possibilities are immediately eliminated.

By contrast, the concrete operational thinker may persist with questions that continue to test some of the same possibilities that previous questions should have eliminated. For example, adolescents may have asked whether the correct picture was in row 1 and received the answer "no," but later ask whether the picture is *x,* which is in row 1.

Thus, formal operational thinkers test their hypotheses with judiciously chosen questions and tests. Often, a single question or test will help them to eliminate an untenable hypothesis. By contrast, concrete operational thinkers often

A common task for all of us is to determine what can logically be inferred from a statement made by someone else. Young children are often told by teachers that if they work hard, they will receive good grades. Regardless of the empirical truth of the claim, the children may believe that good grades are the result of hard work, and that if they do not get good grades, they did not work hard enough. (Establishing the direction of the relationship between variables is an important issue.)

Children in late concrete operations, too, are concerned with understanding the relations between their behavior and their teachers' grading practices. However, they are beginning to question the "truths" of their childhood. First, they now know that there are four possible combinations if two variables are dichotomized (work hard—not work hard; good grades—not good grades).

Behavior	*Consequences*
1. Work hard	Good grades
2. Work hard	Not good grades
3. Not work hard	Good grades
4. Not work hard	Not good grades

Two combinations are consistent with the hypothesis that [a student's] hard work is necessarily related to good grades: (1) they work hard and get good grades, (4) they do not work hard and do not get good grades. When the presumed "cause" is present, the effect is present; when the cause is absent, the effect is absent. There are also two combinations that do not fit the hypothesis of a direct relation between hard work and good grades; (2) they work hard and do not get good grades, and (3) they get good grades without working hard.

The adolescent's notion of possibility allows him or her to take this analysis of combinations one important step further. Each of the four basic combinations of binary variables may be true or it may not. If 1, 2, 3, or 4 are true alone or in combination, there are 16 possible patterns of truth values:

1 or 2 or 3 or 4 is true	4 patterns
1–2 or 1–3 or 1–4 or 2–3 or 2–4 or 3–4 are true	6 patterns
1–2–3 or 1–2–4 or 1–3–4 or 2–3–4 are true	4 patterns
All (1–2–3–4) are true	1 pattern
All are false	1 pattern
Total	16 patterns

The list is critically important because each pattern leads to a different conclusion about the possible relation between two variables.

fail to understand the relation between a hypothesis and a well-chosen test of it—stubbornly clinging to the idea despite clear, logical disconfirmation of it. Another example of a formal operational task is described in Figure 4.4.

Piaget believed that formal operational thought is the best description of how adolescents think (Overton & Montangero, 1991). A summary of the characteristics of formal operational thought is shown in Figure 4.5. As we see next, though, formal operational thought is not a homogeneous stage of development.

Figure 4.4 An example of hypothetical-deductive reasoning.

Early and Late Formal Operational Thought

Not all adolescents are full-fledged formal operational thinkers. Some developmentalists believe that formal operational thought consists of two subperiods: early and late (Broughton, 1983). In **early formal operational thought,** *adolescents' increased ability to think in hypothetical ways produces unconstrained thoughts with unlimited possibilities. In this early period, formal operational thought submerges reality, and there is an excess of assimilation as the world is perceived too subjectively and idealistically.* **Late formal operational thought** *involves a restoration of intellectual balance. Adolescents now test out the products of their reasoning against experience, and a consolidation of formal operational thought takes place. An intellectual balance is restored, as the adolescent accommodates to the cognitive upheaval that has occurred.* Late

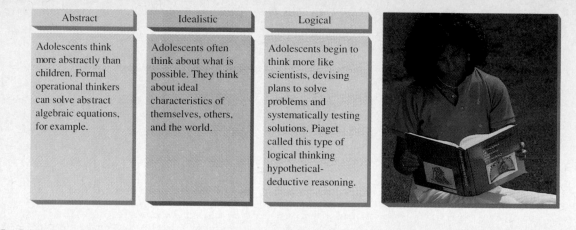

Abstract	Idealistic	Logical
Adolescents think more abstractly than children. Formal operational thinkers can solve abstract algebraic equations, for example.	Adolescents often think about what is possible. They think about ideal characteristics of themselves, others, and the world.	Adolescents begin to think more like scientists, devising plans to solve problems and systematically testing solutions. Piaget called this type of logical thinking hypothetical-deductive reasoning.

Figure 4.5   Primary characteristics of formal operational thought.

formal operational thought may appear during the middle adolescent years. In this view, assimilation of formal operational thought marks the transition to adolescence; accommodation to formal operational thought marks a later consolidation (Lapsley, 1990).

Piaget's (1952) early writings indicated that the onset and consolidation of formal operational thought is completed during early adolescence, from about 11 to 15 years of age. Later, Piaget (1972) revised his view and concluded that formal operational thought is not completely achieved until later in adolescence, between approximately 15 and 20 years of age. As we see next, many developmentalists believe that there is considerable individual variation in adolescent cognition.

Individual Variation in Adolescent Cognition

Piaget's theory emphasizes universal and consistent patterns of formal operational thought. His theory does not adequately account for the unique, individual differences that characterize the cognitive development of adolescents (Overton & Byrnes, 1991). These individual variations in adolescents' cognitive development have been documented in a number of investigations (Bart, 1971; Neimark, 1982; Kaufmann & Flaitz, 1987).

Some individuals in early adolescence are formal operational thinkers; others are not. A review of formal operational thought investigations revealed that only about one of every three eighth-grade students is a formal operational thinker (Strahan, 1983). Some investigators find that formal operational thought increases with age in adolescence (Arlin, 1984; Martorano, 1977); others do not (Strahan, 1987). Many college students and adults do not think in formal operational ways either. For example, investigators have found that from 17 to 67 percent of college students think in formal operational ways (Elkind, 1961; Tomlinson-Keasey, 1972).

Many young adolescents are at the point of consolidating their concrete operational thought, using it more consistently than in childhood. At the same time, many young adolescents are just beginning to think in a formal operational manner. By late adolescence, many adolescents are beginning to consolidate their formal operational thought, using it more consistently. And there often is variation across the content areas of formal operational thought, just as there is in concrete operational thought in childhood. A 14-year-old adolescent may reason at the formal operational level when analyzing algebraic equations but not do so with verbal problem solving or when reasoning about interpersonal relations.

Formal operational thought is more likely to be used in areas in which adolescents have the most experience and knowledge (Carey, 1988; Flavell, 1985). Children and adolescents gradually build up elaborate knowledge through extensive experience and practice in various sports, games, hobbies, and school subjects, such as math, English, and science. The development of expertise in different domains of life may make possible high-level, developmentally mature-looking thought. In some instances, the sophisticated reasoning of formal operational thought may be responsible. In other instances, however, the thought may be largely due to the accumulation of knowledge that allows more automatic, memory-based processes to function. Some developmentalists are wondering if the acquisition of knowledge could account for all cognitive growth. Most, however, argue that *both* cognitive changes in such areas as concrete and formal operational thought *and* the development of expertise through experience are at work in understanding the adolescent's cognitive world. More about knowledge's role in the adolescent's thinking appears in the next chapter.

One recent proposal argues that Piaget's theory of formal operational thought can be better understood by considering the distinction between "knowing that" and "knowing how" (Byrnes, 1988a,b). "Knowing that" has been called conceptual knowledge or declarative knowledge (Hiebert & LeFevre, 1987; Mandler, 1983). It consists of networks of the core concepts in a given domain, such as biology or physics. "Knowing how" is simply a representation of the steps an individual should follow to solve a problem. It has been referred to as procedural knowledge (Anderson, 1990). For example, in the domain of physics, "knowing that" would consist of understanding the relation between the core concepts of "force" and "mass." In contrast, "knowing how" would consist of understanding how to solve introductory physics test problems using formulas and the like.

The argument by James Byrnes (1988a,b) is that Piaget's theory of formal operations can be better understood if it is recast as "knowing that." However, Daniel Keating (1988, 1990b) argues that Piaget's theory is actually about "knowing how," and that considering his view of formal operations in terms of "knowing that" is a misinterpretation. The lively debate about Piaget's theory of formal operations is likely to continue as experts strive to determine just exactly what Piaget meant by formal operational thought and search for the true nature of adolescent cognitive development.

Formal Operational Thought and Language

As the adolescent's thought becomes more abstract and logical, the use of language also changes. This development includes changes in the use of satire and metaphor, in writing skills, and in conversational skills.

A junior high school student sitting in school makes up satirical labels for his teachers. One he calls "the walking wilt Wilkie and his wilking waste." Another he describes as "the magnificent Manifred and his manifest morbidity." The use of nicknames increases during early adolescence, as does their abstractness—"stilt," "spaz," "nerd," and "marshmallow mouth," for example. These examples reflect the aspect of language known as *satire,* which refers to irony, wit, or derision used to expose folly or wickedness. Adolescents use and understand satire more than children (Demorest & others, 1984). The satire of *Mad* magazine, which relies on double meaning, exaggeration, and parody to highlight absurd circumstances and contradictory happenings, finds a more receptive audience among 13- to 14-year-olds than 8- to 9-year olds.

I was 12 years old the first time I read Mad *magazine. It was a time when my best friend and I were already starting to make up crazy nicknames for our teachers and peers. Think back to when you were a young adolescent—were you intrigued by absurdities and contradictory happenings?*

Another aspect of language that comes into use in adolescence is *metaphor,* an implied comparison between two ideas that is conveyed by the abstract meaning contained in the words used. For example, a person's faith and a piece of glass are alike in that they both can be shattered. A runner's performance and a politician's speech are alike in that they both are predictable. Children have a difficult time understanding metaphorical comparisons; adolescents are better able to understand their meaning.

The increased abstractness and logical reasoning of the adolescent's cognition can be witnessed in improved writing ability (Scardamalia, Bereiter, & Goelman, 1982). Organizing ideas is critical to good writing. Logical thinking helps the writer to develop a hierarchical structure, which helps the reader to understand which ideas are general, which are specific, and which are more important than others. Researchers have discovered that children are poor at organizing their ideas prior to writing and have difficulty detecting the salient points in prose passages (Brown & Smiley, 1977). While adolescents are not yet Pulitzer-Prize-winning novelists, they are better than children at recognizing the need for making both general and specific points in their writing. The sentences adolescents string together make more sense than those constructed by children. And adolescents are more likely than children to include an introduction, several paragraphs that represent a body, and concluding remarks when writing an essay (Fischer & Lazerson, 1984).

Most adolescents also are better conversationalists than are children. Adolescents are better at letting individuals take turns in discussions instead of everyone talking at once; they are better at using questions to convey commands ("Why is it so noisy in here?"); they are better at using words like *the* and *a* in ways that enhance understanding ("He is *the* living end! He is not just *a* person); they are better at using polite language in appropriate situations (when a guest comes to the house, for example); and they are better at telling stories that are interesting, jokes that are funny, and lies that convince.

Piaget's Theory and Adolescent Education

Piaget's theory has been widely applied to education, although more extensively with children than adolescents. Piaget was not an educator and never pretended to be. But he did provide a sound conceptual framework from which to view educational problems. What principles of Piaget's theory of cognitive development can be applied to education? David Elkind (1976) described two. First, the foremost issue in education is *communication.* In Piaget's theory, the adolescent's mind is not a blank slate. To the contrary, the adolescent has a host of ideas about the physical and natural world. Adolescents come to school with their own ideas about space, time, causality, quantity, and number. Educators need to learn to comprehend what adolescents are saying and to respond to their ideas. Second, adolescents are, by nature, knowing creatures. The best way to nurture this motivation for knowledge is to allow adolescents to spontaneously interact with the environment. Educators need to ensure that they do not dull adolescents' eagerness to know by providing an overly rigid curriculum that disrupts adolescents' rhythm and pace of learning.

Why have applications to adolescent education lagged behind applications to children's education? Adolescents who are formal operational thinkers are at a level similar to their teachers and to the authors of textbooks. In Piaget's model, it is no longer necessary to pay attention to qualitative changes in cognition. Also, the structure of education itself changes considerably between elementary and secondary levels. For children, the basic focus of education is the classroom. Children may be involved with, at most, several teachers during the day. In secondary schools, the focus shifts to subject-matter divisions of curriculum. Each teacher sees a student for 45 to 60 minutes a day in connection with one content area (English, history, math, for example). Thus, both teachers and texts may become more focused on the development of curriculum than on the developmental characteristics of students. And when teachers *are* concerned about students' developmental characteristics in adolescence, they pay more attention to social-personality dimensions than to cognitive dimensions (Cowan, 1978).

One main argument that has emerged from the application of Piaget's theory to education is that instruction may too often be at the formal operational level, even though the majority of adolescents are not actually formal operational thinkers. That is, the instruction may be too formal and too abstract. Possibly, it should be less formal and more concrete. Perspective on Adolescent Development 4.1 describes a comparison of two teaching formats with different cognitive orientations—one a more formal curriculum, the other a more concrete curriculum. The available data suggest that adolescents construct a view of the world on the basis of observations and experiences and that educators should take this into account when developing a curriculum for adolescents (Burbules & Linn, 1988; Carey, 1986; Danner, 1989; Linn, 1987, 1991).

Beyond Formal Operational Thought

Some critics of Piaget's theory argue that specialized thinking about a specific skill represents a higher stage of thought than formal operational thought. Piaget did not believe that this was so. For him, the change to reasoning about a special skill (such as the kind of thinking engaged in by a nuclear physicist or a medical researcher) is no more than window dressing. According to Piaget, a nuclear physicist may think in ways that an adolescent cannot think, but the adolescent and the nuclear physicist differ only in their familiarity with an academic field of inquiry. They differ in the content of their thought, not in the operations they bring to bear on the content (Piaget, 1970).

Some developmentalists believe that the absolute nature of adolescent logic and buoyant optimism diminish in early adulthood. According to Gisela Labouvie-Vief (1982, 1986), a new integration of thought takes place in early adulthood. She thinks that the adult years produce pragmatic constraints that require an adaptive strategy of less reliance on logical analysis in solving problems. Commitment, specialization, and channeling energy into finding one's niche in complex social and work systems replace the youth's fascination with idealized logic. If we assume that logical thought and buoyant optimism represent the criteria for cognitive maturity, we would have to admit that the cognitive activity of adults is too concrete and pragmatic. But from Labouvie-Vief's view, the adult's understanding of reality's constraints reflects maturity, not immaturity.

Even Piaget (1967) detected that formal operational thought may have its hazards:

> With the advent of formal intelligence, thinking takes wings and it is not
> surprising that at first this unexpected power is both used and abused. . . . Each
> new mental ability starts off by incorporating the world in a process of egocentric
> assimilation. Adolescent egocentricity is manifested by a belief in the
> omnipotence of reflection, as though the world should submit itself to idealistic
> schemes rather than to systems of reality. (pp. 63–64)

Our cognitive abilities are very strong in early adulthood, and they do show adaptation to life's pragmatic concerns. Less clear is whether our logical skills actually decline. Competence as a young adult probably requires doses of both logical thinking skills and pragmatic adaptation to reality. For example, when

Piaget's Theory and the Teaching of Science to Adolescents

Consider a curriculum area that virtually every adolescent is exposed to during the junior high and high school years—science. Most science courses (or at least the majority of units taught in each of them) follow a reasonably formal, straightforward lecture format. Classifications of animals and plants are memorized through exposure to the teacher's lecture and the text.

Some educational experts believe that this format is not the best way to teach science, especially for students who have not yet reached the stage of formal operational thought. Instead, they argue that improved learning and advances in cognitive development are more likely when adolescents observe and collect organisms from natural habitats and then relate the organisms to various subjects covered in the course. In this manner, adolescents are forced to restructure their concrete way of thinking about the world and logically categorize events and objects in more formal, logical ways.

One investigation was specifically designed to test whether the more formal lecture method or the hands-on experience of student participation was superior at promoting cognitive development (Renner & others, 1976). Students in junior high school science courses were taught using either the formal lecture method or the hands-on, participatory method. In the formal classes, the students used standard textbooks, read and recited from the books, and learned concepts about the scientific method. In the experiential, hands-on classes, the junior high science students were given considerable experience in solving laboratory problems, and there was extensive open inquiry and student-directed investigations. There also was a considerable amount of structure in the hands-on strategy, with precise expectations and careful directions being given. The students in both types of classes were tested on Piaget's concrete and formal operational tasks both before and after participation in the classes. Junior high students who were taught in the hands-on, participatory way advanced their formal operational thought more than their counterparts who were taught in a more standard format. It is important to note that the use of concrete materials did not interfere with the transition to formal operational thought, but actually seemed to enhance the move.

Piaget's ideas also have been applied in this manner at the college level. For example, in one investigation in the

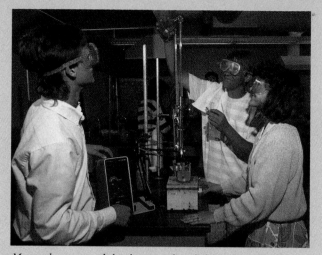

Many educators and developmentalists believe that science and most other areas of secondary education should follow a hands-on, participatory format rather than a straight lecture format. Many adolescents are not yet full-fledged formal operational thinkers in the hypothetical-deductive sense. Possibly through participatory experiences with science, adolescents can restructure their concrete ways of thinking about the world and logically categorize events and objects in more hypothetical-deductive ways. However, some researchers believe that a supportive context and early attention to the development of reasoning are what are needed to improve adolescents' logical thought.

area of humanities, curriculum designed to enhance the transition from concrete to formal operational thought with college freshmen was successful, with 21 of 22 students beginning the year at the concrete level moving to the formal operational level by the end of the term (Wideck, Knefelkamp, & Parker, 1975).

While the main applications of Piaget's theory to the education of adolescents have been to recognize the limitations of adolescents' ability to think logically, some researchers believe that this is the wrong strategy. For example, developmentalist Daniel Keating (1990a) argues that a supportive context and early attention to the development of reasoning are what are needed to improve adolescents' logical thought.

architects design a building, they logically analyze and plan the structure but understand the cost constraints, environmental concerns, and the time it will take to get the job done effectively.

William Perry (1981) also has charted some important changes in the way young adults think differently than adolescents. He believes that adolescents often view the world in a basic dualistic fashion of polarities—right/wrong, black/white, we/they, or good/bad, for example. As youth mature and move into the adulthood years, they gradually become aware of the diversity of opinion and the multiple perspectives that others hold, which shakes their dualistic perceptions. Their *dualistic thinking* gives way to *multiple thinking,* as they come to understand that authorities may not have all of the answers. They begin to carve out their own territory of individualistic thinking, often believing that everyone is entitled to their own opinion and that one's personal opinion is as good as anyone else's. As these personal opinions become challenged by others, multiple thinking yields to *relative subordinate thinking,* in which an analytical, evaluative approach to knowledge is consciously and actively pursued. Only in the shift to *full relativism* does the adult completely comprehend that truth is relative, that the meaning of an event is related to the context in which that event occurs and on the framework that the knower uses to understand that event. In full relativism, the adult recognizes that relativism pervades all aspects of life, not just the academic world. And in full relativism, the adult understands that knowledge is constructed, not given; contextual, not absolute. Perry's ideas, which are oriented toward well-educated, bright individuals (Rybash, Roodin, & Santrock, 1991), have been widely used by educators and counselors in working with young adults in academic settings.

Another candidate for thought that is more advanced than formal operational thought is wisdom, which like good wine, may get better with age. What is this thing we call wisdom? **Wisdom** *is expert knowledge about the practical aspects of life* (Baltes & Baltes, in press; Baltes & others, 1990). This practical knowledge involves exceptional insight into human development and life matters, good judgment, and an understanding of how to cope with difficult life problems. Thus, wisdom, more than standard conceptions of intelligence, focuses on life's pragmatic concerns and human conditions. This practical knowledge system takes many years to acquire, accumulating through intentional, planned experiences and through incidental experiences. Of course, not all older adults solve practical problems in wise ways. In one recent investigation, only 5 percent of adults' responses to life-planning problems were considered wise, and these wise responses were equally distributed across the early, middle, and late adulthood years (Smith & Baltes, in press).

What does the possibility that older adults are as wise or wiser than younger adults mean in terms of the basic issue of intellectual decline in adulthood? Remember that intelligence comes in different forms. In many instances, older adults are not as intelligent as younger adults when speed of processing is involved, and this probably harms their performance on many traditional school-related tasks and standardized intelligence tests. But consideration of general knowledge and something we call wisdom may result in an entirely different interpretation.

Now that we have considered many different ideas about Piaget's theory of adolescent cognition, including the issue of whether there are forms of thought more advanced than formal operational thinking, we turn our attention to evaluating Piagetian contributions and criticisms.

(a)

(b)

(c)

(a) Adolescents' thoughts are more abstract and idealistic than children's thoughts. (b) Young adults' thoughts are more pragmatic, specialized, and multiple (less dualistic) than adolescents' thoughts. (c) Older adults may not be as quick with their thoughts as younger adults, but they may have more general knowledge and wisdom. This elderly woman shares the wisdom of her experiences with a classroom of children.

Culture, Schooling, and Cognitive Development

Consider the following conversation between a researcher and an illiterate Kpelle farmer in the West African country of Liberia (Scribner, 1977):

> Researcher: All Kpelle men are rice farmers. Mr. Smith is not a rice farmer. Is he a Kpelle man?
> Kpelle farmer: I don't know the man. I have not laid eyes on the man myself.

Members of the Kpelle culture who had gone through formal schooling were able to answer the researcher in a logical way, unlike the illiterate Kpelle farmer. Piaget may have underestimated the importance of cultural experiences in cognitive development. Many of the activities examined in research on Piaget's cognitive developmental theory, such as conservation, classification, and logical reasoning, have been found to relate to children's, adolescents', and adults' schooling experience (Cole & Cole, 1989; Lave, 1977; Rogoff, 1990; Rogoff & Morelli, 1989; Sharp, Cole, & Lave, 1979).

Remembering or classifying lists of unrelated objects are often unusual, rarely practiced activities outside of literate or school-related activities (Rogoff, 1990; Rogoff & Morelli, 1989). The categories viewed as most appropriate in literate situations may not be valued in other circumstances. For example, in one investigation of the Kpelle culture, individuals sorted 20 objects into functional groups (a knife with an orange, a potato with a hoe, for example), rather than into the categorical groups the experimenter had in mind (a knife with a hoe, an orange with a potato, for example) (Glick, 1975). When questioned about why they had categorized the objects this way, the Kpelle subjects said that any wise man would know to do things this way. When an exasperated experimenter finally asked, "How would a fool do it?" the Kpelle subjects responded with categories of the type that were initially anticipated—piles with food in one, tools in another, and so on.

Individuals who have more schooling, such as older children and people in Western cultures, may excel on cognitive tasks because not only the skills but also the social contexts of testing resemble the activities practiced in school (Rogoff & Morelli, 1989).

Piagetian Contributions and Criticisms

Piaget was a genius at observing children and adolescents, and some of his insights are surprisingly easy to verify. Piaget showed us some important things to look for in development, including the shift from concrete operational to formal operational thought. He also showed us how we must make our experience fit our cognitive framework, yet simultaneously adapt our cognitive orientation to experience. Piaget also revealed how cognitive change is likely if the situation is structured to allow gradual movement to the next higher level.

Piaget's theory, however, has not gone uncriticized (Gelman & Baillargeon, 1983; Keating, 1991; Kuhn, 1988, 1991; Lapsley, 1990; Overton & Byrnes, 1991; Small, 1990). First, Piaget conceived of stages as unitary structures of thought, so his theory assumes considerable synchrony in development. That is, various aspects of a stage should emerge at about the same time. However, formal op-

In contrast with everyday life, where individuals classify and remember things to accomplish a functional goal, in schools and on tests, they perform to satisfy an adult's request to do so. Individuals who have gone to school are likely to have more experience engaging in cognitive processes at the request of an adult without having a clear, practical goal (Rogoff & Mistry, in press).

Researchers have investigated whether special training can improve the conversation skills of children who live in cultures in which the concept of conservation is not widely practiced. For example, in one study, brief training in procedures similar to the standard conservation task improved the performance of rural aboriginal Australian children on the standard beaker conservation task itself (Dasen, Ngini, & Lavalée, 1979). However, even with special training, the rural aboriginal children lagged behind children from the Australian city of Canberra in the acquisition of conservation by approximately three years, indicating that the aboriginal culture does not provide practice that is relevant to the conservation concept.

The ability to think in scientific ways—to develop hypotheses, systematically evaluate possible solutions, and deduce a correct answer to a difficult problem—is an important dimension of formal operational thought. A majority of adolescents in the United States do not think in formal operational ways when presented with scientific reasoning problems, but in developing countries, an even smaller portion of adolescents and adults do (Neimark, 1982). In one cross-cultural investigation that included the United States, Germany, Austria, and Italy, only 7 percent of the eighth-grade students reasoned in formal operational ways (Karplus, 1981). In one Italian group, the adolescents did especially well on formal operational tasks. Closer observation revealed that these adolescents had been with the same outstanding teacher for three consecutive years, indicating the role that education may play in instilling formal operational thinking. According to observers, in many Third World, developing countries, formal operational thought in the form of scientific thinking is rare. Education in the logic of science and mathematics is an important cultural experience that promotes the development of formal operational thinking. Cultural experiences thus play a much stronger role in formal operational thought than Piaget envisioned.

erational concepts do not always appear in synchrony. For example, idealism may be more full blown at one point, hypothetical-deductive reasoning at another. Second, small changes in procedures involving Piagetian tasks sometimes have significant effects on an adolescent's thoughts. Third, in some cases, adolescents can be trained to reason at a higher level. This poses a special problem for Piaget's theory, which argues that such training only works on a superficial level and is ineffective unless the individual is at a transitional point. Fourth, some cognitive abilities emerge earlier than Piaget envisioned, others later. As we have seen, hypothetical-deductive reasoning does not appear as frequently in early adolescence as Piaget originally believed. And in many developing countries, formal operational thought is rare. Sociocultural Worlds of Adolescence 4.1 presents more information about the role of culture in children's and adolescents' cognitive development. Next, we study an approach that places far more importance than Piaget did on culture's role in adolescent cognition.

An outstanding teacher and education in the logic of science and mathematics are important cultural experiences that promote the development of formal operational thought. Schooling and education likely play more important roles in the development of formal operational thought than Piaget envisioned.

Cognitive Socialization

Adolescents' cognitive development does not occur in a social vacuum. Lev Vygotsky (1896–1934), a Russian psychologist, recognized this important point more than half a century ago. In Vygotsky's view, differences in adolescents' cognitive performance are often related to identifiable features of the *cognitive environment*. He especially stressed that the cognitive growth of children and adolescents is aided by the guidance of individuals who are skilled in the use of the culture's tools. Vygotsky's emphasis on the importance of social interaction and culture in children's and adolescents' cognitive development contrasts with Piaget's description of the child and adolescent as solitary scientists (Rogoff, 1990).

One of Vygotsky's most important concepts is the **zone of proximal development (ZPD),** *which refers to tasks too difficult for individuals to master alone, but that can be mastered with the guidance and assistance of adults or more skilled adolescents.* Thus, the lower level of the ZPD is the level of problem solving reached by the adolescent working independently. The upper limit is the level of additional responsibility the adolescent can accept with the assistance of an able instructor. Vygotsky's emphasis on the ZPD underscored his belief in the importance of social influences on cognitive development. The practical teaching involved in ZPD begins toward the zone's upper limit, where the adolescent is able to reach the goal only through close collaboration with an instructor. With adequate, continuing instruction and practice, the adolescent masters the behavioral sequences necessary to perform the target skill, such as solving an algebraic equation or writing a computer program. As the instruction continues, the performance transfers from the instructor to the adolescent as the teacher gradually reduces the explanations, hints, and demonstrations until the adolescent is able to perform alone. Once the goal is achieved, it may become the foundation for a new ZPD.

To date, Vygotsky's ideas on cognitive socialization have been applied mainly to children's cognitive development. However, some cognitive developmentalists believe that ideas such as Vygotsky's, which emphasize the role of cognitive socialization, have important implications for understanding cognitive growth in adolescence (Keating, 1990a). For example, some researchers have found that small-group discourse is related to improved reasoning about complex problems in adolescence (Newman, in press; Resnick, 1986). The nature of social activities adolescents experience may play important roles in shaping their thinking.

In the cognitive socialization approach, formal education is but one cultural agent that determines adolescents' cognitive growth (Keating, 1990a). Parents, peers, the community, and the technological orientation of the culture are other forces that influence adolescents' thinking. For example, the attitudes toward intellectual competence that adolescents encounter through relationships with their parents and peers affect their motivation for acquiring knowledge. So do the attitudes of teachers and other adults in the community. Media influences, especially through the development of television and the computer, play increasingly important roles in the cognitive socialization of adolescents. For example, does television train adolescents to become passive learners and detract significantly from their intellectual pursuit? We consider television's role in adolescent development in Chapter 9, and in Chapter 5, we examine the computer's role.

The cognitive socialization of adolescents can be improved through the development of more cognitively stimulating environments and additional focus on the role of social factors in cognitive growth. Approaches that take into account adolescents' self-confidence, achievement expectations, and sense of purpose are likely to be just as effective, or even more effective, in shaping adolescents' cognitive growth as more narrow cognitive approaches. For example, a knowledge of physics may be of limited use to inner-city youth with severely limited prospects of employment (Keating, 1990a).

At this point we have studied a number of ideas about cognitive developmental theory, Piaget's ideas, and the cognitive socialization of adolescents. A summary of these ideas is presented in Concept Table 4.1. Our study of the cognitive socialization of adolescents has underscored the important role of culture and stimulating cognitive environments in determining adolescents' cognitive growth. Next, we examine another aspect of adolescents' social cognitive worlds— their thoughts about social matters.

Social Cognition

Developmentalists have recently shown a flourish of interest in how children and adolescents reason about social matters. For many years, the study of cognitive development focused primarily on cognition about nonsocial phenomena, such as logic, number, words, time, and the like. Now there is a lively interest in how children and adolescents reason about their social world as well (Bruner & Bornstein, in press; Lapsley, 1990). Our discussion of social cognition focuses on what social cognition is, egocentrism and perspective taking, implicit personality theory, social cognitive monitoring, whether Piaget's theory adequately explains the adolescent's social cognition, and the discussion of social cognition in the remainder of the book.

Nature of Social Cognition

Social cognition *refers to how individuals conceptualize and reason about their social world—the people they watch and interact with, relationships with those people, the groups in which they participate, and how they reason about themselves and others.* Two main theoretical perspectives have stimulated the development of interest in social cognition—the cognitive developmental view and social information processing.

Concept Table 4.1

Piaget's Theory, Adolescent Cognition, and Cognitive Socialization

Concept	Processes/Related Ideas	Characteristics/Description
Overview and concrete operational thought	Overview	Piaget's widely acclaimed theory stresses biological adaptation through organization, and through assimilation and accommodation. Piaget argued that individuals move through four stages of cognitive development. Adolescents are likely to be either concrete operational or formal operational thinkers.
	Concrete operational thought	According to Piaget, concrete operational thought occurs between approximately 7 and 11 years of age. It is made up of operations and involves reasoning about objects' properties. Conservation and classification skills are characteristics. It is limited by the inability to reason abstractly about objects.
Characteristics of formal operational thought	Its nature	Abstractness and idealism, as well as hypothetical-deductive reasoning, are highlighted in formal operational thought. Formal operational thought involves the ability to reason about what is possible and hypothetical, as opposed to what is real, and the ability to reflect on one's own thoughts.
Early and late formal operational thought	Its nature	Formal operational thought occurs in two phases—an assimilation phase in which reality is overwhelmed (early adolescence) and an accommodation phase in which intellectual balance is restored through a consolidation of formal operational thought (middle years of adolescence).
Individual variation in adolescent cognition	Its nature	Individual variation is extensive, and Piaget did not give this adequate attention. Many young adolescents are not formal operational thinkers but rather are consolidating their concrete operational thought.
Thought and formal operational language	Its nature	Adolescents develop more sophisticated cognitive strategies for handling words and concepts, prose and writing, and communication.
Piaget's theory and adolescent education	Its nature	Piaget's theory has been applied to children's education much more than to adolescents' education. Applications to adolescents' education often follow the belief that instruction is too formal and abstract for adolescents. However, some researchers believe that a supportive context and early attention to reasoning skills promote adolescents' logical thought.
Beyond formal operational thought	Adult cognitive changes	Many life-span developmentalists believe that Piaget was incorrect in assuming that formal operational thought is the highest form of cognition. They argue that more pragmatic, specialized, and multiple (less dualistic) thought takes place in early adulthood and that wisdom may increase throughout the adult years.
Piagetian contributions and criticisms	Evaluating Piaget's theory	Piaget was a genius at observing children and adolescents. He showed us some important things to look for and mapped out some general cognitive changes. Criticisms focus on such matters as stages, which are not as unitary as he believed and do not follow the timetable he envisioned. Culture and education also influence concrete and formal operational thought more than Piaget believed.
Cognitive socialization	Its nature	In Vygotsky's view, differences in adolescents' cognitive performance are often related to identifiable features of the cognitive environment. The cognitive growth of children and adolescents is aided by the guidance of individuals who are skilled in using the tools of the culture. One of Vygotsky's most important concepts is the zone of proximal development. The cognitive socialization approach advocates giving more attention to developing cognitively stimulating environments and to the social factors that influence cognitive growth.

The Cognitive Developmental View

The cognitive developmental view of social cognition is based primarily on the theories of Jean Piaget (1952) and Lawrence Kohlberg (1969, 1976), as well as on the research and thinking of developmental psychologists, such as John Flavell (1981, 1985; Flavell & others, 1968), David Elkind (1976), and Robert Selman (1980). They believe that individuals' social thoughts can be better understood by examining their development.

Kohlberg, in particular, has promoted the role of cognitive developmental theory in understanding different facets of social development. He is known primarily for his contributions to understanding moral development, but he also has expanded Piaget's ideas to account for many social phenomena, not just morality. For example, Kohlberg has applied a cognitive developmental perspective to gender roles, role-taking abilities, peer relations, attachment, and identity.

Like Piaget, Kohlberg believed that biological maturation and environmental experiences interact to produce the individual's stage of thought. Kohlberg said that adolescents attempt to attain intellectual balance or equilibrium. These attempts are influenced by moment-to-moment interactions with people and events in the world. In reaching a new stage of thinking, individuals are able to balance past impressions about the world and themselves with current incoming information. Hence, adolescents who have achieved a stable sense of identity ("I know who I am and where I am going") can handle ostensible threats to their identity ("You aren't working hard enough—you play around too much") without being intellectually blitzed. Over a reasonably long period of time, the balance that has been achieved in a particular stage of thought is disrupted because maturing adolescents gain cognitive abilities that enable them to perceive inconsistencies and inadequacies in their thinking. Just as scientists who are confronted with unexplained events and outcomes must reformulate their theories to explain them, so individuals must shift their former ways of thinking to account for new discrepancies. When individuals are able to balance new information with past impressions, they have reached a new stage in thinking.

Hence, children in elementary school may categorize the identities of themselves and others along a limited number of dimensions—even just one or two, such as "He is a boy, and I am a girl." But as they grow into adolescence, children begin to realize that different people are characterized by traits other than just gender. They recognize, for example, that someone's introverted, quiet style of interaction may shape his or her personal identity just as much or more than his or her "maleness" or "femaleness."

Abstract relations *is developmentalist Kurt Fischer's term for the ability of the adolescent to coordinate two or more abstract ideas; it often appears for the first time between 14 and 16 years of age* (Fischer, 1980). For example, at the age of 16, the adolescent may be able to coordinate the abstraction of conformity with the abstraction of individualism in thinking about his or her personality or the personality of others. Consider the adolescent girl who sees herself as a conformist at school, where she dresses in conventional ways and behaves according to school rules, but views herself as an individualist in social relationships, choosing unconventional friends and wearing unusual clothes in their company. By piecing together these abstractions, she likely views herself as being a different kind of person in the two contexts and senses that, in some ways, she is a contradictory person.

Thus, in the cognitive developmental view, adolescence involves considerable change in how individuals think and reason about themselves and others. Later, we discuss egocentrism and perspective taking in adolescence—two topics

Many adolescent girls spend long hours in front of the mirror, depleting cans of hair spray, tubes of lipstick, and jars of cosmetics. How might this behavior be related to changes in adolescent cognitive and physical development?

that have been important themes of the cognitive developmental view of social cognition. Next, however, we examine a second view of adolescent cognition—social information processing.

Social Information Processing

Social information processing *emphasizes how individuals use cognitive processes, such as attention, perception, memory, thinking, reasoning, expectancies, and so on, to understand their social world.* Two converging theoretical developments led to the interest in social information processing. First, when personality theorist Walter Mischel (1973) introduced *cognitive social learning theory,* he described a number of cognitive processes that mediate experiences between the social world and the individual's behavior. Mischel spoke of plans, memory, imagery, expectations, and other processes as important contributors to how individuals process information about themselves and their social world.

At the same time, a perspective that was to become the dominant view in cognitive psychology was maturing—the view known as information processing, which, like cognitive social learning theory, was discussed in Chapter 2. Some researchers who study social cognition draw heavily from the information-processing perspective as they focus on social memories, social problem solving, social decision making, and so on. Keep in mind, though, that the information-processing perspective is not a developmental perspective, so there is nothing in this view that explains how adolescents process information about themselves and their social world differently than children do. Nonetheless, the information-processing perspective highlights cognitive processes that are central to how individuals understand their social world. Much more about the information-processing perspective appears in Chapter 5. Next, we consider one of the important developmental changes in adolescents' social cognition—egocentrism.

Egocentrism

"Oh my gosh! I can't believe it. Help! I can't stand it!" Tracy desperately yells. "What is wrong? What is the matter?" her mother asks. Tracy responds, "Everyone in here is looking at me." The mother queries, "Why?" Tracy says, "Look, this one hair just won't stay in place," as she rushes to the restroom of the restaurant. Five minutes later, she returns to the restaurant table after she has depleted an entire can of hair spray. During a conversation between two 14-year-old girls, the one named Margaret says, "Are you kidding? I won't get pregnant." And 13-year-old Adam describes himself, "No one understands me, particularly my parents. They have no idea of what I am feeling."

These comments of Tracy, Margaret, and Adam represent the emergence of egocentrism in adolescence. **Adolescent egocentrism** *refers to the heightened self-consciousness of adolescents that is reflected in their belief that others are as interested in them as they themselves are, and in their sense of personal uniqueness.*

Developmental psychologist David Elkind (1967, 1976, 1978) believes that adolescent egocentrism can be dissected into two types of social thinking—imaginary audience and personal fable. The **imaginary audience** *refers to the heightened self-consciousness of adolescents that is reflected in their belief that others are as interested in them as they themselves are. The imaginary audience involves attention-getting behavior—the desire to be noticed, visible, and "on stage."* Tracy's comments and behavior reflect the imaginary audience. Another adolescent may think that others are as aware of a small spot on his trousers as he is, possibly knowing that he has masturbated. Another adolescent, an eighth-grade girl, walks into her classroom and thinks that all eyes are riveted on her

complexion. Adolescents especially sense that they are "on stage" in early adolescence, believing that they are the main actors and all others are the audience.

According to Elkind, the **personal fable** *is the part of adolescent egocentrism involving an adolescent's sense of uniqueness.* The comments of Margaret
and Adam, mentioned earlier, reflect the personal fable. Adolescents' sense of
personal uniqueness makes them feel that no one can understand how they really
feel. For example, an adolescent girl thinks that her mother cannot possibly sense
the hurt that she feels because her boyfriend broke up with her. As part of their
effort to retain a sense of personal uniqueness, adolescents may craft a story about
the self that is filled with fantasy, immersing themselves in a world that is far
removed from reality. Personal fables frequently show up in adolescent diaries.

Developmentalists have increasingly studied adolescent egocentrism in
recent years. The research interest focuses on what the components of egocentrism really are, the nature of self-other relationships, why egocentric thought
emerges in adolescence, and the role of egocentrism in adolescent problems. For
example, David Elkind (1985) believes that adolescent egocentrism is brought
about by formal operational thought. Others, however, argue that adolescent egocentrism is not entirely a cognitive phenomenon. Rather, they think that the
imaginary audience is due both to the ability to think hypothetically (formal operational thought) and the ability to step outside one's self and anticipate the
reactions of others in imaginative circumstances (perspective taking) (Gray &
Hudson, 1984; Lapsley, 1985, 1990, 1991; Lapsley & others, 1986; Lapsley &
Murphy, 1985; Lapsley & Rice, 1988; O'Conner & Nikolic, 1990).

Some developmentalists believe that egocentrism may account for some of
the seemingly reckless behavior of adolescents, including drug use, suicidal
thoughts, and failure to use contraceptives during intercourse (Dolcini & others,
1989; Elkind, 1978). The reckless behavior may stem from the egocentric characteristics of uniqueness and invulnerability. In one recent investigation,
eleventh- and twelfth-grade females who were high in adolescent egocentrism
estimated that they were less likely to get pregnant if they engaged in sex without
contraception than their low adolescent egocentrism counterparts (Arnett, 1990).
As mentioned earlier, some developmentalists believe that perspective taking is
more responsible for adolescent egocentrism than formal operational thought.
Next, we study the nature of perspective taking.

Perspective Taking

Perspective taking *is the ability to assume another person's perspective and understand his or her thoughts and feelings.* Robert Selman (1980) proposed a
developmental theory of perspective taking that has received considerable attention. He believes perspective taking involves a series of five stages, ranging from
three years of age through adolescence (see Figure 4.6). These stages begin with
the egocentric viewpoint in early childhood and end with in-depth perspective
taking in adolescence.

To study adolescents' perspective taking, Selman individually interviews
the adolescents, asking them to comment on such dilemmas as the following:

> Holly is an eight-year-old girl who likes to climb trees. She is the best tree
> climber in the neighborhood. One day while climbing down from a tall tree, she
> falls . . . but does not hurt herself. Her father sees her fall. He is upset and asks
> her to promise not to climb trees any more. Holly promises.
>
> Later that day, Holly and her friends meet Shawn. Shawn's kitten is caught
> in a tree and can't get down. Something has to be done right away or the kitten
> may fall. Holly is the only one who climbs trees well enough to reach the kitten
> and get it down, but she remembers her promise to her father. (Selman, 1976,
> p. 302)

Figure 4.6 Selman's stages of perspective taking.

Stage	Perspective-taking stage	Ages	Description
0	Egocentric viewpoint	3–6	Child has a sense of differentiation of self and other but fails to distinguish between the social perspective (thoughts, feelings) of other and self. Child can label other's overt feelings but does not see the cause-and-effect relation of reasons to social actions.
1	Social-informational perspective taking	6–8	Child is aware that other has a social perspective based on other's own reasoning, which may or may not be similar to child's. However, child tends to focus on one perspective rather than coordinating viewpoints.
2	Self-reflective perspective taking	8–10	Child is conscious that each individual is aware of the other's perspective and that this awareness influences self and other's view of each other. Putting self in other's place is a way of judging other's intentions, purposes, and actions. Child can form a coordinated chain of perspectives but cannot yet abstract from this process to the level of simultaneous mutuality.
3	Mutual perspective taking	10–12	Adolescent realizes that both self and other can view each other mutually and simultaneously as subjects. Adolescent can step outside the two-person dyad and view the interaction from a third-person perspective.
4	Social and conventional system perspective taking	12–15	Adolescent realizes mutual perspective taking does not always lead to complete understanding. Social conventions are seen as necessary because they are understood by all members of the group (the generalized other), regardless of their position, role, or experience.

Subsequently, the interviewer asks the adolescents a series of questions about the dilemma, such as:

> Does Holly know how Shawn feels about the kitten?
> How will Holly's father feel if he finds out she climbed the tree?
> What does Holly think her father will do if he finds out she climbed the tree?
> What would you do in this situation?

By analyzing children's and adolescents' responses to these dilemmas, Selman (1980) concluded that their perspective taking follows the developmental sequence described in Figure 4.6.

Selman's research has shown strong support for the sequential nature of perspective taking, although the ages at which children and adolescents reach the perspective-taking stages overlap considerably. In one investigation, 60 percent of the 10-year-old children were at stage 2 perspective taking, the remaining children at stages 1 and 3 (Selman & Byrne, 1974). This means that, at the threshold of adolescence, 80 percent are likely to be no higher than stage 2 in social perspective taking. In another investigation, only 6 of 28 individuals ages 10 to 13 were at stage 3 or higher, with 78 percent of the early adolescents no higher than stage 2 (Byrne, 1973). Stage 3 was not firmly present until about the age of 16. Selman (1980) acknowledges considerable overlap in the age ranges he applies to the development of interpersonal understanding—for example, stage 2 (6 years 9 months to 15 years 10 months), stage 3 (11 years 3 months to 20+ years). It is the attainment of stage 3 perspective taking that some researchers believe accounts for the imaginary audience and personal fable dimensions of adolescent egocentrism (Lapsley, 1985, 1990).

While adolescents' perspective taking can increase their self-understanding, it also can improve their peer-group status and the quality of their friendships. For example, in one investigation, the most popular children in the third and eighth grades had competent perspective-taking skills (Kurdek & Krile, 1982). Adolescents who are competent at perspective taking are better at understanding the needs of their companions so that they likely can communicate more effectively with them (Hudson, Forman & Brion-Meisels, 1982).

The relation between the self and another individual is complex. Most major developmental theorists believe that development changes in self-other relationships are characterized by movement from egocentrism to perspectivism (Shantz, 1983), but the considerable overlap in the age range at which various levels of perspective taking emerge make generalizations about clear-cut stages difficult (Lapsley, 1990). Next, we turn our attention to another aspect of social cognition that changes during adolescence—implicit personality theory.

Implicit Personality Theory

Implicit personality theory *is the layperson's conception of personality.* Do adolescents conceptualize an individual's personality differently than children do? Adolescents are more likely to interpret an individual's personality in the way that many personality theorists in psychology do than children are (Barenboim, 1981, 1985). Adolescents interpret personality differently than children in three ways. First, when adolescents are given information about another person, they are more likely to consider both previously acquired information and current information, rather than relying only on the concrete information at hand, like children do. Second, adolescents are more likely to detect the situational or contextual variability in personality, rather than thinking that personality is always stable. Third, rather than merely accepting surface traits as a valid description of someone's personality, adolescents are more likely than children to look for deeper, more complex, even hidden causes of personality.

In the following comments obtained in one developmental investigation of how individuals perceive others (Livesley & Bromley, 1973), we can see how the development of an implicit personality theory proceeds:

> Max sits next to me, his eyes are hazel and he is tall. He hasn't got a very big head, he's got a big pointed nose. (p. 213; age seven years, six months)
>
> He smells very much and is very nasty. He has no sense of humor and is very dull. He is always fighting and he is cruel. He does silly things and is very stupid. He has brown hair and cruel eyes. He is sulky and eleven years old and has lots of sisters. I think he is the most horrible boy in the class. He has a croaky voice and always chews his pencil and picks his teeth and I think he is disgusting. (p. 217; age nine years, eleven months)

Andy is very modest. He is even shyer than I am when near strangers and yet is very talkative with people he knows and likes. He always seems good tempered and I have never seen him in a bad temper. He tends to degrade other people's achievements, and yet never praises his own. He does not seem to voice his opinions to anyone. He easily gets nervous. (p. 221; age fifteen years, eight months)

. . . she is curious about people but naive, and this leads her to ask too many questions so that people become irritated with her and withhold information, although she is not sensitive enough to notice it. (p. 225; young adult)

Social Cognitive Monitoring

As part of their increased awareness of themselves and others, which includes both internal thoughts and external behavior, adolescents monitor their social world more extensively. Consider the circumstance of the following adolescent: Bob, a 16-year-old, feels that he does not know as much as he wants or needs to know about Sally, another 16-year-old. He also wants and needs to know more about Sally's relationship with Brian, a 17-year-old. In his effort to learn about Sally, Bob decides that he wants to know more about the groups that Sally belongs to—her student council friends, the clique she belongs to, and so forth. Bob thinks about what he already knows about all these people and groups, and decides he needs to find out how close he is to his goal of understanding them by taking some appropriate, feedback-producing action. What he discovers by taking that action will determine his social-cognitive progress and how difficult his social-cognitive task is. Notice that the immediate aim of this feedback-producing action is not to make progress toward the main goal, but to monitor that progress.

Adolescents engage in a number of cognitive monitoring methods on virtually a daily basis. A student may meet someone new and quickly think, "It's going to be hard to really get to know this guy." Another adolescent may check incoming information about an organization (school, club, group of friends) to determine if it is consistent with the adolescent's impressions of the club or the group. Still another adolescent may question someone or paraphrase what that person has just said about her feelings to ensure that he has understood them correctly.

Cognitive developmentalist John Flavell (1979) believes that adolescents' ability to monitor their social cognition effectively may prove to be an important index of their social maturity and competence. Flavell says that, in many real-life situations, the monitoring problem is not to determine how well you understand what a message means, but rather how much you ought to believe it or do what it says. For example, this aspect of monitoring is especially important in the persuasive appeals to adolescents involving smoking, drinking, engaging in delinquency, having sex, or becoming unthinking followers of this year's flaky cults or movements. Ideas being developed in the area of social cognitive monitoring may someday be parlayed into a method of teaching adolescents to make wise and thoughtful decisions. Next in our discussion of social cognition, we return to Piaget's theory and consider whether it can explain the many social cognitive changes we have been discussing.

Piaget's Theory and Social Cognitive Change

Can Piaget's theory explain the many social cognitive changes that characterize adolescent development? Some critics of Piaget's approach believe that it cannot (Blasi & Hoeffel, 1974; Broughton, 1977; Lapsley, 1990). Formal operational thought is adaptive if the causal structure is known and the deductive rules are correctly followed. Concrete operations is adaptive if the adolescent has a rich and varied social history from which to make the appropriate inductions. What this means is that the kinds of possibilities that concern the typical adolescent—ideological orientation, life plans, social and political commitments, for example—cannot be adequately explained by formal operational thought. The possibilities that spring forth from social life do not require an understanding of perfect logical reasoning in a formal manner, but something else, such as motivation, imagination, desire, and creativity. Rather than formal operational thought producing social cognitive change in adolescence, rich and varied social experiences and communication may be sufficient.

Social Cognition in the Remainder of the Text

Interest in social cognition has blossomed, and the approach has infiltrated many different aspects of the study of adolescent development. In the next chapter, we investigate the topic of social intelligence. In the discussion of families in Chapter 6, the emerging cognitive abilities of the adolescent are evaluated in concert with parent-adolescent conflict and parenting strategies. In the description of peer relations in Chapter 7, the importance of social knowledge and social information processing in peer relations is highlighted. In the overview of the self and identity in Chapter 10, social cognition's role in understanding the self and identity is explored. And in the evaluation of moral development in Chapter 13, considerable time is devoted to discussing Kohlberg's theory, which is a prominent aspect of the study of social cognition in adolescence.

At this point, many different aspects of social cognition have been described. A summary of these ideas is presented in Concept Table 4.2. In the next chapter, we continue our discussion of adolescent cognition, evaluating the nature of information processing and intelligence.

Concept Table 4.2
Social Cognition

Concept	Processes/Related Ideas	Characteristics/Description
Nature of social cognition	What is social cognition?	Social cognition refers to how people conceptualize and reason about their social world, including the relation of the self to others.
	Two major views	The cognitive developmental view, based on the ideas of Piaget, Kohlberg, and others, states that social thoughts are influenced by the individual's development. The social information-processing view is based on cognitive social learning theory and information-processing theory.
Egocentrism and perspective taking	Egocentrism	Elkind proposed that adolescents, especially young adolescents, develop an egocentrism that involves both the construction of an imaginary audience—the belief that others are as preoccupied with the adolescents as they themselves are—and a personal fable—a sense of personal uniqueness. Elkind believes that egocentrism appears because of formal operational thought. Others argue that perspective taking also is involved.
	Perspective taking	Perspective taking is the ability to assume another person's perspective and understand his or her thoughts and feelings. Adolescents are more sophisticated at perspective taking than children, but there is considerable overlap in the ages at which individuals reach higher levels of perspective taking. Selman's model has served as the basis for thinking about perspective taking in adolescence.
Implicit personality theory and social cognitive monitoring	Implicit personality theory	Implicit personality theory refers to the public's or layperson's conception of personality. The implicit personality theories of adolescents are closer to those of scientists who study personality than are children's. Adolescents are more likely to consider the past and present, contextual factors, and deeper causes.
	Social cognitive monitoring	Adolescents engage in much more sophisticated social cognitive monitoring than children do.
Piaget's theory and social cognitive changes	An evaluation	Critics of Piaget's approach argue that formal operational thought does not adequately explain the nature of social cognitive change in adolescence. The inductive aspect of concrete operational thought and a rich and varied social life may be sufficient.
Social cognition in the remainder of the text	Its nature	Interest in social cognition has blossomed, and we study it throughout the text in chapters on intelligence, families, peers, the self and identity, and moral development.

Summary

I. Overview and Concrete Operational Thought

Piaget's widely acclaimed theory stresses biological adaptation through organization and through assimilation and accommodation. Piaget argued that individuals move through four stages of cognitive development. According to Piaget, adolescents are likely to be either concrete operational or formal operational thinkers. Concrete operational thought occurs between approximately 7 and 11 years of age. It is made up of operations and involves reasoning about objects' properties. Conservation and classification skills are characteristics. It is limited by the inability to reason abstractly about objects.

II. Characteristics of Formal Operational Thought

Abstractness and idealism, as well as hypothetical-deductive reasoning, are highlighted in formal operational thought. Formal operational thought involves the ability to reason about what is possible and hypothetical, as opposed to what is real, and the ability to reflect on one's own thoughts.

III. Early and Late Formal Operational Thought and Individual Variation

Formal operational thought occurs in two phases—an assimilation phase in which reality is overwhelmed (early adolescence) and an accommodation phase in which intellectual balance is restored through a consolidation of formal operational thought (middle years of adolescence). Individual variation is extensive, and Piaget did not give this adequate attention. Many young adolescents are not formal operational thinkers but rather are consolidating their concrete operational thought.

IV. Formal Operational Thought and Language

Adolescents develop more sophisticated cognitive strategies for handling words and concepts, prose and writing, and communication.

V. Applications of Piaget's Theory to Education and Beyond Formal Operational Thought

Piaget's theory has been applied to children's education much more than to adolescents' education. Applications to adolescents' education often follow the belief that instruction is too formal and abstract for adolescents. However, some researchers believe that a supportive context and early attention to reasoning skills promote adolescents' logical thought. Many life-span developmentalists believe Piaget was incorrect in assuming that formal operational thought is the highest form of cognition. They argue that more pragmatic, specialized, and multiple (less dualistic) thought takes place in early adulthood and that wisdom may increase throughout the adult years.

VI. Piagetian Contributions and Criticisms

Piaget was a genius at observing children and adolescents. He showed us some important things to look for and mapped out some general cognitive changes. Criticisms focus on such matters as stages, which are not as unitary as he believed and do not follow the timetable he envisioned. Culture and education also influence concrete and formal operational thought more than Piaget believed.

VII. Cognitive Socialization

In Vygotsky's view, differences in adolescents' cognitive performance are often related to identifiable features of the cognitive environment. The cognitive growth of children and adolescents is aided by the guidance of individuals who are skilled in using the tools of the culture. One of Vygotsky's most important concepts is the zone of proximal development. The cognitive socialization approach advocates giving more attention to cognitively stimulating environments and to the social factors that influence cognitive growth.

VIII. Nature of Social Cognition

Social cognition refers to how people conceptualize and reason about their social world, including the relation of the self to others. Two major views of social cognition are the cognitive developmental view—based on the ideas of Piaget, Kohlberg, and others—and social information processing—based on the ideas of cognitive social learning theory and information-processing theory.

IX. Egocentrism and Perspective Taking

Elkind proposed that adolescents, especially young adolescents, develop an egocentrism that involves the construction of an imaginary audience—the belief that others are as preoccupied with the adolescents as they themselves are—and a personal fable—a sense of personal uniqueness. Elkind believes that egocentrism appears because of formal operational thought. Others argue that perspective taking is involved. Perspective taking is the ability to assume another person's perspective and understand his or her thoughts and feelings. Adolescents are more sophisticated at perspective taking than children, but there is considerable overlap in the ages at which individuals reach higher levels of perspective taking. Selman's model has served as the basis for thinking about perspective taking in adolescence.

X. **Implicit Personality Theory and Social Cognitive Monitoring**
Implicit personality theory refers to the layperson's conception of personality. The implicit personality theories of adolescents are closer to those of scientists who study personality than are children's. Adolescents are more likely to consider the past and the present, contextual factors, and deeper causes. Adolescents engage in much more sophisticated social cognitive monitoring than children do.

XI. **Piaget's Theory and Social Cognitive Changes**
Critics of Piaget's approach argue that formal operational thought does not adequately explain the nature of social cognitive change in adolescence. The inductive aspect of concrete operational thought and a rich and varied social life may be sufficient.

XII. **Social Cognition in the Remainder of the Text**
Interest in social cognition has blossomed, and we study it throughout the text in chapters on intelligence, families, peers, the self and identity, and moral development.

Key Terms

operations 117
conservation 117
horizontal décalage 118
classification 118
hypothetical-deductive
  reasoning 120
early formal operational
  thought 121

late formal operational
  thought 121
wisdom 127
zone of proximal
  development 130
social cognition 131
abstract relations 133

social information
  processing 134
adolescent egocentrism
  134
imaginary audience 134
personal fable 135
perspective taking 135
implicit personality
  theory 137

Suggested Readings

Elkind, D. (1976). *Child development and education.* New York: Oxford University Press.
    An excellent, easy-to-read introduction to the implications of Piaget's ideas for educators. Gives practical examples for approaching classroom teaching from the Piagetian perspective.
Flavell, J. H. (1985). *Cognitive development* (2d ed.). Englewood Cliffs, NJ: Prentice-Hall.
    An outstanding statement of the major contemporary ideas about cognitive development by one of the leading scholars in the field. Although inspired by Piaget's work, Flavell goes well beyond it, offering new insights, critical evaluation, and reflections about his own original research, including many ideas about social cognition.

Ginsburg, H., & Opper, S. (1988). *Piaget's theory of intellectual development* (3rd ed.). Englewood Cliffs, NJ: Prentice-Hall.
One of the best explanations and descriptions of Piaget's theory.

Lapsley, D. K. (1990). Continuity and discontinuity in adolescent social cognitive development. In R. Montemayor, G. Adams, & T. Gullota (Eds.), *From childhood to adolescence: A transitional period?* Newbury Park, CA: Sage.
An excellent critique of Piaget's ideas on social cognitive change and extensive coverage of contemporary ideas on adolescent social cognition.

Selman, R. L. (1981). What children understand of intrapsychic processes: The child as a budding personality theorist. In E. K. Weber & E. Weber (Eds.), *Cognitive and affective growth.* Hillsdale, NJ: Erlbaum.
Contains Selman's account of how he thinks the adolescent forms a theory of personality. Includes an overview of his ideas about role taking.

CHAPTER 5

Information Processing and Intelligence

The error of youth is to believe that intelligence is a substitute for experience, while the error of age is to believe that experience is a substitute for intelligence.

Slyman Bryson

Reading *Martina*

Barbara Smith is a sixth-grade student at a middle school. Her favorite activity is tennis, so her mother recently bought her a book entitled, *Martina,* which is about tennis star Martina Navratilova's life. Barbara finished reading the first 11 pages of the book. She placed it on the table in the hall as she left for tennis practice. Her eight-year-old sister, Nancy, saw Barbara leave the book on the table. She grabbed the book and started to read it. Nancy finished the entire book in 12 minutes. In that 12 minutes, she read several sentences in different chapters as she leafed rapidly through the book. She also studied each of the book's photographs and read some of their captions.

After Barbara returned from tennis practice, she showered, ate, and then read another chapter in *Martina,* which Nancy had returned to its place on the table. She sat quietly for 30 minutes and read the next 18 pages of the book. A few of the words were difficult, but Barbara got the idea of what Martina's family background was like and how she started to play tennis in her native country of Czechoslovakia. She especially noted how Martina's father spent long hours playing tennis with her and how she dreamed of being a star.

Nancy, Barbara's younger sister, walked by her room just as Barbara finished reading for the evening. Nancy asked, "Did you like the book? I did." Barbara replied, "You are too little to understand it. Shrimps can't read this kind of book." Their mother heard them begin to argue and ran upstairs to intervene.

She asked Nancy what the book was about. Nancy said, "A tennis player. I can't remember her name, though." Barbara laughed and said, "She doesn't know very much, does she?" The mother reprimanded Barbara for teasing Nancy, then walked out into the hall with Nancy and told her not to worry about what Barbara had said.

The next day, the mother went to Barbara's room while Barbara was at tennis practice and picked up the book about Martina. She sat down and skimmed the book in about one hour, forming a general idea of the book's content. As she read, she made mental notes and developed many concepts about Martina's life both on and off the tennis court.

When we read, we process information and interpret it. So reading serves as a practical example to introduce the topic of information processing in adolescence. To read effectively, adolescents have to perceive and attend to a complex set of visual symbols—words. Note that Barbara and her mother attended more to words and sentences, while Nancy attended more to pictures. Another process in reading is holding the information we process in memory. Note that after about one hour of reading, the mother was able to get the gist of the entire book and hold the book's themes in her memory. But Barbara was able to cover only several chapters of the book in this time frame, and at this point, her memory of what the book was about was much more impoverished than her mother's (Santrock & Yussen, 1992).

I come into the fields and spacious palaces of my memory, where are treasures of countless images of things of every manner.

St. Augustine

T he study of adolescents' information processing is concerned with basic processes, such as attention, memory, and thinking. In the first part of this chapter, we consider these processes and other aspects of information processing. In the second part of the chapter, we discuss the nature of intelligence in adolescence.

Information Processing

Information processing is both a framework for thinking about adolescent development and a facet of that development. As a framework, information processing includes certain ideas about how adolescent minds work and the best methods for studying this. As a facet of development, different aspects of information processing change as children make the transition through adolescence to adulthood. For example, changes in attention and memory are essentially changes in the way individuals process information. In the discussion that follows, we review some basic ideas about the information-processing approach first discussed in Chapter 2 and compare the information-processing approach with other cognitive orientations. Then we examine some basic developmental changes in processing and the nature of attention, memory, and cognitive monitoring in adolescence. Our discussion of information processing continues with an evaluation of its application to adolescent decision making and critical thinking, and concludes with a discussion of the role of computers in adolescents' lives.

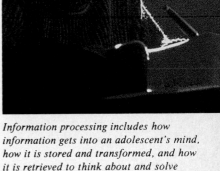

Information processing includes how information gets into an adolescent's mind, how it is stored and transformed, and how it is retrieved to think about and solve problems.

The Information-Processing Perspective

As we discussed in Chapter 2, information processing is concerned with how individuals analyze the many sources of information in the environment and make sense of these experiences. Information processing includes how information gets into adolescents' minds, how it is stored and transformed, and how it is retrieved to think about and solve problems. The development of the computer promoted this approach—the mind as an information-processing system has been compared to the computer as an information-processing system. The information-processing system raises questions about development, such as how do the ways in which we process information change as we make the transition from childhood to adulthood?

How does the information-processing perspective differ from the behavioral perspective (Chapter 2) and the Piagetian cognitive developmental perspective (Chapters 2 and 4)? The behavioral approach focuses on behaviors and the events in the environment that change these behaviors. Traditional principles of behaviorism and learning do little to explain what is going on in the adolescent's mind, although in recent years, cognitive social learning theory has emphasized some cognitive processes. Piagetian theory, in contrast, has much to say about the adolescent's mind. For example, Piaget described the adolescent's thoughts as more abstract, idealistic, and logical than the child's. But the Piagetian description is somewhat general—it does not tell us much about how the adolescent reads or solves math problems. It leaves out some important details about how the adolescent's mind actually works on specific tasks, like solving algebraic equations and writing long essays.

The information-processing perspective tries to correct some of the shortcomings of traditional behaviorism or learning theory and Piagetian cognitive developmental ideas. It describes mental processes and offers details about how these processes work in concrete situations. Where possible, these descriptions include analyses of all the steps necessary to complete some task, the specific mental processes needed for these steps, and precise estimates of how "hard" or "how long" the mind has to work to execute these steps (Klahr, 1989).

Let's examine how an adolescent's mind might work in processing information about an algebraic equation. An event (S) occurs in the environment. Suppose the event is the appearance of the following algebraic equation on the chalkboard at school: "$2x + 10 = 34$. Solve for x." This event contains information that a person can detect and understand. Success in detecting and making sense of it depends on how completely and efficiently the information is processed. Development can be equated with becoming more skillful and efficient at information processing. Once the processing is complete, the person produces an observable response (R). In this model, then, cognitive activity refers to the flow of information through the different steps of processing.

Consider how a well-seasoned algebra student engages cognition. The teacher writes the equation on the board (S). The student looks up and notes that something has been written on the board (*attention*). This "something" is then determined to be a series of numbers, letters, and signs, and—at a higher level of identification—two simple statements: (1) "$2x + 10 = 34$" and (2) "Solve for x" (*perception*). The student must preserve the results of this perceptual analysis over a period of time (*memory*), even if only for the brief interval needed to write the problem on a worksheet.

The student then begins to elaborate on the product of perception and memory (*thinking*). This level of analysis can be described best with an imaginary mental soliloquy (though, of course, the reasoning might take an altogether different track or even a nonverbal form): "Let's see. It's an equation—x is the unknown, and I'm supposed to figure out the value of x. How do I do that?" The final level of analysis (*problem solving*) addresses the question: "How do I do that?" Problem solving then takes the following form: "Okay, $2x + 10 = 34$. First, I have to collect the unknown on one side of the equation and the known values on the other side. To do this, I'll leave the $2x$ where it is—on the left. Then I'll subtract 10 from each side to remove the 10 from the left. This leaves $2x = 24$. Now I have to express the equation as '$x =$ something,' and it's solved. How do I do this? I know! Divide each side by 2 and that will leave $1x$, or x, on the left side. Now I have $x = 12$. That's the answer!" A summary of the processes used in solving the algebraic equation is presented in Figure 5.1.

Figure 5.1 is a necessarily oversimplified representation of information processing that omits a great deal and does not indicate the many routes that the flow of information may take. For example, each hypothetical step (such as perception) may overlap with other steps (for example, memory) or be composed of several substeps. Neither of these features is captured in the diagram, whose purpose is to focus on the basic elements of information processing. In many instances, information processing is dynamic and simultaneous, and many different models of how this processing takes place have been developed. In Chapter

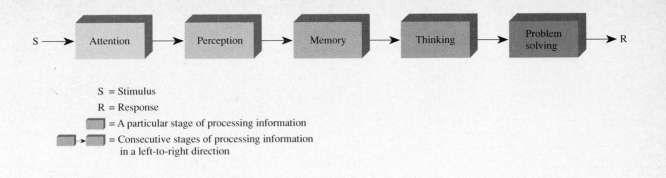

S = Stimulus

R = Response

☐ = A particular stage of processing information

☐ ➤ ☐ = Consecutive stages of processing information
in a left-to-right direction

2, another simplified model of information processing was described (Figure 2.6) to give a sense of the basic processes involved in adolescent cognition.

Figure 5.1 Hypothetical series of steps involved in processing information to solve an algebra problem.

Developmental Changes in Information Processing

Three developmental changes in information processing that distinguish adolescents from children are (1) processing speed, (2) processing capacity, and (3) automaticity, each of which we consider in turn.

Processing Speed

Many things that children and adolescents do are constrained by how much time is available. A child is told to finish writing a letter in five minutes so that the family can leave. A phone message must be written down before the message is forgotten. The teacher gives the adolescent five minutes to finish the assigned algebra problems. The speed with which such tasks is completed improves dramatically across the childhood and adolescent years (Kail, 1988; Stigler, Nusbaum, & Chalip, 1988). The causes of the improvement are not always clear, however. Is a 7-year-old slower to write down a phone message than a 13-year-old because of limitations in the physical act of writing or because of other, more mental limitations, such as the time needed to think of how to spell words correctly or to briefly summarize a message? Do such age differences suggest some maturational, central nervous system differences in maturity? At present, these questions have not been answered.

One recent study found evidence that processing speed continues to improve in early adolescence (Hale, 1990). Ten-year-olds were approximately 1.8 times slower in processing information than young adults on such tasks as reaction time, letter matching, mental rotation, and abstract matching. Twelve-year-olds were approximately 1.5 times slower than young adults, but 15-year-olds processed information on the tasks as fast as young adults.

Processing Capacity

Information-processing capacity can be viewed as a type of energy needed to perform mental work. The difficulty individuals have in dividing attention when they do two things at once is attributed to limits on capacity. So also is the trouble individuals have in performing complex tasks (such as mentally working a complex geometry problem). Although capacity is thought to be limited at all ages, there is no generally accepted measure of an adolescent's capacity, and thus, findings are ambiguous. For example, it is possible that capacity does not change with age but that children must spend more capacity on lower-level processes (such as identifying stimuli), leaving less capacity for higher-level processes (such as dividing attention or performing complex computations) than adolescents.

Automaticity

Some activities are completed with little thought or effort. An able 12-year-old zips through a practice list of multiplication problems with little conscious effort. A 17-year-old adolescent picks up the newspaper and quickly scans the sports section to discover the results of an important basketball game. Both of these examples illustrate relatively automatic information processing. By comparison, imagine a 9-year-old doing long division with three- to five-digit numbers, or an 18-year-old trying to decipher the meaning of a news paragraph in a foreign language studied four years earlier and not studied since. These activities require considerable mental processing and effort. For virtually any given task, such as calculating, reading, or writing, adolescents' **automaticity**—*the ability to perform automatically with little or no effort*—is better than children's (Brown & others, 1983). Automaticity is clearly linked to speed of processing and processing capacity. As an activity is completed faster, it requires less processing capacity. As processing capacity increases, tasks that were previously considered difficult become easier to complete. Next, we consider a developmental model of information processing that includes automaticity and processing capacity.

Case's Developmental Information-Processing Model

Canadian developmentalist Robbie Case (1985) proposed an information-processing model that specifies differences in children's and adolescents' cognition. In Case's view, adolescents make considerable gains in a number of cognitive areas: They have increasingly more cognitive resources available to them because of automaticity, increased information-processing capacity, and more familiarity with a range of content knowledge. Because of the reduced load on the cognitive system, adolescents become capable of holding in mind several different dimensions of a topic of problem, whereas children are more likely to focus on only one (Keating, 1990). Next, we consider two cognitive processes involved in adolescents' processing of information—attention and memory.

Attention and Memory

While the bulk of research on information processing has been conducted with children and adults, the information-processing perspective is important in understanding adolescent cognition. As we saw in the example of the adolescent solving an algebraic equation, attention and memory are two important cognitive processes.

Attention

"Pay attention" is a phrase children and adolescents hear all of the time. Just what is *attention?* **Attention** *is the concentration and focusing of mental effort. Attention also is both selective and shifting.* For example, when adolescents take a test, they must attend to it. This implies that they have the ability to focus their mental effort on certain stimuli (the test questions) while excluding other stimuli, an important aspect of attention called *selectivity.* When selective attention fails adolescents, they have difficulty ignoring information that is irrelevant to their interests or goals (Posner & Rothbart, 1989). For example, if a television set is blaring while the adolescent is studying, the adolescent may have difficulty concentrating.

Not only is attention selective, but it is also *shiftable*. If a teacher asks students to pay attention to a certain question and they do so, their behavior indicates that they can shift the focus of their mental effort from one stimulus to another. If the telephone rings while the adolescent is studying, the adolescent may shift attention from studying to the telephone. An external stimulus is not necessary to shift attention. At any moment, adolescents can shift their attention from one topic to another, virtually at will. They might think about the last time they went to a play, then think about an upcoming music recital, and so on.

In one investigation, 12-year-olds were markedly better than 8-year-olds and slightly worse than 20-year-olds at allocating their attention in a situation involving two tasks (Manis, Keating, & Morrison, 1980). Adolescents may have more resources available (through increased processing speed, capacity, and automaticity), or they may be more skilled at directing these resources.

Memory

There are few moments when adolescents' lives are not steeped in memory. Memory is at work with each step adolescents take, each thought they think, and each word they utter. **Memory** *is the retention of information over time.* It is central to mental life and to information processing. To successfully learn and reason, adolescents need to hold onto information and to retrieve the information they have tucked away. Two important memory systems are short-term memory and long-term memory. **Short-term memory** *is a limited-capacity memory system in which information is retained for as long as 30 seconds, unless the information is rehearsed, in which case it can be retained longer.* **Long-term memory** *is a relatively permanent memory system that holds huge amounts of information for a long period of time.*

A common way to assess short-term memory is to present a list of items to remember, which is often referred to as a memory span task (Fitzgerald, 1991). If you have taken an IQ test, you probably were asked to remember a string of numbers or words. You simply hear a short list of stimuli—usually digits—presented at a rapid pace (one per second, for example). Then you are asked to repeat the digits back. Using the memory span task, researchers have found that short-term memory increases extensively in early childhood and continues to increase in older children and adolescents, but at a slower pace. For example, in one investigation, memory span increased by 1½ digits between the ages of 7 and 13 (Dempster, 1981) (see Figure 5.2). Keep in mind, though, memory span's individual differences, which is why IQ and various aptitude tests are used.

How might short-term memory be used in problem solving? In a series of experiments, Robert Sternberg (1977; Sternberg & Nigro, 1980; Sternberg & Rifkin, 1979) attempted to answer this question by giving third-grade, sixth-grade, ninth-grade, and college students analogies to solve. The main differences occurred between the younger (third and sixth grade) and older (ninth grade and college) students. The older students were more likely to complete the information processing required to solve the analogy task. The children, by contrast, often stopped their processing of information before they had considered all of the necessary steps required to solve the problems. Sternberg believes that incomplete information processing occurred because the children's short-term memory was overloaded. Solving problems such as analogies requires individuals to make continued comparisons between newly encoded information and previously coded information. Sternberg argues that adolescents probably have more storage space in short-term memory, which results in fewer errors on problems like analogies.

In addition to more storage space, are there other reasons adolescents might perform better on memory span tasks and in solving analogies? While many other

In one research investigation, 12-year-olds were much better than 8-year-olds and only slightly worse than 20-year-olds at allocating their attention in a situation involving two tasks (Manis, Keating, & Morrison, 1980). The adolescents' improved attention may have occurred because they had more processing resources available or because they were more skilled at directing those resources.

Figure 5.2 Developmental changes in short-term memory as measured by digit span. In Dempster's (1981) study, memory span increased from an average of about two digits in 2- to 3-year-old children to about five digits in 7-year-old children. Between 7 and 13 years of age, memory span increased by 1½ digits. The dashed lines represent how widely the memory-span scores varied at different ages.

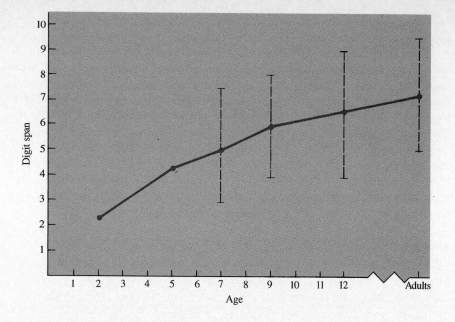

Reading continues to play a powerful role in adolescents' lives, just as it did when they were children. In the last decade, considerable interest has developed in the process of cognitive monitoring as an important aspect of reading. What do we mean by cognitive monitoring?

factors may be involved, information-processing psychologists believe that changes in the speed and efficiency of information processing are important, especially the speed with which information can be identified.

Long-term memory increases substantially in the middle and late childhood years and likely continues to improve during adolescence, although this has not been well documented by researchers. If anything at all is known about long-term memory, it is that it depends on the learning activities engaged in when learning and remembering information (Siegler, 1988). Most learning activities fit under the category of **strategies,** *activities under the learner's conscious control. They sometimes are also called control processes. There are many of these activities, but one of the most important is* organization, *the tendency to group or arrange items into categories.*

Cognitive Monitoring

Attention and memory may occur rather quickly as adolescents examine information or attempt to complete some task. Adolescents may devote little effort and complete the new activity quickly. By contrast, a variety of activities, such as reading, writing, and solving math problems, occur over an extended period of time and require adolescents to mobilize considerable cognitive resources. And when adolescents encounter some difficulty or lapse of attention, they must overcome the temporary hiatus and get back on track. Problem solving and cognitive monitoring are involved in adolescents' ability to guide and control their activities (Voss, 1989). More about problem solving, including creativity in solving problems, appears later in the chapter in the discussion of intelligence. Here we focus on cognitive monitoring.

Cognitive monitoring *is the process of taking stock of what one is currently doing, what will be done next, and how effectively the mental activity is unfolding.* When adolescents engage in an activity like reading, writing, or solving a math problem, they are repeatedly called on to take stock of what they are doing and what they plan to do next (Baker & Brown, 1984; Bereiter & Scardamalia, 1982). In Chapter 4, we saw the importance of social cognitive monitoring in understanding the way adolescents solve social problems. Here we examine the importance of cognitive monitoring in solving problems in the nonsocial aspects of intelligence—reading, writing, math, and so on. For example, when adolescents begin to solve a math problem—especially one that might take a while to finish—they must determine what kind of problem they are working on and a good approach to solving it. And once they undertake a problem solution, they need to check on whether the solution is working or whether some other approach needs to be taken.

Evidence that children and adolescents need advice to help them monitor their cognitive activities is plentiful (Garner, 1987; Mayer, 1987). Parents, teachers, and peers can serve as important cognitive monitoring models and also can interact with adolescents in ways to improve their cognitive monitoring. In one strategy, cognitive monitoring is placed in the hands of peers; that is, instead of adults telling adolescents what to do and checking their performance, this chore is performed by other adolescents.

In addition to cognitive monitoring, two other cognitive activities are especially important in adolescents' everyday cognitive skills—decision making and critical thinking.

Although driver training courses can improve adolescents' cognitive and motor skills related to driving, these courses have not been effective in reducing adolescents' high rate of traffic accidents. An important research agenda is to learn more about how adolescents make decisions in practical situations, such as driving.

Decision Making

Adolescence is a time of increased decision making—about the future, which friends to choose, whether to go to college, which person to date, whether to have sex, whether to take drugs, whether to buy a car, and so on. How competent are adolescents at making decisions? Older adolescents are more competent than younger adolescents, who, in turn, are more competent than children (Keating, 1990). Young adolescents are more likely than children to generate options, to examine a situation from a variety of perspectives, to anticipate the consequences of decisions, and to consider the credibility of sources (Mann, Harmoni, & Power, in press). However, young adolescents are less competent at these decision-making skills than older adolescents.

Transitions in decision making appear at approximately 11 to 12 years of age and at 15 to 16 years of age. For example, in one study, eighth-, tenth-, and twelfth-grade students were presented with dilemmas involving the choice of a medical procedure (Lewis, 1981). The oldest students were most likely to spontaneously mention a variety of risks, to recommend consultation with an outside specialist, and to anticipate future consequences. For example, when asked a question about whether to have cosmetic surgery, a twelfth grader said that different aspects of the situation needed to be examined along with its effects on the individual's future, especially relationships with other people. By contrast, an eighth grader provided a more limited view, commenting on the surgery's effects on getting turned down for a date, the money involved, and being teased at school by peers.

However, the decision-making skills of older adolescents and adults are often far from perfect. And the ability to make competent decisions does not guarantee that such decisions will be made in everyday life, where breadth of experience often comes into play (Jacobs & Potenza, 1990; Keating, 1990). For example, driver-training courses improve adolescents' cognitive and motor skills to levels equal to, or sometimes superior to, those of adults. However, driver training has not been effective in reducing adolescents' high rate of traffic accidents (Potvin, Campagne, & Laberge-Nadeau, 1988). Thus, an important research agenda is to study the ways adolescents make decisions in practical situations.

Adolescents need more opportunities to practice and discuss realistic decision making. Many real-world decisions occur in an atmosphere of stress that includes such factors as time constraints and emotional involvement. One strategy for improving adolescent decision making about real-world choices involving such

matters as sex, drugs, and daredevil driving is for schools to provide more opportunities for adolescents to engage in role-playing and group problem solving
related to such circumstances (Mann, Harmoni, & Power, in press).

In some instances, adolescents' decision making may be blamed when, in
reality, the problem involves society's orientation toward adolescents and the
failure to provide adolescents with adequate choices (Keating, 1990). For example, a mathematically precocious ninth-grade girl may abandon mathematics
not because of poor decision-making skills but because of a stronger motivation
to maintain positive peer relations that would be threatened if she stayed on the
math track. The decision of an adolescent in a low-income inner-city area to
engage in drug trafficking even at considerable risk may not be a consequence of
the adolescent's failure to consider all of the relevant information but may be the
outcome of quite sophisticated thinking about risk-benefit ratios in oppressive
circumstances offering limited or nonexistent options. As cognitive developmentalist Daniel Keating (1990) observed, if we dislike adolescents' choices, perhaps we need to provide them with better options from which to choose.

Critical Thinking

Closely related to making competent decisions is engaging in critical thinking, a
current buzzword in education and psychology (Ennis, 1991; Jones, Idol, &
Brandt, 1991). Although today's definitions of **critical thinking** *vary, they have
in common the notions of grasping the deeper meaning of problems, of keeping
an open mind about different approaches and perspectives, and of deciding for
oneself what to believe or do.* Another, often implicit assumption is that critical
thinking is a very important aspect of everyday reasoning (Galotti, 1989). Adolescents should be encouraged to engage in critical thinking, not just inside the
classroom but outside it as well.

Adolescence is an important transitional period in the development of critical thinking (Keating, 1990). Among the important cognitive changes that allow
improved critical thinking in adolescence are:

- Increased speed, automaticity, and capacity of information processing,
  which free cognitive resources for other purposes
- More breadth of content knowledge in a variety of domains
- Increased ability to construct new combinations of knowledge
- A greater range and more spontaneous use of strategies or procedures
  for applying or obtaining knowledge, such as planning, considering
  alternatives, and cognitive monitoring

While adolescence is an important period in the development of critical-
thinking skills, if a solid basis of fundamental skills (such as literacy and math
skills) is not developed during childhood, such critical-thinking skills are unlikely
to mature in adolescence. For the subset of adolescents who lack such fundamental skills, potential gains in adolescent thinking are not likely.

Considerable interest has recently developed in teaching critical thinking
in schools. Cognitive psychologist Robert J. Sternberg (1985) believes that most
school programs that teach critical thinking are flawed. He thinks that schools
focus too much on formal reasoning tasks and not enough on the critical-thinking
skills needed in everyday life. Among the critical-thinking skills that Sternberg
believes adolescents need in everyday life are: recognizing that problems exist,
defining problems more clearly, handling problems with no single right answer
or any clear criteria for the point at which the problem is solved (such as selecting

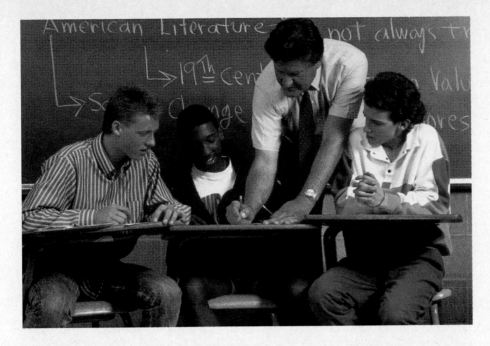

a rewarding career), making decisions on issues of personal relevance (such as deciding to have a risky operation), obtaining information, thinking in groups, and developing long-term approaches to long-term problems.

At this time, there is no agreed-upon curriculum of critical thinking that can be taught in a stepwise, developmental fashion to children and adolescents. Many experts in education and psychology, however, believe that the infusion of a critical-thinking approach into all parts of the curriculum would benefit children and adolescents (Ennis, 1990; McPeck, 1990).

In Chapter 2, we saw that the computer played an important role in the development of the information-processing perspective. While the information-processing perspective has yet to be widely applied to adolescent education, the computer is rapidly becoming an important aspect of adolescent learning.

Computers and Adolescents

At mid-twentieth century, IBM had yet to bring its first computer to market. Now, as we move toward the close of the twentieth century, computers are important influences in adolescents' lives. For some, the computer is a positive tool with the power to transform our schools and revolutionize adolescents' learning. For others, the computer is a menacing force, more likely to undermine than to improve adolescents' education and learning. Let's examine some of computers' possible positive and negative influences.

The influence of the computer on children's and adolescents' learning, motivation, and social behavior is a source of debate and controversy.

Positive Influences of Computers on Adolescents

The potential positive influences of computers on adolescents' development include using computers as personal tutors or as multipurpose tools, and the motivational and social effects of computers (Lepper & Gurtner, 1989).

Computer-assisted instruction *involves using computers as tutors to individualize instruction: to present information, to give students practice, to assess students' level of understanding, and to provide additional instruction if needed.* Computer-assisted instruction requires students' active participation, and in giving immediate feedback to students, is patient and nonjudgmental. Over the past two

For almost 25 years, filmmaker Robert Abel made the screen come alive with special effects, influencing the development of such movies as 2001: A Space Odyssey. Today, Abel is working on creative ways to use computers to educate children and adolescents. His approach blends computers and television. The students, using devices such as a desktop mouse or a touch screen, explore as their curiosity beckons. They can follow a lead from text to photos to music and back again. In an application to art, students see some of Picasso's paintings; then they choose—by clicking with the mouse—various interpretations of the paintings. Abel's combination of computers and television is being tried out in some schools in Los Angeles and should soon be available on a wider basis. Abel's goal is to use the computer/television strategy to turn on students to discover ideas.

decades, the more than 200 research studies on computer-assisted instruction have generally shown that the effects of computer-assisted instruction are positive. More precisely, the effects are more positive with programs involving tutorials rather than drill and practice, with younger rather than older students, and with lower ability than average or unselected populations (Lepper & Gurtner, 1989).

Computers' second important influence on adolescent development involves computers' role in experiential learning. Some experts view computers as excellent mediums for open-ended, exploratory, and experiential learning.

Third, computers can function as a multipurpose tool in helping adolescents to achieve academic goals and to become more creative. They are especially helpful in improving adolescents' writing and communication skills (Collins, 1986). Word-processing programs diminish the drudgery of writing, increasing the probability that adolescents will edit and revise their work. Programs that assist in outlining a paper may help students to organize their thoughts before they write.

Several other themes appear in discussions of computers' positive influence on adolescent development. For one, computer advocates argue that computers make learning more intrinsically motivating (Lepper, 1985). Computer enthusiasts also argue that computers can make learning more fun. In addition, lessons can often be embedded in instructional "games" or puzzles that encourage adolescents' curiosity and sense of challenge. Some computer advocates also argue that increased computer use in schools will lead to increased student cooperation and collaboration, as well as increased intellectual discussion among students. And if computers do increase students' interest, they may free teachers to spend more one-on-one time with students. Finally, computer advocates hope that computers can help to equalize educational opportunity (Becker & Sterling, 1987). Since computers allow students to work at their own pace, they may help students who do not normally succeed in schools. Also, because computers are fair and impartial, they should minimize the adverse influences of teacher prejudice and stereotyping.

Negative Influences of Computers on Adolescents

The potential negative influences of computers on adolescent development include regimentation and dehumanization of the classroom, as well as unwarranted "shaping" of the curriculum. Generalizations and limitations of computer-based teaching may also be potential problems (Lepper & Gurtner, 1989).

Skeptics worry that, rather than increased individualization of instruction, computers bring a much greater regimentation and homogenization of classroom learning experiences. While some students may prefer to work autonomously and may learn most effectively when they are allowed to progress on their own, other students may rely on social interaction with and guidance by the teacher for effective learning. And some computer skeptics worry that computers will ultimately increase inequality, rather than equality, in educational outcomes (Malcom, 1988). School funding in middle-class neighborhoods is usually better than in low-income areas, and the homes of adolescents in middle-class neighborhoods are more likely to have computers than those in low-income neighborhoods. Thus, an increasing emphasis on computer literacy may be inequitable for children from low-income backgrounds because they have likely had fewer opportunities to use computers. Some critics also worry about the dehumanization of the classroom. They argue that school is a social world as well as a cognitive, learning world. From this perspective, children plugged into computers all day long have little opportunity to engage in social interaction.

A further concern is that computers may inadvertently and inappropriately shape the curriculum. Some subjects, such as mathematics and science, seem to be more easily and successfully adapted to computers than such subjects as art and literature. Consequently, there is concern that computers could eventually shape the curriculum in the direction of science and math.

Yet another concern is the transfer of learning and motivation outside the computer domain. If the instructional effectiveness and motivational appeal of computer-based education depend on the use of impressive technical devices, such as color, animation, and sound effects, how effectively will student learning or motivation transfer to other contexts without these technical supports? Will adolescents provided with the editorial assistance of computers still learn the basic skills needed to progress to more complex forms of creative writing later in their careers? Will adolescents using computers in math gain the proficiency to deal with more complicated math in the future, or will their ability to solve complex conceptual problems in the absence of computers have atrophied? Presently, the answers to these important questions about computers' role in adolescent development are not known.

At this point, we have discussed numerous ideas about information processing and a summary of these ideas is presented in Concept Table 5.1. Now we turn our attention to another way of analyzing the adolescent's cognition. We will discover that the study of adolescent intelligence has emphasized individual differences, knowledge, and intelligence tests.

Intelligence

Robert Sternberg recalls being terrified of taking IQ tests as a child. He says that he literally froze when the time came to take such tests. When he was in the sixth grade, he was sent to take an IQ test with the fifth graders and still talks about how embarrassing and humiliating the experience was. Sternberg recalls that maybe he was dumb, but he wasn't *that* dumb. He finally overcame his anxieties about IQ tests and performed much better on them. Sternberg then became so fascinated with IQ tests that he devised his own at the age of 13 and began assessing the intellectual abilities of his classmates until the school psychologist scolded him. Later in our discussion of intelligence, you will discover that Sternberg recently has developed a provocative theory of intelligence. Our exploration of intelligence focuses on the following questions: What is intelligence? How is intelligence measured? Does intelligence have one or many faces? What is the nature of group tests of intelligence? Can aptitude and achievement tests be distinguished? What are some of the major controversies and issues involving intelligence? What are the extremes of intelligence like? We consider each of these in turn.

What Is Intelligence?

Intelligence is a possession that most adolescents value highly, yet it is an abstract concept with few agreed-upon referents. Investigators could agree upon referents for such characteristics as adolescent height, weight, and age, but would be less certain to agree on referents for something like an adolescent's size. Size is a more *abstract* notion than height or weight. An adolescent's size can only be estimated from a set of empirical measures of height and weight. Measuring an adolescent's intelligence is much the same as measuring the adolescent's size, though *much more* abstract; that is, investigators believe that adolescent intelligence exists, but it cannot be measured directly. They cannot peel back an adolescent's scalp and observe the adolescent's intellectual processes in action. The

Concept Table 5.1

Information Processing

Concept	Processes/Related Ideas	Characteristics/Description
The information-processing perspective	Overview	Information processing is concerned with how individuals analyze the many sources of information in the environment and make sense of these experiences. It includes how information gets into the mind, how it is stored and transformed, and how it is retrieved to think about and solve problems.
	Comparison with other approaches	Traditional principles of behaviorism and learning do little to explain what is going on in the mind. Piaget's cognitive developmental theory provides a general outline of changes in cognition but leaves out some important details about the steps involved in analyzing information. The information-processing perspective tries to correct some of these deficiencies.
Developmental changes in information processing	Processing speed, processing capacity, and automaticity	Adolescents process information faster, have greater processing capacity, and show greater automaticity in processing than children.
	Case's information-processing model	According to Case, adolescents have increasingly more cognitive resources available to them because of automaticity, increased capacity, and more familiarity with content knowledge.
Attention and memory	Attention	Attention is the concentration and focusing of mental effort. Attention is both selective and shifting.
	Memory	Memory is the retention of information over time. It can be divided into short-term memory—information held for up to 30 seconds—and long-term memory—information held indefinitely. Strategies, or control processes, especially organization, improve adolescent memory. Increases in storage space, as well as in speed and efficiency of information processing, are likely involved in the adolescent's superior memory when compared to the child's memory.
Cognitive monitoring	Its nature	Cognitive monitoring is the process of taking stock of what one is doing currently, what will be done next, and how effectively the mental activity is unfolding. Parents, teachers, and peers can be effective sources for improving the adolescent's cognitive monitoring.
Decision making and critical thinking	Decision making	Adolescence is a time of increased decision making. Older adolescents are more competent at decision making than younger adolescents, who, in turn, are more competent than children. The ability to make competent decisions does not guarantee that such decisions will be made in everyday life, where breadth of experience comes into play. Adolescents need more opportunities to practice and discuss realistic decision making. In some instances, adolescents' faulty decision making may be blamed when, in reality, the problem is society's orientation toward adolescents and its failure to provide adolescents with adequate choices.
	Critical thinking	Critical thinking involves grasping the deeper meaning of problems, keeping an open mind about different approaches and perspectives, and deciding for oneself what to believe or do. Adolescence is an important transitional period in the development of critical thinking because of such cognitive changes as increased speed, automaticity, and capacity of information processing; more breadth of content knowledge; increased ability to construct new combinations of knowledge; and a greater range and more spontaneous use of strategies. Nonetheless, for critical thinking to develop effectively in adolescence, a solid foundation in basic skills and knowledge in childhood is required. An important agenda is the teaching of critical thinking in schools, which Sternberg believes should focus on the skills needed in everyday life.
Computers and adolescents	Positive effects	Potential positive effects include using computers as personal tutors (computer-assisted instruction) or as multipurpose tools, as well as the motivational and social aspects of computers.
	Negative effects	Potential negative effects include regimentation and dehumanization of the classroom, as well as unwarranted "shaping" of the curriculum. Generalizations and limitations of computer-based teaching may also be a potential problem.

only way to study these intellectual processes is *indirectly,* by evaluating the intelligent acts the adolescent generates. For the most part, psychologists have relied on intelligence tests to provide estimates of adolescents' intelligence.

Throughout much of Western civilization's history, intelligence has been described in terms of knowledge and reasoning (Kail & Pellegrino, 1985). Today, most of us view intelligence in a similar light. In one investigation, individuals were asked to judge which of 250 behaviors were typical of an intelligent individual (Sternberg & others, 1981). Both experts (psychologists researching intelligence) and lay individuals (people of varying backgrounds and education) judged the behaviors similarly. The two groups agreed that intelligence can be divided into two main dimensions. The first is *verbal ability,* reflected in such behaviors as "displays a good vocabulary," "reads with high comprehension," "is knowledgeable about a particular field of knowledge," and "displays curiosity." The second is *problem-solving skills,* reflected in such behaviors as "reasons logically and well," "is able to apply knowledge to problems at hand," and "makes good decisions."

In addition to believing that intelligence involves verbal ability and problem-solving skills, psychologists who study intelligence also emphasize individual differences in intelligence and the assessment of intelligence. **Individual differences** *are the stable, consistent ways adolescents are different from each other.* The study of intelligence has focused extensively on individual differences and their assessment. We can talk about individual differences in the adolescent's personality or any other domain of development, but individual differences in the area of intelligence have received the most attention. For example, an intelligence test indicates whether an adolescent can reason better than most others who have taken the test. **Psychometrics** *is the name psychologists have given to the field that involves the assessment of individual differences.*

As mentioned earlier, **intelligence** *often is defined as verbal ability and problem-solving skills. In addition, however, intelligence involves the ability to learn from and adapt to the experiences of everyday life.*

While intelligence can be generally defined, the way in which intelligence is behaviorally displayed may vary across cultures (Lonner, 1990). For example, in most Western cultures, individuals are considered intelligent if they are both smart (have considerable knowledge and can solve verbal problems) and fast (can process information quickly). However, people in the Buganda culture in Uganda believe that intelligent individuals are wise, slow in thought, and able to say the socially correct thing (Wober, 1974). Thus, investigators cannot always transport a concept (such as intelligence) from one culture to another and assume its behavioral indicators will be the same. To do so is methodologically unsound, ethnocentric, and often culturally insensitive. As we further discuss the most widely used intelligence tests and the nature of intelligence, you will discover that experts still debate what intelligence is.

The Binet and Wechsler Tests

The two individual intelligence tests most widely used with adolescents are the Binet and Wechsler tests, each of which we consider in turn.

The Binet Tests

In 1904 the French Ministry of Education asked psychologist Alfred Binet to devise a method that would determine which students did not profit from typical school instruction. School officials wanted to reduce overcrowding by placing those who did not benefit from regular classroom teaching in special schools. Binet and

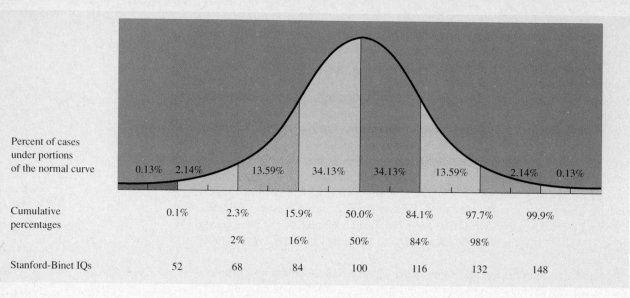

Percent of cases under portions of the normal curve	0.13%	2.14%	13.59%	34.13%	34.13%	13.59%	2.14%	0.13%
Cumulative percentages	0.1%	2.3%	15.9%	50.0%	84.1%	97.7%	99.9%	
		2%	16%	50%	84%	98%		
Stanford-Binet IQs	52	68	84	100	116	132	148	

Figure 5.3 The normal curve and Stanford-Binet IQ scores. The distribution of IQ scores approximates a normal curve. Most of the population falls in the middle range of scores. Notice that extremely high and extremely low scores are very rare. Slightly more than two-thirds of the scores fall between 84 and 116. Only about 1 in 50 individuals has an IQ of more than 132 and only about 1 in 50 individuals has an IQ of less than 68.

his student Theophile Simon developed an intelligence test to meet this request. The test is referred to as the 1905 Scale and consisted of 30 items, ranging from the ability to touch one's nose or ear when asked to the ability to draw designs from memory and to define abstract concepts.

Binet developed the concept of **mental age (MA),** *which is an individual's level of mental development relative to others.* Binet reasoned that a mentally retarded child would perform like a normal child of a younger age. He developed norms for intelligence by testing 50 nonretarded children from the ages of 3 to 11. Children suspected of mental retardation were given the test, and their performance was compared with children of the same chronological age in the normal sample. Average mental age (MA) scores correspond to chronological age (CA), which is age from birth. A bright child has an MA above CA; a dull child has an MA below CA.

The term **intelligence quotient (IQ)** *was devised in 1912 by William Stern. IQ consists of a child's mental age divided by chronological age and multiplied by 100:*

$$IQ = \frac{MA}{CA} \times 100$$

If mental age is the same as chronological age, then the individual's IQ is 100; if mental age is above chronological age, the IQ is more than 100; if mental age is below chronological age, the IQ is less than 100. Scores noticeably above 100 are considered above average; those noticeably below are considered below average. For example, a 16-year-old with a mental age of 20 would have an IQ of 125, while a 16-year-old with a mental age of 12 would have an IQ of 75.

Over the years, the Binet test has been administered to thousands of children and adults of different ages selected at random from different parts of the United States. Test results have shown that intelligence measured by the Binet approximates a normal distribution (see Figure 5.3). **A normal distribution** *is symmetrical, with most test scores falling in the middle of the possible range of scores and few scores appearing toward the extremes of the range.*

The Binet test has been revised many times to incorporate advances in the understanding of intelligence and intelligence testing. The many revisions are called the Stanford-Binet tests (Stanford University is where the revisions were done). Many of the revisions were carried out by Lewis Terman, who applied Stern's IQ concept to the test, developed extensive norms, and provided detailed, clear instructions for each problem on the test.

The current Stanford-Binet is given to individuals from the age of two through adulthood. It includes a wide variety of items, some requiring verbal responses, others nonverbal responses. For example, items that characterize a six-year-old's performance on the test include the verbal ability to define at least six words, such as *orange* and *envelope,* and the nonverbal ability to trace a path through a maze. Items that reflect the average adult's intelligence include defining such words as *disproportionate* and *regard,* explaining a proverb, and comparing *idleness* and *laziness.*

The fourth edition of the Stanford-Binet was published in 1985 (Thorndike, Hagan, & Sattler, 1985). One important addition to this version is the analysis of the individual's responses in terms of four content areas: verbal reasoning, quantitative reasoning, abstract/visual reasoning, and short-term memory. A general composite score also is obtained to reflect overall intelligence. The Stanford-Binet continues to be one of the most widely used individual tests of intelligence.

The Wechsler Scales

Besides the Stanford-Binet, the other most widely used individual intelligence tests are the *Wechsler scales,* developed by David Wechsler. They include the Wechsler Adult Intelligence Scale—Revised (WAIS-R), which is given to older adolescents and adults, and the Wechsler Intelligence Test for Children—Revised (WISC-R), which can be given to children and adolescents ages 6 to 16 (Wechsler, 1949, 1955, 1974, 1981).

The Wechsler scales not only provide an overall IQ score, but the items are grouped according to 11 subtests, 6 of which are verbal and 5 of which are nonverbal. This allows an examiner to obtain separate verbal and nonverbal IQ scores and to see quickly the areas of mental performance in which the individual is below average, average, or above average. The inclusion of a number of nonverbal subtests makes the Wechsler test more representative of verbal *and* nonverbal intelligence; the Binet test includes some nonverbal items but not as many as the Wechsler scales. Several of the subtests on the Wechsler Adult Intelligence Scale—Revised are shown in Figure 5.4.

"You did very well on our IQ test!"

Does Intelligence Have a Single Nature?

Is it more appropriate to think of intelligence as an individual's general ability or as a number of specific abilities?

Spearman's Two-Factor Theory and Thurstone's Multiple-Factor Theory

Long before David Wechsler analyzed intelligence in terms of general and specific abilities (giving an individual an overall IQ but also providing information about specific subcomponents of intelligence), Charles Spearman (1927) proposed that intelligence has two factors. **Two-factor theory** is *Spearman's theory that individuals have both general intelligence, which he called* g, *and a number of specific intelligences, which he called* s. Spearman believed that these two factors accounted for an individual's performance on an intelligence test.

However, some factor approaches abandoned the idea of a general intelligence and searched for specific factors only. **Multiple-factor theory** is *L. L. Thurstone's (1938) theory that intelligence consists of seven primary mental abilities: verbal comprehension, number ability, word fluency, spatial visualization, associative memory, reasoning, and perceptual speed.*

162

Figure 5.4 Subtests of the Wechsler Adult Intelligence Scale—Revised. Notice that the Wechsler scales are divided into verbal subtests and performance subtests.

Simulated items similar to those in the Wechsler Intelligence Scales for Adults and Children. Copyright 1949, 1955, 1974, 1981 and 1989 by The Psychological Corporation. Reproduced by permission. All rights reserved.

Verbal subtests

General information
The individual is asked a number of general-information questions about experiences that are considered normal for individuals in our society.
For example, "How many wings does a bird have?"

Similarities
The individual must think logically and abstractly to answer a number of questions about how things are similar.
For example, "In what way are boats and trains the same?"

Arithmetic reasoning
Problems measure the individual's ability to do arithmetic mentally and include addition, subtraction, multiplication, and division.
For example, "If two buttons cost 14¢, what will be the cost of a dozen buttons?"

Vocabulary
To evaluate word knowledge, the individual is asked to define a number of words. This subtest measures a number of cognitive functions, including concept formation, memory, and language.
For example, "What does the word `biography` mean?"

Comprehension
This subtest is designed to measure the individual's judgment and common sense.
For example, "What is the advantage of keeping money in the bank?"

Digit span
This subtest primarily measures attention and short-term memory. The individual is required to repeat numbers forward and backward.
For example, "I am going to say some numbers and I want you to repeat them backward: 4 7 5 2 8."

Performance subtests

Picture completion
A number of drawings are shown, each with a significant part missing. Within a period of several seconds, the individual must differentiate essential from nonessential parts of the picture and identify which part is missing. This subtest evaluates visual alertness and the ability to organize information visually.
For example, "I am going to show you a picture with an important part missing. Tell me what is missing."

Picture arrangement
A series of pictures out of sequence are shown to the individual, who is asked to place them in their proper order to tell an appropriate story. This subtest evaluates how individuals integrate information to make it logical and meaningful.
For example, "The pictures below need to be placed in an appropriate order to tell a meaningful story."

Object assembly

The individual is asked to assemble pieces into something. This subtest measures visual-motor coordination and perceptual organization.

For example, "When these pieces are put together correctly, they make something. Put them together as quickly as you can."

Block design

The individual must assemble a set of multicolored blocks to match designs that the examiner shows. Visual-motor coordination, perceptual organization, and the ability to visualize spatially are measured.

For example, "Use the four blocks on the left to make the pattern on the right."

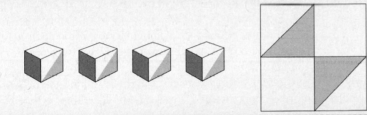

Coding

This subtest evaluates how quickly and accurately an individual can link code symbols and digits. The subtest assesses visual-motor coordination and speed of thought.

For example, "As quickly as you can, transfer the appropriate code symbols to the blank spaces."

Code

Test

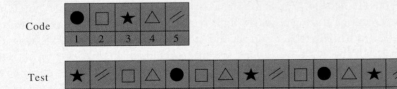

Sternberg's Triarchic Theory

More recently, Robert J. Sternberg (1986, 1990) proposed **triarchic theory,** *a theory of intelligence with three main components: componential intelligence, experiential intelligence, and contextual intelligence.* Consider Ann, who scores high on traditional intelligence tests, such as the Stanford-Binet, and is a star analytical thinker. Consider Todd, who does not have the best test results but has an insightful and creative mind. Consider Art, a street-smart individual who has learned how to deal in practical ways with his world, although his scores on traditional intelligence tests are low.

Sternberg calls Ann's analytical thinking and abstract reasoning *componential intelligence;* it is the closest to what is called intelligence in this chapter and to what commonly is measured by intelligence tests. Sternberg calls Todd's insightful and creative thinking *experiential intelligence* and Art's street-smarts and practical know-how *contextual intelligence* (see Figure 5.5).

In Sternberg's view of componential intelligence, the basic unit in intelligence is a *component,* simply defined as a basic unit of information processing. Sternberg believes that such components include those used to acquire or store information, to retain or retrieve information, to transfer information, to plan, to make decisions, to solve problems, and to carry out problem-solving strategies or translate our thoughts into performance.

The second part of Sternberg's model focuses on experience. According to Sternberg, intelligent individuals have the ability to solve new problems quickly, but they also learn how to solve familiar problems in an automatic, rote way so that their mind is free to handle other problems that require insight and creativity.

The third part of the model involves practical knowledge, such as how to get out of trouble, how to replace a fuse, and how to get along with people. Sternberg calls this *tacit knowledge.* It includes all of the important information about getting along in the real world that is not taught in school. He believes that tacit knowledge is more important for success in life than explicit, or "book," knowledge.

Gardner's Seven Frames of Mind

Another recent attempt to classify intelligence, the brainchild of developmental psychologist Howard Gardner (1983, 1989), includes seven components, or frames of mind, as Gardner refers to them. Gardner's classification encompasses a wide diversity of intelligence. For example, consider a blond, 13-year-old boy who springs into motion during a junior high basketball game in the small town of French Lick, Indiana. Grabbing a rebound, he quickly dribbles the ball the length of the court, all the while processing the whereabouts of his five opponents and four teammates. He throws the ball to an open teammate who scores on an easy lay-up. Years later the young boy had become a 6-foot 9-inch superstar for the Boston Celtics—Larry Bird. Is there intelligence to Bird's movement and perception of the spatial layout of the basketball court?

Now we turn the clock back 200 years. Another 13-year-old boy is playing a piano at a concert hall in front of a large audience. The young adolescent is Ludwig von Beethoven, whose musical genius was evident at a young age. Did Beethoven have a specific type of intelligence, one we might call musical intelligence?

Bird and Beethoven are two different types of individuals with different types of abilities. Gardner argues that Bird's talent reflects his movement intelligence and his ability to analyze the world spatially, and that Beethoven's talent reflects his musical intelligence. Beyond these three forms of intelligence, Gardner

(a)

(b)

(c)

Figure 5.5 Sternberg's triarchic model of intelligence. Sternberg believes that intelligence consists of three main factors: (a) componential intelligence, which primarily involves analytical thinking and abstract reasoning; (b) experiential intelligence, which primarily involves insightful and creative thinking, and (c) contextual intelligence, which primarily involves street-smarts and practical know-how.

argues that we have four other main forms: verbal intelligence, mathematical intelligence, insightful skills for analyzing ourselves, and insightful skills for analyzing others.

Gardner believes that each of the seven intelligences can be destroyed by brain damage, that each involves unique cognitive skills, and that each shows up in exaggerated fashion in both the gifted and in *idiots savants,* which is French for individuals who are mentally retarded but who have unbelievable skill in a particular domain, such as drawing, music, or computing. For example, an individual may be mentally retarded but be able to respond instantaneously with the correct day of the week (for example, Tuesday or Saturday) when given any date in history (such as 4 June, 1926, or 15 December, 1746).

Critics of Gardner's approach point out that there are geniuses in many domains other than music. There are outstanding chess players, prizefighters, writers, politicians, physicians, lawyers, preachers, and poets, for example, yet we do not refer to chess intelligence, prizefighter intelligence, and so on.

In Conclusion

Our discussion of the different approaches to intelligence has shown that theorists often disagree about the definition of intelligence. Two factors explain this disagreement (Kail & Pellegrino, 1985): First, the same data can be analyzed in many ways. Different apparent solutions, which produce different psychological interpretations, can be obtained from the same data. Second, the data obtained in separate studies differ. The critical data for interpretations of whether intelligence is a general ability or a cluster of specific abilities involve correlations (recall our discussion of this in Chapter 2). The pattern of correlations depends on the group tested (schoolchildren, armed service recruits, or criminals, for example), the total number of tests administered, and the specific tests included in the battery. The outcome of such studies is that the abilities thought to make up the core of intelligence may vary across different investigations. Despite these inconsistencies, evidence suggests that intelligence is *both* a general ability and a number of specific abilities.

Group Tests

The Stanford-Binet and Wechsler tests are individually administered intelligence tests. A psychologist approaches the testing situation as a structured interaction between the psychologist and the individual being tested. This provides an opportunity to sample the individual's behavior (Johnson & Goldman, 1990). During testing, the psychologist observes the ease with which rapport is established, the individual's level of energy and enthusiasm, and the degree of frustration tolerance and persistence the individual shows in performing difficult tasks. Each of these observations helps the psychologist to understand the individual.

On some occasions, though, group intelligence tests are administered. Though more economical and convenient than individual tests, group tests have some significant disadvantages. When a test is given to a large group, the examiner cannot establish rapport, determine the level of anxiety, and so on. Most testing experts recommend that, when important decisions are to be made about an individual, a group intelligence test should be supplemented by other information about the individual's abilities (Anastasi, 1988). For example, many children take ability tests at school in a large group. However, a decision about placing a child in a special education class should not be based on such group tests alone. The psychologist should administer an individual intelligence test, such as Stanford-Binet or Wechsler, and collect an extensive amount of additional information about the child's abilities outside of the testing situation.

A group test that many of you have taken in recent years is the Scholastic Aptitude Test (SAT). This test, taken each year by more than 1 million high school seniors, measures some of the same abilities as intelligence tests. However, it does not yield an overall IQ score; rather, the SAT provides separate scores for verbal and mathematical ability. The SAT is similar to the original Binet test in that it was developed to predict success in school.

The SAT is used widely as a predictor of success in college, but it is only one of many pieces of information that determine whether a college admits a student. High school grades, the quality of the student's high school, letters of recommendation, individual interviews with the student, and special circumstances in the student's life that might have impeded academic ability are taken into account along with the SAT scores.

In recent years, a controversy has developed over whether private coaching can raise a student's SAT scores. The student's verbal and mathematical abilities, which the SAT assesses, have been built over years of experience and instruction. Research shows that private coaching on a short-term basis cannot help raise SAT scores substantially. Researchers have found that, on the average, SAT-preparation courses raise a student's scores only 15 points on the SAT's 200 to 800 scale (Kulik, Bangert-Drowns, & Kulik, 1984).

The latest controversy to hit the SAT is the discovery that certain items favor males. In one investigation, the answers of 100,000 students were analyzed (Rosser, 1989). On 23 of 145 questions, one sex did better than the other. Males did better on all but two. Examples of questions that favored males included:

> "Dividends are to stockholders as. . . . " The answer is "royalties are to writers." Fifteen percent more males than females answered this item correctly.
> "The opposite of stamina is. . . . " The answer is "lack of endurance." Twelve percent more males answered this item correctly.

Educational Testing Service, responsible for the SAT's content, is revising the test by throwing out questions that are unusually difficult for females or males.

Aptitude Tests and Achievement Tests

Psychologists distinguish between an **aptitude test,** *which predicts an individual's ability to learn a skill or what the individual can accomplish with training,* and an **achievement test,** *which measures what has been learned or what skills have been mastered.* The distinction between these two types of tests is sometimes blurred, however. Both tests assess an individual's current status, both include similar types of questions, and both produce results that usually are highly correlated.

In each of your college classes, you take tests to measure your mastery of the class's content. These tests are achievement tests. If you major in psychology and decide to apply for graduate school, you may take the Graduate Record Exam Subject Test in Psychology. Your scores on this test would be used with other information (such as college grades and interviews) to predict whether you would be successful at graduate work in psychology. The Graduate Record Exam Subject Test in Psychology may contain questions similar to those from various psychology tests in undergraduate school, but this time the test items are being used to predict your performance in graduate school. Thus, the Graduate Record Exam Subject Test in Psychology falls into the category of aptitude test. The test's *purpose,* not its *content,* determines whether it is an aptitude or an achievement test.

The SAT has the ingredients of both an aptitude test and an achievement test. It is an achievement test in the sense that it measures what you have learned in terms of vocabulary, reading comprehension, algebraic skills, and so on; it is an aptitude test in the sense that it is used to predict your performance in college.

Controversies and Issues in Intelligence

We have seen that intelligence is a complex and slippery concept with many competing definitions, theories, and tests. It is not surprising, therefore, that attempts to understand the nature of intelligence have been filled with controversy. Two controversies that currently share the spotlight are: (1) the degree to which intelligence is due to heredity or to environment and (2) the extent of ethnic differences and the role of culture in intelligence.

The Heredity-Environment Controversy

Psychologist Arthur Jensen (1969) sparked a lively and, at times, hostile debate when he presented his thesis that intelligence is primarily inherited. Jensen believes that environment and culture play only a minimal role in intelligence. In one of his most provocative statements, Jensen claimed that clear-cut genetic differences are present in the average intelligence of races, nationalities, and social classes. When Jensen first stated in the *Harvard Educational Review* in 1969 that lower intelligence probably was the reason that Blacks do not perform as well as Whites in school, he was called naive and racist. He received hate mail by the bushel, and police escorted him to his classes at the University of California at Berkeley.

Jensen examined a number of studies of intelligence, many of which involved comparisons of identical and fraternal twins. Remember that identical twins have identical genetic endowments, so if intelligence is genetically determined, said Jensen, their IQs should be similar. Fraternal twins and ordinary siblings are less similar genetically, so their IQs should be less similar. Jensen found support for his argument in these studies. Investigations of identical twins produced an average correlation of .82, a very high positive association. Investigations of fraternal twins produced an average correlation of .50, a moderately high positive correlation. The difference of .32 is substantial. To show that genetic factors are more important than environmental factors, Jensen compared identical twins reared together with those reared apart. The correlation for those reared together was .89 and for those reared apart was .78, a difference of .11. Jensen argued that, if environmental factors were more important than genetic factors, siblings reared apart, who experienced different environments, should have IQs that differed more than .11. Jensen placed heredity's influence on intelligence at about 80 percent.

The consensus of today's experts on intelligence is that its genetic determination is not as strong as Jensen envisioned. Their estimates fall more in the range of 50 percent genetic determination, 50 percent environmental determination (Plomin, 1989; Plomin, DeFries, & McClearn, 1990). For most individuals, this means that modification of environmental conditions can change their IQ scores considerably (Weinberg, 1989). It also means that programs designed to enrich an adolescent's environment can have a considerable impact, improving school achievement and the acquisition of skills needed for employability. While genetic endowment may always influence the individual's intellectual ability, the environments and opportunities provided to adolescents do make a difference.

Culture and Ethnicity

Are there cultural and ethnic differences in intelligence? Are standard intelligence tests biased, and if so, can culture-fair tests be developed?

Cultural and Ethnic Comparisons. There are cultural and ethnic differences in performance on intelligence tests. For example, in the United States, children and adolescents in Black and Hispanic families score below their counterparts from White families on standardized intelligence tests. Most interest has focused on Black-White comparisons. On the average, Black American schoolchildren score 10 to 15 points lower on standardized intelligence tests than White American schoolchildren (Anastasi, 1988). Keep in mind, though, that we are talking about average scores. Many Black adolescents score higher than many White adolescents because the distributions for Black and White adolescents overlap. Estimates indicate that 15 to 25 percent of Black adolescents score higher than half of all White adolescents.

Patterns of intelligence in Jewish, Chinese, Black, and Puerto Rican children suggest some strengths and weaknesses in children from different ethnic backgrounds (Lesser, Fifer, & Clark, 1965): Jewish children score higher on verbal abilities, lower on numerical and spatial abilities; Chinese children higher on numerical and spatial abilities, lower on verbal abilities; Black children higher on verbal abilities, lower on reasoning and numerical abilities; Puerto Rican children higher on spatial and reasoning abilities, lower on verbal abilities.

How extensively are ethnic differences in intelligence influenced by heredity and environment? The consensus is that the available data do not support a genetic interpretation. For example, in recent decades, as Black Americans have experienced improved social, economic, and educational opportunities, the gap between White and Black children on standardized intelligence tests has begun to diminish. And when children from disadvantaged Black families are adopted by more advantaged middle-class families, their scores on intelligence tests more closely resemble national averages for middle-class than lower-class children (Scarr, 1989; Scarr & Weinberg, 1976).

Cultural Bias and Culture-Fair Tests. Many of the early intelligence tests were culturally biased, favoring urban over rural individuals, middle-class over lower-class individuals, and White over Black individuals. The norms for the early intelligence tests were based almost entirely on White, middle-class standards (Miller-Jones, 1989, 1991). For example, one item on an early test asked what should be done if you find a three-year-old child in the street. The correct answer was "call the police." Adolescents from impoverished inner-city families might not choose this answer if the police force is perceived as unfriendly, and rural adolescents might not choose it since they may not have police nearby. Such items clearly do not measure the knowledge necessary to adapt to one's environment or to be "intelligent" in an inner-city neighborhood or in rural America (Scarr, 1984).

Even if the content of the test items is made appropriate, another problem may exist with intelligence tests. Since many of the questions are verbal in nature, minority groups may encounter problems understanding the language of the questions (Gibbs & Huang, 1989). Minority groups often speak a language that is very different from standard English. Consequently, they may be at a disadvantage when taking intelligence tests oriented toward middle-class White children and adolescents.

Cultural bias is dramatically underscored by tests like the one shown in Table 5.1. The items in this test were developed to reduce the cultural disadvantage that Black children and adolescents might experience on traditional intelligence tests. More information about cultural bias in intelligence testing appears in Sociocultural Worlds of Adolescence 5.1, where you will read about a widely publicized case involving the use of an intelligence test to classify a six-year-old Black child as mentally retarded.

Cultural bias is also dramatically underscored in the life of Gregory Ochoa. When Gregory was a high school student, he and his classmates were given an IQ test. School authorities informed them that the test would allow the school to place them in classes appropriate for their skills. Gregory looked at the test questions. He didn't understand very many of the words. Spanish was spoken at his home, and his English was not very good. Several week later, Gregory was placed in a "special" class. Many of the other students in the class had such last names as Ramirez and Gonzales. The special class was for mentally retarded

Table 5.1   The Chitling Intelligence Test

1. A "gas head" is a person who has a:
   (a) fast-moving car.
   (b) stable of "lace."
   (c) "process."
   (d) habit of stealing cars.
   (e) long jail record for arson.
2. "Bo Diddley" is a:
   (a) game for children.
   (b) down-home cheap wine.
   (c) down-home singer.
   (d) new dance.
   (e) Moejoe call.
3. If a pimp is uptight with a woman who gets state aid, what does he mean when he talks about "Mother's day"?
   (a) second Sunday in May
   (b) third Sunday in June
   (c) first of every month
   (d) none of these
   (e) first and fifteenth of every month

4. A "handkerchief head" is:
   (a) a cool cat.
   (b) a porter.
   (c) an Uncle Tom.
   (d) a hoddi.
   (e) a preacher.
5. If a man is called a "blood," then he is a:
   (a) fighter.
   (b) Mexican-American.
   (c) Negro.
   (d) hungry hemophile.
   (e) red man, or Indian.
6. Cheap chitlings (not the kind you purchase at a frozen-food counter) will taste rubbery unless they are cooked long enough. How soon can you quit cooking them to eat and enjoy them?
   (a) forty-five minutes
   (b) two hours
   (c) twenty-four hours
   (d) one week (on a low flame)
   (e) one hour

Answers: 1. c   2. c   3. e   4. c   5. c   6. c

Source: Adrian Dove, 1968.

Note: The Chitling Intelligence Test was not developed to be a formal, standardized test of intelligence, but rather was constructed to provide a sense of how the experiences of minority group individuals differ from those of White individuals and the way these experiences might influence performance on an intelligence test.

students. Gregory lost interest in school and eventually dropped out. He joined the Navy, where he took high school courses, earning enough credits to attend college. He graduated from San Jose City College as an honor student, continued his education, and became a professor of social work at the University of Washington in Seattle.

Culture-fair tests *are tests of intelligence that attempt to reduce cultural bias.* Two types of culture-fair tests have been devised. The first includes items that are familiar to individuals from all socioeconomic and ethnic backgrounds, or items that at least are familiar to the individuals taking the test. For example, a child might be asked how a bird and a dog are different, on the assumption that virtually all children have been exposed to birds and dogs.

The second type of culture-fair test has all the verbal items removed. Figure 5.6 on page 172 shows a sample from the Raven Progressive Matrices Test, which exemplifies this approach. Even though tests such as the Raven Progressive Matrices are designed to be culture-fair, individuals with more education score higher on them than those with less education.

These attempts to produce culture-fair tests remind us that traditional intelligence tests are probably culturally biased, yet the effort to develop a truly culture-fair test has not yielded a satisfactory alternative. Constructing a culture-fair intelligence test, one that rules out the role of experience emanating from socioeconomic and ethnic background, has been difficult and may be impossible. Consider, for example, that the intelligence of the Iatmul people of Papua, New Guinea, involves the ability to remember the names of 10,000 to 20,000

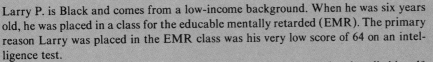

SOCIOCULTURAL WORLDS OF ADOLESCENCE 5.1

Larry P., Intelligent but Not on Intelligence Tests

Larry P. is Black and comes from a low-income background. When he was six years old, he was placed in a class for the educable mentally retarded (EMR). The primary reason Larry was placed in the EMR class was his very low score of 64 on an intelligence test.

Is there a possibility that the intelligence test Larry was given is culturally biased? Psychologists still debate this issue. The controversy has been the target of a major class action challenging the use of standardized IQ tests to place Black elementary school students in classes for the educable mentally retarded. The initial lawsuit, filed on behalf of Larry P., claimed that the IQ test he took underestimated his learning ability. The lawyers for Larry P. argued that IQ tests place too much emphasis on verbal skills and fail to account for the background of Black children. Therefore, it was argued, Larry was incorrectly labeled mentally retarded and may forever be saddled with the stigma of being called retarded.

As part of the lengthy court battle involving Larry P., six Black EMR students were independently retested by members of the Bay Area Association of Black Psychologists in California. The psychologists made sure that they established good rapport with the students and made special efforts to overcome defeatism and distraction on the part of the students. Certain items were rewarded in terms more consistent with the children's social background, and recognition was given to nonstandard answers that showed a logical, intelligent approach to problems. The retesting produced scores of 79 to 104—17 to 38 points higher than the scores the students received when initially tested by school psychologists. The retest scores were above the ceiling for placement in an EMR class.

In Larry's case, it was ruled that IQ tests are biased and that their use discriminates against Blacks and other ethnic minorities. The ruling continued the moratorium on the use of IQ tests in decisions about placement of a child in an EMR class. During the Larry P. trial, it was revealed that 66 percent of elementary school students in EMR classes in San Francisco were Black, whereas Blacks only make up 28.5 percent of the San Francisco school population.

What was the state's argument for using intelligence tests as part of the criteria for placing children in EMR classes? At one point, the state suggested that, because Blacks tend to be poor and poor pregnant women tend to suffer from inadequate nutrition, the brain development of many Black children may have been retarded by their mothers' poor diets during pregnancy. However, from the beginning of the trial, a basic point made by the state was that Blacks are genetically inferior to Whites intellectually.

The decision in favor of Larry P. was upheld by a three-judge appeals panel in 1984, but in another court case, *Pase v. Hannon* in Illinois, it was ruled that IQ tests are not culturally biased.

clans; by contrast, the intelligence of islanders in the widely dispersed Caroline Islands involves the talent of navigating by the stars.

Now that we have considered some of the controversial issues pertaining to intelligence, we turn our attention to yet another much-debated aspect of intelligence—the use and misuse of intelligence tests.

Figure 5.6 Sample item from the Raven Progressive Matrices Test. An individual is presented with a matrix arrangement of symbols, such as the one at the top of this figure, and must then complete the matrix by selecting the appropriate missing symbol from a group of symbols.

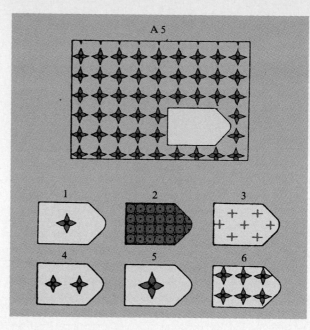

The Use and Misuse of Intelligence Tests

Psychological tests are tools. Like all tools, their effectiveness depends on the knowledge, skill, and integrity of the user. A hammer can be used to build a beautiful kitchen cabinet, or it can be used as a weapon of assault. Like a hammer, psychological tests can be used for positive purposes, or they can be badly abused. Both the test constructor and the test examiner must be familiar with the current state of scientific knowledge about intelligence and intelligence tests (Anastasi, 1988).

Even though they have limitations, tests of intelligence are among psychology's most widely used tools. To be effective, though, intelligence tests must be viewed realistically. They should not be thought of as fixed, unchanging indicators of an individual's intelligence. They should be used in conjunction with other information about an individual and not relied on as the sole indicator of intelligence. For example, an intelligence test should not solely determine whether a child is placed in a special education or gifted class. The adolescent's developmental history, medical background, performance in school, social competencies, and family experiences should be taken into account, too.

The single number provided by many IQ tests can easily lead to stereotypes and expectations about an individual. Many people do not know how to interpret the results of intelligence tests, and sweeping generalizations are too often made on the basis of an IQ score. For example, imagine that you are a teacher in the teacher's lounge the day after school has started in the fall. You mention a student—Johnny Jones—and a fellow teacher remarks that she had Johnny in class last year; she comments that he was a real dunce and points out that his IQ is 78. You cannot help but remember this information, and it may lead to thoughts that Johnny Jones is not very bright so it is useless to spend much time teaching him. In this way, IQ scores are misused, and stereotypes are formed (Rosenthal & Jacobsen, 1968).

Ability tests can help a teacher to divide adolescents into homogeneous groups who function at roughly the same level in math or reading so that they can be taught the same concepts together. However, educators should be extremely cautious about placing adolescents in tracks, such as "advanced," "intermediate," and "low."

Table 5.2   Classifications of Mental Retardation

Level of Functioning	IQ Range	Percentage of All Mentally Retarded Individuals
Mild retardation	50–55 to approximately 70	80
Moderate retardation	35–40 to 50–55	12
Severe retardation	20–25 to 35–40	7
Profound retardation	Below 20–25	1

The Extremes of Intelligence

Intelligence tests have been used to discover the indications of mental retardation or intellectual giftedness—the extremes of intelligence. As we just learned, though, at times intelligence tests have been misused for this purpose. Continuing the theme that an intelligence test should not be used as the sole indicator of mental retardation or giftedness, we now explore the nature of these intellectual extremes.

Mental Retardation

The most distinctive feature of mental retardation is inadequate intellectual functioning. Long before formal tests were developed to assess intelligence, the mentally retarded were identified by a lack of age-appropriate skills in learning and caring for themselves. With the development of intelligence tests, more emphasis has been placed on IQ as an indicator of mental retardation. It is not unusual, however, to find two retarded individuals with the same low IQ, one of whom is married, employed, and involved in the community and the other of whom requires constant supervision in an institution. These differences in social competence led psychologists to include deficits in adaptive behavior in their definition of mental retardation (Matson & Mulick, 1990). **Mental retardation** *is a condition of limited mental ability in which an individual has a low IQ, usually below 70 on a traditional test of intelligence, and has difficulty adapting to everyday life.* About 5 million Americans fit this definition of mental retardation.

The classifications of mental retardation, the IQs associated with them, and the percentage of individuals in each category are presented in Table 5.2. Notice that individuals who score below approximately 70 on a standardized IQ test are categorized as mentally retarded; also notice that most of these individuals are classified as only mildly mentally retarded. *Mildly mentally retarded* individuals (IQ 50–55 to approximately 70) can still learn to read and write. With proper education and training, as adults they can adjust socially, master simple academic and occupational skills, and become self-supporting citizens. *Moderately mentally retarded* individuals (IQ 35–40 to 50–55), with proper education and training, as adults can achieve partial independence in daily self-care, acceptable behavior, and economic usefulness in a family or other sheltered setting. *Severely mentally retarded* individuals (IQ 20–25 to 35–40), with proper education and training, can develop limited personal hygiene and self-help skills, but their motor and speech development are impaired, and they require a great deal of care. Many can learn to perform simple occupational tasks under supervision. *Profoundly mentally retarded* individuals (IQ below 20–25) are extremely deficient in adaptive behavior and can only master the simplest of tasks. Speech impairment is often severe, and these individuals need to remain in custodial care all of their lives.

This mentally retarded adolescent girl has just won a medal in the Special Olympics. In addition to the Special Olympics, what are other ways mentally retarded adolescents' lives can be improved?

What causes mental retardation? The causes are divided into two categories: organic and cultural-familial. **Organic retardation** *is mental retardation caused by a genetic disorder or brain damage;* organic *refers to the tissues or organs of the body, so there is some physical damage in organic retardation.* For example, Down syndrome, a form of mental retardation, occurs when an extra chromosome is present in an individual's genetic makeup. It is not known why the extra chromosome is present, but it may involve the health or age of the female ovum or male sperm. Although those who suffer organic retardation are found across the spectrum of IQ distribution, most have IQs between 0 and 50. **Cultural-familial retardation** *is mental retardation in which there is no evidence of organic brain damage; individuals' IQs range from 50 to 70.* Psychologists seek the cause of this type of retardation in impoverished environments.

Even with organic retardation, though, it is wise to think about the contributions of genetic-environment interaction. Parents with low IQs not only are more likely to transmit genes for low intelligence to their offspring, but also tend to provide them with a less enriched environment (Landesman, in press; Landesman & Ramey, 1989).

Giftedness

Conventional wisdom has identified some individuals in all cultures and historical periods as special or exceptional because they have talents not evident in the majority of the people. *Individuals who are* **gifted** *have above-average intelligence (an IQ of 120 or higher) and/or a superior talent for something.* Most school systems emphasize intellectual superiority and academic aptitude when selecting children for gifted programs, rarely considering competence and potential in the visual and performing arts (drama, dance, art), psychomotor abilities (tennis, golf, basketball), or other special abilities (Reis, 1989).

A classic study of the gifted was begun by Lewis Terman (1925) more than 65 years ago. Terman studied approximately 1,500 children whose Stanford-Binet IQs averaged 150. His goal was to follow these children through their adult lives—the study will not be complete until the year 2010.

The accomplishments of the 1,500 children in Terman's study are remarkable. Of the 800 males, 78 have obtained Ph.D.s (they include two past presidents of the American Psychological Association), 48 have earned M.D.s, and 85 have been granted law degrees. Nearly all of these figures are 10 to 30 times greater than found among 800 men of the same age chosen randomly from the overall population. As children, the gifted individuals in Terman's study were taller, healthier, better adjusted, and more popular with their peers than nongifted children (Wallach & Kogan, 1965). These findings challenge the commonly held belief that the intellectually gifted are emotionally disturbed or socially maladjusted. This stereotype is based on striking instances of mental disturbances in a few gifted individuals. Sir Isaac Newton, Vincent van Gogh, Leonardo da Vinci, Socrates, and Edgar Allan Poe all had emotional problems. However, these are the exception rather than the rule; no relation between giftedness and mental disturbance in general has been found.

In another investigation, 120 individuals with exceptional talents as adults were interviewed about what they believed contributed to their giftedness (Bloom, 1985). The individuals had excelled in six fields—concert pianists and sculptors (arts), Olympic swimmers and tennis champions (psychomotor), and research mathematicians and research neurologists (cognitive). They said that the development of their exceptional accomplishments required special environmental support, excellent teaching, and motivational encouragement. Each experienced years of special attention under the tutelage and supervision of a remarkable series of teachers and coaches. All of these stars devoted exceptional amounts of time to practice and training, easily outdistancing the amount of time spent in all other activities combined. Nine-year-old Robert, a violin prodigy, had little time for television, sports, or other activities, for example. He practiced his talent several hours each day after school and spent weekends taking lessons and going to concerts. The stars also received extensive support and encouragement from their parents. Most stars had at least one parent who devoted a considerable part of each day to developing the child's talents. Raising a star requires levels of energy, commitment, sensitivity, and patience that go beyond what most parents are willing to give (Feldman, 1989a,b). Of course, not all parents want to raise stars, but some who do put unbearable pressure on their children, expecting achievements that far exceed their talents. For every Chris Evert, there are thousands of girls with only mediocre tennis talent whose parents want them to become "another Chris Evert." Such unrealistic expectations always meet with failure and can produce considerable stress in children's lives, and all too often, parents push children into activities that bore them rather than excite them (Hennessey & Amabile, 1988). The importance of family processes in the development of the gifted was recently underscored by the finding that the personal adjustment of gifted individuals at midlife was strongly related to the harmony that existed in their family of origin as they were growing up (Tomlinson-Keasey & Little, 1990).

Creativity

Most of us would like to be both gifted and creative. Why was Thomas Edison able to invent so many things? Was he simply more intelligent than most individuals? Did he spend long hours toiling away in private? Surprisingly, when Edison was a young boy, his teacher told him he was too dumb to learn anything. Other examples of famous individuals whose creative genius went unnoticed when they were young include Walt Disney, who was fired from a newspaper job because he did not have any good ideas; Enrico Caruso, whose music teacher told him that his voice was terrible; and Winston Churchill, who failed one year of secondary school.

    Edison, Disney, Caruso, and Churchill were intelligent individuals, but experts on creativity believe that intelligence and creativity are not the same thing (Winner, 1989). One common distinction is between **convergent thinking,** *which produces one correct answer and is characteristic of the kind of thinking elicited by standardized intelligence tests,* and **divergent thinking,** *which produces many different answers to a question and is more characteristic of creativity* (Guilford, 1967). For example, the following intellectual problem-solving task characteristic of intelligence test items has one correct answer and, thus, requires convergent thinking: "How many quarters will you get in return for 60 dimes?" The following question, however, an example of an item used to assess creative thinking, has many possible answers: "What images does sitting alone in a dark room make you think of?" (Barron, 1989). Answering "the sound of a violin with no strings" or "patience" is considered creative, whereas "a person in a crowd" and "insomnia" are considered common and, thus, not very creative responses.

    Creativity *is the ability to think about something in a novel and unusual way and to come up with unique solutions to problems.* When individuals in the arts and sciences who fit the description of "creative" are asked what enables them to produce their creative works, they say that they generate large amounts of associative content when solving problems and that they have the time and

Some children and adolescents become extraordinarily gifted, reaching the status of "star." Becoming a "star" takes years of special tutelage with remarkable coaches; extensive support by parents; and day after day, week after week, month after month, and year after year of practice.

The Snowflake Model of Creativity and Its Application to Education

Daniel Perkins (1984) describes his view as the *snowflake model of creativity*. Like the six sides of a snowflake, each with its own complex structure, Perkins's model consists of six characteristics common to highly creative individuals (see Figure 5.A). Adolescents who are creative may not have all six characteristics, but the more they have, the more creative they tend to be, says Perkins.

First, creative thinking involves aesthetics as much as practical standards. Aesthetics involves beauty. Outside of literature and the arts, conventional schooling pays little attention to the aesthetics of human inquiry. For example, teachers rarely address the beauty of scientific theories, mathematical systems, and historical syntheses. And how often do teachers comment on the aesthetics of students' work in math and science?

Second, creative thinking involves an ability to excel in finding problems. Creative individuals spend an unusual amount of time thinking about problems. They also explore a number of options in solving a particular problem before choosing which solution to pursue. Creative individuals value good questions because they can produce discoveries and creative answers. A student once asked Nobel laureate Linus Pauling how he came up with good ideas. Pauling said that he developed a lot of ideas and threw away the bad ones. Most assignments in school are so narrow that students have little opportunity to generate, or even select among, different ideas, according to Perkins.

Third, creative thinking involves mental mobility, which allows individuals to find new perspectives and approaches to problems. One example of mental mobility is being able to think in terms of opposites and contraries while seeking a new solution. According to Perkins, most problems that students work on in school are convergent, not divergent. For the most part, the learning problems that students face in school do not allow students the elbow room for exercising mental mobility.

Fourth, creative thinking involves the willingness to take risks. Accompanying risk is the acceptance of failure as part of the creative quest and the ability to learn from failures. Creative geniuses do not always produce masterpieces. For example, Picasso produced more than 20,000 works of art, but much of it was mediocre. The more that adolescents produce, the better their chance of creating something unique. According to Perkins, most schools do not challenge students to take the risks necessary to think creatively and to produce creative work.

Fifth, creative thinking involves objectivity. The popular image of creative individuals usually highlights their subjective, personal insights and commitments; however, without some objectivity and feedback from others, creative individuals would create a private world that was distant from reality and could not be shared or appreciated by others. Creative individuals not only criticize their works—they also seek criticism from others. Schools typically do highlight objectivity, although usually not in the arts.

Sixth, creative thinking involves inner motivation. Creative individuals are motivated to produce something for its own sake, not for school grades or for money. Their cat-

independence to entertain a wide range of possible solutions in an enjoyable setting. How strongly is creativity related to intelligence? A certain level of intelligence is required to be creative in most fields, but many highly intelligent individuals (as measured by IQ tests) are not very creative.

Some experts remain skeptical that we will ever fully understand the creative process. Other experts believe that a psychology of creativity is in reach. Most experts do agree, however, that the concept of creativity as spontaneously bubbling up from a magical well is a myth. Momentary flashes of insight, accompanied by images, make up only a small part of the creative process. At the heart of the creative process are ability and experience that shape an individual's intentional and sustained effort, often over the course of a lifetime. Based on his own research and analysis of the creativity literature, Daniel Perkins developed

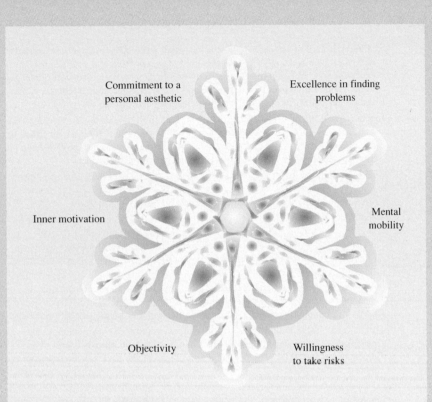

Figure 5.A Snowflake model of creativity. Like a snowflake, Perkins's model of creativity has six parts: commitment to a personal aesthetic, excellence in finding problems, mental mobility, willingness to take risks, objectivity, and inner motivation.

alyst is the challenge, enjoyment, and satisfaction of the work itself. Researchers have found that individuals ranging from preschool children through adults are more creative when they are internally rather than externally motivated. Work evaluation, competition for prizes, and supervision tend to undermine internal motivation and diminish creativity (Amabile & Hennessey, 1988).

a model that takes into account the complexity of the creative process (Perkins, 1984; Perkins & Gardner, 1989). An overview of Perkins's model and its application to children's and adolescents' education is presented in Perspective on Adolescent Development 5.1. As we learn more about creativity, we come to understand how important it is as a human resource, truly being one of life's wondrous gifts.

At this point, we have discussed a number of ideas about intelligence and its extremes. A summary of these ideas is presented in Concept Table 5.2. This chapter concludes Section II on biological and cognitive development. In the next section, we turn our attention to the social contexts in which adolescents develop, beginning with Chapter 6, "Families."

Concept Table 5.2

Intelligence and Its Extremes

Concept	Processes/Related Ideas	Characteristics/Description
What is intelligence?	Its nature	Intelligence is an abstract concept that is measured indirectly. Intelligence is verbal ability, problem-solving skills, and the ability to learn from and adapt to the experiences of everyday life. In the study of intelligence, extensive attention is given to individual differences in intelligence and to the assessment of intelligence. The behavioral indicators of intelligence may vary across cultures.
The Binet and Wechsler tests	The Binet tests	Binet developed the first intelligence test, known as the 1905 Scale. He developed the concept of mental age, while Stern developed the concept of IQ. The Binet has been standardized and revised a number of times. The many revisions are called the Stanford-Binet tests. The test approximates a normal distribution.
	The Wechsler scales	Besides the Stanford-Binet, the Wechsler scales are the most widely used intelligence tests. They include the WAIS-R and the WISC-R. These tests provide an overall IQ, verbal and performance IQ, and information about 11 subtests.
Does intelligence have a single nature?	Four theories	Psychologists debate whether intelligence is a general ability or a number of specific abilities. Spearman's two-factor theory, Thurstone's multiple-factor theory, Sternberg's triarchic theory, and Gardner's seven frames of mind have been attempts to describe the basic factors, or components, of intelligence. Current thinking suggests that intelligence involves both a general factor and specific factors.
Group tests	Their nature	Group tests are convenient and economical, but they do not allow an examiner to monitor the testing and personally interact with the subject. The SAT is a group test used in conjunction with other information to predict academic success in college.
Aptitude tests and achievements tests	Their nature	Aptitude tests predict an individual's ability to learn a skill or the individual's future performance; achievement tests assess what an individual already knows. The distinction between these tests is sometimes blurred; the SAT has the ingredients of both.
Controversies and issues in intelligence	The heredity-environment controversy	In the late 1960s, Jensen argued that intelligence is approximately 80 percent hereditary and that genetic differences exist in the average intelligence of ethnic groups and social classes. Intelligence is influenced by heredity, but not as strongly as Jensen believed. The environments and opportunities provided to adolescents make a difference.
	Culture and ethnicity	There are cultural and ethnic differences in performance on intelligence tests, but the evidence suggests that these differences are not genetically based. In recent decades, as Blacks have experienced more opportunities, the gap between Black-White intelligence test scores has diminished. Early intelligence tests favored White, middle-class, urban individuals. Current tests try to reduce this bias. Culture-fair tests are an alternative to traditional tests; most psychologists believe that they cannot completely replace the traditional tests.
Use and misuse of intelligence tests	Tests as tools	The effectiveness of intelligence tests depends on the knowledge, skill, and integrity of the user. Intelligence tests should be used in conjunction with other information about an individual and not relied on as the sole indicator of intelligence. IQ scores can produce unfortunate stereotypes and expectations about intelligence. Ability tests can help to divide adolescents into homogeneous groups so that they can be taught the same concepts together.
The extremes of intelligence	Mental retardation	A mentally retarded individual has a low IQ, usually below 70 on a traditional IQ test, and has difficulty adapting to everyday life. The four classifications of mental retardation are: mild retardation, moderate retardation, severe retardation, and profound retardation. The two main causes of retardation are organic and cultural-familial.
	Giftedness	A gifted individual has above-average intelligence (an IQ of 120 or higher) and/or superior talent for something.
	Creativity	Creativity is the ability to think about something in a novel or unusual way and to come up with unique solutions to problems.

Summary

I. The Information-Processing Perspective and Developmental Changes in Information Processing

Information processing is concerned with how individuals analyze the many sources of information in the environment and make sense of these experiences. This perspective focuses on how information gets into the mind, how it is stored and transformed, and how it is retrieved to think about and to solve problems. In comparison to other approaches, information-processing approaches provide details about what is going on during mental activity. Adolescents process information faster, have greater processing capacity, and show greater automaticity in processing than children. In Case's model, adolescents have increasingly more cognitive resources available to them because of automaticity, increased capacity, and more familiarity with content knowledge.

II. Attention, Memory, and Cognitive Monitoring

Attention is the concentration and focusing of mental effort. Attention is both selective and shifting. Memory is the retention of information over time. It can be divided into short-term and long-term memory. Strategies, or control processes, especially organization, improve adolescent memory. Increases in storage space, as well as in the speed and efficiency of information processing, are likely involved in the adolescent's superior memory when compared to the child's memory. Cognitive monitoring refers to the process of taking stock of what one is doing currently, what will be done next, and how effectively the mental activity is unfolding. Parents, teachers, and peers can be effective sources for improving the adolescent's cognitive monitoring.

III. Decision Making and Critical Thinking

Adolescence is a time of increased decision making. Older adolescents are more competent at decision making than younger adolescents, who, in turn, are more competent than children. The ability to make competent decisions does not guarantee that such decisions will be made in everyday life, where breadth of experience comes into play. Adolescents need more opportunities to practice and discuss realistic decision making. In some instances, adolescents' faulty decision making may be blamed when, in reality, the problem is society's orientation toward adolescents and the failure to provide adolescents with adequate choices. Critical thinking involves grasping the deeper meaning of problems, keeping an open mind about different approaches and perspectives, and deciding for oneself what to believe or do. Adolescence is an important transitional period in critical thinking because of such cognitive changes as increased speed, automaticity, and capacity of information processing; more breadth of content knowledge; increased ability to construct new combinations of knowledge; and a greater range and more spontaneous use of strategies. Nonetheless, for critical thinking to develop effectively in adolescence, a solid foundation in basic skills and knowledge in childhood is required. An important agenda is the teaching of critical thinking in schools, which Sternberg believes should focus on the skills needed in everyday life.

IV. Computers and Adolescents

Potential positive effects of computers include using computers as personal tutors (computer-assisted instruction) or as multipurpose tools, as well as the motivational and social aspects of computers. Potential negative effects of computers include regimentation and dehumanization of the classroom, as well as unwarranted "shaping" of the curriculum. Generalizations and limitations of computer-based teaching may also be a potential problem.

V. What Is Intelligence?

Intelligence is an abstract concept that is measured indirectly. Psychologists rely on intelligence tests to estimate intellectual processes. Verbal ability, problem-solving skills, and the ability to learn from and adapt to life's everyday experiences are important aspects of intelligence. Extensive effort is devoted to assessing individual differences in intelligence. The field involved in this assessment is called psychometrics. The behavioral indicators of intelligence may vary across cultures.

VI. The Binet and Wechsler Tests

Alfred Binet developed the first intelligence test, known as the 1905 Scale. He developed the concept of mental age, and William Stern developed the concept of IQ. The Binet has been standardized and revised a number of times. The test approximates a normal distribution. Besides the Binet, the most widely used intelligence tests are the Wechsler scales. They include the WAIS-R and the WISC-R. These tests provide an overall IQ, verbal and performance IQs, and information about 11 subtests.

VII. Does Intelligence Have a Single Nature?

Psychologists debate whether intelligence is a general ability or a number of specific abilities. Spearman's two-factor theory, Thurstone's multiple-factor theory, Sternberg's triarchic theory, and Gardner's seven frames of mind have been attempts to describe the basic factors, or components, of intelligence. Current thinking suggests that intelligence involves both a general factor and specific factors.

VIII. Group Tests, Aptitude Tests, and Achievement Tests

Individual tests allow psychologists to monitor the testing situation closely and to personally interact with subjects; group tests are more convenient and economical, but they do not allow examiners such careful evaluation. The SAT is a group test used in conjunction with other information to predict academic success in college. Aptitude tests predict an individual's ability to learn a skill or the individual's future performance; achievement tests assess what an individual already knows. The distinction between these two types of tests is sometimes blurred; the SAT has the ingredients of both.

IX. Controversies and Issues in Intelligence, Culture and Ethnicity

In the late 1960s, Jensen argued that intelligence is approximately 80 percent hereditary and that genetic differences exist in the average intelligence of ethnic groups and social classes. Intelligence is influenced by heredity, but not as strongly as Jensen believed. The environments and opportunities provided to adolescents do make a difference. Ethnic and cultural differences in performance on intelligence tests do exist, but the evidence suggests that these differences are not genetically based. In recent decades, as Blacks have experienced more opportunities, the gap between Black-White intelligence test scores has diminished. Early intelligence tests favored White, middle-class, urban individuals. Current tests try to reduce this bias. Culture-fair tests are an alternative to traditional tests; most psychologists believe that they cannot completely replace the traditional tests.

X. The Use and Misuse of Intelligence Tests

The effectiveness of intelligence tests depends on the knowledge, skill, and integrity of the user. The tests should be used in conjunction with other information about the individual. IQ scores can produce unfortunate stereotypes and expectations about intelligence. Ability tests can help to divide adolescents into homogeneous groups (for example, reading, math) so that they can be taught the same concepts together; however, educators should be extremely cautious about placing adolescents in tracks, such as "advanced" or "low."

XI. The Extremes of Intelligence

A mentally retarded individual has a low IQ, usually below 70 on a traditional intelligence test, and has difficulty adapting to everyday life. The four classifications of mental retardation are: mild retardation, moderate retardation, severe retardation, and profound retardation. The two main causes of retardation are organic and cultural-familial. Both giftedness and creativity are difficult to define. A gifted individual has above-average intelligence (an IQ of 120 or higher) and/or a superior talent for something. Creativity is the ability to think about something in a novel or unusual way and to come up with unique solutions to problems.

Key Terms

automaticity 150
attention 150
memory 151
short-term memory 151
long-term memory 151
strategies 152
cognitive monitoring 152
critical thinking 154
computer-assisted
 instruction 155
individual differences
 159

psychometrics 159
intelligence 159
mental age (MA) 160
intelligence quotient (IQ)
 160
normal distribution 160
two-factor theory 161
multiple-factor theory
 161
triarchic theory 164
aptitude test 167

achievement test 167
culture-fair tests 170
mental retardation 173
organic retardation 174
cultural-familial
 retardation 174
gifted 174
convergent thinking 175
divergent thinking 175
creativity 175

Suggested Readings

Anastasi, A. (1988). *Psychological testing* (6th ed.). New York: Macmillan.
 This widely used text on psychological testing provides extensive information
 about test construction, test evaluation, and the nature of intelligence testing.

Baron, J. B., & Sternberg, R. J. (Eds.). (1987). *Teaching thinking skills: Theory and*
 practice. New York: W. H. Freeman.
 Presents essays by ten eminent psychologists, educators, and philosophers that
 portray the current state of knowledge about critical-thinking skills. Offers
 various exercises and strategies that can be performed both inside and outside the
 classroom to enhance adolescents' critical-thinking skills.

Fancher, R. E. (1985). *The intelligence men: Makers of the IQ controversy.* New York:
 W. W. Norton.
 Includes an extensive portrayal of the history of intelligence testing. Provides
 many insights and detailed descriptions of the lives of the intelligence-test
 makers.

Gardner, H., & Perkins, D. (Eds.). (1989). *Art, mind, and education.* Urbana, IL:
 University of Illinois Press.
 An excellent collection of up-to-date ideas on creativity. Special attention is given
 to education's role in art.

Horowitz, F. D., & O'Brien, M. (Eds.). (1985). *The gifted and the talented.*
 Washington, DC: The American Psychological Association.
 Pulls together what is currently known about the gifted and the talented. Experts
 have contributed chapters on the nature of the gifted and the diverse topics
 involved.

Keating, D. P. (1990). Adolescent thinking. In S. S. Feldman & G. R. Elliott (Eds.), *At*
 the threshold: The developing adolescent. Cambridge, MA: Harvard University
 Press.
 An authoritative, up-to-date overview of a wide-ranging set of ideas about
 adolescent cognition. Especially instructive are the author's discussions of
 adolescents' information-processing skills, decision making, and critical thinking.

The Contexts of Adolescent Development

Man is a knot, a web, a mesh into which relationships are tied.

Saint-Exupéry

A dolescent development takes place in social contexts, which provide the setting and sociohistorical, cultural backdrop for physical, cognitive, and social growth. This third section consists of four chapters: Chapter 6, "Families"; Chapter 7, "Peers"; Chapter 8, "Schools"; and Chapter 9, "Culture."

CHAPTER 6

Families

It is not enough for parents to understand children. They must accord children the privilege of understanding them.

Milton Saperstein, Paradoxes of Everyday Life, *1955*

Variations in Adolescents' Perceptions of Parents

My mother and I depend on each other. However, if something separated us, I think I could still get along O.K. I know that my mother continues to have an important influence on me. Sometimes she gets on my nerves, but I still basically like her, and respect her, a lot. We have our arguments, and I don't always get my way, but she is willing to listen to me.

Amy, age 16

You go from a point at which your parents are responsible for you to a point at which you want a lot more independence. Finally, you are more independent, and you feel like you have to be more responsible for yourself; otherwise you are not going to do very well in this world. It's important for parents to still be there to support you, but at some point, you've got to look in the mirror and say, "I can do it myself."

John, age 18

I don't get along very well with my parents. They try to dictate how I dress, who I date, how much I study, what I do on weekends, and how much time I spend talking on the phone. They are big intruders in my life. Why won't they let me make my own decisions? I'm mature enough to handle these things. When they jump down my throat at every little thing I do, it makes me mad and I say things to them I probably shouldn't. They just don't understand me very well.

Ed, age 17

My father never seems to have any time to spend with me. He is gone a lot on business, and when he comes home, he is either too tired to do anything or plops down and watches TV and doesn't want to be bothered. He thinks I don't work hard enough and don't have values that were as solid as his generation. It is a very distant relationship. I actually spend more time talking to my mom than to him. I guess I should work a little harder in school than I do, but I still don't think he has the right to say such negative things to me. I like my mom a lot better because I think she is a much nicer person.

Tom, age 15

We have our arguments and our differences, and there are moments when I get very angry with my parents, but most of the time they are like heated discussions. I have to say what I think because I don't think they are always right. Most of the time when there is an argument, we can discuss the problem and eventually find a course that we all can live with. Not every time, though, because there are some occasions when things just remain unresolved. Even when we have an unresolved conflict, I still would have to say that I get along pretty good with my parents.

Ann, age 16

The comments of these five adolescents offer a brief glimpse of the diversity that characterizes adolescents' relationships with their parents. While parent-adolescent relationships vary considerably, researchers are finding that, for the most part, the relationships are both (1) extremely important aspects of adolescent development and (2) more positive than once was believed.

When I was a boy of 14, my father was so ignorant I could hardly stand to have the man around. But when I got to be 21, I was astonished at how much he had learnt in 7 years.

Mark Twain

An important contemporary theme of family processes in adolescence is that both autonomy (independence) and attachment (connectedness) to parents are involved in the adolescent's successful adaptation to the world. Historically, the major themes of parent-adolescent relationships were independence and *conflict*. Today, developmentalists are working to correct past overdramatization of independence, detachment from parents, and high conflict during adolescence. These are being replaced with a balanced emphasis on independence, connectedness, and moderate, rather than severe, conflict in the majority of families. Our extensive tour of family processes in adolescence takes us through the basic nature of family processes, parenting techniques, parent-adolescent conflict, autonomy and attachment, sibling relationships, and the changing family in a changing society.

The Nature of Family Processes

Among the important considerations in studying adolescents and their families are reciprocal socialization, synchrony, and the family system; how adolescents construct relationships and how such relationships influence the development of social maturity; and social and historical influences on the family.

Reciprocal Socialization, Synchrony, and the Family As a System

For many years, the socialization of adolescents was viewed as a straightforward, one-way matter of indoctrination. The basic philosophy was that children and adolescents had to be trained to fit into the social world, so their behavior had to be shaped accordingly. However, socialization is much more than molding the child and adolescent into a mature adult. The child and adolescent are not like inanimate blobs of clay that the sculptor forms into a polished statue. **Reciprocal socialization** *is the process by which children and adolescents socialize parents just as parents socialize them.* To get a better feel for how reciprocal socialization works, consider two situations: the first emphasizing the impact of growing up in a single-parent home (parental influences), the second a talented teenage ice skater (adolescent influences). In the first situation, the speaker is 14-year-old Robert:

> I never have seen my father. He never married my mother, and she had to quit school to help support us. Maybe my mother and I are better off that he didn't marry her because he apparently didn't love her . . . but sometimes I get very depressed about not having a father, especially when I see a lot of my friends with their fathers at ball games and such. My father still lives around here, but he has married, and I guess he wants to forget about me and my mother. . . . A lot of times I wish my mother would get married and I could at least have a stepfather to talk with about things and do things with me.

Figure 6.1 Interaction between adolescents and their parents: direct and indirect effects.

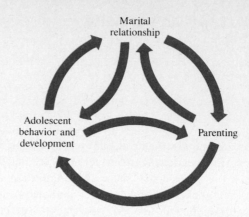

In the second situation, the speaker is 13-year-old Kathy:

> "Mother, my skating coach says that I have a lot of talent, but it is going to take a lot of lessons and travel to fully develop it." Her mother responds, "Kathy, I just don't know. We will have to talk with your father about it tonight when he gets home from work." That evening, Kathy's father tells his wife, "Look, to do that for Kathy, I will have to get a second job, or you will have to get a job. There is no way we can afford what she wants with what I make."

As developmentalists probe the nature of reciprocal socialization, they are impressed with the importance of synchrony in parent-child and parent-adolescent relationships. **Synchrony** *refers to the carefully coordinated interaction between the parent and the child or adolescent, in which, often unknowingly, they are attuned to each other's behavior.* The turn-taking that occurs in parent-adolescent negotiation reflects the reciprocal, synchronous nature of parent-adolescent relationships. In synchronous relationships, the interactions of parents and adolescents can be conceptualized as a dance or a dialogue in which successive actions of the partners are closely coordinated. This coordinated dance or dialogue can assume the form of mutual synchrony (each individual's behavior depends on the partner's previous behavior), or it can be reciprocal in a more precise sense: The actions of the partners can be matched, as when one partner imitates the other or there is mutual smiling (Rutter & Durkin, 1987).

Reciprocal socialization takes place within the social system of a family, which consists of a constellation of subsystems defined by generation, gender, and role (Hooper & Hooper, in press). Divisions of labor among family members define particular subsystems, and attachments define others. Each family member is a participant in several subsystems—some dyadic (involving two people), some polyadic (involving more than two people). The father and adolescent represent one dyadic subsystem, the mother and father another. The mother-father-adolescent represent one polyadic subsystem (Vuchinich, Emery, & Cassidy, 1988).

Figure 6.1 shows an organizational scheme that highlights the reciprocal influences of family members and family subsystems (Belsky, 1981). As can be seen by following the arrows in the figure, marital relations, parenting, and adolescent behavior can have both direct and indirect effects on each other. An example of a direct effect is the influence of the parent's behavior on the adolescent. An example of an indirect effect is how the relationship between the spouses mediates the way a parent acts toward the adolescent. For example, marital conflict might reduce the efficiency of parenting, in which case marital conflict would have an indirect effect on the adolescent's behavior.

In one investigation, 44 adolescents were observed either separately with their mother and father (dyadic settings) or in the presence of both parents (triadic setting) (Gjerde, Block, & Block, 1985). The presence of the father improved mother-son relationships, but the presence of the mother decreased the quality of father-son relations. This may have occurred because the father takes the strain off the mother by controlling the adolescent or because the mother's presence reduces father-son interaction, which may not be high in many instances. Indeed, in one recent investigation, sons directed more negative behavior toward their mothers than their fathers in dyadic situations (Buhrmester & others, in press). However, in a triadic context of adolescent-mother-father, fathers helped "rescue" mothers by attempting to control the sons' negative behavior.

The Developmental Construction of Relationships

Developmentalists have shown an increased interest in understanding how we construct relationships as we grow up. Psychoanalytic theorists have always been interested in how this process works in families. However, the current explanations of how relationships are constructed is virtually stripped of Freud's psychosexual stage terminology and also is not always confined to the first five years of life, as has been the case in classical psychoanalytic theory. Today's **developmental construction views** *share the belief that as individuals grow up they acquire modes of relating to others. There are two main variations within this view, one of which emphasizes continuity and stability in relationships through the life span and one of which emphasizes discontinuity and change in relationships through the life span.*

The Continuity View

In the **continuity view,** *emphasis is on the role that early parent-child relationships play in constructing a basic way of relating to people throughout the life span.* These early parent-child relationships are carried forward to later points in development to influence all subsequent relationships (with peers, with friends, with teachers, and with romantic partners, for example) (Ainsworth, 1979; Bowlby, 1969, 1989; Sroufe, 1985, in press; Urban & others, 1992). In its extreme form, this view states that the basic components of social relationships are laid down and shaped by the security or insecurity of parent-infant attachment relationships in the first year or two of the infant's life. More about the importance of secure attachment in the adolescent's development appears later in the chapter when we discuss autonomy and attachment.

Close relationships with parents also are important in the adolescent's development because these relationships function as models or templates that are carried forward over time to influence the construction of new relationships. Clearly, close relationships do not repeat themselves in an endless fashion over the course of the child's and adolescent's development. And the quality of any relationship depends to some degree on the specific individual with whom the relationship is formed. However, the nature of earlier relationships that are developed over many years often can be detected in later relationships, both with those same individuals and in the formation of relationships with others at a later point in time (Gjerde, Block, & Block, 1991). Thus, the nature of parent-adolescent relationships does not depend only on what happens in the relationship during adolescence. Relationships with parents over the long course of childhood are carried forward to influence, at least to some degree, the nature of parent-adolescent relationships. And the long course of parent-child relationships also could be expected to influence, again at least to some degree, the fabric of the adolescent's peer relationships, friendships, and dating relationships.

How childhood experiences with parents are carried forward and influence the nature of the adolescent's development is important, but the nature of intergenerational relationships is valuable as well. As the life-span perspective has taken on greater acceptance among developmental psychologists, researchers have become interested in the transmission of close relationships across generations (Dunham & Bengtson, 1991; Elder, Caspi, & Downey, 1986; Martin, 1990; Troll, 1985). The middle generation in three generations is especially important in the socialization process. For example, the parents of adolescents can be studied in terms of their relationships with their own parents, when they were children and presently, and in terms of their relationships with their own adolescents, both when the adolescents were children and presently. Life-span theorists point out that the middle-aged parents of adolescents may have to give more help than they receive. Their adolescents probably are reaching the point where they need considerable financial support for education, and their parents, whose generation is living longer than past generations, may also require financial support, as well as more comfort and affection than earlier in the life cycle.

The Discontinuity View

In the **discontinuity view,** *emphasis is on change and growth in relationships over time.* As people grow up, they develop many different types of relationships (with parents, with peers, with teachers, and with romantic partners, for example). Each of these relationships is structurally different. With each new type of relationship, individuals encounter new modes of relating (Buhrmester & Furman, 1986; Piaget, 1932; Sullivan, 1953; Youniss, 1980). For example, Piaget (1932) argued that parent-child relationships are strikingly different from children's peer relationships. Parent-child relationships, he said, are more likely to consist of parents having unilateral authority over children. By contrast, peer relationships are more likely to consist of participants who relate to each other on a much more equal basis. In parent-child relationships, since parents have greater knowledge and authority, their children often must learn how to conform to rules and regulations laid down by parents. In this view, we use the parental-child mode when relating to authority figures (such as with teachers and experts) and when we act as authority figures (when we become parents, teachers, and experts).

By contrast, relationships with peers have a different structure and require a different mode of relating to others. This more egalitarian mode is later called upon in relationships with romantic partners, friends, and coworkers. Because two peers possess relatively equal knowledge and authority (their relationship is reciprocal and symmetrical), children learn a democratic mode of relating that is based on mutual influence. With peers, children learn to formulate and assert their own opinions, appreciate the perspective of peers, cooperatively negotiate solutions to disagreements, and evolve standards for conduct that are mutually acceptable. Because peer relationships are voluntary (rather than obligatory, as in the family), children and adolescents who fail to become skillful in the symmetrical, mutual, egalitarian, reciprocal mode of relating have difficulty being accepted by peers.

While the change, growth variation of the developmental construction view does not deny that prior close relationships (such as with parents) are carried forward to influence later relationships, it does stress that each new type of relationship that children and adolescents encounter (such as with peers, with friends, and with romantic partners) requires the construction of different and ever more sophisticated modes of relating to others. Further, in the change, growth version, each period of development uniquely contributes to the construction of relationship knowledge; development across the life span is not solely determined by a sensitive or critical period during infancy.

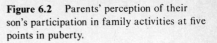

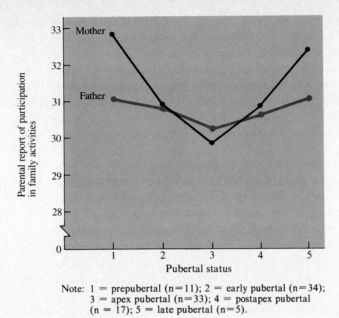

Figure 6.2 Parents' perception of their son's participation in family activities at five points in puberty.

Note: 1 = prepubertal (n=11); 2 = early pubertal (n=34); 3 = apex pubertal (n=33); 4 = postapex pubertal (n = 17); 5 = late pubertal (n=5).

Maturation of the Adolescent and Maturation of Parents

In the quotation presented at the opening of this chapter, Mark Twain remarked that, when he was 14, his father was so ignorant he could hardly stand to be around him, but when Mark got to be 21, he was astonished at how much his father had learned in those seven years! Mark Twain's comments suggest that maturation is an important theme of parent-adolescent relationships. Adolescents change as they make the transition from childhood to adulthood, but their parents also undergo change during their adult years.

Adolescent Changes

Among the changes in the adolescent that can influence parent-adolescent relationships are puberty, expanded logical reasoning, increased idealistic thought, violated expectations, changes in schooling, peers, friendships, dating, and movement toward independence. Several recent investigations have shown that conflict between parents and adolescents, especially between mothers and sons, is the most stressful during the apex of pubertal growth (Hill & others, 1985; Lamborn & Steinberg, 1990; Steinberg, 1981, 1988). For example, as shown in Figure 6.2, mothers were less satisfied with their sons' participation in family activities during the apex of pubertal change (Hill & others, 1985). Observations revealed that the father retains his influence over family decision making throughout the pubertal transition and asserts his authority by requiring the son to be obedient. During pubertal change, mothers and sons interrupt each other more and explain themselves less. Toward the end of pubertal change, sons have grown larger and more powerful. At this time, they are less likely to engage in conflict with their mothers, probably because their mothers defer to them. More about sex differences and similarities in family relations appears later in the chapter. In sum, the adolescent's pubertal status is related to the nature of parent-adolescent relationships.

In terms of cognitive changes, the adolescent can now reason in more logical ways with parents than in childhood. During childhood, parents may be able to get by with saying, "O.K. That is it. We do it my way or else," and the child conforms. But with increased cognitive skills, adolescents no longer are likely to accept such a statement as a reason for conforming to parental dictates. Adolescents want to know, often in fine detail, why they are being disciplined. Even when parents give what seem to be logical reasons for discipline, adolescents' cognitive sophistication may call attention to deficiencies in the reasoning. Such prolonged bouts of discourse with parents are usually uncharacteristic of parent-child relationships but are frequent occurrences in parent-adolescent relationships.

In addition, the adolescent's increasing idealistic thought comes into play in parent-adolescent relationships. Parents are now evaluated vis-à-vis what an ideal parent is like. The very real interactions with parents, which inevitably involve some negative interchanges and flaws, are placed next to the adolescent's schema of an ideal parent. And, as part of their egocentrism, adolescents' concerns with how others view them are likely to produce overreactions to parents' comments. A mother may comment to her adolescent daughter that she needs a new blouse. The daughter might respond, "What's the matter? You don't think I have good taste? You think I look gross, don't you? Well, you are the one who is gross!" The same comment made to the daughter several years earlier in late childhood probably would have elicited a less intense response.

Another dimension of the adolescent's changing cognitive world related to parent-adolescent relations is the expectations parents and adolescents have for each other (Collins, 1985, 1990). The rapid changes of puberty make it difficult to use the individual's past behavior to predict future behavior. For example, preadolescent children are often compliant and easy to manage. As they enter puberty, children begin to question or seek rationales for parental demands (Maccoby, 1984). Parents may perceive this behavior as resistant and oppositional because it departs from the child's usual compliant behavior. Parents often respond to the lack of compliance with increased pressure for compliance. In this situation, expectations that were stabilized during a period of relatively slow developmental change are lagging behind the behavior of the adolescent during the period of rapid pubertal change.

What dimensions of the adolescent's social world contribute to parent-adolescent relationships? Adolescence brings with it new definitions of socially appropriate behavior. In our society, these definitions are associated with changes in schooling arrangements—transitions to middle or junior high school. Adolescents are required to function in a more anonymous, larger environment with multiple and varying teachers. More work is required, and more initiative and responsibility must be shown to adapt successfully. The school is not the only social arena that contributes to parent-adolescent relationships. Adolescents spend more time with peers than when they were children, and they develop more sophisticated friendships than in childhood. Adolescents also begin to push more strongly for independence. In sum, parents are called on to adapt to the changing world of the adolescent's schooling, peer relations, and push for autonomy (Hill, 1980).

Parental Changes

Parental changes that contribute to parent-adolescent relationships involve marital dissatisfaction, economic burdens, career reevaluation and time perspective, and health and body concerns (Hill, 1980; Silverberg & Steinberg, 1990). Marital dissatisfaction is greater when the offspring is an adolescent than a child or an adult. In addition, parents feel a greater economic burden during the rearing of adolescents. Also during this time, parents may reevaluate their occupational achievement, deciding whether they have met their youthful aspirations of success. They may look to the future and think about how much time they have remaining to accomplish what they want. Adolescents, however, look to the future with unbounded optimism, sensing that they have an unlimited amount of time to accomplish what they desire. Health concerns and an interest in body integrity and sexual attractiveness become prominent themes of adolescents' parents. Even when their body and sexual attractiveness are not deteriorating, many parents of adolescents perceive that they are. By contrast, adolescents have reached or are beginning to reach the peak of their physical attractiveness, strength, and health. While both adolescents and their parents show a heightened preoccupation with their bodies, adolescents' outcome probably is more positive.

The changes in adolescents' parents just described characterize development in middle adulthood. Most adolescents' parents either are in middle adulthood or are rapidly approaching middle adulthood. However, in the last two decades, the timing of parenthood has undergone some dramatic shifts. Parenthood is taking place earlier for some, later for others than in previous decades. First, the number of adolescent pregnancies substantially increased during the 1980s. Second, the number of women who postpone childbearing until their thirties and early forties simultaneously increased. Adolescents as parents is discussed in Chapter 12. Here we focus on sociohistorical changes related to postponement of childbearing until the thirties or forties.

There are many contrasts between becoming a parent in adolescence and becoming a parent 15 to 30 years later. Delayed childbearing allows for considerable progress in occupational and educational domains. For both males and females, education usually has been completed, and career development is well established (Parke, 1988).

The marital relationship varies with the timing of parenthood onset. In one investigation, couples who began childbearing in their early twenties were compared with those who began in their early thirties (Walter, 1986). The late-starting couples had more egalitarian relationships, with men participating in child care and household tasks more often.

Is parent-child interaction different for families in which parents delay having children until their thirties or forties? Investigators have found that older fathers are warmer, communicate better, encourage more achievement, and show less rejection with their children than younger fathers. However, older fathers also are less likely to place demands on children, to enforce rules, and to engage in physical play or sports with their children (MacDonald, 1987; Mitteness & Nydegger, 1982; Nydegger, 1981; Parke & others, 1988). These findings suggest that sociohistorical changes are resulting in different developmental trajectories for many families, trajectories that involve changes in the way marital partners and parents and adolescents interact.

Sociocultural, Historical Changes

Family development does not occur in a social vacuum. Important sociocultural and historical influences affect family processes. Family changes may be due to great upheavals in a nation, such as war, famine, or mass immigration. Or they may be due more to subtle transitions in ways of life. The Great Depression in the early 1930s had some negative effects on families. During its height, the depression produced economic deprivation, adult discontent, depression about living conditions, marital conflict, inconsistent child rearing, and unhealthy lifestyles—heavy drinking, demoralized attitudes, and health disabilities—especially in the father (Elder, 1980). Subtle changes in a culture that have significant influences on the family were described by the famous anthropologist Margaret Mead (1978). The changes focus on the longevity of the elderly and the role of the elderly in the family, the urban and suburban orientation of families and their mobility, television, and a general dissatisfaction and restlessness.

Fifty years ago, the older people who survived were usually hearty and still closely linked to the family, often helping to maintain the family's existence. Today, older people live longer, which means that their middle-aged children are often pressed into a caretaking role for their parents or the elderly parents may be placed in a nursing home. Elderly parents may have lost some of their socializing role in the family during the twentieth century as many of their children moved great distances away.

Many of these family moves are away from farms and small towns to urban and suburban settings. In the small towns and farms, individuals were surrounded by lifelong neighbors, relatives, and friends. Today, neighborhood and extended-family support systems are not nearly as prevalent. Families now move all over the country, often uprooting the child from a school and peer group he or she has known for a considerable length of time. And for many families, this type of move occurs every year or two, as one or both parents are transferred from job to job.

Television also plays a major role in the changing family. Many children who watch television find that parents are too busy working to share this experience with them. Children increasingly experience a world their parents are not a part of. Instead of participating in neighborhood peer groups, children come home after school and plop down in front of the television set. And television allows children and their families to see new ways of life. Lower-class families can look into the family lives of the middle class by simply pushing a button.

Another subtle change in families has been an increase in general dissatisfaction and restlessness. Women have become increasingly dissatisfied with their way of life, placing great strain on marriages. With fewer elders and long-term friends close by to help and advise young people during the initial difficult years of marriage and childbearing, marriages begin to fracture at the first signs of disagreement. Divorce has become epidemic in our culture. As women move into the labor market, men simultaneously become restless and look for stimulation outside of family life. The result of such restlessness and the tendency to divorce and remarry has been a hodgepodge of family structures, with far greater numbers of single-parent and stepparent families than ever before in history. Later in the chapter, we discuss such aspects of the changing social world of the adolescent and the family in greater detail.

Parenting Techniques and Parent-Adolescent Conflict

We have seen how the expectations of adolescents and their parents often seem violated as adolescents change dramatically during the course of puberty. Many parents see their child moving from a compliant being to someone who is noncompliant, oppositional, and resistant to parental standards. Parents often clamp down tighter and put more pressure on the adolescent to conform to parental standards. Parents often deal with the young adolescent as if they expect the adolescent to become a mature being within the next 10 to 15 minutes. But the transition from childhood to adulthood is a long journey with many hills and valleys. Adolescents are not going to conform to adult standards immediately. Parents who recognize that adolescents take a long time "to get it right" usually deal more competently and calmly with adolescent transgressions than parents who demand immediate conformity to parental standards. Yet other parents, rather than placing heavy demands on their adolescents for compliance, do virtually the opposite, letting them do as they please in a very permissive manner.

As we discuss parent-adolescent relationships, we will discover that neither high-intensity demands for compliance nor an unwillingness to monitor and be involved in the adolescent's development is likely to be a wise parenting strategy. Further, we will look at another misperception that parents of adolescents sometimes entertain. Parents may perceive that virtually all conflict with their adolescent is bad. We will discover that a moderate degree of conflict with parents in adolescence is not only inevitable but may also serve a positive developmental function.

Parenting Techniques

Parents want their adolescents to grow into socially mature individuals, and they often feel a great deal of frustration in their role as parents. Psychologists have long searched for parenting ingredients that promote competent social development in adolescents. For example, in the 1930s, behaviorist John Watson argued that parents were too affectionate with their charges. Early research focused on a distinction between physical and psychological discipline, or between controlling and permissive parenting. More recently, there has been greater precision in unraveling the dimensions of competent parenting.

Especially widespread is the view of Diana Baumrind (1971, 1991a,b), who believes that parents should be neither punitive nor aloof from their adolescents, but rather should develop rules and be affectionate with them. She emphasizes three types of parenting that are associated with different aspects of the adolescent's social behavior: authoritarian, authoritative, and laissez-faire (permissive). More recently, developmentalists have argued that permissive parenting comes in two forms—permissive-indulgent and permissive-indifferent.

Authoritarian parenting *is a restrictive, punitive style that exhorts the adolescent to follow the parent's directions and to respect work and effort. The authoritarian parent places firm limits and controls on the adolescent and allows little verbal exchange. Authoritarian parenting is associated with adolescents' socially incompetent behavior.* For example, an authoritarian parent might say, "You do it my way or else. There will be no discussion!" Adolescents of authoritarian parents often are anxious about social comparison, fail to initiate activity, and have poor communication skills.

Authoritative parenting *encourages adolescents to be independent but still places limits and controls on their actions. Extensive verbal give-and-take is allowed, and parents are warm and nurturant toward the adolescent. Authoritative parenting is associated with adolescents' socially competent behavior.* An authoritative father, for example, might put his arm around the adolescent in a comforting way and say, "You know you should not have done that. Let's talk about how you can handle the situation better next time." The adolescents of authoritative parents are self-reliant and socially responsible.

Permissive parenting comes in two forms: permissive-indifferent and permissive-indulgent (Maccoby & Martin, 1983). **Permissive-indifferent parenting** *is a style in which the parent is very uninvolved in the adolescent's life. It is associated with adolescents' socially incompetent behavior, especially a lack of self-control.* The permissive-indifferent parent cannot answer the question, "It is 10:00 P.M. Do you know where your adolescent is?" Adolescents have a strong need for their parents to care about them; adolescents whose parents are permissive-indifferent develop the sense that other aspects of the parents' lives are more important than they are. Adolescents whose parents are permissive-indifferent are socially incompetent: They show poor self-control and do not handle independence well.

Authoritative parenting is a highly desirable parenting style; in this style, parents combine warmth, considerable verbal give-and-take, and limit setting when needed.

Figure 6.3   A fourfold scheme of parenting styles.

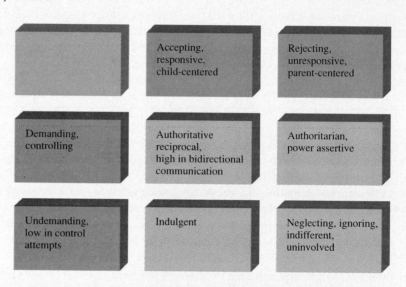

Permissive-indulgent parenting *is a style in which parents are highly involved with their adolescents but place few demands or controls on them. Permissive-indulgent parenting is associated with adolescents' social incompetence, especially a lack of self-control.* Permissive-indulgent parents allow their adolescents to do what they want, and the result is that the adolescents never learn to control their own behavior and always expect to get their way. Some parents deliberately rear their adolescents in this way because they believe that the combination of warm involvement with few restraints will produce a creative, confident adolescent. In one family with permissive-indulgent parents, the 14-year-old son moved his parents out of their master bedroom suite and claimed it—along with their expensive stereo system and color television—as his. The boy is an excellent tennis player but behaves in the manner of John McEnroe, raving and ranting around the tennis court. He has few friends, is self-indulgent, and has never learned to abide by rules and regulations. Why should he? His parents never made him follow any.

In our discussion of parenting styles, we have talked about parents who vary along the dimensions of acceptance, responsiveness, demand, and control. As shown in Figure 6.3, the four parenting styles—authoritarian, authoritative, permissive-indulgent, and permissive-indifferent—can be described in terms of these dimensions.

Several caveats about parenting styles are in order. First, the parenting styles do not capture the important theme of reciprocal socialization and synchrony. Keep in mind that adolescents socialize parents, just as parents socialize adolescents. Second, many parents use a combination of techniques rather than a single technique, although one technique may be dominant. While consistent parenting is usually recommended, the wise parent may sense the importance of being more permissive in certain situations, more authoritarian in others, and yet more authoritative in others. Third, most of the data associating authoritative parenting with social competence is based on children, not adolescents.

In a recent investigation, Diana Baumrind (1991b) analyzed parenting styles and social competence in adolescence. The comprehensive assessment involved observations and interviews with 139 14-year-old boys and girls and their parents. More than any other factor, the responsiveness of the parents (considerateness and supportiveness, for example) was related to the adolescents' social competence. And when parents had problem behaviors themselves (alcohol problems and marital conflict, for example), adolescents were more likely to have problems and show decreased social competence. Other researchers continue to find support for the belief that authoritarian and permissive parenting are less effective strategies than authoritative parenting (Lamborn, Dornbusch, & Kraemer, 1990; Steinberg, 1990; Steinberg & others, 1991).

Parent-Adolescent Conflict

Early adolescence is a time when parent-adolescent conflict escalates beyond parent-child conflict (Montemayor, 1982; Steinberg, 1990, 1991). This increase may be due to a number of factors already discussed involving the maturation of the adolescent and the maturation of parents: the biological changes of puberty, cognitive changes involving increased idealism and logical reasoning, social changes focused on independence and identity, violated expectations, and physical, cognitive, and social changes in parents associated with middle adulthood. While conflict with parents does increase in early adolescence, it does not reach the tumultuous proportions envisioned by G. Stanley Hall at the beginning of the twentieth century (Kupersmidt & others, 1992). Rather, much of the conflict involves the everyday events of family life, such as keeping a bedroom clean, dressing neatly, getting home by a certain time, not talking on the phone forever, and so on. The conflicts rarely involve major dilemmas like drugs and delinquency. In one investigation of 64 high school sophomores, interviews were conducted in their homes on three randomly selected evenings during a three-week period (Montemayor, 1982). The adolescents were asked to tell about the events of the previous day, including any conflicts they had with their parents. Conflict was defined as "either you teased your parent or your parent teased you; you and your parent had a difference of opinion; one of you got mad at the other; you and your parent had a quarrel or an argument; or one of you hit the other." During a period of 192 days of tracking the 64 adolescents, an average of 68 arguments with parents was reported. This represents a rate of .35 arguments with parents per day or about one argument every three days. The average length of the arguments was 11 minutes. Most conflicts were with mothers, and the majority were between mothers and daughters.

Still, a high degree of conflict characterizes some parent-adolescent relationships. One estimate of the percentage of parents and adolescents who engage in prolonged, intense, repeated, unhealthy conflict is about one in five families (Montemayor, 1982). While this figure represents a minority of adolescents, it indicates that 4 to 5 million American families encounter serious, highly stressful parent-adolescent conflict. And this prolonged, intense conflict is associated with

Diana Baumrind developed the important concept of authoritative parenting, which is associated with socially competent adolescent behavior. Recently, Baumrind (1991) also found that parents' responsiveness—which includes considerateness and supportiveness—is related to adolescents' social competence.

Conflict with parents increases in early adolescence. Such conflict usually is moderate, an increase that can serve the positive developmental function of promoting independence and identity. Much of the conflict involves the everyday events of family life—keeping a bedroom clean, dressing neatly, getting home by a certain time, and as shown in the photograph, not talking on the phone forever.

a number of adolescent problems—moving away from home, juvenile delinquency, school dropout rates, pregnancy and early marriage, membership in religious cults, and drug abuse (Brook & others, 1990; Ullman, 1982).

While in some cases these problems may be caused by intense, prolonged parent-adolescent conflict, in others the problems may have originated before the onset of adolescence (Bandura & Walters, 1959). Simply because children are physically much smaller than parents, parents may be able to suppress oppositional behavior. But by adolescence, increased size and strength may result in an indifference to or confrontation with parental dictates. Consider the following circumstance:

> *Interviewer* What sort of things does your mother object to your doing when you are out with your friends?
>
> *Boy* She don't know what I do.
>
> *Interviewer* What about staying out late at night?
>
> *Boy* She says, "Be home at eleven o'clock." I'll come home at one.
>
> *Interviewer* How about using the family car?
>
> *Boy* No. I wrecked mine, and my father wrecked his a month before I wrecked mine, and I can't even get near his. And I got a license and everything. I'm going to hot wire it some night and cut out.
>
> *Interviewer* How honest do you feel you can be to your mother about where you've been and what things you have done?
>
> *Boy* I tell her where I've been, period.
>
> *Interviewer* How about what you've done?
>
> *Boy* No. I won't tell her what I've done. If we're going to have a beer bust, I'm not going to tell her. I'll tell her I've been to a show or something.
>
> *Interviewer* How about your father?
>
> *Boy* I'll tell him where I've been, period.

Some strategies for reducing parent-adolescent conflict are presented in Perspective on Adolescent Development 6.1.

At this point, we have discussed a number of ideas about the nature of adolescents and their families, and a summary of these ideas is presented in Concept Table 6.1. Now we turn our attention to further information about the lives of adolescents and their families.

Strategies for Reducing Parent-Adolescent Conflict

Are there ways parents can reduce parent-adolescent conflict? Laurence Steinberg has studied parent-adolescent conflict for a number of years. Steinberg (with Ann Levine, 1990) believes that the best way for parents to handle parent-adolescent conflict is through collaborative problem solving, the goal of which is to discover a solution that satisfies both the parent and the adolescent. The approach works best when neither the parent nor the adolescent is distracted, when the discussion is restricted to a single issue, and when the adolescent's agreement to try to work out a solution is secured in advance. The collaborative problem-solving approach consists of six basic steps:

1. *Establish ground rules for conflict resolution.* These rules are basically the rules of fighting fairly. Both the parent and the adolescent agree to treat each other with respect—no name-calling or putting each other down, for example—and to listen to each other's point of view. At the beginning of the discussion, the parent should provide a positive note by stating a desire to be fair.
2. *Try to reach a mutual understanding.* Step 2 involves taking turns being understood, which means that both the parent and the adolescent get the opportunity to say what the real problem is and how they feel about it. In this discussion, it is important to focus on the issue, not on personalities.
3. *Try brainstorming.* Step 3 involves both the adolescent and the parent generating as many solutions to the problem as they can. At this point, no idea should be rejected because it is too crazy, too expensive, or too dumb. Set a time limit—something like five or ten minutes—and come up with as many ideas for solving the conflict as both of you can and write them down.
4. *Try to come to an agreement about one or more solutions.* In this fourth step of collaborative problem solving, both the parent and the adolescent select the options they like best. Every option should not be discussed because this can produce endless, sometimes fruitless, debate. In this step, the parent and the adolescent can see where their interests converge. Some give-and-take, some negotiation probably will be needed at this point. Neither the parent nor the adolescent should agree to something they find unacceptable.
5. *Write down the agreement.* While this fifth step may sound formal, it should be followed because memories can become distorted. If either the parent or the adolescent breaks the agreement, the written agreement can be consulted.
6. *Establish a time for a follow-up conversation to examine progress.* Step 6 is just as important as the first five steps. If either the adolescent or the parent is not abiding by the agreement, or if the agreed-upon solution is not working out as well as was hoped, the problem has to be addressed.

The six steps of collaborative problem solving can be applied to a number of parent-adolescent conflicts, including such issues as curfew, choice of friends, keeping a room clean, respect for adults, rules for dating, and so on. In some situations, parents and adolescents may not be able to reach an agreement. When the adolescent's health or safety is at issue, the parent may find it necessary to make a decision that the adolescent does not agree with. However, an adolescent is far more likely to go along with the direction of a parent's decisions if the adolescent is allowed to participate in the decision-making process and sees that the parent is taking the adolescent's needs and desires seriously.

Autonomy and Attachment

It has been said that there are only two lasting bequests that we can leave our offspring—one is roots, the other wings. These words reflect the importance of attachment and autonomy in the adolescent's successful adaptation to the world. Historically, developmentalists have shown much more interest in autonomy than in attachment during the adolescent period. Recently, however, interest has heightened in attachment's role in healthy adolescent development. Adolescents and their parents live in a coordinated social world, one involving autonomy *and* attachment (Steinberg & Lamborn, 1992). In keeping with the historical interest in these processes, we discuss autonomy first.

Concept Table 6.1

The Nature of Family Processes, Parenting Techniques, and Parent-Adolescent Conflict

Concept	Processes/Related Ideas	Characteristics/Description
The nature of family processes	Reciprocal socialization, synchrony, and the family as a system	Reciprocal socialization is the principle which states that adolescents socialize parents, just as parents socialize adolescents. Synchrony is an important dimension of reciprocal socialization and refers to the carefully coordinated interaction between the parent and the child or adolescent in which they are attuned to each other's behavior. The family is a system of interacting individuals with different subsystems—some dyadic, others polyadic. Belsky's model describes direct and indirect effects of interaction between adolescents and their parents.
	The construction of relationships	The developmental construction views share the belief that as individuals grow up they acquire modes of relating to others. There are two main variations within this view, one that emphasizes continuity and stability in relationships through the life span (called the continuity view) and one that emphasizes discontinuity and change in relationships through the life span (called the discontinuity view).
	Maturation of the adolescent and maturation of parents	The adolescent changes involved include puberty, expanded logical reasoning, increased idealistic and egocentric thought, violated expectations, changes in schooling, peers, friendships, dating, and movement toward independence. Parental changes are associated with midlife—marital dissatisfaction, economic burdens, career reevaluation and time perspective, and health and body concerns.
	Sociocultural and historical changes	Sociocultural and historical changes in families may be due to great upheavals, such as war, or more subtle changes, such as television and the mobility of families.
Parenting techniques and parent-adolescent conflict	Parenting techniques	Authoritarian, authoritative, permissive-indifferent, and permissive-indulgent are four main parenting categories. Authoritative parenting is associated with adolescents' social competence more than the other styles. Caveats in understanding parenting styles focus on reciprocal socialization, multiple use of techniques, and few data collected on adolescents.
	Parent-adolescent conflict	Conflict with parents increases in early adolescence. Such conflict usually is moderate, an increase that can serve the positive developmental function of promoting autonomy and identity. However, as much as 20 percent of parent-adolescent relationships involve intense conflict, which is associated with a number of adolescent problems.

Autonomy

The increased independence that typifies adolescence is labeled as rebellious by some parents, but in many instances, the adolescent's push for autonomy has little to do with the adolescent's feelings toward the parents. Psychologically healthy families adjust to adolescents' push for independence by treating the adolescents in more adult ways and including them more in family decision making. Psychologically unhealthy families often remain locked into power-oriented parent control, and parents move even more heavily toward an authoritarian posture in their relationships with their adolescents.

The adolescent's quest for autonomy and a sense of responsibility creates puzzlement and conflict for many parents. Parents begin to see their teenagers slipping away from their grasp. Often, the urge is to take stronger control as the adolescent seeks autonomy and personal responsibility. Heated, emotional exchanges may ensue, with either side calling names, making threats, and doing whatever seems necessary to gain control. Parents can become frustrated because they expected their teenager to heed their advice, to want to spend time with the family, and to grow up to do what is right. To be sure, they anticipated that their teenager would have some difficulty adjusting to the changes adolescence brings, but few parents are able to accurately imagine and predict the strength of adolescents' desires to be with their peers and how much they want to show that it is they, not the parents, who are responsible for their success or failure. As discussed in Perspective on Adolescent Development 6.2, some adolescents show such a strong desire to be away from parents that they leave home.

Expectations for adolescents' autonomy sometimes vary from one culture to another. For example, Western adolescents expect to achieve autonomy earlier than Eastern adolescents. In one recent study of 200 tenth- and eleventh-grade students, Hong Kong youth expected to achieve autonomy earlier than their U.S. Caucasian counterparts (Feldman & Rosenthal, 1990a). And Chinese youth who reside in the United States and Australia have later expectations for autonomy than their Western counterparts (Feldman & Rosenthal, 1990b). With such cultural variations in mind, let us examine more closely what autonomy is.

The Complexity of Adolescent Autonomy

Defining adolescent autonomy is more complex and elusive than it might seem at first. For most individuals, the term *autonomy* connotes self-direction and independence. But what does it really mean? Is it an internal personality trait that consistently characterizes the adolescent's immunity from parental influence? Is it the ability to make responsible decisions for oneself? Does autonomy imply consistent behavior in all areas of adolescent life, including school, finances, dating, and peer relations? What are the relative contributions of peers and other adults to the development of the adolescent's autonomy?

It is clear that adolescent autonomy is *not* a unitary personality dimension that consistently comes out in all behaviors (Hill & Holmbeck, 1986). For example, in one investigation, high school students were asked 25 questions about their independence from their families (Psathas, 1957). Four distinct patterns of adolescent autonomy emerged from analyses of the high school students' responses. One dimension was labeled "permissiveness in outside activities" and was represented by such questions as, "Do you have to account to parents for the way you spend your money?" A second dimension was called "permissiveness in age-related activities" and was reflected in such questions as, "Do your parents help you buy your clothes?" A third independent aspect of adolescent autonomy was referred to as "parental regard for judgment," indicated by responses to items like, "In family discussions, do your parents encourage you to give your opinion?" And a fourth dimension was characterized as "activities with status implications" and was indexed by parental influence on choice of occupation.

Parental Attitudes

A number of investigators have studied the relation between parental attitudes and adolescent autonomy. In general, authoritarian parenting is associated with low adolescent autonomy (Hill & Steinberg, 1976). Democratic parenting (much like authoritative parenting) is usually associated with increased adolescent autonomy (Kandel & Lesser, 1969), although findings in this regard are less consistent.

Developmental Views of Autonomy

Two developmental views of adolescent autonomy have been proposed by David Ausubel and Peter Blos. Ausubel's theory emphasizes the role of parent-child relationships in the adolescent's growth toward maturity. He theorizes that parent-child interactions transform the helpless infant into an independent, self-monitoring individual.

Adolescent Runaways

Her name was Barbara, and she came from the hills of West Virginia. She was homely looking, naive, and not very well socialized. A smooth-talking New York pimp told her she was "foxy" and gave her the name "Country Roads." He broke her into a prostitute's life on the streets of New York. One evening she was stabbed to death by a drunk customer who demanded some things of her she did not want to do.

Sammy was 14 years old, a handsome, blue-eyed blond. An older man in Chicago became a father figure to him, in many ways replacing the father Sammy had never had. The older man was, in fact, one of the first adult males to show considerable interest in Sammy. But after repeated, abusive homosexual assaults, Sammy was found by the police lying unconscious in an alley.

Both Barbara and Sammy were runaways. While many runaways are not exposed to the worst elements of street life, as Barbara and Sammy were, these two examples nevertheless illustrate dangers runaways may encounter. Why do these adolescents run away from their homes? Generally, runaways are very unhappy at home (Adams, 1991). The reasons many of them leave seem legitimate by almost anyone's standards. When they run away, they usually do not leave a clue to their whereabouts—they just disappear.

Many runaways are from families in which a parent or another adult beats them or sexually exploits them. Their lives may be in danger daily. Their parents may be drug addicts or alcoholics. In some cases, the family may be so poor that the parents are unable to feed and clothe their teenagers adequately. The parents may be so overburdened by their material inadequacies that they fail to give their adolescents the attention and understanding they need. So teenagers hit the streets in search of the emotional and material rewards they are not getting at home.

But runaways are not all from our society's lower class. Teenage lovers, confronted by parental hostility toward their relationship, may decide to run off together and make it on their own. Or the middle-class teenager may decide that he has seen enough of his hypocritical parents—people who try to make him live by one set of moral standards, while they live by a loose, false set of ideals. Another teen may live with parents who constantly bicker. Any of these adolescents may decide that they would be happier away from home.

Running away often is a gradual process, as adolescents begin to spend less time at home and more time on the streets or with a peer group. The parents may be telling them that they really want to see them, to understand them; but runaways often feel that they are not understood at home and that the parents care much more about themselves (Ek & Steelman, 1988).

These adolescent girls have run away from home. What is it about family relationships that causes adolescents to run away from home? Are there ways society could better serve runaways?

Adolescent runaways are especially susceptible to drug abuse. In one investigation, as part of the National Longitudinal Study of Youth Survey, runaway status at ages 14 to 15 was associated with drug abuse and alcohol problems four years later at ages 18 to 19 (Windle, 1989). Repeat runaways were more likely to be drug abusers than one-time runaways. Both one-time and repeat runaways were more likely to be school dropouts when this was assessed four years later.

Some provision must be made for runaways' physical and psychological well-being. In recent years, nationwide hotlines and temporary shelters for runaways have been established. However, there are still too few of these shelters, and there is often a noted lack of professional psychological help for the runaways at such shelters.

One exception is the temporary shelter in Dallas, Texas, called Casa de los Amigos (house of friends). At the Casa, there is room for 20 runaways, who are provided with the necessities of life as well as medical and legal assistance. In addition, a professional staff of 13 includes counselors and case managers, assisted by VISTA volunteers and high school and college interns. Each runaway is assigned a counselor, and daily group discussion sessions expose the youth to one another's feelings. Whenever possible, the counselors explore the possibility of working with the runaways' families to see if all of the family members can learn to help each other in more competent ways than in the past. It is hoped that more centers like Casa de los Amigos will appear in cities in the United States so that runaways will not meet the fates that Sammy and Barbara encountered.

Ausubel (1958) states that, during infancy, parents cater to their children's needs and demands. Later, parents expect children to do things for themselves—for example, use the toilet, pick up their toys, control their tempers, and so forth. As they develop cognitively, children begin to realize that they are not completely autonomous from their parents. This perception creates some conflict for children and may lead to a crisis wherein their self-esteem is threatened. One way children can resolve this conflict is **satellization,** *Ausubel's term for children's relinquishment of their sense of self-power and their acceptance of their dependency on their parents.*

However, Ausubel believes that many parents are not capable of developing or maintaining a satellizing relationship with their children. For satellization to occur, children must perceive that their parents love them unconditionally, and they must be able to entrust their care to their parents' hands. Two parenting styles that do not produce satellization are overvaluation and rejection. Parents who overvaluate continually interact with their children as if the children are in control. For example, some parents live vicariously through their children and hope that their children will accomplish goals they did not, such as becoming a baseball player or a doctor. When parents reject, they view the child as an unwanted part of their existence. The child's needs are served unwillingly and only if necessary. Love and acceptance are absent, or at least are perceived by the child as being absent.

As children approach adolescence, satellization is eventually replaced by **desatellization**—*Ausubel's term that describes the adolescent process of breaking away and becoming independent from parents.* Total self-rule is not achieved through desatellization. Rather, adolescents move into a preparatory phase wherein their potential separation from parental rule begins to develop. When final desatellization is reached, individuals have secure feelings about themselves and do not demonstrate the need to prove themselves. They show strong exploratory tendencies and focus their energies on tasks and problem solving rather than self-aggrandizement.

Other desatellization mechanisms may occur during adolescence that are unlike the competent form of desatellization just described. In many instances, however, the other mechanisms may be preliminary steps in the adolescent's attainment of the final stage of desatellization. For example, **resatellization** *is Ausubel's term for a preliminary form of desatellization in which the individual's parents are replaced by other individuals or a group.* Resatellized individuals abdicate their identities to their spouse's identity, or to the identity of a fraternity, sorority, or other social group. As a permanent solution to self/other relationships, resatellization can be detrimental to the adolescent's development. But as a temporary solution, it can provide a testing ground for the development of a more complete, autonomous form of desatellization (Berzonsky, 1978).

Peter Blos (1962, 1989), borrowing from Margaret Mahler's ideas about the development of independence during early childhood, introduced the concept of individuation to the study of adolescence. Like Mahler, Blos believes that there is a critical sharpening of the boundaries of the adolescent's self as distinct from others, especially parents. The **second individuation crisis** *is Blos's term for adolescents' development of a distinctiveness from their parents, which he believes is an attempt to transcend earlier parent-child ties and develop more self-responsibility.* Blos's ideas about individuation are reflected in the following comments of Debbie, a girl in late adolescence:

> Up to a certain age, I believed everything my parents said. Then, in college, I saw all these new ideas, and I said, "Okay, now I'm going to make a new Debbie which has nothing to do with my mother and father. I'm going to start with a clean slate," and what I started to put on it were all new ideas. These ideas were

Adolescents make a strong push for independence. As the adolescent pursues autonomy, the wise parent relinquishes control in those areas in which the adolescent makes competent decisions and continues to monitor and guide the adolescent in those areas in which the adolescent is not making mature choices.

opposite to what my parents believed. But slowly, what's happening is that I'm adding on a lot of the things which they've told me, and I'm taking them as my own, and I'm coming more together with them. (Josselson, 1973, p. 37)

Developmental Transition in Autonomy Involved in Going Away to College

Debbie and many other late adolescents experience a transition in the development of autonomy when they leave home and go away to college. The transition from high school to college involves increased autonomy for most individuals (Montemayor & Flannery, 1991). For some, homesickness sets in; for others, sampling the privileges of life without parents hovering around is marvelous. For the growing number of students whose families have been torn by separation and divorce, though, moving away can be especially painful. Adolescents in such families may find themselves in the roles of comforter, confidant, and even caretaker of their parents as well as their siblings. In the words of one college freshman, "I feel responsible for my parents. I guess I shouldn't, but I can't help it. It makes my separation from them, my desire to be free of others' problems, my motivation to pursue my own identity more difficult." For yet other students, the independence of being a college freshman is not always as stressful. According to 18-year-old Brian, "Becoming an adult is kind of hard. I'm having to learn to balance my own checkbook, make my own plane reservations, do my own laundry, and the hardest thing of all is waking up in the morning. I don't have my mother there banging on the door."

In one recent investigation, the psychological separation and adjustment of 130 college freshmen and 123 college upperclassmen were studied (Lapsley, Rice, & Shadid, 1989). As expected, freshmen showed more psychological dependency on their parents and poorer social and personal adjustment than upperclassmen. Female students also showed more psychological dependency on their parents than male students.

Conclusions

In sum, the ability to attain autonomy and gain control over one's behavior in adolescence is acquired through appropriate adult reactions to the adolescent's desire for control. At the onset of adolescence, the average individual does not have the knowledge to make appropriate or mature decisions in all areas of life. As the adolescent pushes for autonomy, the wise adult relinquishes control in those areas in which the adolescent can make reasonable decisions and continues to guide the adolescent in areas in which the adolescent's knowledge is more limited. Gradually, adolescents acquire the ability to make mature decisions on their own. The discussion that follows reveals in greater detail how it is erroneous to view the development of autonomy apart from connectedness to parents.

Attachment

Adolescents do not simply move away from parental influence into a decision-making world all their own. As they become more autonomous, it is psychologically healthy for them to be attached to their parents.

Secure and Insecure Attachment

Attachment theorists such as British psychiatrist John Bowlby (1969, 1989) and American developmental psychologist Mary Ainsworth (1979, 1988) argue that secure attachment in infancy is central to the development of social competence. In **secure attachment,** *infants use the caregiver, usually the mother, as a secure base from which to explore the environment. Secure attachment is theorized to* *be an important foundation for psychological development later in childhood, adolescence, and adulthood.* In **insecure attachment,** *infants either avoid the caregiver or show considerable resistance or ambivalence toward the caregiver. Insecure attachment is theorized to be related to difficulties in relationships and problems in later development.*

In the last decade, developmentalists have begun to explore the role of secure attachment and related concepts, such as connectedness to parents, in adolescent development. They believe that attachment to parents in adolescence may facilitate the adolescent's social competence and well-being, as reflected in such characteristics as self-esteem, emotional adjustment, and physical health (Armsden & Greenberg, 1987; Kobak, 1992; Kobak & others, 1992; Kobak & Sceery, 1988; Papini, Roggman, & Anderson, 1990; Treboux, Crowell, & Colon-Downs, 1992). For example, adolescents who show more satisfaction with help received from parents report more emotional well-being (Burke & Weir, 1979), and adolescents with secure relationships with their parents have higher self-esteem and more emotional well-being (Armsden & Greenberg, 1987). In contrast, emotional detachment from parents is associated with greater feelings of parental rejection and a lower sense of one's own social and romantic attractiveness (Ryan & Lynch, 1989). Thus, attachment to parents during adolescence may serve the adaptive function of providing a secure base from which adolescents can explore and master new environments and a widening social world in a psychologically healthy manner. Secure attachment to parents may buffer adolescents from the anxiety and potential feelings of depression or emotional distress associated with the transition from childhood to adulthood. In one recent study, when young adolescents had a secure attachment to their parents, they perceived their family as cohesive and reported little social anxiety or feelings of depression (Papini, Roggman, & Anderson, 1990).

Secure attachment or connectedness to parents also promotes competent peer relations and positive, close relationships outside of the family. In one investigation in which attachment to parents and peers was assessed, adolescents who were securely attached to parents also were securely attached to peers; those who were insecurely attached to parents also were more likely to be insecurely attached to peers (Armsden & Greenberg, 1984). In another investigation, college students who were securely attached to their parents as young children were more likely to have securely attached relationships with friends, dates, and spouses than their insecurely attached counterparts (Hazen & Shaver, 1987). And in yet another investigation, older adolescents who had an ambivalent attachment history with their parents, reported greater jealousy, conflict, and dependency, along with less satisfaction in their relationship with their best friend than their securely attached counterparts (Fisher, 1990). There are times when adolescents reject closeness, connection, and attachment to their parents as they assert their ability to make decisions and to develop an identity. But for the most part, the worlds of parents and peers are coordinated and connected, not uncoordinated and disconnected (Haynie & McLellan, 1992).

What are some other ways the worlds of parents and peers are connected? Parents' choices of neighborhoods, churches, schools, and their own friends influence the pool from which their adolescents select possible friends (Cooper & Ayers-Lopez, 1985). For example, choice of schools can lead to differences in grouping policies, academic and extracurricular activities, and classroom organization (open, teacher centered, and so on). In turn, such factors affect which students the adolescent is likely to meet, their purpose in interacting, and eventually who become best friends. For instance, classrooms in which teachers encourage more cooperative peer interchanges have fewer isolates.

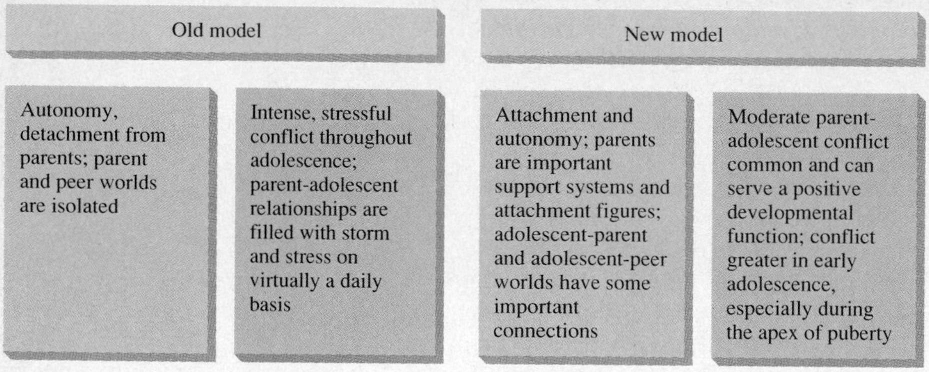

Old model		New model	
Autonomy, detachment from parents; parent and peer worlds are isolated	Intense, stressful conflict throughout adolescence; parent-adolescent relationships are filled with storm and stress on virtually a daily basis	Attachment and autonomy; parents are important support systems and attachment figures; adolescent-parent and adolescent-peer worlds have some important connections	Moderate parent-adolescent conflict common and can serve a positive developmental function; conflict greater in early adolescence, especially during the apex of puberty

Figure 6.4 The old and new models of parent-adolescent relationships.

Parents may model or coach their adolescents in ways of relating to peers. In one study, parents acknowledged that they recommended specific strategies to their adolescents to help them in their peer relations (Rubin & Sloman, 1984). For example, parents discussed with their adolescents ways that disputes could be mediated and how to become less shy. They also encouraged the adolescents to be tolerant and to resist peer pressure. Parents also may coach their adolescents in dating strategies. Sometimes, these discussions are same-sexed, at other times cross-sexed: Mothers may instruct their daughters in how to attract a boy or initiate a relationship, and fathers may instruct their daughters about the type of guys to watch out for, and so on.

Conclusions

In sum, the old model of parent-adolescent relationships suggested that, as adolescents mature, they detach themselves from parents and move into a world of autonomy apart from parents. The old model also suggested that parent-adolescent conflict is intense and stressful throughout adolescence. The new model emphasizes that parents serve as important attachment figures, resources, and support systems as adolescents explore a wider, more complex social world. The new model also emphasizes that, in the majority of families, parent-adolescent conflict is moderate rather than severe and that everyday negotiations and minor disputes are normal, serving the positive developmental function of promoting independence and identity (see Figure 6.4).

So far in our discussion of families, we have focused on parent-adolescent relationships. But there is another aspect to the family worlds of most adolescents—sibling relationships—which we discuss next.

Sibling Relationships

Sandra describes to her mother what happened in a conflict with her sister:

> We had just come home from the ball game. I sat down on the sofa next to the light so I could read. Sally (the sister) said, "Get up. I was sitting there first. I just got up for a second to get a drink." I told her I was not going to get up and that I didn't see her name on the chair. I got mad and started pushing her—her drink spilled all over her. Then she got really mad; she shoved me against the wall, hitting and clawing at me. I managed to grab a handful of hair.

At this point, Sally comes into the room and begins to tell her side of the story. Sandra interrupts, "Mother, you always take her side." Sound familiar? How much does conflict characterize sibling relations? As we examine the roles siblings play in social development, you will discover that conflict is a common dimension of sibling relationships but that siblings also play many other roles in social development (Conger, 1992).

Sibling Roles and Comparisons with Other Social Agents

More than 80 percent of American adolescents have one or more siblings—that is, brothers and sisters. As anyone who has had a sibling knows, the conflict experienced by Sally and Sandra in their relationship with each other is a common interaction style of siblings. However, conflict is only one of the many dimensions of sibling relations. Adolescent sibling relations include helping, sharing, teaching, fighting, and playing, and adolescent siblings can act as emotional supports, rivals, and communication partners (Vandell, 1987).

In some instances, siblings may be stronger socializing influences on the adolescent than parents are (Cicirelli, 1977). Someone close in age to the adolescent—such as a sibling—may be able to understand the adolescent's problems and to communicate more effectively than parents can. In dealing with peers, coping with difficult teachers, and discussing taboo subjects (such as sex), siblings may be more influential in socializing adolescents than parents. Further, in one study, children showed more consistent behavior when interacting with siblings and more varied behavior when interacting with parents (Baskett & Johnson, 1982). In this study, children interacted in much more aggressive ways with their siblings than with their parents. In another study, adolescents reported a higher degree of conflict with their siblings than anyone else (Buhrmester & Furman, 1990).

More than 80 percent of us have one or more siblings. Any of you who have grown up with siblings know that rivalry is a fact of sibling life, as indicated by these two sisters arguing about the phone. But remember, sibling life is not all rivalry. Adolescent siblings also share special moments of caring and trust.

Developmental Changes in Sibling Relationships

While adolescent sibling relations reveal a high level of conflict in comparison to adolescents' relationships with other social agents (parents, peers, teachers, and romantic partners, for example), there is evidence that sibling conflict during adolescence is actually lower than in childhood. In one recent study, the lessened sibling conflict during adolescence was due partly to a drop off in the amount of time siblings spent playing and talking with each other during adolescence (Buhrmester & Furman, 1990). The decline also reflected a basic transformation in the power structure of sibling relationships that seems to occur in adolescence. In childhood, there is an asymmetry of power, with older siblings frequently playing the role of "boss" or caregiver. This asymmetry of power often produces conflicts when one sibling tries to force the other to comply with his or her demands. As younger siblings grow older and their maturity level "catches up" to older siblings', the power asymmetry decreases. As siblings move through adolescence, most learn how to relate to each other on a more equal footing and, in doing so, come to resolve more of their differences than in childhood. Nonetheless, as we said earlier, sibling conflict in adolescence is still reasonably high.

Birth Order

Birth order has been of special interest to sibling researchers, who want to identify the characteristics associated with being born into a particular slot in a family. Firstborns have been described as more adult oriented, helpful, conforming, anxious, and self-controlled, and less aggressive than their siblings. Parental demands and high standards established for firstborns may result in firstborns realizing higher academic and professional achievements than their siblings. For example, firstborns are overrepresented in *Who's Who* and among Rhodes scholars. However, some of the same pressures placed on firstborns for high achievement may be the reason firstborns also have more guilt, anxiety, difficulty in coping with stressful situations, and higher admission to guidance clinics.

Birth order also plays a role in siblings' relationships with each other (Buhrmester & Fuhrman, 1990; Vandell, Minnett, & Santrock, 1987). Older siblings invariably take on the dominant role in sibling interaction, and older siblings report feeling more resentful that parents give preferential treatment to younger siblings.

What are later-borns like? Characterizing later-borns is difficult because they can occupy so many different sibling positions. For example, a later-born might be the second-born male in a family of two siblings or a third-born female in a family of four siblings. In two-child families, the profile of the later-born child is related to the sex of his or her sibling. For example, a boy with an older sister is more likely to develop "feminine" interests than a boy with an older brother. Overall, later-borns usually enjoy better relations with peers than firstborns. Last-borns, who are often described as the "baby" in the family even after they have outgrown infancy, run the risk of becoming overly dependent. Middle-borns tend to be more diplomatic, often performing the role of negotiator in times of dispute (Sutton-Smith, 1982).

The popular conception of the only child is of a "spoiled brat" with such undesirable characteristics as dependency, lack of self-control, and self-centered behavior. But research presents a more positive portrayal of the only child, who often is achievement oriented and displays a desirable personality, especially in comparison to later-borns and children from large families (Falbo & Polit, 1986).

So far our consideration of birth-order effects suggest that birth order might be a strong predictor of adolescent behavior. However, an increasing number of family researchers believe that birth order has been overdramatized and over-emphasized. The critics argue that, when all of the factors that influence adolescence behavior are considered, birth order itself shows limited ability to predict adolescent behavior. Consider just sibling relationships alone. They not only vary in birth order, but also in number of siblings, age of siblings, age spacing of siblings, and sex of siblings.

Consider also the temperament of siblings. Researchers have found that siblings' temperamental traits (such as "easy" and "difficult," for example), as well as differential treatment of siblings by parents, influence how siblings get along (Brody, Stoneman, & Burke, 1987; Stocker, Dunn, & Plomin, 1989). Siblings with "easy" temperaments who are treated in relatively equal ways by parents tend to get along with each other the best, whereas siblings with "difficult" temperaments, or when parents gave one sibling preferential treatment, get along the worst.

Beyond temperament and differential treatment of siblings by parents, think about some of the other important factors in adolescents' lives that influence their behavior beyond birth order. They include heredity, models of competency or incompetency that parents present to adolescents on a daily basis, peer influences, school influences, socioeconomic factors, sociohistorical factors, cultural variations, and so on. When someone says first-borns are always like this, but last-borns are always like that, you now know that they are making overly simplistic statements that do not adequately take into account the complexity of influences on an adolescent's behavior. Keep in mind, though, that, while birth order itself may not be a good predictor of adolescent behavior, sibling relationships and interaction are important dimensions of family processes in adolescence.

We have discussed many aspects of adolescents and their families, but much more remains. Especially important is the nature of the changing family in a changing society.

The Changing Family in a Changing Society

More adolescents are growing up in a greater variety of family structures than ever before in history. Many mothers spend the greater part of their day away from their children. More than one of every two mothers with a child under the age of five, and more than two of every three with a child from 6 to 17 years of age is in the labor force. And the increasing number of children and adolescents who are growing up in single-parent families is staggering (see Figure 6.5). One estimate indicates that 25 percent of the children born between 1910 and 1960 lived in a single-parent family at some time in their childhood or adolescence. However, at least 50 percent of the children born in the 1980s will spend part of their childhood or adolescence in a single-parent family (Glick & Lin, 1986). Further, about 11 percent of all American households now are made up of step-parent families. What are the effects of divorce, of remarriage, and of working parents on adolescents? What role do culture and ethnicity play in parenting? We consider each of these questions in turn.

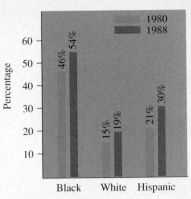

Figure 6.5   Percentage of children under age 18 living with one parent in 1980 and 1988. The percentage of children under age 18 living with one parent increased from 20 percent in 1980 to 24 percent in 1988. The graph reveals the breakdown of single parents in Black, White, and Hispanic families. Note the substantially higher percentage of Black and Hispanic single-parent families.

The Effects of Divorce

What models of how divorce affects adolescents have developmentalists constructed? What are some of the key factors in understanding how divorce influences adolescent development?

Models of Divorce Effects

Two main models have been proposed to explain how divorce affects children's and adolescents' development: the father-absence model and the multiple-factor model. The **father-absence model** *states that, when adolescents from father-absent and father-present families are compared, any differences that occur are attributed to the family structure variations, such as the father being absent in one set of the families.* However, family structure (such as father-present versus father-absent) is only one of many factors that influence the adolescent's development and adjustment in single-parent families. Even when researchers compare the development of adolescents in more precise family structures (such as divorced versus widowed), there are many factors other than family structure that need to be examined to explain the adolescent's development. As we see next, a second model of the effects of divorce on adolescent development goes beyond the overly simplistic family structure father-absence model.

The **multiple-factor model of divorce effects** *takes into account the complexity of the divorce context and examines a number of influences on the adolescent's development, including not only family structure, but also the strengths and weaknesses of the adolescent prior to the divorce, the nature of the events surrounding the divorce itself, the type of custody involved and visitation patterns, socioeconomic status, and post-divorce family functioning.* Researchers are finding that the availability of and use of support systems (relatives, friends, housekeepers), an ongoing positive relationship between the custodial parent and the ex-spouse, authoritative parenting, financial resources, and the adolescent's competencies at the time of the divorce are important factors in how successfully

E. Mavis Hetherington has conducted a number of important research studies on the effects of divorce on children's and adolescents' development. In a recent longitudinal study, Hetherington found that at the onset of adolescence early-maturing girls from divorced families engage in frequent conflict with their mothers, behave in noncompliant ways, have low self-esteem, and experience problems in heterosexual relationships.

the adolescent adapts to the divorce of parents (Barber & Eccles, 1992; Barber & others, 1992; Block, Block, & Gjerde, 1986; Chase-Lansdale & Hetherington, in press; Hetherington, Anderson, & Hagan, 1991; Hetherington & Clingempeel, in press; Santrock & Warshak, 1986; Wallerstein, 1989; Wallerstein & Kelly, 1980). Thus, just as the family structure factor of birth order by itself is not a good predictor of adolescent development, neither is the family structure factor of father absence. In both circumstances—birth order and father absence—there are many other factors that always have to be taken into consideration when explaining the adolescent's development is at issue. Let's further examine what some of those complex factors are in the case of adolescents who experience the divorce of their parents.

Age and Developmental Changes

The age of the child or adolescent at the time of the divorce needs to be considered. Young children's responses to divorce are mediated by their limited cognitive and social competencies, their dependency on parents, and possibly inferior day-care (Hetherington, Hagan, & Anderson, 1989). The cognitive immaturity that creates considerable anxiety for children who are young at the time of their parents' divorce may benefit the children over time. Ten years after the divorce of their parents, adolescents had few memories of their own earlier fears and suffering or their parents' conflict (Wallerstein, Corbin, & Lewis, 1988). Nonetheless, approximately one-third of these children continued to express anger about not being able to grow up in an intact, never-divorced family. Those who were adolescents at the time of their parents' divorce were more likely to remember the conflict and stress surrounding the divorce some 10 years later, in their early adult years. They, too, expressed disappointment at not being able to grow up in an intact family and wondered if their life would not have been better if they had been able to do so. And in one recent study, adolescents who experienced the divorce of their parents during adolescence were more likely to have drug problems than adolescents whose parents were divorced when the adolescents were children or than adolescents living in continuously married families (Needle, Su, & Doherty, 1990).

Recent evaluations of children and adolescents six years after the divorce of their parents by developmental psychologist E. Mavis Hetherington and her colleagues (Hetherington & Clingempeel, in press; Hetherington, Hagan, & Anderson, 1989) found that living in a nonremarried mother-custody home had long-term negative effects on boys, with deleterious outcomes appearing consistently from kindergarten to adolescence. No negative effects on preadolescent girls were found. However, at the onset of adolescence, early-maturing girls from divorced families engaged in frequent conflict with their mothers, behaved in noncompliant ways, had lower self-esteem, and experienced more problems in heterosexual relationships.

Conflict

Many separations and divorces are highly emotional affairs that immerse the adolescent in conflict. Conflict is a critical aspect of family functioning that often outweighs the influence of family structure on the adolescent's development. For example, adolescents in divorced families low in conflict function better than adolescents in intact, never-divorced families high in conflict (Bishop & Ingersoll, 1989; Rutter, 1983; Wallerstein, 1989). Although the escape from conflict that divorce provides may be a positive benefit for adolescents, in the year immediately following the divorce, the conflict does not decline but increases. At this time, adolescents—especially boys—in divorced families show more adjustment problems than adolescents in intact families with both parents present. During the first year after the divorce, the quality of parenting the adolescent experiences is often poor; parents seem to be preoccupied with their own needs and adjustment—experiencing anger, depression, confusion, and emotional instability—which inhibits their ability to respond sensitively to the adolescent's needs. During the second year after the divorce, parents are more effective in their child-rearing duties, especially with daughters (Hetherington & Clingempeel, in press; Hetherington, Cox, & Cox, 1982; Hetherington, Anderson, & Hagan, 1991; Hetherington, Hagan, & Anderson, 1989).

Sex of the Child and the Nature of Custody

The sex of the child or adolescent and the sex of the custodial parent are important considerations in evaluating the effects of divorce on children and adolescents. One research study directly compared 6- to 11-year-old children living in father-custody and mother-custody families (Santrock & Warshak, 1979, 1986). On a number of measures, including videotaped observations of parent-child interaction, children living with the same-sex parent were more socially competent—happier, more independent, higher self-esteem, and more mature—than children living with the opposite-sex parent. Some researchers have recently found support for the same-sex parent-child custodial arrangement (Camara & Resnick, 1988; Furstenberg, 1988), while others have found that, regardless of their sex, adolescents are better adjusted in mother-custody or joint-custody families than in father-custody families (Buchanan & Maccoby, 1990).

In a recent investigation by Christy Buchanan and Eleanor Maccoby (1990), 522 adolescents from 10 to 18 years of age were interviewed by telephone approximately 4½ years after their parents had separated. The adolescents were living in mother-custody, father-custody, or joint-custody families. They were asked about their depression/anxiety, deviant behavior, and grades and effort in school, as well as about various aspects of their family life. The adolescents in father custody reported higher levels of problem behaviors than adolescents in mother- or joint-custody families. Adolescents in joint custody reported the fewest problem behaviors, although other researchers have found no advantage for joint-custody over single-custody arrangements (Kline & others, 1989). It is important to note that in Buchanan and Maccoby's study, adolescents who had been shifted to the father over time were having more problems 4½ years after separation than adolescents who had been with the father all along or adolescents who had never lived with the father. Also, "shifters" (regardless of which type of family they were shifted to) had more problems than adolescents who remained in the same custody across time, and there was a higher proportion of shifters in father custody than other arrangements. In this study, the best predictors of positive adolescent outcomes were the closeness of the adolescent to the custodial parent and the custodial parent's monitoring of the adolescent.

Conclusions

In sum, large numbers of children and adolescents are growing up in divorced families. Most children and adolescents initially experience considerable stress when their parents divorce, and they are at risk for developing problem behaviors. However, divorce can also remove children and adolescents from conflicted marriages. Many children and adolescents emerge from divorce as competent individuals. In recent years, developmentalists have moved away from the view that single-parent families are atypical or pathological, focusing more on the diversity

PERSPECTIVE ON ADOLESCENT DEVELOPMENT 6.3

The Effects of Divorce on Female Adolescents' Heterosexual Behavior

Divorce also influences the adolescent's heterosexual behavior. In an investigation by Mavis Hetherington (1972), adolescent girls with absent fathers acted in one of two extreme ways: They either were very withdrawn, passive, and subdued around males or were overly active, aggressive, and flirtatious. The girls who were inhibited, rigid, and restrained around males were more likely to be from widowed homes; those who sought the attention of males, who showed early heterosexual behavior, and who seemed more open and uninhibited around males were more likely to come from divorced homes.

Several examples of the girls' behavior provide further insight. The girls were interviewed by either a male or a female interviewer. Four chairs were placed in the room, including one for the interviewer. Daughters of the widows more often chose the chair farthest from the male interviewer; daughters of the divorcees more often chose the chair closest to him. There were no differences when the interviewer was female. The girls also were observed at a dance and during activities at a recreation center. At the dance, the daughters of the widows often refused to dance when asked. One widow's daughter spent the entire evening in the restroom. The daughters of the divorcees were more likely to accept the boys' invitation to dance. At the recreation center, the daughters of the divorcees were more frequently observed outside the gym, where boys were playing; the daughters of the widows were more frequently observed in traditional female activities, like sewing and cooking (see Figure 6.A).

Hetherington (1977) continued to study these girls, following them into late adolescence and early adulthood to determine their sexual behavior, marital choices, and marital behavior. The daughters of the divorcees tended to marry younger and select marital partners who were more likely to have poor work histories and drug problems. In contrast, daughters of widows tended to marry males with a more puritanical makeup. In addition, both the daughters of the divorcees and the daughters of the widows reported more sexual adjustment problems than the daughters from the intact homes; for example, the daughters from the homes in which the father was absent had fewer orgasms than daughters from intact homes. The daughters from the intact homes seemed to have worked through their relationships with their fathers and were more psychologically free to deal successfully in their relationships with other males. In contrast, the daughters of the divorcees and the daughters of the widows appeared to be marrying images of their fathers.

Findings such as Hetherington's (1972, 1977) may not hold as the woman's role in society continues to change.

of children's and adolescents' responses to divorce and the factors that facilitate or disrupt the development and adjustment of children and adolescents in these family circumstances (Hetherington, Hagan, & Anderson, 1989). More about the effects of divorce on adolescents appears in Perspective on Adolescent Development 6.3, where a classic investigation by Mavis Hetherington (1972) is discussed. Pay special attention to the observation of the adolescents' behavior in different social contexts, a strategy that needs to be followed much more in investigations of adolescents and their families.

Stepfamilies

The number of remarriages involving children has steadily grown in recent years, although both the rate of increase in divorce and stepfamilies slowed in the 1980s. Stepfather families, in which a woman with custody of children from a previous marriage remarries, make up 70 percent of stepfamilies. Stepmother families make up almost 20 percent of stepfamilies. A small minority are so-called blended families, with both parents bringing children from a previous marriage. A substantial percentage of stepfamilies also produce children of their own.

Research on stepfamilies has lagged behind research on divorced families, but recently a number of investigators have turned their attention to this increas-

Observational variable	Father absent		Father present
	Divorce	Death	
Subject-initiated physical contact and nearness with male peers	3.08	1.71	1.79
Male areas	7.75	2.25	4.71
Female areas	11.67	17.42	14.42

Figure 6.A   The behavior of young, adolescent girls from divorced, widowed, and intact families at a recreation center. Note: The numbers shown are means. Notice that the daughters of divorcees were more likely to initiate contact with males and to spend time in male areas. Notice also that the daughters of the widows were more likely to spend time in female areas of the recreation center.

From E. Mavis Hetherington, "Effects of Faith Absence on Personality Development on Adolescent Daughters" in Developmental Psychology, 7:313–326, 1972. Copyright 1972 by the American Psychological Association. Reprinted by permission.

Also, the findings are from a restricted sample of middle-class families living in one city—the results might not be the same in other subcultures. Nonetheless, Hetherington's results do point to some likely vulnerabilities of adolescent girls growing up in divorced and widowed families. Also, the observations of adolescent behavior in multiple contexts, including laboratory and naturalistic settings provide an excellent model of research on family processes in adolescence. We need more research studies of adolescent development that are based on observations in multiple settings.

ingly common family structure (Anderson, 1992; Bray, 1988; Hetherington & Clingempeel, in press; Hetherington, Hagan, & Anderson, 1989; Lindner, 1992; Lyons & Barber, 1992; Needle, Su, & Doherty, 1990; Santrock & Sitterle, 1987). Following remarriage, children of all ages show a resurgence of problem behaviors. Often younger children eventually form an attachment to a stepparent and accept the stepparent in a parenting role. However, the developmental tasks facing adolescents make them especially vulnerable to the entrance of a stepparent. At the time they are searching for an identity and exploring sexual and close relationships outside the family, a nonbiological parent may increase the stress associated with the accomplishment of these important tasks.

Following the remarriage of the custodial parent, emotional upheaval in girls reemerges and problems in boys often intensify. Over time, preadolescent boys often improve more than girls in stepfather families. Sons who frequently are involved in conflicted, coercive relations with their custodial mothers likely have much to gain from the introduction of a warm, supportive stepfather. In contrast, daughters who frequently have a close relationship with their custodial mothers and considerable independence may find a stepfather disruptive and constraining.

Children's relationships with biological parents are more positive than with stepparents, regardless of whether a stepmother or a stepfather family is involved. Stepfathers often have a distant, disengaged relationship with their step-children. And as a rule, the more complex the stepfamily, the more difficult the children's adjustment. For example, families in which both parents bring children from a previous marriage are associated with the highest level of behavioral problems.

In sum, as with divorce, entrance into a stepfamily involves a disequilibrium in children's and adolescents' lives. Most children and adolescents experience their parent's remarriage as stressful. Remarriage, though, can remove children and adolescents from stressful single-parent circumstances and provide them with additional resources. Many children and adolescents emerge from their remarried family as competent individuals. As with divorced families, it is important to consider the complexity of stepfamilies, the diversity of possible outcomes, and the factors that facilitate children's and adolescents' adjustment in stepfamilies (Hetherington & Clingempeel, in press; Santrock, Sitterle, & Warshak, 1988; Vishner & Vishner, 1992).

Now that we have considered the changing social worlds of adolescents when their parents divorce and remarry, we turn our attention to another aspect of the changing family worlds of adolescents—the situation when both parents work.

Working Parents

Interest in the effects of parental work on the development of children and adolescents has increased in recent years. Our examination of parental work focuses on the following issues: the role of working mothers in adolescents' development, the adjustment of latchkey adolescents, the effects of relocation on adolescent development, and the influence of unemployment on adolescents' lives.

Working Mothers

Most of the research on parental work has focused on young children. Little attention has been given to early adolescence, even though it is during this period that many mothers return to full-time work, in part due to presumed independence of their young adolescents (Hoffman, 1989; Lerner & Hess, 1991; Orthner, 1990). One factor that may be affected by parental work is the amount of time that adolescents have available for various family and community activities. While some studies have found no differences in the number of family activities engaged in by families with and without employed mothers (Dellas, Gaier, & Emihovich, 1979), others have found that adolescents with employed mothers spend less time in family activities (Montemayor, 1984). In another investigation, adolescents with employed mothers spent less time in community-related activities, possibly due to the lack of transportation available because their mothers worked (Keith & others, 1990).

Gender differences have sometimes been associated with parental work patterns. In some studies, no gender differences are found, but in others, maternal employment has greater benefits for adolescent daughters than sons (Law, 1992; Montemayor & Clayton, 1983), and in yet others, adolescent sons benefit academically and emotionally when they identify with the work patterns of their fathers more than their mothers (Armistead, Wierson, & Forehand, 1990; Orthner, Giddings, & Quinn, 1987).

While some investigators have found associations between parental work status and adolescent behavior or well-being, most researchers have not (Bird & Kemerait, 1990; Galambos & Maggs, 1990; Lerner, Jacobson, & del Gaudio, 1992; Orthner, 1990). As one of the leading authorities on maternal employment, Lois Hoffman (1989), states, maternal employment is a fact of modern life. It is not an aberrant aspect of it, but a response to other social changes that meets the needs not met by the previous family ideal of a full-time mother and homemaker. Not only does it meet the parents' needs, but in many ways, it may be a pattern better suited to socializing children for the adult roles they will occupy. This is especially true for daughters, but for sons, too. The broader range of emotions and skills that each parent presents is more consistent with this adult role. Just as the father shares the breadwinning role and the child-rearing role with the mother, so the son, too, will be more likely to share these roles. The rigid gender-role stereotyping perpetuated by the divisions of labor in the traditional family is not appropriate for the demands children of both sexes will have made on them as adults. The needs of the growing child require the mother to loosen her hold on the child, and this task may be easier for the working woman whose job is an additional source of identity and self-esteem.

Latchkey Adolescents

While the mother's working is not associated with negative outcomes for adolescents, a certain set of adolescents from working-mother families bears further scrutiny—those called latchkey adolescents. Latchkey adolescents typically do not see their parents from the time they leave for school in the morning until about 6:00 or 7:00 P.M. They are called latchkey children or adolescents because they often are given the key to their home, take the key to school, and let themselves into the home while their parents are still at work. Many latchkey adolescents are largely unsupervised for two to four hours a day during each school week, or for entire days, five days a week, during the summer months.

Thomas and Lynette Long (1983) interviewed more than 1,500 latchkey children. They concluded that a slight majority of these children had negative latchkey experiences. Some latchkey children may grow up too fast, hurried by the responsibility placed on them (Elkind, 1981). How do latchkey children handle the lack of limits and structure during the latchkey hours? Without limits and parental supervision, it becomes easier for latchkey children and adolescents to find their way into trouble—possibly abusing a sibling, stealing, or vandalizing. The Longs found that 90 percent of the adjudicated juvenile delinquents in Montgomery County, Maryland, were from latchkey families. In another investigation of more than 4,900 eighth graders in Los Angeles and San Diego, those who cared for themselves 11 hours a week or more were twice as likely to have abused alcohol and other drugs than their counterparts who did not care for themselves at all before or after school (Richardson & others, 1989). Adolescent expert Joan Lipsitz (1983), testifying before the Select Committee on Children, Youth, and Families, called the lack of adult supervision of children and adolescents in the after-school hours one of the nation's major problems. Lipsitz called it the "3:00 to 6:00 P.M. problem" because it was during this time frame that the Center for Early Adolescence in North Carolina, where she was director, experienced a peak of adolescent referrals for clinical help.

But while latchkey adolescents may be vulnerable to problems, keep in mind that the experiences of latchkey adolescents vary enormously, just as do the experiences of all children with working mothers (Belle & Burr, 1992). Parents need to give special attention to the ways their latchkey adolescents' lives can be monitored effectively. Variations in latchkey experiences suggest that parental monitoring and authoritative parenting help the adolescent to cope more effectively with latchkey experiences, especially in resisting peer pressure (Galambos & Maggs, 1989; Steinberg, 1986). The degree to which latchkey adolescents are at developmental risk remains unsettled. A positive sign is that researchers are beginning to conduct more precise analysis of adolescents' latchkey experiences in an effort to determine which aspects of latchkey circumstances are the most detrimental and which aspects foster better adaptation (Rodman, Pratto, & Nelson, 1988; Steinberg, 1988).

Relocation

Geographical moves or relocations are a fact of life for many American families. The U.S. Census Bureau estimates that 17 percent of the population changes residences on a yearly basis (U.S. Bureau of the Census, 1986). This figure does not include multiple moves within the same year, so it may even underestimate the mobility of the U.S. population. The majority of these moves are made because of job demands (Cook & others, 1992). Moving can be especially stressful for children and adolescents, disrupting friendship ties and adolescent activities (Brown & Orthner, 1990). The sources of support to which adolescents and their parents turn, such as extended-family members and friends, are often unavailable to recently moved families.

While relocations are often stressful for all individuals involved, they may be especially stressful for adolescents because of their developing sense of identity and the importance of peer relations in their lives. In one recent study, geographical relocation was detrimental to the well-being of 12- to 14-year-old females but not their male counterparts (Brown & Orthner, 1990). The adolescent girls' life satisfaction was negatively related to both recent moves and to a high number of moves in their history, and a history of frequent moves was also associated with the girls' depression. However, the immediate negative effects on the girls disappeared over time. The researchers concluded that female adolescents may require more time to adapt to family relocations. Male adolescents may use sports and other activities in their new locale to ease the effects of relocation.

Unemployment

Unemployment rates and economic distress in the last decade reached levels unknown since the Great Depression. Plant closings, layoffs, and demotions are facts of life for many contemporary parents. What effects do they have on families and adolescents' development? During the Great Depression, unemployment dramatically increased parental stress and undermined the school achievement and health of children and adolescents (Angell, 1936; Elder, 1974). In one recent investigation, the interactions of work status, family integration, and sex of young adolescents on parent-adolescent decision making were studied (Flanagan, 1990 a,b). *Deprived* families reported a layoff or demotion at time 1 but no recovery by two years later. *Recovery* families reported similar work losses at time 1 but reemployment by two years later. *Nondeprived* families reported stable employment across the two-year period. Young adolescents in deprived families reported the highest conflict with parents. Adolescents in recovery families reported high conflict when parents were unemployed, but levels declined when parents were reemployed. In sum, unemployment increases the stress of parents and has negative effects on adolescent development.

Culture and Ethnicity

Cultures vary on a number of issues involving families, such as what the father's role in the family should be, the extent to which support systems are available to families, and how children should be disciplined. Although there are cross-cultural variations in parenting (Whiting & Edwards, 1988), in one study of parenting behavior in 186 cultures around the world, the most common pattern was a warm and controlling style, one that was neither permissive nor restrictive (Roher & Roher, 1981). The investigators commented that the majority of cultures have discovered, over many centuries, a "truth" that only recently emerged in the Western world—namely, that children's and adolescents' healthy social development is most effectively promoted by love and at least some moderate parental control.

Ethnic minority families differ from White American families in their size, structure, and composition, their reliance on kinship networks, and their levels of income and education (Spencer & Dornbusch, 1990). Large and extended families are more common among ethnic minority groups than White Americans (Wilson, 1989). For example, more than 30 percent of Hispanic American families consist of five or more individuals (Keefe & Padilla, 1987). Black American and Hispanic American adolescents interact more with grandparents, aunts, uncles, cousins, and more distant relatives than do White American adolescents.

As we saw earlier in our discussion of divorce, single-parent families are more common among Black Americans and Hispanic Americans than among White Americans. In comparison with two-parent households, single-parent households often have more limited resources of time, money, and energy. This shortage of resources may prompt them to encourage early autonomy among their adolescents (Spencer & Dornbusch, 1990). Also, ethnic minority parents are less well educated and engage in less joint decision making than White American parents. And ethnic minority adolescents are more likely to come from low-income families than White American adolescents (Committee for Economic Development, 1987; McLoyd, in press). Although impoverished families often raise competent youth, poor parents may have a diminished capacity for supportive and involved parenting (McLoyd, in press).

Some aspects of home life can help to protect ethnic minority youth from social patterns of injustice (Spencer & Dornbush, 1990). The community and family can filter out destructive racist messages, parents can provide alternate frames of reference than those presented by the majority, and parents can also provide competent role models and encouragement (Bowman & Howard, 1985; Jones, 1990). And the extended-family system in many ethnic minority families provides an important buffer to stress (Munsch, Wampler, & Dawson, 1992). The extended-family system in Black American and Hispanic American families is addressed in Sociocultural Worlds of Adolescence 6.1.

At this point, we have discussed a number of ideas about autonomy and attachment, sibling relationships, and the changing family in a changing society. A summary of these ideas is presented in Concept Table 6.2. Earlier in this chapter, we found that adolescents' family and peer worlds are more connected than once was believed. In the next chapter, we explore the fascinating world of adolescent peer relations in greater detail.

The Extended Family System in Black American and Hispanic American Families

A fourteen-year-old adolescent, his 6-year-old sister, and their grandmother. The Black cultural tradition of an extended family household has helped many Black parents cope with adverse social conditions.

The Hispanic family reunion of the Limon family in Austin, Texas. Hispanic American children often grow up in families with a network of relatives that runs into scores of individuals.

The Black cultural tradition of an extended family household—in which one or several grandparents, uncles, aunts, siblings, or cousins either live together or provide support—has helped many Black parents cope with adverse social conditions, such as economic impoverishment (Harrison & others, 1990; McAdoo, 1988; Reid, 1991). The extended-family tradition can be traced to the African heritage of many Black Americans, in which a newly married couple does not move away from relatives. Instead, the extended family assists its members with basic family functions. Researchers have found that the extended Black family helps to reduce the stress of poverty and single parenting through emotional support, the sharing of income and economic responsibility, and surrogate parenting (Allen & Majidi-Ahi, 1989; McAdoo, 1988; Wilson, 1989). The presence of grandmothers in the households of many Black adolescents and their infants has been an important support system both for the mothers and their infants (Stevens, 1984).

Active and involved extended-family support systems also help parents of other ethnic groups cope with poverty and its related stress. A basic value in Mexico is represented by the saying "As long as our family stays together, we are strong." Mexican children are brought up to stay close to their families, often playing with siblings rather than with schoolmates or neighborhood children, as American children usually do. Unlike the father in many American families, the Mexican father is the undisputed authority on all family matters and is usually obeyed without question. The mother is revered as the primary source of affection and care. This emphasis on family attachment leads the Mexican to say, "I will achieve mainly because of my family, and for my family, rather than myself." By contrast, the self-reliant American would say, "I will achieve mainly because of my ability and initiative and for myself rather than for my family." Unlike most Americans, families in Mexico tend to stretch out in a network of relatives that often runs to scores of individuals (Busch-Rossnagal & Zayas, 1991).

Both cultures—Mexican and American—have undergone considerable change in recent decades. Whether Mexican adolescents will gradually take on the characteristics of American adolescents, or whether American adolescents will shift closer to Mexican adolescents, is difficult to predict. The cultures of both countries will probably move to a new order more in keeping with future demands, retaining some common features of the old while establishing new priorities and values (Holtzmann, 1982).

Concept Table 6.2

Autonomy and Attachment, Sibling Relationships, and the Changing Family in a Changing Society

Concept	Processes/Related Ideas	Characteristics/Description
Autonomy and attachment	Autonomy	Many parents have a difficult time handling the adolescent's push for autonomy. Autonomy is a complex concept with multiple referents. Democratic parenting is associated with adolescent autonomy. Two important developmental views of autonomy have been proposed by Ausubel (desatellization) and Blos (individuation). A developmental transition in autonomy occurs when individuals leave home and go away to college. The wise parent relinquishes control in areas where the adolescent makes mature decisions and retains more control over areas in which the adolescent's knowledge is more limited.
	Attachment	Adolescents do not simply move away into a world isolated from parents. Attachment to parents increases the probability that the adolescent will be socially competent and explore a widening social world in healthy ways. The social worlds of parents and peers are coordinated and connected.
Siblings	Sibling roles and comparisons with other social agents	Sibling relationships often involve more conflict than relationships with other individuals. However, adolescents also share many positive moments with siblings through emotional support and social communication.
	Developmental changes	While sibling conflict in adolescence is reasonably high, it is, nonetheless, often lower than in childhood.
	Birth order	Birth order has been of special interest and differences between first-borns and later-borns have been reported. The only child often shows greater competence than the stereotype of the spoiled only child suggests. However, an increasing number of family researchers believe that the effects of birth order have been overdramatized and that other factors are more important in predicting the adolescent's behavior.
The changing family in a changing society	Divorce	Two main models of divorce effects have been proposed: the father-absence model and the multiple-factor model. The father-absence model that emphasizes only family structure effects is overly simplistic. The contemporary multiple-factor model takes into account the complexity of the divorce context, including conflict and post-divorce family functioning. Among the important factors in understanding the effects of divorce on adolescents are age and developmental changes, conflict, sex of the child, and the nature of custody. In recent years, developmentalists have moved away from the model of single-parents as atypical or pathological, focusing more on the diversity of adolescents' responses to divorce and the factors that facilitate or disrupt the adjustment of adolescents in these family circumstances.
	Stepfamilies	Just as divorce produces disequilibrium and stress for adolescents, so does remarriage. Over time, preadolescent boys seem to improve more than girls in stepfather families. Adolescence is an especially difficult time for adjustment to the entrance of a stepparent. Children's relationships with biological parents are consistently better than with stepparents, and children's adjustment is adversely affected the more complex the stepfamily becomes.
	Working parents	Overall, the mother working outside the home does not have an adverse effect on the adolescent's development. Latchkey experiences do not have a uniformly negative influence on adolescent development. Parental monitoring and participation in structured activities with competent supervision are important influences on latchkey adolescents' adjustment. Relocation may have a more adverse effect on adolescents than children, but research on this issue is sparse. Unemployment of parents has a detrimental effect on adolescent development.
	Culture and ethnicity	Authoritative parenting is the most common child-rearing pattern around the world. Ethnic minority families differ from White American families in their size, structure, and composition; their reliance on kinship networks; and their levels of income and education.

Summary

I. Reciprocal Socialization, Synchrony, the Family As a System, and the Construction of Relationships

Reciprocal socialization is the principle which states that adolescents socialize parents, just as parents socialize adolescents. Synchrony is an important dimension of reciprocal socialization and refers to the carefully coordinated interaction between the parent and the child or adolescent in which they are attuned to each other's behavior. The family is a system of interacting individuals with different subsystems—some dyadic, others polyadic. Belsky's model describes direct and indirect effects of interaction between adolescents and their parents. The developmental construction views share the belief that as individuals grow up they acquire modes of relating to others. There are two main variations within this view, one of which emphasizes continuity and stability in relationships through the life span (called the continuity view) and one of which emphasizes discontinuity and change in relationships through the life span (called the discontinuity view).

II. Maturation of the Adolescent, Maturation of Parents, and Sociocultural, Historical Changes

The adolescent changes involved include puberty, expanded logical reasoning, increased idealistic and egocentric thought, violated expectations, changes in schooling, peers, friendships, dating, and movement toward independence. Parental changes are associated with midlife—marital dissatisfaction, economic burdens, career reevaluation and time perspective, and health and body concerns. Sociocultural and historical changes in families may be due to great upheavals, such as war, or more subtle changes, such as television and the mobility of families.

III. Parenting Techniques and Parent-Adolescent Conflict

Authoritarian, authoritative, permissive-indifferent, and permissive-indulgent are four main parenting categories. Authoritative parenting is associated with adolescents' social competence more than the other styles. Caveats in understanding parenting styles focus on reciprocal socialization, multiple use of techniques, and few data collected on adolescents. Conflict with parents increases in early adolescence. Such conflict usually is moderate, an increase that can serve the positive developmental function of promoting autonomy and identity. However, as much as 20 percent of parent-adolescent relationships involve intense conflict, which is associated with a number of adolescent problems.

IV. Autonomy and Attachment

Many parents have a difficult time handling the adolescent's push for autonomy. Autonomy is a complex concept with multiple referents. Democratic parenting is associated with adolescent autonomy. Two important developmental views of autonomy have been proposed by Ausubel (desatellization) and Blos (individuation). A developmental transition in autonomy occurs when individuals leave home and go away to college. The wise parent relinquishes control in areas where the adolescent makes mature decisions and retains more control over areas in which the adolescent's knowledge is more limited. Adolescents do not simply move away into a world isolated from parents. Attachment to parents increases the probability that adolescents will be socially competent and explore a widening social world in healthy ways. The social worlds of parents and peers are coordinated and connected.

V. Sibling Relationships

Sibling relationships often involve more conflict than relationships with other people. However, adolescents also share many positive moments with siblings through emotional support and social communication. While sibling conflict in adolescence is reasonably high, it is, nonetheless, often lower than in childhood. Birth order has been of special interest and differences between first-borns and later-borns have been reported. The only child often shows greater competence than the stereotype of the spoiled only child suggests. However, an increasing number of family researchers believe that the effects of birth order have been overdramatized and that other factors are more important in predicting the adolescent's behavior.

VI. Divorce

Two main models of divorce effects have been proposed: the father-absence model and the multiple-factors model. The father-absence model that emphasizes only family structure effects is overly simplistic. The contemporary multiple-factors model takes into account the complexity of the divorce context, including conflict and post-divorce family functioning. Among the important factors in understanding the effects of divorce on adolescents are age and developmental change, conflict, sex of the adolescent, and the nature of custody. In recent years, developmentalists have moved away from the model of single parents as atypical or pathological, focusing more on the diversity of adolescents' responses to divorce and the factors that facilitate or disrupt the adjustment of adolescents in these family circumstances.

VII. Stepfamilies

Just as divorce produces disequilibrium and stress for adolescents, so does remarriage. Over time, preadolescent boys seem to improve more than girls in stepfather families. Adolescence appears to be an especially difficult time for adjustment to the entrance of a stepparent. Children's relationships with biological parents are consistently better than with stepparents, and children's adjustment is adversely affected the more complex the stepfamily becomes.

VIII. Working Parents

Overall, the mother working outside the home does not have an adverse effect on the adolescent's development. Neither do latchkey experiences, although parental monitoring and participation in structured activities with competent supervision are important influences on latchkey adolescents' adjustment. Relocation may have a more adverse effect on adolescents than children, but research on this issue is sparse. Unemployment of parents has a detrimental effect on the adolescent's development.

IX. Culture and Ethnicity

Authoritative parenting is the most common child-rearing pattern around the world. Ethnic minority families differ from White American families in their size, structure, and composition, their reliance on kinship networks, and their levels of income and education.

Key Terms

reciprocal socialization 187
synchrony 188
developmental construction views 189
continuity view 189
discontinuity view 190
authoritarian parenting 195

authoritative parenting 195
permissive-indifferent parenting 195
permissive-indulgent parenting 196
satellization 203
desatellization 203
resatellization 203

second individuation crisis 203
secure attachment 204
insecure attachment 205
father-absence model 209
multiple-factor model of divorce effects 209

Suggested Readings

Farel, A. M. (1982). *Early adolescence: What parents need to know.* Carrboro, NC: Center for Early Adolescence.
This brief, 37-page handbook for the parents of adolescents offers wise advice for responding to the changes of early adolescence.

Hartup, W. W., & Zubin, R. (1986). *Relationships and development.* Hillsdale, NJ: Erlbaum.
This compendium of articles by leading experts gives insight into the new look in carrying forward relationships in families. Pays special attention to the role of development in family relationships.

Hetherington, E. M., Hagan, M. S., & Anderson, E. R. (1989). Marital transitions: a child's perspective. *American Psychologist, 44,* 303–312.
Hetherington is a leading researcher in studying the effects of divorce on children's development. In this article, she and her colleagues review the recent literature on divorce, giving special attention to transitions in divorced and stepparent families.

Journal of Early Adolescence, Spring 1985, vol. 5, no. 1.
The entire issue is devoted to contemporary approaches to the study of families with adolescents. Includes articles by Catherine Cooper and Susan Ayers-Lopez on the connectedness of adolescents and their families, by Raymond Montemayor on parent-adolescent conflict, by John Hill and his colleagues on pubertal status and parent-adolescent relationships, as well as many others.

Journal of Early Adolescence, August 1990, vol. 10, no. 3.
This issue is devoted to the effects of working parents on adolescent development and provides an up-to-date review of what is currently known about this topic.

CHAPTER 7

Peers

A man's growth is seen in the successive choirs of his friends.

Ralph Waldo Emerson, 1841

You Jerk!

"You jerk, what are you trying to do to me," Jess yelled at his teacher. "I got no use for this school and people like you. Leave me alone and quit hassling me."

Jess is 10 years old and has already had more than his share of confrontations with society. He has been arrested three times for stealing, been suspended from school twice, and has a great deal of difficulty getting along with people in social circumstances. He particularly has difficulty with authority figures. No longer able to cope with his outbursts in class, his teacher recommended that he be suspended from school once again. The principal was aware of a different kind of school she thought might help Jess.

Jess began attending the Manville School, a clinic in the Judge Baker Guidance Center in Boston for learning-disabled and emotionally disturbed children 7 to 15 years of age. Jess, like many other students at the Manville School, has shown considerable difficulty in interpersonal relationships, since peer relationships become a crucial aspect of development during the elementary school years. Robert Selman has designed a peer therapy program at the Manville School to help students like Jess to improve their peer relations in classroom settings, group activities, and sports (Selman, Newberger, & Jacquette, 1977). The staff at the Manville School has been trained to help peers provide support and encouragement to one another in such group settings.

Structured programs at the Manville School are designed to help adolescents assist one another to become more cooperative, to develop trust, to become leaders, and to understand conformity. Four school activities were developed to improve students' social reasoning skills in these areas:

First, there is a weekly peer problem-solving session in the classroom in which the peers work cooperatively to plan activities and relate problems. At the end of each week, the peers evaluate their effectiveness in making improvements in areas like cooperation, conflict resolution, and so forth.

Second, the members of a class, numbering from six to eight students, plan a series of weekly field trips—for example, going to the movies or visiting historical sites. While the counselor provides some assistance, peer decision making dominates. When each activity is completed, the students discuss how things went and what might have been done to improve social relations with one another on the outings.

Third, Selman recognizes that there are times when students need to get away from a setting in which they are experiencing intense frustration. When students find themselves in highly frustrating circumstances (for example, they are angry enough to strike out at a classmate), they are allowed to leave the schoolroom and go to a private "time-out" area of the school to regain their composure. In time-out, students also are given the opportunity to discuss the problems with a counselor who has been trained to help adolescents improve their social reasoning skills.

Fourth, during social studies and current events discussion sessions, students evaluate a number of moral and social issues.

We like to read others, but we do not like to be read.

La Rouchefoucauld, Maxims, *1665*

T he power of peer relations in adolescent development is recognized in the structured John Manville School program just described. When you think back to your adolescent years, many of your most enjoyable moments were spent with peers—on the telephone, at school activities, in the neighborhood, on dates, at dances, or just fooling around.

The nature of peer relationships undergoes important changes during adolescence (Buhrmester, 1992). In childhood, the focus of peer relations is often on being liked by classmates and being included in playground games or lunchroom conversations. Being overlooked, or worse yet, being disliked and rejected by classmates, can have damaging effects on children's psychological development that are sometimes carried forward to adolescence. Beginning in early adolescence, teenagers typically prefer to have a smaller number of friendships that are more intense and intimate than those of younger children. Cliques, or crowds, usually take on more important roles in adolescence, as adolescents begin to "hang out" together. At some point in adolescence, individuals usually become interested in dating and romantic relationships. In this chapter, we will examine such fascinating aspects of the society of peers, a society that involves peer relations, friendships, peer groups, and dating, each of which we study in turn.

The Nature of Peer Relations

What are the peer group's functions? How extensively do adolescents conform to their peers? What is the nature of peer popularity, neglect, and rejection? What is the role of social knowledge and social information processing in peer relations? What strategies do developmentalists use to improve the social skills of adolescents who are having difficulty in peer relations? We consider each of these questions in turn.

Peer Group Functions

To many adolescents, how they are seen by peers is the most important aspect of their lives. Some adolescents will go along with anything, just to be included as a member of the group. To them, being excluded means stress, frustration, and sadness. Contrast Bob, who has no close friends, with Steve, who has three close buddies he pals around with all of the time. Sally was turned down by the club at school that she was working to get into for six months, in contrast to Sandra, who is a member of the club and who frequently is told by her peers how "super" her personality is.

Some friends of mine have a 13-year-old daughter. Last year, she had a number of girlfriends—she spent a lot of time on the phone talking with them, and they frequently visited each other's homes. Then her family moved, and this 13-year-old girl had to attend a school with a lower socioeconomic mix of students than at her previous school. Many of the girls at the new school feel that my friends' daughter is "too good" for them, and because of this, she is having difficulty making friends this year. One of her most frequent complaints is, "I don't have any friends. . . . None of the kids at school ever call me. And none of them ever ask me over to their houses. What can I do?"

Peers *are children or adolescents who are about the same age or maturity level.* Same-age peer interaction serves a unique role in U.S. culture (Hartup, 1983). Age grading would occur even if schools were not age graded and adolescents were left alone to determine the composition of their own societies. After all, one can only learn to be a good fighter among age-mates: The bigger guys will kill you, and the little ones are no challenge. One of the most important functions of the peer group is to provide a source of information about the world outside the family. From the peer group, adolescents receive feedback about their abilities. Adolescents learn whether what they do is better than, as good as, or worse than what other adolescents do. Learning this at home is difficult because siblings are usually older or younger.

Children spend an increasing amount of time in peer interaction during middle and late childhood and adolescence (Berndt & Ladd, 1989). In one investigation, children interacted with peers 10 percent of their day at age 2, 20 percent at age 4, and more than 40 percent between the ages of 7 and 11 (Barker & Wright, 1951). In a typical school day, there were 299 episodes with peers per day. By adolescence, peer relations occupy large chunks of an individual's life. In one investigation, over the course of one weekend, young adolescent boys and girls spent more than twice as much time with peers as with parents (Condry, Simon, & Bronfenbrenner, 1968).

What do adolescents do when they are with their peers? In one study, sixth graders were asked what they do when they are with their friends (Medrich & others, 1982). Team sports accounted for 45 percent of boys' nominations but only 26 percent of girls'. General play, going places, and socializing were common listings for both sexes. Most peer interactions occur outside the home (although close to home), occur more often in private than public places, and occur more between children in the same sex than the opposite sex.

Are peers necessary for development? When peer monkeys who have been reared together are separated from one another, they become depressed and less advanced socially (Suomi, Harlow, & Domek, 1970). The human development literature contains a classic example of the importance of peers in social development. Anna Freud (Freud & Dann, 1951) studied six children from different families who banded together after their parents were killed in World War II. Intensive peer attachment was observed; the children were a tightly knit group, dependent on one another and aloof with outsiders. Even though deprived of parental care, they became neither delinquent nor psychotic.

Good peer relations may be necessary for normal social development in adolescence. Social isolation, or the inability to "plug in" to a social network, is linked with many different forms of problems and disturbances, ranging from delinquency and problem drinking to depression (Cairns & Cairns, 1989; Dishion & Skinner, 1989; Kupersmidt & Coie, 1990; Simons, Conger, & Wu, 1992). In one investigation, poor peer relations in childhood were related to dropping out of school and delinquency in late adolescence (Roff, Sells, & Golden, 1972). In another investigation, harmonious peer relations in adolescence were related to positive mental health at midlife (Hightower, 1990).

As you might have detected from our discussion of peer relations thus far, peer influences can be both positive and negative. Both Jean Piaget (1932) and Harry Stack Sullivan (1953) were influential theorists who stressed that it is through peer interaction that children and adolescents learn the symmetrical reciprocity mode of relationships discussed in chapter 6. Children explore the principles of fairness and justice by working through disagreements with peers. They also learn to be keen observers of peers' interests and perspectives in order to smoothly integrate themselves into ongoing peer activities. In addition, Sullivan argued that adolescents learn to be skilled and sensitive partners in intimate relationships by forging close friendships with selected peers. These intimacy skills are carried forward to help form the foundation of later dating and marital relationships, according to Sullivan.

By contrast, some theorists have emphasized the negative influences of peers on children's and adolescents' development. Being rejected or overlooked by peers leads some adolescents to feel lonely or hostile. Further, such rejection and neglect by peers are related to an individual's subsequent mental health and criminal problems. Some theorists have also described the adolescent peer culture as a corrupt influence that undermines parental values and control. Further, peers can introduce adolescents to alcohol, drugs, delinquency, and other forms of behavior that adults view as maladaptive. Next, we further discuss the important role of peers in adolescent development by considering the nature of peer conformity.

Peer Conformity

The words of Solon in Ancient Greece reflect the importance of conformity in adolescents' lives: "Each of you, individually, walketh with the tread of a fox, but collectively, ye are geese." Conformity comes in many forms and affects many aspects of adolescents' lives. Do adolescents take up jogging because everyone else is doing it? Do adolescents let their hair grow long one year and cut it short the next because of fashion? Do adolescents take cocaine if pressured by others, or do they resist the pressure? **Conformity** *occurs when individuals adopt the attitudes or behavior of others because of real or imagined pressure from them.* The pressure to conform to peers becomes very strong during the adolescent years. Consider the comments of Kevin, an eighth grader:

Peer conformity becomes especially strong during the early adolescent years, as reflected in the uniform dress and behavior of these young adolescent "Madonnas."

> I feel a lot of pressure from my friends to smoke and steal and things like that. My parents do not allow me to smoke, but my best friends are really pushing me to do it. They call me a pansy and a momma's boy if I don't. I really don't like the idea of smoking, but my good friend Steve told me in front of some of our friends, "Kevin, you are an idiot and a chicken wrapped up in one little body." I couldn't stand it any more, so I smoked with them. I was coughing and humped over, but I still said, "This is really fun—yeah, I like it." I felt like I was part of the group.

Also, think about the statement by 14-year-old Andrea:

> Peer pressure is extremely influential in my life. I have never had very many friends, and I spend quite a bit of time alone. The friends I have are older. . . . The closest friend I have had is a lot like me in that we are both sad and depressed a lot. I began to act even more depressed than before when I was with her. I would call her up and try to act even more depressed than I was because that is what I thought she liked. In that relationship, I felt pressure to be like her. . . .

Conformity to peer pressure in adolescence can be positive or negative (Camarena, 1991; Foster-Clark & Blyth, 1991; Pearl, Bryan, & Herzog, 1990). Teenagers engage in all sorts of negative conformity behavior—use seedy language, steal, vandalize, and make fun of parents and teachers. However, a great deal of peer conformity is not negative and consists of the desire to be involved in the peer world, such as dressing like friends and wanting to spend huge chunks of time with members of a clique. Such circumstances may involve prosocial activities as well, as when clubs raise money for worthy causes.

In a study focused on negative, neutral, and positive aspects of peer conformity, Thomas Berndt (1979) studied 273 third-grade through twelfth-grade students. Hypothetical dilemmas that were presented to the students required

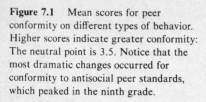

Figure 7.1 Mean scores for peer conformity on different types of behavior. Higher scores indicate greater conformity: The neutral point is 3.5. Notice that the most dramatic changes occurred for conformity to antisocial peer standards, which peaked in the ninth grade.

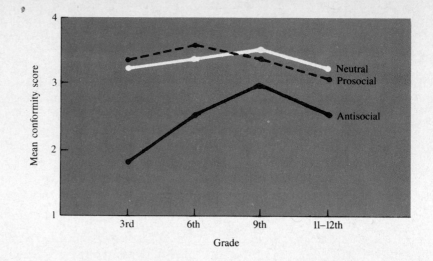

the students to make choices about conformity with friends on prosocial and antisocial behavior and about conformity with parents on neutral and prosocial behaviors. For example, one prosocial item questioned whether students relied on their parents' advice in such situations as deciding about helping at the library or instructing another child to swim. An antisocial question asked a boy what he would do if one of his peers wanted him to help steal some candy. A neutral question asked a girl if she would follow peer suggestions to engage in an activity she wasn't interested in—for example, going to a movie she did not want to see.

Some interesting developmental patterns were found in this investigation. In the third grade, parent and peer influences often directly contradicted each other. Since parent conformity is much greater for third-grade children, children of this age are probably still closely tied to and dependent on their parents. However, by the sixth grade, parent and peer influences were found to be no longer in direct opposition. Peer conformity had increased, but parent and peer influences were operating in different situations—parents had more impact in some situations, while peers had more clout in others. For example, parents were more influential in a discussion of political parties, but peers had more to say when sexual behavior and attitudes were at issue (Hyman, 1959; Vandiver, 1972).

By the ninth grade, parent and peer influences were once again in strong opposition to each other, probably because the conformity of adolescents to the social behavior of peers is much stronger at this grade level than at any other. At this time, adolescent adoption of antisocial standards endorsed by the peer group inevitably leads to conflict between adolescents and parents. Researchers have also found that the adolescent's attempt to gain independence meets with more parental opposition around the ninth grade than at any other time (Douvan & Adelson, 1966; Kandel & Lesser, 1969).

A stereotypical view of parent-child relationships suggests that parent-peer opposition continues into the late high school and college-age years. But Berndt (1979) found that adolescent conformity to antisocial, peer-endorsed behavior decreases in the late high school years, and agreement between parents and peers begins to increase in some areas. In addition, by the eleventh and twelfth grades, students show signs of developing a decision-making style more independent of peer and parental influence. Figure 7.1 summarizes the peer conformity to antisocial, neutral, and prosocial standards found in Berndt's (1979) study.

While most adolescents conform to peer pressure and societal standards, some adolescents are nonconformist or anticonformist. **Nonconformity** *occurs when individuals know what people around them expect, but they do not use*

(a)

(b)

those expectations to guide their behavior. Nonconformists are independent, as when a high school student chooses to not be a member of a clique. **Anticonformity** *occurs when individuals react counter to a group's expectations and deliberately move away from the actions or beliefs the group advocates.* Two contemporary versions of anticonformist teenagers are "skinheads" and "punks."

In sum, peer pressure is a pervasive theme of adolescents' lives. Its power can be observed in almost every dimension of adolescents' behavior—their choice of dress, music, language, values, leisure activities, and so on. Parents, teachers, and other adults can help adolescents to deal with peer pressure (Brown, 1990; Clasen & Brown, 1987). Adolescents need many opportunities to talk with both peers and adults about their social worlds and the pressures involved. The developmental changes of adolescence often bring forth a sense of insecurity. Young adolescents may be especially vulnerable because of this insecurity and the many developmental changes taking place in their lives. To counter this stress, young adolescents need to experience opportunities for success, both in and out of school, that increase their sense of being in control. Adolescents can learn that their social world is reciprocally controlled. Others may try to control them, but they can exert personal control over their actions and influence others in turn (Bandura, 1989, 1991). Next, in our discussion of peer popularity, neglect, and rejection, we discuss further the powerful role that peer relations plays in adolescent development.

Most adolescents conform to the mainstream standards of their peers. However, the rebellious or anticonformist adolescent reacts counter to the mainstream peer group's expectations, deliberately moving away from the actions or beliefs this group advocates. Two contemporary versions of anticonformist teenagers are the (a) "skinheads" and (b) punks.

Peer Popularity, Neglect, and Rejection

Every adolescent wants to be popular—you probably thought about popularity a lot when you were in junior and senior high school. Teenagers commonly think, "What can I do to have all of the kids at school like me?" "How can I be popular with both girls and guys?" "What's wrong with me? There must be something wrong, or I would be more popular." Sometimes, adolescents go to great lengths to be popular; and in some cases, parents go to even greater lengths to try to insulate their adolescents from rejection and to increase the likelihood that they will be popular. Students show off and cut up because it gets attention and makes

Listening skills and effective communication, being yourself, being happy, showing enthusiasm and concern for others, and having self-confidence but not being conceited are related to peer popularity in adolescence.

their peers laugh. Parents set up elaborate parties, buy cars and clothes for their teens, and drive adolescents and their friends all over in the hope that their sons or daughters will be popular.

Researchers have discovered that popular adolescents give out reinforcements, listen carefully, maintain open lines of communication with peers, are happy, act like themselves, show enthusiasm and concern for others, and are self-confident without being conceited (Hartup, 1983). In one recent study, popular youth were more likely to communicate clearly with their peers, elicit their peers' attention, and maintain conversation with peers more than unpopular youth (Kennedy, 1990).

Certain physical and cultural factors also affect adolescents' popularity. Adolescents who are physically attractive are more popular than those who are not (Kennedy, 1990) and, contrary to what some believe, brighter adolescents are more popular than less intelligent ones. Adolescents growing up in middle-class surroundings tend to be more popular than those growing up in lower-class surroundings, presumably in part because they are more in control of establishing standards for popularity (Hollingshead, 1975). But remember that findings such as these reflect group averages—there are many physically attractive teenagers who are unpopular, and some physically unattractive ones who are very well liked. Sociologist James Coleman (1980) points out that, for adolescents in the average range, there is little or no relation between physical attractiveness and popularity. It is only in the extremes (very attractive and very unattractive) that a link between popularity and attractiveness holds.

Recently, developmentalists have distinguished between two types of children and adolescents who often have low acceptance with their peers: those who are neglected and those who are rejected (Asher & Parker, in press; Coie & Koeppl, 1990; East, 1991; Parker & Asher, 1987). **Neglected children and adolescents** *often receive little attention from their peers and have few, if any, friends, but they are not necessarily disliked.* **Rejected children and adolescents** *are disliked by their peers. They are more likely to be disruptive and aggressive than their neglected counterparts.* Rejected children and adolescents often have more serious adjustment problems later in life than those who are neglected (Parker & Asher, 1987). For example, in one recent study, 112 fifth-grade boys were evaluated over a period of seven years until the end of high school (Kupersmidt & Coie, 1990). The key factor in predicting whether rejected children would engage in delinquent behavior or drop out of school later during adolescence was their aggression toward peers in elementary school.

How can neglected children and adolescents be trained to interact more effectively with their peers? The goal of training programs with neglected children and adolescents is often to help them attract attention from their peers in positive ways and to hold their attention by asking questions, by listening in a warm and friendly way, and by saying things about themselves that relate to the peers' interests. They also are taught to enter groups more effectively (Duck, 1988).

The goal of training programs with rejected children and adolescents is often to help them listen to peers and "hear what they say" instead of trying to dominate peer interactions. Rejected children and adolescents are trained to join peers without trying to change what is taking place in the peer group.

Children and adolescents may need to be persuaded or motivated that these strategies work effectively and are satisfying. In some programs, children and adolescents are shown videotapes of appropriate peer interaction; then they are asked to comment on them and to draw lessons from what they have seen. In other training programs, popular children and adolescents are taught to be more accepting of neglected or rejected peers.

One issue that has recently been raised about improving the peer relations of rejected children and adolescents is whether the focus should be on improving their prosocial skills (better empathy, careful listening, improved communication skills, and so on) or on reducing their aggressive, disruptive behavior and improving their self-control (Coie & Koeppl, 1990). Improving the prosocial skills of rejected adolescents does not automatically eliminate their aggressive or disruptive behavior. Aggression often leads to reinforcement because peers give in to aggressive youths' demands. Thus, in addition to teaching better prosocial skills to rejected adolescents, direct steps must also be taken to eliminate their aggressive actions. Further, acquiring positive status with peers may take time to achieve because it is hard for peers to change their opinions if adolescents frequently engage in aggressive conduct. Next, we turn our attention to the role of social cognition in understanding peer relations. Part of this discussion further considers ideas about reducing the aggression of children and adolescents in their peer encounters.

Neglected adolescents receive little attention from their peers, but they are not necessarily disliked. The goal of training programs with neglected adolescents is often to help them attract attention from their peers in positive ways and hold peers' attention by asking questions, by listening in a warm and friendly way, and by saying things about themselves that relate to peers' interests. They also are taught to enter groups more assertively.

Social Knowledge and Social Information Processing

Recall from our discussion of intelligence in Chapter 5 that a distinction can be made between knowledge and process. In studying cognitive aspects of peer relations, the same distinction can be made. Learning about the social knowledge adolescents bring with them to peer relations is important, as is studying how adolescents process information during peer interaction.

As children move into adolescence, they acquire more social knowledge, and there is considerable individual variation in how much one adolescent knows about what it takes to make friends, to get peers to like him or her, and so forth. For example, does the adolescent know that giving out reinforcements will increase the likelihood that he or she will be popular? That is, does Mary consciously know that, by telling Barbara such things as, "I really like that sweater you have on today," and "Gosh, you sure are popular with the guys," she will enhance the likelihood Barbara will want her to be her friend? Does the adolescent know that, when others perceive that he or she is similar to them, he or she

Figure 7.2 Generation of alternative
solutions and adaptive planning by negative
and positive peer status boys. Notice that
negative peer status boys were less likely to
generate alternative solutions and to plan
ahead than their positive peer status
counterparts.

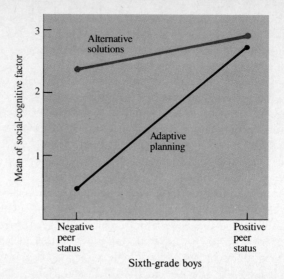

will be liked better by the others? Does the adolescent know that friendship involves sharing intimate conversations and that a friendship likely is improved when the adolescent shares private, confidential information with another adolescent? To what extent does the adolescent know that comforting and listening skills will improve friendship relations? To what extent does the adolescent know what it takes to become a leader? Think back to your adolescent years. How sophisticated were you in knowing about such social matters? Were you aware of the role of nice statements and perceived similarity in determining popularity and friendship? While you may not have been aware of these factors, those of you who were popular and maintained close friendships likely were competent at using these strategies.

From a social cognitive perspective, children and adolescents may have difficulty in peer relations because they lack appropriate social cognitive skills (Dodge & Feldman, 1990; Dodge & others, 1986). One investigation explored the possibility that social cognitive skill deficits characterize children who have peer-related difficulties (Asarnow & Callan, 1985). Boys with and without peer adjustment difficulties were identified, and then a number of social cognitive processes or skills were assessed. These included the boys' ability to generate alternative solutions to hypothetical problems, to evaluate these solutions in terms of their effectiveness, to describe self-statements, and to rate the likelihood of self-statements. It was found that boys without peer adjustment problems generated more alternative solutions, proposed more assertive and mature solutions, gave less intense aggressive solutions, showed more adaptive planning, and evaluated physically aggressive responses less positively than the boys with peer adjustment problems. For example, as shown in Figure 7.2, negative peer status sixth-grade boys were not as likely to generate alternative solutions and were much less likely to adaptively plan ahead than their positive peer status counterparts.

While it is becoming clear that social cognitive knowledge is an important aspect of peer relations, as yet investigators have not developed a precise body of social cognitive knowledge believed to be beneficial to children and adolescents at different developmental levels. However, it seems clear that adolescents who get along better with others, both peers and adults, likely have significantly greater knowledge of social skills than those who are not popular and not well liked.

Now let's examine how social information processing might be involved in peer relations. For example, consider the situation when a peer accidentally trips and knocks a boy's soft drink out of his hand. The boy misinterprets the encounter as hostile, which leads him to retaliate aggressively against the peer. Through repeated encounters of this kind, peers come to perceive the boy as having a habit of acting inappropriately. Kenneth Dodge (1983) argues that children go through five steps in processing information about their social world: decoding of social cues, interpretation, response search, selecting an optimal response, and enactment. Dodge has found that aggressive boys are more likely to perceive another child's actions as hostile when the peer's intention is ambiguous. And when aggressive boys search for cues to determine a peer's intention, they respond more rapidly, less efficiently, and less reflectively than nonaggressive children. These are among the social cognitive factors believed to be involved in children's and adolescents' conflicts with each other (Dodge & Feldman, 1990; Shantz, 1988).

At the beginning of the chapter, we discussed Robert Selman's peer therapy program, and later we looked at methods of improving the peer relations of neglected and rejected children and adolescents. Next, we further consider the increasing interest in improving the social skills of adolescents.

Conglomerate Strategies for Improving Adolescents' Social Skills

Conglomerate strategies, *also referred to as coaching, involve the use of a combination of techniques, rather than a single approach, to improve adolescents' social skills.* A conglomerate strategy might consist of demonstration or modeling of appropriate social skills, discussion, and reasoning about the social skills, as well as the use of reinforcement for their enactment in actual social situations. In one coaching study, students with few friends were selected and trained in ways to have fun with peers (Oden & Asher, 1975). The "unpopular" students were encouraged to participate fully, to show interest in others, to cooperate, and to maintain communication. A control group of students (who also had few friends) was directed in peer experiences but was not coached specifically in terms of improved peer strategies. Subsequent assessment revealed that the coaching was effective, with the coached group members showing more sociability when observed in peer relationships than their noncoached counterparts.

Other recent efforts to teach social skills also have used conglomerate strategies (Varenhorst, 1991). In one investigation, middle-school adolescents were instructed in ways to improve their self-control, stress management, and social problem solving (Weissberg & Caplan, 1989). For example, as problem situations arose, teachers modeled and students practiced six sequential steps: (1) stop, calm down, and think before you act; (2) go over the problem and state how you feel; (3) set a positive goal; (4) think of lots of solutions; (5) plan ahead for the consequences; (6) go ahead and try the best plan. The 240 adolescents who participated in the program improved their ability to devise cooperative solutions to problem situations, and their teachers reported that the students showed improved social relations in the classroom following the program. In another investigation, boys and girls in a low-income area of New Jersey were given instruction in social decision making, self-control, and group awareness (Clabby & Elias, 1988). When compared with boys and girls who did not receive the training, the program participants were more sensitive to the feelings of others, more mindful of the consequences of their actions, and better able to analyze problem situations and act appropriately. Perspective on Adolescent Development 7.1 presents more information about strategies being used with adolescents who have deficient social skills.

The world of peers is one of varying acquaintances: For hours every day, adolescents interact with some adolescents they barely know and with others that they know well. It is to the latter type—friends—that we now turn.

Skill-Streaming the Adolescent

A number of strategies for training the social skills of adolescents have been described by Arnold Goldstein and his colleagues in the book *Skill-Streaming the Adolescent* (1981). These include such behavior management strategies as reinforcement (including social and group reinforcement), punishment (including time-out procedures), modeling, and role-playing. A major focus of the book is how such social skills can be trained in the school setting. One particularly helpful set of strategies involves those pertaining to relationship-based techniques.

Psychologists and educators have known for many years that the better the relationship between a trainer and a student, the more positive and productive the outcome of their interaction. In many instances, relationship-based techniques require the social skills trainer to become aware of broader aspects of the adolescent's life than just those happenings in the classroom. The trainer tries to gain some sense of the adolescent's motivation for behaving in a particular way and attempts to respond to the adolescent's needs. One particular strategy that can be beneficial focuses on empathetic encouragement. In using this strategy, trainers show the adolescent that they understand the adolescent's difficulty, and encourage the adolescent to participate as instructed. A series of steps then are followed:

1. The adolescent is offered the chance to explain in detail the problems being encountered while the trainer listens nondefensively.
2. The trainer indicates that she or he understands the adolescent's behavior.
3. If it is appropriate, the trainer indicates that the adolescent's view is a reasonable interpretation or alternative.
4. The trainer restates his or her view with supporting reasons and likely outcomes.
5. The trainer expresses the appropriateness of delaying a resolution of the problem.
6. The trainer encourages the adolescent to try to participate.

An example is the case of Rose, a somewhat temperamental, disruptive adolescent who was very negative about getting involved in a social skills training program that focused on the importance of asking permission. After attempting to ignore Rose's behavior, which included laughing and making mocking gestures, the trainer finally decided to discuss her behavior in an empathetic manner. Rose was asked to explain why she was acting this way (laughing, mocking). Rose said that she thought that skill training for asking permission was stupid. She said that, in her family, if she wanted permission for anything, she had to wait for a week. At home, then, she simply took what she wanted.

The trainer then told Rose that it was understandable why this skill would not work at home. It might be a skill she would not want to use there. Rose was informed that there might be a lot of situations away from home, such as at school, where the skill could be helpful. She was told that at school there are many times that a student has to ask permission to do certain things, such as leaving the classroom and turning in an assignment late. The trainer indicated that, if Rose just went ahead and did these things without asking permission, she could wind up in a lot of trouble. Rose was told that maybe she should hold off on judging whether this skill involving asking permission was good or bad until she had a chance to try it out. Rose subsequently agreed to try the skill out in a small group, and she became reasonably attentive through the remainder of the social skills training session.

Another helpful strategy described by Goldstein and his colleagues (1981) focuses on the elicitation of peer support. To the degree that peer group goals are important to the adolescent, trainers can use peer pressure to their advantage in working with the adolescent. The trainer's task becomes one of structuring the group activity so that peer support can be mobilized. The trainer also may elicit specific group support for particular behaviors shown by hesitant or less skilled adolescents in the group.

Consider the following circumstances: The trainer noticed that before and after role-playing strategies, a number of negative comments, jokes, and insults were being hurled around by the adolescents. To deal with these sarcastic rejoinders, the trainer decided to teach the skill called "giving a compliment." The trainer made the role-playing task one of giving a true compliment to someone in the class about what he or she was doing in the class. The adolescents had to think about this for awhile but eventually were able to compliment each other on their helpfulness, on communicating better, and so forth. When the next skill was taught, the trainer gave the adolescents the task of giving a compliment to each adolescent who had role-played.

Through strategies such as those described by Goldstein and his associates (1981), skill-deficient adolescents are being helped to live more socially competent lives and to function more maturely in school settings.

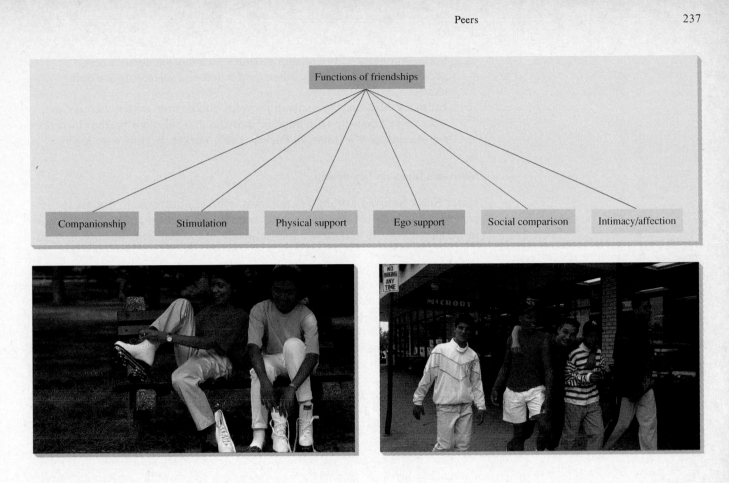

Figure 7.3   The functions of friendships.

Friendships

The important role of friendships in adolescent development is exemplified in the following description by a 13-year-old girl:

> My best friend is nice. She's honest, and I can trust her. I can tell her my innermost secrets and know that nobody else will find out about them. I have other friends, too, but she is my best friend. We consider each other's feelings and don't want to hurt each other. We help each other out when we have problems. We make up funny names for people and laugh ourselves silly. We make lists of which boys are the sexiest and which are the ugliest, which are the biggest jerks, and so on. Some of these things we share with other friends; some we don't.

The Importance of Friendship

Adolescents' friendships serve six functions (see Figure 7.3):

1. Companionship. Friendship provides adolescents with a familiar partner, someone who is willing to spend time with them and join in collaborative activities.
2. Stimulation. Friendship provides adolescents with interesting information, excitement, and amusement.
3. Physical support. Friendship provides time, resources, and assistance.
4. Ego support. Friendship provides the expectation of support, encouragement, and feedback that helps adolescents to maintain an impression of themselves as competent, attractive, and worthwhile individuals.

5. Social comparison. Friendship provides information about where adolescents stand vis-à-vis others and whether adolescents are doing okay.

6. Intimacy/affection. Friendship provides adolescents with a warm, close, trusting relationship with another individual, a relationship that involves self-disclosure (Gottman & Parker, 1987; Parker & Gottman, 1989).

Sullivan's Ideas on Friendship

Harry Stack Sullivan (1953) was the most influential theorist to discuss the importance of adolescent friendships. He argued that there is a dramatic increase in the psychological importance and intimacy of close friends during early adolescence. In contrast to other psychoanalytic theorists' narrow emphasis on the importance of parent-child relationships, Sullivan contended that friends also play important roles in shaping children's and adolescents' well-being and development. In terms of well-being, he argued that all people have a number of basic social needs, including the need for tenderness (secure attachment), playful companionship, social acceptance, intimacy, and sexual relations. Whether or not these needs are fulfilled largely determines our emotional well-being. For example, if the need for playful companionship goes unmet, then we become bored and depressed; if the need for social acceptance is not met, we suffer a lowered sense of self-worth. Developmentally, friends become increasingly depended upon to satisfy these needs during adolescence, and thus the ups-and-downs of experiences with friends increasingly shape adolescents' state of well-being. In particular, Sullivan believed that the need for intimacy intensifies during early adolescence, motivating teenagers to seek out close friends. He felt that, if adolescents failed to forge such close friendships, they would experience painful feelings of loneliness coupled with a reduced sense of self-worth.

Research findings support many of Sullivan's ideas. For example, adolescents report more often disclosing intimate and personal information to their friends than do younger children (Buhrmester & Furman, 1987; Papini & others, 1990). Adolescents also say they depend more on friends than parents to satisfy needs for companionship, reassurance of worth, and intimacy (Furman & Buhrmester, in press). In one recent study, daily interviews with 13- to 16-year-old adolescents over a five-day period were conducted to find out how much time they spent engaged in meaningful interactions with friends and parents (Buhrmester & Carbery, 1992). Adolescents spent an average of 103 minutes per day in meaningful interactions with friends compared to just 28 minutes per day with parents. In addition, the quality of friendship is more strongly linked to feelings of well-being during adolescence than during childhood. Teenagers with superficial friendships, or no close friendships at all, report feeling lonelier and more depressed and anxious, and they have a lower sense of self-esteem than teenagers with intimate friendships (Buhrmester, 1990).

The increased closeness and importance of friendship challenges adolescents to master evermore sophisticated social competencies. Viewed from the developmental constructionist perspective described in Chapter 6, adolescent friendship represents a new mode of relating to others that is best described as a *symmetrical intimate mode*. During childhood, being a good friend involves being a good playmate: Children must know how to play cooperatively and must be skilled at smoothly entering ongoing games on the playground (Putallaz, 1983). By contrast, the greater intimacy of adolescent friendships demand that teenagers learn a number of close relationship competencies, including knowing how to self-disclose appropriately, being able to provide emotional support to friends, and managing disagreements in ways that do not undermine the intimacy of the friendship (Buhrmester, 1990; Paul & White, 1990). These competencies require more sophisticated skills in perspective taking, empathy, and social problem solving than were involved in childhood playmate competencies (Buhrmester & others, 1988; Selman, 1980).

In addition to the role they play in the socialization of social competence, friendship relationships are often important sources of support. Sullivan described how adolescent friends support one another's sense of personal worth. When close friends disclose their mutual insecurities and fears about themselves, they discover that they are not "abnormal" and that they have nothing to be ashamed of. Friends also act as important confidants that help adolescents work through upsetting problems (such as difficulties with parents or the breakup of romance) by providing both emotional support and informational advice (Savin-Williams & Berndt, 1990). In addition, friends can become active partners in building a sense of identity. During countless hours of conversation, friends act as sounding boards as teenagers explore issues ranging from future plans to stances on religious and moral issues.

Intimacy and Similarity in Friendship

In the context of friendship, *intimacy* has been defined in different ways. For example, it has been defined broadly to include everything in a relationship that makes the relationship seem close or intense. In most research studies, though, **intimacy in friendship** is *defined narrowly as self-disclosure or sharing of private thoughts.* Private or personal knowledge about a friend also has been used as an index of intimacy (Selman, 1980; Sullivan, 1953).

The most consistent finding in the last two decades of research on adolescent friendships is that intimacy is an important feature of friendship (Berndt & Perry, 1990). When young adolescents are asked what they want from a friend or how they can tell someone is their best friend, they frequently say that a best friend will share problems with them, understand them, and listen when they talk about their own thoughts or feelings. When young children talk about their friendships, comments about intimate self-disclosure or mutual understanding are rare. In one recent investigation, friendship intimacy was more prominent in 13- to 16-year-olds than in 10- to 13-year-olds (Buhrmester, 1989).

Are the friendships of adolescent girls more intimate than the friendships of adolescent boys? When asked to describe their best friends, girls refer to intimate conversations and faithfulness more than boys do. For example, girls are more likely to describe their best friend as "sensitive just like me," or "trustworthy just like me" (Duck, 1975). The assumption behind this gender difference is that girls are more oriented toward interpersonal relationships. Boys may discourage one another from openly disclosing their problems as part of their masculine, competitive nature (Maccoby, 1991). Boys make themselves vulnerable to being called "wimps" if they can't handle their own problems and insecurities.

Adolescents also regard loyalty or faithfulness as more critical in friendships than children do (Berndt & Perry, 1990). When talking about their best friend, adolescents frequently refer to the friend's willingness to stand up for them when around other people. Typical comments are: "Bob will stick up for me in a fight," "Sally won't talk about me behind my back," or "Jennifer wouldn't leave me for somebody else." In these descriptions, adolescents underscore the obligations of a friend in the larger peer group.

Another predominant characteristic of friendship is that, throughout the childhood and adolescent years, friends are generally similar—in terms of age, sex, ethnicity, and many other factors (Hartup, 1991; Rawlins, 1992). Friends often have similar attitudes toward school, similar educational aspirations, and closely aligned achievement orientations. Friends like the same music, wear the same kind of clothes, and prefer the same leisure activities (Berndt, 1982). If friends have different attitudes about schools, one of them may want to play basketball or go shopping rather than do homework. If one friend insists on completing homework while the other insists on playing basketball, the conflict may weaken the friendship, and the two may drift apart.

Mixed-Age Friendships

While most adolescents develop friendships with individuals who are close to their own age, some adolescents become best friends with younger or older individuals (Savin-Williams & Berndt, 1990). A common fear, especially among parents, is that adolescents who have older friends will be encouraged to engage in delinquent behavior or early sexual behavior. Researchers have found that adolescents who interact with older youths do engage in these behaviors more frequently, but it is not known whether the older youths guide younger adolescents toward deviant behavior or whether the younger adolescents were already prone to deviant behavior before they developed the friendship with the older youths (Billy, Rodgers, & Udry, 1984).

In a longitudinal study of eighth-grade girls, early-maturing girls developed friendships with girls who were chronologically older but biologically similar to them (Magnusson, 1988). Because of their associations with older friends, the early-maturing girls were more likely than their peers to engage in a number of deviant behaviors, such as being truant from school, getting drunk, and stealing. Also, as adults (26 years of age), the early-maturing girls were more likely to have had a child and were less likely to be vocationally and educationally oriented than their later-maturing counterparts. Thus, parents do seem to have reason to be concerned when their adolescents become close friends with individuals who are considerably older than they are.

At this point, we have discussed many ideas about the nature of peer relations and friendships. A summary of these ideas is presented in Concept Table 7.1. Next, we consider another aspect of the adolescent's social world—groups.

Adolescent Groups

During your adolescent years, you were probably a member of both formal and informal groups. Examples of formal groups include the basketball team or drill team, the Girl Scouts or Boy Scouts, the student council, and so on. A more informal group could be a group of peers, such as a clique. Our study of adolescent groups focuses on the functions of groups and how groups are formed, differences between children groups and adolescent groups, cultural variations, and cliques.

Group Function and Formation

Why does an adolescent join a study group? A church? An athletic team? A clique? Groups satisfy adolescents' personal needs, reward them, provide information, raise their self-esteem, and give them an identity. Adolescents might join a group because they think that group membership will be enjoyable and exciting and satisfy their need for affiliation and companionship. They might join a group because they will have the opportunity to receive rewards, either material or psychological. For example, an adolescent may reap prestige and recognition from membership on the school's student council. Groups also are an important source

Concept Table 7.1

Peers and Friends

Concept	Processes/Related Ideas	Characteristics/Description
Peers	Peer group functions	The nature of peer relationships undergoes important changes during adolescence. Peers are individuals who are about the same age or maturity level. Peers provide a means of social comparison and a source of information about the world outside the family. Good peer relations may be necessary for normal social development in adolescence. The inability to "plug in" to a social network in childhood or adolescence is associated with a number of problems and disturbances. Thus, peer influences can be both positive and negative. Both Piaget and Sullivan stressed that peer relations provide the context for learning the symmetrical reciprocity mode of relationships.
	Peer conformity	Conformity occurs when individuals adopt the attitudes or behavior of others because of real or imagined pressure from the others. Conformity to antisocial peer standards peaks around the eighth to ninth grades, then lessens by the twelfth grade. A distinction is made between nonconformists and anticonformists.
	Peer popularity, neglect, and rejection	Listening skills, effective communication, being yourself, being happy, showing enthusiasm and concern for others, and having self-confidence but not being conceited are predictors of peer popularity. Neglected adolescents receive little attention from their peers, while rejected adolescents are disliked by their peers. The risk status of neglected adolescents is unclear. Rejected adolescents are at risk for the development of problems. Training programs focus on improving the peer relations of neglected and rejected adolescents.
	Social knowledge and social information processing	Social knowledge and social information-processing skills are associated with improved peer relations.
	Conglomerate strategies for improving social skills	Conglomerate strategies, also referred to as coaching, involve the use of a combination of techniques, rather than a single approach, to improve adolescents' social skills.
Friendships	Importance of friendship	Adolescents' friendships serve six functions: companionship, stimulation, physical support, ego support, social comparison, and intimacy/affection.
	Sullivan's ideas on friendship	Harry Stack Sullivan was the most influential theorist to discuss the importance of adolescent friendships. He argued that there is a dramatic increase in the psychological importance and intimacy of close friends during early adolescence. Research findings support many of Sullivan's ideas.
	Intimacy and similarity	These are two of the most common characteristics of friendships. Intimacy in friendship is defined narrowly as self-disclosure or sharing of private thoughts. Similarity—in terms of age, sex, ethnicity, and many other factors—is also important to a friendship.
	Mixed-age friendships	Adolescents who become close friends with older individuals engage in more deviant behaviors than adolescents whose best friends are the same age. Early-maturing girls are more likely than their later-maturing counterparts to have older friends, who may encourage deviant behavior.

of information. As adolescents sit in a study group, they learn effective study strategies and valuable information about how to take tests. The groups in which adolescents are members—their family, their school, a club, a team—often make them feel good, raise their self-esteem, and provide them with an identity.

Any group to which adolescents belong has two things in common with all other groups: norms and roles. **Norms** *are rules that apply to all members of a group.* An honor society, for example, may require all members to have a 3.5 grade point average. A school may require its male students to have hair that does not go below the collar of their shirt. A football team may require its members to work on weight lifting in the off-season. **Roles** *are certain positions in a group that are governed by rules and expectations. Roles define how adolescents should behave in those positions.* In a family, parents have certain roles, siblings have other roles, and grandparents have still other roles. On a basketball team, many different roles must be filled: center, forward, guard, rebounder, defensive specialist, and so on.

In a classic study designed to learn more about how adolescent groups are formed, social psychologist Muzafer Sherif and his colleagues (1961) brought together a group of 11-year-old boys at a summer camp called Robbers Cave in Oklahoma. The boys were divided into two groups. In-groupness was promoted by creating competition between the groups of boys. In the first week, one group hardly knew the other group existed. One group became known as the Rattlers (a tough and cussing group whose shirts were emblazoned with a snake insignia) and the other as the Eagles.

Near the end of the first week, each group learned of the other's existence. It took little time for "we-they" talk to surface: "They had better not be on our ball field." "Did you see the way one of them was sneaking around?" Sherif, who disguised himself as a janitor so he could unobtrusively observe the Rattlers and Eagles, then set up competition between the groups in the form of baseball, touch football, and tug-of-war. Counselors juggled and judged events so that the teams were close. Each team perceived the other to be unfair. Raids, burning the other group's flag, and fights resulted. Ethnocentric out-group derogation was observed when the Rattlers and Eagles held their noses in the air as they passed each other. Rattlers described all Rattlers as brave, tough, and friendly and called all Eagles sneaky and smart alecks. The Eagles reciprocated by labeling the Rattlers cry-babies.

After in-groupness and competition transformed the Rattlers and Eagles into opposing "armies," Sherif devised ways to reduce hatred between the groups. He tried noncompetitive contact, but that did not work. Positive relations between the Rattlers and Eagles were attained only when both groups were required to work cooperatively to solve a problem. Three superordinate goals that required the efforts of both groups were: (1) working together to repair the only water supply to the camp, (2) pooling their money to rent a movie, and (3) cooperating to pull the camp truck out of a ditch. All of these dilemmas were created by Sherif.

In addition to recruiting boys for camp to explore the nature of group formation, Sherif has also simply gone out to street corners and hangouts in towns and cities to find out what adolescent groups are like. In one such effort (Sherif & Sherif, 1964), the observers went to a town and began to infiltrate student gathering places. They got to know the adolescent boys and became their confidants by doing such things as buying them a new basketball when their old ball got a hole in it. After the observers gained the adolescents' acceptance, they began to record information about the conversations and activities of the youth. The strategy was to spend several hours with them and then write down what had transpired.

What do adolescent boys do when they get together regularly on their own volition? The Sherifs found that, in each group of adolescents they studied, much time was spent just "hanging around" together, talking and joking. In addition, many of the groups spent a great deal of time participating in, discussing, or attending athletic events and games. The only exceptions were groups from lower-class neighborhoods.

Cars occupied the minds of many of the group members. Whether they owned cars or not, the adolescent boys discussed, compared, and admired cars. Those who did not own cars knew what kinds they wanted. The boys also discussed the problem of having access to a car so they could go somewhere or take a girl out. The adolescents who did have cars spent tremendous amounts of time in and around cars with their buddies. On numerous occasions, the adolescent boys just drove around, looking to see what was going on around town or wanting to be seen by others.

Discussions about girls frequently infiltrated the adolescent boys' conversations. As part of this talk, they focused extensively on sexual activities. They planned, reminisced, and compared notes on girls. Particularly in the middle- and upper-income adolescent groups, looking for opportunities to be with girls and making sure they had dates for the weekend were important group activities.

Much time in every group was spent reflecting on past events and planning for games, parties, and so forth. Thus, despite the fact that the boys just "hung around" a lot, there were times when they constructively discussed how they were going to deal or cope with various events.

Adults were depicted in the adolescents' conversations as a way to obtain needed resources (such as cars, money, and athletic equipment); as figures whose authorization was needed; as obstacles to be overcome; and, occasionally, in terms of obligation.

While the particular activities of the adolescent boys differed from group to group, the general nature of the activities of all the groups was remarkably similar. All the groups were preoccupied with the pleasure of one another's company, the problems of having places to meet with peers apart from adults, relationships with adult authorities, relationships with the opposite sex, and the appurtenances of being an adult male (including a car).

Also, in every group the Sherifs studied, the members engaged in some form of deviant behavior not sanctioned by adults. The most common behavior of this type involved alcoholic beverages. In one of the highest socioeconomic groups, the boys regularly drank, sometimes engaged in illicit sexual activities, and set up a boy-girl swimming party at a motel by forging the registration. The party included not only illegal drinking but the destruction of property as well. The boys paid for the property destruction themselves without ever telling their parents what had happened.

Children Groups and Adolescent Groups

Children groups differ from adolescent groups in several important ways. The members of children groups often are friends or neighborhood acquaintances, and the groups usually are not as formalized as many adolescent groups. During the adolescent years, groups tend to include a broader array of members; in other words, adolescents other than friends or neighborhood acquaintances often are members of adolescent groups. Try to recall the student council, honor society, or football team at your junior high school. If you were a member of any of these organizations, you probably remember that they were made up of many individuals you had not met before and that they were a more heterogeneous group than your childhood peer groups. Rules and regulations were probably well defined, and captains or leaders were formally elected or appointed in the adolescent groups.

A well-known observational study by Dexter Dunphy (1963) indicates that opposite-sex participation in groups increases during adolescence. In late childhood, boys and girls participate in small, same-sex groups. As they move into the early adolescent years, the same-sex groups begin to interact with each other. Gradually, the leaders and high-status members form further groups based on heterosexual relationships. Eventually, the newly created heterosexual groups replace the same-sex groups. The heterosexual groups interact with each other in large crowd activities, too—at dances and athletic events, for example. In late adolescence, the crowd begins to dissolve as couples develop more serious relationships and make long-range plans that may include engagement and marriage. A summary of Dunphy's ideas is presented in Figure 7.4.

244

Figure 7.4 Dunphy's progression of peer group relations in adolescence.

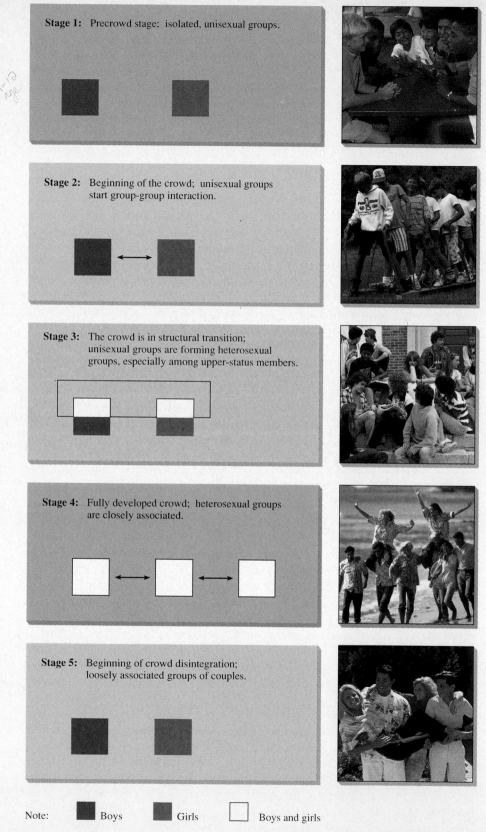

Stage 1: Precrowd stage; isolated, unisexual groups.

Stage 2: Beginning of the crowd; unisexual groups start group-group interaction.

Stage 3: The crowd is in structural transition; unisexual groups are forming heterosexual groups, especially among upper-status members.

Stage 4: Fully developed crowd; heterosexual groups are closely associated.

Stage 5: Beginning of crowd disintegration; loosely associated groups of couples.

Note: ◼ Boys ◼ Girls ☐ Boys and girls

Ethnic and Cultural Variations in Adolescent Peer Groups

Whether adolescents grow up as part of the peer culture in a ghetto or in a middle-class suburban area influences the nature of the groups to which they belong. For example, in a comparison of middle-class and lower-class adolescent groups, lower-class adolescents displayed more aggression toward the low-status members of the group but showed less aggression toward the president of the class or group than their middle-class counterparts (Maas, 1954).

In many schools, peer groups are strongly segregated according to social class and ethnicity. In schools with large numbers of middle- and lower-class students, middle-class students often assume the leadership roles in formal organizations, such as student council, the honor society, fraternity-sorority groups, and so on. Athletic teams are one type of adolescent group in which Black adolescents and adolescents from low-income families have been able to gain parity or even surpass adolescents from middle- and upper-income families in achieving status.

Ethnic minority adolescents, especially immigrants, may rely on peer groups more than White adolescents (Spencer & Dornbusch, 1990). This is especially true when ethnic minority adolescents' parents have not been very successful in their careers. The desire to be accepted by the peer group is especially strong among refugee adolescents, whose greatest threat is not the stress of belonging to two cultures but the stress of belonging to none (Lee, 1988).

For many ethnic minority youth, especially immigrants, peers from their own ethnic group provide a crucial sense of brotherhood or sisterhood within the majority culture. Peer groups may form to oppose those of the majority group and to provide adaptive supports that reduce feelings of isolation. More about the peer groups of ethnic minority adolescents appears in Sociocultural Worlds of Adolescence 7.1.

So far, we have considered adolescents' peer relations in different socio-economic and ethnic minority groups. Are there also some cultures in which the peer group plays a different role than in the United States? In some cultures, children are placed in peer groups for much greater lengths of time at an earlier age than they are in the United States. For example, in the Murian culture of eastern India, both male and female children live in a dormitory from the age of six until they get married (Barnouw, 1975). The dormitory is a religious haven where members are devoted to work and spiritual harmony. Children work for their parents, and the parents arrange the children's marriages. When the children wed, they must leave the dormitory.

Adolescent cliques have been mentioned on several occasions in this chapter. For example, in the discussion of Dunphy's work, the importance of heterosexual relationships in the evolution of adolescent cliques was noted. Let's now examine adolescent cliques in more detail.

Cliques

Most peer group relations in adolescence can be categorized in one of three ways: individual friendships, the crowd, and cliques. The **crowd** *is the largest, most loosely defined, and least personal unit of the adolescent peer society. Crowd members often meet because of their mutual interest in an activity.* For example, crowds get together at large parties or intermingle at school dances. **Cliques** *are smaller in size, involve more intimacy among members, and are more cohesive than crowds. However, they usually are larger in size and involve less intimacy than friendships.* In contrast to crowds, the members of both friendships and cliques come together because of mutual attraction.

Ethnic Minority Adolescents' Peer Relations

As ethnic minority children move into adolescence and enter schools with more heterogeneous school populations, they become more aware of their ethnic minority status. Ethnic minority adolescents may have difficulty joining peer groups and clubs in predominantly White schools. Similarly, White adolescents may have peer relations difficulties in predominately ethnic minority schools. However, schools are only one setting in which peer relations take place; they also occur in the neighborhood and in the community.

Ethnic minority adolescents often have two sets of peer relationships, one at school, the other in the community. Community peers are more likely to be from their own ethnic group in their immediate neighborhood. Sometimes, they go to the same church and participate in activities together, such as Black History Week, Chinese New Year's, or Cinco de Mayo Festival. Because ethnic group adolescents usually have two sets of peers and friends, when researchers ask about their peers and friends, questions should focus on both relationships at school and in the neighborhood and community. Ethnic minority group adolescents who are social isolates at school may be sociometric stars in their segregated neighborhood. Also, because adolescents are more mobile than children, inquiries should be made about the scope of their social networks (Gibbs & Huang, 1989; Mounts, 1992).

One recent investigation studied the school and neighborhood friendship patterns of 292 Black and White adolescents who attended an integrated junior high school (DuBois & Hirsch, 1990). Most students reported having an other-ethnic school friend, but only 28 percent of the students saw such a friend frequently outside of school. Reports of an interethnic school friendship that extended to nonschool settings were more common among Black adolescents than White adolescents and among adolescents who lived in an integrated rather than a segregated neighborhood. Black adolescents were more likely than White adolescents to have extensive neighborhood friendship networks, but Black adolescents said they talked with fewer friends during the school day.

Of special interest to investigators is the degree of peer support for an ethnic minority adolescent's achievement orientation. Some researchers argue that peers often dissuade Black adolescents from doing well in school (Fordham & Ogbu, 1986; Fuller, 1984). However, in one recent investigation, peer support of achievement was relatively high among Asian American adolescents, moderate among Black American and Hispanic American adolescents, and relatively low among Anglo American adolescents (Brown & others, 1990). The low peer support of achievement among Anglo American adolescents possibly is due to their strong individual, competitive, and social comparison orientation.

Adolescent peer relations take place in a number of settings—at school, in the neighborhood, and in the community, for example. Ethnic minority adolescents often have two sets of peer relationships—one at school, the other in the community. A special interest is the degree to which peers support an ethnic minority adolescent's achievement orientation.

Allegiance to cliques, clubs, organizations, and teams exerts powerful control over the lives of many adolescents. Group identity often overrides personal identity. The leader of a group may place a member in a position of considerable moral conflict, asking in effect, "What's more important, our code or your parents?" or "Are you looking out for yourself, or for the members of the group?" Labels like "brother" and "sister" sometimes are adopted and used in group members' conversations with one another. These labels symbolize the intensity of the bond between the members and suggest the high status of membership in the group.

One of the most widely quoted studies of adolescent cliques and crowds is that of James Coleman (1961). Students in 10 different high schools were asked to identify the leading crowds in their schools. They also were asked to name the students who were the most outstanding in athletics, popularity, and different school activities. Regardless of the school sampled, the leading crowds were likely to be composed of male athletes and popular girls. Much less power in the leading crowd was attributed to the bright student. Coleman's finding that being an athlete contributes to popularity for boys was reconfirmed in a more recent investigation by Eitzen (1975).

Think about your high school years—what were the cliques, and which one were you in? While the names of the cliques change, we could go to almost any high school in the United States and find three to six well-defined cliques or crowds. In one recent investigation, six peer group structures emerged: populars, unpopulars, jocks, brains, druggies, and average students (Brown & Mounts, 1989). The proportion of students placed in these cliques was much lower in multi-ethnic schools because of the additional existence of ethnically based crowds.

The exact nature of cliques and crowds depends on the geographical region of the country where the adolescents live. For instance, in towns and cities in Texas, the "kickers" and the "potheads" often create the most controversy. This dichotomy (as well as the dichotomy between groups in most areas) is due to the mixing of cultures—urban and rural, Northern and Southern. The term *kicker* originates from cowboy boots, which were worn mostly by working cowboys. The term has been modified to either "chip kickers" or "cowboys," depending on the purposes of the adolescent using the label. Observers say that the kickers may or may not have anything to do with agriculture, but they usually wear cowboy boots, western shirts and jeans, listen to country/western music, often drive pickups, and carry around tins of snuff in their hip pockets. The other side of the dichotomy has a wider variety of names, depending on the locale: freaks, potheads, slickers, or thugs. Freaks prefer rock music, dress in worn-out clothes, and drive "souped-up" cars.

Sociologists say that adolescents growing up in America usually must decide on which culture to adopt—whether to be a "roper" or a "doper," an "intellectual" or a "going-steady type" (Hawkins, 1979). This decision often reflects some conflict that exists throughout society—in many instances, the students are making a political statement by siding with one clique or crowd rather than another (the kickers and cowboys are on the right, and potheads are on the left). Political statements made during adolescence, though, may not be very strong; sometimes, they boil down to nothing more than which radio station adolescents listen to or which clothes they buy. The split is fairly easy to see in most high schools. In many instances, the two extreme groupings, such as the "ropers" and the "dopers," are not well integrated into the school system itself and are easily distinguished from students who are making good grades and who are social leaders.

Cliques have been portrayed as playing a pivotal role in the adolescent's maintenance of self-esteem and development of a sense of identity (for example, Coleman, 1961; Erikson, 1968). Several theoretical perspectives suggest how clique membership might be linked with the adolescent's self-esteem (Brown & Lohr, 1987). In an extension of Erikson's identity development theory, virtually all 13- to 17-year-olds regard clique membership as salient, and self-esteem is higher among clique members than nonmembers (at least those satisfied with the crowd). The peer group is a "way station" between relinquishing childhood dependence on parents and adult self-definition, achievement, and autonomy. Group affiliation and acceptance by the clique is important in keeping the adolescent's self-concept positive during this long transition period. Social comparison theory also has implications for understanding clique attachment and self-esteem. It implies that, while group members as a whole may have higher self-esteem than nonmembers, there are differences among group members according to the position of their clique in the peer group status hierarchy. This argument is based on the belief that individuals often compare their own attributes with those of significant others to evaluate the adequacy of their ideas or characteristics (Festinger, 1954).

In one recent investigation, Bradford Brown and Jane Lohr (1987) examined the self-esteem of 221 seventh through twelfth graders. The adolescents were either associated with one of the five major school cliques or were relatively unknown by classmates and not associated with any school clique. Cliques included the following: jocks (athletically oriented), populars (well-known students who lead social activities), normals (middle-of-the-road students who make up the masses), druggies/toughs (known for illicit drug use or other delinquent activities), and nobodies (low in social skills or intellectual abilities). The self-esteem of the jocks and the populars was highest, while that of the nobodies was lowest. But one group of adolescents not in a clique had self-esteem equivalent to the jocks and the populars. This group was the independents, who indicated that clique membership was not important to them. Keep in mind that these data are correlational—self-esteem could increase an adolescent's probability of becoming a clique member just as clique membership could increase the adolescent's self-esteem.

So far in our discussion of peers in adolescence, we have discussed the nature of peer relations, friendships, and group behavior. But one aspect of peer relations remains to be discussed—dating.

Dating

While many adolescent boys and girls have social interchanges through formal and informal peer groups, it is through dating that more serious contacts between the sexes occur. Many agonizing moments are spent by young male adolescents worrying about whether they should call a certain girl and ask her out: "Will she turn me down?" "What if she says yes, what do I say next?" "How am I going to get her to the dance? I don't want my mother to take us!" "I want to kiss her, but what if she pushes me away?" "How can I get to be alone with her?" And, on the other side of the coin: "What if no one asks me to the dance?" "What do I do if he tries to kiss me?" Or, "I really don't want to go with him. Maybe I should wait two more days and see if Bill will call me." Think about your junior high, high school, and early college years. You probably spent a lot of time thinking about how you were going to get a particular girl or boy to go out with you. And many of your weekend evenings were probably spent on dates, or on envying others who had dates. Some of you went steady, perhaps even during junior high school; others of you may have been engaged to be married by the end of high school. Our further study of dating focuses on the functions of dating, age of onset and

In the early twentieth century, dating served mainly as a courtship for marriage. What are the functions of dating today?

frequency of dating, what it means to go steady, male and female dating patterns, what attracts adolescents to each other, romantic love, and the developmental construction of dating relationships.

Functions of Dating

Dating is a relatively recent phenomenon. It wasn't until the 1920s that dating as we know it became a reality, and even then, its primary role was for the purpose of selecting and winning a mate. Prior to this period, mate selection was the sole purpose of dating, and "dates" were carefully monitored by parents, who completely controlled the nature of any heterosexual companionship. Often, parents bargained with each other about the merits of their adolescents as potential marriage partners and even chose mates for their children. In recent times, of course, adolescents have gained much more control over the dating process and who they go out with. Furthermore, dating has evolved into something more than just courtship for marriage.

Dating today can serve at least eight functions (Padgham & Blyth, 1991; Paul & White, 1990; Roscoe, Dian, & Brooks, 1987; Skipper & Nass, 1966):

1. Dating can be a form of recreation. Adolescents who date seem to have fun and see dating as a source of enjoyment and recreation.
2. Dating is a source of status and achievement. Part of the social comparison process in adolescence involves evaluating the status of the people one dates: are they the best looking, the most popular, and so forth.
3. Dating is part of the socialization process in adolescence: It helps the adolescent to learn how to get along with others and assists in learning manners and sociable behavior.
4. Dating involves learning about intimacy and serves as an opportunity to establish a unique, meaningful relationship with a person of the opposite sex.
5. Dating can be a context for sexual experimentation and exploration.

6.   Dating can provide companionship through interaction and shared activities in an opposite-sex relationship.
7.   Dating experiences contribute to identity formation and development; dating helps adolescents to clarify their identity and to separate from their families of origin.
8.   Dating can be a means of mate sorting and selection, thereby retaining its original courtship function.

One investigation studied developmental changes in the functions of dating (Roscoe, Dian, & Brooks, 1987). Early (sixth-grade), middle (eleventh-grade), and late (college) adolescents were asked their reasons for dating and their concerns in selecting a dating partner. Early and middle adolescents had an egocentric and immediate gratification orientation toward dating functions (recreation was the most important function, followed by intimacy and status). In contrast, late adolescents placed more emphasis on reciprocity in dating relationships (intimacy was the most important function, followed by companionship, socialization, and recreation). Also, early adolescent concerns in selecting a dating partner stressed status seeking and dependence on others' approval of themselves. In contrast, late adolescents stressed more independence and future orientation in their dating concerns. In sum, the early and middle adolescents were primarily self-focused in their dating relationships, while late adolescents focused more on the reciprocal aspects of dating relationships and on what dating is supposed to be like (Paul & White, 1990).

The sociocultural context exerts a powerful influence on adolescent dating patterns and on mate selection (Xiaohe & Whyte, 1990). Values and religious beliefs of people in various cultures often dictate the age at which dating begins, how much freedom in dating is allowed, whether dates must be chaperoned by adults or parents, and the roles of males and females in dating. For example, Hispanic American and Asian American cultures have more conservative standards regarding adolescent dating than the Anglo American culture. Dating may be a source of cultural conflict for many immigrants and their families who have come from cultures in which dating begins at a late age, little freedom in dating is allowed, dates are chaperoned, and adolescent girls' dating is especially restricted.

Age of Onset and Frequency of Dating

Most girls in the United States begin dating at the age of 14, while most boys begin sometime between the ages of 14 and 15 (Douvan & Adelson, 1966; Sorenson, 1973). Most adolescents have their first date sometime between the ages of 12 and 16. Fewer than 10 percent have a first date before the age of 10, and by the age of 16, more than 90 percent have had at least one date. More than 50 percent of the tenth, eleventh, and twelfth graders in one study averaged one or more dates per week (Dickinson, 1975). About 15 percent of these high school students dated less than once per month, and about three out of every four students had gone steady at least once.

Dating, then, is an important aspect of adolescents' social relationships. Adolescents who do not date very much may feel left out of the mainstream in their high school and community. Clinical and counseling psychologists have developed a number of social skills training programs for individuals who have problems getting a date or who have difficulty during the course of a dating relationship.

Going Steady

At some point in their junior high or high school years, a number of adolescents "go steady" or "go with" each other. Going steady, though, may not mean the same thing to all adolescents. One of my daughter's 13-year-old friends once discussed her history of "going steady." It turned out that, in the course of six months, she had "gone" with five different boys. In two of those situations, the girl agreed to go steady with the boys over the phone and then broke off the relationships before she even had a date with them!

In one investigation of high school juniors and seniors who were going steady, 75 percent felt that their relationship involved a commitment to forgo dating other people, and a full 25 percent felt that they were in love (Schneider, 1966). Forty percent had informally agreed to get married, another 40 percent had considered marriage seriously but had made no commitment, and 20 percent had not considered marriage at all. The longer the couples had gone steady, the more likely they were to have considered marriage seriously. For those who had gone steady for only two months, for example, only 3 percent indicated that they planned to get married. For those who had gone steady for one year or longer, 50 percent said that they planned to get married. Thus, going steady becomes more serious during high school than middle school, and the longer a couple goes steady, the more likely they are to consider marriage.

At some point in their junior or senior high school years, a number of adolescents "go steady" or "go with" each other. Going steady is more serious in high school than middle school. The longer a couple goes steady, the more likely they are to consider marriage.

Male and Female Dating Patterns

It generally has been believed that females are more strongly oriented toward affection in opposite-sex relationships, while males are more interested in sexual matters. With regard to sexual interest, it does appear that, during adolescence, males show a stronger sexual interest than females do, although both males and females show a heightened desire for sexual involvement as the relationship deepens. For example, both male and female adolescents who go steady show a stronger desire for sexual involvement than their counterparts who have only had several dates with the same person (McCabe & Collins, 1979).

With regard to affectional and personality aspects of dating, females show more interest in personality exploration and self-disclosure than males (Douvan & Adelson, 1966; Feiring, 1992; Simon & Gagnon, 1969). However, in one investigation, both males and females said that they begin a dating relationship with an affectional orientation (McCabe & Collins, 1979). And as relationships endure, affection often plays a more prominent role.

What Attracts Adolescents to Each Other?

Does just being around another adolescent increase the likelihood a relationship will develop? Do birds of a feather flock together—that is, are adolescents likely to associate with those who are similar to them? How important is the attractiveness of the other adolescent?

As we have already seen, adolescents' friends are much more like them than unlike them; so are adolescents' dates. Adolescents' dates are likely to share similar attitudes, behavior, and characteristics—clothes, intelligence, personality, political attitudes, ethnic background, values, religious attitudes, life-style, physical attractiveness, and so on. In some limited cases and on some isolated characteristics, opposites attract; for example, an introvert may wish to be with an extravert, a blond may prefer a brunette, a short adolescent may prefer a tall

adolescent, an adolescent from a low-income background may be attracted to an adolescent with money. But overall, adolescents desire to date others with characteristics similar to theirs.

Consensual validation *explains why adolescents are attracted to others who are similar to themselves. Adolescents' own attitudes and behavior are supported, or validated, when someone else's attitudes and behaviors are similar to theirs.* Also, dissimilar others are unlike the adolescent and therefore unknown; thus, the adolescent may be able to gain control over similar others, whose attitudes and behavior the adolescent can predict. Similarity also implies that adolescents enjoy interacting with the other individual in mutually satisfying activities, many of which require a partner with similarly disposed behavior and attitudes.

A characteristic of close relationships that deserves special mention is physical attractiveness. How important is physical attractiveness in determining whether an adolescent will like or love someone? In one experiment, college students assumed that a computer had determined their date on the basis of similar interests, but the dates actually were randomly assigned (Walster & others, 1966). The students' social skills, physical appearance, intelligence, and personality were measured. Then a dance was set up for the matched partners. At intermission, the partners were asked in private to indicate the most positive aspects of their date that contributed to his or her attractiveness. The overwhelming determinant of attractiveness was looks, not other factors such as personality or intelligence. Other research has documented the importance of physical attraction in close relationships. For example, physically attractive individuals have more dates, are more popular with their peers, have more positive encounters with teachers, and report more success in obtaining a marital partner (Simpson, Campbell, & Berscheid, 1986).

Why do adolescents want to be associated with attractive others? As with similarity, being around physically attractive individuals is rewarding. They validate that the adolescent, too, is attractive. As part of the rewarding experience, the adolescent's self-image is enhanced. Looking at attractive individuals is also aesthetically pleasing. The adolescent assumes that, if others are physically attractive, they will have other desirable traits that interest the adolescent.

But not every adolescent can date Rob Lowe or Madonna. How do adolescents deal with this in their dating relationships? While beautiful girls and handsome boys seem to have an advantage, adolescents ultimately tend to seek out someone at their own level of attractiveness. The **matching hypothesis** *states that, although individuals may prefer a more attractive person in the abstract, they end up choosing someone who is close to their level of attractiveness.*

Several additional points help clarify the role of physical beauty and attraction in our close relationships. Much of the research has focused on initial or short-term encounters; attraction over the course of months and years often is not evaluated. As relationships endure, physical attraction probably assumes less importance. Rocky Dennis, as portrayed in the movie *Mask,* is a case in point (see Figure 7.5). Rocky's peers and even his mother initially wanted to avoid Rocky, whose face was severely distorted, but over the course of his childhood and adolescent years, the avoidance turned into attraction and love as people got to know him.

Our criteria for beauty may vary from one culture to another and from one point in history to another, so, although attempts are being made to quantify beauty and to arrive at the ultimate criteria for such things as a beautiful female face, beauty is relative. In the 1940s and 1950s in the United States, a Marilyn Monroe body build (a well-rounded, shapely appearance) and face was the cultural ideal for women. In the 1970s, some women aspired to look like Twiggy and other virtually anorexic females. In the 1990s, the desire for thinness has not ended, but what is culturally beautiful is no longer pleasingly plump or anorexic but, rather, a tall stature with moderate curves. The current image of attractiveness also includes the toning of one's body through physical exercise and healthy eating habits. As we will see next, though, there is more to close relationships than physical attraction.

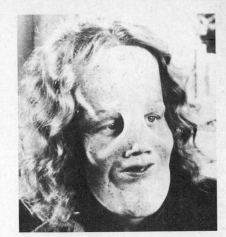

Figure 7.5 Eric Stoltz's portrayal of Rocky Dennis in the movie *Mask*. Rocky was unloved and unwanted as a young child because of his grotesque features. As his mother and peers got to know him, they became much more attracted to him.

Romantic Love

Romantic love *is also called passionate love or Eros; it has strong sexual and infatuation components, and it often predominates in the early part of a love relationship.* The fires of passion burn hot in romantic love. It is the type of love Juliet had in mind when she cried, "O Romeo, Romeo, wherefore art thou Romeo?" It is the type of love portrayed in new songs that hit the charts virtually every week. Romantic love also sells millions of books for such writers as Danielle Steele. Well-known love researcher Ellen Berscheid (1988) says that we mean romantic love when we say we are "in love" with someone. She believes that it is romantic love we need to understand if we are to learn what love is all about.

Romantic love characterizes most adolescent love, and romantic love is also extremely important among college students. In one investigation, unattached college males and females were asked to identify their closest relationship (Berscheid, Snyder, & Omoto, 1989). More than half named a romantic partner, rather than a parent, sibling, or friend.

Romantic love includes a complex intermingling of emotions—fear, anger, sexual desire, joy, and jealousy, for example. Note that not all of these emotions are positive. In one investigation, romantic lovers were more likely to be the cause of a person's depression than were friends (Berscheid & Fei, 1977).

Berscheid (1988; Berscheid, Snyder, & Omoto, 1989) believes that the topic of sexual desire is vastly neglected in the study of romantic love. When asked what romantic love truly is, she concluded, "It's about 90 percent sexual desire." Berscheid said that this still is an inadequate answer but that "to discuss romantic love without also prominently mentioning the role sexual arousal and desire plays in it is very much like printing a recipe for tiger soup that leaves out the main ingredient."

Another type of love is **affectionate love,** *also called companionate love, which occurs when individuals desire to have another person near and have a deep, caring affection for that person.* There is a strong belief that affectionate love is more characteristic of adult love than adolescent love and that the early stages of love have more romantic ingredients than the later stages.

The Developmental Construction of Dating Relationships

Similarity, physical attractiveness, and sexuality are important ingredients of dating relationships. So is intimacy, which is discussed in greater detail in Chapter 10. But to fully understand dating relationships in adolescence, we need to know how experiences with family members and peers contribute to the way adolescents construct their dating relationships, as first discussed in Chapter 6 with regard to the developmental construction view of relationships.

In the continuity version of the developmental construction view, relationships with parents are carried forward to influence the construction of other relationships, such as dating. Thus, adolescents' relationships with opposite-sex parents, as well as same-sex parents, contribute to adolescents' dating. For example, the adolescent male whose mother has been nurturant but not smothering probably feels that relationships with females will be rewarding. By contrast, the adolescent male whose mother has been cold and unloving toward him likely feels that relationships with females will be unrewarding.

Adolescents' observations of their parents' marital relationship also contribute to their own construction of dating relationships. Consider an adolescent girl from a divorced family who grew up watching her parents fight on many occasions. Her dating relationships may take one of two turns: She may immerse herself in dating relationships to insulate herself from the stress she has experienced, or she may become aloof and untrusting with males and not wish to become involved heavily in dating relationships. Even when she does date considerably, she may find it difficult to develop a trusting relationship with males because she has seen promises broken by her parents.

According to Peter Blos (1962, 1989), at the beginning of adolescence, boys and girls try to separate themselves from the opposite-sex parent as a love object. As adolescents separate themselves, they often are self-centered. Blos believes that this narcissism gives adolescents a sense of strength. Especially in early adolescence, this narcissistic self-orientation is likely to produce self-serving, highly idealized, and superficial dating relationships.

There has been little empirical investigation of how parents and friends influence the manner in which adolescents construct dating relationships. As noted in Chapter 6, Hetherington (1972, 1977) found that divorce was associated with a stronger heterosexual orientation of adolescent daughters than was the death of a parent or living in an intact family. Further, the daughters of divorcees had a more negative opinion of males than did the girls from other family structures. And girls from divorced and widowed families were more likely to marry images of their fathers than girls from intact families. Hetherington believes that females from intact families likely have had a greater opportunity to work through relationships with their fathers and therefore are more psychologically free to date and marry someone different than their fathers. Parents also are more likely to be involved or interested in their daughters' dating patterns and relationships than their sons'. For example, in one investigation, college females were much more likely than their male counterparts to say that their parents tried to influence who they dated during adolescence (Knox & Wilson, 1981). They also indicated that it was not unusual for their parents to try to interfere with their dating choices and relationships.

So far we have been discussing the continuity version of the developmental construction view. By contrast, in the discontinuity version of the developmental construction view, early adolescent friendships provide the opportunity to learn modes of relating that are carried over into romantic relationships (Furman & Wehner, 1992; Sullivan, 1953). Sullivan believed that it is through intimate friendships that adolescents learn a mature form of love he referred to as "collaboration." Sullivan felt that it was this collaborative orientation, coupled with sensitivity to the needs of the friend, that forms the basis of satisfying dating and marital relationships. He also pointed out that dating and romantic relationships give rise to new interpersonal issues that youths had not encountered in prior relationships with parents and friends. Not only must teenagers learn tactics for asking partners for dates (and gracefully turning down requests), but they must also learn to integrate sexual desires with psychological intimacy desires. These tactics and integration are not easy tasks and it is not unusual for them to give rise to powerful feelings of frustration, guilt, and insecurity.

In addition to past relationships with parents and friends influencing an adolescent's dating relationships, family members and peers can directly influence dating experiences. For example, sibling relationships influence adolescent dating. In one recent investigation, siblings were important resources for dating (O'Brien, 1990). In this study, adolescents said that they got more support for dating from siblings than from their mothers. In late adolescence, siblings were viewed as more important advisors and confidants than mothers when concerns about dating were involved. Sometimes, adolescents use siblings to their advantage when dealing with parents. In one study, younger siblings pointed to how their older siblings were given dating privileges that they had been denied (Place, 1975). In this investigation, an adolescent would sometimes side with a sibling when the sibling was having an argument with parents in the hope that the sibling would reciprocate when the adolescent needed dating privileges the parents were denying.

Peer relations are also involved in adolescent dating. In Dunphy's research, discussed earlier in the chapter, all large peer crowds in adolescence were heterosexual, and males in these crowds were consistently older than females (Dunphy, 1963). In this research, group leaders also played an important role. Both the leaders of large crowds and smaller cliques were highly involved with the opposite sex. Leaders dated more frequently, were more likely to go steady, and achieved these dating patterns earlier than nonleaders in the cliques. Leaders also were ascribed the task of maintaining a certain level of heterosexual involvement in the group. Peer leaders functioned as dating confidants and advisors, even putting partners together in the case of "slow learners."

At this point, we have discussed a number of ideas about the nature of adolescent groups and dating, and a summary of these ideas is presented in Concept Table 7.2. One setting in which peer relations take place is school. In the next chapter, we study the role of schools in adolescent development.

Concept Table 7.2

Adolescent Groups and Dating

Concept	Processes/Related Ideas	Characteristics/Description
Adolescent groups	Functions of groups	Groups satisfy adolescents' personal needs, reward them, provide information, raise their self-esteem, and give them an identity.
	Group formation	Norms are rules that apply to all members of a group. Roles are rules and expectations that govern certain positions in the group. Sherif's classic study documented how adolescents behave in group settings; superordinate tasks reduced adolescents' intergroup hostility.
	Children groups and adolescent groups	Children groups are less formal, less heterogeneous, and less heterosexual than adolescent groups. Dunphy found that adolescent group development moves through five stages.
	Ethnic and cultural variations	More aggression is directed at low-status members in lower-class groups. In many schools, peer groups are segregated according to ethnic group and social class. However, peer relations take place in diverse settings. Ethnic minority adolescents often have two sets of peers—one at school, one in the community. A special concern is peer support for the ethnic minority adolescent's achievement orientation. Ethnic minority adolescents, especially immigrants, may turn to the peer group more than White adolescents. In some cultures, children are placed in peer groups for greater lengths of time and at a much earlier age than in the United States.
	Cliques	Cliques are in between friendships and crowds in size and intimacy. Almost every secondary school has three to six well-defined cliques. Membership in certain cliques—jock and populars, for example—is associated with increased self-esteem. Independents also have high self-esteem.
Dating	Functions of dating	Dating can be a form of recreation, be a source of social status and achievement, be a part of the socialization process, involve learning about intimacy, provide a context for sexual experimentation, provide companionship, contribute to identity development, and be a means of mate sorting and selection.
	Age of onset, frequency, and going steady	Most adolescents date regularly, with girls beginning, on the average, at age 14 and boys between the ages of 14 and 15. Going steady becomes more serious in late adolescence.
	Male and female dating patterns	Females often show a stronger interest in personality exploration and self-disclosure, males a stronger interest in sexuality.
	What attracts adolescents to each other?	Similarity and physical attraction are important reasons adolescents want to date someone. The matching hypothesis and consensual validation are involved in understanding dating attraction.
	Romantic love	Romantic love, also called passionate love, involves sexuality and passion more than affectionate love. Romantic love is especially prominent in adolescents and college students. Affectionate love is more prominent in middle and late adulthood and is more likely to characterize the later stages of love.
	Developmental construction of dating relationships	The developmental construction view emphasizes how relationships with parents, siblings, and peers influence how adolescents construct their dating relationships. Dunphy's study found that group leaders play an important role in dating.

Summary

I. Peer Group Functions
The nature of peer relationships undergoes important changes during adolescence. Peers are individuals who are about the same age or maturity level. Peers provide a means of social comparison and a source of information about the world outside the family. Good peer relations may be necessary for normal social development in adolescence. The inability to "plug in" to a social network in childhood or adolescence is associated with a number of problems and disturbances. Thus, peer influences can be both positive and negative. Both Piaget and Sullivan stressed that peer relations provide the context for learning the symmetrical reciprocity mode of relationships.

II. Peer Conformity, Popularity, Neglect, and Rejection
Conformity occurs when individuals adopt the attitudes or behavior of others because of real or imagined pressure from the others. Conformity to antisocial peer standards peaks around the eighth to ninth grades, then decreases by the twelfth grade. A distinction is made between nonconformists and anticonformists. Listening skills, effective communication, being yourself, being happy, showing enthusiasm and concern for others, and having self-confidence but not being conceited are predictors of peer popularity. Neglected adolescents receive little attention from their peers, while rejected adolescents are disliked by their peers. The risk status of neglected adolescents is unclear. Rejected adolescents are at risk for the development of problems. Training programs focus on improving the peer relations of neglected and rejected adolescents. One issue involving rejected adolescents is whether to initially improve their prosocial skills or reduce their aggressive behavior and improve their self-control. It is important to remember that rejected adolescents reflect a heterogeneous grouping.

III. Social Knowledge, Social Information Processing, and Conglomerate Strategies for Improving Social Skills
Social knowledge and social information-processing skills are associated with improved peer relations. Conglomerate strategies, also referred to as coaching, involve the use of a combination of techniques, rather than a single approach, to improve adolescents' social skills.

IV. Friendships
The functions of friendship include companionship, stimulation, physical support, ego support, social comparison, and intimacy/affection. Harry Stack Sullivan was the most influential theorist to discuss the importance of adolescent friendships. He argued that there is a dramatic increase in the psychological importance and intimacy of close friends during early adolescence. Research findings support many of Sullivan's ideas. Intimacy and similarity are two of the most common characteristics of friendships. Intimacy in friendships is defined narrowly as self-disclosure or sharing of private thoughts. Similarity—in terms of age, sex, ethnicity, and many other factors—is also important to friendships. Adolescents who become close friends with older individuals engage in more deviant behaviors than their counterparts with same-age friends. Early-maturing girls are more likely than their later-maturing counterparts to have older friends, who may encourage deviant behavior.

V. Group Function and Formation
Groups satisfy adolescents' personal needs, reward them, provide information, raise their self-esteem, and give them an identity. Norms are rules that apply to all members of a group. Roles are rules and expectations that govern certain positions in the group. Sherif's classic study documented how adolescents behave in group settings; superordinate tasks reduced adolescents' intergroup hostility.

VI. Children Groups, Adolescent Groups, Ethnicity, and Culture

Children groups are less formal, less heterogeneous, and less heterosexual than adolescent groups. Dunphy found that adolescent group development moves through five stages. More aggression is directed at low-status members in lower-class groups. In many schools, peer groups are segregated according to ethnic group and social class. However, peer relations take place in diverse settings. Ethnic minority adolescents often have two sets of peers—one at school, one in the community. A special concern is peer support for the ethnic minority adolescent's achievement orientation. Ethnic minority adolescents, especially immigrants, may turn to the peer group more than White adolescents. In some cultures, children are placed in peer groups for greater lengths of time and at a much earlier age than in the United States.

VII. Cliques

Cliques are in between friendships and crowds in size and intimacy. Almost every secondary school has three to six well-defined cliques. Membership in certain cliques—for example, jocks and populars—is associated with increased self-esteem. Independents also have high self-esteem.

VIII. Dating Functions, Age of Onset of Dating, Frequency of Dating, and Going Steady

Dating can be a form of recreation, be a source of social status and achievement, be a part of the socialization process, involve learning about intimacy, provide a context for sexual experimentation, provide companionship, contribute to identity development, and be a means of mate sorting and selection. Most adolescents date regularly, with girls beginning, on the average, at age 14 and boys between the ages of 14 and 15. Going steady becomes more serious in late adolescence.

IX. Dating: Male and Female Patterns, Attraction, Romantic Love, and the Developmental Construction of Dating Relationships

Females often show a stronger interest in personality exploration and self-disclosure, males a stronger interest in sexuality. Similarity and physical attraction are important reasons adolescents want to date someone. The matching hypothesis and consensual validation are involved in understanding dating attraction. Romantic love, also called passionate love, involves sexuality and passion more than affectionate love. Romantic love is especially prominent in adolescents and college students. Affectionate love is more prominent in middle and late adulthood and is more likely to characterize the later stages of love. The developmental construction view emphasizes how relationships with parents, siblings, and peers influence how adolescents construct their dating relationships. Dunphy's study found that group leaders play an important role in dating.

Key Terms

peers 228
conformity 229
nonconformity 230
anticonformity 231
neglected children and
  adolescents 232
rejected children and
  adolescents 232

conglomerate strategies
  235
intimacy in friendship
  239
norms 241
roles 241
crowd 245
cliques 245

consensual validation
  252
matching hypothesis 252
romantic love 253
affectionate love 253

Suggested Readings

Brown, B. B. (1990). Peer groups and peer cultures. In S. S. Feldman & G. R. Elliott (Eds.), *At the threshold: The developing adolescent.* Cambridge, MA: Harvard University Press.
Presents an up-to-date, authoritative discussion of the role of cliques in adolescent development.

Duck, S. (1989). *Relating to others.* Chicago: Dorsey Press.
Presents valuable information about how individuals construct their relationships, including ideas relevant to dating relationships in adolescence.

Goldstein, A. P., Sprafkin, R. P., Gershaw, N. J., & Klein, P. (1981). *Skill-streaming the adolescent.* Champaign, IL: Research Press.
An excellent set of exercises that can be used to improve adolescents' social skills.

Hartup, W. W. (1983). The peer system. In P. H. Mussen (Ed.), *Handbook of child psychology* (Vol. 4, 4th ed.). New York: Wiley.
A detailed look at the development of peer relations from infancy through adolescence by one of the leading researchers on peer relations.

Journal of Early Adolescence, 5 (1985).
The entire issue is devoted to friendships in early adolescence.

Savin-Williams, R. C., & Berndt, T. J. (1990). Friendship and peer relations. In S. S. Feldman & G. R. Elliott (Eds.), *At the threshold: the developing adolescent.* Cambridge, MA: Harvard University Press.
Provides extensive insights into the nature of adolescent friendships.

Schools

The world rests on the breath of the children in the schoolhouse.

The Talmud

From No More "What If" Questions to Authors' Week

Some schools for adolescents are ineffective, others effective, as revealed in the following excerpts (Lipsitz, 1984):

A teacher in a social studies class squelches several imaginative questions, exclaiming, "You're always asking 'what if' questions. Stop asking 'what if.' " When a visitor asks who will become president if the president-elect dies before the electoral college meets, the teacher explodes, "You're as bad as they are! That's another 'what if' question!"

A teacher drills students for a seemingly endless amount of time on prime numbers. After the lesson, not one student can say why it is important to learn prime numbers.

A visitor asks a teacher if hers is an eighth-grade class. "It's called eighth grade," the teacher answers archly, "but we know it's really kindergarten, right class?"

In a predominantly Hispanic school, only the one adult hired as a bilingual teacher speaks Spanish.

In a biracial school, the principal and the guidance counselor cite test scores with pride. They are asked if the difference between the test scores of black and white students is narrowing: "Oh, that's an interesting question!" says the guidance counselor with surprise. The principal agrees. It has never been asked by or of them before.

The preceding vignettes are from middle schools where life seems to be difficult and unhappy for students. By contrast, consider the following circumstances in effective middle schools (Lipsitz, 1984):

Everything is peaceful. There are open cubbies instead of locked lockers. There is no theft. Students walk quietly in the corridors. "Why?" they are asked. "So as not to disturb the media center," they answer, which is self-evident to them, but not the visitor, who is left wondering. . . . When asked, "Do you like this school?" (They) answer, "No, we don't like it. We love it!"

When asked how the school feels, one student answered, "It feels smart. We're smart. Look at our test scores."

Comments from one of the parents of a student at the school are revealing: "My child would have been a dropout. In elementary school, his teacher said to me, 'That child isn't going to give you anything but heartaches.' He had perfect attendance here. He didn't want to miss a day. Summer vacation was too long and boring. Now he's majoring in communications at the University of Texas. He got here and all of a sudden, someone cared for him. I had been getting notes about Roger every other day, with threats about exclusion. Here, the first note said, 'It's just a joy to have him in the classroom.' "

The humane environment that encourages teachers' growth . . . is translated by the teachers . . . into a humane environment that encourages students' growth. The school feels cold when one first enters. It has the institutional feeling of any large school building with metal lockers and impersonal halls. Then one opens the door to a team area, and it is filled with energy, movement, productivity, doing. There is a lot of informal relating among students and between students and teachers. Visible from one vantage point are students working on written projects, putting the last touches on posters, watching a film, and working independently from reading kits. . . . Most know what they are doing, can say why it is important, and go back to work immediately after being interrupted.

Authors' Week is a special activity built into the school's curriculum that entices students to consider themselves in relation to the rich variety of making and doing in peoples' lives. Based on student interest, availability, and diversity, authors are invited . . . to discuss their craft. Students sign up to meet with individual authors. They must have read one individual book by the author. . . . Students prepare questions for their sessions with the authors. . . . Sometimes, an author stays several days to work with a group of students on his or her manuscript.

Excerpts published by permission of Transaction Publishers, from *Successful Schools for Young Adolescents*, by Joan Lipsitz. Copyright © 1983 by Transaction Publishers.

> *The Whole Art of Teaching Is Only the Art of Awakening the Natural Curiosity of Young Minds.*
>
> *Anatole France, 1881*

In this chapter, we explore many different ideas about schools for adolescents. The main questions addressed are: What is the nature of schools for adolescents? What transitions take place in adolescents' schooling? How do school size, classroom characteristics, teacher dimensions, and peer relations at school influence adolescents' development? Have schools done a better job of educating middle-class White students than low-income minority group students?

The Nature of Adolescents' Schooling

Today, virtually all American adolescents under the age of 16 and most 16- to 17-year-olds are in school. More than half of all youth continue their education after graduating from high school by attending technical schools, colleges, or universities. Schools for adolescents are vast and varied settings with many functions and diverse makeups.

Functions of Adolescents' Schools

During the twentieth century, U.S. schools have assumed a more prominent role in the lives of adolescents. From 1890 to 1920, virtually every state developed laws that excluded youth from work and required them to attend school. In this time frame, the number of high school graduates increased by 600 percent. By making secondary education compulsory, the adult power structure placed adolescents in a submissive position and made their move into the adult world of work more manageable. In the nineteenth century, high schools were mainly for the elite, with the educational emphasis on classical, liberal arts courses. By the 1920s, educators perceived that the secondary school curriculum needed to be changed. Schools for the masses, it was thought, should not just involve intellectual training but training for work and citizenship (Murphy, 1987). The curriculum of secondary schools became more comprehensive and grew to include general education, college preparatory, and vocational education courses. As the twentieth century unfolded, secondary schools continued to expand their orientation, adding courses in music, art, health, physical education, and other topics. By the middle of the twentieth century, schools had moved further toward preparing students for comprehensive roles in life (Conant, 1959). Today, secondary schools have retained their comprehensive orientation, designed to train adolescents intellectually but vocationally and socially as well.

While school attendance has consistently increased for more than 150 years, the distress over alienated and rebellious youth brought up the issue of whether secondary schools actually benefit adolescents. In the 1970s, three independent panels agreed that high schools contributed to adolescent alienation and actually restricted the transition to adulthood (Brown, 1973; Coleman & others, 1974; Martin, 1976). These prestigious panels argued that adolescents should be given educational alternatives to the comprehensive high school, such as on-the-job community work, to increase their exposure to adult roles and to decrease their sense of isolation from adults. Partially in response to these reports, a number of states lowered the age at which adolescents could leave school from 16 to 14.

Now, in the last two decades of the twentieth century, the back-to-basics movement has gained momentum. The **back-to-basics movement** *stresses that the function of schools should be the rigorous training of intellectual skills through such subjects as English, mathematics, and science.* Back-to-basics advocates point to the excessive fluff in secondary school curricula, with too many alternative subjects that do not give students a basic education in intellectual subjects. They also believe that schools should be in the business of imparting knowledge to adolescents and should not be concerned about adolescents' social and emotional lives. Critics of the fluff in schools also sometimes argue that the school day should be longer and that the school year should be extended into the summer months. Back-to-basics advocates want students to have more homework, more tests, and more discipline. They usually believe that adolescents should be behind their desks and not roaming around the room, while teachers should be at the head of the classroom, drilling knowledge into adolescents' minds.

Much of the current back-to-basics emphasis is a reaction against the trend toward open education in the 1970s. The open-education approach, which was based on the British educational system, allowed adolescents to learn and develop at their own pace within a highly structured classroom. However, too many school systems that implemented open education in the United States thought it meant tearing down classroom walls and letting adolescents do whatever they wanted. Incorrect application of open education in American schools resulted in a strong backlash against it (Kantrowitz & Wingert, 1989).

Should the main and perhaps only major goal of schooling for adolescents be the development of an intellectually mature individual? Or should schools also focus on the adolescent's maturity in social and emotional development? Should schools be comprehensive and provide a multifaceted curriculum that includes many electives and alternative subjects to a basic core? These provocative questions continue to be heatedly debated ·in educational and community circles (Beane, 1990; Glasser, 1990). Some education analysts believe that secondary schools have become so multifaceted that they are like shopping malls (Powell, Farrar, & Cohen, 1985). The implications of the "shopping mall" analogy for adolescent development are discussed in Perspective on Adolescent Development 8.1.

The debate about the function of schools produces shifts of emphases, much like a swinging pendulum, moving toward basic skills at one point in time, toward options, frills, or comprehensive training for life at another, and so on back and forth (Cross, 1984). What we should strive for, though, is not a swinging pendulum but something like a spiral staircase; that is, we should continually be developing more sophisticated ways of fulfilling the varied and changing functions of schools (see Figure 8.1).

So far in our discussion of the function of schools, we have been examining the nature of U.S. secondary schools. The nature of secondary schools around the world is the focus of Sociocultural Worlds of Adolescence 8.1.

Do Schools Make a Difference?

Schools have a great deal of influence on children and adolescents. By the time students graduate from high school, they have accumulated more than 10,000 hours in the classroom. School influences are more powerful today than in past generations because more individuals are in school longer. For example, in 1900, 11.4 percent of 14- to 17-year-olds were in school. Today, 94 percent of this age group are in school.

Children and adolescents spend many years in schools as members of a small society in which there are tasks to be accomplished; people to be socialized

PERSPECTIVE ON ADOLESCENT DEVELOPMENT 8.1

The "Shopping Mall" High School

Adolescent educators Arthur Powell, Eleanor Farrar, and David Cohen (1985) conducted an in-depth examination of 15 diverse high schools across the United States by interviewing students, teachers, and school personnel, as well as by observing and interpreting what was happening in the schools. The metaphor of the "shopping mall" high school emerged as the authors tried to make sense of the data they had collected.

Variety, choice, and neutrality are important dimensions of what is labeled the "shopping mall" high school. Variety appears in the wide range of courses offered (in one school, 480 courses in the curriculum!), with something for apparently every student. Variety usually stimulates choice. Choice is often cited as a positive aspect of curricula, but the choice often rests in the hands of students, who, in too many instances, make choices based on ignorance rather than information. The investigators found that the diversity of individuals, multiple values, and wide range of course offerings combined to produce neutrality. Because they try to accommodate the needs of different student populations, high schools may become neutral institutions that take few stands on the products and services they offer.

The investigators described the shopping mall high school as possessing "specialty shops" and also as having an "unspecial" dimension. Shopping malls usually have a wide range of stores—from large department stores to exclusive boutiques selling a special line of products and catering to a small, select clientele. Like shopping malls, high schools offer a variety of specialties aimed at providing services to students in "high" and "low" tracks. Students who fall in between—with neither the abilities nor the disabilities to make them unique—make up the domain of the "unspecial." While the unspecial group usually is the largest in number in the school, the allocation of effort and attention to the unspecial usually is the least. Since this difficult-to-define, unspecial group of students lacks strong and influential advocates, minimum requirements may become maximum standards of performance. The investigators stressed that the unspecial students may be the forgotten people in high schools, neither "bright" nor "slow," neither driven nor disruptive. They just get through the system on their own, with too little connectedness to each other or to anyone else.

The investigators argued that the shopping mall high school encourages individualization but does not provide personalization. The shopping mall high school offers the freedom to go through school mainly on one's own, which may result in anonymity and increased numbers of unspecial students. In contrast, private schools and specialty shops in the shopping mall high school provide personalization. They offer connections among people, especially between teacher and student, which increase both teacher and student satisfaction.

A criticism of the "shopping mall" high school label is that, in choosing to focus on the communalities of high schools, the investigators failed to focus on variations in race, social class, ethnicity, and community history that characterize a high school's uniqueness. Nonetheless, the shopping mall is an intriguing metaphor for America's high schools and provides insight into some general characteristics that have emerged (Santilli & Seidman, 1986).

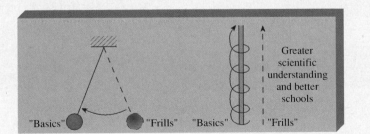

Figure 8.1 The swinging pendulum solution versus the spiral staircase solution.

and to be socialized by; and rules that define and limit behavior, feelings, and attitudes. The experiences children and adolescents have in this society are likely to have a strong influence in such areas as identity development, belief in one's competence, images of life and career possibilities, social relationships, standards of right and wrong, and conceptions of how a social system beyond the family functions.

Cross-Cultural Comparisons of Secondary Schools

Secondary schools in different countries share a number of similar features, but differ on others (Cameron & others, 1983; George, 1987; Thomas, 1988). Here, we examine the similarities and differences in secondary schools in six countries: Australia, Brazil, Germany, Japan, Russia, and the United States.

Most countries mandate that children begin school at 6 to 7 years of age and stay in school until they are 14 to 17 years of age. Brazil only requires students to go to school until they are 14 years of age, while Russia mandates that students stay in school until they are 17. Germany, Japan, Australia, and the United States require school attendance until ages 15 to 16.

Most secondary schools around the world are divided into two or more levels, such as middle school (or junior high school) and high school. However, Germany's schools are divided according to three educational ability tracks: (1) The *main school* provides a basic level of education, (2) the middle school gives students a more advanced education, and (3) the academic school prepares students for entrance to a university. German schools, like most European schools, offer a classical education, which includes courses in Latin and Greek.

Japanese secondary schools have an entrance exam, but secondary schools in the other five countries do not. Only Australia and Germany have comprehensive exit exams.

The United States is the only country in the world in which sports are an integral part of the public school system. Only a few private schools in other countries have their own sports teams, sports facilities, and highly organized sports events.

The juku, *or "cramming school," is available to Japanese children and adolescents in the summertime and after school. It provides coaching to help them improve their grades and their entrance exam scores for high schools and universities. The Japanese practice of requiring an entrance exam for high school is a rarity among the nations of the world.*

The nature of the curriculum is often similar in secondary schools in different countries, although there are some differences in content and philosophy. For example, at least until recently, the secondary schools in Russia have emphasized the preparation of students for work. The "labor education program," which is part of the secondary school curriculum, includes vocational training and on-the-job experience. The idea is to instill in youth a love for manual work and a positive attitude about industrial and work organizations. Russian students who are especially gifted—academically, artistically, or athletically—attend special schools where the students are encouraged to develop their talents and are trained to be the very best in their vocation. With the breakup of the Soviet Union, it will be interesting to follow what changes in education take place in Russia.

In Brazil, students are required to take Portuguese (the native language) and four foreign languages (Latin, French, English, and Spanish). Brazil requires these languages because of the country's international character and emphasis on trade and commerce. Seventh-grade students in Australia take courses in sheep husbandry and weaving, two areas of economic and cultural interest in the country. In Japan, students take a number of Western courses in addition to their basic Japanese courses; these courses include Western literature and languages (in addition to Japanese literature and language), Western physical education (in addition to Japanese martial arts classes), and Western sculpture and handicrafts (in addition to Japanese calligraphy). The Japanese school year is also much longer than that of other countries (225 days versus 180 days in the United States, for example).

In Russia, secondary schools have emphasized the preparation of students for work. Instruction in vocational training and on-the-job experience are emphasized in the labor education programs. With the downfall of the Communist government, it will be interesting to observe whether changes in Russia's schools will take place.

Schools' influence on children and adolescents has been evaluated from two points of view: (1) Is there a difference between the cognitive performances of those who have gone to school and those who have not? (2) Can schools override the negative effects of poverty? Concerning the first question, schooled children and adolescents usually outperform their unschooled counterparts on a variety of cognitive tasks (Cole & Cole, 1989; Farnham-Diggory, 1990). However, investigators do not yet have a complete picture of how schooling affects adolescent social development. Research on the second question, regarding poverty, has been controversial. The disagreement is rooted in the work of sociologists James Coleman and Christopher Jencks (Coleman & others, 1966; Jencks & others, 1972). In such investigations, characteristics of schools were compared with family and economic factors as predictors of school achievement and success. Both Coleman and Jencks argue that the evidence supports their belief that schools have little impact on the cognitive development of poverty-stricken students.

Critics fault Coleman and Jencks on a variety of issues, including the methods they used for collecting their data. One of the most serious criticisms leveled at them is that their analysis is too global, that it was conducted at the level of the school as a whole rather than at the more fine-grained level of everyday happenings in classrooms. In their studies of achievement in school and after, dissenters have compared the effectiveness of schools and classrooms and arrived at the exact opposite conclusion from Coleman and Jencks (Farnham-Diggory, 1990; Klitgaard and Hall, 1975; Rutter & others, 1979). These researchers identify an important idea that is carried through the remainder of this chapter—namely, that academic and social patterns are intricately interwoven. Schools that produced high achievement in lower-income students were identified not only by particular types of curriculum and time involved in teaching, but by many features of the climate of the school, such as the nature of the teachers' expectations and the patterns of interaction between teachers and students. In other words, various aspects of the school as a social system contributed to the achievement of students in the school.

Additional research on whether schools make a difference in a student's achievement suggests that this question cannot be appropriately addressed without considering the extensive variation in schooling. Schools vary even in similar neighborhoods serving similar populations. And they may differ on such dimensions as whether they are integrated or segregated, coed or single sex, parochial or secular, rural or urban, and large or small. Schools are also different in terms of their social climates, educational ideologies, and concepts of what constitutes the best way to promote the adolescent's development.

Schools' Changing Social Developmental Contexts

The social context differs at the preschool, elementary, and secondary level. The preschool setting is a protected environment, whose boundary is the classroom. In this limited social setting, preschool children interact with one or two teachers, almost always female, who are powerful figures in the young child's life. The preschool child also interacts with peers in a dyadic relationship or in small groups. Preschool children have little concept of the classroom as an organized social system, although they are learning how to make and maintain social contacts and communicate their needs. The preschool serves to modify some patterns of behavior developed through family experiences. Greater self-control may be required in the preschool than earlier in development.

The classroom is still the major context for the elementary school child, although it is more likely to be experienced as a social unit than in the preschool. The network of social expression also is more complex now. Teachers and peers have a prominent influence on children during the elementary school years. The teacher symbolizes authority, which establishes the climate of the classroom, conditions of social interaction, and the nature of group functioning. The peer group becomes more salient, with increased interest in friendship, belonging, and status. And the peer group also becomes a learning community in which social roles and standards related to work and achievement are formed.

As children move into middle or junior high schools, the school environment increases in scope and complexity. The social field is the school as a whole rather than the classroom. Adolescents socially interact with many different teachers and peers from a range of social and ethnic backgrounds. Students are often exposed to a greater mix of male and female teachers. And social behavior is heavily weighted toward peers, extracurricular activities, clubs, and the community. The student in secondary schools is usually aware of the school as a social system and may be motivated to conform and adapt to the system or challenge it (Minuchin & Shapiro, 1983).

Transitions in Schooling

As children become adolescents and as adolescents develop and then become adults, they experience many transitions in schooling. We have just seen how the social setting changes from preschools through secondary schools. Additional important considerations involve transitions from elementary school to middle school or junior high school, from high school to college, and from school to work for noncollege youth, either after completing high school or after dropping out of school.

Transition to Middle or Junior High School

The emergence of junior high schools in the 1920s and 1930s was justified on the basis of physical, cognitive, and social changes that characterize early adolescence, as well as on the need for more schools in response to the growing student population. Old high schools became junior high schools, and new, regional high schools were built. In most systems, the ninth grade remained a part of the high school in content, although physically separated from it in a 6–3–3 system (a system whereby students are grouped as follows: first through sixth grade, seventh through ninth grade, and tenth through twelfth grade). Gradually, the ninth grade has been restored to the high school, as many school systems have developed middle schools that include the seventh and eighth grades, or sixth, seventh, and eighth grades. The creation of middle schools has been influenced by the earlier onset of puberty in recent decades. Figure 8.2 reveals the dramatic increase in sixth- through eighth-grade middle schools and the corresponding decrease in seventh- through ninth-grade junior high schools.

One worry of educators and psychologists is that junior highs and middle schools have become simply watered-down versions of high schools, mimicking high schools' curricular and extracurricular schedules (Hill, 1980). The critics argue that unique curricular and extracurricular activities reflecting a wide range of individual differences in biological and psychological development in early adolescence should be incorporated into junior high and middle schools (Mac Iver & others, 1992). The critics also stress that too many high schools foster passivity rather than autonomy and that schools should create a variety of pathways for students to achieve an identity.

The transition to middle school or junior high school from elementary school is a normative experience for virtually all children. However, the transition can

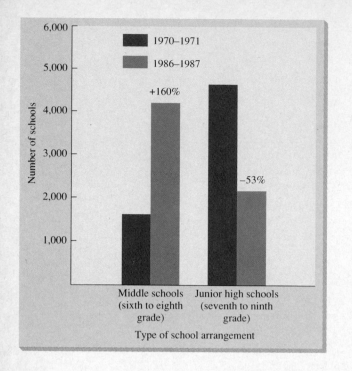

Figure 8.2 The middle school movement.

be stressful because it occurs simultaneously with many other changes—in the individual, in the family, and in school (Eccles & Midgely, 1990; Estrada, 1992; Fenzel, Blyth, & Simmons, 1991; Hawkins & Berndt, 1985; Simmons & Blyth, 1987). These changes include: puberty and related concerns about body image; the emergence of at least some aspects of formal operational thought, including accompanying changes in social cognition; increased responsibility and independence in association with decreased dependency on parents; change from a small, contained classroom structure to a larger, more impersonal school structure; change from one teacher to many teachers and a small, homogeneous set of peers to a larger, more heterogeneous set of peers; and increased focus on achievement and performance, and their assessment. This list includes a number of negative, stressful features, but aspects of the transition can also be positive. Students are more likely to feel grown up, have more subjects from which to select, have more opportunities to spend time with peers and to locate compatible friends, enjoy increased independence from direct parental monitoring, and may be more challenged intellectually by academic work.

When students make the transition from elementary school to middle or junior high school, they experience the **top-dog phenomenon,** *the circumstance of moving from the top position (in elementary school, the oldest, biggest, and most powerful students in the school) to the lowest position (in middle or junior high school, the youngest, smallest, and least powerful students in the school).* Researchers who have charted the transition from elementary to middle or junior high school find that the first year of middle or junior high school can be difficult for many students (Eccles & Midgely, 1990; Hawkins & Berndt, 1985; Simmons & Blyth, 1987). For example, in one investigation of the transition from sixth grade in an elementary school to the seventh grade in a junior high school, adolescents' perceptions of the quality of their school life plunged in the seventh grade (Hirsch & Rapkin, 1987). In the seventh grade, the students were less satisfied with school, were less committed to school, and liked their teachers less. The drop in school satisfaction occurred regardless of how academically successful the students were.

(a)

(b)

Is the transition to sixth- through eighth-grade middle schools easier for students than the transition to seventh- through ninth-grade junior high schools? It is hard to say. The middle school transition does guarantee that more girls will experience pubertal change when they are in the large, impersonal context of the middle school, but middle schools do not reduce the number of times adolescents are "bottom dogs." And with another arrangement, in which the middle school consists of the fifth, sixth, and seventh grades, boys may be subjected to more stress than in the past because their pubertal change coincides with school change (Entwistle, 1988, 1990). The old two-tier system (the 8–4 arrangement: kindergarten through eighth grade, and ninth grade through twelfth grade) probably is the best for minimizing school transition stress because it reduces the number of transitions and because the main transition occurs after many adolescents are already well into puberty.

Roberta Simmons and Dale Blyth (1987) studied students in school systems with a 6–3–3 arrangement and with an 8–4 arrangement. The adolescents in the 8–4 arrangement (who only had to make one change of schools) had higher self-esteem and participated more in extracurricular activities than the adolescents in the 6–3–3 arrangement, who had to change schools twice. The adolescents' grades and sense of anonymity did not differ in the two types of school arrangements. The researchers concluded that all school transitions have a temporary negative influence on student's competence but that, the earlier the school change occurs in adolescence, the more difficult it likely is for students.

The transition from elementary school to middle or junior high school can be stressful. In the last year of elementary school (a), boys and girls are in the "top-dog" position as the biggest, most powerful students in the school. However, in the first year of middle or junior high school (b), boys and girls are in the "bottom-dog" position as the smallest, least powerful students in the school.

Joan Lipsitz (shown here talking with young adolescents) has been an important spokesperson for the needs of adolescents. Former director of the Center for Early Adolescence at the University of North Carolina, she wrote the widely acclaimed book, Successful Schools for Young Adolescents.

Schools that provide more support, less anonymity, more stability, and less complexity improve student adjustment during the transition from elementary to middle or junior high school (Fenzel, 1989; Fenzel, Blyth, & Simmons, 1991). In one investigation, 101 students were studied at three points in time: spring of the sixth grade (pretransition), fall of the seventh grade (early transition), and spring of the seventh grade (late transition) (Hawkins & Berndt, 1985). Two different schools were sampled—one a traditional junior high school, the other a junior high in which the students were grouped into small teams (100 students, four teachers). Students' adjustment was assessed through self-reports, peer ratings, and teacher ratings. Adjustment dropped during the posttransition—for example, seventh-grade students' self-esteem was lower than that of sixth-grade students. Students in the team-oriented junior high reported that they received more support from teachers. Friendship patterns also influenced the students' adjustment. Students who reported more contact with their friends and higher-quality friendships had more positive perceptions of themselves and of their junior high school than their low-friendship counterparts.

What Makes a Successful Middle School?

Joan Lipsitz and her colleagues (1984) searched the nation for the best middle schools. Extensive contacts and observations were made. Based on the recommendations of education experts and observations in schools in different parts of the United States, four middle schools were chosen for their outstanding ability to educate young adolescents. The most striking feature of these middle schools was their willingness and ability to adapt all school practices to the individual differences in physical, cognitive, and social development of their students. The schools took seriously the knowledge investigators have developed about young adolescents. This seriousness was reflected in decisions about different aspects of school life. For example, one middle school fought to keep its schedule of mini-courses on Friday so that every student could be with friends and pursue personal interests. Two other middle schools expended considerable energy on a complex school organization so that small groups of students worked with small groups of teachers who could vary the tone and pace of the school day, depending on students' needs. Another middle school developed an advisory scheme so that each student had daily contact with an adult who was willing to listen, explain, comfort, and prod the adolescent. Such school policies reflect thoughtfulness and personal concern about individuals whose developmental needs are compelling. Another aspect observed was that, early in their existence—the first year in three of the schools and the second year in the fourth school—these effective middle schools emphasized the importance of creating an environment that was positive for the adolescent's social and emotional development. This goal was established not only because such environments contribute to academic excellence but also because social and emotional development are intrinsically valued as important in themselves in adolescents' schooling.

Recognizing that the vast majority of middle schools do not approach the excellent schools described by Joan Lipsitz (1984), in 1989 the Carnegie Corporation issued an extremely negative evaluation of U.S. middle schools. In the report—*Turning Points: Preparing American Youth for the Twenty-First Century*—the conclusion was reached that most young adolescents attend massive, impersonal schools; learn from seemingly irrelevant curricula; trust few adults in school; and lack access to health care and counseling. The Carnegie report recommends:

- Developing smaller "communities" or "houses" to lessen the impersonal nature of large middle schools

- Lowering student-to-counselor ratios from several hundred-to-1 to 10-to-1
- Involving parents and community leaders in schools
- Developing curriculum that produces students who are literate, understand the sciences, and have a sense of health, ethics, and citizenship
- Having teachers team-teach in more flexibly designed curriculum blocks that integrate several disciplines, instead of presenting students with disconnected, rigidly separated 50-minute segments
- Boosting students' health and fitness with more in-school programs and helping students who need public health care to get it

Many of these same recommendations were echoed in a report from the National Governors' Association (*America in Transition,* 1989), which stated that the very structure of middle school education in America neglects the basic developmental needs of young adolescents. Many educators and psychologists strongly support these recommendations (Entwistle, 1990). The Edna Mc-Connell Clark Foundation's Program for Disadvantaged Youth is an example of a multiyear, multisite effort designed to implement many of the proposals for middle school improvement. The foundation has engaged the Center for Early Adolescence at the University of North Carolina to guide five urban school districts in their middle school reform (Scales, 1990). In sum, middle schools throughout the United States need a major redesign if they are to effectively educate adolescents for becoming competent adults in the twenty-first century.

Transition from High School to College

Just as the transition from elementary school to middle or junior high school involves change and possible stress, so does the transition from high school to college (Takahashi & Majima, 1992). In many ways, the two transitions involve parallel changes. Going from a senior in high school to a freshman in college replays the "top-dog" phenomenon of going from the oldest and most powerful group of students to the youngest and least powerful group of students. For many of you, the transition from high school to college was not too long ago. You may vividly remember the feeling of your first days, weeks, and months on campus. You were called a freshman. Dictionary definitions of *freshmen* describe them not only as being in the first year of high school or college but as being novices or beginners. *Senior* not only designates the fourth year of high school or college, but also implies being above others in decision-making power. The transition from high school to college involves a move to a larger, more impersonal school structure, interaction with peers from more diverse geographical and sometimes more diverse ethnic backgrounds, and increased focus on achievement and performance, and their assessment (Belle & Paul, 1989; Upcraft & Gardner, 1989).

But as with the transition from elementary school to middle or junior high school, the transition from high school to college can have positive aspects. Students are more likely to feel grown up, have more subjects from which to select, have more time to spend with peers, have more opportunities to explore different life-styles and values, enjoy greater independence from parental monitoring, and may be more challenged intellectually by academic work.

For many individuals, a major change from high school to college is reduced contact with parents. One investigation revealed that going away to college may not only benefit the individual's independence but also improve relationships with parents (Sullivan & Sullivan, 1980). Two groups of parents and their sons were studied. One group of sons left home to board at college; the other group remained home and commuted daily to college. The students were evaluated both

(a)   (b)

(a) The transition from high school to college shares a number of parallels with the transition from elementary school to middle or junior high school, including the "top-dog" phenomenon. (b) An especially important aspect of the transition to college is reduced interaction with parents.

before they had completed high school and after they were in college. Those who boarded at college were more affectionate toward their parents, communicated better with them, and were more independent from them than their counterparts who remained at home and attended college.

The large number of individuals who go directly to college after completing high school delay formal entry into the adult world of work. You may remember from Chapter 1 the description of *youth*, a post-high-school age period involving a sense of economic and personal "temporariness" (Kenniston, 1970). For many individuals, going to college postpones career or marriage/family decisions. The major shift to college attendance occurred in the post-World-War-II years, as the GI Bill opened up a college education for many individuals. Since the 1960s, college attendance has steadily increased.

Students often go to college expecting something special. As one high school student said, "My main concern is that, without a college education, I won't have much chance in today's world. I want a better life, which to me, means going to college." While high school students usually approach college with high expectations, their transition from high school to college may be less than ideal. In a study of undergraduate education in the United States, the Carnegie Foundation for the Advancement of Teaching pointed out the disturbing discontinuity between public high schools and institutions of higher learning (Boyer, 1986). Almost half of the prospective college students surveyed said that trying to select a college is confusing because there is no sound basis for making a decision. Many high school seniors choose a college almost blindfolded. Once enrolled, they may not be satisfied with their choice and may transfer or drop out, sometimes for the wrong reasons. The transition from high school to college needs to become

		Students %	Parents %
College representatives at "College Nights"	Relevant Accurate	62 73	65 68
High school counselors	Relevant Accurate	57 70	49 62
Comparative guides	Relevant Accurate	53 65	50 59
College publications	Relevant Accurate	32 59	34 49

smoother. As a first step, public schools should take far more responsibility for assisting students in the transition from high school to college. Public high schools could learn considerably from the best private schools, which have always taken this transition seriously, according to the Carnegie Foundation report. Colleges also need to provide more helpful guidance to prospective students, going beyond glossy brochures and becoming more personalized in their interaction with high school students (Fidler & Hunter, 1989). Figure 8.3 suggests that college representatives, high school counselors, comparative guides, and college publications have a long way to go.

Today's college freshmen appear to be experiencing more stress and depression than in the past, according to a UCLA survey of more than 300,000 freshmen at more than 500 colleges and universities (Astin, Green, & Korn, 1987). In 1987, 8.7 percent of the freshmen reported feeling depressed often; in 1988, the figure rose to 10.5 percent. Fear of failing in a success-oriented world is frequently given as a reason for stress and depression among college students. The pressure to succeed in college, get an outstanding job, and make lots of money is pervasive, according to many of the students.

Figure 8.3 Evaluation of major sources of college information by college-bound high school seniors and their parents (percent agreeing).
From the Carnegie Foundation for the Advancement of Teaching, Survey of the Transition from High School to College, 1984–85.

High School Dropouts and Noncollege Youth

Dropping out of high school has been viewed as a serious educational and societal problem for many decades. By leaving high school before graduating, many dropouts have educational deficiencies that severely curtail their economic and social well-being throughout their adult lives. In this section, we study the scope of the problem, the causes of dropping out, and ways to reduce dropout rates.

High School Dropout Rates
Over the past 40 years, the proportion of adolescents who have not finished high school to those who have has decreased considerably (Bachman, 1991). In 1940, more than 60 percent of 25- to 29-year-olds had not completed high school. Today, this figure is approximately 15 percent.

Despite the overall decline in high school dropout rates, the higher dropout rate of ethnic minority students and low-income students, especially in large cities, remains a major concern (Dryfoos, 1990; Eccles, 1991; Goertz, Ekstrom, & Rock, 1991). Although the dropout rates of most ethnic minority students have been declining, the rates remain substantially above those of White students. Thirty-five percent of 20- to 21-year-old Hispanic Americans, 18 percent of 20- to 21-

year-old Black Americans, and 14 percent of 20- to 21-year-old White Americans have dropped out of school. Dropout rates are extremely high for Native Americans: fewer than 10 percent graduate from high school (LaFromboise & Low, 1989). In some inner-city areas, the dropout rate for ethnic minority students is especially high, reaching more than 50 percent in Chicago, for example (Hahn, 1987). Hispanic American dropout rates have declined little if at all in the past decade. While the dropout rate of Black Americans has declined considerably in recent years, it still remains above that of White students.

The Causes of Dropping Out

Students drop out of school for school-related, economic, family-related, peer-related, and personal reasons. School-related problems are consistently associated with dropping out of school (Goertz, Ekstrom, & Rock, 1991; O'Sullivan, 1990). In one investigation, almost 50 percent of the dropouts cited school-related reasons for leaving school, such as not liking school, being suspended, or being expelled (Rumberger, 1983). Twenty percent of the dropouts (but 40 percent of the Hispanic American students) cited economic reasons for dropping out. Many of these students quit school and go to work to help support their families. Socioeconomic status is the main factor in family background that is strongly related to dropping out of school: Students from low-income families are more likely to drop out than those from middle-income families. Many school dropouts have friends who also are school dropouts. Approximately one-third of the girls who drop out of school do so for personal reasons, such as pregnancy or marriage. However, overall, males are more likely to drop out than females.

Many of the factors just mentioned were related to dropping out of school in one large-scale investigation called *The High School and Beyond Study,* in which 30,000 high school sophomores were followed through graduation (Goertz, Ekstrom, & Rock, 1991). High school dropouts were more likely to come from low-income families, be in vocational programs, be males, be an ethnic minority (with the exception of Asian Americans), and be in an urban school district (compared to rural or suburban). In addition, high school dropouts had lower grades in school (especially in reading), more disciplinary problems, lower rates of homework completion, lower self-esteem, lower educational expectations, and a more externalized sense of control.

Reducing the Dropout Rate and Improving the Lives of Noncollege Youth

The dropout rate can be reduced and the lives of noncollege youth improved by strengthening the schools and by bridging the gap between school and work (McCall, 1991; Scales, 1990; Spencer & Dornbusch, 1990; William T. Grant Foundation Commission on Work, Family, and Citizenship, 1988).

Part of the solution lies within schools. Students may work hard through 12 grades of school, attain adequate records, learn basic academic skills, graduate in good standing, and still experience problems in getting started in a productive career. Others may drop out of school because they see little benefit from the type of education they are getting. Although no complete cure-all, strengthening schools is an important dimension of reducing dropout rates. While the education reform movements of the 1980s have encouraged schools to set higher standards for students and teachers, most of the focus has been on college-bound students. But reform movements should not penalize students who will not go to college. One way noncollege-bound youth are being helped is through Chapter 1 of the Education Consolidation and Improvement Act, which provides extra services for low-achieving students. States and communities need to establish clear goals for school completion, youth employment, parental involvement, and youth community service. For example, it should be the goal of every state to reduce the dropout rate to 10 percent or less by the year 2000.

Community institutions, especially schools, need to break down the barriers between work and school. Many youth step off the education ladder long before reaching the level of a professional career, often with nowhere to step next, left to their own devices to search for work. These youth need more assistance than they are now receiving. Among the approaches worth considering are:

- Monitored work experiences, such as through cooperative education, apprenticeships, internships, pre-employment training, and youth-operated enterprises
- Community and neighborhood services, including voluntary service and youth-guided services
- Redirected vocational education, the principal thrust of which should not be preparation for specific jobs but acquisition of basic skills needed in a wide range of work
- Guarantees of continuing education, employment, or training, especially in conjunction with mentoring programs
- Career information and counseling to expose youth to job opportunities and career options as well as to successful role models
- School volunteer programs, not only for tutoring but to provide access to adult friends and mentors

At this point, we have discussed a number of ideas about the nature of adolescent schooling and transitions in schooling. A summary of these ideas is presented in Concept Table 8.1. Next, we describe some dimensions of schools and classrooms, and characteristics of teachers and peers, that influence adolescent development.

Schools and Classrooms, Teachers and Peers

Schools and classrooms vary along many dimensions, including size of school or class and school or class atmosphere, with some schools and classes being highly structured, others more unstructured. Adolescents' lives in school also involve thousands of hours of interactions with teachers and peers.

School Size and Classroom Size

A number of factors led to the increased size of secondary schools in the United States: increasing urban enrollments, decreasing budgets, and an educational rationale of increased academic stimulation in consolidated institutions. But is bigger really better? No systematic relation between school size and academic achievement has been found, but more prosocial and possibly less antisocial behavior occur in small schools (Rutter & others, 1979). Large schools, especially those with more than 500 to 600 students, may not provide a personalized climate that allows for an effective system of social control. Students may feel alienated and not take responsibility for their conduct. This may be especially true for unsuccessful students who do not identify with their school and who become members of oppositional peer groups. The responsiveness of the school may mediate the impact of school size on adolescent behavior. For example, in one investigation,

	Concept Table 8.1	
	The Nature of Schooling and Transitions in Schooling	
Concept	**Processes/Related Ideas**	**Characteristics/Description**
The nature of adolescents' schooling	Functions of schools	In the nineteenth century, secondary schools were for the elite. By the 1920s, they had changed, becoming more comprehensive and training adolescents for work and citizenship, as well as training intellect. The comprehensive high school remains today, but the functions of secondary schools continue to be debated. Supporters of the back-to-basics movement maintain that the function of schools should be intellectual development; others argue for more comprehensive functions, including social and vocational development.
	Do schools make a difference?	Some sociologists have argued that schools have little impact on adolescents' development, but when researchers have conducted more precise, observational studies of what goes on in schools and classrooms, the effects of schooling become more apparent.
	Schools' changing social developmental contexts	The social context differs at the preschool, elementary school, and secondary school levels, increasing in scope and complexity for adolescents.
Transitions in schooling	Transition to middle or junior high school	The emergence of junior high schools in the 1920s and 1930s was justified on the basis of physical, cognitive, and social changes that characterize early adolescence, as well as on the need for more schools in response to the growing student population. Middle schools have become more popular in recent years and coincide with earlier pubertal development. The transition to middle or junior high school coincides with many social, familial, and individual changes in the adolescent's life. The transition involves moving from the "top-dog" to the "bottom-dog" position.
	What makes a successful middle school?	Successful schools for young adolescents take individual differences in development seriously, show a deep concern for what is known about early adolescence, and emphasize social and emotional development as much as intellectual development. In 1989, the Carnegie Corporation recommended a major redesign of middle schools.
	Transition from high school to college	In a number of ways, the transition from high school to college parallels the transition from elementary to middle or junior high school, including the "top-dog" phenomenon. An especially important transition for most adolescents is reduced interaction with parents. A special problem today is the discontinuity between public high schools and colleges.
	High school dropouts and noncollege youth	Dropping out of high school has been a serious problem for decades. Many dropouts have educational deficiencies that curtail their economic and social well-being for much of their adult lives. Some progress has been made in that dropout rates for most ethnic minority groups have declined in recent decades, although dropout rates for inner-city, low-income minorities are still precariously high. Dropping out of school is associated with demographic, family-related, peer-related, school-related economic, and personal factors. The dropout rate could be reduced and the lives of noncollege youth improved by strengthening the schools and by bridging the gap between school and work.

low responsive schools (few rewards for desirable behavior) had higher crime rates than high responsive schools (McPartland & McDill, 1976). While school responsiveness may mediate adolescent conduct, small schools may be more flexible and responsive than larger schools.

Besides the belief that smaller schools provide adolescents with a better education, there also is a belief that smaller classes are better than larger classes. Traditional schools in the United States have 30 to 35 students. Analysis of a large number of investigations revealed that, as class size increases, achievement decreases (Glass & Smith, 1978). The researchers concluded that a pupil who would score at about the sixty-third percentile on a national test when taught individually would score at about the thirty-seventh percentile when taught in a class of 40 students. They also concluded that being taught in a class of 20 students versus a class of 40 students is an advantage of about 10 percentile points on national achievement tests in the subject. These researchers also found that the greatest gains in achievement occurred among students who were taught in classes of 15 students or less. In classes of 20 to 40 students, class size had a less dramatic influence on students' achievement. Although this research has been criticized on methodological grounds, other researchers have reanalyzed the data using different techniques and arrived at the same conclusions (Hedges & Stock, 1983).

Unfortunately, to maximize each adolescent's learning potential, classes would have to be so small that few schools could afford to staff and house them (Klein, 1985; Slavin, 1989a). While class sizes of 15 students or less are not feasible for all subjects, one alternative is to allocate a larger portion of resources to those grade levels or subjects that seem the most critical. For example, some schools are beginning to reduce class size in core academic subjects, such as mathematics, English, and science, while having higher class sizes in elective subjects.

Classroom Structure and Climate

The most widely debated issue in classroom structure and climate focuses on open versus traditional classrooms. The open versus traditional concept is multidimensional. Open classrooms, or open schools, have characteristics such as the following:

- Free choice of activities by students
- Space flexibility
- Varied, enriched learning materials
- Emphasis on individual and small-group instruction
- A teacher who is more a facilitator than a director of learning
- Students who learn to assume responsibility for their learning
- Multi-age groupings of children
- Team-teaching
- Classrooms without walls in which the physical arrangement of the school is more open

Overall, researchers have found that open classrooms are associated with lower language achievement but improved attitudes toward school (Giaconia & Hedges, 1982).

Beyond the overall effects of open versus traditional classrooms, it is important to evaluate how specific dimensions of open classrooms are related to specific dimensions of the adolescent's development. In this regard, researchers have found that individualized instruction (adjusting rate, methods, materials, small-group methods) and role of the adolescent (the degree of activity in learning) are associated with positive effects on the adolescent's self-concept (Giaconia & Hedges, 1982).

The characteristics of the adolescent also need to be considered when evaluating the effects of classroom structure and climate (Linney & Seidman, 1989). For example, some adolescents benefit from structure more than others. **Aptitude-treatment interaction (ATI)** *stresses the importance of both adolescents' attitudes or characteristics and the treatments or experiences adolescents receive in classrooms.* Aptitude *refers to such characteristics as the academic potential and personality characteristics on which students differ;* treatment *refers to educational techniques, such as structured versus flexible classrooms.* Researchers have found that adolescents' achievement level (aptitude) interacts with classroom structure (treatment) to produce the best learning (Cronbach & Snow, 1977). For example, students who are highly achievement oriented usually do well in a flexible classroom and enjoy it; low-achievement-oriented students usually fare worse and dislike such flexibility. The reverse often appears in structured classrooms.

Interactions with Teachers

Virtually everyone's life is affected in one way or another by teachers. You probably were influenced by teachers as you grew up. One day you may have, or already have, children and adolescents whose lives will be guided by many different teachers. You likely can remember several of your teachers vividly. Perhaps one never smiled, another required you to memorize everything in sight, and yet another always appeared vibrant and encouraged question asking. Psychologists and educators have tried to compile a profile of a good teacher's personality traits, but the complexity of personality, education, learning, and individuals makes this a difficult task. Nonetheless, some teacher traits are associated with positive student outcomes more than others—enthusiasm, ability to plan, poise, adaptability, warmth, flexibility, and awareness of individual differences, for example.

Erik Erikson (1968) believes that good teachers produce a sense of industry, rather than inferiority, in their students. Good teachers are trusted and respected by the community and know how to alternate work and play, study and games, says Erikson. They know how to recognize special efforts and to encourage special abilities. They also know how to create a setting in which adolescents feel good about themselves and know how to handle those adolescents to whom school is not important. In Erikson's (1968) own words, adolescents should be "mildly but firmly coerced into the adventure of finding out that one can learn to accomplish things which one would never have thought of by oneself."

Other recommendations for successful teaching with young adolescents have been offered by adolescent educator Stephanie Feeney (1980). She believes that meaningful learning takes place when the developmental characteristics of the age group are understood, when trust has been established, and when adolescents feel free to explore, to experiment, and to make mistakes. The variability and change that characterizes young adolescents make them a difficult age group to instruct. The student who leans on the teacher one day for help may be strutting around independently the next day. Teachers who work successfully with young adolescents probably have vivid memories of their own adolescence and likely have mastered the developmental tasks of those years. Able to recall their youthful vulnerability, they understand and respect their students' sensitivity to criticism, desire for group acceptance, and feelings of being acutely conspicuous. Successful teachers of adolescents are secure in their own identity and comfortable with their sexuality. Possessing clear values, they use power and authority wisely and are sensitive to their students' feelings. Young adolescents respond best to teachers who exercise natural authority—based on greater age, experience, and wisdom—rather than arbitrary authority or abdication of authority by being pals with the adolescent. Young adolescents need teachers who are fair and consistent, who set reasonable limits, and who realize that adolescents need someone to push against while testing those limits.

"You'll find 'Teaching Methods That Never Fail' under fiction."
Reprinted by permission of Ford Button.

Interactions with Peers

The peer group is an important source of status, friendship, and belonging in the school setting. The peer group also is a learning community in which social roles and standards related to work and achievement are formed. At school, adolescents are with each other for at least six hours per day. The school also provides the locus for many of the adolescent's activities after school and on weekends.

James Coleman (1961) conducted a classic investigation of the association patterns of students. He found that social structures vary from school to school. In some schools, the association patterns of students are very intense, while in others, they are more casual. In small schools, more students are members of various cliques than in large schools, where simple pair relationships occur more frequently. There are even differences in group structures among the large schools. In one suburban school that Coleman studied, the social structure was far more complete and fully developed than in another. Probably because of greater community solidarity, middle-class status, and greater parental interest in the schooling process, many more community functions were carried out in and after school in the first school. Clustering social activities around a school helps to strengthen the social system of the students.

Coleman (1961) analyzed the peer associations of boys and girls separately in small schools. Boys achieved status within their schools in a variety of ways. In some schools, the "all-around boy"—athlete, ladies' man, and to some extent, scholar—achieved status, while in other schools, being either an athlete or a scholar was enough to assure high status. However, recall from our discussion of cliques in Chapter 7 that, in most schools, being an intellect does not qualify a student for high status in the peer society.

The association patterns of the girls varied considerably in small schools as well. Elmtown had the largest number of girl cliques, the largest percentage of girls in cliques, and the smallest average clique size. Marketville was the opposite in each of these respects. In Marketville and Maple Grove, middle-class girls from well-educated families formed cliques that dominated social activities, school activities, and adolescent attention. Teachers perceived these cliques as being in control of the student body and clique members as the girls most encouraged by the adults in the community.

Athletic achievement played an important role in the status systems of boys in all ten schools Coleman (1961) studied. Why are athletics so important in the status systems of American high schools? Adolescents identify strongly with their schools and communities. The identification, in part at least, is due to the fact that the school and the community of adolescents are virtually synonymous. They compete as a school against other schools in athletic contests. So the heroes of the system—those with high status—are the boys who win for the school and the community of adolescents. When they win, the entire school and the entire community of adolescents feel better about themselves.

Because boys have had greater opportunity to participate in interscholastic athletics than girls have, they have been more likely to attain high-status positions in schools. However, in the 1970s, the federal government took a major step toward reducing this form of discrimination against female adolescents. Title IX of the 1972 Educational Amendments Act prohibits any educational program from receiving federal funds if sex discrimination is practiced. So far, this act

In the last two decades, female adolescents have made enormous strides in their participation in interscholastic events.

has not produced parity for girls and boys in interscholastic athletics, but girls have made greater strides than ever before in participating in interscholastic events.

While research on male athletic participation has produced consistent findings of its high status in schools, research on female athletic participation has produced mixed findings. In one recent investigation, the type of sport females participated in was studied to determine its relation to status in the school (Kane, 1988). One hundred and twenty-one male students were asked to indicate which female athlete they would like to date—one identified with gender-inappropriate sports (such as basketball) or one identified with gender-appropriate sports (like tennis). As predicted, females associated with gender-appropriate sports were accorded more status than females associated with gender-inappropriate sports.

Since the passage of Title IX, female enrollments in previously male-dominated fields, such as engineering, law, and business, have more than doubled, and reams have been written about sexism in the language, policies, and practices of education. More about gender roles in schools appears later in Chapter 11 ("Gender").

Social Class and Ethnicity in Schools

Sometimes, the major function of schools has appeared to be to train adolescents to contribute to a middle-class society. Politicians who vote on school funding have been from middle-class or elite backgrounds, school board members have often been from middle-class backgrounds, and principals and teachers also have had middle-class upbringing. Critics argue that schools have not done a good job of educating lower-class and ethnic minority children to overcome the barriers that block the enhancement of their position.

Social Class

In *Dark Ghetto,* Kenneth Clark (1965), the only Black to become president of the American Psychological Association, described the ways lower- and middle-class adolescents are treated differently in school. Clark observed that teachers in middle-class schools spent more time teaching students and evaluated students' work more than twice as much as teachers in low-income schools. Clark also observed that teachers in low-income schools made three times as many negative comments to students as did teachers in middle-class schools, who made more positive than negative comments to students. The following observations vividly describe a school in a large, urban slum area:

> It is 2 P.M., beginning of the sixth-period class, and Warren Benson, a young teacher, looks around the room. Eight students are present out of thirty. "Where is everybody?" he demands. "They don't like your class," a girl volunteers. Three girls saunter in. Cora, who is playing a cassette recorder, bumps over to her desk in time with the music. She lowers the volume. "Don't mark us down late," she shouts. "We was right here, you mother f———."
> . . . Here you find students from poverty homes, students who can't read, students with drug problems, students wanting to drop out. . . .

Teachers have lower expectations for adolescents from low-income families than for adolescents from middle-class families (Entwistle, 1990). A teacher who knows that an adolescent comes from a low-income family may spend less time trying to help the adolescent solve a problem and may anticipate that the adolescent will get into trouble. Teachers may perceive that low-income parents are not interested in helping the adolescent, so they may make fewer efforts to communicate with them.

Teachers from low-income backgrounds often have different attitudes toward students from low-income backgrounds than teachers from middle-income backgrounds. Possibly because they have experienced inequities themselves, teachers from low-income backgrounds may be more empathetic to the difficulties faced by adolescents from similar backgrounds. In one study, when asked to rate the most common characteristics of their students from low-income backgrounds, middle-class teachers checked "lazy," "rebellious," and "fun-loving"; teachers from low-income backgrounds checked "happy," "cooperative," "energetic," and "ambitious" (Gottlieb, 1966). Teachers from a low-income background perceive students from a similar background as behaving in adaptive ways, whereas teachers from a middle-class background perceive the same behaviors as falling short of middle-class standards.

Ethnicity

Martin Luther King once said, "I have a dream—that my four little children will one day live in a nation where they will not be judged by the color of their skin but by the content of their character." Like adolescents from low-income backgrounds, adolescents from different ethnic minority groups also have difficulty in schools. In most American schools, Black Americans, Hispanic Americans, Native Americans, and Asian Americans are minorities. Many teachers have been ignorant of the different cultural attitudes, values, and behaviors that non-Anglo adolescents have learned in their communities (Asamen, 1990; Gibbs & Huang, 1989; Hale-Benson, 1989). The social and academic development of ethnic minority students depends on the teacher's expectations; the teacher's experience in working with adolescents from diverse cultural backgrounds; the curriculum; the presence of role models in schools for ethnic minority students; the quality of the relations between school personnel and parents from different ethnic, economic, and educational backgrounds; and the relations between the school and the community. Our further discussion of ethnicity and schools focuses on teacher expectations, the family's role, desegregation and busing, cooperative learning and the jigsaw classroom, and the cultural subordination and exploitation of ethnic minority groups.

Teacher Expectations

Do teachers have lower academic expectations for minority group adolescents? The evidence indicates that teachers look for and reward achievement-oriented behavior in White students more often than in Black students (Scott-Jones & Clark, 1986). When teachers praise Black students for their academic performance, the praise is often qualified: "This is a good paper. It is better than yesterday's." Also teachers criticize gifted Black students more than gifted White students, possibly because they do not expect intellectual competence in Black students (Baron, Tom, & Cooper, 1985).

The following comments of Imani Perry (1988), a 15-year-old Black student, underscore the problems many ethnic minority adolescents face in school:

> Black and Hispanic students have less chance of building strong relationships with teachers because their appearance and behavior may be considered offensive to middle-class White teachers. These students show signs of what White teachers, and some teachers of color, consider disrespect, and they do not get the

nurturing relationships that develop respect and dedication. They are considered less intelligent, as can be seen in the proportion of Blacks and Hispanics in lower-level as opposed to upper-level classes. There is less of a teacher-student contact with "underachievers" because they are guided into peer tutoring programs. . . . The sad part of the situation is that many students believe that this type of teaching is what academic learning is all about. They have not had the opportunity to experience alternative ways of teaching and learning. From my experience in public school, it appears that many minority students will never be recognized as capable of analytical and critical thinking.

Family Influences

Parents' attitudes and behavior can either improve or detract from ethnic minority adolescents' school performance (Jenkins, 1989; Spencer & Dornbusch, 1990). In one investigation that controlled for social class, authoritarian and permissive parenting were both associated with poor grades, while authoritative parenting was associated with better grades (Dornbusch & others, 1987). However, more than parenting styles are involved in understanding ethnic minority adolescents' school performance because many Asian American adolescents' parents follow an authoritarian parenting style, yet many Asian American adolescents, especially Japanese and Chinese American, often excel in school. A special concern is the large number of Black and Hispanic adolescents who grow up in single-parent families. For example, half of Black American adolescents are likely to remain with a single parent through the end of adolescence, in contrast to only 15 percent of White American adolescents (McLoyd, in press). Among ethnic minorities, about 70 percent of Black American and Hispanic American adolescents raised by single mothers are poor (Ford Foundation, 1984). Poor school performance among many ethnic minority youth is related to this pattern of single-parenting and poverty (Dornbusch & others, 1985).

Desegregation and Busing

One of the largest efforts to study ethnicity in school has focused on desegregation and busing. Desegregation attempts to improve the proportions of ethnic minority and White student populations in schools. Efforts to improve this ratio have often involved busing students, usually minority group students, from their home neighborhood to more distant schools. The underlying belief is that bringing different groups together will reduce stereotyped attitudes and improve intergroup relations. But busing tells us nothing about what goes on inside the school once students get there. Minority group adolescents bused to a predominantly white school are often resegregated in the classroom through seating patterns, ability grouping, and tracking systems. Overall, the findings pertaining to desegregation through busing have shown dismal results (Minuchin & Shapiro, 1983).

Improvements in interethnic relations among adolescents in schools depend on what happens after students arrive at the school. In one comprehensive national investigation of factors that contribute to positive interethnic relations, more than 5,000 fifth-grade students and more than 400 tenth-grade students were evaluated (Forehand, Ragosta, & Rock, 1976). Multiethnic curricula, projects focused on ethnic issues, mixed work groups, and supportive teachers and principals led to improved interethnic relations. Next, we examine a strategy to improve interethnic relations in classrooms.

Cooperative Learning and the Jigsaw Classroom

Cooperative learning *involves joint participation by all members of a group in achieving a learning goal. Each member contributes to the learning process.* The strategy of emphasizing cooperation rather than competition in learning has been widely promoted in recent years in American classrooms. A number of researchers have found that cooperative learning is associated with enhanced student outcomes, including increases in self-esteem, better academic performance, friendships among classmates, and improved interethnic perceptions (Aronson, 1986; Johnson & Johnson, 1989; Slavin, 1989b).

When the schools of Austin, Texas, were desegregated through extensive busing, the outcome was increased ethnic tension among Blacks, Mexican Americans, and Anglos, producing violence in the schools. The superintendent consulted with Eliot Aronson, a prominent social psychologist, who was a professor at the University of Texas at Austin at the time. Aronson thought it was more important to prevent ethnic tension than to control it. This led him to observe a number of school classrooms in Austin. What he saw was fierce competition between individuals of unequal status.

Aronson stressed that the reward structure of the classrooms needed to be changed from a setting of unequal competition to one of cooperation among equals, without making curriculum changes. To accomplish this, Aronson developed a form of cooperative learning he called the "jigsaw classroom." How does the jigsaw classroom work? Consider a class of 30 students, some Anglo, some Black, some Hispanic. The lesson to be learned focuses on Joseph Pulitzer's life. The class might be broken up into five groups of six students each, with the groups being as equal as possible in ethnic composition and academic achievement level. The lesson about Pulitzer's life could be divided into six parts, with one part given to each member of the six-person group. The parts might be paragraphs from Pulitzer's biography, such as how the Pulitzer family came to the United States, his childhood, his early work, and so on. The components are like the parts of a jigsaw puzzle. They have to be put together to form the complete puzzle.

Each student in the group is given an allotted time to study. Then the group meets, and each member tries to teach a part to the group. After an hour or so, each member is tested on the entire life of Pulitzer, with each member receiving an individual rather than a group score. Each student, therefore, must learn the entire lesson. Learning depends on the cooperation and effort of other members. Aronson believes that this type of learning increases students' interdependence through cooperatively reaching a common goal.

Cooperative learning is an important addition to learning strategies, but esteemed social psychologist Roger Brown (1986) offers a caveat. According to Brown, academic achievement is as much, or more, an individual "sport" as a team "sport." *Individuals* graduate from high school, enter college, and take jobs, not *groups*. A parent with an advantaged adolescent in a cooperative learning classroom thus may react with increased ethnic hostility when the adolescent brings home a lower grade than is typical. The adolescent may tell his father, "The teacher is getting us to teach each other. In my group, we have this kid named Carlos, who can barely speak English." While cooperative learning is an important strategy for reducing interethnic hostility, caution needs to be exercised in its use because of the unequal status of the participants and achievement's individual orientation. Other ways that the educational and achievement orientation of Hispanic students can be improved are described in Sociocultural Worlds of Adolescence 8.2.

The Subordination and Exploitation of Ethnic Minority Adolescents in Education

American anthropologist John Ogbu (1974, 1986, 1989) proposed the controversial view that ethnic minority youth are placed in a position of subordination and exploitation in the American educational system. He believes that ethnic minority adolescents, especially Black and Hispanic Americans, have inferior educational opportunities, are exposed to teachers and administrators who have low

Dr. Henry Gaskins began an after-school tutorial program for ethnic minority students in 1983 in Washington, D.C. For four hours every weeknight and all day Saturday, 80 students receive one-on-one assistance from Gaskins and his wife, two adult volunteers, and academically talented peers. Those who can afford it contribute five dollars to cover the cost of school supplies. In addition to tutoring in specific subjects, Gaskins's home-based academy helps students to set personal goals and to commit to a desire to succeed. Many of his students come from families in which the parents are high school dropouts and either cannot or are not motivated to help their adolescents achieve in school. In addition, the academy prepares students to qualify for scholarships and college entrance exams. Gaskins was recently awarded the President's Volunteer Action Award at the White House.

Helping Hispanic Youth Stay in School and Go to College

The Hispanic population in the United States is increasing rapidly. Educators are increasingly interested in helping Hispanic adolescents stay in school and succeed in the courses needed for educational and occupational success. As colleges compete to recruit seniors from the small pool of college-eligible and college-ready Hispanics, it is apparent that the pool itself needs to be greatly expanded. Adolescent educator Gloria De Necochea (1988) described seven strategies to help keep Hispanic adolescents in school and get them ready to go to college:

1. Identify students early for a college preparatory curriculum. As early as the sixth grade, both students and parents need to know about the college preparatory curriculum and the long-term consequences of choices.
2. Give more attention to mathematics and science. Mathematics and science are critical for both college admissions and a range of career options, but these subjects pose big barriers for Hispanic students. Success can be increased by teaching the complex academic language necessary to tackle these subjects effectively. This is especially important in grades 7 to 9, where algebra—the gatekeeping course for future scientific and technical courses—is taught.
3. Increase school participation. Counselors and teachers can make college-related information more visible throughout the school. Precollege clubs can be developed. Administrators can invite college representatives, alumni, and individuals in different careers to address students. Critical-thinking skills can be stressed. And teachers can occasionally tailor exams to be more like the structure of the SAT and ACT.
4. Expose students to the world of college. College recruiters, faculty, and financial aid officers are important role models and sources of current information. Visits to colleges enable youth to gain firsthand knowledge about campus life (Justiz & Rendon, 1989).
5. Increase workshops. Study skills, assertiveness training, and survival tips can be taught. College-related topics, such as "How to choose a college" and "What to say to college admissions officers," should be addressed during the senior year.
6. Involve parents. Invitations to all activities should be bilingual and mailed home well in advance of the event. Students can provide child care to increase attendance. Parents should be encouraged to come to workshops and to participate in planning activities.
7. Organize outside support. Better coordination between community organizations and schools could provide a central source for descriptions of available programs at the school and in the community.

These Hispanic youth leaders, participating in a mock legislation session, are positive examples of the increased concern for helping Hispanic youth stay in school and go to college.

academic expectations for them, and encounter negative stereotypes about ethnic minority groups. Ogbu states that ethnic minority opposition to the middle-class White educational system stems from a lack of trust because of years of discrimination and oppression. Says Ogbu, it makes little sense to do well academically if occupational opportunities are often closed to ethnic minority youth and young adults.

Completing high school, or even college, does not always bring the same job opportunities for many ethnic minority youth as for White youth (Entwistle, 1990). In terms of earnings and employment rates, Black American high school graduates do not do as well as their White counterparts. Giving up in school because of a perceived lack of reward (that is, inadequate job opportunities) characterizes many Hispanic American youth as well.

According to American educational psychologist Margaret Beale Spencer and sociologist Sanford Dornbusch (1990), a form of institutional racism prevails in many American schools. That is, well-meaning teachers, acting out of misguided liberalism, often fail to challenge ethnic minority students. Knowing the handicaps these adolescents face, some teachers accept a low level of performance from them, substituting warmth and affection for academic challenge and high standards of performance. Ethnic minority students, like their White counterparts, learn best when teachers combine warmth with challenging standards.

At this point, we have discussed a number of ideas about schools and classrooms, peers and teachers, and social class and ethnicity. A summary of these ideas is presented in Concept Table 8.2. In the next chapter, we continue our discussion of social class and ethnicity, along with many other ideas about cultural influences on adolescent development.

American anthropologist John Ogbu proposed the controversial view that ethnic minority youth are placed in a position of subordination and exploitation in the American school system. He believes that ethnic minority youth, especially Black and Hispanic Americans, have inferior educational opportunities, are exposed to teachers and administrators who have low expectations for them, and encounter negative stereotypes about ethnic minority groups.

A Hispanic American father at his daughter's high school graduation. Parents play an important role in the education of ethnic minority adolescents. Many Black and Hispanic American adolescents grow up in low-income, single-parent families and do not receive the support this Hispanic American girl has been given.

Concept Table 8.2

Schools and Classrooms, Teachers and Peers, Social Class, and Ethnicity

Concept	Processes/Related Ideas	Characteristics/Description
Schools and classrooms, teachers and peers	School size and classroom size	Smaller is usually better when school size and classroom size are at issue. Large schools, especially those with more than 500 to 600 students, may not provide a personalized climate that allows for an effective system of social control. Most class sizes are 30 to 35 students, but class sizes of 15 students or fewer benefit student learning.
	Classroom structure and climate	The open-classroom concept is multidimensional. Specific dimensions of open and traditional classrooms need to be considered, as well as specific outcomes. Overall, open classrooms are associated with lower language achievement but improved attitudes toward school. Individualized instruction and role of the adolescent are associated with positive self-concept. Aptitude-treatment interaction also needs to be considered.
	Interactions with teachers	Teacher characteristics involve many different dimensions, and compiling a profile of a competent teacher of adolescents is difficult. Erikson believes that good teachers create a sense of industry, rather than inferiority, in their students. Competent teachers of adolescents are knowledgeable about adolescent development and sensitive to adolescents' needs.
	Interactions with peers	At school, adolescents are with each other for at least six hours a day, and the school is a setting for many after-school and weekend peer activities. Athletics has played a prominent role in the status hierarchy of male adolescents, but findings for the role of athletics in the status hierarchy of females have been more mixed.
Social class and ethnicity	Social class	Secondary schools have had a strong middle-class bias. Teachers have lower expectations for students from low-income backgrounds, although teachers from these backgrounds see these students' behavior as more adaptive than teachers from middle-class backgrounds.
	Ethnicity	Many teachers have been ignorant of the different cultural values, attitudes, and behaviors that ethnic minority adolescents have learned in their communities. Teachers have lower expectations for ethnic minority students. Parents' attitudes and behavior can either improve or detract from ethnic minority adolescents' school performance. Desegregation through busing has shown virtually no benefits in reducing interethnic group tension. Improvements in interethnic relations among adolescents in schools depend on what happens at school after adolescents arrive. Multiethnic curricula, projects focused on interethnic issues, supportive teachers and administrators, and cooperative learning benefit students from ethnic minority backgrounds. John Ogbu proposed the controversial view that ethnic minority youth are placed in a position of subordination and exploitation in the American educational system. Some experts believe that a form of institutional racism exists in some schools because teachers fail to academically challenge ethnic minority students.

Summary

I. Function of Schools

In the nineteenth century, secondary schools were for the elite. By the 1920s, they had changed, becoming more comprehensive and training adolescents for work and citizenship, as well as training intellect. The comprehensive high school remains today, but the functions of secondary schools continue to be debated. Supporters of the back-to-basics movement maintain that the function of schools should be intellectual development; others argue for more comprehensive functions, including social and vocational development.

II. The Difference Schools Make and Schools' Changing Social Developmental Contexts

Some sociologists have argued that schools have little impact on adolescents' development, but when researchers have conducted more precise observational studies of what goes on in schools and classrooms, the effects of schooling become more apparent. The social context differs at the preschool, elementary school, and secondary school levels, increasing in scope and complexity for adolescents.

III. Transition to Middle or Junior High School, Successful Middle Schools

The emergence of junior high schools in the 1920s and 1930s was justified on the basis of physical, cognitive, and social changes that characterize early adolescence, as well as the need for more schools in response to growing student populations. Middle schools have become more popular in recent years and coincide with earlier pubertal development. The transition to middle or junior high school coincides with many social, familial, and individual changes in the adolescent's life. The transition involves moving from the "top-dog" to "bottom-dog" position. Successful schools for young adolescents take individual differences in development seriously, show a deep concern for what is known about early adolescence, and emphasize social and emotional development as much as intellectual development. In 1989, the Carnegie Corporation recommended a major redesign of middle schools.

IV. Transition from High School to College

In a number of ways, the transition from high school to college parallels the transition from elementary to middle or junior high school, including the "top-dog" phenomenon. An especially important transition for most adolescents is reduced interaction with parents. A special problem today is the discontinuity between public high schools and colleges.

V. High School Dropouts and Noncollege Youth

Dropping out of high school has been a serious problem for decades. Many dropouts have educational deficiencies that curtail their economic and social well-being for much of their adult lives. Some progress has been made in that dropout rates for most ethnic minority groups have declined in recent years, although dropout rates for inner-city, low-income minorities remain precariously high. Dropping out of school is associated with demographic, family-related, peer-related, school-related, economic, and personal factors. The dropout rate could be reduced and the lives of noncollege youth improved by strengthening the schools and by bridging the gap between school and work.

VI. Schools and Classrooms

Smaller is usually better when school size and class size are at issue. Large schools, especially those with more than 500 to 600 students, may not provide a personalized climate that allows for an effective system of social control. Most class sizes are 30 to 35 students, but class sizes of 15 students or fewer benefit student learning. The open-classroom concept is multidimensional. Specific dimensions of open and traditional classrooms need to be considered, as well as specific outcomes. Overall, open classrooms are associated with lower language achievement but improved attitudes toward school. Individualized instruction and role of the adolescent are associated with positive self-concept. Aptitude-treatment interaction also needs to be considered.

VII. Interactions with Teachers

Teacher characteristics involve many different dimensions, and compiling a profile of a competent teacher of adolescents is difficult. Erikson believes that good teachers create a sense of industry, rather than inferiority, in their students. Competent teachers of adolescents are knowledgeable about adolescent development and sensitive to adolescents' needs.

VIII. Interactions with Peers

At school, adolescents are with each other for at least six hours a day, and the school is a setting for many after-school and weekend peer gatherings. Athletics has played a prominent role in the status hierarchy of male adolescents, but findings for the role of athletics in the status hierarchy of females have been more mixed.

IX. Social Class

Secondary schools have had a strong middle-class bias. Teachers have lower expectations for students from low-income backgrounds, although teachers from these backgrounds see these students' behavior as more adaptive than teachers from middle-class backgrounds.

X. Ethnicity

Many teachers have been ignorant of the different cultural values, attitudes, and behaviors that ethnic minority adolescents have learned in their communities. Teachers have lower expectations for ethnic minority students. Parents' attitudes and behavior can either improve or detract from ethnic minority adolescents' school performance. Desegregation through busing has shown virtually no benefits in reducing interethnic group tension. Improvements in interethnic relations among adolescents in schools depend on what happens at school after adolescents arrive. Multiethnic curricula, projects focused on interethnic issues, supportive teachers and administrators, and cooperative learning benefit students from ethnic minority backgrounds. John Ogbu proposed the controversial view that ethnic minority youth are placed in a position of subordination and exploitation in the American educational system. Some experts believe that a form of institutional racism exists in some schools because teachers fail to academically challenge ethnic minority youth.

Key Terms .

back-to-basics movement 264	aptitude-treatment interaction (ATI) 279	cooperative learning 284
top-dog phenomenon 270		

Suggested Readings

Entwistle, D. R. (1990). Schools and the adolescent. In S. S. Feldman & G. R. Elliott (Eds.), *At the threshold: The developing adolescent.* Cambridge, MA: Harvard University Press.
Presents an up-to-date review of ideas about adolescent development and secondary schools.
Feeney, S. (1980). *Schools for young adolescents.* Carrboro, NC: Center for Early Adolescence.
An excellent, easy-to-read overview of what makes a good junior high school teacher.

Harvard Educational Review.
> *The issues of the last three to four years include a number of articles that address the topics raised in this chapter.*

Lipsitz, J. (1984). *Successful schools for young adolescents.* New Brunswick, NJ: Transaction Books.
> *Must reading for anyone interested in better schools for young adolescents. Filled with rich examples of successful schools and the many factors that contribute to success in the education of young adolescents.*

Phi Delta Kappan
> *A leading educational journal that gives a feel for controversial, widely debated ideas in secondary education.*

Review of Educational Research.
> *This journal publishes reviews of educational research, with references to many of the topics in this chapter.*

William T. Grant Foundation Commission on Work, Family, and Citizenship. (1988, February). *The forgotten half: Non-college-bound youth in America.* New York: William T. Grant Foundation.
> *This excellent report on the status of non-college-bound youth in America calls attention to ways American society can help these individuals to more effectively make the school-to-work transition.*

Culture

Our most basic common link is that we all inhabit this planet. We all breathe the same air. We all cherish our children's future.

John F. Kennedy, address, The American University, 1963

Dating Problems of a 16-Year-Old Japanese American Girl and School Problems of a 17-Year-Old Chinese American Boy

Sonya, a 16-year-old Japanese American girl was upset over her family's reaction to her Caucasian American boyfriend. Her parents refused to meet him and more than once threatened to disown her. Her older brothers also reacted angrily to Sonya dating a Caucasian American, warning that they were going to beat him up. Her parents were also disturbed that Sonya's grades, above average in middle school, were beginning to drop.

Generational issues contributed to the conflict between Sonya and her family (Nagata, 1989; Sue, 1990; Sue & Okazaki, 1990). Her parents had experienced strong sanctions against dating Whites when they were growing up and were legally prevented from marrying anyone but a Japanese. As Sonya's older brothers were growing up, they valued ethnic pride and solidarity. The brothers saw her dating a Caucasian as "selling out" her own ethnic group. Sonya's and her family members' cultural values obviously differ.

Michael, a 17-year-old Chinese American high school student, was referred to an outpatient adolescent crisis center by the school counselor for depression and suicidal tendencies (Huang & Ying, 1989). Michael was failing several subjects and was repeatedly absent or late for school. Michael's parents were successful professionals who told the therapist that there was nothing wrong with them or with Michael's younger brother and sister, so what, they wondered, was wrong with Michael? What was wrong was that the parents expected all of their children to become doctors. They were frustrated and angered by Michael's school failures, especially since he was the firstborn son, who in Chinese families is expected to achieve the highest standards of all siblings.

The therapist underscored the importance of the parents putting less pressure for achievement on Michael and gradually introduced more realistic expectations for Michael (who was not interested in becoming a doctor and did not have the necessary academic record anyway). The therapist supported Michael's desire to not become a doctor and empathized with the pressure he had experienced from his parents. As Michael's school attendance improved, his parents noted his improved attitude toward school and supported a continuation of therapy. Michael's case illustrates how the image of Asian American youth as "whiz kids" can become destructive.

Sonya's and Michael's circumstances underscore the importance of culture in understanding adolescent development. The cultural heritage of the families had a strong influence on the conflict Sonya and Michael experienced in their families and on their behavior outside of the family—in Sonya's case, dating; in Michael's case, school. Of course, a family's cultural background does not always produce conflict between adolescents and other family members, but the two cases described here reveal the importance of understanding a family's cultural values, especially those of ethnic minority families.

Consider the flowering of a garden. Though differing in kind, color, form, and shape, yet, as flowers are refreshed by the waters of one spring, revived by the breath of one wind, invigorated by the rays of one sun, their diversity increases their charm and adds to their beauty. How unpleasing to the eye if all the flowers and the plants, the leaves and the blossoms, the fruits, and the trees of the garden were all of the same shape and color! Diversity of hues, form, and shape enriches and adorns the garden.

•

Abud'l-Baha

The sociocultural worlds of adolescents are described throughout this text. Because culture and its social contexts are such pervasive dimensions of adolescent development, this entire chapter is devoted to the study of the many cultural, socioeconomic, and ethnic factors that influence the development of adolescents.

Culture and Its Relevance to the Study of Adolescence

What is culture? Why is culture relevant for the study of adolescence? What is the importance of cross-cultural comparisons? What is the nature of rites of passage? We consider each of these questions in turn.

The Nature of Culture

In Chapter 1, **culture** *is defined as the behavior, patterns, beliefs, and all other products of a particular group of people that are passed on from generation to generation.* The products result from the interaction between groups of people and their environment over many years. For example, in the "Images of Adolescence" section at the beginning of this chapter, we read about how the cultural values of Sonya's parents and brothers conflicted with her dating interests. We also read about how the Chinese American cultural tradition of Michael's parents led to Michael's school-related problems.

Culture is a very broad concept—it includes many different components and can be analyzed in many different ways. We already have analyzed the effects of three important cultural settings on adolescent development—the family, peers, and school. Later in the chapter, we examine how much time adolescents spend in these and other settings.

Two additional important dimensions of culture in adolescents' lives are social class and ethnicity. **Social class,** *also called socioeconomic status or SES, refers to a grouping of people with similar occupational, educational, and economic characteristics.* In the chapter, for example, we evaluate what it is like for an adolescent to grow up in poverty. As was presented in Chapter 1, **ethnicity** *is based on cultural heritage, nationality characteristics, race, religion, and language.* Nowhere are sociocultural changes more profound than in the increasing ethnic diversity of America's adolescents. In the chapter, we look at Black American adolescents, Hispanic American adolescents, Asian American adolescents, and Native American adolescents, and the sociocultural issues involved in their development. The chapter concludes with an overview of how two important dimensions of culture—television and the media—affect adolescent development.

The Relevance of Culture to the Study of Adolescence

If the study of adolescence is to be a relevant discipline in the twenty-first century, increased attention will need to focus on culture and ethnicity. The future will bring extensive contact between people from varied cultural and ethnic backgrounds. Schools and neighborhoods can no longer be the fortresses of one privileged group whose agenda is the exclusion of those with a different skin color or different customs. Immigrants, refugees, and ethnic minority individuals increasingly refuse to become part of a homogeneous melting pot, instead requesting that schools, employers, and governments honor many of their cultural customs. Adult refugees and immigrants may find more opportunities and better-paying jobs, but their children and adolescents may learn attitudes in school that challenge traditional authority patterns at home (Brislin, 1990).

For the most part, the study of adolescents has, so far, been ethnocentric, emphasizing American values, especially middle-class, White, male values. Cross-cultural psychologists point out that many of the assumptions about contemporary ideas in fields like adolescence were developed in Western cultures (Schlegel & Barry, 1991; Segall & others, 1990; Triandis, 1990). One example of **ethnocentrism**—*the tendency to favor one's own group over other groups*—is the American emphasis on the individual or self. Many Eastern countries, such as Japan, China, and India, are group-oriented. So is the Mexican culture. The pendulum may have swung too far in the individualistic direction in many Western cultures.

Research by American social psychologist Donald Campbell and his colleagues (Brewer & Campbell, 1976; Campbell & LeVine, 1968) revealed that people in all cultures have a tendency to:

- Believe that what happens in their culture is "natural" and "correct" and that what happens in other cultures is "unnatural" and "incorrect"
- Perceive their cultural customs as universally valid; that is, what is good for us is good for everyone
- Behave in ways that favor their cultural group
- Feel proud of their cultural group
- Feel hostile toward other cultural groups

In fact, many cultures define the word *human* with reference to their own cultural group. The ancient Greeks distinguished between those who spoke Greek and those whose language was incomprehensible and sounded like "barber" (a repetitive chatter), so they called them *barbarians*. The ancient Chinese labeled themselves "the central kingdom." In many languages, the word for *human* is the same as the name of the tribe. The implication is that people from other cultures are not perceived as fully human (Triandis, 1990).

Global interdependence is no longer a matter of belief or choice. It is an inescapable reality. Adolescents are not just citizens of the United States or Canada. They are citizens of the world, a world that through technological and transportational advances has become increasingly interactive. By understanding the behavior and values of cultures around the world, we may be able to interact more effectively with each other and make this planet a more hospitable, peaceful place on which to live.

Cross-Cultural Comparisons

Early in this century, overgeneralizations about the universal aspects of adolescents were made based on data and experience in a single culture—the middle-class culture of the United States (Havighurst, 1976). For example, it was believed that adolescents everywhere went through a period of "storm and stress" characterized by self-doubt and conflict. However, as we saw in Chapter 1, when Margaret Mead visited the island of Samoa, she found that the adolescents of the Samoan culture were not experiencing much stress.

As we also discovered in Chapter 1, **cross-cultural studies** *involve the comparison of a culture with one or more other cultures, which provides information about the degree to which adolescent development is similar, or* universal, *across cultures, or the degree to which it is culture-specific.* The study of adolescence has emerged in the context of Western industrialized society, with the practical needs and social norms of this culture dominating thinking about adolescents. Consequently, the development of adolescents in Western cultures has evolved as the norm for all adolescents of the human species, regardless of economic and cultural circumstances. This narrow viewpoint can produce erroneous conclusions about the nature of adolescents. To develop a more global, cosmopolitan perspective of adolescents, let us consider adolescents' achievement behavior and sexuality in different cultures, as well as rites of passage.

Achievement

The United States is an achievement-oriented culture, and U.S. adolescents are more achievement oriented than the adolescents in many other countries. Many American parents socialize their adolescents to be achievement oriented and independent. In one investigation of 104 societies, parents in industrialized countries like the United States placed a higher value on socializing adolescents for achievement and independence than parents in nonindustrialized countries like Kenya, who placed a higher value on obedience and responsibility (Bacon, Child, & Barry, 1963).

Anglo American adolescents are more achievement oriented than Mexican and Mexican American adolescents. For example, in one study, Anglo American adolescents were more competitive and less cooperative than their Mexican and Mexican American counterparts (Kagan & Madsen, 1972). In this study, Anglo Americans were more likely to reduce the gains of other students when they could not reach the goals themselves. In other investigations, Anglo American youth were more individual centered, while Mexican youth were more family centered (Holtzmann, 1982). Some developmentalists believe that the American culture is too achievement oriented for rearing mentally healthy adolescents (Elkind, 1981).

While Anglo American adolescents are more achievement oriented than adolescents in many cultures, they are not as achievement oriented as many Japanese, Chinese, and Asian American adolescents (Sue & Okazaki, 1990). For example, as a group, Asian American adolescents demonstrate exceptional achievement patterns. Asian American adolescents exceed the national average for high school and college graduates. Eighty-six percent of Asian Americans, compared to 64 percent of White Americans, are in some higher-education program two years after high school graduation. Clearly, education and achievement are highly valued aspirations of many Asian American youth. More about Asian American youth appears later in this chapter and in Chapter 14, where we discuss achievement.

Sexuality

Culture also plays a prominent role in adolescent sexuality. Some cultures consider adolescent sexual activity normal; others forbid it. Consider the Ines Beag and Mangaian cultures. Ines Beag is a small island off the coast of Ireland. Its

A Nigerian girl, painted for the festival dance of "OBITUN" (coming of age). In many primitive cultures, rites of passage are the avenue through which adolescents gain access to sacred adult practices, knowledge, and sexuality.

inhabitants are among the most sexually repressed in the world. They know nothing about French kissing or hand stimulation of the penis. Sex education does not exist. They believe that, after marriage, nature will take its course. The men think that intercourse is bad for their health. Individuals in this culture detest nudity. Only babies are allowed to bathe nude, and adults wash only the parts of their body that extend beyond their clothing. Premarital sex is out of the question. After marriage, sexual partners keep their underwear on during intercourse! It is not difficult to understand why females in the Ines Beag culture rarely, if ever, achieve orgasm (Messinger, 1971).

By contrast, consider the Mangaian culture in the South Pacific. Boys learn about masturbation as early as age six or seven. At age 13, boys undergo a ritual that introduces them to manhood in which a long incision is made in the penis. The individual who conducts the ritual instructs the boy in sexual strategies, such as how to help his partner achieve orgasm before he does. Two weeks after the incision ceremony, the 13-year-old boy has intercourse with an experienced woman. She helps him to hold back his ejaculation so she can achieve orgasm with him. Soon after, the boy searches for girls to further his sexual experience, or they seek him, knowing that he now is a "man." By the end of adolescence, Mangaians have sex virtually every night.

American adolescents experience a culture more liberal than that of the Ines Beag but one that does not come close to matching the liberal sexual behavior of the Mangaians. The cultural diversity in the sexual behavior of adolescents is testimony to the power of environmental experiences in determining sexuality. As we move up in the animal kingdom, experience seems to take on more power as a determinant of sexuality. While human beings cannot mate in midair like bees or display their plumage as magnificently as peacocks, adolescents can talk about sex with one another, read about it in magazines, and watch it on television and at the movies.

Rites of Passage

Rites of passage *are ceremonies or rituals that mark an individual's transition from one status to another, especially into adulthood.* Some societies have elaborate rites of passage that signal the adolescent's transition to adulthood; others do not. In many primitive cultures, rites of passage are the avenue through which adolescents gain access to sacred adult practices, knowledge, and sexuality (Sommer, 1978). These rites often involve dramatic practices intended to facilitate the adolescent's separation from the immediate family, especially the mother. The transformation usually is characterized by some form of ritual death and rebirth, or by means of contact with the spiritual world. Bonds are forged between the adolescent and the adult instructors through shared rituals, hazards, and secrets to allow the adolescent to enter the adult world. This kind of ritual provides a forceful and discontinuous entry into the adult world at a time when the adolescent is perceived to be ready for the change.

Africa, especially sub-Saharan Africa, has been the location of many rites of passage for adolescents. Under the influence of Western culture, many of the rites are disappearing today, although some vestiges remain. In locations where formal education is not readily available, rites of passage are still prevalent.

Americans do not have formal rites of passage that mark the transition from adolescence to adulthood. Some religious and social groups, however, have initiation ceremonies that indicate an advance in maturity—the Jewish bar mitzvah, the Catholic confirmation, and social debuts, for example. Sociocultural Worlds of Adolescence 9.1 looks at a Jewish boy's bar mitzvah, as well as an Apache girl's coming of age.

SOCIOCULTURAL WORLDS OF ADOLESCENCE 9.1

An Apache Girl and a Jewish Boy Come of Age

Amanda Tiger is an Apache Indian who lives in the American Southwest. She is about to begin a four-day ceremony that signifies her entrance into puberty. The ritual includes special dress and daylong activities. The ceremony is believed to give Amanda and other Apache girls strength, an even temperament, prosperity, and a long life. As Amanda approaches a ceremonial blanket on the ground, she kneels before the sun and is massaged to turn her body into an adult. On the final day of the ceremony, Amanda is sprinkled with pollen to symbolize her newly acquired reproductive powers.

Drew Belzer is a 13-year-old Jewish boy who lives in Dallas, Texas. Aunts, uncles, and cousins from many places come to celebrate Drew's bar mitzvah. In the morning, Drew enters Beth Israel congregation a child. He emerges at the end of the ceremony, in the eyes of his faith, an adult. As a child, Drew listened to the Scripture and learned. As an adult, Drew is allowed to read from the Torah so that he can pass on his family's faith to a new generation. After the religious ceremony at the temple, his relatives and friends join with him to dance, sing, and celebrate his "coming of age."

This young Jewish boy is shown at his bar mitzvah, a Jewish initiation ceremony that takes place when the boy reaches the age of 13. The bar mitzvah gives the boy adult status in the Jewish religion.

The Apache Indians of the American Southwest celebrate a girl's entrance into puberty with a four-day ritual that includes special dress and daylong activities.

School graduation ceremonies come the closest to being culturewide rites of passage in the United States. The high school graduation ceremony has become nearly universal for middle-class adolescents and increasing numbers of adolescents from low-income backgrounds (Fasick, 1988). Nonetheless, high school graduation does not result in universal changes—many high school graduates continue to live with their parents, to be economically dependent on them, and to be undecided about career and life-style matters. Another rite of passage that has characterized increasing numbers of American adolescents is sexual intercourse (Allen & Santrock, in press). By the end of adolescence, more than 70 percent of American adolescents have had sexual intercourse.

(a)

(b)

(a) High school graduation is close to being a culturewide rite of passage among American adolescents. (b) Another rite of passage that has increased in frequency in recent years is sexual intercourse.

The absence in America of clear-cut rites of passage makes the attainment of adult status ambiguous. Many individuals are unsure whether they have reached adult status or not. In Texas, the age for beginning employment is 15, but many younger adolescents and even children are employed, especially Mexican immigrants. The age for driving is 16, but when emergency need is demonstrated, a driver's license can be obtained at age 15. Even at age 16, some parents may not allow their son or daughter to obtain a driver's license, believing that 16-year-olds are too young for this responsibility. The age for voting is 18, and the age for drinking has recently been raised to 21. Exactly when adolescents become adults in America has not been clearly delineated as it has in some primitive cultures, where rites of passage are universal.

Now that we have gained a more global perspective on adolescence, let us turn our attention to American adolescents and examine the social contexts in which they spend time. Then, we study the nature of social class and ethnicity, two cultural dimensions that are important in understanding American adolescents, as well as adolescents in other cultures.

The Settings in Which Adolescents Spend Their Time

What do adolescents do during a typical week? Of course, the answer to this question to some extent depends on adolescents' culture. Adolescents in a small hunter-gatherer culture in Africa spend much of their time in very different ways than American adolescents. Kikuyu adolescents in central Kenya spend two-thirds of their waking hours in chores and family maintenance tasks (Munroe & others, 1983). Girls in rural India spend a similar two-thirds of their time in maintenance tasks, including 1½ hours fetching water, while boys spend two-thirds of their time in leisure (Saraswathi & Dutta, 1988). Contemporary Japanese adolescents spend well over half of their waking hours doing schoolwork. How adolescents spend their waking hours provides insight into the nature of their developmental experiences in a culture and the circumstances that influence what women and men they will become (Larson & Richards, 1989).

Developmental researchers Mihaly Csikszentmihalyi and Reed Larson have extensively studied how much time adolescents spend in different settings, what adolescents spend their time doing, and the people with whom adolescents spend their time (Csikszentmihalyi & Larson, 1984; Larson, 1989). They use the **experience sampling method,** *which consists of participants carrying electronic pagers, usually for a week, and providing reports on their activities when signaled by the pagers at random times.* Of course, the community chosen to be studied does not perfectly mirror adolescents everywhere.

In one study, a heterogeneous sample of 75 ninth- through twelfth-graders, approximately half boys and half girls, and approximately half from a lower-middle-class and half from an upper-middle-class background, in urban and suburban areas near Chicago were beeped at 40 to 50 randomly chosen times (Csikszentmihalyi & Larson, 1984). The paths of the adolescents' lives passed through three main social contexts—home, school, and public settings, such as parks, buses, supermarkets, and friends' homes (see Figure 9.1).

What were the adolescents doing when they were beeped? As indicated in Figure 9.2, they spent 29 percent of their time in productive activities, mainly involving schoolwork. They spent an additional 31 percent in such maintenance activities as eating, resting, bathing, and dressing. They spent the remainder of their time in other activities, such as talking, engaging in sports, and reading, which can be classified primarily as leisure. By far, the largest amount of time

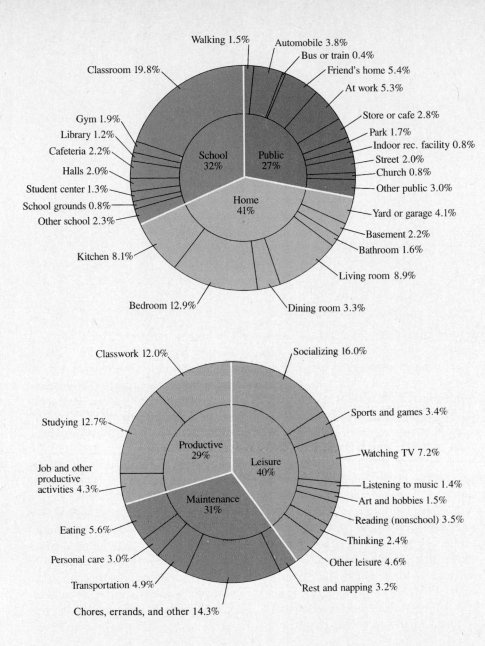

Figure 9.1 Where adolescents spend their time. Graph shows the percentage of self-reports in each location (n = 2,734). In this and the figures that follow, one percentage point is equivalent to approximately one hour per week spent in the given location or activity.

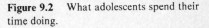

Figure 9.2 What adolescents spend their time doing.

spent in a single activity was studying, which took up 13 percent of the adolescents' waking hours. However, the time spent by the Chicago adolescents in studying is considerably less than the time spent by adolescents in some technologically advanced cultures, such as Japan. In the Chicago sample, combined school and study time added up to 11 hours less per week than for Japanese adolescents. And Japanese adolescents spend 69 more days in school each year than American adolescents. With regard to work, 41 percent of the Chicago adolescents were employed and worked an average of 18 hours per week.

The main leisure activity of the Chicago adolescents was socializing, which took up about one-sixth of their waking hours. They also spent about three times as much time talking with friends and peers as they did with parents and adults. And 13 percent of their talking occurred via the phone! The Chicago adolescents spent far more time socializing and talking than their counterparts in Japan, Germany, and the Soviet Union. The Chicago adolescents also spent some of their

Figure 9.3   People with whom adolescents spend their time.

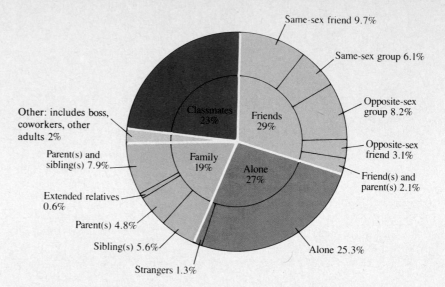

leisure time watching television, engaging in sports, playing games, pursuing hobbies, reading, and listening to music.

What percentage of time do adolescents spend with different people? As shown in Figure 9.3, the Chicago adolescents were not usually in the company of an adult. They were with their family for one-fifth of their waking hours, but only a portion of this time was spent with parents. A full 50 percent of the week's waking hours was spent with peers, partly in the classroom, partly outside of class with friends. One-fourth of their day was spent in solitude.

In a recent study with younger adolescents, Reed Larson and his colleagues beeped 401 fifth- through ninth-grade students in the Chicago area to determine how they were spending their time (Kirshnit, Ham, & Richards, 1989; Larson & Kleiber, 1990; Larson & Richards, 1989). For the youngest participants, play, television viewing, and other home- and family-centered activities filled a major portion of their waking hours. However, a different pattern of time use characterized the older subjects, who were in early adolescence. Talking, listening to music, and other solitary and friend-centered activities became more common in early adolescence. Participation in sports also declined in early adolescence. Perspective on Adolescent Development 9.1 presents more information on the role of sports in adolescent development.

Social Class

Many subcultures exist within countries. For example, the values and attitudes of adolescents growing up in an urban ghetto or rural Appalachia may differ from those of adolescents growing up in a wealthy suburb. In this section, we study the nature of social class; socioeconomic variations in families, schools, and neighborhoods; and adolescents in poverty.

The Nature of Social Class

Earlier in this chapter, social class (also called socioeconomic status or SES) was defined as the grouping of people with similar occupational, educational, and economic characteristics. Social class, or social stratification as it also is sometimes

The Role of Sports in Adolescent Development

For the most part, participation in sports is thought to be constructive and enjoyable for adolescents. Researchers have found that youth sports involvement is associated with positive feelings about one's body and higher self-esteem (Anthrop & Allison, 1983; Hall, Durborow, & Progen, 1986; Kirshnit, Richards, & Ham, 1988; Snyder & Spreitzer, 1976). Because of the potential benefits derived from participation in sports, some developmentalists express concern about the findings that approximately 80 percent of all adolescents drop out of organized sports programs between the ages of 12 and 17 (Kirshnit, Ham, & Richards, 1989; Seefeldt & others, 1978). In addition, girls drop out at higher rates and at earlier ages than boys (Brown, 1985; Butcher, 1985).

Two theories address why adolescents' participation in sports declines (Kirshnit, Ham, & Richards, 1989). First, during adolescence, an interest in sports conflicts with other interests more than it did in childhood (Gould & others, 1982). In this view, adolescents have a limited amount of leisure time, and with increasing age, they have more options from which to choose and more demands on how they should use their free time. In contrast to the idea of time conflicts and constraints, a second theory emphasizes the negative and overly professionalized aspects of organized youth sports programs, including lack of playing time, lack of success, little improvement in skills, pressure to perform or win, and dislike for the coach (Gould & Horn, 1984).

Today's adolescents believe that they have a better chance of obtaining an athletic scholarship than an academic scholarship in college. In 1980, more than 19 percent of high school students thought that they would be most likely to be eligible for an academic scholarship, while 13 percent said that athletics were their best chance. However, in 1990, the high school students reversed their beliefs, with 16 percent thinking that athletics were their best opportunity and only 14 percent thinking that academics were their best chance (Munce, 1990). This national survey of 754,000 juniors and seniors indicates that they were misperceiving reality because colleges award far more academic than athletic scholarships. Undoubtedly, the media portrayal of athletic glamour and the powerful image of big-time athletics contribute to the misperceptions.

Sports rank high in the interests of Black American adolescents, especially males. However, what once seemed to be an opportunity for Black adolescent males to achieve success has now been severely criticized. The concern is that Black families are four times more likely than White families to push their children and adolescents toward sports careers, often to the neglect and detriment of other critically important areas of development—intellectual, personal, and cultural, for example. The tragedy is that only

Dr. Harry Edwards has been instrumental in calling attention to the educational avoidance of many Blacks in sports.

5 percent of high school athletes go on to compete in their sports at the collegiate level, which means that 95 percent of all athletes must face the reality of life after sports at the conclusion of their last high school athletic competition. Of the Black athletes who do attend four-year colleges on athletic scholarships, approximately 70 percent never graduate from the colleges they represent in sports. Of the Black athletes who participate in college football, basketball, and baseball, fewer than 2 percent ever make the roster of a professional team. Among the chosen few, 60 percent are out of professional sports within three to four years and often are financially destitute without either the credentials or the skills for career success.

A number of ongoing efforts by media, academic, civil rights, and sports interests are publicizing and attempting to rectify the tragedies of Black sports involvement. According to Black sociologist and sports researcher Harry Edwards (1990), this does not mean that Blacks should abandon sports but that they need to learn to approach the realities of sports more constructively, especially giving more attention to academic achievement.

called, carries with it certain inequities. Generally, members of society have:
(1) occupations that vary in prestige, and some individuals have more access to
higher-status occupations than others; (2) achieved different levels of educational attainment, and some individuals have more access to better education
than others; (3) different economic resources; and (4) different levels of power to
influence a community's institutions. These differences in the ability to control
resources and to participate in society's rewards produce unequal opportunities
for adolescents.

The number of visibly different social classes depends on the community's
size and complexity (Havighurst, 1987). In most investigators' descriptions of
social classes, two to five categories are included. In a five-class structure, upper,
upper-middle, lower-middle, upper-lower, and lower-lower classes are delineated.
In a two-class structure, lower and middle classes are delineated. Sometimes, the
lower class is described as working-class, blue-collar, or low-income; sometimes,
the middle class is described as managerial-class, white-collar, or middle-income.
Examples of lower-class occupations are factory worker, manual laborer, welfare
recipient, and maintenance worker; examples of middle-class occupations are
salespeople, managers, and professionals (doctors, lawyers, teachers, accountants, and so on).

Socioeconomic Variations in Families, Schools, and Neighborhoods

The families, schools, and neighborhoods of adolescents have socioeconomic
characteristics. Some adolescents have parents who have a great deal of money,
and who work in prestigious occupations. The adolescents live in attractive houses
and neighborhoods, and attend schools where the mix of students is primarily
from middle-and upper-class backgrounds. Other adolescents have parents who
do not have very much money and who work in less prestigious occupations. The
adolescents do not live in very attractive houses and neighborhoods, and attend
schools where the mix of students is mainly from lower-class backgrounds. Such
variations in neighborhood settings can influence adolescents' adjustment (Mason
& Cauce, 1991).

In America and most Western cultures, social class differences in child
rearing exist. Working-class, low-income parents often place a high value on external characteristics, such as obedience and neatness, whereas middle-class parents often place a high value on internal characteristics, such as self-control and
delay of gratification. There also are social class differences in parenting behaviors. Middle-class parents are more likely to explain something, use verbal praise,
accompany their discipline with reasoning, and ask their children and adolescents
questions. By contrast, parents from low-income, working-class households are
more likely to discipline children and adolescents with physical punishment and
criticize them (Heath, 1983; Kohn, 1977).

Social class differences in families also are involved in an important aspect
of the adolescent's intellectual orientation. Most school tasks require students to
use and process language. As part of developing language skills, students must
learn to read efficiently, write effectively, and give competent oral reports. While
variation exists within a social class, middle-class students make use of verbal
skills, especially reading, more than students from low-income backgrounds (also
called working-class students). As shown in Figure 9.4, in one investigation,
working-class adolescents read less and watched television more than middle-
class adolescents (Erlick & Starry, 1973). While television involves some verbal
activity, it is primarily a visual medium, suggesting that working-class adolescents prefer a visual medium to a verbal medium.

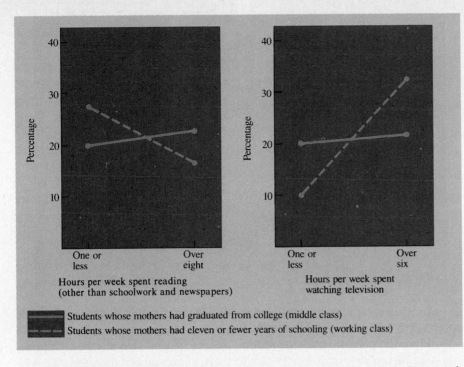

Figure 9.4 The reading and television habits of high school students from working-class families.
"Report of Poll No. 98 of The Purdue Opinion Panel, © 1973, by Purdue Research Foundation, West Lafayette, IN 47907."

Like their parents, children and adolescents from low-income backgrounds are at high risk for experiencing mental health problems (McLoyd, in press, 1990). Social maladaptation and psychological problems, such as depression, low self-confidence, peer conflict, and juvenile delinquency, are more prevalent among poor adolescents than among economically advantaged adolescents (Gibbs & Huang, 1989). Although psychological problems are more prevalent among adolescents from low-income backgrounds, intellectual and psychological functioning among these adolescents varies considerably. For example, a sizeable portion of adolescents from low-income backgrounds perform well in school, in many cases better than some middle-class students. When adolescents from low-income backgrounds are achieving well in school, it is not unusual to find a parent or parents making special sacrifices to provide the necessary living conditions and support that contribute to school success.

Schools in low-income neighborhoods often have fewer resources than schools in high-income neighborhoods. The schools in the low-income areas also are likely to have more students with lower achievement test scores, lower rates of graduation, and smaller percentages of students going to college (Garbarino & Asp, 1981). For example, in one recent profile, 80 percent of urban disadvantaged students scored in the bottom half of standardized tests for reading and math (*The Research Bulletin*, 1991). In some instances, however, federal aid to schools has provided a context for enhanced learning in low-income areas. The school personnel in schools in lower-class neighborhoods often are different than in middle-class settings. Younger, less experienced teachers often are the ones who end up with jobs in schools in lower-class neighborhoods, while older, more experienced teachers are more often found in schools in middle-class neighborhoods.

Poverty

Of special concern to psychologists and educators who work with adolescents is the subculture of the poor—those adolescents from the lower strata of working-

Adolescents from the lowest strata of working-class families are of special concern. Economic poverty makes it very difficult for adolescents to succeed in school and life.

class families. Although the most noticeable aspect of the poor is their economic poverty, other psychological and social characteristics are present.

First, the poor are often powerless. In occupations, they rarely are the decision makers. Rules are handed down to them in an authoritarian way. Second, the poor are vulnerable to disaster. They are not likely to be given advance notice when they are laid off from work and usually do not have financial resources to fall back on when problems arise. Third, their range of alternatives is restricted. Only a limited number of jobs are open to them. Even when alternatives are available, the poor may not know about them or be prepared to make a wise decision because of inadequate education and inability to read well. Fourth, there is less prestige in being poor. This lack of prestige is transmitted to children early in life. The poor child observes other children who wear nicer clothes and live in more attractive houses.

Currently, one in four children and one in five adolescents lives in poverty. The poverty rate for youth in single-parent, female-headed households is much higher (54 percent) than for their counterparts in other families (12.5 percent). Marian Wright Edleman (1987), president of the Children's Defense Fund, has said that today's America represents a cruel paradox. While the rich are getting richer and are often getting more government help, the poor are getting poorer and receiving less help. The decline in federal assistance for children and adolescents has made living in poverty a harsher existence for 13 million children and adolescents, and it has crippled the efforts of many families to struggle out of poverty.

Developmentalists are especially concerned about single mothers in poverty, more than one-third of whom are in poverty compared to only 10 percent of single fathers (U.S. Bureau of the Census, 1987). Developmentalist Vonnie McLoyd (in press; McLoyd & Wilson, 1990) states that, because poor, single mothers are more distressed than their middle-class counterparts, they often show low support, nurturance, and involvement with their children. Among the reasons for the high poverty rate of single mothers are the low pay of women, infrequent awarding of alimony payments, and poorly enforced child support by fathers (Farley, 1990).

At this point, we have discussed a number of ideas about culture, cross-cultural comparisons, the settings in which adolescents spend time, and social class. A summary of these ideas is presented in Concept Table 9.1. Next, we turn our attention to another important aspect of culture—ethnicity.

Concept Table 9.1

Culture and Social Class

Concept	Processes/Related Ideas	Characteristics/Description
Culture and its relevance to the study of adolescence	The nature of culture	Culture refers to the behavior, patterns, beliefs, and all other products of a particular group of people that are passed on from generation to generation. Culture is a broad concept and includes many components—family, peers, school, television and the media, social class, and ethnicity, for example.
	The relevance of culture to the study of adolescence	If the study of adolescence is to be a relevant discipline in the twenty-first century, increased attention will need to focus on culture and ethnicity. The future will bring extensive contact between people from varied cultures and ethnic groups. The world is becoming increasingly interactive and will be even more so in the future. The study of adolescence has been too ethnocentric.
	Cross-cultural comparisons	Cross-cultural studies involve the comparison of a culture with one or more other cultures, which provides information about the degree to which adolescent development is universal or culture-specific. The study of adolescence emerged in the context of Western industrialized society. This narrow viewpoint can produce erroneous conclusions about the nature of adolescents, and a more global, cosmopolitan perspective is needed. Anglo American adolescents are more achievement oriented than adolescents in many cultures, but not as achievement oriented as Japanese, Chinese, and Asian American adolescents. Adolescent sexuality also varies considerably across cultures.
	Rites of passage	Rites of passage are ceremonies that mark an individual's transition from one status to another, especially into adulthood. In primitive cultures, rites of passage are often well-defined, but in contemporary America, they are not. High school graduation and sexual intercourse are rites of passage that many American adolescents experience.
The settings in which adolescents spend their time	Their nature	Using the experience sampling method, which involves beeping adolescents on electronic pagers, researchers found that adolescents spent 29 percent of their time in productive activities, 31 percent in maintenance activities such as eating and resting, and the remainder of their time primarily in leisure. The largest amount of time spent in a single activity was studying (13 percent of their waking hours), but American adolescents spend considerably less time studying than Japanese adolescents. The main leisure activity of the American adolescents was socializing. They spent little time in the company of adults but a full 50 percent of their time with peers. In a recent study, children spent considerable time in play, television viewing, and other home- and family-centered activities; however, young adolescents spent much more time talking, listening to music, and participating in other solitary and friend-centered activities. Participation in sports also declined in adolescence. Nonetheless, sports play an important role in the lives of many adolescents. A special concern is the orientation of Black adolescents and their parents toward sports.
Social class	Its nature	Social class, also called socioeconomic status or SES, is the grouping of people with similar occupational, educational, and economic characteristics. Social class often carries with it certain inequities.
	Socioeconomic variations in families, schools, and neighborhoods	The families, schools, and neighborhoods of adolescents have socioeconomic characteristics that are related to the adolescent's development. Parents from low-income families are more likely to value external characteristics and to use physical punishment and criticism than their middle-class counterparts. Adolescents from low-income backgrounds are at risk for intellectual and mental health problems, although there is considerable variation within each social class.
	Poverty	The subculture of the poor is characterized not only by economic handicaps but also by social and psychological handicaps. Currently, one in five adolescents grows up in poverty. A special concern focuses on adolescents in low-income, single-mother families.

Ethnicity

As mentioned earlier, ethnicity refers to the cultural heritage, national characteristics, race, religion, and language of individuals. Currently, interest in ethnicity is dramatically increasing. First, we discuss the roles of social class, differences, and diversity in understanding ethnic minority adolescents. Then, we examine a number of issues pertaining to ethnic minority adolescents, including adolescence as a special juncture in the lives of these individuals. Finally, we look in more detail at Black American adolescents, Hispanic American adolescents, Asian American adolescents, and Native American adolescents.

Ethnicity, Social Class, Differences, and Diversity

Much of the research on ethnic minority adolescents has been characterized by a failure to tease apart the influences of ethnicity and social class. Ethnicity and social class can interact in ways that exaggerate the influence of ethnicity because ethnic minority individuals are overrepresented in the lower socioeconomic levels of American society (Spencer & Dornbusch, 1990). Consequently, too often researchers have given ethnic explanations of adolescent development that were largely based on socioeconomic status rather than ethnicity. For example, decades of research on group differences in self-esteem failed to consider the socioeconomic status of Black American and White American children and adolescents (Hare & Castenell, 1985). When the self-esteem of Black American adolescents from low-income backgrounds is compared with that of White American adolescents from middle-class backgrounds, the differences are often large but not informative because of the confounding of ethnicity and social class (Bell-Scott & Taylor, 1989; Spencer, 1987).

While some ethnic minority youth are from middle-class backgrounds, economic advantage does not entirely enable them to escape their ethnic minority status (Spencer & Dornbusch, 1990). Middle-class ethnic minority youth still encounter much of the prejudice, discrimination, and bias associated with being a member of an ethnic minority group. Often characterized as a "model minority" because of their strong achievement orientation and family cohesiveness, Japanese Americans still experience stress associated with ethnic minority status (Sue, 1990). While middle-class ethnic minority adolescents have more resources available to counter the destructive influences of prejudice and discrimination, they still cannot completely avoid the pervasive influence of negative stereotypes about ethnic minority groups.

While not all ethnic minority families are poor, poverty contributes to the stressful life experiences of many ethnic minority adolescents. In a recent review, Vonnie McLoyd (in press) concluded that ethnic minority youth experience a disproportionate share of the adverse effects of poverty and unemployment in America today. Thus, many ethnic minority adolescents experience a double disadvantage: (1) prejudice, discrimination, and bias because of their ethnic minority status and (2) the stressful effects of poverty.

Historical, economic, and social experiences produce legitimate differences between various ethnic minority groups, and between ethnic minority groups and the majority White group (Triandis, 1990; Allen & Santrock, 1993). Individuals living in a particular ethnic or cultural group adapt to the values, attitudes, and stresses of that culture. Their behavior, while possibly different from our own, is, nonetheless, often functional for them. Recognizing and respecting these differences is an important aspect of getting along with others in a diverse, multicultural world. Adolescents, as well as each of us, need to take the perspective of individuals from ethnic and cultural groups that are different than ours and think,

"If I were in their shoes, what kind of experiences might I have had?" "How would I feel if I were a member of their ethnic or cultural group?" "How would I think and behave if I had grown up in their world?" Such perspective taking often increases empathy and understanding of individuals from ethnic and cultural groups different from ours.

Unfortunately, the emphasis often placed by society and science on the differences between ethnic minority groups and the White majority has been damaging to ethnic minority individuals. Ethnicity has defined who will enjoy the privileges of citizenship and to what degree and in what ways (Jones, 1990). An individual's ethnic background has determined whether the individual will be alienated, oppressed, or disadvantaged.

The current emphasis on differences between ethnic groups underscores the strengths of various ethnic minority groups and is long overdue. For example, the extended-family support system that characterizes many ethnic minority groups is now recognized as an important factor in coping. And researchers are finding that Black males are better than Anglo males at nonverbal cues, multilingual/ multicultural expression, improvised problem solving, and using body language in communication (Evans & Whitfield, 1988).

For too long, differences between any ethnic minority group and Whites were conceptualized as *deficits* or inferior characteristics on the part of the ethnic minority group. Indeed, research on ethnic minority groups often focused only on a group's negative, stressful aspects. For example, research on Black American adolescent females invariably examined such topics as poverty, unwed motherhood, and dropping out of school. These topics continue to be important and much needed research areas of adolescent development, but research on the positive aspects of Black American adolescent females in a pluralistic society is also much needed and sorely neglected. The self-esteem, achievement, motivation, and self-control of adolescents from different ethnic minority groups deserve considerable study.

Another important dimension of ethnic minority adolescents is their diversity, a point made in Chapter 1 but that deserves a second mention. Ethnic minority groups are not homogeneous; they have different social, historical, and economic backgrounds (Kavanaugh & Kennedy, 1992). For example, Mexican, Cuban, and Puerto Rican immigrants are Hispanics but they had different reasons for migrating, came from varying socioeconomic backgrounds in their native countries, and experience different rates and types of employment in the United States (Ramirez, 1989). The U.S. federal government now recognizes the existence of 511 *different* Native American tribes, each having a unique ancestral background with differing values and characteristics. Asian Americans include the Chinese, Japanese, Philippinos, Koreans, and Southeast Asians, each group having a distinct ancestry and language. The diversity of Asian Americans is reflected in their educational attainment: Some achieve a high level of education, while many others have no education whatsoever (Sue & Okazaki, 1990). For example, 90 percent of Korean American males graduate from high school, but only 71 percent of Vietnamese American males do.

Sometimes, well-meaning individuals fail to recognize the diversity within an ethnic group (Sue, 1990). For example, a sixth-grade teacher went to a human relations workshop and was exposed to the necessity of incorporating more ethnicity into her instructional planning. Since she had two Mexican American adolescents in her class, she asked them to be prepared to demonstrate to the class on the following Monday how they danced at home. The teacher expected both of them to perform Mexican folk dances, reflecting their ethnic heritage. The first boy got up in front of the class and began dancing in a typical American fashion. The teacher said, "No, I want you to dance like you and your family do

Margaret Beale Spencer, shown here talking with adolescents, believes that adolescence is a critical juncture in the identity development of ethnic minority individuals. Most ethnic minority individuals consciously confront their ethnicity for the first time in adolescence.

at home, like you do when you have Mexican American celebrations." The boy informed the teacher that his family did not dance that way. The second boy demonstrated a Mexican folk dance to the class. The first boy was highly assimilated into the American culture and did not know how to dance Mexican folk dances. The second boy was less assimilated and came from a Mexican American family that had retained more of its Mexican heritage.

This example illustrates the diversity and individual differences that exist within any ethnic minority group. Failure to recognize diversity and individual variations results in the stereotyping of an ethnic minority group. Next, we study how adolescence is a special juncture in an ethnic minority individual's development.

Adolescence: A Special Juncture for Ethnic Minority Individuals

For ethnic minority individuals, adolescence is often a special juncture in their development (Spencer, 1991; Spencer & Dornbusch, 1990). Although children are aware of some ethnic and cultural differences, most ethnic minority individuals first consciously confront their ethnicity in adolescence. In contrast to children, adolescents have the ability to interpret ethnic and cultural information, to reflect on the past, and to speculate about the future (Harter, 1990a). As they cognitively mature, ethnic minority adolescents become acutely aware of how the majority White culture evaluates their ethnic group (Comer, 1988; Ogbu, 1989). As one researcher commented, the young Black American child may learn that Black is beautiful but conclude as an adolescent that White is powerful (Semaj, 1985).

Ethnic minority youths' awareness of negative appraisals, conflicting values, and restricted occupational opportunities can influence life choices and plans for the future (Spencer & Dornbusch, 1990). As one ethnic minority youth stated,

"The future seems shut off, closed. Why dream? You can't reach your dreams. Why set goals? At least if you don't set any goals, you don't fail."

For many ethnic minority youth, a special concern is the lack of successful ethnic minority role models (Blash & Unger, 1992). The problem is especially acute for inner-city ethnic minority youth. Because of the lack of adult ethnic minority role models, some ethnic minority youth may conform to middle-class White values and identify with successful White role models. However, for many ethnic minority adolescents, their ethnicity and skin color constrain their acceptance by the White culture. Thus, they face a difficult task: negotiating two value systems—that of their own ethnic group and that of the White society. Some adolescents reject the mainstream, forgoing the rewards controlled by White Americans; others adopt the values and standards of the majority White culture; and still others take the difficult path of biculturality.

The nature of identity development in ethnic minority adolescents is discussed further in Chapter 10, "The Self and Identity." Next, we examine the prejudice, discrimination, and bias experienced by many ethnic minority adolescents.

Prejudice, Discrimination, and Bias

Prejudice *is an unjustified negative attitude toward an individual because of the individual's membership in a group.* The group toward which the prejudice is directed can be made up of people of a particular ethnic group, sex, age, religion, or other detectable difference. Our concern here is prejudice against ethnic minority groups.

In a recent Gallup poll, Americans stated that they believe that the United States is ethnically tolerant and that overt racism is basically unacceptable (*Asian Week,* 1990). However, many ethnic minority individuals continue to experience persistent forms of prejudice, discrimination, and bias (Sue, 1990). Ethnic minority adolescents are taught in schools that often have a middle-class, White bias and in classroom contexts that are not adapted to ethnic minority adolescents' learning styles. They are assessed by tests that are often culturally biased and are evaluated by teachers whose appreciation of their abilities may be hindered by negative stereotypes about ethnic minorities (Spencer & Dornbusch, 1990). Discrimination and prejudice continue to be present in the media, interpersonal interactions, and daily conversations. Crimes, strangeness, poverty, mistakes, and deterioration are often mistakenly attributed to ethnic minority individuals or foreigners (van Dijk, 1987).

As Asian American researcher Stanley Sue (1990) points out, people frequently have opposing views about discrimination and prejudice. On one side are individuals who value and praise the significant strides made in civil rights in recent years, pointing to affirmative action programs as proof of these civil rights advances. On the other side are individuals who criticize American institutions, such as education, because they believe that many forms of discrimination and prejudice still characterize these institutions.

Progress has been made in ethnic minority relations, but discrimination and prejudice still exist, and equality has not been achieved. Much remains to be accomplished (Allen & Santrock, 1993).

Value Conflicts, Assimilation, and Pluralism

Stanley Sue (1990) believes that value conflicts are often involved when individuals respond to ethnic issues. These value conflicts have been a source of consid-

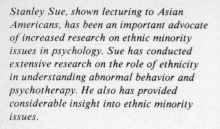

Stanley Sue, shown lecturing to Asian Americans, has been an important advocate of increased research on ethnic minority issues in psychology. Sue has conducted extensive research on the role of ethnicity in understanding abnormal behavior and psychotherapy. He also has provided considerable insight into ethnic minority issues.

erable controversy. According to Sue, without properly identifying the assumptions and effects of the conflicting values, it is difficult to resolve ethnic minority issues.

Let us examine a value conflict that Sue describes—assimilation versus pluralism—and see how it might influence an individual's responses to an ethnic minority issue: One faculty member commented that he was glad that his psychology department was interested in teaching students about ethnic and cultural issues. He felt that, by becoming aware of the cultures of different groups, students would improve their understanding of their own and other cultures. However, another faculty member disagreed. She felt that students' knowledge of ethnic minority issues and different cultures was a relevant concern, but she argued that the department's scarce resources should not be devoted to ethnic and cultural issues. She also believed that, if too much attention was given to ethnic and cultural issues, it might actually increase the segregation of students and even cause friction among ethnic and cultural groups. She commented that we all live in this society, and therefore, we must all learn the same skills to succeed. In Sue's (1990) perspective, a value conflict involving assimilation and pluralism underlies these opposing views about whether a psychology department should devote any or increased funds to teaching students about ethnicity and culture.

Assimilation *refers to the absorption of ethnic minority groups into the dominant group, which often means the loss of some or virtually all of the behavior and values of the ethnic minority group.* Individuals who adopt an assimilation stance usually advocate that ethnic minority groups should become more American. By contrast, **pluralism** *refers to the coexistence of distinct ethnic and cultural groups in the same society.* Individuals who adopt a pluralism stance usually advocate that cultural differences should be maintained and appreciated.

For many years, an assimilation approach was thought to be the best course for American society because the mainstream was believed to be superior in many ways. Even though many individuals today reject the notion that the mainstream culture is intrinsically superior to ethnic minority cultures, the assimilation approach is currently resurfacing with a more complex face. Advocates of the assimilation approach now often use practical and functional arguments rather than intrinsic superiority arguments to buttress their point of view. For example, assimilation advocates stress that educational programs for immigrant children

(Mexican, Chinese, and so on) should stress the learning of English as early as possible, rather than bilingual education. Their argument is that spending time on any language other than English may be a handicap, especially since a second language is not functional in the classroom. By contrast, the advocates of pluralism argue that an English-only approach reasserts the mainstream-is-right-and-best belief. Thus, responses to the ethnic minority issue of bilingual education involve a clash of fundamental values. As Sue asks, how can one argue against the development of functional skills and to some degree the support of Americanization? Similarly, how can one doubt that pluralism, diversity, and respect for different cultures is valid? Sue believes that the one-sidedness of the issue is the main problem. Advocates of assimilation often overlook the fact that a consensus may be lacking on what constitutes functional skills or that a particular context may alter what skills are useful. For example, with an increasing immigrant population, the ability to speak Spanish or Japanese may be an asset, as is the ability to interact with and collaborate with diverse ethnic groups.

Sue believes that one way to resolve value conflicts about sociocultural issues is to conceptualize or redefine them in innovative ways. For example, in the assimilation/pluralism conflict, rather than deal with the assumption that assimilation is necessary for the development of functional skills, one strategy is to focus on the fluctuating criteria of what skills are considered functional or the possibility that developing functional skills does not prevent the existence of pluralism. For instance, the classroom instructor might use multicultural examples when teaching social studies, while also discussing culturally universal (etic) and culturally specific (emic) approaches to American and other cultures.

Now that we have considered a number of ideas about ethnic minority adolescents in general, we turn our attention to specific ethnic minority groups in America, beginning with Black American adolescents.

Black American Adolescents

Black adolescents make up the largest easily visible ethnic minority group. Black adolescents are distributed throughout the social class structure, although they constitute a larger proportion of poor and lower-class individuals than does the majority White group (Gibbs, 1989, 1991; McLoyd, 1989; Reid, 1991). No cultural characteristic is common to all or nearly all Blacks and absent in Whites, unless it is the experience of being Black and the ideology that develops from that experience (Havighurst, 1987).

The majority of Black youth stay in school, do not take drugs, do not get married prematurely and become parents, are employed and eager to work, are not involved in crime, and grow up to lead productive lives in spite of social and economic disadvantage. While much of the writing and research about Black adolescents has focused on low-income youth from families mainly residing in inner cities, the majority of Black youth do not reside in the ghettos of inner cities. At the heart of the new model of studying Black youth is recognition of the growing diversity within Black communities in the United States (Bell-Scott & Taylor, 1989).

While prejudice against Blacks in some occupations still persists, the proportion of males and females in middle-class occupations has been increasing since 1940. A substantial and increasing proportion of Black adolescents are growing up in middle-class families and share middle-class values and attitudes with White middle-class adolescents. Nonetheless, large numbers of Black American adolescents still live in poverty-enshrouded ghettos (Heath, 1989; Taylor, 1990; Wilson, 1989).

A special concern is the experiences of Black adolescents in the inner city. Unattractive jobs and lack of community standards to reinforce work may undermine the well-intentioned efforts of schools.

In one investigation of Black Americans, a mixture of factors was related to the problems of adolescents in the inner city (Wilson, 1987). Increased social isolation in concentrated areas of poverty and little interaction with the mainstream society were related to the difficulties experienced by inner-city Black youth. Unattractive jobs and lack of community standards to reinforce work increased the likelihood that inner-city Black youth turned to either underground illegal activity, idleness, or both.

In the inner city, Black American youth are increasingly unlikely to find legitimate employment, to some extent because of the lack of even low-paying jobs (Spencer & Dornbusch, 1990). The exodus of middle-income Black Americans from the cities to the suburbs has removed leadership, reduced the tax base, decreased the educated political constituency, and diminished the support of churches and other organizations.

In many ethnic minority communities, religious institutions play an important role. Many Black Americans report that their religious beliefs help them to get along with others and to accept the realities of the American occupational system (Spencer & Dornbusch, 1990). In one research study of successful Black American students, a strong religious faith was common (Lee, 1985). In this study, regular church attendance characterized the lives of the successful Black American students, many of whom mentioned Jesus Christ, Martin Luther King, and deacons as important influences in their lives. For many Black American families, the church has served as an important resource and support system, not only in spiritual matters, but in the development of a social network as well.

As mentioned earlier, there is a high percentage of single-parent Black families, many of whom are in low-income categories. These family circumstances tax the coping ability of single parents and can have negative effects on children and adolescents. However, a characteristic of many Black families that helps to offset the high percentage of single-parent households is the extended-family household—in which one or several grandparents, uncles, aunts, siblings, or cousins either live together or provide support. The extended-family system has helped many Black parents to cope with adverse social conditions and economic impoverishment (McAdoo, 1988; McLoyd & Wilson, 1990). The Black extended family can be traced to the African heritage of many Black Americans, where in many cultures, a newly married couple does not move away from relatives. Instead, the extended family assists its members with basic family functions. Researchers have found that the extended family helps to reduce the stress of poverty and single parenting through emotional support, sharing of income and economic responsibility, and surrogate parenting (McAdoo, 1988). The presence of grandmothers in the households of many Black adolescents and their infants has also been an important support system for the teenage mother and the infant (Stevens, 1984).

Hispanic American Adolescents

The number of Hispanics in the United States has increased 30 percent since 1980 to 19 million. Hispanics now account for almost 8 percent of the U.S. population. Most trace their roots to Mexico (63 percent), Puerto Rico (12 percent), and Cuba (5 percent), the rest to Central and South American countries and the Caribbean (Laosa, 1989). By the year 2000, their numbers are expected to swell to 30 million, 15 percent of the U.S. population. And roughly one-third of all Hispanics in the United States marry non-Hispanics, promising a day when the two cultures will be more intertwined.

By far the largest group of Hispanic adolescents consists of those who identify themselves as having a Mexican origin, although many of them were born in the United States (Domino, 1992; Ramirez, 1989). Their largest concentration is in the U.S. Southwest. They represent more than 50 percent of the student population in the schools of San Antonio and close to that percentage in the schools of Los Angeles. Mexican Americans have a variety of life-styles and come from a range of socioeconomic statuses—from affluent professional and managerial status to migrant farm worker and welfare recipient in big city barrios. While coming from families with diverse backgrounds, Hispanic American adolescents have one of the lowest educational levels of any ethnic minority group in the United States (Busch-Rossnagal & Zayas, 1991; Knouse, 1992). Social support from parents and school personnel may be especially helpful in developing stronger academic achievement in Hispanic youth (Field, 1991).

Many Hispanic American adolescents have developed a new political consciousness and pride in their cultural heritage. Some have fused strong cultural links to Mexican and Indian cultures with the economic limitations and restricted opportunities in the barrio. **Chicano** *is the name politically conscious Mexican American adolescents give themselves to reflect the combination of their Spanish-Mexican-Indian heritage and Anglo influences.*

Like for Black adolescents, the church and family play important roles in Hispanic American adolescents' lives. Many, but not all, Hispanic American families are Catholic. And a basic value in Mexico is represented by saying, "As long as our family stays together, we are strong." Mexican children are brought up to stay close to their family, a tradition continued by Mexican Americans. Unlike the father in many Anglo American families, the Mexican father is the undisputed authority on all family matters and is usually obeyed without question. The mother is revered as the primary source of affection and care. This emphasis on family attachment leads the Mexican to say, "I will achieve mainly because of my family, and for my family, rather than myself." By contrast, the self-reliant American would say, "I will achieve mainly because of my ability and initiative, and for myself, rather than for my family." Unlike most American families, Mexican families tend to stretch out in a network of relatives that often runs to scores of individuals. Mexican American families also tend to be large and have a strong extended-family orientation.

The church and family play important roles in the lives of many Hispanic American adolescents. In many Hispanic families, the father is the authority on many matters, whereas the mother is the primary source of affection and care.

Asian American Adolescents

Asian American adolescents are the fastest-growing segment of the American adolescent population, and they, too, show considerable diversity. In the 1970 census, only three Asian American groups were prominent—Japanese, Chinese, and Philippino. But in the last two decades, there has been rapid growth in three other groups—Koreans, Pacific Islanders (Guam and Samoa), and Vietnamese (Huang, 1989).

Adolescents of Japanese or Chinese origin can be found in virtually every large city. While their grasp of the English language is usually good, they have been raised in a subculture in which family loyalty and family influence are powerful (Cooper & others, 1992). This has tended to maintain their separate subcultures. The Japanese American adolescents are somewhat more integrated into the Anglo life-style than are the Chinese American adolescents. However, both groups have been very successful in school. They tend to take considerable advantage of educational opportunities.

Many Asian American adolescents have been very successful in schools, taking advantage of their educational opportunities. Nonetheless, it is always important to keep in mind the diversity that exists within any ethnic minority group.

Native American Adolescents

Approximately 100,000 Native American (American Indian) adolescents are scattered across many tribal groups in about 20 states. About 90 percent are enrolled in school. About 15,000 are in boarding schools, many of which are maintained by the federal government's Bureau of Indian Affairs. Another 45,000 are in public schools on or near Indian reservations. In these schools, the Native American adolescents make up more than 50 percent of the students. The remaining 30,000 are in public schools where they are an ethnic minority. A growing proportion of Native American adolescents have moved to large cities (Havighurst, 1987).

Native American adolescents have experienced an inordinate amount of discrimination. While virtually any minority group experiences some discrimination in being a member of a larger, majority-group culture, in the early years of the United States, Native Americans were the victims of terrible physical abuse and punishment. Injustices that these 800,000 individuals experienced are reflected in the lowest standard of living, the highest teenage pregnancy rate, the highest suicide rate, and the highest school dropout rate of any ethnic group (LaFromboise & Low, 1989).

America: A Nation of Blended Cultures

America has been and continues to be a great receiver of ethnic groups. It has embraced new ingredients from many cultures. The cultures often collide and cross-pollinate, mixing their ideologies and identities. Some of the culture of origin is retained, some of it lost, some of it mixed with the American culture. One after another, immigrants have come to America and been exposed to new channels of awareness and, in turn, exposed Americans to new channels of awareness. Black, Hispanic, Asian American, Native American, and other cultural heritages mix with the mainstream, receiving a new content and giving a new content (Gibbs & Huang, 1989). The ethnicity of Canadian adolescents is discussed in Sociocultural Worlds of Adolescence 9.2. Now that we have considered many cultural dimensions of ethnicity, we examine other important dimensions of the culture that adolescents experience.

The Native American adolescent's quest for identity involves a cultural meshing of tribal customs and the technological, educational demands of modern society.

Television and the Media

Few developments in society over the last 30 years have had a greater impact on adolescents than television. The persuasion capabilities of television are staggering. As they have grown up, many of today's adolescents have spent more time in front of the television set than with their parents or in the classroom. Radio, records, rock music, and music video are other media that are especially important influences in the lives of many adolescents.

Adolescents' Use of Mass Media

If the amount of time spent in an activity is any indication of its importance, then there is no doubt that the mass media play important roles in adolescents' lives (Fine, Mortimer, & Roberts, 1990). Adolescents spend a third or more of their waking hours with some form of mass media, either as a primary focus or as a background for other activities. Estimates of adolescent television viewing range from two to four hours per day with considerable variation around the averages: Some adolescents watch little or no television; others view as much as eight hours

Cultural Dimensions of Canada

Adolescents in Canada are exposed to some cultural dimensions similar to their U.S. counterparts since Canada has long been economically and culturally tied to the United States. For example, Canadian adolescents are inundated with American mass media: popular magazines, radio, and television. However, the cultural worlds of Canadian adolescents differ in certain ways from the cultural worlds of U.S. adolescents. In 1971, Canada was officially redefined by the federal government as bilingual (English/French), yet multicultural. Primarily French-speaking individuals reside mainly in Quebec, primarily English-speaking individuals in the other Canadian provinces. While, officially, Canada is a bilingual nation, it is predominantly the French Canadians who are bilingual. Although Canada's main ethnic ties are British and French, a number of ethnic minorities live there as well—German (6 percent), Italian (3 percent), Ukranian (3 percent), Scandinavian (2 percent), Dutch (2 percent), Indian and Eskimo (1 percent), and Jewish (1 percent), for example. While Canada has become more of a multicultural mosaic, it does not come near to being the ethnic melting pot that the U.S. culture is (Anderson & Frideres, 1981).

a day. Television viewing often peaks in late childhood and then begins to decline at some point in early adolescence in response to competing media and the demands of school and social activities (Huston & Alvarez, 1990; Larson, Kubey, & Colletti, 1989).

As television viewing declines, the use of music media—radio, records and tapes, and music video—increases to four to six hours per day by the middle of adolescence (Fine, Mortimer, & Roberts, 1990; Larson, Kubey, & Colletti, 1989). As adolescents get older, movie attendance increases—more than 50 percent of 12-to-17-year-olds report at least monthly attendance. In recent years, viewing of videocassettes has become a common adolescent activity, with adolescent involvement at 5 to 10 hours per week (Wartella & others, 1990).

Adolescents also use the print media more than children. Newspaper reading often begins at about 11 to 12 years of age and gradually increases until 60 to 80 percent of late adolescents report at least some newspaper reading. In similar fashion, magazine and book reading gradually increase during adolescence. Approximately one-third of high school juniors and seniors say that they read magazines daily, while 20 percent say that they read nonschool books daily, reports that are substantiated by the sales of teen-oriented books and magazines. However, comic-book reading declines steeply between the ages of 10 and 18.

Large, individual differences characterize all forms of adolescent media use (Fine, Mortimer, & Roberts, 1990). In addition to the age differences just described, gender, ethnicity, socioeconomic status, and intelligence are all related to which media are used, to what extent, and for what purposes. For example, female adolescents watch more television and listen to more music than male adolescents; Black American adolescents view television and listen to more music than White American adolescents, with Black females showing the most frequent viewing and listening (Greenberg, 1988). Brighter adolescents and adolescents from middle-class families are more likely to read the newspaper and news magazines, and also are more likely to watch television news than less intelligent adolescents and adolescents from low-income backgrounds (Chafee & Yang, 1990).

The Cosby Show *is an excellent example of how television can present positive models for ethnic minority children and adolescents.*

Television

The messages of television are powerful. What are television's functions? How extensively does television affect adolescents? What is MTV's role in adolescents' lives?

Television's Functions

Television has been called a lot of things, not all of them good. Depending on one's point of view, it is a "window to the world," the "one-eyed monster," or the "boob tube." Scores on national achievement tests in reading and mathematics, while showing a small improvement recently, have generally been lower than in the past decades—and television has been attacked as one of the reasons. Television may take adolescents away from the printed media and books. One study found that children who read books and the printed media watched television less than those who did not (Huston, Siegle, & Bremer, 1983). It is argued that television trains individuals to become passive learners. Rarely, if ever, does television require active responses from the observer. Heavy television use may produce not only a passive learner, but a passive life-style. In one investigation of 406 adolescent males, those who watched little television were more physically fit and physically active than those who watched a lot (Tucker, 1987).

Television also can deceive (Huston, Watkins, & Kunkel, 1989). It can teach adolescents that problems are easily resolved and that everything turns out all right in the end. For example, it takes only about 30 to 60 minutes for detectives to sort through a complex array of clues and discover the killer—and they always find the killer. Violence is pictured as a way of life in many shows, and police are shown to use violence and break moral codes in their fight against evildoers. And the lasting results of violence are rarely brought home to the viewer. An individual who is injured suffers for only a few seconds. In real life, the individual might take months or even years to recover, or perhaps does not recover at all.

A special concern is how ethnic minority groups are portrayed on television. Ethnic minorities have historically been underrepresented and misrepresented on television. Ethnic minority characters—whether Black, Asian, Hispanic, or Native American—have often been presented as less dignified and less positive than White characters (Condry, 1989). In one investigation, television character portrayals of ethnic minorities were examined from 4:00 to 6:00 P.M. and 7:00 to 11:00 P.M., which are heavy adolescent viewing times (Williams & Condry, 1989). The percentage of White characters far exceeded the actual percentage of Whites in the United States; the percentages of Black, Asian, and Hispanic characters fell short of the population statistics. Hispanic characters were especially underrepresented—only 0.6 percent of the characters were Hispanic, while Hispanics comprise 6.4 percent of the U.S. population. Ethnic minorities held lower-status jobs and were more likely than Whites to be cast as criminals or victims.

But there are some positive aspects to television's influence on adolescents. For one, television presents adolescents with a world that is different from the one in which they live. This means that, through television, adolescents are exposed to a wider variety of views and knowledge than when they are informed only by their parents, teachers, and peers. Before television's advent, adolescents' identification models came in the form of parents, relatives, older siblings, neighborhood peers, famous individuals heard about in conversation or on the radio and read about in newspapers or magazines, and the film stars seen in the theater, visited no more than twice a week. Many of the identification figures in the past came from family or peers whose attitudes, clothing styles, and occupational objectives were relatively homogenous. The imagery and pervasiveness of television have exposed children and adolescents to hundreds of different neighborhoods, cultures, clothing fashions, career possibilities, and patterns of intimate relationships.

How Pervasively Does Television Influence Adolescents?

Many reports about the mass media presume large and direct effects of television on children and adolescents. The reports commonly assume that viewing x hours of television violence, commercial appeals, gender-role stereotypes, and pro-sex music videos will almost automatically cause viewers to accept and adopt the attitudes and behaviors they see and hear. So much exposure, it is argued, must produce strong effects, especially among children and adolescents, who are still developing their values and standards (Gore, 1987). However, in some areas, there are few research studies, and in others, direct, causal effects have not been documented (Fine, Mortimer, & Roberts, 1990).

Consider sexuality. There is a widespread assumption that television teaches children and adolescents about sexuality (Bence, 1989, 1991). In a recent survey, two-thirds of adults believed that television encourages adolescents to be sexually active and does not portray sexuality in a realistic way. To some extent, adults' concerns are justified in that, over the past decade, sexual content on television has increased and become more explicit. The consistent sexual messages adolescents learn from television's content are that sexual behaviors usually occur between unmarried couples, that contraception is rarely discussed, and that the negative consequences of sexuality (such as an unwanted pregnancy and sexually transmitted diseases) rarely are shown (Greenberg & others, 1986; Travis, Phillips, & Williams, 1986). Television gives more attention to dramatic events than to thoughtful considerations about sexuality. However, given the concern over television messages about sexuality, there has been little research on how such information influences adolescents. In one investigation, television researcher Rosemarie Truglio (1990) found that adolescents did differentiate between real life and televised portrayals of sexual behavior, although frequent television viewers had more difficulty separating the world of television from real life. She concluded that the socializing influence of television may be greatest for content areas about which adolescents have limited information, such as birth control. To the extent that adolescents accept television's messages about sex (such as a lack of contraception), their sexual behaviors may be influenced by dramatic portrayals of intimate interpersonal relationships.

While there has been little investigation of how televised sex influences adolescent sexuality, many research studies have studied television's influence on aggression. In one longitudinal investigation, the amount of violence watched on television at age eight was significantly related to the seriousness of criminal acts performed as an adult (Huesmann, 1986). In another investigation, long-term exposure to television violence was significantly related to the likelihood of aggression in 1,565 12- to 17-year-old boys (Belson, 1978). Boys who watched the most aggression on television were the most likely to commit a violent crime, swear, be aggressive in sports, threaten violence toward another boy, write slogans on walls, or break windows.

These investigations are *correlational* in nature, so we cannot conclude from them that television *causes* children and adolescents to be more aggressive, only that watching television is *associated* with aggressive behavior. In one experiment, children were randomly assigned to one of two groups: One group watched television shows taken directly from violent Saturday morning cartoon offerings on 11 different days; the second group watched television cartoon shows with all of the violence removed (Steur, Applefield, & Smith, 1971). The children were

During the 1980s, MTV became one of the most popular television networks for adolescents. Why is MTV so popular with adolescents?

then observed during play at their preschool. The preschool children who saw the television cartoon shows with violence kicked, choked, and pushed their playmates more than the preschool children who watched nonviolent television cartoon shows. Because children were randomly assigned to the two conditions (television cartoons with violence versus cartoons with no violence), we can conclude that exposure to television violence *caused* the increased aggression in children in this investigation.

Although some critics have argued that the effects of television violence do not warrant the conclusion that television violence causes aggression (Freedman, 1984), many experts believe that television violence can induce aggressive or antisocial behavior in children (Condry, 1989; Huston, Watkins, & Kunkel, 1989; Liebert & Sprafkin, 1988). Of course, television is not the *only* cause of aggression. There is no *one*, single cause of any social behavior. Aggression, like all other social behaviors, has a number of determinants.

Television and other mass media are no different from other information sources in that there is considerable variation in what adolescents attend to, what sense they make out of it, and the conditions that influence whether they will take action on what has been absorbed (Fine, Mortimer, & Roberts, 1990). Whether televised sexuality or aggression will exert a strong influence on the adolescent's attitudes and behavior likely depends on a complex number of factors that include the needs, abilities, and interests of the adolescent, as well as other characteristics, such as socioeconomic status, the sex of the adolescent, cultural standards and ethnic values, and the adolescent's maturity.

The Media and Music

Anyone who has been around adolescents very long knows that many of them spend huge amounts of time listening to music on the radio, playing records or tapes of their favorite music, or watching music videos on television. Approximately two-thirds of all records and tapes are purchased by the 10- to 24-year-old age group. And one-third of the nation's 8,200 radio stations aim their broadcast rock music at the pool of adolescent listeners.

Music tastes become more specific and differentiated from the beginning to the end of adolescence (Christenson & Roberts, 1991). In early adolescence, individuals often prefer middle-of-the road, top 40 rock music. By high school, however, adolescents frequently identify with much narrower music types, such as heavy metal, new wave, rap, and so on. Boys prefer "harder" forms of rock, girls softer, more romantic forms of "pop."

Music meets a number of personal and social needs for adolescents (Christenson & Roberts, 1991). The most important personal needs are mood control and silence-filling. Somewhat surprisingly, relatively few adolescents say that popular music lyrics are very important to them. Few use music "to learn about the world," although Black American adolescents are more likely to say popular music fulfills this function for them than their White counterparts.

Popular music's social functions range from providing a party atmosphere to expressing rebellion against authority (Lull, 1987). However, the latter function is not as common as popular stereotypes suggest. Music "style" is closely associated with teenage crowds or cliques—"Ropers" prefer country/western music, "Freaks" prefer hard rock, and so on (Frith, 1981). Adolescents who express alienation toward school and frequently commit delinquent acts do prefer hard rock and heavy metal music to other types (Tanner, 1981). Given the popularity of the music media with adolescents, they might be ideal candidates for improving adolescent health behavior. To read about this possibility, turn to Perspective on Adolescent Development 9.2.

The music adolescents enjoy on records, tapes, radio, and television is an important dimension of their culture. Rock music does not seem to be a passing fad, having been around now for more than 35 years. Recently, it has had its share of controversy. Starting in 1983, MTV (the first music video television channel) and music videos in general were targets of debate in the media (Cocks, 1983). About a year later, rock music lyrics were attacked by the Parents Music Resource Center (PMRC). This group charged in a congressional hearing that rock music lyrics were dangerously shaping the minds of adolescents in the areas of sexual morality, violence, drugs, and satanism (Cocks, 1985). The national Parent Teacher Association agreed (Cox, 1985). And Tipper Gore, a PMRC founder, voiced her views about the dangers of rock music lyrics in a book (Gore, 1987).

How pervasively does rock music affect adolescents? In one investigation, a group of young people waiting in line to attend a punk rock concert by the group *Dead Kennedys* were interviewed (Rosenthal, 1985). More than 90 percent agreed with the rebellious sentiments expressed in the *Dead Kennedys'* songs, clearly higher than the population as a whole. However, direction of influence cannot be assessed in this case. That is, young people with particular views are attracted to a particular kind of music, such as punk. At the same time, it may be these particular young people who pay attention to, comprehend, and are vulnerable to the lyrics' influence.

Motivation, experience, and knowledge are factors in the interpretation of lyrics. In one investigation, preadolescents and adolescents often missed sexual themes in lyrics (Prinsky & Rosenbaum, 1987). Adult organizations such as the PMRC interpret rock music lyrics in terms of sex, violence, drugs, and satanism more than adolescents themselves. In this investigation, it was found that, in contrast to these adult groups, adolescents interpreted their favorite songs in terms of love, friendship, growing up, life's struggles, having fun, cars, religion, and other topics in teenage life.

Other recent research has focused on the medium of music video in comparison to other presentations of music (Greenfield & others, 1987). Comparing music videos with audio songs is like comparing the television medium to radio in that music videos and television have been found to detract from imaginative responses. While music video is a compelling medium that attracts attention, it is considered an "easy" medium that requires little mental effort.

At this point we have discussed a number of ideas about ethnicity and television and the media. A summary of these ideas is presented in Concept Table 9.2. This concludes our discussion of culture, and this is the final chapter in Section III of the book, "The Contexts of Adolescent Development." In the next section, Section IV, we turn our attention to the social, emotional, and personality development of adolescents, first studying the self and identity in Chapter 10.

Concept Table 9.2

Ethnicity, Television, and the Media

Concept	Processes/Related Ideas	Characteristics/Description
Ethnicity, social class, differences, and diversity	Ethnicity and social class	Much of the research on ethnic minority adolescents has not teased apart the influences of ethnicity and social class. Because of this failure, too often researchers have given ethnic explanations of adolescent development that were largely based on socioeconomic factors. While not all ethnic minority families are poor, poverty contributes to the stress of many ethnic minority adolescents.
	Differences	Historical, economic, and social experiences produce legitimate differences between many ethnic minority groups, and between ethnic minority groups and the White majority. Recognizing and respecting these differences is an important aspect of getting along with others in a diverse, multicultural world. Too often, differences between ethnic groups and the White majority have been interpreted as deficits on the part of the ethnic minority group. Also, the focus of research has too often been on the negative dimensions of ethnic minority groups. The current emphasis on studying the strengths as well as the weaknesses of ethnic minority adolescents is long overdue.
	Diversity	Another important dimension of ethnic minority groups is their diversity. Ethnic minority groups are not homogeneous; they have different social, historical, and economic backgrounds. Failure to recognize diversity and individual variations results in the stereotyping of an ethnic minority group.
Adolescence: A special juncture for ethnic minority individuals	Its nature	Adolescence is often a special juncture in the development of ethnic minority individuals. Although children are aware of some ethnic and cultural differences, most ethnic minority individuals first consciously confront their ethnicity in adolescence. A problem for many ethnic minority youth is the lack of successful ethnic minority role models.
Prejudice and value conflicts	Prejudice, discrimination, and bias	Prejudice is an unjustified negative attitude toward an individual because of the individual's membership in a group. Our concern here is prejudice against ethnic minority groups. Many ethnic minority adolescents continue to experience persistent prejudice, discrimination, and bias.
	Value conflicts	Value conflicts are often involved when individuals respond to ethnic issues. One prominent value conflict involves assimilation versus pluralism.
Ethnic minority groups	Black American adolescents	Black American adolescents make up the largest easily visible ethnic minority group. They are distributed throughout the social classes, but unusually high numbers still live in poverty-enshrouded ghettos. In the inner city, Black American youth are increasingly unlikely to find legitimate employment. The church and extended-family system play important roles in helping many Black adolescents cope with stress.
	Hispanic American adolescents	Most Hispanic adolescents trace their roots to Mexico, Puerto Rico, or Cuba. Roughly one-third will marry non-Hispanics. Mexican American adolescents are the largest subgroup of Hispanic American adolescents and are concentrated in the U.S. Southwest. Hispanic Americans have one of the lowest educational levels of all ethnic minority groups. The Catholic Church and the extended-family system play important roles in many Hispanic American adolescents' lives. Many Mexican American adolescents have developed a new political consciousness and pride in their cultural heritage.

Concept Table 9.2

Ethnicity, Television, and the Media

Concept	Processes/Related Ideas	Characteristics/Description
	Asian American adolescents	Asian American adolescents are a diverse, fast-growing segment of the adolescent population. Japanese American and Chinese American are the largest subgroups. Family loyalty is powerful, and many Asian American adolescents are very achievement oriented.
	Native American adolescents	Also called American Indian adolescents, they have experienced painful discrimination. Their injustices are reflected in high dropout rates from school, high teenage pregnancy rates, and a high suicide rate.
	America: A nation of blended cultures	America has been and continues to be a great receiver of ethnic groups. The cultures mix their ideologies and their identities. Adolescents in Canada are exposed to some cultural dimensions similar to their counterparts in the United States. While Canada has become more of a cultural mosaic, its main ethnic ties are British and French.
Television and the media	Adolescents' use of mass media	Adolescents spend a third or more of their waking hours with some form of mass media. Estimates of television viewing range from two to four hours a day. Television viewing often declines in adolescence, when the use of music media increases. Adolescents also use the print media more than children. Large individual differences characterize all forms of adolescent media use.
	Television	Television's functions include providing information and entertainment and portraying a world beyond the family, peers, and school. However, television may train adolescents to become passive learners and adopt a passive life-style. Special concerns include the way ethnic minorities are portrayed on television, as well as the way sex and aggression are shown. There have been few studies of how televised sex influences adolescent behavior, but there have been many studies of television violence. Some critics believe that it cannot be stated that television violence causes increases in children's and adolescents' aggression. Many other experts, however, argue that television violence can induce aggressive or antisocial behavior. Nonetheless, television's effects on adolescents vary considerably, depending, in part, on the needs, abilities, interests, and maturity of the adolescent, as well as on such characteristics as socioeconomic status, ethnicity, sex of the adolescent, cultural standards, and values.
	The media and music	Adolescents are heavy consumers of records, tapes, and rock music. Music tastes are more general at the beginning of adolescence; by high school, they are more specific and differentiated. Music meets a number of personal and social needs of adolescents. A special interest is how music media can be used to promote adolescent health behavior. Rock music lyrics have been controversial. A number of factors influence the power of rock music over an adolescent's thoughts and behavior, and the degree of this power is still unknown. Music video is a compelling medium. Rock music does not seem to be a passing fad and is an important dimension of the adolescent culture.

How Effectively Can Music Media Promote Better Adolescent Health Behavior?

What are the arguments that favor using music media to promote improved health behavior in adolescents? Media researchers Peter Christenson and Donald Roberts (1991) recently described such arguments. First, music is often front row and center stage in the adolescent culture. Adolescent involvement and investment in popular music is extensive. Also, because popular music is often produced by youth for youth, messages encased in the pop music culture have less risk of being rejected as unauthentic or of preaching from adult authorities.

Second, pop or rock stars can function as useful spokespersons in health promotion. Many adolescents identify with, admire, and even revere pop music stars. When used carefully and appropriately, pop music stars can be persuasive models. They can be especially effective when they make personal appearances at high school assemblies or make statements directly to live audiences during concerts.

Third, popular music and pop-related subjects can stimulate interpersonal communication among adolescents. Many media messages seldom stimulate meaningful change in adolescent behavior (Flora, 1990). Rather, media campaigns work best when other types of communication or experiences supplement their content. Given the power of the adolescent peer group, combined with the pervasiveness of popular music in the conversations of adolescents, media health messages associated with rock music can stimulate peer conversations about health behavior.

Fourth, a potential advantage of using popular music to convey health messages involves its emotional hold on youth. The main gratification adolescents attribute to music involves its impact on their emotions and moods. Thus, popular music's emotional power possibly can be used in positive ways by incorporating health messages into musical formats, or at least associating the two in the music media.

A fifth advantage of using music media to promote better adolescent health behavior focuses on the visual potential of music videos. Music videos can provide crucial visualizations of health problems (the misery of drug dependency) or health solutions (where and when to seek drug counseling).

Are there any potential problems or cautions that are involved in the use of music media to promote better adolescent health behavior? Christenson and Roberts describe several. The first problem involves authenticity. The very nature of health appeals may make the messages contrived or the messengers insincere, which could lead to rejection of the message, or even to boomerang effects. For example, MTV recently aired a public service announcement promoting automobile seatbelt use. Their choice of rock stars for the public service announcement: the heavy metal rock band Iron Maiden. There may be no good reason to question the sincerity of Iron Maiden on this issue. However, when Christenson and Roberts described this announcement to others, virtually everyone laughed about it. In this particular case, the band's long-standing image as defiant nose-thumbers doesn't square with an image of buckling up for safety. For some heavy metal fans the apparent absurdity of the Iron Maiden-seat belt association may call into question the credibility of the musicians, the authenticity of this particular campaign, and possibly the authenticity of all such campaigns.

Another limitation of popular music in health promotion involves how adolescents listen to music. Although music has a powerful emotional effect on adolescents, it has a relatively weak cognitive effect. While not completely ignored, lyrics are not usually the main attraction of the music, and in some instances, lyrics are either unintelligible or interpreted idiosyncratically, or both. Thus, any verbal content placed in music lyrics needs to be both catchy and unambiguous, without being silly or preachy. Also, important information might be more effectively placed elsewhere than in the lyrics. For example, the message could use a direct voice-over or it could use a print format in materials related to the music.

In sum, do the music media offer any promise in improving adolescent behavior? Yes, they do, but, as highly visible as the media are, it is important to remember that they represent only a small part of the adolescent health picture. However, when any health campaign aimed at adolescents ignores the crucial role of popular music, a lost opportunity is likely the result.

Summary

I. The Nature of Culture and Its Relevance for Adolescents

Culture refers to the behavior, patterns, beliefs, and all other products of a particular group of people that are passed on from generation to generation. Culture is a broad concept and includes many components—family, peers, school, television and the media, social class, and ethnicity, for example. If the study of adolescence is to be a relevant discipline in the twenty-first century, increased attention will need to focus on culture and ethnicity. The future will bring extensive contact between people from varied cultures and ethnic groups. The world is becoming increasingly interactive and will be even more so in the future. The study of adolescence has been too ethnocentric.

II. Cross-Cultural Comparisons

Cross-cultural studies involve the comparison of a culture with one or more other cultures, which provides information about the degree to which adolescent development is universal or culture-specific. The study of adolescence emerged in the context of Western industrialized society. This narrow viewpoint can produce erroneous conclusions about the nature of adolescents, and a more global, cosmopolitan perspective is needed. Anglo American adolescents are more achievement oriented than adolescents in many other cultures, but not as achievement oriented as Japanese, Chinese, and Asian American adolescents. Adolescent sexuality also varies considerably across cultures.

III. Rites of Passage

Rites of passage are ceremonies that mark an individual's transition from one status to another, especially into adulthood. In primitive cultures, rites of passage are often well-defined, but in contemporary America, they are not. High school graduation and sexual intercourse are rites of passage that many American adolescents experience.

IV. The Settings in Which Adolescents Spend Their Time

Using the experience sampling method, which involves beeping adolescents on electronic pagers, researchers found that adolescents spent 29 percent of their time in productive activities, 31 percent in maintenance activities, and the remainder of their time primarily in leisure. The largest amount of time spent in a single activity was studying (13 percent of their waking hours), but American adolescents spend considerably less time studying than Japanese adolescents. The main leisure activity of American adolescents was socializing. They spent little time in the company of adults but a full 50 percent of their time with peers. In a recent study, children spent considerable time in play, television viewing, and other home- and family-centered activities; however, young adolescents spent much more time talking, listening to music, and participating in other solitary and friend-centered activities. Participation in sports also declines in adolescence, although sports plays a significant role in the lives of many adolescents. A special concern is the orientation of Black American adolescents and their parents toward sports.

V. Social Class

Social class, also called socioeconomic status or SES, is the grouping of people with similar occupational, educational, and economic characteristics. Social class often carries with it certain inequities. The families, schools, and neighborhoods of adolescents have socioeconomic characteristics that are related to the adolescent's development. Parents from low-income backgrounds are more likely to value external characteristics and to use physical punishment and criticism than their middle-class counterparts. Adolescents from low-income backgrounds are at risk for intellectual and mental health problems, although there is considerable variation within each social class. The subculture of the poor is characterized not only by economic handicaps but also by social and psychological handicaps. Currently, one in five adolescents grows up in poverty. A special concern focuses on adolescents in low-income, single-mother families.

VI. Ethnicity, Social Class, Differences, and Diversity

Much of the research on ethnic minority adolescents has not teased apart the influences of ethnicity and social class. Because of this failure, too often researchers have given ethnic explanations of adolescent development that were largely based on socioeconomic factors. While not all ethnic minority families are poor, poverty contributes to the stress of many ethnic minority families. Historical, economic, and social experiences produce legitimate differences between many ethnic minority groups, and between ethnic minority groups and the White majority. Recognizing and respecting these differences is an important part of getting along with others in a diverse, multicultural world. Too often, differences between ethnic groups and the White majority have been interpreted as deficits on the part of the ethnic minority group. Also, the focus of research has too often been on the negative characteristics of ethnic minority groups. The current emphasis on studying the strengths as well as the weaknesses of ethnic minority adolescents is long overdue. Another very important dimension of ethnic minority groups is their diversity. Ethnic minority groups are not homogeneous; they have different social, historical, and economic backgrounds. Failure to recognize diversity and individual variations results in the stereotyping of an ethnic minority group.

VII. Adolescence: A Special Juncture for Ethnic Minority Individuals

Adolescence is often a special juncture in the development of ethnic minority individuals. Although children are aware of some ethnic and cultural differences, most ethnic minority individuals first consciously confront their ethnicity in adolescence. A problem for many ethnic minority youth is the lack of successful ethnic minority role models.

VIII. Prejudice and Value Conflicts

Prejudice is an unjustified negative attitude toward an individual because of the individual's membership in a group. Our concern here is prejudice against ethnic minority groups. Many ethnic minority adolescents continue to experience persistent prejudice, discrimination, and bias. Value conflicts are often involved when individuals respond to ethnic issues. One prominent value conflict is assimilation versus pluralism.

IX. Ethnic Minority Groups

Black American adolescents make up the largest easily visible ethnic minority group. They are distributed throughout the social classes, but unusually high numbers still live in poverty-enshrouded ghettos. In the inner city, Black American youth are increasingly unlikely to find legitimate employment. The church and extended-family system play important roles in helping many Black American youth cope with stress. Most Hispanic American adolescents trace their roots to Mexico, Puerto Rico, or Cuba. Roughly one-third will marry non-Hispanics. Mexican American adolescents make up the largest subgroup and are concentrated mainly in the U.S. Southwest. Hispanic Americans have one of the lowest educational levels of all ethnic minority groups. The Catholic Church and the extended-family system play important roles in many Hispanic American adolescents' lives. Many Mexican American adolescents have developed a new political consciousness and pride in their cultural heritage. Asian American adolescents are a diverse, fast-growing segment of the adolescent population. Japanese American and Chinese American are the largest subgroups. Family loyalty is powerful, and many Asian American adolescents are very achievement oriented. Native American adolescents, also called American Indian adolescents, have experienced painful discrimination. Their injustices are reflected in high dropout rates from school, high teenage pregnancy, and a high suicide rate. America has been and continues to be a great receiver of ethnic groups. The cultures mix their ideologies and their identities. Adolescents in Canada are exposed to some cultural dimensions similar to their counterparts in the United States. While Canada has become more of a cultural mosaic, its main ethnic ties are British and French.

X. **Adolescents' Use of Mass Media**

Adolescents spend a third or more of their waking hours with some form of mass media. Estimates of television viewing range from two to four hours a day. Television viewing often declines in adolescence, when the use of music media increases. Adolescents also use the print media more than children. Large individual differences characterize all forms of adolescent media use.

XI. **Television**

Television's functions include providing information and entertainment, and portraying a world beyond the family, peers, and school. However, television may train adolescents to become passive learners and adopt a passive life-style. Special concerns include the way ethnic minorities are portrayed on television, as well as the way sex and aggression are shown. There have been few studies of how televised sex influences adolescent behavior, but there have been many studies of television violence. Some critics believe that it cannot be stated that television violence causes increases in children's and adolescents' aggression. Many other experts, however, argue that television violence can induce aggressive or antisocial behavior. Nonetheless, television's effects on adolescents vary considerably, depending, in part, on the needs, abilities, interests, and maturity of the adolescent, as well as on such characteristics as socioeconomic status, ethnicity, sex of the adolescent, cultural standards, and values.

XII. **The Media and Music**

Adolescents are heavy consumers of records, tapes, and rock music. Rock music lyrics have been controversial. Music tastes are more general at the beginning of adolescence; by high school, they are more specific and differentiated. Music meets a number of personal and social needs of adolescents. A special interest is how music media can be used to promote better adolescent health behavior. A number of factors influence the power of rock music over adolescents' thoughts and behavior, and the degree of this power is still unknown. Music video is a compelling medium. Rock music does not seem to be a passing fad and is an important dimension of the adolescent culture.

Key Terms

culture 295
social class 295
ethnicity 295
ethnocentrism 296
cross-cultural studies
  297

rites of passage 298
experience sampling
  method 300
prejudice 311
assimilation 312

pluralism 312
Chicano 315

Suggested Readings

Condry, J. C. (1989). *The psychology of television.* Hillsdale, NJ: Erlbaum.
Presents a comprehensive overview of the effects of television on children and adolescents.

Fine, G. A., Mortimer, J. T., & Roberts, D. F. (1990). Leisure, work, and the mass media. In S. S. Feldman & G. R. Elliott (Eds.), *At the threshold: The developing adolescent.* Cambridge, MA: Harvard University Press.
An excellent overview of leisure and mass media influences on adolescent development.

Gibbs, J. T., & Huang, L. N. (Eds.) (1989). *Children of color.* San Francisco: Jossey-Bass.
An excellent overview of the nature of adolescence in ethnic minority groups. Separate chapters on Black adolescents, Mexican American adolescents, American Indian adolescents, Southeast Asia refugee adolescents, Chinese American adolescents, and Puerto Rican adolescents.

Journal of Youth and Adolescence (1989), Vol. 18, No. 6.
This entire issue is devoted to an extensive study of young adolescents' activities by Reed Larson and his colleagues.

Schorr, L. B., with Schorr, D. (1988). *Within our reach: Breaking the cycle of disadvantage and despair.* New York: Doubleday/Anchor.
A penetrating thought-provoking analysis of poverty in America.

Sommer, B. B. (1988). *Puberty and adolescence.* New York: Oxford University Press.
Includes extensive descriptions of rites of passage in primitive cultures.

Spencer, M. B., & Dornbusch, S. M. (1990). Challenges in studying minority youth. In S. S. Feldman & G. R. Elliott (Eds.), *At the threshold: The developing adolescent.* Cambridge, MA: Harvard University Press.
A penetrating, thoughtful insight into the dreams and struggles of ethnic minority adolescents in America today.

Social, Emotional, and Personality Development

He who would learn to fly oneday
must learn to stand and walk
and climb and dance:
one cannot fly into flying.

Friedrich Nietzsche,
Thus Spake Zarathustra, *1883*

So far, we have studied the biological, cognitive, and social contexts of adolescent development. In this section, we examine the adolescent's social, emotional, and personality development. Section IV consists of five chapters: Chapter 10, "The Self and Identity"; Chapter 11, "Gender"; Chapter 12, "Sexuality"; Chapter 13, "Moral Development, Values, and Religion"; and Chapter 14 "Achievement, Careers, and Work."

CHAPTER 10

The Self and Identity

"Who are you?" said the Caterpillar.
Alice replied, rather shyly, "I—I hardly know, Sir, just at present— at least I know who I was when I got up this morning, but I must have changed several times since then."

Lewis Carroll,
Alice in Wonderland, 1865

A 15-Year-Old Girl's Self-Description

How do adolescents describe themselves? How would you have described yourself when you were 15 years old? What features would you have emphasized? The following is a self-portrait of one 15-year-old girl:

> What am I like as a person? Complicated! I'm sensitive, friendly, outgoing, popular, and tolerant, though I can also be shy, self-conscious, and even obnoxious. Obnoxious! I'd *like* to be friendly and tolerant all of the time. That's the kind of person I *want* to be, and I'm disappointed when I'm not. I'm responsible, even studious now and then, but on the other hand, I'm a goof-off, too, because if you're too studious, you won't be popular. I don't usually do that well at school. I'm a pretty cheerful person, especially with my friends, where I can even get rowdy. At home I'm more likely to be anxious around my parents. They expect me to get all A's. It's not fair! I worry about how I probably *should* get better grades. But I'd be mortified in the eyes of my friends. So I'm usually pretty stressed-out at home, or sarcastic, since my parents are always on my case. But I really don't understand how I can switch so fast. I mean, how can I be cheerful one minute, anxious the next, and then be sarcastic? Which one is the *real* me? Sometimes, I feel phony, especially around boys. Say I think some guy might be interested in asking me out. I try to act different, like Madonna. I'll be flirtatious and fun-loving. And then everybody, I mean *everybody* else is looking at me like they think I'm totally weird. Then I get self-conscious and embarrassed and become radically introverted, and I don't know who I really am! Am I just trying to impress them or what? But I don't really care what they think anyway. I don't *want* to care, that is. I just want to know what my close friends think. I can be my true self with my close friends. I can't be my real self with my parents. They don't understand me. What do *they* know about what it's like to be a teenager? They still treat me like I'm still a kid. At least at school people treat you more like you're an adult. That gets confusing, though. I mean, which am I, a kid or an adult? It's scary, too, because I don't have any idea what I want to be when I grow up. I mean, I have lots of *ideas*. My friend Sheryl and I talk about whether we'll be stewardesses, or teachers, or nurses, veterinarians, maybe mothers, or actresses. I know I *don't* want to be a waitress or a secretary. But how do you decide all of this? I really don't know. I mean, I think about it a lot, but I can't resolve it. There are days when I wish I could just become immune to myself. (Harter, 1990b, pp. 352–353).

> *When I say "I," I mean something absolutely unique*
> *not to be confused with any other.*
>
> *Ugo Betti,* The Inquiry, *1941*

T he 15-year-old girl's self-description in the "Images of Adolescence" section exemplifies the increased introspective nature of self-portrayal in adolescence and the adolescent's complex search for an identity. This chapter is about the self and identity development in adolescence.

The Self

Adolescents carry with them a sense of who they are and what makes them different from everyone else. They cling to this identity and develop a sense that this identity is becoming more stable. Consider one adolescent male's self-description: "I am male, bright, an athlete, a political liberal, an extravert, and a compassionate individual." And he takes comfort in his uniqueness: "No one else is quite like me. I am 5 feet 11 inches tall and weigh 160 pounds. I grew up in a suburb and attend the state university. I am not married, but one of my friends is. I want to be a sports journalist. I am an expert at building canoes. When I am not studying for exams, I write short stories about sports figures, which I hope to publish someday." Real or imagined, an adolescent's developing sense of self and uniqueness is a motivating force in life. Our exploration of the self begins with information about adolescents' self-understanding and then turns to their self-esteem.

Self-Understanding

Adolescents' self-understanding becomes more introspective, but it is not completely interiorized. Rather, self-understanding is a social-cognitive construction. Adolescents' developing cognitive capacities interact with their sociocultural experiences to influence self-understanding. Among the questions about self-understanding that we examine are: What is self-understanding? What are some important dimensions of adolescents' self-understanding? How integrated is adolescents' self-understanding?

What Is Self-Understanding?

Self-understanding *is the adolescent's cognitive representation of the self, the substance and content of the adolescent's self-conceptions.* For example, a 12-year-old boy understands that he is a student, a boy, a football player, a family member, a video-game lover, and a rock music fan. A 14-year-old girl understands that she is a cheerleader, a student council member, and a movie fan. An adolescent's self-understanding is based, in part, on the various roles and membership categories that define who adolescents are (Harter, 1990a,b). Though not the whole of personal identity, self-understanding provides identity's rational underpinnings (Damon & Hart, 1988).

Dimensions of Adolescents' Self-Understanding

The development of self-understanding in adolescence is complex and involves a number of aspects of the self. Let's examine how the adolescent's self-understanding differs from the child's.

Abstract and Idealistic. Remember from our discussion of Piaget's theory of cognitive development in Chapters 2 and 4 that many adolescents begin to think in more *abstract* and *idealistic* ways. When asked to describe themselves, adolescents are more likely than children to use abstract and idealistic labels. Consider 14-year-old Laurie's abstract description of herself: "I am a human being. I am indecisive. I don't know who I am." Also consider her idealistic description of herself: "I am a naturally sensitive person who really cares about people's feelings. I think I'm pretty good-looking." Not all adolescents describe themselves in idealistic ways, but most adolescents distinguish between the real self and the ideal self, as we see next.

Real and Ideal, True and False Selves. The adolescent's emerging ability to construct ideal selves in addition to actual ones can be perplexing to the adolescent. The capacity to recognize a discrepancy between *real* and *ideal* selves represents a cognitive advance, but humanistic theorist Carl Rogers (1950) believed that, when the real and ideal selves are too discrepant, it is a sign of maladjustment.

Researchers have found that the discrepancy between the real self and the ideal self is greater in middle adolescence than in early or late adolescence (Strachen & Jones, 1982). While, as just mentioned, some theorists consider a strong discrepancy between the ideal and real selves as maladaptive, others argue that this is not always true, especially in adolescence. For example, in one view, an important aspect of the ideal or imagined self is the **possible self,** *what individuals might become, what they would like to become, and what they are afraid of becoming* (Markus & Nurius, 1986). Thus, adolescents' possible selves include both what adolescents hope to be as well as what they dread they will become. In this view, the presence of both hoped-for as well as dreaded selves is psychologically healthy, providing a balance between positive, expected selves and negative, feared selves. The attributes of future positive selves (getting into a good college, being admired, having a successful career) can direct future positive states, while attributes of future negative selves (being unemployed, being lonely, not getting into a good college) can identify what is to be avoided in the future.

Can adolescents distinguish between their *true* and *false* selves? In one research study, they could (Harter & Lee, 1989). Adolescents are most likely to show their false self in romantic or dating situations, and with classmates; they are least likely to show their false self with close friends. Adolescents display a false self to impress others, to try out new behaviors or roles, because others force them to behave in false ways, and because others do not understand their true self (Harter, 1990b). Some adolescents report that they do not like their false-self behavior, but others say that it does not bother them.

Differentiated. Adolescents' self-understanding becomes increasingly *differentiated.* Adolescents are more likely than children to describe the self with contextual or situational variations. For example, 15-year-old Amy describes herself with one set of characteristics in her relationship with her family and another set of characteristics in her relationship with peers and friends. Yet another set of characteristics appears in her description of her romantic relationship. In sum, adolescents are more likely than children to understand that one possesses different selves, depending on one's role or particular context (Harter, 1990a,b).

Contradictions within the Self. Self-understanding in adolescence also involves more *contradictions* within the self. In one investigation, developmentalist Susan Harter (1986) asked seventh-, ninth-, and eleventh-graders to describe themselves. She found that the number of contradictory terms used to describe oneself (moody *and* understanding, ugly *and* attractive, bored *and* inquisitive, caring *and* uncaring, introverted *and* fun-loving, and so on) dramatically increased between the seventh and ninth grades. The contradictory self-descriptions declined in the eleventh grade but still were higher than in the seventh grade. Adolescents develop the cognitive ability to detect these inconsistencies in the self as they strive to construct a general theory of the self or of their personality (Damon, 1991).

Self-Conscious. Adolescents are more likely than children to be *self-conscious* about and *preoccupied* with their self-understanding. As part of their self-conscious and preoccupied self-exploration, adolescents become more introspective. However, the introspection is not always done in social isolation. Sometimes, adolescents turn to their friends for support and self-clarification, obtaining their friends' opinions of an emerging self-definition. As one researcher on self-development commented, adolescents' friends are often the main source of reflected self-appraisals, becoming the social mirror into which adolescents anxiously stare (Rosenberg, 1979). This self-consciousness and self-preoccupation reflect the concept of adolescent egocentrism, which we discussed in Chapter 4.

Self-Protective. Adolescents' self-understanding includes more mechanisms to *protect the self* (Harter 1990a,b). Although adolescents often display a sense of confusion and conflict stimulated by introspective efforts to understand the self, they also call on mechanisms to protect and enhance the self. In protecting the self, adolescents are prone to denying their negative characteristics. For example, in Harter's investigation of self-understanding, positive self-descriptions, such as attractive, fun-loving, sensitive, affectionate, and inquisitive, were more likely to be placed at the core of the self, indicating more importance, whereas negative self-descriptions, such as ugly, mediocre, depressed, selfish, and nervous, were more likely to be placed at the periphery of the self, indicating less importance (Harter, 1986). Adolescents' tendency to protect themselves fits with the earlier description of adolescents' tendency to describe themselves in idealistic ways.

Unconscious. Adolescents' self-understanding involves greater recognition that the self includes *unconscious,* as well as conscious, components, a recognition not likely to occur until late adolescence (Selman, 1980). That is, older adolescents are more likely than younger adolescents to believe that certain aspects of their mental experience are beyond their awareness or control.

Social Comparison. Some developmentalists believe that adolescents are more likely than children to use *social comparison* to evaluate themselves (Ruble & others, 1980). However, adolescents' willingness to *admit* that they engage in social comparison to evaluate themselves declines in adolescence because they view social comparison as socially undesirable. They think that acknowledging their social comparison motives will endanger their popularity (Harter, 1990a). Relying on social comparison information in adolescence may be confusing because of the large number of reference groups. For example, should adolescents compare themselves to classmates in general? To friends? To their own gender? To popular adolescents? To good-looking adolescents? To athletic adolescents? Simultaneously considering all of these social comparison groups can get perplexing for adolescents.

The Fluctuating Self. Given the numerous selves of adolescents, especially their contradictory ones and the tension between true and false selves, it is not surprising that adolescents' selves often *fluctuate* across situations and over time (Harter, 1990a). The 15-year-old girl quoted at the beginning of the chapter in the "Images of Adolescents" section remarked that she could not understand how she could switch so fast—from being cheerful one moment, to anxious the next, and then sarcastic a short time later. One researcher described the fluctuating nature of the adolescent's self with the metaphor of "the barometric self" (Rosenberg, 1986). The adolescent's self continues to be characterized by instability until a more unified theory of self is constructed, usually not until late adolescence or even early adulthood.

Self-Integration

Adolescents' self-understanding becomes more *integrative,* with the disparate parts of the self more systematically pieced together, especially in late adolescence. Older adolescents are more likely to detect inconsistencies in their earlier self-descriptions as they attempt to construct a general theory of self, an integrated sense of identity (Harter, 1990b; Selman, 1980).

Because the adolescent creates multiple self-concepts in adolescence, the task of integrating these varying self-conceptions becomes problematic. At the same time that adolescents are faced with pressures to differentiate the self into multiple roles, the emergence of formal operational thought presses for *integration* and the development of a consistent, coherent theory of self (Harter, 1990b). These budding formal operational skills initially present a liability because they first allow adolescents to *detect* inconsistencies in the self across varying roles, only later providing the cognitive capacity to *integrate* such apparent contradictions. In the "Images of Adolescents" narrative that opened the chapter, the 15-year-old girl could not understand how she could be cheerful yet depressed and sarcastic, wondering "which is the real me." Researchers have found that 14- to 15-year-olds not only detect inconsistencies across their various roles (with parents, friends, and romantic partners, for example) but that they are much more troubled by these contradictions than younger (11- to 12-year-old) and older (17- to 18-year-old) adolescents (Damon & Hart, 1988; Harter, 1986).

At this point, we have discussed a number of characteristics of adolescents' self-understanding. A summary of these characteristics is presented in Figure 10.1. Remember from the introduction of the self that self-conception involves not only self-understanding but also self-esteem.

Self-Esteem

Among the questions we explore regarding adolescents' self-esteem are: What is self-esteem? How is self-esteem measured? Are some domains of self-esteem more salient in adolescence than others? How do relationships with parents and peers influence adolescents' self-esteem? How can adolescents' self-esteem be increased?

What Is Self-Esteem?

Self-esteem *is the evaluative and affective dimension of self-concept. Self-esteem is also referred to as self-worth or self-image.* That is, one adolescent may perceive that she is not merely a student, but a *good* student. Another adolescent may perceive that he is not merely a basketball player, but a *good* basketball player. These self-evaluations often stimulate an emotional reaction. The good student feels proud that she just received an *A* on an exam; the good basketball player is elated that he scored the winning basket in last night's game. Of course, not all self-evaluations are positive. An adolescent may feel sad that she is not a good student. Another adolescent may feel ashamed that he is a poor reader. These are evaluative judgments regarding the adolescent's self-esteem.

Until recently, theorists conceptualized self-esteem as a general, global judgment about the self. However, adolescents make evaluative judgments about many different aspects of their lives. For example, they perceive that they are

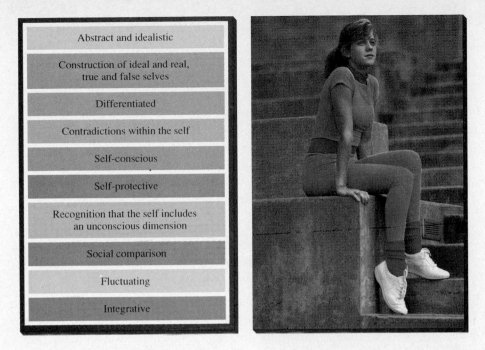

Figure 10.1 Characteristics of
adolescents' self-understanding.

good or bad in physical skills, good or bad in cognitive skills, and good or bad in
social skills. As we see next, interest in the domain-specific aspects of self-esteem
led to the development of new measures of self-esteem.

Measuring Self-Esteem

Psychologists have had a difficult time trying to measure self-worth or self-esteem
(Harter, 1990a; Wylie, 1979; Yardley, 1987). One frequently used method is the
Piers-Harris Scale (Piers & Harris, 1964), which consists of 80 items designed
to measure overall self-esteem. By responding "yes" or "no" to such items as "I
have good ideas," adolescents reveal whether they have high or low self-esteem.

However, as indicated earlier, an adolescent's self-esteem may vary according to different skill domains or areas of competence. The scales developed
by Susan Harter have been welcome additions to the assessment of self-esteem
or self-worth. The Self-Perception Profile for Children is a revision of the original
instrument, the Perceived Competence Scale for Children (Harter, 1982). The
Self-Perception Profile for Children taps five specific domains—scholastic competence, athletic competence, social acceptance, physical appearance, and behavioral conduct—plus general self-worth (Harter, 1985). Harter's scale does an
excellent job of separating children's feelings of self-worth in different skill areas,
and when general self-worth is assessed, questions focus on overall perceptions
of self-esteem rather than specific skill domains. Many developmentalists believe
that the differentiated assessment of self-esteem in various skill domains, as well
as the independent assessment of general self-worth, provides a richer picture
than those measures that yield only a single self-worth score.

The Self-Perception Profile for Children is designed to be used with third-
grade through sixth-grade children. Harter also has developed a separate scale
for adolescents, recognizing important developmental changes in self-percep-
tions. The Self-Perception Profile for Adolescents (Harter, 1989a) taps eight domains—scholastic competence, athletic competence, social acceptance, physical
appearance, behavioral conduct, close friendship, romantic appeal, and job com-

Table 10.1   The Self-Image Questionnaire for Young Adolescents

Scale (item example)

1. Impulse control
   ("I keep an even temper most of the time.")

2. Emotional tone
   ("I feel nervous most of the time.")

3. Body image
   ("I feel proud of my body.")

4. Peer relationships
   ("I think that other people just do not like me.")

5. Family relationships
   ("My parents are usually patient with me.")

6. Mastery and coping
   ("I am fearful of growing up.")

7. Vocational-educational goals
   ("I enjoy learning new things.")

8. Psychopathology
   ("I fear something constantly.")

9. Superior adjustment
   ("I am a leader in school.")

From Anne C. Petersen, et al., "A Self-Image Questionnaire for Young Adolescents (SIQYA): Reliability and Validity Studies" in *Journal of Youth and Adolescence,* 13:100, 1984. Copyright © 1984 Plenum Publishing Corporation. New York, NY. Reprinted by permission of the publisher and authors.

petence—plus global self-worth. Thus, the adolescent version has three skill domains not present in the children's version—job competence, romantic appeal, and close friendship.

Another recently developed measure of self-esteem, one especially designed for young adolescents, is called the Self-Image Questionnaire for Young Adolescents (SIQYA), (Petersen & others, 1984). It is a downward extension of the Offer Self-Image Questionnaire, a widely used measure of older adolescents' self-conceptions, and includes nine separate scales: emotional tone, impulse control, body image, peer relationships, family relationships, mastery and coping, vocational-educational goals, psychopathology, and superior adjustment (see Table 10.1). Adolescents choose the extent to which each of the 98 items describes themselves—from "very well" to "not me at all."

Some assessment experts argue that a combination of several methods should be used in measuring self-esteem. In addition to self-reporting, rating of an adolescent's self-esteem by others and observations of the adolescent's behavior in various settings could provide a more complete and more accurate self-esteem picture. Peers, teachers, parents, and even others who do not know the adolescent can be asked to rate the adolescent's self-esteem. Adolescents' facial expressions and the extent to which they congratulate or condemn themselves are also good indicators of how they view themselves. For example, adolescents who rarely smile or rarely act happy are revealing something about their self-esteem. One investigation that used behavioral observations in the assessment of self-esteem shows some of the positive as well as negative behaviors that can provide clues to the adolescent's self-esteem (see Table 10.2) (Savin-Williams & Demo, 1983). By using a variety of methods (such as self-report and behavioral observations) and obtaining information from various sources (such as the adolescent, parents, friends, and teachers), investigators probably can construct a more accurate picture of the adolescent's self-esteem.

Are Some Domains of Self-Esteem More Salient in Adolescence Than Others?

We have just seen that consideration of different domains is important when evaluating the adolescent's self-esteem. Are some of these domains more important in adolescents' self-evaluations than others? A number of researchers have found that physical appearance is an especially powerful contributor to self-esteem in

Table 10.2   Behavioral Indicators of Self-Esteem

Positive Indicators	Negative Indicators
1. Gives others directives or commands	1. Puts down others by teasing, name-calling, or gossiping
2. Uses voice quality appropriate for situation	2. Uses gestures that are dramatic or out of context
3. Expresses opinions	3. Engages in inappropriate touching or avoids physical contact
4. Sits with others during social activities	4. Gives excuses for failures
5. Works cooperatively in a group	5. Glances around to monitor others
6. Faces others when speaking or being spoken to	6. Brags excessively about achievements, skills, appearance
7. Maintains eye contact during conversation	7. Verbally puts self down; self-depreciation
8. Initiates friendly contact with others	8. Speaks too loudly, abruptly, or in a dogmatic tone
9. Maintains comfortable space between self and others	9. Does not express views or opinions, especially when asked
10. Little hesitation in speech, speaks fluently	10. Assumes a submissive stance

Source: Savin-Williams, R. C. & Demo, D. H., Conceiving or misconceiving the self: Issues in adolescent self-esteem. *Journal of Early Adolescence,* 3, 121–140. Reprinted with permission of H.E.L.P. Books, Inc.

adolescence (Adams, 1977; Harter, 1989b; Lerner & Brackney, 1978; Simmons & Blyth, 1987). For example, in Harter's research, physical appearance consistently correlates the most strongly with global self-esteem, followed by peer social acceptance. Harter (1989b) also has found that the strong association between perceived appearance and general self-worth is not confined to adolescence but holds across the life span, from early childhood through middle age.

Parental and Peer Influences on Self-Esteem

Two important sources of social support that contribute to adolescents' self-esteem are relationships with parents and peers. In the most extensive investigation of parent-child relationships and self-esteem, a measure of self-esteem was given to boys, and the boys and their mothers were interviewed about their family relationships (Coopersmith, 1967). Based on these assessments, the following parenting attributes were associated with boys' high self-esteem:

- Expression of affection
- Concern about the boys' problems
- Harmony in the home
- Participation in joint family activities
- Availability to give competent, organized help to the boys when they needed it
- Setting clear and fair rules
- Abiding by these rules
- Allowing the boys freedom within well-prescribed limits

Remember that because these findings are correlational, researchers cannot say that these parenting attributes *cause* children's high self-esteem. Such factors as expression of affection and allowing children freedom within well-prescribed limits probably are important determinants of children's self-esteem, but researchers still must say that *they are related to* rather than *they cause* children's self-esteem based on the available research data that are correlational.

Peer judgments gain increasing importance among older children and adolescents. In one investigation, peer support contributed more strongly to the self-esteem of young adolescents than children, although parenting support was an important factor in self-esteem for both children and young adolescents (Harter,

Figure 10.2   Four key aspects of improving self-esteem.

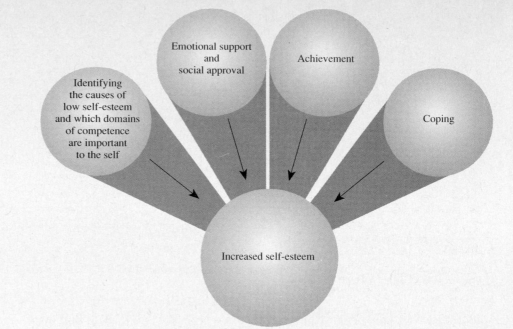

1987). In this study, peer support was a more important factor than parenting support for late adolescents. Two types of peer support were studied: classmate support and close-friend support. Classmate support contributed more strongly to adolescents' self-esteem at all ages than close-friend support. Given that, in most instances, close friends provide considerable support, it may be that their regard is not perceived as enhancing; rather, the adolescent may need to turn to somewhat more objective sources of support to validate his or her self-esteem.

Increasing Adolescents' Self-Esteem

Four ways adolescents' self-esteem can be improved are: (1) identifying the causes of low esteem and the domains of competence important to the self, (2) through emotional support and social approval, (3) through achievement, and (4) through coping (see Figure 10.2).

Identifying adolescents' sources of self-esteem—that is, competence in domains important to the self—is critical to improving self-esteem. Self-esteem theorist and researcher Susan Harter (1990b) points out that the self-esteem enhancement programs of the 1960s, in which self-esteem itself was the target and individuals were encouraged to simply feel good about themselves, were ineffective. Rather, Harter believes that intervention must occur at the level of the *causes* of self-esteem if the individual's self-esteem is to improve significantly.

Adolescents have the highest self-esteem when they perform competently in domains important to the self. Therefore, adolescents should be encouraged to identify and value areas of competence. One strategy is to encourage society to recognize the positive benefits of competence in many different domains, not just academic competence. Another strategy is to acknowledge that education is the primary means for achieving success, and to provide individuals with poor academic skills and low self-esteem better support and more individualized attention. The inspiration of Hispanic high school teacher Jaime Escalante, documented in the movie *Stand and Deliver,* reflects this latter strategy. Escalante was a California high school teacher who spent many evenings and weekends tutoring Hispanic students in math, in addition to effectively teaching the students math in the classroom. Escalante's commitment and motivation were transferred to the Hispanic high school students, many of whom obtained college

Shown here is a scene from the movie Stand and Deliver, *in which Hispanic high school teacher, Jaime Escalante (in the center with a cap), spent many evenings and weekends tutoring Hispanic students in math in addition to effectively teaching the students math in the classroom. Escalante's commitment and motivation was transferred to the students, many of whom obtained college scholarships and passed advanced placement tests in calculus.*

scholarships and passed advanced placement tests in calculus. Insisting that high school and college athletes maintain a respectable grade point average is a policy that endorses the importance of academic achievement and competence in other domains, as is the requirement that students maintain respectable grades to participate in jobs programs.

Emotional support and social approval in the form of confirmation from others also powerfully influence adolescents' self-esteem (Harter, 1990b). Some youth with low self-esteem come from conflicted families or conditions in which they experienced abuse or neglect—situations in which support is unavailable. In some cases, alternative sources of support can be implemented, either informally through the encouragement of a teacher, a coach, or other significant adult, or more formally, through programs such as Big Brothers and Big Sisters. While peer approval becomes increasingly important during adolescence, both adult and peer support are important influences on the adolescent's self-esteem.

Achievement also can improve adolescents' self-esteem (Bednar, Wells, & Peterson, 1989). For example, the straightforward teaching of real skills to adolescents often results in increased achievement and, thus, in enhanced self-esteem. Adolescents develop higher self-esteem because they know the important tasks to achieve goals, and they have experienced performing them or similar behaviors. The emphasis on the importance of achievement in improving self-esteem has much in common with Bandura's cognitive social learning concept of *self-efficacy,* which refers to individuals' beliefs that they can master a situation and produce positive outcomes.

Self-esteem also is often increased when adolescents face a problem and try to cope with it rather than avoid it (Bednar, Wells, & Peterson, 1989; Lazarus, 1991). If coping rather than avoidance prevails, adolescents often face problems realistically, honestly, and nondefensively. This produces favorable self-evaluative thoughts, which lead to the self-generated approval that raises self-esteem. The converse is true of low self-esteem. Unfavorable self-evaluations trigger denial, deception, and avoidance in an attempt to disavow that which has already been glimpsed as true. This process leads to self-generated disapproval as a form of feedback to the self about personal adequacy.

At this point, we have discussed a number of ideas about the self in adolescence, including information about self-understanding and self-esteem. A summary of these ideas is presented in Concept Table 10.1. Next, we turn our attention to an important concept related to the self—identity.

	Concept Table 10.1	
	The Self	
Concept	**Processes/Related Ideas**	**Characteristics/Description**
Self-Understanding	What is self-understanding?	Self-understanding is the adolescent's cognitive representation of the self, the substance and content of the adolescent's self-conceptions. Self-understanding provides the rational underpinnings of personal identity.
	Dimensions of adolescents' self-understanding	Dimensions of adolescents' self-understanding include: abstract and idealistic; construction of ideal and real, true and false selves; differentiated; contradictions within the self; self-conscious; self-protective; recognition that the self includes an unconscious dimension; social comparison; fluctuating; and integrative.
	Self-Integration	Adolescents' self-understanding becomes more integrative, especially in late adolescence. Budding formal operational skills initially present a liability because they allow adolescents to detect inconsistencies in the self across varying roles, only later providing the cognitive capacity to integrate such apparent contradictions. Middle adolescents are more troubled by these discrepancies than young or late adolescents.
Self-Esteem	What is self-esteem?	Self-esteem is the evaluative and affective component of self-concept. Self-esteem is also referred to as self-worth or self-image. Until recently, self-esteem was described in global terms. Today, domain-specific aspects of self-esteem also are considered.
	Measuring self-esteem	Measuring self-esteem is a difficult task. Harter's measures are appealing to many developmentalists because they provide a differentiated assessment of self-esteem in various skill domains, as well as independent assessment of self-worth. Some assessment experts believe that several methods should be used to assess self-esteem, including observations of the adolescent's behavior.
	Are some domains of self-esteem more salient in adolescence than others?	Perceived physical appearance is an especially strong contributor to overall self-esteem, not only in adolescence but in other developmental periods as well. In adolescence, peer acceptance follows physical appearance in contributing to global self-worth.
	Parental and peer influences on self-esteem	In Coopersmith's study, children's self-esteem was associated with such parenting attributes as parental affection and allowing children freedom within well-prescribed limits. These associations are correlational. Peer judgments gain increasing importance among older children and adolescents. In one study of the contribution of peer support to adolescent self-esteem, classmate support was more powerful than close-friend support.
	Increasing adolescents' self-esteem	Four ways to increase adolescents' self-esteem involve: (1) identifying the causes of adolescents' low self-esteem and which domains of competence are important to the self, (2) emotional support and social approval, (3) achievement, and (4) coping.

Identity

By far the most comprehensive and provocative theory of identity development has been told by Erik Erikson. Some experts on adolescence consider Erikson's ideas to be the single most influential theory of adolescent development. Erikson's theory was introduced in Chapter 2. Here that introduction is expanded, beginning with reanalysis of his ideas on identity. Then we examine some contemporary thoughts on identity, the four statuses of identity, developmental changes, identity and gender, family influences on identity, cultural and ethnic aspects of identity, and identity and intimacy.

HARTLAND—*"Reprinted with special permission of King Features Syndicate, Inc."*

Erikson's Ideas on Identity

Who am I? What am I all about? What am I going to do with my life? What is different about me? How can I make it on my own? Not usually considered during childhood, these questions surface as common, virtually universal, concerns during adolescence. Adolescents clamor for solutions to these questions that revolve around the concept of identity, and it was Erik Erikson who first understood how central such questions are to understanding adolescent development. That today identity is believed to be a key concept in adolescent development is a result of Erikson's masterful thinking and analysis.

Revisiting Erikson's Views on Identity and the Human Life Cycle

Identity versus identity confusion *is Erikson's fifth developmental stage, which individuals experience during the adolescent years. At this time, adolescents face finding out who they are, what they are all about, and where they are going in life.* Adolescents are confronted with many new roles, such as vocational and romantic, for example. A **psychological moratorium** *is Erikson's term for the gap between childhood security and adult autonomy that adolescents experience as part of their identity exploration.* As adolescents explore and search their culture's identity files, they often experiment with different roles. Youths who successfully cope with these conflicting identities emerge with a new sense of self that is both refreshing and acceptable. Adolescents who do not successfully resolve this identity crisis suffer what Erikson calls identity confusion. The confusion takes one of two courses: Individuals withdraw, isolating themselves from peers and family, or they immerse themselves in the world of peers and lose their identity in the crowd.

Erikson's ideas about adolescent identity development reveal rich insights into adolescents' thoughts and feelings, and reading one or more of his original writings is worthwhile. A good starting point is *Identity: Youth and Crisis* (1968). Other works that portray identity development are *Young Man Luther* (1962) and *Gandhi's Truth* (1969)—the latter won a Pulitzer Prize. A sampling of Erikson's writings from these books is present in Perspective on Adolescent Development 10.1.

Personality and Role Experimentation

Two core ingredients in Erikson's theory of identity development are personality and role experimentation. As indicated earlier, Erikson believes that adolescents face an overwhelming number of choices and at some point during youth enter

PERSPECTIVE ON ADOLESCENT DEVELOPMENT 10.1

Hitler, Luther, and Gandhi—the Development of Their Identity

Erik Erikson is a master at analyzing famous individuals' lives and discovering historical clues about their identity formation. Erikson also developed ideas for his view of identity development by analyzing the developmental history of clients in his clinical practice. Erikson (1968) believes that an individual's developmental history must be carefully scrutinized and analyzed to obtain clues about identity. He also believes that the best clues for understanding world history appear in the composite of individual life cycles. In the excerpts that follow, Erikson analyzes the lives of Adolf Hitler, Martin Luther, and Mahatma Gandhi.

About Hitler, Erikson commented:

> I will not go into the symbolism of Hitler's urge to build except to say that his shiftless and brutal father had consistently denied the mother a steady residence; one must read how Adolf took care of his mother when she wasted away from breast cancer to get an inkling of this young man's desperate urge to cure. But it would take a very extensive analysis, indeed, to indicate in what way a single boy can daydream his way into history and emerge a sinister genius, and how a whole nation becomes ready to accept the emotive power of that genius as a hope of fulfillment for its national aspirations and as a warrant for national criminality. . . .
>
> The memoirs of young Hitler's friend indicate an almost pitiful fear on the part of the future dictator that he might be nothing. He had to challenge this possibility by being deliberately and totally anonymous; and only out of this self-chosen nothingness could he become everything. (Erikson, 1962, pp. 108–109)

Although the identity crisis of Adolf Hitler led him to turn toward politics in a pathological effort to create a world

Hitler in elementary school. He is in the center of the top row. In Erikson's analysis, what were some of the key experiences that contributed to Hitler's identity development?

order, the identity crisis of Martin Luther in a different era led him to turn toward theology in an attempt to deal systematically with human nothingness or lack of identity:

> In confession, for example, he was so meticulous in the attempt to be truthful that he spelled out every intention as

a period of psychological moratorium. During this moratorium, they try out different roles and personalities before they reach a stable sense of self. They may be argumentative one moment, cooperative the next moment. They may dress neatly one day, sloppily the next day. They may like a particular friend one week, despise the friend the next week. This personality experimentation is a deliberate effort on the part of adolescents to find out where they fit in the world.

As they gradually come to realize that they will be responsible for themselves and their own lives, adolescents search for what those lives are going to be. Many parents and other adults, accustomed to having children go along with what they say, may be bewildered or incensed by the wisecracks, the rebelliousness, and the rapid mood changes that accompany adolescence. It is important for these adults to give adolescents the time and the opportunities to explore different roles and personalities. In turn, most adolescents eventually discard undesirable roles.

Mahatma Gandhi was the spiritual leader of India in the middle of the twentieth century. What factors does Erikson believe contributed to Gandhi's identity development?

And in his Pulitzer-Prize-winning novel on Mahatma Gandhi's life, Erikson describes the personality formation of Gandhi during his youth:

> Straight and yet not stiff; shy and yet not withdrawn; intelligent and yet not bookish; willful and yet not stubborn; sensual and yet not soft. . . . We must try to reflect on the relation of such a youth to his father because the Mahatma places service to the father and the crushing guilt of failing in such service in the center of his adolescent turbulence. Some historians and political scientists seem to find it easy to interpret this account in psychoanalytic terms; I do not. For the question is not how a particular version of the Oedipal complex "causes" a man to be both great and neurotic in a particular way, but rather how such a young person . . . manages the complexes which constrict other men. (Erikson, 1969, p. 113)

In these passages, the workings of an insightful, sensitive mind is shown looking for a historical perspective on personality development. Through analysis of the lives of such famous individuals as Hitler, Luther, and Gandhi, and through the thousands of youth he has talked with in person, Erikson has pieced together a descriptive picture of identity development.

well as every deed; he splintered relatively acceptable purities into smaller and smaller impurities; he reported temptations in historical sequence, starting back in childhood; and after having confessed for hours, would ask for special appointments in order to correct previous statements. In doing this, he was obviously both exceedingly compulsive and, at least unconsciously, rebellious. . . .

At this point, we must note a characteristic of great young rebels: their inner split between the temptation to surrender and the need to dominate. A great young rebel is torn between, on the one hand, tendencies to give in and fantasies of defeat (Luther used to resign himself to an early death at times of impending success), and the absolute need, on the other hand, to take the lead, not only over himself but over all the forces and people who impinge on him. (Erikson, 1968, pp. 155–157)

There are literally hundreds of roles for adolescents to try out, and probably just as many ways to pursue each role. Erikson believes that, by late adolescence, vocational roles are central to identity development, especially in a highly technological society like the United States. Youth who have been well trained to enter a work force that offers the potential of reasonably high self-esteem will experience the least stress during the development of identity. Some youth have rejected jobs offering good pay and traditionally high social status, choosing instead to work in situations that allow them to be more genuinely helpful to their fellow humans, such as in the Peace Corps, in mental health clinics, or in schools for children from low-income backgrounds. Some youth prefer unemployment to the prospect of working at a job they feel they would be unable to perform well or at which they would feel useless. To Erikson, this attitude reflects the desire to achieve a meaningful identity through being true to oneself, rather than burying one's identity in that of the larger society.

"Do you have any idea who I am?"
Drawing by Koren; © 1988 The New Yorker
Magazine, Inc.

The Complexity of Erikson's Theory

The development of an integrated sense of identity is a long, complex, and difficult task. American adolescents are expected to master many different roles. It is the rare, perhaps nonexistent, adolescent who does not have serious doubts about handling at least some of these roles competently. Erikson's view of identity is complex, involving at least seven dimensions (Bourne, 1978):

1. Genetic. Erikson describes identity development as a developmental product or outcome that incorporates the individual's experiences over the first five stages of development. Identity development reflects the way the adolescent has resolved prior stages, such as trust versus mistrust, autonomy versus doubt, initiative versus guilt, and industry versus inferiority.

2. Adaptive. The adolescent's identity development can be viewed as an adaptive accomplishment or achievement. Identity is the adaptation of adolescents' special skills, capacities, and strengths to the society in which they live.

3. Structural. Identity confusion is a breakdown in time perspective, initiative, and ability to coordinate present behavior toward future goals. This kind of breakdown implies a structural deficit.

4. Dynamic. Erikson believes that identity formation begins where the usefulness of identification ends. It arises from childhood identifications with adults but absorbs them in new configurations, which, in turn, are dependent on society's roles for youth.

5. Subjective or experiential. Erikson believes that the individual senses an inner feeling of cohesiveness or lack of assuredness.

6. Psychosocial reciprocity. Erikson emphasizes the mutual relationship of adolescents with their social world and community. Identity development is not just an intrapsychic self-representation but involves relationships with people, community, and society.

7. Existential status. Erikson thinks that adolescents seek the meaning to their life as well as the meaning of life in general, much like an existential philosopher.

Some Contemporary Thoughts on Identity

Contemporary views of identity development suggest several important considerations. First, identity development is a lengthy process, in many instances a more gradual, less cataclysmic transition than Erikson's term *crisis* implies (Baumeister, 1991). Second, as just indicated, identity development is extraordinarily complex (Marcia, 1987, 1989). Identity formation neither begins nor ends with adolescence. It begins with the appearance of attachment, the development of a sense of self, and the emergence of independence in infancy, and reaches its final phase with a life review and integration in old age. What is important about identity development in adolescence, especially late adolescence, is that, for the first time, physical development, cognitive development, and social development advance to the point at which the individual can sort through and synthesize childhood identities and identifications to construct a viable path toward adult maturity. Resolution of the identity issue at adolescence does not mean that identity will be stable through the remainder of life. An individual who develops a healthy identity is flexible and adaptive, open to changes in society, in relationships, and in careers (Adams, Gulotta, & Montemayor, 1992). This openness assures numerous reorganizations of identity's contents throughout the identity-achieved individual's life.

	Identity status			
Position on occupation and ideology	Identity moratorium	Identity foreclosure	Identity diffusion	Identity achievement
Crisis **commitment**	Present Absent	Absent Present	Absent Absent	Present Present

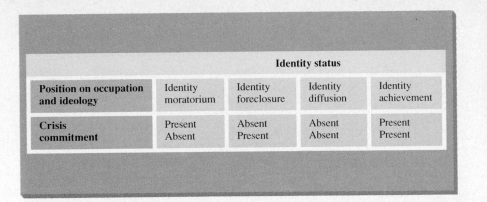

Figure 10.3 The four statuses of identity.

Identity formation does not happen neatly, and it usually does not happen cataclysmically. At the bare minimum, it involves commitment to a vocational direction, an ideological stance, and a sexual orientation. Synthesizing the identity components can be a long and drawn-out process, with many negations and affirmations of various roles and faces. Identity development gets done in bits and pieces. Decisions are not made once and for all, but have to be made again and again. And the decisions may seem trivial at the time: whom to date, whether or not to break up, whether or not to have intercourse, whether or not to take drugs, whether or not to go to college or finish high school and get a job, which major, whether to study or to play, whether or not to be politically active, and so on. Over the years of adolescence, the decisions begin to form a core of what the individual is all about as a human being—what is called his or her identity.

The Four Statuses of Identity

Eriksonian researcher James Marcia (1966, 1980, 1989, 1991) believes that Erikson's theory of identity development contains four statuses of identity, or ways of resolving the identity crisis: identity diffusion, identity foreclosure, identity moratorium, and identity achievement. The extent of an adolescent's crisis and commitment is used to classify the individual according to one of the four identity statuses. **Crisis** *is defined as a period of identity development during which the adolescent is choosing among meaningful alternatives.* Most researchers use the term *exploration* rather than *crisis*, although, in the spirit of Marcia's formulation, the term *crisis* is used here. **Commitment** *is a part of identity development in which adolescents show a personal investment in what they are going to do.*

Identity diffusion *is the term Marcia uses to describe adolescents who have not yet experienced a crisis (that is, they have not yet explored meaningful alternatives) or made any commitments.* Not only are they undecided about occupational and ideological choices, they are also likely to show little interest in such matters. **Identity foreclosure** *is the term Marcia uses to describe adolescents who have made a commitment but have not experienced a crisis.* This occurs most often when parents hand down commitments to their adolescents, usually in an authoritarian way. In these circumstances, adolescents have not had adequate opportunities to explore different approaches, ideologies, and vocations on their own. **Identity moratorium** *is the term Marcia uses to describe adolescents who are in the midst of a crisis, but whose commitments either are absent or are only vaguely defined.* **Identity achievement** *is Marcia's term for adolescents who have undergone a crisis and have made a commitment.* Marcia's four statuses of identity development are summarized in Figure 10.3.

The identity status approach has been sharply criticized by some researchers and theoreticians (Blasi, 1988; Cote & Levine, 1988a,b, 1989; Lapsley

James Marcia, shown talking with college students, developed the concept of identity status. Over three decades, Marcia has greatly advanced our understanding of identity development.

& Power, 1988; Lerner, 1981). They believe that the identity status approach distorts and trivializes Erikson's notions of crisis and commitment. For example, concerning crisis, Erikson emphasized the youth's questioning of the perceptions and expectations of one's culture and developing an autonomous position with regard to one's society. In the identity status approach, these complex questions are dealt with by simply evaluating whether a youth has thought about certain issues and considered alternatives. Erikson's idea of commitment loses the meaning of investing one's own self in certain lifelong projects and is interpreted simply as having made a firm decision or not. Others still believe that the identity status approach is a valuable contribution to understanding identity (Archer, 1989; Marcia, 1989; Waterman, 1989).

Developmental Changes

Early adolescents are primarily in Marcia's identity diffusion or moratorium statuses. At least three aspects of the young adolescent's development are important in identity formation: Young adolescents must (1) establish confidence in parental support, (2) develop a sense of industry, and (3) gain a self-reflective perspective on their future (Marcia, 1987).

Some researchers believe that the most important identity changes take place in youth rather than earlier in adolescence. For example, Alan Waterman (1985, 1989) found that, from the years preceding high school through the last few years of college, the number of individuals who are identity achieved increases, corresponding with a decrease in those who are identity diffused. College upperclassmen are more likely to be identity achieved than college freshmen or high school students. Many young adolescents are identity diffused. These developmental changes are especially true for vocational choice. For religious beliefs and political ideology, fewer college students have reached the identity achieved status, with a substantial number characterized by foreclosure and diffusion. Thus, the timing of identity may depend on the particular role involved, and many college students are still wrestling with ideological commitments (Arehart & Smith, 1990; Harter, 1990a).

Many identity status researchers believe that individuals who develop positive identities follow what are called "MAMA" cycles of *m*oratorium-*a*chievement-*m*oratorium-*a*chievement (Archer, 1989; Marcia, 1991). These cycles may be repeated throughout life (Francis, Fraser, & Marcia, 1989). Personal, family, and societal changes are inevitable, and as they occur, the flexibility and skill required to explore new alternatives and to develop new commitments likely facilitate an individual's coping skills.

Gender

In Erikson's (1968) classic presentation of identity development, the division of labor between the sexes was reflected in his assertion that males' aspirations were mainly oriented toward career and ideological commitments, while females' were centered around marriage and child rearing. In the 1960s and 1970s, researchers found support for Erikson's assertion about gender differences in identity. For example, vocational concerns were more central to the identity of males, affiliative concerns more important to the identity of females (LaVoie, 1976). However, in the last decade, as females have developed stronger vocational interests, sex differences in identity are turning into sex similarities (Archer, 1991; Waterman, 1985).

Some investigators believe that the order of stages proposed by Erikson are different for females and males. One view is that, for males, identity formation precedes the stage of intimacy, while for females, intimacy precedes identity (Douvan & Adelson, 1966). These ideas are consistent with the belief that relationships and emotional bonds are more important concerns of females, while autonomy and achievement are more important concerns of males (Gilligan, 1990). In one recent study, the development of a clear sense of self by adolescent girls was related to their concerns about care and response in relationships (Rogers, 1987). In another investigation, a strong sense of self in college women was associated with their ability to solve problems of care in relationships while staying connected with both self and others (Skoe & Marcia, 1988).

The task of identity exploration may be more complex for females than males in that females may try to establish identities in more domains than males. In today's world, the options for females have increased and thus may at times be confusing and conflicting, especially for females who hope to successfully integrate family and career roles (Archer, 1989; Gilligan, 1990; Marcia, 1989).

Family Influences on Identity

Parents are important figures in adolescents' development of identity. In studies that relate identity development to parenting styles, democratic parents, who encourage adolescents to participate in family decision making, foster identity achievement. Autocratic parents, who control the adolescent's behavior without giving the adolescent an opportunity to express an opinion, encourage identity foreclosure. Permissive parents, who provide little guidance to adolescents and allow them to make their own decisions, promote identity diffusion (Bernard, 1981; Enright & others, 1980; Marcia, 1980).

In addition to studies on parenting styles, researchers also have examined the role of individuality and connectedness in the development of identity. Developmentalist Catherine Cooper and her colleagues (Carlson, Cooper, & Hsu, 1990; Cooper & Grotevant, 1989; Grotevant & Cooper, 1985) believe that a family atmosphere that promotes both individuation and connectedness is important in the adolescent's identity development. **Individuality** *consists of two dimensions— self-assertion (the ability to have and communicate a point of view) and separateness (the use of communication patterns to express how one is different from others).* **Connectedness** *also consists of two dimensions—mutuality (sensitivity to and respect for others' views) and permeability (openness to others' views).*

"*While we're at supper, Billy, you'd make Daddy and Mommy very happy if you'd remove your hat, your sunglasses, and your earring.*"

Drawing by Ziegler; © 1985 The New Yorker Magazine, Inc.

In general, Cooper's research findings reveal that identity formation is enhanced by family relationships that are both individuated, which encourages adolescents to develop their own point of view, and connected, which provides a secure base from which to explore the widening social worlds of adolescence. Other researchers have also found support for the combined influence of individuality and connectedness in promoting the adolescent's identity development (Fullwinder, 1991). However, in one study, when parents were overinvolved in their adolescent daughters' lives, relying on the adolescent daughters for their own emotional needs, the daughters engaged in less identity exploration (Fullwinder, 1991).

Stuart Hauser and his colleagues (Hauser & Bowlds, 1990; Hauser & others, 1984) have also illuminated family processes that promote adolescents' identity development. They have found that parents who use *enabling* behaviors (such as explaining, accepting, and giving empathy) facilitate adolescents' identity development more than parents who use *constraining* behaviors (such as judging and devaluing). In sum, family interaction styles that give adolescents the right to question and to be different, within a context of support and mutuality, foster healthy patterns of identity development (Harter, 1990b).

Cultural and Ethnic Aspects of Identity

Erikson is especially sensitive to the role of culture in identity development. He points out that, throughout the world, ethnic minority groups have struggled to maintain their cultural identities while blending into the dominant culture (Erikson, 1968). Erikson says that this struggle for an inclusive identity, or identity within the larger culture, has been the driving force in the founding of churches, empires, and revolutions throughout history.

As indicated in Chapter 9, adolescence is often a special juncture in the identity development of ethnic minority individuals (Spencer, 1991; Spencer & Dornbusch, 1900; Spencer & Markstrom-Adams, 1990). Although children are

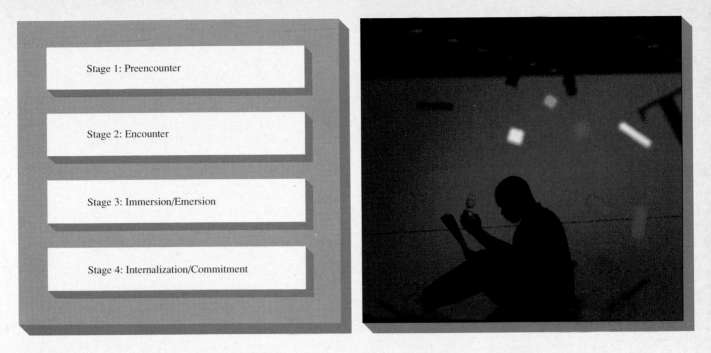

Figure 10.4   Four stages in the development of identity in ethnic minority individuals.

aware of some ethnic and cultural differences, most ethnic minority individuals first consciously confront their ethnicity in adolescence. In one recent investigation, ethnic identity exploration was higher among ethnic minority than White American college students (Phinney & Alipuria, 1990). In this same investigation, ethnic minority college students who had thought about and resolved issues involving their ethnicity had higher self-esteem than their ethnic minority counterparts who had not. Another investigation studied the ethnic identity development of Asian American, Black American, Hispanic American, and White American tenth-grade students in Los Angeles (Phinney, 1989). Adolescents from each of the three ethnic minority groups faced a similar need to deal with their ethnic group identification in a predominately White American culture. In some instances, the adolescents from the three ethnic minority groups perceived different issues to be important in their resolution of ethnic identity. For Asian American adolescents, pressures to achieve academically and concerns about quotas that make it difficult to get into good colleges were salient issues. Many Black American adolescent females discussed their realization that White American standards of beauty (especially hair and skin color) did not apply to them; Black American adolescent males were concerned with possible job discrimination and the need to distinguish themselves from a negative societal image of Black male adolescents. For Hispanic American adolescents, prejudice was a recurrent theme, as were conflicting values between the Hispanic cultural heritage and the majority culture. Sociocultural Worlds of Adolescence 10.1 examines identity development in Native American youth.

Black American psychologists Janet Helms (1985, 1990) and William Cross (1972, 1991), as well as Asian American psychologists Derald Wing Sue and David Sue (1972), believe that a number of stages are involved in the development of an ethnic identity, whether for minorities or Whites (Allen & Santrock, 1993). Helms amended Cross's model of minority identity development to include four stages (see Figure 10.4):

Stage 1: Preencounter. In this first stage, ethnic minority individuals prefer dominant cultural values to those of their own culture. Their role models, lifestyles, and value systems are adopted from the dominant group, while the physical and/or cultural characteristics that single them out as ethnic minority in-

The Development of Identity in Native American Youth

A special concern in the development of identity in Native American adolescents is their negative image, which has been perpetuated for centuries in the majority White culture.

Substandard living conditions, poverty, and chronic unemployment place many Native American youth at risk for school failure and poor health, which can contribute to problems in developing a positive identity (LaFromboise & Low, 1989; Spencer & Markstrom-Adams, 1990). A special concern is the negative image of Native Americans that has been perpetuated for centuries in the majority White American culture. To consider further the development of identity in Native American youth, we examine the experiences of a 12-year-old Hopi Indian boy.

The Hopi Indians are a quiet, thoughtful people who go to great lengths not to offend anyone. In a pueblo north of Albuquerque, a 12-year-old boy speaks: "I've been living in Albuquerque for a year. The Anglos I've met, they're different. I don't know why. In school, I drew a picture of my father's horse. One of the other kids wouldn't believe that it was ours. He said, 'You don't really own that horse.' I said, 'It's a horse my father rides, and I feed it every morning.' He said, 'How come?' I said, 'My uncle and my father are good riders, and I'm pretty good.' He said, 'I can ride a horse better than you, and I'd rather be a pilot.' I told him I never thought of being a pilot."

The 12-year-old Indian boy continues, "Anglo kids, they won't let you get away with anything. Tell them something, and fast as lightning and loud as thunder, they'll say, 'I'm better than you, so there!' My father says it's always been like that."

Native American adolescents are not really angry at or envious of White American adolescents. Maybe they are in awe of their future power; maybe they fear it. White American adolescents cannot keep from wondering if, in some way, they have missed out on something and may end up "losing" (Coles, 1986).

The following words of a Native American vividly capture some important ingredients of the 12-year-old boy's interest in a peaceful identity:

Rivers flow.
The sea sings.
Oceans roar.
Tides rise.
Who am I?

A small pebble
On a giant shore;
Who am I
To ask who I am?
Isn't it enough to be?

dividuals are a source of pain and stress. For example, Black Americans may perceive their own physical features as undesirable and their Black cultural values and ways a handicap to success in American society.

Stage 2: Encounter. While moving to the encounter stage is usually a gradual process, reaching this stage may occur because of an event that makes individuals realize that they will never be members of mainstream White America. A monumental event, such as the assassination of Martin Luther King, Jr., or more personal "identity-shattering" events may serve as triggers. In the encounter stage, ethnic minority individuals begin to break through their denial. For example, Hispanic Americans who feel ashamed of their cultural upbringing may have conversations with Hispanic Americans who are proud of their cultural heritage. Ethnic minority individuals become aware during the encounter stage that not all cultural values of the dominant group are beneficial to them. Conflicting attitudes about the self, minority group culture, and the dominant culture are characteristic of the encounter stage. Ethnic minority individuals want to identify with the minority group but do not know how to develop this identity. The recognition that an identity must be developed and not found leads to the third stage: immersion/emersion.

Stage 3: Immersion/Emersion. At the beginning of this stage—immersion—ethnic minority individuals completely endorse minority views and reject the dominant society. Individuals become strongly motivated to eliminate the oppression of their ethnic minority group. Movement into this stage likely occurs because: (1) individuals begin to resolve some conflicts from the previous stage and develop a better understanding of such societal forces as racism, oppression, and discrimination; and (2) individuals begin to ask themselves, "Why should I feel ashamed of who I am?" The answer at this point often elicits both guilt and anger—the guilt of "selling out" in the past, which is perceived as contributing to the ethnic minority group's oppression, and anger at having been oppressed and "brainwashed" by the dominant group.

In the second phase of this stage—emersion—individuals experience feelings of discontent and discomfort with their rigid views of the immersion phase and develop notions of greater individual autonomy. Emersion allows them to vent the anger that characterized the beginning of this stage, through rap groups, explorations of their own culture, discussions of racial/ethnic issues, and so on. Education and opportunities to expel hostile feelings allow individuals' emotions to level off, so that they can think more clearly and adaptively. They no longer find it necessary to reject everything from the dominant culture and accept everything from their own culture. They now have the autonomy to determine the strengths and weaknesses of their culture, and to decide which parts of the culture will become a part of their identity.

Stage 4: Internalization/Commitment. The main theme of this stage of ethnic minority identity development is that individuals experience a sense of fulfillment regarding the integration of their personal and cultural identities. They have resolved the conflicts and discomforts of the immersion/emersion stage and attained greater self-control and flexibility. They also more objectively examine the cultural values of other ethnic minority individuals and groups, as well as those of the dominant group. At this stage, individuals want to eliminate all forms of oppression. The commitment in this stage refers to the behavioral enactment of the newly realized identity. Individuals take actions—whether large, such as engaging in large-scale political or social activism, or small, such as performing everyday activities that are consistent with their ethnic identity—to eliminate oppression.

Helms (1990) also proposed a model of White ethnic identity, in which White individuals move from a stage of naiveté about racial issues to a sophisticated stage of biculturalism or racial transcendence. Helms's theory assumes that consciousness of ethnic identity in both minority and majority individuals increases understanding of success or failure in cross-ethnic interactions. Helms's five stages of White ethnic identity development are (see Figure 10.5):

Stage 1: Contact. White individuals are oblivious to ethnic/racial/cultural issues. They rarely think of themselves in ethnic or racial terms.

Stage 2: Disintegration. White individuals become aware of the social implications of race and ethnicity on a personal level, caught between the privileges of the White culture and the humane desire to treat ethnic minority individuals fairly.

Stage 3: Reintegration. White persons idealize anything associated with the White culture and denigrate anything associated with ethnic minority cultures. Anger is most common at this stage.

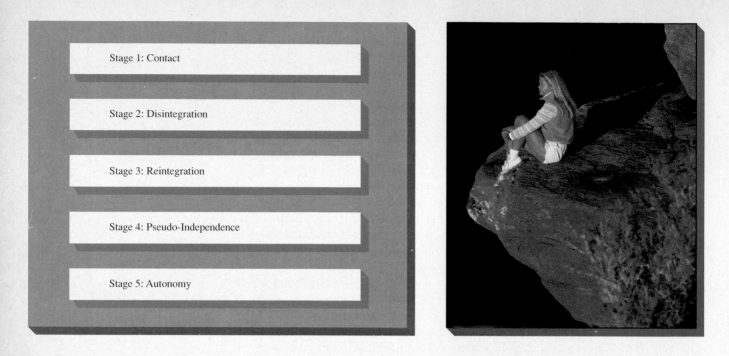

Figure 10.5   Five stages in the ethnic identity development of White individuals.

Stage 4: Pseudo-Independence. White individuals develop an understanding of the privileges of whiteness and recognize a personal responsibility to combat racism.

Stage 5: Autonomy. White individuals develop a bicultural or racially transcendent world view. At this stage, individuals have adopted a positive, nonracist White identity, feeling a kinship with people regardless of their race or ethnic group and seeking to abolish the oppression of ethnic minority groups.

Although the identity development models include distinct stages, the boundaries between the stages are not always abrupt and clearly defined. In many instances, one stage blends into the next. Also, not all individuals experience the entire range of these stages in their lifetimes. Some individuals are born and raised in a family functioning at stage 4 in the White identity development model and may never experience the earlier stages.

Identity and Intimacy

As we go through our adolescence, youth, and early adulthood, most of us are motivated to successfully juggle the development of identity and intimacy. We now examine the development of intimacy in adolescence and then study the nature of loneliness.

Intimacy

Erikson (1968) believes that intimacy should come after individuals are well on their way to establishing a stable and successful individual identity. Intimacy is another life crisis in Erikson's scheme—if intimacy is not developed in early adulthood, the individual may be left with what Erikson calls isolation. **Intimacy versus isolation** *is Erikson's sixth developmental stage, which individuals experience during early adulthood. At this time, individuals face the task of forming intimate relationships with others.* Erikson describes intimacy as finding oneself, yet losing oneself in another. If young adults form healthy friendships and an intimate relationship with another individual, intimacy will be achieved; it not, isolation will result.

An inability to develop meaningful relationships with others can be harmful to an individual's personality. It may lead individuals to repudiate, ignore, or attack those who frustrate them. Such circumstances account for the shallow, almost pathetic attempts of youth to merge themselves with a leader. Many youths want to be apprentices or disciples of leaders and adults who will shelter them from the harm of the "outgroup" world. If this fails, and Erikson believes that it must, sooner or later the individuals recoil into a self-search to discover where they went wrong. This introspection sometimes leads to painful depression and isolation and may contribute to a mistrust of others and restrict the willingness to act on one's own initiative.

Adolescents and young adults show different styles of intimate interaction. Jacob Orlofsky (1976) developed one classification with five styles: intimate, preintimate, stereotyped, pseudointimate, and isolated (Orlofsky, Marcia, & Lessor, 1973). In the **intimate style,** *the individual forms and maintains one or more deep and long-lasting love relationships.* In the **preintimate style,** *the individual shows mixed emotions about commitment, an ambivalence reflected in the strategy of offering love without obligations or long-lasting bonds.* In the **stereotyped style,** *the individual has superficial relationships that tend to be dominated by friendship ties with same-sex rather than opposite-sex individuals.* In the **pseudointimate style,** *the individual maintains a long-lasting heterosexual attachment with little or no depth or closeness.* In the **isolated style,** *the individual withdraws from social encounters and has little or no attachment to same- or opposite-sexed individuals.* Occasionally, the isolate shows signs of developing close interpersonal relationships, but usually, the interactions are stressful. In one investigation, intimate and preintimate individuals were more sensitive to their partners' needs and were more open in their friendships than individuals in the other three intimacy statuses (Orlofsky, Marcia, & Lesser, 1973).

A desirable goal is to develop a mature identity and have positive, close relationships with others. Kathleen White and her colleagues (Paul & White, 1990; White & others, 1986; White & others, 1987) developed a model of relationship maturity that includes this goal at its highest level. Individuals are described as moving through three levels of relationship maturity: self-focused, role-focused, and individuated-connected.

The **self-focused level** *is the first level of relationship maturity, at which one's perspective of another or a relationship is concerned only with how it affects the self.* The individual's own wishes and plans overshadow those of others, and the individual shows little concern for others. Intimate communication skills are in the early developing, experimental stages. In terms of sexuality, there is little understanding of mutuality or consideration of another's sexual needs.

The **role-focused level** *is the second or intermediate level of relationship maturity, at which perceiving others as individuals in their own right begins to develop. However, at this level, the perspective is stereotypical and emphasizes social acceptability.* Individuals at this level know that acknowledging and respecting another is part of being a good friend or a romantic partner. Yet commitment to an individual, rather than the romantic partner role itself, is not articulated. Generalizations about the importance of communication in relationships abound, but underlying this talk is a shallow understanding of commitment.

The **individuated-connected level** *is the highest level of relationship maturity, at which there is evidence of an understanding of one's self, as well as consideration of others' motivation and anticipation of their needs. Concern and caring involve emotional support and individualized expression of interest.* Commitment is made to specific individuals with whom a relationship is shared. At this level, individuals understand the personal time and investment needed to make a relationship work. In White's view, the individuated-connected level is not likely to be reached until adulthood. She believes that most individuals making the transition from adolescence to adulthood are either self-focused or role-focused in their relationship maturity.

Loneliness

We often think of older adults as the loneliest individuals, but surveys have found that the highest levels of loneliness often appear during late adolescence and youth (Cutrona, 1982). Some adolescents feel lonely because they have strong needs for intimacy but have not yet developed the social skills or relationship maturity to satisfy these needs. They may feel isolated and sense that they do not have anyone they can turn to for intimacy. Society's contemporary emphasis on self-fulfillment and achievement, the importance attached to commitment in relationships, and the decline in stable, close relationships are among the reasons feelings of loneliness are common today (de Jong-Gierveld, 1987).

Loneliness is associated with an individual's sex, attachment history, self-esteem, and social skills. A lack of time spent with females, on the part of both males and females, is associated with loneliness. Also, individuals who are lonely often have a poor relationship with their parents. Early experiences of rejection and loss (as when a parent dies) can cause a lasting effect of feeling alone. Lonely individuals often have low self-esteem and tend to blame themselves more than they deserve for their inadequacies. Lonely individuals also are often deficient in social skills (Jones, Hobbs, & Hockenbury, 1982). For example, they show inappropriate self-disclosure, self-attention at the expense of attention to a partner, or an inability to develop comfortable intimacy.

The social transition to college is a time when loneliness may develop, as individuals leave behind the familiar world of hometown and family. Many college freshmen feel anxious about meeting new people and developing a new social life. As one student commented:

> My first year here at the university has been pretty lonely. I wasn't lonely at all in high school. I lived in a fairly small town—I knew everyone and everyone knew me. I was a member of several clubs and played on the basketball team. It's not that way at the university. It is a big place, and I've felt like a stranger on so many occasions. I'm starting to get used to my life here, and the last few months I've been making myself meet people and get to know them, but it has not been easy.

As reflected in the comments of this freshman, individuals usually cannot bring their popularity and social standing from high school into the college environment. There may be a dozen high school basketball stars, National Merit scholars, and former student council presidents on a single dormitory floor. Especially if students attend college away from home, they face the task of forming completely new social relationships.

In one investigation conducted two weeks after the school year began, 75 percent of the 354 college freshmen said that they had felt lonely at least part of the time since arriving on campus (Cutrona, 1982). More than 40 percent said that their loneliness was moderate to severe in intensity. Students who were the most optimistic and had the highest self-esteem were more likely to overcome their loneliness by the end of the freshmen year. Loneliness is not reserved only for college freshmen, though. It is not uncommon to find a number of upper-classmen who are also lonely.

Researchers have developed measures of loneliness. Individuals are asked to respond to such statements as:

"I don't feel in tune with the people around me."
"I can't find companionship when I want it."

Individuals who consistently respond that they never or rarely feel in tune with people around them and rarely or never can find companionship when they want it are likely to fall into the category of moderately or intensely lonely.

According to Robert Weiss (1973), loneliness is virtually always a response to the absence of some particular type of relationship. Weiss distinguished two forms of loneliness—*emotional isolation* and *social isolation*—which correspond to the absence of different types of social provisions. **Emotional isolation** *is a type of loneliness that arises when a person lacks an intimate attachment relationship; single, divorced, and widowed adults often experience this type of loneliness.* In contrast, **social isolation** *is a type of loneliness that occurs when a person lacks a sense of integrated involvement; being deprived of participation in a group or community involving companionship, shared interests, organized activities, and meaningful roles causes a person to feel alienated, bored, and uneasy. Recently relocated married couples often experience social isolation and long for involvement with friends and community.*

It is common for adolescents to experience both types of loneliness. Being left out of clique and crowd activities can give rise to painful feelings of social isolation. Not having an intimate dating or romantic partner can give rise to the loneliness of emotional isolation.

Individuals can reduce their loneliness by either changing their social relations or changing their social needs and desires (Peplau & Perlman, 1982). Probably the most direct and satisfying way for individuals to become less lonely is to improve their social relations by forming new relationships, by using their existing social network more competently, or by creating "surrogate" relationships with pets, television personalities, and the like. A second way to reduce loneliness is to reduce desire for social contact. Over the short run, individuals can accomplish this by selecting activities they can enjoy alone rather than those that require someone's company. Over the long run, though, effort should be made to form new relationships. A third coping strategy that some individuals unfortunately adopt involves distracting themselves from their painful feelings of loneliness by drinking to "drown their sorrows" or by becoming a workaholic. Some of the negative health consequences of loneliness may be the product of such maladaptive coping strategies. If you perceive yourself to be a lonely individual, you might consider contacting the counseling center at your college for advice on ways to reduce your loneliness and to improve your social skills in relationships.

At this point, we have discussed a number of ideas about identity. A summary of these ideas is presented in Concept Table 10.2. In this chapter, we briefly discussed how intimacy and connectedness play especially important roles in the development of female adolescents. In the next chapter, we devote our full attention to the role of gender in adolescent development.

Concept Table 10.2

Identity

Concept	Processes/Related Ideas	Characteristics/Description
Erikson's ideas on identity	Revisiting Erikson's views on identity	Identity versus identity confusion is the fifth stage in Erikson's theory, which individuals experience during adolescence. As adolescents are confronted with new roles, they enter a psychological moratorium.
	Personality and role experimentation	Two core ingredients of Erikson's ideas on identity are personality and role experimentation. There are literally hundreds of roles for individuals to explore and many ways to pursue each role. In technological societies such as the United States, the vocational role is especially important.
	The complexity of Erikson's theory	Erikson's view of identity is complex, involving genetic, adaptive, structural, dynamic, subjective or experiential, psychosocial reciprocity, and existential status dimensions.
Some contemporary thoughts on identity	Lengthy and complex	Identity development is a lengthy process, in many cases more gradual than Erikson implied. Identity development is also extraordinarily complex and gets done in bits and pieces. For the first time in development, individuals during adolescence are physically, cognitively, and socially mature enough to synthesize their lives and pursue a viable path toward adult maturity.
The four statuses of identity and developmental changes	The four statuses	Marcia proposed four identity statuses—identity diffusion, identity foreclosure, identity moratorium, and identity achievement—that are based on crisis (exploration) and commitment. Some experts believe that the identity status approach oversimplifies Erikson's ideas.
	Developmental changes	Some experts believe that the main identity changes take place in youth, rather than earlier in adolescence. College upperclassmen are more likely to be identity achieved than freshmen or high school students, although many college students are still wrestling with ideological commitments. Individuals often follow "moratorium, achievement, moratorium, achievement" cycles throughout life.
Gender, family, culture, and ethnic aspects of identity	Gender	Erikson's classical theory argues that sex differences in identity development exist, with adolescent males having a stronger interest in vocational roles and adolescent females having a stronger interest in marriage and family roles. More recent studies have revealed that, as females have developed stronger vocational interests, sex differences in identity are turning into sex similarities. However, others argue that relationships and emotional bonds are more central to the identity development of females than males and that female identity development is more complex than male identity development.

Summary

I. The Nature of Self-Understanding and Its Dimensions

Self-understanding is the adolescent's cognitive representation of the self, the substance and content of the adolescent's self-conceptions. Self-understanding provides the rational underpinnings of personal identity. Dimensions of adolescents' self-understanding include: abstract and idealistic; construction of ideal and real, true and false selves; differentiated; contradictions within the self; self-conscious; self-protective; recognition that the self includes an unconscious dimension; social comparison; fluctuating; and integrative.

II. Self-Integration

Adolescents' self-understanding becomes more integrative, especially in late adolescence. Budding formal operational skills initially present a liability because they allow adolescents to detect inconsistencies in the self across varying roles, only later providing the cognitive capacity to integrate such apparent contradictions. Middle adolescents are more troubled by these discrepancies than young or late adolescents.

Concept Table 10.2

Identity

Concept	Processes/Related Ideas	Characteristics/Description
	Family influences	Parents are important figures in adolescents' identity development. Democratic parenting facilitates adolescents' identity development; autocratic and permissive parenting do not. Cooper and her colleagues have shown that both individuality and connectedness in family relations are important contributors to adolescent identity development. Hauser has shown that enabling behaviors promote identity development more than constraining behaviors.
	Cultural and ethnic factors	Erikson is especially sensitive to the role of culture in identity development, underscoring how, throughout the world, ethnic minority groups have struggled to maintain their cultural identities while blending into the majority culture. Adolescence is often a special juncture in the identity development of ethnic minority individuals because, for the first time, they consciously confront their ethnic identity. Helms proposed a model of ethnic minority identity development that consists of four stages: preencounter, encounter, immersion/emersion, and internalization/commitment. She also proposed a five-stage model of ethnic identity development in White individuals: contact, disintegration, reintegration, pseudo-independence, and autonomy.
Identity and intimacy	Intimacy	Intimacy versus isolation is Erikson's sixth developmental stage, which individuals experience during early adulthood. As this time, individuals face the task of forming intimate relationships with others. Orlofsky described five styles of intimate interaction: intimate, preintimate, stereotyped, pseudointimate, and isolated. White proposed a model of relationship maturity in which individuals move through three levels: self-focused, role-focused, and individuated-connected.
	Loneliness	Surveys often find that the highest levels of loneliness often appear during late adolescence and youth. Loneliness is associated with an individual's sex, attachment history, self-esteem, and social skills. The social transition to college is a time when loneliness may develop, as individuals leave behind the familiar world of hometown and family. Weiss distinguished between two types of loneliness: emotional isolation and social isolation.

III. The Nature of Self-Esteem and Its Measurement

Self-esteem is the evaluative and affective component of self-concept. Self-esteem is also referred to as self-worth or self-image. Until recently, self-esteem was described in global terms. Today, domain-specific aspects of self-esteem are also considered. Measuring self-esteem is a difficult task. Harter's measures are appealing because they provide a differentiated assessment of self-esteem in various skill domains, as well as independent assessment of self-worth. Some assessment experts believe that several methods should be used to assess self-esteem, including observations of the adolescent's behavior.

IV. Salience of Self-Esteem Domains

Perceived physical appearance is an especially strong contributor to overall self-esteem, not only in adolescence but in other developmental periods as well. In adolescence, peer acceptance follows physical appearance in contributing to global self-worth.

V. Parental and Peer Influences on Self-Esteem

In Coopersmith's study, children's self-esteem was associated with such parenting attributes as parental affection and allowing children freedom within well-prescribed limits. These associations are correlational. Peer judgments gain increasing importance among older children and adolescents. In one study of the contribution of peer support to adolescent self-esteem, classmate support was more powerful than close-friend support.

VI. Increasing Adolescents' Self-Esteem

Four ways to improve adolescents' self-esteem involve: identifying the causes of adolescents' low self-esteem and which domains of competence are important to the self, emotional support and social approval, achievement, and coping.

VII. Erikson's Ideas on Identity

Identity versus identity confusion is the fifth stage in Erikson's theory, which individuals experience during adolescence. As adolescents are confronted with new roles, they enter a psychological moratorium. Two core ingredients of Erikson's theory of identity are personality and role experimentation. There are literally hundreds of roles for adolescents to explore and many ways to pursue each role. In technological societies such as the United States, the vocational role is especially important. Erikson's theory is complex, involving genetic, adaptive, structural, dynamic, subjective or experiential, psychosocial reciprocity, and existential status dimensions.

VIII. Some Contemporary Thoughts on Identity

Identity development is a lengthy process, in many cases more gradual than Erikson envisioned. Identity development is also extraordinarily complex and gets done in bits and pieces. For the first time in development, individuals during adolescence are physically, cognitively, and socially mature enough to synthesize their lives and pursue a viable path toward a mature identity.

IX. The Four Statuses of Identity and Developmental Changes

Marcia proposed four identity statuses—identity diffusion, identity foreclosure, identity moratorium, and identity achievement—that are based on crisis (exploration) and commitment. The identity status approach may oversimplify Erikson's ideas. Some experts believe that the main identity changes take place in youth, rather than earlier in adolescence. College upperclassmen are more likely to be identity achieved than freshmen or high school students, although many college students are still wrestling with ideological commitments. Individuals often follow "moratorium-achievement-moratorium-achievement" cycles throughout life.

X. Gender and Identity

Erikson's classical theory argues that sex differences in identity development exist, with adolescent males having a stronger interest in vocational roles and adolescent females having a stronger interest in marriage and family roles. More recent studies have revealed that, as females have developed stronger vocational interests, sex differences in identity are turning into sex similarities. However, others argue that relationships and emotional bonds are more central to the identity development of females than males and that female identity development is more complex than male identity development.

XI. Family Influences

Parents are important figures in adolescents' identity development. Democratic parenting facilitates identity development in adolescence; autocratic and permissive parenting do not. Cooper and her colleagues have shown that both individuality and connectedness in family relations are important contributors to adolescent identity development. Hauser has shown that enabling behaviors promote identity development more than constraining behaviors.

XII. Cultural and Ethnic Factors in Identity

Erikson is especially sensitive to the role of culture in identity development, underscoring how, throughout the world, ethnic minority groups have struggled to maintain their cultural identities while blending into the dominant culture. Adolescence is often a special juncture in the identity development of ethnic minority individuals because, for the first time, they consciously confront their ethnic identity. Helms proposed a model of ethnic minority identity development that consists of four stages: preencounter, encounter, immersion/emersion, and internalization/commitment. She also proposed a five-stage model of ethnic identity development in White individuals: contact, disintegration, reintegration, pseudo-independence, and autonomy.

XIII. Identity and Intimacy

Intimacy versus isolation is Erikson's sixth developmental stage, which individuals experience during early adulthood. At this time, individuals face the task of forming intimate relationships with others. Orlofsky described five styles of intimate interaction: intimate, preintimate, stereotyped, pseudointimate, and isolated. White proposed a model of relationship maturity in which individuals move through three levels: self-focused, role-focused, and individuated-connected. Surveys often find that the highest levels of loneliness appear during late adolescence and youth. Loneliness is associated with an individual's sex, attachment history, self-esteem, and social skills. The social transition to college is a time when loneliness may develop, as individuals leave behind the familiar world of hometown and family. Weiss distinguished between two types of loneliness: emotional isolation and social isolation.

Key Terms

self-understanding 335
possible self 336
self-esteem 338
identity versus identity
    confusion 345
psychological
    moratorium 345
crisis 349
commitment 349
identity diffusion 349

identity foreclosure 349
identity moratorium 349
identity achievement 349
individuality 351
connectedness 351
intimacy versus
    isolation 356
intimate style 357
preintimate style 357

stereotyped style 357
pseudointimate style 357
isolated style 357
self-focused level 357
role-focused level 357
individuated-connected
    level 357
emotional isolation 359
social isolation 359

Suggested Readings

Erikson, E. H. (1969). *Gandhi's truth*. New York: W. W. Norton.
   In this Pulitzer-Prize-winning novel, Erikson weaves an insightful picture of Gandhi's development of identity.
Harter, S. (1990). Self and identity development. In S. S. Feldman & G. R. Elliott (Eds.), *At the threshold: The developing adolescent*. Cambridge, MA: Harvard University Press.
   An excellent overview of contemporary theory and research on the nature of self and identity development in adolescence by one of the leading researchers in the area of self-understanding.
Lapsley, D., & Power, F. C. (1988). *Self, ego, and identity*. New York: Springer-Verlag.
   An authoritative treatment by leading scholars of issues involved in the nature of the self and identity.
Marcia, J. (1987). The identity status approach to the study of ego identity development. In T. Honess & K. Yardley (Eds.), *Self and identity: Perspectives across the lifespan*. London: Routledge & Kegan Paul.
   Marcia presents his concept of the four statuses of identity and describes the complexity of the identity process.
Paul, E. L., & White, K. M. (1990). The development of intimate relationships in late adolescence. *Adolescence, 25*, 375–400.
   A recent, authoritative overview of intimacy development in late adolescence, including a description of White's model of relationship maturity.

Gender

As the man beholds the woman
As the woman sees the man,
Curiously they note each other,
As each other they only can.

Bryan Procter, The Sexes

Gender Worlds

Controversial currents swirl around today's females and males. Females increasingly struggle to gain influence and change the worlds of business, politics, and relationships with males. The changes are far from complete, but social reformers hope that a generation from now the struggles of the last decades of the twentieth century will have generated more freedom, influence, and flexibility for females. Possibly in the next generation, when today's adolescents become tomorrow's adults, such issues as equal pay, child care, abortion, rape, and domestic violence will no longer be discussed as "women's issues" but, rather, as economic issues, family issues, and ethical issues—reflecting the equal concern of females *and* males. Possibly one of today's adolescent females will become the head of a large corporation several decades from now and the appointment will not make headlines by virtue of her gender. Half the presidential candidates may be women and nobody will notice.

What would it take for today's adolescent females to get from here to there? The choices are not simple ones. When Barbara Bush went to Wellesley College to celebrate motherhood and wifely virtues, she stimulated a national debate among the young on what it means to be a successful woman. The debate was further fueled by TV anchorwoman Connie Chung's announcement that she would abandon the fast track at CBS in a final drive to become a mother at age 44. At the same time, male role models are also in flux. Wall Street star Peter Lynch, the head of Fidelity Investment's leading mutual fund, resigned to have more time with his family and to pursue humanitarian projects (Gibbs, 1990).

When asked to sketch their futures, many of today's youth say they want good careers, good marriages, and two or three children, but they don't want their children to be raised by strangers (Spade & Reese, 1991). Idealistic? Maybe. Some will reach these goals; some will make other choices as they move from adolescence into adulthood, and then through the adult years. Some of today's adolescents will choose to remain single as they move into adulthood and pursue their career goals; others will become married but not have children; and yet others will balance the demands of family and work. In a word, not all of today's females have the same goals; neither do all of today's males. What is important is to develop a society free of barriers and discrimination, one that allows females and males to freely choose, to meet their expectations, and to realize their potential.

> *It is fatal to be man or woman pure and simple;*
> *one must be woman-manly or man-womanly.*
>
> *Virginia Woolf*

T his chapter is about gender, about adolescents' worlds as female and male. Among the questions we explore are: What is gender? Is there an intensification of gender in adolescence? What are the biological, social, and cognitive influences on gender? Are there many gender differences, or are most of what we often consider differences stereotypes? How can gender roles be classified? What is the feminist perspective on gender, and is adolescence a critical juncture in the development of females? We consider each of these questions in turn.

What Is Gender?

Nowhere in adolescents' social development have more sweeping changes occurred in recent years than in the area of gender. What exactly is meant by *gender?* Whereas the term *sex* refers to the biological dimension of being male or female, **gender** *refers to the sociocultural dimension of being male or female.* Few aspects of adolescents' development are more central to their identity and to their social relationships than gender. One aspect of gender bears special mention: **Gender role** *is a set of expectations that prescribes how females and males should think, act, and feel.* For example, should males be more assertive, and should females be more sensitive to others' feelings?

Developmental Changes and Gender Intensification

As females and males experience many physical and social changes during early adolescence, they have to come to terms with new definitions of their gender roles (Belansky & Clements, 1992; Huston & Alvarez, 1990). During early adolescence, individuals develop the adult, physical aspects of their gender. Some theorists and researchers have proposed that, with the onset of puberty, girls and boys experience an intensification in gender-related expectations. The **gender intensification hypothesis** *states that psychological and behavioral differences between boys and girls become greater during early adolescence because of increased socialization pressures to conform to traditional masculine and feminine gender roles* (Galambos, Almeida, & Petersen, in press; Hill & Lynch, 1983; Lynch, 1991). Puberty's role in gender intensification may involve a signaling to socializing others—parents, peers, and teachers, for example—that the adolescent is beginning to approach adulthood and, therefore, should begin to act more in ways that resemble the stereotypical female or male adult. In one recent study, sex differences in gender-role attitudes increased across the early adolescent years (Galambos, Almeida, & Petersen, in press). Gender-role attitudes were measured by the Attitudes toward Women Scale (Galambos & others, 1985), which assesses the extent to which adolescents approve of gender-based division of roles. For example, the adolescent is asked such questions as whether girls should have the same freedom as boys. Other researchers also have reported

The gender intensification hypothesis states that psychological and behavioral differences between boys and girls become greater during early adolescence because of increased socialization pressures to conform to traditional masculine and feminine gender roles. Puberty's role in gender intensification may involve a signaling to socializing others—parents, peers, and teachers, for example—that the adolescent is beginning to approach adulthood and, therefore, should begin to act in ways that resemble the stereotypical female or male adult.

evidence of gender intensification in early adolescence (Hill & Lynch, 1983). As we discuss the biological, social, and cognitive influences on gender, keep in mind that gender intensification characterizes many boys and girls in early adolescence.

Biological, Social, and Cognitive Influences on Gender

How strong is biology's influence on gender? How extensively do children's and adolescents' experiences shape their gender development? How do cognitive factors influence gender development? We explore the answers to each of these questions.

Biological Influences

In our examination of biological influences on gender behavior in adolescence, we first discuss pubertal change, especially its role in increasing sexual interest, and second, we examine Freud's and Erikson's ideas about anatomy and destiny.

Pubertal Change and Sexuality

Biology's influence on gender behavior involves pubertal change. Pubertal change contributes to an increased incorporation of sexuality into the gender attitudes and behavior of adolescents (Crockett, 1991). As their bodies are flooded with hormones, many girls desire to be the very best female possible, and many boys strive to be the very best male possible. The increased incorporation of sexuality into gender behavior means that adolescent girls often display increased stereotypical female behavior and adolescent boys often display increased stereotypical male behavior. In many cases, adolescent girls and boys show these behaviors even more intensely when they interact with opposite-sexed peers, especially with individuals they would like to date. Thus, female adolescents may behave in an affectionate, sensitive, charming, and soft-spoken manner, and male adolescents may behave in an assertive, cocky, cynical, and forceful way, because they perceive that such behaviors enhance their sexuality and attractiveness.

There have been few attempts to relate puberty's sexual changes to gender behavior. Researchers have found that sexual behavior is related to hormonal changes in puberty, at least for boys. For example, in one study, adolescent sex researcher Robert Udry (1990) found that rising androgen levels were related to boys' increased sexual activity. For adolescent girls, androgen levels and sexual activity were associated, but girls' sexual activity was more strongly influenced by the type of friends they had than by their hormone levels. In the same study, Udry investigated whether hormone increases in puberty were related to gender behaviors, such as being affectionate, charming, assertive, and cynical, but found no significant associations.

While puberty's biological changes set the stage for increased incorporation of sexuality into gender behavior, how sexuality becomes a part of gender is determined by such social influences as cultural standards for sex and peer group norms for dating (Brooks-Gunn & Reiter, 1990). In the earlier discussion of gender-role intensification in early adolescence, the main explanation for increased differences in gender behavior was the increased socialization to conform to traditional masculine and feminine roles. However, as mentioned, puberty plays a role in gender intensification since it is a signaling to socializing others—such as parents, peers, and teachers—that the adolescent is beginning to approach adulthood and, therefore, should begin to act in ways that resemble the stereotypical female or male adult.

In sum, gender intensification in adolescence likely includes not only increased social pressures to conform to traditional masculine and feminine roles but also pubertal changes that introduce sexuality into gender behavior. Masculinity and femininity are renegotiated during adolescence, and much of this renegotiation involves sexuality (Bancroft, 1990).

Freud and Erikson—Anatomy Is Destiny

Both Sigmund Freud and Erik Erikson argued that an individual's genitals influence his or her gender behavior and, therefore, that anatomy is destiny. One of Freud's basic assumptions was that human behavior and history are directly related to reproductive processes. From this assumption arose his belief that gender and sexual behavior are essentially unlearned and instinctual. Erikson (1968) extended Freud's argument, claiming that the psychological differences between males and females stem from their anatomical differences. Erikson argued that, because of genital structure, males are more intrusive and aggressive, females more inclusive and passive. Critics of the anatomy-is-destiny view believe that experience is not given enough credit. The critics say that females and males are more free to choose their gender role than Freud and Erikson allow. In response to the critics, Erikson modified his view, saying that females in today's world are transcending their biological heritage and correcting society's overemphasis on male intrusiveness.

Social Influences

In American culture, adults discriminate between the sexes shortly after the infant's birth. The "pink and blue" treatment may be applied to boys and girls before they even leave the hospital. Soon afterward, differences in hairstyles, clothes, and toys become obvious. Adults and peers reward these differences throughout development. And boys and girls learn gender roles through imitation or observational learning by watching what other people say and do. In recent years, the idea that parents are the critical socialization agents in gender-role development has come under fire (Huston, 1983; Huston & Alvarez, 1990). Parents are only one of the sources through which the individual learns gender roles.

Culture, schools, peers, the media, and other family members are others. Yet, especially in the early years of development, parents may be the most important influences on gender development.

Parental Influences

Parents, by action and example, influence their children's and adolescents' gender development. During the transition from childhood to adolescence, parents allow boys more independence than girls, and concern about girls' sexual vulnerability may cause parents to monitor their behavior more closely and ensure that they are chaperoned. Families with young adolescent daughters indicate that they experience more intense conflict about sex, choice of friends, and curfews than families with young adolescent sons (Papini & Sebby, 1988). When parents place severe restrictions on their adolescent sons, it is disruptive to their sons' development (Baumrind, 1991a).

Parents often have different expectations for their adolescent sons and daughters, especially in such academic areas as math and science. For example, many parents believe that math is more important for their sons' futures than for their daughters', and their beliefs influence the value adolescents place on math achievement (Eccles, 1987). More about gender and achievement appears later in the chapter.

Social learning theory has been especially important in understanding social influences on gender. The **social learning theory of gender** *emphasizes that children's and adolescents' gender development occurs through observation and imitation of gender behavior, and through rewards and punishments they experience for gender appropriate and inappropriate behavior.* By observing parents and other adults, as well as peers, at home, at school, in the neighborhood, and in the media, adolescents are exposed to a myriad of models who display masculine and feminine behavior. And parents often use rewards and punishments to teach their daughters to be feminine ("Karen, that dress you are wearing makes you look so pretty") and their sons to be masculine ("Bobby, you were so aggressive in that game. Way to go!").

One major change in the gender role models adolescents have been exposed to in recent years is the increase in working mothers. Most adolescents today have a mother who is employed at least part-time. Although maternal employment is not specific to adolescence, it does influence gender-role development, and its influence likely depends on the age of the child or adolescent involved. Young adolescents may be especially attuned to understanding adult roles, so their mothers' role choices may be important influences on their concepts and attitudes about women's roles (Huston & Alvarez, 1990). Adolescents with working mothers have less stereotyped concepts of female roles (and sometimes male roles as well) than adolescents whose mothers are full-time homemakers. They also have more positive attitudes about nontraditional roles for women. Daughters of employed mothers have higher educational and occupational aspirations than daughters of homemakers (Hoffman, 1989). Thus, working mothers often serve as models who combine traditional feminine home roles with less traditional activities away from home.

Peers

Parents provide the earliest discrimination of gender behavior, but before long, peers join in the societal process of responding to and modeling masculine and feminine behavior. In middle and late childhood, children show a clear preference for being with and liking same-sex peers (Maccoby, 1990; Maccoby & Jacklin, in press). After extensive observations of elementary school playgrounds, two researchers characterized the play settings as "gender school," pointing out that boys teach one another the required masculine behavior and reinforce it, and that girls also teach one another the required feminine behavior and reinforce it (Luria & Herzog, 1985).

In earlier chapters, we learned that adolescents spend increasing amounts of time with peers. In adolescence, peer approval or disapproval is a powerful influence on gender attitudes and behavior. Peers may socialize gender behavior partly by accepting or rejecting others on the basis of their gender-related attributes. Deviance from sex-typed norms often leads to low peer acceptance, but within a broad range of normal behavior, it is not clear that conformity to sex-typed personality attributes is a good predictor of peer acceptance (Huston & Alvarez, 1990).

Schools and Teachers

In a Gallup poll, 80 percent of the respondents agreed that the federal government should promote educational programs intended to reduce such social problems as poverty and unequal educational opportunities for minorities and females (Gallup & Clark, 1987). Discriminatory treatment involving gender involves all ability groups, but in many cases, the stereotypically lower-valued group (by sex, by ethnicity, and so on) is treated similarly to the lower-valued ability group. For example, girls with strong math abilities frequently are given fewer quality instructional interactions from teachers than their male counterparts (Eccles, MacIver, & Lange, 1986). And, ethnic minority females are given fewer teacher interactions than other females, who are given fewer than Black males, who are given fewer than White males (Sadker, Sadker, & Klein, 1986).

In one research study, researchers were trained in an observation system to collect data in more than a hundred fourth-, sixth-, and eighth-grade classrooms (Sadker & Sadker, 1986). At all three grade levels, male students were involved in more interactions than female students, and male students received more attention from teachers. Male students also were given more remediation, more criticism, and more praise than female students.

Historically, education in the United States has been male defined rather than gender balanced. In many instances, traditional male activities, especially White male activities, have been the educational norm. Although females mature earlier, are ready for verbal and math training at a younger age, and have control of small-motor skills earlier than males, educational curricula have been constructed mainly to mirror the development of males. Decisions about the grade in which students should read *Huckleberry Finn,* do long division, or begin to write essays are based primarily on male developmental patterns. Some experts believe that this state of educational affairs means that some girls may become bored or give up, with most girls learning simply to hold back, be quiet, and smile (Shakeshaft, 1986).

A special concern is that most middle and junior high schools consist of independent, masculine learning environments, which appear better suited to the learning style of the average adolescent boy than to that of the average adolescent girl (Huston & Alvarez, 1990). Middle and junior high schools provide a more impersonal environment than elementary schools, which meshes better with the autonomous orientation of male adolescents than the relationship, connectedness orientation of female adolescents.

Mass Media Influences

As already described, adolescents encounter male and female roles in their everyday interactions with parents, peers, and teachers. The messages about

A special concern is that, because they are more impersonal and encourage independence more than elementary schools, most middle and junior high schools are better suited to the learning styles of males.

gender roles carried by the mass media also are important influences on adolescents' gender development (Condry, 1989; Huston & Alvarez, 1990; Morgan, 1987).

Early adolescence may be a period of heightened sensitivity to television messages about gender roles (Huston & Alvarez, 1990). Young adolescents increasingly view programs designed for adults that include messages about gender-appropriate behavior, especially in heterosexual relationships. Cognitively, adolescents engage in more idealistic thoughts than children, and television certainly has its share of idealized characters with whom adolescents can identify and imitate—highly appealing models who are young, glamorous, and successful (Durkin, 1985).

The world of television is highly gender-stereotyped and conveys clear messages about the relative power and importance of women and men (Condry, 1989; Huston & Alvarez, 1990). Males are overrepresented, and females are underrepresented: On virtually every type of program, males outnumber females by approximately two or three to one (Williams & others, 1986). Men and women usually engage in sex-typed occupational and family roles. In the 1970s, female characters appeared more often than males in the contexts of the home, romance, and physical appearance, males more frequently than females in the contexts of work, cars, and sports. By the mid-1980s, when females were portrayed outside the home, their roles were almost as likely to be nontraditional (for example, police officer or attorney) as traditional (for example, secretary or nurse). Men continued to be shown almost entirely in traditional male occupations. In one analysis, women were shown as sexual objects (that is, in scanty clothing or engaged in sexually provocative behavior) in 35 percent of the commercial television programs in 1985 (Williams & others, 1986). Such portrayals are even more frequent on music videos. Male characters are portrayed more often than female characters as aggressive, dominant, competent, autonomous, and active, while female characters are more often portrayed as passive.

Researchers who have studied early adolescent television viewing have found that it influences early adolescents' gender-role attitudes and behavior (Morgan, 1982, 1987). The researchers adopt the assumption that television carries sexist messages and that the more one is exposed, the greater the number of stereotyped messages likely received. In one investigation of eighth-grade boys and girls, heavy television viewing predicted an increased tendency to endorse traditional gender-role divisions of labor with respect to household chores (Morgan, 1987).

If television can communicate sexist messages and influence adolescents' gender behavior, might nonstereotyped gender messages on television reduce sexist behavior? One major effort to reduce gender-role stereotypes was the television series "Freestyle" (Williams, LaRose, & Frost, 1981). The series was designed to counteract the effects of career and ethnic stereotypes on the career interests of 9- to 12-year-olds. The series was somewhat successful in countering gender stereotypes, and girls who saw the series said that they would participate in athletics and engage in mechanical activities more than their counterparts who did not watch the series (Johnston & Ettema, 1982). The producers of the series hoped that it would encourage girls to show a stronger interest in math and science careers, but the results of the research study revealed that it did not.

Cognitive Influences

So far, we have discussed a number of biological and social influences on adolescents' gender behavior. Cognitive theories stress that adolescents actively construct their gender world. In this section, we look at two cognitive theories: the cognitive developmental theory of gender and gender schema theory.

Cognitive Developmental Theory

In the *cognitive developmental theory of gender,* children's gender-typing occurs after they have developed a concept of gender. Once they begin to consistently conceive of themselves as male or female, children often organize their world on the basis of gender. Based on Piaget's theory and initially proposed by developmentalist Lawrence Kohlberg (1966), the cognitive developmental theory of gender proceeds in the following fashion: A young girl decides, "I am a girl. I want to do girl things; therefore, the opportunity to do girl things is rewarding." Having acquired the ability to categorize, children strive toward consistency in using categories and in their behavior.

Kohlberg's cognitive developmental theory emphasizes that the main changes in gender development occur in childhood. By the concrete operational stage (the third stage in Piaget's theory, entered at six to seven years of age), children understand gender constancy—that a male is still a male regardless of whether he wears pants or a skirt, or whether his hair is short or long, for example (Tavris & Wade, 1984).

Are there any cognitive developmental changes in adolescence that might influence gender behavior? The abstract, idealized, logical characteristics of formal operational thought mean that adolescents now have the cognitive capacity to analyze their self and decide what they want their gender identity to be. Adolescence is the developmental period when individuals begin to focus increased attention on vocational and life-style choices. With their increased cognitive skills, adolescents become more aware of the gender-based nature of vocational and life-style behavior. As adolescents pursue an identity—who am I, what am I all about, and where am I going in life—gender roles are one area in which they have choices to make. Recall from the discussion of gender and identity in the last chapter that, as females have developed stronger vocational interests, sex differences that once revealed that adolescent males explore and make commitments to a vocational role more than adolescent females are now turning into similarities. However, as adolescent females pursue an identity, they often show a greater interest in relationships and emotional bonds than adolescent males do. In sum, both the changes ushered in by formal operational thought and the increased interest in identity concerns lead adolescents to examine and redefine their gender attitudes and behavior.

Gender Schema Theory

A **schema** *is a cognitive structure involving a network of associations that organizes and guides an individual's perceptions.* **Gender schema theory** *states that an individual's attention and behavior are guided by an internal motivation to conform to gender-based sociocultural standards and stereotypes* (Bem, 1981; Levy & Carter, 1989; Martin, 1989). Gender schema theory suggests that gender-typing occurs when individuals are ready to encode and organize information along the lines of what is considered appropriate or typical for males and females in society. Gender schema theory emphasizes the active construction of gender but also accepts that societies determine which schema are important and the associations involved. In most cultures, these definitions involve a sprawling network of gender-linked associations, which encompass not only features directly related to female and male persons—such as anatomy, reproductive function, division of labor, and personality attributes—but also features more remotely or metaphorically related to sex, such as an abstract shape's angularity or roundness and the periodicity of the moon. No other dichotomy of life's experiences seems to have as many features linked to it as does the distinction between being male and being female (Doyle & Paludi, 1991).

Concept Table 11.1

The Nature of Gender, Gender Intensification in Adolescence, and Biological, Cognitive, and Social Influences on Gender

Concept	Processes/Related Ideas	Characteristics/Description
What is gender?	The nature of gender and gender roles	Gender refers to the sociocultural dimension of being male or female. Gender role is a set of expectations that prescribes how females or males should think, act, and feel.
Developmental changes and gender intensification	Their nature	As females and males experience many physical and social changes during early adolescence, they have to come to terms with new definitions of their gender roles. During early adolescence, individuals develop the adult, physical aspects of their gender. The gender intensification hypothesis states that psychological and behavioral differences between boys and girls become greater during early adolescence because of increased socialization pressures to conform to traditional masculine and feminine gender roles. Puberty's role in gender intensification may involve a signaling to socializing others that the adolescent is beginning to approach adulthood and, therefore, should begin to act more in ways that resemble the stereotypical female or male adult.
Biological influences on gender	Pubertal change and sexuality	Pubertal change contributes to an increased incorporation of sexuality into the gender attitudes and behavior of adolescents. As their bodies are flooded with hormones, many girls desire to be the very best female possible, and many boys desire to be the very best male possible. Researchers have found that hormonal changes in puberty are related to sexual activity, but puberty's effects are socially mediated. Thus, while puberty's biological changes set the stage for increased incorporation of sexuality into gender behavior, how sexuality influences gender is often mediated by such sociocultural influences as cultural standards for sex and peer group norms for dating. In sum, masculinity and femininity are renegotiated during adolescence, and much of this renegotiation involves sexuality.
	Freud and Erikson-anatomy is destiny	Both Freud and Erikson argued that anatomy is destiny; that is, that psychological differences between males and females stem from their anatomical differences. For example, Erikson stressed that, because of their genital structure, males are more intrusive and aggressive, females more inclusive and passive. The critics say that females and males are more free to choose their gender behavior than Freud and Erikson postulate. Even Erikson has modified his view in this direction.
Social influences on gender	Parental influences	Parents, by action and by example, influence their children's and adolescents' gender development. During the transition to adolescence, parents allow boys more freedom than girls, and families with young adolescent girls report more conflicts about sex, choice of friends, and curfews than families with young adolescent boys. The social learning theory of gender emphasizes that children's and adolescents' gender development occurs through observation and imitation of gender behavior, and through rewards and punishments for gender-appropriate and gender-inappropriate behavior. One major change in the gender role models adolescents have been exposed to in recent years is the increase in working mothers, which influences adolescents' gender development, especially decreasing their stereotyping of gender roles.

As a real-life example of gender schema's influence on adolescents, consider a 17-year-old high school student deciding which hobby to try from among the many available possibilities. The student could ask about how expensive each possibility is, whether it can be done in cold weather, whether or not it can be done during the school week, whether it will interfere with studying, and so on. But the adolescent also is likely to look at the hobby through the lens of gender and ask: "What sex is the hobby? What sex am I? Do they match? If so, I will consider the hobby further. If not, I will reject it." This student may not be consciously aware of his or her gender schema's influence on the decision of which hobby to pursue. Indeed, in many of our everyday encounters, we are not consciously aware of how gender schema affects our behavior.

Concept Table 11.1

The Nature of Gender, Gender Intensification in Adolescence, and Biological, Cognitive, and Social Influences on Gender

Concept	Processes/Related Ideas	Characteristics/Description
	Peers	Adolescents spend increasing amounts of time with peers, and peer approval or disapproval can be a powerful influence on adolescents' gender behavior. Deviance from sex-typed norms often leads to peer disapproval.
	Schools and teachers	Historically, in the United States, education has been male-defined rather than gender-balanced. Males receive more attention in schools than females. A special concern is that most middle and junior high schools are better suited to the learning styles of males than females because of their impersonal, independent environment.
	Mass media	Early adolescence may be a period of heightened sensitivity to television messages about gender roles, especially gender-appropriate behavior in heterosexual relationships. The idealized characters on television may appeal to the idealized nature of adolescent thought. The world of television is highly gender-stereotyped and conveys the message that females are less powerful and less important than males. The sexist messages of television increase young adolescents' endorsement of traditional gender-role divisions of labor. One television series, "Freestyle," attempted to reduce adolescents' gender stereotyping but had mixed results.
Cognitive influences on gender	Cognitive developmental changes	In the cognitive developmental theory of gender, proposed by Kohlberg, children's gender-typing occurs after they have developed a concept of gender. Kohlberg's theory argues that the main gender changes occur in childhood. In addition to Kohlberg's theory, the changes ushered in by formal operational thought—abstract, idealized, and organized thinking—and the increased interest in identity concerns lead adolescents to examine and redefine their gender attitudes and behavior.
	Gender schema theory	Gender schema theory states that an individual's attention and behavior are guided by an internal motivation to conform to gender-based sociocultural standards and stereotypes. In most cultures, adolescents learn a sprawling network of gender-linked associations that they incorporate into their gender schema.

At this point, we have discussed a number of ideas about what gender is, gender intensification, and biological, social, and cognitive influences on gender. A summary of these ideas is presented in Concept Table 11.1. Next, we turn our attention to the nature of gender stereotypes, similarities, differences, and achievement.

Gender Stereotypes, Similarities, Differences, and Achievement

How pervasive is gender stereotyping of adolescents? What are the real differences in adolescents' gender behavior? What is gender's role in achievement? We consider each of these questions in turn.

Gender-Role Stereotyping

Gender-role stereotypes *are broad categories that reflect our impressions and beliefs about males and females.* All stereotypes, whether based on gender, ethnicity, or other groupings, refer to an image of the typical member of a particular social category. The world is extremely complex. Every day, we are confronted with thousands of different stimuli. The use of stereotypes is one way we simplify this complexity. If we simply assign a label (such as the quality of "softness") to someone, we then have much less to consider when we think about the individual. However, once labels are assigned, they are remarkably difficult to abandon, even in the face of contradictory evidence.

Many stereotypes are so general that they are ambiguous. Consider the stereotypes for "masculine" and "feminine." Diverse behaviors can be called on to support each stereotype, such as scoring a touchdown or growing facial hair for "masculine" and playing with dolls or wearing lipstick for "feminine." The stereotype may be modified in the face of cultural change. At one point in history, muscular development may be thought of as masculine; at another point, a more lithe, slender physique may be the stereotype. The behaviors popularly agreed upon as reflecting a stereotype also may fluctuate according to socioeconomic circumstances. For example, a lower socioeconomic group might be more likely than higher socioeconomic groups to include "rough and tough" as part of a masculine stereotype.

Even though the behaviors that are supposed to fit the stereotype often do not, the label itself can have significant consequences for the individual. Labeling a male "feminine" and a female "masculine" can produce significant social reactions to the individuals in terms of status and acceptance in groups, for example (Mischel, 1970).

Stereotyping of females and males is pervasive. A far-ranging study of college students in 30 countries showed that males were widely believed to be dominant, independent, aggressive, achievement oriented, and enduring, while females were widely believed to be nurturant, affiliative, less esteemed, and more helpful in times of distress (Williams & Best, 1982).

In a more recent investigation, males and females who lived in more highly developed countries perceived themselves more similarly than males and females who lived in less developed countries (Williams & Best, 1989). In the more highly developed countries, females are more likely to attend college and be gainfully employed. Thus, as sexual equality increases, stereotypes, as well as actual behavioral differences, between males and females may diminish. In this investigation, females were more likely to perceive similarity between the sexes than males were (Williams & Best, 1989). In addition, the sexes were perceived more similarly in Christian societies than in Muslim societies. Next, we go beyond stereotyping and examine the behavioral similarities of and differences between the sexes.

Gender Similarities and Differences

There is a growing belief in gender research that differences between the sexes have often been exaggerated (Hyde, 1981; Hyde, in press). As mentioned in the discussion of reducing sexist research in psychology in Chapter 2, it is not unusual to find such statements as: "While only 32 percent of the females were found to . . . fully 37 percent of the males were. . . ." This difference of 5 percent likely is a very small difference and may or may not even be statistically significant or capable of being replicated in a separate study (Denmark & others,

1988). And when statements are made about female-male comparisons, such as "Males outperform females in math," this does not mean all females versus all males. Rather, it usually means that the average math achievement scores for males at certain ages are higher than the average math achievement scores for females. The math achievement scores of females and males overlap considerably, so that while an *average* difference may favor males, many females have higher math achievement than many males. Further, there is a tendency to think of differences between females and males as biologically based, when, in fact, they may be socioculturally based.

Let us now examine some of the differences between the sexes, keeping in mind that (1) the differences are averages, not all females versus all males; (2) even when differences are reported, there is considerable overlap between the sexes; and (3) the differences may be due primarily to biological factors, sociocultural factors, or both. First, we examine physical and biological differences, then cognitive and social differences.

From conception on, females are less likely to die or to develop physical or mental disorders than males. Estrogen strengthens the immune system, making females more resistant to infection, for example. Female hormones also signal the liver to produce more "good" cholesterol, which makes their blood vessels more elastic than those of males. Testosterone triggers the production of low-density lipoprotein, which clogs blood vessels. Males have twice the risk of coronary disease as females. Higher levels of stress hormones cause faster clotting in males, but also higher blood pressure than in females. Adult females have about twice the body fat of their male counterparts, most concentrated around breasts and hips. In males, fat is more likely to go to the abdomen. Males grow an average of 10 percent taller than females. Male hormones promote the growth of long bones; female hormones stop such growth at puberty. In sum, there are many physical differences between females and males. But are there as many cognitive differences?

In a classic review of gender differences, Eleanor Maccoby and Carol Jacklin (1974) concluded that males have better math skills and better visuospatial ability (the kind of skills an architect would need to design a building's angles and dimensions), while females have better verbal abilities. Later, Maccoby (1987) revised her conclusion, commenting that the accumulation of research evidence now indicates that the verbal differences in males and females have virtually disappeared but that the math and visuospatial differences are still present.

A number of researchers in the gender area point out that there are more cognitive similarities between females and males than differences. They also believe that the differences that do exist, such as the math and visuospatial differences, have been exaggerated. Males do outperform females in math, but only for a certain portion of the population—the gifted (Hyde, in press; Linn & Hyde, 1991). Further, males do not always outperform females on all visuospatial tasks: Consistent differences occur only in the ability to rotate objects mentally (Linn & Petersen, 1986). Also, as mentioned earlier, considerable overlap exists between females and males, even when differences are reported. Figure 11.1 shows the small average difference on visuospatial tasks that favors males but also clearly reveals the substantial overlap in the visuospatial abilities of females and males. This information, combined with the recent data on convergence in the verbal abilities of males and females (females used to have higher scores on the verbal section of the SAT, but now there are no differences, for example), leads to the conclusion that cognitive differences between females and males do not exist in many areas, are disappearing in other areas, and are small when they do exist (Benbow, 1992; Linn & Hyde, 1991).

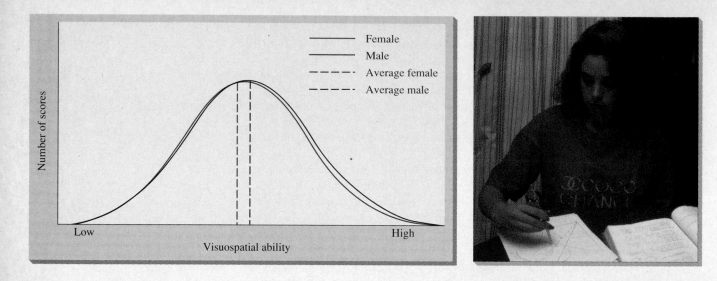

Figure 11.1 The small average difference and substantial overlap between females and males on visuospatial ability. Notice that, while the average male's visuospatial ability is higher than the average female's, the overlap between the sexes is substantial. Not all males have better visuospatial ability than all females. The substantial overlap indicates that, while the average score of males is higher, many females outperform many males on such tasks.

The most consistent gender differences in social behavior are that males are more active and more aggressive than females (Maccoby, 1987; Maccoby & Jacklin, 1974). The difference in aggression appears in children's development and is often present as early as two years of age. With regard to emotions, males and females do not experience different emotions, but they frequently differ in how they express their emotions and in what emotions they feel free to express in public (Doyle & Paludi, 1991). Females grow up to smile more and to "read" emotions better than males (Malatesta, 1990). And by elementary school, girls show more helping and care-giving behavior (Zahn-Waxler, 1990). However, in cultures where boys and girls both care for younger siblings, boys and girls show more similar nurturant behavior (Whiting, 1989). Girls also have a wider social network than boys do (Zahn-Waxler, 1990).

Achievement

For some areas of achievement, gender differences are so large that they can best be described as nonoverlapping. For example, no major league baseball players are female, and 96 percent of all registered nurses are female. In contrast, many measures of achievement-related behaviors yield no gender differences. For example, girls show just as much persistence at tasks. The question of whether males and females differ in their expectations for success at various achievement tasks is not yet settled (Eccles, 1987; Meese, Wigfield, & Eccles, 1990).

Because females are often stereotyped as less competent than males, incorporation of gender-role stereotypes into an adolescent's self-concept could lead girls to have less confidence than boys in their general intellectual abilities and to have lower expectations for success at difficult academic and vocational activities. It also could lead girls to expect to have to work harder to achieve success at these activities than boys expect to have to work. Evidence supports these predictions (Eccles, Harold-Goldsmith, & Miller, 1989). Either of these beliefs could keep girls from selecting demanding educational or vocational options, especially if these options are not perceived as important or interesting.

Gender roles also could produce different expectations for success, depending on the gender stereotyping of the activity. Both educational programs and vocational options are gender stereotyped in the American culture. Many high-level professions, especially those that are math-related and scientific/technical, are thought to be male activities. In contrast, teaching below the college

One of the most consistent differences between males and females is the greater aggression of males. This difference was found in the early 1970s and continues to be evident in recent investigations.

level, working in clerical and related support jobs, and excelling in language-related courses are thought to be female activities by both adolescents and adults (Eccles, 1987; Eccles & Hoffman, 1984; Huston, 1983). Incorporation of these beliefs into self-concept could cause girls to have lower expectations for success in male-typed activities and higher expectations for success in female-typed activities. This pattern could lead girls to select female-typed activities over male-typed activities. Some support for this perspective has been found (Eccles, 1987). At times, though, researchers have found no gender differences in achievement expectations.

An intriguing view about gender roles and achievement argues that, on the basis of an instrumental-achievement (male) versus expressive-affiliation (female) dichotomy, we might expect male superiority in achievement patterns. This is not always the case. In an investigation by Lloyd Lueptow (1984), adolescent girls had both higher levels of achievement-value orientations and higher levels of academic achievement than did adolescent boys. Achievement may be a stronger component of the female gender role than the male gender role. Or a distinction may be necessary between achievement based on excellence and accomplishment (a stronger focus of females) and achievement based on assertion and aggressive competition (a stronger focus of males). That is, females may be stronger achievers, males stronger competitors. Since researchers often have neglected this distinction, the achievement orientation of females may have been underestimated. More about gender and achievement appears in Chapter 14, where we focus on gender and career development.

Male-female ratios in computer classes range from two to one to five to one.

Gender-Role Classification

How have gender roles been viewed historically? What is androgyny and is it the best gender role to adopt? Might adolescent males who identify with a traditional masculine role be prone to problem behaviors? What is gender role transcendence? We consider each of these questions in turn.

A Historical Perspective on Gender Roles

Not that long ago, it was accepted that boys should grow up to be masculine and that girls should grow up to be feminine, that boys are made of frogs and snails and puppy dogs' tails and that girls are made of sugar and spice and all that's nice. Today, diversity characterizes gender roles and the feedback that individuals receive from their culture. A girl's mother might promote femininity, the girl might be close friends with a tomboy, and the girl's teachers at school might encourage her assertiveness.

In the past, the well-adjusted male was expected to be independent, aggressive, and power oriented. The well-adjusted female was expected to be dependent, nurturant, and uninterested in power. Further, masculine characteristics were considered healthy and good by society, while female characteristics were considered undesirable. A classic study in the early 1970s summarized the traits and behaviors that college students believed were characteristic of males and those they believed were characteristic of females. (Broverman & others, 1972). The traits clustered into two groups labeled "instrumental" and "expressive." The instrumental traits paralleled the male's purposeful, competent entry into the outside world to gain goods for his family; the expressive traits paralleled the female's responsibility to be warm and emotional in the home.

Such stereotypes are more harmful to females than to males because the characteristics assigned to males are more valued than those assigned to females.

Table 11.1   The Bem Sex-Role Inventory: Are You Androgynous?

The following items are from the Bem Sex-Role Inventory. To find out whether you score as androgynous, first rate yourself on each item, on a scale from 1 (never or almost never true) to 7 (always or almost always true).

1. self-reliant	16. strong personality	31. makes decisions easily	46. aggressive
2. yielding	17. loyal	32. compassionate	47. gullible
3. helpful	18. unpredictable	33. sincere	48. inefficient
4. defends own beliefs	19. forceful	34. self-sufficient	49. acts as a leader
5. cheerful	20. feminine	35. eager to soothe hurt feelings	50. childlike
6. moody	21. reliable	36. conceited	51. adaptable
7. independent	22. analytical	37. dominant	52. individualistic
8. shy	23. sympathetic	38. soft-spoken	53. does not use harsh language
9. conscientious	24. jealous	39. likable	54. unsystematic
10. athletic	25. has leadership abilities	40. masculine	55. competitive
11. affectionate	26. sensitive to the needs of others	41. warm	56. loves children
12. theatrical	27. truthful	42. solemn	57. tactful
13. assertive	28. willing to take risks	43. willing to take a stand	58. ambitious
14. flatterable	29. understanding	44. tender	59. gentle
15. happy	30. secretive	45. friendly	60. conventional

SCORING

(a) Add up your ratings for items 1, 4, 7, 10, 13, 16, 19, 22, 25, 28, 31, 34, 37, 40, 43, 46, 49, 52, 55, and 58. Divide the total by 20. That is your masculinity score.
(b) Add up your ratings for items 2, 5, 8, 11, 14, 17, 20, 23, 26, 29, 32, 35, 38, 41, 44, 47, 50, 53, 56, and 59. Divide the total by 20. That is your femininity score.
(c) If your masculinity score is above 4.9 (the approximate median for the masculinity scale) and your femininity score is above 4.9 (the approximate femininity median), then you would be classified as androgynous on Bem's scale.

From Janet S. Hyde, *Half the Human Experience: The Psychology of Women,* 3d ed. Copyright © 1985 D. C. Heath and Company, Lexington, MA. Reprinted by permission.

These beliefs and stereotypes have led to the negative treatment of females because of their sex, or what is called *sexism.* Females receive less attention in schools; are less visible in leading roles on television; are rarely depicted as competent, dominant characters in children's books; are paid less than males even when they have more education; and are underrepresented in decision-making roles throughout our society, from corporate executive suites to Congress.

Androgyny

In the 1970s, as both males and females became dissatisfied with the burdens imposed by their strictly stereotyped roles, alternatives to "masculinity" and "femininity" were explored. Instead of thinking of masculinity and femininity as a continuum, with more of one meaning less of the other, it was proposed that individuals could show both *expressive* and *instrumental* traits. This thinking led to the development of the concept of **androgyny,** *the presence of desirable masculine and feminine characteristics in the same individual* (Bem, 1977; Spence & Helmreich, 1978). The androgynous individual might be a male who is assertive (masculine) and nurturant (feminine), or a female who is dominant (masculine) and sensitive to others' feelings (feminine).

Measures have been developed to assess androgyny. One of the most widely used gender measures is the Bem Sex-Role Inventory, constructed by a leading early proponent of androgyny, Sandra Bem. Table 11.1 presents sample items from Bem's Sex-Role Inventory. Based on their responses to the items in the Bem Sex-Role Inventory, individuals are classified as having one of four gender-role

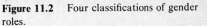

Figure 11.2 Four classifications of gender roles.

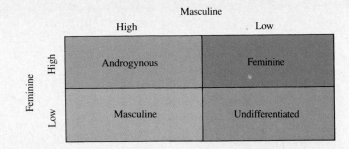

(a)

(b)

orientations: masculine, feminine, androgynous, or undifferentiated (see Figure 11.2). The androgynous individual is simply a male or female who has a high degree of both feminine (expressive) and masculine (instrumental) traits. No new characteristics are used to describe the androgynous individual. An undifferentiated individual is neither high on masculine nor feminine traits. Androgynous individuals are described as more flexible and more mentally healthy than either masculine or feminine individuals. Individuals who are undifferentiated are the least competent. To some degree, though, the context influences which gender role is most adaptive. In close relationships, a feminine or androgynous gender role may be more desirable because of the expressive nature of such relationships. However, a masculine or androgynous gender role may be more desirable in academic and work settings because of the instrumental nature of these settings. The culture in which individuals live also plays an important role in determining what is adaptive. On the one hand, increasing numbers of children and adolescents in the United States and other modernized countries such as Sweden are being raised to behave in androgynous ways. On the other hand, traditional gender roles continue to dominate the cultures of many countries around the world. Sociocultural Worlds of Adolescence 11.1 discusses traditional gender-role practices in Egypt and China.

(a) The femininity dimension of androgyny involves nurturance and sensitivity to others' feelings, as reflected in the gregarious behavior of this group of adolescent girls. (b) The masculine dimension of androgyny involves assertiveness and dominance, as reflected in the behavior of these adolescent boys.

382

Gender Roles in Egypt and China

In recent decades, roles assumed by males and females in the United States have become increasingly similar—that is, androgynous. In many countries, though, gender roles have remained more gender specific. For example, in Egypt, the division of labor between Egyptian males and females is dramatic: Egyptian males are socialized to work in the public sphere, females in the private world of home and child rearing. The Islamic religion dictates that the man's duty is to provide for his family, the woman's duty to care for her family and household (Dickersheid & others, 1988). Any deviations from this traditional gender-role orientation are severely disapproved of.

Egypt is not the only country in which males and females are socialized to behave, think, and feel in strongly gender-specific ways. Kenya and Nepal are two other cultures in which children are brought up under very strict gender-specific guidelines (Munroe, Himmin, & Munroe, 1984). In the People's Republic of China, the female's status has historically been lower than the male's. The teachings of the fifth century B.C. Chinese philosopher Confucius were used to reinforce the concept of the female as an inferior being. Beginning with the 1949 revolution in China, women began to achieve more economic freedom and more equal status in marital relationships. However, even with the sanctions of a socialist government, the old patriarchal traditions of male supremacy in China have not been completely uprooted. Chinese women still make considerably less money than Chinese men in comparable positions, and in rural China, a tradition of male supremacy still governs many women's lives.

Thus, while in China, females have made considerable strides, complete equality remains a distant objective. And in many cultures, such as Egypt and other countries where the Muslim religion predominates, gender-specific behavior is pronounced, and females are not given access to high-status positions.

In China, females and males are usually socialized to behave, feel, and think differently. The old patriarchal traditions of male supremacy have not been completely uprooted. Chinese women still make considerably less money than Chinese men, and, in rural China (such as here in the Lixian village of Sichuan), male supremacy still governs many women's lives.

In Egypt near the Aswan Dam, women are returning from the Nile River, where they have filled their water jugs. How might gender-role socialization for girls in Egypt compare to that in the United States?

PEANUTS reprinted by permission of UFS, Inc.

Can and should androgyny be taught to children and adolescents in school? In one investigation (Kahn & Richardson, 1983), tenth- through twelfth-grade students from three high schools in British Columbia were given a 20-unit course in gender roles. Students analyzed the history and modern development of male and female gender roles and evaluated the function of traditionally accepted stereotypes of males and females. The course centered on student discussion, supplemented by films, videotapes, and guest speakers. The materials included exercises to heighten awareness of one's own attitudes and beliefs, role reversal of typical gender-role behavior, role play of difficult work and family conflict circumstances, and assertiveness training for direct, honest communication.

A total of 59 students participated in the gender-role course. To determine whether the course changed the adolescents' gender-role orientation, these students were compared to 59 students from the same schools who did not take the gender-role course. Prior to the start of the course, all students were given the Bem Sex-Role Inventory. No differences between the two groups were found at that time. After the students completed the course, they and the control group were given the Attitudes toward Women Scale (Spence & Helmreich, 1972). In two of the schools, students who took the gender-role course had more liberal attitudes about the female's role in society than students who did not take the course. In these schools, the students were primarily girls who chose to take the course as an elective. In the third school, students who took the gender-role course actually had more conservative attitudes toward the female's role in society than those who did not. The gender-role class in the third school was required and was made up almost equally of males and females.

Another attempt to produce a more androgynous gender-role orientation in students also met with mixed results (Guttentag & Bray, 1976). The curriculum lasted for one year and was implemented in the kindergarten, fifth, and ninth grades. It involved books, discussion materials, and classroom exercises. The program was most successful with the fifth graders and least successful with the ninth graders, who actually displayed a boomerang effect of more rigid gender-role orientation. The program's success varied from class to class, seeming to be most effective when the teacher produced sympathetic reaction in the peer group. However, some classes ridiculed and rejected the curriculum.

Ethical concerns are aroused when the program involves teaching children and adolescents to depart from socially approved behavior patterns, especially when there is no evidence of extreme sex typing in the groups to whom the interventions are applied. The advocates of androgyny programs believe that traditional sex typing is psychologically harmful for all children and adolescents and that it has prevented many girls and women from experiencing equal opportunity. While some people believe that androgyny is more adaptive than either a traditional masculine or feminine pattern, ignoring the imbalance within our culture that values masculinity more than femininity is impossible (Huston, 1983).

Traditional Masculinity and Problem Behaviors in Adolescent Males

In our discussion of masculinity so far, we have described how the masculine role has been accorded a prominent status in the United States and in most other cultures as well. However, might there be a negative side to traditional masculinity, especially in adolescence? An increasing number of gender theorists and researchers believe there is.

Joseph Pleck and his colleagues (Pleck, 1983; Pleck, Sonnenstein, & Ku, in press) believe that what defines traditional masculinity in many Western societies includes engaging in certain behaviors that, while officially socially disapproved of, validate masculinity. That is, in the male adolescent culture, male adolescents perceive that they are more masculine, and that others will perceive them as more masculine, if they engage in premarital sex, drink alcohol and take drugs, and participate in illegal delinquent activities.

In one recent investigation, the gender role orientation and problem behaviors of 1,680 15–19-year-old males were assessed (Pleck, Sonnenstein, & Ku, in press). In this study—referred to as the National Survey of Adolescent Males— there was strong evidence that problem behaviors in adolescent males were associated with their attitudes toward masculinity. Adolescent males who reported traditional beliefs about masculinity (for example, endorsing such items as "A young man should be tough, even if he's not big," "It is essential for a guy to get respect from others," and "Men are always ready for sex") also were likely to say that they had school difficulties, engaged in alcohol and drug use, participated in delinquent activities, and were sexually active.

The idea that male problem behaviors have something to do with "masculinity" has recently gotten the attention of policy makers. U.S. Department of Health and Human Services Secretary Louis Sullivan (1991) called for action to address a generation whose manhood is measured by the caliber of gun he carries or the number of children he has fathered. In a similar vein, Virginia Governor Douglas Wilder (1991) urged policy makers to get across the message that, contrary to what many of today's youth think, making babies is no act of manhood. Addressing and challenging traditional beliefs about masculinity in adolescent males may have the positive outcome of helping to reduce their problem behaviors.

Gender-Role Transcendence

While androgyny was an improvement over the perspective that femininity and masculinity are opposite ends of gender, it has turned out to be less of a panacea than many of its early proponents envisioned (Doyle & Paludi, 1991). Some theorists, such as Joe Pleck (1981), believe that the concept of androgyny should be replaced with the concept of **gender-role transcendence,** *the belief that when an individual's competence is at issue, it should not be conceptualized on a masculine, feminine, or androgynous basis, but rather on a person basis. Thus, rather than merging their gender roles, Pleck stresses that females and males should go beyond specific gender-role characteristics and stereotypes, and think of people as people.* However, both the concepts of androgyny and gender-role transcendence divert attention from a female's unique needs and the power imbalance between females and males in most cultures.

The Feminist Perspective and Adolescence As a Critical Juncture in the Development of Females

Feminist scholars are developing new perspectives that focus on girls' and women's life experiences and development. We first discuss the nature of the feminist perspective and then turn our attention to Carol Gilligan's provocative thesis that adolescence is a critical juncture in the development of females.

The Feminist Perspective

The feminist perspective emphasizes: (1) girls and women as authorities about their own experiences, or as Harvard psychologist Carol Gilligan (1990) advocates, listening to female voices; (2) female ways of knowing (Belenky & others, 1986); (3) women's career and family roles (Baruch, Biener, & Barnett, 1987; Thompson, 1992); (4) abuse and rape of females (McBride, 1990; Russo, 1990); and (5) female experiences of connectedness and self-determination (Brown & Gilligan, 1990; Chodorow, 1989; Gilligan, Brown, & Rogers, 1990; Josselson, 1987; Lerner, 1989; Miller, 1986).

Jean Baker Miller (1976, 1986) has been an important voice in stimulating examination of psychological issues from a female perspective. She believes that the study of females' psychological development opens up paths to a better understanding of all psychological development. She also concludes that researchers who examine what females have been doing in life usually find that females spend much of their time actively participating in the development of others. In Miller's view, females often try to interact with others in ways that will foster the other person's development along many dimensions—emotionally, intellectually, and socially. Many females are very competent at building other people's strengths, resources, and well-being.

In Miller's, Gilligan's, and other feminists' perspectives, a female's sense of self is often organized around being able to make and then maintain affiliations and relationships. For many females, the threat of disruption of connections is perceived not just as a loss of a relationship, but as something closer to a total loss of self. Many feminist thinkers believe that it is important for females to not only maintain their competency in relationships, but to balance this other-oriented competence with an increased motivation for self-determination. Many females come from environments in which their lives were extensively determined by others as they grew up in a male-dominated culture that dictated what women should be like. Miller believes that, through increased self-determination, coupled with already-developed relationship skills, many females will discover the route to a deserved status of greater power in the American culture. And as feminist scholar Harriet Lerner (1989) concludes in her book *The Dance of Intimacy,* it is important for females to bring to their relationships nothing less than a strong, assertive, independent, and authentic self. She believes that competent

Carol Gilligan with some of the girls she has interviewed about their relationships with others. According to Gilligan, girls experience life differently than boys do; in Gilligan's words, girls have a "different voice." She believes that relationships color every aspect of a female's life. Girls use conversation to expand and understand relationships, and they see people as mutually dependent. Gilligan believes that adolescence is a special juncture in the development of females because it is during this time that girls become aware that their intense interest in intimacy is not prized by the male-dominated culture, even though society values women as caring and altruistic. The dilemma is that girls are presented with a choice that makes them look either selfish or selfless. Gilligan believes that, as adolescent girls experience this dilemma, they increasingly silence their distinctive voice. She thinks that society needs to acknowledge the authenticity and importance of females' distinctive relationship voices.

relationships are those in which the separate "I-ness" of both persons can be appreciated and enhanced while still staying emotionally connected to the significant other.

Gilligan's View of Adolescence As a Critical Juncture in the Development of Females

Carol Gilligan has conducted extensive interviews with girls from 6 to 18 years of age (Brown & Gilligan, 1990; Gilligan, 1990; Gilligan, Brown, & Rogers, 1990). She and her colleagues report that girls consistently reveal detailed knowledge about human relationships that is based on listening and watching what happens between people. According to Gilligan, girls can sensitively pick up different rhythms in relationships and often are able to follow the pathways of feelings. Gilligan believes that girls experience life differently than boys do; in Gilligan's words, girls have a "different voice."

Gilligan also believes that girls come to a critical juncture in their development when they reach adolescence. Gilligan says that, in early adolescence, (usually around 11 to 12 years of age), girls become aware that their intense interest in intimacy is not prized by the male-dominated culture, even though society values women as caring and altruistic. The dilemma, says Gilligan, is that girls are presented with a choice that makes them appear either selfish (if they become independent and self-sufficient) or selfless (if they remain responsive to others). Gilligan states that, as young adolescent girls experience this dilemma, they increasingly "silence" their "different voice." They become less confident and more tentative in offering their opinions, which often persists into adulthood. Some researchers believe that this self-doubt and ambivalence too often translates into depression and eating disorders among adolescent girls.

Some critics argue that Gilligan and her colleagues overemphasize differences in gender. One of those critics is developmentalist Eleanor Maccoby, who says that Gilligan exaggerates the differences in intimacy and connectedness between males and females. Other critics fault Gilligan's research strategy, which rarely includes a comparison group of boys or statistical analysis. Instead, Gilligan conducts extensive interviews with girls and then provides excerpts from the girls' narratives to buttress her ideas. Other critics fear that Gilligan's findings reinforce stereotypes—females as nurturing and sacrificing, for example—that might undermine females' struggle for equality. These critics say that Gilligan's "different voice" perhaps should be called "the voice of the victim." What we should be stressing, say these critics, is more opportunities for females to reach higher levels of achievement and self-determination.

In reply, revisionists such as Gilligan say that their work provides a way to liberate females and transform a society that has far too long discriminated against females. They also say that, if females' approach to life is acknowledged as authentic, women will no longer have to act like men. The revisionists argue that females' sensitivity in relationships is a special gift in our culture. Influenced by Gilligan's and other feminists' thinking, some schools are beginning to incorporate the feminine voice into their curriculum. For example, at the Emma Willard School in Troy, New York, the entire curriculum has been revamped to emphasize cooperation rather than competition, and to encourage girls to analyze and express ideas from their own perspective rather than responding in stereotyped or conformist ways. Perspective on Adolescent Development 11.1 offers more information about the adolescent girls at the Emma Willard School.

Whether you believe the connectionist arguments of Gilligan or the achievement/self-determination arguments of her critics, there is increasing evidence that adolescence is a critical juncture in the psychological development of

Carol Gilligan's Interviews with Adolescent Girls—Their Relational Worlds

Gilligan (1990) believes that adolescence may be an especially critical time in females' development because it poses a problem of connection that is not easily resolved. She says that, as girls grow up in Western culture, they face a tradition in which "human" for the most part has meant "male." Thus, as girls enter adolescence, they face a struggle—with the masculine, autonomous wall of Western culture. To find out more about the struggle and the wall, Gilligan and her colleagues (Gilligan, 1990; Gilligan, Lyons, & Hanmer, 1990; Gilligan, Rogers, & Brown, 1990; Gilligan, Ward, & Taylor, 1988) asked adolescent girls at the Emma Willard School in Troy, New York, and other schools to describe themselves, to talk about important relationships in their lives, to describe experiences of conflict and choice, to discuss their lives in school, and to envision what their future would be like.

Gilligan heard girls speak about storms in relationships and pleasure in relationships, about relational worlds through which at times they moved freely but which at other times seemed blocked or walled. One adolescent girl, Gail, told Gilligan that she had a problem standing between her and her ability to achieve anywhere near her full potential. Gail said that she did not know if she would ever understand what her problem was, but that someday maybe it would go away and then she would be happy. As the interview continued, Gail told Gilligan that she had come up against this big wall in her life, but she still could not explain exactly what the wall was. Later in her adolescence, as a senior in high school, Gail reflected on her years of growing up and said that one of her main problems had been keeping things to herself, especially things that bothered her. She went on to say that she now had a better understanding of why she had felt like she was up against a wall that she could not penetrate. Gail said that she had become aware that, throughout her childhood and adolescent years, she had interpreted her parents as saying to her: "Be as independent and self-sufficient as you can." Thus, Gail felt that she should solve her problems by herself rather than share them with her friends. The wall Gail spoke about was a blocking of her connections with others.

According to Gilligan, girls' wishes to make connections with others are reflected in the pleasure they find in relationships. For example, when Gilligan asked Molly whether she and her friend depended on each other, Molly said that they were so strong for each other because they had such a good time together, because they were so happy when they were around each other. And Susan told Gilligan that she and her mother depended on each other. Susan commented that she liked her mother's sense of humor and that her mother had the ability to detect when she was upset and to calm her down by talking things out with her.

Gilligan also believes that it is in close relationships that adolescent girls are most willing to argue or disagree. One adolescent girl, Anna, told Gilligan that, if you loved someone, you were usually comfortable enough with them to argue with them and say that you wanted them to see your side. Anna said that it was easier to fight with someone you loved because you knew that they would usually forgive you and would still be there after the disagreement.

In an interview with another adolescent girl, Lisa, Gilligan asked, "What is the worst thing that can happen in a relationship?" Lisa said that the worst thing would be not being able to talk to each other, especially if you depended on being able to talk to someone. In sum, Gilligan and her colleagues found that communication in close relationships is especially important in the development of female adolescents.

Carol Gilligan conducted extensive interviews with adolescent girls at the Emma Willard School in Troy, New York. Gilligan believes that early adolescence is a critical juncture in the development of females.

females. In a recent national survey, girls revealed a significantly greater drop in self-esteem during adolescence than boys (American Association of University Women, 1991). At ages 8 and 9, 60 percent of the girls were confident and assertive and felt positive about themselves, compared to 67 percent of the boys. However, over the next 8 years, the girls' self-esteem fell 31 percentage points— only 29 percent of high school girls felt positive about themselves. Across the same age range, boys' self-worth dropped 21 points—leaving 46 percent of the high school boys with high self-esteem, which makes for a gender gap of 17 percentage points.

At this point, we have discussed a number of ideas about gender stereotypes, similarities, differences, and achievement, about gender-role classification, and about the feminist perspective on gender and whether adolescence is a critical juncture in the development of females. A summary of these ideas is presented in Concept Table 11.2. In this chapter, we learned that gender roles are renegotiated during adolescence as boys and girls incorporate sexuality into their gender behavior. The next chapter is devoted exclusively to adolescent sexuality.

Summary

I. The Nature of Gender

Gender refers to the sociocultural dimension of being male or female. Gender role is a set of expectations that prescribes how females or males should think, act, and feel.

II. Developmental Changes and Gender Intensification

As males and females experience many physical and social changes during adolescence, they have to come to terms with new definitions of their gender roles. During early adolescence, individuals develop the adult, physical aspects of their gender. The gender intensification hypothesis states that psychological and behavioral differences between boys and girls become greater during early adolescence because of increased socialization pressures to conform to traditional masculine and feminine gender roles. Puberty's role in gender intensification may involve a signaling to socializing others that the adolescent is beginning to approach adulthood and, therefore, should begin to act more in ways that resemble the stereotypical female or male adult.

III. Biological Influences on Gender

Pubertal change contributes to an increased incorporation of sexuality into the gender attitudes and behavior of adolescents. As their bodies are flooded with hormones, many girls desire to be the very best female possible, and many boys desire to be the very best male possible. Researchers have found that hormonal changes in puberty are related to sexual activity, but puberty's effects are socially mediated. Thus, while puberty's biological changes set the stage for increased incorporation of sexuality into gender behavior, how sexuality influences gender is often mediated by such sociocultural influences as cultural standards for sex and peer group norms for dating. In sum, masculinity and femininity are renegotiated during adolescence, and much of this renegotiation involves sexuality. Both Freud and Erikson argued that anatomy is destiny; that is, that psychological differences between males and females stem from their anatomical differences. For example, Erikson stressed that, because of their genital structure, males are more intrusive and aggressive, females more inclusive and passive. The critics say that females and males are more free to choose their gender behavior than Freud and Erikson postulate. Even Erikson has modified his view in this direction.

Concept Table 11.2

Gender Stereotypes, Similarities, Differences, and Achievement; Gender-Role Classification; and the Feminist Perspective and Adolescence As a Special Juncture in the Development of Females

Concept	Processes/Related Ideas	Characteristics/Description
Gender stereotypes, similarities, differences, and achievement	Stereotypes	Gender-role stereotypes are broad categories that reflect our impressions and beliefs about males and females. These stereotypes are widespread around the world, especially emphasizing the male's power and the female's nurturance. However, in more highly developed countries, females and males are more likely to be perceived as similar.
	Similarities and differences	Many gender researchers believe that a number of differences between females and males have been exaggerated. In considering differences, researchers must recognize that the differences are averages, that there is considerable overlap between the sexes, and that the differences may be due primarily to biological factors, sociocultural factors, or both. There are a number of physical differences between the sexes, but cognitive differences are either small or nonexistent. At the level of the gifted, the average male does outperform the average female in math achievement. In terms of social behavior, males are more aggressive and active than females, but females are usually more adept at "reading" emotions, show more helping behavior, and have a wider social network than males. Overall, though, there are more similarities than differences between females and males.
	Achievement	The question of whether males and females differ in their expectations for success is not yet settled. An often-neglected distinction is that females may be more achievement oriented, males more competitive and assertive.
Gender-role classification	The past	In the past, a well-adjusted male was expected to show instrumental traits, a well-adjusted female expressive traits. Such stereotypes are more harmful to females than to males because the characteristics assigned to men are more valued by society. Widespread sexism is the result.
	Androgyny	In the 1970s, alternatives to traditional masculinity and femininity were explored. It was proposed that individuals could show both expressive and instrumental traits. This thinking led to the development of the concept of androgyny, the presence of desirable masculine and feminine characteristics in the same individual. Gender-role measures often categorize individuals as masculine, feminine, androgynous, or undifferentiated. Androgynous individuals are described as more flexible and mentally healthy, although the particular context and the individual's culture also determine the adaptiveness of a gender-role orientation.
	Traditional masculinity and problem behaviors in adolescent males	What defines traditional masculinity in many Western societies includes engaging in certain behaviors that, while officially socially disapproved of, validate masculinity. Researchers have found that problem behaviors in adolescent males—school difficulties, drug use, and delinquency, for example—are associated with their traditional beliefs in masculinity.
	Gender-role transcendence	One alternative to androgyny is gender-role transcendence, but, like androgyny, it diverts attention from the imbalance of power between females and males.
The feminist perspective and adolescence as a critical juncture in the development of females	The feminist perspective	Feminist scholars are developing new perspectives that focus on girls' and women's experiences and development. Girls' and women's strengths are especially important in relationships and connections with others. A special emphasis is that, while staying emotionally connected to significant others, females can enhance their psychological well-being by developing stronger self-determination.
	Gilligan's view of adolescence as a critical juncture in the development of females	Gilligan argues that girls come to a critical juncture in their development when they reach adolescence. Usually around 11 to 12 years of age, girls become aware that their intense interest in intimacy is not prized by the male-dominated culture, even though society values women as caring and altruistic. The dilemma is that girls are presented with a choice that makes them look either selfish or selfless. Gilligan believes that, as adolescent girls experience this dilemma, they increasingly "silence" their distinctive voice. Gilligan's view has been criticized for, among other reasons, reinforcing the stereotype of females as nurturing and sacrificing.

IV. Social Influences on Gender

Parents, by action and by example, influence their children's and adolescents' gender development. During the transition to adolescence, parents allow boys more freedom than girls, and families with young adolescent girls report more conflicts about sex, choice of friends, and curfews than families with young adolescent boys. The social learning theory of gender emphasizes that children's and adolescents' gender development occurs through observation and imitation of gender behavior, and through rewards and punishments for gender-appropriate and gender-inappropriate behavior. One major change in the gender role models adolescents have been exposed to in recent years is the increase in working mothers, which influences adolescents' gender development, especially decreasing their stereotyping of gender roles. Adolescents spend increasing amounts of time with peers, and peer approval or disapproval can be a powerful influence on adolescents' gender behavior. Deviance from sex-typed norms often leads to peer disapproval. Historically, in the United States, education has been male-dominated rather than gender-balanced. Males receive more attention in schools than females. A special concern is that most middle and junior high schools are better suited to the learning styles of males than females because of their impersonal, independent environment. Early adolescence may be a period of heightened sensitivity to television messages about gender roles, especially gender-appropriate behavior in heterosexual relationships. The idealized characters on television may appeal to the idealized nature of adolescent thought. The world of television is highly gender-stereotyped and conveys the clear message that females are less powerful and less important than males. The sexist messages of television increase young adolescents' endorsement of traditional gender-role divisions of labor. One television series, "Freestyle," attempted to reduce adolescents' gender stereotyping but had mixed effects.

V. Cognitive Influences on Gender

In the cognitive developmental theory of gender, proposed by Kohlberg, children's gender-typing occurs after they have developed a concept of gender. Kohlberg's theory argues that the main gender changes occur in childhood. In addition to Kohlberg's theory, the changes ushered in by formal operational thought—abstract, idealized, and organized thinking—and the increased interest in identity concerns lead adolescents to examine and redefine their gender attitudes and behavior. Gender schema theory states that an individual's attention and behavior are guided by an internal motivation to conform to gender-based sociocultural standards and stereotypes. In most cultures, adolescents learn a sprawling network of gender-linked associations that they incorporate into their gender schema.

VI. Gender Stereotypes, Similarities, Differences, and Achievement

Gender-role stereotypes are broad categories that reflect our impressions and beliefs about males and females. These stereotypes are widespread around the world, especially emphasizing the male's power and the female's nurturance. However, in more highly developed countries, females and males are more likely to be perceived as similar. Many gender researchers believe that a number of differences between females and males have been exaggerated. In considering differences, researchers must recognize that the differences are averages, that there is considerable overlap between the sexes, and that the differences may be due primarily to biological factors, sociocultural factors, or both. There are a number of physical differences between females and males, but cognitive differences are either small or nonexistent. At the level of the gifted, the average male does outperform the average female in math achievement. In terms of social behavior, males are more aggressive and active than females, but females are usually more adept at "reading" emotions, show more helping behavior, and have a wider social network than males. Overall, though, there are more similarities than differences between females and males. The question of whether males and females differ in their expectations for success it not yet settled. An often-neglected distinction is that females may be more achievement oriented, males more competitive and assertive.

VII. Gender-Role Classification

In the past, a well-adjusted male was expected to show instrumental traits, a well-adjusted female expressive traits. Such stereotypes are more harmful to females than to males because the characteristics assigned to men are more valued by society. Widespread sexism is the result. In the 1970s, alternatives to traditional masculinity and femininity were explored. It was proposed that individuals could show both expressive and instrumental traits. This thinking led to the development of the concept of androgyny, the presence of desirable masculine and feminine characteristics in the same individual. Gender-role measures often categorize individuals as masculine, feminine, androgynous, or undifferentiated. Androgynous individuals are described as more flexible and mentally healthy, although the particular context and the individual's culture also determine the adaptiveness of a gender-role orientation. What defines traditional masculinity in many Western societies includes engaging in certain behaviors that, while officially disapproved of, validate masculinity. Researchers have found that problem behaviors in adolescent males—school difficulties, drug use, and delinquency, for example—are associated with their traditional beliefs in masculinity. One alternative to androgyny is gender-role transcendence, but, like androgyny, it diverts attention from the imbalance of power between females and males.

VIII. The Feminist Perspective and Adolescence As a Critical Juncture in the Development of Females

Feminist scholars are developing new perspectives that focus on girls' and women's experiences and development. Girls' and women's strengths are especially important in relationships and connections with others. A special emphasis is that, while staying emotionally connected to significant others, females can enhance their psychological well-being by developing stronger self-determination. Gilligan argues that girls come to a critical juncture in their development when they reach adolescence. Usually around 11 to 12 years of age, girls become aware that their intense interest in intimacy is not prized by the male-dominated culture, even though society values women as caring and altruistic. The dilemma is that girls are presented with a choice that makes them look either selfish or selfless. Gilligan believes that, as adolescent girls experience this dilemma, they increasingly "silence" their distinctive voice. Gilligan's view has been criticized for, among other reasons, reinforcing the stereotype of females as nurturing and sacrificing.

Key Terms

gender 367
gender role 367
gender intensification
   hypothesis 367

social learning theory
   of gender 370
schema 373
gender schema
   theory 373

gender-role
   stereotypes 376
androgyny 380
gender-role
   transcendence 385

Suggested Readings

Bem, S. L. (1985). Androgyny and gender schema theory: Conceptual and empirical integration. In T. B. Sonderegger (Ed.), *Nebraska symposium on motivation*. Lincoln, NE: University of Nebraska Press.
Bem, a leading androgyny expert, describes her views on androgyny and gender schema.

Doyle, J. A., & Paludi, M. A. (1991). *Sex and gender* (2nd ed.). Dubuque, IA: Wm. C. Brown.
An excellent, up-to-date, authoritative overview of the nature of gender issues.

Gilligan, D., Lyons, N., & Hanmer, T. J. (Eds.). (1990). *Making connections: The relational worlds of adolescent girls at the Emma Willard School*. Cambridge, MA: Harvard University Press.
Gilligan's ideas about adolescence as a critical juncture in the development of females are presented, with many excerpts from adolescent interviews.

Huston, A. C., & Alvarez, M. (1990). The socialization context of gender-role development in early adolescence. In R. Montemayor, G. R. Adams, & T. P. Gulotta (Eds.), *From childhood to adolescence: A transitional period?* Newbury Park, CA: Sage.
Huston and Alvarez document why and how gender roles become redefined during early adolescence. Includes discussions of how parents, peers, schools, and television communicate gender information to adolescents.

Reinisch, J. M., Rosenblum, L. A., & Sanders, S. A. (Eds.). (1987). *Masculinity/ femininity*. New York: Oxford University Press.
An outstanding collection of articles by leading experts such as Eleanor Maccoby, John Money, and Jacqueline Eccles. Includes a special section of papers on the development of gender roles.

Sexuality

If we listen to boys and girls at the very moment they seem most pimply, awkward, and disagreeable, we can penetrate a mystery most of us once felt heavily within us, and have now forgotten. This mystery is the very process of creation of man and woman.

Colin Mcinnes, The World of Children

The Mysteries and Curiosities of Adolescent Sexuality

I am 16 years old, and I really like this one girl. She wants to be a virgin until she marries. We went out last night, and she let me go pretty far, but not all the way. I know she really likes me, too, but she always stops me when things start getting hot and heavy. It is getting hard for me to handle. She doesn't know it, but I'm a virgin, too. I feel I am ready to have sex. I have to admit I think about having sex with other girls, too. Maybe I should be dating other girls.

Frank C.

I'm 14 years old. I have a lot of sexy thoughts. Sometimes, just before I drift off to sleep at night, I think about this hunk who is 16 years old and plays on the football team. He is so gorgeous, and I can feel him holding me in his arms and kissing and hugging me. When I'm walking down the hall between classes at school, I sometimes start daydreaming about guys I have met and wonder what it would be like to have sex with them. Last year I had this crush on the men's track coach. I'm on the girls' track team, so I saw him a lot during the year. He hardly knew I thought about him the way I did, although I tried to flirt with him several times.

Amy S.

Is it weird to be a 17-year-old guy and still be a virgin? Sometimes, I feel like the only 17-year-old male on the planet who has not had sex. I feel like I am missing out on something great, or at least that's what I hear. I'm pretty religious, and I sometimes feel guilty when I think about sex. The thought runs through my mind that maybe it is best to wait until I'm married or at least until I have a long-term relationship that matters a lot to me.

Tom B.

I'm 15 years old, and I had sex for the first time recently. I had all of these expectations about how great it was going to be. He didn't have much experience either. We were both pretty scared about the whole thing. It was all over in a hurry. My first thought was, "Is that all there is?" It was a very disappointing experience.

Claire T.

*We are born twice over; the first time for existence, the second for life;
Once as human beings and later as men or as women.*

Jean-Jacques Rousseau

During adolescence, the lives of males and females become wrapped in sexuality. In Chapter 3, we studied the biological basis of sexual maturation, including the timing of these changes and the hormones involved. Here, we focus on the sexual attitudes and experiences of adolescents. Adolescence is a time of sexual exploration and experimentation, of sexual fantasies and sexual realities, of incorporating sexuality into one's identity. Adolescents have an almost insatiable curiosity about sexuality's mysteries. They continually think about whether they are sexually attractive, whether they will grow more, whether anyone will love them, whether their penis or vagina is too small or oddly shaped, and whether it is normal to have sex. Sexual experiences can be enjoyable for some adolescents, painful for others. For most adolescents, they are both enjoyable *and* painful. The curiosity, imagination, expectations, and fantasies adolescents harbor about sex are often extremely enjoyable moments of their lives. The actual sexual experiences of adolescents can be enjoyable, too, but the immaturity, disappointment, and pain that may be involved make adolescent sexuality an ambiguous phenomenon. At a time when sexual identity is a major developmental task of adolescence, the adolescent is confronted with conflicting sexual values and messages. The majority of adolescents manage eventually to develop a mature sexual identity, but for most, there are periods of vulnerability and confusion along life's sexual journey (Kilpatrick, 1992). In this chapter, the coverage of adolescent sexuality includes discussions of sexual attitudes and behavior, adolescent pregnancy, sexually transmitted diseases, sexual knowledge and sex education, and forcible sexual behavior.

Sexual Attitudes and Behavior

Gathering information about sexual attitudes and behavior is not always a straightforward affair. Consider how you would respond if someone asked you, "How often do you have intercourse?" or "How many different sexual partners have you had?" The people most likely to respond to sexual surveys are those with liberal sexual attitudes who engage in liberal sexual behaviors. Thus, research is limited by the reluctance of individuals to candidly answer questions about extremely personal matters and by researchers' inability to get any answer, candid or otherwise, from individuals who simply refuse to talk to strangers about sex (Allen & Santrock, 1993). In addition, when asked about their sexual activity, do individuals respond truthfully or with socially desirable answers? For example, might a ninth-grade boy report that he has had sexual intercourse even if he has not because he is afraid someone will find out that he is sexually inexperienced? With these cautions in mind, we now examine heterosexual attitudes and behavior, homosexual attitudes and behavior, self-stimulation, and contraception.

Heterosexual Attitudes and Behavior

What is the progression of adolescent sexual behaviors? How extensively have heterosexual attitudes and behaviors changed in the twentieth century? What

Table 12.1   The Age at First Experience for Various Sexual Behaviors

	Approximate Age at First Experience	
	Males	**Females**
Necking	14.0	15.0
French kissing	15.0	16.0
Breast fondling	16.0	16.5
Male/female genitals	17.0	17.5
Female/male genitals	17.0	17.5
Intercourse	17.5	18.0
Male oral/female genitals	18.0	18.5
Female oral/male genitals	18.0	18.5

From J. DeLamater and P. MacCorquodale, *Premarital Sexuality.* Copyright © 1979 University of Wisconsin Press, Madison, WI. Reprinted by permission.

sexual scripts do adolescents follow? Are some adolescents more vulnerable to irresponsible sexual behavior than others? We examine each of these questions.

The Progression of Adolescent Sexual Behaviors

Adolescents engage in a rather consistent progression of sexual behaviors (Broderick & Rowe, 1968; DeLamater & MacCorquodale, 1979). Necking usually comes first, followed by petting. Next comes intercourse, or in some cases, oral sex, which has increased substantially in adolescence in recent years. In an investigation of tenth- through twelfth-graders, 25 percent of the males and 15 percent of the females who reported not having intercourse reported having oral sex (Newcomer & Udry, 1985). In one study of the progression of sexual behaviors, 18- to 23-year-olds were asked to remember whether they had engaged in various sexual behaviors, and if they had, to state the age at which they had experienced each of them (DeLamater & MacCorquodale, 1979). As shown in Table 12.1, necking and petting occurred earlier than genital contact or sexual intercourse. Oral sex occurred last. Notice that male adolescents engaged in various sexual behaviors approximately six months to a year earlier than female adolescents. The gradual progression shown in Table 12.1 may be more representative of White Americans than Black Americans. In one study, Black American adolescents were more likely to move toward intercourse at an earlier age and to spend less time in necking, petting, and genital contact before engaging in sexual intercourse (Smith & Udry, 1985).

Adolescent Heterosexual Behavior—Trends and Incidence

Had you been a college student in 1940, you probably would have had a very different attitude toward many aspects of sexuality than you do today, especially if you are female. A review of college students' sexual practices and attitudes from 1900 to 1980 reveals two important trends (Darling, Kallen, & VanDusen, 1984): First, the percentage of young people reporting intercourse has dramatically increased, and, second, the proportion of females reporting sexual intercourse has increased more rapidly than that of males, although the initial base for males was greater. Prior to 1970, about twice as many college males as females reported that they had engaged in sexual intercourse, but since 1970, the proportion of males and females has become about equal. These changes suggest major shifts in the standards governing sexual behavior—that is, movement away from a double standard in which it was more acceptable for males than females to have intercourse.

Table 12.2   Percentage of Young People Sexually Active at Specific Ages

Age	Females	Males
15	5.4%	16.6%
16	12.6	28.7
17	27.1	47.9
18	44.0	64.0
19	62.9	77.6
20	73.6	83.0

Excerpted with permission from *Risking the Future: Adolescent Sexuality, Pregnancy, and Childbearing,* c. 1987 by the National Academy of Sciences. Published by National Academy Press, Washington, D.C.

"Don't encourage him Sylvia."
THE FAR SIDE cartoon by Gary Larson is reprinted by permission of Chronicle Features, San Francisco, CA.

Large portions of American adolescents are sexually active, and their sexual activity increased during the 1980s (Eager, 1992; Kilpatrick, 1992). Trends in adolescents' sexual activity in the 1980s were examined in two studies: one focused on females, the other on males. From 1982 to 1988, the proportion of adolescent girls 15 to 19 years of age who had sexual intercourse increased from 47 percent to 53 percent (Forrest & Singh, 1990). Most of the change is attributable to increases among White and nonpoor adolescents, thus narrowing ethnic and income differences. In a 1988 survey, 58 percent of the adolescent girls reported having had two or more sexual partners. In a survey of male adolescent sexual activity, comparisons were made between 1979 and 1988 (Sonenstein, Pleck, & Ku, 1989). Two-thirds of the 17- to 19-year-old males reported being sexually active in 1979, a figure that increased to three-fourths in 1988. In the most recent national study, 54 percent of the adolescents in grades 9–12 said they have had sexual intercourse (Centers for Disease Control, 1992). In this study, 39 percent of the adolescents reported having had sexual intercourse in the past 3 months.

Other studies have documented that adolescent males are more likely to report having had sexual intercourse and being sexually active than adolescent females (Hayes, 1987). As indicated in Table 12.2, 44 percent of 18-year-old females and 64 percent of 18-year-old males said that they were sexually active. While the gap is closing, males still report that they are sexually active at an earlier age than females. Although, as indicated earlier, sexual activity among White adolescents increased in the 1980s, Black adolescents are still more sexually active than White adolescents (Hayes, 1987). As shown in Table 12.3, Black adolescents are more likely to have had sexual intercourse at every point in adolescence than White or Hispanic adolescents. Notice also that Hispanic girls are the least likely to be sexually active in adolescence.

Among younger adolescents, surveys indicate that 5 to 17 percent of girls 15 years and younger have had sexual intercourse. Among boys the same age, the range is 16 percent to 38 percent (Gilgun, 1984; Jessor & Jessor, 1975; National Research Council, 1987; Ostrov & others, 1985). At age 13, boys also show earlier experience with sexual intercourse than girls—12 percent versus 5 percent (Dreyer, 1982). The pressure on male adolescents in American society to have sexual intercourse is reflected in these figures, even though male adolescents enter puberty, on the average, two years later than female adolescents.

In some areas of the United States, the percentages of sexually active young adolescents may be even greater. In an inner-city area of Baltimore, 81 percent of the males at age 14 said that they already had engaged in sexual intercourse. Other surveys in inner-city, low-income areas also reveal a high incidence of early sexual intercourse (Clark, Zabin, & Hardy, 1984).

Table 12.3   Percentage of Teenagers Who Have Had Sexual Intercourse, by Age, Sex, and Ethnicity, 1983

Sex and Ethnicity	Percentage Who Were Sexually Active, by Age		
	15	17	19
Females			
Total	5%	44%	74%
White	5	42	72
Black	10	59	85
Hispanic	4	40	70
Males			
Total	17%	64%	83%
White	12	60	81
Black	42	86	94
Hispanic	19	67	84

Source: Data from the 1983 National Longitudinal Survey of Youth Center for Human Resource Research, Ohio State University.

In summary, approximately half of all adolescents today have had sexual intercourse by the age of 18, although the percentage varies by sex, ethnicity, and context. Male, Black American, and inner-city adolescents report the highest percentage of sexual intercourse. While sexual intercourse can be a meaningful experience for older, more mature adolescents, many adolescents are not prepared to handle sexual experiences, especially in early adolescence. Adolescents may attempt sexual intercourse without really knowing what to do or how to satisfy their partner, which can lead to frustration and a sense of sexual inadequacy. And many are poorly informed about contraception or fail to use contraceptives.

Adolescent Female and Male Sexual Scripts

As adolescents explore their sexual identities, they engage in sexual scripts (Bancroft, 1990; Gagnon & Simon, 1973; Gordon & Gilgun, 1987). A **sexual script** *is a stereotyped pattern of role prescriptions for how individuals should sexually behave. Females and males have been socialized to follow different sexual scripts.* Differences in female-male sexual scripting can cause problems and confusions for adolescents as they work out their sexual identities. Female adolescents learn to link sexual intercourse with love. They often rationalize their sexual behavior by telling themselves that they were swept away by love. A number of investigators have revealed that adolescent females, more than adolescent males, report being in love as the main reason for being sexually active (Cassell, 1984). Far more females than males have intercourse with partners they love and would like to marry. Other reasons for having sexual intercourse include giving in to male pressure, gambling that sex is a way to get a boyfriend, curiosity, and sexual desire unrelated to loving and caring. Adolescent males may be aware that their female counterparts have been socialized into a love ethic. They also may know the pressure that many girls feel to have a boyfriend. Two classic male lines show how males understand female thinking about sex and love: "You would if you loved me," and "If you really loved me, you would have sex with me." The female adolescent who says, "If you really loved me, you would not put so much pressure on me," shows insight into male sexual motivation.

Some experts on adolescent sexuality, though, believe that we are moving toward a new norm suggesting that sexual intercourse is acceptable, but mainly within the boundary of a loving and affectionate relationship (Dreyer, 1982). As

The adolescent girl shown here learns about sexual scripts of males and females from many different sources, including the romance novel she is reading.

Female adolescents, more than adolescent males, report being in love as the main reason for being sexually active.

part of this new norm, promiscuity, exploitation, and unprotected sexual intercourse are more often perceived as unacceptable by adolescents. One variation of the new norm is that intercourse is acceptable in a nonlove relationship, but physical or emotional exploitation of the partner is not (Cassell, 1984). The new norm suggests that the double standard that once existed does not operate as it did. That is, physical and emotional exploitation of adolescent females by males is not as prevalent today as in prior decades.

Other experts on adolescent sexuality are not so sure that the new norm has arrived (Gordon & Gilgun, 1987; Morrison, 1985). They argue that remnants of the double standard, unfortunately, still flourish. In most investigations, about twice as many boys as girls report positive feelings about sexual intercourse. Females are more likely to report guilt, fear, and hurt. Adolescent males feel considerable pressure from their peers to have experienced sexual intercourse and to be sexually active. I remember vividly the raunchy conversations that filled our basketball locker room in junior high school. By the end of the ninth grade, I was sure that I was the only virgin on the 15-member team, but of course, there was no way I let my teammates know that. As one young adolescent recently remarked, "Look, I feel a lot of pressure from my buddies to go for the score." Further evidence for the male's physical and emotional exploitation of the female was found in a survey of 432 14- to 18-year-olds (Goodchilds & Zellman, 1984). Both male and female adolescents accepted the right of the male adolescent to be sexually aggressive, but let the female set the limits for the male's sexual overtures. Another attitude related to the double standard was the belief that females should not plan ahead to have sexual intercourse but should instead be swept up in the passion of the moment, not taking contraceptive precautions. Unfortunately, while we have chipped away at some parts of the sexual double standard, other aspects appear to remain.

Vulnerable Adolescents and Sexuality

Vulnerable adolescents are most likely to show irresponsible sexual behavior (Gordon & Gilgun, 1987). Adolescents who feel inadequate, who do not have adequate opportunities for education and work, and who feel the need to prove something to themselves through sex are at risk for irresponsible sexual behavior. It is not a coincidence that minority group and low-income adolescents use contraceptives less frequently and have higher pregnancy rates than White, middle-income adolescents. Minority group and low-income adolescents have less access to information and to services. Their irresponsible behavior and lack of social support can lead to pregnancy, sexually transmitted diseases, and psychological stress (Scott-Jones & White, 1990).

Adolescents who do not plan to go to college are less likely to postpone having sex than those who do plan to go (Miller & Simon, 1974). Drinking, drug abuse, and truancy also are associated with sexual activity (Jessor & Jessor, 1975; Rosenbaum & Kandel, 1990). Some investigators consider these behaviors to be part of a general pattern of deviance during adolescence (Jessor & Jessor, 1975). Adolescents who depend heavily on their peers and are less involved with their families are more likely to be sexually involved, with male adolescents' dependence on male peers a strong factor in predicting their sexual activity (Jessor & others, 1983). Negative self-conceptions also can be associated with sexual activity. Some sexually active adolescents may be motivated to have sex because of feelings of low self-worth. Some girls are socialized to believe that sex is one of the few ways they can feel worthwhile about themselves. However, using sex in this way results in exploitation and increased rather than decreased feelings of inadequacy. More information about adolescents who are vulnerable to behaving in sexually irresponsible ways appears later in the chapter in the discussion of contraceptive use and pregnancy.

Homosexual Attitudes and Behavior

Most individuals think that heterosexual behavior and homosexual behavior are distinct patterns that can be easily defined. In fact, however, preference for a sexual partner of the same or opposite sex is not always a fixed decision, made once in life and adhered to forever. For example, it is not unusual for an individual, especially a male, to engage in homosexual experimentation in adolescence, but not engage in homosexual behavior as an adult. And some individuals engage in heterosexual behavior during adolescence, then turn to homosexual behavior as adults (Allen & Santrock, 1993).

Both early and more recent surveys of sexual choice indicate that about 4 percent of males and about 3 percent of females are exclusively homosexual (Hunt, 1974; Kinsey, Pomeroy, & Martin, 1948). As many as 10 percent of adolescents worry about whether or not they are lesbian or gay (Gordon & Gilgun, 1987). Although the incidence of homosexual behavior does not seem to have increased, attitudes toward homosexuality were becoming more permissive, at least until recently. In 1986 the Gallup Poll began to detect a shift in attitudes brought about by public awareness of AIDS (Acquired Immune Deficiency Syndrome). For example, in 1985 slightly more than 40 percent of Americans believed that "homosexual relations between consenting adults should be legal"; by 1986 the figure had dropped to just above 30 percent (Gallup Report, 1987). Individuals who have negative attitudes toward homosexuals also are likely to favor severe controls for AIDS, such as excluding AIDS carriers from the workplace and schools (Pryor & others, 1989).

Adolescence may play an important role in the development of homosexuality. In one investigation, participation in homosexual behavior and sexual arousal by same-sex peers in adolescence were strongly related to an adult homosexual orientation (Bell, Weinberg, & Mammersmith, 1981). When interest in the same sex is intense and compelling, an adolescent often experiences severe conflict (Boxer, 1988; Irvin, 1988). The American culture stigmatizes homosexuality—negative labels such as "fags" and "queers" are given to male homosexuals and "lessies" and "dykes" to female homosexuals. The sexual socialization of adolescent homosexuals becomes a process of learning to hide (Herdt, 1988). Some gay males wait out their entire adolescence, hoping that heterosexual feelings will develop. Many female adolescent homosexuals have similar experiences, although same-sex genital contact is not as common as among males. Many adult females who identify themselves as homosexuals considered themselves predominantly heterosexual during adolescence (Bell, Weinberg, & Mammersmith, 1981).

Why are some individuals homosexual and others heterosexual? Speculation about this question has been extensive, but no firm answers are available. Homosexual and heterosexual males and females have similar physiological responses during sexual arousal and seem to be aroused by the same types of tactile stimulation. Investigators find that, in terms of a wide range of attitudes, behaviors, and adjustments, no differences between homosexuals and heterosexuals are present (Bell, Weinberg, & Mammersmith, 1981). Recognizing that homosexuality is not a form of mental illness, the American Psychiatric Association discontinued its classification of homosexuality as a disorder, except in those cases where the individuals themselves consider the sexual orientation abnormal.

An individual's sexual orientation—heterosexual or homosexual—is most likely determined by a combination of genetic, hormonal, and environmental factors (McWhirter, Reinisch, & Sanders, 1990; Money, 1987; Rowlett, Patel, & Greydanus, 1992). Most experts on homosexuality believe that no one factor alone causes homosexuality and that the relative weight of each factor may vary from one individual to the next. In effect, no one knows exactly what causes an individual to be homosexual. Scientists have a clearer picture of what does *not* cause homosexuality. For example, children raised by gay or lesbian parents or couples are no more likely to be homosexual than are children raised by heterosexual parents. There also is no evidence that male homosexuality is caused by a dominant mother or a weak father, or that female homosexuality is caused by girls choosing male role models. One of the biological factors believed to be involved in homosexuality is prenatal hormone conditions (Ellis & Ames, 1987). In the second to fifth months after conception, the exposure of the fetus to hormone levels characteristic of females may cause the individual (male or female) to become attracted to males. If this prenatal critical-period hypothesis turns out to be correct, it would explain why researchers and clinicians have found that a homosexual orientation is difficult to modify.

Self-Stimulation

As indicated earlier, a heterosexual continuum of necking, petting, and intercourse or oral sex characterizes many adolescents' sexual experiences. Substantial numbers of adolescents, though, have sexual experience outside of this heterosexual continuum through masturbation or same-sex behavior. Most boys have an ejaculation for the first time at about 12 to 13 years of age (Bell, Weinberg & Mammersmith, 1981). Masturbation, genital contact with the same-sex or other-sex partner, or a wet dream during sleep are common circumstances for ejaculation.

Masturbation is the most frequent sexual outlet for many adolescents. In one investigation, masturbation was commonplace among adolescents (Haas, 1979). More than two-thirds of the boys and one-half of the girls masturbated once a week or more. Adolescents today do not feel as guilty about masturbation as they once did, although they still may feel embarrassed or defensive about it (Sorensen, 1973). In past eras, masturbation was denounced as causing everything from warts to insanity. Today, as few as 15 percent of adolescents attach any stigma to masturbation (Hyde, 1985).

Contraceptive Use

The following conversation between an adolescent boy and girl reveals a communication pattern that happens far too often (Gordon, 1987):

> *Susan:* Come in.
> *Skip:* I'm sorry I'm late, Susan. I had to go to the U store and the library and run around and, you know, all kinds of things and I'm sorry. . . .
> *Susan:* Yeah, well I'm glad you came. I called because I want to talk to you.
> *Skip:* Yeah. How was your day today?
> *Susan:* Oh, all right. Did you get much studying done?
> *Skip:* No, I was running around and uh, you know, just thinking, sitting around.
> *Susan:* Yeah. I've been thinking a lot also. I really want to talk with you about last night. (pause)
> *Skip:* Are you sorry or anything?
> *Susan:* No, I'm not sorry—I'm just really worried.
> *Skip:* (surprise) About what?
> *Susan:* You know I'm not using any birth control.
> *Skip:* (shock) You're not using any birth control? (pause) No, I didn't know you weren't using any birth control. How was I supposed to. . . . How could you do that?
> *Susan:* My mother always told me the man would take care of it.
> *Skip:* The man *can* take care of it, but I *wasn't* taking care of it, obviously. It's the woman's responsibility to take care of it—you know that. All women use the pill nowadays.

Table 12.4 Percentage of Adolescent Females Who Used a Contraceptive Method at First Intercourse, and Method Used, by Age

	Age at First Intercourse		
	Under 15	15–17	18–19
No contraceptive method	70%	57%	53%
Pill	14	21	31
Condom	44	44	38
Rhythm	5	4	7
Withdrawal	30	25	15
Diaphragm	0	1	2

Source: Data from National Survey of Family Growth, 1982.

Susan: Not all women use the pill, and why is it my responsibility if we're both involved? Besides, we never really talked about it, and when was I supposed to bring it up, in the middle of . . . I didn't know you were planning to go to bed.

Skip: I didn't plan it. Aw, come on, Susan. You don't plan things like that—they just happen.

Susan: We both must have been thinking about it . . . why didn't we say anything? Aren't we supposed to trust each other?

Skip: Sure we trust each other. Aw, come on, it's not that. It's just not the kind of thing you talk about. Susan, could you see me going up to you and saying, "Susan are you using any. . . ." I can't say that, I can't say it.

Susan: Skip, I'm really scared. I could be pregnant. What are we going to do? (looking at each other scared and questioningly)

Adolescents are increasing their use of contraceptives. The level of contraceptive use at first intercourse for 15- to 19-year-old adolescents improved substantially between 1982 and 1988, rising from 48 percent to 65 percent (Forrest & Singh, 1990). Condom use among 15- to 19-year-old boys increased from 21 percent in 1979 to 58 percent in 1988 (Sonenstein, Pleck, & Ku, 1989). The threat of AIDS and other sexually transmitted diseases is apparently responsible for adolescents' increased use of contraceptives.

While adolescent contraceptive use is increasing, many adolescents still do not use contraception, and when all ages of adolescents are considered, a majority of females do not use contraception at first intercourse (Hofferth, 1990; Treboux & Busch-Rossnagel, 1991). As shown in Table 12.4, 70 percent of adolescent females under the age of 15 did not use any contraceptive method at first intercourse, while 53 percent of 18- to 19-year-old females did not. Older adolescents were more likely to rely on the pill or the diaphragm; younger adolescents were more likely to use a condom or withdrawal.

What factors are related to contraceptive use? Being from a low-income family is one of the best predictors of adolescents' nonuse of contraceptives. Younger adolescents are less likely to use contraceptives than older adolescents (Hofferth, 1990). Not being involved in a steady, committed dating relationship is also associated with a lack of contraceptive use (Chilman, 1979). In addition, adolescents with poor coping skills, lack of a future orientation, high anxiety, poor

Adolescents are increasing their use of contraceptives, although large numbers of sexually active adolescents still do not use contraceptives, especially at first intercourse.

social adjustment, and a negative attitude toward contraceptives are not as likely to use contraceptives (Oskamp & Mindick, 1981). Further, degree of personal concern about AIDS and the perception that a partner would appreciate condom use are associated with more consistent use of condoms by male adolescents (Pleck, Sonenstein, & Ku, 1991). Condom use is inhibited by concerns about embarrassment and reduced sexual pleasure. Educational efforts that include information about AIDS and pregnancy prevention may promote more consistent use of condoms by adolescent males.

While American adolescents' use of contraceptives increased in the 1980s, adolescents in Canada, Great Britain, France, Sweden, and the Netherlands are still more likely to use contraceptives than adolescents in the United States (Forrest, 1990; Jones & others, 1985). U.S. adolescents are especially less likely to use effective contraceptives like the pill than their counterparts in other countries (Forrest, 1990). And as Sociocultural Worlds of Adolescence 12.1 indicates, contraceptive availability differs in these countries. Next, we study one of the outcomes of failure to use contraceptives or to abstain from sexual intercourse—adolescent pregnancy.

Adolescent Pregnancy

Angela is 15 years old and pregnant. She reflects, "I'm three months pregnant. This could ruin my whole life. I've made all of these plans for the future, and now they are down the drain. I don't have anybody to talk with about my problem. I can't talk to my parents. There is no way they can understand." Pregnant adolescents were once virtually invisible and unmentionable. But yesterday's secret has become today's national dilemma. Our exploration of adolescent pregnancy focuses on its incidence and nature, its consequences, cognitive factors that may be involved, adolescents as parents, and ways adolescent pregnancy rates can be reduced.

Jacqueline Forrest has conducted a number of important research studies on adolescent sexuality. Her research has especially provided rich insights into the nature of contraceptive use by adolescents in the United States and other countries.

Incidence and Nature of Adolescent Pregnancy

They are from different ethnic groups and from different places, but their circumstances have the same stressfulness. Each year, more than 1 million American adolescents become pregnant, four out of five of them unmarried. They represent a flaw in America's social fabric. Like Angela, many become pregnant in their early or middle adolescent years, 30,000 of them under the age of 15. In all, this means that 1 of every 10 adolescent females in the United States becomes pregnant each year, with 8 of 10 pregnancies unintended (National Research Council, 1987). In 1989, 36 of every 1,000 girls aged 15–17 in the United States had a baby, an 8 percent rise from 1988 (Sullivan, 1992). As one 17-year-old Los Angeles mother of a one-year-old son said, "We are children having children." The only bright spot in the adolescent pregnancy statistics is that the adolescent pregnancy rate, after increasing during the 1970s, has leveled off and may even be beginning to decline (Hofferth, 1990; National Research Council, 1987).

The adolescent pregnancy rate in the United States is the highest in the Western world. It is more than twice as high as the rates in England, France, or Canada, almost three times as high as the rate in Sweden, and seven times as high as the rate in the Netherlands (Forrest, 1990; Jones & others, 1985) (see Figure 12.1). Though American adolescents are no more sexually active than their counterparts in these other nations, they are many more times likely to become pregnant.

Adolescent pregnancy is a complex American problem, one that strikes many sensitive nerves. The subject of adolescent pregnancy touches on many explosive social issues: the battle over abortion rights, contraceptives and the delicate question of whether adolescents should have easy access to them, and the perennially touchy subject of sex education in the public schools.

Availability of Contraceptive Services in the United States, Canada, England and Wales, France, Sweden, and the Netherlands

How available are contraceptive services in developed countries? In a comparison of the United States, Canada, England and Wales, France, Sweden, and the Netherlands, contraceptive services were least accessible to U.S. adolescents and most accessible to adolescents in England and Wales, Sweden, and the Netherlands (Forrest, 1990; Jones & others, 1985) (see Table 12.A). Except for Sweden, adolescents can obtain prescription contraceptives from both physicians and clinics. In the United States, the physicians are often obstetrician-gynecologists to whom the adolescent has usually not gone before, while in other countries, the physicians are usually general or family practitioners with whom the adolescent often is familiar. The primary health centers that provide contraceptives in Sweden and the health clinics in England and Wales are also places adolescents have often gone before for other care. The clinic system that serves approximately half the adolescents using prescription contraceptives in the United States is not likely to be used for other health services by adolescents. Especially in England and Wales, Sweden, and the Netherlands, health services for adolescents are available in other locations if adolescents are reluctant to obtain services from their regular physician.

Free medical care for contraception is readily available in all but the United States because the other countries have some form of national health system. In contrast, private physician care in the United States is expensive and rarely free except to adolescents on welfare (who in most areas must be poor, unmarried, and already have a child, or be a daughter of a poor, unmarried, single mother). Contraceptive supplies are much more expensive in the United States than the other countries.

Confidentiality was an important issue in each of the six countries, even though the other countries tend to be more open about sexuality than the United States. In the United States and Canada, confidentiality is up to the individual physician or clinic to determine; confidentiality is also up to the physician or clinic for those under age 16 in England and Wales. In all the countries, clinics are more likely than physicians to provide services confidentially. In England and Wales, services to individuals 16 years and older must be confidential, and clinic services in France also are confidential. In Sweden, providers are specifically forbidden to tell parents if an adolescent asks for contraceptives. Clinic services in the Netherlands are also confidential, and physician services must be confidential if the adolescent requests it.

Nonprescription contraceptive sources are also important to consider because the condom is the second most popular method among adolescents. Condoms are readily available in England and Wales, Sweden, and the Netherlands through family-planning clinics, pharmacies, supermarkets, and vending machines. Sources for condoms are more limited in the United States, Canada, and France.

Table 12.A   Characteristics of Current Contraceptive Services in Six Countries

	United States	England and Wales	Canada	France	Sweden	Netherlands
Source of care	Some physicians, mostly specialists Clinics (primarily for low-income women)	General practitioner Clinic A few clinics for youth	Some physicians Clinics (uneven coverage of country)	Some physicians Clinics	Primary health center Clinic for youth	Family doctor Clinic for youth
Same source for regular health care	No	Yes	Yes	Yes	Yes	Yes
Cost	Physician care not free Supplies not free Clinic care and supplies low cost or free	Free care and supplies	Free physician care Some clinics free Supplies not free	Free clinic services and supplies for those under 18; older reimbursed by insurance	Free care and supplies	Free physician care Small fee at clinics Free prescription supplies until recently
Confidentiality	Physician discretion Most clinics provide confidentiality	Physician discretion for age under 16 years Must be confidential for age 16 and older	Physician discretion Most clinics provide confidentiality	Clinic services for under 18 must be confidential	Doctors forbidden to inform parents	Services must be confidential if teen requests it
Condom availability	Limited	Widespread	Limited	Limited	Widespread	Widespread

Source: Jacqueline Darroch Forrest and Susheela Singh, "The Sexual and Reproductive Behavior of American Women, 1982–1988," *Family Planning Perspectives,* Vol. 22, No. 5, September/October 1990 © The Alan Guttmacher Institute.

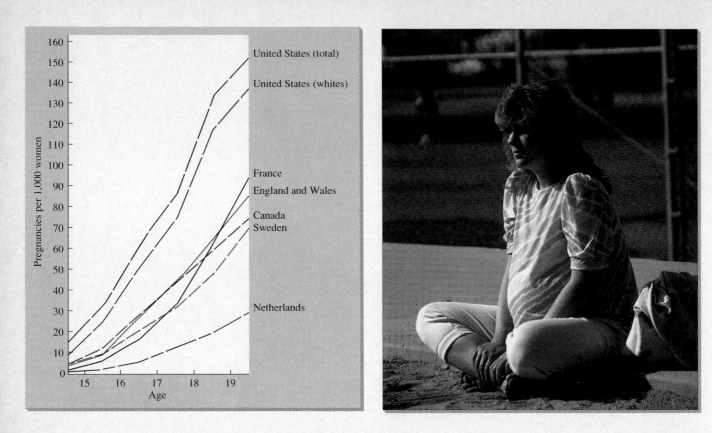

Figure 12.1 Pregnancy rates per 1,000 women by women's age, 1981.

Dramatic changes have swept through the American culture in the last three decades, changes that involve sexual attitudes and social morals. Adolescents actually gave birth at a higher rate in 1957 than they do today, but that was a time of early marriage, with almost one-fourth of 18- to 19-year-olds married. The overwhelming majority of births to adolescent mothers in the 1950s occurred within a marriage and mainly involved females 17 years of age and older. Two to three decades ago, if an unwed adolescent girl became pregnant her parents usually had her swiftly married off in a shotgun wedding. If marriage was impractical, the girl would discreetly disappear, the child would be put up for adoption, and the predicament would never be discussed further. Abortion was not a real option for most adolescent females until 1973, when the Supreme Court ruled that it could not be outlawed.

In today's world of adolescent pregnancies, a different scenario unfolds. If the girl does not choose to have an abortion (some 45 percent of adolescent girls do), she usually keeps the baby and raises it without the traditional involvement of marriage. With the stigma of illegitimacy largely absent, girls are less likely to give up their babies for adoption. Fewer than 5 percent do, compared with about 35 percent in the early 1960s. But while the stigma of illegitimacy has waned, the lives of most pregnant adolescents are anything but rosy.

Consequences of Adolescent Pregnancy

The consequences of America's high adolescent pregnancy rate are cause for great concern. Adolescent pregnancy increases health risks to both the offspring and the mother. Infants born to adolescent mothers are more likely to have low birth weights—a prominent factor in infant mortality—as well as neurological problems and childhood illness (Dryfoos, 1990; Schorr, 1989). Adolescent mothers

Age at first birth	Total %	High school completion by 1983, diploma %	GED %
15	45	24	21
16	49	28	21
17	53	38	15
18	62	52	10
19	77	68	9
Under 20	90	86	4

Figure 12.2 Percentage distribution of women, ages 20 to 26 in 1983, by type of high school completion, according to age at first birth.

often drop out of school, fail to gain employment, and become dependent on welfare. Although many adolescent mothers resume their education later in life, they generally do not catch up with women who postpone childbearing. In the National Longitudinal Survey of Work Experience of Youth, it was found that only half of the 20- to 26-year-old women who first gave birth at age 17 had completed high school by their twenties (the percentage was even lower for those who gave birth at a younger age) (see Figure 12.2) (Mott & Marsiglio, 1985). By contrast, among young females who waited until age 20 to have a baby, more than 90 percent had obtained a high school education. Among the younger adolescent mothers, almost half had obtained a General Equivalency Diploma (GED), which does not often open up good employment opportunities.

These educational deficits have negative consequences for the young females themselves and for their children (Kenney, 1987). Adolescent parents are more likely than those who delay childbearing to have low-paying, low-status jobs, or to be unemployed. The mean family income of White females who give birth before age 17 is approximately half that of families in which the mother delays birth until her middle or late twenties. The difficulties faced by adolescent mothers is clear in the descriptions of three girls in Perspective on Adolescent Development 12.1.

Cognitive Factors in Adolescent Pregnancy

With their developing idealism and ability to think in more abstract and hypothetical ways, young adolescents may get caught up in a mental world far removed from reality, one that may involve a belief that things cannot or will not happen to them and that they are omnipotent and indestructible. These cognitive changes have intriguing implications for adolescents' sex education (Lipsitz, 1980). Having information about contraceptives is not enough—what seems to predict whether or not adolescents will use contraceptives is their acceptance of themselves and their sexuality. This acceptance requires not only emotional maturity but cognitive maturity.

Most discussions of adolescent pregnancy and its prevention assume that adolescents have the ability to anticipate consequences, to weigh the probable outcome of behavior, and to project into the future what will happen if they engage in certain acts, such as sexual intercourse. That is, prevention is based on the belief that adolescents have the cognitive ability to approach problem solving in a planned, organized, and analytical manner. However, many adolescents are just beginning to develop these capacities, and others have not developed them at all (Holmbeck, Gasiewski, & Crossman, 1989).

The personal fable described in Chapter 4 may be associated with adolescent pregnancy. The young adolescent might say, "Hey, it won't happen to me." If adolescents are locked into this personal fable, they may not respond well to

Angela, Michelle, and Stephanie: Three Adolescent Mothers

Before the baby arrived, her bedroom was a dimly lit chapel to the idols of rock music. Now, the rock posters have been removed and the walls painted white. Angela's room has become a nursery for her six-week-old son. Angela, who just turned 15, has difficulty thinking of herself as a mother. She feels as young as she was before the baby and also feels that she has not grown up any faster. She looks like a typical adolescent girl as she sits in her parents' living room, asking her mother for permission to attend a rock concert, asking if she can buy a pet dog, and complaining that she is not allowed to do anything. She mentions that last night she could not get her homework done because it took her so long to feed the baby. She comments, "When I laid him down, he wanted me to pick him back up." She ponders, "Babies are a giant step in life. I should have thought more about what I was doing. I had no idea what this was going to be like."

It is a hot summer day in San Francisco. Michelle, a 14-year-old Black girl, is typing away, practicing her office skills with fervor as beads of sweat trickle down her forehead. She is worried about her future. She feels that she has to get some skills so that she can make some money. She

is right. In three weeks, Michelle is going to have a baby. She comes from a low-income family. She does not know her father's whereabouts, and her mother can barely make ends meet. She says that she used to think, "In 10 years, I will be 24. Now I think, I'll be 24, and my child will be 10."

In the early afternoon, the smells of dirty diapers and grease fill the air in a bleak Minneapolis apartment. The television is tuned to "All My Children." Seventeen-year-old Stephanie has collapsed on the sofa. A few minutes later, above the tone of the television characters' voices, she hears a loud wail. Her one-month-old baby is hungry. In an adjacent bedroom, her other child, 1½-year-old Joey, is recovering from the flu. Stephanie is one of 10 children herself. She first became pregnant at age 15. She says it was an accident. So was her second baby, she says. Stephanie complains that she always feels tired. Before Joey's birth, she dropped out of school. She dreamed of being an airline stewardess. Now her hopes are more down to earth. She would like to pay her bills, buy groceries, and be able to live in a house with her own furniture. Says Stephanie, "It has been a long, long time since I had a good time" (Wallis, 1985).

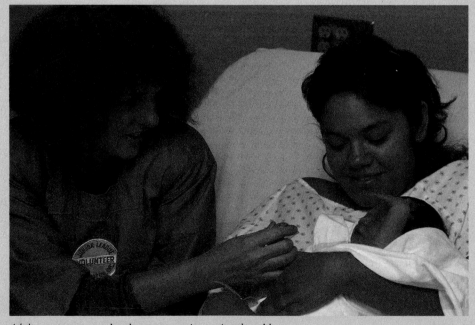

Adolescent pregnancy has become a major national problem. The United States has the highest adolescent pregnancy rate of all Western societies. Why has the adolescent pregnancy rate gotten out of control?

a course on sex education that preaches prevention. A developmental perspective on cognition suggests what can be taught in sex education courses for young adolescents.

Late adolescents (18 to 19 years of age) are to some degree realistic and future oriented about sexual experiences, just as they are about careers and marriage. Middle adolescents (15 to 17 years of age) often romanticize sexuality. But young adolescents (10 to 15 years of age) seem to experience sex in a depersonalized way that is filled with anxiety and denial. This depersonalized orientation toward sex is not likely to lead to preventive behavior.

Consider the outcome if the following are combined: the nature of early adolescent cognition, the personal fable, anxiety about sex, gender-role definitions about what is masculine and what is feminine, the sexual themes of music, the sexual overtones of magazines and television, and a societal standard that says that sex is appropriate for adults but promiscuous for adolescents. That is, society tells adolescents that sex is fun, harmless, adult, and forbidden. The combination of early physical maturation, risk-taking behavior, egocentrism, the inability to think futuristically, and an ambivalent, contradictory culture makes sex difficult for adolescents to handle. Add to this the growing need for adolescents to develop a commitment, especially in a career. Yet youth, especially low-income, minority group youth, face high unemployment rates, which can turn them away from the future and intensively toward the present. Piece together information about early adolescent development, America's sexual ambivalence, and adolescents' vulnerability to economic forces and the result is social dynamite.

Adolescents As Parents

Children of adolescent parents face problems even before they are born. Only one of every five pregnant adolescent girls receives any prenatal care at all during the important first three months of pregnancy. Pregnant adolescents are more likely to have anemia and complications related to prematurity than mothers aged 20 to 24. The problems of adolescent pregnancy double the normal risk of delivering a low-birth-weight baby (one that weighs under 5.5 pounds), a category that places that infant at risk for physical and mental deficits (Dryfoos, 1990; McAnarney, 1988).

Infants who escape the medical hazards of having an adolescent mother may not escape the psychological and social perils. Children born to adolescent mothers do not do as well on intelligence tests and have more behavioral problems than do those born to mothers in their twenties (Broman, 1981; Silver, 1988). Adolescent mothers have less desirable child-rearing practices and less realistic expectations for their infants' development than do older mothers (Field & others, 1980; Osofsky, 1989, 1990). Said one 18-year-old adolescent mother, "Not long after he was born, I began to resent him. I wouldn't play with him the first year. He didn't talk until he was two—he would just grunt. I'm sure some of his slow development is my fault. Now I want to make up for it and try to give him extra attention, but he still is behind his age." Other adolescent mothers may get excited about having "this little adorable thing" and anticipate that their world with their child will be marvelous. But as the infant demands more and more of their attention and they have to take care of the infant instead of going out on dates, their positive expectations turn sour.

So far, we have talked exclusively about adolescent mothers. What role do adolescent fathers play in the adolescent family? The public's perception of the adolescent father is usually of someone irresponsible who rarely if ever is involved in child rearing or support of the adolescent mother. This is a misconception. Researchers have found that adolescent fathers are more willing to participate and do participate more in the adolescent family than is commonly thought (Danziger & Radin, 1989; Robinson, 1988). Researchers find that as many as four of five adolescent fathers have daily contact with their children and that three of four contribute at least some financial support. However, adolescent fathers need considerable support to assure them of their importance in the adolescent family.

Adolescent fathers have lower incomes, less education, and more children than do men who delay having children until their twenties. One reason for these difficulties is that the adolescent father compounds his problem of getting his girlfriend pregnant by dropping out of school (Resnick, Wattenberg, & Brewer, 1992). As soon as he leaves school, the adolescent father moves directly into a low-paying job. Adolescent fathers are saying to themselves, "You need to be a good father. The least you can do is get a job and provide some support."

Many young fathers have little idea of what a father is supposed to do. They may love their baby but do not know how to behave. American society has given them few guidelines and few supports. Programs designed to help adolescent fathers are still relatively rare, but they are increasing. Terry, who is now 21, has a 17-month-old child and is himself the child of adolescent parents. After receiving support from the Teenage Pregnancy and Parenting Project in San Francisco, he is now a counselor there. He reports, "My father was a parent when he was an adolescent. So was my grandfather. I know it will stop with my son" (Stengel, 1985).

Reducing Adolescent Pregnancy

Serious, extensive efforts are needed to help pregnant adolescents and young mothers enhance their educational and occupational opportunities. Adolescent mothers also need extensive help in obtaining competent day-care and in planning for the future (Barnet & others, 1992; Furstenberg, 1991; Furstenberg, Brooks-Gunn, & Chase-Lansdale, 1989; Miller & others, 1992; Paikoff & Brooks-Gunn, 1991). Adolescence expert John Conger (1988) offered the following four recommendations for attacking the high rate of adolescent pregnancy: (1) sex education and family planning, (2) access to contraceptive methods, (3) the life options approach, and (4) broad community involvement and support, each of which we consider in turn.

We badly need age-appropriate family-life education for America's adolescents, including sex education that begins in childhood and continues through adolescence (Potthof, 1992). While still a controversial issue, sex education in the schools is favored by a large majority of parents. Much more about sex education is discussed later in the chapter.

In addition to age-appropriate family-life and sex education, sexually active adolescents need access to contraceptive methods. These needs often can be handled through adolescent clinics that provide comprehensive, high-quality health services (Bilodeau, Forget, & Tetreault, 1992). At four of the nation's oldest adolescent clinics in St. Paul, Minnesota, the overall annual rate of first-time pregnancies has dropped from 80 per 1,000 to 29 per 1,000 (Schorr, 1989). These clinics offer everything from immunizations to sports physicals to treatment for sexually transmitted diseases. Significantly, they also advise adolescents on contraception and dispense prescriptions for birth control (provided parents have agreed beforehand to allow their adolescents to visit the clinic). An important aspect of the clinics is the presence of individuals trained to understand the special needs and confusions of the adolescent age group.

Better sex education, family planning, and access to contraceptive methods alone will not remedy the adolescent pregnancy crisis, especially for high-risk adolescents. Adolescents have to become *motivated* to reduce their pregnancy risk. This motivation will come only when adolescents look to the future and see that they have an opportunity to become self-sufficient and successful (Edelman, 1987). Adolescents need opportunities to improve their academic and career-related skills, job opportunities, life-planning consultation, and extensive mental health services (Dryfoos, 1990; Postrado & Nicholson, 1992).

Finally, for adolescent pregnancy prevention to ultimately succeed, we need broad community involvement and support. This support is a major reason for the success of pregnancy prevention efforts in other developed nations where adolescent pregnancy rates, abortion, and childbearing are much lower than in America despite similar levels of sexual activity (Jones & others, 1985; Wallace & Vienonen, 1989). In Holland, as well as other European countries such as Sweden, sex does not carry the mystery and conflict it does in American society. Holland does not have a mandated sex education program, but adolescents can obtain contraceptive counseling at government-sponsored clinics for a small fee. The Dutch media also have played an important role in educating the public about sex through frequent broadcasts focused on birth control, abortion, and related matters. Dutch adolescents do not consider having sex without contraception.

So far, we have discussed four ways to reduce adolescent pregnancy: sex education and family planning, access to contraceptive methods, life options, and broad community involvement and support. A fifth, very important consideration, especially for young adolescents, is abstention. Abstention is increasingly being included as a theme in sex education classes.

At this point, we have discussed a number of ideas about sexual attitudes and behavior, and adolescent pregnancy. A summary of these ideas is presented in Concept Table 12.1. Next, we examine another problem associated with adolescent sexual activity—sexually transmitted diseases.

Sexually Transmitted Diseases

Tammy, age 15, just finished listening to an expert lecture in her health class. We overhear her talking to one of her girlfriends as she walks down the school corridor: "That was a disgusting lecture. I can't believe all the diseases you can get by having sex. I think she was probably trying to scare us. She spent a lot of time talking about AIDS, which I have heard that normal people do not get. Right? I've heard that only homosexuals and drug addicts get AIDS. And I've also heard that gonorrhea and most other sexual diseases can be cured, so what is the big deal if you get something like that?" Tammy's view of sexually transmitted diseases (formerly called venereal disease or VD)—that they always happen to someone else, that they can be easily cured without any harm done, that they are too disgusting for a nice young person to hear about, let alone get— is common among adolescents. Tammy's view is wrong. Adolescents who are having sex run the risk of getting sexually transmitted diseases.

Sexually transmitted diseases (STDs) *are diseases that are contracted primarily through sexual contact. This contact is not limited to vaginal intercourse but includes oral-genital and anal-genital contact as well.* STDs are an increasing health problem. We begin our discussion by considering two caused by bacterial infections—gonorrhea and syphilis.

Concept Table 12.1

Sexual Attitudes and Behaviors, and Adolescent Pregnancy

Concept	Processes/Related Ideas	Characteristics/Description
Sexual attitudes and behavior	Heterosexual attitudes and behavior	Adolescents engage in a rather consistent progression of sexual behaviors—necking, petting, intercourse, and in some cases, oral sex. The number of adolescents reporting having had intercourse has significantly increased in the twentieth century, and the proportion of females engaging in intercourse has increased more rapidly than that of males. National data indicate that approximately half of all adolescents today have had sexual intercourse by the age of 18, although the percentage varies by sex, ethnicity, and context. Male, Black American, and inner-city adolescents report the highest incidence of sexual activity. As adolescents develop their sexual identity, they follow certain sexual scripts, which are different for females and males. Vulnerable adolescents are more likely to show irresponsible sexual behavior.
	Homosexual attitudes and behavior	About 4 percent of males and 3 percent of females choose to be exclusively homosexual. About 10 percent of adolescents worry about whether they are lesbian or gay. Until recently, there was increasing acceptance of homosexuality, but the AIDS epidemic has reduced this acceptance. The causes of homosexuality are unsettled.
	Self-stimulation	Self-stimulation is part of the sexual orientation of virtually all adolescents and one of their most frequent sexual outlets. Today's adolescents feel less guilty about masturbation than their counterparts earlier in history.
	Contraceptive use	Adolescents are increasing their use of contraceptives, but large numbers still do not use contraception; a majority of adolescent females do not use contraception at first intercourse. Younger adolescents and adolescents from low-income backgrounds are less likely to use contraceptives than their older counterparts from middle-class backgrounds. U.S. adolescents are less likely to have contraceptives available to them and less likely to use contraceptives than adolescents in many developed countries, especially England and Wales, Sweden, and the Netherlands.
Adolescent pregnancy	Incidence and nature of adolescent pregnancy	More than 1 million American adolescents become pregnant each year. Eight of ten adolescent pregnancies are unintended. The only bright spot in adolescent pregnancy statistics is that the adolescent pregnancy rate is leveling off or possibly even declining. America's adolescent pregnancy rate is the highest in the Western world. Dramatic changes have swept through the American culture in the last three decades regarding adolescent sexuality and pregnancy.
	Consequences of adolescent pregnancy	Adolescent pregnancy increases health risks for both the mother and the offspring. Adolescent mothers often drop out of school, fail to gain employment, and become dependent on welfare.
	Cognitive factors in adolescent pregnancy	The personal fable of adolescents may make pregnancy prevention difficult. The nature of early adolescent cognition, the personal fable, anxiety about sex, gender roles, the sexual themes of music and the media, and a societal standard that says that sex is appropriate for adults but not adolescents—all these factors make sex difficult for adolescents to handle.
	Adolescents as parents	The infants of adolescent parents are at risk both medically and psychologically. Adolescent mothers are less effective in rearing their children than older mothers. Adolescent fathers are more involved than the popular stereotype suggests, but many do not know what to do with a baby. Support systems for adolescent fathers are growing but are still far too few. Adolescent fathers have lower incomes, less education, and more children than those who delay having children until their twenties.
	Reducing adolescent pregnancy	Reductions in adolescent pregnancy require sex education and family planning, access to contraceptive methods, the life options approach, broad community involvement and support, and abstention.

Gonorrhea

Gonorrhea *is a sexually transmitted disease that is commonly called the "drip"* *or the "clap." It is reported to be the most common STD in the United States* *and is caused by a bacterium called* gonococcus, *which thrives in the moist* *mucous membranes lining the mouth, throat, vagina, cervix, urethra, and anal* *tract.* The bacterium is spread by contact between the infected moist membranes of one individual and the moist membranes of another. Thus, virtually all forms of sexual contact can spread the gonococcus, although transfer does not occur with every contact. Males have a 10 percent chance of becoming infected with each exposure to gonococcus. Females have more than a 40 percent chance of contracting the disease with each exposure because of the large surface area of the vaginal mucous membrane (Greenberg & others, 1989).

Symptoms of gonorrhea appear in males from three days to a month after contact. The symptoms include discharge from the penis, burning during urination, blood in the urine, aching pain or pressure in the genitals, and swollen and tender lymph glands in the groin. In females, the tragedy is that 80 percent of the infected females show no symptoms in the early stages of the disease, although pelvic inflammation is common at this early point. Untreated in females, the disease causes infection in the reproductive area and pelvic region within two months. Scarring of the fallopian tubes and infertility may result.

Gonorrhea can be successfully treated in its early stages with penicillin or other antibiotics. Despite reporting laws, many gonorrhea cases go unreported. In 1988, 720,000 new cases of gonorrhea were reported by the National Center for Health Statistics. Twenty-seven percent of the recent gonorrhea outbreak was in 15- to 19-year-olds, who represent only 7 percent of the population.

Syphilis

Syphilis *is a sexually transmitted disease caused by the bacterium* Treponema pallidum, *also called a spirochete.* The spirochete needs a warm, moist environment to survive and is transmitted by vaginal, oral-genital, or anal contact. It can also be transmitted from a pregnant woman to her unborn child after the fourth month of pregnancy. If the mother is treated before this time with penicillin, the syphilis will not be transmitted to the child.

Syphilis occurs in four stages: primary, secondary, latent, and tertiary. In the primary stage, a sore or chancre appears at the site of the infection. The sore heals after four to six weeks, giving the impression that the problem has gone away. Untreated, though, the secondary stage appears—it consists of a number of symptoms, including a rash, fever, sore throat, headache, swollen glands, joint pain, poor appetite, and hair loss. Treatment with penicillin can be successful if begun at this stage or earlier. Without treatment, symptoms of the secondary stage go away after six weeks, and the disease enters a latent stage. The spirochetes spread throughout the body, and in 50 to 70 percent of those affected, remain there for years in the same stage. After one or two years, the disease is no longer transmitted through sexual contact but can be passed from a pregnant woman to her unborn child. For 30 to 50 percent of the individuals who reach the latent stage, a final, tertiary stage follows. In this advanced stage, syphilis can cause paralysis, psychological disorders, or even death.

In 1988, 103,000 cases of syphilis were reported to the Public Health Service. In many areas of the United States, syphilis has been increasing. We now turn to two STDs that are caused by viruses—herpes genitalis and AIDS.

Herpes Genitalis

Herpes *is a sexually transmitted disease caused by a family of viruses with different strains. These strains produce diseases such as chicken pox and mononucleosis, as well as herpes simplex, an STD that has two variations.* Type 1 is characterized by cold sores and fever blisters. Type 2 includes painful sores on the lower body—genitals, thighs, and buttocks. Type 1 infections can be transmitted to the lower body, and type 2 infections can be transmitted to the oral area, through oral-genital contact. Approximately 75 percent of individuals exposed to an infected partner develop herpes.

Three to five days after contact, itching and tingling can occur, followed by an eruption of sores and blisters. The attacks can last up to three weeks and may recur in a few weeks or a few years. The blisters and sores in subsequent attacks are usually milder, but while the virus is dormant in the body, it can travel to the brain and other parts of the nervous system. Although rare, this transmission through the nervous system can cause such disorders as encephalitis and blindness. Herpes infections can also be transmitted from a pregnant woman to her offspring at birth, leading to brain damage or even death for the infant. A cesarean section can avert this problem. Women with herpes are also eight times more likely to develop cervical cancer than are unaffected women.

In 1986, the Centers for Disease Control in Atlanta estimated that 98 million Americans were infected with type 1 herpes and 9 million with type 2 herpes. Approximately 600,000 new cases of type 2 herpes appeared annually in the United States during the 1980s.

There is no known cure for herpes, although drugs such as acyclovir can alleviate symptoms. People infected with herpes often experience severe emotional distress, as well as considerable physical discomfort. The virus can be transmitted through condoms and foams, making infected individuals reluctant to associate with others. Herpes victims are often anxious about when attacks will recur, angry about the unpredictability of their lives, and fearful that they will not be able to cope with the pain of the next attack. For these reasons, support groups for victims of herpes have been established. If you or someone you know would like more information about dealing with herpes, the Information Center on Herpes Disease (15 Park Row, New York, New York 10038) is a good resource.

AIDS

No single STD has had a greater impact on sexual behavior, or created more public fear in the last decade, than AIDS. **AIDS (Acquired Immune Deficiency Syndrome)** *is a sexually transmitted disease that is caused by the virus HIV (human immunodeficiency virus), which destroys the body's immune system* (see Figure 12.3). Following exposure, the individual is vulnerable to harm from germs that persons with normal immune systems could destroy.

Stages in the Progression of AIDS

In the first stage of the disease, referred to as HIV+ and asymptomatic, individuals do not show the characteristics of AIDS but can transmit the disease. It is estimated that 20 to 30 percent of those in Stage 1 will develop AIDS within 5 years. In Stage 2—HIV+ and symptomatic—an unknown number of those who had the silent infection develop symptoms, including swelling of the lymph glands, fatigue, weight loss, diarrhea, fever, and sweats. Many who are HIV+

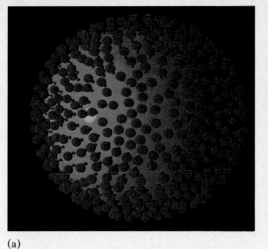

(a)

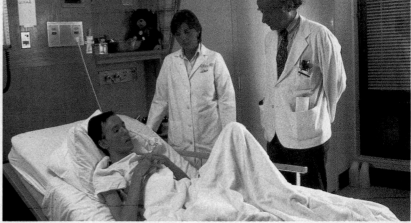

(b)

and symptomatic continue to the final stage—AIDS. A person with AIDS has the symptoms of AIDS plus one or more diseases, such as pneumonia, which is fatal to AIDS patients because of their vulnerable immune systems. Although there is no known cure for AIDS, several drugs are being tested, including AZT or zidovudine, approved by the FDA for treatment of the symptoms of AIDS in 1987.

Figure 12.3 (a) The AIDS virus can remain dormant for months or years. Once activated, though, it reproduces and bursts through the cell. Then the AIDS virus attacks healthy cells. Shown here is a computer-generated model of the AIDS virus. (b) An adolescent with AIDS in a hospital.

Incidence of AIDS in Different Age Groups

In 1981, when AIDS was first recognized in the United States, there were fewer than 60 reported cases. Beginning in 1990, according to Dr. Frank Press, president of the National Academy of Sciences, we annually started losing as many Americans to AIDS as the total number killed in the Vietnam War, almost 60,000 Americans per year. According to federal health officials, 1 to 1.5 million Americans are now asymptomatic carriers of AIDS—those who are infected with the virus and presumably are capable of infecting others but who show no clinical symptoms of AIDS.

The incidence of AIDS is especially high among ethnic minority groups in the United States (Mays, 1991). Although Blacks and Hispanics represented 12.3 percent and 8 percent of the United States population in 1988, 30 percent of the reported AIDS cases were Blacks and 14 percent were Hispanics. Much of the prevention media, as well as the instructions included with packages of retailed condoms, require a high school reading proficiency. It is estimated that approximately 40 percent of adult Hispanics lack this proficiency.

In 1989, researchers attempted to assess AIDS among college students. Tests of 16,861 students found 30 infected with the virus (American College Health Association, 1989). If the 12.5 million students attending college that year were infected in the same proportion, 25,000 students would have the AIDS virus.

Currently, there is a low cumulative prevalence of AIDS cases in adolescence. As of February, 1992, 796 adolescent AIDS cases in the 13- to 16-year age range had been reported to the Centers for Disease Control. However, the average latency time from viral infection to time of illness is about five to seven years (Ahlstrom & others, 1992). Thus, most infected adolescents would not become ill until they are young adults. Some of the differences between AIDS cases in adolescents and adults are the following:

1. A higher percentage of adolescent AIDS cases are acquired by heterosexual transmission.
2. A higher percentage of adolescents are asymptomatic individuals (who will become symptomatic in adulthood).
3. A higher percentage of Black and Hispanic cases occur in adolescence.
4. A special set of ethical and legal issues are involved in testing and informing partners and parents of adolescents.
5. There is less use and availability of contraceptives in adolescence. (Hein, 1990)

In one study, condom use among adolescents who are at the greatest risk of contracting AIDS—for example, intravenous drug users—was significantly below average (Sonenstein, Pleck, & Ku, 1989). Only 21 percent of the adolescents who had used intravenous drugs or whose partners had used intravenous drugs used condoms. Among adolescents who reported having sex with prostitutes, only 17 percent said that they used condoms. And among adolescents who reported having sex with five or more partners in the last year, only 37 percent reported using condoms. Adolescents who reported homosexual intercourse reported the highest condom use—66 percent.

Factors in AIDS Transmission

Experts say that AIDS can be transmitted only by sexual contact, the sharing of needles, or blood transfusion (Rotheram-Borus & Koopman, 1991). Although 90 percent of AIDS cases continue to occur among homosexual males and intravenous drug users, a disproportionate increase among females who are heterosexual partners of bisexual males or of intravenous drug users has been recently noted. This increase suggests that the risk of AIDS may be increasing among heterosexual individuals who have multiple sex partners (Boyer & Hein, 1991; Corless & Pittman-Lindeman, 1989). Table 12.5 describes what's risky and what's not regarding AIDS.

Just asking a date about his or her sexual behavior does not guarantee protection from AIDS and other sexually transmitted diseases. For example, in one recent investigation, 655 college students were asked to answer questions about lying and sexual behavior (Cochran & Mays, 1990). Of the 442 respondents who said that they were sexually active, 34 percent of the males and 10 percent of the females said that they had lied so that their partner would have sex with them. Much higher percentages—47 percent of the males and 60 percent of the females—said that they had been lied to by a potential sexual partner. When asked what aspects of their past they would be most likely to lie about, more than 40 percent of the males and females said that they would understate the number of their sexual partners. Twenty percent of the males but only 4 percent of the females said that they would lie about their results from an AIDS blood test.

Of special interest is the controversy surrounding children and adolescents who have contracted the virus. For example, one 13-year-old hemophiliac contracted AIDS while receiving injections of a clotting agent. He was barred from resuming his seventh-grade classes. In another case in another school district, school officials and doctors met with more than 800 concerned parents to defend their decision to admit a 14-year-old AIDS patient to school. Some parents will not let their children attend schools where an identified AIDS patient is enrolled. Others believe that children and adolescents with the disease should not be so-

Table 12.5   Understanding AIDS: What's Risky, What's Not

The AIDS virus is not transmitted like colds or the flu, but by an exchange of infected blood, semen, or vaginal fluids. This usually occurs during sexual intercourse, in sharing drug needles, or to babies infected before or during birth.

You Won't Get AIDS from:

—Everyday contact with individuals around you at school or the workplace, parties, child-care centers, or stores.

—Swimming in a pool, even if someone in the pool has the AIDS virus.

—A mosquito bite, or from bedbugs, lice, flies, or other insects.

—Saliva, sweat, tears, urine, or a bowel movement.

—A kiss.

—Clothes, telephones, or toilet seats.

—Using a glass or eating utensils that someone with the virus has used.

—Being on a bus, train, or crowded elevator with an individual who is infected with the virus or who has AIDS.

Blood Donations and Transfusions:

—You will not come into contact with the AIDS virus by donating blood at a blood bank.

—The risk of getting AIDS from a blood transfusion had been greatly reduced. Donors are screened for risk factors, and donated blood is tested.

Risky Behavior:

—Having a number of sex partners.

—Sharing drug needles and syringes.

—Engaging in anal sex with or without a condom.

—Performing vaginal or oral sex with someone who shoots drugs or engages in anal sex.

—Engaging in sex with someone you don't know well or with someone who has several sexual partners.

—Engaging in unprotected sex (without a condom) with an infected individual.

Safe Behavior:

—Not having sex.

—Sex with one mutually faithful, uninfected partner.

—Sex with proper protection.

—Not shooting drugs.

Source: U.S. government educational pamphlet: *America Responds to AIDS*, 1988.

ciety's outcasts given current knowledge of how the disease spreads (Task Force on Pediatric AIDS, 1989).

If you or someone you know would like more information about AIDS, you can call the National AIDS Hot Line at 1–800–342–7432, 8 A.M.–2 A.M. EST, 7 days a week.

Sexual Knowledge and Sex Education

Given the high rate of sexually transmitted diseases, a special concern is the knowledge that both adolescents and adults have about these diseases and about other aspects of sexuality. How sexually literate are Americans? What are adolescents' sources of sex education? What is the role of schools in sex education?

Sexual Knowledge

In one investigation, one-third of American females, ages 15 to 17, did not know what time of the month they were most likely to get pregnant (Loewen & Leigh,

The AIDS epidemic has led to an increased awareness of the importance of sex education in adolescence.

1986). In another study, a majority of adolescents believed that pregnancy risk is greatest during menstruation (Zelnick & Kantner, 1977). According to June Reinisch (1990), Director of the Kinsey Institute for Sex, Gender, and Reproduction, U.S. citizens know more about how their automobiles function than how their bodies sexually function.

American adolescents and adults are not sheltered from sexual messages. According to Reinisch, adolescents too often are inundated with sexual messages, but not sexual facts. Sexual information is abundant, but much of it is misinformation. In some cases, even sex education teachers display sexual ignorance. One high school sex education teacher referred to erogenous zones as "erroneous zones," possibly causing students to wonder if their sexually sensitive zones were in error!

Sources of Sex Information

One 14-year-old adolescent recently was asked where he learned about sex. He responded, "In the streets." Asked if this was the only place, he said, "Well, I learned some more from *Playboy* and the other sex magazines." What about school, he was asked. He responded, "No, they talk about hygiene, but not much that could help you out." When asked about his parents' contributions, he replied, "They haven't told me one thing."

Parents are an important missing ingredient in the fight against adolescent pregnancy and sexually transmitted diseases (Franz & others, 1992). A large majority of adolescents say that they cannot talk freely with their parents about sexual matters. Surveys indicate that about 17 percent of adolescents' sex education comes from mothers and only about 2 percent from fathers (Thornburg, 1981). While parents, especially fathers, have been infrequent sources of sex education for adolescents, adolescents report that, when they can talk with their parents openly and freely about sex, they are *less* likely to be sexually active. Contraceptive use by female adolescents also increases when adolescents report that they can communicate about sex with their parents (Fisher, 1987).

In a survey of all 1,152 students at a midwestern high school, students were asked where they learned about various aspects of sex (Thornburg, 1981). As in

Table 12.6 Initial Sources of Sex Information ($N = 1,152$)

	Abortion	Conception	Contraception	Ejaculation	Homosexuality	Intercourse	Masturbation	Menstruation	Petting	Prostitution	Seminal Emissions	Venereal Disease	Totals
Peers	20.6%	27.4%	42.8%	38.9%	50.6%	39.7%	36.3%	21.5%	59.7%	49.7%	35.2%	28.2%	37.1%
Literature	32.0	3.2	23.8	22.1	19.4	15.2	25.0	11.2	10.0	26.8	37.4	21.2	21.9
Mother	21.5	49.4	13.1	8.9	7.5	23.8	11.1	41.5	4.5	7.5	4.2	9.4	17.4
Schools	23.7	16.4	16.7	20.7	16.1	7.6	17.5	15.7	9.0	11.7	21.1	36.8	15.2
Experience	.5	.8	1.0	5.2	2.1	7.5	8.0	7.6	14.0	2.0	.7	1.1	5.4
Father	1.0	1.2	2.4	2.6	4.3	3.9	1.3	1.1	2.2	1.0	1.4	2.1	2.2
Minister	1.0	.9	.0	.7	.0	1.0	.0	.7	.2	1.0	.0	.0	.5
Physician	.3	.7	.2	.9	.0	1.3	.8	.7	.4	.3	.0	1.2	.3
Totals	100.0%	100.0%	100.0%	100.0%	100.0%	100.0%	100.0%	100.0%	100.0%	100.0%	100.0%	100.0%	100.0%

From Thornberg, H. D., "Sources of sex education among early adolescents," *Journal of Early Adolescence,* 1981, 1, p. 174. Reprinted by permission.
Note: "Don't know" responses were eliminated from the table.

other investigations, the most common source of sex information was peers, followed by literature, mothers, schools, and experience (see Table 12.6). While schools are usually thought of as a main source of sex education, only 15 percent of the adolescents' information about sex came from school instruction. In one recent study, college students said that they got more sex education from reading than any other source (Andre, Frevert, & Schuchmann, 1989).

Sex Education in the Schools

A majority of parents favor sex education in the schools. In a national poll conducted for *Time* magazine, 78 percent of parents wanted schools to teach sex education, including information about birth control. Despite the majority opinion, sex education remains swirled in controversy. On one side are groups like Planned Parenthood who argue that sex education should be more open and birth control more available, as in European countries. On the other side are individuals who believe that sex education should be provided by parents and that teaching adolescents about birth control is simply giving them a green light to have sex and be promiscuous. The controversy has led to clashes at school board meetings throughout the nation. In New York City, a program was developed to combat a runaway rate of adolescent pregnancy. Religious groups showed up at a school board meeting with a list of 56 objections. In San Juan Capistrano, California, conservative opponents of sex education in the schools appeared at a school board meeting dressed in Revolutionary War clothes. They even brought a cannon with them. The AIDS epidemic has brought an increased interest in sex education (Brown, DiClemente, & Beausoleil, 1992). To read further about AIDS and sex education, turn to Perspective on Adolescent Development 12.2.

A survey of sex education in the nation's school districts involving cities with populations of 100,000 or more found that three-fourths provided some sex education instruction in high school or junior high school, while two-thirds provided it in elementary school (Sonenstein & Pittman, 1984). This does not mean that every school in the district provided sex education or that the instruction

"I don't like this A in sex education."
© GLENN BERNHARDT

PERSPECTIVE ON ADOLESCENT DEVELOPMENT 12.2

AIDS and Sex Education

In November, 1991, basketball legend Magic Johnson of the Los Angeles Lakers announced that he was HIV-positive. The Monday morning after Johnson told the nation he has HIV, adolescents' conversations were buzzing with comments and questions about Johnson and about AIDS. Within several weeks, condom sales increased and AIDS awareness programs were attracting more people. Sex education instructors reported a dramatic increase in AIDS-related questions from their students. The first question many students asked was, "How did Magic get it?"

Educators continue to debate how best to answer that question, and how best to handle other questions raised by students since Johnson's announcement (Marklein & DeRosa, 1991). Schools also reported a dramatic increase in calls from parents in the months following Johnson's revelation; they wanted to know what the schools were teaching their children and adolescents about AIDS. Some experts on adolescent sexuality hope that Johnson's announcement will prompt more school systems to require sex education and provide more explicit information about contraception. Most states now require some form of AIDS education. However, the nature of the AIDS education programs vary considerably. In Michigan, Minnesota, and Nevada, school districts are required to develop an HIV education program, but students don't have to take it, and most states allow parents the option of taking their children and adolescents out of such courses.

Furthermore, there are clear differences of opinion about what is appropriate for class discussion, and the range of responses to Johnson's announcement underscores the complexity of the issue. Some educators dismiss Johnson's usefulness as a teaching aid. Others fear that the rush to embrace him as a role model is misguided. Still others believe the well-known superstar can have a special influence on adolescents. Yet even others believe that, although Johnson can play an important role in AIDS awareness, his message that "safe sex" is the way to go was the wrong thing to say. They argue that he ought to be communicating abstinence rather than safe sex.

The AIDS epidemic has led an increasing number of school systems to actually distribute condoms to students, and since the Johnson announcement others are considering the distribution. New York City and San Francisco school districts already have condom programs, and Massachusetts is encouraging its districts to adopt them. Los Angeles officials are considering a proposal to make condoms available to 135,000 students in 49 high schools. At the same time, critics of the condom distribution programs argue that abstinence education, not condoms for safe sex, should be the focus of sex education programs in the nation's schools. Given the moral issues that become wrapped up in sexuality, it is likely that such opposing views will continue to be voiced.

---

was comprehensive and competent. Indeed, most school districts integrated material on sex education into other courses, such as health education, biology, physical education, and home economics.

At the junior or senior high school levels, sex education averaged 6 to 10 hours of teaching time, with few school districts providing comprehensive programs involving more than 40 hours of instruction. Almost all of the programs covered physiology, sexually transmitted diseases, pregnancy, and parenthood. About three-fourths included pregnancy prevention information, such as contraception, sources of family-planning services, and the most likely time for pregnancy to occur. Table 12.7 indicates the grade level at which different topics were most likely to be introduced. The progression is usually from physiological facts to reproductive facts and issues and then to more complicated, value-laden issues.

Sex education programs vary from one school to the next. Many schools have no sex education program at all. Among those that do, a sex education program can range from a well-developed, full-semester course on human sexuality to a two-week unit on anatomy and physiology. The most common place for adolescents to be given sex education information is in a tenth-grade biology class. Another factor in quality sex education is the teacher. Most instructors in sex

Table 12.7   Grade-Level Placement of 24 Topics in City Schools

Grades 5–6

Physical differences*   Changes of puberty

Grades 7–8

Intercourse and pregnancy probability*   Communication with opposite sex*
Most likely time in cycle for pregnancy   Media messages about sex
Pregnancy and childbirth   Resistance to peer pressure for sex
Consequences of teen pregnancy*   Sexual decision making*
Sexually transmitted diseases*   Personal values*
Sexual feelings and attraction*   Masturbation
Communication with parents

Grades 9–10

Family-planning sources   Love relationships and commitment*
Contraceptives   Abortion
Gynecological examination   Homosexuality
Responsibilities of parenthood*   Rape and sexual abuse
Teen marriage*

Source: Table 4 Freya L. Sonenstein, et al., "The Availability of Sex Education in Large City School Districts,"
Family Planning Perspectives, Vol. 16, No. 1 January/February 1984 © The Alan Guttmacher Institute.
*Topic offered by at least 80 percent of districts.

education have majored in biology, health education, home economics, or physical education. Few have extensive coursework in human sexuality (Newton, 1982). While teachers do not need a Ph.D. in human sexuality to be an effective sex education instructor, they should be well trained and knowledgeable about sexuality. They should be willing to admit when they do not know the answer to a student's question and to look up the information for the next class. The sex education teacher should be skilled in handling adolescent emotions. Sexuality is a sensitive topic, and adolescents need to be helped to feel at ease in discussing sex.

Sex education programs in schools may not by themselves prevent adolescent pregnancy and sexually transmitted diseases. Researchers have found that sex education classes do improve adolescents' knowledge about human sexuality but do not always change their sexual behavior. When sex education programs are combined with contraceptive availability, the pregnancy rates of adolescents are more likely to drop (Wallis, 1985). This has led to the development of *school-linked* rather than school-based approaches to sex education and pregnancy prevention. In one program pioneered by some Baltimore public schools in cooperation with Johns Hopkins University, family-planning clinics are located adjacent to the schools (Zabin, 1986). The clinics send a nurse and social worker into the schools, where they make formal presentations about the services available from the clinics and about sexuality. They also are available to the students for counseling several hours each day. The same health personnel also conduct after-school sessions at the clinics. These sessions involve further counseling, films, and family-planning information. The results have been very positive. Students who participated in the programs delayed their first intercourse longer than students in a control group. After 28 months, the pregnancy rate had declined by 30 percent in the program schools, while it rose 60 percent in the control-group schools. This program demonstrates that a key dimension of pregnancy prevention is the link between information and support services (Kenney, 1987).

However, some critics argue that school-linked health clinics promote premarital sex and encourage abortion for pregnant adolescents (Glasow, 1988). These critics believe that more effort should be devoted to promoting adolescents' abstention from sex. Supporters of the school-linked clinics argue that sexual activity in adolescence has become a normative behavior and, therefore, that interventions should focus on teaching responsible sexual behavior and providing access to contraception (Dryfoos, 1990).

Responsible sexual behavior is especially lacking in adolescent or adult males who force adolescent females to have sexual intercourse with them. Let's examine the nature of forcible sexual behavior further.

Forcible Sexual Behavior

Most people choose to engage in sexual intercourse or other sexual activities, but, unfortunately, some people force others to engage in sex. **Rape** *is forcible sexual intercourse with a person who does not give consent.* Legal definitions of rape differ from state to state. For example, in some states, husbands are not prohibited from forcing their wives to have intercourse, although this law has been challenged in several states (Greenberg & others, 1989). Because of the difficulties involved in reporting rape, the actual incidence is not easily determined. It appears that rape occurs most often in large cities, where it has been reported that 8 of every 10,000 women 12 years and older are raped each year. Nearly 200,000 rapes are reported each year in the United States. Ninety-five percent of rapes are committed by males.

Why is rape so pervasive in the American culture? Feminist writers believe that males are socialized to be sexually aggressive, to regard females as inferior beings, and to view their own pleasure as the most important objective. Researchers have found the following characteristics common among rapists: aggression enhances the offender's sense of power or masculinity; rapists are angry at females generally; and they want to hurt their victims (Knight, Rosenberg, & Schneider, 1985).

An increasing concern is **date, or acquaintance, rape,** *which is coercive sexual activity directed at someone with whom the individual is at least casually acquainted.* Date rape is an increasing problem in high schools and on college campuses (Clark, Klein, & Beckett, 1992; Klingaman & Vicary, 1992; Lloyd, 1991). In one investigation, almost two-thirds of the college men admitted that they fondled women against their will and one-half admitted to forced sexual activity.

Rape is a traumatic experience for the victim and those close to her or him. The rape victim initially feels shock and numbness, and is often acutely disorganized. Some females show their distress through words and tears; others show more internalized suffering. As victims strive to get their lives back to normal, they may experience depression, fear, and anxiety for months or years. Sexual dysfunctions, such as reduced sexual desire and the inability to reach orgasm, occur in 50 percent of all rape victims (Sprei & Courtoi, 1988). Many rape victims make changes in their life-style, moving to a new apartment or refusing to go out at night. A victim's recovery depends on both her coping abilities and her psychological adjustment prior to the assault. Social support from parents, spouse, and others close to her are important factors in recovery, as is the availability of professional counseling, which sometimes is obtained through a rape crisis center (Koss, 1990).

At this point, we have discussed a number of ideas about sexually transmitted diseases, about sexual knowledge and sex education, and about forcible sexual behavior. A summary of these ideas is presented in Concept Table 12.2.

Concept Table 12.2

Sexually Transmitted Diseases, and Sexual Knowledge and Sex Education

Concept	Processes/Related Ideas	Characteristics/Description
Sexually transmitted diseases	Their nature	Also called STDs, sexually transmitted diseases are contracted primarily through sexual contact. This contact is not limited to vaginal intercourse but includes oral-genital and anal-genital contact as well.
	Gonorrhea	Commonly called the "drip" or the "clap," gonorrhea is reported to be the most common STD in the United States. Gonorrhea is caused by a tiny bacterium called gonococcus. It can be treated with penicillin and other antibiotics.
	Syphilis	Syphilis is caused by the bacterium *Treponema pallidum,* also called a spirochete. Syphilis occurs in four phases: primary, secondary, latent, and tertiary. If detected in the first two phases, it can be successfully treated with penicillin.
	Herpes genitalis	Herpes is caused by a family of viruses with different strains. Herpes simplex has two variations. Type 1 is characterized by cold sores and fever blisters. Type 2 includes painful sores on the lower body—genitals, thighs, and buttocks. There is no known cure for herpes.
	AIDS	AIDS (Acquired Immune Deficiency Syndrome) is caused by the virus HIV (human immunodeficiency virus), which destroys the body's immune system. There is no known cure for AIDS. Three stages characterize the progression of AIDS: HIV+ and asymptomatic, HIV+ and symptomatic, and AIDS. The incidence of AIDS is especially high among ethnic minority groups in the United States. Currently, there is a low cumulative total of AIDS cases in adolescence, but increasing numbers of adolescents are becoming infected with the HIV virus. AIDS can be transmitted only through sexual contact, the sharing of needles, and blood transfusions. AIDS is increasingly occurring as a consequence of heterosexual transmission, especially for heterosexuals who have multiple sex partners.
Sexual knowledge and sex education	Sexual knowledge	American adolescents and adults are not very knowledgeable about sex. Sex information is abundant, but much of it is misinformation.
	Sources of sex information	Adolescents get the most information about sex from peers, followed by literature, mothers, schools, and experience. Less than 2 percent of adolescents' sex education comes from fathers.
	Sex education in the schools	A majority of parents favor sex education in the schools, but controversy still swirls around this topic. Most American schools provide sex education, but it may be as little as a brief segment of a biology class or as much as an entire course on human sexuality. Some experts believe that a promising strategy is school-linked sex education that ties in with community health centers. Critics argue that the school-linked clinics encourage premarital sex and abortion; they believe that more effort should be devoted to promoting adolescents' abstention from sex. Supporters of the school-linked clinics argue that sexual activity has become normative behavior in adolescence and, therefore, that interventions should focus on teaching responsible sexual behavior and providing access to contraception.
	Forcible sexual behavior	Some individuals force others to engage in sexual activity. Rape is forcible sexual intercourse with a person who does not give consent; approximately 95 percent of all rapes are committed by males. Legal definitions of rape vary from state to state. An increasing concern is date, or acquaintance, rape. Rape is a traumatic experience and a woman's recovery depends on her coping resources, as well as on how well she was adjusted prior to the assault.

Moral values are often wrapped up in people's opinions about adolescent sexuality. In the next chapter, we discuss moral development, values, and religion.

Summary

I. Heterosexual Attitudes and Behavior
Adolescents engage in a rather consistent progression of sexual behaviors—necking, petting, intercourse, and in some cases, oral sex. The number of adolescents reporting having had sexual intercourse has significantly increased in the twentieth century, and the proportion of females engaging in intercourse has increased more rapidly than that of males. National data indicate that approximately half of all adolescents today have had sexual intercourse by the age of 18, although the percentage varies by sex, ethnicity, and context. Male, Black American, and inner-city adolescents report the highest incidence of sexual activity. As adolescents develop their sexual identity, they follow certain sexual scripts, which are different for females and males. Vulnerable adolescents are more likely to show irresponsible sexual behavior.

II. Homosexual Attitudes and Behavior
About 4 percent of males and 3 percent of females choose to be exclusively homosexual. About 10 percent of adolescents worry about whether they are lesbian or gay. Until recently, there was increasing acceptance of homosexuality, but the AIDS epidemic has reduced this acceptance. The causes of homosexuality are unsettled.

III. Self-Stimulation
Self-stimulation is part of the sexual orientation of virtually all adolescents and one of their most frequent sexual outlets. Today's adolescents feel less guilty about masturbation than their counterparts earlier in history.

IV. Contraceptive Use
Adolescents are increasing their use of contraceptives, but large numbers still do not use contraception; a majority of adolescents do not use contraception at first intercourse. Younger adolescents and adolescents from low-income backgrounds are less likely to use contraceptives than their older counterparts from middle-class backgrounds. U.S. adolescents are less likely to have contraceptives available to them and less likely to use contraceptives than adolescents in many developed countries, especially England and Wales, Sweden, and the Netherlands.

V. Adolescent Pregnancy: Incidence and Nature
More than 1 million American adolescents become pregnant each year. Eight of ten adolescent pregnancies are unintended. The only bright spot in adolescent pregnancy statistics is that the adolescent pregnancy rate is leveling off or possibly even declining. America's adolescent pregnancy rate is the highest in the Western world. Dramatic changes have swept through the American culture in the last three decades regarding adolescent sexuality and pregnancy.

VI. Adolescent Pregnancy: Consequences, Cognitive Factors in, Adolescents As Parents, and Reducing Adolescent Pregnancy
Adolescent pregnancy increases health risks for both the mother and the offspring. Adolescent mothers often drop out of school, fail to gain employment, and become dependent on welfare. The personal fable of adolescents may make pregnancy prevention difficult. The nature of early adolescent cognition, the personal fable, anxiety about sex, the sexual themes of music and the media, and a societal standard that says that sex is appropriate for adults but not adolescents—all these factors make sex difficult for adolescents to handle. The infants of adolescent parents are at risk both medically and psychologically.

Adolescent mothers are less effective in rearing their children than older mothers. Adolescent fathers are more involved than the popular stereotype suggests, but many do not know what to do with a baby. Support systems for adolescent fathers are growing but are still far too few. Adolescent fathers have lower incomes, less education, and more children than those who delay having children until their twenties. Reducing adolescent pregnancy requires sex education and family planning, access to contraceptive methods, the life options approach, broad community involvement and support, and abstention.

VII. **Sexually Transmitted Diseases: Gonorrhea, Syphilis, Herpes Genitalis, and AIDS**
Sexually transmitted diseases, also called STDs, are diseases that are contracted primarily through sexual contact. This contact is not limited to vaginal intercourse but includes oral-genital and anal-genital contact as well. Gonorrhea, commonly called the "drip" or the "clap," is reported to be the most common STD in the United States. Gonorrhea is caused by a tiny bacterium called gonococcus. It can be treated with penicillin and other antibiotics. Syphilis is caused by the bacterium *Treponema pallidum,* also called a spirochete. Syphilis occurs in four phases: primary, secondary, latent, and tertiary. If detected in the first two phases, it can be successfully treated with penicillin. Herpes is caused by a family of viruses with different strains. Herpes simplex has two variations. Type 1 is characterized by cold sores and fever blisters. Type 2 includes painful sores on the lower body—genitals, thighs, and buttocks. There is no known cure for herpes. AIDS (Acquired Immune Deficiency Syndrome) is caused by the virus HIV (human immunodeficiency virus), which destroys the body's immune system. Three stages characterize the progression of AIDS: HIV+ and asymptomatic, HIV+ and symptomatic, and AIDS. The incidence of AIDS is especially high among ethnic minority groups in the United States. Currently, there is a low cumulative total of AIDS cases in adolescence, but increasing numbers of adolescents are becoming infected with the HIV virus. AIDS can be transmitted only through sexual contact, the sharing of needles, and blood transfusions. AIDS is increasingly occurring as a consequence of heterosexual transmission, especially for heterosexuals who have multiple sex partners.

VIII. **Sexual Knowledge and Sources of Sex Information**
American adolescents and adults are not very knowledgeable about sex. Sex information is abundant, but much of it is misinformation. Adolescents get the most sex information from peers, followed by literature, mothers, schools, and experience. Less than 2 percent of adolescents' sex education comes from fathers.

IX. **Sex Education in the Schools**
A majority of parents favor sex education in the schools, but controversy swirls around this topic. Most American schools provide sex education, but it may be as little as a brief segment of a biology class or as much as a complete course on human sexuality. Some experts believe that a promising strategy is school-linked sex education that ties in with community health centers. Critics argue that the school-linked clinics encourage premarital sex and abortion; they believe that more effort should be devoted to promoting adolescents' abstention from sex. Supporters of the school-linked clinics argue that sexual activity has become normative behavior in adolescence and, therefore, that interventions should focus on teaching responsible sexual behavior and providing access to contraception.

X. **Forcible Sexual Behavior**
Some individuals force others to engage in sexual activity. Rape is forcible sexual intercourse with a person who does not give consent; approximately 95 pecent of rapes are committed by males. Legal definitions of rape vary from state to state. An increasing concern is date, or acquaintance, rape. Rape is a traumatic experience; a female's recovery depends on her coping resources and how well adjusted she was prior to the assault.

Key Terms

sexual script 400
sexually transmitted
  diseases (STDs) 415

gonorrhea 417
syphilis 417
herpes 418

AIDS 418
rape 426
date (acquaintance)
  rape 426

Suggested Readings

Bancroft, J., & Reinisch, J. M. (Eds.). (1990). *Adolescence and puberty*. New York: Oxford University Press.

An excellent, up-to-date source about the nature of adolescent sexuality. Includes chapters about cross-cultural aspects of adolescent sexual activity, the biological basis of sexuality, trends in adolescent sexual behavior, and contraception.

Early adolescent sexuality: Resources for parents, professionals, and young people. (1983). Chapel Hill, NC: Center for Early Adolescence, University of North Carolina.

This compendium of resources provides an excellent annotated bibliography of a wide variety of topics related to sexuality in early adolescence.

Family Planning Perspectives

This journal includes research articles on adolescent pregnancy and contraceptive use. Leaf through the issues of the last several years to discover the nature of research in this field.

Hayes, C. D. (Ed.). (1987). *Risking the future: Adolescent sexuality, pregnancy, and childbearing* (Vol. 1). Washington, DC: National Academy Press.

An excellent source of information about adolescent sexual activity.

Hein, K. (1990). AIDS in adolescence. *Journal of Adolescent Health Care, 10,* 10–35.

An authoritative article on the incidence of AIDS in adolescence and an examination of how AIDS in adolescence differs from AIDS in adulthood.

McWhirter, D. P., Sanders, S. A., & Reinisch, J. M. (1990). *Homosexuality/ heterosexuality: Concepts of sexual orientation*. New York: Oxford University Press.

Includes an in-depth discussion of homosexual attitudes and behavior.

CHAPTER 13

Moral Development, Values, and Religion

It is one of the beautiful compensations of this life that no one can sincerely try to help another without helping himself.

Charles Dudley Warner, 1873

The Morals of a High School Newspaper

Fred, a senior in high school, wanted to publish a mimeographed newspaper for students so that he could express many of his opinions. He wanted to speak out against the war in Vietnam and against some of the school's rules, like the rule forbidding boys to have long hair.

Before Fred started his newspaper, he asked his principal for permission. The principal said that it would be all right if, before every publication, Fred would turn over all his articles for the principal's approval. Fred agreed and turned in several articles for approval. The principal approved all of them, and Fred published two issues of the paper in the next two weeks.

But the principal had not expected that Fred's newspaper would receive so much attention. Students were so excited about the paper that they began to organize protests against the hair regulation and the other school rules. Angry parents objected to Fred's opinions. They phoned the principal, telling him that the newspaper was unpatriotic and should not be published. As a result of the rising excitement, the principal ordered Fred to stop publishing. He gave as a reason that Fred's activities were disruptive to the operation of the school. (Rest, 1986, p. 194)

The preceding story about Fred and his newspaper raises a number of questions related to adolescents' moral development:

Should the principal stop the newspaper?

When the welfare of the school is threatened, does the principal have the right to give orders to students?

Does the principal have the freedom of speech to say "no" in this case?

If the principal stopped the newspaper, would he be preventing full discussion of an important problem?

Is Fred actually being loyal to his school and patriotic to his country?

What effect would stopping the newspaper have on the students' education in critical thinking and judgments?

Was Fred in any way violating the rights of others in publishing his own opinions?

> *Without civic morality, communities perish; without personal morality, their survival has no value.*
>
> *Bertrand Russell*

What moral dilemmas might crop up for adolescents responsible for the school newspaper?

T he story and the questions that followed it in the "Images of Adolescence" section are a common method of investigating adolescents' moral judgments. The strategy is to find out how adolescents think about moral dilemmas. In this chapter, we focus on adolescents' moral development and also discuss the nature of values, religion, and cults in adolescence.

What Is Moral Development?

Moral development is one of the oldest topics of interest to those who are curious about human nature. Today, most people have very strong opinions about acceptable and unacceptable behavior, ethical and unethical behavior, and ways in which acceptable and ethical behaviors are to be fostered in adolescents.

Moral development *concerns rules and conventions about what people should do in their interactions with other people.* In studying these rules, developmentalists examine three domains:

First, how do adolescents *reason* or *think* about rules for ethical conduct? For example, an adolescent can be presented with a story in which someone has a conflict about whether or not to cheat in a particular situation, such as taking an exam in school. The adolescent is asked to decide what is appropriate for the character to do and why. This was the strategy used in the "Images of Adolescence" section regarding Fred's newspaper. The focus is placed on the reasoning adolescents use to justify their moral decisions.

Second, how do adolescents actually *behave* in moral circumstances? For example, with regard to cheating, the emphasis is on observing adolescents' cheating and the environmental circumstances that produced and maintain the cheating. Adolescents might be observed through a one-way mirror as they are taking an exam. The observer might note whether they take out "cheat" notes, look at another student's answers, and so on.

Third, how do adolescents *feel* about moral matters? In the example of cheating, do the adolescents feel enough guilt to resist temptation? If adolescents do cheat, do feelings of guilt after the transgression keep them from cheating the next time they face temptation? The remainder of this discussion of moral development focuses on these three facets—thought, behavior, and feelings.

Moral Thought

How do adolescents think about standards of right and wrong? Piaget had some thoughts about this question. So did Lawrence Kohlberg.

Piaget's Ideas and Cognitive Disequilibrium Theory

Interest in how children and adolescents think about moral issues was stimulated by Piaget (1932), who extensively observed and interviewed children from the ages of 4 to 12. Piaget watched children play marbles to learn how they used and thought about the game's rules. He also asked children questions about ethical issues—theft, lies, punishment, and justice, for example. Piaget concluded that children think in two distinct ways about morality, depending on their developmental maturity. **Heteronomous morality** *is the first stage of moral development in Piaget's theory, occurring at four to seven years of age. Justice and rules are conceived of as unchangeable properties of the world, removed from the control of people.* **Autonomous morality,** *the second stage of moral development in Piaget's theory, is displayed by older children (about 10 years of age and older). The child becomes aware that rules and laws are created by people and that, in judging an action, one should consider the actor's intentions as well as the consequences.* Children 7 to 10 years of age are in a transition between the two stages, evidencing some features of both.

A heteronomous thinker judges the rightness or goodness of behavior by considering the consequences of the behavior, not the intentions of the actor. For example, the heteronomous thinker says that breaking 12 cups accidently is worse than breaking 1 cup intentionally while trying to steal a cookie. For the moral autonomist, the reverse is true. The actor's intentions assume paramount importance. The heteronomous thinker also believes that rules are unchangeable and are handed down by all-powerful authorities. When Piaget suggested to a group of young children that new rules be introduced into the game of marbles, they resisted. By contrast, older children—moral autonomists—accept change and recognize that rules are merely convenient, socially agreed-upon conventions, subject to change by consensus.

The heteronomous thinker also believes in **immanent justice,** *Piaget's concept that, if a rule is broken, punishment will be meted out immediately.* The young child somehow believes that the violation is connected automatically to the punishment. Thus, young children often look around worriedly after committing a transgression, expecting inevitable punishment. Older children, who are moral autonomists, recognize that punishment is socially mediated and occurs only if a relevant person witnesses the wrongdoing and that, even then, punishment is not inevitable.

Piaget argued that, as children develop, they become more sophisticated in thinking about social matters, especially about the possibilities and conditions of cooperation. Piaget believed that this social understanding comes about through the mutual give-and-take of peer relations. In the peer group, where others have power and status similar to the individual, plans are negotiated and coordinated, and disagreements are reasoned about and eventually settled. Parent-child relations, in which parents have the power and children do not, are less likely to advance moral reasoning because rules are often handed down in an authoritarian way.

As discussed in earlier chapters, Piaget believed that adolescents usually become formal operational thinkers. Thus, they are no longer tied to immediate and concrete phenomena but are more logical, abstract, and deductive reasoners. Formal operational thinkers frequently compare the real to the ideal; create contrary-to-fact propositions; are cognitively capable of relating the distant past to the present; understand their roles in society, in history, and in the universe; and can conceptualize their own thoughts and think about their mental constructs as objects. For example, around age 11 or 12, boys and girls spontaneously introduce concepts of belief, intelligence, and faith into their definitions of their religious identities.

Stimulated by Piaget's ideas, Martin Hoffman (1980) developed **cognitive disequilibrium theory,** *which states that adolescence is an important period in moral development, especially as individuals move from the relatively homogeneous grade school to the more heterogeneous high school and college envi-*

ronments, where they are faced with contradictions between the moral concepts they have accepted and experiences outside their family and neighborhood. Adolescents come to recognize that their set of beliefs is but one of many and that there is considerable debate about what is right and what is wrong. Many adolescents and youth start to question their former beliefs and, in the process, develop their own moral system.

Kohlberg's Ideas on Moral Development

One of the most provocative views of moral development was crafted by Lawrence Kohlberg (1958, 1976, 1986). Kohlberg believed that moral development is based primarily on moral reasoning and unfolds in a series of stages. He arrived at his view after about 20 years of research involving unique interviews with children. In the interviews, children were presented with a series of stories in which characters face moral dilemmas. The following is the most popular of the Kohlberg dilemmas:

Lawrence Kohlberg, the architect of a provocative cognitive developmental theory of moral development.

> In Europe, a woman was near death from a special kind of cancer. There was one drug that the doctors thought might save her. It was a form of radium that a druggist in the same town had recently discovered. The drug was expensive to make, but the druggist was charging ten times what the drug cost him to make. He paid $200 for the radium and charged $2,000 for a small dose of the drug. The sick woman's husband, Heinz, went to everyone he knew to borrow the money, but he could only get together $1,000, which is half of what it cost. He told the druggist that his wife was dying and asked him to sell it cheaper or let him pay later. But the druggist said, "No, I discovered the drug, and I am going to make money from it." So Heinz got desperate and broke into the man's store to steal the drug for his wife. (Kohlberg, 1969, p. 379)

This story is one of 11 that Kohlberg devised to investigate the nature of moral thought. After reading the story, interviewees are asked a series of questions about the moral dilemma: Should Heinz have stolen the drug? Was stealing it right or wrong? Why? Is it a husband's duty to steal the drug for his wife if he can get it no other way? Would a good husband steal it? Did the druggist have the right to charge that much when there was no law setting a limit on the price? Why?

From the answers interviewees gave for this and other moral dilemmas, Kohlberg hypothesized three levels of moral development, each of which is characterized by two stages. A key concept in understanding moral development is **internalization,** *the developmental change from behavior that is externally controlled to behavior that is controlled by internal standards and principles.* As children and adolescents develop, their moral thoughts become more internalized. Let us look further at Kohlberg's three levels of moral development.

Kohlberg's Level 1: Preconventional Reasoning
Preconventional reasoning *is the lowest level in Kohlberg's theory of moral development. At this level, the individual shows no internalization of moral values—moral reasoning is controlled by external rewards and punishments.*

- Stage 1. **Punishment and obedience orientation** *is the first stage in Kohlberg's theory of moral development. At this stage, moral thinking is based on punishment.* For example, children and adolescents obey adults because adults tell them to obey.
- Stage 2. **Individualism and purpose** *is the second stage in Kohlberg's theory of moral development. At this stage, moral thinking is based on*

rewards and self-interest. For example, children and adolescents obey when they want to obey and when it is in their best interest to obey. What is right is what feels good and what is rewarding.

Kohlberg's Level 2: Conventional Reasoning

Conventional reasoning *is the second, or intermediate, level in Kohlberg's theory of moral development. At this level, internalization is intermediate. Individuals abide by certain standards (internal), but they are the standards of others (external), such as parents or the laws of society.*

- Stage 3. **Interpersonal norms** *is the third stage in Kohlberg's theory of moral development. At this stage, individuals value trust, caring, and loyalty to others as the basis of moral judgments.* Children and adolescents often adopt their parents' moral standards at this stage, seeking to be thought of by their parents as a "good girl" or a "good boy."
- Stage 4. **Social systems morality** *is the fourth stage in Kohlberg's theory of moral development. At this stage, moral judgments are based on understanding the social order, law, justice, and duty.* For example, adolescents may say that, for a community to work effectively, it needs to be protected by laws that are adhered to by its members.

Kohlberg's Level 3: Postconventional Reasoning

Postconventional reasoning *is the highest level in Kohlberg's theory of moral development. At this level, morality is completely internalized and is not based on others' standards. The individual recognizes alternative moral courses, explores the options, and then decides on a personal moral code.*

- Stage 5. **Community rights versus individual rights** *is the fifth stage in Kohlberg's theory. At this stage, the person understands that values and laws are relative and that standards vary from one person to another.* The person recognizes that laws are important for a society but knows that laws can be changed. The person believes that some values, such as liberty, are more important than the law.
- Stage 6. **Universal ethical principles** *is the sixth and highest stage in Kohlberg's theory of moral development. At this stage, the person has developed a moral standard based on universal human rights.* When faced with a conflict between law and conscience, the person will follow conscience, even though the decision might involve personal risk.

Kohlberg believed that these levels and stages occur in a sequence and are age related: Before age nine, most children reason about moral dilemmas in a preconventional way; by early adolescence, they reason in more conventional ways; and by early adulthood, a small number of individuals reason in postconventional ways. In a 20-year longitudinal investigation, the uses of stages 1 and 2 decreased (Colby & others, 1983). Stage 4, which did not appear at all in the moral reasoning of 10-year-olds, was reflected in 62 percent of the moral thinking of 36-year-olds. Stage 5 did not appear until age 20 to 22 and never characterized more than 10 percent of the individuals. Thus, the moral stages appeared somewhat later than Kohlberg initially envisioned, and the higher stages, especially stage 6, were extremely elusive. Recently, stage 6 was removed from the Kohlberg moral judgment scoring manual, but it still is considered to be theoretically important in the Kohlberg scheme of moral development. A review of data from 45 studies in 27 diverse world cultures provided striking support for the universality of Kohlberg's first four stages, although there was more cultural diversity at stages 5 and 6 (Snarey, 1987).

Influences on the Kohlberg Stages

Kohlberg believed that the individual's moral orientation unfolds as a consequence of cognitive development. Children and adolescents construct their moral thoughts as they pass from one stage to the next, rather than passively accepting a cultural norm of morality. Investigators have sought to understand factors that influence movement through the moral stages, among them modeling, cognitive conflict, peer relations, and role-taking opportunities.

Several investigators have attempted to advance an individual's level of moral development by providing arguments that reflect moral thinking one stage above the individual's established level. These studies are based on the cognitive developmental concepts of equilibrium and conflict. By finding the correct environmental match slightly beyond the individual's cognitive level, a disequilibrium is created that motivates the individual to restructure his or her moral thought. The resolution of the disequilibrium and conflict should be toward increased competence, but the data are mixed on this question. In one of the pioneer studies on this topic, Eliot Turiel (1966) discovered that children preferred a response one stage above their current level over a response two stages above it. However, they actually chose a response one stage below their level more often than a response one stage above it. Apparently, the children were motivated more by security needs than by the need to reorganize thought to a higher level. Other studies indicate that individuals prefer a more advanced stage over a less advanced stage (Rest, Turiel, & Kohlberg, 1969).

A number of investigations have attempted to determine more precisely the effectiveness of various forms of stage modeling and arguments (Lapsley, Enright, & Serlin, 1986; Lapsley & Quintana, 1985). The upshot of these studies is that virtually any plus-stage discussion format, for any length of time, seems to promote more advanced moral reasoning. For example, in one investigation (Walker, 1982), exposure to plus-two stage reasoning (arguments two stages above the child's current stage of moral thought) was just as effective in advancing moral thought as plus-one stage reasoning. Exposure to plus-two stage reasoning did not produce more plus-two stage reasoning but rather, like exposure to plus-one stage reasoning, increased the likelihood that the child would reason one stage above his or her current stage. Other research has found that exposure to reasoning only one-third of a stage higher than the individual's current level of moral thought advances moral thought (Berkowitz & Gibbs, 1983). In sum, current research on modeling and cognitive conflict reveals that moral thought can be moved to a higher level through exposure to models or discussions that are more advanced than the child's or adolescent's.

Like Piaget, Kohlberg believed that peer interaction is a critical part of the social stimulation that challenges individuals to change their moral orientation. Whereas adults characteristically impose rules and regulations on children, the mutual give-and-take in peer interaction provides the child with an opportunity to take the role of another person and to generate rules democratically. Kohlberg stressed that role-taking opportunities can, in principle, be engendered by any peer group encounter. While Kohlberg believed that such role-taking opportunities are ideal for moral development, he also believed that certain types of parent-child experiences can induce the child to think at more advanced levels of moral thinking. In particular, parents who allow or encourage conversation about value-laden issues promote more advanced moral thought in their children and adolescents. Unfortunately, many parents do not systematically provide their children and adolescents with such role-taking opportunities.

Kohlberg's Critics

Kohlberg's provocative theory of moral development has not gone unchallenged (Kurtines & Gewirtz, 1991; Puka, 1991). The criticisms involve the link between moral thought and moral behavior, the quality of the research, inadequate consideration of culture's role in moral development, and underestimation of the care perspective.

Moral Thought and Moral Behavior

Kohlberg's theory has been criticized for placing too much emphasis on moral thought and not enough emphasis on moral behavior. Moral reasons can sometimes be a shelter for immoral behavior. Bank embezzlers and presidents endorse the loftiest of moral virtues when commenting about moral dilemmas, but their own behavior may be immoral. No one wants a nation of cheaters and thieves who can reason at the postconventional level. The cheaters and thieves may know what is right, yet still do what is wrong.

Assessment of Moral Reasoning

Some developmentalists fault the quality of Kohlberg's research and believe that more attention should be paid to the way moral development is assessed. For example, James Rest (1976, 1983, 1986, 1988) argued that alternative methods should be used to collect information about moral thinking instead of relying on a single method that requires individuals to reason about hypothetical moral dilemmas. Rest also said that Kohlberg's stories are extremely difficult to score. To help remedy this problem, Rest developed his own measure of moral development, called the Defining Issues Test (DIT) (the story about Fred and the school newspaper in the "Images of Adolescence" section is one of the moral dilemmas used in Rest's assessment of moral judgment).

The DIT attempts to determine which moral issues individuals feel are more crucial in a given situation by presenting them with a series of dilemmas and a list of definitions of the major issues involved (Kohlberg's procedure does not make use of such a list). In the dilemma of Heinz and the druggist, individuals might be asked whether a community's laws should be upheld or whether Heinz should be willing to risk being injured or caught as a burglar. They might also be asked to list the most important values that govern human interaction. They are given six stories and asked to rate the importance of each issue involved in deciding what ought to be done. Then they are asked to list what they believe are the four most important issues. Rest argued that this method provides a more valid and reliable way to assess moral thinking than Kohlberg's method.

Researchers also have found that the hypothetical moral dilemmas posed in Kohlberg's stories do not match the moral dilemmas many children and adults face in their everyday lives (Walker, de Vries, & Trevethan, 1987; Yussen, 1977). Most of Kohlberg's stories focus on the family and authority. However, when one researcher invited adolescents to write stories about their own moral dilemmas, the adolescents generated dilemmas that were broader in scope, focusing on friends, acquaintances, and other issues, as well as family and authority (Yussen, 1977). The adolescents' moral dilemmas also were analyzed in terms of their content. As shown in Figure 13.1, the moral issue that concerned adolescents more than any other was interpersonal relationships.

Story subject	Grade		
	7	9	12
	Percentage		
Alcohol	2	0	5
Civil rights	0	6	7
Drugs	7	10	5
Interpersonal relations	38	24	35
Physical safety	22	8	3
Sexual relations	2	20	10
Smoking	7	2	0
Stealing	9	2	0
Working	2	2	15
Other	11	26	20

Culture and Moral Development

Yet another criticism of Kohlberg's view is that it is culturally biased (Bronstein & Paludi, 1988; Miller, 1991; Miller & Bersoff, in press). A review of research on moral development in 27 countries concluded that moral reasoning is more culture specific than Kohlberg envisioned and that Kohlberg's scoring system does not recognize higher-level moral reasoning in certain cultural groups (Snarey, 1987). Examples of higher-level moral reasoning that would not be scored as such by Kohlberg's system are values related to communal equity and collective happiness in Israel, the unity and sacredness of all life-forms in India, and the relation of the individual to the community in New Guinea. These examples of moral reasoning would not be scored at the highest level in Kohlberg's system because they do not emphasize the individual's rights and abstract principles of justice. One recent study assessed the moral development of 20 adolescent male Buddhist monks in Nepal (Huebner, Garrod, & Snarey, 1990). The issue of justice, a basic theme in Kohlberg's theory, was not of paramount importance in the monks' moral views, and their concerns about prevention of suffering and the role of compassion are not captured by Kohlberg's theory. More about cultural variations in adolescents' moral thought appears in Sociocultural Worlds of Adolescence 13.1. In sum, moral reasoning is shaped more by the values and beliefs of a culture than Kohlberg acknowledged.

Gender and the Care Perspective

In Chapter 11, we discussed Carol Gilligan's view that relationships and connections to others are critical aspects of female development. Gilligan (1982, 1990, 1992) also has criticized Kohlberg's theory of moral development. She believes that his theory does not adequately reflect relationships and concern for others. The **justice perspective** *is a moral perspective that focuses on the rights of the individual; individuals stand alone and independently make moral decisions. Kohlberg's theory is a justice perspective.* By contrast, the **care perspective** *is a moral perspective that views people in terms of their connectedness with others and emphasizes interpersonal communication, relationships with others, and concern for others. Gilligan's theory is a care perspective.* According to Gilligan, Kohlberg greatly underplayed the care perspective in moral development. She believes that this may have happened because he was a male, because most of his research was with males rather than females, and because he used male responses as a model for his theory.

Figure 13.1 Actual moral dilemmas generated by adolescents.

In one recent study of 20 adolescent Buddhist monks in Nepal, their main concerns were not the issue of justice (as Kohlberg's theory argues) but, rather, the prevention of suffering and the importance of compassion.

Agreement/ Disagreement between American and Indian Hindu Brahman Children and Adolescents about Right and Wrong

Cultural meaning systems vary around the world, and these systems shape children's morality (Damon, 1988; Miller, 1991). Consider a comparison of American and Indian Hindu Brahman children and adolescents (Shweder, Mahapatra, & Miller, 1987). Like people in many other non-Western societies, Indians view moral rules as part of the natural world order. This means that Indians do not distinguish between physical, moral, and social regulation, as Americans do. For example, in India, violations of food taboos and marital restrictions can be just as serious as acts intended to cause harm to others. In India, social rules are seen as inevitable, much like the law of gravity.

As shown in Figure 13.A, there is some, but not much, overlap in the moral concerns of children and adolescents in Indian and American cultures. For Americans accustomed to viewing morality as a freely chosen social contract, Indian beliefs pose a different world view, one that is not easy to reconcile with such treasured ideas as the autonomy of an individualized conscience. The interviews conducted by Richard Shweder and his colleagues (1987) with Indian and American children and adolescents revealed sharp cultural differences in what people judge to be right and wrong. For example, Indian and American children and adolescents disagree about eating beef. On the other hand, there are areas of overlap between the two cultures. For example, both think that breaking promises and ignoring beggars is wrong.

According to moral development theorist and researcher William Damon (1988), where culturally specific practices take on profound moral and religious significance, as in India, the moral development of adolescents focuses extensively on their adherence to custom and convention. In contrast, Western moral doctrine tends to elevate abstract principles, such as justice and welfare, to a higher moral status than customs or conventions. As in India, socialization practices in many Third-World countries actively instill in children and adolescents a great respect for their culture's traditional codes and practices (Edwards, 1987).

Another recent research investigation by Joan Miller and David Bersoff (in press) documented how the majority of Asian Indian children, adolescents, and adults give priority to interpersonal needs in moral conflict situations, whereas the majority of Americans give priority to an individual's justice. Americans were more likely than Indians to downplay the importance of caring in conflict situations, which is likely an outgrowth of the stronger emphasis on an individual's rights in America.

The care perspective is a moral perspective that views people in terms of their connectedness with others and emphasizes interpersonal communication, relationships with others, and concern for others. According to Carol Gilligan, adolescence is a critical juncture in the development of the female's moral voice of caring.

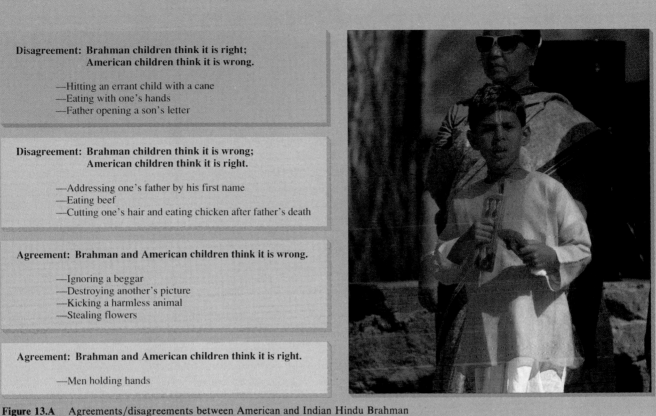

Disagreement: Brahman children think it is right; American children think it is wrong.

—Hitting an errant child with a cane
—Eating with one's hands
—Father opening a son's letter

Disagreement: Brahman children think it is wrong; American children think it is right.

—Addressing one's father by his first name
—Eating beef
—Cutting one's hair and eating chicken after father's death

Agreement: Brahman and American children think it is wrong.

—Ignoring a beggar
—Destroying another's picture
—Kicking a harmless animal
—Stealing flowers

Agreement: Brahman and American children think it is right.

—Men holding hands

Figure 13.A Agreements/disagreements between American and Indian Hindu Brahman children and adolescents about right and wrong.
Source: After Damon, 1988.

In extensive interviews with girls from 6 to 18 years of age, Gilligan and her colleagues found that girls consistently interpret moral dilemmas in terms of human relationships and base these interpretations on listening and watching other people (Gilligan, 1990, 1992; Gilligan, Brown, & Rogers, 1990). According to Gilligan, girls have the ability to sensitively pick up different rhythms in relationships and often are able to follow the pathways of feelings.

Recall from Chapter 11 that Gilligan believes that girls reach a critical juncture in their development when they reach adolescence. Usually around 11 to 12 years of age, girls become aware that their intense interest in intimacy is not prized by the male-dominated culture, even though society values women as caring and altruistic. The dilemma is that girls are presented with a choice that makes them look either selfish or selfless. Gilligan believes that, as adolescent girls experience this dilemma, they increasingly silence their "distinctive voice."

Researchers have found support for Gilligan's claim that females' and males' moral reasoning often centers around different concerns and issues (Bussey &

Maughan, 1982; Galotti, Kozberg, & Appleman, in press; Galotti, Kozberg, & Farmer, 1990; Hanson & Mullis, 1985; Lyons, 1983; Scheidel & Marcia, 1985; Yussen, 1977). However, one of Gilligan's initial claims—that traditional Kohlbergian measures of moral development are biased against females—has been extensively disputed. For example, most research studies using the Kohlberg stories and scoring system do not find sex differences (Walker, 1984, 1991a, b). Thus, the strongest support for Gilligan's claims comes from studies that focus on items and scoring systems pertaining to close relationships, pathways of feelings, sensitive listening, and the rhythm of interpersonal behavior (Galotti, Kozberg, & Farmer, 1990).

While females often articulate a care perspective and males a justice perspective, the gender difference is not absolute, and the two orientations are not mutually exclusive (Donenberg & Hoffman, 1988; Gilligan & Attanucci, 1988; Lyons, 1983, 1990; Rothbart, Hanley, & Albert, 1986). For example, in one study, 53 of 80 females and males showed either a care or a justice perspective, but 27 subjects used both orientations, with neither predominating (Gilligan & Attanucci, 1988). Perspective on Adolescent Development 13.1 presents more information about adolescent girls' care considerations, justice considerations, and mixed considerations of care and justice.

Moral Reasoning and Social Conventional Reasoning

In recent years, researchers have questioned whether reasoning about moral matters is distinct from reasoning about social matters (Nucci, 1982; Smetana, 1985; Turiel, 1978; Ward, 1991). **Social conventional reasoning** *refers to thoughts about social consensus and convention, as opposed to moral reasoning, which stresses ethical issues.* Advocates of the social conventional reasoning approach argue that conventional rules are created to control behavioral irregularities (Enright, Lapsley, & Olson, 1984; Lapsley, Enright, & Serlin, 1986). In this way, the ac-

IN OUR CLASSROOM!!

RULES

1. Keep hands, feet, and objects to yourself
2. Raise your hand.
3. Listen to the teacher.
4. Follow directions the first time.
5. No swearing, teasing, or put downs.

Consequences!

1st. Student's name on the board.
2nd. ✓ = 10 minute time out.
3rd. ✓✓ = 20 minute time out.
4th. ✓✓✓ = Call parent + no recess
5th. ✓✓✓✓ = Sent to the principal's office.

Adolescent Girls—Their Care, Justice, and Mixed Care/Justice Considerations

According to Nona Lyons (1990), an associate of Carol Gilligan, in interpreting moral dilemmas, adolescents may show care considerations, justice considerations, or mixed care/justice considerations. The following comments of adolescent girls from the Emma Willard School in Troy, New York, illustrate these three moral considerations (Lyons, 1990, pp. 38–39):

1. *Justice Considerations.* Justice considerations involve a self-focus that includes respecting and upholding rights, as well as a contract or fairness emphasis in relationships.

   ■ I didn't get my math homework done. . . . We had to hand in the computer tapes, and my friend had an extra computer tape, and I knew the teacher was going to absolutely freak out and scream at me, and I would get into trouble if I didn't hand in a tape. And my friend had an extra one she was offering me, but I couldn't do it. I couldn't take it. . . . I couldn't hand it in when I didn't do it. It would have been like cheating.

   ■ I don't go to chapel anymore because I find that offensive, and I guess that's moral. We have required chapel once a week, and I don't like the idea of being required to go, of being forced into religion. I go to church on my own sometimes. I think that's enough for me, and I don't feel that I need to go to these required services. It was a big decision.

2. *Care Considerations.* Care considerations involve creating and maintaining interdependence and response in relationships.

   ■ I lied to my parents about my grades. I told them that my biology grade was going to be marvelous, and it is not going to be marvelous. . . . Suddenly, my sister, who has always been National Honor Society and all those wonderful things, has gotten horrible grades this past month, and (my parents) called me up and told me this and then wanted to know how mine were. And it was the difference between, knowing my parents, they would go to the ends of the earth if they knew both their children were doing horribly in school—my parents are educational fanatics—and so I've told them that my grades are fine, and there was almost a sigh of relief from my father. And I think that outweighed the idea that I was lying to them. . . . I couldn't bring myself on the phone to say, "Well, Dad, you are looking at two academic failures for the term." And I think that's a moral dilemma.

   ■ My roommate and I were in the same class, and I lost my book, and she lost her book. And then I lost my book and she found hers, and I borrowed her book one night to do my homework. And I noticed my name in it, and I realized that she had taken my book and erased my name and wrote hers over it. And I had to decide whether I should save embarrassing her by confronting her with the problem and just go out and get another book, or whether I should say, "Hey, did you take my book? I know this is my book; give it back."

3. *Mixed Care/Justice Considerations.* Mixed care/justice considerations involve responses to moral dilemmas that include both care and justice components.

   ■ Last year, some friends and I went out, and we were having a little celebration. . . . One girl met a friend of hers, and she wanted to stay longer and talk. . . . The next morning we realized that our friend had gotten busted. . . . I didn't know if I should turn myself in or what. In the end, I really had a hard time deciding what to do because I felt it was really unfair . . . she had gotten busted and we hadn't. And the problem was, if I turned myself in, I would have been responsible for four other people.

tions of individuals can be controlled and the existing social system maintained. Conventional rules are arbitrary. For example, not eating food with one's fingers is a social conventional rule, as is raising one's hand before talking in class.

By contrast, moral rules are not arbitrary. Also, moral rules are not created by social consensus, but rather are obligatory, widely applicable, and somewhat impersonal (Turiel, 1978). Thus, rules pertaining to lying, stealing, cheating, and physically harming another person are moral rules because violation of these rules affronts ethical standards that exist apart from social consensus and convention. In sum, moral judgments are structured as concepts of justice, whereas social conventional judgments are structured as concepts of social organization (Lapsley, Enright, & Serlin, 1986).

So far, we have discussed a number of ideas about the nature of moral thought. One of the criticisms of Kohlberg's cognitive theory of moral development is that he did not give adequate attention to moral behavior. Next, we examine the nature of moral behavior.

Moral Behavior

What are the basic processes that behaviorists and social learning theorists believe are responsible for adolescents' moral behavior? How do cognitive social learning theorists view adolescents' moral development? We look at each of these issues.

Reinforcement, Punishment, Imitation, and Situational Variations in Moral Behavior

Social learning theory emphasizes the moral behavior of adolescents. The familiar processes of reinforcement, punishment, and imitation have been invoked to explain how and why adolescents learn certain moral behaviors and why their behaviors differ from one another. The general conclusions to be drawn are the same as for other domains of social behavior. When adolescents are reinforced for behavior that is consistent with laws and social conventions, they are likely to repeat that behavior. When models who behave "morally" are provided, adolescents are likely to adopt their behavior. And when adolescents are punished for immoral or unacceptable behavior, those behaviors can be eliminated, but at the expense of sanctioning punishment by its very use and of causing emotional side effects for the adolescent.

To these general conclusions can be added several qualifiers. The effectiveness of reinforcement and punishment depends on how consistently they are administered and the schedule that is adopted. The effectiveness of modeling depends on the characteristics of the model (such as power, warmth, uniqueness, and so on) and the presence of cognitive processes, such as symbolic codes and imagery, to enhance retention of the modeled behavior.

What kind of adult moral models are adolescents being exposed to in American society? Do such models usually do what they say? Adolescents are especially tuned in to adult hypocrisy, and evidence indicates that they are right to believe that many adults display a double standard, their moral actions not always corresponding to their moral thoughts. A poll of 24,000 adults sampled views on a wide variety of moral issues. Eight detailed scenarios of everyday moral problems were developed to test moral decision making. A summary of the adults' responses to these moral dilemmas is shown in Table 13.1. Consider the example of whether the adult would knowingly buy a stolen color television set. More than 20 percent said that they would, even though 87 percent said that this act is probably morally wrong. And approximately 31 percent of the adults said that, if they knew they would not get caught, they would be more likely to buy the stolen television. While moral thought is an important dimension of moral development, these data glaringly underscore that what people believe about right and wrong does not always correspond with how they will act in moral situations.

In addition to emphasizing the role of environmental determinants and the gap between moral thought and moral action, social learning theorists also emphasize that moral behavior is situationally dependent. That is, they say that adolescents are not likely to display consistent moral behavior in diverse social settings. In a classic investigation of moral behavior—one of the most extensive ever conducted—Hugh Hartshorne and Mark May (1928–1930) observed the

Table 13.1 The Hypocrisy of Adult Moral Models

Would you:	Percent who said yes, or probably:	Percent who said it is, or probably is, unethical:	Percent who would, or probably would, be more likely to if sure they would not get caught:
Drive away after scratching a car without telling the owner?	44%	89%	52%
Cover for a friend's secret affair?	41	66	33
Cheat on your spouse?	37	68	42
Keep $10 extra change at a local supermarket?	26	85	33
Knowingly buy a stolen color television set?	22	87	31
Try to keep your neighborhood segregated?	13	81	8
Drive while drunk?	11	90	24
Accept praise for another's work?	4	96	8

REPRINTED WITH PERMISSION FROM *PSYCHOLOGY TODAY MAGAZINE.* Copyright © 1981 (Sussex Publishers, Inc.).

moral responses of 11,000 children and adolescents who were given the opportunity to lie, cheat, and steal in a variety of circumstances—at home, at school, at social events, and in athletics. A completely honest or a completely dishonest child or adolescent was difficult to find. Situation-specific moral behavior was the rule. Adolescents were more likely to cheat when their friends pressured them to do so and when the chance of being caught was slim. Other analyses suggest that some adolescents are more likely to lie, cheat, and steal than others, indicating more consistency of moral behavior in some adolescents than in others (Burton, 1984).

Cognitive Social Learning Theory of Moral Development

The **cognitive social learning theory of moral development** *emphasizes a distinction between adolescents'* moral competence—*the ability to produce moral behaviors*—and moral performance—*those behaviors in specific situations* (Mischel & Mischel, 1975). Competence, or acquisition, depends primarily on cognitive-sensory processes; it is the outgrowth of these processes. Competencies include what adolescents are capable of doing, what they know, their skills, their awareness of moral rules and regulations, and their cognitive ability to construct behaviors. Adolescents' moral performance, or behavior, however, is determined by their motivation and the rewards and incentives to act in a specific moral way. Albert Bandura (in press) also believes that moral development is best understood by considering a combination of social and cognitive factors, especially those involving self-control.

One reason that social learning theorists have been critical of Kohlberg's view is that, as mentioned earlier, they believe that he placed too little emphasis on moral behavior and the situational determinants of morality. However, while Kohlberg argued that moral judgment is an important determinant of moral behavior, he, like the Mischels, stressed that the individual's interpretation of both the moral and factual aspects of a situation leads him or her to a moral decision (Kohlberg & Candee, 1979). For example, Kohlberg mentioned that "extra-moral" factors, like the desire to avoid embarrassment, may cause the child to avoid doing what he or she believes to be morally right. In sum, both the Mischels and Kohlberg believe that moral action is influenced by a complex of factors. Overall, the findings are mixed with regard to the association of moral thought and behavior (Arnold, 1989), although one recent investigation with college students found that individuals with both highly principled moral reasoning and high ego strength were less likely to cheat in a resistance-to-temptation situation than their low-principled and low-ego-strength counterparts (Hess, Lonky, & Roodin, 1985).

At this point, we have discussed a number of ideas about the nature of moral development, moral thought, and moral behavior. A summary of these ideas is presented in Concept Table 13.1. As we see next, there is a reemergence of interest in the emotional aspects of moral development.

Moral Feelings

How do adolescents' moral feelings develop? In pursuing the answer to this question, we look at the concepts developed by psychoanalytic theorists, the nature of empathy, and the role of emotions in moral development.

Psychoanalytic Theory

As discussed in Chapter 2, Sigmund Freud's psychoanalytic theory describes the *superego* as one of the three main structures of personality (the id and the ego being the other two). In Freud's classical psychoanalytic theory, an individual's superego—the moral branch of personality—develops in early childhood when the child resolves the Oedipus conflict and identifies with the same-sex parent. According to Freud, one reason why children resolve the Oedipus conflict is to alleviate the fear of losing their parents' love and of being punished for their unacceptable sexual wishes toward the opposite-sex parent. To reduce anxiety, avoid punishment, and maintain parental affection, children form a superego by identifying with the same-sex parent. In Freud's view, through this identification, children internalize the parents' standards of right and wrong that reflect societal prohibitions. Also, children turn inward the hostility that was previously aimed at the same-sex parent. This inwardly directed hostility is then experienced self-punitively (and unconsciously) as guilt. In the psychoanalytic account of moral development, self-punitiveness of guilt keeps children, and later on, adolescents from committing transgressions. That is, children and adolescents conform to societal standards to avoid guilt.

In Freud's view, the superego consists of two main components—the ego-ideal and the conscience—which promote children and adolescents' development of moral feelings. The **ego-ideal** *is the component of the superego that involves ideal standards approved by parents,* whereas the **conscience** *is the component of the superego that involves behaviors not approved of by parents.* An individual's ego-ideal rewards the individual by conveying a sense of pride and personal value when the individual acts according to moral standards. The conscience punishes the individual for acting immorally by making the individual feel guilty and worthless. In this way, self-control replaces parental control.

Erik Erikson (1970) argued that there are three stages of moral development: specific moral learning in childhood, ideological concerns in adolescence, and ethical consolidation in adulthood. According to Erikson, during adolescence, individuals search for an identity. If adolescents become disillusioned with the moral and religious beliefs they acquired during childhood, they are likely to lose, at least temporarily, their sense of purpose and feel that their lives are empty.

Concept Table 13.1

The Nature of Moral Development, Moral Thought, and Moral Behavior

Concept	Processes/Related Ideas	Characteristics/Description
What is moral development?	Its nature	Moral development concerns rules and conventions about what people should do in their interactions with others. The three main domains of moral development are thought, behavior, and feelings.
Moral thought	Piaget's ideas and cognitive disequilibrium theory	Piaget argued that, from four to seven years of age, children are in the stage of heteronomous morality, and from about the age of 10 on, are in the stage of autonomous morality. Formal operational thought may undergird changes in the moral reasoning of adolescents. Cognitive disequilibrium theory states that adolescence is an important period in moral development, especially as individuals move from the relatively homogeneous grade school to the more heterogeneous high school and college environments, where they are faced with contradictions between the moral concepts they have accepted and experiences outside their family and neighborhood. Older adolescents often come to understand that their set of beliefs is but one of many and that there is considerable debate about what is right and what is wrong.
	Kohlberg's ideas on moral development	Kohlberg developed a provocative theory of the development of moral reasoning. He argued that moral development consists of three levels—preconventional, conventional, and postconventional—and six stages (two at each level). Increased internalization characterizes movement to levels 2 and 3. Kohlberg's longitudinal data show a relation of the stages to age, although the highest two stages, especially stage 6, rarely appear. Influences on the Kohlberg stages include cognitive development, modeling, cognitive conflict, peer relations, and role-taking opportunities.
	Kohlberg's critics	Criticisms involve an overemphasis on moral thought and an underemphasis on moral behavior, the quality of the research, inadequate consideration of culture's role in moral development, and underestimation of the care perspective in moral development. Gilligan believes that Kohlberg's theory reflects a justice perspective (individual); she advocates a stronger care perspective (views people in terms of their connectedness with others and emphasizes interpersonal communication). Gilligan also believes that adolescence is a critical juncture in the development of a moral voice for females. Researchers have found support for Gilligan's claim that females' and males' moral reasoning often centers around different concerns, although sex differences in Kohlberg's stages have not been consistently found. Studies that focus more extensively on items pertaining to close relationships and that use scoring systems that emphasize connectedness support Gilligan's claims.
	Moral reasoning and social conventional reasoning	Social conventional reasoning refers to thoughts about social consensus and convention, as opposed to moral reasoning, which stresses ethical issues.
Moral behavior	Reinforcement, punishment, imitation, and situation-specific moral behavior	Behaviorists and social learning theorists argue that adolescents' moral behavior is determined by the processes of reinforcement, punishment, and imitation. Situational variability in moral behavior is stressed.
	Cognitive social learning theory of moral development	The cognitive social learning theory of moral development emphasizes a distinction between moral competence—the ability to produce moral behaviors—and moral performance—those behaviors in specific situations. In general, social learning theorists are critical of Kohlberg's theory, believing that he placed too little emphasis on moral behavior and its situational variability.

This may lead to adolescents' search for an ideology that will give some purpose to their life. For the ideology to be acceptable, it must both fit the evidence and mesh with adolescents' logical reasoning abilities. If others share this ideology, a sense of community is felt. For Erikson, ideology surfaces as the guardian of identity during adolescence because it provides a sense of purpose, assists in tying the present to the future, and contributes meaning to behavior (Hoffman, 1980).

Empathy

Positive feelings, such as empathy, contribute to adolescents' moral development. Feeling **empathy** *means reacting to another's feelings with an emotional response that is similar to the other's response* (Damon, 1988). Although empathy is experienced as an emotional state, it often has a cognitive component—the ability to discern another's inner psychological states, or what we have previously called *perspective taking.*

At about 10 to 12 years of age, individuals develop an empathy for people who live in unfortunate circumstances (Damon, 1988). Children's concerns are no longer limited to the feelings of particular persons in situations they directly observe. Instead, 10- to 12-year-olds expand their concerns to the general problems of people in unfortunate circumstances—the poor, the handicapped, and the socially outcast, for example. This newfound sensitivity may lead older children to behave altruistically, and later, may give a humanitarian flavor to adolescents' development of ideological and political views.

Although every adolescent may be capable of responding with empathy, not all do. Adolescents' empathic behavior varies considerably. For example, in older children and adolescents, empathic dysfunctions can contribute to antisocial behavior. Some delinquents convicted of violent crimes show a lack of feeling for their victims' distress. A 13-year-old boy convicted of violently mugging a number of elderly people, when asked about the pain he had caused one blind woman, said, "What do I care? I'm not her" (Damon, 1988).

The Contemporary Perspective on the Role of Emotions in Moral Development

We have seen that classical psychoanalytic theory emphasizes the power of unconscious guilt in moral development but that other theories, such as that of Damon, emphasize the role of empathy. Today, many developmentalists believe that both positive feelings, such as empathy, sympathy, admiration, and self-esteem, and negative feelings, such as anger, outrage, shame, and guilt, contribute to adolescents' moral development (Damon, 1988). When strongly experienced, these emotions influence adolescents to act in accord with standards of right and wrong. Such emotions as empathy, shame, guilt, and anxiety over other people's violations of standards are present early in development and undergo developmental change throughout childhood and adolescence. These emotions provide a natural base for adolescents' acquisition of moral values, both orienting adolescents toward moral events and motivating them to pay close attention to such events. However, moral emotions do not operate in a vacuum to build adolescents' moral awareness, and they are not sufficient in themselves to generate moral responsivity. They do not give the "substance" of moral regulation—the rules, values, and standards of behavior that adolescents need to understand and act on. Moral emotions are inextricably interwoven with the cognitive and social aspects of adolescents' development. The web of feeling, cognition, and social behavior is also experienced in altruism—the aspect of adolescents' moral development we discuss next.

Altruism

Altruism *is an unselfish interest in helping someone.* While adolescents have often been described as egocentric and selfish, adolescent acts of altruism are, nevertheless, plentiful—the hardworking adolescent who places a one-dollar bill in the church offering plate each week; the adolescent-sponsored car washes, bake sales, and concerts organized to make money to feed the hungry and help mentally retarded children; and the adolescent who takes in and cares for a wounded cat. How do psychologists account for such altruistic acts?

Reciprocity and exchange are involved in altruism (Brown, 1986). Reciprocity is found throughout the human world. Not only is it the highest moral principle in Christianity, but it is also present in every widely practiced religion in the world—Judaism, Hinduism, Buddhism, and Islam. Reciprocity encourages adolescents to do unto others as they would have others do unto them. Human sentiments are wrapped up in this reciprocity. Trust is probably the most important principle over the long run in adolescent altruism. Guilt surfaces if the adolescent does not reciprocate. Anger may result if someone else does not reciprocate. Not all adolescent altruism is motivated by reciprocity and exchange, but self-other interactions and relationships help us to understand altruism's nature. The circumstances most likely to involve altruism by adolescents are empathetic or sympathetic emotion for an individual in need or a close relationship between the benefactor and the recipient (Clark & others, 1987). Altruism occurs more often in adolescence than in childhood, although examples of caring for others and comforting someone in distress occur even during the preschool years (Eisenberg, 1987, 1989, 1991).

Forgiveness *is an aspect of altruism that occurs when the injured person releases the injurer from possible behavioral retaliation* (Enright & the Educational Psychology Study Group, in press). In one recent investigation, individuals from the fourth grade through college and adulthood were asked questions about forgiveness (Enright, Santos, & Al-Mabuk, 1989). The adolescents were especially swayed by peer pressure in their willingness to forgive others. Consider one 12-year-old girl's response to Kohlberg's dilemma of Heinz and the druggist:

> *Interviewer:* "Suppose all of Heinz's friends come to see him and say, 'Please be more mature about this. We want you to be friends with the druggist.' Would it help him to forgive the druggist? Why/why not?"
> *Girl:* "Probably, because Heinz would think they wanted him to. They would influence him."

In response to the same question, a 15-year-old girl said, "Yes, it would be his friends showing him the outside view. They would help him." The adolescent forgiveness theme that emerged was that the injured party often fails to see the best course of action. Outside aid, especially from friends, helps the harmed person to clarify the problem and then forgive.

Emerson once said, "The meaning of good and bad, better and worse, is simply helping or hurting." By developing adolescents' capacity for empathy and altruism, America can become a nation of *good* people who *help* rather than hurt.

Moral Education

The moral education of adolescents has become a widely discussed topic. Many parents worry that their adolescents are growing up without traditional values. Teachers complain that many of their students are unethical. Among the questions about moral education we examine are: What is the hidden curriculum? What is the nature of direct moral education versus indirect moral education? What is values clarification? What is cognitive moral education? How should we foster adolescents' moral growth?

In indirect moral education, children and adolescents are encouraged to define their own and others' values and are helped to define the moral perspectives that support those values. The most widely adopted indirect moral education approaches are values clarification and cognitive moral education.

The Hidden Curriculum

The **hidden curriculum** *is the pervasive moral atmosphere that characterizes schools.* This atmosphere includes school and classroom rules, attitudes toward academics and extracurricular activities, the moral orientation of teachers and school administrators, and text materials. More than half a century ago, educator John Dewey (1933) recognized that, whether or not they offer specific programs in moral education, schools provide moral education through the hidden curriculum. Schools, like families, are settings for moral development. Teachers serve as models of ethical or unethical behavior. Classroom rules and peer relations at school transmit attitudes about cheating, lying, stealing, and consideration of others. The school administration, through its rules and regulations, represents a value system to students.

Direct and Indirect Moral Education

Approaches to moral education can be classified as either direct or indirect (Benninga, 1988). **Direct moral education** *involves either emphasizing values or character traits during specified time slots or integrating those values or traits throughout the curriculum.* **Indirect moral education** *involves encouraging adolescents to define their own and others' values and helping them to define the moral perspectives that support those values.*

In the direct moral education approach, instruction in specified moral concepts can assume the form of example and definition, class discussions and role playing, or rewarding students for proper behavior (Jensen & Knight, 1981). The use of McGuffey Readers during the early part of the twentieth century exemplifies the direct approach. The stories and poems in the readers taught moral behavior and character in addition to academics. A number of contemporary educators advocate a direct approach to moral education. Former U.S. Secretary of Education William Bennett (1986) wrote:

> If a college is really interested in teaching its students a clear lesson in moral responsibility, it should tell the truth about drugs in a straightforward way. This summer, our college presidents should send every student a letter saying they will not tolerate drugs on campus—period. The letter should then spell out precisely

what the college's policy will be toward students who use drugs. Being simple and straightforward about moral responsibility is not the same as being simplistic and unsophisticated.

Bennett also believes that every elementary and secondary school should have a discipline code, making clear to adolescents and parents what the school expects of them. Then the school should enforce the code.

The most widely adopted indirect approaches to moral education are values clarification and cognitive moral education. We consider each of these in turn.

Values Clarification

Values clarification *is an indirect moral education approach that focuses on helping students to clarify what their lives are for and what is worth working for.* In values clarification, students are asked questions or presented with dilemmas and expected to respond, either individually or in small groups. The intent is to help students to define their own values and to become aware of others' values.

In the following values clarification example, students are asked to select from among ten people the six who will be admitted to a fallout shelter during World War III:

> A fallout shelter under your administration in a remote Montana highland contains only enough space, air, food, and water for six people for three months, but ten people wish to be admitted. The ten have agreed by radio contact that, for the survival of the human race, you must decide which six of them shall be saved. You have exactly 30 minutes to make up your mind before Washington goes up in smoke. These are your choices:
> 1. A 16-year-old girl of questionable IQ, a high school dropout, pregnant.
> 2. A policeman with a gun (which cannot be taken from him), thrown off the force recently for brutality.
> 3. A clergyman, 75.
> 4. A woman physician, 36, known to be a confirmed racist.
> 5. A male violinist, 46, who served seven years for pushing narcotics.
> 6. A 20-year-old Black militant, no special skills.
> 7. A former prostitute, female, 39.
> 8. An architect, a male homosexual.
> 9. A 26-year-old law student.
> 10. The law student's 25-year-old wife who spent the last nine months in a mental hospital, still heavily sedated. They refuse to be separated.

In this exercise, no answers are considered right or wrong. The clarification of values is left up to the individual student. Advocates of the values clarification approach argue that it is value-free. Critics argue that, because of its controversial content, it offends community standards (Eger, 1981). Critics also say that, because of its relativistic nature, values clarification undermines accepted values and fails to stress truth and what is right behavior (Oser, 1986).

Cognitive Moral Education

Like values clarification, cognitive moral education also challenges direct moral instruction. **Cognitive moral education** *is an indirect moral education approach that emphasizes that adolescents adopt such values as democracy and justice as their moral reasoning is developed.* In this approach, students' moral standards are allowed to develop through their attention to environmental settings and exercises that encourage more advanced moral thinking. Thus, in contrast to values clarification, cognitive moral education is not value-free. Such values as democracy and justice are emphasized. The advocates of cognitive moral education argue that, when moral standards are imposed—as in the direct moral

William Damon has presented a number of insightful ideas about children's and adolescents' moral development and moral education.

education approach—adolescents can never completely integrate and fully understand moral principles, and that only through participation and discussion can adolescents learn to apply the rules and principles of cooperation, trust, community, and self-reliance.

Lawrence Kohlberg's theory of moral development has extensively influenced the cognitive moral education approach. Contrary to what some critics say, Kohlberg's theory is neither completely relativistic nor completely morally neutral. Higher-level moral thinking is clearly preferred to lower-level moral thinking. And Kohlberg's theory stresses that higher-level thinking can be stimulated through focused discussion of dilemmas. Also, in the 1980s, Kohlberg (1981, 1986) revised his views on moral education by placing more emphasis on the school's moral atmosphere, not unlike John Dewey did many years ago.

Damon's Comprehensive Approach to Moral Education

Developmentalist William Damon (1988) believes that moral education should follow from what is known about the nature of children's and adolescents' moral development. From scientific studies and his own observations of moral development in children and adolescents, Damon believes that the following six principles should serve as the foundation for the development of moral education programs:

1. Adolescents experience classic moral issues facing humans everywhere—issues of fairness, honesty, responsibility, kindness, and obedience, for example—simply by participating in social relationships. Thus, adolescents' moral awareness develops within their normal social experiences. Their moral awareness may need to be guided, informed, and enhanced, but it does not need to be imposed directly in a punitive, authoritarian manner.
2. Adolescents' moral awareness is shaped and supported by natural emotional reactions to observations and events. Such emotional reactions as empathy support moral compassion and altruism. Such reactions as shame, guilt, and fear support obedience and rule adoption. Children's and adolescents' attachment feelings for parents provide an affective foundation for developing respect for authority.
3. Interactions with parents, teachers, and other adults introduce children and adolescents to important social standards and rules. These interactions produce knowledge and respect for the social order, including its principles of organization and legitimate authority. Authoritative adult-adolescent (parent-adolescent or teacher-adolescent) relationships, in which extensive verbal give-and-take and nonpunitive adult control that justifies demands are present, yield the most positive results for adolescents' moral judgment and behavior.
4. Peer relations introduce children and adolescents to the norms of direct reciprocity and to the standards of sharing, cooperation, and fairness. Through peer relations, children and adolescents learn about mutuality, equality, and perspective taking, which promote the development of altruism.
5. Broad variations in social experiences can produce substantial differences in moral reasoning among children and adolescents. One such variation is the different roles and expectations that girls and boys experience, especially in traditional social environments. As discussed earlier in the

chapter, Carol Gilligan (1982, 1990, 1992) believes that the moral development of girls is often oriented more toward relationships and that the moral development of boys is often oriented more toward justice and the individual. There is reason to believe that such orientations can be socially transformed as cultures change. According to Damon, there should be an increased emphasis on both boys and girls learning the principles of care *and* justice.

6. Moral development in schools is determined by the same cognitive and social processes that apply to moral development in other settings. This means that adolescents acquire moral values by actively participating in adult-adolescent and peer relationships that support, enhance, and guide their natural moral tendencies. According to Damon, adolescents' morality is not enhanced by lessons or lectures in which adolescents are passive recipients of information or, even worse, captive and recalcitrant audiences. Further, the quality of social interaction in a school setting communicates a moral message that is more enduring than direct, declarative statements and lectures by teachers. To receive a competent moral education in a democratic society, adolescents need to experience egalitarian interactions that reflect democratic values—among them, equality, fairness, and responsibility.

Damon (1988) believes that, for teachers and parents to contribute positively to an adolescent's moral development, they need to practice *respectful engagement* with the adolescent. Adolescents need guidance, but, for the guidance to register, adolescents need to be productively engaged, and their own initiatives and reactions must be respected.

Damon recognizes that parents alone, or schools alone, are not completely responsible for adolescents' moral development. Adolescents' moral education occurs both in and out of school through adolescents' interactions with parents, peers, and teachers, and through their experiences with society's standards. These interactions are not value-free, and although there is some disagreement about exactly what should be communicated to adolescents in the course of moral education, there is more agreement than is commonly acknowledged. Some fundamental values are shared widely enough to be transmitted without hesitation to adolescents. For example, no one wants adolescents to follow a path of dishonesty, drug abuse, or cruel antisocial behavior, and all of us want adolescents to endorse justice, abide by legitimate authority, consider the needs of others, and be responsible citizens in a democratic society.

Damon's approach contrasts with the permissive approach, which assumes that children's and adolescents' moral growth is enhanced when they are left alone. It also stands in contrast to the indoctrinational approach of direct moral education, which states that children and adolescents can learn moral values by passively listening to the demands of authority figures. Damon's ideas have much in common with cognitive moral education, but they go beyond the traditional view of cognitive moral education, which focuses almost exclusively on the role of schools, peers, and cognition in moral development. Damon's view is more comprehensive because it recognizes the importance of emotions, parent-adolescent relations, and culture in moral development, and integrates these with the influence of schools, peers, and cognition in a meaningful way.

At various times in our discussion of moral development there have been references to adolescents' moral values. Next, we examine adolescents' moral values.

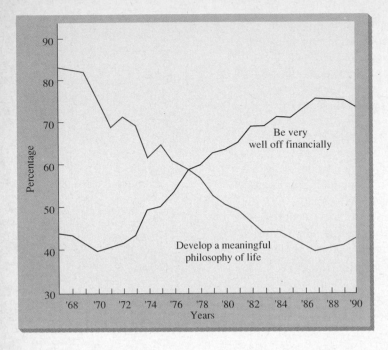

Figure 13.2　Changing freshman life goals, 1968–1990. The percentages indicated are in response to the question of identifying a life goal as "essential" or "very important." There has been a significant reversal in freshman life goals in the last two decades, with a far greater percentage of today's college freshmen stating that a "very important" life goal is to be well-off financially, and far fewer stating that developing a meaningful philosophy of life is a "very important" life goal.

Values, Religion, and Cults

What are adolescents' values like today? How powerful is religion in adolescents' lives? Why do some adolescents run away to join cults? We consider each of these questions in turn.

Values

Adolescents carry with them a set of values that influences their thoughts, feelings, and actions. What were your values when you were an adolescent? Are the values of today's adolescents changing?

Over the past two decades, adolescents have shown an increased concern for personal well-being and a decreased concern for the well-being of others, especially for the disadvantaged (Astin, Green, & Korn, 1987; Astin, Korn, & Berz, 1990). As shown in Figure 13.2, today's college freshmen are more strongly motivated to be well-off financially and less motivated to develop a meaningful philosophy of life than were their counterparts of 20 or even 10 years ago. While, in both 1989 and 1990, student commitment to being very well-off financially began to decline slightly, endorsement of "to be able to make more money" as a "very important" reason for attending college reached a record high in the 1990 survey (73 percent, compared to 72 percent in 1989 and 50 percent in 1971).

However, two aspects of values that increased during the 1960s continue to characterize many of today's youth: self-fulfillment and self-expression (Conger, 1981, 1988). As part of their motivation for self-fulfillment, many adolescents show great interest in their physical health and well-being. Greater self-fulfillment and self-expression can be laudable goals, but if they become the only goals, self-destruction, loneliness, or alienation may result. Young people also need to develop a corresponding sense of commitment to others' welfare. Encouraging adolescents to have a strong commitment to others, in concert with an interest in self-fulfillment, is an important task for America at the close of the twentieth century.

Some signs indicate that today's adolescents are shifting toward a stronger interest in the welfare of society. For example, between 1986 and 1990, there was an increase in the percentage of freshmen who said that they were strongly interested in participating in community action programs (26 percent in 1990 compared to 18 percent in 1986) and in helping to promote racial understanding (38 percent in 1990 compared to 27 percent in 1986). More adolescents are showing an active interest in the problems of homelessness, child abuse, hunger, and poverty (Conger, 1988). The percentage of adolescents who believe that it is desirable to work for a social service organization rose from 11 percent in 1980 to 17 percent in 1989 (Bachman, Johnston, & O'Malley, 1987; Johnston, Bachman, & O'Malley, 1990). Whether these small increments in concern for the community and society will continue to increase in the remainder of the 1990s is difficult to predict.

Religious Beliefs and the Church

Adolescents are more interested in religion and spiritual beliefs than children. Their increasing abstract thought and their search for an identity draw them to religion and spiritual matters (Spilka, 1991a).

The Development of Religious Concepts

In a series of studies, David Elkind (1978) interviewed several hundred Jewish, Catholic, and Protestant boys and girls from 5 to 14 years of age. He asked such questions as "Are you a Catholic?" "Is your family Jewish?" "Are all boys and girls in the world Christians?" He also asked questions like, "What is a Jew?" "How do you become a Catholic?" and "Can you be an American and a Protestant (or Jew, or Catholic) at the same time?" The formal operational thinkers—those who were in early adolescence—had a different way of thinking about religious concepts than the concrete operational thinkers—those in childhood. The formal operational thinkers were more reflective than their younger counterparts. They no longer looked for manifestations of religious identity in an individual's outward behavior but rather in the evidence of innermost beliefs and convictions. For example, one concrete operational thinker said that the way you can tell an individual is a Catholic is by whether the person goes to church or not. By contrast, one formal operational thinker said that you can tell an individual is a Protestant because the person is free to repent and to pray to God.

James Fowler (1976) proposed another perspective on the development of religious concepts. **Individuating-reflexive faith** *is Fowler's stage in late adolescence that is an important time in the development of a religious identity. For the first time in their lives, individuals take full responsibility for their religious beliefs.* Earlier, they relied heavily on their parents' beliefs. During late adolescence, individuals come face-to-face with personal decisions, evaluating such questions as: "Do I consider myself first, or should I consider the welfare of others first?" "Are the doctrines that have been taught to me absolute, or are they more relative than I had been led to believe?" Fowler believes that adolescents' development of moral values is closely related to their development of religious values. He also acknowledges that the stage of individuating-reflexive faith has much in common with Kohlberg's highest level of moral reasoning, postconventional morality.

Spiritual Interest and Church Influences

The sociocultural conditions in which adolescents grow up combine with their developing cognitive capacities to influence their religious identity. The formal

There are some signs that today's adolescents are shifting toward a stronger interest in the welfare of society, as evidenced by this San Antonio youth, who has volunteered his time to paint houses in an impoverished area of the city.

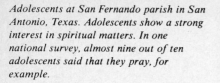

Adolescents at San Fernando parish in San Antonio, Texas. Adolescents show a strong interest in spiritual matters. In one national survey, almost nine out of ten adolescents said that they pray, for example.

operational characteristics of abstract thought and idealism contribute to adolescents' spiritual interest. Adolescents do show a strong interest in spiritual matters. For example, in one national survey, almost 90 percent of adolescents said that they pray (Gallup & Poling, 1980). Compared to children's prayers, adolescents' prayers are more likely to be characterized by responsibility, subjectivity, and intimacy (Scarlett & Perriello, 1990). In the national survey just mentioned, more than 90 percent of adolescents said that they believed in God or a universal spirit. Only 1 in 1,000 had no religious preference or affiliation. At the same time, though, many adolescents say that organized religion has little meaning for them and that the church's doctrines are outmoded. In the national poll just mentioned, only 25 percent said that they had a high degree of confidence in organized religion. About 40 percent said that the honesty and personal ethics of the clergy were average to very low.

One area of religion's influence on adolescent development involves sexual activity. Although variability and change in church teachings make it difficult to characterize religious doctrines simply, most churches discourage premarital sex. Thus, the degree of adolescents' participation in religious organizations may be more important than religious affiliation as a determinant of premarital sexual attitudes and behavior. Adolescents who attend religious services frequently may hear messages about abstaining from sex. Involvement of adolescents in religious organizations also enhances the probability that they will become friends with adolescents who have restrictive attitudes toward premarital sex. In one recent study, adolescents who attended church frequently and valued religion in their lives were less experienced sexually and had less permissive attitudes toward premarital sex than their counterparts who attended church infrequently and said that religion did not play a strong role in their lives (Thornton & Camburn, 1989). However, while religious involvement is associated with a lower incidence of sexual activity among adolescents, adolescents who are religiously involved and sexually active are less likely to use medical methods of contraception (especially the pill) than their sexually active counterparts with low religious involvement (Studer & Thornton, 1987, 1989).

Cults

Barb is 17 years old. She grew up in an affluent family and was given all of the material things she wanted. When she was 15, her parents paid her way to Europe, and for the last three years, she has been attending a private boarding school. Her parents attended a Protestant church on a regular basis, and when Barb was home, they took her with them. Six months ago, Barb joined the "Moonies."

Six unorthodox religious movements have attracted considerable attention from America's youth: Transcendental Meditation (TM), yoga, the charismatic movement, mysticism, faith healing, and various Eastern religions (Gallup & Poling, 1980). More than 27 million Americans have been touched by these religions, either superficially or deeply. In all, there are more than 2,500 cults in the United States. Two to three million youth and young adults are cult members (Levine, 1984; Swope, 1980). Among the more specific religious cults that have attracted the attention of youth are the Unification Church of Sun Myung Moon (the Moonies), the Divine Light Mission of Maharaj Ji, the Institute of Krishna Consciousness, the Children of God, and the Church of Scientology.

The most recent concerns about cults focus on satanism, or devil worship. The nightmarish tale of human sacrifice that unfolded in the spring of 1989 in Matamoros, Mexico, brought national attention to the increasing prevalence of devil worshipping. Some of the bodies in the mass grave had been decapitated. Investigation of the Satanism cult revealed its ties to drugs. The cult's ringleader, Adolpho de Jesus Constanzo, controlled members' lives, getting them to believe that the devil has supernatural, occultlike powers.

Critics of the cults argue that cult leaders are hypocritical, exploit members to gain wealth, brainwash youth, and develop a hypnoticlike spell over members' lives. In some cases, cults have been accused of kidnapping youth and placing them in deprived circumstances to gain control over their minds. Most cults have elaborate training programs in which the cult's preachings are memorized. Cult members are usually required to turn over their wealth to cult leaders. And cult members are often told that they can associate with or marry only other members of the cult (Galanter, 1989).

Why do some adolescents leave home and become members of a cult? Some experts believe that the failures of organized religion and the church, as well as a weakening of family life, are causes (Gallup & Poling, 1980; Levine, 1984; Spilka, 1991b). What kind of youth are most vulnerable to the appeal of cults? Six characteristics have been identified (Swope, 1980):

1. *Idealistic.* Due to the teachings and example of family, religious leaders, peers, educators, and others, there has developed within young people a desire to help others, to improve society, and often to know God better. The cults manipulate this idealism, convincing members that only within their specialized groups can such inclinations be actualized.
2. *Innocent.* Because relationships with religious leaders in the past have been wholesome, the potential recruit naively believes that all who claim to speak in the name of God are sincere and trustworthy. Elmer Gantry and Jim Jones notwithstanding, the trappings of religion are a powerful lure here.
3. *Inquisitive.* On college and high school campuses around the country, intelligent young people, looking for interesting groups to join, are approached by enthusiastic, "together" recruiters who invite them to meetings where, they are told, they will meet other fine young people. It

"We were hoping you'd be home for vacation or whatever Moonies call it when they're not doing what they do."
Drawing by Saxon; © 1967 The New Yorker Magazine, Inc.

The Hare Krishna is one of several religious cults that have attracted the attention of youth.

Concept Table 13.2

Moral Feelings, Altruism, Moral Education, Values, Religion, and Cults

Concept	Processes/Related Ideas	Characteristics/Description
Moral feelings	Psychoanalytic theory	According to psychoanalytic theory, the superego is one of the three main structures of personality. The superego—the moral branch of personality—develops as the child resolves the Oedipus conflict and identifies with the same-sex parent in the early childhood years. Through identification, children and adolescents internalize parents' standards of right and wrong. Individuals conform to societal standards to avoid guilt. In Freud's view, the superego consists of two main components: ego-ideal and conscience. Erikson argues that there are three stages of moral development: specific moral learning in childhood, ideological concerns in adolescence, and ethical consolidation in adulthood.
	Empathy	Feeling empathy means reacting to another's feelings with an emotional response that is similar to the other's response. Empathy often has a cognitive component—perspective taking. Around the beginning of adolescence, individuals begin to show more empathy for people who live in unfortunate circumstances. Individual variation characterizes empathy.
	The contemporary perspective on the role of emotions in moral development	Both positive feelings, such as empathy, sympathy, admiration, and self-esteem, and negative feelings, such as anger, outrage, shame, and guilt, contribute to adolescents' moral development. When strongly experienced, these emotions influence adolescents to act in accord with moral standards. Moral emotions do not operate in a vacuum—they are interwoven with the cognitive and social aspects of adolescents' moral development.
Altruism	Its nature	Altruism is an unselfish interest in helping someone. While adolescents have often been described as selfish and egocentric, adolescent acts of altruism are, nevertheless, plentiful. Reciprocity and exchange are involved in altruism. Forgiveness is an aspect of altruism that occurs when the injured person releases the injurer from possible behavioral retaliation. Adolescents are especially swayed by peer pressure to forgive others.
Moral education	The hidden curriculum	The hidden curriculum is the pervasive moral atmosphere that characterizes any school, regardless of whether there is a specific moral curriculum.
	Direct and indirect moral education	Direct moral education involves either emphasizing values or character traits during specified time slots or integrating those values or traits throughout the curriculum. Indirect moral education involves encouraging adolescents to define their own and others' values and helping them to define the moral perspectives that support those values. The two main approaches to indirect moral education are values clarification and cognitive moral education. Values clarification focuses on helping students to clarify what their lives are for and what is worth working for. Cognitive moral education emphasizes that such values as democracy and justice are adopted through the development of students' moral reasoning. Kohlberg's theory has extensively influenced the cognitive moral education approach.

sounds exciting. Discussion, they are assured, will focus on ecology, world problems, religion, ethics, education—anything in which the recruit has shown some interest.

4. *Independent.* Many young people are recruited into cults when they are away from home—independent for the first time. Parents of such students are not always aware of how their children spend evenings and weekends, and often do not learn that they have left college until several weeks or months after they drop out. Backpackers are particular targets for cult recruiters. These young people are often lonely and susceptible to invitations for free meals and fellowship.

5. *Identity-seeking.* Young adults in every generation experience identity crises as they seek to determine their strengths and weaknesses, value systems, goals, and religious and social beliefs.

Concept Table 13.2

Moral Feelings, Altruism, Moral Education, Values, Religion, and Cults

Concept	Processes/Related Ideas	Characteristics/Description
	Damon's comprehensive approach to moral education	Damon believes that moral education should follow from what is known about the nature of adolescents' moral development. The approach emphasizes: that adolescents' moral awareness develops within their natural social experiences; that adolescents need to be guided but not directly taught moral values in an authoritarian way; that moral awareness is shaped by emotional reactions, such as empathy; that interactions with parents and other adults introduce children and adolescents to important social standards (authoritative parenting is preferred); that peer relations introduce children and adolescents to sharing, cooperation, and fairness; that principles of care and justice should be part of a culture's experiences for boys and girls; and that moral development in the schools is determined by the same cognitive and social processes that apply to moral development in other settings. According to Damon, moral education should involve active participation by the adolescent, not passive reception of rules. Adolescents need to experience egalitarian interactions that reflect democratic values. Damon believes that adults should practice respectful engagement when interacting with adolescents.
Values, religion, and cults	Values	Over the last two decades, adolescents have shown an increased concern for personal well-being and a decreased concern for the welfare of others. Recently, adolescents have shown a slight increase in concern for community and societal issues.
	Religious beliefs and the church	Both Elkind's and Fowler's views illustrate the increased abstractness in thinking that improves adolescents' understanding of the nature of religion. Adolescents show a strong interest in spiritual matters but believe that organized religion does not provide them with the spiritual understanding they are seeking. Adolescents who attend church and value religion in their lives are less experienced sexually and have less permissive attitudes toward sexual activity than their counterparts who have low religious involvement.
	Cults	Cult membership in the United States is extensive. It may appeal to adolescents because of weaknesses in organized religion and families.

6. *Insecure.* Inquisitive young people—looking for new experiences, seeking to clarify their own identities, away from the influence of family, friends, and mentors—develop uneasy feelings of insecurity. Lacking trusted counselors to whom they can turn when upset or disturbed, they are especially vulnerable to smiling, friendly people who show great interest in them and manipulate them through what one cult calls "love bombing."

At this point, we have discussed a number of ideas about moral feelings, altruism, moral education, values, religion, and cults. A summary of these ideas is presented in Concept Table 13.2. In this chapter, we learned that, in the last decade, adolescents were more motivated to be well-off financially. With this value in mind, in the next chapter we turn our attention to the nature of achievement, careers, and work in adolescent development.

Summary

I. What Is Moral Development?

Moral development concerns rules and conventions about what people should do in their interactions with others. The three main domains of moral development are thought, behavior, and feelings.

II. Piaget's Ideas and Cognitive Disequilibrium Theory

Piaget argued that, from four to seven years of age, children are in the stage of heteronomous morality, and from about the age of 10 on, are in the stage of autonomous morality. Formal operational thought may undergird changes in the moral reasoning of adolescents. Cognitive disequilibrium theory states that adolescence is an important period in moral development, especially as individuals move from the relatively homogeneous grade school to the more heterogeneous high school and college environments, where they are faced with contradictions between the moral concepts they have accepted and experiences outside their family and neighborhood. Older adolescents often come to understand that their set of beliefs is but one of many and that there is considerable debate about what is right and what is wrong.

III. Kohlberg's Ideas on Moral Development

Kohlberg developed a provocative theory of the development of moral reasoning. He argued that moral development consists of three levels—preconventional, conventional, and postconventional—and six stages (two at each level). Increased internalization characterizes movement to levels 2 and 3. Kohlberg's longitudinal data show a relation of the stages to age, although the highest two stages, especially stage 6, rarely appear. Influences on the Kohlberg stages include cognitive development, modeling, cognitive conflict, peer relations, and role-taking opportunities.

IV. Kohlberg's Critics

Criticisms of Kohlberg's theory of the development of moral reasoning involve an overemphasis on moral thought and an underemphasis on moral behavior, the quality of the research, inadequate consideration of culture's role in moral development, and underestimation of the care perspective in moral development. Gilligan believes that Kohlberg's theory reflects a justice perspective (individual); she advocates a stronger care perspective (views people in terms of their connectedness with others and emphasizes interpersonal communication). Gilligan also believes that adolescence is a critical juncture in the development of a moral voice for females. Researchers have found support for Gilligan's claim that females' and males' moral reasoning often centers around different concerns, although sex differences in Kohlberg's stages have not been consistently found. Thus, studies that focus more extensively on items pertaining to close relationships and that use scoring systems that emphasize connectedness support Gilligan's claims.

V. Moral Reasoning and Social Conventional Reasoning

Social conventional reasoning refers to thoughts about social consensus and convention, as opposed to moral reasoning, which stresses ethical issues.

VI. Moral Behavior

Behaviorists and social learning theorists argue that adolescents' moral behavior is determined by the processes of reinforcement, punishment, and imitation. Situational variability in moral behavior is stressed. The cognitive social learning theory of moral development emphasizes a distinction between moral competence—the ability to produce moral behaviors—and moral performance—those behaviors in specific situations. In general, social learning theorists are critical of Kohlberg's theory, believing that he placed too little emphasis on moral behavior and its situational variability.

VII. Moral Feelings: Psychoanalytic Theory

According to psychoanalytic theory, the superego is one of the three main structures of personality. The superego—the moral branch of personality—develops as the child resolves the Oedipus conflict and identifies with the same-sex parent in the early childhood years. Through identification, children and adolescents internalize parents' standards of right and wrong. Individuals conform to societal standards to avoid guilt. In Freud's view, the superego consists of two main components: ego-ideal and conscience. Erikson argues that there are three stages of moral development: specific moral learning in childhood, ideological concerns in adolescence, and ethical consolidation in adulthood.

VIII. Moral Feelings: Empathy and the Contemporary Perspective on the Role of Emotions in Moral Development

Feeling empathy means reacting to another's feelings with an emotional response that is similar to the other's response. Empathy often has a cognitive component—perspective taking. Around the beginning of adolescence, individuals begin to show more empathy for people who live in unfortunate circumstances. Individual variation characterizes empathy. Both positive feelings, such as empathy, sympathy, admiration, and self-esteem, and negative feelings, such as anger, outrage, shame, and guilt, contribute to adolescents' moral development. When strongly experienced, these emotions influence adolescents to act in accord with moral standards. Moral emotions do not operate in a vacuum—they are interwoven with the cognitive and social aspects of adolescents' moral development.

IX. Altruism

Altruism is an unselfish interest in helping someone. While adolescents have often been described as selfish and egocentric, adolescent acts of altruism are, nevertheless, plentiful. Reciprocity and exchange are involved in altruism. Forgiveness is an aspect of altruism that occurs when the injured person releases the injurer from possible behavioral retaliation. Adolescents are especially swayed by peer pressure to forgive others.

X. Moral Education: The Hidden Curriculum, and Direct and Indirect Moral Education

The hidden curriculum is the pervasive moral atmosphere that characterizes any school, regardless of whether there is a specific moral curriculum. Direct moral education involves either emphasizing values or character traits during specified time slots or integrating those values or traits throughout the curriculum. Indirect moral education involves encouraging adolescents to define their own and others' values and helping them to define the moral perspectives that support those values. The two main approaches to indirect moral education are values clarification and cognitive moral education. Values clarification focuses on helping students to clarify what their lives are for and what is worth working for. Cognitive moral education emphasizes that such values as democracy and justice are adopted through the development of students' moral reasoning. Kohlberg's theory has extensively influenced the cognitive moral education approach.

XI. Damon's Comprehensive Approach to Moral Education

Damon believes that moral education should follow from what is known about the nature of adolescents' moral development. The approach emphasizes: that adolescents' moral awareness develops within their natural social experiences; that adolescents need to be guided but not directly taught moral values in an authoritarian way; that moral awareness is shaped by emotional reactions, such as empathy; that interactions with parents and other adults introduce children and adolescents to important social standards (authoritative parenting is preferred); that peer relations introduce children and adolescents to sharing, cooperation, and fairness; that principles of care and justice should be part of a culture's experiences for girls and boys; and that moral development in the schools is determined by the same cognitive and social processes that apply to moral development in other settings. According to Damon, moral education should involve active participation by the adolescent, not passive reception of rules. Adolescents need to experience egalitarian interactions that reflect democratic values. Damon believes that adults should practice respectful engagement when interacting with adolescents.

XII. Values, Religion, and Cults

Over the last two decades, adolescents have shown an increased concern for personal well-being and a decreased concern for the welfare of others. Recently, adolescents have shown a slight increase in concern for community and societal issues. Both Elkind's and Fowler's views illustrate the increased abstractness in thinking that improves adolescents' understanding of the nature of religion. Adolescents show a strong interest in spiritual matters but believe that organized religion does not provide them with the spiritual understanding they are seeking. Adolescents who attend church and value religion in their lives are less experienced sexually and have less permissive attitudes toward sexual activity than their counterparts who have low religious involvement. Cult membership in the United States is extensive. It may appeal to adolescents because of weaknesses in organized religion and families.

Key Terms

moral development 435
heteronomous
   morality 436
autonomous
   morality 436
immanent justice 436
cognitive disequilibrium
   theory 436
internalization 437
preconventional
   reasoning 437
punishment and
   obedience
   orientation 437
individualism and
   purpose 437
conventional
   reasoning 438

interpersonal norms 438
social systems
   morality 438
postconventional
   reasoning 438
community rights versus
   individual rights 438
universal ethical
   principles 438
justice perspective 441
care perspective 441
social conventional
   reasoning 444
cognitive social learning
   theory of moral
   development 447

ego-ideal 448
conscience 448
empathy 450
altruism 450
forgiveness 451
hidden curriculum 452
direct moral
   education 452
indirect moral
   education 452
values clarification 453
cognitive moral
   education 453
individuating-reflexive
   faith 457

Suggested Readings

Damon, W. (1988). *The moral child*. New York: Free Press.
   *Presents Damon's intelligent views on the nature of adolescents' moral
   development, including some logical ideas about moral education.*
Gilligan, C. (1982). *In a different voice*. Cambridge, MA: Harvard University Press.
   *Advances Gilligan's provocative view that a care perspective is underrepresented
   in Kohlberg's theory and research.*
Lapsley, D. K., Enright, R. D., & Serlin, R. C. (1986). Moral and social education. In
   J. Worrell and F. Danner (Eds.), *Adolescent development: Issues for education.*
   New York: Academic Press.
   *A thorough overview of what is known about moral education and the more
   recently developed field of social education. Includes thoughtful, detailed
   comments about the nature of moral and social conventional reasoning.*
Lickona, T. (Ed.). (1976). *Moral development and behavior*. New York: Holt, Rinehart
   & Winston.
   *Contemporary essays outlining the major theories, research findings, and
   educational implications of moral development. Included are essays by Kohlberg,
   Hoffman, Mischel, Aronfreed, Bronfenbrenner, and Rest.*
Modgil, S., & Modgil, C. (Eds.). (1986). *Lawrence Kohlberg*. Philadelphia: Falmer.
   *A number of experts evaluate Kohlberg's theory of moral development. Includes a
   concluding chapter by Kohlberg.*

CHAPTER 14

Achievement, Careers, and Work

Whatever you can do, or dream you can, begin it.
Boldness has genius, power, and magic in it.

Johann Wolfgang von Goethe

Kim-Chi and Thuy

Kim-Chi Trinh was only nine years old in Vietnam when her father used his savings to buy passage for her on a fishing boat. It was a costly and risky sacrifice for the family, who placed Kim-Chi on the small boat, among strangers, in the hope that she would eventually reach the United States, where she would get a good education and enjoy a better life.

Kim made it to the United States and coped with a succession of three foster families. When she graduated from high school in San Diego in 1988, she had a straight-A average and a number of college scholarship offers. When asked why she excels in school, Kim-Chi says that she has to do well because she owes it to her parents, who are still in Vietnam.

Kim-Chi is one of a wave of bright, highly motivated Asian Americans who are immigrating to America. Asian Americans are the fastest-growing ethnic minority group in the United States—two out of five immigrants are now Asian. Although Asian Americans make up only 2.4 percent of the U.S. population, they constitute 17 percent of the undergraduates at Harvard, 18 percent at MIT, 27 percent at the University of California at Berkeley, and a staggering 35 percent at the University of California at Irvine (Butterfield, 1990).

Not all Asian American youth do this well, however. Poorly educated Vietnamese, Cambodian, and Hmong refugee youth are especially at risk for school-related problems. Many refugee children's histories are replete with losses and trauma. Thuy, a 12-year-old Vietnamese girl, has been in the United States for two years and resides with her father in a small apartment with a cousin's family of five in the inner city of a West Coast metropolitan area (Huang, 1989). While trying to escape from Saigon, the family became separated, and the wife and two younger children remained in Vietnam. Thuy's father has had an especially difficult time adjusting to the United States, struggling with English classes and being unable to maintain several jobs as a waiter. When Thuy received a letter from her mother saying that her five-year-old brother had died, Thuy's schoolwork began to deteriorate, and she showed marked signs of depression—lack of energy, loss of appetite, withdrawal from peer relations, and a general feeling of hopelessness. At the insistence of the school, she and her father went to the child and adolescent unit of a community mental health center. It took the therapist a long time to establish credibility with Thuy and her father, but eventually, they began to trust the therapist as a good listener who had competent advice about how to handle different experiences in the new country. The therapist also contacted Thuy's teacher, who said that Thuy had been involved in several interethnic skirmishes at school. With the assistance of the mental health clinic, the school initiated interethnic student panels to address cultural differences and discuss reasons for ethnic hostility. Thuy was selected to participate in these panels. Her father became involved in the community mutual assistance association, and Thuy's academic performance began to improve.

The reward of a thing well done is to have done it.

Ralph Waldo Emerson,
Essays, *Second Series, 1844*

A merican adolescents live in an achievement-oriented world with standards that tell them that success is important. The standards suggest that success requires a competitive spirit, a desire to win, a motivation to do well, and the wherewithal to cope with adversity and persist until obstacles are overcome. We saw in the "Images of Adolescence" section the importance of achievement in the lives of two Asian American adolescents, and in this chapter, we examine the achievement orientation of adolescents from many different backgrounds. This chapter is about achievement, about careers, and about work.

Achievement

Some developmentalists worry that the United States is rapidly becoming a nation of hurried, wired people who are raising their youth to become the same way—too uptight about success and failure, and far too worried about how personal accomplishments compare with those of others (Elkind, 1981). In this section, we focus on the importance of adolescence in achievement. We also discuss motivation, achievement motivation, attribution theory and intrinsic-extrinsic motivation, mastery-oriented versus helpless-oriented achievement patterns, and achievement in ethnic minority adolescents.

The Importance of Adolescence in Achievement

Adolescence is a critical juncture in achievement (Henderson & Dweck, 1990). New social and academic pressures force adolescents toward different roles, roles that often involve more responsibility. Achievement becomes a more serious business in adolescence, and adolescents begin to sense that the game of life is now being played for real. They may even begin to perceive current successes and failures as predictors of future outcomes in the adult world. And as demands on adolescents intensify, different areas of their lives may come into conflict. Adolescents' social interests may cut into the time they need to pursue academic matters, or ambitions in one area may undermine the attainment of goals in another, as when academic achievement leads to social disapproval (Ishiyama & Chabassol, 1985; Sue & Okazaki, 1990).

Whether or not adolescents effectively adapt to these new academic and social pressures is determined, in part, by psychological and motivational factors. Indeed, adolescents' achievement is due to much more than their intellectual ability. Students who are less bright than others often show an adaptive motivational pattern—persistent at tasks and confident about their ability to solve problems, for example—and turn out to be high achievers. In contrast, some of the brightest students show maladaptive achievement patterns—give up easily and do not have confidence in their academic skills, for example—and turn out to be low achievers. We now examine what we mean by the term *motivation,* which plays an important role in adolescents' achievement.

Adolescence is a critical juncture in achievement. New social and academic pressures force adolescents toward different roles, roles that often involve more responsibility. Whether or not an adolescent effectively adapts to these new academic and social pressures is determined, in part, by psychological and motivational factors.

Motivation

Motivation focuses on *why* individuals behave the way they do. Why is an adolescent hungry? Why is another adolescent studying so hard? Two important dimensions of the "whys" of behavior are activation and direction. First, when adolescents are motivated, they do something. Their behavior is activated or energized. If adolescents are hungry, they might go to the refrigerator for a snack. If they are motivated to get a good grade on a test, they might study hard. Second, when adolescents are motivated, their behavior also is directed. Why does an adolescent behave one way when there are several options available? For example, if a father reprimands his son for failing to clean up his room before going out, one adolescent might ignore the reprimand, another adolescent might hurry to clean up the room before departing, and a third adolescent might start a verbal argument. Motivation thus focuses on how adolescents direct their behavior or, put another way, the specific behaviors adolescents select in certain situations but not others. To summarize, **motivation** *focuses on* why *individuals behave, think, and feel the way they do, with special consideration of the activation and direction of their behavior.*

Achievement Motivation

Think about yourself and your friends for a moment. Are you more achievement oriented than they are or less so? If researchers asked you and your friends to tell stories about achievement-related themes, could they actually determine which of you is more achievement oriented?

Some adolescents are highly motivated to succeed and spend a lot of energy striving to excel; others are not as motivated to succeed and do not work as hard to achieve. These two types of adolescents vary in their **achievement motivation,** *the desire to accomplish something, to reach a standard of excellence, and to expend effort to excel.* Borrowing from Henry Murray's (1938) theory and measurement of personality, psychologist David McClelland (1955) assessed achievement motivation by showing individuals ambiguous pictures that were likely to stimulate achievement-related responses. Individuals were asked to tell a story about the picture, and their comments were scored according to how strongly the story reflected achievement. Researchers found that individuals whose stories reflected high achievement motivation had a stronger hope for success than fear of failure, were moderate rather than low or high risk takers, and persisted with effort when tasks became difficult (Atkinson & Raynor, 1974). Early research also indicated that independence training by parents promoted achievement, but more recent research reveals that parents need to set high standards for achievement, model achievement-oriented behavior, and reward adolescents for their achievement if their adolescents are to be achievement oriented (Huston-Stein & Higgens-Trenk, 1978). More about the role of parents in adolescents' achievement orientation appears in Perspective on Adolescent Development 14.1.

A concept related to achievement motivation was developed by Matina Horner (1972), who pointed out that much of the research on achievement motivation was based on male experiences. She found that females' achievement-related responses were different from those of males'. She theorized that females do not express the same achievement imagery as males because of **fear of success,** *individuals' worry that they will be socially rejected if they are successful.* Some years later, fear of success, originally believed to be confined to females, was also found to be present in males. Females still worried about social rejection, but males worried that all of their achieving would end up being for an unsatisfying goal (Williams, 1987).

Hurried Adolescents

Adolescents who were called "spoiled" a generation ago took longer to grow up and had more freedom and power than they knew how to handle. Today's adolescents are pressured to achieve more, earlier—academically, socially, sexually. These hurried adolescents, as David Elkind (1981) calls them, must contend with a fear of failure and a feeling that society's promises to them have been broken. Unlike the spoiled adolescents who remain children too long, hurried adolescents grow up too fast, pushed in their early years toward many avenues of achievement.

In adolescence, the symptoms of being hurried become evident, too often taking the form of severe anxiety about academic success. Elkind believes that parent-adolescent contracts—implicit agreements about mutual obligation—can help to alleviate some of this uptightness about achievement. He describes three basic contracts: freedom and responsibility, loyalty and commitment, and achievement and support.

Parents usually give adolescents freedom as long as the adolescents show that they can handle it. In adolescence, though, new types of responsibilities are demanded when individuals begin to date, drive cars, and experiment with drugs. Parents have less control than they did earlier because adolescents can take certain freedoms regardless of parental consent. Yet, parents can still set limits and make clear that some freedoms (such as using the family car) will be withdrawn if adolescents transgress.

A second type of parent-adolescent contract involves loyalty and commitment. Parents usually assume that children will be loyal to them, in the sense of preferring them to other adults. In return, parents show commitment to their children in the time they spend with them and in their concern for their children's well-being. In adolescence, when friendships become more important, parents no longer expect the loyal affection they received when children were young. They do expect, however, that their adolescents will be loyal to their family's values and beliefs. Adolescents, in return, demand that parents not be hypocritical and show commitment to the values they endorse.

A third contract involves achievement and support. Parents demand little in the way of achievement from infants, other than that they learn to sit up, crawl, walk, and talk at appropriate ages. As children grow up and go to school, the achievement-support contract is rewritten. Middle-class families expect achievements in academic subjects, extracurricular activities, and social events. Parents reciprocate with affection for good grades, with material support for lessons, instruments, and uniforms, and with transportation to and from friends' homes and various social activities. In adolescence, parental demands for achievement become more intense, as adolescents prepare for adult maturity.

In a society that emphasizes early achievement, when parents do not couple demands for that achievement with a comparable level of support, there is a disequilibrium in parent-child relations. When the disequilibrium persists, the result is a hurried child or hurried adolescent, achieving ever earlier in adult ways, but also acquiring the tensions that arise from the pressure to achieve. As adolescents, they may be motivated to pay back their parents for what they experienced as childhood inequities. They may come to resent their parents who pushed them to excel in school but who never bothered to look at their work, attend parent conferences, or participate in school functions. They often experience a sense of failure, both in their school performance and in their ability to meet their parents' expectations.

Today, fear of success is a much-debated concept. It has not been able to explain why there are so few females in Congress or so few female orchestra conductors. Nonetheless, many females still report a conflict between traditional femininity and competitive achievement. The final explanation is likely to involve an interaction between achievement motivation and the gender-role socialization practices discussed in Chapter 11. For example, Black American females, who are less likely than White American females to have been traditionally socialized, have lower fear of success (Weston & Mednick, 1970).

Attribution Theory and Intrinsic-Extrinsic Motivation

Shakespeare once wrote, "Find out the cause of this effect, or rather say, the cause of this defect, for the effect defective comes by cause." Attribution theorists have taken Shakespeare's comments to heart. They argue that individuals want to know the causes of people's behavior because the knowledge promotes more effective coping with life's circumstances. **Attribution theory** *states that individuals are motivated to discover the underlying causes of behavior as part of the effort to make sense out of the behavior.* In a way, attribution theorists say, adolescents are like intuitive scientists, seeking the cause behind what happens.

The reasons individuals behave the way they do can be classified in a number of ways, but one basic distinction stands out above all others—the distinction between internal causes, such as the actor's personality traits or motives, and external causes, which are environmental, situational factors such as rewards or task difficulty (Heider, 1958). If adolescents do not do well on a test, do they attribute it to the teacher plotting against them and making the test too difficult (external cause) or to their not studying hard enough (internal cause). The answer to such a question influences how adolescents feel about themselves. If adolescents believe that their performance is the teacher's fault, they will not feel as bad as when they do not spend enough time studying.

An extremely important aspect of internal causes for achievement is *effort*. Unlike many causes of success, effort is under adolescents' control and amenable to change (Jagacinski & Nicholls, 1990; Schunk, 1990; Wisniewski & Gaier, 1990). The importance of effort in achievement is recognized by most children and adolescents. In one recent study, third- to sixth-grade students felt that effort was the most effective strategy for good school performance (Skinner, Wellborn, & Connell, 1990).

Closely related to the concept of internal and external causes of behavior is the concept of intrinsic and extrinsic motivation. Adolescents' achievement motivation—whether in school, at work, or in sports—can be divided into two main types: **intrinsic motivation,** *the internal desire to be competent and to do something for its own sake;* and **extrinsic motivation,** *which is influenced by external rewards and punishments.* If you work hard in college because a personal standard is important to you, intrinsic motivation is involved. But if you work hard in college because you know it will bring you a higher-paying job when you graduate, extrinsic motivation is at work.

A frequent concern is whether to offer a reward to adolescents if they achieve (extrinsic motivation), or whether to let their internal, self-determined motivation operate (intrinsic motivation). If an adolescent is not producing competent work, seems bored, or has a negative attitude, incentives may help to improve motivation. However, external rewards sometimes get in the way of achievement motivation. Educational psychologist Adele Gottfried (1990) has shown that intrinsic motivation is related to higher school achievement and lower academic anxiety in fourth- through eighth-grade students. And in one investigation, students with a strong interest in art spent more time drawing when they expected no reward than their counterparts who knew that they would be rewarded (Lepper, Greene, & Nisbett, 1973) (see Figure 14.1).

In many instances, an adolescent's achievement is motivated by *both* internal and external factors. Some of the most achievement-oriented adolescents are those who have a high personal standard for achievement (internal) as well as a strong sense of competitiveness and a desire to do better than others (external). In one investigation, low-achieving math students who engaged in individual goal setting (internal) and were given comparative information about their peers' achievement (external) worked more math problems and got more of them correct than their counterparts who experienced either condition alone (Schunk, 1983). Other research suggests that social comparison by itself, though, is not a

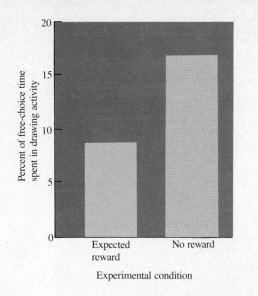

Figure 14.1 Intrinsic motivation and drawing activity. Students with an initial high interest in art spent more time in art activity when no reward was mentioned than did students who expected a reward for their participation (Lepper, Greene, & Nisbett, 1973).

wise strategy (Ames & Ames, 1989). The argument is that social comparison puts the individual in an ego-involved, threatening, self-focused state rather than a task-involved, effortful, strategy-focused state (Nicholls, 1984).

Mastery Orientation Versus Helpless Orientation

Closely related to an emphasis on intrinsic motivation, attributions of internal causes of behavior, and the importance of effort in achievement is a mastery orientation (Nelson-Le Gall, 1990). Valanne Henderson and Carol Dweck (1990) have found that children and adolescents show two distinct responses to difficult or challenging circumstances. The **helpless orientation** *describes children or adolescents who seem trapped by the experience of difficulty. They attribute their difficulty to lack of ability.* They frequently say things like, "I'm not very good at this," even though they may have earlier demonstrated their ability through numerous successes. And once they view their behavior as failure, they often feel anxious about the situation, and their performance worsens even further. The **mastery orientation** *describes children or adolescents who are task oriented. Instead of focusing on their ability, they are concerned about their learning strategies.* Mastery-oriented children and adolescents often instruct themselves to pay attention, to think carefully, and to remember strategies that have worked for them in previous situations. They frequently report feeling challenged and excited by difficult tasks, rather than being threatened by them.

What psychological factors have been found to undergird the mastery and helpless achievement orientations? In one recent investigation, students were followed over the first few months of the seventh grade, their first year of junior high school (Henderson & Dweck, 1990). Students who believed that their intelligence was malleable and who had confidence in their abilities earned significantly higher grades than their counterparts who believed that their intelligence was fixed and who did not have much confidence in their abilities. Students who believed that their intelligence was fixed also had higher levels of anxiety than students who believed that it was changeable. Apparently, then, the way students think about their intelligence and their confidence in their abilities may affect their ability and desire to master academic material. Believing that learning new material increases one's intelligence may actually promote academic mastery.

The mastery orientation describes adolescents who are task oriented. Instead of focusing on their ability, they become concerned about their learning strategies. They often report feeling challenged and excited by difficult tasks, rather than being threatened by them.

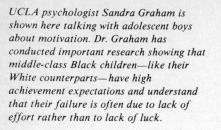

UCLA psychologist Sandra Graham is shown here talking with adolescent boys about motivation. Dr. Graham has conducted important research showing that middle-class Black children—like their White counterparts—have high achievement expectations and understand that their failure is often due to lack of effort rather than to lack of luck.

In summary, a number of psychological and motivational factors influence an adolescent's achievement. Especially important in the adolescent's ability to adapt to new academic and social pressures are achievement motivation, internal attributions of effort, intrinsic motivation, and a mastery achievement orientation. Next, we examine the role of ethnicity in adolescents' achievement.

Achievement in Ethnic Minority Adolescents

The diversity that exists among ethnic minority adolescents, a concept first mentioned in Chapter 9, also is evident in their achievement (Barnard & Lentz, 1992; Manaster, Chan, & Safady, 1992; Slaughter-Defoe & others, 1990; Sue & Okazaki, 1990). For example, the "Images of Adolescence" section that opened the chapter indicated that, while many Asian American adolescents have a very strong achievement motivation, some do not. Later in this section we will return to a discussion of achievement by Asian American adolescents.

Another important point in examining the achievement of ethnic minority adolescents involves differences. Too often, the achievements of ethnic minority group adolescents—especially Black American, Hispanic American, and Native American—have been interpreted as "deficits" by middle-class White standards. Rather than perceiving individuals as *culturally different,* many conclusions unfortunately portray the cultural distinctiveness of Blacks, Hispanics, and Native Americans as deficient in some way (Gibbs & Huang, 1989; Jones, 1990).

As also indicated in Chapter 9, the socioeconomic status of ethnic minority adolescents has not been adequately studied in most investigations. In many instances, when ethnicity *and* social class are investigated in the same study, social class is a much better predictor of achievement than ethnicity. Middle-class adolescents fare better than their lower-class counterparts in a variety of achievement situations—expectations for success, achievement aspirations, and recognition of the importance of effort, for example (Gibbs, 1989).

Black American educational psychologist Sandra Graham (1986, 1987, 1990) conducted a number of investigations that revealed not only stronger social class than ethnic differences in achievement, but also the importance of studying ethnic minority group motivation in the context of general motivational theory. Her inquiries focused on the causes that Black American children and adolescents give for their achievement orientation—why they succeed or fail, for example. She was struck by how consistently middle-class Black American children and adolescents do not fit the stereotype of either deviant or special populations. They, like their middle-class White American counterparts, have high achievement expectations and understand that failure is often due to lack of effort rather than to luck.

The indisputable fact is that too many ethnic minority group individuals are faced with educational, career, and social barriers (Huang & Gibbs, 1989; Jones, 1992). Individuals from ethnic minority groups have benefited from the Civil Rights Act of 1964, but much more progress is needed. We do not have all of the answers to the problems of poverty and racial prejudice in America, but as the Reverend Jesse Jackson commented, hopefully, we have begun to ask some of the right questions. As discussed in Sociocultural Worlds of Adolescence 14.1, some of the right questions are beginning to be asked and answered with regard to Black and Hispanic students enrolled in math and science courses.

At the same time that researchers are concerned about the low achievement of Black American, Hispanic American, and Native American adolescents, they are intrigued by the exceptionally high achievement levels of Japanese, Chinese, and Asian American adolescents (Evans, 1992). To examine the reasons underlying such high achievement, Harold Stevenson and his colleagues conducted extensive investigations of children's math achievement in the first and fifth grades in Japan, China, and the United States (Chen & Stevenson, 1989; Stevenson, Stigler, & Lee, 1986; Stevenson & others, 1990).

The stimulation for this research comes from the poor performance of American students on tests of mathematics and science in comparison to students in other countries. For example, in one cross-national study of math achievement, American eighth- and twelfth-grade students were below the national average in problem solving, geometry, algebra, calculus, and other areas of math (Garden, 1987; McKnight & others, 1987). In contrast, Japanese eighth graders had the highest average scores of children from 20 countries, and in the twelfth grade, Japanese students were second only to Chinese students in Hong Kong. In a recent cross-national comparison of the math and science achievement of 9-to-13-year-olds, Korean and Taiwanese students placed first and second, respectively (Educational Testing Service, 1992). In this cross-national study, 9 to 13 students in the United States finished 13th (out of 15) in science and 15th (out of 16) in math achievement. Critics of the cross-national studies say that such comparisons are flawed because countries, the percentage of children and adolescents who go to school, and the curricula vary widely. Even in the face of such criticisms, most education experts agree that many U.S. adolescents are achieving far below their potential in math.

Why are Chinese and Japanese students consistently among the top achievers in international comparisons and American adolescents among the lowest? One factor probably is the amount of time spent in school and math classes. The Japanese school year consists of 240 days of instruction, and each school week is five and a half days long. The American school year consists of 178 days of instruction, and each school week is five days long. Observations in the children's classrooms also revealed that Japanese teachers spent far more of

Japanese students attend school 240 days out of the year, whereas American students attend school only 178 days out of the year. In the research by Harold Stevenson and his colleagues (1990), the Japanese teachers spent more of their time teaching math than did the American teachers.

476

Modifying the Math Study Strategies of Black American College Students

Professor Treisman confers with students in a math study group at the University of California–Berkeley. Treisman's research revealed the importance of collaborative learning in helping Black students to succeed in math and science courses.

In 1986, Black and Hispanic Americans were awarded just eight of the more than six hundred doctoral degrees in math in the United States. At every level—high school, college, and graduate school—comparatively smaller percentages of Black and Hispanic American students enroll in math and science courses. The rate of enrollment, especially for Black students, declined in the 1980s. With more than one-fourth of America's college-age population expected to be Black or Hispanic in 1995, increasing the number of Black and Hispanic Americans in math and science is critical.

Motivated to discover why the success rate of Black and Hispanic Americans is so low, University of California-Berkeley mathematician Philip Treisman extensively compared 20 Black and 20 Chinese college students who were enrolled in freshman calculus. At Berkeley, as at many American universities, Asian American students often have the highest rate of success in math. Treisman observed the students in the library, their dormitory rooms, and even their homes. He interviewed their families. The differences in the Black and Chinese students were not due to motivation, income, family support, or academic preparation. Even Black students who came with the best test scores and other positive predictors tended to do poorly in math, for example. The most striking observation was that the Black students were virtually isolated in their study of math. Eighteen of the twenty Black students always studied alone— the two who studied together eventually dropped out to marry each other. Many erected a wall between their intellectual and social lives. Treisman found that, for many graduates of inner-city and predominantly ethnic minority high schools, the self-reliance that may have helped them get into a top college—by buffering them from the distractions at their secondary schools—became their downfall at Berkeley. The students had no way to check out their understanding of math or science, no way to check out what Berkeley as an institution required of them.

Within four weeks after arriving at Berkeley, 13 of the 20 Chinese students found study mates, and several others were still searching. The study groups came together after the students had done extensive individual work. Group study was a final, but very important, step. Studying together, the students picked up solutions they had missed. If no student had solved a problem, members of the group recognized its difficulty and thus avoided self-criticism. In these groups, students tested their perceptions of what professors expected, what the university expected, and how many hours they should be studying. They shared tips for handling the bureaucratic maze and for lining up financial aid and housing. They chatted about how to deal with the White community.

Based on his experiences with the Black and Chinese students, Treisman developed a math workshop with three overriding principles: (1) Help ethnic minority students excel, not just avoid failure; (2) emphasize collaborative learning and small-group teaching methods; and (3) require faculty sponsorship. The accomplishments of the math workshop over seven years of operations include: 55 percent of the workshop's 231 Black students (compared with 21 percent of the 234 Black students not in the workshop) have earned a grade of B— or better in first-year calculus. Black students in the workshop have consistently scored a full grade higher than nonworkshop Black students. Among Black workshop participants who entered Berkeley in 1978 or 1979, 44 percent graduated in math-based majors, while only 10 percent of the nonworkshop Black students did.

Freshman mathematics and science courses have too often been the burial ground for the aspirations of Black and Hispanic American students who have entered college with the goal of majoring in some area of math or science. Programs such as Philip Treisman's reveal how the underachievement of Black and Hispanic American students can be turned into accomplishment (Charles A. Dana Foundation Report, 1988).

their time teaching math than did American teachers; approximately one-fourth of total classroom time in the first grade was spent on math instruction in Japan, while American first-grade teachers spent only one-tenth of classroom time on math. Japanese children also spent far more time doing homework than American children—on weekends, 66 minutes versus 18 minutes, respectively. In another investigation, Chinese and Japanese children had a much more positive attitude about homework than American children (Chen & Stevenson, 1989).

In his most recent research on the cross-cultural dimensions of achievement, Stevenson and his colleagues (1990) focused on the family's role in children's achievement in Japan, China, and the United States. Children's academic achievement in American families was not nearly the central concern it was in Chinese and Japanese families. When children entered elementary school, Chinese and Japanese parents provided much greater assistance to their children's academic activities than did American parents. Chinese and Japanese mothers had much higher standards for their children's achievement than did American mothers. Chinese and Japanese mothers also stressed the importance of hard work as a basis for children's achievement, while American mothers were more likely to emphasize innate ability as the reason for their children's achievement level.

In sum, the poor performance of American children in math achievement is due to a number of factors related to cultural dimensions of achievement. Stevenson and his colleagues believe that good teaching, interested parents, and hard work could go a long way toward enhancing American children's and adolescents' math achievement. In another recent investigation, the importance of parents in adolescents' academic achievement was underscored (Leone & Richards, 1989). Students primarily did their homework alone or in classes, but when they did their homework with their parents, they received better grades.

As mentioned at the beginning of this section, many Asian American adolescents do not fit the "whiz-kid, super-achiever" image; instead, they are struggling just to learn English. The whiz-kid image fits many of the adolescents of Asian immigrant families who arrived in the United States in the late 1960s and early 1970s. Many of these immigrants came from Hong Kong, South Korea, India, and the Philippines. The image also fits many of the more than 100,000 Indochinese (primarily Vietnamese) immigrants who arrived in the United States after the Vietnam War in 1975. Both groups included mostly middle- to upper-income professional people who were reasonably well educated and who passed along a strong interest in education and a strong work ethic to their children and adolescents. For thousands of other Asian Americans, including a high percentage of the 600,000 Indochinese refugees who fled Vietnam, Laos, and Cambodia in the late 1970s, the problems are legion. Many in this wave of refugees lived in poor surroundings in their homelands. They came to the United States with few skills and little education. They speak little English and have a difficult time finding a decent job. They often share housing with relatives. Adjusting to school is difficult for their children and adolescents. Some drop out. Some are attracted to gangs and drugs. Better school systems use a range of culturally focused academic programs and social services to help these children and adolescents adapt more effectively to life in America.

At this point, we have discussed a number of ideas about adolescents' achievement. A summary of these ideas is presented in Concept Table 14.1. Achievement serves as a foundation for adolescents' career development, the topic we turn to next.

Concept Table 14.1

Achievement

Concept	Processes/Related Ideas	Characteristics/Description
The importance of adolescence in achievement	Its nature	Adolescence is a critical juncture in achievement. Social and academic pressures force adolescents to cope with achievement in new ways. Whether or not adolescents effectively adapt to these new social and academic pressures is determined, in part, by psychological and motivational factors.
Motivation and achievement motivation	Motivation	Motivation focuses on *why* individuals behave, think, and feel the way they do, with special consideration of the activation and direction of their behavior.
	Achievement motivation	Achievement motivation is the desire to accomplish something, to reach a standard of excellence, and to expend effort to excel. McClelland studied variations of achievement motivation by getting individuals to tell stories involving achievement-related themes. Horner developed the concept of fear of success, which is individuals' worry that they will be socially rejected if they are successful.
Attribution theory, intrinsic-extrinsic motivation, and mastery orientation versus helpless orientation	Attribution theory	Attribution theory states that individuals are motivated to discover the underlying causes of behavior as part of the effort to make sense out of the behavior. One basic distinction in the causes of behavior is between internal causes and external causes. An extremely important aspect of internal causes for achievement is effort.
	Intrinsic-extrinsic motivation	Intrinsic motivation is the internal desire to be competent and to do something for its own sake. Extrinsic motivation is influenced by external rewards and punishments. Adolescents' intrinsic motivation is related to higher school achievement and lower academic anxiety, although in many instances, achievement is influenced by both internal and external factors.
	Mastery orientation versus helpless orientation	The helpless orientation describes individuals who seem trapped by the experience of difficulty. They attribute their difficulty to lack of ability. The mastery orientation describes individuals who remain extremely task oriented. Instead of focusing on their ability, they are concerned about their learning strategies, often instructing themselves to pay attention, to think carefully, and to remember strategies that have worked in previous situations. They frequently report feeling challenged and excited by difficult tasks, rather than being threatened by them. Students who believe that their intelligence is malleable and who have confidence in their abilities earn better grades than their counterparts who believe that their intelligence is fixed and who have low confidence in their abilities.
Achievement in ethnic minority adolescents	Its nature	A special concern is the achievement of adolescents from various ethnic groups. Too often, ethnic differences are interpreted as "deficits" by middle-class White standards. When ethnicity and social class are considered in the same investigation, social class is often a much better predictor of achievement than ethnicity. Middle-class adolescents fare better than their lower-class counterparts in a variety of achievement situations. Psychologists have shown a special interest in the high achievement levels of Japanese, Chinese, and Asian American adolescents. Japanese schools and parents place a much stronger emphasis on education and achievement, especially math achievement, than their American counterparts. However, the diversity that exists among ethnic minority adolescents also is evident in their achievement. For example, while many Asian American adolescents have a very strong achievement motivation, some do not.

Career Development

What are the future occupations of today's adolescents? What theories have been developed to direct our understanding of adolescents' career choices? What roles do exploration, decision making, and planning play in career development? How do sociocultural factors affect career development? We consider each of these questions in turn.

Tomorrow's Jobs for Today's Adolescents

For almost half a century, the U.S. Bureau of Labor Statistics has published the *Occupational Outlook Handbook,* a valuable source for career information. The information that follows comes from the 1990–1991 edition (the handbook is revised every two years):

The long-term shift from goods-producing to service-producing employment will continue. By the year 2000, nearly four out of five jobs will be in industries that provide services, such as banking, insurance, health care, education, data processing, and management consulting. Continued expansion of the service-producing sector generates a vision of a work force dominated by cashiers, retail sales workers, and waiters. However, while the service sector growth will create millions of clerical, sales, and service jobs, it also will create jobs for engineers, accountants, lawyers, nurses, and many other managerial, professional, and technical workers. In fact, the fastest-growing careers will be those that require the most educational preparation.

The range of employment growth in various careers will be diverse. As indicated in Figure 14.2, the greatest growth in jobs will be for technicians and related support occupations. Workers in this group provide technical assistance to engineers, scientists, and other professional workers, as well as operate and program technical equipment. This group also includes the fastest-growing occupation—paralegals. Professional specialty occupations are expected to grow 24 percent from 1988 to 2000. Much of this growth is a result of rising demand for engineers, computer specialists, lawyers, health diagnosing and treating occupations, and preschool, elementary, and secondary school teachers. The greatest decrease in jobs will be in agriculture, forestry, fishing, and related occupations.

Many jobs are becoming more complex and more cognitively demanding. As the amount of what there is to know increases exponentially, technically trained workers such as engineers face a "half-life" of five years; that is, half of what they know when they graduate is obsolete in five years because of rapid technological advances (Goldstein & Gilliam, 1990). Such job demands will require considerable continuing education and training programs for workers in the future.

Theories of Career Development

Three main theories describe the manner in which adolescents make choices about career development: Ginzberg's developmental theory, Super's self-concept theory, and Holland's personality type theory.

Ginzberg's Developmental Theory

Developmental career choice theory *is Eli Ginzberg's belief that children and adolescents go through three career-choice stages: fantasy, tentative, and realistic* (Ginzberg, 1972; Ginzberg & others, 1951). When asked what they want to be when they grow up, young children may answer "a doctor," "a superhero," "a teacher," "a movie star," "a sports star," or any number of other occupations.

Figure 14.2 How employment change will vary widely by broad occupational group.

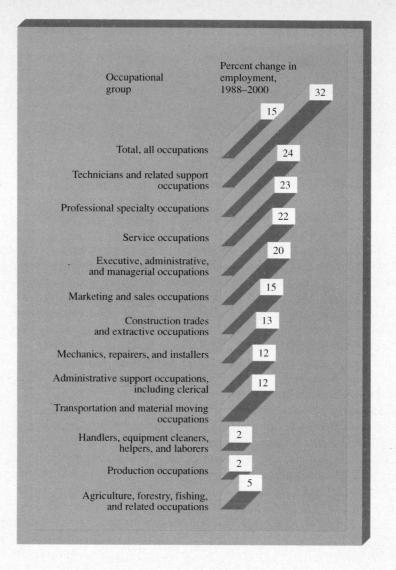

In childhood, the future seems to hold almost unlimited opportunities. Ginzberg argues that, until about the age of 11, children are in the *fantasy stage* of career choice. From the ages of 11 to 17, adolescents are in the *tentative stage* of career development, a transition from the fantasy stage of childhood to the realistic decision making of young adulthood. Ginzberg believes that adolescents progress from evaluating their interests (11 to 12 years of age) to evaluating their capacities (13 to 14 years of age) to evaluating their values (15 to 16 years of age). Thinking shifts from less subjective to more realistic career choices at around 17 to 18 years of age. Ginzberg calls the period from 17 to 18 years of age through the early twenties the *realistic stage* of career choice. During this time, the individual extensively explores available careers, then focuses on a particular career, and finally selects a specific job within the career (such as family practitioner or orthopedic surgeon within the career of doctor).

Critics have attacked Ginzberg's theory on a number of grounds. For one, the initial data were collected from middle-class youth, who probably had more career options open to them. And, as with other developmental theories (such as Piaget's), the time frames are too rigid. Moreover, Ginzberg's theory does not take into account individual differences—some adolescents make mature decisions about careers (and stick with them) at much earlier ages than specified by

Ginzberg. Not all children engage in career fantasies either. In a revision of his theory, Ginzberg (1972) conceded that lower-class individuals do not have as many options available as middle-class individuals do. Ginzberg's general point— that at some point during late adolescence or early adulthood more realistic career choices are made—probably is correct.

Super's Self-Concept Theory

Career self-concept theory *is Donald Super's belief that individuals' self-concept plays a central role in their career choice. Super believes that it is during adolescence that individuals first construct a career self-concept* (Super, 1967, 1976). He emphasizes that career development consists of five different phases. First, at about 14 to 18 years of age, adolescents develop ideas about work that mesh with their already existing global self-concept—this phase is called *crystallization*. Between 18 and 22 years of age, they narrow their career choices and initiate behavior that enables them to enter some type of career—this phase is called *specification*. Between 21 and 24 years of age, young adults complete their education or training and enter the world of work—this phase is called *implementation*. The decision on a specific, appropriate career is made between 25 and 35 years of age—this phase is called *stabilization*. Finally, after the age of 35, individuals seek to advance their careers and to reach higher-status positions— this phase is called *consolidation*. The age ranges should be thought of as approximate rather than rigid. Super believes that career exploration in adolescence is a key ingredient of adolescents' career self-concept. He constructed the Career Development Inventory to assist counselors in promoting adolescents' career exploration.

Holland's Personality Type Theory

Personality type theory *is John Holland's belief that an effort should be made to match an individual's career choice with his or her personality* (Holland, 1973, 1987). According to Holland, once individuals find a career that fits their personality, they are more likely to enjoy that particular career and to stay in a job for a longer period of time than individuals who work at jobs not suited to their personality. Holland believes that six basic personality types need to be considered when matching the individual's psychological makeup to a career (Gottfredson & Holland, 1989; Lowman, 1991):

1. *Realistic.* These individuals show characteristically "masculine" traits. They are physically strong, deal in practical ways with problems, and have very little social know-how. They are best oriented toward practical careers, such as labor, farming, truck driving, and construction.
2. *Intellectual.* These individuals are conceptually and theoretically oriented. They are thinkers rather than doers. They often avoid interpersonal relations and are best suited to careers in math and science.
3. *Social.* These individuals often show characteristically "feminine" traits, particularly those associated with verbal skills and interpersonal relations. They are likely to be best equipped to enter "people" professions, such as teaching, social work, counseling, and the like.
4. *Conventional.* These individuals show a distaste for unstructured activities. They are best suited for jobs as subordinates, such as bank tellers, secretaries, and file clerks.
5. *Enterprising.* These individuals energize their verbal abilities toward leading others, dominating individuals, and selling people on issues or products. They are best counseled to enter careers such as sales, politics, and management.

6. *Artistic.* These individuals prefer to interact with their world through artistic expression, avoiding conventional and interpersonal situations in many instances. These youth should be oriented toward such careers as art and writing.

If all individuals fell conveniently into Holland's personality types, career counselors would have an easy job. But individuals are more varied and complex than Holland's theory suggests. Even Holland (1987) now admits that most individuals are not pure types. Still, the basic idea of matching the abilities and attitudes of individuals to particular careers is an important contribution to the career field (Brown, 1987; Vondracek, 1991). Holland's personality types are incorporated into the Strong-Campbell Vocational Interest Inventory, a widely used measure in career guidance.

Exploration, Decision Making, and Planning

Exploration, decision making, and planning play important roles in adolescents' career choices (Crites, 1989). In countries where equal employment opportunities have emerged—such as the United States, Canada, Great Britain, and France—exploration of various career paths is critical in adolescents' career development. Adolescents often approach career exploration and decision making with considerable ambiguity, uncertainty, and stress (Schulenberg & others, 1988). Many of the career decisions made by youth involve floundering and unplanned changes. Many adolescents do not adequately explore careers on their own and also receive little direction from guidance counselors at their schools. On the average, high school students spend less than three hours per year with guidance counselors, and in some schools, the average is even less (National Assessment of Educational Progress, 1976). In many schools, students not only do not know what information to seek about careers, they do not know how to seek it.

Among the important aspects of planning in career development is awareness of the educational requirements for a particular career. In one investigation, a sample of 6,029 high school seniors from 57 different school districts in Texas was studied (Grotevant & Durrett, 1980). Students lacked knowledge about two aspects of careers: (1) accurate information about the educational requirements of careers they desired and (2) information about the vocational interests predominantly associated with their career choices.

Sociocultural Influences

Not every individual born into the world can grow up to become a nuclear physicist or a doctor—there is a genetic limitation that keeps some adolescents from performing at the high intellectual levels necessary to enter such careers. Similarly, there are genetic limitations that restrict some adolescents from becoming professional football players or professional golfers. But there usually are many careers available to each of us, careers that provide a reasonable match with our abilities. Our sociocultural experiences exert strong influences on career choices from among the wide range available. Among the important sociocultural factors that influence career development are social class, parents and peers, schools, and gender.

"Your son has made a career choice, Mildred. He's going to win the lottery and travel a lot."
© *1985; Reprinted courtesy of Bill Hoest and* Parade Magazine.

Social Class

The channels of upward mobility open to lower-class youth are largely educational in nature. The school hierarchy from grade school through high school, as well as through college and graduate school, is programmed to orient individuals toward some type of career. Less than a hundred years ago, only eight years of education were believed to be necessary for vocational competence, and anything beyond that qualified the individual for advanced placement in higher-status occupations. By the middle of the twentieth century, the high school diploma had already lost ground as a ticket to career success. College rapidly became a prerequisite for entering a higher-status occupation. Employers reason that an individual with a college degree is a better risk than a high school graduate or a high school dropout.

Parents and Peers

Parents and peers also are strong influences on adolescents' career choices. As mentioned earlier in the chapter, David Elkind believes that today's parents are pressuring their adolescents to achieve too much too soon. In some cases, though, adolescents are not challenged enough by their parents. Consider the 25-year-old female who vividly describes the details of her adolescence that later prevented her from seeking a competent career. From early in adolescence, both of her parents encouraged her to finish high school, but at the same time, they emphasized that she needed to get a job to help them pay the family's bills. She was never told that she could not go to college, but both parents encouraged her to find someone to marry who could support her financially. This very bright girl is now divorced and feels intellectually cheated by her parents, who socialized her in the direction of marriage and away from a college education.

From an early age, children see and hear about what jobs their parents have. In some cases, parents even take their children to work with them on jobs. Recently, when we were building our house, the bricklayer brought his two sons to help with the work. They were only 14 years old, yet were already engaging in apprenticeship work with their father.

Unfortunately, many parents want to live vicariously through their son's or daughter's career achievements. The mother who did not get into medical school and the father who did not make it as a professional athlete may pressure their youth to achieve a career status beyond the youth's talents.

Many factors influence parents' role in adolescents' career development (Bogenschneider, 1989). For one, mothers who work regularly outside the home and show effort and pride in their work probably have strong influences on their adolescents' career choices. A reasonable conclusion is that, when both parents work and enjoy their work, adolescents learn work values from both parents.

Peers also can influence adolescents' career development. In one investigation, when adolescents had friends and parents with high career standards, they were more likely to seek higher career status jobs, even if they came from low-income families (Simpson, 1962).

School Influences

Schools, teachers, and counselors can exert a powerful influence on adolescents' career development. School is the primary setting where individuals first encounter the world of work. School provides an atmosphere for continuing self-development in relation to achievement and work. And school is the only institution in society that is presently capable of providing the delivery systems necessary for career education—instruction, guidance, placement, and community connections (Bachhuber, 1992; Vinton, 1992).

A national survey revealed the nature of career information available to adolescents (Chapman & Katz, 1983). The most common single resource was the *Occupational Outlook Handbook* (*OOH*), with 92 percent of the schools having one or more copies. The second major source was the *Dictionary of Occupational Titles* (*DOT*), with 82 percent having this book available for students. Fewer than 30 percent had no established committee to review career information resources. When students talked to counselors, it was more often about high school courses than about career guidance.

School counseling has been criticized heavily, both inside and outside the educational establishment. Insiders complain about the large number of students per school counselor and the weight of noncounseling administrative duties. Outsiders complain that school counseling is ineffective, biased, and a waste of money. Short of a new profession, several options are possible (William T. Grant Foundation Commission, 1988). First, twice the number of counselors are needed to meet all students' needs. Second, there could be a redefinition of teachers' roles, accompanied by retraining and reduction in teaching loads, so that classroom teachers could assume a stronger role in handling the counseling needs of adolescents. The professional counselor's role in this plan would be to train and assist teachers in their counseling and to provide direct counseling in situations the teacher could not handle. Third, the whole idea of school counselors would be abandoned, and counselors would be located elsewhere—in neighborhood social service centers or labor offices, for example. (West Germany forbids teachers to give career counseling, reserving this task for officials in well-developed networks of labor offices.)

The College Board Commission on Precollege Guidance and Counseling (1986) recommends other alternatives. It believes that local school districts should develop broad-based planning that actively involves the home, school, and community. Advocating better-trained counselors, the commission supports stronger partnerships between home and school to increase two-way communication about student progress and better collaboration among schools, community agencies, colleges, businesses, and other community resources.

Hispanic adolescents at a job fair, seeking information about careers. Improving adolescents' awareness of career options and educational requirements is an important agenda for the United States.

Gender

Because many females have been socialized to adopt nurturing roles rather than career or achieving roles, they traditionally have not planned seriously for careers, have not explored career options extensively, and have restricted their career choices to careers that are gender-stereotyped (Baumrind, 1990; Diamond, 1988; Eccles, 1991; Lange, 1992; Lappan & Jingeleski, 1992; Rich & Golan, 1992). The motivation for work is the same for both sexes. However, females and males make different choices because of their socialization experiences and the ways that social forces structure the opportunities available to them (Astin, 1984).

As growing numbers of females pursue careers, they are faced with questions involving career and family: Should they delay marriage and childbearing and establish their career first? Or should they combine their career, marriage, and childbearing in their twenties? Some females in the last decade have embraced the domestic patterns of an earlier historical period. They have married, borne children, and committed themselves to full-time mothering. These "traditional" females have worked outside the home only intermittently, if at all, and have subordinated the work role to the family role.

Many other females, though, have veered from this time-honored path. They have postponed, and even forgotten, motherhood. They have developed committed, permanent ties to the workplace that resemble the pattern once reserved only for males. When they have had children, they have strived to combine a career and motherhood. While there have always been "career" females, today their numbers are growing at an unprecedented rate.

As already mentioned, parents play an important role in their sons' and daughters' career development. In one recent study, 1,500 mothers and their young adolescent sons and daughters were studied to determine the role of maternal expectations, advice, and provision of opportunities in their sons' and daughters' occupational aspirations (Eccles & others, 1991; Harold & Eccles, 1990). Mothers were more likely to encourage their sons to consider the military, to expect their sons to go into the military right after high school, and to discuss the education needed for, and likely income of, different jobs with sons. Expecting marriage right after high school and discussing the problems of combining work and family were topics more common to mother-daughter interactions. Also, mothers were more worried that their daughters would not have a happy marriage, and they were more likely to want their sons to have a job that would support a family.

Further information in this study indicated that mothers worked more with boys on a computer; they also provided boys with more computers, software, and programs. The mothers also bought more math or science books and games for boys, and more often enrolled boys in computer classes. Boys were provided more sports opportunities, while girls were given more opportunities in music, art, and dance. Mothers said that boys have more talent in math and are better suited for careers involving math, while they believed that girls have more talent in English and are better suited for careers related to English. In sum, there were differences in the kinds of advice and opportunities provided and in the expectations, aspirations, and ability assessments held by mothers for their sons and daughters.

Were the maternal advice, provision of opportunities, expectations, and ability assessments associated with adolescents' occupational aspirations in this study? Yes, they were. Mothers tended to provide more math or science books to daughters who aspired to male-typed occupations (nontraditional girls) than to daughters who aspired to female-typed jobs (traditional girls). Mothers talked more about the importance of looking good to their daughters who aspired to more female-typed occupations than to their daughters who aspired to male-typed jobs. They also expected daughters who aspired to more female-typed occupations to be more likely to get married right after high school than their nontraditional counterparts. Further, several of the mothers' and adolescent daughters' family/work-role values were related. For example, mothers' belief that it was better if the man was the breadwinner and the woman took care of the family was related to their adolescent daughters' identical belief. Mothers' belief that working mothers can establish just as warm and secure a relationship with their children as nonworking mothers was related to their adolescent daughters' belief that it is okay for mothers to have full-time careers. Nontraditional girls were more likely to endorse the belief that women are better wives and mothers if they have paid jobs.

In sum, this research study documented that parental socialization practices in the form of provision of opportunities, expectations, and beliefs are important sources of adolescent females' and males' occupational aspirations (Harold & Eccles, 1990).

Gifted Female Adolescents

Some of the brightest and most gifted females do not have achievement and career aspirations that match their talents. One investigation found that high-achieving females had much lower expectations for success than high-achieving males (Stipek & Hoffman, 1980). In the gifted research program at Johns Hopkins University, many mathematically precocious females did select scientific and medical careers, although only 46 percent aspired to a full-time career compared to 98 percent of the males (Fox, Brody, & Tobin, 1979).

To help talented females redirect their life paths, some high schools are using programs developed by colleges and universities. Project CHOICE (Creating Her Options In Career Education) was designed by Case Western University to detect barriers in reaching one's potential. Gifted eleventh-grade females received individualized counseling that included interviews with female role models, referral to appropriate occupational groups, and information about career workshops. A program at the University of Nebraska was successful in encouraging talented female high school students to pursue more prestigious careers (Kerr, 1983). This was accomplished through individual counseling and participation in a "Perfect Future Day," in which girls shared their career fantasies and discussed barriers that might impede their fantasies. Internal and external constraints were evaluated, gender-role stereotypes were discouraged, and high aspirations were applauded. While these programs have short-term success in redirecting the career paths of high-ability females, in some instances, the effects fade over time—six months or more, for example. Improving the career alternatives for all female youth, not just those of high ability, however, should be a priority.

In our discussion of careers, we have studied how adolescents choose the occupation they will work in as adults. Next, we consider another important aspect of their work worlds—their work as adolescents.

Jacqueline Eccles has conducted extensive research on the nature of gender roles in the development of achievement. In her recent research, she has shown how parents influence their sons' and daughters' career choices.

Work

One of the greatest changes in adolescents' lives in recent years has been the increased number of adolescents who work in some part-time capacity and still attend school on a regular basis. Our discussion of adolescents and work includes information about the sociohistorical context of adolescent work, the advantages and disadvantages of part-time work, bridging the gap from school to work, and an added chance for adolescents in the world of work.

Sociohistorical Context of Adolescent Work

Over the past century, the percentage of youth who work full-time as opposed to those who are in school has decreased dramatically. In the late 1800s, fewer than one of every twenty high school age adolescents was in school. Today more than nine of every ten adolescents receive high school diplomas. In the nineteenth century, many adolescents learned a trade from their father or some other adult member of the community.

While prolonged education has kept many contemporary youth from holding full-time jobs, it has not prevented them from working on a part-time basis while going to school (Mortimer, 1991). Most high school seniors have had some work experience. In a national survey of 17,000 high school seniors, three of four reported some job income during the average school week (Bachman, 1982). For 41 percent of the males and 30 percent of the females, this income exceeded $50 a week. The typical part-time job for high school seniors involves 16 to 20 hours of work per week, although 10 percent work 30 hours a week or more.

In 1940, only one of twenty-five tenth-grade males attended school and simultaneously worked part-time. In the 1970s, the number increased to more than one of every four. And, in the 1980s, as just indicated, three of four combined school and part-time work. Adolescents also are working longer hours now than in the past. For example, the number of 14- to 15-year-olds who work more than 14 hours per week has increased substantially in the last three decades. A similar picture emerges for 16-year-olds. In 1960, 44 percent of 16-year-old males who attended school worked more than 14 hours a week, but by the 1980s, the figure had increased to more than 60 percent.

What kinds of jobs are adolescents working at today? About 17 percent who work do so in restaurants, such as McDonald's and Burger King, waiting on

What are the effects of working and going to school on adolescents' grades and integration into school activities?

customers and cleaning up. Other adolescents work in retail stores as cashiers or salespeople (about 20 percent), in offices as clerical assistants (about 10 percent), or as unskilled laborers (about 10 percent). In one recent study, boys reported higher self-esteem and well-being when they perceived that their jobs were providing skills that would be useful to them in the future (Mortimer & others, 1992).

Do male and female adolescents take the same type of jobs, and are they paid equally? Some jobs are held almost exclusively by male adolescents—busboys, gardeners, manual laborers, and newspaper carriers—while other jobs are held almost exclusively by female adolescents—baby-sitters and maids. Male adolescents work longer hours and are paid more per hour than female adolescents (Helson, Elliot, & Leigh, 1989).

Advantages and Disadvantages of Part-Time Work in Adolescence

Does the increase in work have benefits for adolescents? In some cases, yes; in others, no. Ellen Greenberger and Laurence Steinberg (1981, 1986) examined the work experiences of students in four California high schools. Their findings disproved some common myths. For example, generally it is assumed that adolescents get extensive on-the-job training when they are hired for work. The reality is that they got little training at all. Also, it is assumed that youths—through work experiences—learn to get along better with adults. However, adolescents reported that they rarely felt close to the adults with whom they worked. The work experiences of the adolescents did help them to understand how the business world works, how to get and how to keep a job, and how to manage money. Working also helped adolescents to learn to budget their time, to take pride in their accomplishments, and to evaluate their goals. But working adolescents often have to give up sports, social affairs with peers, and sometimes, sleep. And they have to balance the demands of work, school, family, and peers.

Greenberger and Steinberg asked students about their grade point averages, school attendance, satisfaction from school, and the number of hours spent studying and participating in extracurricular activities since they began working. They found that the working adolescents had lower grade point averages than nonworking adolescents. More than one of four students reported that their grades dropped when they began working; only one of nine said that their grades im-

Table 14.1 Unemployment Rates of Youth: 1988 (Percent Unemployed)

Years of Age	Total	White	Black	Hispanic
Total, 16–24:				
16–19	15.3%	13.1%	32.4%	21.9%
20–24	8.7	7.1	19.6	9.8
Nonstudents:				
16–19	16.6%	14.2%	33.6%	21.3%
20–24	9.2	7.4	20.2	10.1
Students:				
16–19	13.9%	11.9%	30.9%	23.2%
20–24	6.3	5.4	15.3	7.6

Source: Bureau of Labor Statistics. *Employment and Earnings,* Volume 36, Number 1, (USGPO, Washington, DC: January 1989), pp. 162–8.

proved. But it was not just working that affected adolescents' grades—more importantly, it was *how long* they worked. Tenth-graders who worked more than 14 hours a week suffered a drop in grades. Eleventh-graders worked up to 20 hours a week before their grades dropped. When adolescents spend more than 20 hours per week working, there is little time to study for tests and to complete homework assignments.

In addition to work affecting grades, working adolescents felt less involved in school, were absent more, and said that they did not enjoy school as much as their nonworking counterparts. Adolescents who worked also spent less time with their families—but just as much time with their peers—as their non-working counterparts. Adolescents who worked long hours also were more frequent users of alcohol and marijuana. More recent research confirms the negative relation between long work hours during the school year and lowered interest and performance in school, drug and alcohol use, and delinquency (Steinberg & Dornbusch, 1991).

Some states have responded to these findings by limiting the number of hours adolescents can work while they are attending secondary school. In 1986, in Pinellas County, Florida, a new law placed a cap on the previously unregulated hours that adolescents could work while school is in session. The allowable limit was set at 30 hours, which—based on research evidence—is still too high.

The Transition from School to Work

In some cases, the media have exaggerated the degree of adolescent unemployment. For example, based on data collected by the U.S. Department of Labor, nine of ten adolescents either are in school, working at a job, or both. Only 5 percent are out of school, without a job, and looking for full-time employment. Most adolescents who are unemployed are not unemployed for long. Only ten percent are without a job for six months or longer. Most unemployed adolescents are school dropouts.

Certain segments of the adolescent population, however, are more likely to be unemployed than others. For example, a disproportionate percentage of unemployed adolescents are Black (Bowman, 1989). As indicated in Table 14.1, the unemployment situation is especially acute for Black American and Hispanic American youth between the ages of 16 and 19. The job situation, however, has improved somewhat for Black American adolescents: In 1969, 44 percent of Black American 16- to 19-year-olds were unemployed; today, that figure is approximately 32 percent.

How can adolescents be helped to bridge the gap between school and work? For adolescents bound for higher education and a professional degree, the educational system provides ladders from school to career. Most youth, though, step off the educational ladder before reaching the level of a professional career. Often, they are on their own in their search for work. Recommendations for bridging the gap from school to work were described briefly in Chapter 8, on schools, but are expanded on here (William T. Grant Foundation Commission, 1988):

1. Monitored work experiences, including cooperative education, internships, apprenticeships, preemployment training, and youth-operated enterprises, should be implemented. These experiences provide opportunities for youth to gain work experience, to be exposed to adult supervisors and models in the workplace, and to relate their academic training to the workplace.

2. Community and neighborhood services, including individual voluntary service and youth-guided services, should be expanded. Youth need experiences not only as workers but as citizens. Service programs not only expose youth to the adult world, but provide them with a sense of the obligations of citizenship in building a more caring and competent society.

3. Vocational education should be redirected. With few exceptions, today's vocational education does not prepare youth adequately for specific jobs. However, its hands-on methods can provide students with valuable and effective ways of acquiring skills they will need to be successful in a number of jobs.

4. Incentives need to be introduced. Low motivation and low expectations for success in the workplace often restrict adolescents' educational achievement. Recent efforts to guarantee postsecondary and continuing education and to provide guaranteed employment, and guaranteed work-related training for students who do well show promise of encouraging adolescents to work harder and be more successful in school.

5. Career information and counseling need to be improved. A variety of information and counseling approaches can be implemented to expose adolescents to job opportunities and career options. These services can be offered both in school and in community settings. They include setting up career information centers, developing the capacity of parents as career educators, and expanding the work of community-based organizations.

6. More school volunteers should be used. Tutoring is the most common form of school volunteer activity. However, adults are needed even more generally—as friends, as mentors for opening up career opportunities, and for assisting youth in mastering the dilemmas of living in a stressful time.

Improving education, elevating skill levels, and providing "hands-on" experience will help adolescents to bridge the gap between school and work. We need to address the needs of youth if we are to retain the confidence of youth who have been brought up to believe in the promise of the American Dream (Grubb, 1989; Wilson, 1989).

An Added Chance

For most youth over the age of 18 who lack a high school diploma, more traditional schooling is probably not the solution. The following recommendations by the William T. Grant Foundation Commission (1988) describe an expanded array of opportunities for youth who are out of school and out of work:

1. Intensive academic skills training should be implemented in all employment training programs where they are not currently offered. The *Job Corps* is an intensive intervention that has been extensively evaluated and fine-tuned. Though it is not for everyone, evaluations have indicated that the Job Corps increases earnings, enables its graduates to be employed longer, and gives society a net return of $1.46 for every tax dollar invested.
2. *State and local youth corps* currently operate in 14 states and 12 cities. They incorporate various dimensions of the Job Corps experience (Hamilton, 1991). Other states and communities operate summer programs. An evaluation of the California Conservation Corps indicated that the work of the corps provided a positive economic return.
3. *Nonresidential preemployment training* is accomplished by a number of national organizations that specialize in preemployment training and basic skills remediation. Their efforts deserve further encouragement and support.
4. The *Job Training Partnership Act's* potential for serving at-risk youth has not been adequately realized. Only 5 percent of eligible youth are currently being served.
5. The *Armed Forces* also can be used more effectively. Although only 9 percent of all recruits lack a high school diploma, the proportion is likely to increase dramatically with the changing youth demographics. The armed forces should expand programs to upgrade the academic and work skills of its members.
6. To obtain maximum effectiveness for added-chance programs, coordination among agencies that serve youth needs to be improved.

At this point, we have discussed many aspects of careers and work. A summary of these ideas is presented in Concept Table 14.2. At various points in the book, we have discussed problems and disturbances of adolescents. For example, in this chapter, we examined the high unemployment rate of inner-city, ethnic minority adolescents. The next chapter is devoted exclusively to adolescents' problems and disturbances.

Concept Table 14.2

Career Development and Work

Concept	Processes/Related Ideas	Characteristics/Description
Tomorrow's jobs for today's adolescents	Their nature	The long-term shift from goods-producing to service-producing employment will continue. By the year 2000, nearly four out of five jobs will be in industries that provide services. The fastest-growing careers will be those that require the most education.
Theories of career development	Ginzberg's developmental theory	Developmental career choice theory is Ginzberg's view that children and adolescents go through three career choice stages: fantasy, tentative, and realistic. Critics charge that Ginzberg's theory is based only on middle-class youth and does not adequately account for individual differences.
	Super's self-concept theory	Career self-concept theory is Super's view that individuals' self-concept plays a central role in their career choice. Super believes that it is during adolescence that individuals first construct a career self-concept.
	Holland's personality type theory	Personality type theory is Holland's view that an effort should be made to match an individual's career choice with his or her personality. Holland believes that six basic personality types can be matched up with various careers: realistic, intellectual, social, conventional, enterprising, and artistic. Critics argue that most individuals are more varied and complex than Holland's theory suggests.
Exploration, decision making, and planning	Their nature	Exploration of career options is a critical aspect of career development in countries where equal employment opportunities exist. Many youth flounder and make unplanned career choice changes. Students also need more knowledge about the education and ability requirements of various careers.
Sociocultural influences	Their nature	Among the important sociocultural factors that influence adolescent career development are social class, parents and peers, schools, and gender. The channels of opportunity for lower-class youth are largely educational in nature. Many factors influence parents' role in adolescents' career development. School counseling has been criticized heavily and recommendations made for its improvement. Because many females have been socialized to adopt nurturing roles rather than career or achievement roles, they have not been adequately prepared for careers. As growing numbers of females pursue careers, they are faced with questions involving career and family. Parents often have different expectations for, give different advice to, and provide different opportunities in career development for their sons and daughters.

Summary

I. The Importance of Adolescence in Achievement

Adolescence is a critical juncture in achievement. Social and academic pressures force adolescents to cope with achievement in new ways. Whether or not adolescents effectively adapt to these new social and academic pressures is determined, in part, by psychological and motivational factors.

II. Motivation and Achievement Motivation

Motivation focuses on *why* individuals behave, think, and feel the way they do, with special consideration of the activation and direction of their behavior. Achievement motivation is the desire to accomplish something, to reach a standard of excellence, and to expend effort to excel. McClelland studied variations of achievement motivation by getting individuals to tell stories involving achievement-related themes. Horner developed the concept of fear of success, which is individuals' worry that they will be socially rejected if they are successful.

III. Attribution Theory and Intrinsic-Extrinsic Motivation

Attribution theory states that individuals are motivated to discover the underlying causes of behavior as part of the effort to make sense out of the

Concept Table 14.2

Career Development and Work

Concept	Processes/Related Ideas	Characteristics/Description
	Gifted female adolescents	A special concern is that some of the brightest and most gifted female adolescents do not have achievement and career aspirations that match their talents. Programs have been designed to help talented female adolescents develop higher career aspirations.
Work	Sociohistorical context of adolescent work	Adolescents are not as likely to hold full-time jobs today as their adolescent counterparts of the nineteenth century. While prolonged education has reduced the number of adolescents holding down full-time jobs, the number of adolescents who work part-time and go to school has increased significantly.
	Advantages and disadvantages of part-time work in adolescence	Advantages of part-time work include learning how the business world works, how to get and keep a job, how to manage money, how to budget time, how to take pride in accomplishments, and how to evaluate goals. Disadvantages include giving up sports, social affairs with peers, and sometimes, sleep, as well as balancing the demands of school, family, peers, and work. Grades, identity with the school, and school participation may be reduced when adolescents work long hours.
	The transition from school to work	In some cases, adolescent unemployment has been exaggerated, but certain segments, such as minority group adolescents, face major unemployment problems. To bridge the gap between school and work, we should monitor work experiences, expand community and neighborhood services, redirect vocational education, introduce incentives, improve career information and counseling, and use more school volunteers.
	An added chance	For youth over 18 who lack a high school diploma, we should improve academic skills training in all employment training programs; upgrade the Job Corps, as well as state and local youth corps; continue nonresidential preemployment training; increase the potential of the Job Training Partnership Act; use the armed forces more effectively; and improve coordination among agencies that serve youth.

behavior. One basic distinction in the causes of behavior is between internal causes and external causes. An extremely important aspect of internal causes for achievement is effort. Intrinsic motivation is the internal desire to be competent and to do something for its own sake. Extrinsic motivation is influenced by external rewards and punishments. Adolescents' intrinsic motivation is related to higher school achievement and lower academic anxiety, although in many instances, achievement is influenced by both internal and external factors.

IV. Mastery Orientation Versus Helpless Orientation

The helpless orientation describes individuals who seem trapped by the experience of difficulty. They attribute their difficulty to lack of ability. The mastery orientation describes individuals who remain extremely task oriented. Instead of focusing on their ability, they are concerned about their learning strategies, often instructing themselves to pay attention, to think carefully, and to remember strategies that have worked in previous situations. They frequently report feeling challenged and excited by difficult tasks, rather than being threatened by them. Students who believe that their intelligence is malleable and who have confidence in their abilities earn better grades than their counterparts who believe that their intelligence is fixed and who have low confidence in their abilities.

V. Achievement in Ethnic Minority Adolescents

A special concern is the achievement of adolescents from various ethnic groups. Too often, ethnic differences are interpreted as deficits by middle-class White standards. When ethnicity and social class are examined in the same investigation, social class is often a much better predictor of achievement than ethnicity. Middle-class adolescents fare better than their lower-class counterparts in a variety of achievement situations. Psychologists have shown a special interest in the high achievement levels of Japanese, Chinese, and Asian American adolescents. Japanese schools and parents place a much stronger emphasis on education and achievement, especially math achievement, than their American counterparts. However, the diversity that exists among ethnic minority adolescents also is evident in their achievement. For example, while many Asian American adolescents have a very strong achievement motivation, some do not.

VI. Tomorrow's Jobs for Today's Adolescents

The long-term shift from goods-producing to service-producing employment will continue. By the year 2000, nearly four out of five jobs will be in industries that provide services. The fastest-growing careers will be those that require the most education.

VII. Theories of Career Development

Developmental career choice theory is Ginzberg's view that children and adolescents go through three career choice stages: fantasy, tentative, and realistic. Critics charge that Ginzberg's theory is based only on middle-class youth and does not adequately account for individual differences. Career self-concept theory is Super's view that individuals' self-concept plays a central role in their career choice. Super believes that it is during adolescence that individuals first construct a career self-concept. Personality type theory is Holland's view that an effort should be made to match an individual's career choice with his or her personality. Holland believes that six basic personality types can be matched up with various careers: realistic, intellectual, social, conventional, enterprising, and artistic. Critics argue that most individuals are more varied and complex than Holland's theory suggests.

VIII. Exploration, Decision Making, and Planning

Exploration of career options is a critical aspect of career development in countries having equal employment opportunities. Many youth flounder and make unplanned career choice changes. Students also need to know more about the education and ability requirements of various careers.

IX. Sociocultural Influences

Sociocultural influences include social class, parents, peers, schools, and gender. The channels of opportunity for lower-class youth are largely educational in nature. Many factors influence parents' role in adolescents' career development. School counseling has been heavily criticized and recommendations made for its improvement. Because many females have been socialized to adopt nurturing roles rather than career or achievement roles, they have not been adequately prepared for careers. As growing numbers of females pursue careers, they are faced with questions involving career and family. Parents often have different expectations for, give different advice to, and provide different opportunities in career development for their sons and daughters. A special concern is that some of the brightest and most gifted female adolescents do not have achievement and career aspirations that match their talents. Programs have been designed to help talented female adolescents develop higher career aspirations.

X. Work: Its Sociohistorical Context and Advantages and Disadvantages of Part-Time Work in Adolescence

Adolescents are not as likely to hold full-time jobs today as their adolescent counterparts of the nineteenth century. While prolonged education has reduced the number of adolescents holding down full-time jobs, the number of adolescents who work part-time and go to school has increased significantly. Advantages of part-time work include learning how the business world works, how to get and keep a job, how to manage money, how to budget time, how to take pride in accomplishments, and how to evaluate goals. Disadvantages include giving up sports, social affairs with peers, and sometimes, sleep, as well as balancing the demands of family, peers, school, and work. Grades, identity with the school, and school participation may be reduced when adolescents work long hours.

XI. The Transition from School to Work and an Added Chance
In some cases, adolescent unemployment has been exaggerated, but certain segments such as minority group adolescents, face major unemployment problems. To bridge the gap between school and work, we should monitor work experiences, expand community and neighborhood services, redirect vocational education, introduce incentives, improve career information and counseling, and use more school volunteers. For youth over 18 who lack a high school diploma, we should improve academic skills training in all employment training programs; upgrade the Job Corps, as well as state and local youth corps; continue nonresidential preemployment training; increase the potential of the Job Training Partnership Act; use the Armed Services more effectively; and improve coordination among agencies that serve youth.

Key Terms

motivation 470
achievement
    motivation 470
fear of success 470
attribution theory 472
intrinsic motivation 472

extrinsic motivation 472
helpless orientation 473
mastery orientation 473
developmental career
    choice theory 479

career self-concept
    theory 481
personality type
    theory 481

Suggested Readings

Ames, C., & Ames, R. (Eds.). (1989). *Research on motivation in education. Goals and cognitions* (Vol. 3). San Diego: Academic Press.
    Presents an excellent overview of adolescents' achievement motivation, with special attention devoted to goals and cognitions.
Applied Psychology: An International Review, 1988, Vol. 37.
    The entire issue of this journal is devoted to gender and career development. Special attention is given to the current status of female career development.
Career Development Quarterly
    This research journal has many articles that pertain to career development in adolescence. Go to your library and look through the issues of the last several years to get a feel for the kinds of issues that are interesting to researchers who study the nature of career development.
Henderson, V. L., & Dweck, C. S. (1990). Motivation and achievement. In S. S. Feldman & G. R. Elliott (Eds.) *At the threshold: The developing adolescent,* Cambridge, MA: Harvard University Press.
    Henderson and Dweck present their model of adolescent achievement, which places a strong emphasis on mastery motivation.
Occupational Outlook Handbook (1990–1991). (1990). Washington, DC: Bureau of Labor Statistics.
    A compendium of tomorrow's jobs for today's adolescents.
William T. Grant Foundation Commission on Work, Family, and Citizenship. (1988). *The forgotten half: Non-college-bound youth in America.* New York: William T. Grant Foundation.
    Also recommended as reading for Chapter 8, "Schools," this report focuses on ways American society can help adolescents at risk for career difficulties. Pay special attention to the transition from school to work and the added chance.

Adolescent Problems, Stress, and Health

There is no easy path leading out of life, and few are the easy ones that lie within it.

Walter Savage Landor,
Imaginary Conversations, *1824*

Modern life is stressful and leaves its psychological scars on too many adolescents, who, unable to cope effectively, never reach their human potential. The need is not only to find better treatments for adolescents with problems, but to find ways to encourage adolescents to adopt healthier life-styles, which can prevent problems from occurring in the first place. This section consists of two chapters: Chapter 15, "Adolescent Problems" and Chapter 16, "Stress and Health."

Adolescent Problems

*They cannot scare me with their
    empty spaces
Between stars—on stars where no
    human race is.
I have it in me so much nearer
    home
To scare myself with my own desert
    places.*

Robert Frost, 1936

Annie and Arnie

Some mornings, Annie, a 15-year-old cheerleader, was too drunk to go to school. Other days, she would stop for a couple of beers or a screwdriver on the way to school. She was tall and blonde and good-looking, and no one who sold her liquor, even at 8:00 in the morning, questioned her age. She got her money from baby-sitting and what her mother gave her to buy lunch. Finally, Annie was kicked off the cheerleading squad for missing practice so often. Soon, she and several of her peers were drinking almost every morning. Sometimes, they skipped school and went to the woods to drink. Annie's whole life began to revolve around her drinking. It went on for two years, and during the last summer, anytime she saw anybody she was drunk. After a while, her parents began to detect Annie's problem. But even when they punished her, she did not stop drinking. Finally, Annie started dating a boy she really liked and who would not put up with her drinking. She agreed to go to Alcoholics Anonymous and has just successfully completed treatment. She has stopped drinking for four consecutive months now, and continued abstinence is the goal.

Arnie is 13 years old. He has a history of committing thefts and physical assaults. The first theft occurred when Arnie was eight—he stole a SONY walkman from an electronics store. The first physical assault took place a year later, when he shoved his seven-year-old brother up against the wall, bloodied his face, and then threatened to kill him with a butcher knife. Recently, the thefts and physical assaults have increased. In the last week, he stole a television set and struck his mother repeatedly and threatened to kill her. He also broke some neighborhood streetlights and threatened youths with a wrench and a hammer. Arnie's father left home when Arnie was three years old. Until the father left, his parents argued extensively, and his father often beat up his mother. Arnie's mother indicates that, when Arnie was younger, she was able to control him, but in the last several years, she has not been able to enforce any sanctions on his antisocial behavior. Arnie's volatility and dangerous behavior have resulted in the recommendation that he be placed in a group home with other juvenile delinquents.

We are all mad at some time or another.

Battista Mantuanus, Ecologues, *1500*

A nnie and Arnie in the "Images of Adolescence" section have serious problems. Their alcohol dependency and delinquency are but two of the many problems and disturbances that can emerge in adolescents' journey to maturity. Throughout this book, we have focused on normal adolescents' development, though there have been many examples of adolescents with problems. In this chapter, we look more closely at some of the major problems that adolescents can develop. To begin, though, we discuss the nature of abnormality.

The Nature of Abnormality

What is abnormal behavior and what causes it? What are the characteristics of adolescent disorders? We examine each of these questions in turn.

What Is Abnormal Behavior?

Defining what is normal and what is abnormal is not a simple task. Among other complications, what is abnormal may vary from one culture to another, and from time to time in the same culture. Early in this century in the United States, masturbation was thought to cause everything from warts to insanity; today, there is a much more accepting attitude toward masturbation, and it is not considered abnormal.

Does being atypical mean that an individual is abnormal? Madonna is atypical but is not considered abnormal because she is an outstanding singer and music video performer. Jennifer Capriati also is not abnormal even though she became a top tennis professional at a young age. And while Joe Montana is a masterful quarterback, that atypicality does not make him abnormal. If being atypical does not make an individual abnormal, what does? **Abnormal behavior** *is behavior that is maladaptive and harmful.* Such behavior fails to promote the well-being, growth, and fulfillment of the adolescent and, ultimately, others (Davison & Neale, 1990). Maladaptive behavior takes many forms—committing suicide; experiencing depression; having bizarre, irrational beliefs; assaulting others; and becoming addicted to drugs, for example. These abnormal behaviors interfere with adolescents' ability to function effectively in the world and can harm the well-being of others.

What Causes Abnormal Behavior?

Causes of adolescents' abnormal, maladaptive, or harmful behavior include biological, psychological, and sociocultural factors.

The Biological Approach

Proponents of the biological approach believe that abnormal behavior is due to a physical malfunction of the body, that if an adolescent behaves uncontrollably, is out of touch with reality, or is severely depressed, biological factors are the culprits. Today, scientists and researchers who adopt the biological approach often focus on brain processes and genetic factors as the causes of abnormal behavior.

The **medical model,** *also called the disease model, was the forerunner of the biological approach. The medical model states that abnormality is a disease or illness precipitated by internal body causes.* From this perspective, abnormalities are called mental *illnesses,* and the individuals are *patients* in *hospitals* and are treated by *doctors.*

The Psychological and Sociocultural Approaches

Although the biological approach provides an important perspective for understanding abnormal behavior, many psychologists believe that it underestimates the importance of psychological and sociocultural factors in abnormal behavior. Emotional turmoil, inappropriate learning, distorted thoughts, and inadequate relationships are of interest in the psychological and sociocultural approaches, rather than brain processes or genes.

Advocates of the psychological and sociocultural approaches also criticize the medical model because they believe that it encourages labeling of mental disturbances. When adolescents are labeled "mentally ill," they may begin to perceive themselves as sick and, thus, not assume responsibility for coping with their problems (Scheff, 1966; Szasz, 1977).

Most experts on abnormal behavior agree that many psychological disturbances are universal, appearing in most cultures (Al-Issa, 1982). However, the frequency and intensity of abnormal behavior often varies across cultures. Variations in disorders are related to social, economic, technological, religious, and other cultural factors (Costin & Draguns, 1989).

An Interactionist Approach

The normality or abnormality of adolescent behavior cannot be determined without considering the complexity of adolescents and the multiple influences on behavior. Neither the biological nor the psychological and sociocultural approaches independently capture this complexity. Adolescents' abnormal behavior is influenced by biological factors (brain processes and heredity, for example), by psychological factors (emotional turmoil and distorted thoughts, for example), and by social factors (inadequate relationships, for example). These factors interact to produce adolescents' abnormal behavior.

Characteristics of Adolescent Disorders

The spectrum of adolescent disorders is wide. The disturbances vary in their severity, developmental level, sex, and social class. Some adolescent disorders are short-lived; others may persist over many years. One 13-year-old adolescent may show a pattern of acting-out behavior that is disruptive to his classroom. As a 14-year-old, he may be assertive and aggressive, but no longer disruptive. Another 13-year-old may show a similar pattern of acting-out behavior. At age 16, she may have been arrested for numerous juvenile offenses and still be a disruptive influence in the classroom.

Some disorders are more likely to appear at one developmental level than another. For example, fears are more common in early childhood, many school-related problems surface for the first time in middle and late childhood, and drug-related problems become more common in adolescence (Achenbach & Edelbrock, 1981). In one study, depression, truancy, and drug abuse were more common among older adolescents, while arguing, fighting, and being too loud were more common among younger adolescents (Edelbrock, 1989).

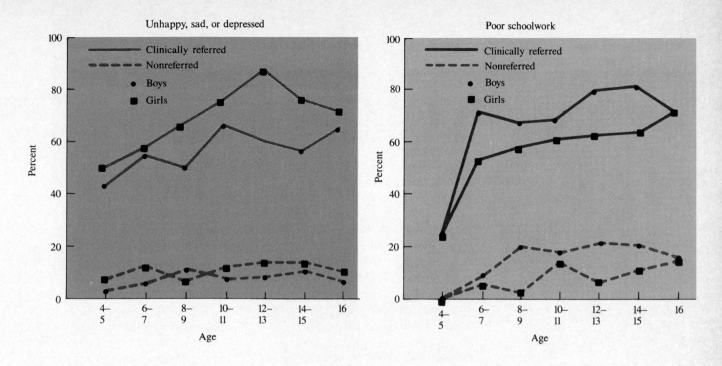

In the large-scale investigation by Thomas Achenbach and Craig Edelbrock (1981), adolescents from a lower-class background were more likely to have problems than those from a middle-class background. Most of the problems reported for adolescents from a lower-class background were undercontrolled, externalizing behaviors—destroying others' things and fighting, for example. These behaviors also were more characteristic of boys than girls. The problems of middle-class adolescents and girls were more likely to be overcontrolled and internalizing—anxiety or depression, for example.

The behavioral problems most likely to cause adolescents to be referred to a clinic for mental health treatment were feelings of unhappiness, sadness, or depression, and poor school performance (see Figure 15.1). Difficulties in school achievement, whether secondary to other kinds of disturbances or primary problems in themselves, account for many clinical referrals of adolescents (Weiner, 1980).

In a recent large-scale national investigation, Achenbach and his colleagues (1991) studied the problems and competencies of 2,600 4- to 16-year-olds assessed at intake into mental health services and 2,600 demographically matched nonreferred children and adolescents. Lower socioeconomic status children and adolescents had more problems and fewer competencies than their higher socioeconomic status counterparts. Children and adolescents had more problems when they had fewer related adults in their homes, had biological parents who were unmarried in their homes, had parents who were separated or divorced, lived in families who received public assistance, and lived in households in which family members had received mental health services. Children and adolescents who had more externalized problems came from families in which parents were unmarried, separated, or divorced, as well as from families receiving public assistance. Now that we have considered some general characteristics of adolescent problems, let's turn our attention to some specific problems beginning with drug abuse.

Figure 15.1 The two items most likely to differentiate between clinically referred and clinically nonreferred children and adolescents.

Drugs and Alcohol

Why do adolescents take drugs? How pervasive is adolescent drug use in the United States? What are the nature and effects of various drugs taken by adolescents? What factors contribute to adolescent drug use? These are among the questions we now evaluate.

Why Do Adolescents Take Drugs?

When Sigmund Freud experimented with cocaine, he was searching for possible medical uses for the substance, among them a use in eye surgery. He soon found that the drug produced an ecstatic feeling and wrote to his fiancée to inform her of how just a small dose provided lofty, wonderful sensations. Over time, Freud stopped taking cocaine, though, because it became apparent that some individuals experienced bad effects from the drug, and several died from overdoses.

Since the beginning of history, humans have searched for substances that would sustain and protect them and also act on their nervous system to produce pleasurable sensations. Individuals are attracted to drugs because drugs help them to adapt to an ever-changing environment. Smoking, drinking, and taking drugs reduce tension and frustration, relieve boredom and fatigue, and in some cases, help adolescents to escape the harsh realities of their world (Avis, 1990). Drugs provide pleasure by giving inner peace, joy, relaxation, kaleidoscopic perceptions, surges of exhilaration, or prolonged heightened sensation. They may help some adolescents to get along better in their world. For example, amphetamines may help the adolescent to stay awake to study for an exam. Drugs also satisfy adolescents' curiosity—some adolescents take drugs because they are intrigued by sensational accounts of drugs in the media, while others may listen to a popular song and wonder if the drugs described can provide them with unique, profound experiences. Drugs are taken for social reasons also, allowing adolescents to feel more comfortable and to enjoy the company of others (Fields, 1992).

But the use of drugs for personal gratification and temporary adaptation carries a very high price tag: drug dependence, personal and social disorganization, and a predisposition to serious and sometimes fatal diseases (Block, 1992). Thus, what is intended as adaptive behavior is maladaptive in the long run. For example, prolonged cigarette smoking, in which the active drug is nicotine, is one of the most serious yet preventable health problems. Smoking has been described by some experts as "suicide in slow motion."

As adolescents continue to take a drug, the drug produces **tolerance,** *which means that a greater amount of the drug is needed to produce the same effect.* The first time adolescents take 5 milligrams of Valium, a very relaxed feeling results, but after taking the pill every day for six months, 10 milligrams may be needed to achieve the same effect.

Addiction *is the body's physical dependence on a drug.* When an addicted adolescent's body is not supplied with an adequate dose of the addictive drug, the adolescent is said to go into withdrawal. **Withdrawal** *is the undesirable intense pain and craving for an addictive drug.* **Psychological dependence** *is a psychological need to take a drug, as when adolescents take drugs to help them cope with problems and stresses in their lives.* In both physical addiction and psychological dependence, the drug plays a powerful role in adolescents' lives. Let us now look at trends in overall drug use by U.S. adolescents.

Table 15.1 Percentage of High School Seniors Who Used Particular Drugs in the Last 30 Days

	Class of 1976	Class of 1977	Class of 1978	Class of 1979	Class of 1980	Class of 1981	Class of 1982	Class of 1983	Class of 1984	Class of 1985	Class of 1986	Class of 1987	Class of 1988	Class of 1989	Class of 1990	Class of 1991
Approximate number of students	15,400	17,100	17,800	15,500	15,900	17,500	17,700	16,300	15,900	16,000	15,200	16,300	16,300	16,700	15,200	15,000
Marijuana/hashish	32.2	35.4	37.1	36.5	33.7	31.6	28.5	27.0	25.2	25.7	23.4	21.0	18.0	16.7	14.0	13.8
Inhalants	—	—	—	3.2	2.7	2.5	2.5	2.5	2.6	3.0	3.2	3.5	3.0	2.7	2.9	2.6
Hallucinogens	—	—	—	5.3	4.4	4.5	4.1	3.5	3.2	3.8	3.5	2.8	2.3	2.9	2.3	2.4
Cocaine	2.0	2.9	3.9	5.7	5.2	5.8	5.0	4.9	5.8	6.7	6.2	4.3	3.4	2.8	1.9	1.4
"Crack"	—	—	—	—	—	—	—	—	—	—	—	1.3	1.6	1.4	0.7	0.7
Other cocaine	—	—	—	—	—	—	—	—	—	—	—	4.1	3.2	1.9	1.7	1.2
Heroin	0.2	0.3	0.3	0.2	0.2	0.2	0.2	0.2	0.3	0.3	0.2	0.2	0.2	0.3	0.2	0.2
Stimulants[a]	7.7	8.8	8.7	9.9	12.1	15.8	13.7	12.4	—	—	—	—	—	—	—	—
Stimulants adjusted[b]	—	—	—	—	—	—	10.7	8.9	8.3	6.8	5.5	5.2	4.6	4.2	3.7	3.2
Sedatives[a]	4.5	5.1	4.2	4.4	4.8	4.6	3.4	3.0	2.3	2.4	2.2	1.7	1.4	1.6	1.4	1.5
Tranquilizers	4.0	4.6	3.4	3.7	3.1	2.7	2.4	2.5	2.1	2.1	2.1	2.0	1.5	1.3	1.2	1.4
Alcohol	68.3	71.2	72.1	71.8	72.0	70.7	69.7	69.4	67.2	65.9	65.3	66.4	63.9	60.0	57.1	54.0
Cigarettes	38.8	38.4	36.7	34.4	30.5	29.4	30.0	30.3	29.3	30.1	29.6	29.4	28.7	28.6	29.4	28.3
Steroids	—	—	—	—	—	—	—	—	—	—	—	—	—	0.8	1.0	0.8

Source: *Smoking, Drinking, and Illicit Drug Use among American Secondary School Students, College Students, and Young Adults, 1975–1991* Volume I. Johnston, L. D., O'Malley, P. M., & Bachman, J. G. (in press). DHHS Publication No. (ADM) 92–
[a]Only drug use which was not under a doctor's orders is included here.
[b]Based on data from a revised question that tries to exclude the inappropriate reporting of nonprescription stimulants.

Trends in Overall Drug Use

The 1960s and 1970s were a time of marked increases in the use of illicit drugs. During the social and political unrest of those years, many youth turned to marijuana, stimulants, and hallucinogens. Increases in adolescent alcohol consumption during this period also were noted (Robinson & Greene, 1988). More precise data about drug use by adolescents have been collected in recent years.

Each year since 1975, Lloyd Johnston, Patrick O'Malley, and Gerald Bachman, working at the Institute of Social Research at the University of Michigan, have carefully monitored drug use by America's high school seniors in a wide range of public and private high schools. They also sample younger adolescents' and adults' drug use. An encouraging finding from the most recent survey (conducted in 1991) of high school seniors is the continued gradual decline in the use of illicit drugs (Johnston, O'Malley, & Bachman, 1992). Among high school seniors, the percentage who used an illicit drug other than marijuana fell from 18 percent to 16 percent between 1990 and 1991, down from a peak of 34 percent in 1981. Nonetheless, the United States still has the highest rate of drug use among the world's industrialized nations. And the University of Michigan survey likely underestimates the percentage of adolescents who use drugs because it does not include high school dropouts, who have a higher rate of drug use than students who are still in high school.

An overview of trends in the 30-day prevalence among adolescents of different types of drugs since 1975 is presented in Table 15.1. Notice the decline in most drug categories. Now we examine a number of these drugs in greater detail.

The number one substance abuse problem among adolescents is alcohol abuse. These adolescents are attending an antidrug rally in Pasadena, California.

"JUST TELL ME WHERE YOU KIDS GET THE IDEA TO TAKE SO MANY DRUGS."

© 1990 by Sidney Harris.

Alcohol

To learn more about the role of alcohol in adolescents' lives, we examine how alcohol influences behavior, the use and abuse of alcohol by adolescents, and risk factors in adolescents' alcohol abuse.

Effects of Alcohol on Adolescents' Behavior

Alcohol is an extremely potent drug. It acts on the body primarily as a depressant and slows down the brain's activities. However, in low doses, alcohol can be a stimulant (Prunell & others, 1987). If used in sufficient quantities, it will damage or even kill biological tissues, including muscle and brain cells. The mental and behavioral effects of alcohol include reduced inhibition and impaired judgment. Initially, adolescents feel more talkative and more confident. However, skilled performances, such as driving, become impaired, and as more alcohol is ingested, intellectual functioning, behavioral control, and judgment become less efficient. Eventually, the drinker becomes drowsy and falls asleep. With extreme intoxication, the drinker may lapse into a coma. Each of these behavioral effects varies according to how the adolescent's body metabolizes alcohol, the individual's body weight, the amount of alcohol ingested, and whether previous drinking has led to tolerance.

Alcohol is the most widely used drug by U.S. adolescents. It has produced many enjoyable moments and many sad ones as well. Alcoholism is the third leading killer in the United States. Each year, approximately 25,000 individuals are killed and 1.5 million injured by drunk drivers. In 65 percent of the aggressive male acts against females, the offender has been under the influence of alcohol (Goodman & others, 1986). In numerous instances of drunk driving and assaults on females, the offenders have been adolescents. More than 13 million individuals are classified as alcoholics, many of whom established their drinking habits during adolescence.

Adolescent Alcohol Use and Abuse

How extensive is alcohol use by adolescents? The recent decline in the use of marijuana and other drugs does not appear to have resulted in a displacement effect in terms of an increase in alcohol use. That is, adolescents do not seem to be drinking more to offset their reduced intake of drugs. Actually, alcohol use by high school seniors has gradually declined—monthly prevalence from 72 percent in 1980 to 60 percent in 1989, for example. The prevalence of drinking five or more drinks in a row during the prior two-week interval—called binge drinking—fell from 41 percent in 1981 to 30 percent in 1991. There remains a substantial sex difference in heavy adolescent drinking—28 percent for females versus 46 percent for males in 1988, although this difference has been gradually diminishing over the last decade. However, there has been much less change in binge drinking among college students. In 1991, 43 percent of college students reported that they engaged in binge drinking, about the same as in 1980 (Johnston, O'Malley, & Bachman, 1992).

Risk Factors in Adolescents' Alcohol Abuse

Among the risk factors in adolescents' abuse of alcohol are heredity, family influences, certain aspects of peer relations, ethnicity, and personality characteristics. There is increasing evidence of a genetic predisposition to alcoholism, although it is important to remember that both genetic and environmental factors are involved (Gabrielli, 1990; Moos, Finney, & Cronkite, 1990).

Adolescent alcohol use is related to parent and peer relations. Adolescents who drink heavily often come from unhappy homes in which there is a great deal

Alcohol abuse is one of adolescents' major problems. Especially disturbing is the high percentage of adolescents who drink heavily. Excessive drinking by adolescents has led to a number of fatal automobile accidents.

of tension, have parents who give them little nurturance, are insecurely attached to their parents, and have parents who sanction alcohol use (Barnes, 1984; Dielman, Shope, & Butchart, 1990; Kwakman & others, 1988). The peer group is especially important in adolescent alcohol abuse (Dielman & others, 1992). In one recent study, exposure to peer use and misuse of alcohol, along with susceptibility to peer pressure, were strong predictors of adolescent alcohol abuse (Dielman & others, 1990). Whether adolescents have older, same-age, or younger peers as friends is also related to alcohol and drug abuse in adolescence. In one study, adolescents who took drugs were more likely to have older friends than their counterparts who did not take drugs (Blyth, Durant, & Moosbrugger, 1985).

Ethnicity also is related to alcohol abuse among adolescents. Alcohol abuse is especially problematic for Native American youth. In one national survey, Native American adolescents had a 42 percent problem-drinking rate, compared to 34 percent for Anglo American adolescents (Donovan & Jessor, 1978). There is no single, concise answer to the problem of alcohol abuse in Native American youth. It is a complex problem that involves cultural, historical, educational, and economic circumstances. Proposed solutions include education and prevention programs that involve the tribal community, programs that include both parents and youth, and economic development programs (Trimble, in press; Watts & Lewis, 1988).

In general, the rate of alcohol use by White American adolescents is higher than for Black and Hispanic American adolescents (Bettes & others, 1990). However, in one study, while fewer Hispanic American and White American adolescents used alcohol, the Hispanic American adolescents who did drink had as many alcohol-related problems as White American adolescents (Barnes & Welte, 1986). As mentioned in earlier discussions of ethnicity, variations in a particular ethnic group must be considered. In one recent study of Hispanic American adolescents in New York City, Dominican adolescents had more alcohol problems than Puerto Rican adolescents (Bettes & others, 1990). This difference may be due to the lower acculturation by the Dominican adolescents, who, for example, are less likely to speak English than the Puerto Rican adolescents.

Figure 15.2   LSD-induced hallucination. Under the influence of hallucinogenic drugs, such as LSD, several users have reported seeing images that have a tunnel effect like the one shown here.

Is there a personality profile that also might provide information about adolescents at risk for alcohol abuse? Alcohol researcher Robert Cloninger (1991) found that three traits present as early as 10 years of age are associated with alcoholism at the age of 28: (1) easily bored, needing constant activity and challenge; (2) driven to avoid negative consequences of actions; and (3) craving immediate external reward for effort. Cloninger advises parents who notice these traits in their children and young adolescents to ensure that their children have a structured, challenging environment and to provide them with considerable support.

A strong family support system is clearly an important preventive strategy in reducing alcohol abuse by adolescents. Are there others? Would raising the minimum drinking age have an effect? In one investigation, raising the minimum drinking age did lower the frequency of automobile crashes involving adolescents, but raising the drinking age alone did not reduce alcohol abuse (Wagennar, 1983). Another effort to reduce alcohol abuse involved a school-based program in which adolescents discussed alcohol-related issues with peers (Wodarski & Hoffman, 1984). At a one-year follow-up, students in the intervention schools reported less alcohol abuse and had discouraged each other's drinking more often than had students in other schools who had not been involved in the peer discussion of alcohol-related issues. Efforts to help the adolescent with a drinking problem vary enormously. Therapy may include working with other family members, peer-group discussion sessions, and specific behavioral techniques. Unfortunately, there has been little interest in identifying different types of adolescent alcohol abusers and then attempting to match treatment programs to the particular problems of the adolescent drinker. Most efforts simply assume that adolescents with drinking problems are a homogeneous group, and do not take into account the varying developmental patterns and social histories of different adolescents. Some adolescents with drinking problems may be helped more through family therapy, others through peer counseling, and yet others through intensive behavioral strategies, depending on the type of drinking problem and the social agents who have the most influence on the adolescent (Baker, 1988).

Hallucinogens

Hallucinogens *are drugs that modify an individual's perceptual experiences and produce hallucinations. Hallucinogens are called psychedelic (mind-altering) drugs.* First, we discuss LSD, which has powerful hallucinogenic properties, and then marijuana, a milder hallucinogen.

LSD

LSD, *lysergic acid diethylamide, is a hallucinogen that, even in low doses, produces striking perceptual changes.* Objects grow and change shape. Color becomes kaleidoscopic. Fabulous images unfold as users close their eyes. Sometimes, the images are pleasurable, sometimes unpleasant or frightening. In one drug trip, an LSD user might experience a cascade of beautiful colors and wonderful scenes; in another drug trip, the images might be frightening and grotesque. Figure 15.2 shows one type of perceptual experience reported by a number of LSD users. LSD's effects on the body may include dizziness, nausea, and tremors. Emotional and cognitive effects may include rapid mood swings or impaired attention and memory (Newcomb & Bentler, 1991a). LSD's popularity in the 1960s and early 1970s was followed by a reduction in use by the mid-1970s as its unpredictable effects became well publicized. However, use of LSD by high school seniors has not decreased since the early 1980s. Also, there has been an upward drift in LSD use by college students. Annual use by college students rose from 3.9 percent in

1989 to 5.1 percent in 1991 (Johnston, Bachman, & O'Malley, 1992). The concerns about "bad trips" from LSD were the concerns of an earlier generation. Today, the negative effects of LSD are little publicized, which may account for its increased use among college students.

Marijuana

Marijuana, *a milder hallucinogen than LSD, comes from the hemp plant* Cannabis sativa, *which originated in central Asia but is now grown in most parts of the world.* Marijuana is made of the hemp plant's dry leaves; its dried resin is known as hashish. The active ingredient in marijuana is THC, which stands for the chemical delta–9–tetrahydrocannabinol. This ingredient does not resemble the chemicals of other psychedelic drugs. Because marijuana is metabolized slowly, its effects may be present over the course of several days.

The physical effects of marijuana include increases in pulse rate and blood pressure, reddening of the eyes, coughing, and dryness of the mouth. Psychological effects include a mixture of excitatory, depressive, and hallucinatory characteristics, making the drug difficult to classify. The drug can produce spontaneous and unrelated ideas; perceptions of time and place can be distorted; verbal behavior may increase or cease to occur at all; and sensitivity to sounds and colors might increase. Marijuana also can impair attention and memory, which suggests that smoking marijuana is not conducive to optimal school performance. When marijuana is used daily in heavy amounts, it also can impair the human reproductive system and may be involved in some birth defects. Marijuana use by adolescents decreased in the 1980s—for example, in 1979, 37 percent smoked marijuana at least once a month, but by 1991, that figure had dropped to 13.8 percent (Johnston, O'Malley, & Bachman, 1992).

Marijuana continues to be a controversial drug in the legal realm. In 1968, under California law, possession of marijuana for personal use was a felony carrying a penalty of one to ten years of prison on first offense and up to life imprisonment on the third offense. That situation changed dramatically in 1976 when a new California law reduced the possession of an ounce or less of marijuana to a misdemeanor with a maximum fine of $100. Laws for marijuana vary from one state to another, and groups such as the National Organization for the Reform of Marijuana Laws (NORML) continue to push for more lenient legal penalties.

Stimulants

Stimulants *are drugs that increase the activity of the central nervous system.* The most widely used stimulants are caffeine, nicotine, amphetamines, and cocaine. Stimulants increase heart rate, breathing, and temperature but decrease appetite. Stimulants increase energy, decrease feelings of fatigue, and lift mood and self-confidence. After the effects wear off, though, the user often becomes tired, irritable, and depressed, and may experience headaches. Stimulants can be physically addictive.

Cigarette smoking (in which the active drug is nicotine) is one of the most serious yet preventable health problems (Miller & Slap, 1989). Smoking is likely to begin in grades seven through nine, although sizable portions of youth are still establishing regular smoking habits during high school and college. Since the national surveys by Johnston, O'Malley, and Bachman began in 1975, cigarettes have been the substance most frequently used on a daily basis by high school seniors. While adolescents' use of cigarettes dropped between 1976 and 1981 (38.8 percent to 29.4 percent in the last 30 days), it has dropped only 1.1 percent since then (to 28.3 percent in 1991) (Johnston, O'Malley, & Bachman, 1992).

"I'll tell you one thing. As soon as I'm thirteen I'm gonna stop!"
Reprinted by permission: Tribune Media Services.

This adolescent is snorting crack cocaine. Crack cocaine is far more addictive and deadly than marijuana, the drug of an earlier generation.

Almost one-third of high school seniors still do not feel that great risk is associated with smoking. Much more about smoking appears in the next chapter, where methods of preventing adolescent smoking are described.

Amphetamines *are widely prescribed stimulants, sometimes appearing in the form of diet pills. They are called pep pills and uppers.* Amphetamine use among high school seniors, college students, and adults has decreased significantly (Johnston, O'Malley, & Bachman, 1992). Use of amphetamines in the last 30 days by high school seniors declined from 10.7 percent in 1982 to 3.2 percent in 1991 (Johnston, O'Malley, & Bachman, 1992). However, use of over-the-counter stay-awake pills, which usually contain caffeine as their active ingredient, has sharply increased. Two other classes of stimulants—"look-alikes" and over-the-counter diet pills—declined in use in recent years. Still, 40 percent of females have tried diet pills by the end of their senior year in high school, and 10 percent have tried them within the last month.

Cocaine *is a stimulant that comes from the coca plant, native to Bolivia and Peru.* For many years, Bolivians and Peruvians chewed on the plant to increase their stamina. Today, cocaine is either snorted or injected in the form of crystals or powder. The effect is a rush of euphoric feelings, which eventually wear off, followed by depressive feelings, lethargy, insomnia, and irritability. As shown in Figure 15.3, cocaine can have a number of damaging effects on the body, resulting in heart attacks, strokes, or brain seizures (Newcomb & Bentler, 1991b). In the case of University of Maryland basketball star Len Bias, it meant death following cardiac arrest.

How many individuals take cocaine? According to a national survey by the National Institute of Drug Abuse (1989), the number of individuals who used cocaine in one month declined from 5,800,000 in 1985 to 2,900,000 in 1988. Unfortunately, though, the number of individuals who used cocaine once a week or more increased from 647,000 to 862,000 in 1988. Emergency-room admissions related to the potent smokable form of cocaine—crack—increased 28-fold, from 549 cases in 1985 to 15,306 in 1988.

Treatment of cocaine addiction has not been very successful. Within six months of leaving treatment, more than 50 percent of cocaine abusers return to the drug, testimony to its powerful addictive characteristics.

Figure 15.3 Cocaine's damaging effects.

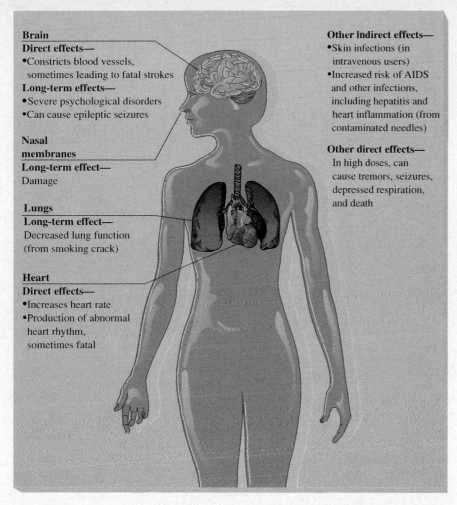

Brain
Direct effects—
•Constricts blood vessels,
sometimes leading to fatal strokes
Long-term effects—
•Severe psychological disorders
•Can cause epileptic seizures

**Nasal
membranes**
Long-term effect—
Damage

Lungs
Long-term effect—
Decreased lung function
(from smoking crack)

Heart
Direct effects—
•Increases heart rate
•Production of abnormal
heart rhythm,
sometimes fatal

Other indirect effects—
•Skin infections (in
intravenous users)
•Increased risk of AIDS
and other infections,
including hepatitis and
heart inflammation (from
contaminated needles)

Other direct effects—
In high doses, can
cause tremors, seizures,
depressed respiration,
and death

How many adolescents use cocaine? Use of cocaine by high school seniors dropped from a peak of 6.7 percent in 1985 to 1.4 percent in 1991 (use at some time in the last 30 days) (Johnston, O'Malley, & Bachman, 1992). Cocaine use by college students has declined considerably—from a peak of 7.9 percent in 1982 to 1.0 in 1991 (use in last 30 days). A growing percentage of high school students are reaching the conclusion that cocaine use entails considerable, unpredictable risk. Still, the percentage of adolescents and young adults who have used cocaine is precariously high. About 1 of every 13 high school seniors has tried cocaine at least once. The trends in perceived availability, perceived risk of trying, and prevalence of use in the past year by high school seniors are shown in Figure 15.4. As can be seen, cocaine use by high school seniors in 1991 dropped to a level similar to that in 1975.

A troublesome part of the cocaine story rests in the dangerous shift in how it is administered, due in large part to the advent of crack cocaine—an inexpensive, purified, smokable form of the drug. Crack use is especially heavy among noncollege-bound youth in urban settings. However, some good news about crack use has appeared in the last few years. In 1991, only 1.5 percent of high school seniors said that they had used crack within the past year, down from 4.1 percent in 1986 (figures for use in the last year) (Johnston, O'Malley, & Bachman, 1992).

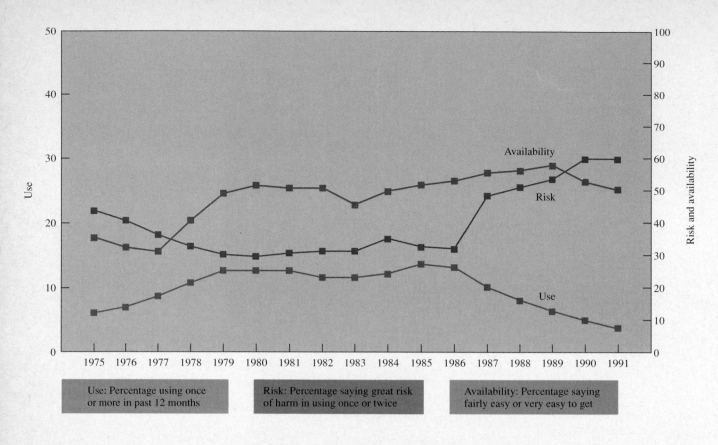

Use: Percentage using once
or more in past 12 months

Risk: Percentage saying great risk
of harm in using once or twice

Availability: Percentage saying
fairly easy or very easy to get

Figure 15.4 Cocaine: Trends in perceived
availability, perceived risk of trying, and
prevalence of use in past year for high
school seniors.

Depressants

Depressants *are drugs that slow down the central nervous system, body functions, and behavior.* Medically, depressants have been used to reduce anxiety and
to induce sleep. Among the most widely used depressants are alcohol, which we
discussed earlier, barbiturates, and tranquilizers. Though used less frequently,
the opiates are especially dangerous depressants.

Barbiturates, *such as Nembutal and Seconal, are depressant drugs that
induce sleep or reduce anxiety.* **Tranquilizers,** *such as Valium and Xanax, are
depressant drugs that reduce anxiety and induce relaxation.* They can produce
symptoms of withdrawal when an individual stops taking them. Since the initial
surveys, begun in 1975, of drug use by high school seniors, use of depressants
has decreased. For example, annual use of barbiturates in 1975 was 10.7 percent;
in 1991, it was only 3.4 percent. Over the same time period, tranquilizer use also
decreased, from 10.6 percent to 3.6 percent annual use.

Opiates, *which consist of opium and its derivatives, depress the activity of
the central nervous system. They are commonly known as narcotics.* Many drugs
have been produced from the opium poppy, among them morphine and heroin
(which is converted to morphine when it enters the brain). For several hours after
taking an opiate, an individual feels euphoria, pain relief, and an increased appetite for food and sex; however, the opiates are among the most physically addictive drugs. The body soon craves more heroin and experiences very painful
withdrawal unless more is taken. Recently, another hazardous consequence of
opiate addiction has surfaced. Most heroin addicts inject the drug intravenously.

When addicts share their needles with others, blood from the needles can be passed on. When this blood comes from an individual with AIDS, the virus can be spread from one user to another. Heroin is widely perceived by adolescents as having a greater risk of harm for the user. Its low use reflects this perception. Annual use by high school seniors was 1 percent in 1975, a percentage that dropped even further by 1991 (to 0.4 percent).

At this point, we have discussed a number of depressants, stimulants, and hallucinogens. Their medical uses, duration of effects, overdose symptoms, health risks, physical addiction risk, and psychological dependence risk are summarized in Figure 15.5.

The Roles of Development, Parents, Peers, and Schools in Adolescent Drug Abuse

Earlier, we discussed the factors that place adolescents at risk for alcohol abuse. Researchers also have examined the factors that are related to drug use in adolescence, especially the roles of development, parents, peers, and schools.

Most adolescents become drug users at some point in their development, whether limited to alcohol, caffeine, and cigarettes, or extended to marijuana, cocaine, and hard drugs. A special concern involves adolescents using drugs as a way of coping with stress, which can interfere with the development of competent coping skills and responsible decision making. Researchers have found that drug use in childhood or early adolescence has more detrimental long-term effects on the development of responsible, competent behavior than when drug use occurs in late adolescence (Newcomb & Bentler, 1989). When they use drugs to cope with stress, young adolescents often enter adult roles of marriage and work prematurely without adequate socioemotional growth and experience greater failure in adult roles.

How early are adolescents beginning drug use? National samples of 8th- and 9th-grade students were included in the Institute for Social Research survey of drug use for the first time in 1991 (Johnston, O'Malley, & Bachman, 1992). Early on in the increase in drug use in the United States (late 1960s, early 1970s), drug use was much higher among college students than among high school students, who in turn had much higher rates of drug use than middle or junior high school students. However, today the rates for college and high school students are similar, and the rates for young adolescents are not as different from older adolescents as might be anticipated (see Table 15.2).

Drinking in the past year was reported by 54 percent of the 8th graders, 72 percent of the 10th graders, and 78 percent of the 12th graders. Thirteen percent of the 8th graders said they had engaged in binge drinking. Cigarette smoking had already been tried by 44 percent of the 8th graders, with 14 percent of them (average age of 13) smoking in the past 30 days. Relatively few students had initiated cocaine use by the eighth grade (2.3 percent use ever) or the 10th grade (4.1 percent ever). An age differentiation also appeared for marijuana use, which tends to be one of the first illegal drugs tried by adolescents. Of the 8th graders, only 6 percent reported using marijuana in the prior year, compared with 17 percent of the 10th graders and 24 percent of the high school seniors. Inhalant drugs, such as glues, aerosols, and butane, are rather commonly used by young adolescents—9 percent of the 8th graders reported use of inhalant drugs in the prior year, for example, while only 7 percent of the 10th and 12th graders reported such use.

514

Figure 15.5 Psychoactive drugs: Their use, effects, and addictive characteristics.

One glass of wine equals one can of beer in alcoholic content.

Cocaine is extracted from coca plants.

Cannabis paraphernalia, drug equipment or gadgets, is usually sold in "head shops" for use in smoking marijuana.

	Medical uses	Duration of effects	Short-term effects
Depressants			
Alcohol	Pain relief	3–6 hours	Relaxation, depresses brain activity, slows behavior, reduces inhibitions
Barbiturates	Sleeping pill	1–16 hours	Relaxation, induces sleep
Tranquilizers	Anxiety reduction	4–8 hours	Relaxation, slows behavior
Opiates (narcotics)	Pain relief	3–6 hours	Euphoric feelings, drowsiness, nausea
Stimulants			
Amphetamines	Weight control,	2–4 hours	Increases alertness, excitability; decreases fatigue, irritabilty
Cocaine	Local anesthetic	1–2 hours	Increases alertness, excitability, euphoric feelings; decreases fatigue, irritabilty
Hallucinogens			
LSD	None	1–12 hours	Strong hallucinations, distorted time perception
Marijuana	Treatment of the eye disorder glaucoma	2–4 hours	Euphoric feelings, relaxation, mild hallucinations, time distortion, attention and memory impairment

Overdose	Health risks	Risk of physical addiction	Risk of psychological dependence
Disorientation, loss of consciousness, even death at high blood-alcohol levels	Accidents, brain damage, liver disease, heart disease, ulcers, birth defects	Moderate	Moderate
Breathing difficulty, coma, possible death	Accidents, coma, possible death	High	High
Breathing difficulty, coma, possible death	Accidents, coma, possible death	Low	Low–moderate
Convulsions, coma, possible death	Accidents, infectious diseases such as AIDS	Very high	Very high

Heroin, a semisynthetic narcotic, appears as a white powder in its pure form, but illicit heroin varies in color from white to dark brown because of impurities and additives.

Overdose	Health risks	Risk of physical addiction	Risk of psychological dependence
Extreme irritability, feelings of persecution, convulsions	Insomnia, hypertension, malnutrition, possible death	Moderate	High
Extreme irritability, feelings of persecution, convulsions, cardiac arrest, possible death	Insomnia, hypertension, malnutrition, possible death	Moderate–high	High

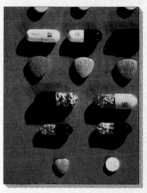

Amphetamines are stimulants used to increase alertness and energy.

Overdose	Health risks	Risk of physical addiction	Risk of psychological dependence
Severe mental disturbance, loss of contact with reality	Accidents	None	Very low
Fatigue, disoriented behavior	Accidents, respiratory disease	None	Low–moderate

Shown here is a private, illegal laboratory for manufacturing LSD.

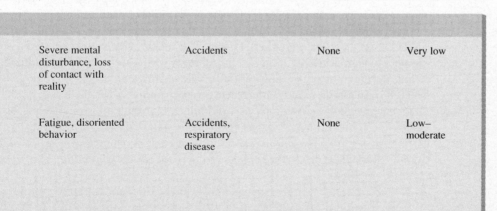

Table 15.2 Comparison of Drug Use Rates for 8th-, 10th-, and 12th-Grade Students in the United States in 1991

	Lifetime Use			Use in the Past Year			Use in the Past 30 Days		
	8th	10th	12th	8th	10th	12th	8th	10th	12th
Approximate number of students	17,500	14,800	15,000	17,500	14,800	15,000	17,500	14,800	15,000
Marijuana/hashish	10.2	23.4	36.7	6.2	16.5	23.9	3.2	8.7	13.8
Inhalants	17.6	15.7	17.6	9.0	7.1	6.6	4.4	2.7	2.4
Hallucinogens	3.2	6.1	9.6	1.9	4.0	5.8	0.8	1.6	2.2
Cocaine	2.3	4.1	7.8	1.1	2.2	3.5	0.5	0.7	1.4
"Crack"	1.3	1.7	3.1	0.7	0.9	1.5	0.3	0.3	0.7
Other cocaine	2.0	3.8	7.0	1.0	2.1	3.2	0.5	0.6	1.2
Heroin	1.2	1.2	0.9	0.7	0.5	0.4	0.3	0.2	0.2
Stimulants	10.5	13.2	15.4	6.2	8.2	8.2	2.6	3.3	3.2
Tranquilizers	3.8	5.8	7.2	1.8	3.2	3.6	0.8	1.2	1.4
Alcohol	70.1	83.8	88.0	54.0	72.3	77.7	25.1	42.8	54.0
Cigarettes	44.0	55.1	63.1	—	—	—	14.3	20.8	28.3
Steroids	1.9	1.8	2.1	1.0	1.1	1.4	0.4	0.6	0.8

Source: Johnston, L. D. (1992 January 25) *Most Forms of Drug Use Decline Among High School and College Students.* Ann Arbor, MI: University of Michigan News & Information Services.

Parents, peers, and social support play important roles in preventing adolescent drug abuse (Cohen, Brook, & Kandel, 1991; Conger, Conger, & Simons, 1992; Dishion, 1992; Kandel, 1991). A developmental model of adolescent drug abuse has been proposed by Judith Brook and her colleagues (Brook & Brook, in press; Brook & others, 1990; Brook & others, 1989). They believe that the initial step in adolescent drug abuse is laid down in the childhood years, when children fail to receive nurturance from their parents and grow up in conflict-ridden families. These children fail to internalize their parents' personality, attitudes, and behavior, and later carry this absence of parental ties into adolescence. Adolescent characteristics, such as lack of a conventional orientation and inability to control emotions, are then expressed in affiliations with peers who take drugs, which, in turn, leads to drug use. In recent studies, Brook and her colleagues have found support for their model (Brook & others, 1990).

Positive relationships with parents and others are important in reducing adolescents' drug use (Hughes, Power, & Francis, 1992). In one study, social support (which consisted of good relationships with parents, siblings, adults, and peers) during adolescence substantially reduced drug abuse (Newcomb & Bentler, 1988). In another study, adolescents were most likely to take drugs when both their parents took drugs (such as tranquilizers, amphetamines, alcohol, or nicotine) and their peers took drugs (Kandel, 1974).

In a recent review of the role that schools can play in the prevention of drug abuse, Joy Dryfoos (1990) concluded that a consensus is beginning to be reached:

1. Early intervention in schools is believed to be more effective than later intervention. This intervention works best when implemented before the onset of drug use. Middle school is often mentioned as an excellent time for the inclusion of drug abuse programs in schools.
2. Nonetheless, school-based drug abuse prevention requires a kindergarten through twelfth-grade approach, with age-appropriate components available (Hopkins & others, 1988). When school prevention programs are provided, the students need follow-up and continuous attention.

PERSPECTIVE ON ADOLESCENT DEVELOPMENT 15.1

The Life Skills Training Program

Gilbert Botvin's Life Skills Training Program was selected as one of fourteen showcase programs by the American Psychological Association's Task Force on Promotion, Prevention, and Intervention Alternatives in Psychology (Price & others, 1988). Botvin's (1986) program was the only drug prevention/intervention program selected out of a field of 300 nominees.

According to Botvin, substance use is a socially learned, purposive, and functional behavior. His approach involves attempts to reduce pressure to smoke, to develop general personal competence, and to learn specific skills to resist peer pressure. The Life Skills Training curriculum consists of five main components:

1. Students are given information about the short-term and long-term consequences of substance abuse; biofeedback demonstrates the immediate effects of cigarette smoking.
2. Decision-making skills are taught to foster students' critical thinking. Counterarguments to advertising appeals are formulated.
3. Coping skills are taught so that students deal with stress more effectively.

4. Social skills training for resisting peer pressure is implemented. The training sessions include such topics as dealing with shyness, coping with dating, and assertiveness skills.
5. Self-improvement is emphasized by helping students to develop a positive self-image using learning principles.

The Life Skills Training Program consists of 20 sessions and is designed primarily for middle school and junior high school students. It is directed by a classroom teacher who uses a Teacher's Manual and receives one day of in-service training. Older peers (eleventh- and twelfth-graders) are also used as teachers after extensive training and on-site monitoring by the Life Skills Training staff.

Botvin has conducted a number of evaluations of the Life Skills Training Program and demonstrated that the program is effective in reducing cigarette smoking, alcohol use, and marijuana use. The greatest success has occurred when the sessions are led by older peers (Botvin, 1987).

Counseling about drug abuse should be available throughout the school years.
3. Teacher training is an important element in school-based programs. The best-designed drug abuse curriculum is ineffective in the hands of an inadequately prepared teacher. School systems need to provide time and resources for in-service training and supervision.
4. School skills training, especially focused on coping skills and resistance to peer pressure, is the most promising of the new wave of school-based curricula (Tobler, 1986). However, the effectiveness of these social skills training programs over the long term and whether or not they are as effective with high-risk youth as with others are not known.
5. Peer-led programs are often more effective than teacher-led or counselor-led programs, especially when older students (senior high) are the leaders and role models for younger students (junior high and middle school).
6. Most of the school-based programs have been general programs directed at all students, rather than specific programs targeted at high-risk adolescents. More programs aimed at the high-risk group are needed.
7. The most effective school-based programs are often part of community-wide prevention efforts that involve parents, peers, role models, media, police, courts, businesses, youth-serving agencies, as well as schools (NIAAA, 1984).

Perspective on Adolescent Development 15.1 presents more information on a successful school-based program to prevent substance abuse.

Concept Table 15.1

The Nature of Abnormality: Drugs and Alcohol

Concept	Processes/Related Ideas	Characteristics/Description
The nature of abnormality	What is abnormal behavior?	Abnormal behavior is behavior that is maladaptive and harmful. Such behavior fails to promote the well-being, growth, and fulfillment of the adolescent and, ultimately, others.
	What causes abnormal behavior?	In the biological approach, mental disorders have biological causes. The forerunner of this approach was the medical model, which describes individuals as patients with mental diseases in hospitals, where they are treated by doctors. Today's biological approach emphasizes the role of brain processes and heredity in mental disorders. Proponents of the psychological and sociocultural approaches believe that the biological approach understates the importance of psychological and sociocultural factors in abnormal behavior. They also emphasize that the medical model encourages the labeling of mental disorders. In the interactionist approach, biological, psychological, and social factors often interact to produce abnormal behavior.
	Characteristics of adolescent disorders	The spectrum of adolescent disorders is wide, varying in severity, developmental level, sex, and social class. Middle-class and female adolescents are more likely to have internalizing problems; lower-class and male adolescents are more likely to have externalizing problems. Overall, adolescents from lower socioeconomic circumstances have more problems than their counterparts from higher socioeconomic circumstances.
Drugs and alcohol	Why do adolescents take drugs?	Drugs have been used since the beginning of human existence for pleasure, for utility, out of curiosity, and for social reasons. As an adolescent continues to take a drug, the drug produces tolerance, which means that a greater amount of the drug is needed to produce the same effect. Addiction is the body's physical dependence on a drug. When an addicted adolescent's body is not supplied with an adequate dose of the addictive drug, the adolescent is said to go into withdrawal, the undesirable intense pain and craving for an addictive drug. Psychological dependence is a psychological need to take a drug.
	Trends in overall drug use	The 1960s and 1970s were a time of marked increase in the use of illicit drugs. An encouraging finding is that, beginning in the mid-1980s, there was a downturn in illicit drug use by high school seniors. Nonetheless, the United States still has the highest adolescent drug-use rate of any industrialized nation.

At this point, we have discussed a number of ideas about the nature of abnormality and about drugs and alcohol. A summary of these ideas is presented in Concept Table 15.1. Next, we consider another pervasive disturbance in adolescence—juvenile delinquency.

Juvenile Delinquency

Thirteen-year-old Arnie in the "Images of Adolescence" section that opened this chapter has a history of thefts and physical assaults. Arnie is a juvenile delinquent. What is a juvenile delinquent? What are the antecedents of delinquency? What types of interventions have been used to prevent or reduce delinquency? We consider each of these questions in turn.

Concept Table 15.1

The Nature of Abnormality: Drugs and Alcohol

Concept	Processes/Related Ideas	Characteristics/Description
	Alcohol	Alcohol is primarily a depressant, although in low dosages it can act as a stimulant. It has produced many enjoyable as well as many sad moments for adolescents. Many automobile deaths and aggressive attacks on females are associated with alcohol use. Alcohol is the most widely used drug by adolescents. Alcohol abuse is a major adolescent problem. Alcohol use by U.S. high school seniors has slightly declined in recent years, but heavy drinking is still common. Among the risk factors in adolescent alcohol abuse are heredity, family influences, certain aspects of peer relations, ethnicity, and personality characteristics.
	Hallucinogens	Hallucinogens are drugs that modify an individual's perceptual experiences and produce hallucinations. Hallucinogens include LSD (a powerful hallucinogen) and marijuana (a milder hallucinogen). Adolescents decreased their use of marijuana in the 1980s, but LSD use has not decreased in recent years.
	Stimulants	Stimulants are drugs that increase the activity of the central nervous system. The most widely used stimulants are caffeine, nicotine, amphetamines, and cocaine. Nicotine in cigarettes is the substance most frequently used by adolescents on a daily basis. Smoking habits are often formed during adolescence, and while cigarette smoking declined in the 1980s, it remains a dangerous habit. There has been a decrease in amphetamine use, although adolescents have increased their use of over-the-counter stay-awake pills. Cocaine use by adolescents dropped in the late 1980s, but a dangerous form of the drug—crack cocaine—is increasingly used.
	Depressants	Depressants are drugs that slow down the central nervous system, body functions, and behavior. Among the most widely used depressants are alcohol, barbiturates, and tranquilizers. An especially dangerous depressant is heroin, an opiate. The use of depressants by adolescents declined in the 1980s.
	The roles of development, parents, peers, and schools in adolescent drug abuse	Drug use in childhood or early adolescence has more detrimental long-term effects than when its onset occurs in late adolescence. Parents, peers, and social support play important roles in preventing adolescent drug abuse. Considerable interest has developed in the role of schools in preventing adolescent drug abuse. Early intervention, a kindergarten through twelfth-grade approach, teacher training, social skills training, peer-led programs, programs aimed at high-risk groups, and community-wide prevention efforts are important components of successful school-based programs.

What Is Juvenile Delinquency?

The term **juvenile delinquency** *refers to a broad range of behaviors, from socially unacceptable behavior (such as acting out in school) to status offenses (such as running away) to criminal acts (such as burglary)* (Quay, 1987). For legal purposes, a distinction is made between index offenses and status offenses. **Index offenses** *are criminal acts, whether they are committed by juveniles or adults. They include such acts as robbery, aggravated assault, rape, and homicide.* **Status offenses,** *such as running away, truancy, drinking under age, sexual promiscuity, and uncontrollability, are less serious acts. They are performed by youth under a specified age, which classifies them as juvenile offenses* (Dryfoos, 1990). States often differ in the age used to classify an individual as a juvenile or an adult. Approximately three-fourths of the states have established age 18 as a

Table 15.3 Percentage of 10- to 17-Year-Olds Arrested
by Type of Offense in 1986

	Percentage of 10- to 14-Year-Olds	Percentage of 15- to 17-Year-Olds
Total arrests	2.9%	10.9%
Serious crimes	1.3%	3.6%
Larceny/theft	0.8	2.0
Burglary	0.3	0.8
Motor vehicle theft	—	0.4
Aggravated assault	—	0.3
Robbery	—	0.2
Other arrests	1.6%	7.3%
Liquor law violations	—	1.1
Vandalism	0.2	0.5
Disorderly conduct	0.1	0.5
Other assaults	0.2	0.5
Drug abuse	—	0.5
Runaways	0.3	0.7

From *Adolescents at Risk: Prevalence and Prevention* by Joy G. Dryfoos. Copyright © 1990 by Joy G. Dryfoos.
Used with permission of Oxford University Press, Inc.

maximum for defining juveniles. Two states use age 19 as the cutoff, seven states
use age 17, and four states use age 16. Thus, running away from home at age 17
may be an offense in some states but not others.

In addition to the legal classifications of index offenses and status offenses,
many of the behaviors considered delinquent are included in widely used classifications of abnormal behavior. **Conduct disorder** *is the psychiatric diagnostic
category used when multiple behaviors occur over a six-month period. These
behaviors include truancy, running away, fire setting, cruelty to animals, breaking
and entering, excessive fighting, and others. When three or more of these behaviors co-occur before the age of 15 and the child or adolescent is considered
unmanageable or out of control, the clinical diagnosis is conduct disorder.*

In sum, most children or adolescents at one time or another act out or do
things that are destructive or troublesome for themselves or others. If these behaviors occur often in childhood or early adolescence, psychiatrists diagnose them
as conduct disorders (Myers & Burket, 1992). If these behaviors result in illegal
acts by juveniles, society labels them as *delinquents.*

How many juvenile delinquents or children and adolescents with conduct
disorder are there? Figures are somewhat sketchy and depend on the criteria
used. The most concrete figures are legally defined, but many adolescents who
engage in delinquent behavior are never arrested. Table 15.3 was compiled from
the Unified Crime Reports that gather data on all arrests in the United States
every year according to type of crime and age (Flanagan & Jamieson, 1987). As
indicated in the table, about 3 percent of 10- to 14-year-olds and 11 percent of
15- to 17-year-olds were arrested in 1986 for an offense. Based on self-reported
patterns of behavior, a large number of adolescents—as many as 20 percent—
are at risk for committing offenses that could result in arrests. Overall, the prevalence of delinquency has probably not changed much in the last decade (Dryfoos, 1990).

Antecedent	Association with delinquency	Description
Identity	Negative identity	Erikson believes delinquency occurs because the adolescent fails to resolve a role identity.
Self-control	Low degree	Some children and adolescents fail to acquire the essential controls that others have acquired during the process of growing up.
Age	Early initiation	Early appearance of antisocial behavior is associated with serious offenses later in adolescence. However, not every child who acts out becomes a delinquent.
Sex	Males	Boys engage in more antisocial behavior than girls do, although girls are more likely to run away. Boys engage in more violent acts.
Expectations for education and school grades	Low expectations and low grades	Adolescents who become delinquents often have low educational expectations and low grades. Their verbal abilities are often weak.
Parental influences	Monitoring (low), support (low), discipline (ineffective)	Delinquents often come from families in which parents rarely monitor their adolescents, provide them with little support, and ineffectively discipline them.
Peer influences	Heavy influence, low resistance	Having delinquent peers greatly increases the risk of becoming delinquent.
Socioeconomic status	Low	Serious offenses are committed more frequently by lower-class males.
Neighborhood quality	Urban, high crime, high mobility	Communities often breed crime. Living in a high-crime area, which also is characterized by poverty and dense living conditions, increases the probability that a child will become a delinquent. These communities often have grossly inadequate schools.

Figure 15.6 The antecedents of juvenile delinquency.

Adapted from Adolescents at Risk: Prevalence and Prevention *by Joy G. Dryfoos. Copyright 1990 by Joy G. Dryfoos. Used with permission of Oxford University Press, Inc.*

What Are the Antecedents of Delinquency?

Predictors of delinquency include: identity (negative identity), self-control (low degree), age (early initiation), sex (males), expectations for education (low expectations, little commitment), school grades (low achievement in early grades), peer influence (heavy influence, low resistance), socioeconomic status (low), parental role (lack of monitoring, low support, and ineffective discipline), and neighborhood quality (urban, high crime, high mobility). A summary of these antecedents of delinquency is presented in Figure 15.6. We now examine several of these antecedents in greater detail: identity, self-control, family processes, and social class/community.

Identity

According to Erik Erikson's (1968) theory of development, adolescence is the stage when the crisis of identity versus identity diffusion should be resolved. Not surprisingly, Erikson's ideas about delinquency are linked to adolescent's ability to positively resolve this crisis. Erikson believes that the biological changes of puberty initiate concomitant changes in the social expectations placed on adolescents by family, peers, and schools. These biological and social changes allow for two kinds of integration to occur in adolescents' personality: (1) the establishment of a sense of consistency in life and (2) the resolution of role identity, a sort of joining of adolescents' motivation, values, abilities, and styles with the role demands placed on adolescents.

Erikson believes that delinquency is characterized more by a failure of adolescents to achieve the second kind of integration, involving the role aspects of identity. He comments that adolescents whose infant, childhood, or adolescent experiences have somehow restricted them from acceptable social roles or made them feel that they cannot measure up to the demands placed on them may choose a negative course of identity development. Some of these adolescents may take on the role of the delinquent, enmeshing themselves in the most negative currents of the youth culture available to them. Thus, for Erikson, delinquency is an attempt to establish an identity, although it is a negative one.

Self-Control

Juvenile delinquency also can be described as the failure to develop sufficient behavioral self-control. Some children fail to develop the essential controls that others have acquired during the process of growing up. Most youths have learned the difference between acceptable and unacceptable behavior, but juvenile delinquents have not. They may fail to distinguish between acceptable and unacceptable behavior, or they may have learned this distinction but failed to develop adequate control in using the distinction to guide their behavior. An understanding of delinquency thus requires study of different aspects of the development of self-control—for example, delay of gratification and self-imposed standards of conduct. Failure to delay gratification is related to cheating and to a general lack of social responsibility often revealed in delinquent behavior (Mischel & Gilligan, 1964).

Delinquents also may have developed inadequate standards of conduct. Adolescents about to commit an antisocial act must invoke self-critical thoughts to inhibit the tendency to commit the illegal action. These self-critical standards are strongly influenced by adolescents' models. Thus, adolescents whose parents, teachers, and peers exhibit self-critical standards usually develop the self-control needed to refrain from an illegal or antisocial act. Other adolescents, however, may be exposed to models who praise antisocial acts. For example, adolescents whose peer models praise or engage in antisocial deeds may follow their example, especially if family models of high conduct are lacking.

The expected consequences of negative actions also influence the adolescents' decision to engage in or refrain from delinquent behavior. When youth expect some sort of reward for delinquent behavior, they are more likely to perform the antisocial act than if they expect punishment. The expected rewards can take many different forms—the acquisition of stolen goods, for example, or high status in the gang or in neighborhood peer groups.

Whether or not adolescents engage in juvenile delinquency may also be affected by the competence they have achieved in different aspects of life. Consider youth who do well in academic subjects at school, who actively participate in socially desirable clubs, or who develop athletic skills. These youth are likely to develop a positive view of themselves and receive reinforcement from others for prosocial behavior. Most delinquents, however, have achieved few ego-enhancing competencies. Antisocial behavior is one way they can demonstrate self-competence and receive reinforcement from the delinquent subculture.

Family Processes

While there has been a long history of interest in defining the family factors that contribute to delinquency (Glueck & Glueck, 1950; McCord, McCord, & Gudeman, 1960; Rutter, 1971), the most recent focus has been on the nature of family support and family management practices. Disruptions or omissions in the parents' applications of family support and management practices are consistently linked with antisocial behavior by children and adolescents (Novy & others, 1992; Rosenbaum, 1989). These family support and management practices include monitoring adolescents' whereabouts, using effective discipline for antisocial behavior, calling on effective problem-solving skills, and supporting the development of prosocial skills (Offord & Boyle, 1988).

The parents of delinquents are less skilled in discouraging antisocial behavior than the parents of nondelinquents. Parental monitoring of adolescents is especially important in whether adolescents become delinquents. In one investigation, parental monitoring of adolescents' whereabouts was the most important family factor in predicting delinquency (Patterson & Stouthamer-Loeber, 1984). "It's 10 P.M., do you know where your children are?" seems to be an important question for parents to answer affirmatively. Family discord and inconsistent and inappropriate discipline also are associated with delinquency.

An important question is whether family experiences cause delinquency, are the consequences of delinquency, or are merely associated or correlated with delinquency (Rutter & Garmezy, 1983). The associations may simply reflect some third factor, such as genetic influences; may be the result of the disturbing effect of the child's behavior on the family; or may indicate that family stress may produce delinquency through some environmental effect. In a review of research on the family-delinquency link, Michael Rutter and Norman Garmezy (1983) concluded that family influences do have some kind of environmental influence on delinquency. The research by Gerald Patterson and his colleagues (Patterson, DeBaryshe, & Ramsey, 1989) documents that inadequate parental supervision, involving poor monitoring of adolescents, and inconsistent, inappropriate discipline are key family factors in determining delinquency.

Social Class/Community

Although juvenile delinquency is less exclusively a lower-class problem than it was in the past, some characteristics of the lower-class culture are likely to promote delinquency (Jenkins & Bell, 1992; Kennedy, 1991; Mednick, Baker, & Carothers, 1990). The norms of many lower-class peer groups and gangs are antisocial, or counterproductive to the goals and norms of society at large (McCord, 1990). Getting into and staying out of trouble in some instances becomes a prominent feature of the lives of some adolescents from lower-class backgrounds (Miller, 1958). Status in the peer group may be gauged by how often the adolescent can engage in antisocial conduct, yet manage to stay out of jail. Since lower-class adolescents have less opportunity to develop skills that are socially desirable, they may sense that they can gain attention and status by performing antisocial actions. Being "tough" and "masculine" are high-status traits for lower-class boys, and these traits are often gauged by adolescents' success in performing delinquent acts and getting away with them.

The nature of a community may contribute to delinquency (Chesney-Lind, 1989). A community with a high crime rate allows adolescents to observe many models who engage in criminal activities and may be rewarded for their criminal accomplishments. Such communities often are characterized by poverty, unemployment, and feelings of alienation from the middle class. The quality of schools,

A recent, special concern in low-income areas is escalating gang violence.

funding for education, and organized neighborhood activities are other community factors that may be related to delinquency. Are there caring adults in the schools and neighborhood who can convince adolescents with delinquent tendencies that education is the best route to success? When family support becomes inadequate, then such community supports take on added importance in preventing delinquency.

Even if adolescents grow up in high-crime communities, their peer relations may influence whether or not they become delinquents. In one investigation of 500 delinquents and 500 nondelinquents in Boston, Massachusetts, a much higher percentage of the delinquents had regular associations with delinquent peers (Glueck & Glueck, 1950).

A recent, special concern in low-income areas is escalating gang violence, which is being waged on a level more lethal than ever before. Knives and clubs have been replaced by grenades and automatic weapons, frequently purchased with money made from selling drugs. The lure of gang membership is powerful, especially for children and adolescents who are disconnected from family, school, work, and the community. Children as young as 9 to 10 years of age cling to the fringes of neighborhood gangs, eager to prove themselves worthy of membership by the age of 12. Once children are members of a gang, it is difficult to get them to leave. Recommendations for preventing gang violence include identifying disconnected children in elementary schools and initiating counseling with the children and their families (Calhoun, 1988; Huff, 1990). More about life in gangs and an effort in Detroit, Michigan, that has made a difference in reducing gang participation appears in Sociocultural Worlds of Adolescence 15.1.

Prevention and Intervention

Brief descriptions of the varied attempts to reduce delinquency would fill a large book. These attempts include forms of individual and group psychotherapy, family therapy, behavior modification, recreation, vocational training, alternative schools, survival camping and wilderness canoeing, incarceration and probation, "Big Brothers" and "Big Sisters," community organizations, and Bible reading (Gold & Petronio, 1980). However, surprisingly little is known about what actually does help to reduce delinquency, and in many instances, prevention and intervention have not been successful (Leitenberg, 1986; Lundman, 1984; Rabkin, 1987).

Frog and Dolores

He goes by the name of Frog. He is the cocky prince of the barrio in East Los Angeles. He has street-smarts. Frog happily smiles as he talks about raking in $200 a week selling crack cocaine. He proudly details his newly acquired membership in a violent street gang, the Crips. Frog brags about using his drug money to rent a convertible on weekends, even though at less than 5 feet in height, he can barely see over the dashboard. Frog is 13 years old.

With the advent of crack, juvenile arrests in New York City tripled from 1983 to 1987 and almost quadrupled in the same time frame in Washington, D.C. Adults who founded the crack trade recognized early on that young adolescents do not run the risk of mandatory jail sentences that courts hand out to adults. Being a lookout is the entry-level position for 9- and 10-year-olds. They can make as much as $100 a day warning dealers that police are in the area. The next step up the ladder is as a runner, a job that can pay as much as $300 a day. A runner transports drugs to the dealers on the street from makeshift factories where cocaine powder is cooked into rock-hard crack. And, at the next level, older adolescents can reach the status of dealer. In a hot market like New York City, they can make over $1,000 a day.

The escalating drug-related gang violence is difficult to contain or reduce. Police crackdowns across the country seem to have had a minimal impact. In a recent weekend-long raid of drug-dealing gangs in Los Angeles, police arrested 1,453 individuals, including 315 adolescents. Half had to be released for lack of evidence. The Los Angeles County juvenile facilities are designed to house 1,317. Today more than 2,000 adolescents are overflowing their facilities.

Counselors, school officials, and community workers report that turning around the lives of children and adolescents involved in drug-related gang violence is extremely difficult. When impoverished children can make $100 a day, it is hard to wean them away from gangs. Federal budgets for training and employment programs, which provide crucial assistance to disadvantaged youth, have been reduced dramatically.

However, in Detroit, Michigan, Dolores Bennett has made a difference. For 25 years, she has worked long hours trying to find things to keep children from low-income families busy. Her activities have led to the creation of neighborhood sports teams, regular fairs and picnics, and an informal job-referral service for the children and youth in the neighborhood. She also holds many casual get-togethers for the youth in her small, tidy, yellow frame house. The youth talk openly and freely about their problems and their hopes, knowing that Dolores will listen. Dolores says that she has found being a volunteer to be priceless. On the mantel in her living room are hundreds of pictures of children and adolescents with whom she has worked. She points out that most of them did not have someone in their homes who would listen to them and give them love. America needs more Dolores Bennetts.

Dolores Bennett, volunteer in a low-income area of Detroit, Michigan, talks with and listens to two of her "children."

Successful programs that prevent or reduce delinquency do not focus on delinquency alone, but rather include other components, such as education or life skills training. Successful programs also have multiple components (but no one component is a "magic bullet"), begin early in the child's development, often involve schools, focus on institutions, also focus on giving individual attention to delinquents, and include maintenance.

While few successful models of delinquency prevention and intervention have been identified, many experts on delinquency agree that the following points deserve closer examination as prevention and intervention possibilities (Dryfoos, 1990):

1. Programs should be broader than just focusing on delinquency (O'Donnell, Manos, & Chesney-Lind, 1987). For example, it is virtually impossible to improve delinquency prevention without considering the quality of education available to high-risk youth.
2. Programs should have multiple components because no one component has been found to be the "magic bullet" that decreases delinquency.
3. Programs should begin early in the child's development to prevent learning and conduct problems (Berrueta-Clement & others, 1986).
4. Schools play an important role. Schools with strong governance, fair discipline policies, student participation in decision making, and high investment in school outcomes by both students and staff have a better chance of curbing delinquency (Hawkins & Lam, 1986; Hawkins & Lishner, 1987).
5. Efforts should often be directed at institutional rather than individual change. Especially important is upgrading the quality of education for disadvantaged children.
6. While point 5 is accurate, researchers have found that intensive individual attention and personalized planning also are important factors in working with children at high risk for becoming delinquent.
7. Program benefits often "wash out" after the program stops. Thus, maintenance programs and continued effort are usually necessary.

In her recent review of delinquency prevention, Joy Dryfoos (1990) also outlined what has *not* worked in preventing delinquency. Ineffective attempts include preventive casework, group counseling, pharmacological interventions (except for extremely violent behavior), work experience, vocational education, "scaring straight" efforts, and the juvenile justice system. Current school practices that are ineffective in reducing delinquency include suspension, detention, expulsion, security guards, and corporal punishment.

So far, we have discussed a number of ideas about juvenile delinquency as well as substance abuse by adolescents. Next, we consider two additional problems in adolescence—depression and suicide.

Depression and Suicide

As mentioned earlier in the chapter, one of the most frequent characteristics of adolescents referred for psychological treatment is sadness or depression, especially among girls. In this section, we discuss the nature of adolescent depression and adolescent suicide.

Depression

Major depression *in adults is a mood disorder in which an individual feels deeply unhappy, demoralized, self-derogatory, and bored. An individual with major depression does not feel well, loses stamina easily, has a poor appetite, and is listless and unmotivated.* In adolescence, the features of depression are mixed with a broader array of behaviors than in adult depression. For example, during adolescence, aggression, antisocial behavior, school failure, anxiety, and poor peer relations are often associated with depression, which makes its diagnosis more difficult (Kendall, Cantwell, & Kazdin, 1989; Reinherz & others, 1990; Strober, McCracken, & Hanna, 1991; Yaylayan & others, 1992).

How frequently does depression occur in adolescence? In one recent study of 1,710 urban and rural high school students aged 14–18, 20 percent met the adult criteria for having had major depression at some point in their lifetime (Lewinsohn & others, 1991). At the time they were interviewed, 2.9 percent of the adolescents met the criteria for major depression. The 20 percent lifetime prevalence rate of depression in adolescents is somewhat higher than other researchers have reported; the 2.9 percent current rate of depression for adolescents is in line with what other researchers have found. In the study by Peter Lewinsohn and his colleagues (1991), adolescent girls showed much higher rates of depression than adolescent males, which is supported by other researchers (Petersen & Sarigiani, 1989; Weissman & Klerman, 1991). Most experts on depression believe that depression becomes more common in adolescence than in childhood.

Why does depression occur in adolescence? As with other disorders, biogenetic and socioenvironmental causes have been proposed. Some psychologists believe that understanding adolescent depression requires information about experiences in both adolescence and childhood. For example, John Bowlby (1980, 1989) believes that insecure mother-infant attachment, a lack of love and affection in child rearing, or the actual loss of a parent in childhood creates a negative cognitive set. This schema built up during early experiences can cause children to interpret later losses as yet other failures to produce enduring close, positive relationships. From Bowlby's developmental construction view, early experiences, especially those involving loss, produce a cognitive schema that is carried forward to influence the way later experiences are interpreted. When these new experiences involve further loss, the loss serves as the immediate precipitant of depression.

In a longitudinal study of nonclinical children, the relationship between parent-child interaction during preschool and depression symptoms of the child at age 18 was examined (Gjerde and Block, 1990). The findings were significant only for the mother-daughter dyad. When mothers combined authoritarian control with nurturance in early childhood, at age 18, their daughters were more

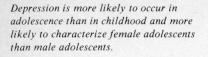

Depression is more likely to occur in adolescence than in childhood and more likely to characterize female adolescents than male adolescents.

likely to show depression. In this "double-bind" circumstance, the daughters were prevented from moving beyond the mother-daughter dyad toward an independent and autonomous engagement with the wider world. While girls often find it more difficult to break ties with their mothers than boys, a maternal orientation of combined authoritarian control and nurturance is likely to interfere even further with transformation of the mother-daughter relationship from one of high dependency on the mother to one that permits the daughter's individuation and psychological separation.

Another cognitive view stresses that individuals become depressed because, early in their development, they acquire a cognitive schema characterized by self-devaluation and lack of confidence about the future (Beck, 1976; Clark & Beck, 1989; Kovacs, 1989). These habitual negative thoughts magnify and expand depressed adolescents' negative experiences. Depressed adolescents, then, may blame themselves far more than is warranted. In one recent study of female college students, depressed females consistently evaluated their performance more negatively than was warranted (Clark & Nelson, 1990).

Another factor thought to be important in understanding adolescent depression is **learned helplessness,** *which occurs when individuals are exposed to aversive stimulation, such as prolonged stress or pain, over which they have no control. This experience fosters a sense of hopelessness and a general belief that nothing can be done to improve the situation* (Seligman, 1975). In other words, depressed adolescents may be apathetic because they cannot reinstate the rewards they previously experienced. For example, an adolescent girl may not be able to make her boyfriend come back to her. Martin Seligman (1989), who originally proposed the concept of learned helplessness, has speculated that depression is so common among adolescents and young adults today because of widespread hopelessness, brought about by an increased emphasis on self, independence, and individualism and a decreased emphasis on connectedness to others, family, and religion.

Follow-up studies of depressed adolescents indicate that the symptoms of depression experienced in adolescence predict similar problems in adulthood (Garber & others, 1988; Kandel & Davies, 1986). This means that adolescent depression needs to be taken seriously. It does not just automatically go away. Rather, adolescents who are diagnosed as having depression are more likely to

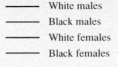

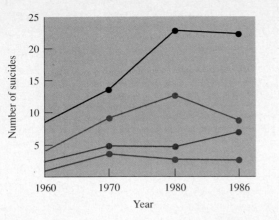

White males
Black males
White females
Black females

1960   1970   1980   1986
Year

Figure 15.7 Suicide rates for 15- to 24-year-old individuals in the United States (rates per 100,000 individuals).

experience the problem on a continuing basis in adulthood than adolescents not diagnosed as having depression. And, as we see next, some of the same factors involved in adolescent depression are likely to be involved in adolescent suicide attempts.

Suicide

Suicide occurs rarely in childhood and early adolescence, but beginning at about age 15, the suicide rate increases dramatically. Between the ages of 15 and 19, White American males have a rate of 18 suicides per 100,000; between the ages of 20 and 24, they have a rate of 28 suicides per 100,000. Suicide rates for Black American adolescents and female adolescents are lower, with the rate for Black American female adolescents the lowest. Figure 15.7 shows the suicide rates of the 15 to 24 age groups. Suicide accounts for about 12 percent of the mortality in the adolescent and young adult age group (Brent, 1989). The suicide rate has tripled since the 1950s (Lann & Moscicki, 1989).

While males are about three times more likely to commit suicide than females, females are more likely to attempt suicide (Maltsberger, 1988). The explanation for this is that males use more active methods when attempting suicide, such as shooting, while females use more passive methods, such as sleeping pills.

Estimates indicate that six to ten suicide attempts occur for every suicide in the general population. For adolescents, the figure is as high as 50 attempts for every life taken. As many as two of every three college students have thought about suicide on at least one occasion. In one recent study, such thoughts began to surface in a serious vein at about nine years of age and increased thereafter (Bolger & others, 1989).

Why do adolescents attempt suicide? While there is no simple answer to this important question, it is helpful to think about suicide in terms of immediate (proximal) and earlier (distal) experiences. Immediate, highly stressful circumstances, such as the loss of a boyfriend or girlfriend, failing in class at school, or an unwanted pregnancy, can trigger a suicide attempt (Blumenthal & Kupfer, 1988; Neiger & Hopkins, 1988; Lester, 1989). In addition, drugs have been more involved in suicide attempts in recent years than in the past (Rich, Young, & Fowler, 1986). Earlier experiences are also often involved in suicide attempts, as reflected in a long history of family instability and unhappiness (Cole, 1991; Hodgman, 1992; Rubenstein & others, 1989; Shapiro & Freedman, 1989; Stork, 1989; Strang & Orlofsky, 1990; Tishler, 1992) or a lack of supportive friendships (Rubenstein & others, 1989). In an investigation of suicide in gifted women, previous suicide attempts, anxiety, conspicuous instability in work and relationships,

Table 15.4   The Early Warning Signs of Suicide among Adolescents

1. The adolescent makes suicide threats, such as: "I wish I was dead"; "My family would be better off without me"; "I don't have anything to live for."

2. A prior suicide attempt, no matter how minor. Four out of five people who commit suicide have made at least one previous attempt.

3. Preoccupation with death in music, art, and personal writing.

4. Loss of a family member, pet, or boyfriend/girlfriend through death, abandonment, breakup.

5. Family disruptions, such as unemployment, serious illness, relocation, divorce.

6. Disturbances in sleeping and eating habits, and in personal hygiene.

7. Declining grades and lack of interest in school or activities that previously were important.

8. Dramatic changes in behavior patterns, such as a very gregarious adolescent becoming very shy and withdrawn.

9. Pervasive sense of gloom, helplessness, and hopelessness.

10. Withdrawal from family members and friends; feelings of alienation from significant others.

11. Giving away prized possessions and otherwise getting affairs in order.

12. Series of accidents or impulsive, risk-taking behaviors; drug or alcohol abuse; disregard for personal safety; taking dangerous dares. (With regard to drug or alcohol abuse, there has been a dramatic increase in recent years in the number of adolescent suicides committed while the adolescent is under the influence of alcohol or drugs.)

Reprinted from *Living with 10- to 15-Year-Olds: A Parent Education Curriculum.* Copyright by the Center for Early Adolescence, Carrboro, NC, 1982, rev. ed. 1987. Used with permission.

depression, or alcoholism were present in the women's lives (Tomlinson-Keasey, Warren, & Elliott, 1986). These factors are similar to those found to predict suicide in gifted men (Shneidman, 1971).

Genetic factors also may be involved in suicide. The closer an individual's genetic relation to someone who has committed suicide, the more likely that the individual will also commit suicide (Wender & others, 1986).

Table 15.4 provides valuable information about the early warning signs of suicide among adolescents. In addition, Table 15.5 explains what to do and what not to do when you suspect an adolescent is contemplating suicide. Perspective on Adolescent Development 15.2 discusses whether school programs prevent or promote suicide.

The Interrelation of Problems and Disorders in Adolescence and Programs for Reducing Problems

This and other chapters have described the major problems adolescents are at risk for developing. In many instances, adolescents have more than one problem. In this section, we examine the interrelation of problems and disturbances in adolescence and then explore some important ideas for reducing adolescent problems.

The Interrelation of Problems and Disorders in Adolescence

Very-high-risk youth *have multiple problem behaviors and make up as many as 10 percent of the adolescent population (Dryfoos, 1990). This group includes adolescents who have been arrested or have committed serious offenses, have*

PERSPECTIVE ON ADOLESCENT DEVELOPMENT 15.2

Do School Programs Prevent or Promote Suicide?

If adolescents are exposed to the topic of suicide, might they possibly be more likely to consider it for themselves than if the subject had been ignored? Many advocates of suicide prevention programs believe that the instruction is not harmful, but some researchers feel that the instruction may sometimes increase suicide attempts. In a national survey, talking about suicide in class was related to an increase in ninth- and tenth-graders' suicide considerations (Shaffer & others, 1988). A small number of disturbed adolescents may interpret the message in suicide prevention instruction the wrong way. Many suicide prevention advocates, though, believe that discussing suicide does not increase adolescents' vulnerability to suicide (Berman, 1991).

Suicide prevention programs vary enormously in their content and their frequency of instruction. Some consist of just one lecture, others consist of a series of lectures, yet others may set up a suicide hot line and a crisis center, while others may blanket the halls of schools with suicide prevention posters. However, no data are yet available as to whether the programs are effective or what portions of the programs may be effective.

The overwhelming majority of adolescents are not motivated to attempt suicide. Therefore, some experts on adolescent suicide believe that it does not make sense to hold suicide prevention classes for all students. A special concern is identifying which adolescents are in need of suicide prevention instruction and linking them to available resources. An increasing number of school systems follow this strategy. For example, a student at risk for committing suicide might be visibly depressed and have written several suicide notes in the past. This type of student would immediately be referred to professionals, who would then work with the high-risk adolescent and his or her parents.

Table 15.5 What to Do and What Not to Do When You Suspect an Adolescent Is Likely to Attempt Suicide

What to Do

1. Ask direct, straightforward questions in a calm manner: "Are you thinking about hurting yourself?"
2. Assess the seriousness of the suicidal intent by asking questions about feelings, important relationships, who else the person has talked with, and the amount of thought given to the means to be used. If a gun, pills, rope, or other means have been obtained and a precise plan developed, the situation is clearly dangerous. Stay with the person until some type of help arrives.
3. Be a good listener and be very supportive without being falsely reassuring.
4. Try to persuade the adolescent to obtain professional help and assist him or her in getting this help.

What Not to Do

1. Do not ignore the warning signs.
2. Do not refuse to talk about suicide if an adolescent approaches you about the topic.
3. Do not react with horror, disapproval, or repulsion.
4. Do not give false reassurances by saying things like, "Everything is going to be okay." Also do not give out simple answers or platitudes like, "You have everything to be thankful for."
5. Do not abandon the adolescent after the crisis has gone by or after professional help has commenced.

Reprinted from *Living with 10- to 15-Year-Olds: A Parent Education Curriculum.* Copyright by the Center for Early Adolescence, Carrboro, NC, 1982, rev. ed. 1987. Used with permission.

dropped out of school or are behind their grade level, are users of heavy drugs, drink heavily, regularly use cigarettes and marijuana, and are sexually active but do not use contraception. Many, but not all, of these highest-risk youth "do it all."

High-risk youth *include as many as another 15 percent of adolescents who participate in many of the same behaviors as very-high-risk youth but with slightly lower frequency and less deleterious consequences. They commit less serious delinquent offenses; are heavy users of alcohol, cigarettes, and marijuana; often engage in unprotected intercourse; and are frequently behind in school. This group of high-risk youth are often engaged in two to three problem behaviors.*

Researchers are increasingly finding that problem behaviors in adolescence are interrelated (Barnes, Welte, & Dintcheff, 1992). An overview of the interrelation of adolescent problem behaviors suggests that (Dryfoos, 1990):

1. Delinquency is related to early sexual activity, early pregnancy, substance abuse, and dropping out of school.
2. Early initiation of smoking and drinking is associated with later, heavier use of cigarettes and alcohol, as well as the use of marijuana and other illicit drugs.
3. Heavy substance abuse is related to early sexual activity, lower grades, dropping out, and delinquency.
4. Early initiation of sexual activity is associated with the use of cigarettes, alcohol, marijuana, and other illicit drugs; lower grades; dropping out of school; and delinquency.
5. Early childbearing is related to early sexual activity, heavy drug use, low academic achievement, dropping out of school, and delinquency.
6. School failure leads to dropping out of school. Lower grades are associated with substance abuse and early childbearing. Truancy and misbehavior in school are associated with substance abuse, dropping out of school, and delinquency.

Common Components of Programs That Successfully Prevent or Reduce Adolescent Problems

Joy Dryfoos (1990) recently analyzed the programs that have been successful in preventing or reducing adolescent problems and outlined 11 common program components. Of these 11 components, the first two—the importance of providing individual attention to high-risk adolescents and the need to develop broad, community-wide interventions—had the widest applications. This finding supports the idea that successful programs meet the needs of high-risk adolescents at the personal level within the context of broader changes in the environment. Dryfoos's 11 program components are:

1. *Intensive Individualized Attention.* In a number of different successful programs, a high-risk adolescent is attached to a responsible adult who gives the adolescent attention and deals with the adolescent's specific needs. In a successful substance abuse program, a student assistance counselor was available full-time for individual counseling and referral for treatment. In a successful delinquency program, a family worker gave extensive care to a predelinquent and the family to help them to make the changes needed in their lives to avoid repeated delinquent acts. A common concern of parents who have an adolescent showing problem behaviors is whether to seek therapy for the adolescent. To read about

the guidelines for deciding when to seek therapy for an adolescent, turn to Perspective on Adolescent Development 15.3.

2. *Community-wide Multiagency Collaborative Approaches.* The basic philosophy of community-wide programs is that a number of different programs and services have to be in place (Dryfoos, 1992). One successful substance abuse program implemented a community-wide health promotion campaign that used local media and community education in concert with a substance abuse curriculum in the schools. In a successful delinquency program, a neighborhood development approach involved local residents in neighborhood councils, who worked with the schools, police, courts, gang leaders, and the media.

3. *Early Identification and Intervention.* Reaching adolescents and their families before adolescents develop problems, or at the beginning of their problems, is a successful strategy. One preschool program serves as an excellent model for the prevention of delinquency, pregnancy, substance abuse, and dropping out of school. Operated by the High Scope Foundation in Ypsilanti, Michigan, the Perry Preschool has a long-term, positive impact on its students (Berrueta-Clement & others, 1986). This enrichment program, directed by David Weikart, services disadvantaged Black American children. They attend a high-quality, two-year preschool program and receive weekly home visits from program personnel. Based on official police records, by age 19, individuals who had attended Perry Preschool were less likely to have been arrested and reported fewer adult offenses than a control group. The Perry Preschool students also were less likely to drop out of school, and teachers rated their social behavior as more competent than a control group who did not receive the enriched preschool experience.

4. *Locus in the Schools.* Many of the successful programs were located in the schools. This is not surprising because the acquisition of basic skills is the bottom line for most high-risk children and adolescents. Programs in which the school principal was one of the key elements were especially effective. In some instances, the principal was an important factor in school reorganization, in the development of school teams for delinquency and substance abuse prevention, in facilitating school-based clinics, and as a liaison with student assistance counselors.

PERSPECTIVE ON ADOLESCENT DEVELOPMENT 15.3

Some Guidelines for Seeking Therapy When an Adolescent Shows Problem Behaviors

Determining whether an adolescent needs professional help when she or he engages in problem behaviors is not an easy task. Adolescents, by nature, tend to have mercurial moods and engage in behaviors that are distasteful to adults and run counter to their values. In many cases, though, such behaviors are only part of the adolescent's search for identity, are very normal, and do not require professional help. Too often when an adolescent first shows a problem behavior, such as drinking or stealing, parents panic and fear that their adolescent is going to turn into a drug addict or a hardened criminal. Such fears are usually not warranted—virtually every adolescent drinks alcohol at some point in their transition from childhood to adulthood, and likewise, virtually every adolescent engages in at least one or more acts of juvenile delinquency. By overreacting to such initial occurrences of adolescent problem behaviors, parents can exacerbate their relationship with the adolescent and thereby contribute to increased parent-adolescent conflict.

What are the circumstances under which parents should seek professional help for their adolescent's problems? Laurence Steinberg and Ann Levine (1990) recently developed five guidelines for determining when to get professional help if an adolescent is showing problem behaviors:

- If the adolescent is showing severe problem behaviors, such as depression, anorexia nervosa, drug addiction, repeated delinquent acts, or serious school-related problems, parents should not try to treat these problems alone and probably should seek professional help for the adolescent.
- If the adolescent has a problem, but the parents do not know what the problem is, they may want

to seek professional help for the adolescent. An example is an adolescent who is socially withdrawn and doesn't have many friends, which could be due to extreme shyness, depression, stress at school, drug involvement, or any of a number of other reasons. If parents do not know what the adolescent's problem is, how can they help the adolescent? Professionals can often make specific diagnoses and provide recommendations for helping the adolescent.

- If parents have tried to solve the adolescent's problem but have not been successful and the problem continues to disrupt the adolescent's life, then parents may wish to seek professional help for the adolescent. Frequent truancy, chronic running away, or repeated, hostile opposition to authority are examples of such problems.
- If parents realize they are part of the adolescent's problem, they may wish to seek professional help for the family. Constant, intense, bitter fighting that disrupts the everyday living of the family is a good example. Rarely is one individual the single cause of extensive family dissension. A therapist can objectively analyze the family's problems and help the family members to see why they are fighting so much and to find ways to reduce the fighting.
- When the family is under extensive stress (from the death of a family member or a divorce, for example) and the adolescent is not coping well (for example, becomes depressed or drinks a lot), professional help may be needed.

5. *Administration of School Programs by Agencies Outside of Schools.* In each problem area of adolescence, agencies or organizations outside of the schools often had the main responsibility for implementing programs in the schools. In one strategy, university-based researchers (such as James Comer at Yale and Cheryl Perry at Minnesota) obtained grants to develop a school-based program. In another strategy, nonprofit youth services and research organizations (such as Public/Private Ventures or the Academy for Educational Development) implemented demonstration projects in schools or communities with support from foundations or government agencies. And in yet another strategy, local health or youth service agencies collaborated with schools and obtained money from foundations or a state health agency.

6. *Location of Programs Outside of Schools.* Not every successful program is located within a school. Some programs may be more effective if they are community-based rather than school-based. Some youth are "turned off" by school, and they may be better served by programs in community centers, churches, businesses, or youth service centers. Some of these programs may be beneficial to very-high-risk youth, such as homeless and runaway adolescents, especially in providing them with overnight shelter.

7. *Arrangements for Training.* Many of the successful programs hire special staff members, who require training to develop a program. In many cases, they are asked to use a certain strategy (such as behavior modification) or a new curriculum (such as life skills training). School-based programs often involve the implementation of new concepts, such as cooperative learning. Many of the model programs have teams, made up of support personnel (social worker, psychologist, counselor), the school principal, parents, (in some instances), and occasionally students. These teams also need training to carry out the plan of the program.

8. *Social Skills Training.* A number of successful programs use social skills training as part of their strategy. Social skills training often involves teaching youth about their own risky behavior, providing them with the skills to cope with high-risk situations and to resist negative peer influence, and helping them to make healthy decisions about their futures. Role-playing, rehearsal, peer instruction, and media analysis are examples of social skills training techniques. However, few of the social skills training programs have demonstrated success with very-high-risk youth.

9. *Use of Peers in Intervention.* Successful program developers are aware of the importance of peers in adolescent development. The most successful programs use older peers—either as classroom instructors in social skills training, or as tutors and mentors—to influence or help younger peers. In some programs, the peer tutors are paid. Students who are selected to act as peer mentors often gain the most from the experience.

10. *Use of Parents in Interventions.* Many programs report less success in involving parents than they would like. However, a number of successful programs have demonstrated that parents can play an important role in intervention. Two approaches that have produced positive results involve: (1) home visits that provide parent education and support, and (2) use of parents as classroom aides. Parents have also been recruited as members of school teams and advisory committees.

11. *Involvement of the World of Work.* Successful programs often use innovative approaches to introduce career planning, expose youth to work experiences, and prepare them to enter the labor force. Successful programs have a variety of work-related components, such as a combination of life-planning curricula with school remediation and summer job placement, creation of opportunities for volunteer community service, and payment to high-risk youth to become tutors for younger children.

At this point, we have discussed a number of ideas about juvenile delinquency, depression, and suicide, the interrelation of problems and disturbances, and programs for reducing problems. A summary of these ideas is presented in Concept Table 15.2. In the next chapter, we will study the nature of stress and health in adolescents' lives, including such problems as eating disorders and smoking.

Concept Table 15.2

Juvenile Delinquency, Depression, Suicide, the Interrelation of Problems and Disorders,
and Programs for Reducing Problems

Concept	Processes/Related Ideas	Characteristics/Description
Juvenile delinquency	What is juvenile delinquency?	Juvenile delinquency refers to a broad range of behaviors, from socially unacceptable behavior to status offenses to criminal acts. For legal purposes, a distinction is made between index offenses (criminal acts, whether they are committed by juveniles or adults) and status offenses (performed by youth under a certain age). Conduct disorder is the psychiatric diagnosis category used when multiple behaviors—such as truancy, running away, and breaking and entering—occur before the age of 15, and the child or adolescent is considered unmanageable. Figures on the number of juvenile delinquents are sketchy, although 3 percent of 10- to 14-year-olds and 11 percent of 15- to 17-year olds were arrested for an offense in one recent year. Self-reported patterns suggest that approximately 20 percent of adolescents engage in delinquent behavior.
	What are the antecedents of delinquency?	Predictors of delinquency include a negative identity, a low degree of self-control, early initiation of delinquency, being a male, low expectations for education and little commitment to education, heavy peer influence and low resistance to peer pressure, failure of parents to adequately monitor their adolescents, ineffective discipline by parents, and living in an urban, high-crime, mobile neighborhood.
	Prevention and intervention	Successful programs do not focus on delinquency alone (rather, they include other components, such as education), have multiple components (but no one component is a "magic bullet"), begin early in the child's development, often involve schools, focus on institutions while also giving individualized attention to delinquents, and include maintenance.
Depression and suicide	Depression	In adolescence, the features of depression often are mixed with school failure, aggression, anxiety, antisocial behavior, or poor peer relations, making diagnosis difficult. Biogenetic and socioenvironmental causes have been proposed. Bowlby's developmental construction view, exaggerated self-blame, and learned helplessness are among the explanations of adolescent depression. Depression in adolescence is more frequent among girls than boys.
	Suicide	The suicide rate has tripled since the 1950s. White males are most likely to commit suicide, Black females the least likely. Females are more likely than males to attempt suicide but use more passive means, such as sleeping pills, whereas males use more active means, such as shooting. There is no simple answer to why adolescents commit suicide. As with depression, proximal and distal factors often are involved.
The interrelation of problems and disorders in adolescence and programs for reducing problems	The interrelation of problems and disorders in adolescence	Very-high-risk youth have multiple problem behaviors and make up as many as 10 percent of adolescents. They include adolescents who have been arrested or have committed serious offenses, have dropped out of school or are behind their grade level, and users of heavy drugs, drink heavily, regularly use cigarettes and marijuana, and are sexually active but do not use contraception. High-risk youth include as many as 15 percent of adolescents who participate in the same behaviors as very-high-risk youth but with slightly lower frequency and less deleterious consequences. Researchers are increasingly finding that problem behaviors in adolescence are interrelated.
	Common components of programs that successfully prevent or reduce adolescent problems	Of the 11 common components in successful prevention and intervention programs, Dryfoos concluded that two had the widest application: the importance of providing individual attention to high-risk adolescents and the need to develop broad, community-wide interventions. Others include early identification and intervention, locus in the schools, administration of school programs by agencies outside of schools, location of programs outside of schools, arrangements for training, social skills training, use of peers in interventions, use of parents in interventions, and involvement of the world of work.

Summary

I. What is Abnormal Behavior?

Abnormal behavior is behavior that is maladaptive and harmful. Such behavior fails to promote the well-being, growth, and fulfillment of the adolescent and, ultimately, others.

II. Causes of Abnormal Behavior

In the biological approach, mental disorders have biological causes. The forerunner of this approach was the medical model, which describes individuals as patients with mental diseases in hospitals, where they are treated by doctors. Today's biological approach emphasizes the role of brain processes and heredity in mental disorders. Proponents of the psychological and sociocultural approaches believe that the biological approach understates the importance of psychological and sociocultural factors in abnormal behavior. They also emphasize that the medical model encourages the labeling of mental disorders. In the interactionist approach, biological, psychological, and social factors often interact to produce abnormal behavior.

III. Characteristics of Adolescent Disorders

The spectrum of adolescent disorders is wide, varying in severity, developmental level, sex, and social class. Middle-class and female adolescents are more likely to have internalizing problems; lower-class and male adolescents are more likely to have externalizing problems. Overall, adolescents from lower socioeconomic circumstances have more problems than their counterparts from higher socioeconomic circumstances.

IV. Why Do Adolescents Take Drugs?

Drugs have been used since the beginning of human existence for pleasure, for utility, out of curiosity, and for social reasons. As an adolescent continues to take a drug, the drug produces tolerance, which means that a greater amount of the drug is needed to produce the same effect. Addiction is the body's physical dependence on a drug. When an addicted adolescent's body is not supplied with an adequate dose of the addictive drug, the adolescent is said to undergo withdrawal, the undesirable, intense pain and craving for an addictive drug. Psychological dependency is a psychological need to take a drug.

V. Trends in Overall Drug Use

The 1960s and 1970s were a time of marked increase in the use of illicit drugs. An encouraging finding is that, beginning in the mid-1980s, there was a downturn in illicit drug use by high school seniors. Nonetheless, the United States still has the highest adolescent drug-use rate of any industrialized nation.

VI. Alcohol

Alcohol is primarily a depressant, although in low dosages, it can act as a stimulant. Alcohol has produced many enjoyable as well as many sad moments for adolescents. Many automobile deaths and aggressive attacks on females are associated with alcohol use. Alcohol is the most widely used drug by adolescents. Alcohol abuse is a major adolescent problem. Alcohol use by U.S. high school seniors has slightly declined in recent years, but heavy drinking is still common. Among the risk factors in adolescent alcohol abuse are heredity, family influences, certain aspects of peer relations, ethnicity, and personality characteristics.

VII. Hallucinogens

Hallucinogens are drugs that modify an individual's perceptual experiences and produce hallucinations. Hallucinogens include LSD (a powerful hallucinogen) and marijuana (a milder hallucinogen). Adolescents decreased their use of marijuana in the 1980s, but LSD use has not decreased in recent years.

VIII. Stimulants

Stimulants are drugs that increase the activity of the central nervous system. The most widely used stimulants are caffeine, nicotine, amphetamines, and cocaine. Nicotine in cigarettes is the substance most frequently used by adolescents on a daily basis. Smoking habits are often formed during adolescence, and while cigarette smoking declined in the 1980s, it remains a dangerous habit. There has been a decrease in amphetamine use, although adolescents have increased their use of over-the-counter stay-awake pills. Cocaine use by adolescents dropped in the late 1980s, but a dangerous form of the drug—crack cocaine—is increasingly used.

IX. Depressants
Depressants are drugs that slow down the central nervous system, body functions, and behavior. Among the most widely used depressants are alcohol, barbiturates, and tranquilizers. An especially dangerous depressant is heroin, an opiate. The use of depressants by adolescents declined in the 1980s.

X. The Roles of Development, Parents, Peers, and Schools in Adolescent Drug Abuse
Drug use in childhood or early adolescence has more detrimental long-term effects than when its onset occurs in late adolescence. Parents, peers, and social support play important roles in preventing adolescent drug abuse. Considerable interest has developed in the role of schools in preventing adolescent drug abuse. Early intervention, a kindergarten through twelfth-grade approach, teacher training, social skills training, peer-led programs, programs aimed at high-risk groups, and community-wide prevention efforts are important components of successful school-based programs.

XI. What Is Juvenile Delinquency?
Juvenile delinquency refers to a broad range of behaviors, from socially unacceptable behavior to status offenses to criminal acts. For legal purposes, a distinction is made between index offenses (criminal acts, whether they are committed by juveniles or adults) and status offenses (performed by youth under a certain age). Conduct disorder is the psychiatric diagnosis category used when multiple behaviors—such as truancy, running away, and breaking and entering—occur before the age of 15, and the child or adolescent is considered unmanageable. Figures on the number of juvenile delinquents are sketchy, although 3 percent of 10- to 14-year-olds and 11 percent of 15- to 17-year-olds were arrested for an offense in one recent year. Self-reported patterns suggest that approximately 20 percent of adolescents engage in delinquent behavior.

XII. The Antecedents of Delinquency
The antecedents of delinquency include a negative identity, a low degree of self-control, early initiation of delinquency, being a male, low expectations for education and little commitment to education, heavy peer influence and low resistance to peer pressure, failure of parents to adequately monitor their adolescents, ineffective discipline by parents, and living in an urban, high-crime, mobile neighborhood.

XIII. Prevention and Intervention
Successful programs do not focus on delinquency alone (rather, they include other components, such as education), have multiple components (but no one component is a "magic bullet"), begin early in the child's development, often involve schools, focus on institutions while also giving individualized attention to delinquents, and include maintenance.

XIV. Depression
In adolescence, the features of depression are often mixed with school failure, aggression, anxiety, antisocial behavior, or poor peer relations, making diagnosis difficult. Biogenetic and socioenvironmental causes have been proposed. Bowlby's developmental construction view, exaggerated self-blame, and learned helplessness are among the explanations of adolescent depression. Depression in adolescence is more common among girls than boys.

XV. Suicide
The suicide rate has tripled since the 1950s. White males are more likely to commit suicide, Black females the least likely. Females are more likely than males to attempt suicide but use more passive means, such as sleeping pills, whereas males use more active means, such as shooting. There is no simple

answer to why adolescents commit suicide. As with depression, proximal and distal factors often are involved.

XVI. The Interrelation of Problems and Disorders in Adolescence
Very-high-risk youth have multiple problem behaviors and make up as many as 10 percent of adolescents. They include adolescents who have been arrested or have committed serious offenses, have dropped out of school or are behind in grade level, are users of heavy drugs, drink heavily, regularly use cigarettes and marijuana, and are sexually active but do not use contraception. High-risk youth include as many as 15 percent of adolescents who participate in the same behaviors as very-high-risk youth but with slightly lower frequency and less deleterious consequences. Researchers are increasingly finding that problem behaviors in adolescence are interrelated.

XVII. Common Components of Programs That Successfully Prevent or Reduce Adolescent Problems
Of the 11 common components in successful prevention and intervention programs, Dryfoos concluded that two had the widest application: the importance of providing individual attention to high-risk adolescents and the need to develop broad, community-wide interventions. Others include early identification and intervention, locus in the schools, administration of school programs by agencies outside of schools, location of programs outside of schools, arrangements for training, social skills training, use of peers in interventions, use of parents in interventions, and involvement of the world of work.

Key Terms

abnormal behavior 501
medical model 502
tolerance 504
addiction 504
withdrawal 504
psychological dependence
    504
hallucinogens 508
LSD 508

marijuana 509
stimulants 509
amphetamines 510
cocaine 510
depressants 512
barbiturates 512
tranquilizers 512
opiates 512

juvenile delinquency 519
index offenses 519
status offenses 519
conduct disorder 520
major depression 527
learned helplessness 528
very-high-risk youth 530
high-risk youth 532

Suggested Readings

Blumenthal, S. J., & Kupfer, D. J. (1988). Overview of early detection and treatment strategies for suicidal behavior in young people. *Journal of Youth and Adolescence, 17,* 1–23.
    A contemporary, up-to-date overview of what is known about suicide prevention in adolescence.
Coleman, J. (Ed.). (1987). *Working with troubled adolescents.* Orlando, FL: Academic Press.
    Includes chapters on adolescent individuation and family therapy, social skills training for adolescents, helping adolescents to improve their identity, and suicide.
Dryfoos, J. G. (1990). *Adolescents at risk: Prevalence and prevention.* New York: Oxford University Press.
    An outstanding contribution to our understanding of problems and disturbances. Dryfoos describes the common components of successful prevention and intervention efforts.
McCord, J. (1990). Problem behaviors. In S. S. Feldman & G. R. Elliott (Eds.), *At the threshold: The developing adolescent.* Cambridge, MA: Harvard University Press.
    Presents a broad overview of adolescent problems.
Quay, H. C. (Ed.). (1987). *Handbook of juvenile delinquency.* New York: Wiley.
    A collection of articles by leading experts about many dimensions of delinquency.

CHAPTER 16

Stress and Health

Look to your health and if you have it value it next to a good conscience; for health is a blessing we mortals are capable of.

Izaak Walton
The Compleat Angler, *1653*

Alan's Stress, Sarah's Obesity, and Brian's Exercise

I never thought it would be so hard to grow up. I feel a lot of pressure. My parents put a lot of pressure on me. They say they don't, but they do. I'm afraid to bring home a B on my report card. They want me to be perfect. I feel anxious every day about achieving. I want to be able to get into one of the top colleges, but I don't know if it's worth all of this anxiety and nervous feelings I have inside of me. I don't want to feel this way. Sometimes, my heart starts pounding really fast when I get nervous, and I'm not always able to settle myself down. I remember when I was in elementary school I was a lot happier. I didn't seem to care as much about what other people thought, and I was more fun to be around. The competition for grades wasn't as tough then. In the last several years, I've noticed how much more intense the push for good grades is. I wish someone could help me cope better with all of these pressures.

Alan, age 16

Food is a major problem in my life. Let's face it—I'm fat. Fat and ugly. I don't like myself, and I know other people don't like me either. I'm only 5 feet 4 inches tall and I weigh 166 pounds. I hate being fat, but I can't seem to lose weight. In the last year, I haven't grown in height, but I have gained 20 pounds. Some girls just think they are fat, and they really aren't. I heard this one girl talking yesterday about how fat she was. No way. She is about 5 feet tall and probably doesn't weigh over 100 pounds. She should be in my body. It seems like the fatter I get, the more I want to eat. I hear about all of these diets, but from what I know, none of them work in the long run. I've thought about going on one hundreds of times, especially right after I've pigged out. But I just get up the next day and start pigging out again. I'm a hopeless case.

Sarah, age 15

A lot of kids in my class are in pitiful physical shape. They never exercise, except in gym class, and even then a lot of them hardly ever break a sweat. During lunch hour, I see some of the same loafers hanging out and smoking a bunch of cigarettes. Don't they know what they are doing to their bodies? All I can say is that I'm glad I'm not like them. I'm on the basketball team, and during the season, the coach runs us until we are exhausted. In the summer, I still play basketball and do a lot of swimming. Just last month, I started lifting weights. I don't know what I would do without exercise. I couldn't stand to be out of shape.

Brian, age 14

A cheerful spirit is a good medicine, but a downcast spirit dries up the bones.

Proverbs 17:22

S tress, obesity, and exercise—the themes of Alan's, Sarah's, and Brian's comments, respectively, in the "Images of Adolescence" section—are issues in the burgeoning interest in adolescents' stress and health. Before turning to detailed discussions of health and stress, we examine the new approach to preventing illness and promoting health.

Health Psychology and Behavioral Medicine

Around 2600 B.C., Oriental physicians, and later around 500 B.C., Greek physicians, recognized that good habits were essential for good health. Instead of blaming magic or the gods for illness, they realized that human beings are capable of exercising some control over their health. The physician's role was as guide, assisting the patient in restoring a natural and emotional balance.

As we approach the twenty-first century, once again we recognize the power of our life-styles and psychological states in promoting our health. **Health psychology** *is a multidimensional approach to health that emphasizes psychological factors, life-style, and the nature of the health-care delivery system.* To underscore the increasing interest in psychology's role in health, a new division of the American Psychological Association, called health psychology, was formed in 1978 (Matarazzo, 1979). **Behavioral medicine** *is a field closely related to health psychology; it attempts to combine medical and behavioral knowledge to reduce illness and to promote health.* The interests of health psychologists and behavioral medicine researchers are broad: They include examination of why children, adolescents, and adults do or do not comply with medical advice, how effective media campaigns are in reducing adolescent smoking, psychological factors in losing weight, the role of exercise in reducing stress, and access to health care (Garrick & Loewenstein, 1989; Irwin & Orr, 1991).

Causes of Death in Adolescence

What are the leading causes of death in adolescence? What roles do age, socioeconomic status, ethnicity, and sex play in adolescent death? We examine each of these questions.

Leading Causes of Death

Medical improvements have increased the life expectancy of today's adolescents compared to their counterparts who lived earlier in the twentieth century. Still, life-threatening factors continue to exist in adolescents' lives.

The three leading causes of death in adolescence are accidents, suicide, and homicide (Kovar, 1991; Millstein & Litt, 1990; Wetzel, 1989). More than half of all deaths in adolescents ages 10 to 19 are due to accidents, and most of those involve motor vehicles, especially for older adolescents. Risky driving habits, such as speeding, tailgating, and driving under the influence of alcohol or other drugs, may be more important causes of these accidents than is lack of driving experience (Jonah, 1985). In about 50 percent of the motor vehicle fatalities involving an adolescent, the driver has a blood alcohol level of 0.10 percent, twice the level needed to be "under the influence" in some states. A high rate of intoxication is also often present in adolescents who die as pedestrians or while using recreational vehicles (Millstein & Irwin, 1988).

Suicide accounts for 6 percent of the deaths in the 10 to 14 age group, a rate of 1.3 per 100,000 population; in the 15 to 19 age group, suicide accounts for 12 percent of deaths, or 9 per 100,000 population. As reported in Chapter 15, since the 1950s, the adolescent suicide rate has tripled.

Homicide is yet another leading cause of death in adolescence. During 1988, 5,771 youths between the ages of 15 and 24 died in homicides. Homicide is especially high among Black American male adolescents: Black adolescent males are three time more likely to be killed by guns than natural causes (Simons, Finlay, & Yang, 1991). Let us now further examine some sociodemographic factors in adolescent death.

Age, Socioeconomic Status, Ethnicity, and Sex

The mortality rate for adolescents in 1984 was 31 per 100,000 population between the ages of 12 and 14, 66 per 100,000 between the ages of 15 and 17, and 102 per 100,000 between the ages of 18 and 19.

Between the early part of adolescence (ages 10 to 14) and the late part of adolescence (ages 15 to 19), adolescent mortality rates more than triple as causes of mortality change, with a shift toward more violent causes of death (Millstein & Litt, 1990). Youth who live in impoverished, high-density metropolitan areas are especially likely to be victims in homicides. Marked ethnic differences emerge in a number of areas of adolescent mortality. Black American adolescent males are especially likely to be involved in homicides, while White American adolescent males are much more likely to commit suicide. In late adolescence, homicide is the leading cause of death for Black American males. Male adolescents die at a rate more than twice that of their female peers, primarily because of their involvement in motor vehicle accidents. Now that we have considered the leading causes of death in adolescence, we turn our attention to the nature of health and illness in adolescence.

Health and Illness

While America has become a health-conscious nation, and we are aware of the importance of nutrition and exercise in our lives, many of us still smoke, eat junk food, have extra flab hanging around our middle, and spend too much of our lives as couch potatoes. This description fits too many adolescents as well as adults.

Adolescents often reach a level of health, strength, and energy they never will match during the remainder of their lives. They also have a sense of uniqueness and invulnerability that leads them to think that illness and disorder will not enter their lives. And they possess a time perspective that envisions the future as having few or no boundaries. Adolescents believe that they will live forever and recoup any lost health or modify any bad habits they might develop. Given this combination of physical and cognitive factors, is it any wonder that so many adolescents have poor health habits?

Cognitive Factors in Adolescents' Health Behavior

Among the cognitive factors in adolescents' health behavior are concepts of health behavior, beliefs about health, health knowledge, and decision making.

Concepts of Health Behavior

Concepts of health and illness develop in concert with Piaget's stages of cognitive development (Burbach & Peterson, 1986). Young children perceive health and illness in simplistic terms, describing vague feelings and depending on others to determine when they are ill. As children get older, they develop a concept of health and begin to understand that health has multiple causes. In early adolescence, some individuals still do not recognize the multiple causes of health, and relatively concrete thinking about illness predominates. By late adolescence, many individuals have become formal operational thinkers and view health in more hypothetical and abstract ways. They are now more likely to describe health in terms of psychological, emotional, and social components, and to consider their personal behavior important for their health (Millstein, 1991; Millstein & Irwin, 1987).

Beliefs about Health

Adolescents' health beliefs include beliefs about vulnerability and behavior (Millstein & Litt, 1990). Adolescents, as well as adults, underestimate their vulnerability to harm (Kamler & others, 1987). While they usually recognize that behaviors such as substance abuse and unprotected sexual intercourse are potential health hazards, they often underestimate the potentially negative consequences of these behaviors. They also anticipate, sometimes incorrectly, that the risks associated with certain behaviors will decrease as they get older (Millstein & Irwin, 1985).

Health Knowledge

Adolescents are generally poorly informed about health issues and have significant misperceptions about health (Centers for Disease Control, 1988). Younger adolescents have less factual knowledge about a variety of health topics, including sexually transmitted diseases and drug abuse, than older adolescents.

Decision Making

In Chapter 5, we discussed how young adolescents are better at decision making than children but are worse at decision making than older adolescents. The decision-making skills of older adolescents and adults, however, are far from perfect. And the ability to make decisions does not guarantee that such decisions will be made in everyday life, where breadth of experience comes into play (Jacobs & Potenza, 1990; Keating, 1990). For example, driver-training courses improve adolescents' cognitive and motor skills to levels equal to, or sometimes superior to, those of adults. However, driver training has not been effective in reducing adolescents' high rate of traffic accidents (Potvin, Champagne, & Laberge-Nadeau, 1988). Thus, an important research agenda is to study the way adolescents make decisions in practical health situations.

Sociocultural Factors in Adolescents' Health Behavior

Sociocultural factors influence health through their roles in setting cultural norms about health, through social relationships that provide emotional support, and through the encouragement of healthy or unhealthy behaviors (Millstein & Litt, 1990).

Cultural and Ethnic Variations

In considering the health of ethnic minority group adolescents, it is important to recognize that there are large within-group differences in living conditions and life-styles and that these differences are influenced by social class, status as an immigrant, social skills, language skills, occupational opportunities, and social resources, such as the availability of meaningful social support networks. At present, there is little research information about the role of ethnicity in adolescents' health beliefs and behavior. However, researchers do know what some of the important health issues are for various ethnic minority adolescents and adults. To learn about some of these issues, turn to Sociocultural Worlds of Adolescence 16.1.

Family and Peers

The family is an important aspect of social support for adolescents' health. Positive health behaviors are best achieved when adolescents develop a sense of autonomy within a supportive family context (Allen, Aber, & Leadbetter, in press; Turner & others, 1991). In addition to providing social support, parents and older siblings are important models for children's and adolescents' health.

Peers and friends also play important roles in adolescents' health behavior. A number of research studies have documented the association between unhealthy behaviors in adolescents and their friends, but the association may not be causal. For example, adolescents may choose friends who support their negative health behaviors. A special concern in adolescents' health behaviors is peer pressure. Adolescents who have a limited capacity to resist dares often engage in risk-taking behaviors at the urging of their peers (Berndt & Perry, 1990).

Health Services

While adolescents have a greater number of acute health conditions than do adults, they use private physician services at a lower rate than any other age group (Children's Defense Fund, 1986). And adolescents often underutilize other health-care systems as well (Millstein, 1988). Health services are especially unlikely to meet the health needs of younger adolescents, ethnic minority adolescents, and adolescents living in poverty. Among the chief barriers to better health services for adolescents are cost, poor organization, and availability of health services, as well as confidentiality of care (Klerman, 1991; Resnick, 1991). Also, few health-care providers receive any special training for working with adolescents. Many say that they feel unprepared to provide services such as contraceptive counseling and accurate evaluation of what constitutes abnormal behavior in adolescence (Irwin, 1986). Health-care providers may transmit to their patients their discomfort in discussing such topics as sexuality, which may lead to adolescents' unwillingness to discuss sensitive issues with them.

Now that we have considered some important aspects of health and illness—cognitive factors, sociocultural factors, and health services—we turn our attention to some specific health problems in adolescence as part of our discussion on promoting health.

Felipe Castro and Delia Magana (1988) developed a course in health promotion in ethnic minority children, adolescents, and adults, which they teach at UCLA. A summary of some of the issues they discuss follows:

For Black Americans, historical issues of prejudice and racial segregation are important considerations. The chronic stress of discrimination and poverty continue to negatively affect the health of many Black Americans. Personal and support systems are viable ways to improve the health of Black Americans. Their extended-family network may be especially helpful in coping with stress (Boyd-Franklin, 1989; McAdoo, 1988).

For many Hispanic Americans, some of the same stressors mentioned for Black Americans are associated with migration to the United States by Puerto Ricans, Mexicans, and Latin Americans. Language is likely a barrier for unacculturated Hispanics in doctor-patient communications. In addition, there is increasing evidence that diabetes occurs at an above-average rate in Hispanics (Gardner & others, 1984), making this disease a major health problem that parallels the above-average rate of high blood pressure among Blacks.

For Asian Americans, it is important to consider their broad diversity in national backgrounds and life-styles. They range from highly acculturated Japanese Americans, who may be better educated than many Anglo Americans and have excellent access to health care, to the many Indochinese refugees, who have few economic resources and poor health status.

Cultural barriers to adequate health care include the aforementioned financial resources and language skills. In addition, members of ethnic minority groups are often unfamiliar with how the medical system operates, confused about the need to see numerous people, and uncertain about why they have to wait so long for service (Snowden & Cheung, 1990).

Other barriers may be specific to certain cultures, reflecting different ideas regarding what causes disease and how disease should be treated. For example, Chinese Americans have access to folk healers in every Chinatown in the United States. Depending on their degree of acculturation to Western society, a Chinese American may go to a folk healer first, or to a Western doctor first, but invariably consults a folk healer for follow-up care. Chinese medicines are usually used for home care. These include ginseng tea for many ailments, boiled centipede soup for cancer, and eucalyptus oil for dizziness resulting from hypertension.

Native Americans view Western medicine as a source of crisis intervention, a quick fix for broken legs or other symptoms. They do not view Western medicine as a source for treatment of the causes of disease or for preventive intervention. For example, they are unlikely to attend a seminar on the prevention of alcohol abuse. They also are reluctant to become involved in care that requires a long hospitalization or that necessitates surgery.

Both Navajo Indians and Mexican Americans rely on family members to make decisions about treatment choices. Doctors who expect such patients to decide on the spot whether or not to undergo treatment will likely embarrass the patient or force the patient to give an answer that may lead to cancelled appointments if the family members veto the decision.

Mexican Americans also believe that some illnesses are due to natural causes, while others are due to supernatural causes. Depending on their level of acculturation, they may be disappointed and confused by doctors who do not show an awareness of how to treat diseases with supposed supernatural origins.

Health-care professionals can increase their effectiveness with culturally diverse populations by improving their knowledge of what patients bring to the health-care setting in the way of attitudes, beliefs, and folk health practices. Such information should be integrated into the Western-prescribed treatment rather than ignored at the risk of alienating the patient.

The Health Status of Black American, Hispanic American, Asian American, and Native American Adolescents

THE FAR SIDE   By GARY LARSON

The real reason dinosaurs became extinct

THE FAR SIDE cartoon by Gary Larson is
reprinted by permission of Chronicle Features,
San Francisco, CA.

*At the heart of preventing smoking is a
stronger educational and policy effort to
keep children and adolescents from
starting to use tobacco products.*

Promoting Health

Adolescents' health profile can be improved by reducing the incidence of certain
health-impairing life-styles, such as smoking and overeating, and by engaging in
health-improving life-styles that include good nutrition and exercise.

The Dangers of Cigarette Smoking

The year 1988 marked the seventy-fifth anniversary of the introduction of Camel
cigarettes. Selected magazines surprised readers with elaborate pop-up advertisements for Camels. Camel's ad theme was "75 years and still smokin'." Co-
incidentally, 1988 was also the seventy-fifth anniversary of the American Cancer
Society.

In 1989, the surgeon general and his advisory committee issued a report
called *Reducing the Health Consequences of Smoking: 25 Years of Progress*. It
was released 25 years after the original warnings that cigarettes are responsible
for major health problems, especially lung cancer. New evidence was presented
to show that smoking is even more harmful than previously thought. The report
indicated that, in 1985, for example, cigarette smoking accounted for more than
one-fifth of all deaths in the United States—20 percent higher than previously
believed. Thirty percent of all cancer deaths are attributed to smoking, as are 21
percent of all coronary heart disease deaths, and 82 percent of chronic pulmonary
disease deaths.

At the heart of preventing smoking is a stronger educational and policy
effort to keep children and adolescents from starting to use tobacco products.
Smoking begins primarily during childhood and adolescence. Adolescent smoking
reached its peak in the mid-1970s, then began to decline through 1980. However,
rates of adolescent smoking have dropped only 1 percent since 1981 (Johnston,
O'Malley, & Bachman, 1992). This means that it is important to keep children
from initiating smoking, a difficult task since there are fewer restrictions on children's access to cigarettes today than there were in 1964, and the existing restrictions are rarely reinforced (U.S. Public Health Service, 1989).

Traditional school health programs have often succeeded in educating
adolescents about the long-term health consequences of smoking but have had
little effect on adolescent smoking behavior. That is, adolescent smokers know as
much about the health risks of smoking as do nonadolescent smokers, but this
knowledge has had little impact on reducing their smoking behavior (Miller &
Slap, 1989). The need for effective intervention has prompted investigators to
focus on those factors that place young adolescents at high risk for future smoking,
especially social pressures from peers, family members, and the media.

A number of research teams have developed strategies for interrupting behavioral patterns that lead to smoking (Bruess & Richardson, 1992; Chassin &
others, 1984; Perry, 1991; Perry & others, 1988). In one investigation, high school
students were recruited to help seventh-grade students resist peer pressure to
smoke (McAlister & others, 1980). The high school students encouraged the
younger adolescents to resist the influence of high-powered ads suggesting that
liberated women smoke by saying, "She is not really liberated if she is hooked
on tobacco." The students also engaged in role-playing exercises called "chicken."
In these situations, the high school students called the younger adolescents
"chicken" for not trying a cigarette. The seventh-graders practiced resistance to
the peer pressure by saying, "I'd be a real chicken if I smoked just to impress
you." Following several sessions, the students in the smoking prevention group
were 50 percent less likely to begin smoking compared to a group of seventh-
grade students in a neighboring junior high school, even though the parents of
both groups of students had the same smoking rate.

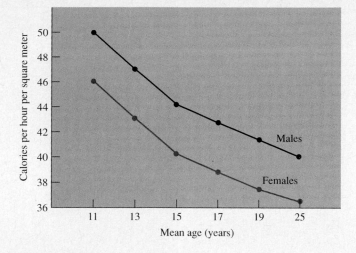

Figure 16.1 Basal metabolic rates (BMR) for adolescent females and males.

One comprehensive health approach that includes an attempt to curb cigarette smoking by adolescents was developed by clinical psychologist Cheryl Perry and her colleagues (Perry & others, 1988). Three programs were developed based on peer group norms, healthy role models, and social skills training. Elected peer leaders were trained as instructors. In seventh grade, adolescents were offered "Keep It Clean," a six-session course emphasizing the negative effects of smoking. In eighth grade, students were involved in "Health Olympics," an approach that included exchanging greeting cards on smoking and health with peers in other countries. In ninth grade, students participated in "Shifting Gears," which included six sessions focused on social skills. In the social skills program, students critiqued media messages and created their own positive health videotapes. At the same time as the school intervention, a community-wide smoking cessation program, as well as a diet and health awareness campaign, were initiated. After five years, students who were involved in the smoking and health program were much less likely to smoke cigarettes, use marijuana, or drink alcohol than their counterparts who were not involved in the program.

The tobacco industry does prey on adolescents' motivation to feel grown up by including "cool" people who smoke in their advertisements—successful young women smoking Virginia Slims cigarettes, handsome Marlboro men in rich surroundings with beautiful women at their side, for example. The advertisements encourage adolescents to associate cigarette smoking with a successful, active life-style. Legislators are working on the introduction of more stringent laws to further regulate the tobacco industry, since smoking is the only industry in America that will have killed 3 million of its best customers between 1964 and the year 2000, according to the 1989 report of the U.S. Department of Public Health.

Nutrition

The recommended range of energy intake for adolescents takes into account the different needs of adolescents, their growth rate, and their level of exercise. Males have higher energy needs than females. Older adolescent girls also have slightly lower energy needs than younger adolescent girls. Some adolescents' bodies burn energy faster than others. **Basal metabolism rate (BMR)** *is the minimum amount of energy an individual uses in a resting state.* As shown in Figure 16.1, BMR gradually declines from the beginning of adolescence through the end of adolescence.

Selected meal	Calories	Percent of calories from fat
Burger King Whopper, fries, vanilla shake	1,250	43
Big Mac, fries, chocolate shake	1,100	41
McDonald's Quarter-Pounder with cheese	418	52
Pizza Hut 10-inch pizza with sausage, mushrooms, pepperoni, and green pepper	1,035	35
Arby's roast beef plate (roast beef sandwich, two potato patties, and coleslaw), chocolate shake	1,200	30
Kentucky Fried Chicken dinner (three pieces chicken, mashed potatoes and gravy, coleslaw, roll)	830	50
Arthur Treacher's fish and chips (two pieces breaded, fried fish, french fries, cola drink)	900	42
Typical restaurant "diet plate" (hamburger patty, cottage cheese, etc.)	638	63

Figure 16.2   Fat and calorie intake of selected fast-food meals.

Concern is often expressed over adolescents' tendency to eat between meals. However, the choice of foods is much more important than the time or place of eating. Fresh vegetables and fruits as well as whole-grain products are needed to complement the foods high in energy value and protein that adolescents commonly choose (Rees & Mahan, 1988).

A special concern in American culture is the amount of fat in our diet. Many of today's adolescents virtually live on fast-food meals, which contributes to the increased fat levels in their diet. Most fast-food meals are high in protein, especially meat and dairy products. But the average American adolescent does not have to worry about getting enough protein. What should be of concern is the vast number of adolescents who consume large quantities of fast foods that not only are high in protein but high in fat. The American Heart Association recommends that the daily limit for calories from fat should be approximately 30 percent. Compare this figure with the figures in Figure 16.2. Clearly, many fast-food meals contribute to excess fat intake by adolescents.

Eating Disorders

A tall, slender, 16-year-old girl goes into the locker room of a fitness center, throws her towel across the bench, and looks squarely in the mirror. She yells, "You fat pig. You are nothing but a fat pig." America is a nation obsessed with food, spending extraordinary amounts of time thinking about, eating, and avoiding food. Eating disorders are complex, involving genetic inheritance, physiological factors, cognitive factors, and environmental experiences (Stunkard, 1989). In one investigation, girls who in early adolescence felt most negatively about their bodies were more likely to develop eating problems two years later (Attie & Brooks-Gunn, 1989). The three most prominent eating disorders are obesity, anorexia nervosa, and bulimia. We consider each of these in turn.

Obesity

Adolescent obesity involves genetic inheritance, physiological mechanisms, cognitive factors, and environmental influences (Brownell, 1990; Logue, 1986; McGlynn, 1990). Some adolescents may have inherited a tendency to be overweight. Only 10 percent of children who do not have obese parents become obese themselves, whereas about 40 percent of children who have one obese parent become obese, and about 70 percent of children who have two obese parents become obese. The extent to which this is due to genes or experiences with parents cannot be determined in research with humans, but animals can be bred to have a propensity for fatness.

Another factor in the weight of adolescents is **set point,** *the weight maintained when no effort is made to gain or lose weight.* Set point is influenced by adolescents' basal metabolism rate, discussed earlier. Researchers have discovered that individuals with a slow metabolism are most likely to gain weight (Brownwell & Stein, 1989). And, as indicated in Figure 16.1, BMR drops sharply from the beginning to the end of adolescence. During the adult years, BMR continues to decline, but at a much slower rate than in adolescence. To some extent, a declining BMR helps to explain why there are more fat older adolescents than fat younger adolescents. Scientists are working on drugs that they hope will be able to raise the BMR of overweight adolescents, although as we will see shortly, something else is able to raise metabolism rate and burn calories.

Adolescents' insulin levels also are important factors in eating behavior and obesity. American health psychology researcher Judith Rodin (1984) argues that what adolescents eat influences their insulin levels. When adolescents eat complex carbohydrates, such as cereals, bread, and pasta, insulin levels go up but fall off gradually. When adolescents consume simple sugars, such as candy bars and Cokes, insulin levels rise and then fall, often sharply—producing the sugar low with which many of us are all too familiar.

Glucose levels in the blood also are affected by these complex carbohydrates and simple sugars, and in similar ways. The consequence is that adolescents are more likely to eat within the next several hours after eating simple sugars than after eating complex carbohydrates. And the food adolescents eat at one meal influences how much they will eat at the next meal. So consumption of doughnuts and candy bars, in addition to providing only minimal nutritional value, sets up an ongoing sequence of what and how much adolescents crave the next time they eat.

Rodin also believes that exercise is an important part of weight loss and weight maintenance for adolescents. She points out that, no matter what adolescents' genetic background, aerobic exercise increases metabolic rate, which helps to burn calories. Exercise not only burns up calories but continues to raise metabolic rate for several hours *after* the exercise. Exercise actually lowers the body's set point for weight, making it much easier to maintain a lower weight (Bennett & Gurin, 1982).

Many obese adolescents feel that everything would be great in their lives if only they could lose weight. As one adolescent commented, "Losing weight would make my parents happy, my peers at school would like me, and I could concentrate on other things." A typical example is Debby, who at age 17 had been obese since she was 12. She came from a middle-class family in which her parents pressured her to lose weight, repeatedly sending her to reducing centers and to physicians. One summer, Debby was sent to a diet camp, where she went from 200 to 150 pounds. On returning home, she was terribly disappointed when her parents pressured her to lose more. With increased tension and parental preoccupation with her weight, she gave up all efforts at dieting, and her weight rose rapidly. Debby isolated herself and continued her preoccupation with food. Later, clinical help was sought and, fortunately, Debby was able to work through her hostility toward her parents and understand her self-destructive behavior. Eventually, she gained a sense of self-control and became willing to reduce for herself and not for her parents or her peers.

Medical personnel and psychologists have become increasingly concerned with the health hazards associated with obesity (Sigman & Flanery, 1992). Eating patterns established in childhood and adolescence are highly associated with

No matter what an adolescent's genetic background, aerobic exercise increases metabolic rate, which helps burn calories. Exercise can actually lower the body's set point for weight, making it much easier to maintain a lower weight.

Anorexia nervosa has become a prominent problem in adolescent females.

obesity in adulthood—80 percent of obese adolescents become obese adults. Obesity is estimated to characterize 25 percent of today's American adolescents (Brone & Fisher, 1988). As we see next, a more infrequent condition has received considerable attention in recent years.

Anorexia Nervosa and Bulimia

Fifteen-year-old Jane gradually eliminated foods from her diet to the point where she subsisted by eating *only* applesauce and eggnog. She spent hours observing her own body, wrapping her fingers around her waist to see if it was getting any thinner. She fantasized about becoming a beautiful fashion model and wearing designer bathing suits. But even when she reached 85 pounds, Jane still felt fat. She continued to lose weight, eventually emaciating herself. She was hospitalized and treated for **anorexia nervosa,** *an eating disorder that involves the relentless pursuit of thinness through starvation.* Eventually, anorexia nervosa can lead to death, as it did for popular singer Karen Carpenter.

Anorexia nervosa primarily afflicts females during adolescence and the early adulthood years; only about 5 percent of anorexics are males (Leon & others, 1989; Stein & Reichert, 1990). Most adolescents with this disorder are White and come from well-educated, middle- and upper-income families. Although anorexics avoid eating, they have an intense interest in food. They cook for others, they talk about food, and they insist on watching others eat. Anorexics have a distorted body image, perceiving that they will become attractive only when they become skeletal in appearance. As self-starvation continues and the fat content of the body drops to a bare minimum, menstruation usually stops. Behavior is often hyperactive (Polivy & Thomsen, 1987).

Numerous causes of anorexia have been proposed, including societal, psychological, and physiological factors (Attie & Brooks-Gunn, 1989; Fisher & Brone, 1991; Litt, 1991; Stern & others, 1989). The societal factor most often held responsible is the current fashion image of thinness. Psychological factors include motivation for attention, desire for individuality, denial of sexuality, and a way of coping with overcontrolling parents. Anorexics sometimes have families that place high demands for achievement on them. Unable to meet their parents' high standards, they feel unable to control their own lives. By limiting their food intake, anorexics gain some sense of self-control. Physiological causes involve the hypothalamus, which becomes abnormal in a number of ways when an adolescent becomes anorexic (Garfinkel & Garner, 1982). But the bottom line is that, at this time, the exact causes of anorexia nervosa are uncertain.

Bulimia *is an eating disorder in which the individual consistently follows a binge-and-purge eating pattern.* The bulimic goes on an eating binge and then purges by self-induced vomiting or by using a laxative. Sometimes, the binges alternate with fasting, at other times with normal eating. Like anorexia nervosa, bulimia is primarily a female disorder. Bulimia has become prevalent among college women. Some estimates indicate that as many as one in two college women binge and purge at least some of the time. However, recent estimates reveal that true bulimics—those who binge and purge on a regular basis—make up less than 2 percent of the college female population (Stunkard, 1987). Another recent survey of 1,500 high school and university students found that 4 percent of the high school students and 5 percent of the university students were bulimic (Howatt & Saxton, 1988). While anorexics can control their eating, bulimics cannot. Depression is a common characteristic of bulimics (Levy, Dixon, & Stern, 1989). Bulimia can produce gastric and chemical imbalances in the body. Many of the causes proposed for anorexia nervosa also are offered for bulimia (Leon, 1991; Thelan & others, 1990).

Now that we have considered the dangers of smoking, the nature of nutrition, and eating problems in adolescence, we turn our attention to one of the most important factors in helping adolescents to keep from gaining too much weight or in losing weight and maintaining the weight loss—exercise. As we learned earlier, exercise not only burns calories, but it continues to raise the basal metabolism rate for several hours *after* the exercise.

Exercise

In 1961, President John F. Kennedy offered the following recommendation: "We are underexercised as a nation. We look instead of play. We ride instead of walk.

Our existence deprives us of the minimum physical activity essential for living." A special interest in recent years involves **aerobic exercise,** *sustained exercise— jogging, swimming, or cycling, for example—that stimulates heart and lung activity.* Studies of the effects of exercise on health have focused on the role of exercise in preventing heart disease. Most health experts recommend that we should try to raise our heart rate to 60 percent of our maximum rate. Maximum heart rate is calculated as 220 minus your age, so if you are 20, you should aim for an exercise heart rate of 120 ($220 - 20 = 200 \times 0.60 = 120$). Some health experts recommend that, regardless of other risk factors (smoking, high blood pressure, being overweight, heredity), if we exercise enough to burn more than 2,000 calories per week, we can cut our risk of heart attack by an impressive two-thirds (Sherwood, Light, & Blumenthal, 1989). Burning up 2,000 calories a week through exercise requires a lot of effort, however, far more than most of us are willing to expend. Burning 300 calories a day through exercise would require one of the following: swimming or running for about 25 minutes, walking for 45 minutes at about 4 miles an hour, or participating in aerobic dancing for 30 minutes.

Many of our patterns of health are long-standing. Our experiences as children and adolescents contribute to our health practices as adults. Are today's children and adolescents getting enough exercise? In a national assessment comparing 6- to 17-year-olds' physical fitness in 1980 and 1989, ratings of "satisfactory" on the entire test, which included sprints, sit-ups, push-ups, and long jumps, dropped from 43 percent in 1980 to 32 percent in 1989.

Some health experts blame television for the poor physical condition of American adolescents. In one investigation, adolescents who watched little television were much more physically fit than their heavy-television-viewing counterparts (Tucker, 1987). The more adolescents watch television, the more they are likely to be overweight. No one is quite sure whether this is because they spend their leisure time in front of a television set, because they eat a lot of junk food they see advertised on television, or because less physically fit youth find physical activity less reinforcing than watching television.

The family plays an important role in children's and adolescents' exercise program. A wise strategy is for families to take up vigorous physical activities that parents and children can enjoy together. Running, swimming, cycling, and hiking are especially recommended. However, in encouraging children and adolescents to exercise more, parents should not encourage them beyond their physical limits or expose them to intense competitive pressures that take the fun out of sports and exercise. For example, long-distance running may be too strenuous for young children and can result in bone injuries. Recently, the number of children participating in strenuous events such as marathons and triathalons has increased. Doctors are beginning to see injuries in children that previously they only saw in adults, such as stress fractures and tendonitis (Risser, 1989). If left to their own devices, how many eight-year-old children would want to prepare for a marathon?

Some of the blame for the poor physical condition of U.S. children and adolescents falls on U.S. schools, many of which fail to provide physical education class on a daily basis. One extensive investigation of behavior in physical education classes at four different schools revealed how little vigorous exercise takes place in these classes (Parcel & others, 1987). Boys and girls moved through space only 50 percent of the time they were in the classes, and they moved continuously an average of only 2.2 minutes. In sum, not only do adolescents' school week include inadequate physical education classes, but the majority of adolescents do not exercise vigorously even when they are in physical education classes. Further, while we hear a lot about the exercise revolution among adults, most

children and adolescents report that their parents are poor role models when it comes to vigorous physical exercise (Feist & Brannon, 1989).

Does it make a difference if children and adolescents are pushed to exercise more vigorously in school? One recent investigation provided an affirmative answer to this question (Tuckman & Hinkle, 1988). One hundred fifty-four boys and girls were randomly assigned to either three 30-minute running programs per week or to regular attendance in physical education classes. Although the results sometimes varied by sex, for the most part, those in the running program had increased cardiovascular health and showed increased creativity. For example, the running-program boys had less body fat, and the running-program girls had more creative involvement in their classrooms.

An exciting possibility is that physical exercise might provide a buffer to adolescents' stress. In one investigation of 364 females in grades 7 through 11 in Los Angeles, the negative impact of stressful events on health declined as exercise levels increased, suggesting that exercise can be a valuable resource for combating adolescents' life stresses (Brown & Siegel, 1988). In another investigation, adolescents who exercised regularly coped more effectively with stress and had more positive identities than adolescents who engaged in little exercise (Grimes & Mattimore, 1989).

In the fourth century B.C., Aristotle commented that the quality of life is determined by its activities. In today's world, we know that exercise is one of the principal activities that improves the quality of life, both adolescents' and adults'.

Toward Healthier Adolescent Lives

Adolescents' health involves far more than trips to a doctor when sick and treatments for disease. Researchers are becoming increasingly aware that adolescents' behavior determines whether they will develop a serious illness or whether they will be healthy (Minkler, 1989). Health psychologists and behavioral medicine specialists believe that the next major step in improving the general health of American adolescents will be primarily behavioral, not medical.

What should be America's health goals for adolescents? A number of recommendations are being made for the year 2000. Among them are the following

Concept Table 16.1

Health Psychology and Behavioral Medicine, Leading Causes of Death in Adolescence,
Health and Illness, and Promoting Health

Concept	Processes/Related Ideas	Characteristics/Description
Health psychology and behavioral medicine	Their nature	Today, we recognize the power of life-style and psychological states in promoting adolescents' health. Health psychology is a multidimensional approach to health that emphasizes psychological factors, life-style, and the nature of the health-care delivery system. Behavioral medicine is a field closely related to health psychology; it attempts to combine medical and behavioral knowledge to reduce illness and to promote health.
Causes of death in adolescence	Leading causes	The three leading causes of death in adolescence are accidents (most of which involve motor vehicles), suicide, and homicide.
	Age, socioeconomic status, ethnicity, and sex	The mortality rate for adolescents is higher among older than younger adolescents. Homicide rates are especially high among Black males who live in urban, low socioeconomic status neighborhoods. Male adolescents die at a rate more than twice that of their female peers.
Health and illness	Cognitive factors	Cognitive factors in adolescents' health behavior include: concepts of health behavior, which develop in concert with Piaget's stages (adolescents' health concepts are more abstract and are more likely to emphasize multiple determinants of health than children's); beliefs about health (adolescents and adults underestimate their vulnerability to health problems and illness); health knowledge (adolescents are generally poorly informed about health issues and have significant misperceptions about health); and decision making (adolescents are better at making decisions about health than children but worse at making such decisions than adults).
	Sociocultural factors	Sociocultural factors influence health through their roles in setting cultural norms about health, through social relationships that provide emotional support, and through the encouragement of healthy or unhealthy behaviors. There are large within-group differences in living conditions and life-styles that affect the health of ethnic minority adolescents, and these differences are influenced by social class, status as an immigrant, social skills, language skills, occupational opportunities, and social resources. Family influences also are important. Positive health is best achieved when adolescents develop a sense of autonomy within a supportive family framework. In addition to social support, parents and older siblings are important models for health. Peers and friends also play important roles in adolescents' health behavior.

objectives of the federal government and the Society for Public Health Education
(Breslow, 1990; Schwartz & Eriksen, 1989):

- The development of preventive services targeting such diseases as
  cancer, heart disease, unintended pregnancy, and AIDS
- Health promotion, including behavior modification and health
  education; stronger programs for dealing with adolescents' smoking,
  alcohol and drug abuse, nutrition, physical fitness, and mental health
- Satisfaction of the health needs of special populations, such as a better
  understanding of health prevention in Black American and Hispanic
  American populations

At this point, we have discussed a number of ideas about health psychology
and behavioral medicine, the causes of death in adolescence, health and illness,
and promoting health. A summary of these ideas is presented in Concept Table
16.1. Next, we consider another important factor in adolescents' health—stress
and how to cope with it.

Concept Table 16.1

Health Psychology and Behavioral Medicine, Leading Causes of Death in Adolescence, Health and Illness, and Promoting Health

Concept	Processes/Related Ideas	Characteristics/Description
	Health services	While adolescents have a greater number of acute health conditions than do adults, they use private physician services and other health-care systems at lower rates than any other age group. Health services are especially unlikely to meet the needs of younger adolescents, ethnic minority adolescents, and adolescents living in poverty. Among the chief barriers to better health services for adolescents are cost, poor organization, availability, and confidentiality of care. Also, few health-care providers receive any special training in working with adolescents.
Promoting health	Dangers of cigarette smoking	In 1989, the surgeon general released a report that presented new evidence to show that smoking is even more harmful than previously thought. Traditional school health programs have had little impact on reducing smoking. Current prevention efforts with adolescents focus on coping with social pressures from family, peers, and the media.
	Nutrition	The recommended range of energy intake for adolescents takes into account their different needs, their growth rate, and their level of exercise. Some adolescents' bodies burn energy faster than others. A key concept is basal metabolism rate (BMR), the minimum amount of energy an individual uses in a resting state. Many adolescents have too much fat in their diet.
	Eating disorders	These prominent eating disorders in adolescence are obesity, anorexia nervosa, and bulimia. Heredity, set point, BMR, insulin level, glucose level in the blood, and exercise are key aspects of understanding the nature of adolescents' obesity. A large percentage of obese adolescents become obese adults. Anorexia nervosa is an eating disorder that involves relentless pursuit of thinness through starvation. It especially affects adolescent females. Bulimia involves a binge-and-purge pattern on a regular basis. Societal, psychological, and physiological factors have been proposed as causes of these eating disorders.
	Exercise	Experts agree that children and adolescents are not getting enough exercise. Television and U.S. schools have been criticized for contributing to the poor exercise patterns of adolescents. Most adolescents also say that their parents are poor role models in the realm of exercise. An exciting possibility is that exercise can serve as a buffer to stress.
	Toward healthier adolescent lives	Recommendations for the year 2000 include: preventive services, health promotion, and satisfaction of the health needs of special adolescent populations, such as Black American and Hispanic American adolescents.

Stress

Stress is a sign of the times. No one really knows whether today's adolescents experience more stress than their predecessors, but it does seem that their stressors have increased. Among the stress-related questions we examine are: What is stress? What is the body's response to stress? What environmental factors are involved in stress? Do personality factors influence stress? How do cognitive factors influence stress? How do sociocultural factors influence stress?

What Is Stress?

Stress is not easy to define. Initially, the term *stress* was loosely borrowed from physics. Humans, it was thought, are in some ways similar to physical objects, such as metals, that resist moderate outside forces but lose their resiliency at some point of greater pressure. But unlike metal, adolescents can think and reason and experience a myriad of social circumstances that make defining stress more complex in psychology than in physics (Hobfoll, 1989). In adolescents, is stress the threats and challenges the environment places on them, as when we say, "Sally's world is so stressful, it is overwhelming her"? Is stress adolescents' response to such threats and challenges, as when we say, "Bob is not coping well with the problems in his life; he is experiencing a lot of stress and his body is falling apart"? Because debate continues on whether stress is the threatening events in adolescents' worlds or their responses to those events, a broad definition of stress is best: **Stress** *is the response of individuals to the circumstances and events, called stressors, that threaten them and tax their coping abilities.*

The Body's Response to Stress

According to the Austrian-born founder of stress research, the late Hans Selye (1974, 1983), stress simply is the wear and tear in the body due to the demands placed on it. Any number of environmental events or stimuli produce the same stress response in the body. Selye observed patients with different problems: the death of someone close, loss of income, arrest for embezzlement. Regardless of which problem the patient had, similar symptoms appeared: loss of appetite, muscular weakness, and decreased interest in the world.

The **general adaptation syndrome (GAS)** *is Selye's concept that describes the common effects on the body when demands are placed on it. The GAS consists of three stages: alarm, resistance, and exhaustion.* First, in the *alarm stage,* the individual enters a temporary state of shock, a time when resistance to stress is below normal. The individual detects the presence of stress and tries to eliminate it. Muscle tone is lost, temperature decreases, and blood pressure drops. Then, a rebound called *countershock* occurs, in which resistance to stress begins to pick up; the adrenal cortex enlarges, and hormone release increases. The alarm stage is short. Not much later, the individual moves into the *resistance stage,* during which resistance to stress is intensified, and an all-out effort is made to combat stress. In the resistance stage, the individual's body is flooded with stress hormones; blood pressure, heart rate, temperature, and respiration all increase. If the all-out effort to combat stress fails and stress persists, the individual moves into the *exhaustion stage,* at which time wear and tear on the body increases, the person may collapse in a state of exhaustion, and vulnerability to disease increases. Figure 16.3 provides an illustration of Selye's general adaptation syndrome.

Not all stress is bad, though. **Eustress** *is Selye's concept that describes the positive features of stress.* Competing in an athletic event, writing an essay, or pursuing someone who is attractive requires the body to expend energy. Selye does not say that we should avoid these fulfilling experiences in life, but he does emphasize that we should minimize the wear and tear on our bodies.

One of the main criticisms of Selye's view is that human beings do not always react to stress in the uniform way he proposed. There is much more to understanding stress in humans than knowing their physical reactions to it. We also need to know about their personality, their physical makeup, their perceptions, and the context in which the stressor occurred (Hobfoll, 1989).

Environmental Factors

Many factors, big and small, can produce stress in adolescents' lives. In some instances, extreme events, such as war, an automobile accident, or the death of a friend, produce stress. In others, the everyday pounding of being overloaded with school and work, of being frustrated in unhappy family circumstances, or of living in poverty produce stress. What makes some situations stressful and others less stressful for adolescents?

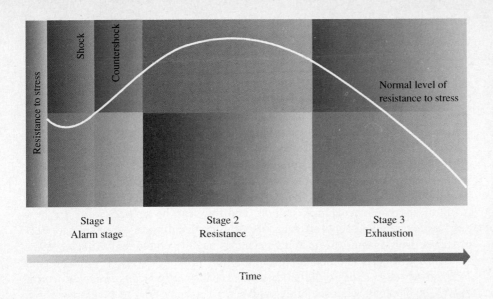

Stage 1
Alarm stage

Stage 2
Resistance

Stage 3
Exhaustion

Time

Figure 16.3 Selye's general adaptation syndrome. The general adaptation syndrome (GAS) describes an individual's general response to stress. In the first stage (alarm), the body enters a temporary state of shock, a time when resistance to stress is below normal. Then, a rebound called countershock occurs, in which resistance to stress begins to pick up. Not much later, the individual moves into the second stage (resistance), during which resistance to stress is intensified in an all-out effort to combat stress. If the effort fails and stress persists, the individual moves into the third and final stage (exhaustion), when wear and tear on the body worsens, the person may collapse in a state of exhaustion, and vulnerability to disease increases.

From Hans Selye, The Stress of Life. *Copyright © 1976 McGraw-Hill Book Company, New York, NY. Reprinted by permission of McGraw-Hill, Inc.*

Overload, Conflict, and Frustration

Sometimes, circumstances become so intense that adolescents no longer can cope. Adolescents are known for their interest in listening to loud music, but when noise remains at a high level for a prolonged period of time—such as a loud siren—the individual's adaptability becomes overloaded at some point. This overload can occur with work, too. An adolescent may say, "There are not enough hours in the day to do all I have to do."

The buzzword for overload in today's world is **burnout,** *a hopeless, helpless feeling brought on by relentless work-related stress.* Burnout leaves its sufferers in a state of physical and emotional exhaustion (Pines & Aronson, 1988). On a number of campuses, college burnout is the most common reason students leave school before earning their degrees, reaching a rate of 25 percent at some schools. Dropping out of college for a semester or two used to be considered a sign of weakness. Now sometimes called "stopping out" because the student fully intends to return, it may be encouraged for some students who are feeling overwhelmed by stress. Before recommending "stopping out" though, most counselors suggest examining ways the overload could be reduced and possible coping strategies that would allow the student to remain in school. The simple strategy of taking a reduced class load or a better-balanced load sometimes works, for example. Most college counseling services have professionals who can effectively work with students to alleviate the sense of being overloaded and overwhelmed by life.

Stimuli not only overload adolescents—they can also be a source of conflict. Conflict occurs when adolescents must decide between two or more incompatible stimuli. Three major types of conflict are approach/approach, avoidance/avoidance, and approach/avoidance. The **approach/approach conflict** *is when the individual must choose between two attractive stimuli or circumstances.* Should an adolescent go out with the tall, thin, good-looking person or with the rich, more stockily built person? Should the adolescent decide to take a summer job as a lifeguard or as a salesperson? The approach/approach conflict is the least stressful of the three types of conflict because either choice leads to a positive result.

The **avoidance/avoidance conflict** *is when the individual must choose between two unattractive stimuli or circumstances. Adolescents want to avoid both, but they must choose one.* Will the adolescent go to the dentist to have a bad tooth pulled or endure the toothache? Is the adolescent going to go through the stress of an oral presentation in class or not show up and get a zero? Obviously, these conflicts are more stressful than having the luxury of choosing between two approach circumstances. In many instances, adolescents delay their decision about an avoidance/avoidance conflict until the last possible moment.

The **approach/avoidance conflict** *involves a single stimulus or circumstance that has both positive and negative characteristics.* For example, an adolescent may really like a particular individual and even be thinking about getting married. The possibility of steady love and affection is attractive, but, on the other hand, marriage at this time might hinder college and a career. The adolescent looks at a menu and faces a dilemma—the double chocolate delight would be sumptuous, but is it worth the extra pound of weight? The adolescent's world is full of approach/avoidance conflicts, and they can be very stressful. In these circumstances, adolescents often vacillate before deciding. As the adolescent approaches decision time, avoidance tendencies usually dominate (Miller, 1959).

Frustration is another circumstance that produces stress for adolescents. **Frustration** *refers to any situation in which the individual cannot reach a desired goal.* If adolescents want something and cannot have it, they feel frustrated. Adolescents' worlds are full of frustrations that build up to make their lives stressful— not having enough money to buy a car, not getting a good job, not getting an A average, being late for school because of traffic, and not being able to get a date with a particular person. Failures and losses are especially frustrating—for example, not getting grades that are high enough to get into the desired college or losing someone the adolescent is close to through death. Sometimes, the frustrations adolescents experience are major life events—as in the divorce of their parents or the suicide of a friend. Others are an accumulation of daily hassles.

Life Events and Daily Hassles

Adolescents can experience a spectrum of stresses, ranging from ordinary to severe. At the ordinary end are experiences that occur in most adolescents' lives and for which there are reasonably well-defined coping patterns. For example, most parents are aware that siblings are jealous of one another and that, when one sibling does well at something, the other sibling(s) will be jealous. They know how jealousy works and know ways to help adolescents cope with it. More severe stress occurs when children or adolescents become separated from their parents. Healthy coping patterns for this stressful experience are not spelled out well. Some adolescents are well cared for, others are ignored when there is a separation caused by divorce, death, illness, or foster placement (Kreppner, 1989; Sakurai, 1989). Even more severe are the experiences of adolescents who have lived for years in situations of neglect or abuse (Williamson & Borduin, 1989). Victims of incest also experience severe stress, with few coping guidelines.

In many instances, more than one stress occurs at a time in adolescents' lives. Researchers have found that, when several stresses are combined, the effects may be compounded (Brenner, 1984; Rutter & Garmezy, 1983; Rutter & Schopler, 1987). For example, in one investigation, British psychiatrist Michael Rutter (1979) found that boys and girls who were under two chronic life stresses were four times as likely to eventually need psychological services as those who had to cope with only one chronic stress. A similar multiplier effect was found for boys and girls who experienced more than one short-term strain at a time.

Recently, psychologists have emphasized that life's daily experiences as well as life's major events may be the culprits in stress. Enduring a tense family and living in poverty do not show up on scales of major life events in adolescents' development, yet the everyday pounding adolescents experience in these living

Economic factors can produce stress. In recent investigations, economic hardship in Iowa brought on by crisis in the agricultural industry was associated with inconsistent parenting, as well as increased drug use, delinquency, and depression (Clark-Lempers, Lempers, & Netusil, 1990; Lempers, Clark-Lempers, & Simons, 1989).

conditions can add up to a highly stressful life and, eventually, psychological disturbance or illness (Bowker & Hymel, 1991; Compas, 1989; Compas & Wagner, 1991; Conger & others, 1989; Ebata, 1991; Greene, 1989; Lazarus & Folkman, 1984; Lempers, Clark-Lempers, & Simons, 1989). In one recent investigation, 16- to 18-year-old adolescents who experienced the most daily hassles had the most negative self-images (Tolan, Miller, & Thomas, 1988).

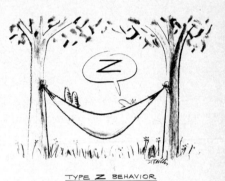

TYPE **Z** BEHAVIOR

Drawing by D. Reilly; © 1987 The New Yorker Magazine, Inc.

Personality Factors—Type-A Behavior Pattern

Are aspects of adolescents' personalities associated with adolescents' stress and health? In recent years, researchers have focused the most attention in this area on the **Type-A behavior pattern,** *a cluster of characteristics—excessively competitive, hard-driven, impatient, irritable, and hostile—thought to be related to coronary problems.* Most research on the Type-A behavior pattern has been conducted with adults (Friedman & Rosenman, 1974; Siegman & Dembrowski, 1989). Recently, researchers have examined the different components of Type-A behavior to determine a more precise link with coronary risk. People who are hostile or consistently turn anger inward are more likely to develop heart disease (Williams, 1989). Hostile, angry individuals have been labeled "hot reactors," meaning that they have intense physiological reactions to stress—their hearts race, their breathing hurries, and their muscles tense up, which could lead to heart disease. Behavioral medicine researcher Redford Williams believes that everyone has the ability to control anger and to develop more trust in others, which he thinks will reduce the risk for heart disease.

Researchers have recently examined the Type-A behavior pattern in children and adolescents and found that Type-A children and adolescents have more illnesses, cardiovascular symptoms, muscle tension, and sleep disturbances (Murray & others, 1988; Thoresen & others, 1985). Some researchers have found that Type-A children and adolescents are more likely to have Type-A parents; this association is strongest for fathers and sons (Weidner & others, 1988). In one investigation, when Type-A parents were observed interacting with their sons and daughters, the parents often criticized their offsprings' failures and compared their performances to those of others (Eagleston & others, 1986). Such stressful family circumstances may set the tone for ineffective ways of coping with stress and a tendency to develop cardiovascular symptoms.

In one recent study, the components of Type-A behavior that were associated with a low level of competent functioning were being impatient and being aggressively competitive.

As in research on adults, when studying children and adolescents, it is important to determine which components of the Type-A behavior pattern are associated more strongly with coronary-prone behavior and low levels of competence than others. In one recent study of 990 adolescents, the components of the Type-A behavior pattern that were associated with a low level of competent functioning (low self-esteem, low achievement standard, and external locus of control) were being impatient and aggressively competitive (Keltikangas-Järvinen & Raikkonen, 1990). Another important question about the Type-A behavior pattern in children and adolescents involves its stability over the childhood and adolescent years. In one study, the Type-A behavior pattern was more stable in adolescence than in childhood (Steinberg, 1986). And in another recent study, the most stable component of the Type-A behavior pattern over time was the impatience-aggression component (Keltikangas-Järvinen, 1990). Nonetheless, researchers still have not documented whether Type-A children or adolescents grow up to become Type-A adults and have more coronary problems as adults.

Cognitive Factors

Most of us think of stress as environmental events that place demands on our lives, such as losing one's notes from a class, being yelled at by a friend, failing a test, or being in a car wreck. While there are some common ways that adolescents and adults experience stress, not everyone perceives the same events as stressful. For example, one adolescent may perceive an upcoming interview for college admission as threatening, while another adolescent may perceive it as challenging. One adolescent may perceive a D grade on a paper as threatening, while another adolescent may perceive the same grade as challenging. To some degree, then, what is stressful for adolescents depends on how they cognitively appraise and interpret events. This view has been most clearly presented by stress researcher Richard Lazarus (1966, 1990). **Cognitive appraisal** *is Lazarus's term that describes individuals' interpretation of events in their lives as harmful, threatening, or challenging, and their determination of whether they have the resources to effectively cope with the event.*

In Lazarus's view, events are appraised in two steps: primary appraisal and secondary appraisal. In **primary appraisal,** *adolescents interpret whether an event involves harm or loss that has already occurred, a threat to some future danger, or a challenge to be overcome. Harm* is adolescents' appraisal of the damage the event has already inflicted. For example, if an adolescent skipped school yesterday and missed an exam, the harm has already been done. *Threat* is adolescents' appraisal of potential future damage an event may bring. For example, missing the exam may lower the teacher's opinion of the adolescent and increase the probability that the adolescent will get a low grade in the course at the end of the semester. *Challenge* is adolescents' appraisal of the potential to overcome the adverse circumstances of an event and ultimately profit from the event. For example, the adolescent who skipped school and missed the exam may develop a commitment to never get into that situation again and thus become a better student.

After adolescents cognitively appraise an event for its harm, threat, or challenge, Lazarus says that they subsequently engage in secondary appraisal. In **secondary appraisal,** *adolescents evaluate their resources and determine how effectively they can be used to cope with the event.* This appraisal is called *secondary* because it comes after primary appraisal and depends on the degree to which the event has been appraised as harmful, threatening, or challenging. Coping involves a wide range of potential strategies, skills, and abilities for effectively managing stressful events. For example, if the adolescent who missed the exam learns that the teacher will give a makeup exam two days later, the adolescent may not experience much stress. However, if the teacher says that the adolescent has to write a lengthy term paper for missing the test, the adolescent may cognitively appraise the situation and determine that this additional requirement places considerable demands on his or her time and wonder whether this requirement can be met. In this case, the adolescent's secondary appraisal indicates a more stressful situation than simply having to take a makeup test several days later (Sears & others, 1988).

Lazarus believes that adolescents' experience of stress is a balance of primary and secondary appraisal. When harm and threat are high, and challenge and resources are low, stress is likely to be high; when harm and threat are low, and challenge and resources are high, stress is more likely to be moderate or low.

Sociocultural Factors

Among the sociocultural factors involved in stress are acculturative stress and socioeconomic status, each of which we consider in turn.

Acculturative Stress

Acculturation *refers to cultural change that results from continuous, first-hand contact between two distinctive cultural groups.* **Acculturative stress** *is the negative consequence of acculturation.* Members of ethnic minority groups have historically encountered hostility, prejudice, and lack of effective support during crises, which contributes to alienation, social isolation, and heightened stress (Huang & Gibbs, 1989). As upwardly mobile ethnic minority families have attempted to penetrate all-White neighborhoods, interracial tensions often mount. Similarly, racial tensions and hostility often emerge among the various ethnic minorities as they each struggle for limited housing and employment opportunities, seeking a fair share of a limited market. Clashes become inevitable as Hispanic family markets spring up in Black urban neighborhoods, as Vietnamese

(a)

(c)

(b)

Confronted with overt or covert attempts at segregation, many ethnic minority groups have developed their own communities and social structures, which include (a) Black churches, one of which is attended by this church youth group; (b) Indian "bands" and tribal associations, as reflected in this Native American celebration, and (c) Mexican American kin systems, as reflected in this large extended family gathering.

extended families displace Puerto Rican apartment dwellers, and as the increasing enrollment of Asian students on college campuses is perceived as a threat to affirmative action policies by other non-White ethnic minority students.

While race relations in the United States have historically been conceptualized as Black/White, this is no longer the only combination of racial animosity. As the numbers of Hispanics and Asians have increased dramatically, and as Native Americans have crossed the boundaries of their reservations, the visibility of these groups has brought them in contact not only with the mainstream White society, but with one another as well. Depending on the circumstances, this contact has sometimes been harmonious, sometimes antagonistic.

Although the dominant White society has tried on many occasions to enslave or dispossess entire populations, these ethnic minority groups have survived and flourished. In the face of severe stress and oppression, they have shown remarkable resilience and adaptation. Confronted with overt or covert attempts at segregation, they have developed their own communities and social structures, including Black churches, Vietnamese mutual assistance associations, Chinese American family associations, Japanese-language schools, Indian "bands" and tribal associations, and Mexican American kin systems, at the same time they learn to negotiate with the dominant White culture in America. They essentially have mastered two cultures and have developed impressive competencies and coping strategies for adapting to life in America. The resilience and adaptation of ethnic minority groups can teach us much about coping and survival in the face of overwhelming adversity.

Sociologist Deborah Belle, shown here interviewing a young girl, has documented how poverty imposes considerable stress on children. Chronic life conditions, such as inadequate housing, dangerous neighborhoods, burdensome responsibilities, and economic uncertainties are potent stressors in the lives of the poor.

Socioeconomic Status

Poverty imposes considerable stress on adolescents and their families (Belle, 1990). Chronic life conditions, such as inadequate housing, dangerous neighborhoods, burdensome responsibilities, and economic uncertainties are potent stressors in the lives of the poor. The incidence of poverty is especially pronounced among ethnic minority adolescents and their families. For example, Black women heading families face a risk of poverty that is more than 10 times that of White men heading families. Puerto Rican female family heads face a poverty rate that is almost 15 times that found among White male family heads (National Advisory Council on Economic Opportunities, 1980). Many individuals who become poor during their lives remain poor for one or two years. However, Blacks and female family heads are at risk for experiencing persistent poverty. The average poor Black child experiences poverty for almost 20 years (Wilson & Neckerman, 1986).

Poverty is related to threatening and uncontrollable events in adolescents' lives (Belle, 1990; Russo, 1990). For example, poor females are more likely to experience crime and violence than middle-class females (Belle & others, 1981). Poverty also undermines sources of social support that play a role in buffering the effects of stress.

Coping with Stress

If you think back to the first two weeks of this class, you may remember students who used to sit near you who do not come to class anymore. Every semester, several students stop showing up for classes, often after the first exam. They never talk to the instructor about their performance in the class, and they do not go through the proper procedures for dropping the class. The result of their immediate stress avoidance is having to face the delayed stressful circumstance of getting an F on their record at the end of the semester. Students also sometimes strike out in anger when faced with stress. One student who flunked one of my classes came to my office and delivered a few choice epithets after he received his grade. The next day, he returned to apologize, saying that he deserved the F and that he had also failed two other classes. The behaviors of these two types

PERSPECTIVE ON ADOLESCENT DEVELOPMENT 16.1

A Cognitive Stress-Reduction Program for Adolescents

Many adolescent stressors occur on a persistent, daily basis. Academic pressure and competition, career and higher-education goals, dating anxieties, peer pressure, parental expectations, and parent-adolescent conflict often require coping and adaptation by adolescents (Omizo, Omizo, & Suzuki, 1988). For some adolescents, the stress becomes overwhelming because they engage in extensive cognitive distortions (Johnson, 1986). Most cognitive stress-reduction programs have been conducted with adults. Might a cognitive stress-reduction program also work with adolescents under considerable stress?

In one recent cognitive stress-reduction program, 16-to 17-year-old males were randomly assigned to either a cognitive intervention program or a waiting list control group (Hains & Szyjakowski, 1990). The training procedure had three phases: conceptualization, skill acquisition and rehearsal, and application. Each phase began with a one-hour group session, followed by two individual sessions.

In the *conceptualization phase,* adolescents were told that the purpose of the project was to help them identify irrational cognitions (self-defeating cognitions) that often promote stress and anger, and to learn how to restructure these cognitions. Then the adolescents were trained to monitor their irrational cognitions. In the *skill acquisition and rehearsal phase,* adolescents were shown how to challenge, examine the evidence for, and restructure the self-defeating cognitions that they had learned to identify during the conceptualization phase. In addition to the cognitive restructuring training, adolescents also were taught how to use self-instructions as a means of further coping with stress-provoking events. Then, the therapist and the adolescent discussed what rational responses or self-instructions could be used as substitute thoughts in certain situations. In the *application phase,* adolescents continued to practice their coping skills and prepared for potential stressful events.

The adolescents in the stress-reduction program subsequently had lower anxiety and anger, improved self-esteem, and increased positive cognitions in a hypothetical stressful situation. These treatment gains were maintained at a 10-week follow-up.

of students—those who avoid stress and those who discharge anger—are two often ineffective ways of coping with stress. What are the best strategies for coping with stress?

Removal of Stress, Defense Mechanisms, and Problem-Focused Coping

Stress is so abundant in American society that adolescents are often confronted with more than one stressor at the same time. A college student might be taking an extra course load, not have enough money to eat regularly, and be having problems in a relationship. As mentioned earlier in the chapter, researchers have found that, when several stressors are simultaneously experienced, the effects can be compounded (Rutter & Garmezy, 1983). For example, in one investigation, individuals who were under two chronic life stressors were four times more likely to eventually need psychological services as those who only had to cope with one chronic stressor (Rutter, 1979). Thus, the student with the school, financial, and relationship stressors would likely benefit from removal of one of the stressors, such as dropping one class and taking a normal course load.

Richard Lazarus (1966, 1990) believes that coping takes one of two forms. **Problem-focused coping** *is Lazarus's term for the cognitive strategy used in coping with stress by individuals who face their troubles and try to solve them.* For example, if you are having trouble with a class, you might go to the study skills center at your college or university and enter a training program to learn how to study more effectively. You have faced your problem and attempted to do something about it. More about cognitive strategies for reducing adolescents' stress appears in Perspective on Adolescent Development 16.1.

Emotion-focused coping *is Lazarus's term for coping with stress in which individuals respond to stress in an emotional manner, especially using defensive appraisal.* Emotion-focused coping involves using defense mechanisms, as discussed in Chapter 2. In emotion-focused coping, adolescents might avoid something, rationalize what has happened to them, deny that it is occurring, or laugh it off. Adolescents who use emotion-focused coping might avoid going to school, saying that school does not matter, deny that they are having a problem, and laugh and joke about it with their friends. In one investigation, depressed individuals used more avoidant coping strategies than nondepressed individuals (Ebata & Moos, 1989).

There are times when emotion-focused coping is adaptive. For example, denial is one of the main protective psychological mechanisms that enables adolescents to cope with the flood of feelings that occur when the reality of death or dying becomes too great. In other circumstances, emotion-focused coping is not adaptive. Adolescents who deny that they are not doing well in school, when in reality they are flunking two classes, are not responding adaptively. Neither are adolescents who deny that the person they were dating does not love them anymore, when in reality that person is going steady with someone else. However, denial can be used to avoid the destructive impact of shock by postponing the time when adolescents have to deal with stress. Over the long term, though, adolescents should use problem-focused rather than emotion-focused coping (Blanchard-Fields & Robinson, 1987; Ebata, 1991). Would thinking positively also help adolescents to cope with stress?

Positive Thinking and Self-Efficacy

"Don't worry, be happy" goes the words of the popular tune by Bobby McFerrin, "Cause when you worry, your face will frown, and that will bring everybody down. . . ." Is McFerrin's cheerful optimism a good coping strategy for adolescents? Most of the time, adolescents *do* want to avoid negative thinking when handling stress. A positive mood improves adolescents' ability to process information more efficiently, makes them more altruistic, and gives them higher self-esteem. An optimistic attitude is superior to a pessimistic one in most instances, producing a sense that adolescents are controlling their environment, or what cognitive social learning theorist Albert Bandura (1986, 1989) calls *self-efficacy*. A negative mood increases adolescents' chances of getting angry, feeling guilty, and magnifying their mistakes. Several months before 17-year-old Michael Chang became the youngest male to win the French Open Tennis Championships in 1989, sports psychologist Jim Loehr (1989) pieced together videotaped segments of the most outstanding points Chang had played during the past year. Chang periodically watched the videotape, always seeing himself winning and in a positive mood and never seeing himself making mistakes.

For a number of years, seeing reality as accurately as possible was described as the best path to health for adolescents. Recently, though, researchers have found increasing evidence that maintaining some positive illusions about one's self and the world is healthy. Happy adolescents often have high opinions of themselves, give self-serving explanations for events, and have exaggerated beliefs about their ability to control the world around them (Snyder, 1988; Taylor & others, 1988).

Illusions, whether positive or negative, are related to adolescents' self-esteem. Adolescents may have thoughts about themselves that are too grandiose or too negative, and both have negative consequences. Rather, the ideal overall orientation may be an optimal margin of illusion in which adolescents see themselves as slightly more positive than they actually are (see Figure 16.4). For some ad-

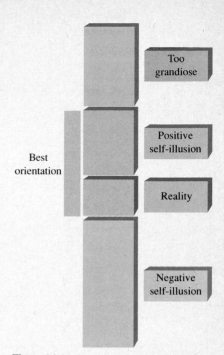

Figure 16.4 Reality and self-illusion. In Baumeister's model of self-illusion, the most healthy adolescents often have self-illusions that are slightly more positive than reality dictates. Having too grandiose an opinion of one's self or thinking negatively about one's self can have negative consequences. For some adolescents, seeing things too accurately may be too depressing. Overall, in most contexts, a reality orientation or a slightly positive self-illusion may be most effective.

olescents, seeing things too accurately can lead to depression. Seeing one's suffering as meaningless and random does not help adolescents to cope and move forward, even if the suffering *is* random and meaningless. An absence of positive illusions may also thwart adolescents from undertaking the risky and ambitious projects that yield the greatest rewards (Baumeister, 1989).

In some cases, though, a strategy of defensive pessimism may actually work best in handling stress. By imagining negative outcomes, adolescents prepare themselves for forthcoming stressful circumstances (Norem & Cantor, 1986). For example, an honors student may be worried that she will flunk the next test. For her, thoughts of failure may not be paralyzing but instead may motivate her to do everything necessary to ensure that she will do well on the test. By imagining potential problems, she may develop relevant strategies for dealing with or preventing negative outcomes. Positive *and* negative thinking, then, are involved in coping with stress.

At this point, we have found that such factors as removing stress, reducing the use of defense mechanisms, increasing problem-focused coping, thinking positively, and following a self-efficacy strategy can help adolescents to cope with stress. As we see next, psychologists increasingly believe that support systems are also extremely valuable in helping adolescents to cope with stress.

Support Systems

Adolescents' physical and social worlds are more crowded, polluted, noisy, and achievement-oriented than those of their counterparts who lived a century ago. In such a world, support systems are often needed to buffer stress. Close, positive attachments to others—especially to family and friends—consistently show up as important buffers to stress in adolescents' lives (East, 1989; Gottlieb, 1991; O'Brien, 1990; Youniss & Smollar, 1985). In one recent study, adolescents coped with stress better when they had a close affective relationship with their mothers (Wagner, Cohen, & Brook, 1991). In one recent investigation, peers were the most likely source of overall support for adolescents, followed by mothers (O'Brien, 1990). In this study, peers provided more support than siblings in all categories and more than both parents in all areas except financial support, future/career planning, and personal values. Siblings provided more support for dating than mothers. Patterns of support seeking were generally similar across gender, but when differences did exist, female adolescents were more likely than their male counterparts to go to peers and mothers for support. In future/career planning, life-style, dating support, and personal values, male adolescents were as likely to seek support from fathers as from mothers.

Multiple Coping Strategies

As we have seen, there are many different ways for adolescents to cope effectively—and ineffectively—with stress. An important point about effective coping strategies is that adolescents can often use more than one to help them deal with stress. For example, the advice to an adolescent who is experiencing a great deal

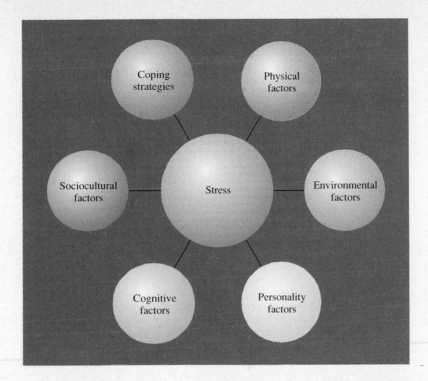

Figure 16.5 Factors involved in adolescents' stress. Among the most important factors involved in understanding adolescents' stress are: physical factors (the body's response to stress), environmental factors, personality factors, cognitive factors, sociocultural factors, and coping strategies.

of stress might include: develop a more trusting attitude, reduce your anger, set aside time for play and relaxation, make sure you have one or two friends in whom you can confide, quit smoking, lose weight, exercise several times a week, use problem-focused coping strategies, and develop more positive images of yourself. One of these alone may not be able to turn the tide against stress, but a combination of them may be effective.

As with other aspects of adolescents' lives, adolescents' stress is not determined by a single factor but, rather, by multiple factors (Susman, 1991). Among the most important factors that determine whether adolescents will experience stress are physical factors (such as the body's response to stress), environmental factors (such as overload, conflict, and frustration, as well as life events and daily hassles), personality factors (such as the impatience and anger involved in the Type-A behavior pattern), cognitive factors (such as cognitive appraisal), sociocultural factors (such as acculturative stress and poverty), and adolescents' coping strategies (such as removing stress, reducing defense mechanisms, increasing problem-focused coping, developing positive thinking and self-efficacy, enlisting the help of support systems, and using multiple coping strategies). A summary of these factors involved in stress is presented in Figure 16.5.

At this point, we have discussed a number of ideas about stress and coping. A summary of these ideas is presented in Concept Table 16.2. You have arrived at the end of *Adolescence*'s 16 chapters, but following this chapter is a brief "Epilogue" that contains some stimulating thoughts about adolescents.

Concept Table 16.2

Stress and Coping

Concept	Processes/Related Ideas	Characteristics/Description
Stress	What is stress?	Stress is the response of individuals to the circumstances and events, called stressors, that threaten them and tax their coping abilities.
	The body's response to stress	Selye's general adaptation syndrome (GAS) describes the common effects of stress on adolescents' bodies. The GAS consists of three stages: alarm, resistance, and exhaustion. Not all stress is bad—Selye calls good stress eustress. Critics argue that we also need to know about such factors as adolescents' coping strategies for stress.
	Environmental factors	Stress is produced because stimuli become so intense and prolonged that adolescents cannot cope. Three types of conflict are approach/approach, avoidance/avoidance, and approach/avoidance. Frustration occurs when adolescents cannot reach a desired goal. Stress may be produced by major life events or by daily hassles in adolescents' lives.
	Personality factors—Type-A behavior pattern	The Type-A behavior pattern refers to a cluster of characteristics—excessively competitive, hard-driven, impatient, irritable, and hostile—thought to be related to coronary problems. Researchers who examined the Type-A behavior pattern in children and adolescents found that Type-A children and adolescents have more illnesses, cardiovascular symptoms, muscle tension, and sleep disturbances, and that Type-A children and adolescents are more likely to have Type-A parents.
	Cognitive factors	Lazarus believes that adolescents' stress depends on how they cognitively appraise and interpret events. Cognitive appraisal is Lazarus's term that describes individuals' interpretation of events in their lives as harmful, threatening, or challenging (primary appraisal), and their determination of whether they have the resources to effectively cope with the event (secondary appraisal).
	Sociocultural factors	Acculturation refers to cultural change that results from continuous, first-hand contact between two distinctive cultural groups. Acculturative stress refers to the negative consequences of acculturation. Members of ethnic minority groups have historically encountered hostility, prejudice, and lack of effective support during crises, which contributes to alienation, social isolation, and heightened stress. Poverty also imposes considerable stress on adolescents and their families. Chronic life conditions, such as inadequate housing, dangerous neighborhoods, burdensome responsibilities, and economic uncertainties are potent stressors in the lives of the poor. The incidence of poverty is especially pronounced among ethnic minority adolescents and their families.
Coping with stress	Removal of stress, defense mechanisms, and problem-focused coping	Most adolescents are confronted with more than one stressor. Removing one stressor can be very beneficial. In most cases, problem-focused coping is better than emotion-focused coping and the use of defense mechanisms, especially in coping with stress over the long term.
	Positive thinking and self-efficacy	Most of the time, adolescents should think positively and avoid negative thoughts. An optimistic attitude produces a sense of self-efficacy. Positive self-illusions can improve some adolescents' lives, but it is important to guard against unrealistic expectations. A strategy of defensive pessimism helps some adolescents to cope more effectively.
	Support systems	Close, positive attachments to others—especially to family and friends—consistently show up as important buffers to stress in adolescents' lives.
	Multiple coping strategies	Adolescents often can and should use more than one coping strategy in dealing with stress.

Summary

I. Health Psychology and Behavioral Medicine
Today, we recognize the power of life-style and psychological states in promoting adolescents' health. Health psychology is a multidimensional approach to health that emphasizes psychological factors, life-style, and the nature of the health-care delivery system. Behavioral medicine is a field closely related to health psychology; it attempts to combine medical and behavioral knowledge to reduce illness and to promote health.

II. Causes of Death in Adolescence
The three leading causes of death in adolescence are accidents (most of which involve motor vehicles), suicide, and homicide. The mortality rate for adolescents is higher among older than younger adolescents. Homicide rates are especially high among Black males who live in urban, low socioeconomic status neighborhoods. Male adolescents die at a rate more than twice that of their female peers.

III. Cognitive Factors in Health and Illness
Cognitive factors in adolescents' health behavior include: concepts of health behavior, which develop in concert with Piaget's stages (adolescents' health concepts are more abstract and are more likely to emphasize multiple determinants of health than children's); beliefs about health (adolescents and adults underestimate their vulnerability to health problems and illness); health knowledge (adolescents are generally poorly informed about health issues and have significant misperceptions about health); and decision making (adolescents are better at making decisions about health than children but worse at making such decisions than adults).

IV. Sociocultural Factors in Health and Illness
Sociocultural factors influence health through their roles in setting cultural norms about health, through social relationships that provide emotional support, and through the encouragement of healthy or unhealthy behaviors. There are large within-group differences in living conditions and life-styles that affect the health of ethnic minority adolescents, and these differences are influenced by social class, status as an immigrant, social skills, language skills, occupational opportunities, and social resources. Family influences also are important. Positive health is best achieved when adolescents develop a sense of autonomy within a supportive family framework. In addition to social support, parents and older siblings are important models of health. Peers and friends also play important roles in adolescents' health behavior.

V. Health Services
While adolescents have a greater number of acute health conditions than do adults, they use private physician services and other health-care systems at lower rates than any other age group. Health services are especially unlikely to meet the needs of younger adolescents, ethnic minority adolescents, and adolescents living in poverty. Among the chief barriers to better health services for adolescents are cost, poor organization, availability, and confidentiality of care. Also, few health-care providers receive any special training in working with adolescents.

VI. Dangers of Cigarette Smoking
In 1989, the surgeon general released a report that presented new evidence to show that smoking is even more harmful than previously thought. Traditional school health programs have had little impact on reducing smoking. Current prevention efforts with adolescents focus on coping with social pressures from family, peers, and the media.

VII. Nutrition

The recommended range of energy intake for adolescents takes into account their different needs, their growth rate, and their level of exercise. Some adolescents' bodies burn energy faster than others. A key concept is basal metabolism rate (BMR), the minimum amount of energy an individual uses in a resting state. Many adolescents have too much fat in their diet.

VIII. Eating Disorders, Exercise, and Toward Healthier Adolescent Lives

Three prominent eating disorders in adolescence are obesity, anorexia nervosa, and bulimia. Heredity, set point, BMR, insulin level, glucose level in the blood, and exercise are key aspects of understanding the nature of obesity in adolescence. A large percentage of obese adolescents become obese adults. Anorexia nervosa involves relentless pursuit of thinness through starvation. Adolescent females are especially susceptible to this eating disorder. Bulimia involves a binge-and-purge pattern on a regular basis. Societal, psychological, and physiological explanations of these eating disorders have been proposed. Experts agree that children and adolescents are not getting enough exercise. Television and U.S. schools have been criticized for contributing to the poor exercise patterns of adolescents. Most adolescents also say that their parents are poor role models in the realm of exercise. An exciting possibility is that exercise can serve as a buffer to stress. Recommendations for the year 2000 include: preventive services, health promotion, and satisfaction of the health needs of special adolescent populations, such as Black American and Hispanic American adolescents.

IX. The Nature of Stress, the Body's Response to Stress, and Environmental Factors

Stress is the response of individuals to the circumstances and events, called stressors, that threaten them and tax their coping abilities. Selye's general adaptation syndrome (GAS) describes the common effects of stress on adolescents' bodies. The GAS consists of three stages: alarm, resistance, and exhaustion. Not all stress is bad—Selye calls good stress eustress. Critics argue that we also need to know about such factors as adolescents' coping strategies for stress. Stress is produced because stimuli become so intense and prolonged that adolescents cannot cope. Three types of conflict are approach/approach, avoidance/avoidance, and approach/avoidance. Frustration occurs when adolescents cannot reach a desired goal. Stress may be produced by major life events or by daily hassles in adolescents' lives.

X. Personality Factors (Type-A Behavior Pattern) and Cognitive Factors in Stress

The Type-A behavior pattern refers to a cluster of characteristics—excessively competitive, hard-driven, impatient, irritable, and hostile—thought to be related to coronary problems. Researchers who examined the Type-A behavior pattern in children and adolescents found that Type-A children and adolescents have more illnesses, cardiovascular symptoms, muscle tension, and sleep disturbances, and that Type-A children and adolescents are more likely to have Type-A parents. Lazarus believes that adolescents' stress depends on how they cognitively appraise and interpret events. Cognitive appraisal is Lazarus's term that describes individuals' interpretation of events in their lives as harmful, threatening, or challenging (primary appraisal), and their determination of whether they have the resources to effectively cope with the event (secondary appraisal).

XI. Sociocultural Factors in Stress

Acculturation refers to cultural change that results from continuous, first-hand contact between two distinctive cultural groups. Acculturative stress refers to the negative consequences of acculturation. Members of ethnic minority groups have historically encountered hostility, prejudice, and lack of effective support during crises, which contributes to alienation, social isolation, and heightened stress. Poverty also imposes considerable stress on adolescents and their families. Chronic life conditions, such as inadequate housing, dangerous neighborhoods, burdensome responsibilities, and economic uncertainties, are potent stressors in the lives of the poor. The incidence of poverty is especially pronounced among ethnic minority adolescents and their families.

XII. Coping with Stress

Most adolescents are confronted with more than one stressor. Removing one stressor can be very beneficial. In most cases, problem-focused coping is better than emotion-focused coping and the use of defense mechanisms, especially in coping with stress over the long term. Most of the time, adolescents should think positively and avoid negative thoughts. An optimistic attitude produces a sense of self-efficacy. Positive self-illusions can improve some adolescents' lives, but it is important to guard against unrealistic expectations. A strategy of defensive pessimism helps some adolescents to cope more effectively. Close, positive attachments to others—especially to family and friends—consistently show up as important buffers to stress in adolescents' lives. Adolescents can and should use more than one coping strategy in dealing with stress.

Key Terms

health psychology 543
behavioral medicine 543
basal metabolism rate
  (BMR) 549
set point 551
anorexia nervosa 553
bulimia 553
aerobic exercise 554
stress 558
general adaptation
  syndrome (GAS) 558

eustress 558
burnout 559
approach/approach
  conflict 559
avoidance/avoidance
  conflict 559
approach/avoidance
  conflict 560
frustration 560
Type-A behavior pattern
  561

cognitive appraisal 562
primary appraisal 563
secondary appraisal 563
acculturation 563
acculturative stress 563
problem-focused
  coping 566
emotion-focused
  coping 567

Suggested Readings

Brenner, A. (1984). *Helping children cope with stress.* Lexington, MA: D.C. Heath.
  An excellent, insightful portrayal of children's and young adolescents' ways of coping with stress. Includes many case examples.
Brone, R. J., & Fisher, C. B. (1988). Determinants of adolescent obesity: A comparison with anorexia nervosa. *Adolescence, 23,* 155–169.
  Describes similarities in the factors contributing to obesity and anorexia nervosa, especially family factors.
Bruch, H., Czyzewski, D., & Suhr, M. A. (1988). *Conversations with anorexics.* New York: Basic Books.
  Describes fifty years of clinical experiences with anorexics. Conversations encourage the adolescent to actively explore the past and search for solutions in the present.
Journal of School Health
  Includes a number of articles about children's nutrition, health, illness, and exercise. Leaf through the issues of the last several years to get a feel for the type of interventions being used in school settings to improve children's health.
Millstein, S. G., & Litt, I. F. (1990). Adolescent health. In S. S. Feldman & G. R. Elliott (Eds.), *At the threshold: The developing adolescent.* Cambridge, MA: Harvard University Press.
  An excellent, very contemporary review of research on adolescent health.
Williams, S. R., & Worthington, B. S. (1988). *Nutrition through the life cycle.* St. Louis, MO: Times Mirror/Mosby.
  Brings together information about nutrition and eating behavior at different periods in the human life cycle. Separate chapters focus on nutrition in childhood and nutrition in adolescence.

EPILOGUE

We have come to the end of this book. I hope you can now look back and say that you learned a lot about adolescents, not only other adolescents but yourself as an adolescent and how your adolescent years contributed to who you are today. The insightful words of philosopher Søren Kierkegaard capture the importance of looking backward to understand ourselves: "Life is lived forward, but understood backwards." I also hope that those of you who become the parents of adolescents or work with adolescents in some capacity—whether teacher, counselor, or community leader—feel that you now have a better grasp of what adolescence is all about. I leave you with the following montage of thoughts and images that convey the power, complexity, and beauty of adolescence in the human life cycle:

In no order of things is adolescence the time of simple life. Adolescents feel like they can last forever, think they know everything, and are quite sure about it. They clothe themselves with rainbows and go brave as the zodiac, flashing from one end of the world to the other both in mind and body. In many ways, today's adolescents are privileged, wielding unprecedented economic power. At the same time, they move through a seemingly endless preparation for life. They try on one face after another, seeking to find a face of their own. In their most pimply and awkward moments, they become acquainted with sex. They play furiously at "adult games" but are confined to a society of their own peers. They want their parents to understand them and hope that their parents will accord them the privilege of understanding them. Their generation of young people is the fragile cable by which the best and the worst of their parents' generation is transmitted to the present. In the end, there are only two lasting gifts parents can leave youth—one is roots, the other is wings.

John W. Santrock

575

Glossary

abnormal behavior This is behavior that is maladaptive and harmful. *501*

abstract relations This is Fischer's term for the ability of an adolescent to coordinate two or more abstract ideas; it often appears for the first time between 14 and 16 years of age. *133*

accommodation This occurs when individuals adjust to new knowledge. *55*

acculturation This refers to cultural change that results from continuous first-hand contact between two cultural groups. *563*

acculturative stress This is the negative consequence of acculturation. *563*

achievement motivation This is the desire to accomplish something, to reach a standard of excellence, and to expend effort to excel. *470*

achievement test This type of test measures what has been learned, or what skills have been mastered. *167*

addiction This occurs when the body is physically dependent on a drug. *504*

adolescence Because of the combined factors of age and sociohistorical influences, this developmental period is defined as the transition between childhood and adulthood that involves biological, cognitive, and social changes. *29*

adolescent egocentrism This refers to the heightened self-consciousness of adolescents that is reflected in their belief that others are as interested in them as they themselves are and in their sense of a personal uniqueness. *134*

adolescent generalization gap Adelson created this term to mean that widespread generalizations about adolescents have developed that are based on information about a limited, often highly visible group of adolescents. *18*

adoption study In this type of study, investigators seek to discover whether the behavior and psychological characteristics of adopted adolescents are more like their adoptive parents, who provided a home environment, or their biological parents, who contributed to their heredity. *91*

aerobic exercise This is sustained exercise, such as jogging or swimming, that stimulates the heart and lung activity. *554*

affectionate love Also called companionate love, this love occurs when an individual desires to have another person near and has a deep, caring affection for that person. *253*

AIDS Acquired Immune Deficiency Syndrome is a primarily sexually transmitted disease caused by the HIV virus, which destroys the body's immune system. *418*

altruism This is an unselfish interest in helping someone. *450*

amphetamines Called pep pills or uppers, these are widely prescribed stimulants, sometimes in the form of diet pills. *510*

anal stage This second Freudian stage of development occurs between 1 1/2 and 3 years of age. At this stage, the child's greatest pleasure involves the anus or the eliminative functions associated with it. *47*

androgens These are the main class of male sex hormones. *99*

androgyny In this state, there is the presence of desirable masculine and feminine characteristics in the same individual. *380*

anorexia nervosa This eating disorder involves the relentless pursuit of thinness through starvation. *553*

anticonformity This occurs when individuals react counter to a group's expectations and deliberately move away from the actions or beliefs the group advocates. *231*

approach/approach conflict This occurs when an individual must choose between two attractive stimuli or circumstances. *559*

approach/avoidance conflict This occurs when there is a single stimulus or circumstance, but it has both positive and negative characteristics. *560*

aptitude test This type of test predicts an individual's ability to learn a skill, or what the individual can accomplish with training. *167*

aptitude-treatment interaction (ATI) This interaction stresses the importance of both the attitudes and the characteristics of the adolescent, such as academic potential or personality traits, and the treatments or experiences, such as the educational techniques, that the adolescent receives. *279*

assimilation This occurs when individuals incorporate new information into existing knowledge. *55*

assimilation This refers to the absorption of ethnic minority groups into the dominant group, which often means the loss of some or virtually all of the behavior and values of the ethnic minority group. *312*

attention Concentration and the focusing of mental effort is called attention. Attention is both selective and shifting. *150*

attribution theory Individuals are motivated to discover the underlying causes of behavior as part of the effort to make sense out of behavior. *472*

authoritarian parenting This is a restrictive, punitive style that exhorts the adolescent to follow the parent's directions and to respect work and effort. Firm limits and controls are placed on the adolescent, and little verbal exchange is allowed. This style is associated with adolescents' socially incompetent behavior. *195*

authoritative parenting This style encourages adolescents to be independent but still places limits and controls on their actions. Extensive verbal give-and-take is allowed, and parents are warm and nurturant toward the adolescent. This style is associated with adolescents' socially competent behavior. *195*

automaticity This is the ability to perform automatically with little or no effort. *150*

autonomous morality Piaget's second stage of moral development is displayed by older children (about 10 years of age or older). At this stage, the child becomes aware that rules and laws are created by people and that, in judging an action, one should consider the actor's intentions as well as the consequences. *436*

autonomy versus shame and doubt Erikson's second stage occurs in approximately the second year of life. *50*

avoidance/avoidance conflict This occurs when an individual must make a choice between two unattractive stimuli, both of which he or she wants to avoid. *559*

back-to-basics movement This philosophy stresses that the function of schools should be the rigorous training of intellectual skills through such subjects as English, mathematics, and science. *264*

barbiturates Such drugs as Nembutal and Seconal are depressant drugs that induce sleep or reduce anxiety. *512*

basal metabolism rate (BMR) The minimum amount of energy an individual uses in a resting state is the BMR. *549*

behavior genetics This field of study is concerned with the degree and nature of behavior's heredity basis. *90*

behavioral medicine This field is closely related to health psychology in that it attempts to combine medical and behavioral knowledge to reduce illness and promote health. *543*

behaviorism This emphasizes the scientific study of observable behavioral responses and their environmental determinants. *62*

biological processes These processes involve changes in an individual's physical nature. *28*

bulimia In this eating disorder, the individual consistently follows a binge-purge eating pattern. *553*

burnout This is a hopeless, helpless feeling brought on by relentless work-related stress. *559*

canalization This is the process by which characteristics take a narrow path or developmental course since, apparently, preservative forces help buffer a person from environmental extremes. *90*

care perspective This is a moral perspective that views people in terms of their connectedness with others and emphasizes interpersonal communication, relationships with others, and concern for others. *441*

career self-concept theory Super believes that individuals' self-concepts play a central role in their career choice and that in adolescence individuals first construct their career self-concept. *481*

case study This is an in-depth look at an individual; it is used mainly by clinical psychologists when the unique aspects of a person's life cannot be duplicated, either for practical or ethical reasons. *71*

Chicano Reflecting the combination of their Spanish-Mexican-Indian heritage and Anglo influences, Chicano is the name politically conscious Mexican American adolescents give themselves. *315*

chronosystem This system involves the patterning of environmental events and transitions over the life course and their sociohistorical contexts. *66*

classification Class inclusion reasoning is Piaget's concept of concrete operational thought that requires children to systematically organize objects into hierarchies of classes and subclasses. *118*

cliques These units are smaller, involve more intimacy, and are more cohesive than crowds. They are, however, larger and involve less intimacy than friendships. *245*

cocaine This stimulant comes from the coca plant, which is native to Bolivia and Peru. *510*

cognitive appraisal Using this term, Lazarus describes individuals' interpretations of events in their lives as harmful, threatening, or challenging and their determination of whether they have the resources to cope effectively with the event. *562*

cognitive developmental theory This is mainly represented by Piaget's theory, which emphasizes that individuals go through four stages of cognitive development in sequence. Piaget's theory emphasizes the organization and adaptation of thought. *55*

cognitive disequilibrium theory Hoffman's theory states that adolescence is an important period in moral development, in which, because of broader experiences associated with the move to high school or college, individuals recognize that their set of beliefs is but one of many and that there is considerable debate about what is right and wrong. *436*

cognitive monitoring This is the process of taking stock of what one is currently doing, what will be done next, and how effectively the mental activity is unfolding. *152*

cognitive moral education This is an indirect moral education approach that emphasizes that adolescents adopt such values as democracy and justice as their moral reasoning is developed. *453*

cognitive processes Changes in an individual's thought, intelligence, and language are involved in cognitive processes. *28*

cognitive social learning theory of moral development This emphasizes a distinction between adolescents' *moral competence*—the ability to produce moral behaviors—and *moral performance*—behaviors in specific situations. *447*

cohort effects Effects may occur due to an individual's time of birth or generation that have nothing to do with the individual's actual age. *77*

commitment A part of identity development, this is when adolescents show a personal investment in what they are going to do. *349*

community rights versus individual rights In Kohlberg's fifth stage, the person understands that values and laws are relative and that standards vary from one person to another. *438*

computer-assisted instruction This teaching strategy involves using computers as tutors to individualize instruction: to present information, to give students practice, to assess students' level of understanding, and to provide additional information if needed. *155*

concrete operational stage Piaget's third stage lasts from approximately 7 to 11 years of age. In this stage, children can perform operations. Logical reasoning replaces intuitive thought as long as the reasoning can be applied to specific, concrete examples. *58*

conduct disorder This is a psychiatric diagnostic term used when multiple behaviors, such as truancy, cruelty to animals, and excessive fighting, co-occur before the age of 15 in a six-month period. *520*

conformity This occurs when individuals adopt the attitudes or behaviors of others because of real or imagined pressure from them. *229*

conglomerate strategies These strategies, also referred to as coaching, involve the use of a combination of techniques to improve adolescents' social skills. *235*

connectedness This consists of two dimensions: mutuality (sensitivity to and respect for others' views) and permeability (openness to others' views). *351*

conscience This is Freud's component of the superego that involves behaviors not approved of by parents. *448*

consensual validation This explains why adolescents are attracted to others who are similar to themselves. The adolescent's own attitudes and behavior are supported when someone else's attitudes and behavior are similar to theirs. *252*

conservation This is Piaget's term for an individual's ability to recognize that the length, number, mass, quantity, area, weight, and volume of objects do not change through transformations that alter their appearance. *117*

contexts Development occurs in settings called contexts. These settings are influenced by historical, economic, social, and cultural factors. *21*

continuity of development Development is a gradual, cumulative change from conception to death. *32*

continuity view In this view, the emphasis is on the role that early parent-child relationships play in constructing a basic way of relating to others throughout the life span. *189*

conventional reasoning This is Kohlberg's second, or intermediate, level, in which internalization is immediate and individuals abide by the standards of others, such as parents or the laws of society. *438*

convergent thinking This type of thinking produces only one correct answer and is characteristic of the type of thinking elicited by standardized intelligence tests. *175*

cooperative learning This technique involves joint participation by all members of a group in achieving learning goals. Each member contributes to the learning process. *284*

correlational strategy The goal in this strategy is to describe the strength of the relation between two or more events or characteristics. *74*

creativity This is the ability to think about something in a novel and unusual way and to come up with unique solutions to problems. *175*

crisis This is a period of identity development during which the adolescent is choosing among meaningful alternatives. *349*

critical thinking This style of thinking involves grasping the deeper meaning of problems, keeping an open mind about different approaches and perspectives, and deciding for oneself what to do or believe. *154*

cross-cultural studies Studies of this type compare a culture with one or more other cultures. Such studies provide information about the degree to which adolescent development is similar, or universal, across cultures or about the degree to which it is culture-specific. *22, 297*

cross-sectional approach This is a research strategy in which individuals of different ages are compared all at one time. *76*

crowd This is the largest, most loosely defined, and least personal unit of adolescent peer society. Crowds often meet because of their mutual interest in an activity. *245*

cultural-familial retardation This form of retardation is characterized by no evidence of organic brain damage, but the individual's IQ ranges from 50 to 70. *174*

culture This refers to the behavior patterns, beliefs, and all other products of a particular group of people that are passed on from generation to generation. *22, 295*

culture-fair tests These are tests of intelligence that attempt to reduce cultural bias. *170*

date, or acquaintance, rape This is coercive sexual activity directed at someone with whom the individual is at least casually acquainted. *426*

defense mechanisms This is a psychoanalytic term for unconscious methods used by the ego to distort reality in order to protect itself from anxiety. *45*

dependent variable This is the factor that is measured in an experiment; it may change because of the manipulation of the independent variable. *75*

depressants These are drugs that slow the central nervous system, body functions, and behavior. *512*

desatellization This is Ausubel's term that describes the adolescent process of breaking away and becoming independent from parents. *203*

development A pattern of movement or growth begins at conception and continues through the life cycle. Most development involves growth, although it also includes decay (as in death and dying). *28*

developmental career choice theory Ginzberg believes that children and adolescents go through three career-choice stages: fantasy, tentative, and realistic. *479*

developmental construction view This is the belief that as individuals grow up they acquire modes of relating to others. *189*

difficult child This is a child who tends to react negatively and fuss a lot. This child engages in irregular daily routines and is slow to accept new experiences. *92*

direct moral education This involves either emphasizing values or character traits during specified time slots or integrating those values or traits throughout the curriculum. *452*

discontinuity of development Development occurs in distinct stages throughout the life span. *32*

discontinuity view In this view, the emphasis is on change and variety in relationships over time. *190*

divergent thinking This type of thinking produces many different answers to one question and is more characteristic of creativity than traditional intelligence. *175*

early adolescence This period roughly corresponds to the middle school or junior high school years and includes most pubertal changes. *29*

early adulthood This is the developmental period that usually begins in the late teens or early twenties and lasts through the thirties. *30*

early childhood Early childhood is the developmental period that extends from the end of infancy to about five or six years of age. Early childhood is sometimes called the preschool years. *28*

early formal operational thought In this portion of the stage, adolescents' increased ability to think in hypothetical ways produces unconstrained thought with unlimited possibilities. In this early period, formal operational thought submerges reality, and there is an excess of assimilation as the world is perceived too subjectively and idealistically. *121*

easy child This is a child who is generally in a positive mood, quickly establishes regular routines, and adapts easily to new experiences. *92*

ecological theories These emphasize the role of social contexts in development. *65*

ego The Freudian structure of personality that deals with the demands of reality is the ego. *44*

ego-ideal This is Freud's component of the superego that involves ideal standards approved by parents. *448*

emic approach In this approach, the goal is to describe behavior in one culture or ethnic group in terms that are meaningful and important to the people in that group, without regard to other cultures or ethnic groups. *72*

emotion-focused coping This is Lazarus's term for coping with stress in which individuals respond to stress in an emotional manner, especially using defensive appraisal. *567*

emotional isolation Often experienced by single, divorced, or widowed adults, this type of loneliness arises when a person lacks an intimate attachment relationship. *359*

empathy This means reacting to another's feelings with an emotional response that is similar to the other's response. *450*

epigenetic principle This is Erikson's term for the process that guides development through the life cycle. This principle states that anything that has growth has a blueprint, with each part having a special time of ascendancy until all of the parts have arisen to form a functioning whole. *50*

erogenous zones The parts of the body that have especially strong pleasure-giving qualities at each stage of development are called erogenous zones. *47*

estradiol This is an estrogen that plays an important role in female pubertal development. *99*

estrogens These are the main class of female sex hormones. *99*

ethnic identity A person develops a sense of membership based on the shared language, religion, customs, values, history, and race of an ethnic group. *22*

ethnicity Derived from the Greek word for nation, ethnicity is based on cultural heritage, nationality characteristics, race, religion, and language. *22, 295*

ethnocentrism A tendency to favor one's group over other groups is called ethnocentrism. *296*

etic approach The goal in this approach is to describe behaviors so that generalizations can be made across cultures. *73*

eustress This is Selye's concept of the positive effects of stress. *558*

exosystem This system is involved when experiences in another social setting—in which the individual does not have an active role—influence what the individual experiences in an immediate context. *65*

experience sampling method This research method consists of participants carrying electronic pagers, usually for a week, and providing reports on their activities when signaled by the pagers at random times. *300*

experiment This is a precisely regulated setting in which one or more of the factors believed to influence the behavior being studied are manipulated and all others are held constant. *75*

experimental strategy This strategy allows investigators to precisely determine behavior's causes by performing an experiment. *75*

extrinsic motivation This is when behavior is influenced by external rewards and punishments. *472*

father-absence model This model states that, when father-absent and father-present families are compared, any differences that occur are attributed to the family structure variation. *209*

fear of success This occurs when individuals worry that they will be socially rejected if they are successful. *470*

fixation This defense mechanism occurs when an individual remains locked into an earlier developmental stage because his or her needs are under- or over-gratified. *47*

forgiveness This is an aspect of altruism that occurs when an injured person releases the injurer from possible behavioral retaliation. *451*

formal operational stage Piaget's fourth and final stage appears between the ages of 11 and 15. In this stage, individuals move beyond the world of actual, concrete experiences and think in more abstract and more logical ways. *58*

fraternal twins Called dyzygotic twins, these twins develop from separate eggs, making them genetically less similar than identical twins. *90*

frustration This refers to any situation in which an individual cannot reach a desired goal. *560*

gender In contrast to the biological dimension, gender is the sociocultural definition of male and female. *23, 367*

gender intensification hypothesis According to this hypothesis, psychological and behavioral differences between boys and girls become greater during early adolescence because of increased social pressures to conform to traditional masculine and feminine gender roles. *367*

gender role This is a set of expectations that prescribes how females and males should think, act, and feel. *367*

gender schema theory This theory states that an individual's attention and behavior are guided by an internal motivation to conform to gender-based sociocultural standards and stereotypes. *373*

gender-role stereotypes These are broad categories that reflect our impressions and beliefs about males and females. *376*

gender-role transcendence This is the belief that, when an individual's competence is at issue, it should not be conceptualized on a masculine, feminine, or androgynous basis but, rather, on a personal basis. Thus, rather than merging their gender roles, females and males should go beyond specific gender-role characteristics and stereotypes and think of people as people. *385*

general adaptation syndrome (GAS) Selye describes, in three stages, the common effects on the body when demands are placed on it: alarm, resistance, and exhaustion. *558*

generativity versus stagnation Erikson's seventh developmental stage is experienced in middle adulthood. *51*

genital stage This fifth and final Freudian stage occurs from puberty on. This stage is one of sexual reawakening, in which the source of sexual pleasure becomes someone outside of the family. *49*

genotype This is a person's genetic heritage, the actual genetic material. *89*

gifted At the opposite end of the intelligence spectrum from retardation, gifted individuals have above-average intelligence, usually at 120 or higher, and a superior talent for something. *174*

gonads These are the sex glands—the testes in males and the ovaries in females. *99*

gonorrhea Reported to be the most common STD in the United States, this sexually transmitted disease is caused by a bacterium called *gonococcus,* which thrives in the moist mucous membranes lining the mouth, throat, vagina, cervix, urethera, and anal tract. This disease is commonly called the "drip" or the "clap." *417*

goodness-of-fit model This model states that an adolescent's adaptation is best when there is a congruence, or match, between the adolescent's temperament and the demands of the social environment. *92*

hallucinogens Called psychedelic or mind-altering drugs, these are drugs that modify an individual's perceptual experiences and produce hallucinations. *508*

health psychology This is a multidimensional approach to health that emphasizes psychological factors, life-style, and the nature of the health-care delivery system. *543*

helpless orientation Children or adolescents who attribute their difficulty to lack of ability seem to be trapped by the experience of difficulty. *473*

heritability This is the statistical estimate of the degree to which physical, cognitive, and social differences among individuals are due to their genetic differences. Heritability is measured by correlational statistical procedures. *91*

herpes This is a sexually transmitted disease that is caused by a family of viruses with different strains. These strains produce such diseases as chicken pox, mononucleosis, and herpes simplex, which has two variations. *418*

heteronomous morality Piaget's first stage of moral development occurs at four to seven years of age. At this stage, justice and rules are conceived of as unchangeable properties of the world, removed from the control of people. *436*

hidden curriculum This is the pervasive moral atmosphere that characterizes schools. *452*

high-risk youth About 15 percent of the adolescent population, these youths often engage in two or three problem behaviors but with less seriousness and less frequency than do very-high-risk youths. *532*

horizontal décalage Piaget used this concept to describe how similar abilities do not appear at the same time within a stage of development. *118*

hormones The powerful chemical substances secreted by the endocrine glands and carried through the body by the blood stream are called hormones. *99*

hypothalamus This is the structure in the higher portion of the brain that monitors eating, drinking, and sex. *99*

hypotheses A theory gives rise to hypotheses, which are assumptions that can be tested to determine their accuracy. *43*

hypothetical-deductive reasoning This is Piaget's formal operational thought concept that adolescents have the cognitive ability to develop hypotheses, or best guesses, about ways to solve problems, such as algebraic equations. They then systematically deduce, or conclude, which is the best path to follow in solving the equations. *120*

id The Freudian structure that consists of instincts, which are an individual's reserve of psychic energy, is the id. *44*

identical twins Called monozygotic twins, these twins develop from a single fertilized egg that splits into two genetically identical replicas, each of which becomes a person. *90*

identity achievement This is Marcia's term for adolescents who have undergone a crisis and have made a commitment. *349*

identity diffusion Marcia uses this term to describe adolescents who have not yet experienced a crisis or made any commitments. *349*

identity foreclosure This is Marcia's term to describe adolescents who have made a commitment but have not experienced a crisis. *349*

identity moratorium Marcia uses this term to describe adolescents who are in the midst of a crisis but whose commitments either are absent or are only vaguely defined. *349*

identity versus identity confusion In Erikson's fifth developmental stage, adolescents face finding out who they are, what they are all about, and where they are going in life. *51, 345*

imaginary audience The imaginary audience involves attention-getting behavior—the desire to be noticed, visible, and "on stage." *134*

immanent justice This is Piaget's concept that, if a rule is broken, punishment will be meted out immediately. *436*

implicit personality theory This is the layperson's conception of personality. *137*

independent variable This is the manipulated, influential, experimental factor in an experiment. *75*

index offenses Whether they are committed by juveniles or adults, these are criminal acts, such as robbery, rape, and homicide. *519*

indirect moral education This involves encouraging adolescents to define their own and others' values and helping them define the moral perspectives that support those values. *452*

individual differences These are the stable, consistent ways in which adolescents are different from each other. *159*

individual-connected level This is the highest level of relationship maturity, at which there is evidence of an understanding of one's self, as well as consideration of others' motivation and anticipation of their needs. Concern and caring involve emotional support and individualized expression of interest. *357*

individualism and purpose In Kohlberg's second stage, moral thinking is based on rewards and self-interest. *437*

individuality This consists of two dimensions: self-assertion (the ability to have and communicate a point of view) and separateness (the use of communication patterns to express how one is different from others). *351*

individuating-reflexive faith In Fowler's stage in late adolescence, which is an important time in the development of a religious identity, individuals take full responsibility for their religious beliefs. *457*

industry versus inferiority Erikson's fourth stage of development occurs in the elementary school years. *51*

infancy This is the developmental period that extends from birth to 18–24 months. *28*

information-processing theory This theory is concerned with how individuals process information about their world—how information enters the mind, how it is stored and transformed, and how it is retrieved to perform such complex activities as problem solving and reasoning. *58*

initiative versus guilt This third of Erikson's stages occurs during the preschool years. *50*

insecure attachment In this attachment pattern, infants either avoid the caregiver or show considerable resistance or ambivalence toward the caregiver. This pattern is theorized to be related to difficulties in relationships and problems in later development. *205*

integrity versus despair This is Erikson's eighth and final stage, which individuals experience during late adulthood. *51*

intelligence Often defined as verbal ability and problem-solving skills, intelligence involves the ability to learn from and adapt to the experiences of everyday life. *159*

intelligence quotient (IQ) Devised in 1912 by William Stern, IQ consists of a child's mental age divided by chronological age and multiplied by 100. *160*

internalization This is the concept of developmental change from behavior that is externally controlled to behavior that is controlled by internal standards and principles. *437*

interpersonal norms In Kohlberg's third stage, individuals value trust, caring, and loyalty to others as the basis for moral judgment. *438*

intimacy in friendship In most research, this is defined narrowly as self-disclosure or sharing of private thoughts. *239*

intimacy versus isolation Individuals experience Erikson's sixth developmental stage during the early adulthood years. *51, 356*

intimate style In this style, Orlofsky says that an individual forms and maintains one or more deep and long-lasting love relationships. *357*

intrinsic motivation This is the internal desire to be competent and to do something for its own sake. *472*

inventionist view Inventionists state that adolescence is a sociohistorical creation. Especially important in the development of the inventionist view were the sociohistorical circumstances at the beginning of the twentieth century, when legislation was enacted that ensured the dependency of youth and that made their move into the economic sphere more manageable. *15*

isolated style Orlofsky attributes this style to individuals who withdraw from social encounters and have little or no attachment to same- or opposite-sex individuals. *357*

justice perspective This is a moral perspective that focuses on the rights of the individual; individuals stand alone and independently make moral decisions. *441*

juvenile delinquency This term refers to a broad range of socially and legally unacceptable behaviors. *519*

laboratory This is a controlled setting in which many of the complex factors of the "real world" are removed. *70*

late adolescence This refers to approximately the latter half of the second decade of life. Career interests, dating, and identity exploration are often more pronounced in late adolescence. *29*

late adulthood This is the developmental period that begins at approximately 60 to 70 years of age and continues until death. *30*

late formal operational thought This period involves a restoration of intellectual balance. Adolescents now test the products of their reasoning against experience, and a consolidation of formal operational thought takes place. An intellectual balance is restored as the adolescent accommodates to the cognitive upheaval that has occurred. *121*

latency stage In this fourth Freudian stage, which lasts from about age 6 to age 12, the child concentrates on such activities as going to school and getting along with society. Stressful problems of the previous phallic stages are repressed. *48*

learned helplessness This occurs when an individual is exposed to aversive stimulation, such as prolonged stress or pain, over which they have no control. *528*

longitudinal approach This is a research strategy in which the same individuals are studied over a period of time, usually several years or more. *76*

long-term memory This memory system is relatively permanent, and it holds huge amounts of information for a long period of time. *151*

LSD Lysergic acid diethylamide is a hallucinogen that, even in low doses, produces striking perceptual changes. *508*

macrosystem This system involves the culture in which individuals live. Culture refers to behavior patterns, beliefs, and all other products of a particular group of people that are passed from generation to generation. *66*

major depression In adults this is a mood disorder in which the individual feels deeply unhappy, demoralized, self-derogatory, and bored. An individual with major depression does not feel well, loses stamina easily, has a poor appetite, and is listless and unmotivated. *527*

marijuana Originally from central Asia but now grown in most parts of the world, this mild hallucinogen comes from the hemp plant *Cannabis sativa*. *509*

mastery orientation Children or adolescents who are task oriented are concerned about their learning strategies rather than focusing on their abilities. *473*

matching hypothesis This states that, although individuals may prefer a more attractive person in the abstract, they end up choosing someone who is close to their level of attractiveness. *252*

maturation Each of us has a genetic blueprint, and maturation is the orderly sequence of changes dictated by that blueprint. *30*

medical model Also called the disease model, this model was the forerunner of the biological approach, and it states that abnormality is a disease or an illness precipitated by internal body causes. *502*

memory This is the retention of information over time. *151*

menarche This is a girl's first menstruation. *97*

mental age (MA) According to Binet, this is an individual's level of mental development in relation to that of others. *160*

mental retardation This is a condition of limited mental ability in which an individual has a low IQ, usually below 70 on a traditional test of intelligence, and has difficulty adapting to everyday life. *173*

mesosystem This system involves relationships between microsystems or connections between contexts, such as the family experience to the school experience. *65*

microsystem In Bronfenbrenner's ecology theory, this system is the setting, or context, in which an individual lives. This system includes the person's family, peers, school, and neighborhood. The most direct interactions with social agents occur in the microsystem. *65*

middle adulthood This period is entered at approximately 35 to 45 years of age and is exited between approximately 55 and 65 years of age. *30*

middle and late childhood This developmental period extends from about 6 to 11 years of age and is also called the elementary school years. *29*

moral development This concerns rules and conventions about what people *should* do in their interactions with other people. *435*

motivation This focuses on why individuals behave, think, and feel the way they do, with special consideration of the activation and direction of their behavior. *470*

multiple-factor model of divorce effects This model takes into account the complexity of the divorce context and examines a number of influences in the adolescent's development, including such things as type of custody, socioeconomic status, post-divorce family functioning, and strengths and weaknesses of the adolescent prior to the divorce. *209*

multiple-factor theory Thurstone theorized that intelligence consists of seven primary mental abilities: verbal comprehension, number ability, word fluency, spatial visualization, associative memory, reasoning, and perceptual speed. *161*

naturalistic observation This is a method in which scientists observe behavior in real-world settings and make no effort to manipulate or control the situation. *70*

nature-nurture controversy *Nature* refers to an organism's biological inheritance, *nurture* to environmental experiences. In an ongoing debate, "nature" proponents claim biological inheritance is the most important influence on development; "nurture" proponents argue that environmental experiences are most important. *32*

neglected children and adolescents These children or adolescents receive little attention from their peers and have few, if any, friends, but they are not necessarily disliked. *232*

nonconformity This occurs when individuals know what people around them expect, but they do not use those expectations to guide their behavior. *230*

normal distribution This is a symmetrical pattern of scores in which most test scores fall in the middle of the possible range of scores and few scores appear toward either the upper or lower extremes of the range. *160*

norms These are rules that apply to all members of a group. *241*

Oedipus complex In this Freudian concept, the young child develops an intense desire to replace the parent of the same sex and enjoy the affections of the opposite-sex parent. *47*

operant conditioning A form of learning in which the consequences of behavior lead to change in the probability of that behavior's occurrence is called operant conditioning. *63*

operations Piaget said that thought involves mental actions, called operations, that allow an individual to do mentally what was done before physically. A concrete operational thinker can engage in mental actions that are reversible. *117*

opiates Consisting of opium and its derivatives, these depress the activity of the central nervous system. *512*

oral stage This is the first Freudian stage of development. It occurs during the first 18 months of life and is defined by the infant's pleasure centering around the mouth. *47*

organic retardation This form of mental retardation involves some physical damage and is caused by a genetic disorder or brain damage. *174*

peers Children or adolescents who are at about the same age or maturity level are called peers. *228*

permissive-indifferent parenting This is a style in which the parent is very uninvolved in the adolescent's life. It is associated with adolescents' socially incompetent behavior, especially lack of self-control. *195*

permissive-indulgent parenting This is a style in which parents are highly involved with their adolescents but place few demands or controls on them. This is associated with adolescents' social incompetence, especially lack of self-control. *196*

personal fable According to Elkind, this is the part of adolescent egocentrism that involves an adolescent's sense of uniqueness. *135*

personality type theory Holland believes that an effort should be made to match an individual's career choice with his or her personality. *481*

perspective taking This is the ability to assume another person's perspective and understand his or her thoughts and feelings. *135*

phallic stage This third Freudian stage of development occurs between the ages of three and six. Its name comes from the Latin word *phallus*, which means "penis." During this stage, the child's pleasure focuses on the genitals, and the child discovers that self-manipulation is enjoyable. *47*

phenotype This is the way a person's genotype is expressed in observed and measurable characteristics. *89*

pituitary gland An important endocrine gland, the pituitary controls growth and regulates other glands. *99*

pleasure principle This is the Freudian concept that the id always seeks pleasure and avoids pain. *44*

pluralism This refers to the coexistence of distinct ethnic and cultural groups in the same society. *312*

possible self An aspect of the ideal or imagined self, this is what individuals might become, what they would like to become, and what they are afraid of becoming. *336*

postconventional reasoning This is Kohlberg's highest level, in which morality is completely internalized and not based on others' standards. *438*

preconventional reasoning In this, the lowest level in Kohlberg's theory, the individual shows no internalization of moral values—moral reasoning is controlled by external rewards and punishments. *437*

preintimate style This is Orlofsky's style in which an individual shows mixed emotions about commitment, an ambivalence reflected in the strategy of offering love without obligations or long-lasting bonds. *357*

prejudice This is an unjustified negative attitude toward an individual because of the individual's membership in a group. *311*

prenatal period This is the time period from conception to birth. *28*

preoperational stage From about two to seven years of age, Piaget believed, children begin to represent the world with words, images, and symbols. In this second stage, symbolic thought goes beyond simple connections of sensory information and motoric actions. *55*

primary appraisal In this state, adolescents interpret whether an event involves harm or loss that has already occurred, a threat of future danger, or a challenge to be overcome. *563*

problem-focused coping This is Lazarus's term for the cognitive coping strategy used by individuals who face their troubles and try to solve them. *566*

projection Individuals use this defense mechanism to attribute their own shortcomings, problems, and faults to others. *46*

pseudointimate style In this style, Orlofsky says individuals maintain long-lasting heterosexual attachments with little or no depth or closeness. *357*

psychological dependence This is a psychological need to take a drug, as in adolescents taking drugs to help them cope with stress. *504*

psychological moratorium This is Erikson's term for the gap between childhood security and adult autonomy that adolescents experience as part of their identity exploration. *345*

psychometrics The name that psychologists have given to the field that involves the assessment of individual differences is psychometrics. *159*

puberty This is a period of rapid change that occurs primarily in early adolescence. The change is to physical maturation and involves hormonal and bodily changes. *97*

punishment The opposite of reinforcement, punishment is the consequence that decreases the probability that a behavior will occur. *63*

punishment and obedience orientation At this first stage in Kohlberg's theory of moral development, moral thinking is based on punishment. *437*

questionnaire This is similar to a highly structured interview except that respondents read the questions and mark their answers on paper rather than respond verbally to an interviewer. *71*

random assignment This occurs when researchers assign subjects to experimental and control conditions by chance, thus reducing the likelihood that the results of the experiment will be due to preexisting differences between the two groups. *75*

rape This is forcible sexual intercourse with a person who does not give consent. *426*

rationalization This defense mechanism is used when the real motive for an individual's behavior is not accepted by the ego and is replaced by a "cover" motive. *46*

reaction formation An individual can use this defense mechanism to express an unacceptable impulse by transforming it into its opposite. *46*

reaction range This describes the range of phenotypes for each genotype, suggesting the importance of the environment's restrictiveness or enrichment. *90*

reality principle This Freudian concept is the one by which the ego tries to bring individual pleasures within the boundaries of reality. *44*

reciprocal socialization This is the process by which children and adolescents socialize parents, just as parents socialize them. *187*

regression This defense mechanism occurs when an individual behaves in a way that characterizes a previous developmental level. *47*

reinforcement This is the consequence that increases the probability a behavior will occur. *63*

rejected children and adolescents These children and adolescents are disliked by their peers. They are more likely to be disruptive and aggressive than their neglected counterparts. *232*

repression Freud named this the most powerful and pervasive defense mechanism. It pushes unacceptable id impulses out of awareness and back into the unconscious mind. *45*

resatellization This is Ausubel's term for a preliminary form of desatellization in which the individual's parents are replaced by other individuals or a group. *203*

rites of passage These are ceremonies or rituals that mark an individual's transition from one status to another, especially into adulthood. *298*

role-focused level This is the second or intermediate level of relationship maturity, at which perceiving others as individuals in their own right begins to develop. However, at this level, the perspective is stereotypical and emphasizes social acceptability. *357*

roles These are certain positions in a group that are governed by rules and expectations. Roles define how adolescents should behave in those positions. *241*

romantic love Also called passionate love or Eros, this love has strong sexual and infatuation components, and it often predominates in the early part of a love relationship. *253*

satellization This is Ausubel's term for children's relinquishment of their sense of self-power and their acceptance of their dependency on their parents. *203*

schema This is a cognitive structure involving a network of associations that organizes and guides an individual's perceptions. *373*

scientific method This approach can be used to discover accurate information about behavior and development and includes the following steps: identify and analyze the problem, collect data, draw conclusions, and revise theories. *69*

second individuation crisis This is Blos's term for adolescents' development of a distinctiveness from their parents, which he believes is an attempt to transcend earlier parent-child ties and develop more self-responsibility. *203*

secondary appraisal In this state, adolescents evaluate their resources and determine how effectively they can be used to cope with an event. *563*

secure attachment In this attachment pattern, infants use their primary caregiver, usually the mother, as a secure base from which to explore the environment. Secure attachment is theorized to be an important foundation for psychological development later in childhood, adolescence, and adulthood. *204*

self-esteem Also referred to as self-worth or self-image, this is the evaluative and affective dimension of self-concept. *338*

self-focused level This is the first level of relationship maturity, at which one's perspective of another or of a relationship is concerned only with how it affects the self. *357*

self-understanding This is an adolescent's cognitive representation of the self, the substance and content of the adolescent's self-concept. *335*

sensorimotor stage In the first of Piaget's stages, infants construct an understanding of the world by coordinating sensory experiences with motoric actions—hence, the name. This stage lasts from birth to about two years of age. *55*

sequential approach This is the term used to describe a combined cross-sectional, longitudinal design. *77*

set point This is the weight maintained when no effort is made to gain or lose weight. *551*

sexual script This is a stereotyped pattern of role prescriptions for how individuals should behave sexually. Females and males have been socialized to follow different sexual scripts. *400*

sexually transmitted diseases (STDs) These are diseases that are contracted primarily through sexual contact. This contact is not limited to vaginal intercourse but includes oral-genital contact and anal-genital contact as well. *415*

short-term memory In this limited-capacity system, information can be retained for as long as 30 seconds without rehearsal. *151*

slow-to-warm-up child This child has a low activity level, is somewhat negative, shows low adaptability, and displays a low intensity of mood. *92*

social class Also called socioeconomic status or SES, this refers to a grouping of people with similar occupational, educational, and economic characteristics. *295*

social cognition This refers to how individuals conceptualize and reason about their social world—the people they watch and interact with, relationships with those people, the groups in which they participate, and how they reason about themselves and others. *131*

social conventional reasoning This refers to thoughts about social consensus and convention as opposed to moral reasoning, which stresses ethical issues. *444*

social desirability This is a response set in which individuals tell the interviewer what they think is most socially acceptable or desirable rather than what they truly feel or think. *71*

social information processing This emphasizes how individuals use cognitive processes, such as attention, perception, memory, thinking, reasoning, expectancies, and so on, to understand their social world. *134*

social isolation Recently relocated married couples often experience this type of loneliness, which occurs when a person lacks a sense of integrated involvement: being deprived of participation in a group or community involving companionship, shared interests, organized activities, and meaningful roles. *359*

social learning theory This view emphasizes a combination of behavior, environment, and cognition as the key factors in development. *63*

social learning theory of gender This theory emphasizes that children's and adolescents' gender development occurs through observation and imitation of gender behavior and through rewards and punishments they experience for gender appropriate and inappropriate behavior. *370*

social policy This is a national government's course of action designed to influence the welfare of its citizens. *25*

social processes These processes involve changes in an individual's relationships with other people, in emotions, in personality, and in the role of social contexts in development. *28*

social systems morality In Kohlberg's fourth stage, moral judgments are based on understanding the social order, laws, justice, and duty. *438*

stability-change issue This issue addresses whether development is better characterized mainly by stability or by change. The stability-change issue involves the degree to which we become older renditions of our early experience or whether we can develop into someone different from who we were at an earlier point in development. *33*

standardized tests These require an individual to answer a series of written or oral questions. They have two features: first, psychologists usually total an individual's scores to yield a single score, or set of scores, that reflects something about the individual and, second, psychologists compare the individual's score with the scores of a large group to determine how the individual responded relative to others. *72*

status offenses Performed by youths under a specified age, these are juvenile offenses that are not as serious as index offenses. These offenses may include such acts as drinking under age, truancy, and sexual promiscuity. *519*

stereotype A broad category that reflects our impressions and beliefs about people is a stereotype. All stereotypes refer to an image of what the typical member of a particular group is like. *18*

stereotyped style Orlofsky attributes this style to individuals who have superficial relationships that tend to be dominated by friendship ties with same-sex rather than opposite-sex individuals. *357*

stimulants These are drugs that increase the activity of the central nervous system. *509*

storm-and-stress view Hall, in this view, conceptualizes adolescence as a turbulent time charged with conflict and mood swings. *14*

strategies These are the activities that are under the learner's conscious control. They may also be called control processes and there are many of them. One of the most important is organization, which is the tendency to arrange items into categories. *152*

stress Stressors are circumstances and events that threaten or tax an individual's coping ability. Stress is the response to stressors. *558*

sublimation This is the defense mechanism in which the individual replaces a socially distasteful course of action with a socially useful one. *46*

superego The Freudian structure that is the moral branch of personality, the branch that takes into account whether something is right or wrong, is the superego. *44*

synchrony Synchrony is the carefully coordinated interaction between a parent and child or adolescent in which, often unknowingly, they are attuned to each other's behavior. *188*

syphilis This sexually transmitted disease is caused by the bacterium *Treponema pallidum*, also called a spirochete. *417*

temperament An individual's behavioral style and characteristic way of responding is referred to as his or her temperament. *91*

testosterone This is an androgen that plays an important role in male pubertal development. *99*

theory A theory is a coherent set of ideas that helps explain data and make predictions. *43*

tolerance This means that a greater amount of a drug is needed to produce the same effect. *504*

top-dog phenomenon This is the circumstance of moving from the top position (in elementary school, the oldest, biggest, and most powerful students) to the lowest position (in middle or junior high school, the youngest, smallest, and least powerful students). *270*

tranquilizers Valium and Xanax are depressant drugs that reduce anxiety and induce relaxation. *512*

triarchic theory Sternberg proposed intelligence with three main components: componential intelligence, experiential intelligence, and contextual intelligence. *164*

trust versus mistrust This is Erikson's first psychosocial stage, and it is experienced in the first year of life. *50*

twin study This is a research strategy in which the behaviors of identical twins are compared with the behaviors of fraternal twins. *90*

two-factor theory Spearman theorized that individuals have both general intelligence, which he called *g*, and a number of specific intelligences, which he called *s*, both of which account for performance on an intelligence test. *161*

Type-A behavior pattern An individual with this cluster of characteristics is excessively competitive, hard-driven, impatient, and hostile. This pattern is thought to be related to coronary problems. *561*

universal ethical principles In Kohlberg's sixth stage, the person has developed a moral standard based on universal human rights. *441*

values clarification This is an indirect moral education approach that focuses on helping students clarify what their lives are for and what is worth working for. *453*

very-high-risk youth As many as 10 percent of the adolescent population, these youths have multiple problem behaviors that include serious offenses. *530*

wisdom According to Baltes, this is expert knowledge about the practical aspects of life. *127*

withdrawal This is the undesirable intense pain and craving for an addictive drug. *504*

youth Kenniston's term for the transitional period between adolescence and adulthood, youth is a time of economic and personal temporariness. *29*

zone of proximal development (ZPD) This is Vygotsky's concept of tasks that are too difficult for an individual to master alone but that can be mastered with the guidance of adults or more highly skilled adolescents. *130*

References

Aber, L., Allen, L., Mitchell, C., & Seidman, E. (1992, March). *Neighborhood social isolation and adolescent academic achievement: Gender and race-specific patterns and processes.* Paper presented at the meeting of the Society for Research on Adolescence, Washington, DC.

Achenbach, T. M., & Edelbrock, C. S. (1981). Behavioral problems and competencies reported by parents of normal and disturbed children aged four through sixteen. *Monographs of the Society for Research in Child Development, 46* (1, Serial No. 188).

Achenbach, T. M., Howell, C. T., Quay, H. C., & Conners, C. K. (1991). National survey of problems and competencies among four- to sixteen-year-olds. *Monographs of the Society for Research in Child Development,* Serial No. 225 (Vol. 56, No. 3).

Adams, G. (1977). Physical attractiveness research. *Human Development, 20,* 217–239.

Adams, G. R. (1991). Physical attractiveness and adolescent development. In R. M. Lerner, A. C. Petersen, & J. Brooks-Gunn (Eds.), *Encyclopedia of adolescence* (Vol. 2). New York: Garland.

Adams, G. R. (1991). Runaways, negative consequences for. In R. M. Lerner, A. C. Petersen, & J. Brooks-Gunn (Eds.), *Encyclopedia of adolescence* (Vol. 2). New York: Garland.

Adams, G. R., Gulotta, T. P., & Montemayor, R. (Eds.). (1992). *Adolescent identity formation.* Newbury Park, CA: Sage.

Adelson, J. (1979, January). Adolescence and the generalization gap. *Psychology Today,* pp. 33–37.

Adelson, J., & Doehrman, M. J. (1980). The psychodynamic approach to adolescence. In J. Adelson (Ed.), *Handbook of adolescent psychology.* New York: Wiley.

Ahlstrom, P. A., Richmond, D., Townsend, C., & D'Angelo, L. (1992, March). *The course of HIV infection in adolescence.* Paper presented at the meeting of the Society for Adolescent Medicine, Washington, DC.

Ainsworth, M. D. S. (1979). Infant-mother attachment. *American Psychologist, 34,* 932–937.

Ainsworth, M. D. S. (1988, August). *Attachments beyond infancy.* Paper presented at the meeting of the American Psychological Association, Atlanta, GA.

Al-Issa, I. (Ed.). (1982). *Culture and psychopathology.* Baltimore, MD: University Park Press.

Allen, J. P., Aber, J. L., & Leadbetter, B. J. (in press). Adolescent problem behaviors: The influence of attachment and autonomy. *Psychiatric Clinics of North America.*

Allen, L., & Majidi-Ahi, S. (1989). Black American adolescents. In J. T. Gibbs & L. N. Huang (Eds.), *Children of color.* San Francisco: Jossey-Bass.

Allen, L., & Santrock, J. W, (1993). *Psychology: The contexts of behavior.* Dubuque, IA: Wm. C. Brown.

Amabile, T. M., & Hennessey, B. A. (1988). The motivation for creativity in children. In A. K. Boggiano & T. Pittman (Eds.), *Achievement motivation: A social-developmental perspective.* New York: Cambridge University Press.

America in Transition. (1989). Washington, DC: National Governors' Association Task Force on Children.

American College Health Association. (1989, May). *Survey of AIDS on American college and university campuses.* Washington, DC: American College Health Association.

Ames, C., & Ames, R. (Eds.). (1989). *Research on motivation in education. Goals and cognitions.* (Vol. 3). San Diego: Academic Press.

Anastasi, A. (1988). *Psychological testing* (6th ed.). New York: Macmillan.

Anderson, A. B., & Frideres, J. S. (1981). *Ethnicity in Canada.* Toronto: Butterworths.

Anderson, E. R. (1992, March). *Consistency of parenting in stepfather families.* Paper presented at the meeting of the Society for Research on Adolescence, Washington, DC.

Anderson, J. R. (1990). *Cognitive psychology and its implications* (3rd ed.). New York: W. H. Freeman.

Andre, T., Frevert, R. L., & Schuchmann, D. (1989). From whom did college students learned what about sex? *Youth and Society, 20,* 241–268.

Angell, R. C. (1936). *The family encounters the depression.* New York: Charles Scribner's Sons.

Anthrop, J., & Allison, M. T. (1983). Role conflict and the high school female athlete. *Research Quarterly, 54,* 104–111.

Archer, S. L. (1989). The status of identity: Reflections on the need for intervention. *Journal of Adolescence, 12,* 345–359.

Archer, S. L. (1991). Identity development, gender differences in. In R. M. Lerner, A. C. Petersen, & J. Brooks-Gunn (Eds.), *Encyclopedia of adolescence* (Vol. 1). New York: Garland.

Arehart, D. M., & Smith, P. H. (1990). Identity in adolescence: Influences on dysfunction and psychosocial task issues. *Journal of Youth and Adolescence, 19,* 63–72.

Aristotle. (1941). *Rhetorica* (W. R. Roberts, Trans.). In R. McKeon (Ed.), *The basic works of Aristotle.* New York: Random House.

Arlin, P. K. (1984). *Arlin Test of Formal Reasoning.* East Aurora, NY: Slosson Educational Publications.

Armsden, G., & Greenberg, M. T. (1984). *The inventory of parent and peer attachment: Individual differences and their relationship to psychological well-being in adolescence.* Unpublished manuscript, University of Washington.

Armsden, G., & Greenberg, M. T. (1987). The inventory of parent and peer attachment: Individual differences and their relationship to psychological well-being in adolescence. *Journal of Youth and Adolescence, 16,* 427–454.

Arnett, J. (1990). Contraceptive use, sensation seeking, and adolescent egocentrism. *Journal of Youth and Adolescence, 19,* 171–180.

Arnold, M. L. (1989, April). *Moral cognition and conduct: A quantitative review of the literature.* Paper presented at the biennial meeting of the Society for Research in Child Development, Kansas City.

Aronson, E. (1986, August). *Teaching students things they think they know all about: The case of prejudice and desegregation.* Paper presented at the meeting of the American Psychological Association, Washington, DC.

Asamen, J. K. (1990). Afro-American students and academic achievement. In G. L. Berry & J. K. Asamen (Eds.), *Black students.* Newbury Park, CA: Sage.

Asarnow, J. R., & Callan, J. W. (1985). Boys with peer adjustment problems: Social cognitive processes. *Journal of Consulting and Clinical Psychology, 53,* 80–87.

Asher, S. R., & Parker, J. G. (in press). The significance of peer relationship problems in childhood. In B. H. Schneider, G. Attili, J. Nadel, & R. P. Weisberg (Eds.), *Social competence in developmental perspective.* Amsterdam: Kluwer Academic Publishing.

Asian Week. (1990, June 29). Poll finds racial tension decreasing. p. 4.

Astin, A. W., Green, K. C., & Korn, W. S. (1987). *The American freshman: Twenty-year trends.* Los Angeles: UCLA Higher Education Research Institute.

Astin, A. W., Korn, W. S., & Berz, E. R. (1990). *The American freshman: National norms for fall 1989*. Los Angeles: Higher Education Research Institute, UCLA.

Astin, H. S. (1984). The meaning of work in women's lives: A sociopsychological model of career choice and work behavior. *The Counseling Psychologist, 12*, 117–126.

Atkinson, J. W., & Raynor, I. O. (1974). *Motivation and achievement*. Washington, DC: V. H. Winston & Sons.

Attie, I., & Brooks-Gunn, J. (1989). Development of eating problems in adolescent girls: A longitudinal study. *Developmental Psychology, 25*, 70–79.

Ausubel, D. P. (1958). *Theory and problems of child development*. New York: Grune & Stratton.

Avis, H. (1990). *Drugs and life*. Dubuque, IA: Wm. C. Brown.

Bachhuber, T. (1992). 13 ways to pass along real information to students. *Journal of Career Planning and Employment, 27*, 67–70.

Bachman, J. G. (1982, June 28). *The American high school student: A profile based on national survey data*. Paper presented at a conference entitled, "The American High School Today and Tomorrow," Berkeley, CA.

Bachman, J. G. (1991). Dropouts, school. In R. M. Lerner, A. C. Petersen, & J. Brooks-Gunn (Eds.), *Encyclopedia of adolescence* (Vol. 1). New York: Garland.

Bachman, J. G., Johnston, L. D., & O'Malley, P. M. (1987). *Monitoring the future*. Ann Arbor, MI: Institute for Social Research, University of Michigan.

Bacon, M. K., Child, I. L., & Barry, H. (1963). A cross-cultural study of correlates of crime. *Journal of Abnormal and Social Psychology, 66*, 291–300.

Baer, D. M. (1989, April). *Behavior analysis of human development*. Paper presented at the biennial meeting of the Society for Research in Child Development, Kansas City, MO.

Baker, L., & Brown, A. L. (1984). Metacognitive skills and reading. In P. D. Pearson (Ed.), *Handbook of reading research, Part 2*. New York: Longman.

Baker, T. B. (1988). Models of addiction. *Journal of Abnormal Psychology, 97*, 115–117.

Baltes, P. B., & Baltes, M. M. (Eds.). (in press). *Successful aging*. New York: Cambridge University Press.

Baltes, P. B., Smith, J., Staudinger, U. M., & Sowarda, D. (1990). Wisdom: One facet of successful aging? In M. Perlmutter (Ed.), *Late-life potential*. Washington, DC: Gerontological Association of America.

Bancroft, J. (1990). The impact of sociocultural influences on adolescent sexual development: Further considerations. In J. Bancroft & J. M. Reinisch (Eds.), *Adolescence and puberty*. New York: Oxford University Press.

Bandura, A. (1965). Influence of models' reinforcement contingencies on the acquisition of imitative responses. *Journal of Personality and Social Psychology, 1*, 589–595.

Bandura, A. (1977). *Social learning theory*. Englewood Cliffs, NJ: Prentice-Hall.

Bandura, A. (1986). *Social foundations of thought and action: A social cognitive theory*. Englewood Cliffs, NJ: Prentice-Hall.

Bandura, A. (1989). Social cognitive theory. In R. Vasta (Ed.), *Six theories of child development*. Greenwich, CT: JAI Press.

Bandura, A. (1991). Self-efficacy, impact of self-beliefs on adolescent life paths. In R. M.

Lerner, A. C. Petersen, & J. Brooks-Gunn (Eds.), *Encyclopedia of adolescence* (Vol. 2). New York: Garland.

Bandura, A., & Walters, R. M. (1959). *Adolescent aggression*. New York: Ronald Press.

Barber, B. L., Clark, J. J., Clossick, M. L., & Wamboldt, P. (1992, March). *The effects of parent-adolescent communication on adjustment: Variations across divorced and intact families*. Paper presented at the meeting of the Society for Research on Adolescence, Washington, DC.

Barber, B. L., & Eccles, J. S. (1992). Long-term influence of divorce and single parenting on adolescent family- and work-related values, behaviors, and aspirations. *Psychological Bulletin, 111*, 108–126.

Barenboim, C. (1981). The development of person perception in childhood and adolescence: From behavioral comparisons to psychological constructs to psychological comparisons. *Child Development, 52*, 129–144.

Barenboim, C. (1985, April). *Person perception and interpersonal behavior*. Paper presented at the biennial meeting of the Society for Research in Child Development, Toronto.

Barker, R., & Wright, H. F. (1951). *One boy's day*. New York: Harper.

Barnard, C., & Lentz, G. (1992). Making diversity a reality within our profession. *Journal of Career Planning and Employment, 27*, 30–35.

Barnes, G. M. (1984). Adolescent alcohol abuse and other problem behaviors: Their relationships and common parental influences. *Journal of Youth and Adolescence, 13*, 329–348.

Barnes, G. M., & Welte, J. W. (1986). Adolescent alcohol use: Subgroup differences and relations to other problem behaviors. *Journal of Adolescent Research, 1*, 79–94.

Barnes, G. M., Welte, J. W., & Dintcheff, B. (1992, March). *Trends and patterns of alcohol use among 5th–12th grade students in New York state*. Paper presented at the meeting of the Society for Research on Adolescence, Washington, DC.

Barnet, B., Joffe, A., Duggan, A., & Repke, J. (1992, March). *Depressive symptoms, stress, and social support in pregnant and postpartum adolescents*. Paper presented at the meeting of the Society for Adolescent Medicine, Washington, DC.

Barnouw, V. (1975). *An introduction to anthropology*. Vol. 2, *Ethnology*. Homewood, IL: Dorsey Press.

Baron, R., Tom, D., & Cooper, H. (1985). Social class, race, and teacher expectations. In J. Dusek & G. Joseph (Eds.), *Teacher expectancies*. Hillsdale, NJ: Erlbaum.

Barron, F. (1989, April). The birth of a notion: Exercises to tap your creative potential. *Omni*, pp. 112–119.

Bart, W. M. (1971). The factor structure of formal operations. *The British Journal of Educational Psychology, 41*, 40–77.

Bartlett, J. C., & Santrock, J. W. (1986). *Developmental psychology*. Dubuque, IA: Wm. C. Brown.

Baruch, G. K., Biener, L., & Barnett, R. C. (1987). Women and gender in research on work and family. *American Psychologist, 42*, 130–136.

Baskett, L. M., & Johnston, S. M. (1982). The young child's interaction with parents versus siblings. *Child Development, 53*, 643–650.

Baumeister, R. F. (1989). *Masochism and the self*. Hillsdale, NJ: Erlbaum.

Baumeister, R. F. (1991). Identity crisis. In R. M. Lerner, A. C. Petersen, & J. Brooks-Gunn (Eds.), *Encyclopedia of adolescence* (Vol. 1). New York: Garland.

Baumrind, D. (1971). Current patterns of parental authority. *Developmental Psychology Monographs, 4*(1, Pt. 2).

Baumrind, D. (1990). Parenting styles and adolescent development. In R. M. Lerner, A. C. Petersen, & J. Brooks-Gunn (Eds.), *Encyclopedia of adolescence* (Vol. 2). New York: Garland.

Baumrind, D. (1991a). Effective parenting during the early adolescent transition. In P. A. Cowan & E. M. Hetherington (Eds.), *Advances in family research* (Vol. 2). Hillsdale, NJ: Erlbaum.

Baumrind, D. (1991b). Parenting styles and adolescent development. In J. Brooks-Gunn, R. Lerner, & A. C. Petersen (Eds.), *Encyclopedia of adolescence* (Vol. 2). New York: Garland.

Beane, J. A. (1990, May). Rethinking the middle school curriculum. *Middle School Journal, 21*, 1–5.

Beck, A. (1976). *Cognitive therapy and the emotional disorders*. New York: International Universities Press.

Becker, H. J., & Sterling, C. W. (1987). Equity in school computer use: National data and neglected considerations. *Journal of Educational Computing Research, 3*, 289–311.

Bednar, R. L., Wells, M. G., & Peterson, S. R. (1989). *Self-esteem*. Washington, DC: American Psychological Association.

Beilin, H. (1989). Piagetian theory. In R. Vasta (Ed.), *Six theories of child development: Revised formulations and current issues*. Greenwich, CT: JAI Press.

Belansky, E. S., & Clements, P. (1992, March). *Adolescence: A crossroads for gender-role transcendence or gender-role intensification*. Paper presented at the meeting of the Society for Research on Adolescence, Washington, DC.

Belenky, M. F., Clinchy, B. M., Goldberger, N. R., & Tarule, J. M. (1986). *Women's ways of knowing*. New York: Basic.

Bell, A. P., Weinberg, M. S., & Mammersmith, S. K. (1981). *Sexual preferences: Its development in men and women*. New York: Simon & Schuster.

Belle, D. (1990). Poverty and women's mental health. *American Psychologist, 45*, 385–389.

Belle, D., & Burr, R. (1992, March). *The after-school experiences of young people: A contextual and longitudinal analysis*. Paper presented at the meeting of the Society for Research on Adolescence, Washington, DC.

Belle, D., Longfellow, C., Makosky, V., Saunder, E., & Zelkowitz, P. (1981). Income, mothers' mental health, and family functioning in a low-income population. In American Academy of Nursing, *The impact of changing resources on health policy*. Kansas City, MO: American Nurses' Association.

Belle, D., & Paul, E. (1989, April). *Structural and functional changes accompanying the transition to college*. Paper presented at the biennial meeting of the Society for Research in Child Development, Kansas City.

Bell-Scott, P., & Taylor, R. L. (1989). Introduction: The multiple ecologies of black adolescent development. *Journal of Adolescent Research, 4*, 117–118.

Belsky, J. (1981). Early human experience: A family perspective. *Developmental Psychology, 17*, 3–23.

Belson, W. (1978). *Television violence and the adolescent boy*. London: Saxon House.

Bem, S. L. (1977). On the utility of alternative procedures for assessing psychological androgyny. *Journal of Consulting and Clinical Psychology, 45*, 196–205.

Bem, S. L. (1981). Gender schema theory: A cognitive account of sex-typing. *Psychological Review, 88*, 354–364.

Benbow, C. P. (1992). Academic achievement in mathematics and science of students between ages 13 and 23: Are there differences in the top one percent of mathematical ability? *Journal of Educational Psychology*, 84, 51–61.

Bence, P. (1989, April). *Adolescent dating behavior and TV soaps: Guided by "The Guiding Light"?* Paper presented at the biennial meeting of the Society for Research in Child Development, Kansas City, MO.

Bence, P. (1991). Television, adolescents and. In R. M. Lerner, A. C. Petersen, & J. Brooks-Gunn (Eds.), *Encyclopedia of adolescence* (Vol. 2). New York: Garland.

Bennett, W. I., & Gurin, J. (1982). *The dieter's dilemma: Eating less and weighing more.* New York: Basic Books.

Bennett, W. J. (1986). *First lessons: A report on elementary education in America.* Washington, DC: U.S. Government Printing Office.

Benninga, J. S. (1988, February). An emerging synthesis in moral education. *Phi Delta Kappan*, pp. 415–418.

Bereiter, C., & Scardamalia, M. (1982). From conversation to composition: The role of instruction in a developmental process. In R. Glaser (Ed.), *Advances in instructional psychology.* Hillsdale, NJ: Erlbaum.

Berkowitz, M., & Gibbs, J. (1983). Measuring the developmental features of moral discussion. *Merrill-Palmer Quarterly*, 29, 399–410.

Berman, L. (1991). Suicide cases. Special issue: Assessment and prediction of suicide. *Suicide and Life-Threatening Behavior*, 21, 18–36.

Bernard, H. S. (1981). Identity formation in late adolescence: A review of some empirical findings. *Adolescence*, 16, 349–358.

Berndt, T. J. (1979). Developmental changes in conformity to peers and parents. *Developmental Psychology*, 15, 608–616.

Berndt, T. J. (1982). The features and effects of friendship in early adolescence. *Child Development*, 53, 1447–1460.

Berndt, T. J., & Ladd, G. W. (1989). *Peer relationships in child development.* New York: Wiley.

Berndt, T. J., & Perry, T. B. (1990). Distinctive features and effects of early adolescent friendships. In R. Montemayor (Ed.), *Advances in adolescent research.* Greenwich, CT: JAI Press.

Berrueta-Clement, J., Schweinhart, L., Barnett, W., & Weikart, D. (1986). The effects of early educational intervention on crime and delinquency in adolescence and early adulthood. In J. Burchard & S. Burchard (Eds.), *Prevention of delinquent behavior.* Newbury Park, CA: Sage.

Berry, J. W. (1980). Introduction to methodology. In H. C. Triandis & J. W. Berry (Eds.), *Handbook of cross-cultural psychology: Methodology* (Vol. 2). Boston: Allyn & Bacon.

Berry, J. W., Poortinga, V. H., Segall, M. H., & Dasen, P. R. (in press). *Cross-cultural psychology: Theory, method, and applications.* Cambridge, England: Cambridge University Press.

Berscheid, E. (1988). Some comments on love's anatomy: Or, whatever happened to old-fashioned lust? In R. J. Sternberg & M. L. Barnes (Eds.), *Anatomy of love.* New Haven, CT: Yale University Press.

Berscheid, E., & Fei, J. (1977). Sexual jealousy and romantic love. In G. Clinton & G. Smith (Eds.), *Sexual jealousy.* Englewood Cliffs, NJ: Prentice-Hall.

Berscheid, E., Snyder, M., & Omoto, A. M. (1989). Issues in studying close relationships. In C. Hendrick (Ed.), *Close relationships.* Newbury Park, CA: Sage.

Berzonsky, M. D. (1978). Formal reasoning in adolescence: An alternative view. *Adolescence*, 13, 279–290.

Bettes, B. A., Dusenbury, L., Kerner, J., James-Ortiz, S., & Botvin, G. J. (1990). Ethnicity and psychosocial factors in alcohol and tobacco use in adolescence. *Child Development*, 61, 557–565.

Bijou, S. W. (1989). Behavior analysis. In R. Vasta (Ed.), *Six theories of child development: Revised formulations and current issues.* Greenwich, CT: JAI Press.

Billy, J. O. G., Rodgers, J. L., & Udry, J. R. (1984). Adolescent sexual behavior and friendship choice. *Social Forces*, 62, 653–678.

Bilodeau, A., Forget, G., & Tétreaul11t, J. (1992, March). *Preventing teenage pregnancy: A pilot project in two low-income communities of eastern Montreal.* Paper presented at the meeting of the Society for Research on Adolescence, Washington, DC.

Bird, G. W., & Kemerait, L. N. (1990). Stress among early adolescents in two-earner families. *Journal of Early Adolescence*, 10, 344–365.

Bishop, S. M., & Ingersoll, G. M. (1989). Effects of marital conflict and family structure on the self-concepts of pre- and early adolescents. *Journal of Youth and Adolescence*, 18, 25–38.

Blanchard-Fields, F., & Robinson, S. (1987, April). *Controllability and adaptive coping from adolescence through older adulthood.* Paper presented at the biennial meeting of the Society for Research in Child Development, Baltimore.

Blash, R., & Unger, D. G. (1992, March). *Cultural factors and the self-esteem and aspirations of African-American adolescent males.* Paper presented at the meeting of the Society for Research on Adolescence, Washington, DC.

Blasi, A. (1988). Identity and the development of the self. In D. Lapsley & F. C. Power (Eds.), *Self, ego, and identity: Integrative approaches.* New York: Springer-Verlag.

Blasi, A., & Hoeffel, E. C. (1974). Adolescence and formal operations. *Human Development*, 17, 344–363.

Block, J. (1992, March). *Parental and personality antecedents of early menarche.* Paper presented at the meeting of the Society for Research on Adolescence, Washington, DC.

Block, J. H., Block, J., & Gjerde, P. (1986). The personality of children prior to divorce: A prospective study. *Child Development*, 57, 827–840.

Block, R. W. (1992). Chemical dependency in the adolescent. In D. E. Greydanus & M. L. Wolraich (Eds.), *Behavioral pediatrics.* New York: Springer-Verlag.

Bloom, B. S. (Ed.). (1985). *Developing talent in young people.* New York: Ballantine.

Blos, P. (1962). *On adolescence.* New York: Free Press.

Blos, P. (1989). The inner world of the adolescent. In A. H. Esman (Ed.), *International annals of adolescent psychiatry* (Vol. 1). Chicago: University of Chicago Press.

Blumenthal, S. J., & Kupfer, D. J. (1988). Overview of early detection and treatment strategies for suicidal behavior in young people. *Journal of Youth and Adolescence*, 17, 1–14.

Blyth, D. A., Bulcroft, R., & Simons, R. G. (1981, August). *The impact of puberty on adolescents: A longitudinal study.* Paper presented at the meeting of the American Psychological Association, Los Angeles.

Blyth, D. A., Durant, D., & Moosbrugger, L. (1985, April). *Perceived intimacy in the social relationships of drug- and nondrug-using adolescents.* Paper presented at the meeting of the Society for Research in Child Development, Toronto.

Bogenschneider, K. (1989, April). *Maternal employment in two-parent intact families, parenting style and adolescents' academic achievement: A process approach.* Paper presented at the biennial meeting of the Society for Research in Child Development, Kansas City.

Bolger, N., Downey, G., Walker, E., & Steininger, P. (1989). The onset of suicidal ideation in childhood and adolescence. *Journal of Youth and Adolescence*, 18, 175–190.

Botvin, G. (1986). Substance abuse prevention efforts: Recent developments and future directions. *Journal of School Health*, 56, 369–374.

Botvin, G. (1987, April 28). *Infancy to adolescence: Opportunities for success.* Paper presented to the Select Committee on Children, Youth, and Families, Washington, DC.

Bourne, E. (1978). The state of research on ego identity: A review and appraisal (Part I). *Journal of Youth and Adolescence*, 7, 223–251.

Bowker, A., & Hymel, S. (1991, April). *Coping with daily hassles in early adolescence.* Paper presented at the biennial meeting of the Society for Research in Child Development, Seattle.

Bowlby, J. (1969). *Attachment and loss* (Vol. 1). London: Hogarth.

Bowlby, J. (1980). *Attachment and loss.* Vol. 3: *Loss, sadness and depression.* New York: Basic Books.

Bowlby, J. (1989). *Secure attachment.* New York: Basic Books.

Bowman, P. (1989, April). *Job search discouragement among black adolescents: Familial and educational antecedents.* Paper presented at the biennial meeting of the Society for Research in Child Development, Kansas City.

Bowman, P. J., & Howard, C. (1985). Race-related socialization, motivation, and academic achievement: A study of black youths in three-generation families. *Journal of the American Academy of Child Psychiatry*, 24, 134–141.

Boxer, A. M. (1988, August). *Developmental continuities of gay and lesbian youth.* Paper presented at the meeting of the American Psychological Association, Atlanta, GA.

Boyd-Franklin, N. (1989). *Black families in therapy: A multisystems approach.* New York: Guilford.

Boyer, C. B., & Hein, K. (1991). AIDS and HIV infection in adolescents: The role of education and antibody testing. In R. M. Lerner, A. C. Petersen, & J. Brooks-Gunn (Eds.), *Encyclopedia of adolescence* (Vol. 1). New York: Garland.

Boyer, E. L. (1986, December). Transition from school to college. *Phi Delta Kappan*, pp. 283–287.

Bray, J. H. (1988). The effects of early remarriage on children's development: Preliminary analyses of the developmental issues in stepfamily research project. In E. M. Hetherington & J. D. Arasteh (Eds.), *Impact of divorce, single-parenting, and stepparenting on children.* Hillsdale, NJ: Erlbaum.

Brenner, A. (1984). *Helping children cope with stress.* Lexington, MA: Lexington Books.

Brent, D. A. (1989). Suicide and suicidal behavior in children and adolescents. *Pediatrics in Review*, 10, 269–275.

Breslow, L. (1990). The future of public health: Prospects in the United States for the 1990s. In *Annual Review of Public Health* (Vol. 11). Palo Alto, CA: Annual Reviews.

Brewer, M. B., & Campbell, D. T. (1976). *Ethnocentrism and intergroup attitudes.* New York: Wiley.

Brislin, R. (1991, August). *Directions in cross-cultural psychology.* Paper presented at the meeting of the American Psychological Association, San Francisco.

Brislin, R. W. (1990). Applied cross-cultural psychology: An introduction. In R. W. Brislin (Ed.), *Applied cross-cultural psychology.* Newbury Park, CA: Sage.

Broderick, C., & Rowe, G. (1968). A scale of preadolescent heterosexual development. *Journal of Marriage and the Family, 30,* 97–101.

Broman, S. (1981). Long-term development of children born to teenagers. In K. G. Scott, T. Field, & E. Robertson (Eds.), *Teenage parents and their offspring.* New York: Grune & Stratton.

Brone, R. J., & Fisher, C. B. (1988). Determinants of adolescent obesity: A comparison with anorexia nervosa. *Adolescence, 23,* 155–169.

Bronfenbrenner, U. (1979). Contexts of child rearing: Problems and prospects. *American Psychologist, 34,* 844–850.

Bronfenbrenner, U. (1986). Ecology of the family as a context for human development: Research perspectives. *Developmental Psychology, 22,* 723–742.

Bronfenbrenner, U. (1989, April). *Ecology of the family as a context for human development.* Paper presented at the biennial meeting of the Society for Research in Child Development, Kansas City, MO.

Bronstein, P. A., & Paludi, M. (1988). The introductory course from a broader human perspective. In P. A. Bronstein & K. Quina (Eds.), *Teaching a psychology of people.* Washington, DC: American Psychological Association.

Brook, D. W., & Brook, J. S. (in press). Family processes associated with alcohol and drug use and abuse. In E. Kaufman & P. Kaufman (Eds.), *Family therapy of drug and alcohol abuse: Ten years later.* New York: Gardner Press.

Brook, J. S., Brook, D. W., Gordon, A. S., Whiteman, M., & Cohen, P. (1990). The psychological etiology of adolescent drug use: A family interactional approach. *Genetic Psychology Monographs, 116,* no. 2.

Brook, J. S., Gordon, A. S., Brook, A., & Brook, D. (1989). The consequences of marijuana use on intrapersonal and interpersonal functioning in black and white adolescents. *Genetic, Social, and General Psychology Monographs, 115,* 349–369.

Brooks-Gunn, J. (1987). Pubertal processes: Their relevance to developmental research. In V. B. Van Hasselt & M. Hersen (Eds.), *Handbook of adolescent psychology.* New York: Pergamon.

Brooks-Gunn, J. (1988). Antecedents and consequences of variations in girls' maturational timing. In M. D. Levine & E. R. McAnarney (Eds.), *Early adolescent transitions.* Lexington, MA: Lexington Books.

Brooks-Gunn, J. (1991). Maturational timing variations in adolescent girls, antecedents of. In R. M. Lerner, A. C. Petersen, & J. Brooks-Gunn (Eds.), *Encyclopedia of adolescence.* New York: Garland.

Brooks-Gunn, J. (1992, March). *Revisiting theories of "storm and stress": The role of biology.* Paper presented at the meeting of the Society for Research on Adolescence, Washington, DC.

Brooks-Gunn, J., & Reiter, E. O. (1990). The role of pubertal processes. In S. S. Feldman & G. R. Elliott (Eds.), *At the threshold: The developing adolescent.* Cambridge, MA: Harvard University Press.

Brooks-Gunn, J., & Ruble, D. N. (1982) The development of menstrual-related beliefs and behaviors during early adolescence. *Child Development, 53,* 1567–1577.

Brooks-Gunn, J., & Warren, M. P. (1989, April). *How important are pubertal and social events for different problem behaviors and contexts.* Paper presented at the biennial meeting of the Society for Research in Child Development, Kansas City, MO.

Brooks-Gunn, J., & Warren, M. P. (1989). The psychological significance of secondary sexual characteristics in 9- to 11-year-old girls. *Child Development, 59,* 161–169.

Broughton, J. (1977). Beyond formal operations: Theoretical thought in adolescence. *Teachers College Record, 79,* 87–96.

Broughton, J. (1983). The cognitive developmental theory of adolescent self and identity. In B. Lee & G. Noam (Eds.), *Developmental approaches to self.* New York: Plenum.

Broverman, I., Vogel, S., Broverman, D., Clarkson, F., & Rosenkranz, P. (1972). Sex-role stereotypes: A current appraisal. *Journal of Social Issues, 28,* 59–78.

Brown, A. C., & Orthner, D. K. (1990). Relocation and personal well-being among early adolescents. *Journal of Early Adolescence, 10,* 366–381.

Brown, A. L., Bransford, J. D., Ferrara, R. A., & Campione, J. C. (1983). Learning, remembering, and understanding. In P. H. Mussen (Ed.), *Handbook of child psychology* (4th ed., Vol. 3). New York: Wiley.

Brown, A. L., & Smiley, S. S. (1977). Rating the importance of structural units of prose passages: A problem of metacognitive development. *Child Development, 48,* 1–8.

Brown, B. A. (1985). Factors influencing the process of withdrawal by female adolescents from the role of competitive age group swimmer. *Sociology of Sport Journal, 2,* 111–129.

Brown, B. B. (1990). Peer groups and peer cultures. In S. S. Feldman & G. R. Elliott (Eds.), *At the threshold: The developing adolescent.* Cambridge, MA: Harvard University Press.

Brown, B. B., & Lohr, M. J. (1987). Peer-group affiliation and adolescent self-esteem: An integration of ego-identity and symbolic-interaction theories. *Journal of Personality and Social Psychology, 52,* 47–55.

Brown, B. B., & Mounts, N. (1989, April). *Peer group structures in single vs. multiethnic high schools.* Paper presented at the biennial meeting of the Society for Research in Child Development, Kansas City.

Brown, B. B., Steinberg, L., Mounts, N., & Philipp, M. (1990, March). *The comparative influence of peers and parents on high school achievement: Ethnic differences.* Paper presented at the meeting of the Society for Research in Adolescence, Atlanta, GA.

Brown, D. (1987). The status of Holland's theory of vocational choice. *Career Development Quarterly, 36,* 13–24.

Brown, F. (1973). *The reform of secondary education: Report of the national commission on the reform of secondary education.* New York: McGraw-Hill.

Brown, J. D., & Siegel, J. D. (1988). Exercise as a buffer of life stress: A prospective study of adolescent health. *Health Psychology, 7,* 341–353.

Brown, L. K., DiClemente, R. J., & Beausoleil, N. I. (1992). Comparison of Human Immunodeficiency Virus related knowledge, attitudes, intentions, and behaviors among sexually active and abstinent young adolescents. *Journal of Adolescent Health Care, 13,* 140–145.

Brown, L. M., & Gilligan, C. (1990, March). *The psychology of women and the development of girls.* Paper presented at the meeting of the Society for Research on Adolescence, Atlanta, GA.

Brown, R. (1986). *Social psychology* (2nd ed.). New York: Macmillan.

Brownell, K. D. (1990, August). *Dieting, weight, and body image: Where culture and physiology collide.* Paper presented at the meeting of the American Psychological Association, Boston, MA.

Brownwell, K. D., & Stein, L. J. (1989). Metabolic and behavioral effects of weight loss and regain: A review of the animal and human literature. In A. J. Stunkard & A. Baum (Eds.), *Perspectives on behavioral medicine.* Hillsdale, NJ: Erlbaum.

Bruess, C. E., & Richardson, G. E. (1992). *Decisions for health* (3rd ed.). Dubuque, IA: Wm. C. Brown.

Bruner, J. (1966). *Toward a theory of instruction.* Cambridge, MA: Harvard University Press.

Bruner, J. (1989, April). *The state of developmental psychology.* Paper presented at the biennial meeting of the Society for Research in Child Development, Kansas City, MO.

Bruner, J. (1991, April). *Sociocultural determinants of the concept of mind.* Paper presented at the biennial meeting of the Society for Research in Child Development, Seattle.

Bruner, J. S., & Bornstein, M. H. (in press). On interaction. In M. H. Bornstein & J. S. Bruner (Eds), *Interaction in cognitive development.* Hillsdale, NJ: Erlbaum.

Buchanan, C. M. (1989, April). *Hormone concentrations and variability: Associations with reported moods and energy in adolescent girls.* Paper presented at the biennial meeting of the Society for Research in Child Development, Kansas City, MO.

Buchannon, C. M., & Maccoby, E. E. (1990, March). *Characteristics of adolescents and their families in three custodial arrangements.* Paper presented at the meeting of the Society for Research in Adolescence, Atlanta, GA.

Buhrmester, D. (1989). *Changes in friendship, interpersonal competence, and social adaptation during early adolescence.* Unpublished manuscript, Department of Psychology, UCLA, Los Angeles.

Buhrmester, D. (1990). Friendship, interpersonal competence, and adjustment in preadolescence and adolescence. *Child Development, 61,* 1101–1111.

Buhrmester, D. (1992, January). *Developmental changes in peer relations and friendships.* Colloquium, Program in Psychology and Human Development, University of Texas at Dallas.

Buhrmester, D., Camparo, L., Christensen, A., Gonzalez, L. S., & Hinshaw, S. P. (in press). Mothers and fathers interacting in dyads and triads with normal and hyperactive sons. *Developmental Psychology.*

Buhrmester, D., & Carbery, J. (1992, March). *Daily patterns of self-disclosure and adolescent adjustment.* Paper presented at the biennial meeting of the Society for Research on Adolescence, Washington, DC.

Buhrmester, D., & Furman, W. (1987). The development of companionship and intimacy. *Child Development, 58,* 1101–1113.

Buhrmester, D., & Furman, W. (1990). Perceptions of sibling relationships during middle childhood and adolescence. *Child Development, 61,* 1387–1398.

Buhrmester, D., Furman, W., Wittenberg, M., & Reis, H. (1988). Five domains of interpersonal competence in peer relationships. *Journal of Personality and Social Psychology, 55,* 991–1008.

Burbach, D. J., & Peterson, L. (1986). Children's concept of physical illness. *Health Psychology, 5,* 307–325.

Burbules, N. C., & Linn, M. C. (1988). Response to contradiction: Scientific reasoning during adolescence. *Journal of Educational Psychology, 80,* 67–75.

Burke, R. J., & Weir, T. (1979). Helping responses of parents and peer and adolescent well-being. *Journal of Psychology, 102,* 49–62.

Burton, R. V. (1984). A paradox in theories and research in moral development. In W. W. Kurtines & J. L. Gewirtz (Eds.), *Morality, moral behavior, and moral development.* New York: Wiley.

Busch-Rossnagal, N. A., & Zayas, L. U. (1991). Hispanic adolescents. In R. M. Lerner, A. C. Peterson, & J. Brooks-Gunn (Eds.), *Encyclopedia of adolescence* (Vol. 1). New York: Garland.

Bussey, K., & Maughan, B. (1982). Gender differences in moral reasoning. *Journal of Personality and Social Psychology, 42,* 701–706.

Butcher, J. (1985). Longitudinal analysis of adolescent girls' participation in physical activity. *Sociology of Sport Journal, 2,* 130–143.

Butterfield, F. (1990, January 21). Why they excel. *Parade Magazine,* pp. 4–6.

Byrne, D. (1973). *The development of role-taking in adolescence.* Unpublished doctoral dissertation, Harvard University Graduate School of Education.

Byrnes, J. P. (1988a). Formal operations: A systematic reformulation. *Developmental Review, 8,* 66–87.

Byrnes, J. P. (1988b). What's left is closer to right. *Developmental Review, 8,* 385–392.

Cairns, R. B., & Cairns, B. D. (1989, April). *Risks and lifelines in adolescence.* Paper presented at the biennial meeting of the Society for Research in Child Development, Kansas City.

Calhoun, J. A. (1988, March). *Gang violence.* Testimony to the House Select Committee on Children, Youth, and Families, Washington, DC.

Callahan, R. (1962). *Education and the cult of efficiency.* Chicago: University of Chicago Press.

Camara, K. A., & Resnick, G. (1988). Interparental conflict and cooperation: Factors moderating children's postdivorce adjustment. In E. M. Hetherington & J. D. Arasteh (Eds.), *Impact of divorce, single-parenting, and stepparenting on children.* Hillsdale, NJ: Erlbaum.

Camarena, P. M. (1991). Conformity in adolescence. In R. M. Lerner, A. C. Petersen, & J. Brooks-Gunn (Eds.), *Encyclopedia of adolescence* (Vol. 1). New York: Garland.

Cameron, J., Cowan, L. Holmes, B., Hurst, P., & McLean, M. (Eds.). (1983). *International handbook of educational systems.* New York: Wiley.

Campbell, D. T., & LeVine R. A. (1968). Ethnocentrism and intergroup relations. In R. Abelson & others (Eds.), *Theories and cognitive consistency: A sourcebook.* Chicago: Rand McNally.

Carey, S. (1986). *Conceptual change in childhood.* Boston: MIT Press.

Carey, S. (1988). Are children fundamentally different kinds of thinkers and learners than adults? In K. Richardson & S. Sheldon (Eds.), *Cognitive development to adolescence.* Hillsdale, NJ: Erlbaum.

Carlson, C., Cooper, C., & Hsu, J. (1990, March). *Predicting school achievement in early adolescence: The role of family process.* Paper presented at the meeting of the Society for Research in Adolescence, Atlanta.

Carnegie Corporation. (1989). *Turning points: Preparing American youth for the 21st century.* New York: Carnegie Corporation.

Case, R. (1985). *Intellectual development: Birth to adulthood.* New York: Academic Press.

Cassell, C. (1984). *Swept away: Why women fear their own sexuality.* New York: Simon & Schuster.

Castro, F. G., & Magana, D. (1988). A course in health promotion in ethnic minority populations. In P. A. Bronstein & K. Quina (Eds.), *Teaching a psychology of people.* Washington, DC: American Psychological Association.

Centers for Disease Control. (1988). HIV-related beliefs, knowledge, and behaviors among high school students. *Morbidity and Mortality Weekly Reports, 37,* 717–721.

Centers for Disease Control. (1992, January). *The CDC survey of adolescent sexual activity.* Atlanta, GA: Centers for Disease Control.

Chafee, S. H., & Yang, S. M. (1990). Communication and political socialization. In O. Ichilov (Ed.), *Political socialization, citizen education, and democracy.* New York: Columbia University Press.

Chapman, W., & Katz, M. R. (1983). Career information systems in secondary schools: A survey and assessment. *Vocational Guidance Quarterly, 31,* 165–177.

Charles A. Dana Foundation Report. (1988, Spring). *Dana award winner's innovations in educating minority students in math and science attract nationwide attention.* New York: Charles A. Dana Foundation, pp. 1–5.

Chase-Lansdale, P. L., & Hetherington, E. M. (in press). The impact of divorce on life-span development: Short- and long-term effects. In P. B. Baltes, D. L. Featherman, & R. M. Lerner (Eds.), *Life-span development and behavior.* Hillsdale, NJ: Erlbaum.

Chassin, L., Presson, C. C., Sherman, S. J., Corty, E., & Olshavsky, R. W. (1984). Predicting the onset of cigarette smoking in adolescents: A longitudinal study. *Journal of Applied Social Psychology, 14,* 224–243.

Chen, C., & Stevenson, H. W. (1989). Homework: A cross-cultural examination. *Child Development, 60,* 551–561.

Chesney-Lind, M. (1989). Girls' crime and woman's place: Toward a feminist model of female delinquency. *Crime and Delinquency, 35,* 5–30.

Chess, S., & Thomas, A. (1977). Temperamental individuality from childhood to adolescence. *Journal of Child Psychiatry, 16,* 218–226.

Children's Defense Fund. (1986). *Building health programs for teenagers.* Washington, DC: Children's Defense Fund.

Children's Defense Fund. (1991). *The adolescent and young adult fact book.* Washington, DC: Children's Defense Fund.

Chilman, C. (1979). *Adolescent sexuality in a changing American society: Social and psychological perspectives.* Washington, DC: Public Health Service, National Institute of Mental Health.

Chodorow, N. (1978). *The reproduction of mothering.* Berkeley, CA: Univeristy of California Press.

Chodorow, N. J. (1989). *Feminism and psychoanalytic theory.* New Haven, CT: Yale University Press.

Christenson, P. W., & Roberts, D. F. (1991, August). *Music media in adolescent health promotion: Problems and prospects.* Paper presented at the meeting of the American Psychological Association, San Francisco.

Cicirelli, V. (1977). Family structure and interaction: Sibling effects on socialization. In M. McMillan & M. Sergio (Eds.), *Child psychiatry: Treatment and research.* New York: Brunner/Mazel.

Clabby, J. G., & Elias, M. J. (1988). Improving social problem-solving and awareness. *William T. Grant Foundation Annual Report,* p. 18.

Clark, D. A., & Beck, A. T. (1989). Cognitive theory and therapy of anxiety and depression. In P. C. Kendall & D. Watson (Eds.), *Anxiety and depression.* San Diego: Academic Press.

Clark, K. (1965). *Dark ghetto.* New York: Harper.

Clark, M., Klein, J., & Beckett, J. (1992, March). *Correlates of courtship violence.* Paper presented at the meeting of the Society for Research on Adolescence, Washington, DC.

Clark, M. S., Powell, M. C., Ovellette, R., & Milberg, S. (1987). Recipient's mood, relationship type, and helping. *Journal of Personality and Social Psychology, 43,* 94–103.

Clark, S. D., Zabin, L. S., & Hardy, J. B. (1984). Sex, contraception, and parenthood: Experience and attitudes among urban black young men. *Family Planning Perspectives, 16,* 77–82.

Clark, V. F., & Nelson, W. M. (1990). Negative expectations and self-evaluations in dysphoria. *Journal of Youth and Adolescence, 19,* 57–62.

Clark-Lempers, D. S., Lempers, J. D., & Netusil, A. J. (1990). Family financial stress, parental support, and young adolescents' academic achievement and depressive symptoms. *Journal of Early Adolescence, 10,* 21–36.

Clasen, D. R., & Brown, B. B. (1987). Understanding peer pressure in the middle school. *Middle School Journal, 19,* 21–23.

Cloninger, C. R. (1991, January). *Personality traits and alcoholic predisposition.* Paper presented at the conference of the National Institute on Drug Abuse, University of California at Los Angeles.

Cochran, S. D., & Mays, V. M. (1990). Sex, lies, and HIV. *New England Journal of Medicine, 322 (11),* 774–775.

Cocks, J. (1983, December 26). Sing a song of seeing. *Time,* p. 54.

Cocks, J. (1985, September 30). Rock is a four-letter word. *Time,* pp. 70–71.

Cohen, P., Brook, J. S., & Kandel, D. B. (1991). Drug use, predictors and correlates of. In R. M. Lerner, A. C. Petersen, & J. Brooks-Gunn (Eds.), *Encyclopedia of adolescence* (Vol. 1). New York: Garland.

Coie, J. D., & Koeppl, G. K. (1990). Adapting intervention to the problems of aggressive and disruptive rejected children. In S. R. Asher & J. D. Coie (Eds.), *Peer rejection in childhood.* New York: Cambridge University Press.

Colby, A., Kohlberg, L., Gibbs, J., & Lieberman, M. (1983). A longitudinal study of moral judgment. *Monographs of the Society for Research in Child Development, 48*(21, Serial No. 201).

Cole, D. A. (1991). Suicide, adolescent. In R. M. Lerner, A. C. Petersen, & J. Brooks-Gunn (Eds.), *Encyclopedia of adolescence* (Vol. 2). New York: Garland.

Cole, M., & Cole, S. R. (1989). *The development of children.* New York: Scientific American.

Coleman, J. S. (1961). *The adolescent society.* New York: Free Press.

Coleman, J. S. (1980). The peer group. In J. Adelson (Ed.), *Handbook of adolescent psychology.* New York: Wiley.

Coleman, J. S., Campbell, E. Q., Hobson, C. J., McPartland, J., Mood, A. M., Weinfeld, F. D., & York, R. L. (1966). *Equality of educational opportunity.* Washington, DC: U.S. Government Printing Office.

Coleman, J. S., et al. (1974). *Youth: Transition to adulthood.* Report of the Panel on Youth of the President's Science Advisory Committee. Chicago: University of Chicago Press.

Coles, R. (1970). *Erik H. Erikson: The growth of his work.* Boston: Little, Brown.

Coles, R. (1986). *The political life of children.* Boston: Little, Brown.

College Board Commission on Precollege Guidance and Counseling. (1986). *Keeping the options open.* New York: College Entrance Examination Board.

Collins, A. (1986). Teaching reading and writing with personal computers. In J. Oransanu (Ed.), *A decade of reading research: Implications for practice.* Hillsdale, NJ: Erlbaum.

Collins, W. A. (1985, April). *Cognition, affect, and development in parent-child relationships.* Paper presented at the biennial meeting of the Society for Research in Child Development, Toronto.

Collins, W. A. (1990). Parent-child relationships in the transition to adolescence: Continuity and change in interaction, affect, and cognition. In R. Montemayor, G. R. Adams, & T. P. Gulotta (Eds.), *From childhood to adolescence: A transitional period?* Newbury Park, CA: Sage.

Comer, J. P. (1988). Educating poor minority children. *Scientific American, 259,* 42–48.

Committee for Economic Development. (1987). *Children in need: Investment strategies for the educationally disadvantaged.* Washington, DC: Committee for Economic Development.

Compas, B. (1989, April). *Vulnerability and stress in childhood and adolescence.* Paper presented at the biennial meeting of the Society for Research in Child Development, Kansas City.

Compas, B. E., & Wagner, B. M. (1991). Psychosocial stress during adolescence: Intrapersonal and interpersonal processes. In M. E. Colten & S. Gore (Eds.), *Adolescent stress: Causes and consequences.* Hawthorne, NY: Aldine de Gruyter.

Conant, J. B. (1959). *The American high school today.* New York: McGraw-Hill.

Condry, J. C. (1989). *The psychology of television.* Hillsdale, NJ: Erlbaum.

Condry, J. C., Simon, M. L., & Bronfenbrenner, U. (1968). *Characteristics of peer- and adult-oriented children.* Unpublished manuscript, Cornell University, Ithaca, NY.

Conger, J. J. (1981). Freedom and commitment: Families, youth, and social change. *American Psychologist, 36,* 1475–1484.

Conger, J. J. (1988). Hostages to the future: Youth, values, and the public interest. *American Psychologist, 43,* 291–300.

Conger, K. J. (1992, March). *Sibling relationship quality as a mediator and moderator of the relationship between parental mood and behavior and adolescent self-esteem.* Paper presented at the meeting of the Society for Research on Adolescence, Washington, DC.

Conger, R. D., Conger, K. J., & Simons, R. L. (1992, March). *Family economic stress, parenting behavior, and adolescent drinking.* Paper presented at the meeting of the Society for Research on Adolescence, Washington, DC.

Conger, R. D., Elder, G. H., Lasley, F., Lorenz, F., Norem, R., & Simons, R. L. (1989, April). *Preliminary findings from the Iowa Youth and Families Project.* Paper presented at the biennial meeting of the Society for Research in Child Development, Kansas City.

Cook, T. D., Schleef, D. J., Miller, L. L., & Stockdill, B. C. (1992, March). *Moving as a strategy of family management.* Paper presented at the meeting of the Society for Research on Adolescence, Washington, DC.

Cooper, C. R., & Ayers-Lopez, S. (1985). Family and peer systems in early adolescence: New models of the role of relationships in development. *Journal of Early Adolescence, 5,* 9–22.

Cooper, C. R., Baker, H., Polichar, D., & Welsh, M. (1992, March). *Ethnic perspectives on individuality and connectedness in adolescents' relationships with families and peers.* Paper presented at the meeting of the Society for Research on Adolescence, Washington, DC.

Cooper, C. R., & Grotevant, H. D. (1989, April). *Individuality and connectedness in the family and adolescents' self and relational competence.* Paper presented at the meeting of the Society for Research in Child Development, Kansas City.

Coopersmith, S. (1967). *The antecedents of self-esteem.* San Francisco: W. H. Freeman.

Corless, I. B., & Pittman-Lindeman, M. (1989). *AIDS: Principles, practices, and politics.* New York: Hemisphere.

Cosby, F. J. (1991). *Juggling.* New York: Free Press.

Costin, F., & Draguns, J. G. (1989). *Abnormal psychology: Patterns, issues, interventions.* New York: John Wiley.

Cote, J. E., & Levine, C. (1988a). A critical examination of the ego identity status paradigm. *Developmental Review, 8,* 147–184.

Cote, J. E., & Levine, C. (1988b). On critiquing the identity status paradigm: A rejoinder to Waterman. *Developmental Review, 8,* 209–218.

Cote, J. E., & Levine, C. (1989). *An empirical investigation of the validity of the ego status paradigm.* Unpublished manuscript, University of Western Ontario.

Cowan, P. (1978). *Piaget with feeling.* New York: Holt, Rinehart & Winston.

Cox, T. (Host). (1985, September 29). "At issue" [Television talk show]. Channel 2, Los Angeles.

Cremin, L. (1961). *The transformation of the school.* New York: Knopf.

Crites, J. O. (1989). Career differentiation in adolescence. In D. Stern & D. Eichorn (Eds.), *Adolescence and work.* Hillsdale, NJ: Erlbaum.

Crockett, L. J. (1991). Sex roles and sex-typing in adolescence. In R. M. Lerner, A. C. Petersen, & J. Brooks-Gunn (Eds.) *Encyclopedia of adolescence* (Vol. 2). New York: Garland.

Cronbach, L. J., & Snow, R. E. (1977). *Aptitudes and instructional methods.* New York: Irvington.

Cross, K. P. (1984, November). The rising tide of school reform reports. *Phi Delta Kappan,* pp. 167–172.

Csikszentmihalyi, M., & Larson, R. (1984). *Being adolescent.* New York: Basic Books.

Curtiss, S. (1978). *Genie.* New York: Academic Press.

Cutrona, C. E. (1982). Transition to college: Loneliness and the process of social adjustment. In L. A. Peplau & D. Perlman (Eds.), *Loneliness: A sourcebook of current theory, research, and therapy.* New York: Wiley.

Damon, A. (1977). *Human biology and ecology.* New York: W. W. Norton.

Damon, W. (1988). *The moral child.* New York: Free Press.

Damon, W. (1991). Self-concept, adolescent. In R. M. Lerner, A. C. Petersen, & J. Brooks-Gunn (Eds.), *Encyclopedia of adolescence* (Vol. 2). New York: Garland.

Damon, W., & Hart, D. (1988). *Self-understanding in childhood and adolescence.* New York: Cambridge University Press.

Danner, F. (1989). Cognitive development in adolescence. In J. Worrell & F. Danner (Eds.), *The adolescent as decision maker.* New York: Academic Press.

Danziger, S. K., & Radin, N. (1989, April). *Absent does not equal uninvolved: Predictors of fathering in teen mother families.* Paper presented at the meeting of the Society for Research in Child Development, Kansas City.

Darling, C. A., Kallen, D. J., & VanDusen, J. E. (1984). Sex in transition, 1900–1984. *Journal of Youth and Adolescence, 13,* 385–399.

Dasen, P. R., Ngini, L., & Lavalée, M. (1979). Cross-cultural training studies of concrete operations. In L. H. Eckenberger, W. J. Lonner, & Y. H. Poortinga (Eds.), *Cross-cultural contributions to psychology.* Boston: Allyn & Bacon.

Davison, G. C., & Neale, J. M. (1990). *Abnormal psychology* (5th ed.). New York: John Wiley.

DeFour, D. C., & Paludi, M. A. (in press). Integrating scholarship on ethnicity into the psychology of women course. *Teaching of Psychology.*

de Jong-Gierveld, J. (1987). Developing and testing a model of loneliness. *Journal of Personality and Social Psychology, 53,* 119–128.

DeLamater, J., & MacCorquodale, P. (1979). *Premarital sexuality.* Madison, WI: University of Wisconsin Press.

De Necochea, G. (1988, May). Expanding the Hispanic college pool. *Change,* pp. 61–62.

Dellas, M., Gaier, E. L., & Emihovich, C. A. (1979). Maternal employment and selected behaviors and attitudes of preadolescents and adolescents. *Adolescence, 14,* 579–589.

Demorest, A., Meyer, C., Phelps, E., Gardner, H., & Winner, E. (1984). Words speak louder than actions: Understanding deliberately false remarks. *Child Development, 55,* 1527–1534.

Dempster, F. N. (1981). Memory span: Sources of individual and developmental differences. *Psychological Bulletin, 89,* 63–100.

Denmark, F. L., & Paludi, M. A. (Eds.). (in press). *Handbook on the psychology of women.* Westport, CT: Greenwood.

Denmark, F. L., Russo, N. F., Frieze, I. H., Sechzur, J. (1988). Guidelines for avoiding sexism in psychological research: A report of the Ad Hoc Committee on nonsexist research. *American Psychologist, 43,* 582–585.

Dewey, J. (1933). *How we think: A restatement of the relation of reflective thinking to the educative process.* Lexington, MA: D. C. Heath.

Diamond, E. E. (1988). Women's occupational plans and decisions: An introduction. *Applied Psychology: An International Review, 37,* 97–102.

Dickerscheid, J. D., Schwarz, P. M., Noir, S., & El-Taliawy, T. (1988). Gender concept development of preschool-aged children in the United States and Egypt. *Sex Roles, 18,* 669–677.

Dickinson, G. E. (1975). Dating behavior of black and white adolescents before and after desegregation. *Journal of Marriage and the Family, 37,* 602–608.

Dielman, T., Schulenberg, J., Leech, S., & Shope, J. T. (1992, March). *Reduction of susceptibility to peer pressure and alcohol use/misuse through a school-based prevention program.* Paper presented at the meeting of the Society for Research on Adolescence, Washington, DC.

Dielman, T. E., Shope, J. T., & Butchart, A. T. (1990, March). *Peer, family, and intrapersonal predictors of adolescent alcohol use and misuse.* Paper presented at the meeting of the Society for Research in Adolescence, Atlanta, GA.

Dishion, T. J. (1992, March). *Parental factors in early adolescent substance use: Correlational and experimental evidence.* Paper presented at the meeting of the Society for Research on Adolescence, Washington, DC.

Dishion, T. J., & Skinner, M. S. (1989, April). *A process model for the role of peer relations in adolescent social adjustment.* Paper presented at the biennial meeting of the Society for Research in Child Development, Kansas City.

Dodge, K. A. (1983). Behavioral antecedents of peer social status. *Child Development, 54,* 1386–1399.

Dodge, K. A., & Feldman, E. (1990). Issues in social cognition and sociometric status. In S. R. Asher & J. D. Coie (Eds.), *Peer rejection in childhood.* New York: Cambridge University Press.

Dodge, K. A., Pettit, G. S., McClaskey, C. L., & Brown, M. M. (1986). Social competence in children. *Monographs of the Society for Research in Child Development, 51*(2, Serial No. 213).

Dolcini, M. M., Coh, L. D., Adler, N. E., Millstein, S. G., Irwin, C. E., Kegeles, S. M., & Stone, G. C. (1989). Adolescent egocentrism and feelings of invulnerability: Are they related? *Journal of Early Adolescence, 9,* 409–418.

Domino, G. (1992). Acculturation of Hispanics. In S. B. Knouse, P. Rosenfeld, & A. Culbertson (Eds.), *Hispanics in the workplace.* Newbury Park, CA: Sage.

Donovan, J. E., & Jessor, R. (1978). Adolescent problem drinking: Psychosocial correlates in a national sample study. *Journal of Studies on Alcohol, 39,* 1506–1524.

Dooley, D., Whalen, C. K., & Flowers, J. V. (1978). Verbal response styles of children and adolescents in a counseling analog setting: Effects of age, sex, and labeling. *Journal of Counseling Psychology, 25,* 85–95.

Dornbusch, S. M., Carlsmith, J. M., Bushwall, S. J., Ritter, P. I., Leidman, P. H., Hastorf, A. H., & Gross, R. T. (1985). Single parents, extended households, and the control of adolescents. *Child Development, 56,* 326–341.

Dornbusch, S. M., Petersen, A. C., & Hetherington, E. M. (1991). Projecting the future of research on adolescence. *Journal of Research on Adolescence, 1,* 7–18.

Dornbusch, S. M., Ritter, P, L., Leiderman, P. H., Roberts, D. F., & Fraleigh, M. J. (1987). The relation of parenting style to adolescent school performance. *Child Development, 58,* 1244–1257.

Douvan, E., & Adelson, J. (1966). *The adolescent experience.* New York: Wiley.

Dove, A. (1968, July 15). Taking the chitling test. *Newsweek,* pp. 51–52.

Doyle, J. A., & Paludi, M. A. (1991). *Sex and gender: The human experience* (2nd ed.). Dubuque, IA: Wm. C. Brown.

Draguns, J. G. (1991). Freud, Anna. In R. M. Lerner, A. C. Petersen, & J. Brooks-Gunn (Eds.), *Encyclopedia of adolescence* (Vol. 1). New York: Garland.

Dreyer, P. H. (1982). Sexuality during adolescence. In B. B. Wolman (Ed.), *Handbook of developmental psychology.* Englewood Cliffs, NJ: Prentice-Hall.

Dryfoos, J. G. (1990). *Adolescents at risk: Prevalence and prevention.* New York: Oxford University Press.

Dryfoos, J. G. (1992, March). *Integrating services for adolescents: The community schools.* Paper presented at the meeting of the Society for Research on Adolescence, Washington, DC.

DuBois, D. L., & Hirsch, B. J. (1990). School and neighborhood friendship patterns of blacks and whites in early adolescence. *Child Development, 61,* 524–536.

Duck, S. W. (1975). Personality similarity and friendship choices by adolescents. *European Journal of Social Psychology, 5,* 351–365.

Duck, S. W. (1988). Child and adolescent friendships. In P. Marsh (Ed.), *Eye to eye: How people interact.* Topsfield, MA: Salem House.

Duckett, E., & Richards, M. H. (1992, March). *Maternal employment, family relations, and young adolescents' emotional attachment.* Paper presented at the meeting of the Society for Research on Adolescence, Washington, DC.

Dunham, C. C., & Bengtson, V. L. (1991). Generational continuity and change. In R. M. Lerner, A. C. Petersen, and J. Brooks-Gunn (Eds.), *Encyclopedia of adolescence* (Vol. 1). New York: Garland.

Dunphy, D. C. (1963). The social structure of urban adolescent peer groups. *Society, 26,* 230–246.

Durkin, K. (1985). Television and sex-role acquisition 1: Content. *British Journal of Social Psychology, 24,* 101–113.

Eager, R. M. (1992). Child and adolescent sexuality: Perspectives and recommendations. In D. E. Greydanus & M. L. Wolraich (Eds.), *Behavioral pediatrics.* New York: Springer-Verlag.

Eagleston, J. R., Kirmil-Gray, K., Thoresen, C. E., Widenfield, S. A., Bracke, P., Helft, L., & Arnow, B. (1986). Physical health correlates of Type A behavior in children and adolescents. *Journal of Behavioral Medicine, 9,* 341–362.

East, P. L. (1989). Early adolescents' perceived interpersonal risks and benefits: Relations to social support and psychological functioning. *Journal of Early Adolescence, 9,* 374–395.

East, P. L. (1991). Peer status groups. In R. M. Lerner, A. C. Petersen, & J. Brooks-Gunn (Eds.), *Encyclopedia of adolescence* (Vol. 2). New York: Garland.

Ebata, A. T. (1991). Stress and coping in adolescence. In R. M. Lerner, A. C. Petersen, & J. Brooks-Gunn (Eds.), *Encyclopedia of adolescence* (Vol. 2). New York: Garland.

Ebata, A. T., & Moos, R. H. (1989, April). *Coping and adjustment in four groups of adolescents.* Paper presented at the biennial meeting of the Society for Research in Child Development, Kansas City.

Eccles, J. (1987). Gender roles and achievement patterns: An expectancy value perspective. In J. M. Reinisch, L. A. Rosenblum, & S. A. Sanders (Eds.), *Masculinity/femininity.* New York: Oxford University Press.

Eccles, J., & Hoffman, L. W. (1984). Sex roles, socialization, and occupational behavior. In H. W. Stevenson & A. E. Siegel (Eds.), *Research in child development and public policy* (Vol. 1). Chicago: University of Chicago Press.

Eccles, J., MacIver, D., & Lange, L. (1986). *Classroom practices and motivation to study math.* Paper presented at the annual meeting of the American Educational Research Association, San Francisco.

Eccles, J., & Midgley, C. (1990). Changes in academic motivation and self-perception during early adolescence. In R. Montemayor, G. R. Adams, & T. P. Gulotta (Eds.), *From childhood to adolescence: A transitional period?* Newbury Park, CA: Sage.

Eccles, J. S. (1991). Academic achievement. In R. M. Lerner, A. C. Petersen, & J. Brooks-Gunn (Eds.), *Encyclopedia of adolescence* (Vol. 1). New York: Garland.

Eccles, J. S., & Buchanan, C. M. (1992, March). *Hormones and behavior at early adolescence: A theoretical overview.* Paper presented at the meeting of the Society for Research on Adolescence, Washington, DC.

Eccles, J. S., Harold-Goldsmith, R., & Miller, C. L. (1989, April). *Parents' stereotypic belief about gender differences and adolescence.* Paper presented at the biennial meeting of the Society for Research in Child Development, Kansas City.

Eccles, J. S., Jacobs, J., Harold, R., Yoon, K., Aberbach, A., & Dolan, C. F. (1991, August). *Expectancy effects are alive and well on the home front: Influences on, and consequences of, parents' beliefs regarding their daughters' and sons' abilities and interests.* Paper presented at the meeting of the American Psychological Association, San Francisco.

Edelbrock, C. S. (1989, April). *Self-reported internalizing and externalizing problems in a community sample of adolescents.* Paper presented at the meeting of the Society for Research in Child Development, Kansas City, MO.

Edelman, M. W. (1987). *Families in peril: An agenda for social change.* New York: Alan Guttmacher Institute.

Educational Testing Service. (1992, February). *Cross-national comparisons of 9–13 year olds' science and math achievement.* Princeton, NJ: Educational Testing Service.

Edwards, C. P. (1987). Culture and the construction of moral values. In J. Kagan & S. Lamb (Eds.), *The emergence of morality in young children.* Chicago: University of Chicago Press.

Edwards, H. (1990). The sociology of sport. In J. E. Farley, *Sociology.* Englewood Cliffs, NJ: Prentice-Hall.

Eger, M. (1981). The conflict in moral education: An informal case study. *Public Interest, 63,* 62–80.

Eisenberg, N. (1987). The relation of altruism and other moral behaviors to moral cognition: Methodological and conceptual issues. In N. Eisenberg (Ed.), *Contemporary topics in developmental psychology.* New York: Wiley.

Eisenberg, N. (1989, April). *Sources of variation in prosocial moral reasoning.* Paper presented at the biennial meeting of the Society for Research in Child Development, Kansas City.

Eisenberg, N. (1991). Prosocial development in adolescence. In R, M. Lerner, A. C. Petersen, & J. Brooks-Gunn (Eds.), *Encyclopedia of adolescence* (Vol. 2), New York: Garland.

Eitzen, D. S. (1975). Athletics in the status system of male adolescents: A replication of Coleman's *The adolescent society. Adolescence, 10,* 267–276.

Ek, C. A., & Steelman, L. C. (1988). Becoming a runaway. *Youth and Society, 19,* 334–358.

Elder, G. H. (1974). *Children of the Great Depression.* Chicago: University of Chicago Press.

Elder, G. H. (1975). Adolescence in the life cycle. In S. E. Dragastin & G. H. Elder (Eds.), *Adolescence in the life cycle: Psychological change and social context.* New York: Wiley.

Elder, G. H. (1980). Adolescence in historical perspective. In J. Adelson (Ed.), *Handbook of adolescent psychology.* New York: Wiley.

Elder, G. H., Caspi, A., & Downey, G. (1986). Problem behavior and family relationships: Life course and intergenerational themes. In A. Sorensen, F. Weinert, & L. Sherrod (Eds.), *Human development and the life course.* Hillsdale, NJ: Erlbaum.

Elkind, D. (1961). Quantity conceptions in junior and senior high school students. *Child Development, 32,* 551–560.

Elkind, D. (1967). Egocentrism in adolescence. *Child Development, 38,* 1025–1034.

Elkind, D. (1976). *Child development and education: A Piagetian perspective.* New York: Oxford University Press.

Elkind, D. (1978). Understanding the young adolescent. *Adolescence, 13,* 127–134.

Elkind, D. (1981). *The hurried child.* Reading, MA: Addison-Wesley.

Elkind, D. (1985). Reply to D. Lapsley and M. Murphy's *Developmental Review* paper. *Developmental Review, 5,* 218–226.

Ellis, L., & Ames, M. A. (1987). Neurohormonal functioning and sexual orientation: A theory of homosexuality-heterosexuality. *Psychological Bulletin, 101,* 233–258.

Ennis, R. H. (1990). The extent to which critical thinking is subject-specific: Further clarification. *Educational Leadership, 19,* 13–16.

Ennis, R. H. (1991). Critical thinking: Literature review and needed research. In L. Idol & B. F. Jones (Eds.), *Educational values and cognitive instruction.* Hillsdale, NJ: Erlbaum.

Enright, R. D., & the Educational Psychology Study Group. (in press). The moral development of forgiveness. In W. Kurtines & J. Gewirtz (Eds.), *The moral development of forgiveness.* Hillsdale, NJ: Erlbaum.

Enright, R. D., Lapsley, D., & Olson, L. (1984). Moral judgment and the social cognitive development research program. In S. Modgil & C. Modgil (Eds.), *Lawrence Kohlberg: Consensus and controversy.* Slough, England: NFER Press.

Enright, R. D., Lapsley, D. K., Dricas, A. S., & Fehr, L. A. (1980). Parental influence on the development of adolescent autonomy and identity. *Journal of Youth and Adolescence, 9,* 529–546.

Enright, R. D., Levy, V. M., Harris, D., & Lapsley, D. K. (1987). Do economic conditions influence how theorists view adolescents? *Journal of Youth and Adolescence, 16,* 541–559.

Enright, R. D., Santos, M. J. D., & Al-Mabuk, R. (1989). The adolescent as forgiver. *Journal of Adolescence, 12,* 95–110.

Entwistle, D. R. (1988). Adolescents change schools. *Contemporary Psychology, 33,* 585–586.

Entwistle, D. R. (1990). Schools and the adolescent. In S. S. Feldman & G. R. Elliott (Eds.), *At the threshold: The developing adolescent.* Cambridge, MA: Harvard University Press.

Epstein, H. T. (1974). Phrenoblysis: Special brain and mind growth periods. *Developmental Psychobiology, 7,* 217–224.

Epstein, H. T. (1978). Growth spurts during brain development: Implications for educational policy and practice. In J. S. Chall & A. F. Mirsky (Eds.), *Education and the brain.* Chicago: University of Chicago Press.

Epstein, H. T. (1980). EEG developmental stages. *Developmental Psychobiology, 13,* 629–631.

Erikson, E. H. (1950). *Childhood and society.* New York: Norton.

Erikson, E. H. (1962). *Young man Luther.* New York: Norton.

Erikson, E. H. (1968). *Identity: Youth and crisis.* New York: W. W. Norton.

Erikson, E. H. (1969). *Gandhi's truth.* New York: Norton.

Erikson, E. H. (1970). Reflections on the dissent of contemporary youth. *International Journal of Psychoanalysis, 51,* 11–22.

Erlick, A. C., & Starry, A. R. (1973, June). *Sources of information for career decisions.* Report of Poll No. 98, Purdue Opinion Panel.

Estrada, P. (1992, March). *Socio-emotional and educational functioning in poor urban youth during the transition to middle school: The role of peer and teacher social support.* Paper presented at the meeting of the Society for Research on Adolescence, Washington, DC.

Evans, B. J., & Whitfield, J. R. (Eds.) (1988). *Black males in the United States: An annotated bibliography from 1967 to 1987.* Washington, DC: American Psychological Association.

Evans, M. E. (1992, March). *Achievement and achievement-related beliefs in Asian and Western contexts: Cultural and gender differences.* Paper presented at the meeting of the Society for Research on Adolescence, Washington, DC.

Eveleth, P. B., & Tanner, J. M. (1990). *Worldwide variation in human growth* (2nd ed.). Cambridge, England: Cambridge University Press.

Falbo, T., & Polit, D. F. (1986). A quantitative review of the only-child literature: Research evidence and theory development. *Psychological Bulletin, 100,* 176–189.

Farley, J. E. (1990). *Sociology.* Englewood Cliffs, NJ: Prentice-Hall.

Farnham-Diggory, S. (1990). *Schooling.* Cambridge, MA: Harvard University Press.

Fasick, F. A. (1988). Patterns of formal education in high school as rites of passage. *Adolescence, 23,* 457–468.

Faust, M. S. (1977). Somatic development of adolescent girls. *Monographs of the Society for Research in Child Development, 42*(1, Serial No. 169).

Feeney, S. (1980). *Schools for young adolescents: Adapting the early childhood model.* Carrboro, NC: Center for Early Adolescence.

Feiring, C. (1992, March). *Concepts of romance in mid-adolescence.* Paper presented at the meeting of the Society for Research on Adolescence, Washington, DC.

Feist, J., & Brannon, L. (1989). *An introduction to behavior and health.* Belmont, CA: Wadsworth.

Feldman, D. H. (1989a). Creativity: Proof that development occurs. In W. Damon (Ed.), *Child development today and tomorrow.* San Francisco: Jossey-Bass.

Feldman, D. H. (1989b, April). *The development of extraordinary artistic ability.* Discussion at the biennial meeting of the Society of Research for Child Development, Kansas City, MO.

Feldman, S. S., & Elliott, G. R. (1990). Progress and promise of research on normal adolescent development. In S. S. Feldman & G. Elliott (Eds.), *At the threshold: The developing adolescent.* Cambridge, MA: Harvard University Press.

Feldman, S. S., & Rosenthal, D. A. (1990a). The acculturation of autonomy expectations in Chinese high schoolers residing in two Western nations. *International Journal of Psychology, 25,* 259–281.

Feldman, S. S., & Rosenthal, D. A. (1990b). *The influence of family variables and adolescents' values on age expectations of behavioral autonomy: A cross-cultural study of Hong Kong, Australian, and American youth.* Unpublished manuscript, Stanford Center for the Study of Families, Stanford, CA.

Fenzel, L. M. (1989). Role strains and the transition to middle school: Longitudinal trends and sex differences. *Journal of Early Adolescence, 9,* 211–226.

Fenzel, L. M. (1992, March). *The effects of parents' participation on the social and academic adjustment of African-American middle school students.* Paper presented at the meeting of the Society for Research on Adolescence, Washington, DC.

Fenzel, L. M., Blyth, D. A., & Simmons, R. G. (1991). School transitions, secondary. In R. M. Lerner, A. C. Petersen, & J. Brooks-Gunn (Eds.), *Encyclopedia of adolescence* (Vol. 2). New York: Garland.

Festinger, L. (1954). A theory of social comparison processes. *Human Relations, 7,* 117–150.

Fidler, P. P., & Hunter, M. S. (1989). How seminars enhance student success. In M. L. Upcraft & J. N. Gardner (Eds.), *The freshman year experience.* San Francisco: Jossey-Bass.

Field, J. (1981). Whither quantitative history? A review of some recent work in the economic and social history of education. *Historical Methods, 14,* 85–95.

Field, L. D. (1991, April). *The role of social support in Hispanic adolescents' academic achievement.* Paper presented at the biennial meeting of the Society for Research in Child Development, San Francisco.

Field, T. M., Widmayer, S. M., Stringer, S., & Ignatoff, E. (1980). Teenage lower-class, black mothers and their preterm infants: An intervention and developmental follow-up. *Child Development, 51,* 426–436.

Fields, R. (1992). *Drugs and alcohol in perspective.* Dubuque, IA: Wm. C. Brown.

Fine, G. A., Mortimer, J. T., & Roberts, D. F. (1990). Leisure, work, and the mass media. In S. S. Feldman & G. R. Elliott (Eds.), *At the threshold: The developing adolescent.* Cambridge, MA: Harvard University Press.

Fischer, K. W. (1980). A theory of cognitive development: The control and construction of hierarchies of skills. *Psychological Review, 87,* 477–531.

Fischer, K. W., & Lazerson, A. (1984). *Human development.* San Francisco: W. H. Freeman.

Fisher, C. B., & Brone, R. J. (1991). Eating disorders in adolescence. In R. M. Lerner, A. C. Petersen, & J. Brooks-Gunn (Eds.), *Encyclopedia of adolescence* (Vol, 1). New York: Garland.

Fisher, D. (1990, March). *Effects of attachment on adolescents' friendships.* Paper presented at the meeting of the Society for Research in Adolescence, Atlanta, GA.

Fisher, T. D. (1987). Family communication and the sexual behavior and attitudes of college students. *Journal of Youth and Adolescence, 16,* 481–495.

Fitzgerald, J. M. (1991). Memory. In R. M. Lerner, A. C. Petersen, & J. Brooks-Gunn (Eds.), *Encyclopedia of adolescence* (Vol. 2). New York: Garland.

Flanagan, C. A. (1990a). Change in family work status: Effects on parent-adolescent decision making. *Child Development, 61,* 163–177.

Flanagan, C. A. (1990b). Families and schools in hard times. In V. C. McLoyd & C. A. Flanagan (Eds.), *Economic stress: Effects on family life and child development.* San Francisco, CA: Jossey-Bass.

Flanagan, T., & Jamieson, K. (Eds.). (1988). *Sourcebook of criminal justice statistics— 1987.* Washington, DC: U.S. Government Printing Office, U.S. Department of Justice Statistics.

Flavell, J. H. (1979). Metacognition and cognitive monitoring: A new area of psychological inquiry. *American Psychologist, 34,* 906–911.

Flavell, J. H. (1980, Fall). A tribute to Piaget. *Society for Research in Child Development Newsletter, 1.*

Flavell, J. H. (1981). Monitoring social-cognitive enterprises: Something else that may develop in the area of social cognition. In J. H. Flavell & L. Ross (Eds.), *Social cognitive development: Frontiers and possible futures.* New York: Cambridge University Press.

Flavell, J. H. (1985). *Cognitive development* (2nd ed.). Englewood Cliffs, NJ: Prentice-Hall.

Flavell, J. H., Botkin, P. T., Fry, C. L., Wright, J. W., & Jarvis, P. E. (1968). *The development of role-taking and communication skills in children.* New York: Wiley.

Ford Foundation. (1984). *Ford Foundation Letter, 15* (5).

Fordham, S., & Ogbu, J. U. (1986). Black students' school success: Coping with the burden of "acting white." *Urban Review, 18,* 176–206.

Forehand, G., Ragosta, J., & Rock. D. (1976). *Conditions and processes of effective school desegregation.* Princeton, NJ: Educational Testing Service.

Forrest, J. D. (1990). Cultural influences on adolescents' reproductive behavior. In J. Bancroft & J. M. Reinisch (Eds.), *Adolescence and puberty.* New York: Oxford University Press.

Forrest, J. D., & Singh, S. (1990). The sexual and reproductive behavior of American women, 1982–1988. *Family Planning Perspectives, 22,* 206–214.

Foster-Clark, F. S., & Blyth, D. A. (1991). Peer relations and influences. In R. M. Lerner, A. C. Petersen, & J. Brooks-Gunn (Eds.), *Encyclopedia of adolescence* (Vol. 2). New York: Garland.

Fowler, J. W. (1976). Stages in faith: The structural-developmental approach. In T. Hennessy (Ed.), *Values and moral development.* New York: Paulist Press.

Fox, L. H., Brody, L., & Tobin, D. (1979). *Women and mathematics.* Baltimore, MD: Intellectually Gifted Study Group, Johns Hopkins University.

Francis, J., Fraser, G., & Marcia, J. E. (1989). *Cognitive and experimental factors in Moratorium-Achievement (MAMA) cycles.* Unpublished manuscript, Department of Psychology, Simon Fraser University, Burnaby, British Columbia.

Franz, W. K., Phillips, R., Karther, D., & Swinker, M. (1992, March). *The effects of a videotaped, family-based, in-home sexuality education program.* Paper presented at the meeting of the Society for Research on Adolescence, Washington, DC.

Freedman, J. L. (1984). Effects of television violence on aggressiveness. *Psychological Bulletin, 96,* 227–246.

Freeman, D. (1983). *Margaret Mead and Samoa.* Cambridge, MA: Harvard University Press.

Fregly, M. J., & Luttge, W. G. (1982). *Human endocrinology: An interactive text.* New York: Elsevier Science.

Freud, A. (1958). *The ego and the mechanisms of defense.* New York: International Universities Press.

Freud, A. (1966). Instinctual anxiety during puberty. In *The writings of Anna Freud: The ego and the mechanisms of defense.* New York: International Universities Press.

Freud, A., & Dann, S. (1951). Instinctual anxiety during puberty. In A. Freud, *The ego and its mechanisms of defense.* New York: International Universities Press.

Freud, S. (1917). *A general introduction to psychoanalysis.* New York: Washington Square Press.

Friedman, M., & Rosenman, R. (1974). *Type-A behavior and your heart.* New York: Knopf.

Frisch, R., & Revelle, R. (1970). Height and weight at menarche and a hypothesis of critical body weights and adolescent events. *Science, 169,* 397–399.

Frisch, R. E. (1991). Puberty and body fat. In R. M. Lerner, A. C. Petersen, & J. Brooks-Gunn (Eds.), *Encyclopedia of adolescence.* New York: Garland.

Frith, S. (1981). *Sound effects: Youth, leisure, and the politics of rock 'n' roll.* New York: Pantheon.

Fuller, M. (1984). Black girls in a London comprehensive school. In M. Hammersley & P. Woods (Eds.), *Life in school: The sociology of pop culture.* New York: Open University Press.

Fullwinder, N. (1991, April). *Adolescent identity development within the context of a triangulated family system.* Paper presented at the biennial meeting of the Society for Research in Child Development, Seattle.

Furman, W., & Buhrmester, D. (1985). Children's perceptions of the qualities of sibling relationships. *Child Development, 56,* 448–461.

Furman, W., & Buhrmester, D. (in press). Age and sex differences in perceptions of networks of personal relationships. *Child Development.*

Furman, W., & Wehner, E. A. (1992, March). *Adolescent romantic relationships: A behavioral systems conceptualization.* Paper presented at the meeting of the Society for Research on Adolescence, Washington, DC.

Furstenberg, F. F. (1988). Child care after divorce and remarriage. In E. M. Hetherington & J. D. Arasteh (Eds.), *Impact of divorce, single-parenting, and stepparenting on children.* Hillsdale, NJ: Erlbaum.

Furstenberg, F. F. (1991). Pregnancy and childbearing: Effects on teen mothers. In R. M. Lerner, A. C. Petersen, & J. Brooks-Gunn (Eds.), *Encyclopedia of adolescence* (Vol. 2). New York: Garland.

Furstenberg, F. F., Brooks-Gunn, J., & Chase-Lansdale, L. (1989). Teenage pregnancy and childbearing. *American Psychologist, 44,* 313–320.

Furth, H. G., & Wachs, H. (1975). *Thinking goes to school.* New York: Oxford University Press.

Gabrielli, W. (1990, June). *Alcoholism from a biological perspective.* Paper presented at the meeting of the American Psychological Society, Dallas, TX.

Gagnon, J. H., & Simon, W. (1973). *Sexual conduct.* Chicago: Aldine.

Galambos, N. L., Almeida, D. M., & Petersen, A. C. (in press). Masculinity, femininity, and sex role attitudes in early adolescence: Exploring gender intensification. *Child Development.*

Galambos, N. L., & Maggs, J. L. (1989, April). *The after-school ecology of young adolescents and self-reported behavior.* Paper presented at the biennial meeting of the Society for Research in Child Development, Kansas City.

Galambos, N. L., & Maggs, J. L. (1990). Putting mothers' work-related stress in perspective. *Journal of Early Adolescence, 10,* 313–328.

Galambos, N. L., Petersen, A. C., Richards, M., & Gitleson, I. B. (1985). The Attitudes toward Women Scale for Adolescents (AWSA): A study of reliability and validity. *Sex Roles, 13,* 343–356.

Galanter, M. (1989). *Cults: Faith, healing, and coercion.* New York: Oxford University Press.

Gallagher, J. J. (1989). Children and social policy: Section introduction. *American Psychologist, 44,* 386.

Gallup, A. M., & Clark, D. L. (1987). The 19th annual Gallup poll of the public's attitude toward the public schools. *Phi Delta Kappan, 69,* 17–30.

Gallup, G., & Poling, D. (1980). *The search for America's faith.* New York: Abington.

Gallup Report. (1987). *Legalized gay relations.* Gallup Report, No. 254, p. 25.

Galotti, K. M. (1989). Approaches to studying formal and everyday reasoning. *Psychological Bulletin, 105,* 331–351.

Galotti, K. M., Kozberg, S. F., & Appleman, D. (in press). Younger and older adolescents' thinking about commitments. *Journal of Experimental Child Psychology.*

Galotti, K. M., Kozberg, S. F., & Farmer, M. C. (1990, March). *Gender and developmental differences in adolescents' conceptions of moral reasoning.* Paper presented at the meeting of the Society for Research in Adolescence, Atlanta, GA.

Garbarino, J., & Asp, C. E. (1981). *Successful schools and competent students.* Lexington, MA: Lexington Books.

Garber, J., Kriss, M. R., Koch, M., & Lindholm, L. (1988). Recurrent depression in adolescents: A follow-up study. *Journal of the American Academy of Child and Adolescent Psychiatry, 27,* 49–54.

Garden, R. A. (1987). The second IEA mathematics study. *Comparative Education Review, 31,* 47–68.

Gardner, H. (1983). *Frames of mind.* New York: Basic Books.

Gardner, H. (1989). Beyond a modular view of mind. In W. Damon (Ed.), *Child development today and tomorrow.* San Francisco: Jossey-Bass.

Gardner, L. I., Stern, M. P., Haffner, S. M., Gaskill, S. P., Hazuda, H. P., Relethford, J. H., & Eifter, C. W. (1984). Prevalence of diabetes in Mexican Americans: Relationships to percent of gene pool derived from native American sources. *Diabetes, 33,* 86–92.

Garfinkel, P. E., & Garner, D. M. (1982). *Anorexia nervosa.* New York: Brunner/Mazel.

Garland, A., Schaffer, D., & Whittle, B. (1988). A national survey of school-based adolescent suicide prevention programs. *Journal of the American Academy of Child and Adolescent Psychiatry, 28,* 931–934.

Garner, R. (1987). *Metacognition and reading comprehension.* Norwood, NJ: Ablex.

Garnets, L., Jones, J. M., Kimmel, D., Sue, S., & Tavris, C. (1991). *Psychological perspectives on human diversity.* Washington, DC: American Psychological Association.

Garrick, T. R., & Loewenstein, R. J. (1989). Behavioral medicine in the general hospital. *Psychosomatics, 30,* 123–134.

Garrison, K. C. (1968). Physiological changes in adolescence. In J. F. Adams (Ed.), *Understanding adolescence.* Boston: Allyn & Bacon.

Garwood, S. G., Phillips, D., Hartman, A., & Zigler, E. F. (1989). As the pendulum swings: Federal agency programs for children. *American Psychologist, 44,* 434–440.

Gelman, R., & Baillargeon, R. (1983). A review of some Piagetian concepts. In P. H. Mussen (Ed.), *Handbook of child psychology.* New York: Wiley.

George, R. (1987). *Youth policies and programs in selected countries.* Washington, DC: William T. Grant Foundation.

Giaconia, R. M., & Hedges, L. V. (1982). Identifying features of effective open education. *Review of Educational Research, 52,* 579–602.

Gibbs, J. T. (1989). Black American adolescents. In J. T. Gibbs & L. N. Huang (Eds.), *Children of color.* San Francisco: Jossey-Bass.

Gibbs, J. T. (1991). Black adolescents at-risk: Approaches to prevention. In R. M. Lerner, A. C. Petersen, & J. Brooks-Gunn (Eds.), *Encyclopedia of adolescence* (Vol. 1). New York: Garland.

Gibbs, J. T., & Huang, L. N. (1989). A conceptual framework for assessing and treating minority youth. In J. T. Gibbs & L. N. Huang (Eds.), *Children of color.* San Francisco, CA: Jossey-Bass.

Gilgun, J. F. (1984). Sexual abuse of the young female in life course perspective (Doctoral dissertation, Syracuse University). *Dissertation Abstracts International, 45,* 3058.

Gilligan, C. (1982). *In a different voice.* Cambridge, MA: Harvard University Press.

Gilligan, C. (1990). Teaching Shakespeare's sister. In C. Gilligan, N. Lyons, and T. Hanmer (Eds.), *Making connections: The relational worlds of adolescent girls at Emma Willard School.* Cambridge: Harvard University Press.

Gilligan, C. (1991, April). *How should "we" talk about development?* Paper presented at the biennial meeting of the Society for Research in Child Development, Seattle.

Gilligan, C. (1992, May). *Joining the resistance: Girls' development in adolescence.* Paper presented at the symposium on development and vulnerability in close relationships, Montreal, Quebec.

Gilligan, C., & Attanucci, J. (1988). Two moral orientations. In C. Gilligan, J. V. Ward, J. M. Taylor, & B. Bardige (Eds.), *Mapping the moral domain.* Cambridge, MA: Harvard University Press.

Gilligan, C., Brown, L. M., & Rogers, A. G. (1990). Psyche embedded: A place for body, relationships, and culture in personality theory. In A. I. Rabin, R. A. Zucker, R. A. Emmons, & S. Frank (Eds.), *Studying persons and lives.* New York: Springer.

Gilligan, C., Lyons, N. P., & Hanmer, T. J. (Eds). (1990). *Making connections: The relational worlds of adolescent girls at the Emma Willard School.* Cambridge, MA: Harvard University Press.

Gilligan, C., Rogers, A., & Brown, L. M. (1990). Soundings into development. In C. Gilligan, N. P. Lyons, & T. J. Hanmer (Eds.), *Making connections: The relational worlds of adolescent girls at the Emma Willard School.* Cambridge, MA: Harvard University Press.

Gilligan, C., Ward, J., & Taylor, J. (Eds.). (1988). *Mapping the moral domain: A contribution of women's thinking to psychology and education.* Cambridge, MA: Harvard University Graduate School of Education.

Ginzberg, E. (1972). Toward a theory of occupational choice: A restatement. *Vocational Guidance Quarterly, 20,* 169–176.

Ginzberg, E., Glnzberg, S. W., Axelrad, S., & Herman, J. L. (1951). *Occupational choice.* New York: Columbia University.

Gjerde, P. F., & Block, J. (1989, April). *Depressive symptoms and personality in adolescence.* Paper presented at the meeting of the Society for Research in Child Development, Kansas City, MO.

Gjerde, P. F., & Block, J. (1990, March). *The preschool context of 18-year-olds with depressive symptoms: A prospective study.* Paper presented at the meeting of the Society for Research in Adolescence, Atlanta, GA.

Gjerde, P. F., Block, J., & Block, J. E. (1985). *Parental interactive patterns in dyads and triads: Prospective relationships to adolescent personality characteristics.* Unpublished manuscript, University of California, Berkeley.

Gjerde, P. F., Block, J., & Block, J. H. (1991). The preschool family context of 18-year-olds with depressive symptoms: A prospective study. *Journal of Research on Adolescence, 1,* 63–92.

Glasow, R. D. (1988). *School-based clinics: The abortion connection.* Washington, DC: National Right to Life Educational Trust Fund.

Glass, G. V., & Smith, M. L. (1978, September). *Meta-analysis of research on the relationship of class size and achievement.* San Francisco: Far West Educational Laboratory.

Glasser, W. (1990, March). Interview: Developing quality middle schools. *Middle School Journal, 21,* 1–4.

Glick, J. (1975). Cognitive development in cross-cultural perspective. In F. Horowitz (Ed.), *Review of child development research* (Vol. 4), Chicago: University of Chicago Press.

Glick, P. C., & Lin, S. (1986). Recent changes in divorce and remarriage. *Journal of Marriage and the Family, 48,* 737–747.

Glueck, S., & Glueck, E. (1950). *Unraveling juvenile delinquency.* Cambridge, MA: Harvard University Press.

Goertz, M. E., Ekstrom, R. B., & Rock, D. (1991). Dropouts, high school: Issues of race and sex. In R. M. Lerner, A. C. Petersen, & J. Brooks-Gunn (Eds.), *Encyclopedia of adolescence* (Vol. 1). New York: Garland.

Goethals, G. W., & Klos, D. S. (1970). *Experiencing youth.* Boston: Little, Brown.

Gold, M., & Petronio, R. J. (1980). Delinquent behavior in adolescence. In J. Adelson (Ed.), *Handbook of adolescent psychology.* New York: Wiley.

Goldsmith, H. H. (1988, August). *Does early temperament predict late development?* Paper presented at the meeting of the American Psychological Association, Atlanta, GA.

Goldsmith, H. H., & Gottesman, I. I. (1981). Origins of variation in behavioral style: A longitudinal study of temperament in young twins. *Child Development, 52,* 91–103.

Goldstein, A. P., Sprafkin, R. P., Gershaw, N. J., & Klein, P. (1981). *Skill-streaming the adolescent.* Champaign, IL: Research Press.

Goldstein, I. R., & Gilliam, P. (1990). Training system issues in the year 2000. *American Psychologist, 45,* 134–143.

Goodchilds, J. D., & Zellman, G. L. (1984). Sexual signalling and sexual aggression in adolescent relationships. In N. M. Malamuth & E. D. Donnerstein (Eds.), *Pornography and sexual aggression.* New York: Academic Press.

Goodman, R. A., Mercy, J. A., Loya, F., Rosenberg, M. L., Smith, J. C., Allen, N. H., Vargas, L., & Kolts, R. (1986). Alcohol use and interpersonal violence: Alcohol detected in homicide victims. *American Journal of Public Health, 76,* 144–149.

Gordon, K. A. (1987). *Great expectations: Unprotected intercourse scenario.* Princeton, NJ: Princeton University, McCosh Health Center.

Gordon, S., & Gilgun, J. F. (1987). Adolescent sexuality. In V. B. Van Hasselt & M. Hersen (Eds.), *Handbook of adolescent psychology.* New York: Pergamon.

Gore, T. (1987). *Raising PG kids in an X-rated society.* Nashville, TN: Abingdon Press.

Gottfredson, G. D., & Holland, J. L. (1989). *Dictionary of Holland occupational titles* (2nd ed.). Odessa, FL: Psychological Assessment Resources.

Gottfried, A. (1990). Academic intrinsic motivation on young elementary school children. *Journal of Educational Psychology, 82,* 525–538.

Gottlieb, B. H. (1991). Social support in adolescence. In M. E. Colten & S. Gore (Eds.), *Adolescent stress: Causes and consequences.* Hawthorne, NY: Aldine de Gruyter.

Gottlieb, D. (1966). Teaching and students: The views of Negro and white teachers. *Sociology of Education, 37,* 345–353.

Gottman, J. M., & Parker, J. G. (Eds.). (1987). *Conversations with friends.* New York: Cambridge University Press.

Gould, D., Feltz, D. L., Hort, T., & Weiss, M. (1982). Reasons for discontinuing involvement in competitive youth swimming. *Journal of Sport Behavior, 5,* 155–165.

Gould, D., & Horn, T. (1984). Participation motivation in young athletes. In J. M. Silva & R. S. Weinberg (Eds.), *Psychological foundations of sport.* Champaign, IL: Human Kinetics Publishers.

Graham, S. (1986, August). *Can attribution theory tell us something about motivation in blacks?* Paper presented at the meeting of the American Psychological Association, Washington, DC.

Graham, S. (1987, August). *Developing relations between attributions, affect, and intended social behavior.* Paper presented at the meeting of the American Psychological Association, New York.

Graham, S. (1990). Motivation in Afro-Americans. In G. L. Berry & J. K. Asamen (Eds.), *Black students: Psychosocial issues and academic achievement.* Newbury Park, CA: Sage.

Gray, W. M., & Hudson, L. M. (1984). Formal operations and the imaginary audience. *Developmental Psychology, 20,* 619–627.

Greenberg, B. S. (1988). *Mass media and adolescents: A review of research reported from 1980–1987.* Manuscript prepared for the Carnegie Council on Adolescent Development.

Department of Communication, Michigan State University, East Lansing, MI.

Greenberg, B. S., Stanley, C., Siemicki, M., Heeter, C., Soderman, A., & Linsangan, R. (1986). *Sex content on soaps and prime-time television series most viewed by adolescents.* Project CAST Report #2. East Lansing, MI: Michigan State Department of Telecommunication.

Greenberg, J. S., Bruess, C. E., Mullen, K. D., & Sands, D. W. (1989). *Sexuality* (2nd ed.). Dubuque, IA: Wm. C. Brown.

Greenberger, E., & Steinberg, L. (1981). *Project for the study of adolescent work: Final report.* Report prepared for the National Institute of Education, U.S. Department of Education, Washington, DC.

Greenberger, E., & Steinberg, L. (1986). *When teenagers work: The psychological social costs of adolescent employment.* New York: Basic Books.

Greene, A. L. (1989, April). *Differentiating developmental contributors and contexts of adolescent stress.* Paper presented at the biennial meeting of the Society for Research in Child Development, Kansas City.

Greene, B. (1988, May). The children's hour. *Esquire Magazine,* pp. 47–49.

Greenfield, P. M., Bruzzone, L., Koyamatsu, K., Satuloff, W., Nixon, K., Brodie, M., & Kingsdale, D. (1987). What is rock music doing to the minds of our youth? A first experimental look at the effects of rock music lyrics and music videos. *Journal of Early Adolescence, 7,* 315–329.

Grimes, B., & Mattimore, K. (1989, April). *The effects of stress and exercise on identity formation in adolescence.* Paper presented at the biennial meeting of the Society for Research in Child Development, Kansas City.

Grotevant, H. D., & Cooper, C. R. (1985). Patterns of interaction in family relationships and the development of identity exploration in adolescence. *Child Development, 56,* 415–428.

Grotevant, H. D., & Durrett, M. E. (1980). Occupational knowledge and career development in adolescence. *Journal of Vocational Behavior, 17,* 171–182.

Grubb, W. N. (1989). Preparing youth for work. In D. Stern & D. Eichorn (Eds.), *Adolescence and work.* Hillsdale, NJ: Erlbaum.

Guilford, J. P. (1967). *The structure of intellect.* New York: McGraw-Hill.

Guttentag, M., & Bray, H. (1976). *Undoing sex stereotypes: Research and resources for educators.* New York: McGraw-Hill.

Haas, A. (1979). *Teenage sexuality: A survey of teenage sexual behavior.* New York: Macmillan.

Hahn, A. (1987, December). Reaching out to America's dropouts: What to do? *Phi Delta Kappan,* pp. 256–263.

Hains, A. A., & Szyjakowski, M. (1990). A cognitive stress-reduction intervention program for adolescents. *Journal of Counseling Psychology, 37,* 79–84.

Hale, S. (1990). A global developmental trend in cognitive processing speed. *Child Development, 61,* 653–663.

Hale-Benson, J. (1989). The school learning environment and academic success. In G. L. Berry & J. K. Asamen (Eds.), *Black students.* Newbury Park, CA: Sage.

Hall, E. G., Durborow, B., & Progen, J. (1986). Self-esteem of female athletes and nonathletes relative to sex role type and sport type. *Sex Roles, 15,* 379–390.

Hall, G. S. (1904). *Adolescence* (Vols. I & II). Englewood Cliffs, NJ: Prentice-Hall.

Hamburg, B. (1974). Early adolescence: A specific and stressful stage of the life cycle. In G. Coelho, D. A. Hamburg, & J. E. Adams (Eds.), *Coping and adaptation.* New York: Basic Books.

Hamilton, S. F. (1991). Vocational training. In R. M. Lerner, A. C. Petersen, & J. Brooks-Gunn (Eds.), *Encyclopedia of adolescence* (Vol. 2). New York: Garland.

Hanson, R. A., & Mullis, R. L. (1985). Age and gender differences in empathy and moral reasoning among adolescents. *Child Study Journal, 15,* 181–188.

Hare, B. R., & Castenell, L. A. (1985). No place to run, no place to hide: Comparative status and future prospects of black boys. In M. B. Spencer, G. K. Brookins, & W. R. Allen (Eds.), *Beginnings: The social and affective development of black children.* Hillsdale, NJ: Erlbaum.

Harmon, D. S. (1984). Brain growth theory and educational psychology. *Psychological Reports, 55,* 59–66.

Harold, R. D., & Eccles, J. S. (1990, March). *Maternal expectations, advice, and provision of opportunities: Their relationships to boys' and girls' occupational aspirations.* Paper presented at the meeting of the Society for Research in Adolescence, Atlanta, GA.

Harrison, A. O., Wilson, M. N., Pine, C., Chan, S. Q., & Buriel, R. (1990). Family ecologies of ethnic minority children. *Child Development, 61,* 347–362.

Harter, S. (1982). The perceived competence scale for children. *Child Development, 53,* 87–97.

Harter, S. (1985). *Self-Perception Profile for Children.* Denver, CO: Department of Psychology, University of Denver.

Harter, S. (1986). Processes underlying the construction, maintenance, and enhancement of the self-concept of children. In J. Suls & A. Greenwald (Eds.), *Psychological perspective on the self* (Vol. 3). Hillsdale, NJ: Erlbaum.

Harter, S. (1987). The determinants and mediational role of global self-worth in children. In N. Eisenberg (Ed.), *Contemporary issues in developmental psychology.* New York: Wiley.

Harter, S. (1989a). Causes, correlates, and the functional role of global self-worth: A life-span perspective. In J. Kolligian & R. Sternberg (Eds.), *Perceptions of competence and incompetence across the life-span.* New Haven, CT: Yale University Press.

Harter, S. (1989b). *Self-Perception Profile for Adolescents.* Denver, CO: Department of Psychology, University of Denver.

Harter, S. (1990a). Processes underlying adolescent self-concept formation. In R. Montemayor, G. R. Adams, & T. P. Gulotta (Eds.), *From childhood to adolescence: A transitional period?* Newbury Park, CA: Sage.

Harter, S. (1990b). Self and identity development. In S. S. Feldman & G. R. Elliott (Eds.), *At the threshold: The developing adolescent.* Cambridge, MA: Harvard University Press.

Harter, S., & Lee, L. (1989). *Manifestations of true and false selves in adolescence.* Paper presented at the meeting of the Society for Research in Child Development, Kansas City, MO.

Hartshorne, H., & May, M. S. (1928–1930). *Moral studies in the nature of character: Studies in deceit* (Vol. 1); *Studies in self-control* (Vol. 2); *Studies in the organization of character* (Vol. 3). New York: Macmillan.

Hartup, W. W. (1983). Peer relations. In P. H. Mussen (Ed.), *Handbook of child psychology* (4th ed., Vol. 4). New York: Wiley.

Hartup, W. W. (1991). Friendships. In R. M. Lerner, A. C. Petersen, & J. Brooks-Gunn (Eds.), *Encyclopedia of adolescence* (Vol. 1). New York: Garland.

Hauser, S. T., & Bowlds, M. K. (1990). Stress, coping, and adaptation. In S. S. Feldman & G. R. Elliott (Eds.), *At the threshold: The developing adolescent.* Cambridge, MA: Harvard University Press.

Hauser, S. T., Powers, S. I., Noam, G. G., Jacobson, A. M., Weisse, B., & Follansbee, D. J. (1984). Familial contexts of adolescent ego development. *Child Development, 55,* 195–213.

Havighurst, R. J. (1976). A cross-cultural view. In J. F. Adams (Ed.), *Understanding adolescence.* Boston: Allyn & Bacon.

Havighurst, R. J. (1987). Adolescent culture and subculture. In V. B. Van Hasselt & M. Hersen (Eds.), *Handbook of adolescent psychology.* New York: Pergamon.

Hawkins, D., & Lam, T. (1986). Teacher practices, social development, and delinquency. In J. Burchard & S. Burchard (Eds.), *Prevention of delinquent behavior.* Newbury Park, CA: Sage.

Hawkins, D., & Lishner, D. (1987). School and delinquency. In E. Johnson (Ed.), *Handbook on crime and delinquency prevention.* Westport, CT: Greenwood Press.

Hawkins, J. A., & Berndt, T. J. (1985, April). *Adjustment following the transition to junior high school.* Paper presented at the biennial meeting of the Society for Research in Child Development, Toronto.

Hawkins, R. (1979, October 29). "Ropers" and "dopers." *Dallas Morning News,* p. 1.

Hayes, C. (Ed.). (1987). *Risking the future: Adolescent sexuality, pregnancy, and childbearing* (Vol. 1). Washington, DC: National Academy Press.

Haynie, D., & McLellan, J. (1992, March). *Continuity in parent and peer relationships.* Paper presented at the meeting of the Society for Research on Adolescence, Washington, DC.

Hazen, C., & Shaver, P. (1987). Romantic love conceptualized as an attachment process. *Journal of Personality and Social Psychology, 51,* 511–524.

Heath, S. B. (1983). *Ways with words.* Cambridge, England: Cambridge University Press.

Heath, S. B. (1989). Oral and literate traditions among black Americans living in poverty. *American Psychologist, 44,* 367–373.

Hedges, L. V., & Stock, W. (1983, Spring). The effects of class size: An examination of rival hypotheses. *American Educational Research Journal,* pp. 63–85.

Heider, F. (1958). *The psychology of interpersonal relations.* New York: Wiley.

Hein, K. (1990). AIDS in adolescence. *Journal of Adolescent Health Care, 10,* 10–35.

Helson, R., Elliot, T., & Leigh, J. (1989). Adolescent antecedents of women's work patterns. In D. Stern & D. Eichorn (Eds.), *Adolescence and work.* Hillsdale, NJ: Erlbaum.

Henderson, V. L., & Dweck, C. S. (1990a). Motivation and achievement. In S. S. Feldman & G. R. Elliott (Eds.), *At the threshold: The developing adolescent.* Cambridge, MA: Harvard University Press.

Henderson, V. L., & Dweck, C. S. (1990b, April). *Predicting individual differences in school anxiety in early adolescence.* Paper presented at the meeting of the Society for Research in Child Development, Kansas City, MO.

Hennessey, B. A., & Amabile, T. M. (1988). The conditions of creativity. In R. J. Sternberg (Ed.), *The nature of creativity.* New York: Cambridge University Press.

Herdt, G. H. (1988, August). *Coming out processes as an anthropological rite of passage.* Paper presented at the meeting of the America Psychological Association, Atlanta, GA.

Hess, L., Lonky, E., & Roodin, P. A. (1985, April). *The relationship of moral reasoning and ego strength to cheating behavior.* Paper presented at the meeting of the Society for Research in Child Development, Toronto.

Hetherington, E. M. (1972). Effects of father-absence on personality development in adolescent daughters. *Developmental Psychology, 7,* 313–326.

Hetherington, E. M. (1977). *My heart belongs to daddy: A study of the remarriages of daughters of divorcees and widows.* Unpublished manuscript, University of Virginia.

Hetherington, E. M. (1989). Coping with family transitions: Winners, losers, and survivors. *Child Development, 60,* 1–14.

Hetherington, E. M., Anderson, E. R., & Hagan, M. S. (1991). Divorce: Effects on adolescents. In R. M. Lerner, A. C. Petersen, & J. Brooks-Gunn (Eds.)., *Encyclopedia of adolescence* (Vol. 1.). New York: Garland.

Hetherington, E. M., & Clingempeel, W. G. (in press). Coping with marital transitions: A family systems perspective. *Society for Research in Child Development Monographs.*

Hetherington, E. M., Cox, M., & Cox, R. (1982). Effects of divorce on children and parents. In M. E. Lamb (Ed.), *Nontraditional families.* Hillsdale, NJ: Erlbaum.

Hetherington, E. M., Hagan, M. S., & Anderson, E. R. (1989). Marital transitions: A child's perspective. *American Psychologist, 44,* 303–312.

Hetherington, E. M., Lerner, R. M., & Perlmutter, M. (Eds.). (1989). *Child development in life-span perspective.* Hillsdale, NJ: Erlbaum.

Hetherington, E. M., Lindner, M., Miller, N. B., & Clingempeel, G. W. (1991, April). *Work, marriage, parenting, and children's adjustment in nondivorced and remarried families.* Paper presented at the biennial meeting of the Society for Child Development, Seattle.

Hiebert, J., & LeFevre, P. (Eds.). (1987). *Conceptual and procedural knowledge; The case of mathematics.* Hillsdale, NJ: Erlbaum.

Hightower, E. (1990). Adolescent interpersonal and familial precursors of positive mental health at midlife. *Journal of Youth and Adolescence, 19,* 257–275.

Hill, J. P. (1980a). The early adolescent and the family. In M. Johnson (Ed.), *The 79th yearbook of the National Society for the Study of Education.* Chicago: University of Chicago Press.

Hill, J. P. (1980b). *Understanding early adolescence: A framework.* Carrboro, NC: Center for Early Adolescence.

Hill, J. P., & Holmbeck, G. N. (1986). Attachment and autonomy during adolescence. *Annals of Child Development, 3,* 145–189.

Hill, J. P., Holmbeck, G. N., Marlow, L., Green, T. M., & Lynch, M. E. (1985). Pubertal status and parent-child relations in families of seventh-grade boys. *Journal of Early Adolescence, 5,* 31–44.

Hill, J. P., & Lynch, M. E. (1983). The intensification of gender-related role expectations during early adolescence. In J. Brooks-Gunn & A. C. Petersen (Eds.), *Girls at puberty: Biological and psychosocial perspectives.* New York: Plenum.

Hill, J. P., & Steinberg, L. D. (1976, April 26–30). *The development of autonomy in adolescence.* Paper presented at the Symposium on Research on Youth Problems, Fundacion Orbegoza Eizaquirre, Madrid, Spain.

Hirsch, B. J., & Rapkin, B. D. (1987). The transition to junior high school: A longitudinal study of self-esteem, psychological symptomatology, school life, and social support. *Child Development, 58,* 1235–1243.

Hobfoll, S. E. (1989). Conservation of resources: A new attempt at conceptualizing stress. *American Psychologist, 44,* 513–524.

Hodgman, C. H. (1992). Child and adolescent depression and suicide. In D. E. Greydanus & M. L. Wolraich (Eds.), *Behavioral pediatrics.* New York: Springer-Verlag.

Hofferth, S. L. (1990). Trends in adolescent sexual activity, contraception, and pregnancy in the United States. In J. Bancroft & J. M. Reinisch (Eds.), *Adolescence and puberty*. New York: Oxford University Press.

Hofferth, S. L., & Hayes, C. D. (Eds.). (1987). *Risking the future: Adolescent sexuality, pregnancy, and childbearing* (Vol. 2). Washington, DC: National Academy Press.

Hoffman, L. W. (1989). Effects of maternal employment in the two-parent family. *American Psychologist, 44*, 283–292.

Hoffman, M. L. (1980). Moral development in adolescence. In J. Adelson (Ed.), *Handbook of adolescent psychology*. New York: Wiley.

Holland, J. L. (1973). *Making vocational choices: A theory of careers*. Englewood Cliffs, NJ: Prentice-Hall.

Holland, J. L. (1987). Current status of Holland's theory of careers: Another perspective. *Career Development Quarterly, 36*, 24–30.

Hollingshead, A. B. (1975). *Elmtown's youth and Elmtown revisited*. New York: Wiley.

Holmbeck, G. N., Gasiewski, E., & Crossman, R. (1989, April). *Cognitive development, egocentrism, and adolescent contraceptive knowledge, attitudes, and behavior*. Paper presented at the biennial meeting of the Society for Research in Child Development, Kansas City.

Holmes, L. D. (1987). *Quest for the real Samoa: The Mead-Freeman controversy and beyond*. South Hadley, MA: Bergin & Garvey.

Holtzmann, W. (1982). Cross-cultural comparisons of personality development in Mexico and the United States. In D. Wagner & H. W. Stevenson (Eds.), *Cultural perspectives on child development*. San Francisco: W. H. Freeman.

Hood, K. E. (1991). Menstrual cycle. In R. M. Lerner, A. C. Petersen, & J. Brooks-Gunn (Eds.), *Encyclopedia of adolescence*. New York: Garland.

Hooper, F. H., & Hooper, J. O. (in press). The family as a system of reciprocal relations: Searching for a developmental life-span perspective. In G. Brody & I. E. Siegel (Eds.), *Family research journeys* (Vol. 1). Hillsdale, NJ: Erlbaum.

Hopkins, R., Mauss, A., Kearney, K., & Weisheit, R. (1988). Comprehensive evaluation of a model alcohol education curriculum. *Journal of Studies on Alcohol, 49*, 38–49.

Horner, M. (1972). Toward an understanding of achievement-related conflicts in women. *Journal of Social Issues, 28*, 157–175.

Horney, K. (1967). *Feminine psychology*. New York: Norton.

Horowitz, F. D., & O'Brien, M. (1989). In the interest of the nation: A reflective essay on the state of knowledge and the challenges before us. *American Psychologist, 44*, 441–445.

Howatt, P. M., & Saxton, A. M. (1988). The incidence of bulimic behavior in a secondary and university school population. *Journal of Youth and Adolescence, 17*, 221–231.

Huang, L. N. (1989). Southeast Asian refugee children and adolescents. In J. T. Gibbs & L. N. Huang (Eds.), *Children of color*. San Francisco: Jossey-Bass.

Huang, L. N., & Gibbs, J. T. (1989). Future directions: Implications for research, training, and practice. In J. T. Gibbs & L. N. Huang (Eds.), *Children of color*. San Francisco: Jossey-Bass.

Huang, L. N., & Ying, Y. (1989). Chinese American children and adolescents. In J. T. Gibbs & L. N. Huang (Eds.), *Children of color*. San Francisco: Jossey-Bass.

Hudson, L. M., Forman, E. R., & Brion-Meisels, S. (1982). Role-taking as a predictor of prosocial behavior in cross-age tutors. *Child Development, 53*, 1320–1329.

Huebner, A. M., Garrod, A. C., & Snarey, J. (1990, March). *Moral development in Tibetan Buddhist monks: A cross-cultural study of adolescents and young adults in Nepal*. Paper presented at the meeting of the Society for Research in Adolescence, Atlanta, GA.

Huesmann, L. R. (1986). Psychological processes promoting the relation between exposure to media violence and aggressive behavior by the viewer. *Journal of Social Issues, 42*, 125–139.

Huff, C. R. (Ed.). (1990). *Gangs in America*. Newbury Park, CA: Sage.

Hughes, S. O., Power, T. G., & Francis, D. J. (1992, March). *Attachment, autonomy, and adolescent drinking: Differentiating abstainers, experimenters, and heavy users*. Paper presented at the meeting of the Society for Research on Adolescence, Washington, DC.

Hunt, M. (1974). *Sexual behavior in the 1970s*. Chicago: Playboy Press.

Huston, A. C. (1983). Sex-typing. In P. H. Mussen (Ed.), *Handbook of child psychology* (4th ed., Vol. 4). New York: Wiley.

Huston, A. C. (1991) Children in poverty: Developmental and policy issues. In A. C. Huston (Ed.), *Children in poverty: Child development and public policy*. New York: Cambridge University Press.

Huston, A. C., & Alvarez, M. (1990). The socialization context of gender-role development in early adolescence. In R. Montemayor, G. R. Adams, & T. P. Gulotta (Eds.), *From childhood to adolescence: A transitional period?* Newbury Park, CA: Sage.

Huston, A. C., Siegle, J., & Bremer, M. (1983, April). *Family environment television use by preschool children*. Paper presented at the biennial meeting of the Society for Research in Child Development, Detroit, MI.

Huston, A. C., Watkins, B. A., & Kunkel, D. (1989). Public policy and children's television. *American Psychologist, 44*, 424–433.

Huston-Stein, A., & Higgens-Trenk, A. (1978). Development of females from childhood through adulthood. Career and feminine role orientations. In P. Baltes (Ed.), *Lifespan development and behavior* (Vol. 1). New York: Academic Press.

Hyde, J. S. (1981). How large are cognitive gender differences? A meta-analysis using w^2 and d. *American Psychologist, 36*, 892–901.

Hyde, J. S. (1985) *Half the human experience* (3rd ed.). Lexington, MA: D. C. Heath.

Hyde, J. S. (in press). Meta-analysis and the psychology of women. In F. L. Denmark & M. A. Paludi (Eds.), *Handbook on the psychology of women*. Westport, CT: Greenwood Press.

Hyman, H. M. (1959). *Political socialization*. New York: Free Press.

Inoff-Germain, G., Arnold, G. S., Nottelmann, E. D., Susman, E. J., Cutler, G. B., & Chrousos, G. P. (1988). Relations between hormone levels and observational measures of aggressive behavior of young adolescents in family interactions. *Developmental Psychology 24*, 124–139.

Irvin, F. S. (1988, August). *Clinical perspectives on resilience among gay and lesbian youth*. Paper presented at the annual meeting of the American Psychological Association, Atlanta, GA.

Irwin, C. E. (1986). Why adolescent medicine? *Journal of Adolescent Health Care, 7*, 2S–12S.

Irwin, C. E., & Orr, D. P. (1991). Health research in adolescence, future directions of the. In R. M. Lerner, A. C. Petersen, & J. Brooks-Gunn (Eds.), *Encyclopedia of adolescence* (Vol. 1). New York: Garland.

Ishiyama, F. I., & Chabassol, D. J. (1985). Adolescents' fear of social consequences of academic success as a function of age and sex. *Journal of Youth and Adolescence, 14*, 37–46.

Jacobs, J. E., & Potenza, M. (1990, March). *The use of decision-making strategies in late adolescence*. Paper presented at the meeting of the Society for Research in Adolescence, Atlanta, GA.

Jagacinski, C. M., & Nicholls, J. G. (1990). Reducing effort to protect perceived ability: "They'd do it but I wouldn't." *Journal of Educational Psychology, 82*, 15–21.

Jencks, C. S., Smith, M., Acland, H., Bane, M. J., Cohen, D., Gintis, H., Heyns, B., & Michelson, S. (1972). *Inequality: A reassessment of the effects of family and schooling in America*. New York: Basic Books.

Jenkins, E. J., & Bell, C. C. (1992). Adolescent violence: Can it be curbed? *Adolescent Medicine, 3*, 71–86.

Jenkins, L. E. (1989). The black family and academic achievement. In G. L. Berry & J. K. Asamen (Eds.), *Black students*. Newbury Park, CA: Sage.

Jensen, A. R. (1969). How much can we boost IQ and scholastic achievement? *Harvard Educational Review, 39*, 1–123.

Jensen, L. C., & Knight, R. S. (1981). *Moral education: Historical perspectives*. Washington, DC: University Press of America.

Jessor, L., & Jessor, R. (1975). Transition from virginity to nonvirginity among youth: A social-psychological study over time. *Developmental Psychology, 11*, 473–484.

Jessor, R., Costa, F., Jessor, L., & Donovan, J. E. (1983). Time of first intercourse: A prospective study. *Journal of Personality and Social Psychology, 44*, 608–620.

Johnson, D., & Johnson, R. T. (1989). *A meta-analysis of cooperation, competition, and individualistic learning* (2nd ed.). Hillsdale, NJ: Erlbaum.

Johnson, J. H. (1986). *Life events as stressors in childhood and adolescence*. Newbury Park, CA: Sage Publications.

Johnson, J. H., & Goldman, J. (Eds.). (1990). *Developmental assessment in clinical child psychology*. Elmsford, NY: Pergamon.

Johnston, J., & Ettema, J. S. (1985). *Positive images: Breaking stereotypes with children's television*. Newbury Park, CA: Sage.

Johnston, L., Bachman, J. G., & O'Malley, P. M. (1990). *Monitoring the future*. Ann Arbor, MI: Institute of Social Research, University of Michigan.

Johnston, L. D., O'Malley, P. M., & Bachman, J. G. (1990, February 13). *Drug use continues to decline*. News Release, Institute for Social Research, University of Michigan, Ann Arbor.

Johnston, L. D., O'Malley, P. M., & Bachman, J. G. (1992, January 25). *The 1991 survey of drug use by American high school and college students*. Ann Arbor, MI: Institute of Social Research.

Jonah, B. (1985). *Adolescent risk and risk-taking behavior among young drivers: Relevant research*. Paper presented at the conference on adolescent risk-taking behavior, University of British Columbia, Department of Pediatrics, Vancouver, BC.

Jones, E. R., Forrest, J. D., Goldman, N., Henshaw, S. K., Lincoln, R., Rosoff, J. I., Westoff, C. G., & Wulf, D. (1985). Teenage pregnancy in developed countries: Determinants and policy implications. *Family Planning Perspectives, 17*, 53–63.

Jones, B. F., Idol, L., & Brandt, R. S. (1991). Dimensions of thinking. In B. F. Jones & L. Idol (Eds.), *Dimensions of thinking and cognitive instruction*. Hillsdale, NJ: Erlbaum.

Jones, J. M. (1990, August). *Psychological approaches to race: What have they been and what should they be?* Paper presented at the meeting of the American Psychological Association, Boston.

Jones, M. C. (1965). Psychological correlates of somatic development. *Child Development, 36,* 899–911.

Jones, S. (1992). Providing minority students with the competitive edge. *Journal of Career Planning and Employment, 27,* 36–40.

Jones, W. H., Hobbs, S. A., & Hockenbury, D. (1982). Loneliness and social skills deficits. *Journal of Personality and Social Psychology, 42,* 682–689.

Josselson, R. (1973). Psychodynamic aspects of identity formation in college women. *Journal of Youth and Adolescence, 2,* 3–52.

Josselson, R. (1987). *Finding herself.* San Francisco: Jossey-Bass.

Juster, S. M., & Vinovskis, M. A. (1991). Nineteenth-century America, adolescence in. In R. M. Lerner, A. C. Petersen, & J. Brooks-Gunn (Eds.), *Encyclopedia of adolescence* (Vol. 1). New York: Garland.

Justiz, M. J., & Rendon, L. I. (1989). Hispanic students. In M. L. Upcraft & J. N. Gardner (Eds.), *The freshman experience.* San Francisco: Jossey-Bass.

Kagan, J. (1984). *The nature of the child.* New York: Basic Books.

Kagan, S., & Madsen, M. C. (1972). Experimental analysis of cooperation and competition of Anglo-American and Mexican children. *Developmental Psychology, 6,* 49–59.

Kahn, S. E., & Richardson, A. (1983). Evaluation of a course in sex roles for secondary school students. *Sex Roles, 9,* 431–440.

Kail, R. (1988). Reply to Stigler, Nusbaum, and Chalip. *Child Development, 59,* 1154–1157.

Kail, R., & Pellegrino, J. W. (1985). *Human intelligence.* New York: W. H. Freeman.

Kamler, J., Irwin, C. E., Stone, G. C., & Millstein, S. G. (1987). *Optimistic bias in adolescent hemophiliacs.* Paper presented at the meeting of the Society for Research in Pediatrics, Anaheim, CA.

Kandel, D., & Lesser, G. S. (1969). Parent-adolescent relationships and adolescence independence in the United States and Denmark. *Journal of Marriage and the Family, 31,* 348–358.

Kandel, D. B. (1974). The role of parents and peers in marijuana use. *Journal of Social Issues, 30,* 107–135.

Kandel, D. B. (1991). Drug use, epidemiology and developmental stages of involvement. In R. M. Lerner, A. C. Petersen, & J. Brooks-Gunn (Eds.), *Encyclopedia of adolescence* (Vol. 1). New York: Garland.

Kandel, D. B., & Davies, M. (1986). Adult sequelae of adolescent depressant symptoms. *Archives of General Psychiatry, 43,* 255–262.

Kane, M. J. (1988). The female athletic role as a status determinant within the social systems of high school adolescents. *Adolescence, 23,* 253–264.

Kantrowitz, B., & Wingert, P. (1989, April 17). How kids learn. *Newsweek,* pp. 4–10.

Karplus, R. (1981). Education and formal thought—a modest proposal. In I. Siegel, D. Brodzinsky, & R. Golinkoff (Eds.), *Piagetian theory and research: New directions and applications.* Hillsdale, NJ: Erlbaum.

Kaufmann, A. S., & Flaitz, J. (1987). Intellectual growth. In V. B. Van Hasselt & M. Hersen (Eds.), *Handbook of adolescent psychology.* New York: Pergamon Press.

Kavanaugh, K. H., & Kennedy, P. H. (1992). *Promoting cultural diversity.* Newbury Park, CA: Sage.

Keating, D. P. (1988). Byrnes' reformulation of Piaget's formal operations: Is what's left what's right? *Developmental Review, 8,* 376–384.

Keating, D. P. (1990a). Adolescent thinking. In S. S. Feldman & G. R. Elliott (Eds.), *At the threshold: The developing adolescent.* Cambridge, MA: Harvard University Press.

Keating, D. P. (1990b). Structuralism, deconstruction, reconstruction: The limits of reasoning. In W. F. Overton (Ed.), *Reasoning, necessity, and logic: Developmental perspectives.* Hillsdale, NJ: Erlbaum.

Keating, D. P. (1991). Cognition, adolescent. In R. M. Lerner, A. C. Petersen, & J. Brooks-Gunn (Eds.), *Encyclopedia of adolescence* (Vol. 1). New York: Garland.

Keefe, S. E., & Padilla, A. M. (1987). *Chicano ethnicity.* Albuquerque, NM: University of New Mexico Press.

Keith, J. G., Nelson, C. S., Schlabach, J. H., & Thompson, C. J. (1990). The relationship between parental employment and three measures of early adolescent responsibility. *Journal of Early Adolescence, 10,* 399–415.

Keltikangas-Järvinen, L. (1990). Continuity of Type-A behavior during childhood, preadolescence, and adolescence. *Journal of Youth and Adolescence, 19,* 753–775.

Keltikangas-Järvinen, L., & Raikkonen, K. (1990). Healthy and maladjusted Type-A behavior in adolescents. *Journal of Youth and Adolescence, 19,* 1–18.

Kendall, P. C., Cantwell, D. P., & Kazdin, A. E. (1989). Depression in children and adolescents: Assessment issues and recommendations. *Cognitive Therapy and Research, 13,* 109–146.

Kennedy, J. H. (1990). Determinants of peer social status: Contributions of physical appearance, reputation, and behavior. *Journal of Youth and Adolescence, 19,* 233–244.

Kennedy, R. E. (1991). Delinquency. In R. M. Lerner, A. C. Petersen, & J. Brooks-Gunn (Eds.), *Encyclopedia of adolescence* (Vol. 2). New York: Garland.

Kenney, A. M. (1987, June). Teen pregnancy: An issue for schools. *Phi Delta Kappan,* pp. 728–736.

Kenniston, K. (1970). Youth: A "new" stage of life. *The American Scholar, 39,* 631–654.

Kenyatta, J. (1965). *Facing Mt. Kenya.* New York: Vintage Books.

Kerr, B. A. (1983). Raising the career aspirations of gifted girls. *Vocational Guidance Quarterly, 32,* 37–43.

Kett, J. F. (1977). *Rites of passage.* New York: Basic Books.

Kilpatrick, A. C. (1992). *Long-range effects of childhood and adolescent sexual experiences: Myths, mores, and menaces.* Hillsdale, NJ: Erlbaum.

Kinsey, A. C., Pomeroy, W. B., & Martin, C. E. (1948). *Sexual behavior in the human male.* Philadelphia: Saunders.

Kirshnit, C. E., Ham, M., & Richards, M. H. (1989). The sporting life: Athletic activities during early adolescence. *Journal of Youth and Adolescence, 18,* 601–615.

Kirshnit, C. E., Richards, M. H., & Ham, M. (1988). *Athletic participation and body image during early adolescence.* Paper presented at the meeting of the American Psychological Association, Atlanta, GA.

Klahr, D. (1989). Information-processing approaches. In R. Vasta (Ed.), *Six theories of child development: Revised formulations and current issues.* Greenwich, CT: JAI Press.

Klein, K. (1985, April). The research on class size. *Phi Delta Kappan,* pp. 578–580.

Klerman, L. V. (1991a). Health services for adolescents, barriers to. In R. M. Lerner, A. C. Petersen, & J. Brooks-Gunn (Eds.), *Encyclopedia of adolescence* (Vol. 1). New York: Garland.

Klerman, L. V. (1991b). The association between adolescent parenting and childhood poverty. In A. C. Huston (Ed.), *Children in poverty: Child development and public policy.* New York: Cambridge University Press.

Kline, M., Tschann, J. M., Johnston, J. R., & Wallerstein, J. S. (1989). Children's adjustment in joint and sole physical custody families. *Developmental Psychology, 24,* 430–438.

Klingaman, L., & Vicary, J. R. (1992, March). *Risk factors associated with date rape and sexual assault of young adolescent girls.* Paper presented at the meeting of the Society for Research on Adolescence, Washington, DC.

Klitgaard, R. E., & Hall, G. R. (1975). Are there unusually effective schools? *Journal of Human Resources, 10,* 90–106.

Knouse, S. B. (1992). Hispanics and work: An overview. In S. B. Knouse, R. Rosenfeld, & A. Culbertson (Eds.), *Hispanics in the workplace.* Newbury Park, CA: Sage.

Knox, D., & Wilson, K. (1981). Dating behaviors of university students. *Family Relations, 30,* 255–258.

Kobak, R. (1992, March). *Autonomy as self-regulation: An attachment perspective.* Paper presented at the meeting of the Society for Research on Adolescence, Washington, DC.

Kobak, R., Ferenz-Gillies, R., Everhart, E., & Seabrook, L. (1992, March). *Maternal attachment strategies and autonomy among adolescent offspring.* Paper presented at the meeting of the Society for Research on Adolescence, Washington, DC.

Kobak, R. R., & Sceery, A. (1988). Attachment in late adolescence: Working models, affect regulation, and representations of self and others. *Child Development, 59,* 135–146.

Koff, E., & Rierdan, J. (1991). Menarche and body image. In R. M. Lerner, A. C. Petersen, & J. Brooks-Gunn (Eds.), *Encyclopedia of adolescence.* New York: Garland.

Kohlberg, L. (1958). *The development of modes of moral thinking and choice in the years 10 to 16.* Unpublished doctoral dissertation, University of Chicago.

Kohlberg, L. (1966). A cognitive-developmental analysis of children's sex-role concepts and attitudes. In E. E. Maccoby (Ed.), *The development of sex differences.* Palo Alto, CA: Stanford University Press.

Kohlberg, L. (1969). Stage and sequence: The cognitive-developmental approach to socialization. In D. A. Goslin (Ed.), *Handbook of socialization theory and research.* Chicago: Rand McNally.

Kohlberg, L. (1976). Moral stages and moralization: The cognitive-developmental approach. In T. Lickona (Ed.), *Moral development and behavior.* New York: Holt, Rinehart & Winston.

Kohlberg, L. (1981). *The philosophy of moral development.* New York: Harper & Row.

Kohlberg, L. (1986). A current statement on some theoretical issues. In S. Modgil & C. Modgil (Eds.), *Lawrence Kohlberg.* Philadelphia: Falmer.

Kohlberg, L., & Candee, D. (1979). *Relationships between moral judgment and moral action.* Unpublished manuscript. Harvard University.

Kohn, M. L. (1977). *Class and conformity* (2nd ed.). Homewood, IL: Dorsey.

Kovacs, M. (1989). Affective disorders in children and adolescents. *American Psychologist, 44,* 209–215.

Kovar, M. G. (1991). Health of adolescents in the United States: An overview. In R. M. Lerner, A. C. Petersen, & J. Brooks-Gunn (Eds.), *Encyclopedia of adolescence* (Vol. 1). New York: Garland.

Kreppner, K. (1989, April). *A longitudinal study of changes in socialization and interaction patterns in families.* Paper presented at the biennial meeting of the Society for Research in Child Development, Kansas City.

Kuhn, D. (1988). Cognitive development. In M. H. Bornstein & M. E. Lamb (Eds), *Developmental psychology: An advanced textbook* (2nd ed.). Hillsdale, NJ: Erlbaum.

Kuhn, D. (1991). Reasoning, higher-order in adolescence, In R. M. Lerner, A. C. Petersen, & J. Brooks-Gunn (Eds.), *Encyclopedia of adolescence* (Vol. 2). New York: Garland.

Kulick, J. A., Bangert-Drowns, R. L., & Kulik, C. C. (1984). The effectiveness of coaching for aptitude tests. *Psychological Bulletin, 95,* 179–188.

Kulin, H. E. (1991). Puberty, hypothalamic-pituitary changes of. In R. M. Lerner, A. C. Petersen, & J. Brooks-Gunn (Eds.), *Encyclopedia of adolescence* (Vol. 2). New York: Garland.

Kupersmidt, J. B., Burchinal, M. R., Leff, S. S., & Patterson, C. J. (1992, March). *A longitudinal study of perceived support and conflict with parents from middle childhood through early adolescence.* Paper presented at the meeting of the Society for Research on Adolescence, Washington, DC.

Kupersmidt, J. B., & Coie, J. D. (1990). Preadolescent peer status, aggression, and school adjustment as predictors of externalizing problems in adolescence. *Child Development, 61,* 1350–1363.

Kupersmidt, J. B., Coie, J. D., & Dodge, K. A. (1990). Predicting disorder from peer social problems. In S. R. Asher & J. D. Coie (Eds.), *Peer rejection in childhood.* New York: Cambridge University Press.

Kurdek, L. A., & Krile, D. (1982). A developmental analysis of the relation between peer acceptance and both interpersonal understanding and perceived social self-competence. *Child Development, 53,* 1485–1491.

Kurtines, W. M., & Gewirtz, J. (Eds.). (1991). *Moral behavior and development: Advances in theory, research, and application.* Hillsdale, NJ: Erlbaum.

Kwakman, A. M., Zuker, F. A. J. M., Schippers, G. M., & de Wuffel, F. J. (1988). Drinking behavior, drinking attitudes, and attachment relationships of adolescents. *Journal of Youth and Adolescence, 17,* 247–253.

Labouvie-Vief, G. (1982). Dynamic development and mature autonomy: A theoretical prologue. *Human Development, 25,* 161–191.

Labouvie-Vief, G. (1986, August). *Modes of knowing and life-span cognition.* Paper presented at the annual meeting of the American Psychological Association, Washington, DC.

LaFromboise, T. D., & Low, K. G. (1989). American Indian children and adolescents. In J. T. Gibbs & L. N. Huang (Eds.), *Children of color.* San Francisco: Jossey-Bass.

Lamborn, S. D., Dornbusch, S. M., & Kraemer, E. (1990, March). *Parental monitoring strategies in an ethnically mixed sample.* Paper presented at the meeting of the Society for Research in Adolescence, Atlanta, GA.

Lamborn, S. D., & Steinberg, L. D. (1990, March). *Emotional autonomy redux: Revisiting Ryan and Lynch.* Paper presented at the meeting of the Society for Research on Adolescence, Atlanta, GA.

Lampl, M., & Emde, R. N. (1983). Episodic growth in infancy: A preliminary report on length, head circumference, and behavior. *New directions for child development.* San Francisco: Jossey-Bass.

Landesman, S., & Ramey, C. (1989). Developmental psychology and mental retardation: Integrating scientific principles with treatment practices. *American Psychologist, 44,* 409–415.

Landesman, S. L. (in press). Stage (and restaging) the trio of service, evaluation, and research. *American Journal of Mental Retardation.*

Lange, L. D. (1992, March). *Gender differences in college stress, academic motivation, and career intent during late adolescence.* Paper presented at the meeting of the Society for Research on Adolescence, Washington, DC.

Lann, I. S., & Moscicki, E. K. (1989). Introduction. *Suicide and Life-Threatening Behavior, 19,* xi–xiii.

Laosa, L. M. (1989, April). *Current research on Hispanic immigration and children's development: Theory and methods.* Paper presented at the biennial meeting of the Society for Research in Child Development, Kansas City.

Lappan, R. T., & Jingeleski, J. (1992). Circumscribing vocational aspirations in junior high school. *Journal of Counseling Psychology, 39,* 81–90.

Lapsley, D. K. (1985). Elkind on egocentrism. *Developmental Review, 5,* 227–236.

Lapsley, D. K. (1990). Continuity and discontinuity in adolescent social cognitive development. In R. Montemayor, G. Adams, & T. Gulotta (Eds), *From childhood to adolescence: A transitional period?* Newbury Park, CA: Sage.

Lapsley, D. K. (1991). Egocentrism theory and the "new look" at the imaginary audience and personal fable in adolescence. In R. M. Lerner, A. C. Petersen, & J. Brooks-Gunn (Eds.), *Encyclopedia of adolescence.* New York: Garland.

Lapsley, D. K., Enright, R. D., & Serlin, R. C. (1985). Toward a theoretical perspective on the legislation of adolescence. *Journal of Early Adolescence, 5,* 441–466.

Lapsley, D. K., Enright, R. D., & Serlin, R. C. (1986). Moral and social education. In J. Worrell & F. Danner (Eds.), *Adolescent development: Issues in education.* New York: Academic Press.

Lapsley, D. K., Milstead, M., Quintana, S. M., Flannery, D., & Buss, R. R. (1986). Adolescent egocentrism and formal operations: Tests of a theoretical assumption. *Developmental Psychology, 22,* 800–807.

Lapsley, D. K., & Murphy, M. N. (1985). Another look at the theoretical assumptions of adolescent egocentrism. *Developmental Review, 5,* 201–217.

Lapsley, D. K., & Power, F. C. (Eds.). (1988). *Self, ego, and identity.* New York: Springer-Verlag.

Lapsley, D. K., & Quintana, S. M. (1985). Recent approaches in children's elementary moral and social education. *Elementary School Guidance and Counseling Journal, 19,* 246–251.

Lapsley, D. K., & Rice, K. G. (1988a). History, puberty, and the textbook consensus on adolescent development. *Contemporary Psychology, 33,* 210–213.

Lapsley, D. K., & Rice, K. G. (1988b). The "new look" at the imaginary audience and personal fable: Toward an integrative model of adolescent ego development. In D. K. Lapsley & F. C. Power (Eds.), *Self, ego, and identity: Integrative approaches.* New York: Springer-Verlag.

Lapsley, D. K., Rice, K. G., & Shadid, G. E. (1989). Psychological separation and adjustment to college. *Journal of Counseling Psychology, 36,* 286–294.

Larson, R. (1989). Beeping children and adolescents: A method for studying time use and daily experience. *Journal of Youth and Adolescence, 18,* 511–530.

Larson, R., & Kleiber, D. (1990). Free-time activities as factors in adolescent adjustment. In P. Tolan & B. Cohler (Eds.), *Handbook of clinical research and practice with adolescents.* New York: Oxford University Press.

Larson, R., Kubey, R., & Colletti, J. (1989). Changing channels: Early adolescent media choices and shifting investments. *Journal of Youth and Adolescence, 18,* 583–599.

Larson, R., & Richards, M. H. (1989). Introduction: The changing life space of early adolescence. *Journal of Youth and Adolescence, 18,* 501–509.

Lave, J. (1977). Tailor-made experiments and evaluating the intellectual consequences of apprenticeship training. *Quarterly News Letter of the Institute of Comparative Human Development, 1,* 1–3.

LaVoie, J. (1976). Ego identity formation in middle adolescence. *Journal of Youth and Adolescence, 5,* 371–385.

Law, T. C. (1992, March). *The relationship between mothers' employment status and perception of child behavior.* Paper presented at the meeting of the Society for Research on Adolescence, Washington, DC.

Lazarus, R. S. (1966). *Psychological stress and the coping process.* New York: McGraw-Hill.

Lazarus, R. S. (1990, August). *Progress on a cognitive-motivational-relational theory of emotion.* Paper presented at the meeting of the American Psychological Association, Boston, MA.

Lazarus, R. S. (1991). *Emotion and adaptation.* New York: Oxford University Press.

Lazarus, R. S., & Folkman, S. (1984). *Stress, appraisal, and coping.* New York: Springer.

Lee, C. B. T. (1970). *The campus scene: 1900-1970.* New York: McKay.

Lee, C. C. (1985). Successful rural black adolescents: A psychological profile. *Adolescence, 20,* 129–142.

Lee, E. (1988). Cultural factors in working with Southeast Asian refugee adolescents. *Journal of Adolescence, 2,* 167–179.

Leitenberg, H. (1986). Primary prevention in delinquency. In J. Burchard & S. Burchard (Eds.), *Prevention of delinquent behavior.* Newbury Park, CA: Sage.

Lempers, J. D., Clark-Lempers, D., & Simons, R. L. (1989). Economic hardship, parenting, and distress. *Child Development, 60,* 25–39.

Leon, G. R. (1991). Bulimia nervosa. In R. M. Lerner, A. C. Petersen, & J. Brooks-Gunn (Eds.), *Encyclopedia of adolescence* (Vol. 1). New York: Garland.

Leon, G. R., Perry, C. L., Mangelsdorf, C., & Tell, G. J. (1989). Adolescent nutritional and psychological patterns and risk for the development of an eating disorder. *Journal of Youth and Adolescence, 18,* 273–282.

Leone, C. M., & Richards, M. H. (1989). Classwork and homework in early adolescence: The ecology of achievement. *Journal of Youth and Adolescence, 18,* 531–548.

Lepper, M., Greene, D., & Nisbett, R. E. (1973). Undermining children's intrinsic interest with extrinsic rewards. *Journal of Personality and Social Psychology, 28,* 129–137.

Lepper, M. R. (1985). Microcomputers in education: Motivational and social issues. *American Psychologist, 40,* 1–18.

Lepper, M. R., & Gurtner, J. (1989). Children and computers: Approaching the twenty-first century. *American Psychologist, 44,* 170–178.

Lerner, H. G. (1989). *The dance of intimacy.* New York: Harper & Row.

Lerner, J. V., & Hess, L. E. (1991). Maternal employment influences on adolescent development. In R. M. Lerner, A. C. Petersen, & J. Brooks-Gunn (Eds.), *Encyclopedia of adolescence* (Vol. 2). New York: Garland.

Lerner, J. V., Jacobson, L., & del Gaudio, A. (1992, March). *Maternal role satisfaction and family variables as predictors of adolescent adjustment.* Paper presented at the meeting of the Society for Research on Adolescence, Washington, DC.

Lerner, R. M. (1981). Adolescent development: Scientific study in the 1980s. *Youth and Society, 12,* 251–261.

Lerner, R. M. (1987). A life-span perspective for early adolescence. In R. M. Lerner & T. T. Foch (Eds.), *Biological-psychosocial interactions in early adolescence.* Hillsdale, NJ: Erlbaum.

Lerner, R. M. (1991). Continuities and changes in the scientific study of adolescence. *Journal of Research on Adolescence, 1,* 1–6.

Lerner, R. M., & Brackney, B. E. (1978). The importance of inner and outer body parts attitudes in the self-concept of late adolescents. *Sex Roles, 4,* 225–237.

Lerner, R. M., & Karabenick, S. A. (1974). Physical attractiveness, body attitudes, and self-concept in late adolescence. *Journal of Youth and Adolescence, 3,* 307–316.

Lerner, R. M., & Lerner, J. V. (1983). Temperament-intelligence reciprocities in early childhood: A contextual model. In M. Lewis (Ed.), *Origins of intelligence.* New York: Plenum.

Lerner, R. M., Petersen, A. C., & Brooks-Gunn, J. (Eds.). (1991). *Encyclopedia of adolescence.* New York: Garland.

Lesser, G., Fifer, G., & Clark, D. (1965). Mental abilities of children from different social classes and cultural groups. *Monographs of the Society for Research in Child Development, 30* (4, Whole No. 102).

Lester, D. (1989). *Can we predict suicide?* New York: AMS.

Levine, S. V. (1984, August). Radical departures. *Psychology Today,* pp. 18–27.

Levy, A. B., Dixon, K. N., & Stern, S. L. (1989). How are depression and bulimia related? *American Journal of Psychiatry, 146,* 162–169.

Levy, G. D., & Carter, D. B. (1989). Gender schema, gender constancy, and gender-role knowledge: The roles of cognitive factors in preschoolers' gender-role stereotype attributions. *Developmental Psychology, 25,* 444–449.

Lewinsohn, P., Hops, H., Roberts, R. E., Seeley, J. R., & Andrews, J. A. (1991, August). *Adolescence depression: I. Prevalence and incidence.* Paper presented at the meeting of the American Psychological Association, San Francisco, CA.

Lewis, C. G. (1981). How adolescents approach decisions: Changes over grades seven to twelve and policy implications. *Child Development, 52,* 538–554.

Liebert, R. M., & Sprafkin, J. (1988). *The early window* (3rd ed.). New York: Pergamon.

Lindner, M. S. (1992, March). *When dad and mom and adolescent makes four: Adolescents' perceptions of relationships with three parents.* Paper presented at the meeting of the Society for Research on Adolescence, Washington, DC.

Linn, M. C. (1987). Establishing a research base for scientific education: Challenges, trends, and recommendations. *Journal of Research in Science Teaching, 24,* 191–216.

Linn, M. C. (1991). Scientific reasoning, adolescent. In R. M. Lerner, A. C. Petersen, & J. Brooks-Gunn (Eds.), *Encyclopedia of adolescence* (Vol. 2). New York: Garland.

Linn, M. C., & Hyde, J. S. (1991). Cognitive and psychosocial gender differences, trends in. In R. M. Lerner, A. C. Petersen, & J. Brooks-Gunn (Eds.), *Encyclopedia of adolescence.* New York: Garland.

Linn, M. C., & Peterson, A. C. (1986). A meta-analysis of gender differences in spatial ability: Implications for mathematics and science achievement. In J. S. Hyde & M. C. Linn (Eds.), *The psychology of gender: Advances through meta-analysis.* Baltimore, MD: Johns Hopkins University Press.

Linney, J. A., & Seidman, E. (1989). The future of schooling. *American Psychologist, 44,* 336–340.

Lipsitz, J. (1980, March). *Sexual development in young adolescents.* Invited speech given at the American Association of Sex Educators, Counselors, and Therapists.

Lipsitz, J. (1983, October). *Making it the hard way: Adolescents in the 1980s.* Testimony presented at the Crisis Intervention Task Force, House Select Committee on Children, Youth, and Families, Washington, DC.

Lipsitz, J. (1984). *Successful schools for young adolescents.* New Brunswick, NJ: Transaction Books.

Litt, I. F. (1991). Eating disorders, medical complications of. In R. M. Lerner, A. C. Petersen, & J. Brooks-Gunn (Eds.), *Encyclopedia of adolescence* (Vol. 1). New York: Garland.

Livesley, W. J., & Bromley, D. B. (1973). *Person perception in childhood and adolescence.* New York: Wiley.

Loehr, J. (1989, May). *Personal communication.* Saddlebrook, FL: U.S. Tennis Association Training Camp.

Loewen, I. R., & Leigh, G. K. (1986). *Timing of transition to sexual intercourse: A multivariate analysis of white adolescent females ages 15–17.* Paper presented at the meeting of the Society for the Scientific Study of Sex, St. Louis, MO.

Logue, A. W. (1986). *Eating and drinking.* New York: W. H. Freeman.

Long, T., & Long, L. (1983). *Latchkey children.* New York: Penguin.

Lonner, W. (1991, August). *Representation of cross-cultural psychology in mainstream publications.* Paper presented at the meeting of the American Psychological Association, San Francisco.

Lonner, W. J. (1990). An overview of cross-cultural testing and assessment. In R.W. Brislin (Ed.), *Applied cross-cultural psychology.* Newbury Park, CA: Sage.

Lowman, R. L. (1991). *The clinical practice of career assessment.* Washington, DC: American Psychological Association.

Lueptow, L. (1984). *Adolescent sex roles and social change.* New York: Columbia University Press.

Lull, J. (1987). Listener's communicative uses of popular music. In J. Lull (Ed.), *Popular music and communication.* Newbury Park, CA: Sage.

Lundman, R. (1984). *Prevention and control of juvenile delinquency.* New York: Oxford University Press.

Luria, A., & Herzog, E. (1985, April). *Gender segregation across and within settings.* Paper presented at the biennial meeting of the Society for Research in Child Development, Toronto.

Lynch, M. E. (1991). Gender intensification. In R. M. Lerner, A. C. Petersen, & J. Brooks-Gunn (Eds.), *Encyclopedia of adolescence* (Vol. 1). New York: Garland.

Lyons, J. M., & Barber, B. L. (1992, March). *Family environment effects on adolescent adjustment: Differences between intact and remarried families.* Paper presented at the meeting of the Society for Research on Adolescence, Washington, DC.

Lyons, N. P. (1983). Two perspectives: On self, relationships, and morality. *Harvard Educational Review, 53,* 125–145.

Lyons, N. P. (1990). Listening to voices we have not heard. In C. Gilligan, N. P. Lyons, & T. J. Hanmer (Eds.), *Making connections.* Cambridge, MA: Harvard University Press.

Maas, H. S. (1954). The role of members in clubs of lower-class and middle-class adolescents. *Child Development, 25,* 241–251.

Maccoby, E. E. (1984). Middle childhood in the context of the family. In W. A. Collins (Ed), *Development during middle childhood.* Washington, DC: National Academy Press.

Maccoby, E. E. (1987, November). Interview with Elizabeth Hall: All in the family. *Psychology Today,* pp. 54–60.

Maccoby, E, E. (1990, June). *Gender and relationships: A developmental account.* Paper presented at the meeting of the American Psychological Society, Dallas, TX.

Maccoby, E. E. (1991, April). Discussant, symposium on the development of gender and relationships. Symposium presented at the biennial meeting of the Society for Research in Child Development, Seattle.

Maccoby, E. E., & Jacklin, C. N. (1974). *The psychology of sex differences.* Palo Alto, CA: Stanford University Press.

Maccoby, E. E., & Jacklin, C. N. (in press). Gender segregation in childhood. In H. Reese (Ed.), *Advances in child development and behavior* (Vol. 20). New York: Academic Press.

Maccoby, E. E., & Martin, J. A. (1983). Socialization in the context of the family: Parent-child interaction. In P. H. Mussen (Ed.), *Handbook of child psychology* (4th ed., Vol. 4). New York: Wiley.

MacDonald, K. (1987). Parent-child physical play with rejected, neglected, and popular boys. *Developmental Psychology, 23,* 705–711.

Mac Iver, D., Urdan, T., Beck, J., Midgley, C., Reuman, D., Tasko, A., Fenzel, L. M., Arhar, J., & Kramer, L. (1992, March). *Changing schools and classrooms in the middle grades: Research on new partnerships, processes, practices, and programs.* Paper presented at the meeting of the Society for Research on Adolescence, Washington, DC.

Magnusson, D. (1988). *Individual development from an interactional perspective: A longitudinal study.* Hillsdale, NJ: Erlbaum

Malatesta, C. (1990, May 28). Commentary. *Newsweek,* p. 61.

Malcom, S. M. (1988). Technology in 2020: Educating a diverse population. In R. S. Nickerson & P. P. Zodhiates (Eds.), *Technology in education: Looking toward 2020.* Hillsdale, NJ: Erlbaum.

Malina, R. M. (1990). Physical growth and performance during the transitional years (9–16). In R. Montemayor, G. R. Adams, & T. P. Gulotta (Eds.), *From childhood to adolescence: A transitional period?* Newbury Park, CA: Sage.

Malina, R. M. (1991). Growth spurt, adolescent. II. In R. M. Lerner, A. C. Petersen, & J. Brooks-Gunn (Eds.), *Encyclopedia of adolescence* (Vol. 1). New York: Garland.

Malinowski, B. (1927). *Sex and repression in savage society.* New York: Meridian.

Maltsberger, J. T. (1988). *Suicide risk.* New York: Human Services Press.

Manaster, G. J., Chan, J. C., & Safady, R. (1992). Mexican-American migrant students' academic success. *Adolescence, 105,* 123–136.

Mandler, J. M. (1983). Representation. In P. H. Mussen (Ed.), *Handbook of child psychology* (4th ed., Vol. 3). New York: Wiley.

Manis, F. R., Keating, D. P., & Morrison, F. J. (1980). Developmental differences in the allocation of processing capacity. *Journal of Experimental Child Psychology, 29,* 156–169.

Mann, L., Harmoni, R., & Power, C. N. (in press). Adolescent decision making: The development of competence. *Journal of Adolescence.*

Marcia, J. E. (1966). Identity six years after: A follow-up study. *Journal of Youth and Adolescence, 5,* 145–160.

Marcia, J. E. (1980a). Ego identity development. In J. Adelson (Ed.), *Handbook of adolescent psychology.* New York: Wiley.

Marcia, J. E. (1980b). Identity in adolescence. In J. Adelson (Ed.), *Handbook of adolescent psychology.* New York: Wiley.

Marcia, J. E. (1987). The identity status approach to the study of ego identity development. In T. Honess & K. Yardley (Eds.), *Self and identity: Perspectives across the lifespan.* London: Routledge & Kegan Paul.

Marcia, J. E. (1989). Identity and intervention. *Journal of Adolescence, 12,* 401–410.

Marcia, J. E. (1991). Identity and self-development. In R. M. Lerner, A. C. Petersen, & J. Brooks-Gunn (Eds.), *Encyclopedia of adolescence* (Vol. 1). New York: Garland.

Marín, G., & Marín, B. V. (1991). *Research with Hispanic populations.* Newbury Park, CA: Sage.

Marklein, M. B., & DeRosa, R. (1991, November 19). Magic's HIV affects health educators' game plans. *USA Today,* p. 8D.

Markus, H., & Nurius, P. (1986). Possible selves. *American Psychologist, 41,* 954–969.

Martin, B. (1990). The transmission of relationship difficulties from one generation to the next. *Journal of Youth and Adolescence, 19,* 181–199.

Martin, C. L. (1989, April). *Beyond knowledge-based conceptions of gender schematic processing.* Paper presented at the biennial meeting of the Society for Research in Child Development, Kansas City.

Martin, J. (1976). *The education of adolescents.* Washington, DC: U.S. Office of Education.

Martorano, S. (1977). A developmental analysis of performance on Piaget's formal operations tasks. *Developmental Psychology, 13,* 666–672.

Mason, C. A., & Cauce, A. M. (1991, August) *An ecological model of adjustment in African American adolescents.* Paper presented at the meeting of the American Psychological Association, San Francisco.

Matarazzo, J. D. (1979). Health psychology: APA's newest division. *The Health Psychologist, 1,* 1.

Matson, J. L., & Mulick, J. A. (Eds.). (1990). *Handbook of mental retardation* (2nd ed.). Elmsford, NY: Pergamon.

Mayer, R. (1987). *Educational psychology: A cognitive approach.* Boston, MA: Little, Brown.

Mays, V. M. (1991, August). *The role of sexual orientation and ethnic identification in HIV health risk.* Paper presented at the meeting of the American Psychological Association, San Francisco.

McAdoo, H. P. (Ed.). (1988). *Black families* (2nd ed.). Newbury Park, CA: Sage.

McAlister, A., Perry, C., Killen, J., Slinkard, L. A., & Maccoby, N. (1980). Pilot study of smoking, alcohol, and drug abuse prevention. *American Journal of Public Health, 70,* 719–721.

McAnarney, E. R. (1988). Early adolescent motherhood: Crisis in the making? In M. D. Levine & E. R. McAnarney (Eds.), *Early adolescent transitions.* Lexington, MA: D. C. Heath.

McBride, A. B. (1990). Mental health effects of women's multiple roles. *American Psychologist, 45,* 381–384.

McCabe, M. P., & Collins, J. K. (1979). Sex role and dating orientation. *Journal of Youth and Adolescence, 8,* 407–425.

McCall, R. B. (1991). Underachievers and dropouts. In R. M. Lerner, A. C. Petersen, & J. Brooks-Gunn (Eds.), *Encyclopedia of adolescence* (Vol. 2). New York: Garland.

McCall, R. B., Meyers, E. D., Hartman, J., & Roche, A. F. (1983). Developmental changes in head circumference and mental performance growth rates: A test of Epstein's phrenoblysis hypothesis. *Developmental Psychobiology, 16,* 457–468.

McClelland, D. C. (1955). Some social consequences of achievement motivation. In M. R. Jones (Ed.), *Nebraska Symposium on Motivation.* Lincoln, NE: University of Nebraska Press.

McCord, J. (1990). Problem behaviors. In S. S. Feldman & G. R. Elliott (Eds.), *At the threshold: The developing adolescent.* Cambridge, MA: Harvard University Press.

McCord, W., McCord, J., & Gudeman, J. (1960). *Origins of alcoholism.* Palo Alto, CA: Stanford University Press.

McGlynn, G. (1990). *Dynamics of fitness: A practical approach* (2nd ed.). Dubuque, IA: Wm. C. Brown.

McHugh, M., Koeske, R., & Frieze, I. H. (1986). Issues to consider in conducting nonsexist psychological research: A guide for researchers. *American Psychologist 41,* 879–890.

McKnight, C. C., Crosswhite, F. J., Dossey, J. A., Kifer, E., Swafford, J. O., Travers, K. J., & Cooney, T. J. (1987). *The underachieving curriculum: Assessing U.S. school mathematics from an international perspective.* Champaign, IL: Stipes.

McLoyd, V. (1989, April). *Facing the future in hard times: Choices, perceptions, and behavior of black adolescents.* Paper presented at the biennial meeting of the Society for Research in Child Development, Kansas City.

McLoyd, V. (1990). Minority children: An introduction to the special issue. *Child Development, 61,* 263–266.

McLoyd, V. (in press). The declining fortunes of black children: Psychological distress, parenting, and socioeconomic development in the context of economic hardship. *Child Development.*

McLoyd, V. C., & Wilson, L. (1990). Maternal behavior, social support, and economic conditions as predictors of distress in children. In V. C. McLoyd & C. A. Flanagan (Eds.), *Economic stress: Effects on family life and child development.* San Francisco: Jossey-Bass.

McLoyd, V. C., & Wilson, L. (1991). The strain of living poor: Parenting, social support, and child mental health. In A. C. Huston (Ed.), *Children in poverty: Child development and public policy.* New York: Cambridge University Press.

McPartland, J. M., & McDill, E. L. (1976). *The unique role of schools in the causes of youthful crime.* Baltimore: Johns Hopkins University Press.

McPeck, J. E. (1990). Critical thinking and subject specificity: A reply to Ennis. *Educational Leadership, 19,* 10–12.

McWhirter, D. P., Reinisch, J. M., & Sanders, S. A. (Eds.). (1990). *Homosexuality/heterosexuality.* New York: Oxford University Press.

Mead, M. (1928). *Coming of age in Samoa.* New York: Morrow.

Mead, M. (1978, Dec. 30–Jan. 5). The American family: An endangered species. *TV Guide.*

Mednick, B. R., Baker, R. L., & Carothers, L. E. (1990). Patterns of family instability and crime: The association of timing of the family's disruption on subsequent adolescent and young adult criminality. *Journal of Youth and Adolescence, 19,* 201–219.

Medrich, E. A., Rosen, J., Rubin, V., & Buckley, S. (1982). *The serious business of growing up.* Berkeley: University of California Press.

Meese, J. L., Wigfield, A., & Eccles, J. S. (1990). Predictors of math anxiety and its influence on young adolescents' course enrollment intentions and performance in mathematics. *Journal of Educational Psychology, 82,* 60–70.

Messinger, J. C. (1971). Sex and repression in an Irish folk community. In D. S. Marshal & R. C. Suggs (Eds.), *Human sexual behavior: Variations in the ethnographic spectrum* (pp. 3–37). New York: Basic Books.

Miller, B. C., Card, J. J., Paikoff, R. L., & Peterson, J. L. (1992). *Preventing adolescent pregnancy.* Newbury Park, CA: Sage.

Miller, J. B. (1976). *Toward a new psychology of women.* Boston: Beacon Press.

Miller, J. B. (1986). *Toward a new psychology of women* (2nd ed.). Boston: Beacon Press.

Miller, J. G. (1991). A cultural perspective on the morality of beneficience and interpersonal responsibility. In S. Ting-Toomey & F. Korzenny (Eds.), *International and intercultural communication annual, 15.* Newbury Park, CA: Sage.

Miller, J. G., & Bersoff, D. M. (in press). Culture and moral judgment: How are conflicts between justice and interpersonal responsibilities resolved? *Journal of Personality and Social Psychology.*

Miller, N. E. (1959). Liberalization of basic S-R concepts: Extension to conflict behavior, motivation, and social learning. In S. Koch (Ed.), *Psychology: A study of science.* New York: McGraw-Hill.

Miller, P. Y., & Simon, W. (1974). Adolescent sexual behavior: Context and change. *Social Problems, 22,* 58–76.

Miller, S. K., & Slap, G. G. (1989). Adolescent smoking: A review of prevalence and prevention. *Journal of Adolescent Health Care, 10,* 129–135.

Miller, W. B. (1958). Lower-class culture as a generating milieu of gang delinquency. *Journal of Social Issues, 14,* 5–19.

Miller-Jones, D. (1989). Culture and testing. *American Psychologist, 44,* 360–366.

Miller-Jones, D. (1991). Informal reasoning in inner-city children. In J. Voss, D. Perkins, & J. Segal (Eds.), *Informal reasoning and education.* Hillsdale, NJ: Erlbaum.

Millstein, G. B. (1988). *The potential of school-linked centers to promote adolescent health and development.* Washington, DC: Carnegie Council on Adolescent Development.

Millstein, S. G. (1991). Health beliefs. In R. M. Lerner, A. C. Petersen, & J. Brooks-Gunn (Eds.), *Encyclopedia of adolescence* (Vol. 1). New York: Garland.

Millstein, S. G., & Irwin, C. E. (1985). Adolescent assessment of behavioral risk: Sex differences and maturation effects. *Pediatric Research, 19,* 112A.

Millstein, S. G., & Irwin, C. E. (1987). Concepts of health and illness: Different constructs or variation on a same theme? *Health Psychology, 6,* 515–524.

Millstein, S. G., & Irwin, C. E. (1988). Accident-related behaviors in adolescents: A biopsychosocial view. *Alcohol, Drugs, and Driving, 4*, 21–29.

Millstein, S. G., & Litt, I. F. (1990). Adolescent health. In S. S. Feldman & G. R. Elliott (Eds.), *At the threshold: The developing adolescent.* Cambridge, MA: Harvard University Press.

Minkler, M. (1989). Health education, health promotion, and the open society: An historical perspective. *Health Education Quarterly, 16,* 17–30.

Minuchin, P. P., & Shapiro, E. K. (1983). The school as a context for social development. In P. H. Mussen (Ed.), *Handbook of child psychology* (4th ed., Vol. 4). New York: Wiley.

Mirel, J. E. (1991). Twentieth-century America, adolescence in. In R. M. Lerner, A. C. Petersen, & J. Brooks-Gunn (Eds.), *Encyclopedia of adolescence* (Vol. 2). New York: Garland.

Mischel, W. (1970). Sex-typing and socialization. In P. H. Mussen (Ed.), *Manual of child psychology* (3rd ed., Vol. 2). New York: Wiley.

Mischel, W. (1973). Toward a cognitive social learning reconceptualization of personality. *Psychological Review, 80,* 252–283.

Mischel, W. (1984). Convergences and challenges in the search for consistency. *American Psychologist, 39,* 351–364.

Mischel, W., & Gilligan, C. (1964). Delay of gratification, motivation for the prohibited gratification, and responses to temptation. *Journal of Abnormal and Social Psychology, 69,* 411–417.

Mischel, W., & Mischel, H. (1975, April). *A cognitive social-learning analysis of moral development.* Paper presented at the meeting of the Society for Research in Child Development, Denver.

Mitteness, L. S., & Nydegger, C. N. (1982, October). *Dimensions of parent-child relations in adulthood.* Paper presented at the meeting of the American Gerontological Association.

Money, J. (1987). Sin, sickness, or status? Homosexual gender identity and psychoneuroendocrinology. *American Psychologist, 42,* 384–389.

Montemayor, R. (1982). The relationship between parent-adolescent conflict and the amount of time adolescents spend with parents, peers, and alone. *Child Development, 53,* 1512–1519.

Montemayor, R. (1984). Maternal employment and adolescents' relations with parents, siblings, and peers. *Journal of Youth and Adolescence, 13,* 543–557.

Montemayor, R., Adams, G. R., & Gulotta, T. P. (Eds.). (1990). *From childhood to adolescence: A transitional period?* Newbury Park, CA: Sage.

Montemayor, R., & Clayton, M. D. (1983). Maternal employment and adolescent development. *Theory into Practice, 22,* 112–118.

Montemayor, R., & Flannery, D. J. (1990). Making the transition from childhood to early adolescence. In R. Montemayor, G. R. Adams, & T. P. Gullotta (Eds.), *From childhood to adolescence: A transitional period?* Newbury Park, CA: Sage.

Montemayor, R., & Flannery, D. J. (1991). Parent-adolescent relations in middle and late adolescence. In R. M. Lerner, A. C. Petersen, & J. Brooks-Gunn (Eds.), *Encyclopedia of adolescence* (Vol. 2). New York: Garland.

Moos, R. H., Finney, J. W., & Cronkite, R. C. (1990). *Alcoholism treatment: Context, process, and outcome.* New York: Oxford University Press.

Morgan, M. (1982). Television and adolescents' sex-role stereotypes: A longitudinal study. *Journal of Personality and Social Psychology, 43,* 947–955.

Morgan, M. (1987). Television, sex-role attitudes, and sex-role behavior. *Journal of Early Adolescence, 7,* 269–282.

Morrison, D. M. (1985). Adolescent contraceptive behavior: A review. *Psychological Bulletin, 98,* 538–568.

Morrow, L. (1988, August 8). Through the eyes of children. *Time,* pp. 32–33.

Mortimer, J. T. (1991). Employment. In R. M. Lerner, A. C. Petersen, & J. Brooks-Gunn (Eds.), *Encyclopedia of adolescence* (Vol. 1). New York: Garland.

Mortimer, J. T., Finch, M., Shanahan, M., & Ryu, S. (1992). Work experience, mental health, and behavioral adjustment in adolescence. *Journal of Research on Adolescence, 2,* 24–57.

Mott, F. L., & Marsiglio, W. (1985, September/October). Early childbearing and completion of high school. *Family Planning Perspectives,* p. 234.

Mounts, N. S. (1992, March). *An ecological analysis of peer influence on adolescent academic achievement and delinquency.* Paper presented at the meeting of the Society for Research on Adolescence, Washington, DC.

Munce, D. (1990, November). *High school students' perceptions of the likelihood of obtaining college athletic and academic scholarships: A national survey.* Unpublished data, National Research Center for College and University Admissions, Summit, MO.

Munroe, R. H., Himmin, H. S., & Munroe, R. L. (1984). Gender understanding and sex-role preference in four cultures. *Developmental Psychology, 20,* 673–682.

Munroe, R. H., Koel, A., Munroe, R. L., Bolton, R., Michelson, C., & Bolton, C. (1983). Time allocation in our societies. *Ethnology, 22,* 355–370.

Munsch, J., Wampler, R. S., & Dawson, M. (1992, March). *Coping with school-related stress in multi-ethnic sample of early adolescents.* Paper presented at the meeting of the Society for Research on Adolescence, Washington, DC.

Murphy, J. (1987). Educational influences. In V. B. Van Hasselt & M. Hersen (Eds.), *Handbook of adolescent psychology.* New York: Pergamon.

Murray, D. M., Matthews, K. A., Blake, S. M., Prineas, R. J., & Gillum, R. F. (1988). Type-A behavior in children: Demographic, behavioral, and physiological correlates. In B. G. Melamed & others (Eds.), *Child health psychology.* Hillsdale, NJ: Erlbaum.

Murray, H. A. (1938). *Explorations in personality.* New York: Oxford University Press.

Muuss, R. E. (1989). *Theories of adolescence* (15th ed.). New York: Random House.

Myers, W. C., & Burket, R. C. (1992). Current perspectives on adolescent conduct disorder. *Adolescent Medicine, 3,* 61–70.

Nagata, D. K. (1989). Japanese American children and adolescents. In J. T. Gibbs & L. N. Huang (Eds.), *Children of color.* San Francisco: Jossey-Bass.

National Advisory Council on Economic Opportunity (1980). *Critical choices for the 80s.* Washington, DC: U.S. Government Printing Office.

National Assessment of Educational Progress. (1976). *Adult work skills and knowledge* (Report No. 35-COD-01). Denver, CO: National Assessment of Educational Progress.

National Institute of Drug Abuse (1989, July). *Survey of drug use in the United States.* Washington, DC: U.S. Government Printing Office.

National Institute on Alcohol Abuse and Alcoholism (NIAAA). (1984). *Prevention plus: Involving schools, parents, and the community in alcohol and drug education.* Washington, DC: Department of Health and Human Services.

National Research Council. (1987). *Risking the future: Adolescent sexuality, pregnancy, and childbearing.* Washington, DC: National Academy Press.

Needle, R. H., Su, S. S., & Doherty, W. J. (1990). Divorce, remarriage, and adolescent substance use: A prospective longitudinal study. *Journal of Marriage and the Family, 52,* 157–169.

Neiderhiser, J. M., McGuire, S., Plomin, R., Reiss, D., & Hetherington, E. M. (1992, March). *Genetic and environmental influences on teacher reports of cognitive and social competence on the Harter.* Paper presented at the meeting of the Society for Research on Adolescence, Washington, DC.

Neiger, B. L., & Hopkins, R. W. (1988). Adolescent suicide: Character traits of high-risk teenagers. *Adolescence, 23,* 469–475.

Neimark, E. D. (1982). Adolescent thought: Transition to formal operations. In B. B. Wolman (Ed.), *Handbook of developmental psychology.* Englewood Cliffs, NJ: Prentice-Hall.

Nelson-Le Gall, S. (1990). Academic achievement orientation and help-seeking behavior in early adolescent girls. *Journal of Early Adolescence, 10,* 176–190.

Newcomb, M. D., & Bentler, P. M. (1988). Impact of adolescent drug use and social support on problems of young adults: A longitudinal study. *Journal of Abnormal Psychology, 97,* 64–75.

Newcomb, M. D., & Bentler, P. M. (1989). Substance use and abuse among children and teenagers. *American Psychologist, 44,* 242–248.

Newcomb, M. D., & Bentler, P. M. (1991a). Cocaine use among adolescents and young adults, antecedents/predictors of. In R. M. Lerner, A. C. Petersen, & J. Brooks-Gunn (Eds.), *Encyclopedia of adolescence* (Vol. 1). New York: Garland.

Newcomb, M. D., & Bentler, P. M. (1991b). Hallucinogens. In R. M. Lerner, A. C. Petersen, & J. Brooks-Gunn (Eds.), *Encyclopedia of adolescence* (Vol. 1). New York: Garland.

Newcomer, S. F., & Udry, J. R. (1985). Oral sex in an adolescent population. *Archives of Sexual Behavior, 14,* 41–46.

Newman, F. M. (in press). Higher-order thinking in the teaching of social studies: Connections between theory and practice. In D. Perkins, J. Segal, & J. Voss (Eds.), *Informal reasoning and education.* Hillsdale, NJ: Erlbaum.

Newton, D. E. (1982). The status of programs in human sexuality: A preliminary study. *The High School Journal, 6,* 232–239.

Nicholls, J. G. (1984). Conceptions of ability and achievement motivation. In R. E. Ames & C. Ames (Eds.), *Motivation in education.* New York: Academic Press.

Nitz, K., & Lerner, J. V. (1991). Temperament during adolescence. In R. M. Lerner, A. C. Petersen, & J. Brooks-Gunn (Eds.), *Encyclopedia of adolescence* (Vol. 2). New York: Garland.

Norem, J. K., & Cantor, N. (1986). Anticipatory and post-hoc cushioning strategies: Optimism and defensive pessimism in "risky" situations. *Cognitive Therapy Research, 10,* 347–362.

Nottelmann, E. D., Susman, E. J., Blue, J. H., Inoff-Germain, G., Dorn, L. D, Loriaux, D. L., Cutler, G. B., & Chrousos, G. P. (1987). Gonadal and adrenal hormone correlates of adjustment in early adolescence. In R. M. Lerner & T. T. Foch (Eds.), *Biological-psychological interactions in early adolescence.* Hillsdale, NJ: Erlbaum.

Novy, D. M., Gaa, J. P., Frankiewicz, R. G., Liberman, D., & Amerikaner, M. (1992). The association between patterns of family functioning and ego development of the juvenile offender. *Adolescence, 27,* 25–36.

Nucci, L. (1982). Conceptual development in the moral and conventional domains: Implications for values education. *Review of Educational Research, 52,* 93–122.

Nydegger, C. N. (1981, October). *The ripple effect of parental timing.* Paper presented at the meeting of the American Gerontological Association.

O'Brien, R. W. (1990, March). *The use of family members and peers as resources during adolescence.* Paper presented at the meeting of the Society for Research in Adolescence, Atlanta, GA.

O'Conner, B. P., & Nikolic, J. (1990). Identity development and formal operations as sources of adolescent egocentrism. *Journal of Youth and Adolescence, 19,* 149–158.

Occupational Outlook Handbook (1990–1991 Ed.). (1990). Washington, DC: Bureau of Labor Statistics.

Oden, S. L., & Asher, S. R. (1975, April). *Coaching children in social skills for friendship making.* Paper presented at the meeting of the Society for Research in Child Development, Denver, CO.

O'Donnell, C., Manos, M., & Chesney-Lind, M. (1987). Diversion and neighborhood delinquency programs in open settings. In E. Morris & C. Braukmann (Eds.), *Behavioral approaches to crime and delinquency.* New York: Plenum.

Offer, D., & Church, R. B. (1991a). Generation gap. In R. M. Lerner, A. C. Petersen, & J. Brooks-Gunn (Eds.), *Encyclopedia of adolescence* (Vol. 1). New York: Garland.

Offer, D., & Church, R. B. (1991b). Turmoil, adolescent. In R. M. Lerner, A. C. Petersen, & J. Brooks-Gunn (Eds.), *Encyclopedia of adolescence* (Vol. 2). New York: Garland.

Offer, D., Ostrov, E., Howard, K. I., & Atkinson, R. (1988). *The teenage world: Adolescents' self-image in ten countries.* New York: Plenum.

Offord, D. R., & Boyle, M. H. (1988). The epidemiology of antisocial behavior in early adolescents, aged 12 to 14. In M. D. Levine & E. R. McAnarney (Eds.), *Early adolescent transitions.* Lexington, MA: Lexington Books.

Ogbu, J. U. (1974). *The next generation: An ethnography of education in an urban neighborhood.* New York: Academic Press.

Ogbu, J. U. (1986). The consequences of the American caste system. In U. Neisser (Ed.), *The school achievement of minority children: New perspectives.* Hillsdale, NJ: Erlbaum.

Ogbu, J. U. (1989, April). *Academic socialization of black children: An inoculation against future failure?* Paper presented at the meeting of the Society for Research in Child Development, Kansas City, MO.

Omizo, M. M., Omizo, S. A., & Suzuki, L. A. (1988). Children and stress: An exploratory study of stressors and symptoms. *The School Counselor, 35,* 267–274.

Orlofsky, J. (1976). Intimacy status: Relationship to interpersonal perception. *Journal of Youth and Adolescence, 5,* 73–88.

Orlofsky, J., Marcia, J., & Lesser, I. (1973). Ego identity status and the intimacy vs. isolation crisis of young adulthood. *Journal of Personality and Social Psychology, 27,* 211–219.

Orthner, D. K. (1990). Parental work and early adolescence: Issues for research and practice. *Journal of Early Adolescence, 10,* 246–259.

Orthner, D. K., Giddings, M., & Quinn, W. (1987). *Youth in transition: A study of adolescents from Air Force and civilian families.* Washington, DC: U.S. Air Force.

Oser, F. K. (1986). Moral education and values education: The discourse perspective. In M. C. Wittrock (Ed.), *Handbook of research on teaching.* New York: Macmillan.

Oskamp, S., & Mindick, B. (1981). Personality and attitudinal barriers to contraception. In D. Byrne & W. A. Fisher (Eds.), *Adolescents, sex, and contraception.* New York: McGraw-Hill.

Osofsky, J. D. (1989, April). *Affective relationships in adolescent mothers and their infants.* Paper presented at the biennial meeting of the Society for Research in Child Development, Kansas City.

Osofsky, J. D. (1990, Winter). Risk and protective factors for teenage mothers and their infants. *SRCD Newsletter,* pp. 1–2.

Ostrov, E., Offer, D., Howard, K. I., Kaufman, B., & Meyer, H. (1985). Adolescent sexual behavior. *Medical Aspects of Human Sexuality, 19,* 28, 30–31, 34–36.

O'Sullivan, R. G. (1990). Validating a method to identify at-risk middle school students for participation in a dropout prevention program. *Journal of Early Adolescence, 10,* 209–220.

Overton, W. F., & Byrnes, J. P. (1991). Cognitive development. In R. M. Lerner, A. C. Petersen, & J. Brooks-Gunn (Eds.), *Encyclopedia of adolescence* (Vol. 1). New York: Garland.

Overton, W. F., & Montangero, J. (1991). Piaget, Jean. In R. M. Lerner, A. C. Petersen, & J. Brooks-Gunn (Eds), *Encyclopedia of adolescence* (Vol. 2). New York: Garland.

Pacheco, S., & Valdez, L. F. (1989, August). *The present state and future directions of Hispanic psychology.* Paper presented at the meeting of the American Psychological Association, New Orleans.

Padgham, J. J., & Blyth, D. A. (1991). Dating during adolescence. In R. M. Lerner, A. C. Petersen, & J. Brooks-Gunn (Eds.), *Encyclopedia of adolescence* (Vol. 1). New York: Garland.

Paikoff, R. L., & Brooks-Gunn, J. (1990). Physiological processes: What role do they play during the transition to adolescence? In R. Montemayor, G. R. Adams, & T. P. Gulotta (Eds.), *From childhood to adolescence: A transitional period?* Newbury Park, CA: Sage.

Paikoff, R. L., & Brooks-Gunn, J. (1991). Pregnancy, interventions to prevent. In R. M. Lerner, A. C. Petersen, & J. Brooks-Gunn (Eds.), *Encyclopedia of adolescence* (Vol. 2). New York: Garland.

Paikoff, R. L., Buchanan, C. M., & Brooks-Gunn, J. (1991). Hormone-behavior links at puberty, methodological links in the study of. In R. M. Lerner, A. C. Petersen, & J. Brooks-Gunn (Eds.), *Encyclopedia of adolescence.* New York: Garland.

Papini, D. R., Farmer, F. F., Clark, S. M., Micka, J. C., & Barnett, J. K. (1990). Early adolescent age and gender differences in patterns of emotional self-disclosure to parents and friends. *Adolescence, 25,* 959–976.

Papini, D. R., Roggman, L. A., & Anderson, J. (1990). *Early adolescent perceptions of attachment to mother and father: A test of the emotional distancing hypothesis.* Paper presented at the meeting of the Society for Research in Adolescence, Atlanta, GA.

Papini, D., & Sebby, R. (1988). Variations in conflictual family issues by adolescent pubertal status, gender, and family member. *Journal of Early Adolescence, 8,* 1–15.

Parcel, G. S., Simons-Morton, G. G., O'Hara, N. M., Baranowski, T., Kolbe, L. J., & Bee, D. E. (1987). School promotion of healthful diet and exercise behavior: An integration of organizational change and social learning theory interventions. *Journal of School Health, 57,* 150–156.

Parish, T. S. (1987). Family and environment. In V. B. Van Hasselt & M. Hersen (Eds.), *Handbook of adolescent psychology.* New York: Pergamon Press.

Parke, R. D. (1988). Families in life-span perspective: A multilevel developmental approach. In E. M. Hetherington, R. M. Lerner, & M. Perlmutter (Eds.), *Child development in life-span perspective.* Hillsdale, NJ: Erlbaum.

Parke, R. D., MacDonald, K., Beitel, A., & Bhavangri, N. (1988). The interrelationships among families, fathers, and peers. In R. D. Peters (Ed.), *New approaches in family research.* New York: Brunner/Mazel.

Parker, J. G., & Asher, S. R. (1987). Peer relations and later personal adjustment: Are low accepted children at risk? *Psychological Bulletin, 102,* 357–389.

Parker, J. G., & Gottman, J. M. (1989). Social and emotional development in a relational context: Friendship interaction from early childhood to adolescence. In T. J. Berndt & G. W. Ladd (Eds.), *Peer relations in child development.* New York: Wiley.

Patterson, G. R. (1982). *Coercive family processes.* Eugene, OR: Castalia Press.

Patterson, G. R., Bank, L., & Stoolmiller, M. (1990). The preadolescent's contribution to disrupted family process. In R. Montemayor, G. R. Adams, & T. P. Gulotta (Eds.), *From childhood to adolescence: A transitional period?* Newbury Park, CA: Sage.

Patterson, G. R., Capaldi, D., & Bank, L. (1991). An early starter model for predicting delinquency. In D. Pepler & K. Rubin (Eds.), *The development and treatment of childhood aggression.* Hillsdale, NJ: Erlbaum.

Patterson, G. R., DeBaryshe, B. D., & Ramsey, E. (1989). A developmental perspective on antisocial behavior. *American Psychologist, 44,* 329–335.

Patterson, G. R., & Stouthamer-Loeber, M. (1984). The correlation of family management practices and delinquency. *Child Development, 55,* 1299–1307.

Paul, E. L., & White, K. M. (1990). The development of intimate relationships in late adolescence. *Adolescence, 25,* 375–400.

Pearl, R., Bryan, T., & Herzog, A. (1990). Resisting or acquiescing to peer pressure to engage in misconduct: Adolescents' expectations of probable consequences. *Journal of Youth and Adolescence, 19,* 43–55.

Peplau, L. A., & Perlman, D. (Eds.). (1982). *Loneliness: A sourcebook of current theory, research, and therapy.* New York: Wiley.

Perkins, D. N. (1984, September). Creativity by design. *Educational Leadership,* pp. 18–25.

Perkins, D. P., & Gardner, H. (1989). Why "Zero"? A brief introduction to Project Zero. In H. Gardner & D. P. Perkins (Eds.), *Art, mind, and education.* Ithaca, NY: The University of Illinois Press.

Perry, C., Hearn, M., Murray, D., & Klepp, K. (1988). *The etiology and prevention of adolescent alcohol and drug abuse.* Unpublished manuscript, University of Minnesota.

Perry, C. L. (1991). Smoking and drug prevention with early adolescents, programs for. In R. M. Lerner, A. C. Petersen, & J. Brooks-Gunn (Eds.), *Encyclopedia of adolescence* (Vol. 2). New York: Garland.

Perry, I. (1988). A black student's reflection on public and private schools. *Harvard Educational Review, 58,* 332–336.

Perry, W. G. (1981). Cognitive and ethical growth. The making of meaning. In A. W. Chickering (Ed.), *The modern American college: Responding to the new realities of diverse students and a changing society.* San Francisco: Jossey-Bass.

Peskin, H. (1967). Pubertal onset and ego functioning. *Journal of Abnormal Psychology, 72,* 1–15.

Petersen, A. C. (1979, January). Can puberty come any faster? *Psychology Today,* pp. 45–56.

Petersen, A. C. (1987, September). Those gangly years. *Psychology Today,* pp. 28–34.

Petersen, A. C., & Crockett, L. (1985). Pubertal timing and grade effects on adjustment. *Journal of Youth and Adolescence, 14,* 191–206.

Petersen, A. C., & Sarigiani, P. A. (1989, April). *The development of depression in adolescence: Why more girls?* Paper presented at the biennial meeting of the Society for Research in Child Development, Kansas City.

Petersen, A. C., Schulenberg, J. E., Abramowitz, R. H., Offer, D., & Jarcho, H. D. (1984). A self-image questionnaire for young adolescents (SIQYA): Reliability and validity studies. *Journal of Youth and Adolescence, 13,* 93–111.

Petersen, A. C., & Taylor, B. (1980). The biological approach to adolescence: Biological change and psychological adaptation. In J. Adelson (Ed.), *Handbook of adolescent psychology.* New York: Wiley.

Phinney, J. S. (1989). Stages of ethnic identity development in minority group adolescents. *Journal of Early Adolescence, 9,* 34–49.

Phinney, J. S., & Alipuria, L. L. (1990). Ethnic identity in college students from four ethnic groups. *Journal of Adolescence, 13,* 171–183.

Phinney, J. S., Chavira, V., & Williamson, L. (1992). Acculturation attitudes and self-esteem among high school and college students. *Youth and Society, 25,* 299–312.

Phinney, J. S., Espinoza, C., & Onwughalu, M. N. (1992, March). *Accommodation and conflict: The relationship of ethnic identity and American identity among Asian American, Black, and Hispanic adolescents.* Paper presented at the meeting of the Society for Research on Adolescence, Washington, DC.

Piaget, J. (1932). *The moral judgment of the child.* New York: Harcourt Brace Jovanovich.

Piaget, J. (1952a). Jean Piaget. In C. A. Murchison (Ed.), *A history of psychology in autobiography* (Vol. 4). Worcester, MA: Clark University Press.

Piaget, J. (1952b). *The origins of intelligence in children.* New York: International Universities Press.

Piaget, J. (1954). *The construction of reality in the child.* New York: Basic Books.

Piaget, J. (1967). The mental development of the child. In D. Elkind (Ed.), *Six psychological studies by Piaget.* New York: Random House.

Piaget, J. (1970). Piaget's theory. In P. H. Mussen (Ed.), *Carmichael's manual of child psychology* (3rd ed., Vol. 1). New York: Wiley.

Piaget, J. (1972). Intellectual evolution from adolescence to adulthood. *Human Development, 15,* 1–12.

Piers, E. V., & Harris, D. V. (1964). Age and other correlates of self-concept in children. *Journal of Educational Psychology, 55,* 91–95.

Pines, A., & Aronson, E. (1988). *Career burnout: Causes and cures.* New York: Free Press.

Place, D. M. (1975). The dating experience for adolescent girls. *Adolescence, 38,* 157–173.

Plato. (1968). *The republic* (B. Jowett, Trans.). Bridgeport, CT: Airmont.

Pleck, J. (1981). *Three conceptual issues in research on male roles.* Working paper no. 98, Wellesley College Center for Research on Women, Wellesley, MA.

Pleck, J. H. (1983). The theory of male sex role identity: Its rise and fall, 1936–present. In M. Lewin (Ed.), *In the shadow of the past: Psychology portrays the sexes.* New York: Columbia University Press.

Pleck, J. H., Sonenstein, F. L., & Ku, L. C. (1991). Adolescent males' condom use: Relationships between perceived cost-benefits and consistency. *Journal of Marriage and the Family, 53,* 733–745.

Pleck, J. H., Sonnenstein, F. L., & Ku, L. C. (in press). Problem behaviors and masculine ideology in adolescent males. In R. Ketterlinus & M. E. Lamb (Eds.), *Adolescent problem behaviors.* Hillsdale, NJ: Erlbaum.

Plomin, R. (1989). Environment and genes: Determinants of behavior. *American Psychologist, 44,* 105–111.

Plomin, R. (1990). The role of inheritance in behavior. *Science, 248,* 183–188.

Plomin, R. (1991a). Genetic change. In R. M. Lerner, A. C. Petersen, & J. Brooks-Gunn (Eds.), *Encyclopedia of adolescence* (Vol. 1). New York: Garland.

Plomin, R. (1991b, April). *The nature of nurture: Genetic influence on "environmental" measures.* Paper presented at the biennial meeting of the Society for Research in Child Development, Seattle.

Plomin, R., DeFries, J. C., & McClearn, G. E. (1990). *Behavioral genetics: A primer.* New York: W. H. Freeman.

Polivy, J., & Thomsen, L. (1987). Eating, dieting, and body image. In E. A. Blechman & K. D. Brownell (Eds.), *Handbook of behavioral medicine for women.* Elmsford, NY: Pergamon.

Posner, M., & Rothbart, M. (1989, August). *Attention: Normal and pathological development.* Paper presented at the meeting of the American Psychological Association, New Orleans.

Postrado, L. T., & Nicholson, H. J. (1992). Effectiveness in delaying the initiation of sexual intercourse of girls aged 12–14. *Youth and Society, 23,* 356–379.

Potthof, S. J. (1992, March). *Modeling family planning expertise to predict oral contraceptive discontinuance in teenagers.* Paper presented at the meeting of the Society for Research on Adolescence, Washington, DC.

Potvin, L., Champagne, F., & Laberge-Nadeau, C. (1988). Mandatory driver training and road safety: The Quebec experience. *American Journal of Public Health, 78,* 1206–1212.

Powell, A. G., Farrar, E., & Cohen, D. K. (1985). *The shopping mall high school: Winner and losers in the educational marketplace.* Boston: Houghton Mifflin.

Price, R., Cowen, E., Lorion, R., & Ramos-McKay, J. (Eds.). (1988). *14 ounces of prevention.* Washington, DC: American Psychological Association.

Prinsky, L. E., & Rosenbaum, J. L. (1987). Leer-ics or lyrics? *Youth and Society, 18,* 384–394.

Prunell, M., Boada, J., Feria, M., & Benitez, M. A. (1987). Antagonism of the stimulant and depressant effects of ethanol in rats by naloxone. *Psychopharmacology, 92,* 215–218.

Pryor, J. B., Reeder, G. D., Vinacco, R., & Kott, T. L. (1989). The instrumental and symbolic functions of attitudes toward persons with AIDS. *Journal of Applied Social Psychology, 19,* 377–404.

Psathas, G. (1957). Ethnicity, social class, and adolescent independence. *Sociological Review, 22,* 415–523.

Pugh, D. (1983, November 11). Bringing an end to mutilation. *New Statesman,* pp. 8–9.

Puka, B. (1991). Toward the redevelopment of Kohlberg's theory: Preserving essential structure, removing controversial content. In W. M. Kurtines & J. Gewirtz (Eds.), *Moral behavior and development: Advances in theory, research, and application.* Hillsdale, NJ: Erlbaum.

Putallaz, M. (1983). Predicting children's sociometric status from their behavior. *Child Development, 54,* 1417–1426.

Quay, H. (Ed.). (1987). *Handbook of juvenile delinquency.* New York: Wiley.

Quina, K. (1986). *Teaching research methods: A multidimensional feminist curricular transformation plan.* Wellesley College Center for Research on Women, Working Paper no. 164.

Rabin, D. S., & Chrousos, G. P. (1991). Androgens, gonadal. In R. M. Lerner, A. C. Petersen, & J. Brooks-Gunn (Eds.), *Encyclopedia of adolescence* (Vol. 1). New York: Garland.

Rabkin, J. (1987). *Epidemiology of adolescent violence: Risk factors, career patterns, and intervention programs.* Paper presented at the conference on adolescent violence, Stanford University, Stanford, CA.

Ramirez, M. (1990). *Psychotherapy and counseling with minorities.* Riverside, NJ: Pergamon.

Ramirez, O. (1989). Mexican American children and adolescents. In J. T. Gibbs & L. N. Huang (Eds.), *Children of color.* San Francisco: Jossey-Bass.

Rawlins, W. K. (1992). *Friendship matters.* Hawthorne, NY: Aldine.

Rees, J. M., & Mahan, M. K. (1988). Nutrition in adolescence. In S. R. Williams & B. S. Worthington-Roberts (Eds.), *Nutrition throughout the life cycle,* St. Louis: Times Mirror/Mosby.

Reid, P. T. (1991). Black female adolescents, socialization of. In R. M. Lerner, A. C. Petersen, & J. Brooks-Gunn (Eds), *Encyclopedia of adolescence* (Vol. 1). New York: Garland.

Reinherz, H. Z., Frost, A. K., Stewart-Berghauer, G., Pakiz, B., Kennedy, K., & Schille, C. (1990). The many faces of correlates of depressive symptoms in adolescents. *Journal of Early Adolescence, 10,* 455–471.

Reinisch, J. M. (1990). *The Kinsey Institute new report on sex: What you must know to be sexually literate.* New York: St. Martin's Press.

Reis, S. M. (1989). Reflections on policy affecting the education of gifted and talented students. *American Psychologist, 44,* 399–408.

Renner, J. W., Stafford, D., Lawson, A., McKinnon, J., Friot, F., & Kellog, D. (1976). *Research, teaching, and learning with the Piaget model.* Norman, OK: University of Oklahoma Press.

Resnick, L. B. (1986). *Education and learning to think.* Washington, DC: National Research Council.

Resnick, M. D. (1991). Health services for adolescents in the United States, the financing of. In R. M. Lerner, A. C. Petersen, & J. Brooks-Gunn (Eds.), *Encyclopedia of adolescence* (Vol. 1). New York: Garland.

Resnick, M. D., Wattenberg, E., & Brewer, R. (1992, March). *Paternity avowal/disavowal among partners of low income mothers.* Paper presented at the meeting of the Society for Research on Adolescence, Washington, DC.

Rest, J. R. (1976). New approaches in the assessment of moral judgment. In T. Lickona (Ed.), *Moral development and behavior.* New York: Holt, Rinehart & Winston.

Rest, J. R. (1983). Morality. In P. H. Mussen (Ed.), *Handbook of child psychology* (4th ed., Vol. 3). New York: Wiley.

Rest, J. R. (1986). *Moral development: Advances in theory and research.* New York: Praeger.

Rest, J. R. (1988, November). *With the benefits of hindsight.* Paper presented at the thirteenth annual conference of the Association for Moral Education, Pittsburgh, PA.

Rest, J. R., Turiel, E., & Kohlberg, L. (1969). Relations between level of moral judgment and preference and comprehension of the moral judgments of others. *Journal of Personality, 37,* 225–252.

Rich, C. L., Young, D., & Fowler, R. C. (1986). San Diego suicide study. *Archives of General Psychiatry, 43,* 577–582.

Rich, Y., & Golan, R. (1992). Career plans for male-dominated occupations among female seniors in religious and secular high schools. *Adolescence, 27,* 123–136.

Richardson, J. L., Dwyer, K., McGrugan, K., Hansen, W. B., Dent, C., Johnson, C. A., Sussman, S. Y., Brannon, B., & Glay, B. (1989). Substance use among eighth-grade students who take care of themselves after school. *Pediatrics, 84,* 556–566.

Rierdan, J., Koff, E., & Stubbs, M. (1989). A longitudinal analysis of body image as a predictor of the onset and persistence of adolescent girls' depression. *Journal of Early Adolescence, 9,* 454–466.

Risser, W. L. (1989). Exercise for children. *Pediatrics in Review, 10,* 131–140.

Robinson, B. R. (1988). *Teenage fathers.* Lexington, MA: Lexington Books.

Robinson, D. P., & Greene, J. W. (1988). The adolescent alcohol and drug problem: A practical approach. *Pediatric Nursing, 14,* 305–310.

Rodin, J. (1984, December). Interview: A sense of control. *Psychology Today,* pp. 38–45.

Rodman, H., Pratto, D. J., & Nelson, R. S. (1988). Toward a definition of self-care children: A commentary on Steinberg (1986). *Developmental Psychology, 24,* 292–294.

Roff, M., Sells, S. B., & Golden, M. W. (1972). *Social adjustment and personality development in children.* Minneapolis, MN: University of Minnesota Press.

Rogers, A. (1987). *Questions of gender differences: Ego development and moral voice in adolescence.* Unpublished manuscript, Department of Education, Harvard University.

Rogers, C. R. (1950). The significance of the self regarding attitudes and perceptions. In M. L. Reymart (Ed.), *Feelings and emotions.* New York: McGraw-Hill.

Rogoff, B. (1990). *Apprenticeship in thinking.* New York: Oxford University Press.

Rogoff, B., & Mistry, J. J. (in press). The social and motivational context of children's memory skills. In R. Fivish & J. Hudson (Eds.), *What young children remember and why.* Cambridge, England: Cambridge University Press.

Rogoff, B., & Morelli, G. (1989). Perspectives on children's development from cultural psychology. *American Psychologist, 44,* 343–348.

Rohner, R. P., & Rohner, E. C. (1981). Parental acceptance-rejection and parental control: Cross-cultural codes. *Ethnology, 20,* 245–260.

Root, M. P. (Ed.). (1992). *Racially mixed people in America.* Newbury Park, CA: Sage.

Roscoe, B., Dian, M. S., & Brooks, R. H. (1987). Early, middle, and late adolescents' views on dating and factors influencing partner's selection. *Adolescence, 22,* 59–68.

Rose, R. J., Koskenvuo, M., Kaprio, J., Sarna, S., & Langinvainio, H. (1988). Shared genes, shared experiences, and similarity of personality: Data from 14,228 adult Finnish co-twins. *Journal of Personality and Social Psychology, 54,* 161–171.

Rosenbaum, E., & Kandel, D. B. (1990). Early onset of adolescent sexual behavior and drug involvement. *Journal of Marriage and the Family, 52,* 783–798.

Rosenbaum, J. L. (1989). Family dysfunction and female delinquency. *Crime and Delinquency, 35,* 31–44.

Rosenberg, M. (1979). *Conceiving the self.* New York: Basic Books.

Rosenberg, M. (1986). Self-concept from middle childhood through adolescence. In J. Suls & A. G. Greenwald (Eds.), *Psychological perspective on the self* (Vol. 3). Hillsdale, NJ: Erlbaum.

Rosenhan, D. L., & Seligman, M. E. P. (1989). *Abnormal psychology* (2nd ed.). New York: Norton.

Rosenthal, R. (1985). *Lyric cognition and the potential for protest among punk rockers.* Unpublished manuscript, University of Hartford, Hartford, CT.

Rosenthal, R., & Jacobsen, L. (1968). *Pygmalion in the classroom.* New York: Rinehart & Winston.

Rosser, P. (1989). *SAT gender gap: Identifying the causes.* Washington, DC: Center for Women's Policy Studies.

Rothbart, M. K., Hanley, D., & Albert, M. (1986). Gender differences in moral reasoning. *Sex Roles, 15,* 645–653.

Rotheram-Borus, M. J., & Koopman, C. (1991). AIDS and adolescents. In R. M. Lerner, A. C. Petersen, & J. Brooks-Gunn (Eds.), *Encyclopedia of adolescence* (Vol. 1). New York: Garland.

Rousseau, J. J. (1962). *The Emile of Jean Jacques Rousseau* (W. Boyd, Ed. and Trans.). New York: Teachers College Press, Columbia University. (Original work published 1762)

Rowe, D. C., & Rodgers, J. E. (1989). Behavioral genetics, adolescent deviance, and "d": Contributions and issues. In G. R. Adams, R. Montemayor, & T. P. Gulotta (Eds), *Biology of adolescent behavior and development.* Newbury Park, CA: Sage.

Rowlett, J. D., Patel, D., & Greydanus, D. E. (1992). Homosexuality. In D. E. Greydanus & M. L. Walraich (Eds.), *Behavioral pediatrics.* New York: Springer-Verlag.

Rubenstein, J., Heeren, T., Houseman, D., Rubin, C., & Stechler, G. (1989). Suicidal behavior in "normal" adolescents: Risk and protective factors. *American Journal of Orthopsychiatry, 59,* 59–71.

Rubin, Z., & Mitchell, C. (1976). Couples research as couples counseling. *American Psychologist 31,* 17–25.

Rubin, Z., & Sloman, J. (1984). How parents influence their children's friendships. In M. Lewis (Ed.), *Beyond the dyad.* New York: Plenum.

Ruble, D. N., Boggiano, A. K., Feldman, N. S., & Loebl, J. H. (1980). Developmental analysis of the role of social comparison in self-evaluation. *Developmental Psychology, 16,* 105–115.

Rumberger, R. W. (1983). Dropping out of high school: The influence of race, sex, and family background. *American Educational Research Journal, 20,* 199–220.

Russo, N. F. (1990). Overview: Forging research priorities for women's mental health. *American Psychologist, 45,* 368–374.

Rutter, D. R., & Durkin, K. (1987). Turn-taking in mother-infant interaction: An examination of vocalization and gaze. *Developmental Psychology, 23,* 54–61.

Rutter, M. (1971). Parent-child separation: Psychological effects on the children. *Journal of Child Psychology and Psychiatry, 12,* 233–256.

Rutter, M. (1979). Protective factors in children's response to stress and disadvantage. In M. W. Kent & J. E. Rolf (Eds.), *Primary prevention in psychopathology* (Vol. 3). Hanover, NH: University Press of New England.

Rutter, M. (1983, April). *Influences from family and school.* Paper presented at the meeting of the Society for Research in Child Development, Detroit.

Rutter, M., & Garmezy, N. (1983). Developmental psychopathology. In P. H. Mussen (Ed.), *Handbook of child psychology* (4th ed., Vol. 4). New York: Wiley.

Rutter, M., Maughan, B., Mortimore, P., & Ouston, J. (1979). *Fifteen thousand hours: Secondary schools and their effects on children.* Cambridge, MA: Harvard University Press.

Rutter, M., & Schopler, E. (1987). Autism and pervasive developmental disorders: Concepts and diagnostic issues. *Journal of Autism and Developmental Disorders, 17,* 159–186.

Ryan, R. M., & Lynch, J. H. (1989). Emotional autonomy versus detachment: Revisiting the vicissitudes of adolescence and young adulthood. *Child Development, 60,* 340–356.

Rybash, J., Roodin, P., & Santrock, J. W. (1991). *Adult development and aging* (2nd ed.). Dubuque, IA: Wm. C. Brown.

Sadker, M., & Sadker, D. (1986, March). Sexism in the classroom: From grade school to graduate school. *Phi Delta Kappan,* pp. 512–515.

Sadker, M., Sadker, D., & Klein, S. S. (1986). Abolishing misperceptions about sex equity in education. *Theory into Practice, 25,* 219–226.

Sakurai, M. (1989, April). *Risk and resiliency in adolescence: The protective role of relationships.* Paper presented at the biennial meeting of the Society for Research in Child Development, Kansas City.

Santilli, S. A., & Seidman, I. E. (1986). The shopping mall high school. *Equity and Excellence, 23,* 138–141.

Santrock, J. W. (1992). *Life-span development* (4th ed.). Dubuque, IA: Wm. C. Brown.

Santrock, J. W., & Sitterle, K. (1987). Parent-child relationships in stepmother families. In K. Pasley & M. Ihinger-Tallman (Eds.), *Remarriage and stepparenting.* New York: Guilford.

Santrock, J. W., Sitterle, K. A., & Warshak, R. A. (1988). Parent-child relationships in stepfather families. In P. Bronstein & C. P. Cowan (Eds.), *Fatherhood today.* New York: Wiley.

Santrock, J. W., & Warshak, R. A. (1979). Father custody and social development in boys and girls. *Journal of Social Issues, 35,* 112–125.

Santrock, J. W., & Warshak, R. A. (1986). Development, relationships, and legal/clinical considerations in father-custody families. In M. E. Lamb (Ed.), *The father's role: Applied perspectives.* New York: Wiley.

Santrock, J. W., & Yussen, S. R. (1992). *Child development* (5th ed.). Dubuque, IA: Wm. C. Brown.

Saraswathi, T., & Dutta, R. (1988). *Invisible boundaries: Grooming for adult roles.* New Delhi, India: Northern Book Center.

Savin-Williams, R. C., & Berndt, T. J. (1990). Friendship and peer relations. In S. S. Feldman & G. R. Elliot (Eds.), *At the threshold: The developing adolescent.* Cambridge, MA: Harvard University Press.

Savin-Williams, R. C., & Demo, D. H. (1983). Conceiving or misconceiving the self: Issues in adolescent self-esteem. *Journal of Early Adolescence, 3,* 121–140.

Scales, P. (1990). Developing capable young people: An alternative strategy for prevention programs. *Journal of Early Adolescence, 10,* 420–438.

Scales, P. C. (1992). *A portrait of young adolescents in the 1990s: Implications for promoting healthy growth and development.* Carrboro, NC: Center for Early Adolescence.

Scardamalia, M., Bereiter, C., & Goelman, H. (1982). The role of production factors in writing ability. In M. Nystrand (Ed.), *What writers know: The language, process, and structure of written discourse.* New York: Academic Press.

Scarlett, W. G., & Perriello, L. (1990, March). *The development of prayer in adolescence.* Paper presented at the meeting of the Society for Research in Adolescence, Atlanta, GA.

Scarr, S. (1984, May). [Interview.] *Psychology Today*, pp. 59–63.

Scarr, S. (1989, April). *Transracial adoption.* Discussion at the biennial meeting of the Society for Research in Child Development, Kansas City.

Scarr, S., & Kidd, K. K. (1983). Developmental behavior genetics. In P. H. Mussen (Ed.), *Handbook of child psychology* (Vol. 2, 4th ed). New York: Wiley.

Scarr, S., & Weinberg, R. A. (1976). IQ test performance of black children adopted by white families. *American Psychologist, 31,* 726–739.

Scarr, S., & Weinberg, R. A. (1980). Calling all camps! The war is over. *American Sociological Review, 45,* 859–865.

Scarr, S., & Weinberg, R. A. (1983). The Minnesota adoption studies: Genetic differences and malleability. *Child Development, 54,* 253–259.

Schaie, K. W. (1973). Methodological problems in descriptive developmental research on adulthood and aging. In J. R. Nesselroade & H. W. Reese (Eds.), *Life-span developmental psychology: Methodological issues.* New York: Academic Press.

Schaie, K. W. (1989) Introduction. In K. W. Schaie & C. Schooler (Eds.), *Social structure and aging: Psychological processes.* Hillsdale, NJ: Erlbaum.

Schaie, K. W. (1991). Developmental designs revisited. In S. H. Cohen & H. W. Reese (Eds.), *Life-span developmental psychology: Methodological innovation.* Hillsdale, NJ: Erlbaum.

Scheff, T. J. (1966). *Being mentally ill: A sociological theory.* Chicago: Aldine.

Scheidel, D. G., & Marcia, J. E. (1985). Ego identity, intimacy, sex-role orientation, and gender. *Developmental Psychology, 21,* 149–160.

Schlegel, A., & Barry, H. (1991). *Adolescence: An anthropological inquiry.* New York: Free Press.

Schneider, A. J. (1966). *Measurement of courtship progress of high school upperclassmen currently going steady.* Unpublished dissertation, Pennsylvania State University.

Schneidman, E. S. (1971). Suicide among the gifted. *Suicide and Life-Threatening Behavior, 1,* 23–45.

Schoggen, P. (1991). Ecological psychology: One approach to development in context. In R. Cohen & A. W. Siegel (Eds.), *Context and development.* Hillsdale, NJ: Erlbaum.

Schorr, L. B. (1989, April). *Within our reach: Breaking the cycle of disadvantage.* Paper presented at the biennial meeting of the Society for Research in Child Development, Kansas City.

Schulenberg, J. E., Shimizu, K., Vondracek, F. W., & Hostetler, M. (1988). Factorial invariance of career indecision dimensions across junior high and high school males and females. *Journal of Vocational Behavior, 33,* 63–81.

Schunk, D. H. (1983). Developing children's self-efficacy and skills: The roles of social comparative information and goal setting. *Contemporary Educational Psychology, 8,* 76–86.

Schunk, D. H. (1990). Introduction to the special section on motivation and efficacy. *Journal of Educational Psychology, 82,* 3–6.

Schwartz, B. (1990). The creation and destruction of value. *American Psychologist, 45,* 7–15.

Schwartz, R., & Eriksen, M. (1989). Statement of the Society for Public Health Education on the national health promotion/disease prevention objectives for the year 2000. *Health Education Quarterly, 16,* 3–7.

Scott-Jones, D., & Clark, M. L. (1986, March). The school experiences of black girls: The interaction of gender, race, and socioeconomic status. *Phi Delta Kappan,* pp. 520–526.

Scott-Jones, D., & White, A. B. (1990). Correlates of sexual activity in early adolescence. *Journal of Early Adolescence, 10,* 221–238.

Scribner, S. (1977). Modes of thinking and ways of speaking: Culture and logic reconsidered. In P. N. Johnson-Laird & P. C. Wason (Eds.), *Thinking: Readings in cognitive science.* New York: Cambridge University Press.

Sears, D. O., Peplau, L. A., Freedman, J. L., & Taylor, S. E. (1988). *Social psychology* (6th ed.). Englewood Cliffs, NJ: Prentice-Hall.

Seefeldt, V., Blievernicht, D., Bruce, R., & Gilliam, T. (1978). *Joint legislative study on youth sport programs, phase II: Agency-sponsored sports.* Lansing, MI: Michigan State Legislature.

Segall, M. H., Dasen, P. R., Berry, J. W., & Poortinga, Y. H. (1990). *Human behavior in global perspective.* New York: Pergamon.

Seligman, M. E. P. (1975). *Learned helplessness.* New York: W. H. Freeman.

Seligman, M. E. P. (1989). Why is there so much depression today? In the *G. Stanley Hall Lecture Series.* Washington, DC: American Psychological Association.

Selman, R., & Byrne, D. (1974). A structural developmental analysis of levels of role-taking in middle childhood. *Child Development, 45,* 803–806.

Selman, R. L. (1976). Social-cognitive understanding. In T. Lickona (Ed.), *Moral development and behavior.* New York: Holt, Rinehart & Winston.

Selman, R. L. (1980). *The growth of interpersonal understanding.* New York: Academic Press.

Selman, R. L., Newberger, C. M., & Jacquette, D. (1977, April). *Observing interpersonal reasoning in a clinic/educational setting: Toward the integration of developmental and clinical child psychology.* Paper presented at the meeting of the Society for Research in Child Development, New Orleans.

Selye, H. (1974). *Stress without distress.* Philadelphia: W. B. Saunders.

Selye, H. (1983). The stress concept: Past, present, and future. In C. L. Cooper (Ed.), *Stress research.* New York: Wiley.

Semaj, L. T. (1985). Afrikanity, cognition, and extended self-identity. In M. B. Spencer, G. K. Brookins, & W. R. Allen (Eds.), *Beginnings: The social and affective development of black children.* Hillsdale, NJ: Erlbaum.

Shakeshaft, C. (1986, March). A gender at risk. *Phi Delta Kappan,* pp. 499–503.

Shantz, C. (1983). The development of social cognition. In P. H. Mussen (Ed.), *Handbook of child psychology* (4th ed., Vol. 3). New York: Wiley.

Shantz, C. O. (1988). Conflicts between children. *Child Development, 59,* 283–305.

Shapiro, E. R., & Freedman, J. (1989). Family dynamics of adolescent suicide. In A. H. Esman (Ed.), *International annals of adolescent psychiatry.* Chicago: University of Chicago Press.

Sharp, D. W., Cole, M., & Lave, C. (1979). Education and cognitive development: The evidence from experimental research. *Monographs of the Society for Research in Child Development, 4,* (1–2, Serial No. 178).

Sherif, C. (1982). Needed concepts in the study of gender identity. *Psychology of Women Quarterly, 6,* 375–398.

Sherif, M., Harvey. O. J., White, B. J., Hood, W. R., & Sherif, C. W. (1961). *Intergroup conflict and cooperation: The Robber's Cave experiment.* Norman, OK: Institute of Group Relations, University of Oklahoma.

Sherif, M., & Sherif, C. W. (1964). *Reference groups: Exploration into conformity and deviation of adolescents.* New York: Harper.

Sherwood, A., Light, K. C., & Blumenthal, J. A. (1989). Effects of aerobic exercise training on hemodynamic responses during psychosocial stress in normotensive and borderline hypertensive Type-A men: A preliminary report. *Psychosomatic Medicine, 51,* 123–136.

Shweder, R., Mahapatra, M., & Miller, J. (1987). Culture and moral development. In J. Kagan & S. Lamb (Eds.), *The emergence of morality in young children.* Chicago: University of Chicago Press.

Siegler, R. S. (1988). Individual differences in strategy choices: Good students, not-so-good students, and perfectionists. *Child Development, 59,* 833–851.

Siegman, A. W., & Dembrowski, T. (Eds.). (1989). *In search of coronary-prone behavior: Beyond Type-A.* Hillsdale, NJ: Erlbaum.

Sigman, G, S., & Flanery, R, C. (1992). Eating disorders. In D. E. Greydanus & M. L. Wolraich (Eds.), *Behavioral pediatrics.* New York: Springer-Verlag.

Silver, S. (1988, August). *Behavior problems of children born into early-childbearing families.* Paper presented at the meeting of the American Psychological Association, Atlanta, GA.

Silverberg, S. B., & Steinberg, L. (1990). Psychological well-being of parents with early adolescent children. *Developmental Psychology, 26,* 658–666.

Simmons, R. G., & Blyth, D. A. (1987). *Moving into adolescence.* Hawthorne, NY: Aldine.

Simon, W., & Gagnon, J. H. (1969). On psychosexual development. In D. Goslin (Ed.), *Handbook of socialization theory and research.* Chicago: Rand McNally.

Simons, J. M., Finlay, B., & Yang, A. (1991). *The adolescent and young adult fact book.* Washington, DC: Children's Defense Fund.

Simons, R., Conger, R., & Wu, C. (1992, March). *Peer group as amplifier/moderator of the stability of adolescent antisocial behavior.* Paper presented at the meeting of the Society for Research on Adolescence, Washington, DC.

Simpson, J. A., Campbell, B., & Berscheid, E. (1986). The association between love and marriage: Kephart (1967) twice revisited. *Personality and Social Psychology Bulletin, 12,* 363–372.

Simpson, R. L. (1962). Parental influence, anticipatory socialization, and social mobility. *American Sociological Review, 27,* 517–522.

Skinner, B. F. (1938). *The behavior of organisms: An experimental analysis.* New York: Appleton-Century-Crofts.

Skinner, B. F. (1948). *Walden two.* New York: Macmillan.

Skinner, E. A., Wellborn, J. G., & Connell, J. P. (1990). What it takes to do well in school and whether I've got it: A process model of perceived control and children's engagement and achievement in school. *Journal of Educational Psychology, 82,* 22–32.

Skipper, J. K., & Nass, G. (1966). Dating behavior: A framework for analysis and an illustration. *Journal of Marriage and the Family, 28,* 412–420.

Skoe, E. E., & Marcia, J. E. (1988). *Ego identity and care-based moral reasoning in college women.* Unpublished manuscript, Acadia University.

Slaughter-Defoe, D. T., Nakagawa, K., Takanishi, R., & Johnson, D. J. (1990). Toward cultural/ecological perspectives on schooling and achievement in Africa- and Asian-American children. *Child Development, 61,* 363–383.

Slavin, R. (1989a). Achievement effects of substantial reductions in class size. In R. E. Slavin (Ed.), *School and classroom organization.* Hillsdale, NJ: Erlbaum.

Slavin, R. (1989b). Cooperative learning and student achievement. In R. Slavin (Ed.), *School and classroom organization.* Hillsdale, NJ: Erlbaum.

Small, M. (1990). *Cognitive development.* San Diego: Harcourt Brace Jovanovich.

Smetana, J. (1985). Preschool children's conceptions of transgressions: Effects of varying moral and conventional domain-related attributes. *Developmental Psychology, 21,* 18–29.

Smith, E., & Udry, J. (1985). Coital and noncoital sexual behaviors of white and black adolescents. *American Journal of Public Health, 75,* 1200–1203.

Smith, J., & Baltes, P. B. (in press). A study of wisdom-related knowledge: Age-cohort differences in responses to life-planning problems. *Developmental Psychology.*

Snarey, J. (1987, June). A question of morality. *Psychology Today,* pp. 6–8.

Snowden, L. R., & Cheung, F. K. (1990). Use of inpatient mental health services by members of ethnic minority groups. *American Psychologist, 45,* 347–355.

Snyder, C. R. (1988, August). *Reality negotiation: From excuses to hope.* Paper presented at the meeting of the American Psychological Association, Atlanta, GA.

Snyder, E. E., & Spreitzer, E. (1976). Correlates of sports participation among adolescent girls. *Research Quarterly, 47,* 804–809.

Solantaus, T. (1992, March). *The global world: A challenge to young people's development and well-being?* Paper presented at the meeting of the Society for Research on Adolescence, Washington, DC.

Sommer, B. B. (1978). *Puberty and adolescence.* New York: Oxford University Press.

Sonenstein, F. L., & Pittman, K. J. (1984, January/February). The availability of sex education in large city school districts. *Family Planning Perspectives,* p. 19.

Sonenstein, F. L., Pleck, J. H., & Ku, L. C. (1989). Sexual activity, condom use, and AIDS awareness among adolescent males. *Family Planning Perspectives, 21*(4), 152–158.

Sorensen, R. C. (1973). *Adolescent sexuality in contemporary America.* New York: World.

Spearman, C. (1927). *The abilities of man.* New York: Macmillan.

Spence, J. T., & Helmreich, R. (1972). The Attitudes Toward Women Scale. An objective instrument to measure the rights and roles of women in contemporary society. *JSAS Catalog of Selected Documents in Psychology, 2,* 66.

Spence, J. T., & Helmreich, R. (1978). *Masculinity and femininity: Their psychological dimensions.* Austin, TX: University of Texas Press.

Spencer, M. B. (1987). Black children's ethnic identity formation: Risk and resilience of castelike minorities. In J. S. Phinney & M. J. Rotheram (Eds.), *Children's ethnic socialization: Pluralism and development.* Newbury Park, CA: Sage.

Spencer, M. B. (1990). Development of minority children: An introduction. *Child Development, 61,* 267–269.

Spencer, M. B. (1991). Identity, minority development of. In R. M. Lerner, A. C. Petersen, & J. Brooks-Gunn (Eds.), *Encyclopedia of adolescence* (Vol. 1). New York: Garland.

Spencer, M. B. (1992, March). *Neighborhood features, self-esteem, and achievement orientation.* Paper presented at the meeting of the Society for Research on Adolescence, Washington, DC.

Spencer, M. B., & Dornbusch, S. M. (1990). Challenges in studying minority youth. In S. S. Feldman & G. R. Elliott (Eds.), *At the threshold: The developing adolescent.* Cambridge, MA: Harvard University Press.

Spencer, M. B., & Markstrom-Adams, C. (1990). Identity processes among racial and ethnic minority children in America. *Child Development, 61,* 290–310.

Spilka, B. (1991a). Cults, adolescence and. In R. M. Lerner, A. C. Petersen, & J. Brooks-Gunn (Eds.), *Encyclopedia of adolescence* (Vol. 1). New York: Garland.

Spilka, B. (1991b). Religion and adolescence. In R. M. Lerner, A. C. Petersen, & J. Brooks-Gunn (Eds.), *Encyclopedia of adolescence* (Vol. 2). New York: Garland.

Sroufe, L. A. (1985) Attachment classification from the perspective of infant-caregiver relationships and infant temperament. *Child Development, 56,* 1–14.

Sroufe, L. A. (in press). Pathways to adaptation and maladaptation: Psychopathology as developmental deviation. In D. Cicchetti (Ed.), *Developmental psychopathology: Past, present, and future.* Hillsdale, NJ: Erlbaum.

Stedman, L., & Smith, M. (1983). Recent reform proposals for American education. *Contemporary Education Review, 2,* 85–104.

Stein, D. M., & Reichert, P. (1990). Extreme dieting behaviors in early adolescence. *Journal of Early Adolescence, 10,* 108–121.

Steinberg, L. (1986). Stability (and instability) of Type-A behavior from childhood to young adulthood. *Developmental Psychology, 22,* 393–402.

Steinberg, L. (1991). Parent-adolescent relations. In R. M. Lerner, A. C. Petersen, & J. Brooks-Gunn (Eds.), *Encyclopedia of adolescence* (Vol. 2). New York: Garland.

Steinberg, L., & Lamborn, S. D. (1992, March). *Autonomy redux: Adolescent adjustment as a joint function of emotional autonomy and relationship security.* Paper presented at the meeting of the Society for Research on Adolescence, Washington, DC.

Steinberg, L., Mounts, N. S., Lamborn, S. D., & Dornbusch, S. M. (1991). Authoritative parenting and adolescent adjustment across varied ecological niches. *Journal of Research on Adolescence, 1,* 19–36.

Steinberg, L. D. (1981). Transformations in family relations at puberty. *Developmental Psychology, 17,* 833–840.

Steinberg, L. D. (1986). Latchkey children and susceptibility to peer pressure: An ecological analysis. *Developmental Psychology, 22,* 433–439.

Steinberg, L. D. (1988). Reciprocal relation between parent-child distance and pubertal maturation. *Developmental Psychology, 24,* 122–128.

Steinberg, L. D. (1990, August). *Adolescent development in ecological perspective.* Paper presented at the meeting of the American Psychological Association, Boston, MA.

Steinberg, L. D., & Dornbusch, S. M. (1991). Negative correlates of part-time employment during adolescence: Replication and education. *Developmental Psychology, 27,* 304–313.

Steinberg, L. D., & Levine, A. (1990). *You and your adolescent.* New York: Harper Perennial.

Stengel, R. (1985, December 9). The missing-father myth. *Time,* p. 90.

Stern, S. L., Dixon, K. N., Jones, D., Lake, M., Nemzer, E., & Samsone, R. (1989). Family environment in anorexia nervosa and bulimia. *International Journal of Eating Disorders, 8,* 25–31.

Sternberg, R. J. (1977). *Intelligence, information processing, and analogical reasoning: The componential analysis of human abilities.* Hillsdale, NJ: Erlbaum.

Sternberg, R. J. (1985, December). Teaching critical thinking, Part 2: Possible solutions. *Phi Delta Kappan,* 277–280.

Sternberg, R. J. (1986). *Intelligence applied.* San Diego: Harcourt Brace Jovanovich.

Sternberg, R. J. (1990, April). *Academic and practical cognition as different aspects of intelligence.* Paper presented at the Twelfth West Virginia Conference on Life-Span Developmental Psychology, Morgantown, WV.

Sternberg, R. J., Conway, B. E., Ketron, J. L., & Berstein, M. (1981). People's conceptions of intelligence. *Journal of Personality and Social Psychology, 41,* 37–55.

Sternberg, R. J., & Nigro, C. (1980). Developmental patterns in the solution of verbal analogies. *Child Development, 51,* 27–38.

Sternberg, R. J., & Rifkin, B. (1979). The development of analogical reasoning processes. *Journal of Experimental Child Psychology, 27,* 195–232.

Steur, F. B., Applefield, J. M., & Smith, R. (1971). Televised aggression and the interpersonal aggression of preschool children. *Journal of Experimental Child Psychology, 11,* 442–447.

Stevens, J. H. (1984). Black grandmothers' and black adolescent mothers' knowledge about parenting. *Developmental Psychology, 20,* 1017–1025.

Stevenson, H. W. (1991, April). *Academic achievement and parental beliefs: A longitudinal study in Japan, Taiwan, and the United States.* Paper presented at the biennial meeting of the Society for Research in Child Development, Seattle.

Stevenson, H. W., Lee, S., Chen, C., Stigler, J., Hsu, C., & Kitamura, G. (1990). Contexts of achievement. *Monograph of the Society for Research in Child Development* (Serial No. 221, Vol. 55, Nos. 1–2).

Stevenson, H. W., Stigler, J. W., & Lee, S. (1986). Achievement in mathematics. In H. W. Stevenson, H. Azuma, & K. Hakuta (Eds.), *Child development and education in Japan.* San Francisco: W. H. Freeman.

Stigler, J. W., Nusbaum, H. C., & Chalip, O. (1988). Developmental changes in speed of processing: Central limiting mechanism or skill transfer? *Child Development, 59,* 1144–1153.

Stipek, D. J., & Hoffman, J. M. (1980). Children's achievement-related expectancies as a function of academic performance histories and sex. *Journal of Educational Psychology, 72,* 861–865.

Stocker, C., & Dunn, J. (1991). Sibling relationships in adolescence. In R. M. Lerner, A. C. Petersen, & J. Brooks-Gunn (Eds.), *Encyclopedia of adolescence* (Vol. 2). New York: Garland.

Stork, J. (1989). Suicide and adolescence. In A. H. Esman (Ed.), *International annals of adolescent psychiatry*. Chicago: University of Chicago Press.

Strachen, A., & Jones, D. (1982). Changes in identification during adolescence: A personal construct theory approach. *Journal of Personality Assessment, 46*, 139–148.

Strahan, D. B. (1983). The emergence of formal operations in adolescence. *Transcendence, 11*, 7–14.

Strahan, D. B. (1987). A developmental analysis of formal reasoning in the middle grades. *Journal of Instructional Psychology, 14*, 67–73.

Strang, S. P., & Orlofsky, J. L. (1990). Factors underlying suicidal ideation among college students: A test of Teicher and Jacobs' model. *Journal of Adolescence, 13*, 39–52.

Strober, M., McCracken, J., & Hanna, G. (1991). Affective disorders. In R. M. Lerner, A. C. Petersen, & J. Brooks-Gunn (Eds.), *Encyclopedia of adolescence* (Vol. 1). New York: Garland.

Stubbs, M. L., Rierdan, J., & Koff, E. (1989). Developmental differences in menstrual attitudes. *Journal of Early Adolescence, 9*, 480–498.

Studer, M., & Thornton, A. (1987). Adolescent religiosity and contraceptive usage. *Journal of Marriage and the Family, 49*, 117–128.

Studer, M., & Thornton, A. (1989). The multifaceted impact of religiosity on adolescent sexual experience and contraceptive usage: A reply to Shornack and Ahmed. *Journal of Marriage and the Family, 51*, 1085–1089.

Stunkard, A. J. (1987). The regulation of body weight and the treatment of obesity. In H. Weiner & A. Baum (Eds.), *Eating regulation and discontrol*. Hillsdale, NJ: Erlbaum.

Stunkard, A. J. (1989). Perspectives on human obesity. In A. J. Stunkard & A. Baum (Eds.), *Perspectives on behavioral medicine*. Hillsdale, NJ: Erlbaum.

Sue, S. (1990, August). *Ethnicity and culture in psychological research and practice*. Paper presented at the meeting of the American Psychological Association, Boston.

Sue, S., & Okazaki, S. (1990). Asian-American educational achievements. *American Psychologist, 45*, 913–920.

Sullivan, H. S. (1953). *The interpersonal theory of psychiatry*. New York: W. W. Norton.

Sullivan, K., & Sullivan, A. (1980). Adolescent-parent separation. *Developmental Psychology, 16*, 93–99.

Sullivan, L. (1991, May 25). US secretary urges TV to restrict "irresponsible sex and reckless violence." *Boston Globe*, p. A1.

Sullivan, L. (1992, January 13). Press release, U.S. Health and Human Services, Washington, DC.

Suomi, S. J., Harlow, H. F., & Domek, C. J. (1970). Effect of repetitive infant-infant separations of young monkeys. *Journal of Abnormal Psychology, 76*, 161–172.

Super, D. E. (1967). *The psychology of careers*. New York: Harper & Row.

Super, D. E. (1976). *Career education and the meanings of work*. Washington, DC: U.S. Office of Education.

Susman, E. J. (1991). Stress and the adolescent. In R. M. Lerner, A. C. Petersen, & J. Brooks-Gunn (Eds.), *Encyclopedia of adolescence* (Vol. 2). New York: Garland.

Susman, E. J., & Dorn, L. D. (1991). Hormones and behavior in adolescence. In R. M. Lerner, A. C. Petersen, & J. Brooks-Gunn (Eds.), *Encyclopedia of adolescence*. New York: Garland.

Sutton-Smith, B. (1982). Birth order and sibling status effects. In M. E. Lamb & B. Sutton-Smith (Eds.), *Sibling relationships: Their nature and significance across the life span*. Hillsdale, NJ: Erlbaum.

Swope, G. W. (1980). Kids and cults: Who joins and why? *Media and Methods, 16*, 18–21.

Szasz, T. (1977). *Psychiatric slavery: When confinement and coercion masquerade as cure*. New York: Free Press.

Takahashi, K., & Majima, N. (1992, March). *The functions of pre-established social relationships during a life transition among college freshmen*. Paper presented at the meeting of the Society for Research on Adolescence, Washington, DC.

Talwar, R., Nitz, K., & Lerner, R. M. (1990). Relations among early adolescent temperament, parent and peer demands, and adjustment: A test of the goodness-of-fit model. *Journal of Adolescence, 13*, 279–298.

Tanner, J. (1981). Pop music and peer groups: A study of Canadian high school students' responses to pop music. *Canadian Review of Sociology and Anthropology, 18*, 1–13.

Tanner, J. M. (1970). Physical growth. In P. H. Mussen (Ed.), *Manual of child psychology* (Vol. 1, 3rd ed.). New York: Wiley.

Tanner, J. M. (1991). Growth spurt, adolescent. I. In R. M. Lerner, A. C. Petersen, & J. Brooks-Gunn (Eds.), *Encyclopedia of adolescence*. New York: Garland.

Task Force on Pediatric AIDS. (1989). Pediatric AIDS and human immunodeficiency virus infection. *American Psychologist, 44*, 258–264.

Tavris, C. (1991). The mismeasure of women. In L. Garnets, J. M. Jones, D. Kimmel, S. Sue, & C. Tavris (Eds.), *Psychological perspectives on human diversity in America*. Washington, DC: American Psychological Association.

Tavris, C., & Wade, C. (1984). *The longest war: Sex differences in perspective* (2nd ed.). San Diego: Harcourt Brace Jovanovich.

Taylor, D. (1985). *Women: A world report*. New York: Oxford University Press.

Taylor, R. L. (1990). Black youth: The endangered generation. *Youth and Society, 22*, 1–4.

Taylor, S. E., Collins, R., Skokan, L., & Aspinwall, L. (1988, August). *Illusions, reality, and adjustment in coping with victimizing events*. Paper presented at the meeting of the American Psychological Association, Atlanta, GA.

Terman, L. (1925). *Genetic studies of genius: Vol. 1. Mental and physical traits of a thousand gifted children*. Stanford, CA: Stanford University Press.

Thelan, M. H., Farmer, J., Mann, L. Mc., & Puritt, J. (1990). Bulimia and interpersonal relationships. *Journal of Counseling Psychology, 17*, 85–90.

The Research Bulletin. (1991, Spring). *Disadvantaged urban eighth graders*. Washington, DC: Hispanic Policy Development Project.

Thomas, A., & Chess, S. (1977). *Temperament and development*. New York: Brunner/Mazel.

Thomas, A., & Chess, S. (1987). Commentary. In H. H. Goldsmith, A. H. Buss, R. Plomin, M. K. Rothbart, A. Thomas, A. Chess, R. R. Hinde, & R. B. McCall. Roundtable: What is temperament? Four approaches. *Child Development, 58*, 505–529.

Thomas, A., & Chess, S. (1991). Temperament in adolescence and its functional significance. In R. M. Lerner, A. C. Petersen, & J. Brooks-Gunn (Eds.), *Encyclopedia of adolescence* (Vol. 2). New York: Garland.

Thomas, G. (Ed.). (1988). *World education encyclopedia*. New York: Facts on File Publications.

Thompson, L. (1992). Feminist methodology in family studies. *Journal of Marriage and the Family, 54*, 3–18.

Thoresen, C. E., Eagleston, J. R., Kirmil-Gray, K., & Bracke, P. E. (1985, August). *Exploring the Type-A behavior pattern in children and adolescents*. Paper presented at the meeting of the American Psychological Association, Los Angeles.

Thornburg, H. D. (1981). Sources of sex education among early adolescents. *Journal of Early Adolescence, 1*, 171–184.

Thorndike, R. L., Hagan, E. P., & Sattler, J. M. (1985). *Stanford-Binet* (4th ed.). Chicago: Riverside.

Thornton, A., & Camburn, D. (1989). Religious participation and sexual behavior and attitudes. *Journal of Marriage and the Family, 51*, 641–653.

Thurstone, L. L. (1938). *Primary mental abilities*. Chicago: University of Chicago Press.

Tishler, C. L. (1992). Adolescent suicide: Assessment of risk, prevention, and treatment. *Adolescent Medicine, 3*, 51–60.

Tobler, N. (1986). Meta-analysis of 143 adolescent drug prevention programs: Quantitative outcome results of program participants compared to a control or comparison group. *Journal of Drug Issues, 16*, 537–567.

Toepfer, C. F. (1979). Brain growth periodization: A new dogma for education. *Middle School Journal, 10*, 20.

Tolan, P., Miller, L., & Thomas, P. (1988). Perception and experience of types of social stress and self-image among adolescents. *Journal of Youth and Adolescence, 17*, 147–163.

Tomlinson-Keasey, C. (1972). Formal operations in females from 11 to 54 years of age. *Developmental Psychology, 6*, 364.

Tomlinson-Keasey, C., & Little, T. D. (1990). Predicting educational attainment, occupational achievement, intellectual skill, and personal adjustment among gifted men and women. *Journal of Educational Psychology, 82*, 442–455.

Tomlinson-Keasey, C., Warren, L. W., & Elliott, J. E. (1986). Suicide among gifted women: A prospective study. *Journal of Abnormal Psychology, 95*, 123–130.

Travis, L., Phillips, S., & Williams, T. M. (1986, June). *Television portrayal of sex and romance: What might children be learning?* Paper presented at the meeting of the Canadian Psychological Association, Toronto, Canada.

Treboux, D., Crowell, J. A., & Colon-Downs, C. (1992, March). *Self-concept and identity in late adolescence: Relation to working models of attachment*. Paper presented at the meeting of the Society for Research on Adolescence, Washington, DC.

Treboux, D. A., & Busch-Rossnagel, N. A. (1991). Sexual behavior, sexual attitudes, and contraceptive use, age differences in adolescent. In R. M. Lerner, A. C. Petersen, & J. Brooks-Gunn (Eds.), *Encyclopedia of adolescence* (Vol. 2). New York: Garland.

Triandis, H. C. (1990). Theoretical concepts that are applicable to the analysis of ethnocentrism. In R. W. Brislin (Ed.), *Applied cross-cultural psychology*. Newbury Park, CA: Sage.

Trimble, J. E. (1989, August). *The enculturation of contemporary psychology.* Paper presented at the meeting of the American Psychological Association, New Orleans.

Trimble, J. E. (in press). Ethnic specification, validation prospects, and the future of drug use research. *International Journal of Addiction.*

Troll, L. (1985). *Development in early and middle adulthood* (2nd ed.). Monterey, CA: Brooks-Cole.

Truglio, R. T. (1990, April). *What is television teaching adolescents about sexuality?* Paper presented at the meeting of the Society for Research in Adolescence, Atlanta, GA.

Tucker, L. A. (1987). Television, teenagers, and health. *Journal of Youth and Adolescence, 16,* 415–425.

Tuckman, B. W., & Hinkle, J. S. (1988). An experimental study of the physical and psychological effects of aerobic exercise on schoolchildren. In B. G. Melamed & others (Eds.), *Child health psychology.* Hillsdale, NJ: Erlbaum.

Turiel, E. (1966). An experimental test of the sequentiality of developmental stages in the child's moral judgments. *Journal of Personality and Social Psychology, 3,* 611–618.

Turiel, E. (1978). Social regulations and domains of social concepts. In W. Damon (Ed.), *New directions for child development: Social cognition* (Vol. 1). San Francisco: Jossey-Bass.

Turner, R. A., Irwin, C. E., Tschann, J. M., & Millstein, S. G. (1991, April). *Autonomy, relatedness and the initiation of health risk behaviors in early adolescence.* Paper presented at the biennial meeting of the Society for Research in Child Development, Seattle.

Tyack, D. (1976). Ways of seeing: An essay on the history of compulsory schooling. *Harvard Educational Review, 46,* 355–389.

Udry, J. R. (1990). Hormonal and social determinants of adolescent sexual initiation. In J. Bancroft & J. M. Reinisch (Eds.), *Adolescence and puberty.* New York: Oxford University Press.

Ullman, C. (1982). Cognitive and emotional antecedents of religious conversion. *Journal of Personality and Social Psychology, 43,* 183–192.

Upcraft, M. L., & Gardner, J. N. (1989). *The freshman year experience.* San Francisco: Jossey-Bass.

Urban, J., Carlson, E., Egeland, B., & Sroufe, A. (1992, March). *Continuity in behavioral patterns across childhood.* Paper presented at the meeting of the Society for Research on Adolescence, Washington, DC.

U.S. Bureau of the Census. (1986). *Geographical mobility: March 1980 to March 1985* (Current Population Reports Series P-20, No. 368). Washington, DC: U.S. Government Printing Office.

U.S. Bureau of the Census. (1987). Money income and poverty status of families and persons in the United States, 1986. *Current population reports: Consumer income,* Series P-60, No. 157. Washington, DC: U.S. Government Printing Office.

U.S. Department of Health and Human Services, Public Health Service. (1989). *Reducing the health consequences of smoking: 25 years of progess.* Washington, DC: U.S. Government Printing Office.

Vandell, D. L. (1987). Baby sister/baby brother: Reactions to the birth of a sibling and patterns of early sibling relations. In F. F. Schachter & R. K. Stone (Eds.), *Practical concerns about siblings.* New York: Haworth Press.

Vandell, D. L., Minnett, A., & Santrock, J. W. (1987). Age differences in sibling relationships during middle childhood. *Applied Developmental Psychology, 8,* 247–257.

van Dijk, T. A. (1987). *Communicating racism.* Newbury Park, CA: Sage.

Vandiver, R. (1972). *Sources and interrelation of premarital sexual standards and general liberality and conservatism.* Unpublished doctoral dissertation, Southern Illinois University.

Varenhorst, B. B. (1991). Peer counseling: A human resource program. In R. M. Lerner, A. C. Petersen, & J. Brooks-Gunn (Eds.), *Encyclopedia of adolescence* (Vol. 2). New York: Garland.

Vinton, D. (1992). Helping students find time for the job search. *Journal of Career Planning and Employment, 27,* 71–74.

Visher, E. B., & Visher, J. (1992). Why stepfamilies need your help. *Contemporary Pediatrics, 9,* 146–165.

Vondracek, F. W. (1991). Vocational development and choice in adolescence. In R. M. Lerner, A. C. Petersen, & J. Brooks-Gunn (Eds.), *Encyclopedia of adolescence* (Vol. 2). New York: Garland.

Voss, J. F. (1989). Problem solving and the educational process. In A. Lesgold & R. Glaser (Eds.), *Foundations of a psychology of education.* Hillsdale, NJ: Erlbaum.

Vuchinich, S., Emery, R. E., & Cassidy, J. (1988). Family members as third parties in dyadic family conflict: Strategies, alliances, and outcomes. *Child Development, 59,* 1293–1302.

Waddington, C. H. (1957). *The strategy of the genes.* London: Allen & Son.

Wagennar, A. C. (1983). *Alcohol, young drivers, and traffic accidents.* Lexington, MA: D. C. Heath.

Wagner, B. M., Cohen, P., & Brook, J. S. (1991, March). *Parent-adolescent relationships as moderators of the effects of stressful live events during adolescence.* Paper presented at the meeting of the Society for Research in Adolescence, Atlanta.

Walker, L. (1982). The sequentiality of Kohlberg's stages of moral development. *Child Development, 53,* 1330–1336.

Walker, L. J. (1984). Sex differences in the development of moral reasoning. A critical review. *Child Development, 51,* 131–139.

Walker, L. J. (1991a). Sex differences in moral development. In W. M. Kurtines & J. Gewirtz (Eds.), *Moral behavior and development* (Vol. 2). Hillsdale, NJ: Erlbaum.

Walker, L. J. (1991b, April). *The validity of an ethic of care.* Paper presented at the Society for Research in Child Development meeting, Seattle.

Walker, L. J., de Vries, B., & Trevethan, S. D. (1987). Moral stages and moral orientation in real-life and hypothetical dilemmas. *Child Development, 58,* 842–858.

Wall, J. A. (1992, March). *Situational resistance to peer pressure in a Hispanic sample.* Paper presented at the meeting of the Society for Research on Adolescence, Washington, DC.

Wallace, H. M., & Vienonen, M. (1989). Teenage pregnancy in Sweden and Finland: Implications for the United States. *Journal of Adolescent Health Care, 10,* 231–236.

Wallach, M. A., & Kogan, N. (1965). *Modes of thinking in young children.* New York: Holt, Rinehart & Winston.

Wallerstein, J. S. (1989). *Second chances.* New York: Ticknor & Fields.

Wallerstein, J. S., Corbin, S. B., & Lewis, J. M. (1988). Children of divorce: A 10-year study. In E. M. Hetherington & J. D. Arasteh (Eds.), *Impact of divorce, single parenting, and stepparenting on children.* Hillsdale, NJ: Erlbaum.

Wallerstein, J. S., & Kelly, J. B. (1980). *Surviving the breakup: How children actually cope with divorce.* New York: Basic Books.

Wallis, C. (1985, December 9). Children having children. *Time,* pp. 78–88.

Walster, E., Aronson, E., Abrahams, D., & Rottman, L. (1966). Importance of physical attractiveness in dating behavior. *Journal of Personality and Social Psychology, 4,* 508–516.

Walter, C. A. (1986). *The timing of motherhood.* Lexington, MA: D.C. Heath.

Ward, S. L. (1991). Moral development in adolescence. In R. M. Lerner, A. C. Petersen, & J. Brooks-Gunn (Eds.), *Encyclopedia of adolescence* (Vol. 2). New York: Garland.

Wartella, E., Heintz, K., Aidman, A., & Mazzarella, S. (1990). Television and beyond: Children's video media in one community. *Communications Research, 17,* 45–64.

Waterman, A. S. (1985). Identity in the context of adolescent psychology. In A. S. Waterman (Ed.), *Identity in adolescence: Processes and contents.* San Francisco: Jossey-Bass.

Waterman, A. S. (1989). Curricula interventions for identity change: Substantive and ethical considerations. *Journal of Adolescence, 12,* 389–400.

Waterman, A. S., & Archer, S. L. (1991). Erikson, Erik Homberger. In R. M. Lerner, A. C. Peterson, & J. Brooks-Gunn (Eds.), *Encyclopedia of adolescence* (Vol. 1). New York: Garland.

Watts, T. D., & Lewis, R. C. (1988). Alcoholism and native American youth: An overview. *Journal of Drug Issues, 18,* 69–86.

Wechsler, D. (1949). *Wechsler Intelligence Scale for Children.* New York: Psychological Corporation.

Wechsler, D. (1955). *Wechsler Adult Intelligence Scale Manual.* New York: Psychological Corporation.

Wechsler, D. (1974). *Wechsler Intelligence Scale for Children—Revised.* New York: Psychological Corporation.

Wechsler, D. (1981). *Wechsler Adult Intelligence Scale—Revised.* New York: Psychological Corporation.

Weidner, G., Sexton, G., Matarazzo, J. D., Pereira, C., & Friend, R. (1988). Type-A behavior in children, adolescents, and their parents. *Developmental Psychology, 24,* 118–121.

Weinberg, R. A. (1989). Intelligence and IQ: Landmark issues and great debates. *American Psychologist, 44,* 98–104.

Weiner, I. B. (1980). Psychopathology in adolescence. In J. Adelson (Ed.), *Handbook of adolescent psychology.* New York: Wiley.

Weiss, R. S. (1973). *Loneliness: The experience of emotional and social isolation.* Cambridge, MA: MIT Press.

Weissberg, R., & Caplan, M. (1989, April). *A follow-up study of a school-based social competence program for young adolescents.* Paper presented at the meeting of the Society for Research in Child Development, Kansas City, MO.

Weissman, M. M., & Klerman, G. L. (1991). Depression in adolescence, gender differences in. In R. M. Lerner, A. C. Petersen, & J. Brooks-Gunn (Eds.), *Encyclopedia of adolescence* (Vol. 1). New York: Garland.

Wender, P. H., Kety, S. S., Rosenthal, D., Schulsinger, F., Ortmann, J., & Lunde, I. (1986). Psychiatric disorders in the biological and adoptive families of adopted individuals with affective disorders. *Archives of General Psychiatry, 43,* 923–929.

Weston, P. J., & Mednick, M. T. (1970). Race, social class, and the motive to avoid success in women. *Journal of Cross-Cultural Psychology, 1,* 284–291.

Wetzel, J. R. (1989). *American youth: A statistical snapshot.* Washington, DC: William T. Grant Foundation.

White, K. M., Speisman, J. C., Costos, D., & Smith, A. (1987). Relationship maturity: A conceptual and empirical approach. In J. Meacham (Ed.), *Interpersonal relations: Family, peers, friends.* Basel, Switzerland: Karger.

White, K. M., Speisman, J. C., Jackson, D., Bartis, S., & Costos, D. (1986). Intimacy maturity and its correlates in young married couples. *Journal of Personality and Social Psychology, 50,* 152–162.

White, S. H. (1985, April). *Risings and fallings of developmental psychology.* Paper presented at the biennial meeting of the Society for Research in Child Development, Toronto.

Whiting, B. B. (1989, April). *Culture and interpersonal behavior.* Paper presented at the biennial meeting of the Society for Research in Child Development, Kansas City, MO.

Whiting, B. B., & Edwards, C. P. (1988). *Children of different worlds.* Cambridge, MA: Harvard University Press.

Whiting, B. B., & Whiting, J. W. M. (1991). Preindustrial world, adolescent in. In R. M. Lerner, A. C. Petersen, & J. Brooks-Gunn (Eds.), *Encyclopedia of adolescence* (Vol. 2). New York: Garland.

Wideck, C., Knefelkamp, L., & Parker, C. (1975). The counselor as a developmental instructor. *Counselor Education and Supervision, 14,* 286–295.

Wilder, D. (1991, March 28). To save the Black family, the young must abstain. *Wall Street Journal,* p. A14.

Williams, F., LaRose, R., & Frost, F. (1981). *Children, television, and sex-role stereotyping.* New York: Praeger.

Williams, J. (1987). *Psychology of women: Behavior in a biosocial context* (3rd ed.). New York: W. W. Norton.

Williams, J. E., & Best, D. L. (1982). *Measuring sex stereotypes: A thirty-nation study.* Newbury Park, CA: Sage.

Williams, J. E., & Best, D. I. (1989). *Sex and psyche: Self-concept viewed cross-culturally.* Newbury Park, CA: Sage.

Williams, M. F., & Condry, J. C. (1989, April). *Living color: Minority portrayals and cross-racial interactions on television.* Paper presented at the biennial meeting of the Society for Research in Child Development, Kansas City, MO.

Williams, R. B. (1989). Biological mechanisms mediating the relationship between behavior and coronary-prone behavior. In A. W. Siegman & T. Dembrowski (Eds.), *In search of coronary-prone behavior: Beyond Type-A.* Hillsdale, NJ: Erlbaum.

Williams, T. M., Baron, D., Phillips, S., David, L., & Jackson, D. (1986, August). *The portrayal of sex roles on Canadian and U.S. television.* Paper presented at the conference of the International Association for Mass Media Research, New Delhi, India.

Williamson, J. M., & Borduin, C. (1989, April). *A multivariate examination of adolescent physical abuse, sexual abuse, and neglect.* Paper presented at the biennial meeting of the Society for Research in Child Development, Kansas City.

William T. Grant Foundation Commission on Work, Family, and Citizenship. (1988, February). *The forgotten half: Noncollege-bound youth in America.* New York: William T. Grant Foundation.

Willis, S. L. (1989). Cohort differences in cognitive aging: A sample case. In K. W. Schaie & C. Schooler (Eds.), *Social structure and aging: Psychological processes.* Hillsdale, NJ: Erlbaum.

Willis, S. L., & Schaie, K. W. (1986). Training the elderly on the ability factors of spatial orientation and inductive reasoning. *Psychology and Aging, 1,* 239–247.

Wilson, A. B. (1989). Dreams and aspirations in the status attainment model. In D. Stern & D. Eichorn (Eds.), *Adolescence and work.* Hillsdale, NJ: Erlbaum.

Wilson, J. W. (1987). *The truly disadvantaged: The inner city, the underclass, and public policy.* Chicago: University of Chicago Press.

Wilson, M. N. (1989). Child development in the context of the black extended family. *American Psychologist, 44,* 380–383.

Wilson, W. J., & Neckerman, K. M. (1986). Poverty and family structure: The widening gap between evidence and public policy issues. In S. Danziger & D. Weinberg (Eds.), *Fighting poverty.* Cambridge, MA: Harvard University Press.

Windle, M. (1989). Substance use and abuse among adolescent runaways: A four-year follow-up study. *Journal of Youth and Adolescence, 18,* 331–341.

Winner, E. (1989). Development in the visual arts. In W. Damon (Ed.), *Child development today and tomorrow.* San Francisco: Jossey-Bass.

Wisniewski, S. A., & Gaier, E. L. (1990). Casual attributions for losing as perceived by adolescents. *Adolescence, 25,* 239–247.

Wober, M. (1974). Towards an understanding of the Kiganda concept of intelligence. In J. W. Berry & P. R. Dasen (Eds.), *Culture and cognition.* London: Methuen.

Wodarski, J. S., & Hoffman, S. D. (1984). Alcohol education for adolescents. *Social Work in Education, 6,* 69–92.

Wong, H. Z. (1982). Asian and Pacific Americans. In L. Snowden (Ed.), *Reaching the underserved: Mental health needs of neglected populations.* Newbury Park, CA: Sage.

Wright, M. R. (1989). Body image satisfaction in adolescent girls and boys. *Journal of Youth and Adolescence, 18,* 71–84.

Wylie, R. (1979). *The self concept.* Vol. 2.: *Theory and research on selected topics.* Lincoln, NE: University of Nebraska Press.

Xiaohe, X., & Whyte, M. K. (1990). Love matches and arranged marriages. *Journal of Marriage and the Family, 52,* 709–722.

Yankelovich, D. (1974). *The new morality: A profile of American youth in the 1970s.* New York: McGraw-Hill.

Yardley, K. (1987). What do you mean "Who am I?": Exploring the implications of a self-concept measurement with subjects. In K. Yardley & T. Honess (Eds.), *Self and Identity: Psychosocial perspectives.* New York: Wiley.

Yaylayan, S., Viesselman, J. O., Weller, E. B., & Weller, R. A. (1992). Depressive mood disorders in adolescents. *Adolescent Medicine, 3,* 41–50.

Youniss, J. (1980). *Parents and peers in the social environment: A Sullivan Piaget perspective.* Chicago: University of Chicago Press.

Youniss, J., & Smollar, J. (1985). *Adolescent relations with mothers, fathers, and friends.* Chicago: University of Chicago Press.

Yussen, S. R. (1977). Characteristics of moral dilemmas written by adolescents. *Developmental Psychology, 13,* 162–163.

Zabin, L. S. (1986, May/June). Evaluation of a pregnancy prevention program for urban teenagers. *Family Planning Perspectives,* p. 119.

Zahn-Waxler, C. (1990, May 28). Commentary. *Newsweek,* p. 61.

Zelnik, M., & Kantner, J. F. (1977). Sexual and contraceptive experiences of young unmarried women in the United States, 1976 and 1971. *Family Planning Perspectives, 9,* 55–71.

Credits

Photographs

Section Openers

Section 1: © Lanpher Productions, Inc.; **Section 2:** © Steve Leonard/Black Star; **Section 3:** © David W. Hamilton/The Image Bank; **Section 4:** © David Burnett/Contact Press Images; **Section 5:** © Mel Di Giacomo/The Image Bank

Chapter 1

Opener: © Gabe Palmer/The Stock Market; **p. 8:** © Owen Franken/Stock Boston; **p. 12:** Historical Pictures Service; **p. 14:** Courtesy of the Institute for Intercultural Studies, Inc, New York; **p. 17a:** © Historical Pictures Service; **p. 17b:** © Topham/The Image Works; **p. 17c:** © Joe Munroe/Photo Researchers Inc.; **p. 17d:** © Jean Claude Lejeune; **p. 17e:** © David R. Frazier Photolibrary; **p. 18a:** © Alan Oddie/PhotoEdit; **p. 18b:** © Carl Purcell, 1989; **p. 22:** © Frank Siteman/The Picture Cube; **p. 23:** Courtesy of Rhoda Unger/Photograph by Will Cofnuk; **p. 24 left:** © Bob Daemmrich/The Image Works; **p. 24 bottom:** © Dianne Carter; **p. 26:** © Lee Celano/SIPA-Press; **1,3 top to bottom:** © Elyse Lewin/Image Bank, © Jim Matheny/Light Images, © D. Esgero/Image Bank, © James L. Shaffer, © Michael Salas/Image Bank, © Joe Sohm/The Image Works, © Helena Frost Associates, Ltd., © Landrum Shettles

Chapter 2

Opener: © Richard Hutchings/InfoEdit; **p. 44:** The Bettmann Archive; **2.2:** Scala/Art Resource, New York; **p. 48:** © Michael Siluk/The Image Works; **p. 49:** © Barton Silverman/NYT Pictures; **p. 51:** The Bettmann Archive; **2.3 left top to bottom:** © William Hopkins, © Suzanne Sasz/Photo Researchers, Inc., © Kathleen Loewenberg, © Alan Becker/The Image Bank; **right top to bottom:** © Sam Zarember/The Image Bank, © Brett Froomer/The Image Bank, © Alan Carey/The Image Works, © Art Kane/The Image Bank; **p. 55:** © Yves DeBraine/Black Star; **p. 57 left:** © W. L. Hamilton/Superstock; **p. 57 right:** Courtesy of Nancy Chodorow/Photo by Jean Margolis; **2.4 left to right:** © Julie O'Neil, © G. Zucker/Stock Boston, © L. Enkelis/Stock Boston, © M. L. Baer/Tom Stack Associates; **p. 63 top:** © Joe McNally/Sygma; **p. 63 bottom:** Courtesy of Albert Bandura; **p. 65:** Courtesy of Urie Bronfenbrenner/Cornell University; **p. 66:** © Jay Dickman; **p. 73a:** © Anthony Bannister/Earth Scenes; **p. 73b:** © Chagnon/Anthrophoto; **p. 78:** Courtesy of Dr. Florence Denmark/Photo by Robert Wesner

Chapter 3

Opener: © J. P. Horlin/The Image Bank; **p. 91:** © Tony Freeman/PhotoEdit; **3.2:** © Joe Devenney/The Image Bank; **3.A:** © Paul Conklin/Monkmeyer Press; **3.6:** © Jeff Persons/Stock Boston; **p. 105:** © Guiseppe Molteni/The Image Bank; **p. 106:** Courtesy of Jeanne Brooks-Gunn/Photograph by Mark Sherman; **p. 108:** Courtesy of Roberta Simmons

Chapter 4

Opener: © R. Heinzen/Superstock; **4.1:** © Paul Fusco/Magnum Photos, Inc; **4.3:** © Richard Hutchings/Photo Researchers; **4.5:** © Jeff Smith/The Image Bank; **p. 124:** © Michael Siluk; **p. 126:** © David R. Frazier Photolibrary; **p. 127a:** © Ellis Herwig/Stock Boston; **p. 127b:** © Stacy Pick/Stock Boston; **p. 127c:** © Elizabeth Crews; **p. 130:** © M & E Bernheim/Woodfin Camp and Associates; **p. 134:** © Howard Dratch/The Image Works; **4.6:** © Bob Daemmrich/Stock Boston

Chapter 5

Opener: © Will and Deni McIntyre/Photo Researchers, Inc; **p. 147:** Courtesy of Texas Instruments; **p. 151:** © Susan Lapides; **p. 152:** © Jeff Persons/Stock Boston; **p. 153:** © Susan Lapides; **p. 155 top:** © Jeffry W. Myers/Stock Boston; **p. 155 right:** © Bob Daemmrich/Stock Boston; **p. 156:** © James Wilson/Woodfin Camp and Associates; **5.5A:** © Charles Gupton/Stock Boston; **5.5B:** © Bob Daemmrich/The Image Works; **5.5C:** © David W. Hamilton/The Image Bank; **p. 173:** © Jan Doyle; **p. 175:** © Mike Penney/David Frazier Photolibrary

Chapter 6

Opener: © Richard Hutchings/Photo Researchers, Inc; **p. 195:** © R. Llewellyn/Superstock; **p. 197:** Courtesy of Diana Baumrind; **p. 198:** © Jeffry W. Myers/Stock Boston; **p. 202:** David Wells/The Image Works; **p. 204:** © David Wells/The Image Works; **6.4:** © R. Llewellyn/Superstock; **p. 207:** © James G. White; **p. 210:** Courtesy of Mavis Hetherington; **6.A:** © James G. White; **p. 218 left:** © Erika Stone/Peter Arnold, Inc; **p. 218 bottom:** © Bob Daemmrich/The Image Works

Chapter 7

Opener: © Jean Claude Lejeune; **p. 229:** Nils Jorgensen/Rex Features; **p. 231a:** © Mark Richards/SIPA Press; **p. 231b:** © Gio Barto/The Image Bank; **p. 232:** © Tony Freeman/PhotoEdit; **p. 233:** © Bill Stanton/Rainbow; **7.3 right:** © P. R. Productions/Superstock; **7.3 left:** © David M. Grossman/Photo Researchers, Inc; **7.4 top to bottom:** © Mary Kate Denny/PhotoEdit, © Jean Claude Lejeune, © Peter Vandermark/Stock Boston, © David De Lossy/The Image Bank, © Myrleen Ferguson/PhotoEdit; **p. 246:** © Jan Doyle; **p. 249:** © Ellis Herwig/The Picture Cube; **p. 251:** © Bob Daemmrich/The Image Works; **7.5:** Courtesy of the Academy of Motion Pictures

Chapter 8

Opener: © Bob Daemmrich/The Image Works; **p. 266:** © H. Yamaguchi/Gamma Liaison; **p. 267:** © Tass/Sovfoto; **8.2:** © Peter Vandermark/Stock Boston; **p. 271a:** © M. Antman/The Image Works; **p. 271b:** © James G. White Photography; **p. 272:** Courtesy of Dr. Joan Lipsitz; **p. 274a:** © Patsy Davidson/The Image Works; **p. 274b:** © Toby Rankin/The Image Bank; **8.3B:** © Bob Daemmrich/The Image Works; **p. 282:** © Mary Messenger; **p. 285:** © Joan Marcus; **p. 286:** © Bob Daemmrich/The Image Works; **p. 287 top:** © Jose Carrillo; **p. 287 bottom:** © Bob Daemmrich/The Image Works

Chapter 9

Opener: © Steve Schapiro/Gamma Liaison; **p. 298:** © George Holton/Photo Researchers, Inc; **p. 299 left:** © Bill Gillette/Stock Boston; **p. 299 right:** © Blair Seitz/Photo Researchers, Inc; **p. 300a:** © Michael Siluk; **p. 300b:** © Roger Sandler/Black Star; **p. 303:** Courtesy of Dr. Harry Edwards; **p. 306:** © R. Mayer/H. Armstrong Roberts, Inc.; **p. 310:** Courtesy of Margaret Beale Spencer; **p. 312:** Courtesy of Stanley Sue; **p. 314:** © Scott Thode/International Stock Photo; **p. 315 top:** © Spencer Grant/The Picture Cube; **p. 315 bottom:** © Elizabeth Crews; **p. 316:** © Gio Barto/The Image Bank; **p. 318:** © The Everett Collection; **p. 320:** © James L. Shaffer

Chapter 10

Opener: © Richard Hutching/Photo Researchers, Inc.; **10.1:** © Michael Melford/The Image Bank; **p. 343:** © 1988 by Warner Bros. Inc., Photo by Tony Friedkin; **p. 346:** The Bettmann Archive; **p. 347:** © Paul Popper Ltd.; **10.3:** © David R. Frazier Photolibrary; **p. 350:** Courtesy of James Marcia; **10.4:** © Gregory Heisler/The Image Bank; **p. 354:** © Manley/Superstock; **10.5:** © Dan Coffey/The Image Bank

Chapter 11

Opener: © Gio Barto/The Image Bank; **p. 368:** © Tony Freeman/PhotoEdit; **p. 371:** © K. Horan/Stock Boston; **11.1:** © Jose Carrillo; **p. 378 bottom:** © James L. Shaffer; **p. 379:** © James L. Shaffer; **p. 381a:** © James L. Shaffer; **p. 381b:** © Jan Doyle; **p. 382 left:** © Catherine Gehm; **p. 382 right:** © Bernard Pierre Wolff/Photo Researchers, Inc.; **p. 386:** © Keith Carter; **p. 387:** © Charles Gupton/Stock Boston

Chapter 12

Opener: © Day Williams/Photo Researchers, Inc.; **p. 401 top:** © B. L. Productions/Superstock; **p. 401 bottom:** © Richard Anderson; **p. 406:** © Bernard Gotfryd/Woodfin Camp and Associates; **p. 407:** Courtesy of Jacqueline Forrest; **12.1:** © William Hopkins Photography; **12.2:** © D. Fineman/Sygma; **p. 412:** © Dan Ford Connolly/Picture Group; **12.3A:** © Division of Computer Research and Technology, National Institute of Health/Photo Researchers, Inc.; **12.3B:** © Rick Friedman/The Picture Cube; **p. 422:** © James D. Wilson/Woodfin Camp and Associates

Chapter 13

Opener: © Randall Hyman/Stock Boston; **p. 435:** © David R. Frazier Photolibrary; **p. 437:** Courtesy of Professor Lawrence Kohlberg, Harvard University; **13.1:** © Janeart Ltd./The Image Bank; **p. 441 bottom:** © Margaret Finefrock/Unicorn Stock Photos; **p. 442:** © Bob Daemmrich/Stock Boston; **13.A:** © David R. Frazier Photolibrary; **p. 444:** © James L. Shaffer; **p. 452:** © David R. Frazier Photolibrary; **p. 454:** © John Foraste/Brown University; **13.2:** © D. W. Productions/The Image Bank; **p. 457:** © Bob Daemmrich/The Image Works; **p. 458:** © Bob Daemmrich/The Image Works; **p. 459:** © Catherine Ursillo/Photo Researchers, Inc.

Chapter 14

Opener: © Comstock; **p. 469:** © Joe MacNally/Sygma; **p. 473:** © Comstock; **p. 474:** Courtesy of Dr. Sandra Graham; **p. 475:** © Robert A. Isaacs/Photo Researchers, Inc.; **p. 476:** © Jane Scherr; **p. 485:** © Bob Daemmrich/The Image Works; **p. 487:** Courtesy of Jacqueline Eccles; **p. 488:** © Richard Anderson

Chapter 15

Opener: © Alan Carey/The Image Works; **p. 505:** © John T. Barr/Gamma Liaison; **p. 507:** © Jeff Greenberg; **p. 510:** © Mark Antman/The Image Works; **15.5 top left:** © Derik Murray/The Image Bank; **15.5 all others:** Courtesy of the Drug Enforcement Agency, U.S. Department of Justice; **15.6:** © Barbara Burnes/Photo Researchers, Inc; **p. 524:** © Edward Lettau/Photo Researchers, Inc; **p. 525:** © Andrew Sacks/Time Magazine; **p. 526:** © Mike Kagan/Monkmeyer Press; **p. 528:** © Mark W. Walker/The Picture Cube; **p. 533:** © Bob Daemmrich/The Image Works

Chapter 16

Opener: © Mel Di Giacomo/The Image Bank; **p. 548:** © Carl Purcell; **16.2:** R. Heinzen/Superstock; **p. 551:** © Tim Davis/Photo Researchers, Inc.; **p. 552:** © George Zimbel/Monkmeyer Press; **p. 555:** © Robert Brenner/PhotoEdit; **p. 561:** © Steve Burr Williams/The Image Bank; **p. 562:** © Richard Hutchings/PhotoEdit; **p. 564a:** © Robert Brenner/PhotoEdit; **p. 564b:** © Spencer Grant/Photo Researchers, Inc.; **p. 564c:** © F. Wood/Superstock; **p. 565:** Courtesy of Deborah Bell

Epilogue

Opener: © A. Upitis/The Image Bank

Line Art and Text

Chapter 1

Excerpt, pp. 12–13: Source: G. S. Hall, *Adolescence,* (2 vols.), New York: Appleton, 1904. **Fig. 1.1:** Source: Data from U.S. Department of Commerce, Bureau of the Census, *Current Population Reports by Age, Sex, and Ethnic Origin, 1980–1988.*

Chapter 2

Fig. 2.1: From *Psychology: A Scientific Study of Human Behavior,* 5th ed., by L. W. Wrightsman, C. K. Sigelman, and F. H. Sanford. Copyright © 1979, 1975, 1970, 1965, 1961 by Wadsworth, Inc. Reprinted by permission of Brooks/Cole Publishing Co., Pacific Grove, CA 93950. **Fig. 2.8:** Albert Bandura, *SOCIAL FOUNDATIONS OF THOUGHT & ACTION: A Social Cognitive Theory,* © 1986, p. 24. Reprinted by permission of Prentice-Hall, Inc., Englewood Cliffs, N.J. **Fig. 2.9:** J. Garbarino in Kopp/Krakow, *The Child,* © 1982, by Addison-Wesley Publishing Company, Inc. Reprinted with permission of the publisher. **Excerpt, p. 78:** From Florence Denmark, et al., "Guidelines for Avoiding Sexism in Psychological Research: A Report of the Ad Hoc Committee on Nonsexist Research" in *American Psychologist,* 43:582–585, 1988. Copyright 1988 by the American Psychological Association. Reprinted by permission.

Chapter 3

Fig. 3.1: From I. Gottesman, "Genetic Aspects of Intellectual Behavior" in *Handbook of Mental Deficiency,* edited by Norman R. Ellis. Copyright © 1963 McGraw-Hill Book Company, New York, NY. Reprinted by permission of Norman R. Ellis. **Fig. 3.2 left:** Adapted from *Human Biology and Economy* by Albert Damon, second edition, by permission of W.W. Norton & Company, Inc. Copyright © 1977, 1969 by W.W. Norton & Company, Inc. **Fig. 3.A left:** From M. Matousek and J. Peterson, "Frequency Analysis of the EEG in Normal Children and Adolescents" in *Automation of Clinical Electroencephalographs,* edited by P. Kellaway and I. Peterson. Copyright © 1973 Raven Press, New York, NY. Reprinted by permission. **Fig. 3.3:** From A. F. Roche, "Secular Trends in Stature, Weight, and Maturation" in *Monographs of The Society for Research in Child Development,* 44, Serial No. 179, 1977. Copyright © 1977 The Society for Research in Child Development, Inc. Reprinted by permission. **Fig. 3.4:** Source: E. D. Nottlemann, et al., "Hormone Level and Adjustment and Behavior during Early Adolescence," May 1985, page 38. Paper presented at the annual meeting of the American Association for the Advancement of Science, Los Angeles, CA. **Fig. 3.6 left:** From J. M. Tanner, et al., "Standards from Birth to Maturity for Height, Weight, Height Velocity, and Weight Velocity: British Children 1965" in *Archives of Diseases in Childhood,* 41, 1966. Copyright © 1966 British Medical Association, London, England. Reprinted by permission. **Figs. 3.8 and 3.10:** From M. N. Morris and J. R. Udry, "Validation of a Self-Administered Instrument to Assess Stage of Adolescence Development" in *Journal of Youth and Adolescence,* 9:271–280, 1980. Copyright © 1980 Plenum Publishing Corporation, New York, NY. Reprinted by permission of the publisher and authors. **Fig. 3.11:** Simmons, R. G., Blyth, D. A.,

and McKinney, K. L. "The Social and Psychological Effects of Puberty on White Females." In J. Brooks-Gunn & A. Petersen (Eds.), *Girls at Puberty: Biological & Psychosocial Perspectives,* 1983, p. 249, fig. 3. Copyright © 1983 Plenum Publishing Corporation, New York, NY. Reprinted by permission of the publisher and authors.

Chapter 4

Fig. 4.4: Excerpt from *Piaget With Feeling* by Philip Cowan, copyright © 1978 by Holt, Rinehart and Winston, Inc., reprinted by permission of the publisher. **Fig. 4.6 right:** From R. L. Selman, "The Development of Social-Cognitive Understanding: A Guide to Educational and Clinical Practice" in *Moral Development and Behavior: Theory, Research and Social Issues,* edited by Thomas Lickona. Copyright © 1986 Holt, Rinehart & Winston, Inc., New York, NY. Reprinted by permission of Dr. Thomas Lickona.

Chapter 5

Fig. 5.2: From Frank N. Dempster, "Memory Span: Sources of Individual and Developmental Differences" in *Psychological Bulletin,* 89, 63–100, 1981. Copyright 1981 by the American Psychological Association. Reprinted by permission. **Fig. 5.6:** Reproduced from *THE RAVEN STANDARD PROGRESSIVE MATRICES.*

Chapter 6

Fig. 6.2: Source: Hill, J. P., Holmbeck, G. N., Marlow, L., Green, T. M., & Lynch, M. E. Pubertal status and parent-child relations in families of seventh-grade boys. *Journal of Early Adolescence,* 5, 31–44. Reprinted by permission of H.E.L.P. Books, Inc. **Fig. 6.3:** From E. E. Maccoby and J. A. Martin, "Socialization in the Context of the Family: Parent-Child Interaction" in *Handbook of Child Psychology,* 4th ed., Vol. 4, edited by P. H. Mussen. Copyright © 1983 John Wiley & Sons, Inc., New York, NY. Reprinted by permission of John Wiley & Sons, Inc.

Chapter 7

Fig. 7.2: From J. R. Asarnow and J. W. Callan, "Boys with Peer Adjustment Problems: Social Cognitive Processes" in *Journal of Consulting and Clinical Psychology,* 53:80–87, 1985. Copyright 1985 by the American Psychological Association. Reprinted by permission. **Fig. 7.4 left:** Source: Data from Dexter C. Dunphy, "The Social Structure of Urban Adolescent Peer Groups" in *Sociometry,* Vol. 26, 1963. American Sociological Association, Washington, DC.

Chapter 8

Fig. 8.2 left: William M. Alexander & C. Kenneth McEwin from *Schools in the Middle: Status & Progress.* Printed June 1989. © National Middle School Association. **Excerpt, pp. 272–273:** This report was prepared by the Carnegie Council on Adolescent Development's Task Force on Education of Young Adolescents. The Carnegie Council is a program of Carnegie Corporation of New York. **Fig. 8.3 left:** From the Carnegie Foundation for the Advancement of Teaching, *Survey of the Transition from High School to College, 1984–85.*

Chapter 9

Figs. 9.1, 9.2, and 9.3: Three figures from *Being Adolescent: Conflict and Growth in the Teenage Years* by M. Csikszentmihalyi and Reed Larson. Copyright © 1984 by Basic Books, Inc. Reprinted by permission of Basic Books, a division of HarperCollins Publishers.

Chapter 10

Excerpt, p. 334: Reprinted by permission of the publishers from *At the Threshold: The Developing Adolescent* by S. Shirley Feldman and Glen R. Elliott, Cambridge, Mass.: Harvard University Press, Copyright © 1990 by the President and Fellows of Harvard College.

Chapter 11

Fig. 11.1: From Janet S. Hyde, et al., "Gender Differences in Mathematics Performance" in *Psychological Bulletin,* 107:139–155, 1990. Copyright © 1990 by the American Psychological Association. Reprinted by permission.

Chapter 12

Excerpt, pp. 404–405: From Student SECH Advisor Program, Princeton University Health Services, Princeton, New Jersey. Permission granted by Karen A. Gordon, Director of Health Education, 1987. **Fig. 12.1 left:** Reprinted with permission from *Family Planning Perspectives,* Volume 17, Number 2, 1985. **Fig. 12.2 left:** Source: Table 3, Frank L. Mott and William Marsiglio, "Early Childbearing and Completion of High School," *Family Planning Perspectives,* Volume 17, No. 5, September/October 1985 © The Alan Guttmacher Institute.

Chapter 13

Fig. 13.1 left: From Steven R. Yussen, "Characteristics of Moral Dilemmas Written by Adolescents" in *Developmental Psychology,* 13:162–163, 1977. Copyright 1977 by the American Psychological Association. Reprinted by permission. **Excerpt, p. 445:** Reprinted by permission of the publishers from *Making Connections,* edited by

Carol Gilligan, Nona P. Lyons and Trudy J. Hanmer, Cambridge, Mass.: Harvard University Press, Copyright © 1990 by the President and Fellows of Harvard College, © 1989 by Emma Willard School, © 1989 Prologue and Preface by Carol Gilligan. **Fig. 13.2A:** *The American Freshman: Twenty-Five Year Trends, Dey, Astin, Korn.* Higher Education Research Institute, UCLA. Used by permission. **Excerpt, pp. 459–461:** From G. W. Swope, "Kids and Cults: Who Joins and Why?" in *Media and Methods,* 16:18–21, 1980. Copyright © 1980 American Society of Educators, Philadelphia, PA. Reprinted by permission.

Chapter 14

Fig. 14.1: From Mark Lepper, et al., "Undermining Children's Intrinsic Interest with Extrinsic Rewards" in *Journal of Personality and Social Psychology,* 1973. Copyright 1973 by the American Psychological Association. Reprinted by permission. **Fig. 14.2:** Source: Data from Bureau of Labor Statistics.

Chapter 15

Poem, p. 499: From *The Poetry of Robert Frost* edited by Edward Connery Lathem. Copyright 1936 by Robert Frost. Copyright © 1964 by Lesley Frost Ballantine. Copyright © 1969 by Holt, Rinehart and Winston. Reprinted by permission of Henry Holt and Company, Inc. **Fig. 15.1:** From T. Achenbach and C. S. Edelbrock. "Behavioral Problems and Competencies Reported by Parents of Normal and Disturbed Children Aged Four through Sixteen" in *Monographs of the Society for Research in Child Development,* 46, No. 1, 1981, Copyright © 1981 The Society for Research in Child Development, Inc. Reprinted by permission. **Fig. 15.4:** Source:

L. D. Johnston, P. M. O'Malley, & J. G. Bachman (1991) *Drug Use among American High School Seniors, College Students and Young Adults, 1975–1990,* Vol I: *High School Seniors* (DHHS Pub No (ADM) 91–1813) and Vol II: *College Students and Young Adults* (DHHS Pub No (ADM) 91–1835). **Fig. 15.7:** Source: Data from U.S. Bureau of the Census, 1960–1989.

Chapter 16

Fig. 16.1: From Lee L. Langley, *Physiology of Man.* Copyright © 1971 Van Nostrand Reinhold, New York, NY. Reprinted by permission of the author. **Fig. 16.2 left:** From Virginia Demoss, "Good, the Bad and Edible" in *Runner's World,* June 1980. Copyright Virginia Demoss. Reprinted by permission. **Lyrics, p. 567:** Bobby McFerrin/Prob Noblem Music. Reprinted by permission.

Fineline

6.2, 7.2, 9.2, 9.3, 15.1

GBR Graphics

1.1, 2.10, 2.11, 3.4, 5.1, 6.3, 8.1, 10.2, 10.4, 10.5, 14.2, 15.4, 15.7

Hans & Cassady

1.2, 1.4, 4.2, 5.A, 6.5, 15.3, 16.3, 16.4

Illustrious, Inc.

3.2, 3.5, 3.6, 3.A, 4.1, 4.3, 4.6, 6.A, 6.4, 7.3, 7.4, 8.2, 8.3, 10.1, 10.3, 11.1, 12.1, 12.2, 13.1, 13.2, 13.A, 15.5, 15.6, 16.2

PC&F Incorporated

2.3, 2.4, 2.6, 2.8, 2.9

Name Index

Subject Index